W9-CEW-266

Microsoft®

Windows Server® 2008 Administrator's Companion

Charlie Russel
Sharon Crawford

PUBLISHED BY
Microsoft Press
A Division of Microsoft Corporation
One Microsoft Way
Redmond, Washington 98052-6399

Library of Congress Control Number: 2008923625

Printed and bound in the United States of America.

1 2 3 4 5 6 7 8 9 QWT 3 2 1 0 9 8

Distributed in Canada by H.B. Fenn and Company Ltd.

A CIP catalogue record for this book is available from the British Library.

Microsoft Press books are available through booksellers and distributors worldwide. For further information about international editions, contact your local Microsoft Corporation office or contact Microsoft Press International directly at fax (425) 936-7329. Visit our Web site at www.microsoft.com/mspress. Send comments to mspinput@microsoft.com.]

Acquisitions Editor: Martin DelRe
Developmental Editor: Karen Szall
Project Editor: Melissa von Tschudi-Sutton
Editorial Production: Custom Editorial Productions, Inc.
Technical Reviewer: Randall Galloway; Technical Review services provided by Content Master, a member of CM Group, Ltd.
Cover: Tom Draper Design

Body Part No. X14-65790

Contents at a Glance

Part IV

Secure the Network

Part V

Use Support Services and Features

Part VI

Tune, Maintain, and Repair

Table of Contents

Part III

Administer the Network

Part V
Use Support Services and Features

Part VI

Tune, Maintain, and Repair

Acknowledgments

No book of this size or scope ever comes only from the authors' hands. We are indebted to many people for their efforts to help us succeed.

From Microsoft Canada, Roger Benes played a crucial and very much appreciated role in helping to make critical connections for us. Plus he's a good and valued friend.

Also from Microsoft Canada, we're indebted to Mark Dikinson, who took that connection to the next step, and to Sasha Krsmanovic, Charlie's super MVP Lead, for always being there when we really needed an answer.

Building and running the kind of hardware it takes to do a book like this is a challenge, even with the ability to virtualize. Hewlett-Packard Canada was extremely generous in lending us a wonderful, fully loaded ML350G5 server to use for this book. It's a great server and we love it. We're indebted to Gordon Pellose and Alan Rogers at HP Canada; SanSan Strozier of HP in the United States; Sharon Fernandez of Hill & Knowleton, HP's public relations firm in Canada; and especially David Chin, also of Hill & Knowleton, for making the loan possible and being generous with their time and expertise.

We also had the use of another excellent Hewlett-Packard server, a DL380G5, thanks to Greg Rankich of Xtreme Consulting Group, Inc. and Dan Cox of Hewlett-Packard USA. A great help to us and much appreciated.

Creating and testing Storage Area Networks is hard to do without a SAN, and we are indebted to Dylan Locsin and Chris Carrier of EqualLogic for generously allowing us to borrow an amazing PS3800XV SAN array. A very well-built and powerful SAN, it served us well and we're grateful for the help.

All the screen captures in this book were made using HyperSnap from Hyperionics. Capturing screens in Server Core was a special challenge, but Greg Kochiniak of Hyperionics created a special build of HyperSnap just for Server Core. Now that's customer support!

We also had help from several other experts to create the content in this book. For three of the security chapters, Susan Bradley, a Microsoft MVP and forensic accountant, was invaluable, jumping in to help and meeting tight deadlines. A fourth security chapter came from Dana Epp, a Security MVP and developer of AuthAnvil, our preferred authentication solution. The clustering chapter was primarily the work of Mark Cooper, of Microsoft, who did an excellent job. For the Active Directory chapters, we couldn't have had a better author than Stan Reimer, who agreed to a ridiculous schedule and then met it with quality. Marco Shaw, a fellow Microsoft MVP for AdminFrameworks, knows way more about PowerShell than we ever will and contributed the scripting chapter. Finally, Kurt Dillard did an excellent and much appreciated job on the IIS chapter.

We very much appreciate the great people who make working with Microsoft Learning a real pleasure. It starts with Martin DelRe, whom we've known for many years now, and who really pulled out all the stops when we needed a hand at the end. Thank you, Martin; you're a true professional. Our project editor was Melissa von Tschudi-Sutton, who has been a pleasure to work with throughout this long process. This is our second book with Melissa and we hope it won't be the last. We deeply appreciate her enthusiasm, feedback, editorial insights, and patience. Especially her patience, which we sorely tried at times.

Randall Galloway was our technical editor, and we much valued his efforts and comments throughout the process. Our indexer at Hyde Park Publishing Services and desktop publisher at Custom Editorial Productions, Inc. did an excellent and much-appreciated job. The editorial team of Megan Smith-Creed and Becka McKay performed a meticulous and sensitive edit, for which we're very grateful. And last but absolutely not the least, the production and support people at Microsoft Learning, without whom this book would not exist. It is a pleasure to work with a team of professionals of this caliber. Thank you.

As always, we thank the people from past collaborations whose contributions to everything we write can't be overstated: Rudolph S. Langer and David J. Clark.

Introduction

To improve is to change; to be perfect is to change often. –*Winston Churchill*

Change is inevitable, constant, and inescapable. You can brood about it or you can take the optimist's view—and Churchill was nothing if not an optimist—and accept that improvement isn't possible without change. And even though upgrading servers and clients can be a significant challenge for an administrator, it also represents an opportunity to improve how your network functions. And you can be sure that Windows Server 2008 contains many tools to help you move in the direction of change for the better.

Meet the Family

Windows Server is available in five primary versions. Three of those are available without Windows Server Hyper-V, bringing the total number of editions to eight:

- Windows Server 2008 Standard
- Windows Server 2008 Enterprise
- Windows Server 2008 Datacenter
- Windows Server 2008 for Itanium-Based Systems
- Windows Web Server 2008
- Windows Server 2008 Standard without Hyper-V
- Windows Server 2008 Enterprise without Hyper-V
- Windows Server 2008 Datacenter without Hyper-V

For the five primary editions, the table below shows the features available in each one.

Edition	Server Core	Windows Deployment Services	Server Manager	Terminal Services Gateway and RemoteApp	Active Directory Rights Management	Network Access Protection	Hyper-V	Internet Information Services 7.0
Standard	Yes	Yes	Yes	Yes	Yes	Yes	Yes	Yes
Enterprise	Yes	Yes	Yes	Yes	Yes	Yes	Yes	Yes
Datacenter	Yes	Yes	Yes	Yes	Yes	Yes	Yes	Yes
Web	Yes	No	Yes	No	No	No	No	Yes
Itanium	No	No	Yes	No	No	No	No	Yes

The next table provides some general guidance on hardware requirements. The actual requirements will vary depending on your system and particularly on the applications and features that you use. Processor performance is dependent upon not only the clock frequency of the processor, but also the number of cores and the size of the processor cache. Disk space requirements for the system partition are approximate. Itanium-based and x64-based operating systems will vary from these disk size estimates. Additional available hard disk space may be required if you are installing over a network.

Component	Requirement
Processor	Minimum: 1 GHz (x86 processor) or 1.4 GHz (x64 processor)
	Recommended: 2 GHz or faster.
Memory	Minimum: 512 MB RAM Recommended: 2 GB RAM or more
	Optimal: 2 GB RAM for full installation or 1 GB RAM for Server Core installation
	Maximum for 32-bit systems: 4 GB (Standard) or 64 GB (Enterprise and Datacenter)
	Maximum for 64-bit systems: 32 GB (Standard) or 2 TB (Enterprise, Datacenter, and Itanium-based Systems)
Available Disk Space	Minimum: 10 GB
	Recommended: 40 GB or more
	Computers with RAM in excess of 16 GB will require more disk space for paging, hibernation, and dump files.
Drive	DVD-ROM drive
Display	Super VGA (800 x 600) or higher resolution monitor
Other	Keyboard
	Mouse or other pointing device

Note An Intel Itanium 2 processor is required for Windows Server 2008 for Itanium-Based Systems.

New in Windows Server 2008

Of course, there are lots of new features in Windows Server 2008, though many of them are not obvious at first glance. Some of the highlights include:

- Server Manager, the expanded Microsoft Management Console (MMC), provides a one-stop interface for server configuration and monitoring with wizards to streamline common server management tasks.

- Windows PowerShell, a new optional command-line shell and scripting language, enables administrators to automate routine system administration tasks across multiple servers.
- Group Policy preference extensions allow the configuration of settings that are simpler to deploy and manage than logon scripts.
- Windows Reliability and Performance Monitor provides diagnostic tools to give you ongoing visibility into your server environment, both physical and virtual, to pinpoint and resolve issues quickly.
- Optimized server administration and data replication increase control over servers in remote locations, such as a branch office.
- Server Core allows minimal installations where only the server roles and features you need are installed, reducing maintenance needs and decreasing the available attack surface of the server.
- Failover clustering wizards make it easy for even IT generalists to implement high-availability solutions. Internet Protocol version 6 (IPv6) is now fully integrated.
- The new Windows Server Backup incorporates faster backup technology and simplifies data or operating system restoration.
- Windows Server 2008 Hyper-V allows you to virtualize server roles as separate virtual machines (VMs) running on a single physical machine, without the need to buy third-party software.
- Multiple operating systems–Windows, Linux, and others–can be deployed in parallel on a single server using Hyper-V.
- Terminal Services (TS) RemoteApp and TS Web Access allow programs that are accessed remotely to be opened with just one click and appear as if they are running seamlessly on the end user's local computer.
- Microsoft Web publishing platform unifies IIS 7.0, ASP.NET, Windows Communication Foundation, and Windows SharePoint Services.
- Network Access Protection helps ensure your network and systems aren't compromised by unhealthy computers, isolating and/or remediating those computers that don't comply with the security policies you set.
- User Account Control provides new authentication architecture for protection against malicious software.
- Read Only Domain Controller (RODC) allows a more secure method for local authentication of users in remote and branch office locations using a read-only replica of your primary AD database.

- BitLocker Drive Encryption provides enhanced protection against data theft and exposure of server hardware if lost or stolen, and it provides more secure data deletion when your servers are eventually decommissioned.

And, as the saying goes, there's more—much more.

What's In This Book

Windows Server 2008 Administrator's Companion consists of thirty-seven chapters arranged in an order roughly corresponding to each stage in the development of a Windows Server 2008 network.

Chapters 1 through 4 are all about planning. Perhaps you've heard Edison's famous quote, "Genius is one percent inspiration and ninety-nine percent perspiration." Modify that slightly and you have a good motto for network building: A good network is one percent implementation and ninety-nine percent preparation. The first chapter is an overview of Windows Server 2008, its components, and its features. This is followed by chapters on directory services and namespace planning. The last chapter in this section covers specific issues that need to be addressed when planning your deployment.

Chapters 5 through 9 cover installation and initial configuration. These chapters take you through the process of installing Windows Server 2008 and configuring hardware. Also included are chapters on installing server roles and installing Server Core.

Chapters 11 through 21 cover day-to-day tasks, including managing file resources and using scripts for administration.

Chapters 22 through 26 are all about security—how make a plan and how to implement a security plan.

Chapters 27 through 31 cover additional features including virtualization and terminal services—both of which add exciting new capabilities to Windows Server 2008.

The final chapters on tuning, maintenance, and repair cover important material on network health. There's a chapter on the Windows Server Backup and another on performance monitoring. There are also chapters on the important topics of disaster planning and prevention. If, despite your best efforts, the network falters, here's where you'll find information on troubleshooting and recovery. In addition, we include a chapter on the registry—the brains of Windows Server 2008—and some advice if you're contemplating brain surgery.

At the end of the book, you'll find supplemental material about interface changes and support tools.

Within the chapters themselves, we've tried to make the material as accessible as possible. You'll find descriptive and theoretical information, as well as many step-by-step examples for how to implement or configure a particular feature. These are supplemented with graphics that make it easy to follow the written instructions.

In addition, we've made extensive use of the reader aids common to all books in the Administrator's Companion series.

Note Notes generally represent alternate ways to perform a task or some information that needs to be highlighted. Notes may also include tips on performing tasks more quickly or in a not-so-obvious manner.

Important Text highlighted as Important should always be read carefully. This is information that can save time or prevent a problem or both.

Real World

Everyone benefits from the experiences of others. Real World sidebars contain elaboration on a particular theme or background based on the adventures of IT professionals just like you.

Under the Hood

When wizards perform their magic or other procedures are done offstage, Under The Hood sidebars describe what is going on that can't be seen.

We encourage you to take advantage of additional books offered by Microsoft Learning. Other Windows Server 2008 titles that allow in-depth studies of specific areas include *Windows Server 2008 Active Directory Resource Kit*, *Windows Server 2008 Security Resource Kit*, and *Windows Group Policy Resource Kit: Windows Server 2008 and Windows Vista*.

System Requirements

The following are the minimum system requirements to run the companion CD provided with this book:

- Microsoft Windows XP, with at least Service Pack 2 installed and the latest updates installed from Microsoft Update Service
- CD-ROM drive
- Internet connection

- Display monitor capable of 1024 x 768 resolution
- Microsoft Mouse or compatible pointing device
- Adobe Reader for viewing the eBook (Adobe Reader is available as a download at *http://www.adobe.com*)

About the Companion CD

The companion CD contains the fully searchable electronic version of this book and additional sample chapters from other titles that you might find useful. We've also included scripts from Chapter 9 and Chapter 15.

Digital Content for Digital Book Readers: If you bought a digital-only edition of this book, you can enjoy select content from the print edition's companion CD.
Visit ***http://go.microsoft.com/fwlink/?LinkId=113195*** to get your downloadable content. This content is always up-to-date and available to all readers.

Support

Every effort has been made to the accuracy of this book and companion CD content. Microsoft Press provides corrections to this book through the Web at *http://www.microsoft.com/mspress/support/search.aspx*

If you have comments, questions, or ideas regarding the book or companion CD content, please send them to Microsoft Press using either of the following methods:

E-mail: mspinput@microsoft.com

Postal mail:

Microsoft Press
Attn: Windows Server 2008 Administrator's Companion Editor
One Microsoft Way
Redmond, WA 98052-6399

Please note that product support is not offered through the preceding mail addresses. For support information, please visit the Microsoft Help and Support Web site at *http://support.microsoft.com*.

Part I
Prepare

Chapter 1

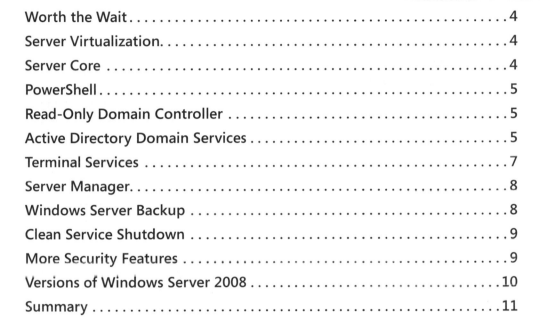

Introduction to Windows Server 2008

It's quite clear just from the name that Windows Server 2008 arrives five years after Windows Server 2003. In human time, that's not a very long spell, but in computer time, it's practically an eon.

You might reasonably ask, why so long? You may attribute it to Windows Vista. Windows Vista, released more than five years after *its* predecessor, Windows XP, includes many new and reworked features in networking, management, administration, and especially security that help explain its delay. Windows Server 2008, built on the same code base, couldn't take advantage of these new features until Windows Vista itself was finalized.

Worth the Wait

Windows Server 2008 may have been a while in coming, but it is clearly worth the wait, offering desperately needed help to IT departments under increasing pressure to do more with fewer people and less money. The new features and improved functionality in Windows Server 2008 are aimed at reducing administration and management costs without compromising security or ease of use. These are not showy changes—after all, there's little glamour associated with read-only domain controllers, policy-based networking, Windows PowerShell, or even major upgrades to Terminal Services. These features and many more are, however, music to an overworked administrator's ears.

Server Virtualization

Virtual servers are a new hot-button topic, though virtualization has been around for a number of years. What's new is built-in virtualization in Windows Server 2008. Underutilization of servers is much more common than you might think. Often, servers are dedicated to a specific purpose that uses perhaps ten or twenty percent of the servers' capabilities. The rest, though bought and paid for, remains idle. Being able to virtualize numerous servers on a single computer is an easy way to maximize a server's utility, reducing management and administrative costs in the process. Chapter 29, "Virtualization," covers all the ways virtualization can help you make efficient use of hardware resources.

Server Core

With Windows Server 2008 you can install a low-overhead, high-security, minimal environment called a Server Core. The Server Core installation option installs only the subset of the binary files that are required by the supported server roles and leaves out the graphical interface. Administrators use a command prompt or scripting techniques for local administration of the server. Or they administer the Server Core installation using Microsoft Management Console (MMC) from another computer running Windows Server 2008 by selecting the Server Core computer as a remote computer to manage.

Servers without a graphical user interface (GUI) offer smaller targets for hackers and require much less space (about 1 GB) to install. You can configure a virtualized server core installation to run roles such as DHCP Server, DNS Server, Internet Information Services 7, Printer Server, File Services, Active Directory Domain Services, Active Directory Lightweight Directory Services, and more. Chapter 9, "Installing and Configuring Server Core," covers the installation and configuration of Server Core.

Note Server Core is not a separate edition of Windows Server 2008; it's an installation option available in all versions except the Web and Itanium editions.

PowerShell

Long awaited, Windows PowerShell is a new Windows command-line shell that includes an interactive prompt and a scripting environment that can be used separately or in combination. Windows PowerShell introduces the concept of a cmdlet (pronounced "command-let"), a simple, single-function, command-line tool built into the shell. Each cmdlet can be used separately, but their strength lies in using them in combination. Windows PowerShell includes more than one hundred basic core cmdlets that you can combine to automate complex tasks. You can even write your own cmdlets for even more customized scripts.

PowerShell and its permutations are covered in Chapter 15, "Using Scripts for Consistent Administration."

Read-Only Domain Controller

A major challenge faced by many IT departments is the management and security of branch office systems. Branch offices are frequently too small to have their own IT departments and too distant for administrators to put in personal appearances. A branch office may have poor physical security but still requires a domain controller to run one or more essential applications. Or the domain controller may be the only server in the branch office and therefore required to perform multiple roles.

A Read-Only Domain Controller (RODC) addresses many of the problems inherent in branch office locations. An RODC holds the same Active Directory attributes and objects as one would find on a writeable domain controller. The difference is that you cannot make modifications directly to an RODC. Instead, changes must be made on a writeable DC and replicated back to the RODC, preventing a change made at the branch office from backfeeding into the entire forest. Also, since no changes originate at the RODC, no changes have to be pulled from the RODC during replication.

You can find much more about Read-Only Domain Controllers in Chapter 16, "Installing and Configuring Directory Services."

Active Directory Domain Services

Lots of changes have been made in Active Directory Domain Services (AD DS) that administrators will find highly useful. A few of them are described here.

Restartable Active Directory Domain Services

Most administrators will agree: Features that reduce the number of times a domain controller has to be rebooted are all to the good. In Windows Server 2008, administrators can apply updates, even security updates, without a reboot–stopping Active Directory and restarting as needed.

In Windows Server 2003, an offline defragmentation requires a restart using Directory Services Restore Mode. In Windows Server 2008, you can perform offline operations much more quickly by simply stopping and then restarting Active Directory Domain Services.

For more details, see Chapter 17, "Managing Active Directory."

Fine-Grained Password Policies

In Windows 2000 and Windows Server 2003, you could stipulate just one password policy and account lockout rule (in the Default Domain Policy), which was then applied to all users in the domain. Different password and account lockout settings for different sets of users required that you either create a password filter of some kind or deploy additional domains. These are time-consuming and therefore expensive solutions.

In Windows Server 2008, you can use fine-grained password policies to set multiple password policies within a single domain. For example, you can have stricter rules for passwords and more stringent account lockout policies to protect accounts with greater privileges.

You'll find more on fine-grained passwords in Chapter 23, "Implementing Security."

Data Mining Tool

Data Mining has long been a tool for extracting information from data for business analysts. In Windows Server 2008, the Data Mining tool provides a way to compare data from snapshots or backups taken at different times to help you make better decisions about which data to restore.

Prior to Windows Server 2008, if objects or organizational units were deleted, it was usually impossible to know the extent and number of deletions without restoring a full backup. This required restarting Active Directory in Directory Services Restore Mode. Additionally, you had no practicable way to compare backups done at different times. The Data Mining Tool doesn't recover deleted objects, but it allows you to examine changes and decide what corrections are needed.

You can find more on the Data Mining Tool in Chapter 34, "Using Backup."

Terminal Services

If not exactly an ugly stepsister, Terminal Services has never been the sort to attract the attention of a Prince or Princess Charming. Now, all of a sudden, it's transformed into the Cinderella of Windows Server 2008. Many new features have been added, including some of the very best in Windows Server 2008, and old features have been improved.

Terminal Services enables access from almost any computing device to a server running Windows-based programs or the full Windows desktop. Users can connect to a terminal server to run programs and use network resources on that server.

Terminal Services Gateway

Terminal Services Gateway (TS Gateway) is a service within the Terminal Services role that allows remote users to connect to the network from the Internet, over an encrypted connection, without having to set up VPN connections. In previous versions of Windows Server, users couldn't connect to remote computers across firewalls and NATs because the port used for RDP connections, port 3389, is usually blocked for security reasons. In Terminal Services Gateway, RDP traffic is sent to port 443, typically open for Internet connectivity and therefore open to remote connections.

Terminal Services RemoteApp

Terminal Services RemoteApp (TS RemoteApp) is arguably the most noteworthy addition to Windows Server 2008. With TS RemoteApp, computers running Windows Server 2008, Windows Vista, Windows XP (SP2), or Windows Server 2003 (SP1) can access one or more Windows-based applications, which will then run in their own resizable windows with appropriate entries in the taskbar. If a program uses a notification area icon, the icon appears in the notification area. Popup windows are redirected to the local desktop. A user can easily start multiple programs at the same time. If a user is running more than one RemoteApp on the same terminal server, the RemoteApps will share the same Terminal Services session.

Terminal Services Easy Print, also new in Windows Server 2008, ensures that users can dependably print from a RemoteApp or from a terminal server desktop session to the printer on their client computer.

Terminal Services Web Access

With TS Web Access, users can visit a Web site (either from the Internet or from an intranet) to access a list of available RemoteApps. When a user starts a RemoteApp, a Terminal Services session is started on the terminal server that hosts the application.

Terminal Services Session Broker

Terminal Services Session Broker includes a new feature, TS Session Broker Load Balancing. This feature allows you to distribute the session load among servers in a load-balanced terminal server farm. This solution is easier to use than Windows Network Load Balancing (NLB), and is optimal for terminal server farms of two to five servers.

Terminal Services Drain Mode

If you're going to be using these new Terminal Services features, the time will come when you need to take a server offline for maintenance even though users are remotely connected. In Windows Server 2003, you could use a command-line tool to disable remote connections but users were then unable to reconnect to their existing sessions so any unsaved work was lost. Not desirable.

To remedy this problem, Windows Server 2008 includes Terminal Services Drain Mode, which prevents new users from logging onto the server while allowing currently logged-on users to reconnect to their existing sessions. New logon requests are redirected to another server. TS server drain mode is integrated with TS Session Broker Load Balancing, so a server in a load balanced farm can be taken offline without any change to the end user experience.

These and other enhancements to Terminal Services are detailed in Chapter 30, "Deploying Terminal Services."

Server Manager

Server Manager is a new one-stop console that provides a view of the server, including information about the server configuration, status of installed roles, and wizards for adding and removing roles and features. Server Manager is the place to view Device Manager, Event Viewer, and Performance Monitor, perform a backup, and configure services. It's much easier to use than Manage Your Server and puts more information at your fingertips.

Server Manager replaces Manage Your Server, Configure Your Server, and Add Or Remove Windows Components. Chapter 8, "Installing Server Roles and Features," covers the many uses of Server Manager.

Windows Server Backup

At long last, a new and faster backup feature replaces the rather creaky backup technology in previous versions of Windows Server, which has been essentially unchanged since Windows NT. Designed to work with USB or FireWire disks, backups are image-based and can be automated or done manually. Backups of all kinds are covered in Chapter 37.

Clean Service Shutdown

In Windows Server 2003, when you initiate a shutdown, the operating system gives applications 20 seconds in which to close themselves in an orderly fashion. If an application fails to close in that time, a message is displayed allowing you to force the application to close. A forced closure can result in data loss. Windows Server 2008 waits for applications as long as they keep signaling that they still need time to shut down properly.

More Security Features

Many of the new or improved features discussed thus far play a role in security. The following sections discuss some features that appeared first in Windows Vista but have an even more important role in Windows Server 2008.

Address Space Load Randomization

Address Space Load Randomization (ASLR) is another one of the non-glamorous but exceedingly worthwhile features that are rife in Windows Server 2008. In previous versions of Windows (until Windows Vista and now Windows Server 2008) system executables and DLLs always load at the same location, allowing malware to find APIs residing at fixed addresses. ASLR makes certain that no two subsequent instances of an operating system load the same system drivers in the same place. Instead, early in the boot process a location is randomly chosen by Memory Manager from one of the 256 64-Kb-aligned addresses in the 16 Mb region at the top of the user-mode address space. DLLs that have the new dynamic-relocation flag are loaded into memory starting at the randomly selected location and working down.

With this simple change, all done in the background, the chances of software-with-evil-intent locating a system service on its own have gone from a sure thing to a very poor bet indeed.

BitLocker Drive Encryption

BitLocker is a security feature introduced with Windows Vista as a way to protect the system volume on client computers—particularly portable computers—if a computer is lost or stolen. A drive encrypted by BitLocker, for example, can't be removed from one computer and installed in another in an attempt to bypass Windows security.

In Windows Server 2008, BitLocker is particularly valuable for servers in branch offices where physical security may be more difficult. BitLocker encrypts all data stored on the system volume (and configured data volumes) including the Windows operating system, hibernation and paging files, applications, and data used by applications. The data is "locked" so that even if the operating system is not running or the disk drive is physically removed, the data remains encrypted.

You'll find more on the configuration and use of BitLocker in Chapter 23, "Implementing Security."

Windows Firewall

The new Windows Firewall is part of the new role-based management. Based on the version in Windows Vista, Windows Firewall is bidirectional and set to On by default, no matter which roles you've configured. When you enable and disable roles and features, Windows Firewall automatically configures itself so that only required ports are opened.

You'll find more information on the new firewall operations in Chapter 23.

Network Access Protection

Network Access Protection (NAP) is a new set of operating system components that monitor the health of client computers when they attempt to connect or to communicate on a network. If client computers are determined to be noncompliant, they can be limited to a restricted network until health requirements are met.

NAP does not protect against malicious users. Rather, it enforces compliance with health policies determined by the administrator. For example, a health policy can require that all computers logging onto the network have the most recent Windows updates, be running the newest antivirus signatures, and so forth. This is particularly important for portable computers or home computers that are otherwise beyond the control of the network much of the time. A computer found to be noncompliant at logon can be redirected to a limited network served by remediation servers that can provide what's needed to bring the computer into compliance.

Chapter 24, "Administering Network Access Protection," is all about using NAP to best advantage.

Versions of Windows Server 2008

Windows Server 2008 is offered in the following 32-bit and 64-bit editions:

- Windows Server 2008 Web Edition
- Windows Server 2008 Standard Edition
- Windows Server 2008 Enterprise Edition
- Windows Server 2008 Datacenter Edition

Windows Server 2008 will be the last 32-bit Windows server operating system. Since virtually all servers sold are 64-bit compliant, give serious thought to switching to a 64-bit environment. The increase in address space results in a significant increase in performance. Also, a 64-bit version takes advantage of the hardware to offer additional security features. At the server, driver availability is no longer a problem. While it's true that a 64-bit system will no longer run 16-bit applications, if you have an essential 16-bit program you can run it in a virtual machine and no one will be the wiser.

Summary

This chapter introduced you to some of the improvements in Windows Server 2008. The next three chapters cover subjects important to planning your deployment of Windows Server 2008. The next chapter covers the concepts and structure of Active Directory Domain Services.

Chapter 2

Introducing Directory Services

Francis Bacon (1561–1626) was probably the last person to know everything. Granted, he was an extraordinary polymath, but then a great deal less was known in the seventeenth century. These days we have far too much information to keep track of, so we must rely on directories. Directories—defined as listings that help you locate things—include bus schedules, book indexes, and telephone books. In fact, telephone directories are the source of the analogy for two searching capabilities that are necessary in computer directories. One type is the "white pages" Search By attribute, in which you know a name or some other fact about the object and you search using that piece of information. The second type of search, called a "yellow pages" search, is done by category. With either type of search, you don't have to know much about an object to locate it.

Directories are essential to a computer network's functioning. The lack of coherent, accessible directories is felt acutely on a network of any size. True directory services—a global catalog of network services and resources—are missing from Microsoft Windows NT networks. Although the directory functions available in version 4 do provide the all-important single logon and single point of administration that corporate environments need, they have serious deficiencies when large numbers of users are involved. Attempts to organize documents in folders and directories work up to a point, but as the number of objects scales up, management becomes both complex and onerous.

Understanding Directory Services

In a typical Windows NT computing environment, a user could log on to the network with a user name, such as *crussel*, and a password. Assuming that permissions are correctly granted, crussel could click Network Neighborhood or open a mapped drive and browse for needed files.

All this works very well until the scope of the network changes. The company adds e-mail, and crussel gains another identity (charlie.russel@example.local). The additional services, databases, and administrative tools—each one identifying Charlie Russel slightly differently—need to be accessible by the same user. When you consider that this is just one of hundreds or even thousands of users, it's easy to see how errors can arise that can be very difficult to resolve. As the number of objects in a network grows, directory services—a centralized place for storing administrative data used to manage the entire computer system—become essential.

Directory services differs from a directory in that it consists of both the directory information source and the services that make the information available to users. Being both a management tool and an end-user tool, directory services must address the following needs:

- Access to all the servers, applications, and resources through a single logon point. (User access is granted or blocked using permissions.)
- Multimaster replication. All information is distributed throughout the system and replicated on multiple servers.
- "White pages" searches based on attributes—for example, by filename or file type.
- "Yellow pages" searches based on classification—for example, all the printers on the third floor or all the servers in the Hartford office.
- The ability to remove dependency on physical locations for purposes of administration. That is, it should be possible to delegate administration of the directory, either partially or completely.

Although Microsoft occasionally used the term "directory services" in connection with Windows NT, Windows NT did not provide a true, hierarchical directory service. In Windows NT, the directory functions were divided among a host of services based on domains. The Domain Name System (DNS) Server provided the translation of names into IP numbers and was integrated with Dynamic Host Configuration Protocol (DHCP) servers used to dynamically allocate Transmission Control Protocol/Internet Protocol (TCP/IP) addresses. The Windows Internet Name Service (WINS) was used for Network Basic Input/Output System (NetBIOS) name resolution and was required on Windows NT networks for file sharing and some applications. Security was implemented through access control lists (ACLs), the Security Accounts Manager (SAM) database, and other services.

Microsoft Windows 2000 Server was the first product in which the Active Directory service replaced the Windows NT collection of directory functions with an integrated implementation that includes DNS, DHCP, Lightweight Directory Access Protocol (LDAP), and Kerberos. (You'll learn more about these later in this chapter.)

Real World Directory Services and X.500

X.500 is a standard for directory services established by the International Telecommunications Union (ITU). The International Organization for Standardization/International Electrotechnical Commission (ISO/IEC) also publishes the same standard. The X.500 standard defines the information model used in directory services. In this model, all information in a directory is stored in entries, each of which belongs to at least one object class. The actual information in an entry is determined by attributes contained in that entry.

The original 1988 X.500 standard focused heavily on the protocols to be implemented. Directory Access Protocol (DAP) specifies how user applications access the directory information. Directory Service Protocol (DSP) is used to propagate user directory requests between directory servers when the local directory server can't satisfy the request.

No extant directory service completely implements the X.500 standard, but all are modeled on the basic specifications of X.500, as is Active Directory. You can find an excellent introduction to directories and X.500 at *http://www.nlc-bnc.ca/9/1/p1-244-e.html.*

Active Directory in Microsoft Windows Server 2008

Active Directory Domain Services (AD DS) has numerous advantages, not the least of which is that it can handle any size of installation, from a single server with a few hundred objects to thousands of servers and millions of objects. Active Directory also greatly simplifies the process of locating resources across a large network. The Active Directory Service Interfaces (ADSI) and the new Active Directory Application Mode (ADAM) introduced in Windows Server 2003 R2, allow developers to "directory-enable" their applications, giving users a single point of access to multiple directories, whether those directories are based on LDAP, NDS, or NT Directory Services (NTDS).

Active Directory integrates the Internet concept of a namespace with the operating system's directory services. This combination allows the unification of multiple namespaces in, for example, the mixed software and hardware environments of corporate networks—even across operating system boundaries. The ability to subsume individual corporate directories into a general-purpose directory means that Active Directory can greatly reduce the costs of administering multiple namespaces.

Active Directory is not an X.500 directory. Instead, it uses LDAP as the access protocol and supports the X.500 information model without requiring systems to host the entire

X.500 overhead. LDAP is based on TCP/IP and is considerably simpler than the X.500 DAP. Like X.500, LDAP bases its directory model on entries, where the distinguished name (discussed in the next section) is used to refer to an entry without ambiguity. But rather than use the highly structured X.500 data encoding, LDAP adopts a simple, string-based approach for representing directory entries. LDAP uses many of the directory-access techniques specified in the X.500 DAP standard but requires fewer client resources, making it more practical for mainstream use over a TCP/IP link.

Active Directory also directly supports Hypertext Transfer Protocol (HTTP). Every object in Active Directory can be displayed as a Hypertext Markup Language (HTML) page in a Web browser. Directory-support extensions to Microsoft Internet Information Services (IIS) translate HTTP requests for directory objects into HTML pages for viewing in any HTML client.

Active Directory allows a single point of administration for all published resources, which can include files, peripheral devices, host connections, databases, Web access, users, other arbitrary objects, services, and so forth. Active Directory uses the Internet DNS as its locator service, organizes objects in domains into a hierarchy of organizational units (OUs), and allows multiple domains to be connected into a tree structure. The concepts of primary domain controller (PDC) and backup domain controller (BDC) that went away in Windows Server 2000 are back—but with a change (of course). Now the BDC role is filled by the Read-Only Domain Controller (RODC), discussed at length in Chapter 16, "Installing and Configuring Directory Services." Starting with Windows Server 2003 R2, the Active Directory Federation Services (ADFS) extends the Active Directory to enable identity management across organizational and platform boundaries.

Terminology and Concepts in Active Directory

Some of the terms used to describe concepts in Active Directory have been around for a while in other contexts, so it's important to understand what they mean when used specifically in reference to Active Directory. This section covers these basic terms and concepts.

Namespace and Name Resolution

"Namespace" is perhaps an unfamiliar term for a very familiar concept. Every directory service is a *namespace*—a circumscribed area in which a name can be resolved. A television listing forms a namespace in which the names of television shows can be resolved to channel numbers. A computer's file system forms a namespace in which the name of a file can be resolved to the file itself.

Active Directory forms a namespace in which the name of an object in the directory can be resolved to the object itself. *Name resolution* is the process of translating a name into some object or information that the name represents.

Attribute

Each piece of information that describes some aspect of an entry is called an *attribute*. An attribute consists of an *attribute type* and one or more *attribute values*. An example of an attribute type might be "telephone number," and an example of a telephone number attribute value might be "425-555-0123."

Object

An *object* is a particular set of attributes that represents something concrete, such as a user, a printer, or an application. The attributes hold data describing the thing that is identified by the directory object. Attributes of a user might include the user's given name, surname, and e-mail address. The classification of the object defines which types of attributes are used. For example, the objects classified as "users" might allow the use of attribute types such as "common name," "telephone number," and "e-mail address," while the object class "organization" allows attribute types such as "organization name" and "business category." An attribute can take one or more values, depending on its type.

Every object in Active Directory has a unique *identity*. Objects can be moved or renamed, but their identity never changes. Objects are known internally by their identity, not their current name. An object's identity is a globally unique identifier (GUID), which is assigned by the Directory System Agent (DSA) when the object is created. The GUID is stored in an attribute, *objectGUID*, that is part of every object. The *objectGUID* attribute can't be modified or deleted. When storing a reference to an Active Directory object in an external store (for example, a database), use *objectGUID* because, unlike a name, it won't change.

Container

A *container* resembles an object in that it has attributes and is part of the Active Directory namespace. However, unlike an object, a container doesn't represent anything concrete. It is a holder of objects and of other containers.

Tree and Subtree

A *tree* in Active Directory is just an extension of the idea of a directory tree. It's a hierarchy of objects and containers that demonstrates how objects are connected, or the path from one object to another. Endpoints on the tree are usually objects.

A *subtree* is any unbroken path in the tree, including all the members of any containers in that path. Figure 2-1 shows a tree structure for microsoft.com. Any of the unbroken paths (for example, from nw.sales.seattle.microsoft.com to microsoft.com) is a subtree. Trees and forests are discussed in more detail in Chapter 3, "Planning Namespace and Domains."

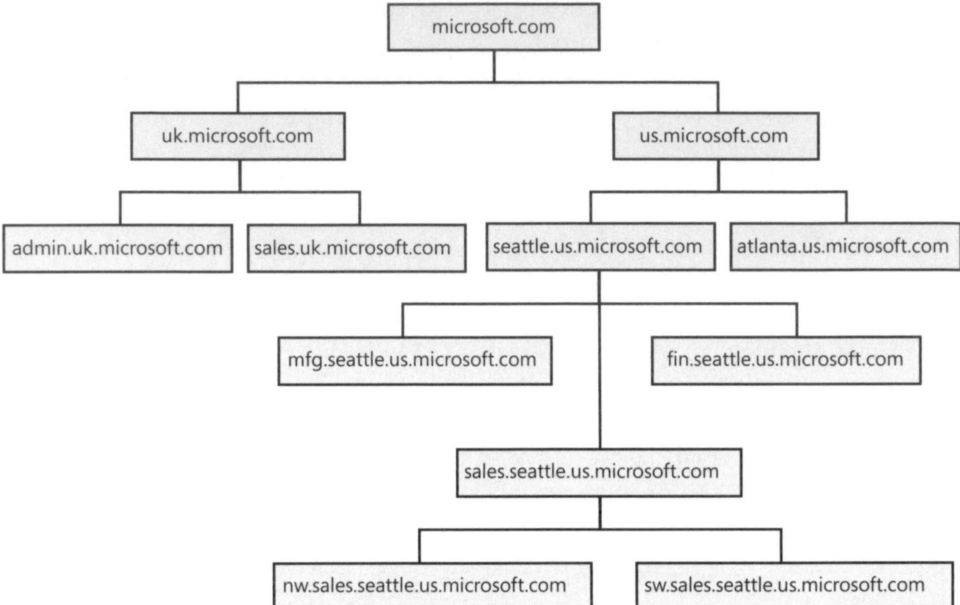

Figure 2-1 A tree structure with subtrees.

Distinguished Name

Every object in Active Directory has what's called a *distinguished name* (DN). In this context, "distinguished" means the qualities that make the name distinct. The DN identifies the domain that holds the object as well as the complete path through the container hierarchy used to reach the object. A typical DN might be CN=Charlie Russel, OU=Engineering, DC=example, DC=local. This DN identifies the "Charlie Russel" user object in the Engineering OU, in the example.local domain.

> **Note** CN stands for common name, OU stands for organizational unit, and DC stands for domain controller. Some attributes are derived from the X.500 model; an administrator can define others.

Active Directory also uses a *relative distinguished name* (RDN), which is the part of the DN that is an attribute of the object itself. In the previous example, the RDN of the user object is CN=Charlie Russel. The RDN of the parent object is OU=Engineering.

The "DC=" portion of a DN allows X.500 directories to plug in to the DNS namespace, which is also what Active Directory does. The root of the global namespace for Active Directory is the DNS namespace. Thus, DNS domain names merge within the Active Directory naming scheme. For example, example.local is a valid, internal, DNS domain name and can be the name of an Active Directory domain as well. This DNS integration means that Active Directory fits naturally into Internet and intranet environments. You can connect Active Directory servers directly to the Internet to simplify secure communications and electronic commerce with customers and partners.

Schema

"Schema" is a term commonly used in database work. In the context of Active Directory, the *schema* consists of definitions of the pieces that make up your Active Directory: the objects, attributes, containers, and so forth. Active Directory has a default schema that defines the most common object classes, such as users, groups, computers, OUs, security policies, and domains.

The Active Directory schema can be updated dynamically. That is, an application can extend the schema with new attributes and classes and use the extensions immediately. Creating or altering the schema objects stored in the directory causes schema updates. ACLs protect schema objects so that only authorized users (members of the Schema Admins group) can modify the schema.

The Active Directory Architecture

As mentioned previously, Active Directory isn't, strictly speaking, an X.500 directory service, although like all existing directory services, it's derived from that standard. The sections that follow enumerate some characteristics of the Active Directory architecture.

The Directory System Agent

The DSA is the process that provides access to the physical store of directory information located on a hard disk. The DSA is part of the Local System Authority (LSA) subsystem in all versions of Windows Server since Windows Server 2000. Clients access the directory information using one of the following mechanisms:

- LDAP clients connect to the DSA using LDAP. Active Directory supports LDAP v3, defined by RFC 2251; and LDAP v2, defined by RFC 1777. Clients of Microsoft Windows 2000 or later use LDAP v3 to connect to the DSA.
- Messaging Application Programming Interface (MAPI) clients, such as Microsoft Exchange, connect to the DSA using the MAPI remote procedure call (RPC) interface.
- Active Directory DSAs connect to each other to perform replication using a proprietary RPC interface.

Naming Formats

Active Directory supports several name formats to accommodate both users and applications:

- **RFC 822 names** Familiar to most users as Internet e-mail addresses, such as crussel@example.local. Active Directory provides a "friendly name" in RFC 822 form for all objects. Thus, a user can use a friendly name both as an e-mail address and as the name used to log on.
- **HTTP URLs** Familiar to most users who have Web browsers. A typical Uniform Resource Locator (URL) takes the form *http://domain/path-to-page*, where *domain* refers to a server running Active Directory services and *path-to-page* is the path through the Active Directory hierarchy to the object of interest. The URL for Charlie Russel is *http://AServer.example.local/Division/Product/Engineering/charlie.russel.*
- **LDAP names** More complicated than Internet names but usually hidden within an application. LDAP names use the X.500 attributed naming convention. An LDAP URL specifies the server holding Active Directory services and the attributed name of the object–for example, ldap://AServer.example.local/CN=charlie.russel,OU=engineering,OU=Product,OU=Division,O=MegaIntl,C=US.
- **UNC names** The Uniform Naming Convention used in networks based on Windows Server 2008 servers to refer to shared volumes, printers, and files–for example, \\example.local\Division.Product.Engineering.Volume\WordDocs\aprilreport.doc.

The Data Model

The Active Directory data model is derived from the X.500 data model. The directory holds objects that represent various items, described by attributes. The universe of objects that can be stored in the directory is defined in the schema. For each object class, the schema defines what attributes an instance of the class must have, what additional attributes it can have, and what object class can be a parent of the current object class.

Schema Implementation

The Active Directory schema is implemented as a set of object class instances stored in the directory. This is very different from directories that have a schema but store it as a text file that is read at startup. Storing the schema in the directory has many advantages. For example, user applications can read it to discover what objects and properties are available.

The Security Model

Active Directory is part of the Windows Server 2000 and later trusted computing base (TCB) and is a full participant in the security infrastructure. The distributed security model is based on the MIT Kerberos authentication protocol (version 5). Kerberos authentication accommodates both public-key and private-key security, using the same ACL support model as the underlying Windows Server 2008 operating system. ACLs protect all objects in Active Directory. They determine who can see the object, what attributes each user can see, and what actions each user can perform on the object. If a user is not allowed to see an object or an attribute, the fact of its existence is never made known to that user.

An ACL, in turn, is made up of access control entries (ACEs) stored with the object the ACL protects. In Windows 2000 and later, an ACL is stored as a binary value, called a *security descriptor*. Each ACE contains a security identifier (SID), which identifies the *principal* (user or group) to which the ACE applies and provides information about what type of access the ACE grants or denies.

ACLs on directory objects contain ACEs that apply to the object as a whole and ACEs that apply to the individual attributes of the object. This allows an administrator to control not only which users can see an object, but also what properties those users can see. For example, all users might be granted read access to the e-mail and telephone number attributes for all other users, but access to the security properties of users might be denied to all but members of a special security administrators group. Also, individual users might be granted write access to personal attributes such as the telephone and mailing addresses on their own user objects.

Active Directory is the store for the security system, including user accounts, groups, and domains. This store replaces the registry account database and is a trusted component within the LSA.

Delegation and Inheritance

Delegation is one of the most important security features of Active Directory. An administrator can authorize a user to perform a specified set of actions in some identified subtree of the directory. This is called *delegated administration*. Delegated administration allows very fine-grained control over who can do what and enables administrators to delegate authority without granting elevated privileges. This also eliminates the need for domain administrators with broad authority over large segments of the user population.

Administrators grant rights for specific operations on specific object classes by adding ACEs to the container's ACL. For example, to allow user Charlie Russel to be an administrator of the Engineering OU, you add ACEs to the ACL in Engineering as follows:

```
"Charlie Russel";Grant ;Create, Modify, Delete;Object-Class User
"Charlie Russel";Grant ;Create, Modify, Delete;Object-Class Group
"Charlie Russel";Grant ;Write;Object-Class User; Attribute Password
```

Now Charlie Russel can create new users and groups in Engineering and set the passwords for existing users, but he can't create other object classes and he can't affect users in other containers (unless, of course, ACEs grant him that access in the other containers).

Inheritance allows a given ACE to be propagated from the container in which it was applied to all children of the container. Inheritance can be combined with delegation to grant administrative rights to a whole subtree of the directory in a single operation.

Naming Contexts and Partitions

Active Directory is made up of one or more naming contexts or partitions. A *naming context* is any contiguous subtree of the directory. Naming contexts are the units of partitioning. A single server always holds at least three naming contexts:

- The schema
- The configuration (replication topology and related data)
- One or more user naming contexts (subtrees containing the actual objects in the directory)

The Global Catalog

The DN of an object includes enough information to locate a replica of the partition that holds the object. Many times, however, the user or application does not know the DN of the target object, or which partition might contain the object. The global catalog (GC) allows users and applications to find objects in an Active Directory domain tree, given one or more attributes of the target object.

The global catalog contains a partial replica of every naming context in the directory. It contains the schema and configuration naming contexts as well. This means that the GC holds a replica of every object in Active Directory, but with only a small number of their attributes. The attributes in the GC are those most frequently used in search operations (such as a user's first and last names, logon name, and so on) and those required to find a full replica of the object. The GC lets users quickly find objects of interest without knowing what domain holds them and without requiring a contiguous extended namespace in the enterprise.

The global catalog is built automatically by the Active Directory replication system. The replication topology for the GC is also generated automatically. The properties replicated into the GC include a base set defined by Microsoft. Administrators can specify additional properties to meet the needs of their installation.

In Windows 2000, when processing a logon event for a user in a native-mode domain, a domain controller has to contact a Global Catalog (GC) server to expand a user's Universal Group membership. This means that users in a remote office can experience logon failures if the network connection to the rest of the organization is cut off.

In Windows Server 2008, domain controllers can be configured to cache Universal Group membership lookups when processing user logon events, so users can log on even when a GC isn't available. You'll find specifics on the administration and deployment of Active Directory in Chapter 16 and in Chapter 17, "Managing Active Directory."

Summary

As you have no doubt gathered, Active Directory is a powerful tool and, like most powerful tools, it can be the source of great trouble if mishandled. Allow time for careful thought and planning before deploying Active Directory. First consider the design of a logical and efficient directory. A poor tree design can negatively affect the productivity and even the stability of the network. Chapter 3 covers how to plan your namespace and domains for both maximum utility and longevity.

Chapter 3

Planning Namespace and Domains

Planning has somehow acquired a poor reputation these days. It's associated in some people's minds with long, boring meetings and is even viewed as a way to avoid taking action. Nevertheless, planning and preparation are essential, whether you're constructing a network or just painting a room.

If you're coming to the concept of a namespace for the first time, you'd be well advised to spend the necessary time and energy up front—you'll be repaid later with reduced support costs, more flexibility, and less reorganization.

Planning the namespace of a large or even medium-sized organization is an iterative process. You won't get it right the first—or probably even the second—time. But you need to start somewhere, and then consult and collaborate with key players in your organization, and refine and consult again until you have a namespace that will work for your organization. As you work through the process, many of the opinions you receive will depend on company politics and personal agendas, making the whole process more difficult than it should be. Your job is to understand and protect the best interests of the organization as a whole.

Analyzing Naming Convention Needs

To plan your namespace and domain structure, you need to analyze your organization and attempt to understand its underlying naming needs. This requires both a thorough understanding of the type of organization you have and who the players are, as well as some educated guesses about where the organization is going.

Trees and Forests

There are two basic namespace types—tree and forest. By understanding the differences between these models, and how they align with your organization, you can choose the model that best reflects the needs of your organization. Although you can change models later, that requires considerable effort and will have an impact on the overall use of names in the namespace. So take the time in the planning stage to understand what your organization really needs—which can be different from what the organization thinks it wants.

Trees

A tree namespace, like that shown in Figure 3-1, is a single, contiguous namespace, with each name in the namespace directly descended from a single root name. This straightforward naming design is appropriate for an organization that is essentially cohesive and has a single name underlying what can be many divisions and diverse businesses. Many small to midsize businesses fit well within this model. Even very large businesses might be a comfortable fit for a tree structure if the organization is fairly centralized and has a single, recognizable name.

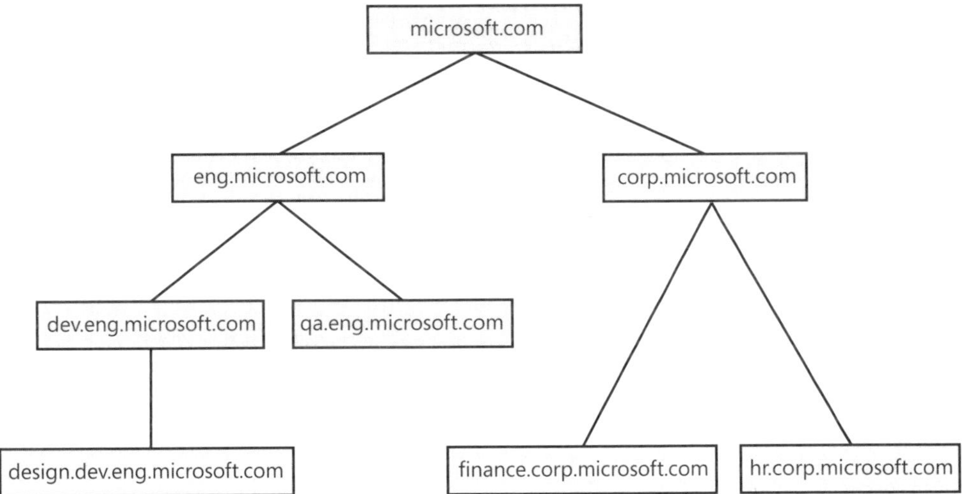

Figure 3-1 A tree structure yields a single, contiguous namespace, with all names derived from a single root.

As you can see from the figure, with a tree-structured namespace, each branch of the tree has a name that is directly descended from the root of the tree. This structure makes it easy to find any leaf or branch of the tree by tracing down the structure of its name.

Forests

A forest namespace, like that shown in Figure 3-2, is a collection of essentially equal trees, with no single root to the namespace. The forest namespace is appropriate for an organization that has multiple lines of business, each with its own separate and identifiable name. These are usually larger businesses, especially those that have grown by acquisition. They typically don't have a single, central Information Systems group that manages the entire organization, and each of the divisions for the most part has a separate identity and infrastructure.

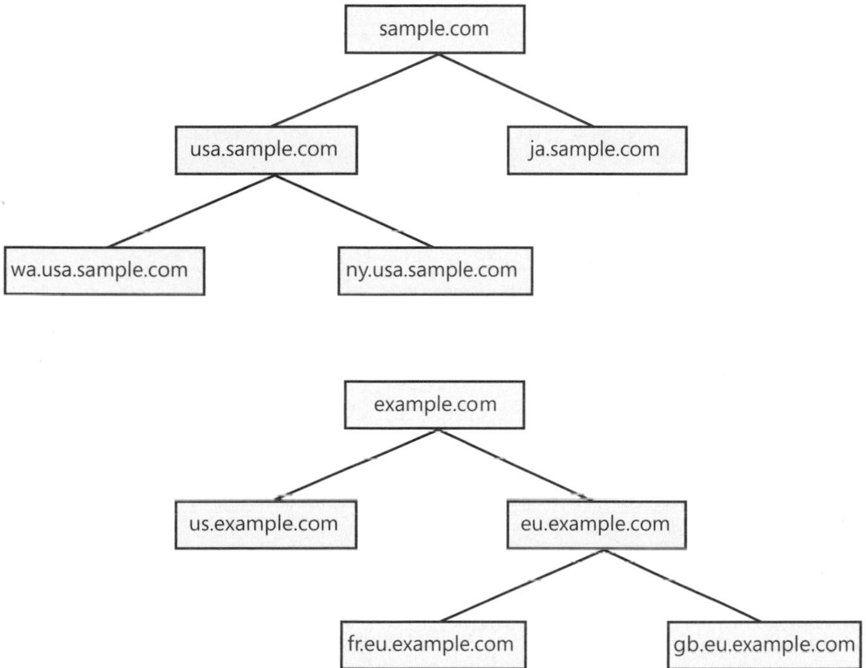

Figure 3-2 A forest is a collection of individual trees that are not part of a contiguous namespace.

As you can see from the figure, with a forest namespace you have a peer group of trees, each its own contiguous namespace, but the trees do not fit into an overall, contiguous namespace. In other words, you can't directly trace the names of all the leaves back to a single root.

Defining a Naming Convention

Whether you're going to have a single tree or a forest of trees for your overall namespace, you first need to decide what to name the various branches of the tree. These are probably the most delicate and politically sensitive decisions you have to make as you lay out your overall naming structure. Be prepared to suffer through some long and painful meetings as you get the critical players involved in the decision process. Nevertheless, spend the time to do this—it will save you untold amounts of grief later.

There are essentially two types of naming conventions—organizational and geographical. Both have their proponents, and an argument can be made for either choice. Keep in mind that people can get amazingly emotional about what their division or department is called and about its relative weight in the organization. Such political disagreements can be not only bitter but also prolonged beyond any reasonable expectation.

The Organizational Naming Convention

Using an organizational naming convention, you model your namespace on the way your company or organization is structured. Thus, the root of your tree might be *microsoft.com*, with the first level under that consisting of *admin.microsoft.com*, *finance.microsoft.com*, *mfg.microsoft.com*, *eng.microsoft.com*, and so forth.

The following list shows some advantages and disadvantages of an organizational model:

Advantages

- Reflects company organization
- Is easily understood
- Has a natural growth path
- Permits resources to be organized by business function

Disadvantages

- Is difficult to adjust when organizational structures and names change
- Can be politically sensitive
- Is difficult to support as divisions split and merge
- Can be difficult to implement if divisions of the organization have multiple geographical locations

Real World Sites

Sites, provided by the Active Directory service, can reduce or eliminate the problem the organizational naming structure has with divisions that have multiple locations. A company can create a site for each island of computers with local area network (LAN) connectivity. For example, the main office would be one site while a branch office would be another site. Any domains that span more than one site automatically adjust their replication parameters to optimize the use of the slow wide area network (WAN) link between the sites. Clients are also automatically directed to local domain controllers for service requests, further decreasing the use of your WAN links.

The Geographical Naming Convention

Using a geographical naming convention, you model your namespace on the geographical divisions of the organization. For example, with the same root of *microsoft.com*, you might have a first level consisting of *noram.microsoft.com*, *europe.microsoft.com*, *asia.microsoft.com*, *africa.microsoft.com*, and so on. Underneath this first level, you might break each entry down to the individual country or state/province, depending on the size and complexity of your organization.

The following list shows some advantages and disadvantages of the geographical naming convention:

Advantages

- Is apolitical in nature
- Uses names that tend to be persistent
- Offers greater flexibility and granularity

Disadvantages

- Doesn't reflect the nature of the organization
- Might require additional domains to meet security needs

Note Sites can be useful for optimizing the use of slow WAN links on networks using a geographical naming convention. Although there usually aren't any domains that span multiple sites in networks using the geographical naming convention, using sites further optimizes the use of WAN links by tuning interdomain replication of Active Directory.

Mixed Naming Conventions

Finally, you can opt to use a mixture of the organizational and geographical naming conventions, especially in a forest namespace where different corporate cultures have grown up and have their own agendas. The catch, of course, is that this can lead to confusion and make support more difficult because there is no consistency in how things are done. You should make every effort to rationalize the structure of your namespace when you create it. Your overall support job will be easier in the end.

Even if you adopt a purely geographic naming convention across the whole organization, chances are you'll find it advantageous at the lowest level of the tree to create organizational units (OUs) or domains that reflect the different business functions of the organization. This is because groups working in similar areas or on related projects tend to need access to resources of a similar nature. The needs on the manufacturing plant floor are different from those in accounting, for example. These common needs identify natural areas of administrative support and control.

Determining Name Resolution

After defining your naming convention, the second decision you need to make is whether you want the namespace you use internally to be the same as the one you present to the outside world. While your initial expectation might be that they should be the same, there can be compelling reasons for using different internal and external namespaces.

Using the Same Internal and External Namespaces

When you have a single namespace, you and your computers have the same names on the internal network as they do on the public Internet. This consistency means that you get a single name from the appropriate Internet registration authority and you maintain a single Domain Name System (DNS) namespace, although only a subset of the names is visible from outside the company. Your network structure will end up looking something like Figure 3-3.

When you use the same name for internal and external namespaces, you must ensure that the ability to resolve names from outside your company is limited to computers outside your firewall that are supposed to be externally visible. Make sure that no Active Directory servers reside outside the firewall. However, you also need to make sure that your internal computers can resolve names and access resources on both sides of the firewall.

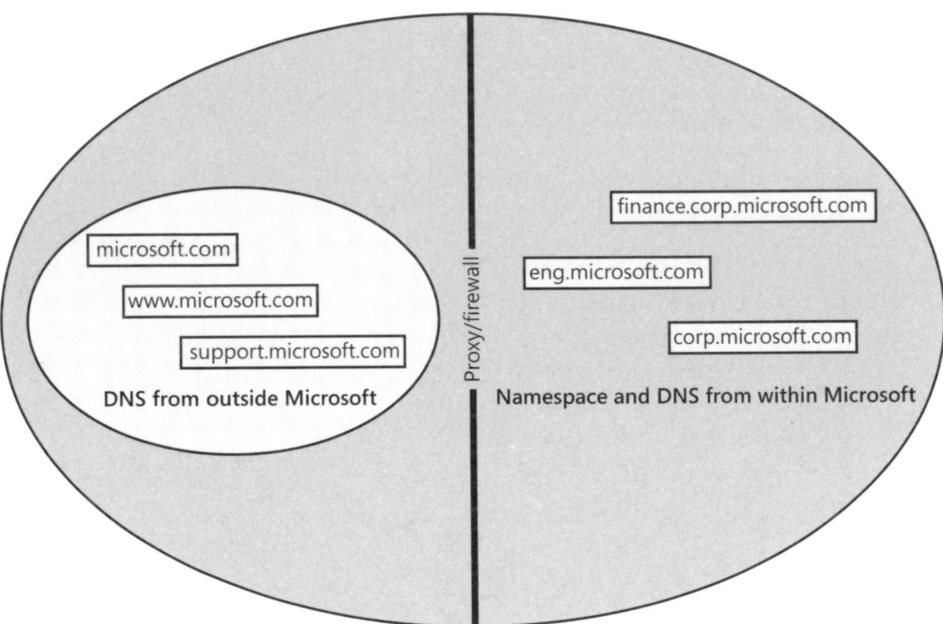

Figure 3-3 With the same internal and external namespace, your DNS must have different zones depending on where the request is coming from.

The following list shows some advantages and disadvantages of using the same internal and external namespace:

Advantages

- Provides consistent naming internally and externally
- Allows single name registration
- Enables users to have a single logon identity and e-mail identity

Disadvantages

- Needs a complex proxy server configuration
- Requires maintenance of different zones with the same names
- Requires users to be aware of the different views they'll have of resources, depending on where they are accessing the resources from

Using Different Internal and External Namespaces

If you set up different internal and external namespaces, your public presence might be *microsoft.com*, while internally you use *msn.com*. All resources that reside outside the company network have names that end in *microsoft.com*, such as *www.microsoft.com*. Within the company network, however, you use a separate namespace that has *msn.com* as its root, as shown in Figure 3-4.

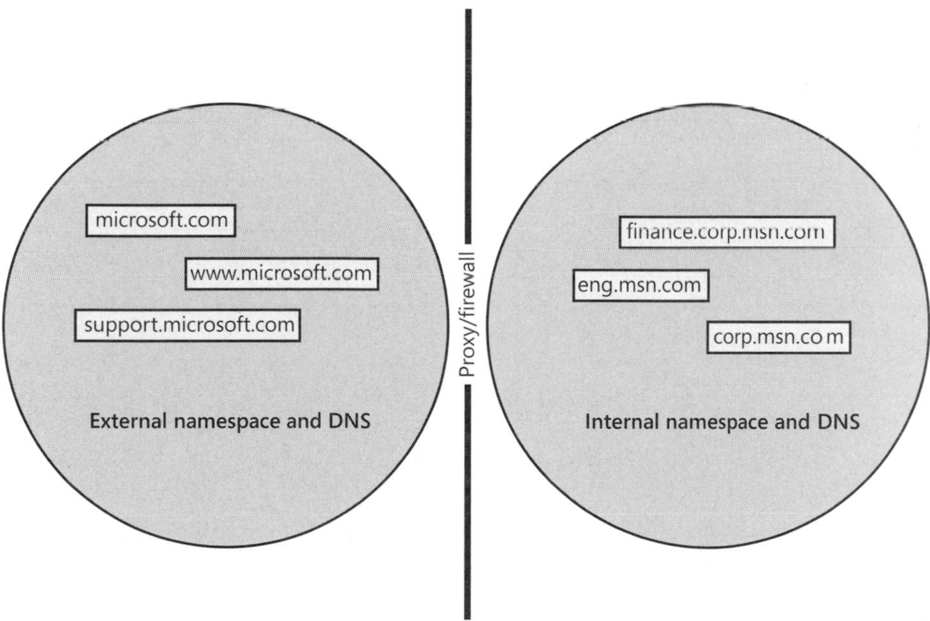

Figure 3-4 Public/private network with separate namespaces.

With different internal and external namespaces, your DNS names for computers that are publicly available are different from those that are visible only from inside your firewall. One consideration with this scenario: you must register both the public and private names with the appropriate Internet name registration authority. You might think you don't need to register the internal-only name because you don't intend to expose it to the public Internet. What you're really doing, however, is making sure that no one else uses the same name because this can cause name resolution problems for your internal clients.

Note One way around the problem of an internal-only name, especially where you might have difficulty gaining control of the domain name because it's legitimately owned by someone else, is to use a nonexistent root domain name for it, such as .lan (for example, *microsoft.lan*). This strategy lets you have an internal name that is appropriate for that portion of the namespace without running into a conflict with someone else's domain name. The default in Windows Server 2008 is to use *.local* as the internal root domain name. In this book, we'll use *example.local* as our primary domain throughout.

The following list shows some advantages and disadvantages of using different internal and external namespaces:

Advantages

- Provides a clear distinction between what is internal and what is external
- Offers easier management and proxy configuration
- Makes it easier for users to understand the differences between the internal and external namespaces

Disadvantages

- Requires that two names be registered
- Means that users' logon names are different from their e-mail names

Planning a Domain Structure

After you settle on the overall design of your namespace, you need to design your domain structure to support it. Each branch of the namespace can be broken down to either a domain or an OU. Whether a branch is a domain or an OU depends on a variety of considerations, including the need for replication, security policy, resource availability, quality of the connection, and so forth.

Domains vs. Organizational Units

Windows Server 2008 network trees consist of domains and OUs. Each provides for administrative boundaries between branches on the tree, but they have different implications and resource requirements.

Domains

The core unit of the Windows Server 2008 Active Directory is the domain, just as it is in Windows Server 2003 and Microsoft Windows NT 4. All network objects exist as part of a domain, and the security policy is uniform throughout a domain. Unlike Windows NT, security in Windows 2000, Windows Server 2003, and Windows Server 2008 is based on Kerberos version 5, and the trust relationships are *transitive*. This means that if domain A trusts domain B and domain B trusts domain C, domain A also trusts domain C.

Planning You can still set up one-way Windows NT 4–style trust relationships. More important, the relationships between Windows Server 2008 domains and legacy Windows NT domains are based on the one-way, nontransitive trust relationships inherent in Windows NT. It is essential that you consider these relationships when planning your domain structure.

Starting with Windows 2000, the concept of a primary domain controller (PDC) and one or more backup domain controllers (BDCs) was finally history. Domain controllers in Windows 2000 and later were multimaster and peer-based. Each controller of a domain had identical authority over the domain, and if any controller went offline, the others continued to administer and authenticate the domain. Any domain controller could originate a change to the domain and then propagate the change to the other domain controllers in the domain.

Notice the past tense? Backup domain controllers have returned, with a new name—Read-Only Domain Controllers (RODC). But the concept is the same—a read-only domain controller cannot originate changes in the Active Directory. We'll talk about Read-Only Domain Controllers Active Directory and domain controllers in more detail in Chapter 16, "Installing and Configuring Directory Services."

Note Although all full domain controllers are created equal in Windows Server 2008, one is more equal than the others if you're still supporting Windows NT computers on your domain (for example, if you're running in a domain or forest functional level that supports Windows NT 4 domain controllers). In this special case, one domain controller emulates the Windows NT 3.*x* and Windows NT 4 primary domain controller (PDC) functionality. By default, the first domain controller in a domain gets this job, but you can transfer the PDC Emulator role to another domain controller if you need to. See Chapter 17, "Managing Active Directory," for more details about this and other Operations Master roles in the domain.

The domain is also the unit of replication within Active Directory. Changes in the domain replicate throughout the domain, even when the domain spans multiple sites or locations. This allows domain controllers at distant sites to originate changes to the domain and have the changes replicated across the domain. Of course, if a remote site has only a read-only domain controller, it can't originate changes.

Although access rights are transitive across domain boundaries, administrative rights are, by default, limited to the domain. You can therefore grant administrative rights to a key user in a particular domain without worrying about compromising the overall security of the organization, because the administrative rights stop at the domain boundary unless explicitly granted to other domains.

Organizational Units

The OU concept was first introduced in Windows 2000. It has some of the characteristics of a domain, but without the resource overhead of one. An OU is contained within a domain and acts as a container for directory service objects. It forms a branch of the contiguous LDAP (Lightweight Directory Access Protocol) namespace, though not necessarily of the DNS namespace, and it can in turn contain other OUs. Thus, the domain *corp.microsoft.com* can contain other domains, such as *finance.corp.microsoft.com*, and it can also contain OUs such as the "hr" OU of *corp.microsoft.com*. Here, the LDAP name would be "OU=hr,DC=finance,DC=corp,DC=microsoft,DC=com", but the DNS name, unless explicitly changed, would still be *corp.microsoft.com*.

The OU provides a convenient administrative boundary, and you can delegate rights and privileges for administration to users in an OU without compromising the rest of the domain. However, an OU does not require a separate domain controller, nor is it involved in replication.

Designing a Domain Structure

After you design your namespace and everyone involved agrees to it, you're ready to start designing and implementing your domain structure. The design of your domain structure will closely match the design of your namespace, though you might make a decision that certain namespace boundaries require only OUs, not full domains. Base your choice between an OU and a domain on whether you need a separate security policy (for example, a policy defining account lockout or password complexity) for the entities within the namespace boundary. If a particular namespace boundary doesn't require a security policy that is different from that of its parent, you'll probably find an OU to be an appropriate division because it requires fewer resources to implement.

Designing a Single-Domain Tree Structure

To create a single, contiguous namespace and therefore a pure domain tree structure, create the domains in hierarchical order, starting at the top of the tree. This top domain is your *root domain* and has either all the users in it (for smaller, single-domain models) or no users at all (if you use a structural domain as the root domain). For those familiar with the Windows NT 4 domain models, this structure roughly corresponds to the "single master" domain model, with one important difference. Users need not, and most often should not, reside in a single-master domain, but should reside in their actual appropriate place in the domain hierarchy.

As you branch down the tree of your namespace, you create domains or OUs for each branch of the tree. The decision about whether to create an OU or a domain controller depends on your overall security model, the quality of the connection to the location, and a variety of other factors, including political considerations from the original namespace planning.

Note The single-tree structure described here is also *forest*—a forest with a single tree in it, but nonetheless a forest.

Designing a Multiple-Domain Tree Structure

The forest-of-trees structure is most often used to accommodate an existing namespace that is noncontiguous and can't easily be made contiguous. You end up with multiple root domains, all on the same level. Below each of these root domains is a contiguous namespace for that tree. Each branch of the LDAP namespace is either a domain (with its attendant requirement of one or more domain controllers) or an OU. You generally create each tree from the top down, and each branch of the tree automatically has a transitive trust relationship with the other branches of the tree.

All trees in a forest share the same schema, configuration, and global catalog, with transitive Kerberos trust relationships among all domains in the forest. The trust hierarchy within each tree follows the DNS naming hierarchy. The trust hierarchy in the forest as a whole, however, follows the order in which trees join the forest, with two-way, transitive trusts created between each pair of trees in the forest. This is transparent to the users but can be modified by the administrator to improve management and referrals.

Domain Security Guidelines

Within each domain, the security requirements, policy, and configuration are consistent. If you need to change the security requirements and policy for a subunit within a domain, create that subunit as a child domain, not as an OU. Keep this limitation in mind as you plan your overall namespace–you need a separate branch of the namespace to have a separate security policy.

What is security policy? What does it entail? Part IV deals exclusively with security matters, so for the moment, here is a summary of what the security policy includes:

- Logon requirements
- Certificates
- Password-aging and minimum-length requirements
- Smart card or other authentication add-ons
- Computer and time-of-day restrictions

Many of these security measures will be the same throughout your organization, but certain areas can require significantly greater security than the rest of the organization. If so, plan for areas that require extra care to be in a separate domain so that their more restrictive security isn't imposed on the entire organization.

Creating Organizational Units

In situations where you don't need to create separate domains for security reasons but you do want to be able to delegate administrative functions, create a separate OU instead of a child domain. Thus, you might have a domain called *noram.example.com* that you want to divide into business units within the region. You can create separate sales, support, education, human resources, manufacturing, and finance domains under *noram.example.com*. However, the overhead of separate domains and their required controllers for each of these units isn't necessary—primarily because they all share a single security policy. So, simply create OUs for each of them. If you later need to convert one or more of them to a domain, you can, though the process is not as simple as it should be.

OUs make useful boundaries for administrative purposes. Various administrative tasks and privileges can be delegated to the administrator for a specific OU, freeing up the domain administrator and giving the OU local control of its own resources.

Planning Multiple Domains

When your organization is complex enough, or simply large enough, that you know you'll have to create multiple domains, spend the extra time up front planning exactly how to implement them. Time spent on the front end will be repaid many times over.

Draw your planned domain structure, and compare it to your planned (or existing) namespace. Decide what simply *must* be a domain and what can comfortably be an OU. Identify which servers are to be your domain controllers. Keep in mind that the concepts of PDC (primary domain controller) and BDC (backup domain controller) from Windows NT are back, at least in part. Domain controllers that are read-only domain controllers can't initiate changes to the domain, but all other domain controllers are treated equally. Changes made to any domain controller that isn't a read-only domain controller are propagated to all other controllers within the domain. If you make simultaneous changes against multiple controllers, Active Directory uses update sequence numbers and the timestamps of the changes to resolve conflicts.

Planning a Contiguous Namespace

When planning a contiguous namespace, and thus a single-tree forest structure, you first create the root domain for the namespace. In this namespace, create the primary administrative accounts but leave the creation of other accounts until later. User and computer accounts should reside in the leaf of the tree where they are going to do the majority of their work. This arrangement is the opposite of Windows NT, where if you were running multiple domains, you often had to create all your user accounts at the highest level of the domain because of the nature of trust relationships.

If you're migrating from an existing Windows NT environment, you might have your users in a single-master or multiple-master domain. You can continue this arrangement, and it might be the easiest way to migrate from an existing environment. See Chapter 6, "Upgrading to Windows Server 2008," for a more detailed discussion about upgrading domains.

Determining the Need for a Multi-Tree Forest

If you already have an environment with multiple root domains–or one without a contiguous namespace–you have to create a multi-tree forest rather than a single forest, single-tree environment.

The first step is to take a long, hard look at your noncontiguous namespaces. Do you see an opportunity to consolidate them into fewer contiguous namespaces? Now is definitely the time to do this. It's much harder to consolidate them later, and you'll have a harder political battle as well.

Creating the Forest

If you decide that you simply have no way to get to a single, contiguous namespace–meaning that you need to create a multi-tree forest–decide exactly where the root of each tree in the forest will reside. Think about the physical locations of your potential domain controllers, the layout of your network, the bandwidth to various sites, and the current existence of Windows NT 4 domains and controllers. After you have a good physical and logical map of your network, you're in a position to plan your domain strategy.

Create your root-level domains first and then start building your trees. This order isn't an absolute requirement–if you miss a tree or something changes, you can go back and add another tree to your forest. However, it's generally better to create the roots first, if only to get your tree-to-tree trusts in order.

Best Practices After you create the root of a tree, you can't easily rename or delete it. In Windows Server 2008, you can change domain names using Rendom.exe, but it's not a task to undertake frequently. So don't rush into settling on a domain structure—planning it in detail will save you headaches in the long run.

More Info For detailed descriptions of Active Directory and how it works, see *Active Directory for Microsoft Windows Server 2003 Technical Reference* by Stan Reimer and Mike Mulcare (Microsoft Press, 2003) or the *Microsoft Windows Server 2003 Deployment Kit* (Microsoft Press, 2003).

Summary

Planning your namespace and domain structure is an *essential* first step to a successful implementation of Windows Server 2008. It's an iterative process that requires careful planning and a clear understanding of the political realities in the organization. A Windows Server 2008 namespace can have a single, contiguous, and hierarchical structure with a forest that is a single tree, or it can be a forest of multiple trees in a noncontiguous namespace. All domain controllers, except read-only domain controllers, within a domain have the same authority over the domain, and there can be multiple OUs within a domain for delegation purposes. In Chapter 4, "Planning Deployment," you continue to focus on planning; in Chapter 5, "Getting Started," you move from planning your installation to actually doing it.

Chapter 4

Planning Deployment

We've worked with system administrators whose idea of deployment is to insert the DVD into the new server and start installing. Well, that's always fun, which is a good thing, since you're likely to be doing it over and over again. In our experience, inserting the DVD (or however you actually do the installation) is the last step in the process. By the time you install, you should have already done all the planning, negotiating, and preparing that are the most important parts of a successful deployment.

Deployment involves a good deal more than merely installing an operating system, even a network operating system. We'll get to the specifics of deployment—application installation and configuration, file and print services, the Active Directory service, communications, security, and other functions—in later chapters. In this chapter, we're going to focus on all the work that you must do before you ever insert that first DVD into a drive—planning the hardware and software infrastructure on which you will base your Microsoft Windows Server 2008 network.

Successful deployment of a network depends primarily on planning. Successful planning, in turn, depends on gathering and analyzing data as well as doing a certain amount of prophesizing and just plain old guessing about what the future of the organization will be. The decisions you make during the early stages of deployment will have your fingerprints all over them, for good or ill. Your vision of the future will prevail for years to come in the operation of the organization, and you'll undoubtedly be held accountable if the vision turns out to be a nightmare. Therefore, the more planning you devote to deployment, the better off everyone will be.

Three elements are essential for an effective Information Technology (IT) strategy:

- An analysis of how your business requirements and IT capabilities match up today. Where is your technological structure adequate, and where is it lacking?
- A projection of your business and IT goals. You need one-year, three-year, five-year, and ten-year plans for business needs, and the IT functionality and services to meet those needs.
- A roadmap that provides a path to your business and IT goals.

This chapter discusses all three of these elements and examines how they are interrelated.

Throughout this chapter, we focus on the what, the why, and the how. We have deliberately avoided suggesting any of the many software applications—either from Microsoft or from third parties—that are designed to help in the process. We'll leave that for the sales folks. We think the most important thing is to thoroughly understand the processes involved. Deciding on tools to help should be part of that process.

How Information Technology Functions

Most people, when talking about IT departments in general, would agree with the statement that the purpose of an IT department is to serve current business needs as well as to advance long-term goals. Some would even agree that the IT department should be a key business *asset*, a business driver and a force for competitive advantage. Unfortunately, when those same people start making decisions about their own IT departments, it often seems like no decisions or thought have taken place at all—the network appears to have sprouted like mushrooms after a rain, without the benefit of anything resembling an overall vision.

Changing the situation is complicated by a number of factors:

- Legacy hardware and software
- Incompatible operating systems and applications that were adopted to solve specific divisional or departmental problems
- Rapidly changing technologies and user requirements
- Resistance to change by those who have grown comfortable with older technologies
- Too little staff, time, and money to plan and execute a network upgrade

This last item is virtually universal. However, if these factors plague your organization, it's time to start struggling against the status quo. The situation can't and won't change overnight, but a carefully thought-out plan with clear priorities can do a great deal to move things forward.

Identifying Business Needs

Identifying business needs is a topic of such scope that it can seem overwhelming. A good place to start is with individual departments or areas. For example, consider the needs of your sales, human resources, and marketing departments. What does each area need to do now, and what services will be of benefit in the future?

Consider basic operations (such as accounts payable and inventory) that have to be taken care of daily, as well as less frequent operations (the launching of a new product). What kinds of flexibility need to be built into the IT systems? What sorts of changes must be anticipated to deal with increased Internet activity or increased access for users in remote locations?

The research you perform into the organization's business requirements can also help you overcome resistance–and there's always some resistance–to changes in the infrastructure. As people participate in your research and share your understanding of the organization's current issues and opportunities, more of them will come to have a personal stake in supporting your Windows Server 2008 deployment.

Getting Specific

Start with a list, ranked in order of importance, of enterprise functions that are necessary to meet your organization's business goals. That list should include the following:

- A total cost of ownership (TCO) analysis identifying potential areas where upgrades to the IT infrastructure can result in cost reductions
- A return on investment (ROI) analysis identifying the financial opportunities that can result from upgrades to the IT infrastructure
- Additional business that can result from the infrastructure upgrade
- Potential risks from not updating the IT infrastructure

These are complicated issues with much overlap, so you might have to construct this list more than once. Depending on the size of your operation, it might be easier to subdivide the list into manageable bites, each one of which constitutes a project of its own, with the sum of these smaller lists creating an overall planning and justification framework for the entire organization.

Seeing into the Future

To make your network successful, you need to take a high-level look at where your organization will be in one, three, five, and even ten years. Will the organization become more centralized or less? Will it expand geographically, or will it contract? Will you have more knowledge workers who require the free flow of information on networks to do their jobs? Will you need to deal with "boundaryless" workers who spend time in the office but also telecommute, belong to virtual teams, or even work in their clients' offices? Workers with such needs can make the usual means of information distribution completely inadequate. How will these workers get what they need? How will you balance conflicting demands for access and security?

Computer networks themselves are subject to rapid change because the experience of working on a network changes users' perceptions of what is possible and consequently their view of what is needed. When it becomes possible to have access to real-time sales figures or inventory counts, the demand for access grows rapidly.

Even modest changes can have a substantial impact on your IT infrastructure. By anticipating changes and planning for them, you ensure that your network can evolve to meet future needs.

Assessing Current Systems

It's a rare company that has a complete inventory of its hardware and software. It's an even rarer company that knows the rate at which its hardware and software infrastructure changes. You can't meet grand goals for the future without knowing the facts about the present. Even if you're sure you want to go to Chicago, you don't have much hope of getting there unless you know whether you're currently in Savannah or Seattle. The sections that follow detail the steps for analyzing what you have so that you can determine what you need and how to implement changes.

Documenting the Network

Knowing what hardware and software you have deployed and *how that equipment is being used* is vital when designing your network and determining the best way to implement it. After all, you're probably not tearing out the entire current network and replacing it with brand new, state-of-the-art equipment. (And if you are, that's not as easy as it sounds either.)

Instead, you'll likely be phasing out or repurposing legacy hardware and software over a period of weeks, months, or even years. During this time, the existing hardware and software will still have to be supported. A careful and thorough audit of your existing network can be of great use in determining where potential problems (and opportunities) lie.

The Organizational and Physical Infrastructure

Make a drawing of the physical network, including workstations, servers, routers, wiring closets, and hubs. This picture will clarify where the network can be expanded (and where it can't), what the best traffic routing is, and whether servers and other hardware are optimally placed. At the same time, an organizational chart showing all members of the IT staff and the responsibilities assigned to each one can help clarify lines of communication and show where they might be lacking. Make sure that all critical tasks are assigned at every site, organizational unit (OU), or location. You don't want to establish a server at a remote location and have no one there who can manage anything beyond a reboot.

Traffic Patterns

Gather network traffic reports to determine the optimum placement of routers, hubs, and switches; bandwidth requirements for workstations and workgroups; and future needs for network management software. Network analysis utilities are available to help you determine your overhead (or background) network traffic. Traffic patterns are also important in determining appropriate wide area network (WAN) connectivity speeds or the speed to be used on risers connecting floors in a building.

Network Addresses

As you upgrade the network using Active Directory, you'll probably be assigning new network names to most of the nodes on the network. Add the node addresses to the hardware drawing you made earlier so that you can analyze what addresses to assign and what steps will be necessary to make the transition from the old naming system to the new one.

Operating System Connectivity

Many networks are connected to other systems such as UNIX. You'll need to determine what tools are necessary to maintain the connectivity you want or migrate these platforms to Windows Server 2008. In addition, hardware placement–routers, switches, and gateways–can all be critical to optimum connectivity and may need upgrading as well.

> **Note** Windows Server 2008 includes Network File System (NFS) client and server components for UNIX connectivity, along with the Subsystem for UNIX Applications (SUA) that facilitates the migration of UNIX applications to Windows. See Chapter 27, "Interoperability," for more details.

External Connectivity

Just as most companies don't know what hardware they have, many networks have undocumented external connectivity. Most companies know about their Internet, WAN, and fax services, but often there are completely undocumented telephone lines used for dial-up networking or remote network management, and often there are undocumented (and usually unauthorized) wireless connections. Document *all* connections. Do a thorough sweep for rogue wireless access points. Now is the time to get them under control.

Existing Network Operating Systems

Documenting the operating system on each server and workstation on the network is an essential ingredient to a successful operating system upgrade or migration. You'll need to determine what the upgrade or migration must support and what preparatory steps are needed.

Existing Applications and Services

You'll need an inventory of all the software running on all servers and workstations. When you have this list, take a closer look at both the typical and the atypical resource requirements for each program. For example, a particular program might generate a modest amount of traffic most of the time except for weekly downloads of 200 MB from a WAN server, and the accounting department's requirements are vastly different at year end than they are in midquarter. Where applications are running on servers or operating systems that you will be migrating, make sure that you understand the migration path for the application as well as the operating system.

In addition, subdivide and classify the inventory of applications and services into the following categories:

- **Strategic** Software and services that are essential to business operations and that have the most relevance to current and future goals.
- **Tactical** Applications and services that are valuable to the business but are not providing optimal benefit.
- **Legacy** Software and services that are still used by some groups or departments but are nearing the end of their useful life. Your plan must call for removing these components before they fall into the obsolete category.
- **Obsolete** Applications and services that are not beneficial to the business and also are a hindrance. The goal of IT is to remove these elements as soon as possible.

Every component belongs in one of these categories, and making the assignments can clarify your thinking and help give shape to your plan. Don't attempt to make the assignments in a vacuum, however. Involve the parts of the organization that use an application or service in the process. This is especially important if you think the application is either a legacy or obsolete application. An important part of the process of helping your users let go of those legacy applications is getting them to understand where the application fits in the overall strategic direction of the organization and getting them involved in finding a better way to solve the problem that the legacy application is there to solve.

Legacy applications are especially good candidates for virtualization. As you identify applications that fit into this category, think about how you could effectively combine and rationalize the servers that are supporting them to virtualize them.

Server Load

You'll need your physical inventory of the servers on your network to also include the effective load of the servers. This will help you identify candidates for virtualization and server consolidation. By consolidating workloads onto under-utilized servers, and moving other workloads onto virtualized servers, you can significantly reduce your overall management load and make more effective use of your resources. Windows Server 2008 includes new virtualization capabilities that are covered in Chapter 29, "Working with Windows Virtualization."

Making a Roadmap

A study commissioned by Microsoft several years ago identified six characteristics of successful IT departments. None of these conclusions is startling, but they bear repeating. Companies with successful IT departments will do the following:

- **Make IT a business-driven line function, not a technology-driven staff function.** In other words, the function of the technology people must be firmly connected to business strategies and the everyday work that advances these strategies.
- **Base technology funding decisions on the same considerations as any other corporate expenditure.** Cost/benefit and ROI analyses must be as much a part of every IT investment decision as they are in the decision to buy a new building.
- **Insist on simplicity and flexibility throughout the technology environment.** Reduce the number of technologies and platforms deployed, and aim for maximum flexibility and ease of implementation.
- **Demand near-term business results from development efforts.** Incremental project rollouts are preferred, as is packaged software over custom software wherever possible. When custom development is necessary, focus on the 20 percent of the functionality that typically adds 80 percent of the value.
- **Drive constant year-to-year operational productivity improvements.** Measure performance against internal and external benchmarks and standards, and strive for constant improvements.
- **Aim for an IT department that is smart about business and a business organization that is smart about IT.** Simply stated, in the better-performing companies the IT and business organizations work together. They speak the same language, talk to each other, and understand each other's capabilities and needs.

These are all grand statements that are difficult to argue with in the abstract but hard to implement in the real world. However, we all have to start somewhere, and keeping these aims in mind and working toward implementing them can only benefit the enterprise overall.

After you analyze your present situation as well as the business goals you need to achieve, the next step is to design a roadmap that will take you where you want to go. The roadmap will include a definition of the goals, a risk assessment, and an implementation plan.

Defining Goals

Your deployment goals must be specific, achievable, and measurable. That bears repeating: deployment goals *must be specific, achievable, and measurable.* Spell out the problems that have to be solved and how you will address constraints such as end-user requirements, costs, schedules, and reliability.

Your plan must then address specifically what you want to accomplish at each stage and how you will measure whether you have done what you set out to do. When deploying Windows Server 2008 in a particular department, approach the task as a vendor to that department. At a minimum, you need to do the following:

- Determine who has to agree to the scope of the project and who can sign off at the end of it.
- Determine the scope of the project: what needs to be installed, what needs to be configured, and what the users need to be able to do at the end of the project. Involve as many people in the department as possible.
- Reach an agreement as to what will constitute completion of the project. For example, a project might be considered complete when all workstations are connected to the network with specified software installed, all users can log on, and data can be retrieved under all conditions in *n* seconds or fewer. Again, be specific and be measurable.
- Define a method that will test all areas of the project. Get a sign-off on the method. Allow ample time for testing. Regular, short-loop testing as you go will save much time and aggravation later.
- When the project is complete, get a sign-off that it is in fact complete. Address additions and changes that were not in the original scope as a new project—a different phase of the deployment. It's very important that every stage have a point of closure.

Some of these steps seem obvious, but it's surprising how often people have no idea whether their upgrade to the system has actually accomplished anything and, if it has, whether the results are what was wanted and needed. All too often the IT people go away dusting off their hands and congratulating themselves, while the actual "customers" are far from satisfied.

Real World The Endless Project

In our early days in the IT world, we worked on a migration project that went horribly wrong. A large company that had been almost exclusively using mainframes and had virtually no IT infrastructure or experience outside of mainframes decided to roll out personal computers to every department. At the same time, they were installing a large enterprise software suite that would change how virtually every process in the company was performed. The software suite was dependent on those personal computers, as well as new UNIX database servers.

While the list of problems and lessons to be learned from the fiasco that resulted could fill an entire book, the real lesson was about goals and scope. Rather than building out the project in stages, with a thorough and well-thought-out test and verification plan at every stage, the project was scoped to do the entire company essentially at once, with no clear and agreed-upon end points that could allow sign-off. As a result, the project never really finished. It ended up way over budget, with unhappy users, unhappy IT staff, and unhappy management—and an expensive and poorly thought-out infrastructure that has never met the needs of its users. Don't let your project be like this one. Do what it takes to make sure that you control scope at each stage of the project, and that your goals are specific, achievable, and measurable for each stage, with a clear and unambiguous end point that *realistically* meets those goals.

Assessing Risk

You can't predict everything that can go wrong in a deployment, but you can be sure that something will. Typical problems include sudden changes in business needs or user requirements, costs running higher than expected, and the almost inevitable schedule slippage.

You can manage risks proactively or reactively. Anticipating and preventing a problem is obviously better than reacting to trouble after it pops up. Take time to identify your resources and responses to each risk you identified. Then do the same for the risks that you haven't identified ahead of time—because there will surely be something you didn't anticipate. It might be the new server tripping a circuit breaker that you didn't realize was overloaded or a legacy application that everyone forgot about but that is still running a critical part of the business. It might even be a key member of your team accepting a job offer two weeks before the implementation date. You won't know what this unanticipated problem is until it's already on top of you. But if you take the time to identify your resources and responses, you'll still be better off than if you're caught totally by surprise and haven't spent some time thinking through what to do.

Few things can hurt you more during deployment than a poorly thought-out schedule. A schedule that considers risks can go a long way toward minimizing the likelihood of serious problems. The following precautions will help you minimize schedule-related perils:

- **Develop high-risk components first.** Any areas that are already an ongoing tangle—such as messaging or your Web server—must be developed first and independently. New components that haven't been part of your network before must also be tested separately and understood completely before you install them where they can affect critical operations.
- **Include a fudge factor for unforeseen circumstances.** Nothing ever works exactly as you expect. The "five-minute install" turns out to require a change in hardware to work correctly. The quick change of hardware requires a half-hour of configuration. Estimate how much time each stage of deployment will take, and then double it.
- **Update the project plan and schedule.** When circumstances change and milestones are reached, notify everyone involved in the project by updating and distributing the plan and schedule. If you find yourself two days behind after the first stage of the deployment, don't just plan on working faster to catch up. Instead, update the plan and determine whether the delay is due to a defect in the plan (and therefore likely to multiply over time) or merely a one-time failing. Optimism is a fine quality, but being realistic is more important.

More Info Risk management is a complex subject, but highly important for IT staff to understand, particularly in the area of network security. Microsoft's Security Risk Management Guide provides expert advice in this area. You can download it from *http://www.microsoft.com/downloads/details.aspx?FamilyID=c782b6d3-28c5-4dda-a168-3e4422645459&displaylang=en.*

Summary

These first chapters have no doubt given you lots to think about—and certainly plenty to do. Nevertheless, no matter how much groundwork you lay, you must eventually put some of your plans into practice—if only to see how you can improve them. Part II starts with the next chapter, where you will begin the process of actually installing and configuring Windows Server 2008.

Part II
Install and Configure

Chapter 5

Getting Started

Installing Windows interactively is a time-consuming task on a single system; installing Windows interactively to five computers is a mind-numbing experience; installing twenty servers interactively is just plain stupid. Actually, we'd argue that installing more than one or two servers manually is a less than intelligent use of your time. In this chapter, we'll cover the basics of how to install Windows Server 2008—and how to automate some or all of that process to make your life easier.

Reviewing System Requirements

Before attempting to install Windows Server 2008, you should carefully review the system requirements to ensure that your computer hardware meets the minimum levels required. Table 5-1 shows the official minimum requirements for Windows Server 2008 for a new, fresh installation onto "bare metal"—along with our commentary on those minimum requirements.

Table 5-1 Windows Server 2008 Hardware Requirements

Hardware	Requirements	Comments
Processor	32-bit – 1GHz 64-bit, x64 – 1.4 GHz 64-bit, Itanium – Itanium 2	2 GHz or greater is more realistic.
RAM	512 Mb	1 GB of RAM is a more realistic minimum. 2 GB is recommended. For Server Core, 1 GB of RAM is normally sufficient for typical infrastructure workloads.

Table 5-1 Windows Server 2008 Hardware Requirements

Hardware	Requirements	Comments
Disk	10 GB	No less than 40 GB of hard disk space on the system drive, please. And if your server has greater than 16 GB of RAM, increase the minimum to at least 50 GB.
Optical Drive	DVD-ROM	A CD-ROM drive is no longer sufficient, though it's still technically possible to get special CD-ROM–based installation media. For network installations, no optical drive is required.
Video	800 x 600	1024 x 768 is a more realistic minimum. Some screens will be difficult to use at a resolution below 1024 x 768.
Other	Keyboard and Mouse	
Network	Not required	Who are they kidding? A supported network card is required for joining a domain or almost anything you'll want to do with Windows Server 2008.

Notice what is *not* on the list of required hardware–a floppy drive! Finally, in Windows Server 2008, we can get rid of the floppy requirement, even if we need to load drivers for our hard disk controller. Drivers can now be loaded from CD or DVD, from a USB flash drive, or from floppy disk.

Real World 64-Bit and Signed Drivers

A major change in Windows Server 2008 is the requirement for signed drivers in all 64-bit versions. This requirement means that you *must* do your homework and make sure that your vendors provide full support for their hardware in 64-bit Windows Server 2008. We've continued to be surprised at the slow response from even major vendors to providing signed 64-bit drivers, so if you need to use hardware cards or peripherals that aren't part of the server you ordered from your server vendor, be sure to verify the availability of a supported, signed driver for that hardware card or peripheral before installing a 64-bit version of Windows Server 2008.

If a driver isn't available, your only options are to either find an alternative hardware vendor that does provide a driver, or run a 32-bit version Windows Server 2008 that does have a driver. Personally, we're choosing to change hardware vendors where we find deficiencies in 64-bit driver support. And we're telling our old hardware vendors exactly why we're dropping them, too.

Designing a Deployment Environment

Unless you are performing a single installation of Windows Server 2008, it is helpful to design a deployment environment that allows you to deploy Windows efficiently to the client and server systems in your organization. The following sections discuss how to design a deployment environment that provides the deployment speed and control you need while maintaining an acceptable level of complexity.

Choosing an Installation Method

Windows installation is now entirely image-based. Rather than copying individual files to the hard drive of the target computer, the new Windows Server 2008 installation uses Windows Image (WIM) files to put a complete image of Windows Server 2008 on the system disk of the target server. And this image-based installation is the same whether you're using a local DVD or installing over the network using Windows Deployment Services (WDS).

The move to an image-based install has several advantages, including:

- Actual installation times are noticeably shorter, regardless of the source of the install.
- Adding or removing Windows components doesn't require access to the original install media—all the files are already on the server.
- Deployment of pre-patched images, or images with custom sets of drivers, is simplified.

When you deploy Windows Server 2008 to one or two servers, it is easy to use standard DVD media and just do the install. If this is an upgrade installation, jump ahead to Chapter 6, "Upgrading to Windows Server 2008." If you're installing onto a new server and using standard DVD media read, "Installing Windows Server 2008" later in this chapter. For details on using Windows Deployment Services to automate the deployment of Windows Server 2008, read "Automating Server Deployment" later in this chapter.

Installing Windows Server 2008

Installing Windows Server 2008 from standard distribution media onto a clean server with no operating system on it requires just seven screens at the very beginning; the entire rest of the installation will complete without further interruption. You don't need to enter any network information, computer name, domain name, or any other information except the actual Product Identification (PID) code associated with the installation and the language to install.

Under the Hood PID-less Installs

Windows Server 2008 normally requires you to enter a PID for installation. But you can simply skip entering the PID and then you'll have to select exactly which version of Windows Server 2008 you're installing. You'll get a couple of extra prompts and warnings, but if you only want to run a demonstration or evaluation environment for 60 days or less, just skip entering the PID. You'll have a fully functional Windows Server 2008 installation for those 60 days. And you can even extend the 60 days twice for an additional 60 days each time using the *slmgr -rearm* command.

If you decide to convert a server installed without a PID to a fully activated Windows Server 2008 server, you need to enter a PID for the *exact* same version of Windows Server 2008 that you said you were installing when you initially installed. That means if you used retail media to install the server, you must provide a retail key. If you selected Windows Server 2008 Standard, you need to provide a retail Windows Server 2008 Standard key. You can't change which version is installed without completely reinstalling Windows Server 2008.

To enter a product key for a server installed without a PID, use the *slmgr.vbs -ipk* command.

Use the following steps to install Windows Server 2008 onto a bare server using standard DVD media:

1. Turn on the server and immediately insert the Windows Server 2008 DVD for the architecture Windows Server 2008 you want to install. If the primary hard disk hasn't got a bootable operating system on it, you'll go directly into the Windows Server 2008 installation process. If the disk has a bootable operating system on it, you might be prompted to Press Any Key To Boot From CD Or DVD. If so, press a key.
2. When the initial Install Windows screen shown in Figure 5-1 appears, select the language and other regional settings to use for this installation.

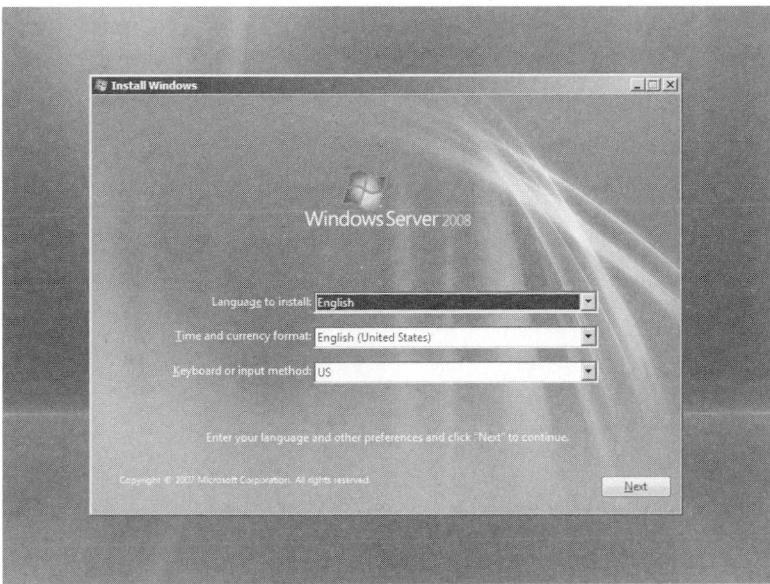

Figure 5-1 The initial page of the Install Windows Wizard

3. Click Next to open the page shown in Figure 5-2. From here you can choose to repair a corrupted Windows Server 2008 installation or get additional information before installing.

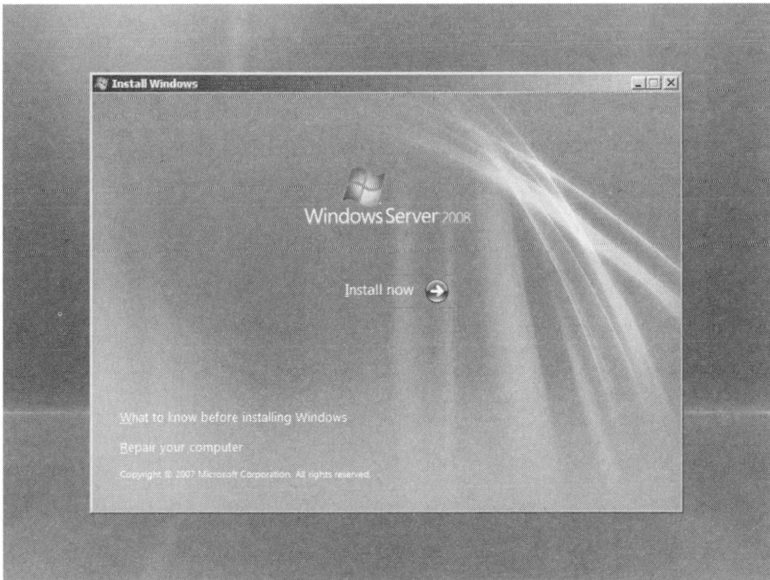

Figure 5-2 The Install Now page of the Install Windows Wizard

4. Click Install Now to open the Type Your Product Key For Activation page of the Install Windows Wizard, as shown in Figure 5-3.

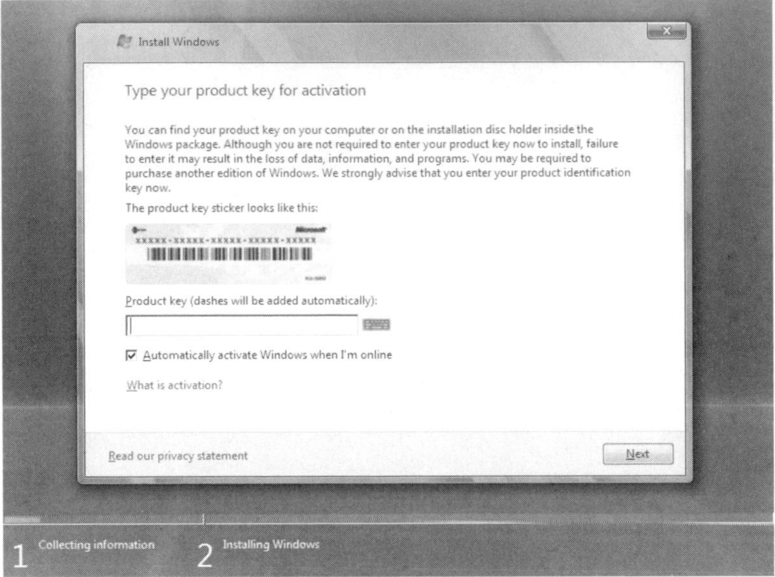

Figure 5-3 The Type Your Product Key For Activation page of the Install Windows Wizard

5. Enter a product key for this installation of Windows Server 2008. (See the Under The Hood sidebar for information on installing without entering a product key.)

6. Leave the Automatically Activate Windows When I'm Online check box selected unless you need to control when activation occurs.

7. Click Next to open the Select The Operating System You Want To Install page of the Install Windows Wizard, as shown in Figure 5-4. If you're installing without entering a product key, you'll see a much longer list of possible versions.

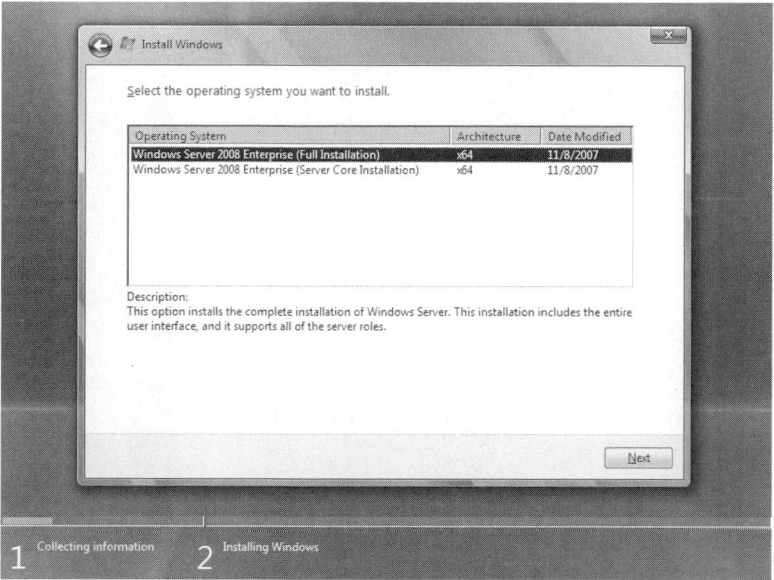

Figure 5-4 The Select The Operating System You Want To Install page of the Install Windows Wizard

8. Select either Full Installation or Server Core Installation. This selection is irrevocable: You can't change an installation at a later time from Full to Server Core, or from Server Core to Full. (For details on installing and configuring Windows Server 2008 Server Core, see Chapter 9, "Installing and Configuring Server Core.")

9. Click Next to open the Please Read The License Terms page. Select I Accept The License Terms. You don't have a choice—either accept them or the installation terminates.

10. Click Next to open the Which Type Of Installation Do You Want page. The only choice when you boot from a DVD is Custom (Advanced), so click that to open the Where Do You Want To Install Windows page shown in Figure 5-5.

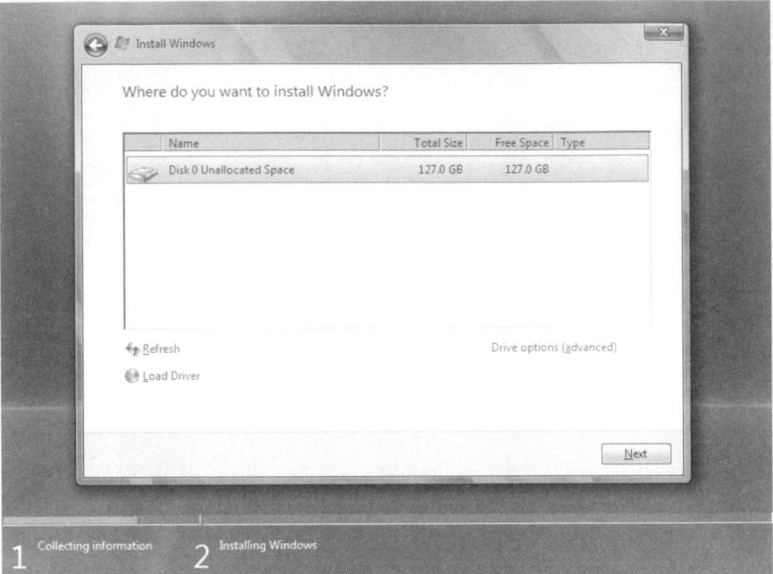

Figure 5-5 the Where Do You Want To Install Windows page of the Install Windows Wizard

11. The first disk on your computer will be highlighted. You can select any disk shown, or if the disk you want to install on isn't displayed, you can load any required driver at this point by clicking Load Driver. Clicking Drive Options (Advanced) will give you additional options to repartition or format the selected drive.
12. When you've selected the drive to install on, click Next and the installation will begin. You won't be prompted again until the installation completes and you're prompted for a password for the Administrator account.

Under the Hood **Drive Options**

The default selected drive when you're installing Windows Server 2008 is the first drive as enumerated by the BIOS. You can change the selection if the drive you want isn't selected, or add drivers for additional controllers if the drive you want isn't visible. For those familiar with earlier versions of Windows, you'll be glad to know that Windows Server 2008 *finally* adds support for something besides a floppy drive for loading storage drivers during installation! As shown in Figure 5-6, you can load drivers from floppy disk, from CD or DVD, or from a USB flash drive.

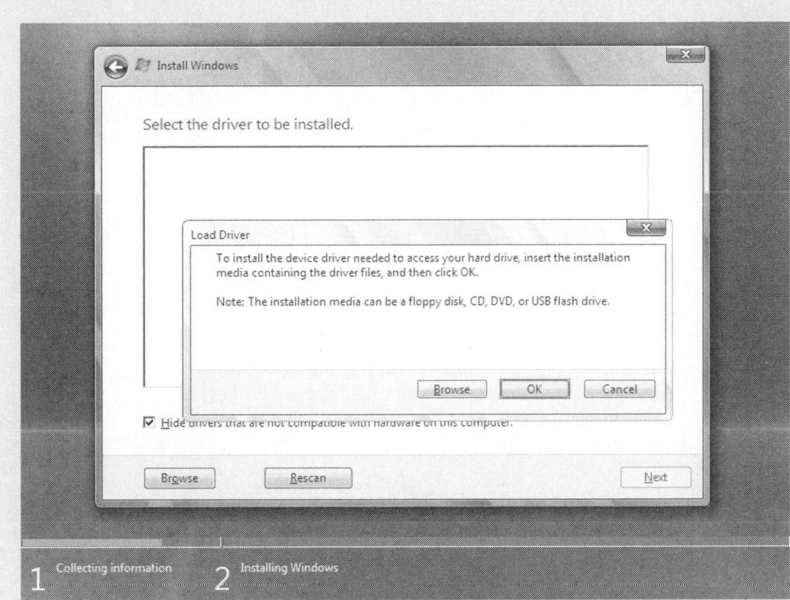

Figure 5-6 Windows Server 2008 supports loading storage drivers from floppy disk, optical drive, or USB drive.

If you need to change partitions on a drive, format it, or even extend it to add additional space, just click Drive Options (Advanced) to display additional options for managing and configuring your disks during installation, as shown in Figure 5-7.

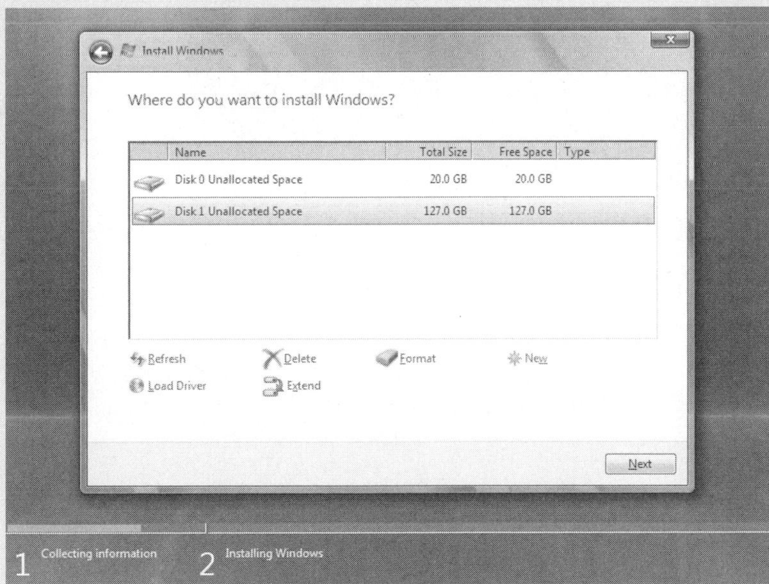

Figure 5-7 Advanced Drive Options are available during installation of Windows Server 2008.

An important addition to the capabilities of the Windows Server 2008 installation process is the ability to extend a partition. While this is not a feature that matters in completely new installations, it can be a useful feature if you're recycling a computer. You can extend a partition onto available unallocated space on the same disk.

Note If you need to open a Command Prompt window during the installation process, just press Shift+F10. Now you can manually run Diskpart.exe or any other tool available at this point in the process to manually load a driver or fine-tune partitioning.

After the installation completes, Windows Server 2008 will restart and proceed to the logon screen. You'll need to enter a new password for the Administrator account, as shown in Figure 5-8, and then log on to new server.

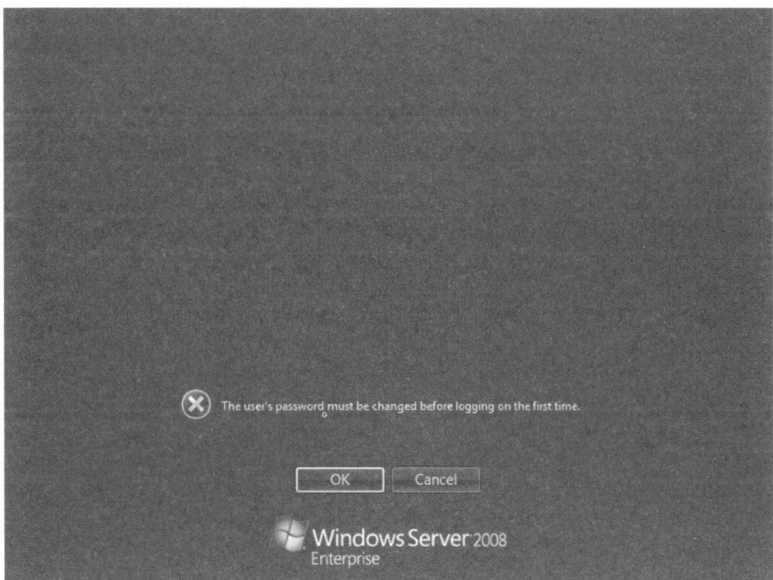

Figure 5-8 Setting the initial password for the Administrator account

After you log on you'll see the Initial Configuration Tasks Wizard, which makes the initial setup of your new server easy. See Chapter 7, "Configuring a New Installation," for all the information on this wizard and the other initial steps in configuring a server.

Server Core Installations

An exciting change in Windows Server 2008 is the ability to install in Server Core mode. This minimal interface version of Windows Server 2008 has fewer available roles and features, and few graphical features. It installs into a noticeably smaller hard disk space, and has a smaller memory overhead. But most important, it presents a smaller attack surface, making it more secure. Also, because it has fewer running services and fewer installed components, ongoing maintenance and updates (and the risks associated with them) are reduced. For complete details and scripts for installing and configuring Server Core, see Chapter 9.

Default Settings in Initial Configuration

Because the installation of Windows Server 2008 asks fewer questions during the process, it has to set some defaults that you will later configure using the Initial Configuration Tasks Wizard. Table 5-2 lists those initial defaults.

Table 5-2 Initial Installation Defaults

Setting	Default Value
Time Zone	GMT-8 (Pacific Time, US/Canada)
Networking	DHCP configured
Computer Name	Generated name
Domain/Workgroup	WORKGROUP
Automatic Updates	Not configured
Windows Error Reporting (WER)	Off
Customer Experience Improvement Program (CEIP)	Not participating
Roles	None
Features	None
Remote Desktop	Disabled
Windows Firewall	On

Automating Server Deployment

If you're installing one or two servers, using a DVD and sitting at the console to do it probably makes sense—especially if you're not also setting up for a big client deployment. But if you've got a dozen servers to install and configure, you're not going to want to do that sitting at the console. You want a way to automate the installation.

Real World Standardizing IT

We've heard it said many times that you can't standardize information technology. Simply not true. And if you want to have any hope at all of getting your IT processes under control, you need to start standardizing them. Well-documented methodologies for standardizing many of the processes of IT are available, including the Information Technology Infrastructure Library (ITIL) and Microsoft Operations Framework (MOF). And if you don't know what these are, it's way past time to start reading about them. A useful place to start is the white paper "MOF: An Actionable and Prescriptive Approach to ITIL," available for download at *http://www.microsoft.com/technet/solutionaccelerators/cits/mo/mof/mofitil.mspx*.

Deployment is one of the most obvious places to start standardizing. By utilizing the tools in Windows Server 2008, you can create standard images of both servers and clients to deploy automatically.

A key advantage to automating deployment is that each automated deployment is assured of being the same, simplifying ongoing maintenance and updating.

The mechanism for automating deployments in Windows Server 2008 is the Windows Deployment Services (WDS) role. WDS is an extension and enhancement to the Remote Installation Services (RIS) of earlier versions of Windows Server.

Under the Hood Changes from RIS

While WDS is built on RIS, it offers many advantages and changes. The changes from RIS to WDS on Windows Server 2008 include:

- Support for Windows Vista and Windows Server 2008 deployments
- Support for Windows PE as a bootable operating system
- Support for Windows Image (.wim) format files
- Support for multicast deployment
- A new graphical interface

WDS is available on Windows Server 2003, but has a somewhat more limited feature set. There is no support for multicast deployment, the TFTP server is more limited, and reporting capabilities are also more limited.

Windows Deployment Services has three different sets of components:

- **Server Components** A new Trivial File Transfer Protocol (TFTP) server, an improved Pre-Boot Execution Environment (PXE) server, and the image repository.

- **Client Components** A graphical interface that runs as part of the Windows Pre-Installation Environment (Windows PE).
- **Management Components** The various tools used to manage the WDS server and its components. This includes both the graphical Wdsmgmt.msc console, and the command-line Wdsutil.exe utility.

Installing and Configuring WDS

The Windows Deployment Services role is installed with the same Add Role Wizard as other Windows Server 2008 server roles. There are two Role Services to choose from: Deployment Server and Transport Server. Install only the Transport Server if you want to do multicasting but don't want the full WDS feature set. For most situations, you'll want to install both, however.

Installation Steps

To install the Windows Deployment Services role, follow these steps:

1. Open Server Manager if it isn't already open.
2. Highlight Roles in the left pane and select Add Roles from the Action menu to open the Add Roles Wizard.
3. Click Next to open the Select Server Roles page, as shown in Figure 5-9.

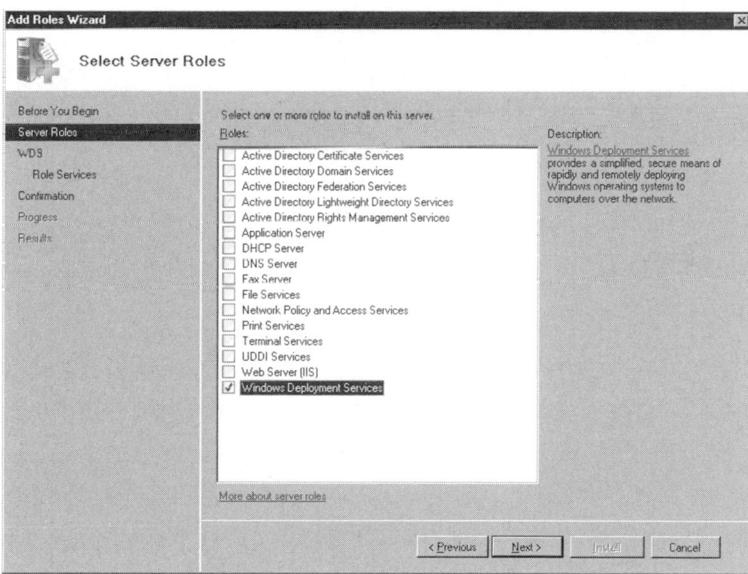

Figure 5-9 The Select Server Roles page of the Add Roles Wizard

4. Select Windows Deployment Services and click Next to open the Overview of Windows Deployment Services page. From this page you can read some basic information on the requirements for WDS and links to documents on configuring and managing WDS.
5. Click Next to open the Select Role Services page, as shown in Figure 5-10. For most installations, select both Deployment Server and Transport Server Role Services.

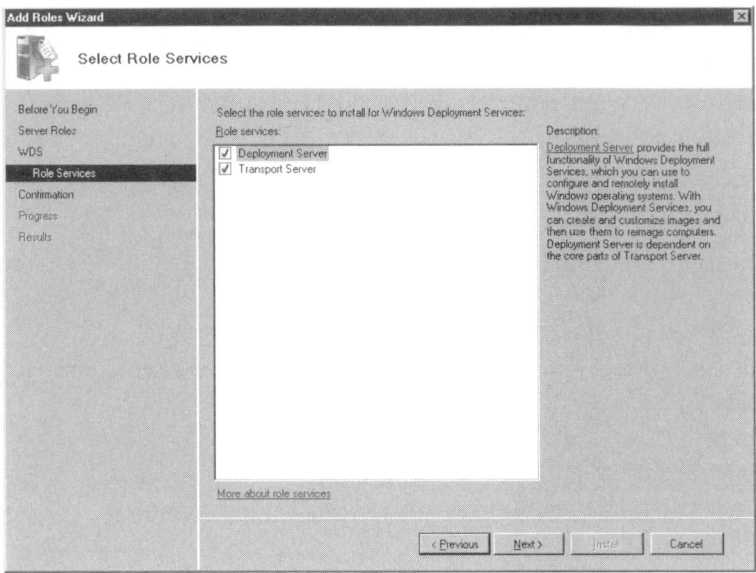

Figure 5-10 The Select Role Services page of the Add Roles Wizard

6. Click Next to open the Confirm Installation Selections page.
7. Click Install to begin the installation, and click Close when the installation completes.

Initial Configuration

Once WDS is installed, it still needs basic configuration before it is enabled. You need to do initial configuration and add images to use for deployment before the Pre-boot Execution Enviroment PXE server gets enabled and WDS is actually ready to deploy operating systems. Follow these steps to configure WDS to deploy Windows Server 2008 versions:

1. Open the Windows Deployment Services console if it isn't already open.

Note The command line to open the Windows Deployment Services console is *Wdsmgmt.msc*.

2. Select the server that you want to configure, as shown in Figure 5-11, and then select Configure Server from the Action menu.

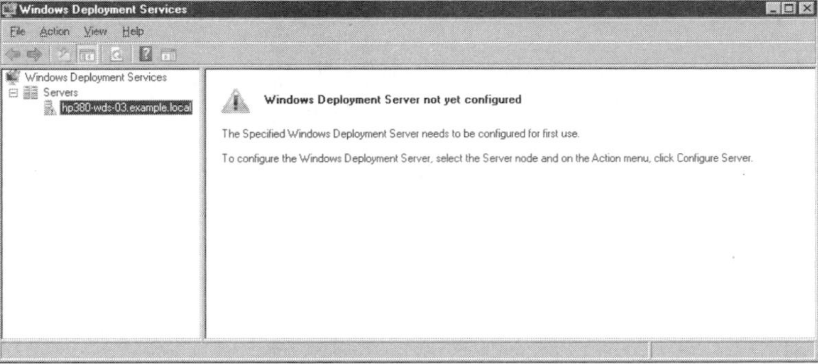

Figure 5-11 The Windows Deployment Services console

3. On the Welcome Page of the Windows Deployment Services Configuration Wizard, read the minimum requirements for WDS.

4. If your environment meets the minimum requirements, click Next to open the Remote Installation Folder Location page, as shown in Figure 5-12. Enter the location to store images or click Browse to find the location.

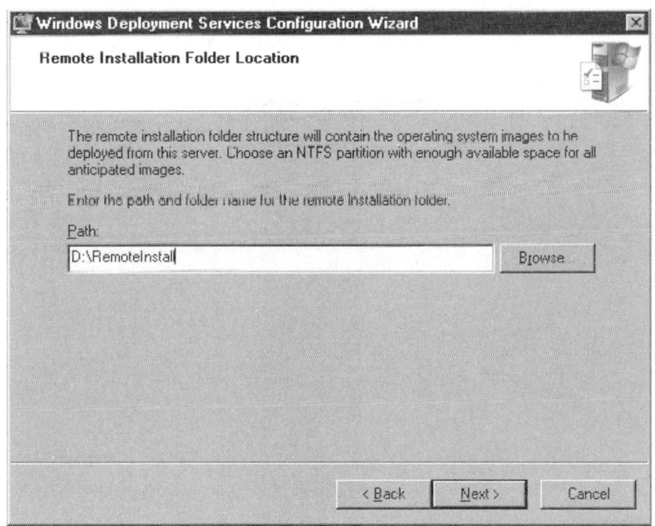

Figure 5-12 The Remote Installation Folder Location page of the Windows Deployment Services Configuration Wizard

5. Click Next to open the PXE Server Initial Settings page shown in Figure 5-13. The default is to not respond to PXE requests, which doesn't make a whole lot of sense. Select Respond Only To Known Client Computers if you intend to pre-stage computers in Active Directory. Select Respond To All (Known And Unknown) Client Computers if you don't plan to pre-stage clients. If you don't pre-stage, you can set WDS to require approval of unknown clients. (Known clients–those pre-staged in Active Directory Users and Computers– will not require approval.)

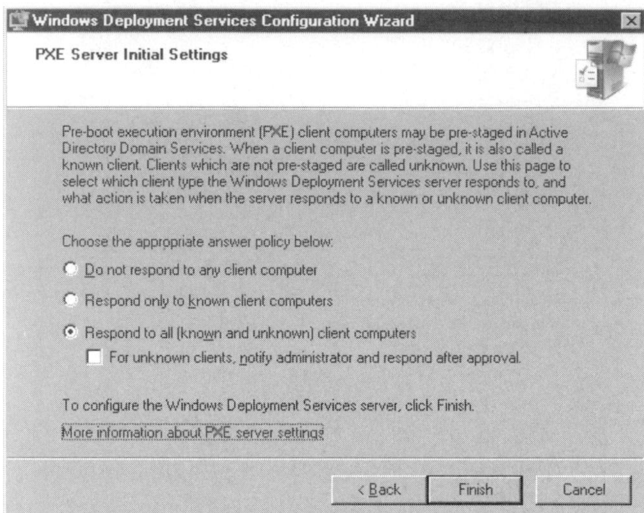

Figure 5-13 The PXE Server Initial Settings page of the Windows Deployment Services Configuration Wizard

6. Click Finish to open the Configuration Complete page of the Windows Deployment Services Configuration Wizard, as shown in Figure 5-14.

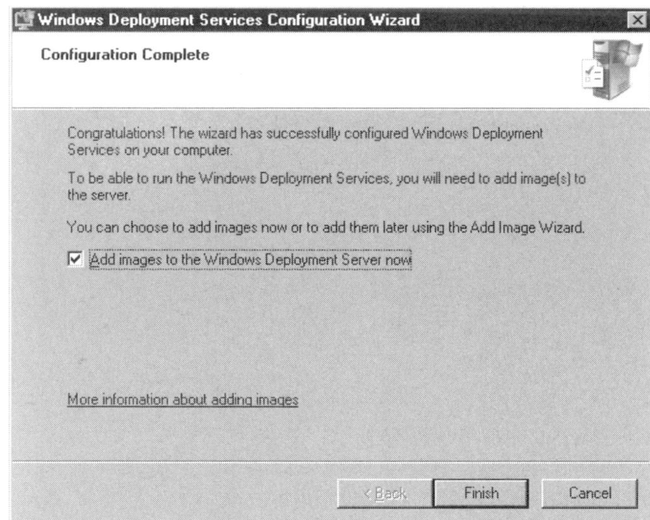

Figure 5-14 The Configuration Complete page of the Windows Deployment Services Configuration Wizard

7. Select Add Images To The Windows Deployment Server Now, and click Finish to open the Add Image Wizard.

8. On the Windows Image Files Location page, shown in Figure 5-15, enter the location of Windows images to use. This location must be a local drive or directory.

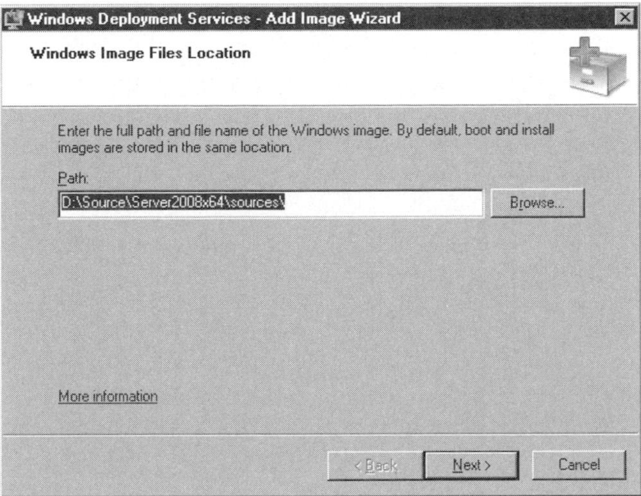

Figure 5-15 The Windows Image Files Location page of the Windows Deployment Services – Add Image Wizard

The location of Windows Server 2008 and Windows Vista install and boot images is in the Sources subdirectory of the installation media.

9. Click Next to open the Image Group page. Enter a descriptive name for your first image group. (The default isn't terribly useful.)
10. Click Next to open the Review Settings page, as shown in Figure 5-16.

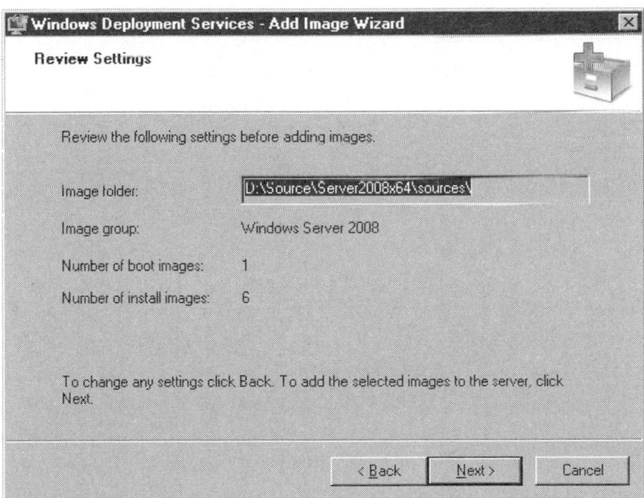

Figure 5-16 The Review Settings page of the Windows Deployment Services – Add Image Wizard

11. Click Next to begin adding the images. When all the selected images have been added, click Finish to complete the wizard.

Setting Additional Properties

Once you've done basic configuration of your WDS server, you can fine-tune the settings for the server by opening the Properties dialog box in the Windows Deployment Services management console. The following sections describe the eight tabs in the Properties dialog box:

General

- No settings available, but shows basic information on the server, including name, installation folder, and deployment mode.

PXE Response Settings

- PXE Response Policy.
- Do Not Respond To Any Client Computer.
- Respond Only to Known Client Computers.
- Respond to All (Known and Unknown) Client Computers.
- For Unknown Clients, Notify Administrator And Respond After Approval.
- PXE Response Delay (In Seconds). The default is zero.

Directory Services

- New Client Naming Policy. This has a frankly silly naming default based on the user name. You'll want to change that for server deployments.

> **Important** The maximum length of a computer name is 15 characters. Up to 63 characters can be generated by the default policies, which generates issues when trying to join the domain. Choose a naming convention that ensures that all names are 15 characters or fewer.

- Client Account Location. The domain or OU where client computer accounts are created.

Boot

- Default Boot Program (Optional). Allows you to specify a boot program different from the default for each architecture.
- Default Boot Image (Optional). Allows you to specify a specific default image for each architecture.

Client

- Enable Unattended Installation. When checked, allows fully unattended installation using unattend XML files.

- Client Account Creation. Allows you to disable automatic joining to the domain.

DHCP

- Use to configure DHCP if it's running locally on the WDS server.

Network Settings

- Multicast IP Addresses. Specify DHCP if your DHCP server supports it, or specify the IP address range for multicast. (The default value is 239.0.0.1 – 239.0.0.254.)
- UDP Port Range. The default value is 64001 – 65000. Don't change it.
- Network Profile. Set this to match the speed of your network.

Advanced

- Options Used By This Windows Deployment Services Server. Allows you to specify domain controllers and global catalog servers (not recommended) or allow WDS to dynamically discover them.
- DHCP Authorization. Select whether to authorize the WDS server as a DHCP server.

Adding Additional Images

The initial configuration allows you to specify images to use in WDS, but you can add additional images for different architectures and different operating systems. Or specify images that include preinstalled applications and server roles that you want to use across a range of WDS clients.

Adding Standard Images

To add standard operating system images with no special customizations or default behavior, you can follow these steps:

1. Open the Windows Deployment Services console if it isn't already open.
2. Expand the server name of the WDS server you want to add images to in the left-hand pane, and select Install Images (to add new installation images) or Boot Images (to add a new boot image).
3. For a boot image, select Add Boot Image from the Action menu. For an installation image, select the Image Group you want to add the image to and then select Add Install Image from the Action menu.
4. On the Image File page of the Windows Deployment Services – Add Image Wizard, shown in Figure 5-17, browse to the image you want to add, select it, and click Open to return to the Image File page.

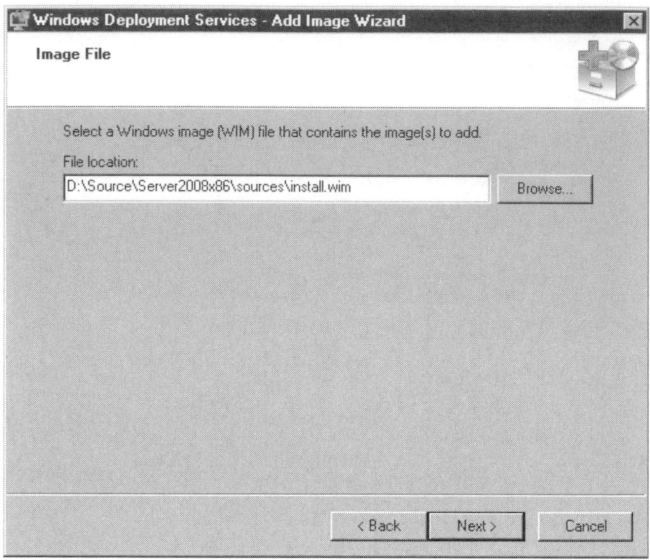

Figure 5-17 The Image File page of the Windows Deployment Services – Add Image Wizard

5. Click Next to open List of Available Images page. Clear any images that you don't want to install.

6. Click Next to open the Summary page. If everything looks as you expected, click Next to add the image and then click Finish when the wizard completes.

Creating a Capture Image

A capture image is a boot image that allows you to create an image of a specific computer, enabling you to create custom deployment (install) images. To create a capture image, follow these steps:

1. Open the Windows Deployment Services console if it isn't already open.

2. Expand the server name of the WDS server you want to add images to in the left-hand pane, and select Boot Images.

3. Highlight the boot image you want to use to make your Capture Boot Image and select Create Capture Boot Image from the Action menu to open the Create Capture Image Wizard shown in Figure 5-18.

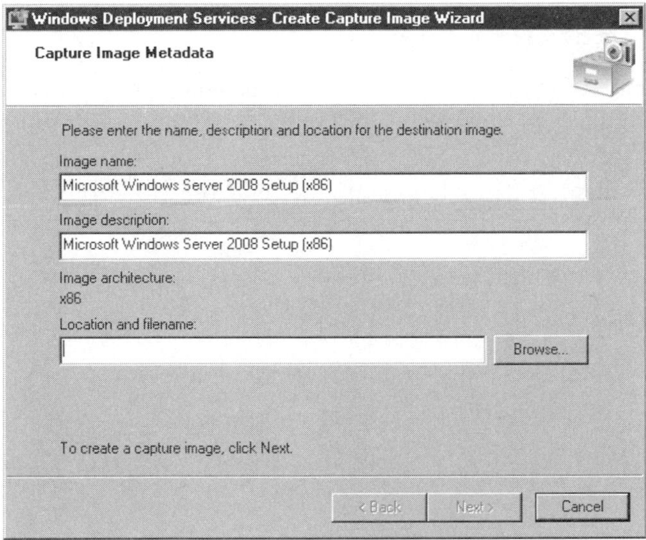

Figure 5-18 The Capture Image Metadata page of the Create Capture Image Wizard

4. Fill in the fields on the Capture Image Metadata page and click Next.
5. Click Finish when the capture image is complete.
6. Highlight Boot Images and select Add Boot Image from the Action menu.
7. Browse to the capture image you just created and click Next.
8. Follow the instructions of the Add Image Wizard to complete the capture.

> **Note** To avoid issues with duplicate names and SIDs on the network, you need to use Sysprep.exe to prepare computers that are used to capture images from. An unsupported alternative to Sysprep is Newsid.exe, available for download at *http://www.microsoft.com/technet/sysinternals/Utilities/NewSid.mspx*.

Adding Custom Images

After you've created a custom install image, you can use the same procedures to add it to your deployments as any other image. This image can include preinstalled drivers for custom network cards, and pre-installed applications, simplifying the distribution and deployment of standard server images.

Troubleshooting Installations

Installing Windows Server 2008 is a relatively painless if somewhat boring process. However, when the installation fails for some reason or another, life gets less boring. Most installation errors are caused by hardware failures or incompatibilities, so standard troubleshooting techniques for hardware problems apply. Some of the more common issues we've seen include:

- Failure to boot from a network distribution point
- Corrupt file during installation
- Failure to find a hard disk
- Stop errors

In the following sections we'll cover each of these problem scenarios and how to resolve them.

Failure to Boot from a Network Distribution Point

When installing Windows Server 2008 from a network distribution point, you're depending on the PXE code of network card to connect to the distribution share and download the Windows Pre-Installation Environment boot environment onto the server, and from that environment to copy down the bootable Windows Server 2008 image you've chosen for the server. All of this depends on your networking environment, and on drivers for the hardware in the server you're trying to deploy to. Some of the possible problems include:

- Failure to connect to the PXE Server.
- Failure to load WinPE.
- WinPE can't connect to the distribution server.
- Image corruption.

Let's look at each of these to identify possible causes.

Failure to Connect to the PXE Server

The most common cause of a failure to connect to the PXE server is that the PXE boot code isn't enabled in the BIOS. The quick check for this is to see if your network card is trying to boot, as shown in Figure 5-19. While each network card has a slightly different display as it attempts to PXE boot, they all are essentially similar. If you don't see this screen, check your BIOS settings on the computer and verify that network boot is enabled.

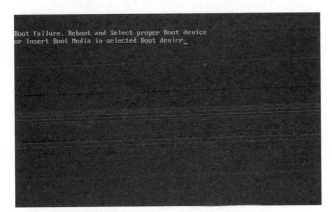

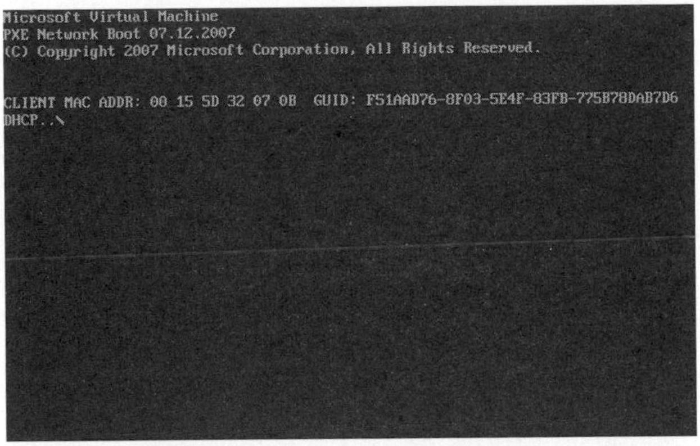

Figure 5-19 A network boot attempt to connect to a PXE server

A second possibility is a connectivity problem with the PXE server: It's trying to boot from the PXE server but doesn't succeed, as shown in Figure 5-20. This could be a network cabling issue, or a problem with the PXE server itself. Check network connectivity and verify that the PXE boot server is working correctly.

Figure 5-20 A failure to boot from a PXE server

Failure to Load WinPE

After the PXE client on the network card of your new computer connects to the PXE server, it will download the necessary files to boot WinPE. No hard disk is involved: WinPE loads entirely into memory. If the computer begins downloading WinPE, but then fails to successfully load it, check for network issues. It's also possible that there's a problem with the memory on the computer, but this is less likely to show up here than at other stages in the process.

WinPE Can't Connect to the Distribution Server

After WinPE is loaded on the new computer, the next task is for it to connect to the Windows Deployment Server and download the appropriate Windows Server 2008 image onto the hard disk of the new computer. If it can't connect to the WDS server, the most likely cause is a missing network card driver in WinPE. You'll need to create a custom boot image that includes the necessary network card drivers, or use a different network card.

Image Corruption

Another possible failure scenario is that all the networking steps and WinPE steps appear to work correctly, and the Windows Server 2008 image starts downloading from the WDS server, but either fails during the download or fails when the new computer attempts to reboot into the downloaded image. This can be caused by a bad image on the WDS server or by networking issues that cause corruption during the image download. Network image distribution is an intense process that stresses the networking components at all stages of the path from the WDS server to the computer that is being deployed, and a failure or weakness at any stage of the process can cause a corruption. Verify your networking components and check for updated network card firmware from the manufacturer.

Corrupt File During Installation

Even when you are installing from a DVD, a corrupt image is a possible failure scenario. The likelihood of a defective Microsoft DVD is relatively small, but it can happen, and damage to the DVD can also render it unreadable. If a DVD has been burned from a downloaded .ISO image, a bad download or a bad DVD burn are both possibilites, and both can cause a corrupt image. Another possible failure that can manifest itself as a corrupt or missing file during the installation is a bad memory module. If you get an error during installation from a DVD, try the following:

1. If the DVD is a production DVD, attempt the installation with a different DVD.
2. If the DVD is a self-burned DVD, replace it with a production DVD, or attempt to re-burn the image at half the speed of the failing DVD.
3. If the DVD is a self-burned DVD, and a re-burn at half speed doesn't resolve the problem, re-download the .ISO file.
4. If none these options works, verify that the cables inside your server's case are properly seated. Replace the DVD drive with a different drive.
5. Run a thorough memory test.

Real World CRC Verification of Downloads

Cyclic Redundancy Code (CRC) is a method of uniquely identifying a file. Many download sources provide a CRC checksum that can be compared against the downloaded file on your local hard disk. You'll need a CRC tool to execute against the downloaded file. There are many free CRC tools available, including CRC305.exe, which is available as a download to MSDN and TechNet subscribers in the Tools, SDKs, and DDKs section of Subscriber Downloads.

The CRC305 tool supports checking both image files and the actual CD/DVD disk. Whenever you use a self-burned DVD, we strongly recommend verifying the CRC value when the reference CRC is known. In our experience, corrupt DVD images, either from a bad download or a badly burned DVD, are the most common cause of installation failures of Windows Server 2008.

Failure to Find a Hard Disk

During installation, Windows Server 2008 inspects your computer and tries to find a hard disk that it can install to. If it can't find a hard disk, it doesn't have the necessary driver for your disk controller, and you'll be prompted to provide a driver during the installation, as shown in Figure 5-21.

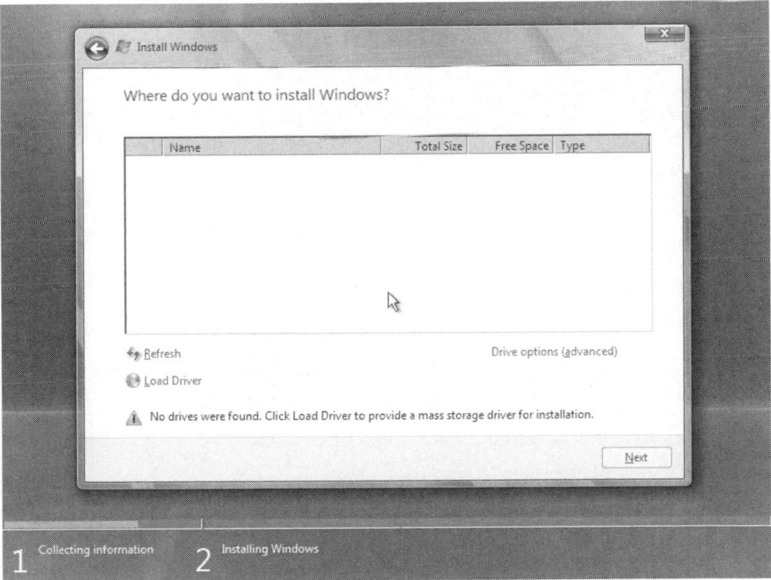

Figure 5-21 The Install Windows Wizard prompts you to load a driver when no drives are found.

Windows Server 2008 supports loading drivers from a USB storage device, a CD or DVD disk, or a floppy disk. This is a huge improvement over earlier versions of Windows Server that would only support loading mass storage drivers from a floppy disk.

You can also use this technique if you have multiple mass storage devices on your computer and the one you want to install Windows Server 2008 on isn't shown in the list of drives available.

Stop Errors

A fatal error during the installation of Windows Server 2008 can sometimes cause the server to reboot unexpectedly and repeatedly. The error generated is called a *stop error* and each kind of error has a different code, allowing you to troubleshoot the cause of the error.

If the stop error flashes by too quickly on the screen and the computer automatically reboots, you can force Windows to not automatically restart on a failure. As the system is restarting, press F8 immediately as it starts to boot to access the Advanced Boot Options page shown in Figure 5-22.

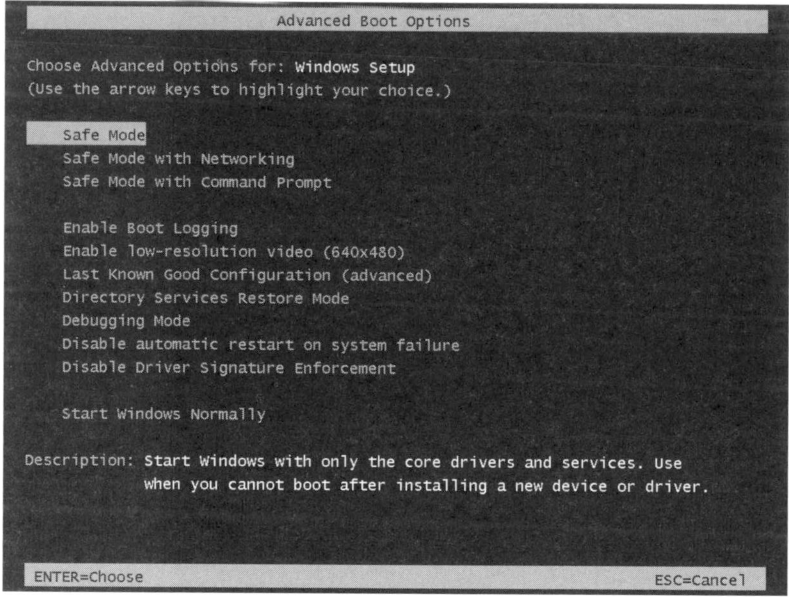

Figure 5-22 The Advanced Boot Options page

Select Disable Automatic Restart On System Failure and then continue the boot process. Now when the system fails it will stop at the failure screen and you can write down the stop error and search for it.

Summary

In this chapter we've covered installing Windows Server 2008 to a new computer, either by booting from an installation DVD or by using a PXE boot image and deploying across a network. Windows Server 2008 uses an image-based installation and provides the Windows Deployment Server as a built-in Server Role to allow for both standard and custom network deployments.

In the next chapter we'll cover the process of upgrading an earlier version of Windows Server to Windows Server 2008.

Chapter 6

Upgrading to Windows Server 2008

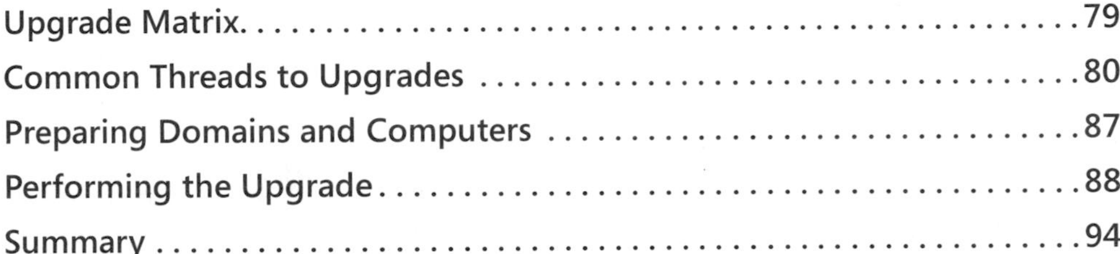

The easiest way to install Windows Server 2008 on a computer and still preserve existing domain information, programs, and computer settings is to perform an upgrade installation. This process is easy for 32-bit member servers and stand-alone servers, but when domain controllers are involved, or you have to change architectures, you need to do some advance planning.

Upgrade Matrix

The general rule is that you can upgrade from a computer running any edition of Windows Server 2003 to the equivalent edition of Windows Server 2008. You cannot, however, change architectures during the upgrade. And there is no direct upgrade support for Itanium systems–you'll need to do a clean installation. Table 6-1 shows the specific supported paths.

Table 6-1 Upgrade Paths for Windows Server 2008

Current operating system	Supported upgrade
Windows Server 2003 Standard Edition (SP1)	Windows Server 2008 Standard (Full)
Windows Server 2003 Standard Edition (SP2)	Windows Server 2008 Enterprise (Full)
Windows Server 2003 R2 Standard Edition	

Table 6-1 **Upgrade Paths for Windows Server 2008**

Current operating system	Supported upgrade
Windows Server 2003 Standard x64 Edition (SP1) Windows Server 2003 Standard x64 Edition (SP2) Windows Server 2003 R2 Standard x64 Edition	Windows Server 2008 Standard (Full, x64 Architecture) Windows Server 2008 Enterprise (Full, x64 Architecture)
Windows Server 2003 Enterprise Edition (SP1) Windows Server 2003 Enterprise Edition (SP2) Windows Server 2003 R2 Enterprise Edition	Windows Server 2008 Enterprise (Full)
Windows Server 2003 Enterprise x64 Edition (SP1) Windows Server 2003 Enterprise x64 Edition (SP2) Windows Server 2003 R2 Enterprise x64 Edition	Windows Server 2008 Enterprise (Full, x64 Architecture)
Windows Server 2003 Datacenter Edition (SP1) Windows Server 2003 Datacenter Edition (SP2) Windows Server 2003 R2 Datacenter Edition	Windows Server 2008 Datacenter (Full)
Windows Server 2003 Datacenter x64 Edition (SP1) Windows Server 2003 Datacenter x64 Edition (SP2) Windows Server 2003 R2 Datacenter x64 Edition	Windows Server 2008 Datacenter (Full, x64 Architecture)

As you can see from the table, there is no upgrade path to Server Core, only full editions of Windows Server 2008. And you can upgrade only to the exact same architecture as you are currently running.

Common Threads to Upgrades

Before we get started on the details of how to actually perform an upgrade, there are a few common threads that affect most environments. The basic issues that need to be planned for ahead of time are:

- Pre-upgrade steps
- Architecture
- Active Directory
- Hardware support
- Software support

In the following sections we'll discuss these issues to identify and plan for in your environment before and during an upgrade of an existing server.

Pre-upgrade Steps

First and foremost, before you upgrade any server, do a full, complete, and verified backup. We don't care what you use for a backup program or a backup media. But whatever you choose, be certain that you have verified the backup by restoring—either by restoring the entire backup to identical hardware or by restoring files from the backup to a test area of the original server. If you haven't tested your backup, it simply doesn't count as a verified backup. And what you're about to do could easily result in the need to completely rebuild the server from bare metal.

We've done quite a few upgrades during the writing of this book, and we've not had a single catastrophic failure yet. But we still make sure we have a verified backup. A verified backup is especially important if you have critical line of business applications that would be a major problem to reinstall and restore data to.

So you've got a verified backup. What other steps do you need to take before you attempt your upgrade?

- **Convert FAT Volumes** Windows Server 2008 will install only onto an NTFS partition. FAT volumes are still supported for non-system disks, but are strongly discouraged.
- **Free Disk Space** You will need at least 10 GB of free disk space on the system volume that you're upgrading. Frankly, we think that a minimum of 20 GB of free space is a more realistic minimum.
- **Update Firmware** It's a good idea to update the firmware on your server to the latest revision. Older firmware can have compatibility issues with Windows Server 2008 that are resolved in more current releases of the firmware
- **Obtain Updated Drivers** Obtaining updated drivers is especially important for x64-based servers. Windows Server 2008 supports only digitally signed drivers for x64 versions of Windows Server 2008.
- **Disconnect UPS Devices** The automatic detection mechanism of Windows Server 2008 can cause problems with the UPS automatic shutdown mechanisms. You can reconnect the UPS serial cable after the installation is complete.
- **Disable Antivirus Software** Virus-protection software can interfere with any installation, and with Windows Server 2008 upgrades even more than most. At the very least, antivirus software will make the upgrade much slower, and it is highly likely to cause a failure of the upgrade. Do not re-enable your antivirus software until you have verified that it supports Windows Server 2008.

- **Prepare Your Active Directory** If you're upgrading a domain controller, you'll need to ensure that the Active Directory has been properly prepared. See the section on Active Directory later in this chapter.

Architecture

The vast majority of Windows Server 2003 servers are running 32-bit versions of Windows Server 2003. However, many of these servers, if purchased within the last two years, are fully capable of running an x64 version of Windows Server 2008. There are significant advantages to using x64 versions of Windows Server 2008, including support for more RAM (32 GB in the x64 version of Windows Server 2008 Standard, and 2 TB in the x64 versions of Windows Server 2008 Enterprise and Datacenter). If you've got an x64-capable server running Windows Server 2003, and you have 64-bit signed drivers for all your hardware, now is a good time to make the shift to 64-bit. We think you'll find x64 versions of Windows Server 2008 faster, more stable, and more secure than 32-bit versions in many cases.

Real World x64 and Signed Drivers

Why all this emphasis on making sure you have digitally signed drivers if you're installing an x64 version of Windows Server 2008? Because Microsoft decided that with the release of Windows Server 2008, they would neither support nor allow unsigned drivers to run in kernel mode on any x64 version of the operating system. Even if you've been running an x64 Edition of Windows Server 2003, you need to verify that you have updated digitally signed drivers or you will experience problems.

We think this shift is a very good thing indeed, and will make Windows Server 2008 a more secure and stable operating system. It will still be possible for an OEM to write a bad driver, and digitally sign it, but at least you'll be certain that all the drivers running on your system are signed and come from who they claim to come from.

We actually think Microsoft should have considered imposing this requirement on existing 32-bit servers that are being upgraded to Windows Server 2008, but we also understand the screams of anguish that would have caused, and the problems it could create for the huge installed base of existing 32-bit servers. And with a clear statement from Microsoft that this is the *last* version of Windows Server that will have 32-bit versions, the decision makes some sense. However, it just further emphasizes our position that existing 32-bit Windows Server 2003 installations that can support x64 versions of Windows Server 2008 should be converted now.

Active Directory

Windows Server 2008 Active Directory requires a new version of the AD schema if any of your Windows Server 2008 servers will be domain controllers. Before attempting to add the Active Directory Domain Services role to a Windows Server 2008 in your existing Windows 2000 or Windows Server 2003 AD, you need to prepare the forest (and possibly the domain) to accept the new Windows Server 2008 domain controller. If you are not installing the AD DS role on any of your Windows Server 2008 computers, you do not need to upgrade the schema.

To upgrade the Active Directory schema to support a Windows Server 2008 domain controller, you need to follow these steps:

1. Log on to the server hosting the Schema Master Flexible Single Master Operations (FSMO) role. You must log on with an account that is a member of the Schema Admins security group.

   Note For a quick PowerShell way to identify the current FSMO role owners, see the Under The Hood sidebar titled "Using PowerShell to Find the FSMO Role Owners."

2. Copy the contents of the \sources\adprep folder on the Windows Server 2008 DVD to the server.

   Note You must use the same architecture version of adprep as the server version hosting the schema master role. So if your current schema master is on a 32-bit Windows Server 2003, copy the files from a 32-bit version of Windows Server 2008 installation media.

   Note Adprep is a one-time tool and can be run directly from the DVD if desired.

3. Open a command prompt window.
4. Navigate to the folder where you copied the contents of the adprep folder.
5. Run the following command:

   ```
   Adprep /forestprep
   ```

6. For environments in which you will be installing a read-only domain controller (RODC), also run the following command:

   ```
   Adprep /rodcprep
   ```

7. When the operation has completed and replicated, you can continue to prepare the domain to support a Windows Server 2008 domain controller.
8. Log on to the server hosting the Infrastructure Master FSMO role for the domain you are preparing. You must log on with an account that is a member of the Domain Admins security group.
9. Copy the contents of the \sources\adprep folder on the Windows Server 2008 DVD to the server.

> **Note** You must use the same architecture version of adprep as the server version hosting the schema master role. So if your current schema master is on 32-bit Windows Server 2003, copy the files from a 32-bit version of Windows Server 2008 installation media.

10. Open a command prompt window.
11. Navigate to the folder where you copied the contents of the adprep folder.
12. Run the following command:

```
Adprep /domainprep /gpprep
```

13. When the operation has completed and replicated, you can add a Windows Server 2008 domain controller to your existing domain.

Under the Hood Using PowerShell to Find the FSMO Role Owners

There are lots of ways to find the FSMO roles, but one of the easiest is to use PowerShell to ask. The following can be run interactively from the command line, or included in a script, and can be run from any computer in the domain that has PowerShell on it.

```
# ScriptName: Get_FSMO_Owners.ps1
$Forest =
    [system.directoryservices.activedirectory.forest]::getcurrentforest()
$Domain =
    [system.directoryservices.activedirectory.domain]::getcurrentdomain()

$Forest | format-list SchemaRoleOwner, NamingRoleOwner
$Domain | format-list PDCRoleOwner, InfrastructureRoleOwner, RIDRoleOwner
```

The result of running this script is seen in Figure 6-1.

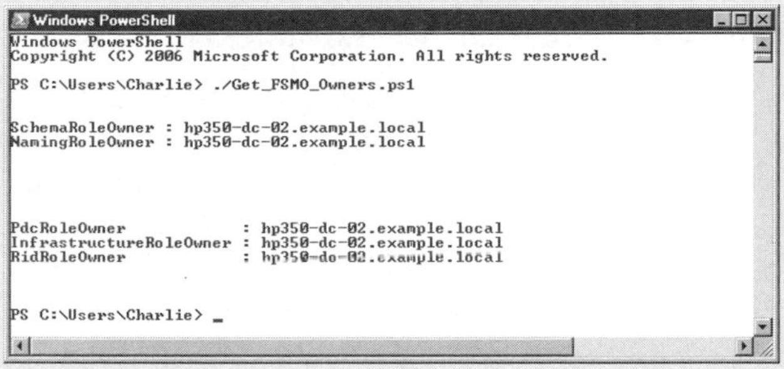

```
Windows PowerShell
Windows PowerShell
Copyright (C) 2006 Microsoft Corporation. All rights reserved.

PS C:\Users\Charlie> ./Get_FSMO_Owners.ps1

SchemaRoleOwner : hp350-dc-02.example.local
NamingRoleOwner : hp350-dc-02.example.local



PdcRoleOwner                : hp350-dc-02.example.local
InfrastructureRoleOwner : hp350-dc-02.example.local
RidRoleOwner                : hp350-dc-02.example.local

PS C:\Users\Charlie> _
```

Figure 6-1 Using PowerShell to get the current FSMO role holders

Hardware Support

Windows Server 2008 supports three different architectures: 32-bit x86, 64-bit x64, and 64-bit ia64. Each architecture has separate drivers and supported hardware. You can't use drivers for one architecture on another architecture. Furthermore, there are significantly greater limitations on supported hardware for ia64 systems, with no support for most consumer- or client-oriented hardware or features, such as sound cards or wireless adapters. Windows Server 2008 for Itanium-Based Systems is designed solely for very large-scale server applications.

As already stated, x64 versions of Windows Server 2008 support only digitally signed drivers for all hardware. Before attempting to upgrade an x64 Edition of Windows Server 2003, ensure that you have signed drivers for all critical hardware on the server.

If your existing server is running a 32-bit version of Windows Server 2003 and supports only 32-bit Windows Server 2008, you should still verify that there are updated drivers for any critical hardware on the server. The minimum supported processor is an x86 processor of at least 1 GHz processor speed, and the minimum RAM required is 512 MB. These numbers are significantly higher than those for Windows Server 2003, which required only a minimum of a 133 MHz processor and 128 MB of RAM. If your existing Windows Server 2003 server doesn't have at *least* the minimum requirements, don't try to upgrade it. Even if the upgrade is successful, the experience won't be satisfactory. Instead, consider migrating the roles of the server to a new server. Or migrating the server to a virtual machine.

Real World Leveraging Virtualization for Legacy Servers

An exciting new capability in Windows Server 2008 is Hyper-V. This new hypervisor-based native virtualization allows you to migrate existing legacy servers to run as virtual machines on Windows Server 2008. Unfortunately, Hyper-V is running late and did not ship at the time Windows Server 2008 released to manufacturing. We have detailed coverage of Hyper-V and other virtualization solutions in Chapter 29, "Working with Windows Virtualization."

Even though Hyper-V isn't part of the initial release of Windows Server 2008, you can still take advantage of virtualization to migrate your existing legacy hardware servers that aren't really powerful enough to migrate to Windows Server 2008 natively. You can use Microsoft Virtual Server 2005 R2 SP1 and convert the physical server to a virtual machine. System Center Virtual Machine Manager 2007 supports direct physical to virtual (P2V) conversions, and there are other, third-party tools that can facilitate the conversion as well. When converted to a virtual machine, legacy servers that weren't hardware capable of running Windows Server 2008 will actually be faster and have sufficient processor speed and RAM to support an upgrade. Or you can continue to have them run a legacy version of Windows Server if there is no urgent need to upgrade.

If your current server is running an x64 Edition of Windows Server 2003, it already meets the minimum processor and RAM requirements for upgrading to Windows Server 2008. You will need a DVD drive if your server doesn't currently have one (or you'll need to order a special CD distribution of Windows Server 2008). And you will need significantly more hard disk space. Other than those changes, however, you should have no issues, assuming you have updated digitally signed drivers for your hardware.

Software Support

Software that runs on Windows Server 2003 should run on Windows Server 2008. However, there can be compatibility issues. Always verify that the manufacturer supports Windows Server 2008 before upgrading. Also, if migrating from a 32-bit version of Windows Server 2003 to an x64 version of Windows Server 2008, you need to verify that any 32-bit applications running on the Windows Server 2003 server will support running in the 32-bit Windows on Windows64 (WOW64) environment that x64 versions of Windows Server 2008 use to support 32-bit applications.

Under the Hood **WOW64**

The hardware architecture of x64 Windows is actually an extension of the existing x86 hardware supported by 32-bit Windows. As such, it has native support for all of the 32-bit command set of 32-bit Windows Server, and can actually run a 32-bit version of Windows Server 2008 natively. When running an x64 version of Windows Server 2008, this native 32-bit support is used to provide a highly efficient and lightweight 32-bit operating subsystem for 32-bit applications. If the application doesn't require a hardware driver or use low-level, kernel mode calls, it should run natively in WOW64 as fast or even faster than it did in 32-bit Windows Server.

Applications written to take advantage of greater than 2 GB of virtual memory address space when running in 32-bit Windows will automatically see a full 4 GB of virtual memory address space. This means that applications that are memory constrained even when running with the /3GB switch in Windows Server 2003 will now have 4 GB of memory available in WOW64. This is often enough to make a significant speed increase for memory-constrained applications.

Applications running in WOW64 see a different view of the registry and parts of the Windows file system to keep them separate from 64-bit applications. This allows a staged migration to native 64-bit versions of applications as they become available, because they can run side by side with 32-bit versions.

64-bit versions of Windows Server 2008 do not support *any* 16-bit applications at all. If you have a legacy 16-bit application (or a 32-bit application that has a 16-bit installer), you will need to either maintain the existing server that supports it or migrate the server to a physical or virtual server running a 32-bit version of Windows Server.

Regardless of what version of Windows Server 2008 you're upgrading to, you should always verify that your key business applications will be fully supported on Windows Server 2008 before upgrading. When you've completed an upgrade, the only way to return to a previous version of Windows Server is to do a complete reinstallation.

Preparing Domains and Computers

Before you can upgrade a domain controller to Windows Server 2008, you should follow the steps detailed in the "Active Directory" section earlier in this chapter to prepare the forest and domain to accept a Windows Server 2008 domain controller. If you are only upgrading to Windows Server 2008 on a member server–or are upgrading a stand-alone server–you don't need to prepare the domain. However, it's useful to note that upgrading the forest and domain well before you actually install a Windows Server 2008 domain controller causes no issues.

Before you upgrade, do a basic cleanup of the system drive of the computer you'll be upgrading. Remove any temporary files and clean up log file directories. (Save the logs on another drive if you need to retain them.) Defragment the drive. We use a third-party disk defragmentation utility, PerfectDisk from Raxco. We think it does a better job overall, and it has the ability to do a boot-time defragmentation of system files that would otherwise be busy and couldn't be defragmented. Of course, none of this will prevent your system drive from becoming seriously fragmented during the upgrade. But every little bit helps.

Another thing to do when getting a server ready to upgrade is to remove any files that you don't absolutely need on the system drive to give it the maximum possible space. You need roughly 15 GB of free disk space on the drive to complete the upgrade.

Finally, stop any unnecessary services or applications, especially any antivirus applications or anything that is a real-time monitoring service. Remove any USB storage devices or other USB devices (except the mouse and keyboard–it's hard to get away from those).

Upgrading Clients

If you have any pre-Windows XP SP2 clients on the network, now would be a really good time to upgrade them. Windows 95 and its relatives, Windows 98 and Windows ME, are past their end-of-life support and should be removed from the network. If any of the computers are relatively modern and will support it, you can do a clean install of Windows XP onto them. Avoid doing an upgrade. Yes, it's technically possible in some cases. But it's very much a bad idea.

If you have clients that will support Windows Vista, by all means upgrade them. Windows Vista works better with Windows Server 2008 because they share a common networking stack and other features. Windows Vista also supports User Account Control (UAC) and includes the new bidirectional Windows Firewall, thereby improving overall security.

Performing the Upgrade

Now that you've planned the upgrade and prepared the domain and forest for an upgrade, you're ready to start upgrading. The only direct upgrade paths supported are from the same architecture of Windows Server 2003 to Windows Server 2008. If you have a Windows 2000 Server that needs upgrading, you'll need to do it in two steps: once to Windows Server 2003, and then again to Windows Server 2008. If you do that, use integrated media that includes *at least* Service Pack 1 (SP1) for Windows Server 2003, though integrated Service Pack 2 (SP2) is preferable.

Important If the computer you're considering upgrading is currently running Windows NT4, consider migrating the Windows NT4 workloads to a virtual machine and rebuilding the server from scratch. We really don't like upgrades from all the way back to Windows NT.

Upgrading To Windows Server 2008

To upgrade to Windows Server 2008 on a server running Windows Server 2003, follow these steps:

1. Upgrade the server to the latest Windows Server 2003 service pack. (Windows Server 2003 SP2 is the current level.)
2. Close all open programs, disable all virus-protection programs, and insert the Windows Server 2008 DVD into the DVD drive.
3. If the Windows Server 2008 setup program doesn't automatically start, run setup.exe on the DVD drive.
4. On the initial page of the Install Windows Wizard, click Install Now.
5. On the Get Important Updates For Installation page, shown in Figure 6-2, choose whether to go online to get updates or continue without updating. See the Real-World sidebar "Updates During Installation?" for an explanation of the tradeoffs.

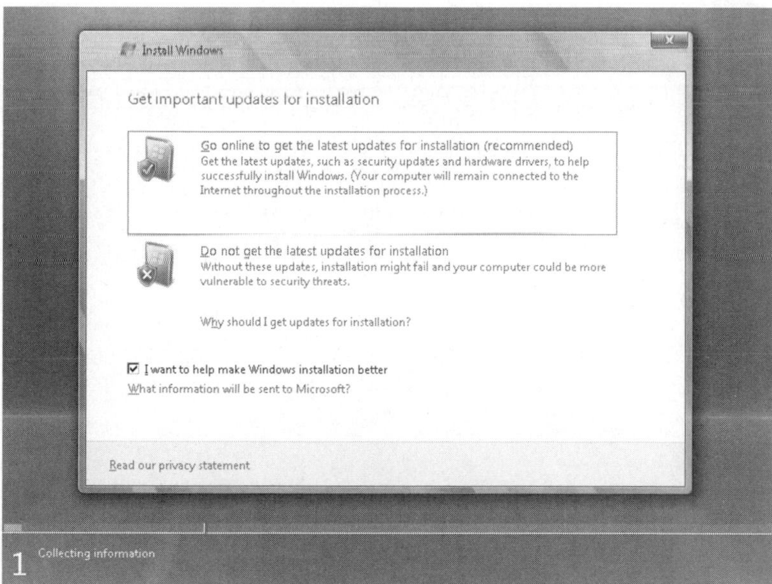

Figure 6-2 The Get Important Updates For Installation page of the Install Windows Wizard

6. If you're willing to have information about how the installation proceeds sent to Microsoft, select I Want To Help Make Windows Installation Better. We think this is a good idea.
7. Select whether to apply updates. If you choose to apply updates, the Install Windows Wizard will search for updates, as shown in Figure 6-3.

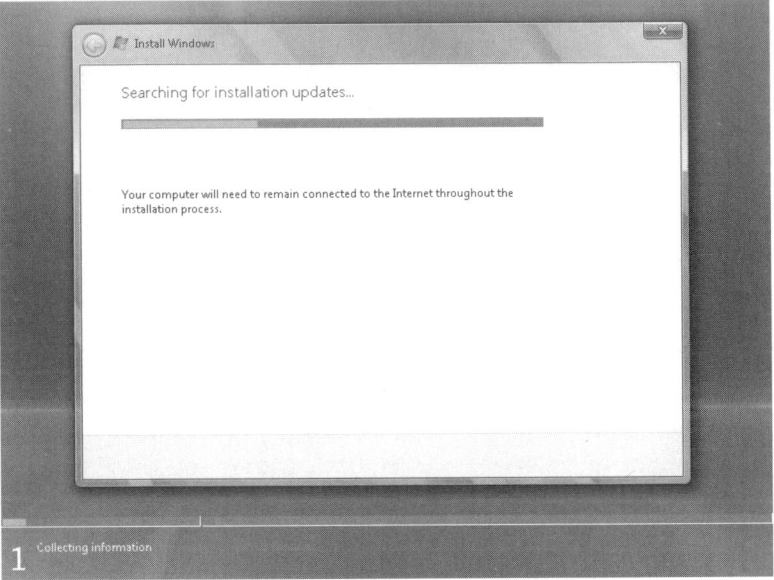

Figure 6-3 The Searching For Installation Updates page of the Install Windows Wizard

8. On the Type Your Product Key For Activation page, enter a valid product key for the upgrade and click Next. You can bypass entering a key and run Windows Server 2008 for 60 days. If you don't enter a key, you'll see the warning shown in Figure 6-4. Click No to continue without a key; click Yes to go back to the Type Your Product Key For Activation page.

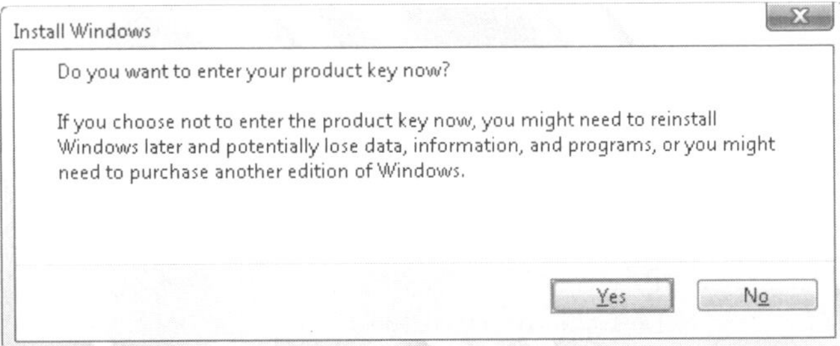

Figure 6-4 If you try to proceed without entering a product key, you'll see a warning.

9. Choose the version of Windows Server 2008 to install. If you've entered a license key, you'll only have versions that are specifically covered by that license key, as shown in Figure 6-5. If you didn't enter a key, you'll see the screen shown in Figure 6-6.

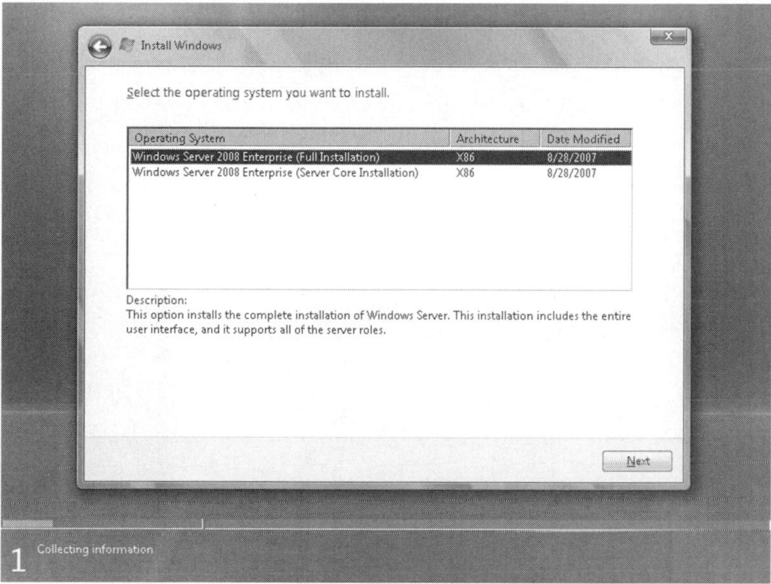

Figure 6-5 The Select The Operating System You Want To Install page of the Install Windows Wizard

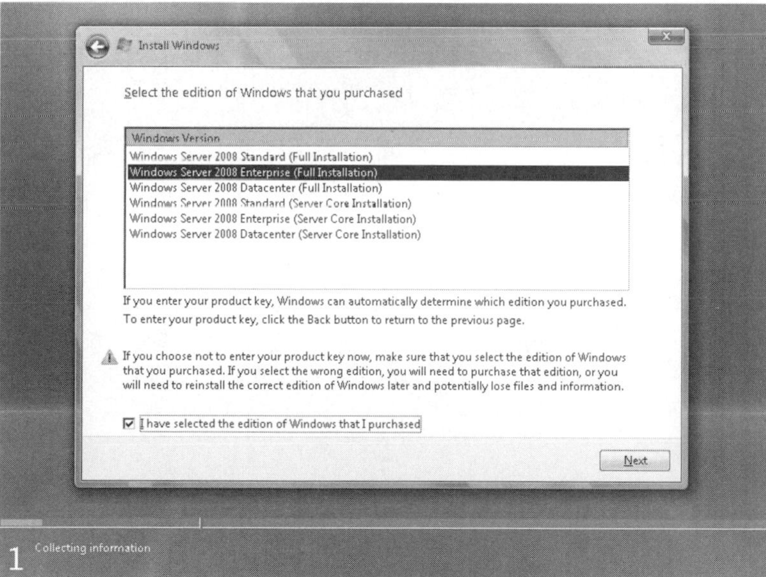

Figure 6-6 The Select The Edition Of Windows That You Purchased page of the Install Windows Wizard

10. You must choose a Full Installation version of Windows Server 2008 for an upgrade installation, and you must choose a version of Windows Server 2008 that is part of the supported upgrade matrix in Table 6-1 earlier in this chapter. Click Next. (If you are installing without a license key, you'll need to confirm that you're selected the correct edition of Windows Server 2008.)
11. On the Please Read The License Terms page, select I Accept The License Terms. You don't have a choice, though it *is* a good idea to actually read the terms occasionally. Click Next.
12. If all the conditions for an upgrade are met, you'll see the Upgrade option available on the What Type Of Installation Do You Want page, as shown in Figure 6-7.

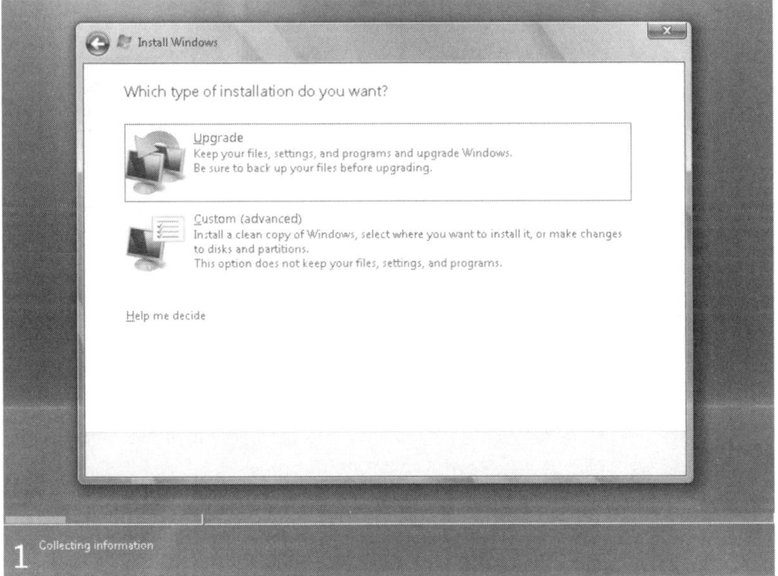

Figure 6-7 The What Type Of Installation Do You Want page of the Install Windows Wizard

13. Click Upgrade to perform an upgrade installation. You'll see a compatibility report. Ours is shown in Figure 6-8, but yours is likely to be different, depending on what the Install Windows Wizard finds. Read the report carefully, and take note of any issues that are reported. If there are no critical problems, you can click Next to perform the upgrade.

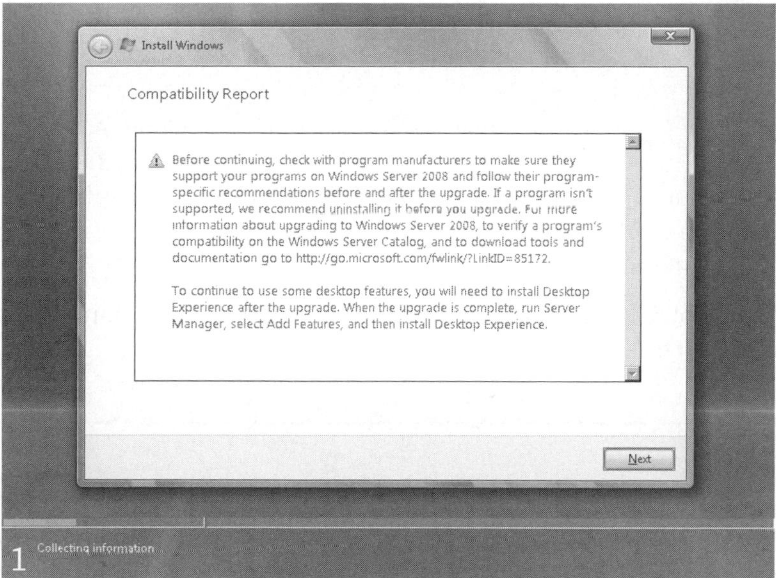

Figure 6-8 The Compatibility Report page of the Install Windows Wizard

That's it. The installation will proceed, usually rebooting several times during the process.

Real World Updates During Installation?

To update during installation or not, that is the question. And there are valid arguments on both sides. The advantage to allowing updates is that any critical fixes that Microsoft identifies after Windows Server 2008 ships that could affect the success of your upgrade will be automatically downloaded and included in the installation. Great—this certainly improves the chances that the installation will proceed without issues.

The downside is that you need to keep the server connected to the Internet for the entire duration of the installation. Now in some environments, that probably isn't an issue, but in others it's a direct violation of the policy that requires all computers to be completely disconnected from any external networks until completely built and all updates installed. Which isn't a bad idea at all if you have an environment that supports it, such as one with Windows Server Update Services (WSUS) or other update distribution mechanism.

So, which to choose? We have a hard time deciding ourselves, but ultimately choose the download updates scenario for ourselves. Your choice will depend on your policies and environment.

Forest and Domain Functional Levels

Windows Server 2008 supports three domain functional levels–Windows 2000 Native, Windows Server 2003, and Windows Server 2008–and three forest functional levels: Windows 2000 Native, Windows Server 2003, and Windows Server 2008. If you're upgrading a domain controller in an existing Active Directory domain and forest to Windows Server 2008, your domain and your forest *must* be at one of these levels. All support for legacy and interim domain functional levels that allowed the continued existence of Windows NT4 domain controllers is gone.

For a full discussion of the features and limitations of each domain and forest functional level, see Chapter 16. "Installing and Configuring Directory Services."

Summary

In this chapter we've covered the basic concerns about and steps for upgrading an existing Windows Server 2003 computer to Windows Server 2008. We've identified the supported upgrade paths, and what preparation you need to make to your environment before upgrading. Upgrades are a good way to maintain your existing installed applications and services and make sense for key line of business applications where doing a fresh install would be a nuisance or cause significant downtime. But in most cases, you'll want to do a clean, fresh install whenever possible because it allows you the greatest flexibility in choosing the type and architecture of installation. In the next chapter, we'll cover the steps to do a clean, fresh install of Windows Server 2008.

Chapter 7

Configuring a New Installation

Once the Windows Server 2008 setup finishes, there are still several steps that need to be completed before the server is actually ready to perform its role on your network. Not even the initial Administrator password or computer name are configured as part of the default setup. No roles are installed, the network is locked down, and all but the most basic required services are disabled. You're going to have to do some basic configuration on the server before it can be used. You'll need to verify that setup completed without error, assign the Administrator password, and configure the rest of the basic setup, including adding devices, configuring the server's name and network settings, and setting up the server to fulfill its role in life (or at least, its role on your network). We'll assume you're setting up a new server, but if this is an upgrade from a previous version of Windows Server, you'll still have some of the same tasks to perform, though others will be already done as part of the upgrade.

Note This chapter is focused entirely on a normal, graphical, Windows Server 2008 installation. It doesn't cover a Windows Server 2008 Core installation, which is a more specialized setup, and has an entire chapter dedicated to it. See Chapter 9, "Installing and Configuring Server Core," for full details on configuring a Core server.

Overview of the Tasks

Most of the tasks in this chapter are short and simple so that you can get the server up and running quickly after setup completes. At minimum, you'll need to perform the following tasks on a fresh server installation:

- Assign the initial Administrator account password.
- Install any hardware drivers required.
- Set the time zone.
- Configure the networking.
- Assign a name to the server.
- Join the server to a domain or assign a workgroup.
- Configure automatic updates and automatic feedback settings.
- Check for updates and install them.

There are additional tasks on the Initial Configuration Tasks (ICT) Wizard that you'll likely want to perform as part of your initial setup. These are:

- Add server roles.
- Add server features.
- Enable Remote Desktop.
- Configure Windows Firewall.

The first and last two of these you can leave for the moment. We'll cover adding server roles in the next chapter, and Windows Firewall is enabled automatically. Fine-tuning the Windows Firewall configuration is covered in Chapter 23, "Implementing Security." The other two tasks in this list, however, need a bit of attention. We think that every server should have at least one feature installed immediately–Windows PowerShell. We'll cover that in this chapter. And we also think that getting out of the server room is a good idea, so we'll turn on Remote Desktop in this chapter. Once that's done, you can do anything else you need to do from the comfort of your own workstation.

The setup program for Windows Server 2008 is completely new, and Microsoft has made every effort to ask as few questions of the user as possible during that initial install. The price for that simplicity, however, is to require the user to configure more settings after the setup completes. We think it's a reasonable tradeoff. For one thing, you don't need to pay attention during the setup at all–you can start a new setup, work through those first few screens, and then go away. When you come back, Windows Server 2008 will be installed and you can now configure it according to your needs.

Microsoft has an internal expression for the experience that their customers have when they first install a software package–the Out Of Box Experience (OOBE, pronounced "ewe-B").

Initial Logon

For Windows Server 2008, the OOBE starts by requiring you to set the initial Administrator password before you can log on, as shown in Figure 7-1.

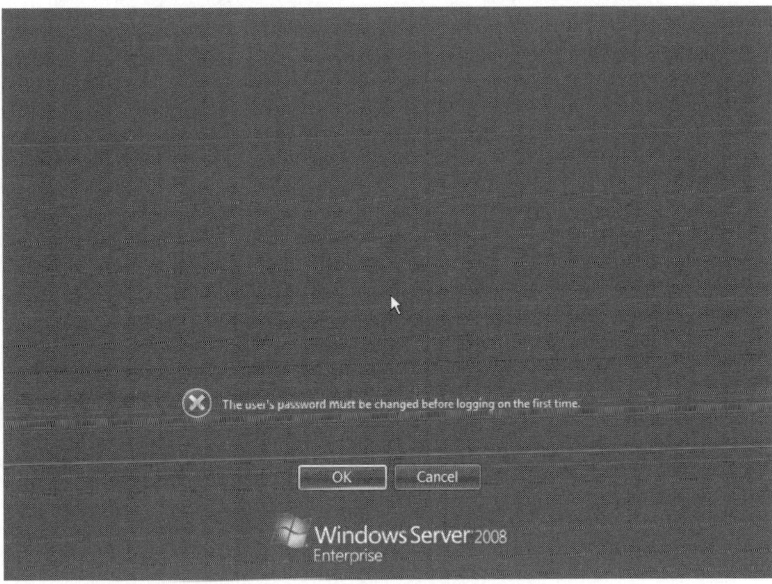

Figure 7-1 Setting the initial password for Windows Server 2008

Once you've set the initial password for the Administrator account, and logged on to the console, you get your first look at the ICT Wizard, as shown in Figure 7-2.

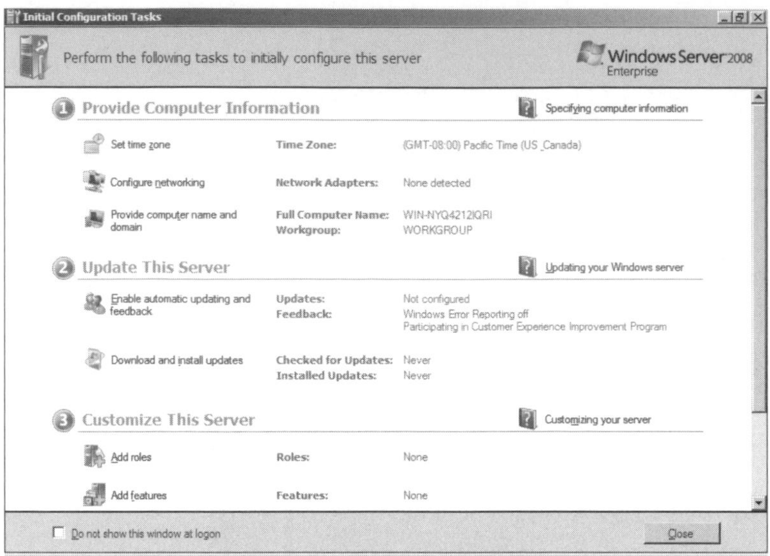

Figure 7-2 The Initial Configuration Tasks Wizard

Configure Hardware

We think the ICT Wizard has a huge hole in it–one that we really don't understand. Before you can configure your server, we think it just makes sense to get your hardware working. As you can see in Figure 7-2, we didn't have a lot of choice–our network card isn't supported without adding a driver, so the ICT Wizard thought we didn't have any network adapters installed at all. Microsoft makes every effort to get as many drivers as possible on the installation DVD, but the reality is that new hardware will continue to be released after Windows Server 2008 ships, and some of that hardware will require drivers that aren't on the DVD.

So for us, the first step is to open Device Manager and check for devices that are missing or not working. They'll be identified clearly, as our network adapter is in Figure 7-3. You can install the drivers now, or if it's not a device that you need for initial configuration, you can wait until after you've finished the ICT Wizard.

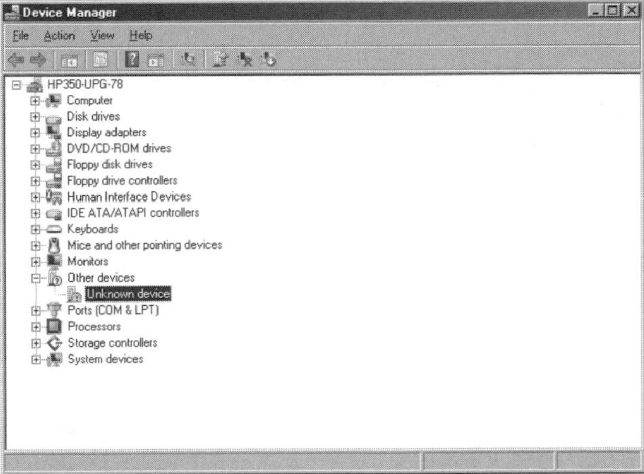

Figure 7-3 An unknown device in Device Manager

Once you've got your hardware working, you can proceed to configuring the basic computer settings in the ICT Wizard.

Configuring Basic Computer Information

The first section of the ICT Wizard covers basic computer configuration: time zone, networking and computer name, and joining the computer to a domain. This section of setup will require a reboot of your server when you set the server name and join to a domain, so save that for last in the section.

Setting the Time Zone

During the initial installation, Windows will pick a time zone (probably not the one you're in unless you live on the west coast of North America) and will also set the current date and time based on your computer's BIOS. To set the date and time, as well as setting the current time zone, click the link on the ICT Wizard to open the Date And Time dialog box shown in Figure 7-4. Once you've set your server's clock and time zone, click Apply and then click OK to return to the ICT Wizard.

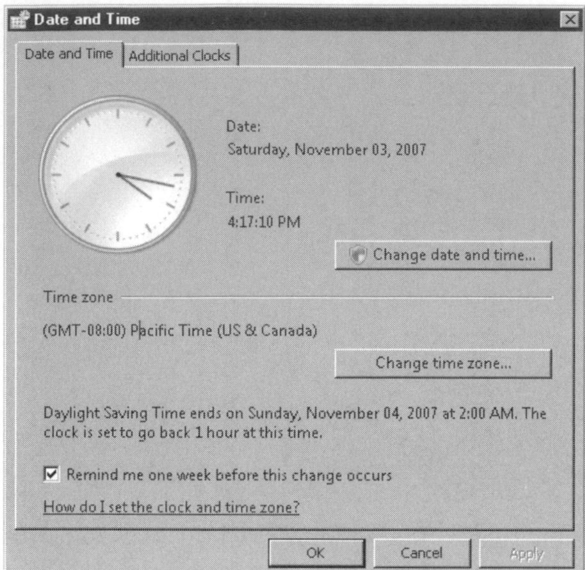

Figure 7-4 The Date And Time dialog box

Real World **Additional Clocks**

Windows Server 2008 lets you configure two additional clocks as part of the Date And Time dialog box. The clock display in the notification area is turned on by default, but if it's off for some reason, you can turn it on by right-clicking in the notification area to bring up the Taskbar And Start Menu Properties dialog box, clicking the Notification Area tab, and selecting the Clock check box. This will enable the clock display. If you've configured additional clocks, the time in those time zones will be visible when you hover the mouse cursor over the clock.

If you regularly work with folks in another time zone, you eventually get used to the time difference and don't need additional clocks on your server. And, after all, you shouldn't be sitting at the server console in most cases anyway. But we still find it handy, and since we work with folks in Europe and Australia fairly often, we turn on two additional clocks: one set to Greenwich Mean Time (GMT), and the other set to GMT+10 hours, for Sidney, Australia. This ensures that when we call at a totally unreasonable hour, we have absolutely no excuse.

Configuring Networking

Next on the list is configuring your networking. By default, your new server has enabled both IPv4 and IPv6, and if you've got a DHCP server running on the network, it has automatically configured addresses for each. If no DHCP server was available, the server has configured a *link-local* address–an autoconfiguration IP address that is unique on the network, but that won't be forwarded by routers to another network. For servers, we highly recommend that at least the IPv4 address be a fixed address. In most scenarios, the IPv6 address can be a stateless autoconfiguration address, or a DHCP supplied site-local address, as described in Chapter 18, "Administering TCP/IP."

To configure the networking and set a fixed IP address for the server, follow these steps:

1. Click Configure Networking in the Initial Configuration Tasks Wizard to open the Network Connections Control Panel application shown in Figure 7-5. (The command line for this is Ncpa.cpl.)

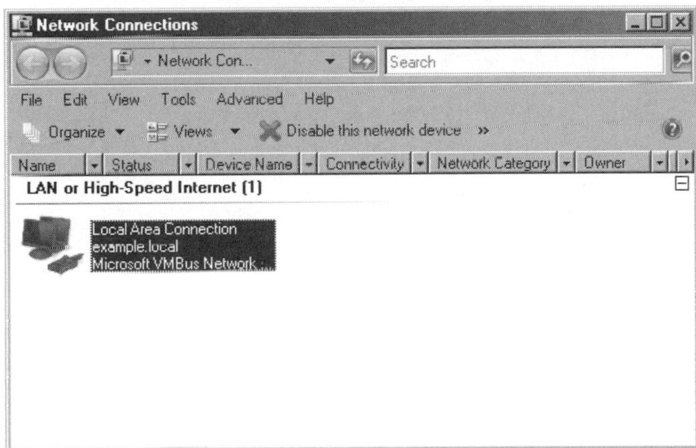

Figure 7-5 The Network Connections Control Panel application

2. Right-click the connection you want to configure and select Properties from the shortcut menu to open the Local Area Connection Properties dialog box, shown in Figure 7-6.

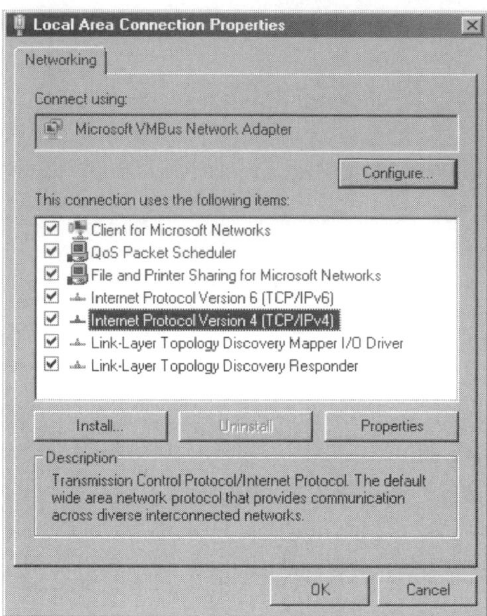

Figure 7-6 The Local Area Connection Properties dialog box

3. Select Internet Protocol Version 4 (TCP/IPv4) and click Properties.
4. Select Use The Following IP Address, as shown in Figure 7-7.

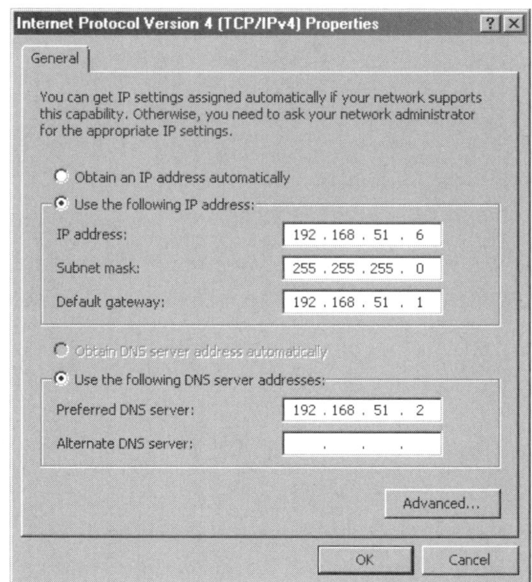

Figure 7-7 The Internet Protocol Version 4 (TCP/IP) Properties dialog box

5. Enter an IP Address, a Subnet Mask, and a Default Gateway appropriate to your network.
6. Specify the Preferred DNS Server for your network. (This should be a domain controller if you're using Active Directory–integrated DNS.) You can also enter a secondary DNS server if appropriate on your network.
7. Click Advanced only if you need to set any additional properties of this network connection. You can specify additional IP addresses, alternate gateways, additional DNS settings, and WINS server settings. The defaults for these advanced settings are sufficient in most networks, especially for this initial configuration. Click OK to return to the main Properties page.
8. Click OK to close the Internet Protocol Version 4 (TCP/IP) Properties dialog box, and then click Close to complete the configuration of the connection.
9. Close the Network Connections window by clicking the X button in the upper right corner of the window to return to the ICT Wizard page.

Note If you have multiple network cards on your server, renaming them something more meaningful than Local Area Connection and Local Area Connection 2 can simplify configuration of later Server Roles.

Setting the Computer Name and Domain

Once you have your networking configured, you're ready to give the computer a name and join it to the domain. If this is the first computer in the domain, you won't be setting the domain at this time–that will happen later when you add and configure Active Directory Domain Services (AD DS).

The Windows Server 2008 setup process automatically assigns a random and meaningless name to a new server. While this name is certainly unique on the network, it's not a useful final name, so you'll want to change it.

Real World Naming Computers

It's a good idea to use a computer name that is both DNS-compatible and NetBIOS-compatible so that all types of clients see the same name for your computer. (And yes, we're going to have to live with NetBIOS for a while still–there are just too many applications, including Microsoft applications, that simply don't work properly without it.) To do this, keep the name to 15 characters or fewer and don't use asterisks or periods. To obtain the best application compatibility, use dashes instead of spaces and underscores.

Beyond that, you should use a naming convention that has some internal consistency. We've seen all sorts of naming conventions, from the literary obscurities of naming them after romantic poets or science-fiction characters, to Norse or Greek gods, to colors (with the server fronts all painted to match the color name of the server). But honestly, we like names that actually help identify functionality, location, address, hardware, domain, or some combination of these. So our Example network here includes computers with the following names:

- hp350-dc-02 (It's running on an H-P ML350 G5, it's a domain controller, and its IP address is 192.168.51.2.)
- hp350-ts-05 (The terminal server running on an H-P 350 at 192.168.51.5.)
- dl380-core-08 (An H-P DL380, running Server Core, and at an IP address of 192.168.51.8.)

We know it's a boring way to name things, but we think it makes more sense than trying to remember that Hermes is the Microsoft Exchange server and Zeus is a domain controller.

You can save a reboot if you change the computer name and domain at the same time. Both require a reboot that will prevent other tasks from being completed, but fortunately they can be paired. To set the name and domain, follow these steps:

1. Click Provide Computer Name And Domain on the ICT Wizard to open the System Properties dialog box shown in Figure 7-8.

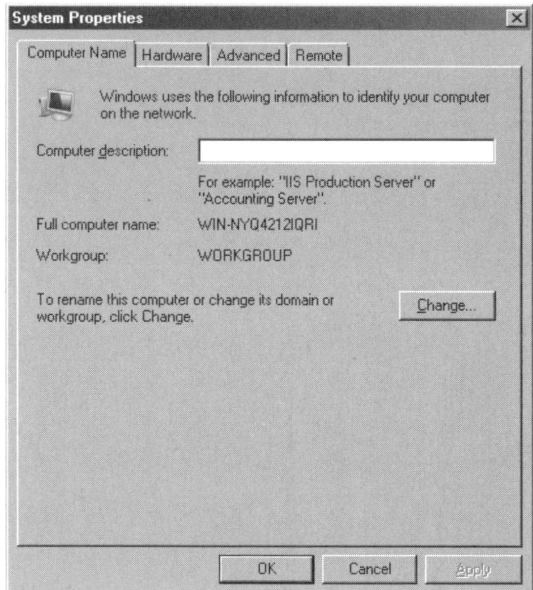

Figure 7-8 The System Properties dialog box

2. You can enter a description for this computer if you want, but it's hardly ever visible and thus not terribly useful.
3. Click Change to open the Computer Name/Domain Changes dialog box shown in Figure 7-9.

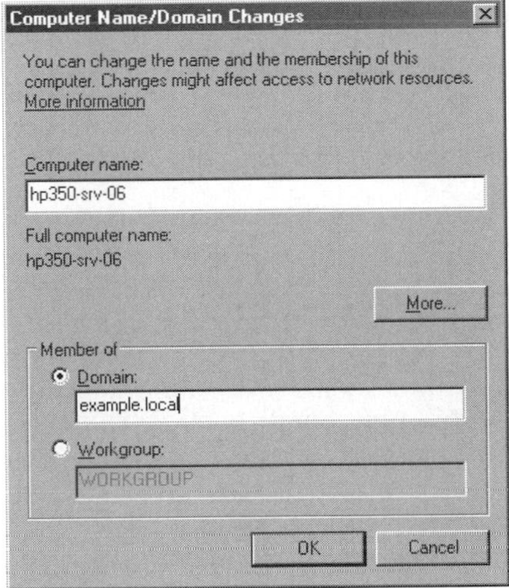

Figure 7-9 The Computer Name/Domain Changes dialog box

4. Enter a computer name consistent with your naming convention, and then click Domain to enter a domain you want to join.
5. Click OK, and you'll be prompted for credentials to perform the change, as shown in Figure 7-10. These need to be administrative-level credentials on the domain you're joining this server to, or an account that has been granted the right to join computers to the domain.

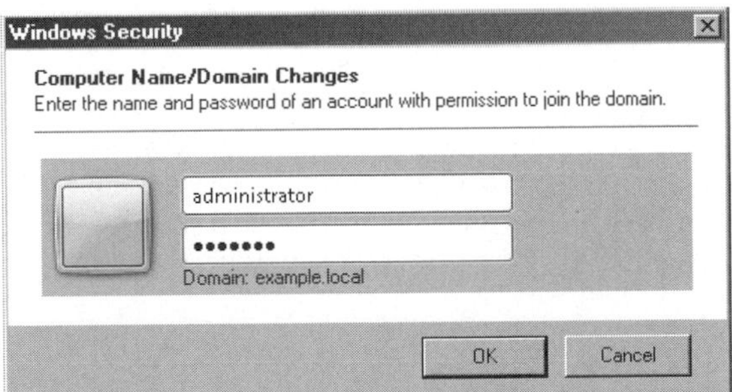

Figure 7-10 You must provide administrative credentials for the domain you want to join.

6. Click OK. If there aren't any problems, you'll get a Welcome message like that shown in Figure 7-11.

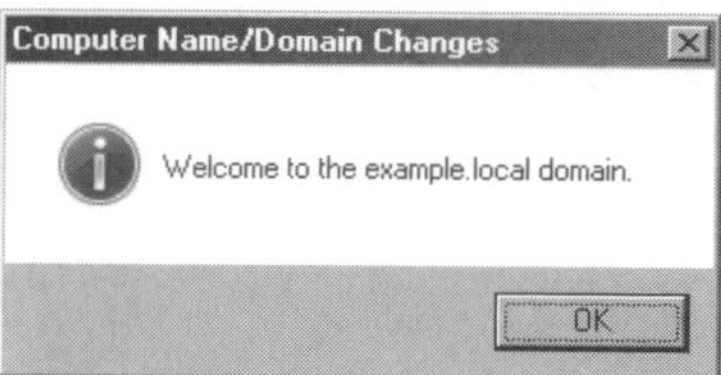

Figure 7-11 The Welcome message lets you know you're now joined to the domain.

7. Click OK to acknowledge the Welcome message. You'll be warned that you need to restart the server before the changes take full effect. Click OK again, and then click OK a couple more times and the server will reboot.

Important It's tempting at this point to try to delay the reboot to see if you can squeeze a few more things in before having to wait for the server to shut down and restart. And we understand the temptation—we're big fans of minimizing the number of reboots required and doing as many things as we can when we know we're going to have to reboot. But this is the one time we think you shouldn't do it. You need to get that new name and security in place before anything else happens.

Updating and Feedback Settings

The next group of settings on the ICT Wizard is used to set how updates are handled and what feedback is sent to Microsoft. The default behavior, if you don't do anything at all, is to not automatically download any updates, to not send any error reports to Microsoft, but to automatically report what roles are installed on the server. This is not the right settings in most cases, we believe, so let's do the configuration now.

Enable Updates and Feedback

The first setting in this section of the ICT Wizard is to actually configure what settings are used for updates and feedback. There are three basic choices that you can make when you click Enable Automatic Updating And Feedback on the ICT Wizard:

- Windows and Microsoft Update settings
- Windows Error Reporting settings
- Customer Experience Improvement Program settings

To configure these settings, follow these steps:

1. On the Initial Configuration Tasks Wizard, click Enable Automatic Updating And Feedback to open the dialog box shown in Figure 7-12.

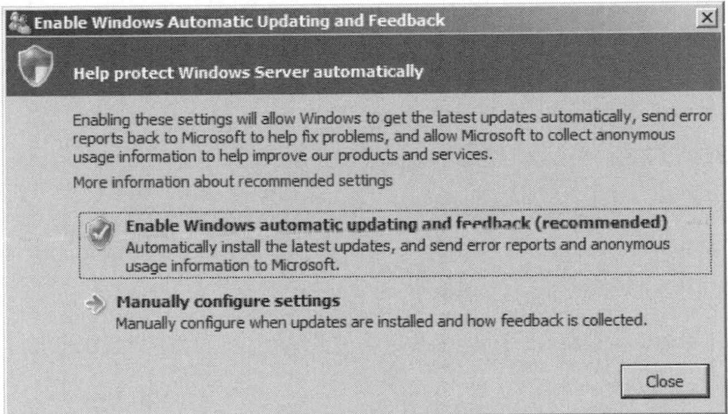

Figure 7-12 The Enable Windows Automatic Updating And Feedback dialog box

2. Unless you really want your server to be automatically downloading and installing updates with no warning, and with automatic reboots, again without warning, do *not* select Enable Windows Automatic Updating And Feedback.
3. Click Manually Configure Settings to open the dialog box shown in Figure 7-13.

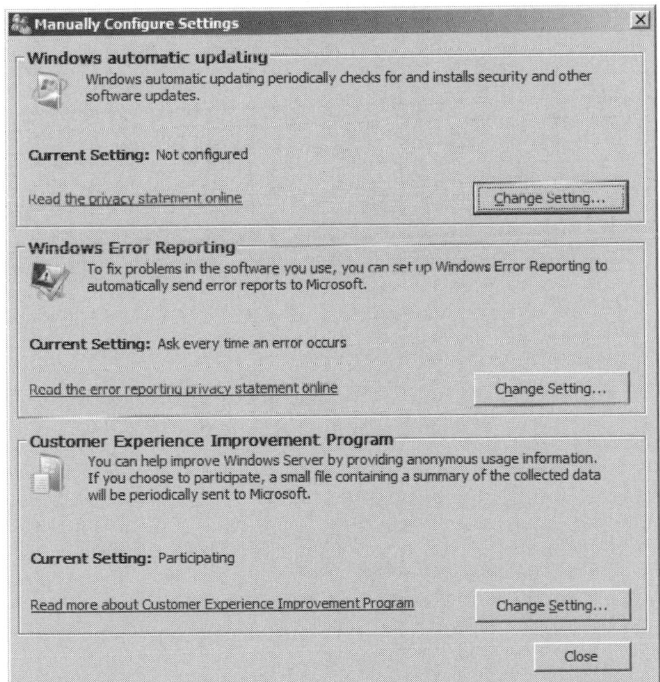

Figure 7-13 The Manually Configure Settings dialog box

4. To configure how the Windows and Microsoft updates are handled on this server, click Change Settings in the Windows Automatic Updating section to open the dialog box shown in Figure 7-14.

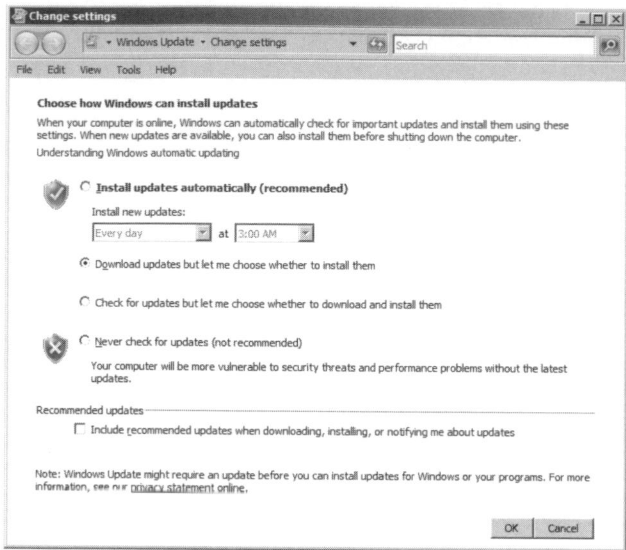

Figure 7-14 The Choose How Windows Can Install Updates dialog box

5. Make your selection from the following choices:

   - Install Updates Automatically (Recommended)

     This may be Microsoft's recommended setting but we think it's a really, really bad idea on a server. See the Real World sidebar on automatic updates for more information.

   - Download Updates But Let Me Choose Whether To Install Them

     This is our recommended setting. Downloads happen automatically in the background during times of low bandwidth usage. Once the download has completed, the next administrator to log on to the server will see a prompt to install the update in the notification area.

   - Check For Updates But Let Me Choose Whether To Download And Install Them

     When an update is available that applies to the server, the next administrator who logs on to the server will see a prompt in the notification area. If the update is one you want installed, you'll need to begin downloading it before you can install it. Unless bandwidth is very expensive, this seems like a less efficient way to work.

- Never Check For Updates (Not Recommended)

  Unless your environment uses a non-Microsoft patching solution, we think this setting is a really bad idea. Most urgent and critical updates should be installed in a timely fashion to protect your server. If you use this setting, you'll have to manually connect to Windows Update periodically to see if any updates are available. Or use a third-party solution.

  You can also choose to have recommended updates included with the updates covered by the settings you make. These are updates that are less important than the Critical or Important updates normally covered by automatic updating.

6. When you've made your selections, click OK to return to the Manually Configure Settings dialog box shown earlier in Figure 7-13.
7. Click Change Settings in the Windows Error Reporting section to open the Windows Error Reporting Configuration dialog box shown in Figure 7-15.

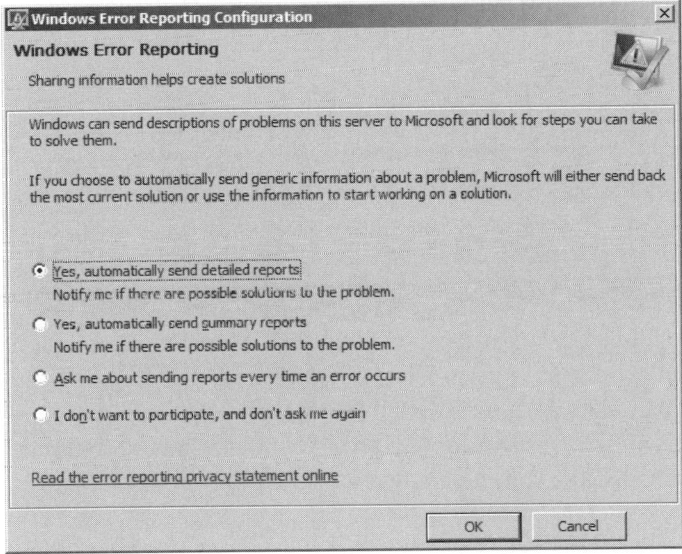

Figure 7-15 The Windows Error Reporting Configuration dialog box

8. Select how you want error reports handled. We think that automatically sending at least summary reports, and preferably detailed reports, is good for all of us. See the Under the Hood sidebar for more information on what is sent and why we care. Once you've made your selection, click OK to return to the Manually Configure Settings dialog box, shown earlier in Figure 7-13.

9. Click Change Settings in the Customer Experience Improvement Program (CEIP) section to open the Customer Experience Improvement Program Configuration dialog box shown in Figure 7-16.

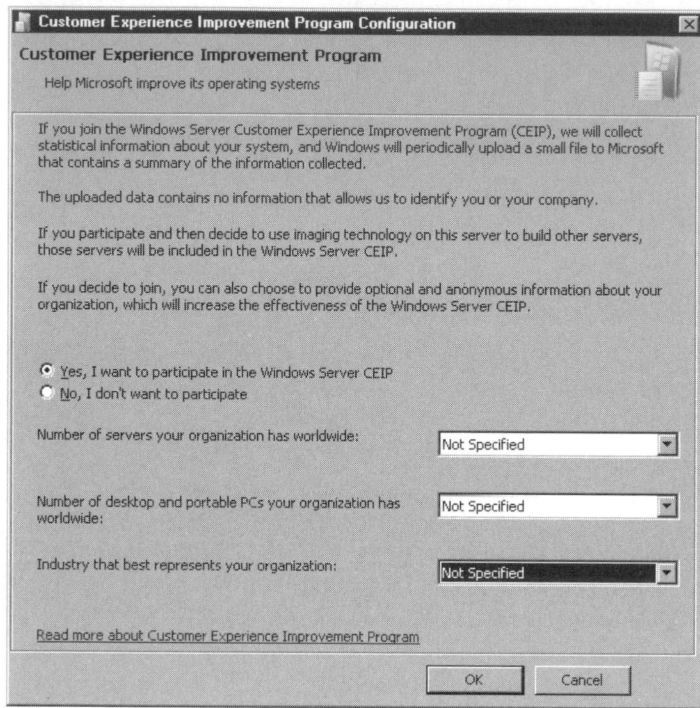

Figure 7-16 The Customer Experience Improvement Program Configuration dialog box

10. The default is to automatically participate in the CEIP. No personal or organizationally identifiable information is sent to Microsoft. None. But they do gather information about your hardware and the Server Roles installed on the server, and if you include details about your organization's servers, workstations, and industry, that information is linked to the collected data.

11. Make your selections, and click OK , then click Close to return to the ICT Wizard.

Real World Automatic Updates on a Server

We strongly believe in the importance of regularly and promptly updating your servers whenever critical security updates are available. We devote an entire chapter (Chapter 25) to patching. We'd like to think that servers and workstations never need patching or updating, but the reality is that they do, and when a new vulnerability is found, there is often very little time at all before there are publicly available exploits that can take that vulnerability and turn it into a mess for your network. Given that, why do we feel so strongly that Microsoft is *wrong* to default to automatically applying updates on Windows Server 2008? Because we think that where and when and how updates are applied is *your* decision, not theirs. And we especially think that users have a right to know when a server is going to be rebooted. Not only could that automatic reboot put you in violation of your Service Level Agreement, but in this global world we all live and work in, what makes 3 AM (the default installation and reboot time) in the local time zone necessarily a good time to reboot in the time zone of your branch offices, or for your salespeople who might be anywhere in the world? They could well have critical files open that they're working on.

So take control of your updating environment and just say no to fully automatic updates. By all means, download the updates if that makes sense for how you pay for bandwidth. Or set up a Windows Server Update Services (WSUS) server on your network and configure it to control how and when updates are offered and applied to your servers. Or use System Center Configuration Manager if you have a big enough network to justify it. Or use a third-party product such as Shavlik NetChk Protect to manage your updating. But don't set your servers to automatically update themselves and reboot as required. Bad idea.

Under the Hood Windows Error Reporting

Windows Error Reporting dates back to the old Dr. Watson errors that we all learned to hate in the earlier days of Windows. But it's come a long way since then. One of the major changes, introduced in Windows XP, was the sending of the crash dumps back to Microsoft when a program crashed or stopped responding. (This is called Online Crash Analysis, or OCA, and it found a lot of bugs!) You were asked each time if you wanted to send the crash dump, and a lot of people did, fortunately, because the result has been a far more stable and solid Windows, along with much better drivers. Microsoft CEO Steve Ballmer is reliably reported to have observed that "about 20 percent of the bugs cause 80 percent of all errors, and—this is stunning to me—*one percent of bugs cause half of all errors.*" By identifying those 20 percent of the bugs, and focusing efforts on them, we all benefit from more stable, crash-free software.

It is important to note, however, that crash dumps may contain personally identifiable information. If you're in the middle of entering your credit card number when the program you're working in crashes, chances are that the credit card number, or some portion of it, is likely to be inside that crash dump. Microsoft has made repeated and we think credible assurances that they will not use any personal information in those crash dumps in any way. You can read their Privacy Statement at *http://oca.microsoft.com/en/dcp20.asp*. In fact, we urge you to read it. It's clear and we think as unambiguous as possible when lawyers are involved. And we found it reassuring. We've all benefited from the errors that have been reported in the past to help make the software we use better and more reliable.

Getting Updates

The final option in this section of the ICT Wizard is to go online and download updates right now. Just click Download And Install Updates. The Windows Update dialog box shown in Figure 7-17 opens.

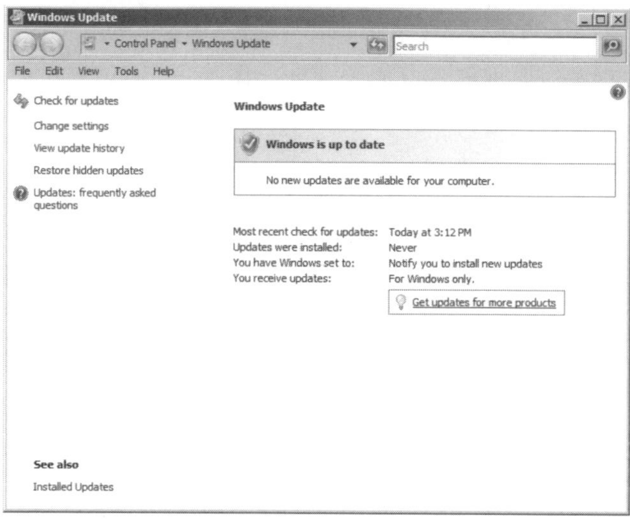

Figure 7-17 The Windows Update dialog box

If there are updates available, they'll be displayed and you can choose to install them now. An important link on this page, however, is Get Updates For More Products. By clicking this link, you can choose to use the Microsoft Update Service instead of the Windows Update Service. The Microsoft Update Service includes most Microsoft products, including those that you'd normally install on Windows Server. If you don't include these, you could be setting yourself up to have unpatched vulnerabilities on the server applications you use. So, unless you are using some other mechanism to ensure that your other Microsoft applications on the server are getting timely updates, we suggest you choose to use Microsoft Update Services.

Customizing the Server

The final section of the ICT Wizard is used to add roles and features to the server, enable remote access, and configure Windows Firewall. Finally, we can now get down to actually setting the server up to do some real work. All the rest of this has just been getting ready.

We're not going to cover the Add Roles option in the ICT Wizard because the whole next chapter is dedicated to installing and configuring Server Roles. We could also save installing features for that chapter, which we'll cover there as well, but we think that one feature that Microsoft doesn't install by default should be installed on every server–Windows PowerShell. So we'll cover installing that here.

Adding the Windows PowerShell Feature

Windows PowerShell is the new command-line shell and scripting language released by Microsoft in 2006. It is available as a download at *http://www.microsoft.com/technet/scriptcenter/topics/msh/download.mspx* for earlier versions of Windows, but is included as a feature in Windows Server 2008. (Just not one that is installed automatically.) And, unfortunately, it is not available at all on Server Core.

Windows PowerShell has completely replaced Cmd.exe as our everyday command shell. and it should for you too. Even if you don't write a bunch of PowerShell scripts right away, just using PowerShell as your command-line shell will get you started.

Before you can use PowerShell, however, you need to add the PowerShell feature to your new Windows Server 2008 installation. The ICT Wizard has an Add Features link, so let's use it to add PowerShell right now, by following these steps:

1. Click Add Features on the Initial Configuration Tasks Wizard to open the Add Features Wizard, shown in Figure 7-18.

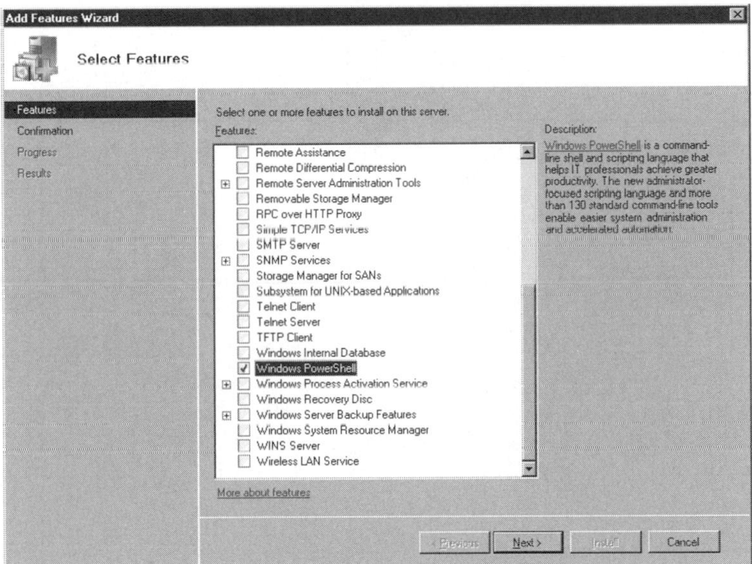

Figure 7-18 The Select Features page of the Add Features Wizard

2. Scroll down to near the bottom of the Features list, and select Windows PowerShell.
3. Click Next to open the confirmation page. You'll see a list of features that are going to be installed, and a warning that this might require a reboot. Don't worry, the server won't reboot as long as this is the only feature you're installing.

4. Click Install to begin the actual installation. When the installation completes, you'll see the Installation Results page. Any problems will be highlighted here, or it will simply report that the installation was successful. Click Close to exit the Add Features Wizard.

Now, you're almost done. There are a couple of little configuration steps that will simplify your use of PowerShell, so let's take care of that right now.

First, let's pin PowerShell to the Start menu to make it easier to use. After all, Cmd is there, so why shouldn't PowerShell be? To pin PowerShell to the Start menu, follow these steps:

1. Click Start.
2. Click All Programs and then Click Windows PowerShell 1.0.
3. Right-click Windows PowerShell and select Pin To Start Menu, as shown in Figure 7-19.

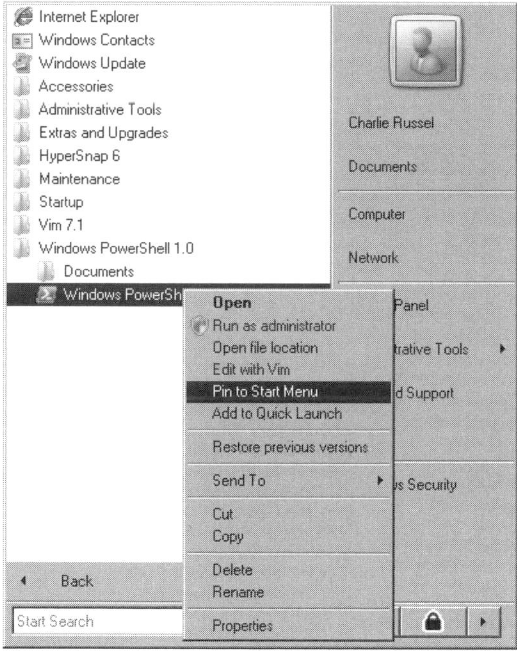

Figure 7-19 Adding Windows PowerShell to the Start Menu

4. While you're there, add PowerShell to your Quick Launch toolbar also. Now you have easy access to PowerShell without having to dig into the menus to get to it.

By default, PowerShell installs in the safest way possible, prohibiting you from running any scripts or configuration files. This lets you use the command line, but severely limits your ability to customize or do much of anything with PowerShell beyond simple shell commands.

This restriction is called the *execution policy* of the shell. There are four levels of execution policy available:

- **Restricted** Does not allow any scripts to be run, and won't load configuration files. This is the default value.
- **AllSigned** Allows the running of scripts or configuration files signed by a trusted publisher. Even scripts that you write yourself must be signed.
- **RemoteSigned** Allows the running of scripts or configuration files that were created on the local network to run without being signed, but any script that was downloaded from the Internet must be signed by a trusted publisher.
- **Unrestricted** Allows the running of any script or configuration file, regardless of where it came from. Scripts or configuration files that originated on the Internet will prompt you before you can run them, however.

We think the default value of Restricted is a bit much, and frankly we're just not willing to have to get a code-signing certificate just to run our own scripts, so even AllSigned is a bit much. In an environment that fully supports code-signing certificates, and where you want to restrict which scripts can be run to only those that are approved and signed, AllSigned makes sense. But for most locations, we think RemoteSigned is a good compromise. To change the execution policy to RemoteSigned, follow these steps:

1. Click Start, right-click the Windows PowerShell, and then select Run As Administrator.
2. Select Continue at the User Account Control prompt to open PowerShell with administrative privileges.
3. At the PowerShell prompt, run the following command:

   ```
   Set-ExecutionPolicy RemoteSigned
   ```

4. To confirm that the change has taken effect, you can use the `Get-ExecutionPolicy` command, shown in Figure 7-20.

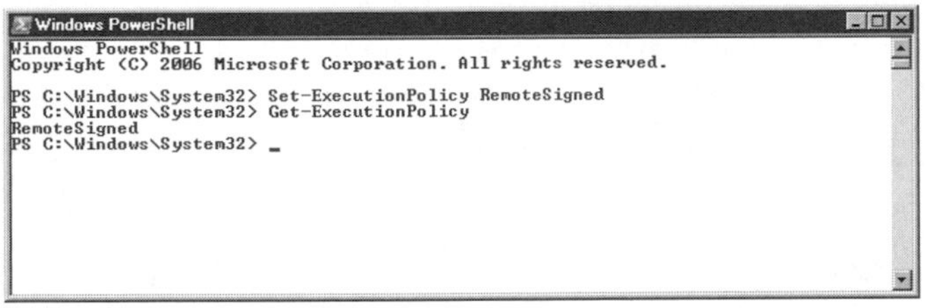

```
Windows PowerShell
Windows PowerShell
Copyright (C) 2006 Microsoft Corporation. All rights reserved.

PS C:\Windows\System32> Set-ExecutionPolicy RemoteSigned
PS C:\Windows\System32> Get-ExecutionPolicy
RemoteSigned
PS C:\Windows\System32> _
```

Figure 7-20 Setting the PowerShell Execution Policy

Enable Remote Desktop

Next on the ICT Wizard list is a link to Enable Remote Desktop. Remote desktop allows administrators to connect directly to the server without having to sit down at the console in the server room. Windows Server 2008 introduces version 6.1 of the Remote Desktop Protocol (RDP). The Remote Desktop Client version 6.1 is included in Windows Vista Service Pack (SP) 1 and Windows XP SP3, and version 6 clients are downloadable from Microsoft Knowledge Base Article 925876 at *http://support.microsoft.com/kb/925876*.

Version 6 and later of RDP includes many improvements over earlier versions, including 32-bit color, server authentication, resource redirection, font smoothing, and Terminal Services RemoteApps. For remote administration of a server, the most important improvement is server authentication, which ensures that you are actually connecting to the computer you think you are.

To enable Remote Desktop to the new server, follow these steps:

1. Click Enable Remote Desktop on the Initial Configuration Tasks Wizard to open the System Properties dialog box. The Remote tab should be selected by default, as shown in Figure 7-21.

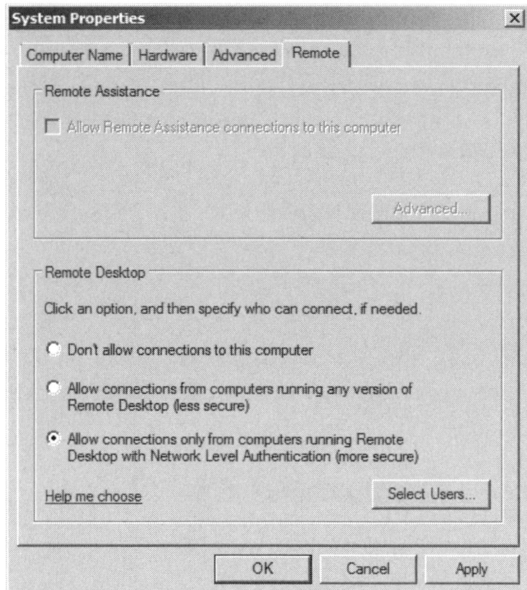

Figure 7-21 The Remote tab of the System Properties dialog box

2. Select the level of Remote Desktop client you want to enable. If all your clients will be running at least Windows XP SP2 or later, select Allow Connections Only From Computers Running Remote Desktop With Network Level Authentication (More Secure).

3. Click OK and you'll see a notice that a Windows Firewall exception has been enabled to allow Remote Desktop to work. Click OK again to return to the System Properties dialog box.

4. Click OK and Remote Desktop is enabled.

Configuring Windows Firewall

The last stop on the ICT Wizard is the Configure Windows Firewall link. By default, Windows Firewall is enabled on all new servers. This is a very different version of Windows Firewall than the one that came with the first release of Windows Server 2003. The new Windows Firewall is location-aware, with different rules for Domain traffic, Private Network traffic, and Public Network traffic. And it's bidirectional, controlling both incoming and outgoing traffic. We'll cover Windows Firewall in detail in Chapter 23, "Implementing Security." For the moment, it's primarily important only to know that Windows Firewall is on by default. Any Windows Server 2008 roles or features that you enable through Server Manager or the ICT Wizard will automatically update Windows Firewall as necessary, but if you have third-party line-of-business applications that need firewall exceptions enabled, you'll need to do that manually.

To configure Windows Firewall on the new server, follow these steps:

1. Click Configure Windows Firewall on the Initial Configuration Tasks Wizard to open the Windows Firewall dialog box shown in Figure 7-22.

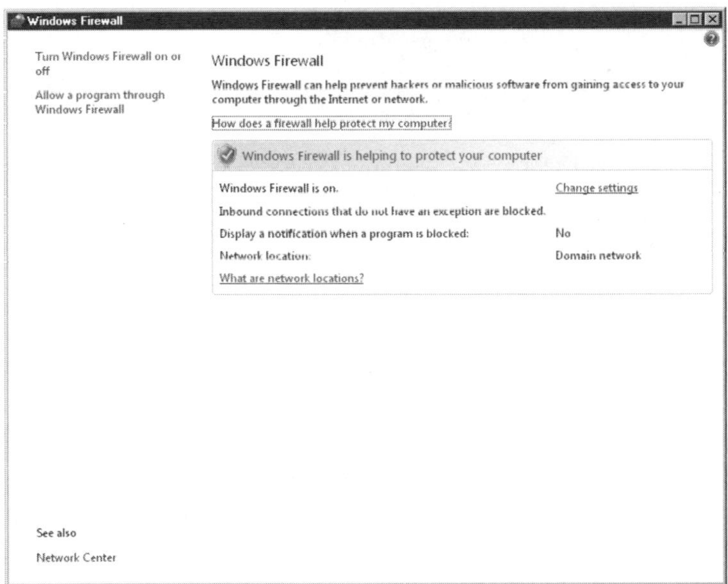

Figure 7-22 The Windows Firewall dialog box

2. Click Change Settings to open the General tab of the Windows Firewall Settings dialog box. On this page you can enable or disable the firewall, or set the firewall to block all incoming connections.

3. Click the Exceptions tab of the Windows Firewall Settings dialog box to allow specific programs or features to pass through the Windows Firewall, as shown in Figure 7-23.

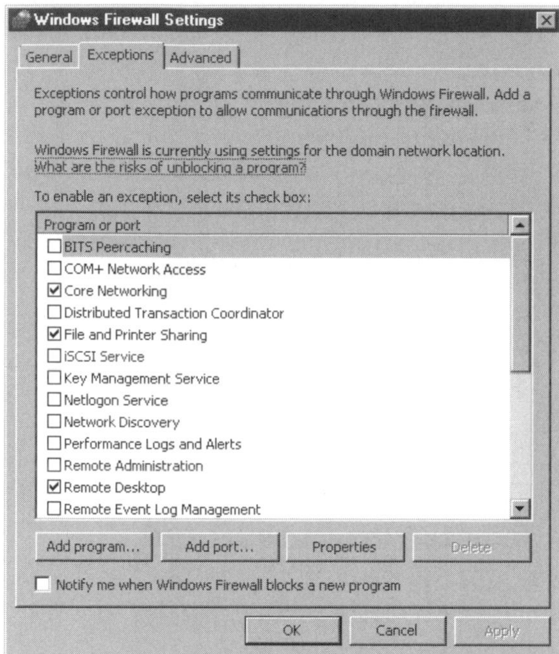

Figure 7-23 The Exceptions tab of the Windows Firewall Settings dialog box

4. Select Windows Firewall Remote Management to allow remote configuration of the Windows Firewall on this server. Other exceptions you might consider at this point include Windows Remote Management and Remote Service Management.

5. Click OK to close the Windows Firewall Settings dialog box and then close the Windows Firewall dialog box to return to the ICT Wizard.

Closing the Initial Configuration Tasks Wizard

Once you've finished all the steps in the ICT Wizard, you can select the Do Not Show This Window At Logon check box and click Close. This will close the ICT Wizard and you'll never see it again. When the wizard closes, the Server Manager console will open, allowing you to continue to configure your server for additional roles and features, along with providing easy access to all your daily management tasks on the server.

If you're not quite sure you're completely done with the ICT Wizard, we suggest you leave the box cleared and close the ICT Wizard. This will still automatically open the Server Manager, but the next time you log on to the server you'll see the ICT Wizard.

All the functions on the ICT Wizard are available elsewhere, but we think it's a useful and well-designed feature that pulls together all the initial steps you're likely to need to do on a new server into a single, logical place. If you've closed the ICT Wizard and turned it off, and then realize that you need something on it and can't find it easily, you can always get it back by running Oobe.exe from the command line.

Summary

In this chapter we've covered the basic initial configuration tasks you're likely to do on most new Windows Server 2008 computers. We've focused on using the graphical Initial Configuration Tasks Wizard that automatically runs on a new server, because we think this is a logical and well-thought-out wizard, but all the tasks on the ICT Wizard can also be performed from a command line or by using individual wizards. If you're running Windows Server Core, you won't have a choice–you'll need to use the command line or scripts to perform your initial configuration, and we'll cover Server Core in Chapter 9. Meanwhile, in Chapter 8 we'll cover using Server Manager to add Server Roles, Role Services, and Features.

Chapter 8

Installing Server Roles and Features

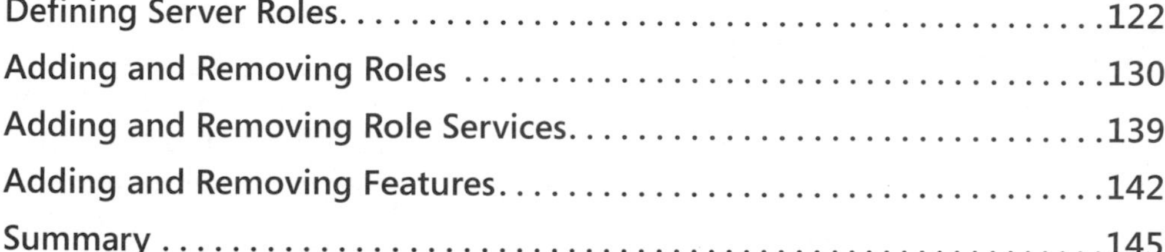

Previous versions of Windows Server used a freeform method for adding and removing the various features and abilities of Windows Server. This method could easily allow unnecessary services to be enabled, exposing the server to risk. Equally, it was possible to disable a critical feature or ability of Windows Server, causing other services or features not to work correctly. Troubleshooting these issues was time-consuming and frustrating, and the overall security of the server could be compromised. The Configure Your Server Wizard and the Manage Your Server Wizard of Windows Server 2003 were an attempt to resolve some of these issues by providing a simple interface that allowed for a single place to add or remove roles and manage those that were already on the server.

Windows Server 2008 takes these old wizards and completely replaces them with the new Server Manager. The goal of Server Manager is to be *the* one place where you can add or remove roles, role services, and features on the server, while giving you access to all the management of the roles and features that are installed. Server Manager is your "one-stop shop" for all management tasks on Windows Server 2008. Or at least, that's the theory. Frankly, we find the Server Manager a huge improvement for adding and removing roles, role services, and features, but less satisfactory for day-to-day management. We continue to use the stand-alone consoles for the roles we need to manage. They're faster, and we find navigation easier with them, but we still go to Server Manager for some management tasks. And for adding roles, role services, or features, Server Manager is quite a useful tool, although there is also a command-line equivalent.

Note Server Manager is not available on Server Core installations of Windows Server 2008. Server Core uses different tools for configuration. To set up a Windows Server 2008 Core server, jump ahead to Chapter 9, "Installing and Configuring Server Core."

In this chapter, we'll cover how to use the graphical Server Manager console and the command line ServerManagerCmd.exe to add and remove roles, role services, and features.

Defining Server Roles

Windows Server 2008 makes a distinction between a server role, a role service, and a feature. *Server roles* are broad groupings of common functionality that help define what a server is used for. Thus a file server would have the File Services role installed, and a terminal server would have the Terminal Services role installed.

Each of those broadly defined roles has available one or more role services. A *role service* is a particular functionality that is only available for the role for which it is a role service. Thus for a file server with the File Services role installed, there are the following role services that can be installed as part of the File Services role: File Server, Distributed File System (and its subsidiary services, DFS Namespaces and DFS Replication), File Server Resource Manager, Services for Network File System, Windows Search Service, and Windows Server 2003 File Services (including its two subsidiary services, the File Replication Service and the Indexing Service). For the Terminal Services role, the following role services are available: Terminal Server, TS Licensing, TS Session Broker, TS Gateway, and TS Web Access.

Table 8-1 lists the roles and role services available in Windows Server 2008.

Table 8-1 Windows Server 2008 Roles and Role Services

Role	Role Service	Install ID
Active Directory Certificate Services		AD-Certificate
	Certification Authority	ADCS-Cert-Authority
	Certification Authority Web Enrollment	ADCS-Web-Enrollment
	Online Responder Service	ADCS-Online-Cert
	Network Device Enrollment Service	ADCS-Device-Enrollment
Active Directory Domain Services		None (installed with Dcpromo.exe)
	Active Directory Domain Controller	ADDS-Domain-Controller

Table 8-1 **Windows Server 2008 Roles and Role Services**

Role	Role Service	Install ID
	Identity Management for UNIX	ADDS –Identity-Mgmt
	Server for Network Information Services	ADDS-NIS
	Password Synchronization	ADDS-Password-Sync
	Administration Tools	ADDS-IDMU-Tools
Active Directory Federation Services		
	Federation Service	ADFS -Federation
	Federation Service Proxy	ADFS-Proxy
	AD FS Web Agents	ADFS-Web-Agents
	Claims-Aware Agent	ADFS-Claims
	Windows Token-Based Agent	ADFS-Windows-Token
Active Directory Lightweight Directory Services		ADLDS
Active Directory Rights Management Services		
	Active Directory Rights Management Server	
	Identity Federation Support	
Application Server		Application-Server
	Application Server Foundation	AS-AppServer-Foundation
	Web Server (IIS) Support	AS-Web-Support
	COM+ Network Access	AS-Ent-Services
	TCP Port Sharing	AS-TCP-Port-Sharing
	Windows Process Activation Service Support	AS-WAS-Support
	HTTP Activation	AS-HTTP-Activation
	Message Queuing Activation	AS-MSMQ-Activation
	TCP Activation	AS-TCP-Activation
	Named Pipes Activation	AS-Named-Pipes
	Distributed Transactions	AS-Dist-Transaction
	Incoming Remote Transactions	AS-Incoming-Trans
	Outgoing Remote Transactions	AS-Outgoing-Trans

Table 8-1 **Windows Server 2008 Roles and Role Services**

Role	Role Service	Install ID
	WS-Atomic Transactions	AS-WS-Atomic
DHCP Server		DHCP
DNS Server		DNS
Fax Server		Fax
File Services		
	File Server	FS-FileServer
	Distributed File System	FS-DFS
	DFS Namespaces	FS-DFS-Namespace
	DFS Replication	FS-DFS-Replication
	File Server Resource Manager	FS-Resource-Manager
	Services for Network File System	FS-NFS-Services
	Windows Search Service	FS-Search-Service
	Windows Server 2003 File Services	FS-Win2003-Services
	File Replication Service	FS-Replication
	Indexing Service	FS-Indexing-Service
Hyper-V		Hyper-V
Network Policy and Access Services		NPAS
	Network Policy Server	NPAS-Policy-Server
	Routing and Remote Access Services	NPAS-RRAS-Services
	Remote Access Service	NPAS-RRAS
	Routing	NPAS-Routing
	Health Registration Authority	NPAS-Health
	Host Credential Authorization Protocol	NPAS-Host-Cred
Print Services		Print-Services
	Print Server	Print-Server
	LPD Service	Print-LPD-Service
	Internet Printing	Print-Internet
Terminal Services		Terminal-Services
	Terminal Server	TS-Terminal-Server
	TS Licensing	TS-Licensing
	TS Session Broker	TS-Session-Broker
	TS Gateway	TS-Gateway

Table 8-1 **Windows Server 2008 Roles and Role Services**

Role	Role Service	Install ID
	TS Web Access	TS-Web-Access
UDDI Services		
	UDDI Services Database	
	UDDI Services Web Application	
Web Server (IIS)		Web-Server
	Web Server	Web-WebServer
	Common HTTP Features	Web-Common-Http
	Static Content	Web-Static-Content
	Default Document	Web-Default-Doc
	Directory Browsing	Web-Dir-Browsing
	HTTP Errors	Web-Http-Errors
	HTTP Redirection	Web-Http-Redirect
	Application Development	Web-App-Dev
	ASP.NET	Web-Asp-Net
	.NET Extensibility	Web-Net-Ext
	ASP	Web-ASP
	CGI	Web-CGI
	ISAPI Extensions	Web-ISAPI-Ext
	ISAPI Filters	Web-ISAPI-Filter
	Server Side Includes	Web-Includes
	Health and Diagnostics	Web-Health
	HTTP Logging	Web-Http-Logging
	Logging Tools	Web-Log-Libraries
	Request Monitor	Web-Request-Monitor
	Tracing	Web-Http-Tracing
	Custom Logging	Web-Custom-Logging
	ODBC Logging	Web-ODBC-Logging
	Security	Web-Security
	Basic Authentication	Web-Basic-Auth
	Windows Authentication	Web-Windows-Auth
	Digest Authentication	Web-Digest-Auth
	Client Certificate Mapping Authentication	Web-Client-Auth
	IIS Client Certificate Mapping Authentication	Web-Cert-Auth

Table 8-1 Windows Server 2008 Roles and Role Services

Role	Role Service	Install ID
	URL Authorization	Web-Url-Auth
	Request Filtering	Web-Filtering
	IP and Domain Restrictions	Web-IP-Security
	Performance	Web-Performance
	Static Content Compression	Web-Stat-Compression
	Dynamic Content Compression	Web-Dyn-Compression
	Management Tools	Web-Mgmt-Tools
	IIS Management Console	Web-Mgmt-Console
	IIS Management Scripts and Tools	Web-Scripting-Tools
	Management Service	Web-Mgmt-Service
	IIS 6 Management Compatibility	Web-Mgmt-Compat
	IIS 6 Metabase Compatibility	Web-Metabase
	IIS 6 WMI Compatibility	Web-WMI
	IIS 6 Scripting Tools	Web-Lgcy-Scripting
	IIS 6 Management Console	Web-Lgcy-Mgmt-Console
	FTP Publishing Service	Web-Ftp-Publishing
	FTP Server	Web-Ftp-Server
	FTP Management Console	Web-Ftp-Mgmt-Console
Windows Deployment Services		WDS
	Deployment Server	WDS-Deployment
	Transport Server	WDS-Transport

Features are Windows Server 2008 functionality that doesn't require a specific role to be installed. Features are useful across a wide variety of server role configurations. Features include broad, general-purpose functionality, such as Windows PowerShell, as well as narrow but non-role-specific functionality such as Internet Storage Name Server (iSNS) or Message Queuing. Table 8-2 lists the features available in Windows Server 2008.

Table 8-2 **Windows Server 2008 Features**

Feature	**Install ID**
NET Framework 3.0 Features	NET-Framework
.NET Framework 3.0	NET-Framework-Core
XPS Viewer	NET-XPS-Viewer
WCF Activation	NET-Win-CFAC
HTTP Activation	NET-HTTP-Activation
Non-HTTP Activation	NET-Non-HTTP-Activ
BitLocker Drive Encryption	BitLocker
BITS Server Extensions	BITS
Connection Manager Administration Kit	CMAK
Desktop Experience	Desktop-Experience
Failover Clustering	Failover-Clustering
Group Policy Management	GPMC
Internet Printing Client	Internet-Print-Client
Internet Storage Name Server	ISNS
LPR Port Monitor	LPR-Port-Monitor
Message Queuing	MSMQ
Message Queuing Services	MSMQ-Services
Message Queuing Server	MSMQ-Server
Directory Service Integration	MSMQ-Directory
Message Queuing Triggers	MSMQ-Triggers
HTTP Support	MSMQ-HTTP-Support
Multicasting Support	MSMQ-Multicasting
Routing Service	MSMQ-Routing
Windows 2000 Client Support	MSMQ-Win2000
Message Queuing DCOM Proxy	MSMQ-DCOM
Multipath I/O	Multipath-IO
Network Load Balancing	NLB
Peer Name Resolution Protocol	PNRP
Quality Windows Audio Video Experience	qWave
Remote Assistance	Remote-Assistance
Remote Differential Compression	RDC
Role Server Administration Tools	RSAT

Table 8-2 **Windows Server 2008 Features**

Feature	Install ID
Role Administration Tools	RSAT-Role-Tools
Active Directory Certificate Services Tools	RSAT-ADCS
Certification Authority Tools	RSAT-ADCS-Mgmt
Online Responder Tools	RSAT-Online-Responder
Active Directory Domain Services Tools	RSAT-ADDS
Active Directory Domain Controller Tools	RSAT-ADDC
Server for NIS Tools	RSAT-SNIS
Active Directory Lightweight Directory Services Tools	RSAT-ADLDS
Active Directory Rights Management Services Tools	RSAT-RMS
DHCP Server Tools	RSAT-DHCP
DNS Server Tools	RSAT-DNS-Server
Fax Server Tools	RSAT-Fax
File Services Tools	RSAT-File-Services
Distributed File System Tools	RSAT-DFS-Mgmt-Con
File Server Resource Manager Tools	RSAT-FSRM-Mgmt
Hyper-V	Hyper-V
Services for Network File System Tools	RSAT-NFS-Admin
Network Policy and Access Services Tools	RSAT-NPAS
Print Services Tools	RSAT-Print-Services
Terminal Services Tools	RSAT-TS
Terminal Server Tools	RSAT-TS-RemoteApp
TS Gateway Tools	RSAT-TS-Gateway
TS Licensing Tools	RSAT-TS-Licensing
UDDI Services Tools	RSAT-UDDI
Web Server (IIS) Tools	RSAT-Web-Server
Windows Deployment Services Tools	RSAT-WDS
Feature Administration Tools	RSAT-Feature-Tools
BitLocker Drive Encryption Tools	RSAT-BitLocker
BITS Server Extensions Tools	RSAT-Bits-Server
Failover Clustering Tools	RSAT-Clustering
Network Load Balancing Tools	RSAT-NLB

Table 8-2 Windows Server 2008 Features

Feature	Install ID
SMTP Server Tools	RSAT-SMTP
WINS Server Tools	RSAT-WINS
Removable Storage Manager	Removable-Storage
RPC over HTTP Proxy	RPC-over-HTTP-Proxy
Simple TCP/IP Services	Simple-TCPIP
SMTP Server	SMTP-Server
SNMP Services	SNMP-Services
SNMP Service	SNMP-Service
SNMP WMI Provider	SNMP-WMI-Provider
Storage Manager for SANs	Storage-Mgr-SANS
Subsystem for UNIX-based Applications	Subsystem-UNIX-Apps
Telnet Client	Telnet-Client
Telnet Server	Telnet-Server
TFTP Client	TFTP-Client
Windows Internal Database	Windows-Internal-DB
Windows PowerShell	PowerShell
Windows Process Activation Service	WAS
Process Model	WAS-Process-Model
.NET Environment	WAS-NET-Environment
Configuration APIs	WAS-Config-APIs
Windows Server Backup Features	Backup-Features
Windows Server Backup	Backup
Command-line Tools	Backup-Tools
Windows System Resource Manager	WSRM
WINS Server	WINS-Server
Wireless LAN Service	Wireless-Networking

As you can see from Tables 8-1 and 8-2, there are a lot of roles, role services, and features you can install. All of them can be installed from either the Server Manager console or from an elevated command prompt (using ServerManagerCmd.exe). The one oddity is that Active Directory Domain Services (AD DS) is installed from the Server Manager, but doesn't actually *do* anything until you run the command line Dcpromo.exe. When you do run Dcpromo.exe, it first checks to see whether the AD DS role is installed, and if it isn't, it installs the role and then begins the promotion of the server to be a domain controller.

Adding and Removing Roles

Adding and removing roles from Windows Server 2008 can be done from either the Server Manager console or the command line. Both methods perform the same tasks and follow the same logic for which services get installed. It's a whole lot easier, however, to use the GUI for this, so unless you're installing lots of servers that all have the same configuration, we strongly suggest just using Server Manager for this. (We can't believe we said that–we're the quintessential command-line types for almost everything. But this is one time where graphical just makes sense.)

Real World Roles: An Unnecessary Restriction or a Smart Improvement?

When we first ran across the new requirement to always use Server Manager to install roles, role services, and features, we were not very happy about it. In fact, we complained loudly and with a good deal of enthusiasm to more than one set of ears inside Microsoft. It probably didn't help that at that point the feature was pretty much broken; it didn't yet have a command line; and you could only install a single role, role service, or feature at a time. But we still saw it as an unnecessary and unproductive dumbing down of Windows Server. Everyone we said this to kept telling us to be patient. Well, we *hate* to admit it, but they were right. The new Server Manager–controlled adding and removing of roles, role services, and features is just a whole lot better and smarter about what it does. Not only does it always get the right *minimum* level of dependent services, but it also automatically configures Windows Firewall with the right exceptions. And if you're installing roles from Server Manager, it's trivially easy to add just the role services you need. Plus, you can add a whole bunch of roles and role services all at the same time. Or a whole bunch of features all at once–making it fairly quick and easy to set up a new server just the way you want it.

We do find, however, that if you add more than one role or feature at a time, the likelihood of having to reboot the server goes up noticeably. That's annoying, certainly. And you can't add features in the same pass as adding roles and role services. Again, an annoyance, but not a huge one.

Finally, one last annoyance. If you're adding roles or features one at a time, you can almost always avoid a reboot. But if you remove a role or feature, you are very likely to have to reboot.

Add a Role

You can use either the graphical Server Manager console to add a role or you can use the command-line utility ServerManagerCmd.exe.

Using the Server Manager Console

To add a role from the Server Manager console, follow these steps:

1. Open the Server Manager console if it isn't open already.
2. Select Add Roles from the Action menu to open the Before You Begin page of the Add Roles Wizard, as shown in Figure 8-1.

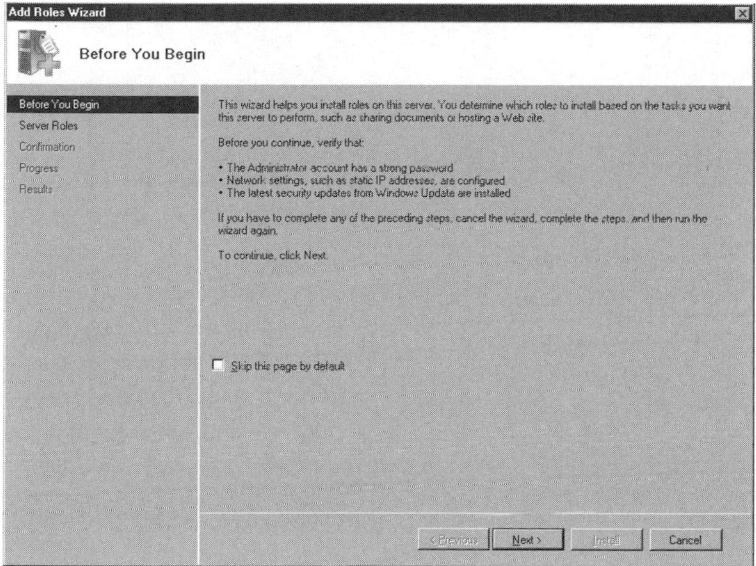

Figure 8-1 The Before You Begin page of the Add Roles Wizard

3. Read the advice on the Before You Begin page. It's actually good advice and a useful reminder. If you've read the page, understand all its implications, and don't ever want to see the page again, select the Skip This Page By Default check box. (Personally, we like to leave it unchecked.)
4. Click Next to open the Select Server Roles page, as shown in Figure 8-2.

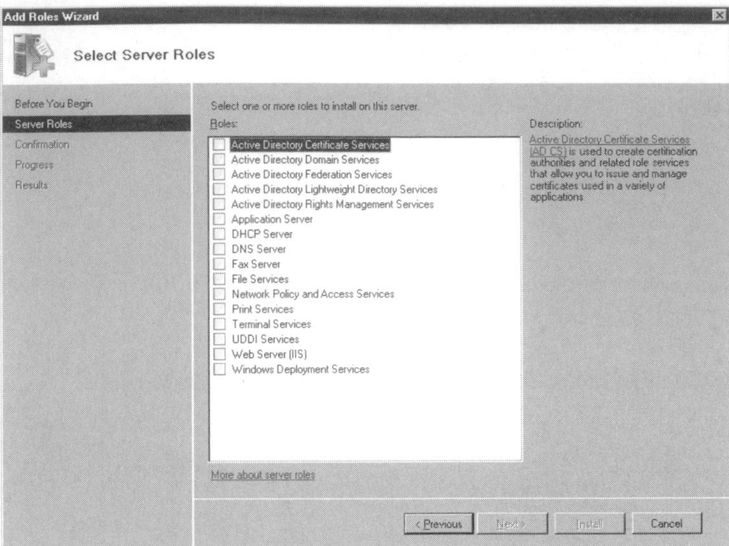

Figure 8-2 The Select Server Roles page of the Add Roles Wizard

5. Select the server roles you want to add. You can select more than one, but doing so makes it much more likely that you'll have to reboot before the installation completes.
6. Click Next to open the page for first role that will be installed, as shown in Figure 8-3 (if you selected Terminal Services in the previous step). This page describes the role that is being installed, and includes a Things To Note section that contains cautions or advisories specific to the role being installed. There is also a link to an Additional Information page with up-to-date information on the role being installed.

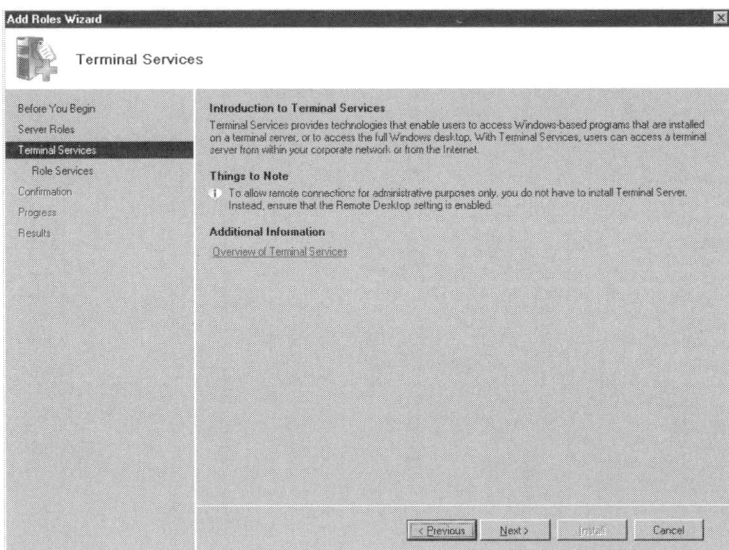

Figure 8-3 The Terminal Services page of the Add Roles Wizard

7. Once you've read any Things To Note, click Next to open the Select Role Services page shown in Figure 8-4.

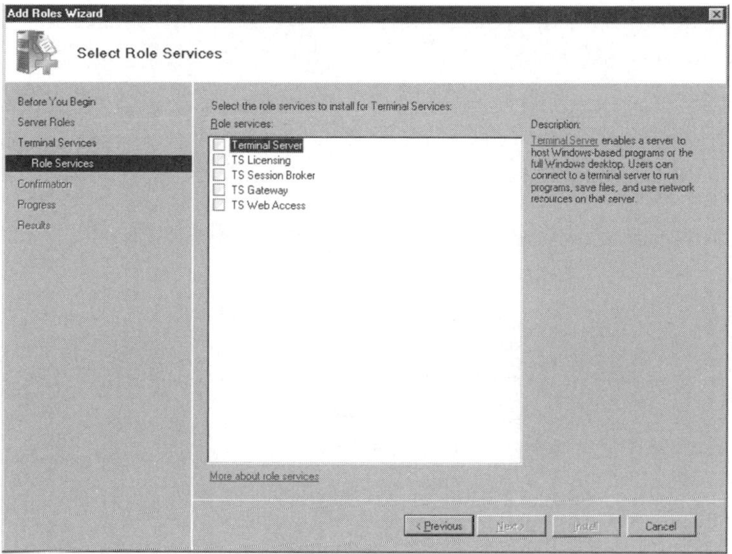

Figure 8-4 The Select Role Services page of the Add Roles Wizard

8. Select the role services you want to add at this time. If you select a role service that has a dependency on another role, role service, or feature, you'll see a pop-up dialog box describing the additional role services that will be installed, as shown in Figure 8-5.

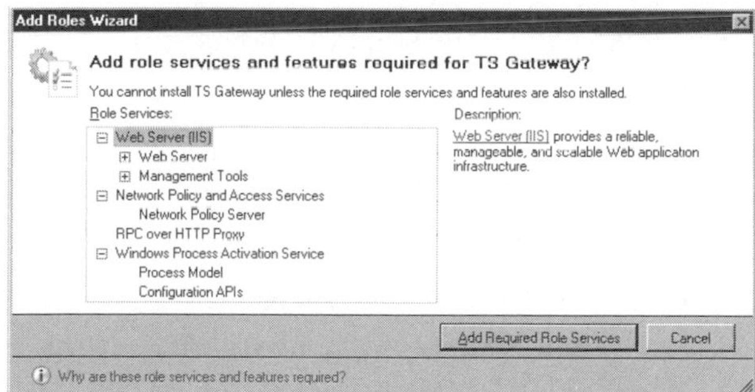

Figure 8-5 The Add Role Services And Features Required For TS Gateway page of the Add Roles Wizard

9. Click Add Required Role Services to continue and return to the Select Role Services page or click Cancel if you want to change your role services selection.

10. Click Next to open the next page in the Add Roles Wizard. From here to the end of the wizard, the specific pages will vary depending on what roles and role services you've selected.

11. After the Add Roles Wizard has all the information necessary to proceed, it will open the Confirm Installation Selections page. This is your last chance to make sure you've selected the roles and role services you expected, and configured any necessary settings appropriate for your environment. If everything looks correct, click Install to begin the installation.

12. After the installation completes, you'll see the Installation Results page, shown in Figure 8-6. If the installation requires a restart, or there are any other warnings or errors, you'll see that on this page. Click Close to complete the wizard.

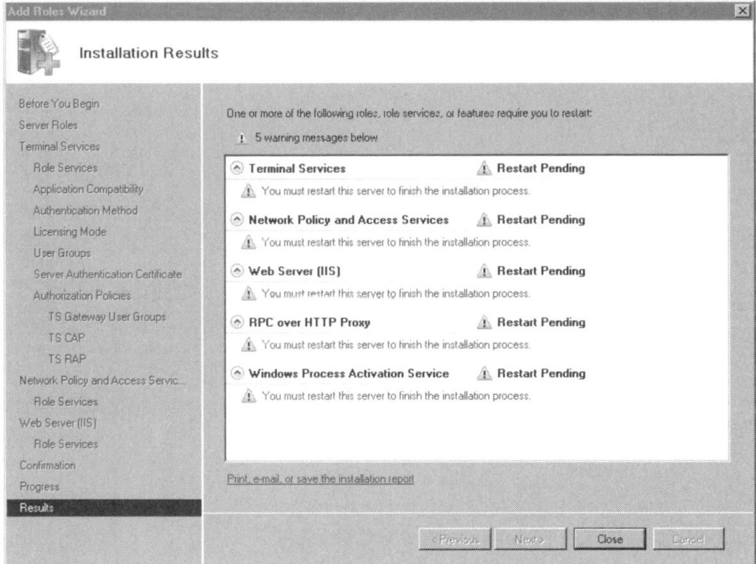

Figure 8-6 The Installation Results page

13. If your installation required a restart, you'll be prompted to restart the server. You might as well do it now because you can't install anything else while a restart is pending.

14. If your installation require a restart, be sure to log back on with the same account you used to add the role. The installation can't complete until you log back on with that account. The Resume Configuration Wizard will open and complete the installation of the roles and role services you selected, as shown in Figure 8-7. Click Close when the installation is complete.

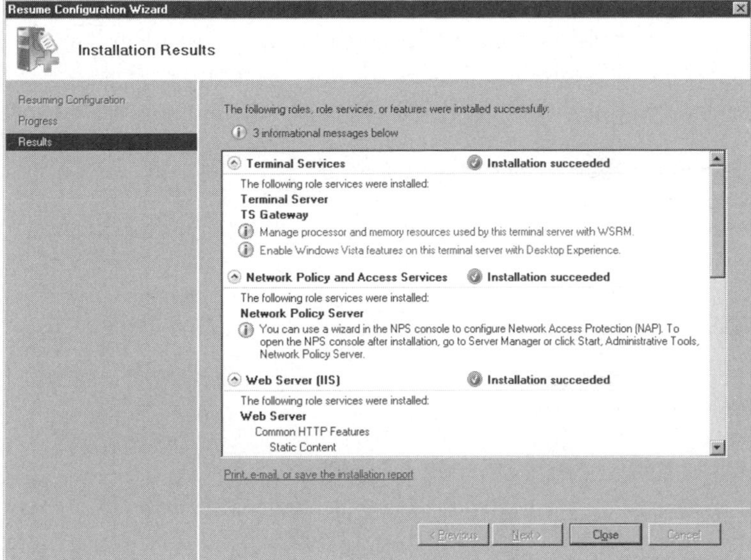

Figure 8-7 The Installation Results page of the Resume Configuration Wizard

Using the Command Line

To add a role using the command line, follow these steps:

1. Open an elevated command window by right-clicking the Command Prompt shortcut on the Start Menu and selecting Run As Administrator.
2. Type **ServerManagerCmd /?** to see a list of command-line options for the command.
3. To install the Terminal Services role with the Terminal Server role service, use the following command:

```
ServerManagerCmd -install Terminal-Services TS-Terminal-Server -restart
```

4. When you include the *–restart* command-line parameter, the server will automatically restart (without warning or delay) if that's required for the installation.

Removing a Role

You can use either the graphical Server Manager console to remove a role, or you can use the command-line utility ServerManagerCmd.exe. Both have the same functionality: They remove only the explicit role selected. They will not usually remove any roles or role services that were added during the initial role installation to support the role being removed–unless the role, role service, or feature *requires* the role that is being removed. That's a bit confusing, isn't it? OK, how about a specific example that makes it a bit clearer: Let's say you installed the Terminal Services role with all its role services. You'll also have Network Policy And Access Services installed, along with Web Server (IIS). You can uninstall the entire Terminal Services role and neither the Network Policy And Access Services nor Web Server (IIS) roles will removed. But if you remove the Web Server (IIS) role, it will also remove the RPC over HTTP Proxy feature, as shown in Figure 8-8.

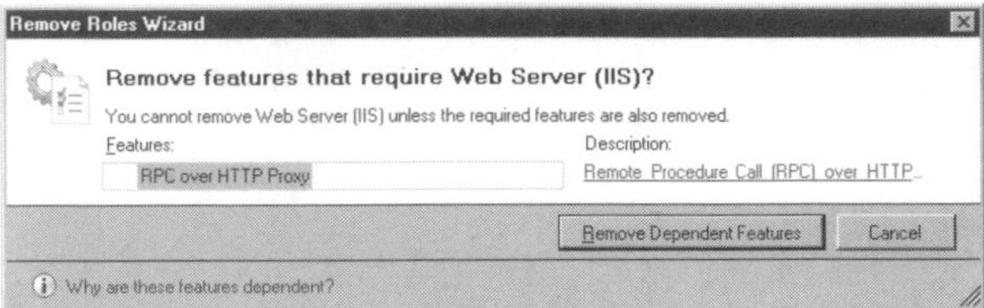

Figure 8-8 Removing the Web Server (IIS) role forces removal of the RPC over HTTP Proxy feature

Using the Server Manager Console

Using the Server Manager console to remove a role is usually a better solution than using the command line. When using the Server Manager console, you can see what other roles and role services are also installed, making it easy to remove any roles and role services that aren't needed but won't be automatically removed.

To remove a role using the Server Manager console, follow these steps:

1. Open the Server Manager Console if it isn't already open.
2. Select Remove Roles from the Action menu to open the Before You Begin page of the Remove Roles Wizard.
3. Read the advice on the Before You Begin page. It's actually good advice and a useful reminder. If you've read the page, understand all its implications, and don't ever want to see the page again, select the Skip This Page By Default check box. Personally, we leave it unchecked.
4. Click Next to open the Remove Server Roles page, as shown in Figure 8-9. Clear the roles you want to remove.

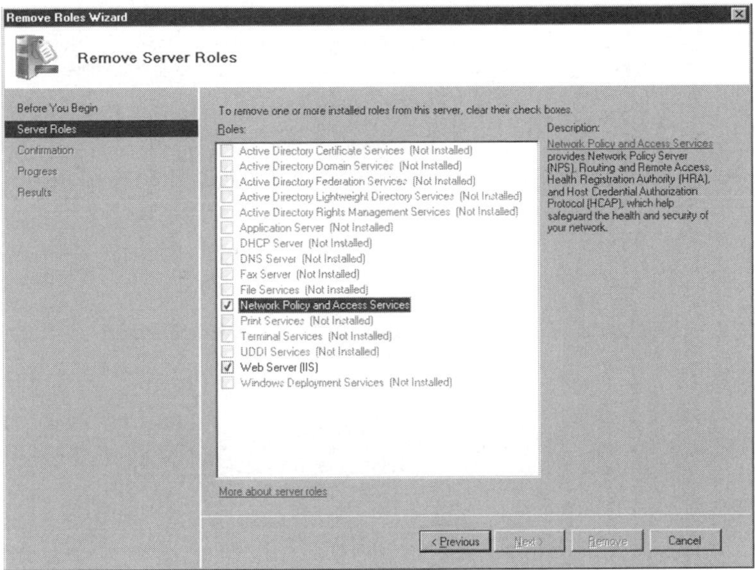

Figure 8-9 The Remove Server Roles page of the Remove Roles Wizard

5. If there are any dependent features, you'll be prompted to remove them also, as shown earlier in Figure 8-8.
6. When you've cleared the check boxes for any roles you want to remove, click Next to open the Confirm Removal Selections page, as shown in Figure 8-10. This page will often include one or more informational messages. Be sure you understand all implications of removing the role or roles.

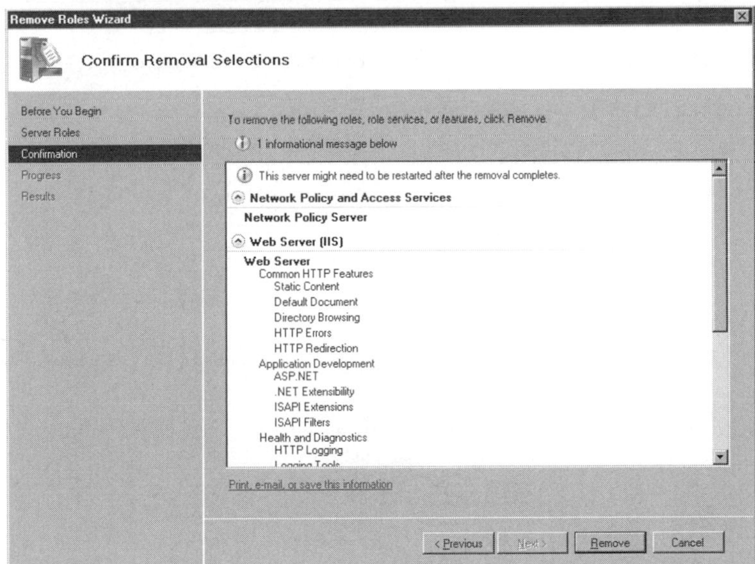

Figure 8-10 The Confirm Removal Selections page of the Remove Roles Wizard

---

Note You can print, e-mail, or save the information in the Confirm Removal Selections page by clicking below the informational window.

7. Click Remove to actually begin the removal.
8. When the removal has completed, you'll see the Removal Results page, as shown in Figure 8-11. If any of the roles or features require a restart, you'll see a message warning you that a restart is pending. In our experience, removing just about anything requires a restart.

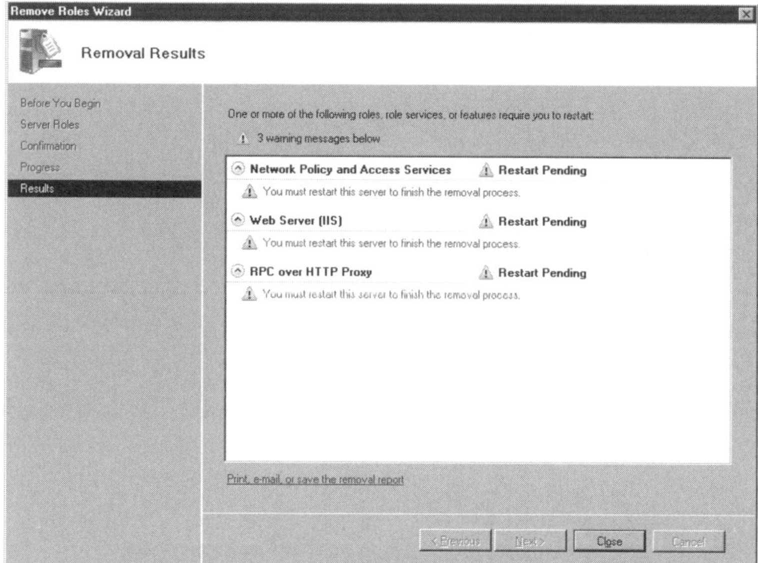

Figure 8-11 The Removal Results page of the Remove a Role Wizard

9. Click Close and then click Yes if prompted for a restart.
10. If your removal requires a restart, be sure to log back on with the same account you used to remove the role. The removal can't complete until you log back on with that account. The Resume Configuration Wizard will open and complete the removal of the roles you selected. Click Close when the removal is complete.

Using the Command Line

In general, we think using the command line to remove a role is not all that great an idea. You can't really see what's going to happen, and there are very few use cases for mass role removal across enough servers to make automation a necessary tool. But if you really feel the need, the command-line syntax is exactly the same as for adding a role. To remove a role from the command line, use the following command:

```
ServerManagerCmd -remove <Install ID> -restart
```

You can find the <*Install ID*> for all roles and role services in Table 8-1.

Adding and Removing Role Services

In many situations, you'll add or remove role services as a part of adding and removing the roles they are services for. But often enough you'll start out with one set of role services for a particular role, and at some point discover the need to add a role service or even remove a role service for something that's no longer needed.

The process of adding and removing role services is much the same as adding and removing roles, and follows many of the same steps. The command-line tool for adding and removing role services is the same as that for roles: ServerManagerCmd.exe.

Adding Role Services

Adding a role service requires that the role for that service be installed. You can't add the Services For Network File System role service without having the File Services role installed. (You can, of course, add the Network File System role service as part of the process of adding the File Services role.)

You can use either the command line or the graphical Server Manager console to add a role service. To add the Services For Network File System role service to the File Services role, follow these steps:

1. Open the Server Manager console if it isn't already open.
2. Select the File Services role in the left pane of the Server Manager console, as shown in Figure 8-12.

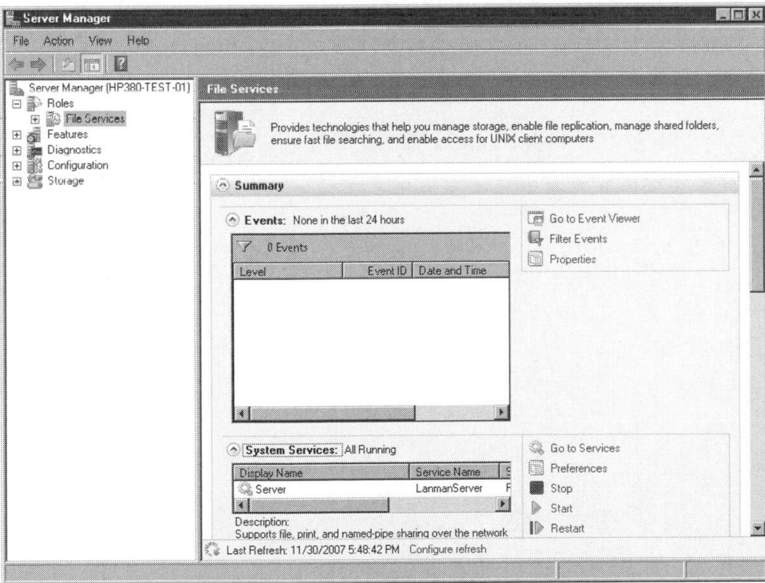

Figure 8-12 The Server Manager console, showing the File Services role

3. Select Add Role Services from the Action menu to open the Select Role Services page, as shown in Figure 8-13.

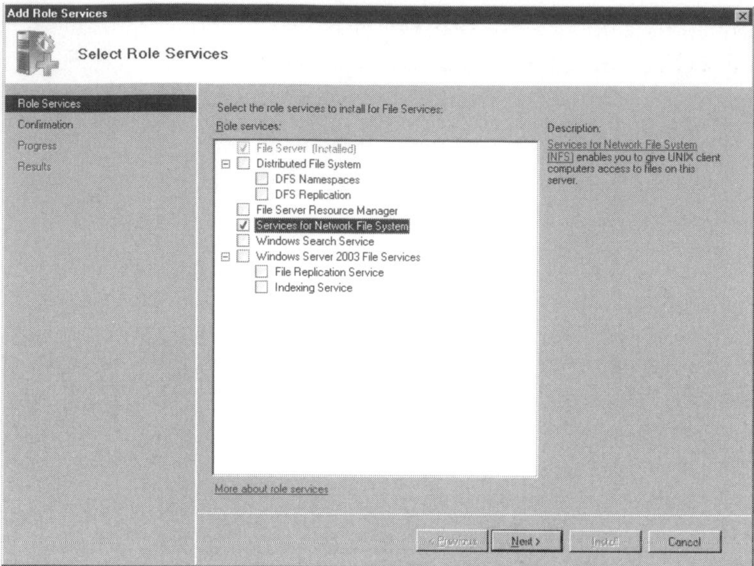

Figure 8-13 The Select Role Services page of the Add Role Services Wizard

4. Click Next to open the Confirm Installation Selections page.
5. Click Install to begin the installation.
6. After the installation is complete, the Installation Results page will open, as shown in Figure 8-14. If no restart is required, click Close to complete the installation.

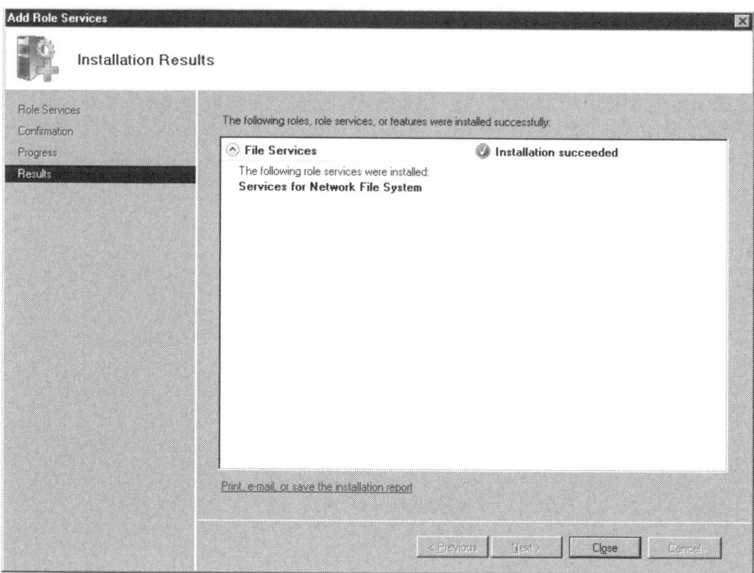

Figure 8-14 The Installation Results page of the Add Role Services Wizard

To perform the same installation of the Services For Network File System role service using the command line, the command line is:

```
Servermanagercmd -install FS-NFS-Services
```

Removing Role Services

Removing a role service doesn't necessarily remove the role. You can remove the Services For Network File System role service without affecting other role services of the File Services role.

You can use either the command line or the graphical Server Manager console to remove role services. As with removing roles, we have a hard time understanding why anyone would use the command line to remove a role service, but there's no particular reason not to. To remove the Services For Network File System role service of the File Services role, follow these steps:

1. Open the Server Manager console if it isn't already open.
2. Select the File Services role in the left pane of the Server Manager console.
3. Select Remove Role Service from the Action menu to open the Select Role Services page of the Remove Role Services Wizard, as shown in Figure 8-15.

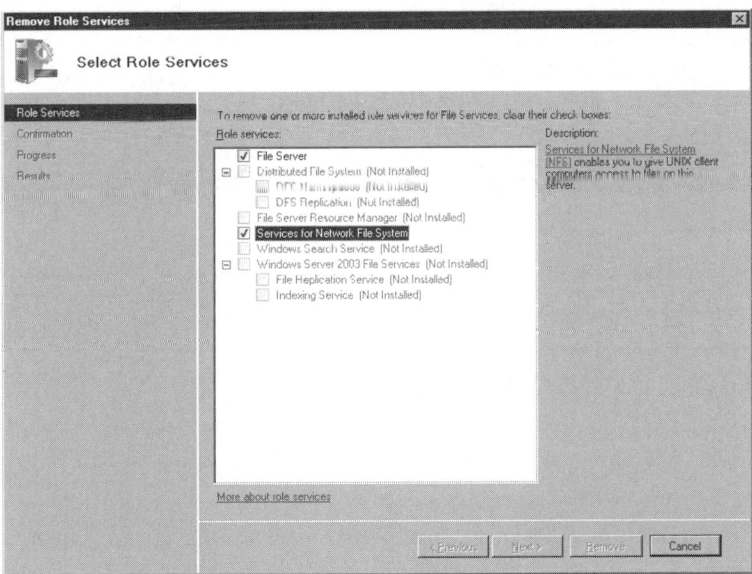

Figure 8-15 The Select Role Services page of the Remove Role Services Wizard

4. Clear Services For Network File System and click Next to open the Confirm Removal Selections page.
5. Click Remove to begin the removal process. When the process completes, you'll see the Removal Results page, as shown in Figure 8-16.

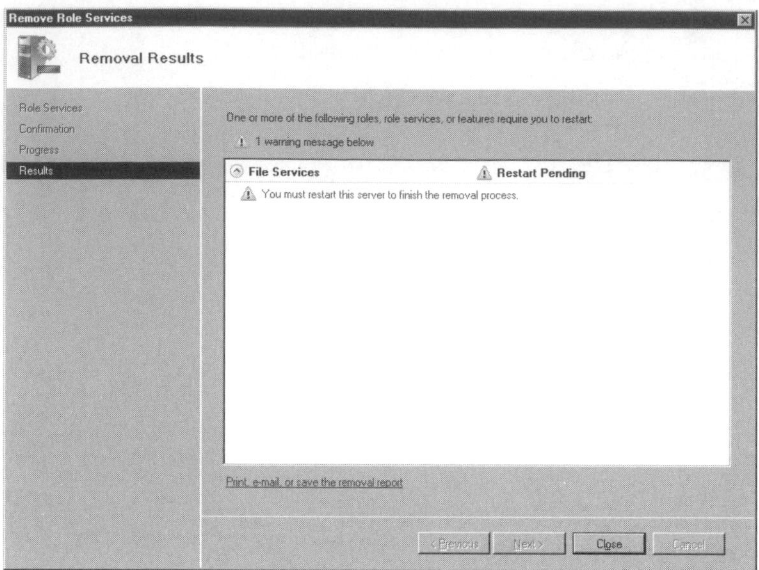

Figure 8-16 The Removal Results page of the Remove Role Services Wizard

6. Click Close to exit the wizard. Click Yes to restart the server if prompted.
7. If removing the role services requires a restart, be sure to log back on with the same account you used to remove the role service. The removal can't complete until you log back on with that account. The Resume Configuration Wizard will open and complete the removal of the role service you selected. Click Close when the removal is complete.

To perform the same removal of the Services For Network File System role service using the command line, use the following command:

```
Servermanagercmd -remove FS-NFS-Services -restart
```

Adding and Removing Features

You add and remove features using the same two tools that you use with roles and role services. The difference is that features are generally independent of the particular roles installed on a server. One of the first things we do with any server is to install some basic features that we find useful—or, in the case of PowerShell, essential—on any server we work with. These basic features are PowerShell, the Subsystem for UNIX Applications (SUA), and the Telnet Client.

Adding Features

Adding a feature to Windows Server 2008 usually doesn't require other features or roles, though there are exceptions. The exceptions include Message Queuing, which has several subsidiary features dependent on the main Message Queuing feature, and the .NET Framework 3.0 features, which also has several subsidiary features.

To install the three basic features we have on every server, follow these steps:

1. Open the Server Manager console if it isn't already open.
2. Select Features in the left pane of the Server Manager console.
3. Select Add Features from the Action menu to open the Select Features page of the Add Features Wizard, as shown in Figure 8-17.

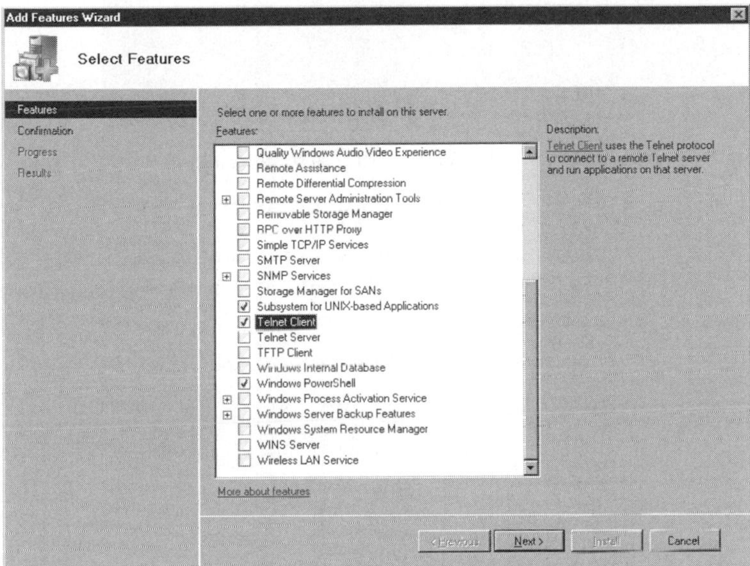

Figure 8-17 The Select Features page of the Add Features Wizard

4. Select the features you want to install and click Next to begin the installation process.
5. When the process completes, you'll see the Installation Results page (see Figure 8-18). If this page shows that one or more of your features has a pending restart, you'll need to restart the server before continuing.

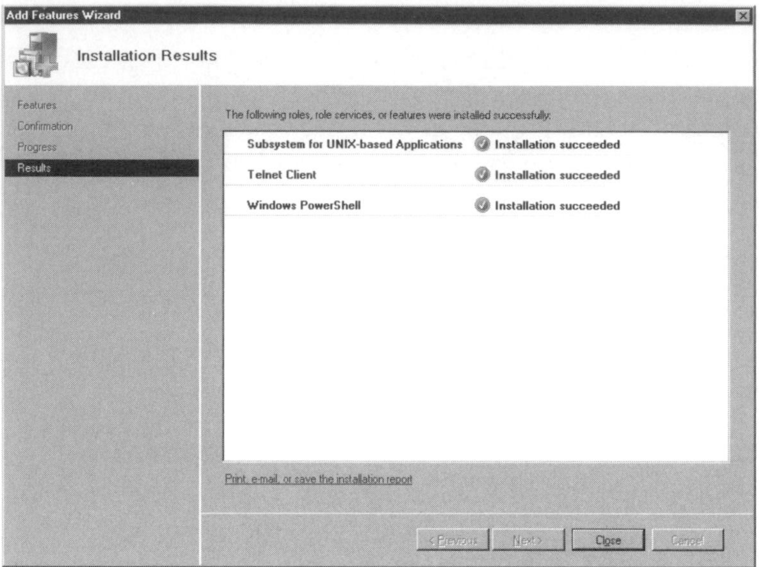

Figure 8-18 The Installation Results page of the Add Features Wizard

6. Click Close to exit the wizard. Click Yes to restart the server if prompted.
7. If your installation requires a restart, be sure to log back on with the same account you used to add the features. The installation isn't complete until you log back on with that account. The Resume Configuration Wizard will open and complete the installation of the features you selected. Click Close when the installation is complete.

To install the same three features using the command line, use the following command:

```
servermanagercmd -install Telnet-Client PowerShell Subsystem-UNIX-Apps
```

In our experience, these three features can be installed together without requiring a server restart. We've added the preceding command line to our standard build configuration, ensuring that the tools we need and expect are available on all servers.

Removing Features

Removing a feature from Windows Server 2008 usually doesn't affect other features or roles, though there are exceptions, including Message Queuing, which has several subsidiary features that depend on the main Message Queuing feature, and the .NET Framework 3.0 features, which also has several subsidiary features.

To remove the Telnet Client feature, follow these steps:

1. Open the Server Manager console if it isn't already open.

2. Select Features in the left pane of the Server Manager console and then highlight the feature you want to remove.
3. Select Remove Features from the Action menu to open the Select Features page of the Remove Features Wizard.
4. Clear the check box of the feature you want to remove and click Next to begin the removal process.
5. When the process completes, you'll see the Removal Results page. If this page shows a pending restart, you'll need to restart the server before continuing.
6. Click Close to exit the wizard. Click Yes to restart the server if prompted.
7. If your removal requires a restart, be sure to log back on with the same account you used to add the features. The removal isn't complete until you log back on with that account. The Resume Configuration Wizard will open and complete the removal of the features you selected. Click Close when the wizard is finished.

To remove the Telnet Client feature using the command line, use the following command:

```
servermanagercmd -remove Telnet-Client
```

Summary

In this chapter we've covered the basic steps for adding and removing roles, role services, and features on Windows Server 2008. As we continue in the book, we'll be using these same basic steps to install and configure the functionality we need in Windows Server 2008. An exception to this process is the new Server Core installation option of Windows Server 2008. Server Core uses different tools and has a more limited subset of available roles and features. In the next chapter we'll cover the basic steps to installing and configuring Server Core, and also build some scripts to make it easier.

Chapter 9

Installing and Configuring Server Core

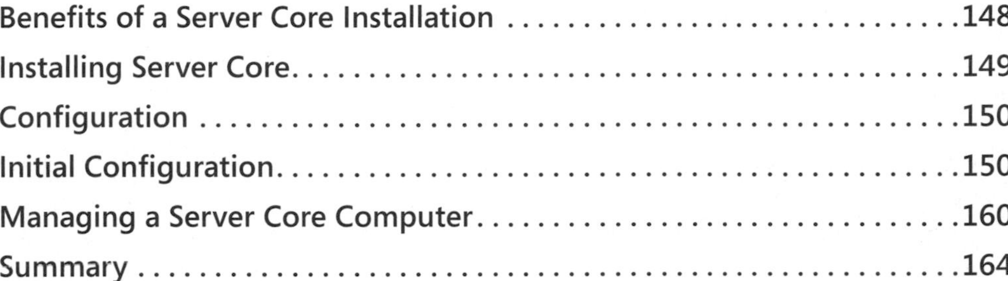

The usual progression for an operating system (or an application, for that matter) is to grow and add features, sometimes well beyond what any of us want or need. Windows Server 2008 reverses that trend with a completely new installation option–Server Core. When you install Windows Server 2008, regardless of which edition you're installing, you have the option of choosing a full installation, with everything, or just the Server Core portion.

Server Core is just the essentials, with little or no graphical interface. The logon provider has the same graphical look, but then, when you've logged in, all you see is a single command-shell window, as shown in Figure 9-1.

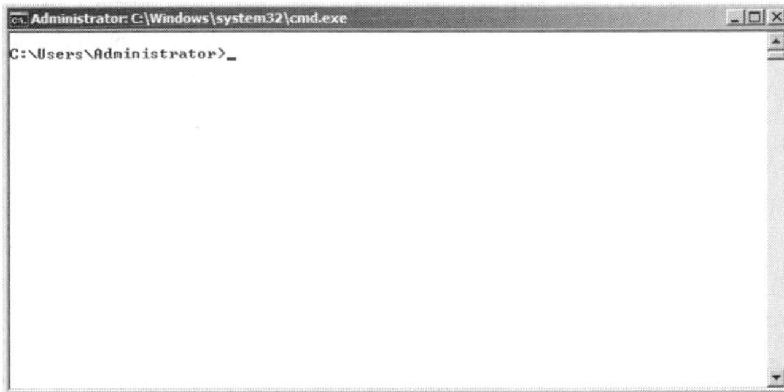

Figure 9-1 The Windows Server 2008 Core desktop.

Note For improved readability in screen shots used here and in the rest of the book, we've changed the default color scheme for Command Prompt windows to dark blue text on a white background.

Benefits of a Server Core Installation

All Windows Server 2008 editions support Server Core, with the exception of Compute Cluster Edition. And installing Server Core doesn't give you a break on the cost of the license–it's exactly the same license and media as the full Windows Server 2008 installation. At install time, you simply choose which edition you are installing. So, if you don't save any money, and you don't have special media, and you have reduced functionality, why in the world would you choose Server Core over the full product? It's simple, really: security and resources. Let's take a look at those two in a bit more depth before we go on to the details of how to actually install and configure Server Core.

Security

In the old days, whenever you installed Windows Server, it automatically installed just about everything that was available, and turned on all the services that you were likely to need. The goal was to make installation as simple as possible, and this seemed like a good idea at the time. Sadly, the world is not a friendly place for computers any more, and that approach is no longer safe or wise. The more services that exist, and the more services that are enabled, the more attack vectors the bad guys have to work with. To improve security, limiting the available attack surfaces is just good common sense.

In Server Core, Microsoft has completely removed all managed code, and the entire .NET Framework. This leaves a whole lot fewer places for possible attack. This does, obviously, impose some severe limits on what you can and can't do with a Server Core installation. And it also means that there isn't any PowerShell possible, which in our opinion is easily the biggest limitation of Server Core–but one that we hope will be resolved in a later version of Windows Server.

The default installation of Server Core has only less than 40 services running. A typical full Windows Server 2008 installation, with one or two roles enabled, is likely to have 60 or even 70 or more services running. Not only does the reduced number of services limit the potential attack surface that must be protected, but it also limits the number of patches that are likely to be required over the life of the server, making it easier to maintain.

Resources

The second major benefit to running Server Core is the reduced resources required for the base operating system. While the official requirements for installing Windows Server 2008 are the same for Core as for a full installation, the effective numbers are significantly less, in our experience–with the exception of the disk space required (only 2 to 3 GB of HD space for a running Core installation). Plus with the limited subset of tasks that you can perform, we think Server Core is ideal for running those infrastructure tasks that everyone runs, and that don't require much interaction over time. Tasks such as DHCP, DNS, and, increasingly, virtualization. Now if it just had PowerShell...

Installing Server Core

Installing Windows Server 2008 Server Core is ultimately the same as installing the full graphical version of Windows Server 2008. The installation engine is the same, and the only difference occurs during the install, when you have to choose which version of Windows Server 2008 to install, as shown in Figure 9-2.

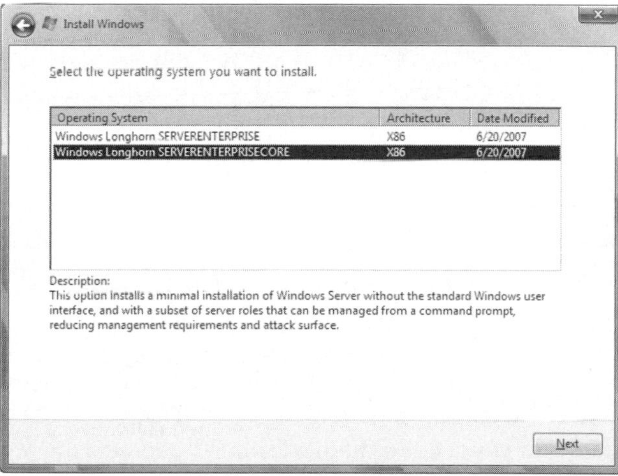

Figure 9-2 During initial installation, you make an irrevocable choice between Server and Server Core.

Once installation completes, you're presented with the initial logon screen. Log on as Administrator, with no password, and you'll be immediately prompted to change the password and then logged on to the desktop, as shown earlier in Figure 9-1. All initial configuration takes place from the command line, though once you've configured the basics, you'll be able to use familiar management consoles remotely.

You can use an unattend.xml file to automate the initial install and configuration of your Server Core installation. For details on the settings and syntax of unattend.xml, see *http://go.microsoft.com/fwlink/?LinkId=81030*.

Configuration

You can do all configuration tasks for Server Core at the command line, and all the initial tasks must be done at either the command line or as part of the installation process by using an unattend.xml script. Once you're performed these initial configuration tasks, you can then use regular Windows management consoles to manage the additional settings. Unfortunately, there isn't a single command shell for the tasks, but a collection of old favorites, each with a different behavior and syntax.

Initial Configuration

The initial steps you'll need to perform on a Server Core installation will depend somewhat on your intended use of the installation, but we think that the following ones are the most obvious:

- Set a fixed IP address.
- Change the server name to match your internal standards.
- Join the server to a domain.
- Change the default resolution of the console.
- Enable remote management through Windows Firewall.
- Enable remote desktop.
- Activate the server.

We'll walk through these steps for you, and leave you with a couple of basic scripts that you can modify to automate these tasks for your environment. Table 9-1 contains the settings we'll be using during this install scenario.

Table 9-1 Settings for Initial Server Core Configuration (Example)

Setting	Value
IP Address	192.168.51.4
Gateway	192.168.51.1
DNS Server	192.168.51.2
Server Name	Hp350-core-04

Table 9-1 **Settings for Initial Server Core Configuration (Example)**

Setting	**Value**
Domain To Join	example.local
Default Desktop Resolution	1024x768
Remote Management	Enable for Domain Profile
Windows Activation	Activate

Set IP Address

To set the IP address for the server, you need to use the **netsh** command-line tool. Follow these steps to configure TCP/IP:

1. From the command window, use **netsh** to get the "name" (index number) of the network card.

   ```
   netsh interface ipv4 show interfaces
   ```

2. The result will be something like the following:

   ```
   C:\Users\administrator>netsh interface ipv4 show interfaces

   Idx  Met   MTU   State        Name
   ---  ---  -----  -----------  -------------------
     2   10   1500  connected    Local Area Connection
     1   50 4294967295  connected    Loopback Pseudo-Interface 1
   ```

   The Idx value for your real network card (2, in this case) will be used as the name value in future commands for **netsh**.

3. Now, using the Idx value from step 2, run the following **netsh** command:

   ```
   netsh interface ipv4 set address name="<Idx>" source=static
       address=<IP Address> mask=<netmask>
       gateway=<IP Address of default gateway>
   ```

> **Note** The **netsh** lines above, and in examples below, are actually one long command line, but we had to break them (and indent subsequent lines) because of the limitations of the printed page. And it's not just **netsh** that is a problem—most of the commands you end up having to use with Server Core are long and will be artificially broken in this chapter.

4. Next, specify the DNS server for the adapter, using **netsh** again:

```
netsh interface ipv4 add dnsserver name="<Idx>"
   address=<IP Address of DNS Server> index=1
```

5. For secondary DNS servers, repeat the command in step 4, increasing the index value by one each time.

Renaming the Server and Joining to a Domain

The next step in initial configuration is assigning the name of the server and joining it to a domain. During initial installation of Windows Server 2008, an automatically generated name is assigned to the server and the server is placed in the WORKGROUP workgroup. You'll want to change this to align the computer name with your corporate naming policy and join the server to the correct domain and Organizational Unit. Our naming policy here has three parts: the model of server, the functional role, and a number reflecting its IP address. Thus the Server Core computer we're building in this chapter is named hp350-core-04: it's a Hewlett Packard ML 350 G5 server, it is running Server Core, and the final octet of its IP address is four. Your server naming convention will undoubtedly be different, but the important thing is to be consistent. Our domain for this book is example.local.

To change the name of the server and join it to the example.local domain, follow these steps:

1. From the command prompt, use the **netdom** command to change the name of the server:

   ```
   netdom renamecomputer %COMPUTERNAME% /newname:<newname>
   ```

2. After you change the name, you must reboot the server.

   ```
   shutdown /t 0 /r
   ```

3. After the server restarts, log on to the Administrator account.
4. Use the **netdom** command again to join the domain.

   ```
   netdom join %COMPUTERNAME% /DOMAIN:<domainname>
      /userd:<domain admin account> /password:*
   ```

5. You'll be prompted for the password for the domain administrative account you used. Enter the password. When the domain join has succeeded, you'll again need to reboot the server.

   ```
   shutdown /t 0 /r
   ```

6. After the server restarts, log back on to a domain administrator's account. (You'll need to click Change User because the server will default to the local administrator account.)

Under the Hood Scripting Initial Configuration

If you set up more than one or two Server Core computers, you'll quickly get tired of doing all this interactively from the command prompt. We know we did. You have the choice of either using an unattend.xml file to set options during the install or using simple scripts to automate the process. Both work, and both have their adherents, but we tend to use scripts after the fact. You can modify the following three scripts (which you'll also find on the companion CD) for your environment to automate the initial TCP/IP, server name, and domain join steps.

The first script sets the IP address, sets the DNS server, and changes the server name.

```
echo off
REM filename: initsetup1.cmd
REM
REM initial setup for a Server 2008 Server Core installation.
REM command file 1 of 3
REM
REM Created: 4 September, 2007
REM ModHist: 5/9/07 - switched to variables (cpr)
REM
REM Copyright 2007 Charlie Russel and Sharon Crawford. All rights reserved.
REM   You may freely use this script in your own environment, modifying it
REM   to meet your needs. But you may not re-publish it without permission.

REM first, set a fixed IP address. You'll need to know the index number
REM of the interface you're setting, but in a default Server Core install,
REM with only a single NIC, the index should be 2. To find the index,
REM you can run:
REM      netsh interface ipv4 show interfaces
REM

SETLOCAL
REM Change the values below to match your needs
SET IPADD=192.168.51.4
SET IPMASK=255.255.255.0
SET IPGW=192.168.51.1
SET DNS1=192.168.51.2
SET NEWNAME=hp350-core-04

netsh interface ipv4 set address name="2" source=static
   address=%IPADD% mask=%IPMASK% gateway=%IPGW%

REM Next, set DNS to point to DNS server for example.local.
REM   192.168.51.2 in this case
netsh interface ipv4 add dnsserver name="2" address=%DNS1% index=1
```

```
REM Now, we need to change the computer name. After we're done, the server
REM must be restarted, and we can continue with the next batch of commands.
REM we use the /force command here to avoid prompts
netdom renamecomputer %COMPUTERNAME% /newname:%NEWNAME% /force

@echo If everything looks OK, the it's time to reboot
pause
REM now, shutdown and reboot. No need to wait.
shutdown /t 0 /r
```

The second script we use is to actually join the server to the domain.

```
@echo off
REM Filename: initsetup2.cmd
REM
REM initial setup for a Server 2008 Server Core installation.
REM command file 2 of 3
REM
REM Created: 4 September, 2007
REM ModHist:
REM
REM Copyright 2007 Charlie Russel and Sharon Crawford. All rights reserved.
REM   You may freely use this script in your own environment, modifying it
REM   to meet your needs. But you may not re-publish it without permission.

SETLOCAL
SET DOMAIN=example.local
SET DOMADMIN=Administrator

REM Join the domain using the netdom join command. Prompts for password
REM of domain administrator account set above

netdom join %COMPUTERNAME% /DOMAIN:%DOMAIN% /userd:%DOMADMIN% /password:*

REM now, shutdown and reboot. No need to wait, and that's all we can do
REM at this time

shutdown /t 0 /r
```

Finally, use the third script to enable remote management and activate the server.

```
echo off
REM initsetup3.cmd
REM
REM initial setup for a Server 2008 Server Core installation.
REM command file 3 of 3
REM
REM Created: 4 September, 2007
REM ModHist:
REM
```

```
REM Copyright 2007 Charlie Russel and Sharon Crawford. All rights reserved.
REM   You may freely use this script in your own environment, modifying it
REM   to meet your needs. But you may not re-publish it without permission.

REM Use netsh to enable remote management through the firewall for the
REM domain profile. This is the minimum to allow using remote MMCs to work
REM from other computers in the domain.

netsh advfirewall set domainprofile settings remotemanagement enable

REM allow remote administration group
netsh advfirewall firewall set rule group="Remote Administration" new
    enable=yes

REM Allow remote desktop
REM (also works with group="Remote Desktop" instead of name=)
netsh advfirewall firewall set rule name="Remote Desktop (TCP-In)" new
    enable=yes

REM Enable Remote Desktop for Administration, and allow
REM downlevel clients to connect
cscript %windir%\system32\scregedit.wsf /AR 0
cscript %windir%\system32\scregedit.wsf /CS 0

REM Now, run the activation script
REM No output means it worked
Slmgr.vbs -ato
```

Setting Desktop Display Resolution

To set the display resolution for the Server Core desktop, you need to manually edit the registry. We'd give you a script to do it, but it is dependent on correctly identifying the specific GUID for your display adapter. Not something we want to automate. So, to change the resolution on your Server Core desktop, follow these steps:

1. Open `regedit`.
2. Navigate to HKLM\System\CurrentControlSet\Control\Video.
3. One or more GUIDs is listed under Video. Select the one that corresponds to your video card. Hint: They each have a device description under the 0000 key that can sometimes help.
4. Under the GUID for your video card select the 0000 key, and add a DWORD DefaultSettings.XResolution. Edit the value to the X axis resolution you want. For a width of 1024 pixels, use 400 hexadecimal, as shown in Figure 9-3.

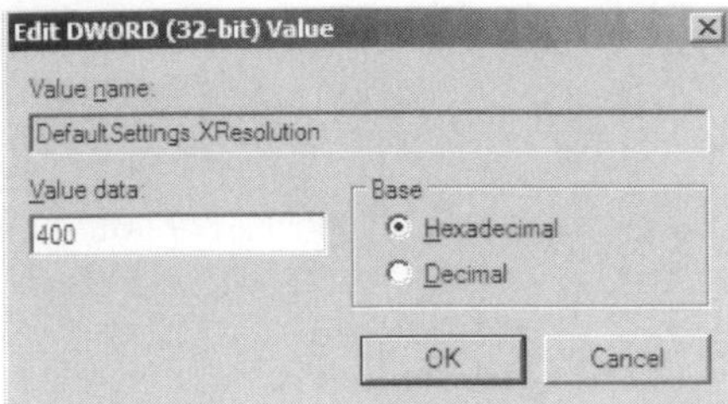

Figure 9-3 Editing the display resolution value for the X axis

5. Add a DWORD DefaultSettings.YResolution. For height of 768 pixels, use 300 hexadecimal.

> **Note** In some cases, these keys will already exist. If they do, you can simply change their value as necessary.

6. Exit the registry editor and log off using the following:

```
shutdown /l
```

7. Once you log back on, the new display settings will take effect.

Enabling Remote Management

To allow access to the familiar graphical administration tools, you need to enable them to work through Windows Firewall. This requires another set of **netsh** commands. Use the following steps to enable remote administration and Remote Desktop:

1. From the command prompt, use the **netsh** command to enable remote management:

```
netsh advfirewall set domainprofile settings remotemanagement enable
```

2. Now, enable the Remote Administration group of firewall rules.

```
netsh advfirewall firewall set rule group="Remote Administration" new
    enable=yes
```

3. Finally, life is easier when you can connect using remote desktop, so let's enable that, too:

```
netsh advfirewall firewall set rule name="Remote Desktop (TCP-In)" new
    enable=yes
```

You should now be able to do additional management using familiar graphical tools from another server but connecting to the Server Core computer.

Activating the Server

The final step in basic configuration of the Server Core computer is to activate it. This requires using a Visual Basic script, which is provided. Use the following command:

```
Slmgr.vbs -ato
```

Note All the basic initial setup commands for Server Core are included in the three scripts described in the Under The Hood sidebar, and are also available on the CD that comes with the book.

Installing Roles

Windows Server 2008 Core doesn't support all the possible roles and features of the full graphical Windows Server, but it does support the most important infrastructure roles. We think one of the most compelling scenarios for Server Core is as a remote site server to enable basic functionality at a remote site where there isn't anyone on site to administer it. By combining the DHCP Server, DNS Server, File Services, and Print Services roles with a read-only Active Directory Domain Services role, you have a "branch office in a box" solution–just add a remote access device such as a VPN router and you're in business.

The File Services role is added by default as part of the base Server Core installation, but you can add additional role services to support additional functionality.

The command used to install a role in Server Core is Ocsetup.exe. The exact same command is used to uninstall a role, but with the */uninstall* command-line parameter. The full syntax for `Ocsetup` is:

```
Ocsetup </?|/h|/help>
Ocsetup <component> [/uninstall][/passive][/unattendfile:<file>] [/quiet]
   [/log:<file>][/norestart][/x:<parameters>]
```

The important thing to remember about `Ocsetup` is that it is quite unforgiving. It is case-sensitive, and even a slight mistake in the case of the component name will cause the command to fail.

A script to install the roles for this solution, except the domain controller role, would look like this:

```
@REM filename: SetupBranch.cmd
@REM
@REM Setup file to install roles for a branch office server
@REM
@REM Created: 5 September, 2007
@REM ModHist:
@REM
```

```
@REM Copyright 2007 Charlie Russel and Sharon Crawford. All rights reserved
@REM   You may freely use this script in your own environment,
@REM   modifying it to meet your needs.
@REM   But you may not re-publish it without permission.

@REM Using "start /w" with ocsetup forces ocsetup to wait until it
@RME completes before
going on to the next task.

@REM Install DNS and DHCP
@echo Installing DNS and DHCP roles...
start /w ocsetup DNS-Server-Core-Role
start /w ocsetup DHCPServerCore

@REM Now, install File Role Services
@echo Now installing File Role Services...
start /w ocsetup FRS-Infrastructure
start /w ocsetup DFSN-Server
start /w ocsetup DFSR-Infrastructure-ServerEdition

@REM Uncomment these two lines to add NFS support
@REM start /w ocsetup ServerForNFS-Base

@REM start /w ocsetup ClientForNFS-Base

@REM Install Print Server Role

@echo Installing Print Server Role
start /w ocsetup Printing-ServerCore-Role

@REM Uncomment next for LPD support
@REM start /w ocsetup Printing-LPDPrintService
```

Note You can't include the **DCPromo** command in the script above because installing the Print Server role requires a reboot, which locks out **DCPromo**.

You cannot use **DCPromo** interactively to create a domain controller–you must create an unattend.txt file to use with it. The basic minimum unattend.txt file is:

```
[DCInstall]
InstallDNS = Yes
ConfirmGC = yes
CriticalReplicationOnly = No
RebootOnCompletion = No
ReplicationSourceDC = hp350-dc-02.example.local
ParentDomainDNSName = example.local
ReplicaOrNewDomain = ReadOnlyReplica
ReplicaDomainDNSName = example.local
```

```
SiteName=Default-First-Site-Name
SafeModeAdminPassword = <passwd> UserDomain = example
UserName = Administrator
Password = <passwd>
```

Important The passwords fields must be correct, and will be automatically stripped from the file for security reasons. For Server Core, you must specify a *ReplicationSourceDC* value. You should set *ReplicaOrNewDomain* to the value shown here—*ReadOnlyReplica*—to create a read-only domain controller.

To install the read-only Domain Controller role, follow these steps:

1. Use Notepad or your favorite ASCII text editor (we use GVim, which works quite well in Server Core) to create an unattend.txt file with the necessary settings for the domain you will be joining. The specific filename of the unattend file is not important because you specify it on the command line.
2. Change to the directory that contains the unattend file. If the server has any pending restarts, you *must* complete them before promoting the server to domain controller.
3. Run DCPromo with the following syntax:

   ```
   Dcpromo /unattend:<unattendfilename>
   ```

4. If there are no errors in the unattend file, DCPromo will proceed and promote the server to be a read-only domain controller, as shown in Figure 9-4.

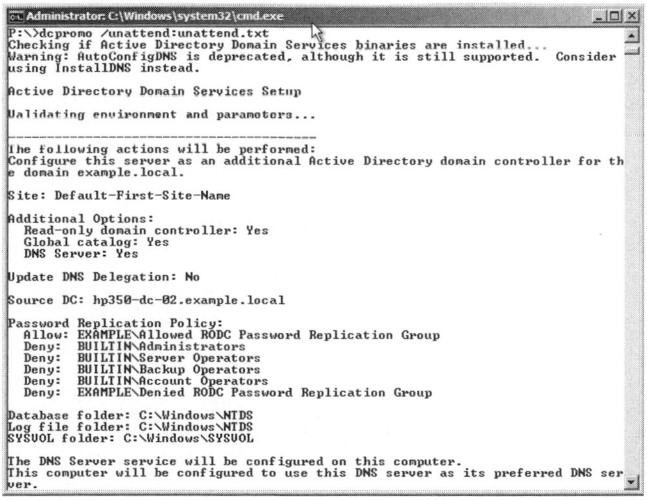

```
Administrator: C:\Windows\system32\cmd.exe
P:\>dcpromo /unattend:unattend.txt
Checking if Active Directory Domain Services binaries are installed...
Warning: AutoConfigDNS is deprecated, although it is still supported.  Consider
using InstallDNS instead.

Active Directory Domain Services Setup

Validating environment and parameters...

----------------------------------------
The following actions will be performed:
Configure this server as an additional Active Directory domain controller for th
e domain example.local.

Site: Default-First-Site-Name

Additional Options:
  Read-only domain controller: Yes
  Global catalog: Yes
  DNS Server: Yes

Update DNS Delegation: No

Source DC: hp350-dc-02.example.local

Password Replication Policy:
  Allow: EXAMPLE\Allowed RODC Password Replication Group
  Deny:  BUILTIN\Administrators
  Deny:  BUILTIN\Server Operators
  Deny:  BUILTIN\Backup Operators
  Deny:  BUILTIN\Account Operators
  Deny:  EXAMPLE\Denied RODC Password Replication Group

Database folder: C:\Windows\NTDS
Log file folder: C:\Windows\NTDS
SYSVOL folder: C:\Windows\SYSVOL

The DNS Server service will be configured on this computer.
This computer will be configured to use this DNS server as its preferred DNS ser
ver.
```

Figure 9-4 Use DCPromo to create a read-only domain controller with an unattend file.

Listing Roles

The Oclist.exe command provides a complete list of the available Server Core roles, role services, and features, as well as their current state. Use `Oclist` to get the exact, case-sensitive list of the features and roles you want to install.

Managing a Server Core Computer

Managing a Server Core computer is a different experience for most system administrators. None of the graphical tools you're used to using is available *on the server.* But once you've configured the Server Core computer for remote management, as described under "Initial Configuration" earlier in the chapter, you can create management consoles that point to the Server Core computer, which allow you to do all your tasks from a graphical console.

More Info For details on how to create custom MMCs, see Chapter 14, "Managing Daily Operations."

There are four basic ways to manage a Server Core installation. They are:

1. Locally using a command prompt.
2. Remotely using Remote Desktop. The shell in Remote Desktop will have only the same functionality (a command prompt) as being logged on locally.
3. Remotely using Windows Remote Shell.
4. Remotely using an MMC snap-in from a computer running Windows Vista or Windows Server 2008.

Some tasks are a bit tricky in Server Core–we're used to usually doing them exclusively from the GUI. An obvious task is changing the password on your account. For that, use the `net user <username> *` command. Some of the tasks that can be a problem, and their solutions, are shown in Table 9-2.

Table 9-2 Common Task Workarounds in Server Core

Task	Solution/Workaround
Enable automatic updates	Cscript %windir%\system32\scregedit.wsf /AU [value] Where values are: 1 – disable automatic updates 4 – enable automatic updates /v – view current setting

Table 9-2 Common Task Workarounds in Server Core

Task	Solution/Workaround
Enable Remote Desktop for Administrators	Cscript %windir%\system32\scregedit.wsf /AR [value] Where values are: 0 – enable Remote Desktop 1 – disable Remote Desktop /v – view current setting
Enable Terminal Server clients from Windows versions prior to Windows Vista	Cscript %windir%\system32\scregedit.wsf /CS [value] Where values are: 0 – enable prior versions 1 – disable prior versions /v – view current setting
Allow IPSec Monitor remote management	Cscript %windir%\system32\scregedit.wsf /IM [value] Where values are: 0 – disable remote management 1 – enable remote management /v – view current setting
Configure DNS SRV record weight and priority	Cscript %windir%\system32\scregedit.wsf /DP [value] Where DNS SRV priority values are: 0-65535. (Recommended value = 200) /v – view current setting Cscript %windir%\system32\scregedit.wsf /DW [value] Where DNS SRV weight values are: 0-65535. (Recommended value = 50) /v – view current setting
Update User passwords	Net user <username> [/domain] *
Installing .msi files	Use the /q or /qb switches from the command line with the full .msi filename. /q is quiet; /qb is quiet but with a basic user interface
Changing the time zone, date, or time	timedate.cpl
Change internationalization settings	intl.cpl
Using Disk Management console	From the command line of the Server Core installation: Net start VDS Then run Disk Management remotely.
Get Windows version information	Winver is not available. Use systeminfo.exe instead.
Get Help (regular Windows Help and Support files are not viewable in Server Core)	Cscript %windir%\system32\scregedit.wsf /cli

Using Windows Remote Shell

You can use Windows Remote Shell to remotely execute commands on a Server Core computer. But before you can run Windows Remote Shell, you need to first enable it on the target Server Core computer. To enable Windows Remote Shell, use the following command:

```
winrm quickconfig
```

To run a command remotely, use the `WinRS` command from another computer using the following command:

```
winrs -r:<ServerName> <command string to execute>
```

Using Terminal Server RemoteApp

One neat trick that we like is to use the new TS RemoteApp functionality of Windows Server 2008 to publish a Command Prompt window for the Server Core computer directly onto our desktop. This is simpler and more direct, and saves screen real estate, which is always a benefit. To create an RDP package that you can put on your desktop, follow these steps:

1. On a Windows Server 2008 server that has the Terminal Services role enabled, open the TS RemoteApp Manager, as shown in Figure 9-5.

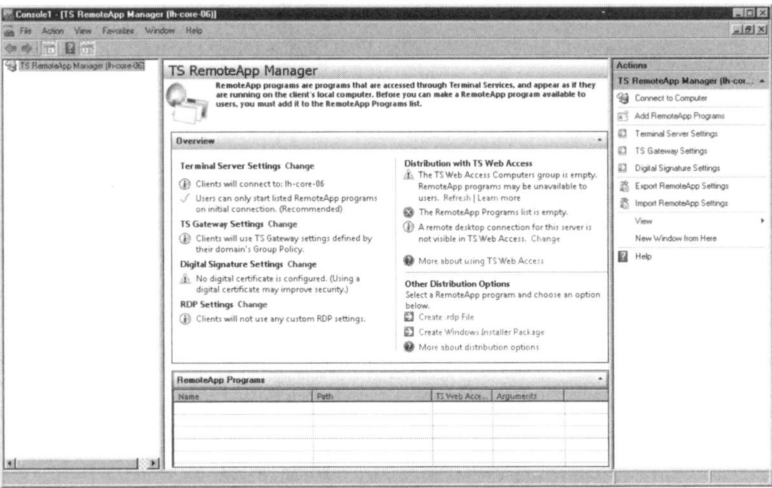

Figure 9-5 Use the TS RemoteApp Manager to create a remote cmd.exe window.

2. Connect to the Server Core computer you want to build an RDP package for.

3. Click Add RemoteApp Programs in the actions pane to open the RemoteApp Wizard.

4. Click Next to open the Choose Programs To Add To The RemoteApp Programs List page, shown in Figure 9-6.

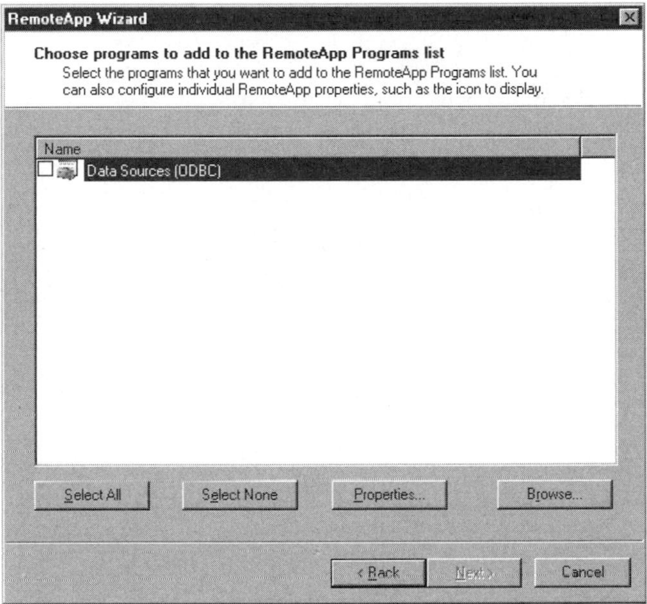

Figure 9-6 The Choose Programs To Add To The RemoteApp Programs List page of the RemoteApp Wizard

5. Click Browse, and navigate to \\<ServerName>\c$\windows\system32\cmd.exe. Click Open.

6. Click Next and then click Finish to add the remote program and return to the TS RemoteApp Manager.

7. Select cmd.exe in the RemoteApp programs pane and click Create .rdp File in the actions pane.

8. Click Next, and specify any additional package settings for the RDP package. Note the location where the package will be saved.

9. Click Next twice and then click Finish to create the RDP package.

10. Copy the package to the computer where you will use it.

Now you can open a Command Prompt window directly onto the Server Core computer simply by double-clicking the RDP package you created and saved.

Summary

In this chapter we've covered some basic steps for setting up and configuring the new Server Core installation option of Windows Server 2008. We think this is an exciting new way to get the power of Windows Server while maintaining very high levels of security and ease of management. And yes, we know that sounds a bit like marketing hype, but we actually think that Server Core is an important step forward.

In the next chapter, we'll cover managing and configuring your printers using the Printer Management console.

Chapter 10

Managing Printers

As much as everyone would like to have a paperless office, it appears we'll all be much grayer (or balder, or both) before that completely comes to pass. Office paper consumption peaked in 1999 and since then the quantities of waste in the office paper-recycling bin have leveled off and in some places have actually begun to shrink. However, even if fewer people are printing out their e-mails before reading them, paper remains at the center of many business operations.

The cost of basic printers has declined dramatically, but companies are investing in sophisticated high-speed printers that allow users to handle jobs that once required an outside print shop. These are expensive both to buy and to use. Therefore, printer sharing remains an important function of enterprise networks. Setting up multiple users to share printers reduces cost and can increase printing output. You can direct routine work to low-cost-per-page printers, schedule long print jobs for off hours, and limit access to high-end printers.

Planning Printer Deployment

When you are planning the deployment of printers and print servers, it's important to establish printer- and location-naming conventions, evaluate whether to upgrade or migrate existing print servers, and prepare for print server failures.

Best Practices When possible, connect printers to the print server via a network connection. Network printers are faster and require fewer resources on the print server than do locally attached printers, and you can also place the printers anywhere you can run a network cable (or wireless connection).

Establishing Printer Naming Conventions

An effective printer-naming convention is important to ensure that users can easily identify printers on the network. When creating a printer-naming convention, consider the following:

- The *printer name* can be any length up to 220 characters, which is plenty of room for any scheme you devise. Of course, the name should also be as short as possible without sacrificing clarity.
- The *share name* is the name that all clients see when they browse for a printer, use the Add Printer Wizard, or use the Net Use command. It can be up to 80 characters long, but again should be shorter for readability. Some older applications cannot print to printers with fully qualified printer share names (the computer name and printer share name combined) that exceed 31 characters, or to print servers where the default printer's share name exceeds 31 characters. Clients using other operating systems might also have trouble with names longer than 31 characters or names containing spaces or other special characters. But whether you have to deal with such applications or not, shorter is generally better.
- The agreement of relevant management is necessary before deploying a naming convention to ensure compliance.

Creating a Location-Naming Convention

In small organizations, finding printers is easy—just stand up and look around or ask the person sitting next to you. This doesn't work as well in larger organizations where printers have varying capabilities and might be widely scattered. Under these circumstances, users need to be able to browse or search for printers in Active Directory based on the criteria they want, including printer features and printer location.

Location names are similar in form to domain names and use the *name/name/name...* syntax. They start with the most general location name and become progressively more specific. For example, a multinational corporation might have the location name structure shown in Figure 10-1. Each part name can have a maximum of 32 characters and can contain any characters except the forward slash (/), which Windows reserves as a delimiter.

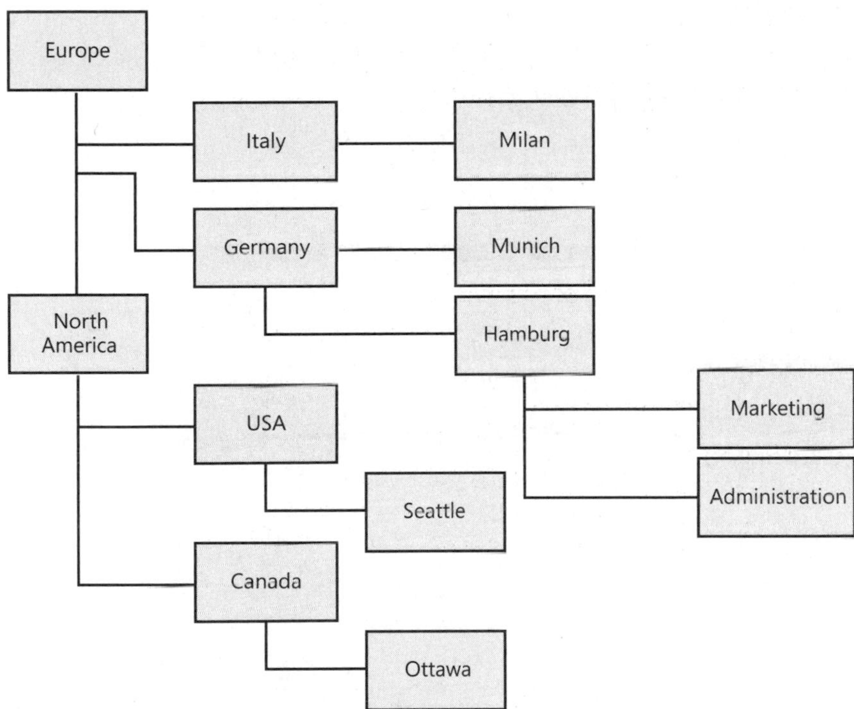

Figure 10-1 A sample location name structure

Like choosing domain names, creating a printer location-naming scheme is political, so get the appropriate sign-off. Keep the naming convention simple and easy to understand for end users—after all, they need to be able to look at the location name and answer the age-old question, "Where's my printout?" Design/ArtStudio/HPDesignJet5500 is one example of a location name.

After creating a printer location–naming convention, enable printer location tracking in Active Directory, as discussed in the "Enabling Printer Location Tracking" section of this chapter.

If you're not using the printer location tracking feature of Active Directory, you can still include location information with printers, although this approach has some limitations. To enter location information, type the location name in the General tab of the printer's Properties dialog box. Be careful and consistent with location names. Make sure that all administrators use the same name for a particular location, and keep the names short and easy to remember: Users need to know the exact location names when they search for printers if Active Directory's location-browsing capabilities are unavailable.

Creating a Print Server

You can install the Print Service role on any server. To do so, open Server Manager, select Roles in the console tree, and then follow these steps:

1. In the results pane, click Add Roles. The Add Roles Wizard starts.
2. Click Next until you come to the Select Server Roles page. (See Figure 10-2.)

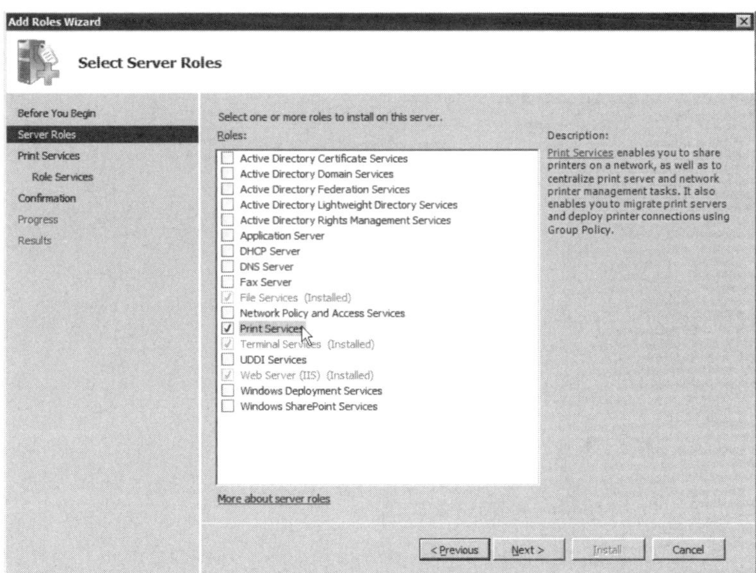

Figure 10-2 Selecting the Print Services role

3. Select Print Services and then click Next until the Installation Results page appears. (See Figure 10-3.)

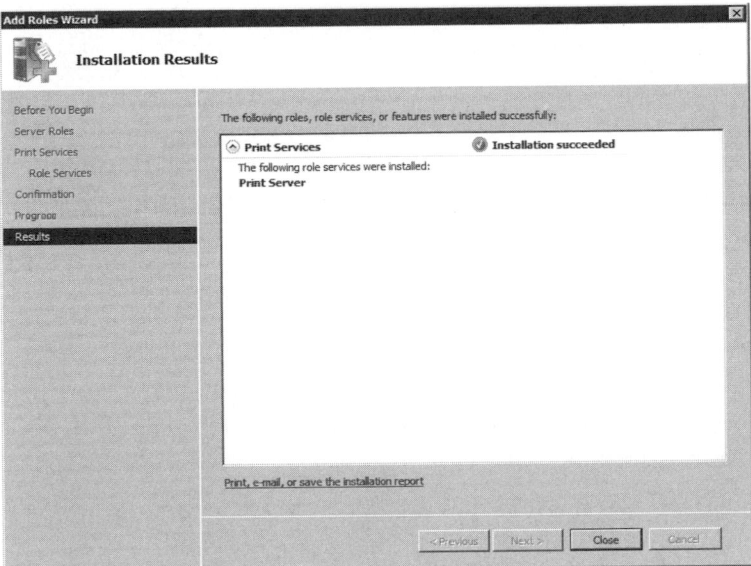

Figure 10-3 The Print Server is installed.

Enabling Printer Location Tracking

To use printer location tracking, the network must meet the following conditions:

- The network must have an IP addressing scheme that approximates the network's physical layout.
- The Active Directory structure must contain more than one site or more than one subnet. If you do not have multiple IP subnets, you can use the Active Directory Sites And Subnets console to create subnets from address ranges within a subnet that correspond to physical locations.
- The client computers must be able to query Active Directory. (They must support Lightweight Directory Access Protocol version 2 or later.)
- Each site is on a separate subnet.
- Each subnet that clients need to access has its own subnet object in Active Directory.
- The network has a printer location naming convention.

More Info For information about how to install Directory Services and create the appropriate subnets for the enterprise, see Chapter 16 "Installing and Configuring Directory Services."

Best Practices Keep printers and print servers on the same network segment as the users of the printer if you expect a high print volume. This approach minimizes the impact to users on other parts of the network. In any case, minimize the number of network hops a print job needs to take to get from users to their default printer.

To enable users to easily search Active Directory for printers by location, create a location-naming convention as discussed in the "Creating a Location-Naming Convention" section of this chapter, and then follow these steps to set up printer location tracking:

1. Open Active Directory Sites And Services from Server Manager, the Administrative Tools menu, or by entering **dssite.msc** in the Start Search box.
2. In the Sites node, right-click the first site and choose Properties from the shortcut menu.
3. Click the Location tab and type the location name for the site, as shown in Figure 10-4, or click Browse to select the location from the location tree for the enterprise.
4. Browse to select the location from the location tree for the enterprise.

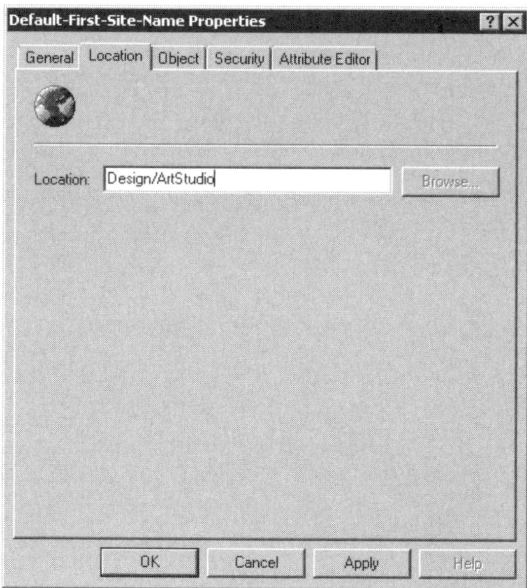

Figure 10-4 Specifying the location name for a subnet

5. Click OK and repeat steps 2 and 3 for each site and subnet on the network.
6. Create a new Group Policy object that applies to all computers on which you enable printer location tracking: Open the Group Policy Management Console in Server Manager from the Administrative Tools menu or by entering gpmc.msc in the Start Search box. Right-click the domain name and select Create A GPO In This Domain, And Link It Here.
7. Name the GPO and click OK. Right-click the GPO, and choose Edit to open the Group Policy Management Editor.
8. In the console tree, select Computer Configuration, select Administrative Templates folder, and then select Printers.
9. Double-click the Pre-Populate Printer Search Location Text policy (See Figure 10-5.), select Enabled, and click OK.

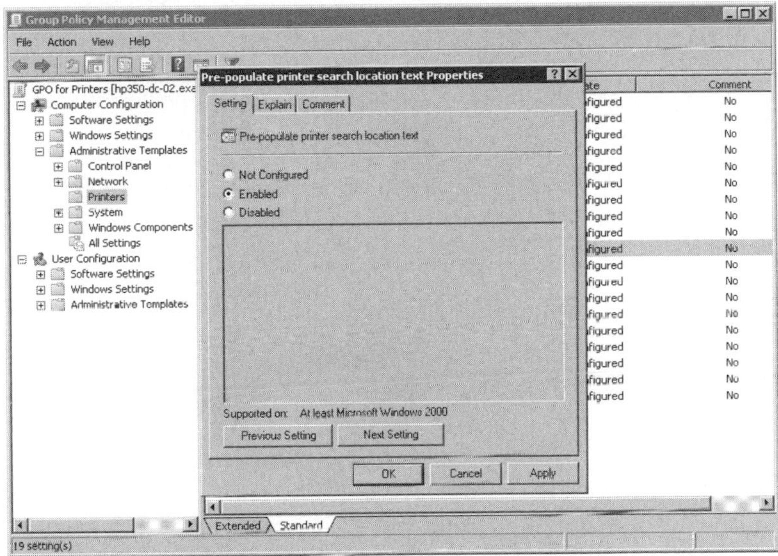

Figure 10-5 Enabling printer location tracking

10. Close the Group Policy Management Editor console.
11. Open the Print Management Console or the Printers And Faxes folder for your print server, right-click a printer, choose Properties, and then type the location in the Location text box, or click Browse to select the location from the location tree for the enterprise. Repeat this for all printers in Active Directory, or use the Prncnfg.vbs script to automate this procedure.
(Type **cscript %WINDIR%\system32\prncnfg.vbs /?** at a command prompt for command line reference information.)

Note Be more specific in the Location box for printers than simply providing the location of the subnet. For example, add a room number or name.

12. Test printer location tracking by searching Active Directory by location from a client computer.

Migrating Print Servers

If you need to replace an older print server or combine multiple print servers into one, you can use the Printer Migration Wizard or the Printbrm.exe command-line tool. You can export print queues, printer settings, printer ports, and language monitors and then import them to another print server.

Using the Print Migration Wizard

To use the Print Migration Wizard, follow these steps:

1. Select Print Management from the Administrative Tools menu.
2. In the Print Management tree, right-click the computer that contains the printer queues to export, and then click Export Printers To A File.
3. Review the list of files to be exported, and then click Next.
4. On the Select The File Location page, designate the location to save the printer settings (see Figure 10-6) and then click Next to save the printers. Click Finish when the operation completes.

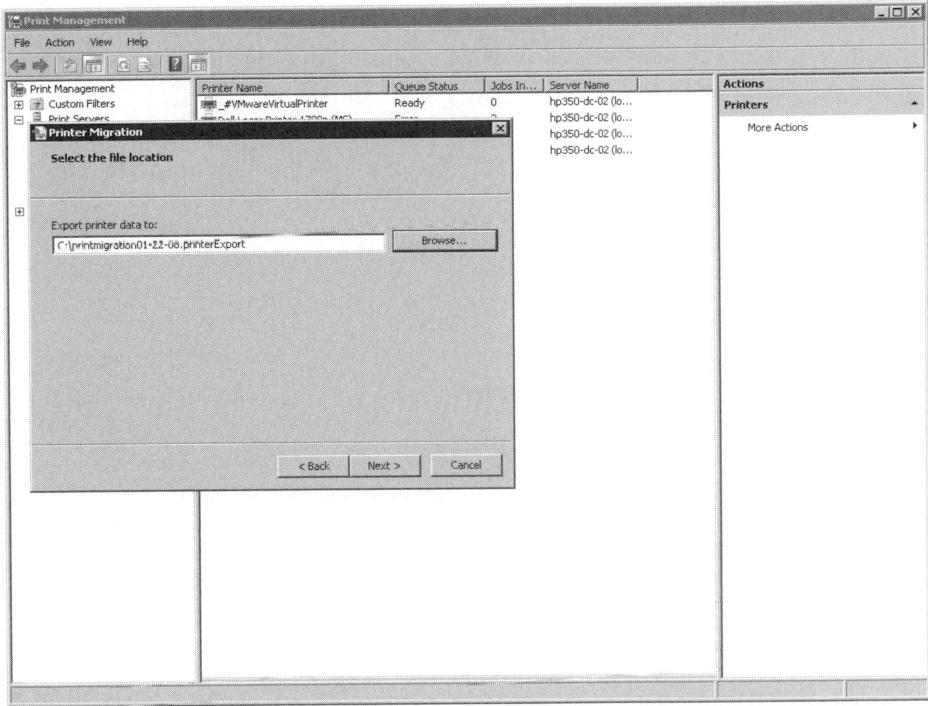

Figure 10-6 Specifying a location to save printer files

5. Right-click the destination computer on which to import the printers, and select Import Printers From A File.
6. On the Select The File Location page, designate the location of the printer settings file, and then click Next. Review the objects that will be imported and click Next.
7. Select the import options on the Select Import Options page as follows:
   - **Import Mode** What to do if a specific print queue already exists on the destination computer.
   - **List In The Directory** Should the imported print queues be published in Active Directory Domain Services.
   - **Convert LPR Ports To Standard Port Monitors** Should Line Printer Remote (LPR) printer ports in the printer settings file be converted to the faster Standard Port Monitor when importing printers.
8. Click Next to import the printer settings.

Using the Command Line

Migrating print servers is even easier when you use the command line by following these steps:

1. Click Start, click All Programs, click Accessories, right-click Command Prompt, and then click Run As Administrator.
2. Type the following:

```
CD %WINDIR%\System32\Spool\Tools
Printbrm -s \\<sourcecomputername> -b -f <filename>.printerExport
```

3. Type the following:

```
Printbrm -s \\<destinationcomputername> -r -f <filename>.printerExport
```

The basic syntax for this command is the following:

<sourcecomputername>*The UNC name for the source computer.*

<filename>*The filename for the printer settings file. Use the .printerExport or .cab file extension.*

<destinationcomputername>*The UNC name for the destination computer.*

> **Note** For the complete syntax for this command, type **printbrm /?** at a command prompt.

Installing Printers

Installing a printer is a familiar task for most computer users–if the printer has a USB or IEEE 1394 (Firewire) connection, attach it to the server and insert the driver disk. To install a printer using a network connection (the best way to connect a printer), you can add a printer manually, as described in this section, or have Print Management automatically detect all printers on the same subnet as a Print Server.

To set up a network-based printer through a standard TCP/IP printer port, connect the printer to the network and set up the printer with the proper TCP/IP settings. If you configure the printer to use DHCP, create a DHCP reservation for the printer so that its address does not change, and then follow these steps:

1. Open Print Management from the Administrative Tools menu.
2. Select the appropriate print server, right-click Printers, and choose Add Printer.
3. On the Printer installation page, select an installation method from the following:

Search The Network For Printers

a. The Network printer search window opens and searches for printers.

b. When the search is complete, highlight the printer to be installed and select Next.

> **Note** If you can't find a printer by using the search function, use one of the other installation methods in this section.

Add A TCP/IP Or Web Services Printer By IP Address Or Hostname

a. Supply the printer's network name or IP address. Click Next and the wizard will search for the port.

Add A New Printer Using An Existing Port

a. Select an existing port from the drop-down list and then click Next.

b. Designate an existing driver to use or select Install A New Driver. Click Next.

> **Note** If you choose to install a new driver, you'll need to supply the printer manufacturer and printer model, and then supply the printer installation disk if needed.

c. In the Printer Name And Sharing Settings dialog box, you can change the printer name and share name, add a location and other comments, and choose to publish the printer to the directory. Click Next.

d. The printer is ready to install. Review the settings and click Next to finish the installation.

Create A New Port And Add A New Printer

a. Select the type of port to create and click Next.

b. Enter a port name and click Ok.

c. Select whether to use an existing driver or install a new one. Click Next.

d. In the Printer Name And Sharing Settings dialog box, you can change the printer name and share name, add a location and other comments, and choose to publish the printer to the directory. Click Next.

e. The printer is ready to install. Review the settings and click Next to finish the installation.

Deploying Printers with Group Policy

You can automatically deploy printers to users or computers using Group Policy. This technique of installing a printer is most practical in a situation where the same printers are used by most of the computers or users, such as a classroom or branch office.

Note To deploy printer connections using Group Policy, your environment must meet the requirement that the AD DS schema must use the Windows Server 2003 R2 or later schema version.

Client computers running Windows 2000, Windows XP, or Windows Server 2003 must use the PushPrinterConnections.exe tool in either a start-up script (for per-computer connections) or in a logon script (for per-user connections). See the section "Adding PushPrinterConnections Using Group Policy" later in this chapter.

To automatically deploy printers, follow these steps:

1. Select Print Management from the Administrative Tools menu.
2. Under the appropriate print server, click Printers.
3. In the results pane, right-click the printer to deploy, and then select Deploy With Group Policy.
4. In the Deploy With Group Policy dialog box, select Browse and then choose a GPO to store the printer connections. Click OK.
5. Specify whether to deploy the printer connections to users, or to computers:
   - To deploy to groups of users so that the users can access the printers from any computer they log onto, select the Users That This GPO Applies To (Per User) check box.
   - To deploy to groups of computers so that all users of the computers can access the printers, select the The Computers That This GPO Applies To (Per Machine) check box.
6. Click Add.
7. Repeat steps 4 to 6 to add the printer connection setting to another GPO, if necessary.
8. Click OK.

Note For per-user connections, Windows adds the printer connections when the user logs on. For per-computer connections, Windows adds the printer connections only when the client computer restarts. If you remove the printer connection settings from the GPO, PushPrinterConnections.exe removes the corresponding printers from the client computer on the next restart or user logon.

Adding PushPrinterConnections Using Group Policy

To deploy printer connections to computers running Windows XP, Windows 2000, or Windows Server 2003, you must add the PushPrinterConnections.exe utility to a computer startup script for per-computer connections or to a user logon script for per-user connections. Group Policy is the most efficient way to handle this task.

To add the PushPrinterConnections.exe file to startup or logon scripts, follow these steps:

1. Select Group Policy Management from the Administrative Tools menu.
2. In the console tree, right-click the domain or Organizational Unit (OU) that stores the computer or user accounts to which you want to deploy the PushPrinterConections.exe utility and select Create A GPO In This Domain, And Link It Here (shown in Figure 10-7). Type a name for the new GPO and then click OK.

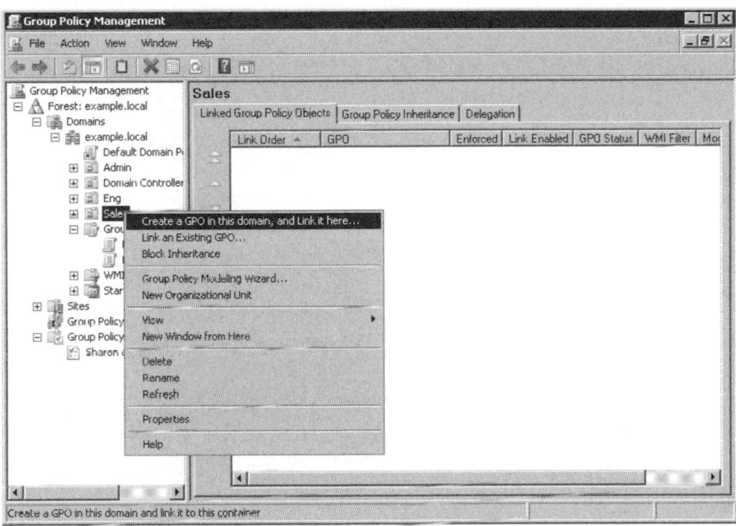

Figure 10-7 Creating a new Group Policy Object

3. Right-click the GPO you created and then click Edit.
4. In the Group Policy Management Editor tree, navigate to the following:
   - If the printer connections are deployed per-computer, go to Computer Configuration, Windows Settings, Scripts (Startup/Shutdown).
   - If the printer connections are deployed per-user, go to User Configuration, Windows Settings, Scripts (Logon/Logoff).

Note Client computers running Windows 2000 do not support per-machine connections.

5. Right-click Startup or Logon, and then select Properties.
6. In the Logon Properties or Startup Properties dialog box, click Show Files to open the Startup or Logon window.
7. Copy the PushPrinterConnections.exe file from the %WINDIR%\System32 folder to the Startup or Logon window. This adds the utility to the GPO, where it will replicate to other domain controllers along with the rest of the Group Policy settings.
8. In the Logon Properties or Startup Properties dialog box, click Add. The Add Script dialog box appears.
9. Type **PushPrinterConnections.exe** in the Script Name box.
10. To enable logging of client computers running Windows Server 2003, Windows XP, or Windows 2000, type **–log** in the Script Parameters box. Log files are written to %WINDIR%\temp\ppcMachine.log for per-computer connections and %temp%\ppcUser.log for per-user connections on the computer to which the policy is applied.
11. Click OK in the Add Script dialog box, and then click OK in the Startup Properties or Logon Properties dialog box.

Use the Group Policy Management Console to link the PushPrinterConnections.exe GPO to any other OUs or domains.

Excluding Windows Vista and Windows Server 2008 Computers from PushPrinterConnections.exe

The PushPrinterConnections.exe file automatically detects computers running Windows Vista or Windows Server 2008 and exits automatically, so it's safe to deploy this file in logon or startup scripts to all client computers in your organization. If the logon or startup times of client computers running Windows Vista or Windows Server 2008 are too slow, you can exclude these clients using WMI filters. Just follow these steps:

1. Open Group Policy Management from the Administrative Tools menu.
2. In the console tree, go to the domain, right-click WMI Filters, and select New.
3. Enter a Name and Description in the appropriate fields, and then click Add.

4. The WMI Query dialog box opens. To make a filter selecting all client computers running pre-Windows Vista versions of Windows, type the following in the query section:

```
Select * from Win32_OperatingSystem where BuildNumber < 6000
```

5. Click OK in the WMI Query dialog box, and then click Save in the New WMI Filter dialog box.
6. Select the Group Policy that has the PushPrinterConnections.exe file, select the WMI filter you created from the WMI Filtering list box, and then click Yes.

Managing Print Jobs from Windows

To manage print jobs, open Print Management from the Administrative Tools menu, and then follow the instructions under the appropriate task in the following list.

Temporarily Stopping Print Jobs

To temporarily stop *a* document from printing, right-click the appropriate printer and select Open Printer Queue. Right-click the document and choose Pause from the shortcut menu. To resume printing, right-click the document and then choose Resume.

To temporarily stop *all* documents from printing, right-click the appropriate printer and select Pause Printing. To resume printing all documents, right-click the printer and select Resume Printing.

Canceling Print Jobs

To cancel one or more print jobs, right-click the appropriate printer and select Open Printer Queue. Right-click the job to be canceled and choose Cancel from the shortcut menu. (You can also cancel a print job by selecting it and pressing the Delete key.)

To cancel *all* print jobs in the print queue, select Cancel All Documents from the Printer menu.

Restarting a Print Job

To restart a print job (force the document to print from the beginning again), right-click the document and choose Restart from the shortcut menu.

Note Sometimes a print job appears stuck in the queue and you cannot delete it. If this occurs, turn the printer off and then on again, or stop the Print Spooler service on the print server and then restart it.

Changing a Print Job Priority

To change the priority or scheduling of a print job, right-click the print job, choose Properties, and then click the General tab. Use the Priority slider (shown in Figure 10-8) to adjust the priority of the document, with 1 being the lowest priority and 99 the highest priority.

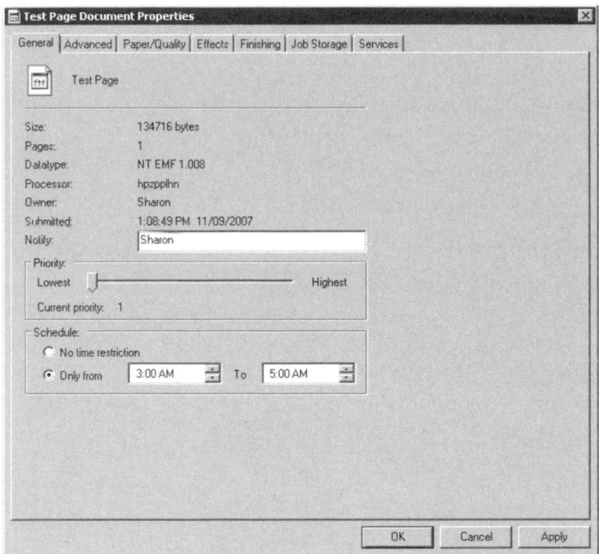

Figure 10-8 Setting a print job's priority and a specific time to print

To specify that the document should be printed only during a certain period, select the Only From option on the same page and choose the time range to allow the document to print.

Note The Schedule feature is useful if you have large print jobs but don't want to tie up a printer during peak working hours.

Moving Print Jobs

To move all documents from one printer to another printer that can use the same printer driver, right-click the printer, choose Properties, click the Ports tab, select the port that the second printer is on, and then clear the check box next to the original port.

Note A print job that has already started printing can't be moved. To move it, you must restart it.

Managing Printers from the Command Line

Windows Server 2008 makes command-line administration practical for Windows administrators. You can perform almost all administration tasks from a command line—printers included. Use the following list of commands and scripts to get started.

- **Print** Prints the specified text file to the specified printer.
- **Lpr** Prints the specified text file to the specified LPD print queue.
- **Net print** Displays information about the specified print queue or print job. Can also hold, release, or delete print jobs.
- **Lpq** Displays information about the specified LPD print queue.
- **Net start** Starts the specified service. You can use the `Net start spooler` and `Net stop spooler` commands to start or stop the spooler service.

> **Note** To view a list of parameters, type the command followed by **/?** at a command prompt, or use the Windows Server 2008 Help And Support Center.

- **Cscript %Windir%\System32\Prnmngr.vbs** Adds, deletes, or lists printers on a Windows print server.
- **Cscript %Windir%\System32\Prnjobs.vbs** Lets you view and manage the print jobs of printer shares on a Windows print server.
- **Cscript %Windir%\System32\Prncfg.vbs** Allows you to view and change the settings of printers on a Windows print server.
- **Cscript %Windir%\System32\Prnqctl.vbs** Pauses or resumes printing, clears the print queue, or prints test pages.
- **Cscript %Windir%\System32\Prnport.vbs** Administers all things related to printer ports.
- **Cscript %Windir%\System32\Prndrvr.vbs** Adds, deletes, or lists printer drivers on a Windows print server.

For more on using scripts for command-line administration, see Chapter 15, "Using Scripts for Consistent Administration."

Setting Security Options

Security options come into play when you have a range of printers that are separate but not at all equal. For example, you might not want everyone to print to the five-dollar-a-page dye-sublimation printer purchased for the art staff. At a more basic level, security settings can preserve printer properties or printing priorities from unauthorized changes.

To set permissions on a printer, right-click the printer, choose Properties, and then use the Security tab to assign permissions to groups of users. Click Advanced to exert finer control over permissions or to enable auditing. You can view the results of the audit settings in the security log.

A printer has three levels of permissions: Print, Manage Documents, and Manage Printers. These are defined as follows:

- **Print** Users or groups with Print permission can connect to the printer; print documents; and pause, restart, or delete their own documents from the print queue. Windows by default grants members of the Everyone group the Print permission.
- **Manage Documents** Users or groups with Manage Documents permission have the Print permission along with the ability to change the settings for all documents in the print queue and to pause, restart, and delete any user's documents from the print queue. Windows grants the Creator/Owner group the Manage Documents permission level by default.
- **Manage Printers** Users or groups with Manage Printers permission have the Manage Documents and Print permissions along with the ability to modify printer properties, delete printers, change printer permissions, and take ownership of printers. The Manage Printers permission level is the equivalent of Full Control permission in Windows NT. Windows grants this permission level to print operators, server operators, and administrators by default.

Changing Printer Availability and Group Priorities

You can set up a printer so that print jobs submitted by some users print before jobs submitted by other users; for example, you can give priority to managers or groups with tight deadlines. You can also reserve a printer for exclusive use by certain groups during certain times; for example, you can reserve a printer outside of normal business hours so that the groups you specify can print large, high-priority print jobs.

To control availability or group priority, create two or more logical printers for a single physical printer, give each logical printer a different priority and/or make it available at different times, and give different sets of users or groups permission to print to each logical printer.

To perform this procedure, follow these steps:

1. Open Print Management from the Administrative Tools Menu. Navigate to the printer server where you want to create the logical printer, right-click Printers, and then select Add Printer. The Printer Installation Wizard starts.
2. Select Add A New Printer Using An Existing Port, select the port that the physical printer is on, and then click Next.
3. Choose Use An Existing Printer Driver On The Computer and select the driver from the drop-down list. Click Next.
4. Give the printer a descriptive name that describes its function or who uses it. Click Next twice and finish the installation process.
5. Right-click the new printer in Printer Management and select Properties.
6. Click the Security tab and assign permissions to the users or groups that will have special access to this printer.
7. Click the Advanced tab (shown in Figure 10-9). If the logical printer is to be available only at certain times, select Available From and set the times.

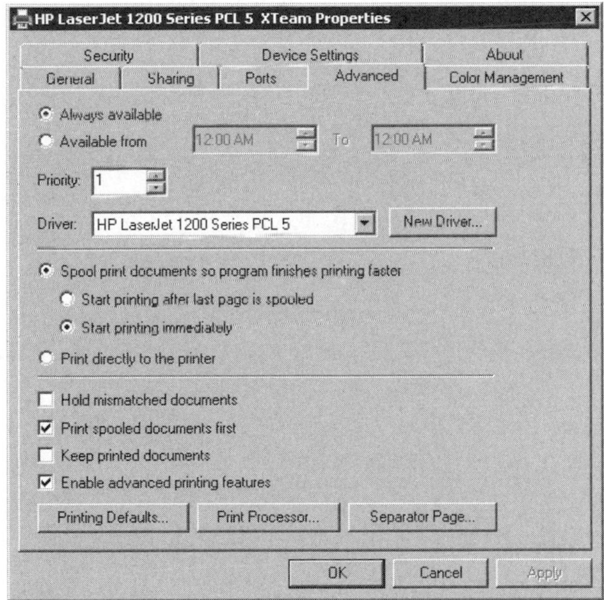

Figure 10-9 The Advanced tab of a printer's Properties dialog box

8. To change the priority of the users and groups who use this logical printer, type a number in the Priority text box. The priority range goes from 1, which is the lowest priority, to 99, which is the highest priority.
9. Click OK, and repeat the process for all other logical printers you created for the printer.

Specifying a Separator Page

Use a separator page with busy printers to help prevent one user from picking up the next user's print job in addition to his or her own. Windows Server 2008 comes with four default separator pages located in the %WINDIR%\System32 folder:

- **Pcl.sep** Switches the printer to Printer Control Language (PCL) and then prints a separator page
- **Pscript.sep** Switches the printer to PostScript and does not print a separator page
- **Sysprint.sep** Switches the printer to PostScript and then prints a separator page
- **Sysprintj.sep** Switches the printer to PostScript with Japanese character support and then prints a separator page

If your printer does not support these languages, create a custom separator page, as discussed in the "Custom Separator Pages" sidebar later in this chapter. To specify a separator page, follow these steps:

1. In the Print Management Console, right-click the printer to modify and select Properties.
2. Click the Advanced tab.
3. Click Separator Page to select a page to insert between printed documents to help separate the print jobs.

Custom Separator Pages

To create a custom separator page, create a text file in Notepad or any text editor, save it with the .sep file extension, and then create your separator page. On the first line, type the escape character to use (for example, \), and then the text that is to appear on the separator page. (See Table 10-1 for a listing of commands you can use on a separator page.) The following example shows a simple print separator page that prints the user name, job number, date, and time of the print job using the backslash (\) character as the escape character:

```
\
\U\LUser Name: \N
\U\LJob : \I
\U\LDate: \D
\U\LTime: \T
\E
```

Table 10-1 Separator Page Commands

Command	Function
\	Escape character used by the separator file interpreter to delimit commands. Can be any character, but this table uses \ as an example.
\H*n*	Sends the *n* control sequence to the printer. See your printer manual for the correct control sequence to use with your printer.
\Wn	Specifies the width of the separator page, beyond which Windows omits all characters. The default width is 80 and the maximum width is 256.
n	Skips the number of lines you specify by *n*. Valid numbers are 0 through 9, with 0 acting as a carriage return, moving printing to the next line.
\F*pathname*	Prints the contents of file specified by *pathname* directly to the printer. The file must be rendered in the appropriate language for the printer.
\L	Prints all characters following the \L command until the next escape character.
\N	Prints the user name of the user that submitted the print job.
\I	Prints the print job number.
\D	Prints the date when the print job is printed, using the date format used by the print server.
\T	Prints the time when the print job is printed, using the time format used by the print server.
\U	Disables block printing of characters in the separator file until explicitly enabled.
\B\S	Prints characters in single-width block text until the separator file interpreter encounters a \U command.
\B\M	Prints characters in double-width block text until the separator file interpreter encounters a \U command.
\E	Ejects the current page.

Modifying Print Spooling by Printer

Print spooling, or storing a print job on disk before printing, is the primary means by which users perceive printing performance and the actual printing speed. You can change the way print spooling works to correct printing problems or to hold printed documents in the printer queue in case a user needs to print the document again.

To change the spool settings for a printer, right-click the printer to modify, select Properties, and then use the following settings on the Advanced tab to modify the spool settings.

Spool Print Documents So Program Finishes Printing Faster

Spools the print documents to the print server, freeing the client to perform other tasks more quickly.

- To reduce the time it takes to print a document, select Start Printing Immediately.
- To ensure that the entire document is available to the printer when printing begins, select Start Printing After Last Page Is Spooled. This step might correct some printing problems and helps high-priority documents print before low-priority documents.

Print Directly To The Printer

Turns off spooling, causing a performance hit on the server (though it might fix some printing problems).

Hold Mismatched Documents

Holds documents in the queue that do not match the current printer settings (for example, documents that require legal size paper when letter paper is currently in the printer). Other documents in the print queue are unaffected by held documents.

Print Spooled Documents First

Prints the highest priority document that is already spooled first, ahead of higher priority documents that are still spooling. This step speeds overall printer throughput by preventing the printer from waiting for documents to spool.

Keep Printed Documents

Keeps a copy of print jobs in the printer queue in case users need to print the document again. In this circumstance, the user can resubmit the document directly from the queue rather than printing from his or her application a second time.

Modifying Spooling on a Print Server

By default, all warning events are logged in the Event Log on the Print Services page in Server Manager. To stop logging these events, follow these steps:

1. Open Control Panel and select Printers.

2. Point to a blank place in the window and right-click. Select Run As Administrator and then select Server Properties. (See Figure 10-10.)

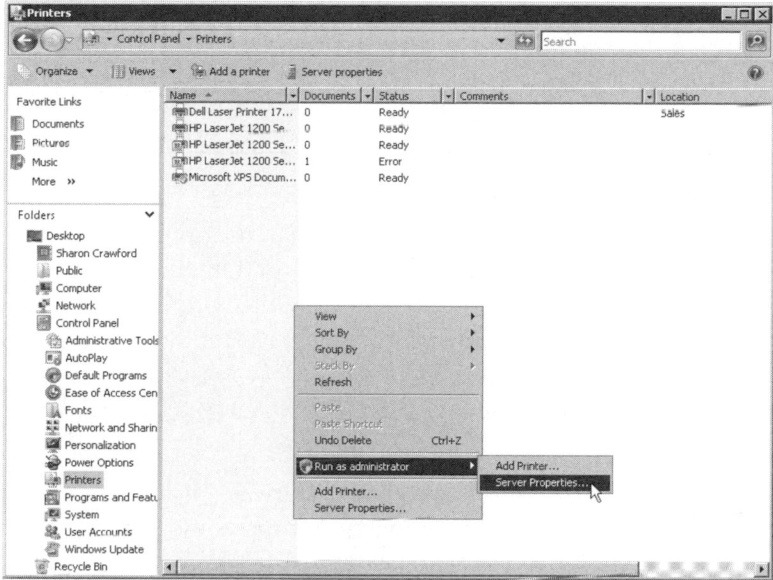

Figure 10-10 Opening print server properties as an administrator

3. Click the Advanced tab and clear the Show Informational Notifications For Network Printers check box.

4. Click OK to finish.

Optimizing Print Server Performance

For best performance, use a fast, dedicated drive or disk array just for the print spool folder, and do not place any system files—especially the swap file–on this drive. File sharing has a higher priority than printer sharing, so expect reduced print performance if you use both services on a server. Be sure to place print servers on the same network segment as the users and printers, and be sure that the drive is big enough to hold all the documents in the print queue. (If you choose to hold printed documents, you might need a large drive or disk array.)

Changing the Print Spooling Folder Location

By default, print jobs are spooled to WINDIR%\System32\Spool\PRINTERS, which is not usually the optimal location. To change the location, follow these steps:

1. Open Control Panel\Hardware And Sound and select Printers.
2. Point to a blank pace in the window and right-click. Select Run As Administrator and then select Server Properties.
3. Click the Advanced tab and type in the new location for the spool folder. Click OK to finish.

Managing Printer Drivers

When you install a printer, Windows installs the version of the driver that corresponds to the processor architecture used by the server (x86, x64, or Itanium). To use the printer from a client computer that uses different processor architecture than the server, you must install additional drivers. For example, if the server is running a 32-bit version of Windows but the client computer is running Windows XP Professional x64 Edition, you must install x64 drivers on the server for all printers to which you want the client computer to be able to print.

You might also need to remove or reinstall problematic drivers, or set up a printer pool where two or more printers act as one printer to improve speed and availability.

To install printer drivers that Windows automatically downloads onto a client computer when a user connects to the printer, follow these steps:

1. Open Print Management from the Administrative Tools menu. In the Print Management Console, right-click the Drivers folder on the appropriate print server and choose Manage Drivers.
2. Use the Drivers tab of the Print Server Properties dialog box to manage drivers:
   - To install drivers, click Add and then use the Add Printer Driver Wizard to install drivers for the appropriate operating system and processor architecture.
   - To remove an obsolete or problematic driver, select it and click Remove.
   - To view the details of a printer driver, select the driver and click Properties.

Note When installing new drivers for multiple operating system versions and/or processor architectures, use drivers that are designed to work together so that printer settings you specify on the print server can be applied to client computers when they connect to the printers. Some printer manufacturers provide multiple-platform driver packages just for this purpose.

> **Windows Automatically Checks for New Drivers**
>
> Windows Server 2008 and Windows Vista automatically download printer drivers when connecting to a Windows printer share. Windows XP, Windows 2003, and Windows 2000 clients automatically check for updated versions of the printer drivers at startup and download newer versions from the print server, if present.

Creating Printer Pools

A *printer pool* is useful for handling a large volume of printing at a single location, particularly with a mix of large and small documents. For example, someone with a single-page memo probably won't be happy to be stuck in the queue behind a print job that is the corporate equivalent of *War and Peace*.

If multiple printers share a single driver, you can add them to a printer pool, which then appears to users as a single printer. The advantage of using a printer pool is that clients simply print to the single logical printer on the print server, which then sends the print job to the first available printer. If one printer in a printer pool goes offline, Windows sends the print jobs to the other printers in the printer pool, eliminating downtime for users. Printer pools also simplify administration because you manage all printers in a printer pool with one logical printer; if you modify the properties for the single logical printer, all physical printers in the printer pool use the same settings.

> **Note** Place physical printers in a printer pool near each other to make finding a completed print job easier.

To set up a printer pool, follow these steps:

1. In Print Management, right-click the logical printer on which to enable printer pooling and choose Properties.
2. Click the Ports tab.
3. Select the Enable Printer Pooling check box.
4. To add an additional printer to the printer pool, select the port to which the printer is connected.

   If the printer is a network printer and you have not yet added it to the print server, click Add Port to add a new Standard TCP/IP printer port for the printer. (See "Installing Printers" earlier in this chapter for more information.)

5. To change the transmission retry settings for a port, select the port and click Configure Port.

> **Note** All printers in a printer pool must be able to use the same printer driver—if you add an incompatible printer to a printer pool, documents might not print correctly.

Preparing for Print Server Failure

If at all possible, it is wise to have a secondary print server to back up the primary print server. When the primary print server fails, the administrator can send e-mail instructing users to choose ReserveServer2 (for example) for printing. This option is easiest for the administrator but, inevitably, some users have difficulty connecting to another printer. If you planned the print server downtime, you can use Print Management to deploy printer connections to the backup server and remove connections to the offline server.

Create an alias on a backup print server so that clients see the backup server instead of the primary server. The backup print server must connect to the same network printers as the primary print server and use the same share names. Use the Print Migration Wizard to copy the configuration of the primary server to the backup server. (See "Using the Print Migration Wizard" earlier in this chapter.) To switch users, follow these steps:

1. Open Registry Editor (Regedit.exe) and navigate to the following registry key:

   ```
   HKEY_LOCAL_MACHINE\System\CurrentControlSet\Services\LanmanServer\Parameters
   ```

2. Create a new String Value named **OptionalNames** with the primary server name as the data.
3. Create a new DWORD Value named **DisableStrictNameChecking** with a value of **1**.

> **Important** The DisableStrictNameChecking registry value makes it possible for someone on the internal network to use the *OptionalNames* parameter to impersonate a computer, although name resolution would be unreliable unless the impersonator also "poisoned" the DNS and/or WINS server.

4. Create a DNS Alias (CNAME) record mapping the primary server's DNS name to the backup server's DNS name.
5. If you are using WINS on the network, create a DHCP reservation for the backup print server so that its IP address does not change, and then create a new static mapping in WINS mapping the primary print server's NetBIOS name to the backup print server's IP address. (See Chapter 18, "Administering TCP/IP," for more information about administering WINS, DHCP, and DNS.)

6. Restart the server.
7. To bring the primary print server back online, delete the new registry values, DNS alias, and WINS registration and then restart the server.

Note If a printer fails on the print server but the server itself does not, you can easily move users to another printer that can use the same printer driver. (Recent printers in the same model line can often use the same driver.) To do so, right-click the printer, choose Properties, click Ports, and then select the port of the printer to which you want to redirect users of the failed printer. This port can be a local port, a network port, or a printer share on another print server. You can also create a printer pool to automate the failover of one printer to another that uses the same driver. If your network requires an extremely high level of print performance and reliability, set up a print server cluster. This provides additional capacity and automatic fail-over should one server stop responding. For information about clustering, see Chapter 21, "Using Clusters."

Troubleshooting Printers

The procedure for troubleshooting printing problems, as in troubleshooting any type of problem, is first to isolate and identify the problem and then to determine a course of action to fix it. This section helps you diagnose printer problems, helps you locate the printing subsystem where the error is occurring, and provides some specific suggestions for solving the problem.

Starting at the Server

Printing problems usually fall into one of the following categories:

Physical problems

Includes problems with the actual printer and connections. This includes paper jams, low toner or ink, and so forth.

Print server problems

Includes problems with printer drivers, permissions levels, and software status.

Network connectivity problems

Includes communication failures between servers and clients resulting from incorrect protocols or network settings. (Troubleshoot these problems on either the client or the server, depending on where the connectivity problem exists.)

Client problems

Includes problems with printer drivers, permissions, and applications.

Determine which category the problem is in before getting into details, if possible. Often you can clear a problem from the server and avoid a trip to the client computer. This is extremely desirable when the client computer and printer are several floors or even several buildings away. Keep trying alternatives until you isolate the problem as precisely as possible, and then apply the most common fixes until you solve the problem.

If you already know where the problem is, jump straight to the heading in this section that applies and continue.

More Info If you cannot resolve the problems by using the information provided here, use the Microsoft Knowledge Base on the Microsoft Web site at *http://support.microsoft.com*.

Document Prints Incorrectly

When a document prints but appears garbled or has some other defect, a compatibility problem exists between the client, the printer driver, and the printer. Make sure that the client is using the proper client printer driver and that the server is using the proper printer driver. If the client is using an x64 edition of Windows, obtain a native x64 version of the printer driver for the specific printer model you are using instead of using a printer driver written for a similar model.

Install a duplicate logical printer to test whether the printer driver is corrupt. If this is not the problem, change the spool settings on the client driver. If multiple clients experience the same problem, change the server's printer driver. Specifically, change the following options on the Advanced tab of the printer's Properties dialog box. (See "Modifying Print Spooling by Printer" earlier in this chapter for a more detailed procedure.)

- To ensure that the entire document is available to the printer when printing begins, select the Start Printing After Last Page Is Spooled option.
- If you continue to have printing problems, choose the Print Directly To The Printer option to turn off spooling. This action causes a performance reduction on the server.
- Clear the Enable Advanced Printing Features check box on the print server to turn off metafile spooling, which disables some printer options such as page order, booklet printing, and pages per sheet (if available on the printer).

Note If the printer has multiple trays with different forms, match the form to the tray so that documents using the form always print properly. Under the Form To Tray Assignment heading, select each tray and choose the form that the tray holds. If the printer supports Page Protection and has 1 MB or more of available optional memory, click the Device Settings tab and turn on this option to ensure that complex pages print properly. When you turn this option on, the printer creates each page in memory before beginning to print.

Document Fails to Print

If the document does not print at all, try these troubleshooting tasks one at a time:

- If an error states that the appropriate printer driver is not available for download, install the printer drivers on the print server that correspond to the client computer's operating system and processor architecture. (See "Managing Printer Drivers" earlier in this chapter for more information.)
- An error stating that the print device was unavailable might indicate a network connectivity problem, or the user might not have Print permissions on the printer. (See "Setting Security Options" earlier in this chapter for more information.)
- If you experience a lot of disk access and the document fails to print, verify that the drive holding the client's spool folder contains enough free disk space to hold the spooled document. (See "Modifying Print Spooling by Printer" earlier in this chapter for more information.)
- Determine whether you can see and connect to the print server across the network. Copy a file to the print server to see whether you can access the print server. (Generally, if you cannot access the print server, you cannot access any attached printers.)
- Print a test document from Microsoft Notepad. If you can print with Notepad, the printer drivers are correct and the application is likely the problem.
- If you can't print with Notepad, try printing from the command line by typing the following command: `echo test>` [printer port name], where *printer port name* is the share name of the network printer.

Printing from a Particular Application Fails

Some applications experience problems when printing in Windows. Some of the issues you might encounter are as follows:

- An "Access denied" error message when configuring a printer inside an application occurs when you do not have sufficient privileges to change the printer's configuration. To change advanced printer settings, you need to have Manage Printers permissions.
- If an MS-DOS program does not print, quit the program. Some MS-DOS programs don't print until you close them. Also, use the `net use` command to map a local port to the shared printer. (For more information, see Microsoft Knowledge Base Article 314499 on the Microsoft Web site at *http://support.microsoft.com/kb/314499*.)

More Info For other issues, consult the Printers.txt file on the installation CD-ROM for the client operating system if the system is Windows 2003, Windows XP, or Windows 2000. You can also check the Microsoft Knowledge Base at *http://support.microsoft.com*.

Deleting Stuck Documents

If documents won't print or you can't delete documents in the print queue, the print spooler could be stalled. This also affects any fax services the server is running. To restart the Print Spooler service, follow these steps:

1. Launch Server Manager. In the console tree, select Configuration and then Services.
2. Right-click Print Spooler in the right pane and select Restart.
3. To specify a recovery process to perform if the Print Spooler service fails, double-click Print Spooler and click the Recovery tab. Click the action that you want in First Failure, Second Failure, and Subsequent Failures, and then click OK.
4. To view the services (such as remote procedure call) on which the print spooler depends, double-click the Print Spooler service, and then click the Dependencies tab. You can also use this tab to view the services that depend on the print spooler to function properly.

Note To restart the print spooler from a command prompt, type **`net stop "print spooler"`** and then **`net start "print spooler"`**.

Check the Print Server Status

Check the print server status remotely. Use the following list to check the print server status:

- Check for stalled documents or error messages in the print queue or on the printer configuration Web page (if present). If the printer is out of paper or toner or if there is a paper jam, an error message frequently appears here.
- Check that sufficient free disk space exists on the drive holding the spool folder.
- If documents print garbled, the printer might be using the wrong data type (EMF or raw). Try using the raw data type to see whether this corrects the problem. Clear the Enable Advanced Printing Features check box on the Advanced tab of the printer's Properties dialog box. (See "Modifying Print Spooling by Printer" earlier in this chapter for more information.)
- Check to see if any documents are printing. If no documents are in the print queue, print a test page or document from the print server to verify that the print server is printing properly.

- If some documents in the print queue do not print and you cannot delete them, the print spooler might be stalled. Restart the Print Spooler service to see whether this corrects the problem. Add another logical printer (printer driver) for the printer to rule out the possibility of a corrupt printer driver.

Note To prevent documents with certain languages from printing slowly, install on the print servers the fonts for all languages that the clients will use to print. To do this, copy the fonts to the %WINDIR%\Fonts folder on the print server and open the Fonts folder (or reboot the server).

Starting at the Client

If the problem is not at the print server, proceed to the client computer and the printer.

Print from the Client Computer Experiencing the Problem

Print from the client computer and take note of error messages. These messages often uncover the cause of the problem or at least indicate some possibilities. If the document prints properly, you might have a simple user error. Otherwise, the problem could be with a particular program, or there might be a compatibility problem with the printer driver.

Check the Printer

If you ruled out the clients and the server as the source of the problem but you still cannot print any documents on the printer, take a close look at the printer. Pause the print queue and then go check the actual printer. Are any errors reported on the printer? If you find any paper jams or if the printer is low on toner or needs servicing, the printer usually reports an error message. Make sure that the ready or online light is illuminated and that the printer cable is securely attached, or that the network cable is properly plugged in and the light next to the network port is illuminated (if available).

If you still can't print to the printer, print a test page directly from the printer. Most printers support this capability. If the test page prints, configure a different print server with the printer. If you can print from a different print server, you have a problem with the original print server. Use the Ping.exe program to access the printer's IP address.

Summary

Almost all networks need comprehensive and reliable print services. Aside from failure of the network or lost access to the Internet, no problem will create as much angst and frustration as the inability to print. Meeting present printing needs while also preparing for expansions and changes are all essential in devising a viable printer strategy.

In the next chapter, we move on to another critical area: managing groups and user accounts.

Chapter 11

Managing Users and Groups

Networks have become so ubiquitous that they are completely taken for granted. It's only when the network goes missing that anyone notices. And do they notice! The cries of panic and dismay can be heard at great distances because the central task of a network is to provide users with everything they need and clear away clutter that hampers their progress. What they need includes access to the files, folders, applications, printers, and Internet connections that users require to do their jobs. What they don't need is any trouble getting at these items.

The network administrator has additional needs, including shielding need-to-know material from those who don't need to know, protecting the network from malicious or otherwise dangerous users, and protecting the users from themselves. The key to meeting all these needs is the configuration of organizational units, groups, users, and Group Policies–the topics of this chapter and Chapter 13, "Group Policy."

Understanding Groups

By definition, groups in the Microsoft Windows Server 2008 family are Active Directory Domain Service (AD DS) or local computer objects that can contain users, contacts, computers, or other groups. In general, however, a group is usually a collection of user accounts. The point of groups is to simplify administration by allowing the network administrator to assign rights and permissions to groups rather than to individual users.

Windows Server 2008 allows two group types: security and distribution. Almost all groups used by Windows Server 2008 are *security groups* because they're the only groups through which permissions can be assigned. Each security group is also assigned a *group scope*, which defines how permissions are assigned to the group's members. Programs that can search Active Directory can also use security groups for nonsecurity purposes, such as sending e-mail to a group of users. *Distribution groups*, on the other hand, are not security-enabled and can be used *only* with e-mail applications to send e-mail to sets of users.

Later in the chapter, you will find sections on user rights and how they are defined and assigned to groups. Chapter 12, "Managing File Resources," follows with a discussion on permissions and how they are assigned.

Assigning Group Scopes

When a group is created, it is assigned a group scope that in turn defines how permissions are assigned. The three possible group scopes–global, domain local, and universal–are defined in the following sections.

Global Scope

A group with a global scope is truly global in the sense that permissions can be granted for resources located in any domain. However, members can come only from the domain in which the group is created, and in that sense the group is not global. Global groups are best used for directory objects that require frequent maintenance, such as user and computer accounts. Global groups can be members of universal and domain local groups in any domain, and they can have the following members:

- Other global groups in the same domain
- Individual accounts from the same domain

Domain Local Scope

A domain local group is the inverse of a global group–members can come from any domain but the permissions can be assigned only for resources in the domain in which the group is created. The members of a domain local group have a common need to access certain resources in a particular domain. Domain local groups can have one or more of the following members:

- Other domain local groups in the same domain
- Global groups from any domain
- Universal groups from any domain
- Individual accounts from any domain
- A mixture of any of the above

Universal Scope

A universal security group can have members from any domain and can be assigned permissions to resources in any domain. Universal groups can have the following members, which can be drawn from any domain:

- Other universal groups
- Global groups
- Individual accounts

Consolidate groups that span domains using groups with universal scope. To do this, add the accounts to groups with global scope and nest these groups within groups having universal scope. Universal groups must be used with discretion because of the negative impact they can have on network performance, as described in the Real World sidebar, "How Groups Affect Network Performance."

How Groups Affect Network Performance

The importance of planning groups becomes even more apparent when you consider the negative effect your group organization can have on network performance. When a user logs on to the network, the domain controller determines the user's group memberships and assigns a security token to the user. The token includes the security identifiers (SIDs) of all the groups that the user belongs to, in addition to the user account ID. The more security groups the user belongs to, the longer it takes to assemble the token and the longer it takes the user to log on.

In addition, the security token, once assembled, is sent to every computer the user accesses. The target computer compares all the SIDs in the token against the permissions for all the shared resources available at that computer. A large number of users added to a large number of shared resources (including individual folders) can take up a lot of bandwidth and processing time. One solution is to limit membership in security groups. Use distribution groups for categories of users that don't require specific permissions or rights.

Groups with universal scope have a performance impact of their own because all such groups, along with their members, are listed in the global catalog. When there's a change to the membership in a group with universal scope, this fact must be relayed to every global catalog server in the domain tree, adding to the replication traffic on the network. Groups with global or domain local scope are also listed in the global catalog, but their individual members are not, so the solution is to limit the membership of universal groups primarily to global groups.

Planning Organizational Units

Organizational units (OUs) are, as the name implies, organizing tools for collections of objects within a domain. An OU can contain any collection of Active Directory objects, such as printers, computers, groups, as well as other organizational units.

When a domain gets very complicated, one solution is to split the domain into multiple domains. OUs provide an alternative administrative substructure that is infinitely more flexible. They can be arranged hierarchically within a domain, and administrative control can be delegated for functions in a single OU or an entire subtree of OUs. (An OU is the smallest entity to which you can delegate administrative control or assign Group Policy settings.) At the same time, OUs can be modified, moved, renamed, and even deleted easily. Another plus is that unlike a domain, a subtree of OUs doesn't require a separate domain controller.

Organizational Units or New Domain?

Unfortunately, there's no firm rule you can apply to decide when an expanding network should be divided into separate domains and when new OUs might be sufficient. If any of the following applies to your network, multiple domains might be the answer:

- Decentralized administration is needed.
- The network encompasses competing business units or joint ventures.
- Parts of the network are separated by *very* slow links (analog modems, for example), so complete replication would create severe traffic problems. (If the link is merely slow, you can use multiple sites within a single domain because replication is less frequent.)
- Different account policies are needed. Because account policies are applied at the domain level, greatly differing policies might call for separate domains.

The following situations call for the use of OUs:

- Localized and/or tightly controlled administration is needed.
- The structure of the organization requires the arrangement of network objects into separate containers.
- The structure that you want to separate is likely to change at some point.

So, in general, when the situation calls for a flexible and even fluid structure, OUs are the answer.

OUs are containers only. They don't confer membership and aren't security principals. Rights and permissions are granted to users through group membership. After your groups are constructed, use OUs or organize group objects and assign Group Policy settings. The use of Group Policy is covered in Chapter 13.

Creating Organizational Units

OUs are easily created and appear as folders in a domain structure. You create an OU by following these steps:

1. Choose Active Directory Users And Computers from the Administrative Tools menu.
2. Right-click the domain, select New, and then select Organizational Unit to open the dialog box shown in Figure 11-1.

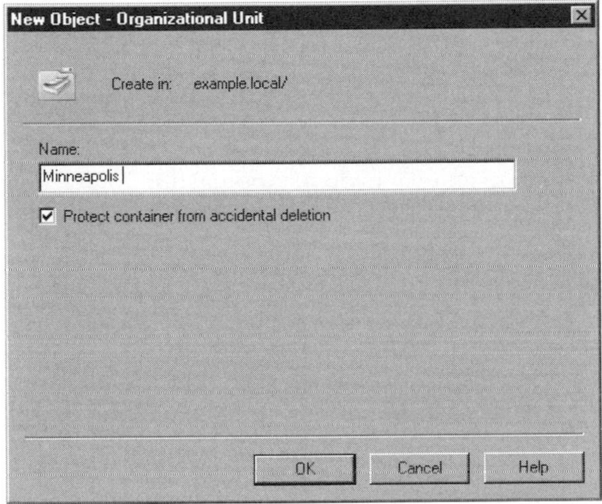

Figure 11-1 Creating a new organizational unit

3. In the Organizational Unit dialog box, type the name for the OU, and then click OK.

Note By default, the Protect This Container From Accidental Deletion box is selected. This option updates the security descriptor of the object and, potentially, its parent, which denies all administrators or users of this domain and domain controller the ability to delete this object. It does not, however, protect against accidental deletion of a subtree that contains the protected object. So for better protection, enable this setting for all the protected object's containers up to the domain naming context head.

Moving Organizational Units

One of the most useful aspects of OUs is that they can be moved from one container to another, or even one domain to another. To move an OU, follow these steps:

1. Choose Active Directory Users And Computers from the Administrative Tools menu.
2. Right-click the OU to be moved, and select Move from the shortcut menu.
3. In the Move dialog box, select the new location for the OU and click OK.

Important Moving OUs is easy in Windows Server 2008, but moving OUs that have Group Policy Objects linked to them can have unexpected results. Carefully consider the consequences of an OU move to the overall design of your Group Policy and verify the final behavior after the move.

Deleting Organizational Units

OUs can also be deleted easily. However, exercise caution when deleting an OU because the contents of the OU are also removed. That means you can inadvertently delete all the resources and user accounts contained in an OU if you act too hastily. To delete an OU, follow these steps:

1. Choose Active Directory Users And Computers from the Administrative Tools menu.
2. Right-click the OU and select Delete.
3. Confirm the deletion by clicking Yes twice.

Planning a Group Strategy

When you look at your network and the various group types, and then factor in your specific needs, you can end up feeling as though you're working on some infernal logic puzzle: Claire lives in a blue house, Lynn collects stamps, Owen drives a station wagon, and Wally eats cheese. Which one has red hair? Nevertheless, as in so many other aspects of network administration, planning is *the* essential step.

Determining Group Names

When planning your groups, determine a naming scheme that is appropriate for your organization. You have to consider two factors:

- **Group names must be instantly recognizable** Administrators searching Active Directory don't have to guess at their meaning.
- **Comparable groups must have similar names** In other words, if you have a group for engineers in each domain, give all the groups parallel names, such as NorAmer Engineers, SoAmer Engineers, and Euro Engineers.

Using Global and Domain Local Groups

Develop a strategy for using the different groups. For example, users with common job responsibilities belong in a global group. Thus, add user accounts for all graphic artists to a global group called Graphic Artists. Other users with common needs are assigned to other global groups. Then you must identify resources that users need access to and create a domain local group for each resource. If, for example, you have several color printers and plotters that are used by specific departments, you can make a domain local group called Printers&Plotters.

Next, decide which global groups need access to the resources you identified. Continuing the example, add the global group Graphic Artists to the domain local group Printers&Plotters, along with other global groups that need access to the printers and plotters. Permission to use the resources in Printers&Plotters is assigned to the Printers&Plotters domain local group.

Keep in mind that global groups can complicate administration in multiple-domain situations. Global groups from different domains must have their permissions set individually. Also, assigning users to domain local groups and granting permissions to the group does not give members access to resources outside the domain.

Using Universal Groups

When using universal groups, keep the following guidelines in mind:

- Avoid adding individual accounts to universal groups, to keep replication traffic down.
- Add global groups from multiple domains to universal groups to give members access to resources in more than one domain.
- Universal groups can be members of domain local groups and other universal groups, but they can't be members of global groups.

Implementing the Group Strategy

After you plan your strategy and test it using a variety of scenarios, you're ready to begin putting the structure into place.

Creating Groups

Use Active Directory Users And Computers to create and delete groups. Create groups in the Users container or in an OU that you create for the purpose of containing groups. To create a group in the Sales OU, follow these steps:

1. Choose Active Directory Users And Computers from the Administrative Tools menu.
2. Expand the domain in which you want to create the group.
3. Right-click the Sales container, point to New, and choose Group from the shortcut menu to open the dialog box shown in Figure 11-2.

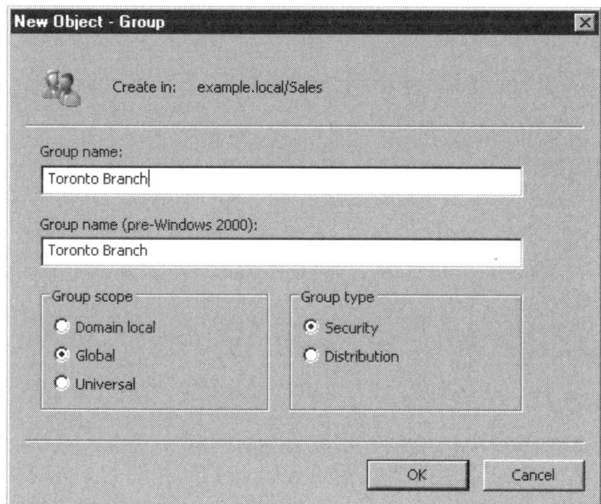

Figure 11-2 Creating a new group

4. Fill in the required information:
   - The group name must be unique in the domain.
   - The group name as it would be seen by pre-Windows 2000 operating systems is filled in automatically. Note that pre-Windows 2000 operating systems are no longer supported, but they might exist in some legacy situations.
   - For Group Scope, click Domain Local, Global, or Universal.
   - For Group Type, click Security or Distribution.

5. Click OK when you're finished. The new group appears in Sales. You might have to wait a few minutes for the group to be replicated to the global catalog before adding members.

Note Groups that are created directly in the Users container (the default behavior) can't have Group Policies applied to them. By using OUs and managing your groups within them, you have much greater control over how Group Policy is applied.

Deleting Groups

Don't create groups until and unless you need them, and when groups are no longer necessary be sure to promptly delete them from the system. Unnecessary groups are a security risk because it is all too easy to unintentionally grant permissions where you shouldn't.

Each group, like each user, has a unique security identifier (SID). The SID is used to identify the group and the permissions assigned to the group. When the group is deleted, the SID is deleted and not used again. If you delete a group and decide later to re-create it, you have to configure the users and permissions as if for a new group.

To delete a group, right-click its name in Active Directory Users And Computers and choose Delete from the shortcut menu. Deleting a group deletes only the group and the permissions associated with the group. It has no effect on the accounts of users who are members of the group.

Adding Users to a Group

After you create a group, you need to add members to it. As mentioned earlier in the chapter, groups can contain users, contacts, other groups, and computers. To add members to a group, follow these steps:

1. Choose Active Directory Users And Computers from the Administrative Tools menu.
2. In the console tree, click the container that includes the objects you want to add to the group.
3. Highlight the accounts you want to add. (You can use the Shift and Ctrl keys to select multiple accounts.)
4. Right-click the highlighted accounts, and select Add To A Group from the shortcut menu. This opens the Select Groups dialog box. Select Object Types And Locations to narrow the search.

5. Enter the name of the group, click Check Names, and then click OK.

You can also approach adding users to a group from another angle by following these steps:

1. Right-click a group name and select Properties.
2. Click the Members tab and then click Add. Make sure the Object Types and Locations fields are pointing to the positions you want.
3. Click Advanced, and then click Find Now. All the potential group members appear in the lower pane.
4. Highlight the accounts to be added and click OK.

> **Note** A contact is an account without security permissions and is typically used to represent external users for the purpose of e-mail. You can't log on to the network as a contact.

Changing the Group Scope

Over time, you might find that you need to change the scope of a particular group. For example, you might need to change a global group to a universal group so that users from another domain can be part of the group. However, the types of changes that can be made to a group scope are quite limited, and you might need to delete the group and create a new one to get the configuration you need.

To change a group scope, right-click the group name in Active Directory Users And Computers and choose Properties from the shortcut menu. Make the necessary changes on the General tab, and click OK when you're finished. The following rules apply to changing a group scope:

- A global group can be changed to a universal group if the global group is not already a member of another global group.
- A domain local group can be changed to a universal group if the domain local group does not already contain another domain local group.
- A universal group can be converted to a global group, as long as no other universal groups are members.

Creating Local Groups

A local group is a collection of user accounts on a single computer. The user accounts must be local to the computer, and members of local groups can be assigned permissions for resources only on the computer where the local group was created.

Local groups can be created on any computer running Windows Server 2000 or later except a domain controller. In general, local groups on a computer that is part of a domain should be used sparingly. Local groups don't appear in AD DS, so you must administer local groups separately on each computer. Local groups can be created at the console or remotely.

Creating a Local Group at the Console

1. Right-click Computer on the Start menu, and choose Manage from the shortcut menu.
2. In the console tree, expand System Tools and then Local Users And Groups.
3. Right-click the Groups folder and select New Group from the shortcut menu.
4. In the New Group dialog box, type the group name. You can include a description of the group if you want.
5. Click Add to add members to the group. (You can add members now or later.)
6. Click Create when you're finished. The new group is added to the list of groups in the details pane.

Creating a Local Group Remotely

1. Click Start and then click Run. Type in **mmc /a** and click OK.
2. On the File menu, select Add/Remove Snap-in.
3. In the Add or Remove Snap-ins dialog box (shown in Figure 11-3) highlight Local Users And Groups and then click Add.

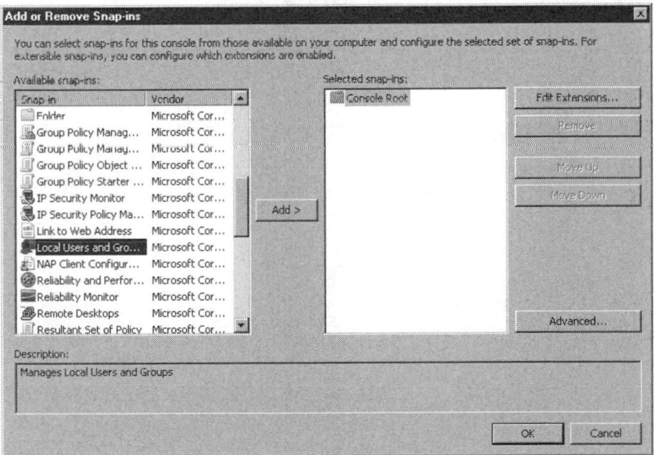

Figure 11-3 Selecting the Local Users And Groups snap-in

4. In the Choose Target Machine dialog box, select Another Computer and type in the computer name or IP address. Click Finish and then click OK.
5. In the console tree, select Local Users And Groups. Right-click Groups and select New Group.
6. Create the group.

Managing Default Groups and User Rights

When you create an Active Directory domain with one or more Windows Server 2008 domain controllers, default groups are automatically created in both the Users and Builtin containers. Many of these groups also have rights that are automatically assigned to members of the group. The default groups in the Builtin container have the scope of Builtin Local. You can't change their group scope or their group type.

The Users container holds groups that are defined with Global Scope and groups that are defined with Domain Local scope. Groups in these containers can be moved to other groups and Organizational Units within the domain but can't be moved to other domains.

Builtin Local Groups

Member servers and stand-alone servers running Windows 2000 Server (Service Pack 3 or later), Windows 2000 Professional (Service Pack 3 or later), Windows XP Professional (Service Pack 1 or later), or Windows Vista have default local groups that give rights to perform tasks on a single computer. The specific groups will differ slightly from one computer to another. Table 11-1 shows default local groups on a Windows 2008 Server that is not a domain controller.

Table 11-1 Default Local Groups

Local group	Description
Administrators	Members can perform all administrative tasks on the computer. The default Administrator account created when the operating system installed is a member of the group. When a server (not a domain controller) or a client running Windows Vista, Windows XP Professional, or Windows 2000 Professional joins a domain, the Domain Admins group (described in Table 11-3) is made part of this group.
Backup Operators	Members can log on to the computer, back up and restore the computer's data, and shut down the computer. Members cannot change security settings but can override them for purposes of backup and restore. No default members.

Table 11-1 Default Local Groups

Local group	Description
Cryptographic Operators	Members can perform cryptographic operations. No default members.
Event Log Readers	Members can read event logs from the local computer. No default members.
Guests	Members can perform only tasks for which an administrator has granted rights. Members can use only resources for which an administrator has specifically granted permission. The guest account is a default member of this group.
Distributed COM Users	Members can start, activate, and use DCOM objects on this computer. No default members.
IIS_IUSRS	Used by Internet Information Services.
Network Configuration Operators	Members can change TCP/IP settings and renew and release addresses. No default members.
Performance Monitor Users	Members can monitor performance counters on a specific server locally and remotely. No default members.
Performance Log Users	Members can administer performance logs, counters, and alerts on a specific server, locally or remotely. No default members.
Power Users	This group is included for backward compatibility but by default members have no more rights or permissions than standard user accounts. If you need to retain this group with rights and permissions that were present in previous versions of Windows, apply a security template granting the rights and permissions.
Print Operators	Members can manage printers and print queues on a specific server. No default members.
Remote Desktop Users	Members are allowed to connect remotely. No default members.
Replicator	Do not add user accounts of actual users to this group. If necessary, you can add a "dummy" user account to this group to permit you to log on to Replicator services on a domain controller and manage replication of files and directories.
Users	Members of this group can log on to the computer, access the network, save documents, and shut down the computer. Members cannot install programs or make system changes. When a member server, Windows 2000 Professional, or Windows XP Professional computer joins a domain, the Domain Users group is added to this group. The Interactive and Authenticated Users groups are also members of the users group, so all user accounts are automatically members of the Users group.

Note If you don't want members of the Domain Users group to have access to a particular workstation or member server, remove Domain Users from that computer's local Users group. Similarly, if you don't want the members of Domain Admins to administer a particular workstation or member server, remove Domain Admins from the local Administrators group.

Builtin Domain Local Groups

Default domain local groups provide users with rights and permissions to perform tasks on domain controllers and in Active Directory Domain Services. The domain local groups have predefined rights and permissions that are granted to users and global groups that you add as members. Table 11-2 shows the most commonly used default domain local groups.

Table 11-2 Commonly Used Default Domain Local Groups

Domain local group	Description
Account Operators	Members can create, delete, and manage user accounts and groups. Members cannot modify the Administrators, Domain Admins, and Domain Controllers groups, or any of the Operators groups. Members can log on locally to domain controllers and shut them down. No default members.
Administrators	Members are automatically granted every right and permission on all domain controllers and the domain itself. The Administrator account, Domain Admins group, and Enterprise Admins group are members.
Allowed RODC Password Replication Group	Members of this group can have their passwords replicated to a Read Only Domain Controller (RODC). No default members. This group appears in the Builtin list when an RODC is created in the domain.
Backup Operators	Members can back up and restore data on all domain controllers, and can log on to domain controllers and shut them down. This group has no default members, and membership should be granted with care. This group is not the same as the Default Local Group Backup Operators.
Certificate Service DCOM Access	Members can publish certificates for users and computers. No default members.
Cryptographic Operators	Members can perform cryptographic operations. No default members.

Table 11-2 **Commonly Used Default Domain Local Groups**

Domain local group	Description
Denied RODC Password Replication Group	Members of this group can not have their passwords replicated to an RODC. Default members are Cert Publishers, Domain Admins, Domain Controllers, Enterprise Admins, Group Policy Creator Owners, Read Only Domain Controllers, and Schema Admins. This group appears in the Builtin list when an RODC is created in the domain.
Distributed COM Users	Members can launch, activate, and use Distributed COM objects. No default members.
Event Log Readers	Members can read event logs from a local computer. No default members.
Guests	By default, members have the same access as members of the User group except for the Guest account, which is restricted further. The Guests and Domain Guests groups are members by default.
IIS_IUSRS	Built-in group used by Internet Information Services.
Incoming Forest Trust Builders (appears only in forest root domain)	Members can allow an incoming forest trust to let users in another forest access resources in the home forest. No default members.
Network Configuration Operators	Members can renew and release addresses on domain controllers and change TCP/IP settings. No default members.
Performance Monitor Users	Members can monitor performance counters on domain controllers either locally or from remote clients without being administrators or members of the Performance Log Users group. No default members.
Performance Log Users	Members can manage performance logs, counters, and alerts on domain controllers either locally or remotely without being administrators. No default members.
Pre–Windows 2000 Compatible Access	Provided for backward compatibility for computers running Windows NT 4. Add users to this group only if they are running Windows NT 4 or earlier. No default members.
Print Operators	Members can manage all aspects of domain printer operation and configuration. No default members.
Remote Desktop Users	Members can remotely log on to domain controllers. No default members.
Replicator	Supports file replication.
Server Operators	Members can perform most administrative tasks on domain controllers, except the manipulation of security options. No default members.

Table 11-2 Commonly Used Default Domain Local Groups

Domain local group	Description
Terminal Servers License Servers	Members can update user accounts in Active Directory to track and report Terminal Server per user Client Access Licenses usage. No default members.
Users	Members can log on to the computer, access the network, save documents, and shut down the computer. Members cannot install programs or make system changes. Authenticated Users and Domain Users are members by default.
Windows Authorization Access	Members have access to the computed *tokenGroupsGlobalAnd-Universal* attribute on *User* objects.

Note In Windows NT, all domain users are members of the Everyone group. This group is controlled by the operating system and appears on any network with Windows NT servers. In Windows 2000 Server and later, the equivalent group is called Authenticated Users. Unlike Everyone, Authenticated Users contains no anonymous users or guests. The Everyone group survives as a *special identity*. You don't see it when you administer groups, and it cannot be placed in a group. When a user logs on to the network, the user is automatically added to Everyone. You can't see or change the membership of the special identities, which also include the Network and Interactive groups.

Builtin Global Groups

Default global groups are created to encompass common types of accounts. By default, these groups do not have inherent rights; an administrator must assign all rights to the group. However, some members are added to these groups automatically, and you can add more members based on the rights and permissions you assign to the groups. Rights can be assigned directly to the groups or by adding the default global groups to domain local groups. Table 11-3 describes the default global groups that are commonly used.

Table 11-3 Commonly Used Default Global Groups

Global group	Description
DnsUpdateProxy (installed with DNS)	Members are DNS clients that can provide dynamic updates to DNS on behalf of other clients. No default members.
Domain Admins	This group is automatically a member of the domain local Administrators group, so members of Domain Admins can perform administrative tasks on any computer in the domain. This group is automatically a member of the Administrators group and the Denied RODC Password Replication group. The Administrator account is a member of this group by default.
Domain Computers	All controllers and workstations in the domain are members.

Table 11-3 Commonly Used Default Global Groups

Global group	Description
Domain Controllers	All domain controllers in the domain are members. This group is automatically a member of the Denied RODC Password Replication group.
Domain Guests	The Guest account is a member by default. This group is automatically a member of the domain local Guests group.
Domain Users	The Administrator account and all user accounts are members. The Domain Users group is automatically a member of the domain local Users group.
Group PolicyCreator Owners	Members can create and modify group policy for the domain. The Administrator account is a default member of the group. Group PolicyCreator Owners group is automatically a member of the Denied RODC Password Replication group.

Note If you have users with fewer rights and permissions than the typical user, add these users to Domain Guests and remove them from Domain Users.

Defining User Rights

What users can and cannot do depends on the rights and permissions that have been granted to them. Rights generally apply to the system as a whole. The ability to back up files or to log on to a server, for example, is a right that the administrator giveth or taketh away. Rights can be assigned individually, but most often they are characteristics of groups, and a user is assigned to a particular group on the basis of the rights that the user needs.

Permissions indicate the access that a user (or group) has to specific objects, such as files, directories, and printers. For example, the question of whether a user can read a particular directory or access a network printer is a permission. Permissions are discussed at length later in this chapter.

Rights, in turn, are divided into two types: privileges and logon rights. *Privileges* include such functions as the ability to run security audits or force shutdown from a remote system—obviously not tasks that are done by most users. *Logon rights* are self-explanatory: They involve the ability to connect to a computer in specific ways. Rights are automatically assigned to the default groups in Windows Server 2008, although they can be assigned to individual users as well as groups. Assignment by group is preferred, so whenever possible, assign rights by group membership to keep administration simple. When membership in groups defines rights, rights can be removed from a user by simply removing the user from the group. Tables 11-4 and 11-5 list the logon rights and privileges and the groups to which they are assigned by default.

Table 11-4 Logon Rights Assigned To Groups By Default

Name	Description	Groups assigned the right on domain controllers	Groups assigned the right on workstations and servers
Access This Computer From The Network	Permits connection to the computer through the network	Administrators, Authenticated Users, Everyone, Pre-Windows 2000 Compatible Access, Enterprise Domain Controllers	Administrators, Backup Operators, Users, Everyone
Allow Logon Locally	Permits logging on to the computer interactively	Administrators, Account Operators, Backup Operators, Print Operators, Server Operators	Administrators, Backup Operators, Users
Allow Log On Through Terminal Services	Allows logging on as a Terminal Services client	Administrators	Administrators, Remote Desktop Users

Table 11-5 Privileges Assigned to Groups by Default

Privilege	Description	Groups assigned the privilege by default
Act As Part Of The Operating System	Allows a process to authenticate as any user. A process that requires this privilege must use the LocalSystem account, which already includes this privilege.	None
Add Workstations To Domain	Allows a user to add new workstations to an existing domain.	Authenticated Users on domain controllers
Adjust Memory Quotas For A Process	Allows user to set the maximum amount of memory a process can use.	Administrators, Local Service, and Network Service
Back Up Files And Directories	Allows backing up the system; overrides specific file and folder permissions.	Administrators, Server Operators (on domain controllers), Backup Operators
Bypass Traverse Checking	Allows a user to go through directory trees (folder structures) even if the user doesn't have permission to access the directories being passed through.	Administrators, Authenticated Users, Everyone and Pre-Windows 2000 Compatible Access on domain controllers; on servers and workstations, Administrators, Backup Operators, Users, Everyone, Local Service, Network Service

Table 11-5 **Privileges Assigned to Groups by Default**

Privilege	Description	Groups assigned the privilege by default
Change The System Time	Allows the setting of the computer's internal clock.	Administrators and Server Operators on domain controllers; Administrators on servers and workstations, Local Service
Create A Pagefile	Allows the creation and modification of a pagefile.	Administrators
Create Global Objects	Allows the creation of global objects in a Terminal Services session.	Administrators, Service, Local Service, Network Service
Debug Programs	Allows the user to attach a debugger to a process.	Administrators
Enable User And Computer Accounts To Be Trusted For Delegation	Permits a user to set the Trusted For Delegation setting on an object.	Administrators on domain controllers; not assigned on member servers or workstations
Force Shutdown From A Remote System	Allows the shutdown of a computer from a remote location on the network.	Administrators and Server Operators on domain controllers; Administrators on member servers and workstations
Impersonate A Client After Authentication	Allows an account to impersonate another account.	Administrators
Increase Scheduling Priority	Allows the use of Task Manager to change the scheduling priority of a process.	Administrators
Load And Unload Device Drivers	Installs and removes Plug and Play device drivers.	Administrators and Print Operators on domain controllers; Administrators on other computers
Manage Auditing And Security Log	Allows a user to specify auditing options and to view and clear the security log in Event Viewer. Audit Directory Service Access must be turned on for object access auditing to be performed. Administrators can always view and clear the security log.	Administrators
Modify Firmware Environment Variables	Allows the configuration of nonvolatile RAM on computers that support this function.	Administrators

Table 11-5 Privileges Assigned to Groups by Default

Privilege	Description	Groups assigned the privilege by default
Profile A Single Process	Allows performance sampling on a process.	Administrators; on member servers and workstations, Administrators and Users
Profile System Performance	Allows performance sampling of the system.	Administrators
Remove Computer From Docking Station	Allows the removal of a laptop from a docking station using Eject PC on the Start menu.	Administrators and Users
Restore Files And Directories	Allows restoring files and folders to a system; overrules specific file and folder permissions.	Administrators, Backup Operators, and Server Operators on domain controllers; Administrators and Backup Operators on workstations and servers
Shut Down The System	Shuts down the local computer.	Administrators, Backup Operators, Print Operators, and Server Operators on domain controllers; Administrators and Backup Operators on member servers; Administrators, Backup Operators, and Users on workstations
Synchronize Directory Service Data	Allows a user to initiate a synchronization of Active Directory.	None
Take Ownership Of Files Or Other Objects	Allows a user to take ownership of any security object, including files and folders, printers, registry keys, and processes.	Administrators

Assigning User Rights to a Group

Rights are assigned and removed most easily at a domain level using Group Policy. Suppose you have a group of users who should be able to log on locally to servers running Windows Server 2008 but you don't want them to be members of any groups that have this logon right by default. One way to approach this situation is to create a group called Logon Rights, add the users to the group, and assign the right to log on locally to the Logon Rights group. To assign a right to a particular group, follow these steps:

1. Start Group Policy Management from the Administrative Tools menu.
2. Expand the domain name. Right-click Group Policy Objects and then select New from the shortcut menu.
3. In the New GPO dialog box, type a name for the new policy, as shown in Figure 11-4. Click OK.

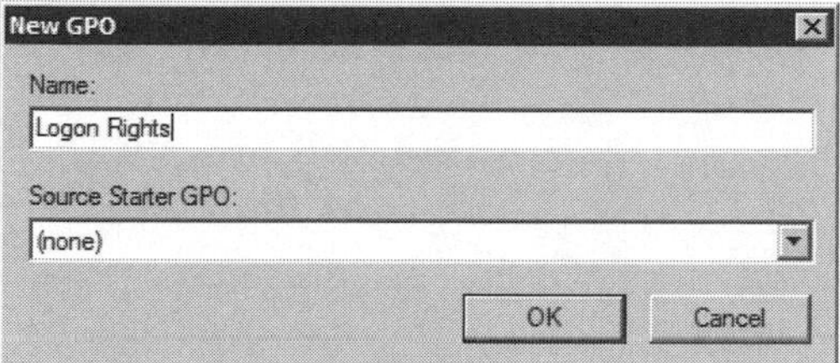

Figure 11-4 Creating a new Group Policy Object

4. Right-click the new Group Policy Object and select Edit to open the Group Policy Management Editor.
5. Expand Computer Configuration, then Policies, then Windows Settings, then Security Settings, Local Policies, and then User Rights Assignment.
6. In the details pane, double-click Allow Log On Locally.
7. Select Define These Policy Settings and then click Add User Or Group.
8. Type the name of the group to be granted this right (or click Browse to search for the group). Click OK. (You will need to add an Administrative account or group as well.)
9. Click OK and close the Group Policy Management editor.

The same process can remove rights, except that you click Remove rather than Add User Or Group in step 7. Using this method, you can also assign rights to an individual user.

Assigning Rights Locally

Rights can be assigned or removed locally, though you must bear in mind that a defined domain-level policy overrides a local policy setting. To assign a policy locally, follow these steps:

1. Choose Local Security Policy from the Administrative Tools menu.
2. Under Security Settings, click Local Policies and then click User Rights Assignment.
3. In the detail pane, double-click the policy you want to assign to open the policy's Properties window.
4. Click Add User Or Group to select an individual or a group in the Select Users, Computers, Or Groups dialog box. Make sure the object type and location fields are pointing to the locations you want. Click Advanced, and then click Find Now. All the potential group members appear in the lower pane.
5. Highlight the accounts to be added and click OK.

If the Add User Or Group and Remove buttons aren't available in the Properties window, the policy has been set at the domain level and can't be overridden locally.

Creating User Accounts

Every person who has access to the network requires a user account. A user account makes it possible to do the following:

- Authenticate the identity of the person connecting to the network
- Control access to domain resources
- Audit actions performed using the account

Windows Server 2008 creates only two normal predefined accounts on a domain controller: the Administrator account, which is granted all rights and permissions, and the Guest account, which has limited rights. On domain controllers there is also a KRBTGT key distribution account, and on non-DCs there are built in special accounts for Help and Support and Remote Assistance. All other accounts are created by an administrator and are either domain accounts, which are valid throughout the domain by default, or local accounts, which are usable only on the computer on which they are created.

Naming User Accounts

In Active Directory Domain Services, each user account has a *principal name*. The name consists of two parts, the *security principal name* and the *principal name suffix*. For existing Windows NT user accounts, the security principal name is by default the same as the name used to log on to the Windows NT domain. For new Windows Server 2008 user accounts, an administrator assigns the security principal name. The default principal name suffix is the DNS name of the root domain in the domain tree. So a user identified as EduardoP in a Windows NT domain has a principal name such as EduardoP@example.com in Windows Server 2000 and later.

Account Options

Planning account options for users simplifies the process of creating accounts. Consider the following account options:

- **Logon Hours** By default, a user can log on at any hour of the day or night. For security reasons, you might want to restrict access by some or all users to certain times of the day or certain days of the week.
- **Log On To** By default, users can log on to all workstations. For security reasons, you can limit logon access to a particular computer or computers.
- **Account Expiration** You can decide whether you want to set accounts to expire. For obvious reasons, it makes sense to set an expiration date for temporary employees to coincide with the end of their contracts.

You can set other options—*many* other options—in user accounts; these are detailed in the section "Setting User Account Properties" later in the chapter. The preceding three options are the most likely to be applied across large numbers of users.

Real World Establishing a Naming Convention

Assign the security principal name using a consistent naming convention so that you and your users can remember user names and find them in lists. Consider the following options for user names:

- **First name plus last initial** Examples are MichaelG and SusanM. In the case of duplicate first names, you can add numbers (MichaelG1 and MichaelG2) or enough letters to provide identification (IngridMat and IngridMur).
- **First name plus a number** Examples are Dave112 and Dave113. This approach can be a problem, especially for people with first names that appear frequently in the population. This approach can make it hard to remember your *own* user name, much less any others.
- **First initial plus last name** An example is MSmith. If you have both a John Smith and a Jeff Smith, you could use JoSmith and JeSmith or JSmith1 and JSmith2.
- **Last name plus an initial** This convention is useful in a large network. When you have multiple users with the same last name, add a few letters as in SmithLi or SmithLo.

No matter which approach you choose, you must not only accommodate the existing users on your network but you must also be able to integrate future users. Then, whether the company's next hire is U Ti or Chomondely St. J. Montmorency-Glossup, your user-name convention can still handle it.

Passwords

All your users must have well-chosen passwords and be required to change them periodically. Passwords should be chosen according to the guidelines in the Real World sidebar "Rules for Good Passwords." Set accounts to lock out when invalid passwords are entered. (Allow three attempts, to leave room for typographical errors by the user.)

Real World Rules for Good Passwords

A good password has the following characteristics:

- It is not a rotation or reuse of the characters in a logon name. (How many brain cells does it take to figure this one out?)
- It contains at least two alphabetic characters and one nonalphabetic character.
- It is at least eight characters long.
- It isn't the user's name or initials, the initials of his or her children or significant other, or any of these items combined with other commonly available personal data such as a birth date, telephone number, or license plate number.

Among the best passwords are alphanumeric acronyms of phrases that have a meaning to the user but are not likely to be known to others. This makes the password easy for the user to remember, while at the same time making it hard for an outsider to guess. Another good password isn't a word at all, but a *passphrase* —an entire phrase or sentence, complete with spaces and punctuation.

It pays to educate your users about passwords and password privacy, but most of all, it pays to heed your own advice: Make sure the password you select for administration is a good password, and change it frequently. Doing so will help you avoid the consequences of having somebody break into your system and wreak havoc in your very own kingdom. If users dial in to the network from home or other remote sites, include more security than domain-level password authorization.

Creating a Domain User Account

You can create domain user accounts in the default Users container or you can make an OU to hold domain user accounts. To add a domain user account, follow these steps:

1. Choose Active Directory Users And Computers from the Administrative Tools menu.
2. Right-click the container in which you want to create the account, point to New, and then choose User from the shortcut menu.
3. Provide the user's first and last name, as shown in Figure 11-5. The Full Name box is filled in automatically. The full name must be unique in the OU where the user account is created.

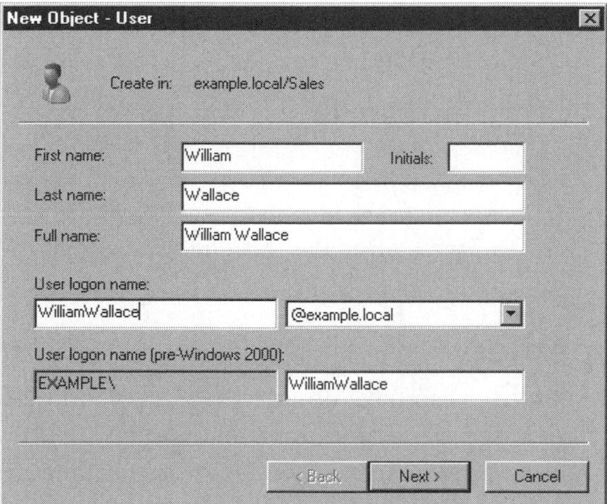

Figure 11-5 Creating a new user

4. Provide the user logon name based on your naming convention. This name must be unique in Active Directory. The pre–Windows 2000 logon name is filled in automatically. This is the name used to log on from computers running older Windows operating systems such as Windows NT. Click Next.
5. Provide a password, and set password policies. Click Next. A confirmation screen appears.
6. If the details of the account you are about to create are correct, click Finish. Otherwise, click Back to make corrections.

At this point, the new user account is added to the OU with default settings. It's unlikely that the default settings are exactly what you want, so you need to adjust the properties of the new account, as described in the section "Setting User Account Properties" later in the chapter.

Creating a Local User Account

A local account can't log on to the domain and therefore has access only to the resources on the computer where it's created and used. To create a local user account, on a client with Windows Vista, follow these steps:

1. Right-click Computer from the Start menu, and choose Manage from the shortcut menu.
2. In the console tree, click Local Users And Groups. Right-click Users, and choose New User from the shortcut menu.

3. In the New User dialog box, supply the user name, full name, and description.
4. Provide a password, and set password policies. Click Create. At this point, the new user account is created with default settings. Local accounts can belong to locally created groups (on the single computer).

Note To create a local user account on a Windows XP machine, use the steps above except in step 1, right-click My Computer on the Start menu.

Setting User Account Properties

The Properties window for a domain user can have up to 13 tabs, depending on the domain's setup; Table 11-6 describes these tabs. Information entered in the Properties window can be used as the basis for a search in Active Directory. For example, you can find a user's telephone number or department by searching for the user's last name. To set the properties for a domain user account, follow these steps:

1. Choose Active Directory Users And Computers from the Administrative Tools menu.
2. Open the OU where the domain user account was created.
3. Double-click the user account to open the Properties window.
4. Click the tab for the properties you want to set. Make the changes, and click OK when you're finished.

Table 11-6 Tabs in the Properties Window for a Domain User Account

Tab	Description
General	Documents the user's name, description, office location, telephone number, e-mail address, and Web page address
Address	Documents the user's physical address
Account	Documents the logon name, logon restrictions, password options, and whether the account expires
Profile	Shows the user's profile path, the path of any script that runs when the user logs on, the path to a home folder, and any automatic drive connections
Telephones	Lists additional telephone numbers such as for a pager, cellular phone, or Internet phone
Organization	Documents the user's title, department, company, manager, and direct reports

Table 11-6 Tabs in the Properties Window for a Domain User Account

Tab	Description
Remote Control	Configures the degree to which an administrator can view or control the user's Terminal Services sessions
Terminal Services Profile	Documents the user's Terminal Services profile
COM+	Documents the user's participation in COM+ partition sets
Member Of	Lists the user's group memberships
Dial-in	Documents the user's dial-in access
Environment	Settings for the user's Terminal Services environment
Sessions	Terminal Services disconnect and reconnect settings

Note Select Advanced Features from the View menu in Active Directory Users and Computers to see additional tabs for Published Certificates, Object, and Security.

Testing User Accounts

As you develop different types of user accounts, it's advisable to test them. Create a dummy account with the memberships and restrictions you're planning to use. Then log on to a client computer and see whether the account produces the results you expect by doing the following:

- Test restrictions to logon hours and passwords by attempting to bypass them.
- Test home folders and profiles (discussed in "Using Home Folders," later in this chapter) to see whether they are actually created.
- Test roaming profiles by logging on from various computers.
- Test group memberships by performing a task that membership in the group is supposed to allow (or deny), such as logging on to a server.

The time to discover an unfortunate setting is in a test environment. Test Group Policy settings using Resultant Set of Policy, discussed in Chapter 13.

Managing User Accounts

On a large, busy network, managing user accounts is a continual process of additions, deletions, and changes. Although these tasks aren't difficult, they can be time-consuming and need to be managed carefully.

Finding a User Account

On small networks, it's easy enough to locate a user under Active Directory Users And Computers. On a larger network, more advanced search techniques must be brought to bear.

To search for a particular user account, choose Active Directory Users And Computers from the Administrative Tools menu, and on the toolbar, click the Find icon, shown here.

This opens the Find Users, Contacts, And Groups dialog box. Click the drop-down arrow in the Find list box and you see that you can also use this tool to search for computers, printers, shared folders, OUs, and more. (See Figure 11-6.)

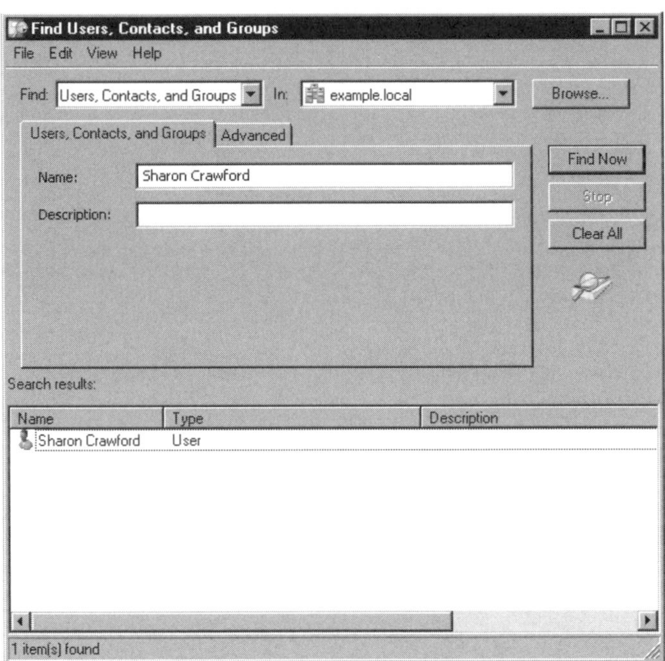

Figure 11-6 The Find tool allows for fairly specific searches.

Select the scope of your search in the In list box. Type a name or part of a name, and click Find Now. A search for a portion of a name returns all users, contacts, and groups with that element in their names.

Choose another option in Find and the possible search parameters adjust. For example, choose Common Queries in the Find list and you have an easy way to search for disabled accounts or users with nonexpiring passwords.

For even more in-depth searches, click the Advanced tab and select criteria from the Field drop-down list. Searches can be made on virtually every bit of information in a user, contract, group, or other object record. Figure 11-7 shows a search for a printer that can print double-sided in color on legal-sized paper *and* prints at least four pages per minute *and* has a resolution of 600 dpi or greater. A tall order, but if it exists, it will be found.

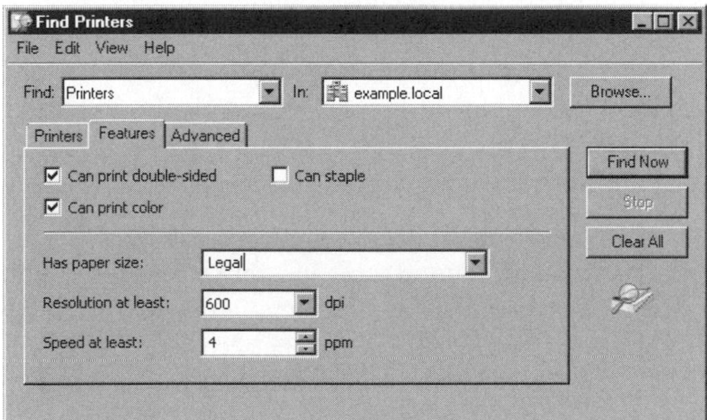

Figure 11-7 Searching for printers in Active Directory using very specific criteria

Disabling and Enabling a User Account

If you need to deactivate a domain user account for some period of time but not delete it permanently, you can disable it. Find the user account, right-click the user name, and select Disable Account from the shortcut menu, as shown in Figure 11-8.

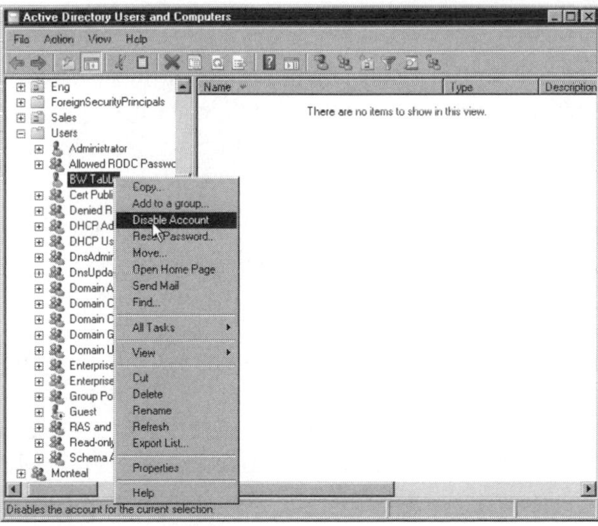

Figure 11-8 Disabling a user account

An informational box opens telling you that the object has been disabled. Enable a disabled account by reversing the process and choosing Enable Account from the shortcut menu.

Deleting a User Account

Each user account in the domain has an associated SID that is unique and never reused, which means that a deleted account is completely deleted. If you delete Jeremy's account and later change your mind, you have to re-create not only the account but also the permissions, settings, group memberships, and other properties that the original user account had. For that reason, if you have any doubt about whether an account might be needed in the future, it's best to disable it and not perform the deletion until you're sure it won't be needed again.

However, accounts do have to be deleted at regular intervals. Just find the user account, right-click the user name, and select Delete from the shortcut menu. An Active Directory dialog box prompts you to confirm the deletion. Click Yes and the account is deleted.

Moving a User Account

Moving a user account from one container to another is similarly easy. Find the user account in Active Directory. Right-click and select Move from the shortcut menu. In the Move dialog box, select the destination container and click OK. Or just drag the account to its new destination container. To select multiple user accounts to move at once, use the Ctrl and Shift keys.

Renaming a User Account

On occasion, a user account might need to be renamed. For example, if you have an account configured with an assortment of rights, permissions, and group memberships for a particular position and a new person is taking over that position, you can change the first, last, and user logon names to fit the new person. To rename an existing user account, follow these steps:

1. Find the existing user account. Right-click the user name and choose Rename from the shortcut menu. (You can also slowly click the user name twice.)
2. Press the Delete key and then the Enter key to open the Rename User dialog box.
3. Type the changes, and click OK. The account is renamed, and all permissions and other settings remain intact. Other data in the account's Properties window—such as address, phone number, and so forth—have to be changed as well. If a home folder exists, it will not be renamed for the new user and will have to be created separately.

Resetting a User's Password

For passwords to be effective, they must not be obvious or easy to guess. However, when passwords are not obvious or easy to guess, they are often forgotten. When a user forgets her password, you can reset it. The best practice is to reset it to a simple password and require the user to change the password the next time she logs on to the network.

To reset a password, follow these steps:

1. Find the user account whose password you need to reset.
2. Right-click the account name and choose Reset Password from the shortcut menu.
3. In the Reset Password dialog box, shown in Figure 11-9, type the new password twice. If you are making the change because the user has forgotten the account password and has tried to log on repeatedly, you may have to select the Unlock The User's Account box. Click OK to implement the change.

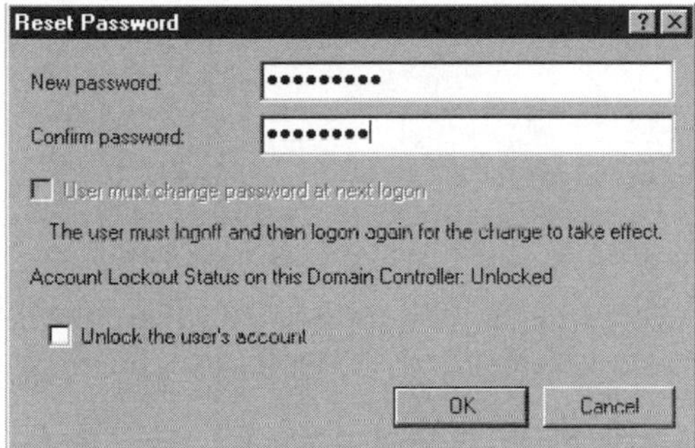

Figure 11-9 Resetting a user's password

Unlocking a User Account

If a user violates a group policy, such as exceeding the limit for bad logon attempts or failing to change an expired password, Active Directory Domain Services locks the account. When an account is locked, it cannot be used to log on to the system. When the penitent comes pleading for reinstatement and after you deliver a few firm words on the importance of following password rules, take the following steps to unlock the user account:

1. Find the locked account in Active Directory Users And Computers. Right-click the account and choose Properties from the shortcut menu.
2. In the Properties window, click the Account tab.
3. Clear the Account Is Locked Out check box. Click OK.

By default, Group Policy does not lock accounts because of failed logon attempts—you make this setting for security reasons. See Chapter 13 for more about Group Policy.

More Info For instructions about how to delegate the right to unlock locked accounts, see Chapter 14, "Managing Daily Operations."

Using Home Folders

Home directories or folders are repositories you can provide on a network server for users' documents. Placing home folders on a network file server has several advantages:

- Backup of user documents is centralized.
- Users can access their home folders from any client computer.
- Home folders can be accessed from clients running any Microsoft operating system (including MS-DOS and all versions of Windows).

The contents of home folders are not part of user profiles, so they don't affect network traffic when users log on. (A home folder can also be on a client computer, but that defeats much of its purpose.)

Creating Home Folders on a Server

To create a home folder on a network file server, follow these steps:

1. On the server, create a new folder for the home folders and name it **Home Folders**. Right-click the new folder, and choose Properties from the shortcut menu.
2. Click the Sharing tab and then click the Share button.
3. In the File Sharing dialog box, type in **Users** (as shown in Figure 11-10) and click Add.

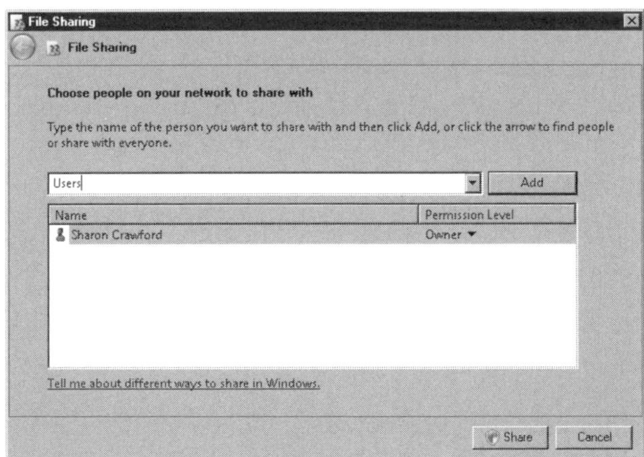

Figure 11-10 Sharing the Home Folders with the Users group

4. In the Permission Level list for Users, select Co-owner and then click Share.

> **Note** Store home folders on a partition formatted with NTFS. Home folders on a FAT partition can be secured only by assigning shared folder permissions on a user-by-user basis.

Providing Home Folders to Users

To provide a user with a home folder, you must add the path for the folder to the user account's properties. Follow these steps to give a user access to a home folder:

1. Find the user account in Active Directory Users And Computers. Right-click the user name and choose Properties from the shortcut menu.
2. Click the Profile tab. In the Home Folder panel, click Connect and specify a drive letter to use to connect to the file server.
3. In the To box, specify the UNC name for the connection–for example, **\\server_name\shared_folder\user_logon_name**. If you use the variable *%username%*, as shown in Figure 11-11, the home folder will be created with the user's logon name.

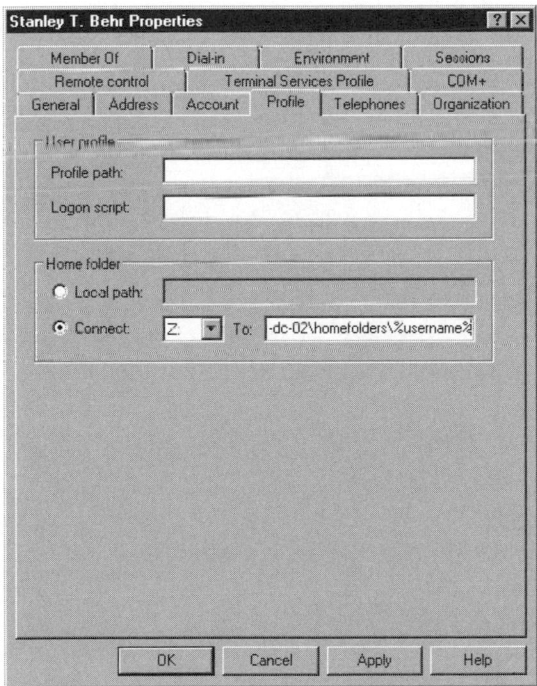

Figure 11-11 Specifying a home folder

Maintaining User Profiles

A *profile* is an environment specifically customized for a user. The profile contains the desktop and program settings for the user. Every user has a profile, whether the administrator configures one or not, because a default profile is automatically created for each user who logs on to a computer. Profiles offer a number of advantages:

- Multiple users can use the same computer, with the settings for each user restored at logon time to the same state as when she logged off.
- Desktop changes made by one user do not affect any other user.
- If user profiles are stored on a server, they can follow users to any computer on a network running Windows Server 2008, Windows Vista, Windows Server 2003, Windows XP Professional, or Windows 2000.

From an administrator's standpoint, the information in the profile can be a valuable tool for setting up default user profiles for all users on the network or for customizing default profiles for different departments or job classifications. You can also set up *mandatory* profiles that allow a user to make changes to the desktop while logged on but not to save any of the changes. A mandatory profile always looks exactly the same every time a user logs on. There are three types of profiles:

- **Local profiles** Profiles made on a computer when a user logs on. The profile is specific to a user, local to that computer, and stored on the local computer's hard disk.
- **Roaming profiles** Profiles created by an administrator and stored on a server. These profiles follow a user to any computer on a network running Windows Server 2008, Windows Vista, Windows Server 2003, Windows XP Professional, or Windows 2000.
- **Mandatory profiles** Roaming profiles that can be changed only by an administrator.

Real World What's Stored in a Profile?

All profiles start out as a copy of the Default User profile that is installed on every computer running Windows Server 2008, Windows Vista, Windows Server 2003, Windows XP Professional, or Windows 2000. Registry data for Default User is in the Ntuser.dat file contained in the Default User profile. Inside each profile for Windows Server 2008 and Windows Vista are the following folders:

- **Contacts** Contains the user's individually configured contacts

- **Desktop** Contains the user's personalized desktop settings
- **Documents** User's documents
- **Downloads** Downloaded files
- **Favorites** User-selected favorites on Internet Explorer
- **Links** Shortcuts to Documents, Music, Pictures, Public folder, Recently Changed, and Searches
- **Music** Stored music files
- **Pictures** Stored pictures
- **Saved Games** Incomplete games that have been saved
- **Searches** Recent and saved searches
- **Videos** Stored videos

Inside each profile for Windows Server 2008, Windows Vista, Windows Server 2003, Windows XP Professional, or Windows 2000 are the following folders:

- **Desktop** Desktop files, folders, shortcuts, and the desktop appearance
- **Favorites** Shortcuts to favorite locations, particularly Web sites
- **Local Settings** Application data, History, and Temporary files
- **Shared Documents** User documents and My Pictures, which contains user graphics files

Depending on the operating system, you might also find the following:

- **Application Data** Program-specific settings determined by the program manufacturer, plus specific user security settings
- **Cookies** Messages sent to a Web browser by a Web server and stored locally to track user information and preferences
- **NetHood** Shortcuts to My Network Places
- **PrintHood** Shortcuts to items in the Printers folder
- **Recent** Shortcuts to the most recently accessed folders and files
- **SendTo** Items on the Send To menu
- **Start Menu** Items on the user's Start menu
- **Templates** Application templates

By default, only some of the folders are visible in Windows Explorer. The other folders are hidden. To see them, select Folder Options, click the View tab, and select Show Hidden Files And Folders.

Local Profiles

Local profiles are created on computers when individual users log on. On a computer upgraded from Windows NT 4, the profile is stored in the Profiles folder on the system root partition. On computers running Windows 2008 Server and Windows Vista, local profiles are in the Users folder on the C: drive, as shown in Figure 11-12. On a computer with a new installation of Windows Server 2003, Windows XP Professional, Windows 2000 Server, or Windows 2000 Professional, the user profile is in the Documents And Settings folder.

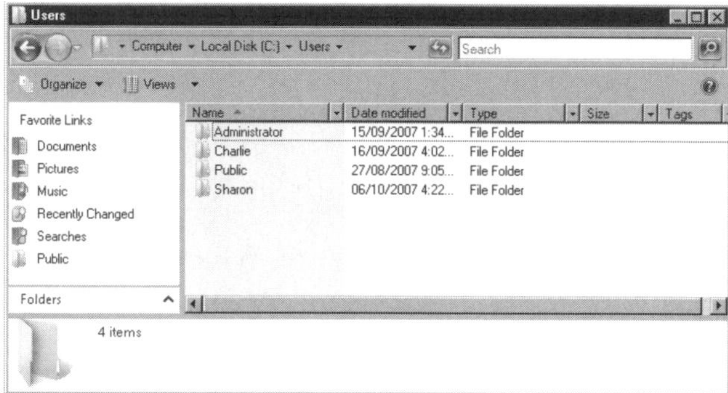

Figure 11-12 A user's local profile set up at the first logon event

The first time a user logs on to a computer, a profile folder is generated for the user, and the contents of the Default User folder are copied into it. Any changes made to the desktop by the user are saved in that user's profile when he logs off.

If a user has a local account on the computer as well as a domain account and logs on at different times using both accounts, the user will have two profile folders on the local computer: one for when the user logs on to the domain using the domain user account and one for when the user logs on locally to the computer. The local profile is shown with the logon name. The domain profile is also shown with the logon name but has the domain name appended to it.

Roaming Profiles

Roaming profiles are a great advantage for users who frequently use more than one computer. A roaming profile is stored on a server and, after the user's logon attempt is authenticated in the directory service, the profile is copied to the local computer. Once the roaming profile is set up, the user will have the same desktop, application configuration, and local settings at any computer running Windows Server 2003, Windows XP Professional, Windows 2000, or Windows NT 4. When the user logs on to a Windows Vista or Windows Server 2008 computer, a separate roaming profile will be generated. Figure 11-

13 shows two profiles for the user name stanley. The first is a profile that can roam among pre-Windows Vista computers. The second, stanleyV2, is the roaming profile that loads when the user logs on to a Windows Vista or Windows 2008 computer.

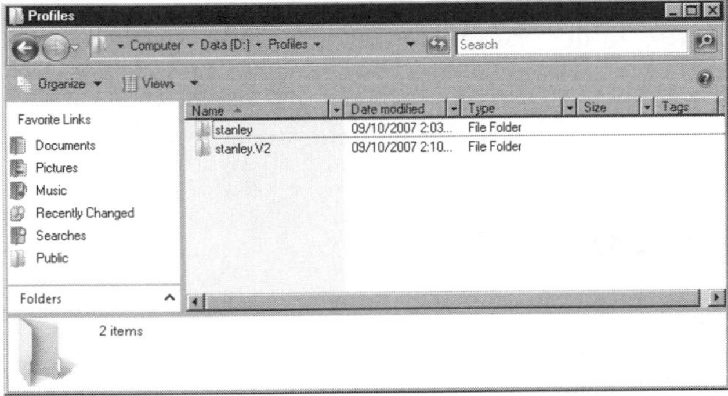

Figure 11-13 Roaming profiles for the same user that will load according to the operating system being used

Here's how it works. You assign a location on a server for user profiles and create a folder shared with users who are to have roaming profiles. You type a path to that folder in the user's Properties window. The next time the user logs on to a computer, the profile from the server is downloaded to the local computer. When the user logs off, the profile is saved both locally and in the user profile path location. Specifying the user profile path is all it takes to turn a local profile into a roaming profile, available on any computer running a compatible operating system.

When the user logs on again, the profile on the server is compared to the copy on the local computer, and the more recent copy is loaded for the user. If the server isn't available, the local copy is used. If the server isn't available and this is the first time the user has logged on to the computer, a user profile is created locally using the Default User profile. When a profile isn't downloaded to a local computer because of server problems, the roaming profile is not updated when the user logs off.

Note It's best to put user profiles on a member server rather than on a domain controller to speed up the process of authentication and to avoid using a domain controller's processing power and bandwidth for the downloading of profiles. In addition, place the profiles on a server that is backed up regularly so that copies of roaming profiles are as recent as possible.

Setting Up Roaming Profiles

Setting up roaming profiles is easy—you assign a location on a server and follow these steps:

1. Create a shared folder for the profiles on the server. Share the folder with the Groups or OUs that will have roaming profiles.
2. On the Profile tab in the user account Properties window, go to the Profile path field and provide a path to the shared folder, such as: **\\server_name\shared_profile_folder\%username%**.

Figure 11-14 shows an example of a path for a roaming profile. When you use the variable *%username%*, Windows Server 2008 automatically replaces the variable with the user account name.

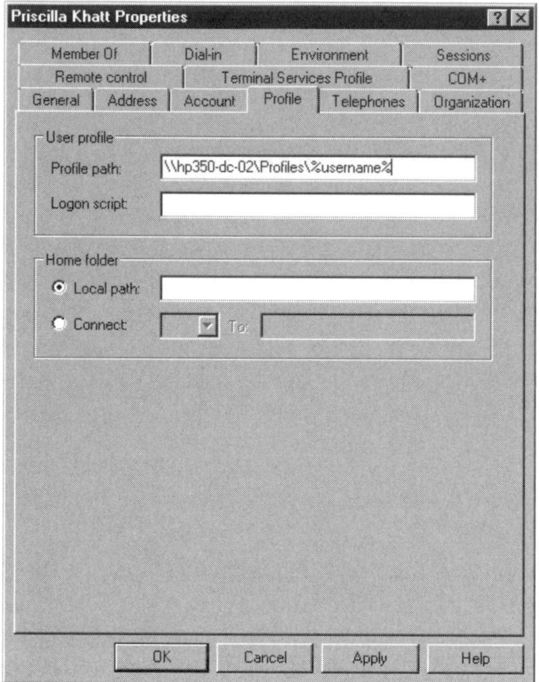

Figure 11-14 Setting a path for a roaming profile

After you create a shared profile folder on a server and supply a profile path in the user account, a roaming profile is enabled. The user's configuration of her desktop is copied and stored on the server and is available to the user from any computer. Most of the time, though, you don't want to send your users off to fend for themselves. Life is easier for them, and for you, if users are assigned a customized profile that is already set up with appropriate shortcuts, network connections, and Start menu items. For this, you need to set up customized profiles.

Creating Customized Roaming Profiles

Creating customized roaming profiles is a simple—albeit multistep—process:

1. Create a user account with a descriptive name such as District Managers or Sales Staff. This is just a "blank" user account that you use to create a template for the customized configuration.
2. Log on using the template account, and create the desktop settings you want, including applications, shortcuts, appearance, network connections, printers, and so forth.
3. Log off the template account. Windows Server 2008 creates a user profile on the system root drive in the Documents And Settings folder.
4. Log on again using an administrator account. Find the accounts that are going to have this customized roaming profile.
5. In each account, click the Profile tab, and in the Profile Path box, type **\\server_name\profile_folder\%username%**. Click OK.
6. In Control Panel, select System.
7. Under Tasks, click Advanced System Settings, and then in the User Profiles section, click Settings. Highlight the template account and click Copy To.
8. In the Copy To dialog box, type the path of the profiles folder on the server, **\\server_name\roaming_profiles_folder\username**. Note that this time you must use the actual name of the roaming profile or the profile will be stored under the name of whoever is logged on.
9. In the Permitted To Use area, click Change to give the appropriate group permission to use the profile. Click OK to copy the template profile.

Using Mandatory Profiles

If you're going to all the trouble of assigning customized profiles, you undoubtedly want to make the profiles mandatory. To change a profile into a mandatory profile, you need only rename the hidden file Ntuser.dat to Ntuser.man.

Note If you don't see the Ntuser file in the individual's profiles folder, choose Folder and Search Options from the Organize menu and click the View tab. In Advanced Settings, select Show Hidden Files And Folders.

Assigning a Logon Script to a User Profile

Logon scripts can be assigned by profile or through Group Policy. (Group Policy is covered in Chapter 13.) To assign a script to a profile, follow these steps:

1. Choose Active Directory Users And Computers from the Administrative Tools menu.
2. In the console tree, click the appropriate container. Right-click the user account and choose Properties.
3. Click the Profile tab, and type the name of the logon script in the Logon Script box.
4. Click OK when you're finished.

Windows Server 2008 always looks for logon scripts in the same place—on the authenticating domain controller at the path *%SystemRoot%*\SYSVOL*sysvol**domain_name*\scripts. Scripts in this folder can be typed in the Logon Script path by name only. If you use folders inside the Scripts folder, you must show that part of the path in the Logon Script path. Table 11-7 shows the special variables that can be used when creating logon scripts. Logon scripts can also be created in VBScript and JScript. If Windows PowerShell is deployed in your environment, you can use PowerShell scripts as well. Replication of logon scripts to all domain controllers is automatic on servers running Windows 2000 Server or later.

Table 11-7 Logon Script Variables

Variable	Description
%homedrive%	Letter of the drive containing the user's home directory on the user's local workstation
%homepath%	Full path of the user's home directory
%os%	User's operating system
%processor_architecture%	Processor type on the user's workstation
%processor_level%	Processor level of the user's workstation
%userdomain%	Domain where the user's account is defined
%username%	Account user name

Writing and using scripts is covered in Chapter 15, "Using Scripts for Consistent Administration." For additional information on scripting and sample scripts, the TechNet Script at: *http://www.microsoft.com/technet/scriptcenter/default.mspx* is an excellent resource.

Summary

The success of a network operation is measured by both the availability of some information and resources and the restriction and protection of others. Windows Server 2008 offers the network administrator the tools and functionality to meet the information needs of users, while protecting sensitive information stored on or passed through the network. This chapter has explored the options available to the administrator for configuring groups, group scope, and user accounts through Windows Server 2008. The next chapter covers the management of file resources including shares, permissions, and collaboration.

Chapter 12

Managing File Resources

On most networks, users have their own files, whether stored locally or on a server, but it's a rare network that doesn't use at least some shared files and folders. Windows Server 2008 supports four kinds of file resource sharing. The type or types you use depends on what has to be shared and by how many people.

- **Shared Folders** Shared folders are essentially the same old shared folders that we've all used and seen many times. Starting in Windows Server 2003 SP1, there is an important change, however. The default share permissions for a folder are read-only for the Everyone group. And since Windows Server 2003, the Everyone group does *not* include anonymous users.
- **Active Directory Shared Folders** Active Directory Shared Folders are any shared folders that are published in Active Directory. To create an Active Directory Shared Folder, the underlying folder must first be shared on the host computer.
- **DFS Folders** DFS folders are another way to mask the underlying complexities of the network and file locations to simplify the user's view of file resources.
- **NFS Shared Folders** Starting in Windows Server 2003 R2, Microsoft Services for NFS are an installable component of Windows. Services for NFS include NFS Server and NFS Client, along with the various supporting utilities, including the User Name Mapping Server. Services for NFS are discussed in Chapter 27, "Interoperability."

Share Permissions vs. File Permissions

There are two kinds of permissions involved in any shared folder—those on the actual share, and those imposed by the underlying file system. These permissions are *subtractive*. This means that only the most restrictive permission will win. Simultaneously managing permissions on both the share and the file system can often be confusing, and keeping track of the details of both is difficult. In most situations, you use the underlying NTFS file permissions to control access and you set the share permissions to Full Control for everyone for most normal shares. The NTFS file permissions give much greater granularity and control over exactly what level of access is granted. However, in some cases using a more restrictive share permission is useful. When you do that, you indicate in the share name that the share is restricted.

Note NFS-based access control for UNIX-based file systems is implemented by granting permissions to specific client computers and groups, using network names.

Share Permissions

Shares can be entire volumes or a folder tree. Until a volume or folder is shared over the network, users can't see it or gain access to it. By default, the Everyone group is granted read access to all files in the folder, to all subfolders of that folder, and so on, assuming users have sufficient file system permissions. After a volume or folder is shared, restrictions can be added or removed in the form of *share permissions*. These permissions apply only at the drive or folder level—not at the file level—and are limited to allowing or denying Full Control, Read, and Change, as shown in Table 12-1.

Table 12-1 Share Permissions

Share	Type of Permission
Read	Allows viewing of file and subfolder names, viewing data in files, and running programs
Change	Allows the access under Read, plus allows adding files and subdirectories to the shared folder, changing data in files, and deleting files and subdirectories
Full Control	Allows all the access under Change, plus allows changing file permissions and taking ownership (NTFS volumes only)

Share permissions determine the maximum access allowed over the network. They don't affect a user who logs on locally or a terminal server user of the computer.

File Permissions

File permissions, unlike share permissions, control user access regardless of where it originates. Local users, Terminal Services users, and network users are all treated equally. Because FAT and FAT32 file systems don't support any restriction on access to files, it's important to use only the NTFS file system. NTFS uses access control lists (ACLs) to limit access to resources. NTFS permissions can be assigned to both files and folders, and they apply network-wide and locally.

On an NTFS volume, you can set permissions down to the file level. This means that for any file, you can give individual users different types of access. Although you can set such detailed permissions, this way lies madness for all but the most meticulous control freaks (who are, arguably, already mad).

Always try to operate with the simplest possible permissions. Set as few restrictions as possible. Assign permissions to groups, not individuals. Don't set file-by-file permissions unless doing so is unavoidable. Managing the minutiae of permissions can easily and quickly soak up all your time and much of your life's blood as well, unless you guard against it.

Under the Hood User Account Control

For ten years or more, smarty-pants types (such as ourselves) have been warning administrators not to do everything using the Administrator account. Save that account for when you need it, we said. Use a standard user account most of the time, we implored. Of course, no one paid the slightest bit of attention, and here's the inevitable result: User Account Control.

User Account Control (UAC) is a new security feature introduced in Windows Vista. It's based on the security theory of least privilege. The idea is that users should have the absolute minimum privilege necessary to perform assigned tasks. This may sound as though it contradicts our advice to operate with the simplest possible permissions, but in fact it does not. Shares and permissions remain the way to allow or restrict access to files and folders.

The goal of UAC is to reduce the exposure of the operating system by requiring that all users run in standard user mode, minimizing the ability of users to make changes that could destabilize their computers or expose the network to undetected virus infections on their computers.

Problems Implementing UAC

Prior to Windows Vista, the Windows usage model has been one of assumed administrative rights. Software developers assumed their programs could access and modify any file, registry key, or operating system setting. Even when Windows NT introduced security and differentiated between granting access to administrative and standard user accounts, users were guided through a setup process that encouraged them to use the built-in Administrator account or one that was a member of the Administrators group. A second problem is that even standard users sometimes need to perform tasks that require administrative rights, such as installing software and opening ports in the firewall.

The UAC solution is to require administrative rights less frequently, enable legacy applications to run with standard user rights, make it easier for standard users to access administrative rights when they need them, and enable administrative users to run as if they were standard users.

For a detailed explanation of how UAC does all these things, see *http://www.microsoft.com/technet/technetmag/issues/2007/06/UAC/default.aspx*.

NTFS Permissions

As we noted earlier, the underlying ability to assign enforceable permissions to files and folders is part of the NTFS file system. As you work with files and folders on NTFS, you need to understand how the permissions work and how they are different for a file and for the folder that contains the file.

What Permissions Mean

NTFS permissions affect access both locally and remotely. Share permissions, on the other hand, apply only to network shares and don't restrict access on the part of any local user (or terminal server user) of the computer on which you've set the share permissions. Windows 2003 Server has a set of standard folder permissions that are combinations of specific kinds of access. The individual permissions are Full Control, Modify, Read & Execute, List Folder Contents, Read, and Write. Each of these permissions consists of a group of special permissions. Table 12-2 shows the special permissions and the standard permissions to which they apply.

Table 12-2 Special Permissions for Folders

Special Permission	Full Control	Modify	Read & Execute	List Folder Contents	Read	Write
Traverse Folder/ Execute File	Yes	Yes	Yes	Yes	No	No
List Folder/Read data	Yes	Yes	Yes	Yes	Yes	No
Read Attributes	Yes	Yes	Yes	Yes	Yes	No

Table 12-2 **Special Permissions for Folders**

Special Permission	Full Control	Modify	Read & Execute	List Folder Contents	Read	Write
Read Extended Attributes	Yes	Yes	Yes	Yes	Yes	No
Create Files/Write data	Yes	Yes	No	No	No	Yes
Create Folders/ Append data	Yes	Yes	No	No	No	Yes
Write Attributes	Yes	Yes	No	No	No	Yes
Write Extended Attributes	Yes	Yes	No	No	No	Yes
Delete Subfolders and Files	Yes	No	No	No	No	No
Delete	Yes	Yes	No	No	No	No
Read Permissions	Yes	Yes	Yes	Yes	Yes	Yes
Change Permissions	Yes	No	No	No	No	No
Take Ownership	Yes	No	No	No	No	No
Synchronize	Yes	Yes	Yes	Yes	Yes	Yes

Note These settings remain unchanged from Windows Server 2003.

Although Read & Execute and List Folder Contents appear to have identical permissions, in fact these permissions are inherited differently. Read & Execute is inherited by both files and folders and is always present when you view file or folder permissions. List Folder Contents is inherited by folders only and will appear only when viewing folder permissions.

Standard file permissions include Full Control, Modify, Read & Execute, Read, and Write. As with folders, each of these permissions controls a group of special permissions. Table 12-3 shows the special permissions associated with each standard permission.

Table 12-3 **Special Permissions for Files**

Special Permission	Full Control	Modify	Read & Execute	Read	Write
Traverse folder/ execute file	Yes	Yes	Yes	No	No
List Folder/Read Data	Yes	Yes	Yes	Yes	No
Read Attributes	Yes	Yes	Yes	Yes	No

Table 12-3 Special Permissions for Files

Special Permission	Full Control	Modify	Read & Execute	Read	Write
Read Extended Attributes	Yes	Yes	Yes	Yes	No
Create Files/Write Data	Yes	Yes	No	No	Yes
Create Folders/ Write Data	Yes	Yes	No	No	Yes
Create Folders/ Append Data	Yes	Yes	No	No	Yes
Write Attributes	Yes	Yes	No	No	Yes
Write Extended Attributes	Yes	Yes	No	No	Yes
Delete Subfolders And Files	Yes	No	No	No	No
Delete	Yes	Yes	No	No	No
Read Permissions	Yes	Yes	Yes	Yes	Yes
Change Permissions	Yes	No	No	No	No
Take Ownership	Yes	No	No	No	No

Note These settings remain unchanged from Windows Server 2003.

Important Groups or users granted Full Control on a folder can delete any files and subfolders no matter what the permissions are on the individual files or subfolders. Any user or group assigned Take Ownership can become the owner of the file or folder and then change permissions and delete files or even entire subfolder trees, no matter what the permissions were before that user or group become the owner.

How Permissions Work

If you take no action at all, the files and folders inside a shared folder have the same permissions as the share. Permissions for both directories and files can be assigned to the following:

- Groups and individual users on this domain
- Global groups, universal groups, and individual users from domains that this domain trusts
- Special identities, such as Everyone and Authenticated Users

The important rules for permissions can be summarized as follows:

- By default, a folder inherits permissions from its parent folder. Files inherit their permissions from the folder in which they reside.
- Users can access a folder or file only if they were granted permission to do so or they belong to a group that has been granted permission.
- Permissions are cumulative, but the *explicit* Deny permission trumps all others. For example, suppose the Engineering group has Read access to a folder, the Project group has Modify permission for the same folder, and Alex is a member of both groups. Alex has the higher level of permission, which is Modify. However, if the Engineering group permission is changed to explicitly Deny, Alex is unable to use the folder despite his membership–and ostensibly higher level of access–in the Project group.
- Explicit permissions take precedence over inherited permissions. Inherited Deny will not prevent access if an object has an explicit Allow permission.
- The user who creates a file or folder owns the object and can set permissions to control access.
- An administrator can take ownership of any file or folder.

Considering Inheritance

Just to complicate matters a bit more, there are two types of permissions: explicit and inherited. *Explicit* permissions are the ones you set on files or folders you create. *Inherited* permissions are those that flow from a parent object to a child object. By default, when you create a file or a subfolder, it inherits the permissions of the parent folder. If the Allow and Deny boxes are shaded when you view the permissions for an object, the permissions are inherited.

If you don't want the child objects to inherit the permissions of the parent, you can block inheritance at the parent level or child level. *Where* you block inheritance is important. If you block at the parent level, no subfolders will inherit permissions. If you block selectively at the child level, some folders will inherit permissions and others will not.

To make changes to inherited permissions, follow these steps:

1. Right-click the folder and select Properties.
2. Click the Security tab and then click Advanced.
3. On the Permissions tab of the Advanced Security Settings For dialog box, highlight the permission you want to change and click Edit.
4. Clear the check box for Include Inheritable Permissions From This Object's Parent.

You'll be given the option to copy existing permissions to the object or to remove all inherited permissions. (See Figure 12-1.) The object will no longer inherit permissions from the parent object and you can change permissions or remove users and groups from the Permissions list.

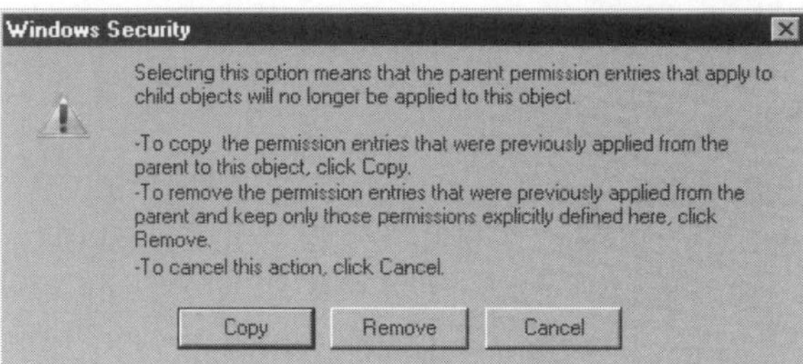

Figure 12-1 Removing inherited permissions

You can also change inherited permissions by changing the permissions of the parent folder or by explicitly selecting the opposite permission—Allow or Deny—to override the inherited permission. Figure 12-2 shows a folder with inherited and non-inherited permissions.

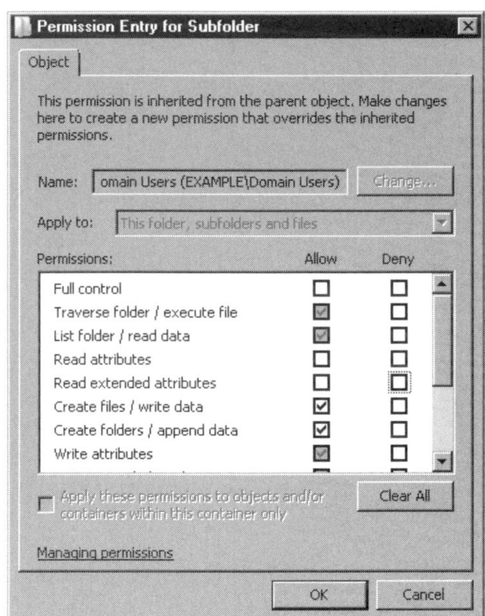

Figure 12-2 Permissions on this folder are a mix of inherited and explicit.

Configuring Folder Permissions

Before sharing a folder, set all the permissions on the folder. When setting folder permissions, you're also setting permissions on all the files and subfolders that are now in the folder or will be placed there in the future. To set permissions, you'll need to perform one or more of the following actions:

- To assign permissions to a folder, right-click the folder and choose Properties from the shortcut menu. Then click the Security tab.
- To remove an individual or group from the list, click Edit. Select the group or user name and click Remove.
- To add a user or group to the list of those with permissions, click Edit and then click Add. This opens the Select Users, Or Groups dialog box. Enter the object name or click Advanced. Be sure that the object type and location are correct. Click Advanced and then click Find Now to return a list of all the existing objects of the type you selected. (See Figure 12-3.) Highlight the ones you want (use Ctrl+Click to select multiple objects) and click OK.

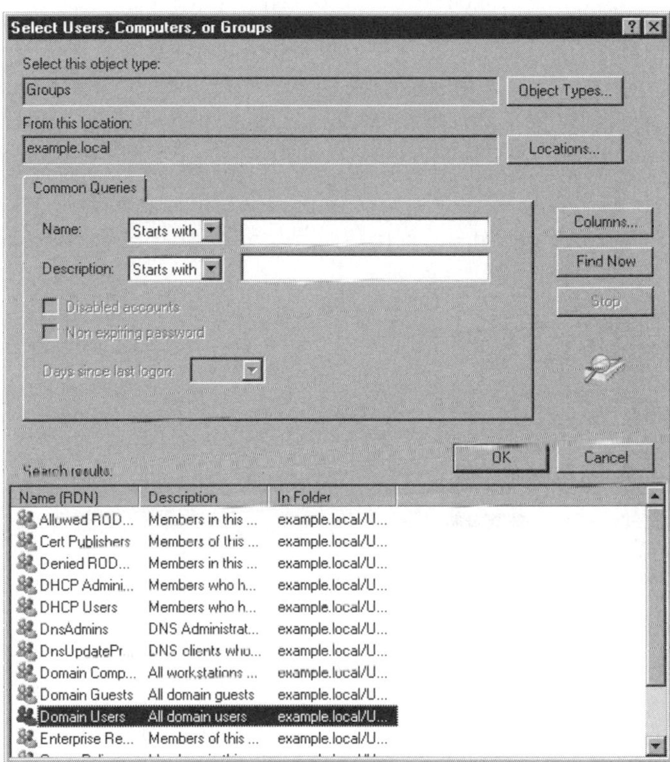

Figure 12-3 Finding all the selected objects in the location specified

Assigning Permissions to Files

Permissions for individual files are assigned in the same way as permissions for folders. There are, however, some special considerations:

- Remember to grant permissions to groups rather than to individuals.
- Create domain-based groups, and assign file permissions to them rather than assigning permissions directly to local groups.

Configuring Special Permissions

In some circumstances, you might find it necessary to set, change, or remove special permissions on either a file or folder. To access special permissions, follow these steps:

1. Right-click the file or folder and choose Properties from the shortcut menu.
2. Click the Security tab.
   - To add a user or group, click Edit and then click Add. Enter the object name or use the Advanced button and the Add button to return a list of all the objects in the categories specified.
   - To view or modify existing special permissions, click Edit. Highlight the group or user name to display the relevant permissions.
   - To remove special permissions, click Advanced. In the Advanced Security Settings For dialog box, click Edit. Select the name of the user or group and click Edit. Select the Deny box for any inherited special permission you wish to remove. For other permissions, you need only to clear the Allow check box.
3. In the Permission Entry For dialog box shown in Figure 12-4, select from the Apply To drop-down list where you want the permissions applied. Apply To is available for folders only.

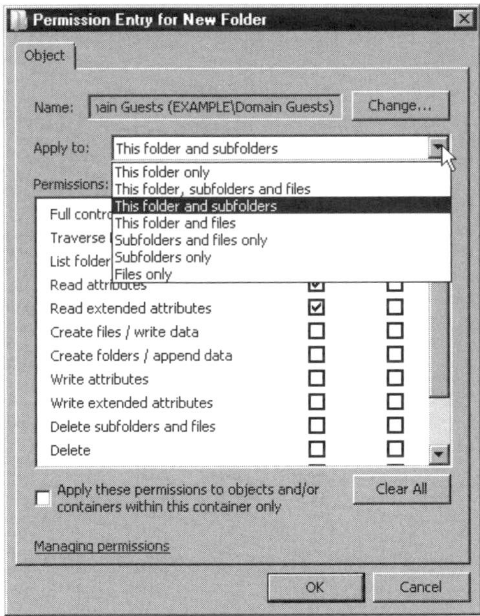

Figure 12-4 Selecting where the permissions are applied

4. If the permissions are not to be inherited, check the box for Apply These Permissions To Objects And/Or Containers Within This Container Only.
5. Click OK to close the dialog box.

Important The check box for Apply These Permissions To Objects And/Or Containers Within This Container Only has significant and wide-ranging consequences. Table 12-4 enumerates those consequences when the box is selected and Table 12-5 lists the effects when the box is not selected.

Table 12-4 Outcome When Apply These Permissions Within This Container Only Is Selected

Selected in Apply To	Applies to Current Folder?	Applies to Subfolders in Current Folder	Applies to Files in Current Folder?	Applies to Subsequent Subfolders?	Applies to Files in Subsequent Subfolders?
This Folder Only	X				
This Folder, Subfolders And Files	X	X	X		
This Folder And Subfolders	X	X			
This Folder And Files	X		X		
Subfolders And Files Only		X	X		
Subfolders Only		X			
Files Only			X		

Table 12-5 Outcome When Apply These Permissions Within This Container Only Is Not Selected

Selected in Apply Onto	Applies to Current Folder?	Applies to Subfolders in Current Folder	Applies to Files in Current Folder?	Applies to Subsequent Subfolders?	Applies to Files in Subsequent Subfolders?
This Folder Only	X				
This Folder, Subfolders, And Files	X	X	X	X	X

Table 12-5 Outcome When Apply These Permissions Within This Container Only Is Not Selected

Selected in Apply Onto	Applies to Current Folder?	Applies to Subfolders in Current Folder	Applies to Files in Current Folder?	Applies to Subsequent Subfolders?	Applies to Files in Subsequent Subfolders?
This Folder And Subfolders	X	X		X	
This Folder And Files	X		X		X
Subfolders And Files Only		X	X	X	X
Subfolders Only		X		X	
Files Only			X		X

Ownership and How It Works

Every object on an NTFS volume or in Active Directory has an owner. By default, the owner is the person who created the file or folder. The owner controls how permissions are set on the object and to whom permissions are granted. Even if the owner is denied access, the owner can always change permissions on an object. The only way to prevent this is for the ownership to change.

Ownership of an object can change in one of the following ways:

- An administrator can take ownership. The Administrators group has the Take Ownership of Files or Other Objects user right.
- Any user or group that has the Take Ownership permission on the object can change the object's ownership.
- Any user or group that has the Restore Files and Directories user right can change the object's ownership.
- The owner can transfer ownership to another user.

Note These last three methods do not work unless User Account Control is turned off or the user has an administrator's credentials.

Taking Ownership of an Object

To take ownership of an object, you must first be logged on as an Administrator or as a user with Take Ownership permission, or as a user with the Restore Files And Directories user right. Then follow these steps:

1. Right-click the object and select Properties from the shortcut menu. Click the Security tab.
2. Click Advanced and then click the Owner tab. Click Edit.
   - To change the owner to a user or group that is not listed, click Other Users And Groups. In the Enter The Object Name To Select box, type the name of the user or group, click Check Names, and then click OK
   - To change the owner to a user or group that is listed, in the Change Owner To box, click the new owner.
3. To change the owner of all subcontainers and objects within the tree, select the Replace Owner On Subcontainers And Objects check box.

Transferring Ownership

The owner of an object can transfer ownership by following these steps:

1. Right-click the object and select Properties. Click the Security tab.
2. Click Advanced and then click the Owner tab. Click Edit.
3. If the proposed new owner is in the Change Owner To list, select the name and click OK. Otherwise, click Other Users Or Groups to open the Select User, or Group dialog box.
4. Locate the new owner and then click OK.
5. Select the new owner in the Change Owner To list (Figure 12-5) and click OK.

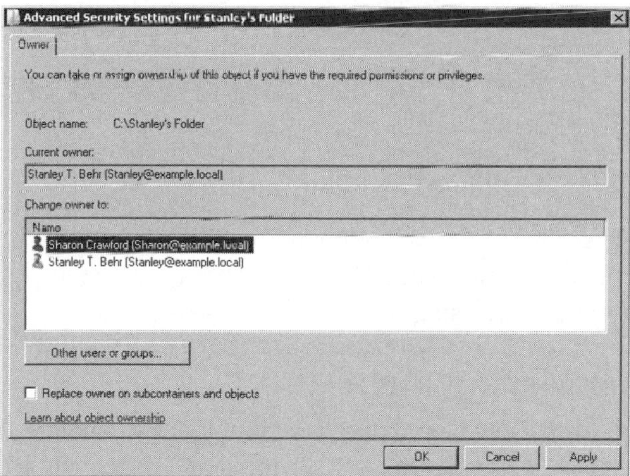

Figure 12-5 Selecting a new owner

Share-Level Permissions

As stated earlier in this chapter, it's generally best to use NTFS file permissions *instead* of share-level permissions to control access to shared resources over the network. Using share-level permissions alone gives you significantly less control over the specific permissions being granted, and they're less secure than file system permissions because they apply only to users connecting over the network.

However, there are some exceptions to this rule. For example, you might want to permit all authenticated users to access a volume in a certain subfolder but allow only a certain group to access the root directory. In this instance, you can create two file shares: one at the subfolder level with no share-level security (Full Control for Everyone), and one at the root folder level with share-level security to allow only the specified group access.

Somewhat more useful is the ability to hide file shares by adding the dollar sign character ($) to the end of the share name. This notation allows any user to connect to the share–provided that she knows the share name. After users connect, they're still bound by NTFS security permissions, but this approach can be handy for storing advanced tools so that an administrator can access them from a user's system or user account. File security isn't really an issue–you just don't want users messing around with the files.

Shared Folders

As with most things in Windows Server 2008, there are several ways to configure and administer shared folders. You can right-click a folder in Windows Explorer and choose Share from the shortcut menu; you can use the Share And Storage Management tool from the Administrative Tools menu; or you can use the command line.

Each approach has its advantages, but using the command line is best for quickly creating or modifying a share. Using Share And Storage Management is best when you want access to more management functions in a single place.

Using Share And Storage Management

The Share And Storage Management console provides a central place to manage folders and volumes that are shared on the network. Share And Storage Management is on the Administrative Tools menu. Using the Provision A Shared Folder Wizard, you can easily share a folder or volume and assign all the necessary properties to it. Just follow these steps:

1. Open Share And Storage Management on the Administrative Tools menu.
2. Select Provision Share in the Actions pane.
3. Type in the location for the folder or click Browse to locate it (Figure 12-6). Click Next.

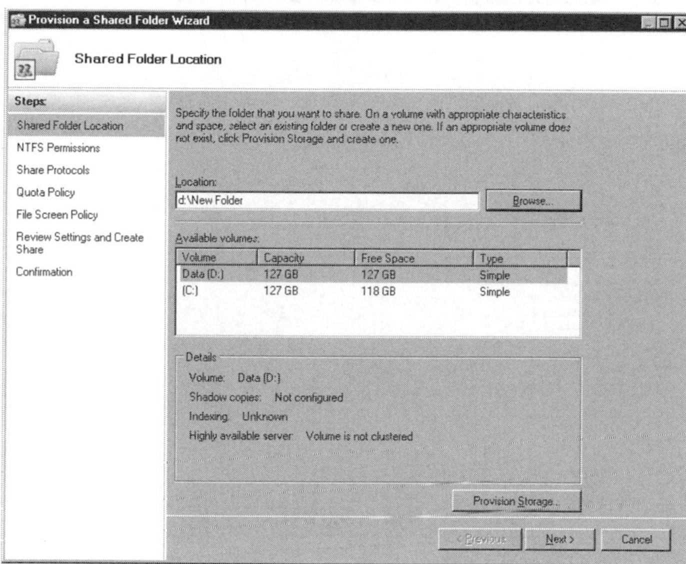

Figure 12-6 Identifying the name and location of the proposed share

4. On the NTFS Permissions page, you can change the NTFS permissions on the folder or leave them as they are. Click Next.
5. On the Share Protocols page, choose the protocol that users will use to access the share. Unless you have NFS installed on the computer, the default is SMB (Server Message Block), a native-to-Windows protocol used for shares since Windows NT. Click Next.
6. On the SMB Settings page, you can view the User Limit, Access-Based Enumeration, and Offline Settings for the folder. Click Advanced to change any of these. Click Next.
7. On the SMB Permissions page, select the share permissions you want and then click Next.
8. On the Quota Policy page, you can set a quota to limit the space used by the shared folder. (See Chapter 19, "Implementing Disk Management" and Chapter 20, "Managing Storage" for more on quotas.) Click Next.

9. On the File Screen Policy page, you can apply a file screen to limit the types of files the shared folder can contain. Choose a template from the drop-down list (as shown in Figure 12-7) and a summary of the file screen properties appears. Click Next.

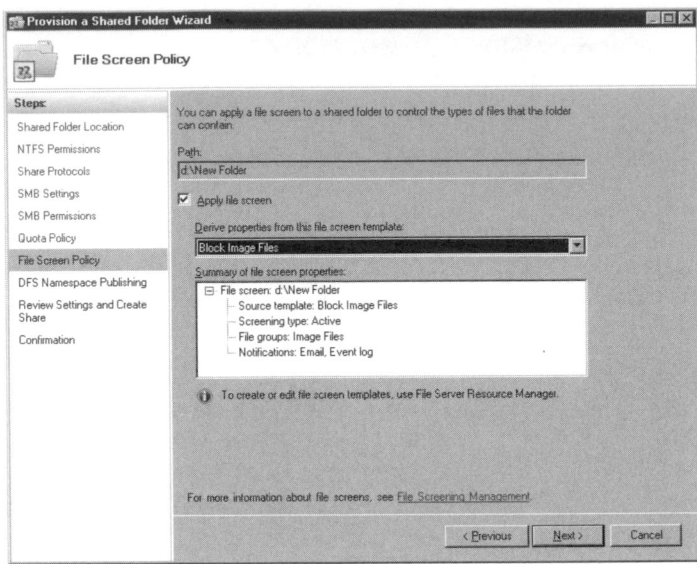

Figure 12-7 Choosing a file screen policy

10. On the DFS Namespace Publishing page, you can choose to publish the share to a DFS namespace. (Using and creating a DFS namespace is described later in this chapter.) Click Next.

11. On the Review Settings And Create Share page, review the settings. Click Previous to change settings. If the settings are correct, click Create.

Share And Storage Management also lets you change existing permissions on a folder, view connections to a folder, and disconnect a user if necessary. Highlight the shared folder in the list of shares and click the action you want to take in the Actions pane.

Removing a Folder Share

To stop sharing a folder, you can use Share And Storage Management. Just highlight the share and right-click to chose Stop Sharing. Or, from the command line type the following:

```
net share <sharename> /delete
```

From the command line, you won't even get prompted to confirm. Use caution when you remove a share. It will disconnect any open files that users might be using and could cause loss of data.

Special Shares

In addition to shares created by a user or administrator, the system creates a number of special shares that shouldn't be modified or deleted. These include the administrative shares: the ADMIN$ share and the hidden shares for each hard drive volume (C$, D$, E$, and so on). These shares allow administrators to connect to drives that are otherwise not shared. These shares are not visible by default and can be connected only by administrators.

Special shares exist as part of the operating system's installation. Depending on the computer's configuration, some or all of the following special shares might be present (and none of them should be modified or deleted):

- **ADMIN$** Used during the remote administration of a computer. The path is always the location of the folder in which Windows was installed (that is, the system root). Only Administrators, Backup Operators, and Server Operators can connect to this share.
- **driveletter$** The root folder of the named drive. Only Administrators, Backup Operators, and Server Operators can connect to these shares on Windows servers. On Windows XP Professional, Windows 2000 Professional, and Windows Vista computers, only Administrators and Backup Operators can connect to these shares.
- **IPC$** Used during remote administration and when viewing shared resources. This share is essential to communication and can't be deleted.
- **NETLOGON** Used while processing domain logon requests. Do not remove.
- **SYSVOL** Required on all domain controllers. Do not remove.
- **PRINT$** A resource that supports shared printers.

To connect to an unshared drive on another computer, you need to be logged on using an account with the necessary rights. Use the address bar in any window and type the address using the following syntax:

```
\\computer_name\[driveletter]$
```

To connect to the system root folder (the folder in which Windows is installed) on another computer, use the following syntax:

```
\\computer_name\admin$
```

Note Adding a dollar sign ($) to the end of a share name hides the share from *all* users. To access a hidden share, you need to specify it explicitly; you can't browse the network for the share.

Using the Command Line: Net Share

For the command-line literate, *net share* is the easiest and most efficient way to manage network shares. The *net share* command has the following syntax:

```
NET SHARE
sharename
   sharename=drive:path [/GRANT:user,[READ | CHANGE | FULL]]
                        [/USERS:number | /UNLIMITED]
                        [/REMARK:"text"]
                        [/CACHE:Manual | Documents| Programs | None ]
   sharename [/USERS:number | /UNLIMITED]
             [/REMARK:"text"]
             [/CACHE:Manual | Documents | Programs | None]
{sharename | devicename | drive:path} /DELETE
```

Simply typing *net share* at the command line with no parameters will give you a list of currently shared folders. Typing *net share* <*sharename*> will give you the parameters in effect for the share name.

Two other useful net commands for dealing with shares are *net view* and *net session*. Typing *net view* will give you a list of computers on the network or the resources available on a particular computer, while typing *net session* will list the sessions on the current computer or the details of a session with a particular computer. These two commands have the following syntax:

```
NET VIEW
[\\computername [/CACHE] | /DOMAIN[:domainname]]
NET VIEW /NETWORK:NW [\\computername]

NET SESSION
[\\computername] [/DELETE]
```

Note The net commands work with both NetBIOS names and IP addresses, and where the user is specified, they can use both DOMAIN\User and e-mail address formats. This makes them both very flexible and useful.

Publishing Shares in Active Directory

You can publish relatively permanent file shares in Active Directory, making them easier for users to find in a large network. To do so, follow these steps:

1. Open Active Directory Users And Computers on the Administrative Tools menu.
2. Right-click the domain where the share is to be published, select New, and then select Shared Folder from the shortcut menu.
3. In the New Object dialog box, enter the name of the shared folder and then the network path, as shown in Figure 12 -8.

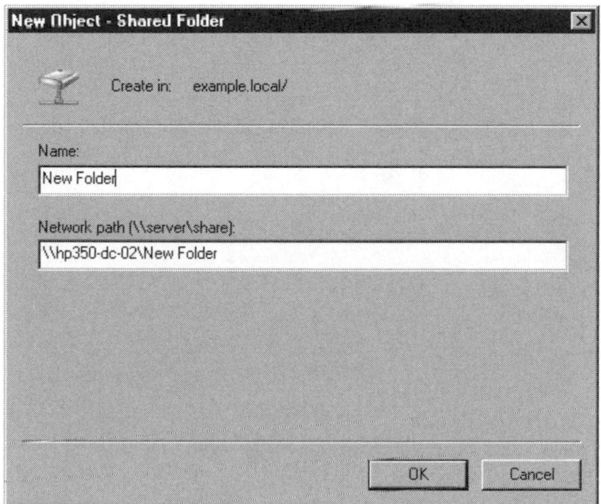

Figure 12-8 Publishing a shared folder to Active Directory

4. Click OK when finished.

Distributed File System (DFS)

Distributed File System (DFS) allows administrators to group shared folders located on different servers and present them to users as a virtual tree of folders known as a *namespace*. A namespace has many benefits, including increased availability of data, load sharing, and simplified data migration. DFS Replication allows administrators to replicate folders in a bandwidth-efficient manner using the remote differential compression (RDC) algorithm that replicates only the changed blocks within a file.

DFS Namespaces and DFS Replication are useful for the following purposes:

- Organizing a large number of file shares scattered across multiple servers into a contiguous namespace so that users can find the files they need
- Improving the availability and performance of file shares, especially in network environments with multiple sites, where DFS namespaces can redirect users to the closest available server

- "Caching" data at a branch office so that users can access files at a local file server, which then efficiently replicates with a central file server across a WAN connection
- Centralizing backup from branch offices by replicating all data from the branch office to a central server that is backed up regularly
- Keeping two or more file shares in sync over LAN or WAN links

---

Note You can use DFS to create a loosely coupled collaboration environment where DFS replication replicates data between multiple servers. However, DFS Replication does not include the ability to "check out" files, or replicate files that are in use, such as multi-user databases. Therefore, use Windows SharePoint Services in environments where users regularly attempt to edit the same file at the same time from different locations.

DFS Terminology

Much of the terminology in DFS is very specific to the DFS environment. Acquainting yourself with these terms will save a lot of confusion later.

- **Namespace** A namespace is a virtual view of shared folders. The folders can be in a variety of locations but appear to the user as a single tree.
- **Namespace server** A namespace server hosts a namespace. The namespace server can be a member server or a domain controller.
- **Namespace root** The namespace root is the shared folder that serves as the root for a particular namespace. Because DFS is a virtual file system, the namespace root can be any shared folder on an NTFS partition.
- **Folders** Folders in a DFS namespace can provide structural depth to a hierarchy or can contain folder targets that map to shares.
- **Folder target** A folder target is the UNC path of a shared folder or another namespace that is associated with a folder in a namespace. The folder target is where data and content is stored.

Note Folders can contain folder targets or other folders, but not both at the same level in the hierarchy.

DFS clients automatically choose a folder target in their site, if available, reducing inter-site network utilization. If more than one target is available on the client's site, each client randomly selects a target, spreading the load evenly across all available servers. If a target goes down, the client automatically picks a different target. (This process is called *client failover.*) When the original target comes back online, the client automatically switches back to the preferred target if the namespace server and the client support client failback. In this way, targets provide fault tolerance, load balancing, and site awareness. You can use DFS Replication to keep folder targets synchronized.

Namespace Type

There are two types of DFS Namespaces: stand-alone and domain-based. A stand-alone namespace (for example, \\srv1\public) stores all namespace information on the registry of the namespace server instead of in Active Directory. Any server running Windows 2000 Server or later can host a stand-alone namespace, regardless of whether the server belongs to a domain (though servers running Windows Server 2003 and Windows 2000 Server do not support all features of DFS Namespaces). Stand-alone namespaces can host more folders (up to 50,000 folders with targets) than domain-based namespaces (which can hold up to 5000 folders with targets), but the only way to provide redundancy for a stand-alone namespace root is to use a server cluster. You cannot use multiple namespace servers to host a stand-alone namespace as you can with a domain-based namespace. However, you can replicate folders in a stand-alone namespace as long as all replication members belong to the same Active Directory forest.

Domain-based namespace roots (for example, \\example.local\public) differ from stand-alone namespace roots in a couple of ways. First, you must host domain-based namespace roots on a member server or domain controller of an Active Directory domain. Second, domain-based namespace roots automatically publish the DFS topology in Active Directory. This arrangement provides fault tolerance and network performance optimization by directing clients to the nearest target.

Choose a stand-alone namespace if the network does not use Active Directory, if the namespace contains more than 5000 folders with targets, or if you want to host the namespace on a server cluster. Otherwise, choose a domain-based namespace to use multiple namespace servers for redundancy and to take advantage of Active Directory for site-aware client referrals. You can also combine the two—for example, you can create a domain-based namespace that includes a stand-alone root as a folder.

Before creating namespaces, design the namespace hierarchy in a similar manner to the way you designed the domain structure for the organization. (See Chapter 3, "Planning Namespace and Domains" for more information.) Create a namespace structure that is logical, easy to use (by end users!), and matches the organization design, and then get the key stakeholders in the project to sign off on the design. Enlist some representative users from the organization to review the namespace design and provide feedback.

Table 12-6 lists guidelines for namespace servers.

Table 12-6 Guidelines for Namespace Servers

Server Hosting Stand-Alone Namespaces	Server Hosting Domain-Based Namespaces
Only servers running Windows Server 2008 support access-based enumeration for stand-alone or domain-based (Windows Server 2008 mode) namespaces.	Only servers running Windows Server 2008 can host domain-based namespaces in Windows Server 2008 mode.
NTFS volume required.	NTFS volume required.
Domain controller or member server.	Domain controller or member server in the domain in which the namespace is configured.
Can be hosted by a failover cluster to increase availability.	Can use multiple namespace servers to increase availability.
	The namespace can't be a clustered resource in a failover cluster. However, you can place the namespace on a server that also functions as a node in a failover cluster if you configure the namespace to use only local resources on that server.

Namespace Server Requirements

A namespace server is a domain controller or member server that hosts a namespace. The number of namespaces you can host on a server is determined by the operating system running on the namespace server.

The following servers can host multiple namespaces:

- Windows Server 2008 Enterprise
- Windows Server 2008 Datacenter
- Windows Server 2003 R2, Enterprise Edition
- Windows Server 2003 R2, Datacenter Edition
- Windows Server 2003, Enterprise Edition
- Windows Server 2003, Datacenter Edition

Servers running the following operating systems can host only a single namespace:

- Windows Server 2008 Standard
- Windows Server 2003 R2, Standard Edition
- Windows Server 2003, Web Edition

- Windows Server 2003, Standard Edition
- Any version of Windows 2000 Server

Namespace Client Requirements

To access the DFS folder structure, you need a DFS client. Users can access file shares that are part of a DFS namespace without a DFS client; however, the user does not benefit from any of the DFS features, such as hierarchical namespaces, multiple folder targets, and site-aware client referrals.

The following operating systems include full support for DFS namespaces, including support for client failback to the preferred folder target:

- Windows Server 2008
- Windows Vista Business, Windows Vista Enterprise, Windows Vista Ultimate
- Windows Server 2003 R2
- Windows Storage Server 2003 R2
- Windows Server 2003 with SP2, or SP1 and the Windows Server 2003 client failback hotfix
- Windows XP Professional with SP3, or SP2 and the Windows XP client failback hotfix

The client failback hotfixes are described in Microsoft Knowledge Base article 898900 at *http://support.microsoft.com/kb/898900*.

Users who are running the following operating systems can access namespaces, but if a folder target becomes unavailable and then later comes back online, the computer will not fail back (return) to the preferred folder target:

- Windows Storage Server 2003
- Windows XP Professional
- Windows Preinstallation Environment (Windows PE) (Windows PE can access stand-alone namespaces, but it cannot access domain-based namespaces.)
- Windows 2000 Server
- Windows 2000 Professional
- Windows NT Server 4.0 with Service Pack 6a
- Windows NT Workstation 4.0 with Service Pack 6a

To use DFS to best advantage, clients with the ability to fail back are preferred.

DFS Replication

Before deploying DFS Replication, verify that all the following tasks have been done:

- Extend (or update) the Active Directory Domain Services (AD DS) schema to include Windows Server 2003 R2 or Windows Server 2008 schema additions.

> **Note** Chapter 2, "Introducing Directory Services" includes a description of the schema and how it works. For information about extending the AD DS schema, see *http://msdn.microsoft.com/en-us/library/ms676900.aspx.*

- Place replicated folders for failover clusters in the local storage of a node. The DFS Replication service will not coordinate with cluster components, and the service will not fail over to another node.
- Install the File Services role with the DFS Replication role service on all servers that will act as members of a replication group.
- Ensure that all members of the replication group are running Windows Server 2008 or Windows Server 2003 R2.
- Install DFS Management on a server to manage replication. This server cannot run a Server Core installation of the Windows Server 2008 operating system.
- Make sure that all servers in a replication group are located in the same forest. You can't enable replication across servers in different forests.
- Store replicated folders on NTFS volumes.
- Verify that your antivirus software is compatible with DFS Replication.

File Replication Service

File Replication Service (FRS), introduced in Windows Server 2000, replicates files and folders that are stored in DFS folders or in the SYSVOL folder on domain controllers. FRS in Windows Server 2008 is an optional role service of the File Services server role that allows replication of content with other servers that use FRS instead of DFS Replication.

DFS Replication replaces FRS for replication of DFS folders on servers running Windows Server 2003 R2 or Windows Server 2008. In domains that use the Windows Server 2008 domain functional level, DFS Replication replaces FRS for the SYSVOL folder as well.

Neither DFS Replication nor FRS support file support checkout or merging. If two or more users modify the same file simultaneously on different servers, DFS Replication uses a conflict resolution method that keeps the most recently modified copy of the file (or the earliest creator when dealing with folders). DFS Replication moves the other copies to a conflict folder on the losing server but does not replicate this folder by default, unlike FRS, so the folder remains on the local server. To avoid conflicts, use Windows SharePoint Services when users in multiple locations need to collaborate on the same files at the same time. (Windows SharePoint Services allows users to check out files.)

DFS Replication, like FRS, is a multimaster replication engine that detects changes in a file by monitoring the update sequence number (USN) journal and replicating the changed file once the file is closed. Unlike FRS, DFS Replication uses a version vector exchange protocol to determine what parts of the file are different, and then uses the RDC protocol to replicate only changed blocks of files larger than 64 KB. This makes DFS Replication much more efficient at replication than FRS, which is particularly important when replicating with servers across a WAN link. DFS Replication does not replicate files that make use of EFS encryption.

Replication Topologies

DFS Replication can make use of several of topologies: hub and spoke, full mesh, and custom. These topologies are familiar to most network administrators, but here is a quick review:

- **Hub and spoke** This topology is also known as a star topology. Each server replicates with a central server, minimizing the use of WAN links. This topology is similar to an Ethernet network, which uses a hub or switch as the center of the network. Choose this topology to reduce network usage when the replication group has more than 10 members, or when members of the replication group are in a site connected via a WAN connection.
- **Full mesh** All servers replicate with all other servers. Choose this topology when the replication group has fewer than 10 servers and all links have low enough costs (performance or monetary) to allow each server to replicate with every other server. The full mesh topology minimizes the time it takes to propagate changes to all members of the replication group and increases reliability by replicating with all members of the replication group, but it also increases network traffic from replication.
- **Custom** This topology allows you to manually specify replication connections.

Installing DFS Management

To manage a DFS namespace and DFS Replication, you must first install DFS Management. Open Server Manager and install the File Services role on the server. Then follow these steps:

1. In Server Manager, select Roles
2. Scroll down to File Services and click Add Role Services to open the Add Role Services Wizard.

3. Select Distributed File System, as shown in Figure 12-9, and click Next.

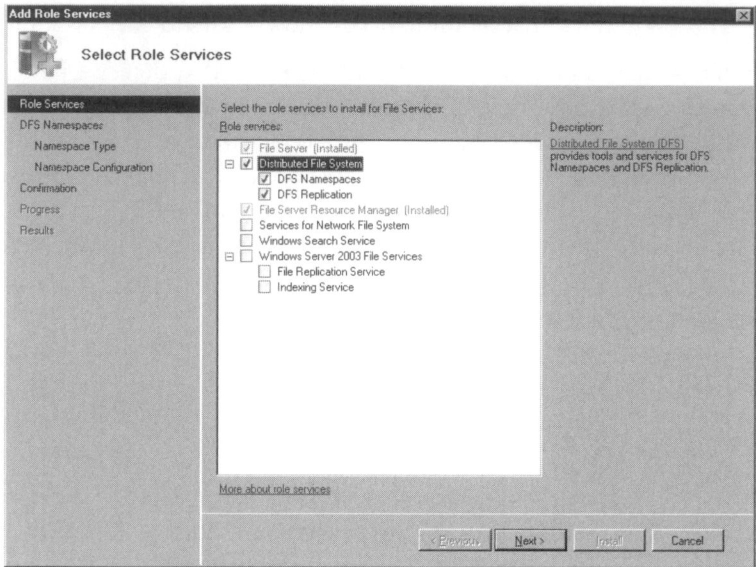

Figure 12-9 Selecting file services to install

4. On the Create A DFS Namespace page, select Create A Namespace Now and provide a name. Alternatively, you can choose to create the namespace later. Click Next.
5. On the Select Namespace Type page, select the type of namespace you are creating.
6. On the Configure Namespace page, click Add to add folders to the namespace. In this process, shown in Figure 12-10, you can browse for folder targets and place the targets in the folders you choose.

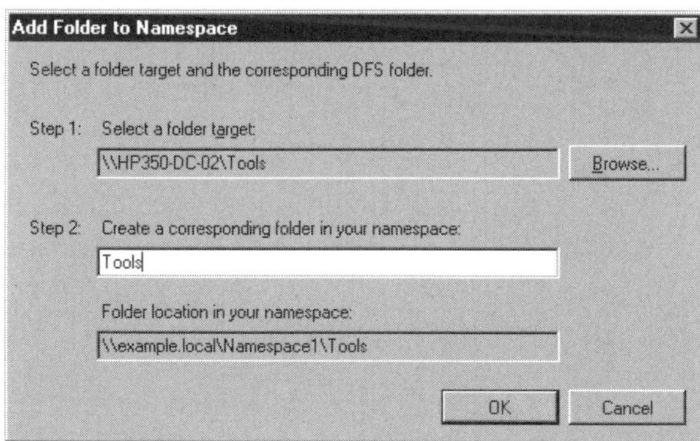

Figure 12-10 Adding a folder to the namespace

7. When you have finished adding shares to the namespace, click Next.
8. Review the selections and click Install.

Creating or Opening a Namespace Root

The first step in working with DFS Namespaces is to create a namespace or open an existing namespace root. If you created a namespace root when installing DFS Management, you can use this procedure to open it; otherwise, follow these steps to create one:

1. Launch DFS Management from the Administrative Tools folder. Navigate to DFS Management and then to Namespaces node.
2. To open an existing namespace root, right-click Namespaces and choose Add Namespace To Display. To create a new namespace root, right-click Namespaces and choose New Namespace. The New Namespace Wizard appears.
3. On the Namespace Server page, type the name of the server that you want to host the namespace root, and then click Next. If the DFS service is disabled, click Yes in the Warning dialog box to start the DFS service and set its start-up setting to Automatic.
4. On the Namespace Name And Settings page, type the name to use for the namespace root. This name appears as the share name to users–for example, \\example.local\public. The New Namespace Wizard creates the namespace root in the %SYSTEMDRIVE%:\DFSRoots*name* folder and gives all users read-only permissions. To change these settings, click Edit Settings. Click next.
5. On the Namespace Type page (shown in Figure 12-11), choose whether to create a domain-based namespace or a stand alone namespace:
   - Select Domain-Based Namespace to store the namespace on multiple servers in Active Directory. An example of a domain-based namespace is \\example.local\public.
   - Select the Stand-Alone Namespace option to create the namespace on a single server or server cluster. An example of a stand-alone namespace is \\srv1\public. Click Next.

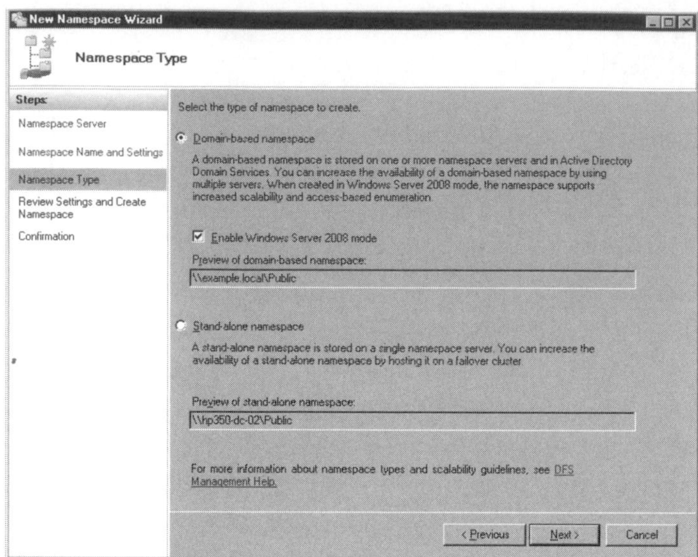

Figure 12-11 Choosing the namespace type

6. On the Review Settings And Create Namespace page, click Create. The New Namespace Wizard creates the namespace root. Correct any errors using the Previous button and then click Close.

To create a namespace from a command prompt, use the *Dfsutil /Addftroot* or *Dfsutil / Addstdroot* commands. For example, to create the same namespace as shown in Figure 12-11, follow these steps:

1. Open the Command Prompt window. Start the DFS service and set the start-up type to Automatic if it is not already by typing the following commands:

```
Sc Start Dfs
Sc Config Dfs Start= Auto
```

2. Create a folder and file share for the namespace root by typing the following commands:

```
Md E:\Public
Net Share Public=E:\Public
```

3. Create the domain-based namespace root by typing the following command:

```
Dfsutil /Addftroot /Server:Srv1 /Share:Public
```

Adding Namespace Servers

The namespace root is the most important part of the namespace. Without it, clients cannot access any DFS folders. Because of this, the first step in creating a more fault-tolerant namespace is to add namespace servers to the namespace root. If possible, add at least one namespace server on each site where users need access to the DFS namespace:

1. In the DFS Management console, navigate to Namespaces, right-click the domain-based namespace root you want to replicate, and then choose Add Namespace Server.
2. In the Add Namespace Server dialog box, type the path to the namespace server and then click OK. Windows creates the namespace root on the target server in the %SYSTEMDRIVE%:\DFSRoots*name* folder and gives all users read-only permissions. To change these settings, click Edit Settings.
3. If the DFS service is disabled, click Yes in the Warning dialog box to start the DFS service and set its start-up setting to Automatic.
4. To add a namespace server to a namespace from a command prompt, create the appropriate shared folder, verify that the DFS service is started and the start-up type is set to Automatic, and then use the `Dfsutil /Addftroot` command. For example, open a command prompt window and then type **Dfsutil /Addftroot /Server:Srv2/Share:Public**

Adding DFS Folders

DFS folders allow users to navigate from the namespace root to other file shares on the network without leaving the DFS namespace structure. To create a DFS folder, follow these steps:

1. Right-click the namespace root to which you want to add a folder, and then choose New Folder. This displays the New Folder dialog box, shown in Figure 12-12.

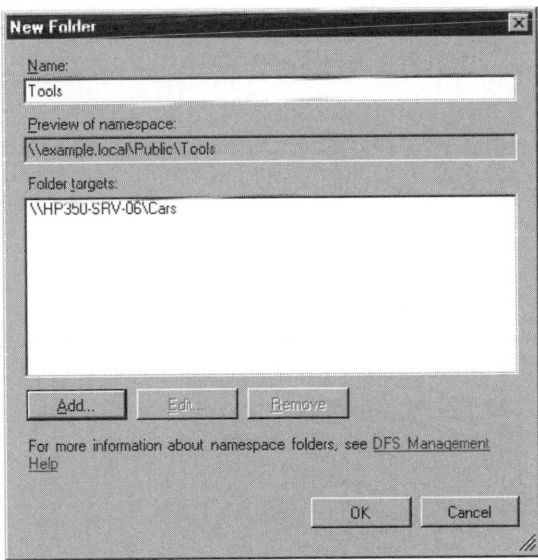

Figure 12-12 Creating a new folder

2. Type a name for the folder in the Name box. To create a folder that contains other DFS folders, click OK without adding any target folders. This creates a layer of structure to the namespace.
3. To add target folders, click Add and then type the shared folder's UNC or DNS path, or click Browse to browse to the shared folder.
4. Add any additional folder targets and then click OK.

If you added multiple folder targets, click Yes in the Replication dialog box to create a replication group for the folder targets or click No to set up a replication group later (or not at all). If you click Yes, the Replicate Folder Wizard appears with some settings already entered. For more information, see "Creating a Replication Group" later in this chapter.

To create a DFS folder from a command prompt, create the appropriate file shares, and then use the *Dfscmd /Map* command. (You cannot add DFS folders without folder targets from a command prompt.) For example, open the Command Prompt window and then type the following commands:

```
Dfscmd /Map \\Example.local\Public\Software \\Dc1\Software
Dfscmd /Add \\Example.local\Public\Software \\Srv2\Software
```

Note To publish a DFS folder or namespace root in Active Directory so that users can find the folder or namespace when searching Active Directory for shared folders, right-click the appropriate container in the Active Directory Users And Computers console, choose New, choose Shared Folder, and then type the path of the namespace or DFS folder in the Network Path box.

Changing Advanced Settings

The default settings for DFS Management are appropriate for most installations, but if you need to change advanced namespace settings such as the referral order, to change how namespace servers poll domain controllers for DFS metadata, or to delegate DFS management permissions, use the information in following sections.

Changing Namespace Referral Settings

To change the cache duration, the order in which domain controllers or namespace servers refer clients to namespace servers and folder targets, or the failback settings for an entire namespace, right-click a namespace root or folder, choose Properties, and click the Referrals tab (Figure 12-13).

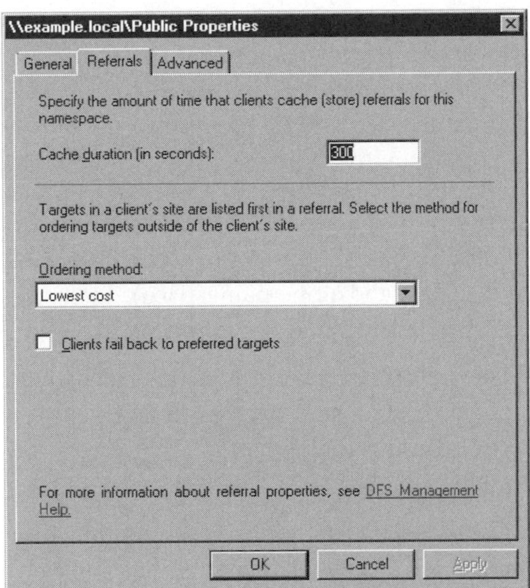

Figure 12-13 The Referrals tab of a namespace Properties dialog box

Use the following list to complete the process:

- In the Cache Duration box, specify how long clients should cache referrals before polling the domain controller or namespace server for a new referral.
- In the Ordering Method box, choose how domain controllers and namespace servers should refer clients to folder targets and namespace servers.
- Select the Clients Fail Back To Preferred Targets option to make a client switch back to using its preferred server when it comes back online.

The preferred server is based on site and any custom referral ordering settings you specify on folder targets. This setting is supported by clients running Windows XP with Service Pack 2 and the post-SP2 Windows XP client failback hotfix, Windows Server 2003 with Service Pack 1 and the Windows Server 2003 client failback hotfix and Windows Server 2003 R2. See Knowledge Base article 898900 at *http://support.microsoft.com/kb/898900/* for information on how to obtain this hotfix.

Overriding Referral Settings on Individual Folders

DFS folders inherit referral settings from the namespace root unless you specifically override them. To override the referral settings for a folder, right-click the appropriate folder, choose Properties, click the Referrals tab, and then specify the settings you want to override.

To explicitly set a single folder target as the preferred target or set the folder target as a target of last resort, select the folder in the console tree. Right-click a folder target in in the Results pane and select Properties from the shortcut menu. Click the Advanced tab, select the Override Referral Ordering check box, and then specify the priority for the target folder.

Delegating Management Permissions

DFS Management sets the permissions on the namespace object in Active Directory or in the registry of the namespace server (when using a stand-alone namespace). To change the ability of users to perform common management tasks, use the following list:

- **Create and manage namespaces** To view, add, or remove groups that can manage namespaces, right-click the Namespaces node, choose Delegate Management Permissions, and then use the Select Users Or Groups dialog box.
- **Manage individual namespaces and replication groups** To view groups that can manage a namespace or replication group, select the namespace or replication group and then click the Delegation tab. To remove management permissions for a group, right-click the group and choose Remove. To give management permissions for the namespace to a group, right-click the namespace, choose Delegate Management Permission, type the name of the group in the Select Users Or Groups dialog box, and then click OK.
- **Create and manage replication groups** To view, add, or remove groups that can manage replication, right-click the Replication node, choose Delegate Management Permissions, and then use the Delegate Management Permissions dialog box.

Changing Namespace Polling Settings

To change how namespace servers poll domain controllers for the latest namespace metadata in a domain-based namespace, right-click the appropriate namespace, choose Properties, click the Advanced tab, and then choose one of the following polling methods:

- **Optimize For Consistency** Polls the primary domain controller (PDC) emulator for new namespace data every hour and after each change to the namespace. Use this setting when the network contains 16 or fewer namespace servers to minimize the time it takes to propagate namespace changes to all namespace servers. This is the default setting.
- **Optimize For Scalability** Polls the nearest domain controller every hour for changes to the namespace. Use this setting when the network contains more than 16 namespace servers to reduce the load on the PDC emulator. However, choosing this setting increases the amount of time it takes to propagate namespace changes to all namespace servers. Servers running Windows 2000 Server do not support this setting and continue to use the Optimize For Consistency polling method.

To enable the Optimize For Scalability polling method from a command prompt, use the `Dfsutil /Rootscalability` command. For example, open the Command Prompt window, then type **Dfsutil /Root:Example.local\Public /Rootscalability /Enable**

Backing Up and Restoring the DFS Folder Targets

The DFS Namespaces database for domain-based DFS is stored in Active Directory, and you can back it up and restore it using Active Directory–aware backup methods. To back up the listing of folder targets for a stand-alone namespace root, type the following text at a command prompt (replacing *ServerName* and *Namespace* with the name of the appropriate server name and namespace root):

```
DFScmd /View \\ServerName\Namespace /Batch >DFS_backup.bat
```

To restore this DFS structure, re-create the DFS namespace and then run the batch file you created.

> **Note** In addition to backing up the DFS topology, back up the contents of the actual file shares routinely. Always test the backup before relying on it. You can use the `Dfsradmin Replicationgroup` command to export DFS Replication settings such as replication group members and connections.

Using DFS Replication

An easy-to-use, fault-tolerant, and high-performance file system is not worth much if the data you want to access is unavailable or out of date. To ensure that files are available to users even if a server goes down, create additional folder targets (as described earlier in this chapter) and use DFS Replication to keep the folder targets in sync. You can also use DFS Replication to synchronize folders that are not part of a DFS namespace—for example, to replicate data from a branch office to a server in the main office that you back up regularly and reliably.

Creating a Replication Group

A *replication group* is defined as two or more servers that participate in replication. Replication groups define the replication topology used by members for replication. To create a replication group, follow these steps:

1. Click Start, point to Administrative Tools, and then click DFS Management.
2. In the console tree, right-click the Replication node and then click New Replication Group.
3. Follow the instructions in the New Replication Group Wizard.

Conflict Resolution During the Initial Replication

If other members of the replication group have data in the replicated folders, Windows takes the following actions during the initial replication:

- If an identical file already exists on the target server (any server other than the primary member), the primary member does not replicate the file.
- If a file already exists on a target server but the file is not identical to the version on the primary member, Windows moves the file on the target server to the local conflict folder and then replicates the primary member's version of the file, even if this file is older than the version on the target server.
- If a file exists on a target server that is not present on the primary member, Windows does not replicate it during the initial replication but does replicate it during subsequent replications to other members, including the primary member.

After the initial replication, the primary member role goes away and replication is multiple-master-based. Do not delete, rename, or move files on the primary member or any member that has already replicated until the first replication is complete. (Look for Event 4104 in the DFS Replication log.) Deleting, renaming, or moving files before the first replication is complete can cause the files to reappear if they existed on a target that had not yet replicated.

Replicating a DFS Folder

To create a replicated folder in a new replication group that replicates a DFS folder, follow these steps:

1. Right-click the appropriate folder under the Namespaces node of DFS Management and choose Replicate Folder. The Replicate Folder Wizard appears.
2. On the Replication Group And Replicated Folder Name page, confirm the name for the replication group and for the replicated folder. (The name for the replication group must be unique on the domain. To add to an existing replication group, use the instructions in the following sections.)
3. On the Replication Eligibility page, review the target folders that will be replicated. Click Next.
4. On the Primary Member page, select the server that holds the data that you want to use as the seed for the initial replication.
5. On the Topology Selection page, select one of the following replication topologies:

- **Hub And Spoke** Spoke servers replicate with one or two central hub servers. Hub servers replicate with all other hub servers by using the full mesh topology, as well as with designated spoke servers. Choose this topology in large network environments and environments with multiple branch offices. This topology requires a minimum of three members.
- **Full Mesh** All servers replicate with all other servers. Choose this topology when the replication group has fewer than 10 servers and all links have low enough costs (performance or monetary) to allow each server to replicate with every other server instead of a central hub server.
- **No Topology** This option does not specify a topology and postpones replication until you specify a replication topology manually. To specify a replication topology after creating the replication group, right-click the replication group in the DFS Management snap-in and then choose New Topology.

6. On the Hub Members page that appears if you chose Hub And Spoke Topology, specify the hub servers.
7. On the Hub And Spoke Connections page that appears if you chose Hub And Spoke topology, verify that the wizard lists the proper spoke servers. To change the required hub server with which a spoke member replicates preferentially, or the optional hub member with which a spoke member replicates if the required hub member is unavailable, select the spoke server, click Edit, and then specify the required hub and the optional hub.
8. On the Replication Group Schedule And Bandwidth page, choose when to replicate and the maximum amount of bandwidth you want DFS Replication to use.
9. To create a custom schedule, choose Replicate During The Specified Days And Times and then click Edit Schedule. You can create a custom schedule that uses Coordinated Universal Time (UTC) or the local time of the receiving server.
10. On the Review Settings And Create Replication Group page, review the settings, and then click Create. Review any errors and then click Close. Windows then replicates topology and replication settings to all domain controllers. A replication group member polls its nearest domain controller regularly. (By default, replication group members perform a lightweight poll every 5 minutes for Subscription objects under the local computer container and a full poll every hour.) The replication group member receives the settings after Windows updates the domain controller. To change the replication polling interval, use the *Dfsrdiag* command.

To replicate a DFS folder from a command prompt, use the *Dfsradmin* command. For example, open the Command Prompt window and then follow these steps:

1. Create a folder for the DFS Staging folder by typing the following commands on each member of the replication group:

```
Md E:\Documents\DfsrPrivate\Staging
Attrib +H /S /D E:\Documents\DfsrPrivate
```

> **Note** Use the *Dfsradmin Bulk* command or a batch file to perform a list of commands from a text file. See the accompanying CD for examples.

2. Create a new replication group by typing the following command:

```
Dfsradmin Replicationgroup New /Rgname:Example.local\Public\Documents
```

3. Add members to the replication group by typing the following commands:

```
Dfsradmin Member New /Rgname:Example.local\Public\Documents /Memname:Dc1 /
Force
Dfsradmin Member New /Rgname:Example.local\Public\Documents /Memname:Srv1 /
Force
```

4. Create a new replicated folder by typing the following command:

```
Dfsradmin Replicatedfolder New /Rgname:Example.local\Public\Documents/
Rfname:Documents
         /Replicatedfolderdfspath:\\Example.local\Public\Documents /Force
```

5. Add members to the replicated folder by typing the following commands:

```
Dfsradmin Membership Set /Rgname:Example.local\Public\Documents /
Rfname:Documents
         /Memname:Dc1 /Membershiplocalpath:E:\Documents
         /Membershipstagingpath:E:\Documents\Dfsrprivate\Staging /
Isprimary:True
         /Membershipenabled:True /Force
   Dfsradmin Membership Set /Rgname:Example.local\Public\Documents /
   Rfname:Documents
         /Memname:Srv1 /Membershiplocalpath:E:\Documents\
         /Membershipstagingpath:E:\Documents\Dfsrprivate\Staging
         /Membershipenabled:True /Force
```

6. Create replication connections by typing the following commands:

```
Dfsradmin Connection New /Rgname:Example.local\Public\Documents
   /Connectionsendingmembername:Dc1 /
Connectionreceivingmembername:Srv1
   /Connectionenabled:True
Dfsradmin Connection New /Rgname:Example.local\Public\Documents
   /Connectionsendingmembername:Srv1 /
Connectionreceivingmembername:Dc1
   /Connectionenabled:True
```

Creating a Branch Office Replication Group

To create a replication group that replicates a single branch server with a single hub server, follow these steps:

1. In the DFS Management snap-in, right-click Replication and choose New Replication Group. The New Replication Group Wizard appears.

   Note Creating replicated folders within an existing replication group is faster than creating a new replication group for each replicated folder because the replication group automatically applies its schedule, topology, and bandwidth throttling settings to the new replicated folder.

2. On the Replication Group Type page, choose Replication Group For Data Collection.
3. On the Name And Domain page, type a name for the replication group that is unique on the domain, specify in which domain to host the replication group, and (optionally) type a description of the replication group.
4. On the Branch Server page, type the name of the branch server that holds the data that you want to replicate with the hub server.
5. On the Replicated Folders page, click Add, and in the Add Folder To Replicate dialog box specify the local folder on the branch server to replicate with the hub server. Click OK when you are finished.
6. On the Hub Server page that appears if you chose Replication Group For Data Collection on the Replication Group Type page, type the name of the hub server that serves as a replication target for the replicated folders.
7. On the Target Folder On Hub Server page, specify the local folder on the hub server in which you want to place replicated data from the branch server. This folder is usually located in a folder or volume that you back up regularly.
8. On the Replication Group Schedule And Bandwidth page, choose when to replicate and the maximum amount of bandwidth you want to allow DFS Replication to use. To create a custom schedule, choose Replicate During The Specified Days And Times and then click Edit Schedule. You can create a custom schedule that uses Coordinated Universal Time (UTC) or the local time of the receiving server.
9. On the Review Settings And Create Replication Group page, review the settings, and then click Create. Review for errors and then click Close.

Windows then replicates topology and replication settings to all domain controllers. A replication group member polls its nearest domain controller regularly. (By default, replication group members perform a lightweight poll every 5 minutes for Subscription objects under the local computer container and a full poll every hour.) It receives the settings after Windows updates the domain controller. To change the replication polling interval, use the **Dfsrdiag** command.

To create a replication group from a command prompt, use the **Dfsradmin** command. For example, open a command prompt window and then follow these steps:

1. Create a folder for the DFS Staging folder by typing the following commands on each member of the replication group:

```
Md C:\Data\Utilities\Dfsrprivate\Staging
Attrib +H /S /D C:\Data\Utilities\Dfsrprivate
```

> **Note** Use the **Dfsradmin Bulk** command or a batch file to perform a list of commands from a text file. See the accompanying CD for examples.

2. Create a new replication group by typing the following command:

```
Dfsradmin Replicationgroup New /Rgname:Utilities
```

3. Add members to the replication group by typing the following commands:

```
Dfsradmin Member New /Rgname:Utilities /Memname:Dc1
Dfsradmin Member New /Rgname:Utilities /Memname:Srv1
```

4. Create a new replicated folder by typing the following command:

```
Dfsradmin Replicatedfolder New /Rgname:Utilities /Rfname:Utilities
```

5. Add members to the replicated folder by typing the following commands:

```
Dfsradmin Membership Set /Rgname:Utilities /Rfname:Utilities /
Memname:Dc1
   /Membershiplocalpath:C:\Data\Utilities
   /Membershipstagingpath:C:\Data\Utilities\Dfsrprivate\Staging /
Isprimary:True
   /Membershipenabled:True /Force
Dfsradmin Membership Set /Rgname:Utilities /Rfname:Utilities /
Memname:Srv1
   /Membershiplocalpath:C:\Data\Utilities
   /Membershipstagingpath:C:\Data\Utilities\Dfsrprivate\Staging
   /Membershipenabled:True /Force
```

6. Create replication connections by typing the following commands:

```
Dfsradmin Connection New /Rgname:Utilities /
Connectionsendingmembername:Dc1
   /Connectionreceivingmembername:Srv1 /Connectionenabled:True
Dfsradmin Connection New /Rgname:Utilities /
Connectionsendingmembername:Srv1
   /Connectionreceivingmembername:Dc1 /Connectionenabled:True
```

Note You can seed a branch member by backing up the replicated folder on the primary member and then restoring it on a target server before setting up replication. This reduces the amount of data that Windows must send over the WAN connection during the initial replication.

Creating a Multipurpose Replication Group

To create a replication group that replicates any number of servers with any number of other servers, follow these steps:

1. In the DFS Management snap-in, right-click Replication and choose New Replication Group. The New Replication Group Wizard appears.
2. On the Replication Group Type page, choose Multipurpose Replication Group.
3. On the Name And Domain page, type a name for the replication group that is unique on the domain, specify in which domain to host the replication group, and optionally type a description of the replication group.
4. On the Replication Group Members page, add the servers on which you want to replicate content.
5. On the Topology Selection page, choose a replication technology.
6. On the Hub Members page that appears if you chose Hub And Spoke Topology, specify the hub servers.
7. On the Hub And Spoke Connections page that appears if you chose Hub And Spoke Topology, verify that the wizard lists the proper spoke servers. To change the required hub server with which a spoke member replicates preferentially, or the optional hub member with which a spoke member replicates if the required hub member is unavailable, select the spoke server, click Edit, and then specify the required hub and the optional hub.
8. On the Replication Group Schedule And Bandwidth page, choose when to replicate and the maximum amount of bandwidth you want to allow DFS Replication to use. To create a custom schedule, choose Replicate During The Specified Days And Times and then click Edit Schedule. You can create a custom schedule that uses Coordinated Universal Time (UTC) or the local time of the receiving server.
9. On the Primary Member page, select the server that holds the data that you want to use as the seed for the initial replication.
10. On the Folders To Replicate page, click Add and in the Add Folder To Replicate dialog box, specify the folder to replicate. Click OK when you are finished.

11. On the Local Path Of *Folder* On Other Members page, select a replication member that you want to participate in replication of the specified folder, click Edit, and in the Edit Local Path dialog box, enable replication and specify the local folder on the target server in which to place replicated data from the hub server. Repeat this step for every replicated folder you specify in the Replicated Folders page.
12. On the Review Settings And Create Replication Group page, review the settings and then click Create. Review any errors and then click Close.

Windows then replicates topology and replication settings to all domain controllers. A replication group member polls its nearest domain controller regularly. (By default, replication group members perform a lightweight poll every 5 minutes for Subscription objects under the local computer container and a full poll every hour.) It receives the settings after Windows updates the domain controller. To change the replication polling interval, use the `Dfsrdiag` command.

Note To create a multipurpose replication group from the command-line, see "Creating a Branch Office Replication Group" earlier in this chapter—the command-line procedure is identical.

Managing Replication Groups

Select a replication group, and then use the Memberships, Connections, Replicated Folders, and Delegation tabs of the DFS Management console to manage the replication group, as discussed in the following sections.

Note Click a column heading to change how Windows groups items in the view. To add or remove columns, right-click the column heading and choose Add/Remove Columns.

Use the following options on the Memberships tab to view and manage the member servers for each replicated folder:

- To disable a member of the replication group, right-click the member and then choose Disable. Disable members that do not need to replicate a specific replicated folder. Do not disable members temporarily and then enable them–doing so causes roughly one kilobyte of replication traffic per file in the replicated folder, and overwrites all changes on the disabled member. (See the "Conflict Resolution During the Initial Replication" sidebar for more information.)
- To delete a member of the replication group, right-click it and then choose Delete.
- To add a member server that participates in replication, right-click the replication group in the DFS Management console, choose New Member, and then use the

New Member Wizard to specify the local path of the replicated folders, connections, and schedule.

- To change the size of the conflict or staging folders or to disable the retention of deleted files, right-click the member, choose Properties, click the Advanced tab, and then use the Quota boxes. The conflict folder stores the "losing" files that Windows deletes when it encounters two versions of the same file during replication as well as the most recently deleted files in the replicated folder, and the staging folder queues replication data.

> **Note** The default size of the staging folder is 4096 MB, but by increasing the size of the staging folder, you can increase the performance of replication group members that replicate with a large number of replication partners or that contain large files that change often. Look for event ID 4208 in the DFS Replication event log; if this event appears multiple times in an hour, increase the staging folder size 20 percent until the event no longer appears frequently.

- To create a report showing the replication health as well as RDC efficiency, right-click the replication group, choose Create Diagnostic Report, and then use the Diagnostic Report Wizard to create the report. (See Figure 12-14 for an example of a health report.)

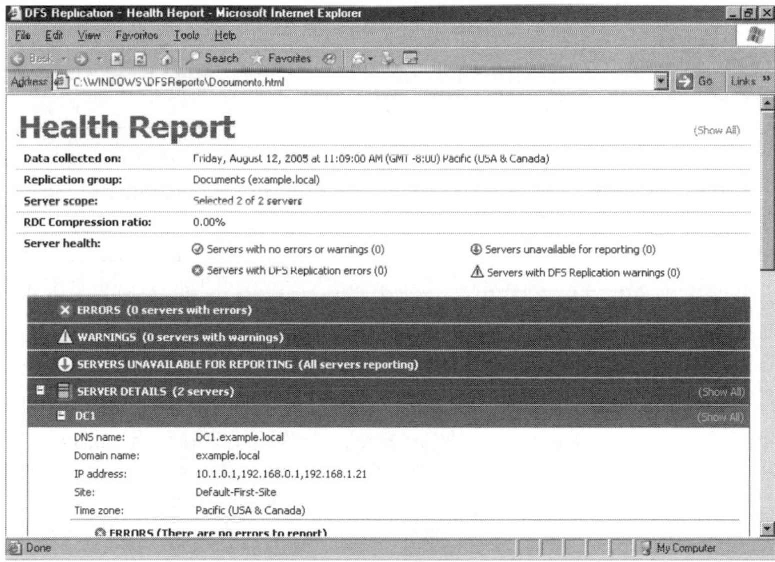

Figure 12-14 An example of a health report

- To verify the replication topology, right-click the replication group and then choose Verify Topology.

- On the Connections tab, view and manage all replication connections. To add a new replication connection between two members of a replication group, right click the replication group and choose New Connection. In the New Connection dialog box, specify the sending member, the receiving member, the schedule, and whether to create a one-way or two-way replication connection.
- Use the following options on the Replicated Folders tab to view and manage all replicated folders:
  - To add a new replicated folder to the replication group, right-click the replication group in the DFS Management console, choose New Replicated Folder, and then use the New Replicated Folder Wizard to specify the primary member and the local folders to replicate.
  - To omit certain file types or subfolders from replication, click the Replicated Folders tab, right-click the replicated folder, choose Properties, and then use the File Filter and Subfolder Filter boxes on the General tab.
  - To share a replicated folder on the network and optionally add the folder to a DFS namespace, right-click the replicated folder, choose Share And Publish In Namespace, and then use the Share Or Publish Replicated Folder Wizard.

  Note RDC increases processor utilization on the server, so you might want to disable it on servers with slow processors or high-speed links, and in environments that replicate only new content or files smaller than 64 KB. To disable RDC on a connection, click the Connections tab, right-click the member, choose Properties, and then clear the Use Remote Differential Compression (RDC) check box. You can also change the minimum file size that RDC engages from the 64 KB default size by using the `Dfsradmin ConnectionSet` command. Monitor RDC statistics and CPU utilization before and after disabling RDC to verify that you reduce processor utilization enough to warrant the increased network traffic.

- On the Delegation tab, view and manage administrative permissions. See the Delegating Management Permissions section of this chapter for information about the Delegation tab.

Note To change the replication polling interval, which controls how often a server checks for updated files, use the `Dfsrdiag` command.

Summary

Windows Server 2008 offers many ways to manage your file resources to make them secure and accessible. In the next chapter, we move on to creating and managing Group Policy.

Chapter 13

Group Policy

The job of a network administrator becomes increasingly complex with each passing year. You are expected to deliver and maintain customized desktop configurations to mobile users, information workers, or others assigned to strictly defined tasks, such as data entry. Changes to standard operating system images are periodically required. Security settings and updates must be promptly delivered to the computers and devices. New users need to be productive quickly without costly training. In the event of a computer failure or disaster, service must be restored with a minimum of data loss and interruption.

Group Policy can reduce lost productivity caused by the usual suspects—users who accidentally delete system configuration files, misplace vital folders, or inadvertently introduce a virus to the network. Also, Group Policy can help increase productivity by making it easier for users to find what they need to work more efficiently. Group Policy does this by allowing the administrator to delineate the elements of the user's desktop environment by specifying which programs are available, which programs appear on the desktop, and which options are available on the Start menu.

What's New in Server 2008

The two major changes in Windows Server 2008 Group Policy are Starter Group Policy Objects and Group Policy preference extensions. There are also some interface changes, but mostly of a minor nature.

In this chapter you'll find Group Policy basics with extended coverage of Starter GPOs and client-side extensions.

Components of Group Policy

Group Policy consists of the following configurable components:

- **Security Settings** Configures security for users, computers, and domains.
- **Scripts** Specifies scripts for computer startup and shutdown, as well as for user logon and logoff events.
- **Preference items** Configures unenforced settings for users and computers.
- **Folder Redirection** Places special folders such as Documents or specified application folders on the network.
- **Software Settings** Assigns applications to users. (See Chapter 28, "Managing Software," for more about publishing software on the network.)

Group Policy Objects

A collection of policy settings is called a Group Policy Object (GPO). A GPO contains both policies that affect computers and policies that affect users. Computer-related policies include security settings, application settings, assigned applications, and computer startup and shutdown scripts. User-related policies define application settings, folder redirection, assigned and published applications, user logon and logoff scripts, and security settings. In cases of conflicting policies, computer-related settings usually override user-related settings.

GPOs are stored at the domain level and are associated with an Active Directory object—a site, domain, or organizational unit (OU). One or more GPOs can apply to a site, domain, or OU, just as a single GPO can be linked to multiple sites, domains, and OUs.

Important Linking GPOs across domains will seriously diminish network performance.

Order of Implementation

Group policies are processed in the following order:

1. Local GPO.
2. GPOs linked to the site, in the order specified by the administrator. See the Linked Group Policy Objects folder in the Group Policy Management Console (GPMC). The GPO with the lowest link order is processed last and therefore has the highest precedence.
3. Domain GPOs in the order specified by the administrator. The GPO with the lowest link order is processed last and therefore has the highest precedence.
4. Organizational unit GPOs, from largest to smallest organizational unit (parent to child organizational unit).

In this sequence, the last writer wins. If multiple GPOs attempt contradictory settings, the GPO with highest precedence wins.

Order of Inheritance

As a rule, Group Policy settings are passed from parent containers down to child containers. This practice means that a policy applied to a parent container applies to all the containers—including users and computers—that are below the parent container in the Active Directory tree hierarchy. However, if you specifically assign a Group Policy for a child container that contradicts the parent container policy, the child container's policy overrides the parent Group Policy.

If two policies are not contradictory, both can be implemented. For example, if a parent container policy calls for an application shortcut to be on a user's desktop and the child container policy calls for another application shortcut, both appear. Policy settings that are disabled are inherited as disabled. Policy settings that are not configured in the parent container are not inherited.

Overriding Inheritance

Several options are available for changing how inheritance is processed. One option prevents child containers from overriding any policy setting set in a higher level GPO. In GPMC, this option is known as *enforcing the GPO link*. This option is not set by default and must be turned on in each GPO where it's wanted.

Enforcing a GPO Link

To enforce a GPO link, open GPMC and follow these steps:

1. Select the GPO in the console tree.

2. On the Scope tab, right-click the link and select Enforced on the shortcut menu to enable or disable enforcement for the link.
3. Click OK.

Blocking Inheritance

A second option for changing how inheritance is processed as Block Inheritance. When you select this option, the child container does not inherit any policies from parent containers. In the event of a conflict between these two options, the Enforced/No Override option always takes precedence.

Simply stated, Enforced/No Override is a link property, Block Policy Inheritance is a container property, and Enforced takes precedence over Block Policy Inheritance. To block inheritance, follow these steps:

1. Start Group Policy Management Console.
2. In the console tree, navigate to the domain or OU for which you want to block inheritance.
3. Right-click the domain or OU and select Block Inheritance.

Important Explicit permissions take precedence over inherited permissions—even an inherited Deny. So if you explicitly grant access to an object, the inherited Deny will not prevent access.

Creating a Group Policy Object

Creating an Active Directory domain also creates a Default Domain Policy and a Default Domain Controllers Policy. In general, to simplify administration and policy modeling, it is better to have more GPOs with fewer settings each than just a few GPOs that have many settings each. To create a GPO, follow these steps:

1. Start Group Policy Management Console.
2. Right-click Group Policy Objects in the domain to which you want the new GPO to apply. Select New from the shortcut menu.
3. In the New GPO dialog box, enter a name for the new GPO and click OK.

Editing a Group Policy Object

To edit an existing GPO, follow these steps:

1. Start Group Policy Management Console.
2. Expand the Group Policy Objects folder under the domain where the policy exists.

3. Right-click the policy and select Edit to open the Group Policy Management Editor.
4. Expand Policies under Computer Configuration or User Configuration and edit the settings.

Important As a best practice, you shouldn't edit the Default Domain Policy or the Default Domain Controllers Policy, with two exceptions: Account policy settings must be configured in the Default Domain Policy, and applications on domain controllers that require changes to Audit Policy or User Rights will have to have those settings made in the Default Domain Controllers Policy.

Deleting a Group Policy Object

To delete a GPO, follow these steps:

1. Start Group Policy Management Console.
2. In the console tree, expand the Group Policy Objects folder in the forest and domain that contains the GPO to be deleted.
3. Right-click the GPO and click Delete on the shortcut menu.
4. When prompted to confirm the deletion, as shown in Figure 13-1, click Yes.

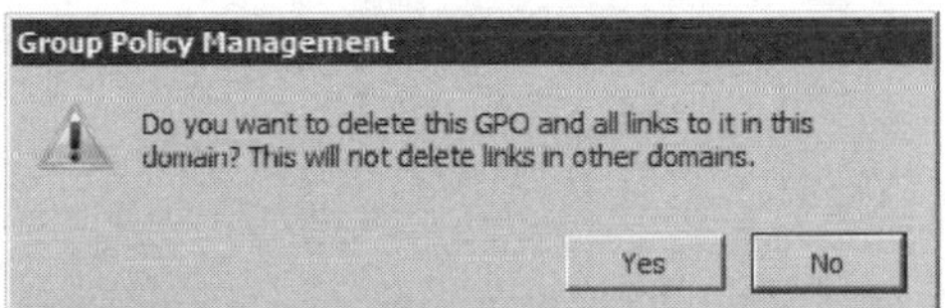

Figure 13-1 Confirming the deletion of a GPO

When you delete a GPO, GPMC attempts to delete all links to that GPO in the domain. If you do not have sufficient rights to delete a link, the GPO will be deleted, but the link will remain. The link to a deleted GPO appears in GPMC as Not Found. To delete Not Found links, you must have permission on the site, domain, or organizational unit containing the link.

Searching for a Group Policy Object

To search for a GPO, follow these steps:

1. Start Group Policy Management Console.
2. Double-click the forest containing the domain you want to search.
3. Right-click the domain and select Search from the shortcut menu.

4. In the Search For Group Policy Objects dialog box, shown in Figure 13-2, select where you want to search and add as much search criteria as you know.
5. Click Add.

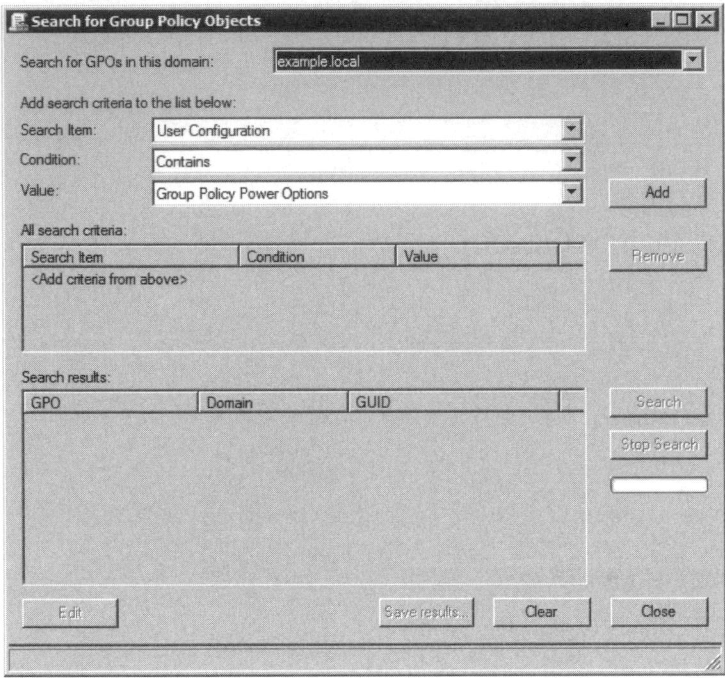

Figure 13-2 Searching for a GPO

6. Click Search.

Using Starter GPOs

A Starter GPO derives from a GPO and provides a way to store a number of administrative templates in a single object. Starter GPOs can be easily imported and exported, making them ideal for distribution to others.

Creating a Starter GPO

Making a Starter GPO couldn't be simpler. Just follow these steps:

1. Start Group Policy Management Console.
2. Navigate to the Starter GPOs folder under the domain where the GPO is to be created.
3. Right-click Starter GPOs and select New from the shortcut menu.

4. In the New Starter GPO dialog box, enter a name for the Starter GPO and a comment, which is optional.
5. Click OK.

Editing a Starter GPO

Starter GPOs contain all the administrative template settings not configured. To configure the settings for a Starter GPO, follow these steps:

1. Start Group Policy Management Console.
2. Navigate to the Starter GPOs folder.
3. In the Results pane, right-click the starter GPO you want to edit and select Edit from the shortcut menu. The Starter GPO opens in the Group Policy Starter GPO Editor.
4. Expand Administrative Templates under Computer Configuration or User Configuration and configure the settings.

Creating a New GPO from a Starter GPO

When you create a new GPO from a Starter GPO, the new GPO contains all the Administrative template policy settings and their values defined in the Starter GPO. To use a Starter GPO as the basis for a new GPO, follow these steps:

1. Start Group Policy Management Console.
2. Expand the Starter GPO folder.
3. Right-click the Starter GPO you want to use and select New GPO From Starter GPO from the shortcut menu.
4. In the New GPO dialog box, provide a name for the new GPO and click OK.

Generating a Report of Starter GPO Settings

Rather than clicking through many screens of settings, you can generate a report of the settings in a Starter GPO by following these steps:

1. Start Group Policy Management Console.
2. Expand the Starter GPOs folder.
3. Right-click the Starter GPO from which you want the report. Select Save Report from the shortcut menu.
4. In the Save Starter GPO Report dialog box, select a location for the report. Accept the report name or type in a new one. Click Save.

You can open the saved report to view or print it.

Importing and Exporting a Starter GPO

To use the Starter GPO in another environment, you export it by saving it as a cabinet file. After transferring it to the other environment, you import it by loading the cabinet file.

To export a Starter GPO, follow these steps:

1. Start Group Policy Management Console.
2. Expand the Starter GPO folder.
3. Highlight the GPO to export and click Save As Cabinet.
4. In the Save Starter GPO As Cabinet dialog box, select the location for the new cabinet file. Click Save.

To import a Starter GPO, reverse the previous process by following these steps:

1. Start Group Policy Management Console.
2. Expand the Starter GPO folder.
3. Click Load Cabinet, and then click Browse For CAB.
4. Browse to the Starter GPO Cabinet you want to import. Click the filename and then click Open.
5. Click OK to complete the import process.

Group Policy Preferences

Group Policy Preferences are a new feature in Windows Server 2008 to help you configure, deploy, and manage operating system and application settings that you cannot manage by using Group Policy. Examples include mapped drives, scheduled tasks, and Start menu settings. Using Group Policy Preferences is often a better alternative than logon scripts for configuring these settings. Group Policy Preferences are built in to Group Policy Management Console.

Networks customarily have two types of settings: enforced settings (Group Policy) and optional settings (preferences). Enforced settings can't be changed by users. Preferences, on the other hand, can be changed by users. By specifically deploying preferences, you can create configurations that are more suitable for your organization than the operating system's default settings. Deploying preferences is usually done through logon scripts or default user profiles.

So what are the differences between Group Policy Preferences and Group Policy? The primary difference is that Group Policy is enforced and Group Policy Preferences are not. However, there are other key differences, shown in Table 13-1.

Table 13-1 Group Policy vs. Group Policy Preferences

Group Policy Settings	**Group Policy Preferences**
Settings are enforced.	Preferences are not enforced.
User interface is disabled.	User interface is not disabled.
Adding policy settings requires application support and constructing administrative templates.	Preference items for files and registry settings are easily created.
Requires Group Policy–aware applications.	Supports non-Group Policy–aware applications.
Filtering is based on Windows Management Instrumentation (WMI) and requires writing WMI queries.	Supports item-level targeting.
Alternative user interface is provided for most policy settings.	Uses a familiar, easy-to-use interface for configuring most settings.

Figure 13-3 shows a decision tree for choosing between Group Policy settings and Group Policy Preferences.

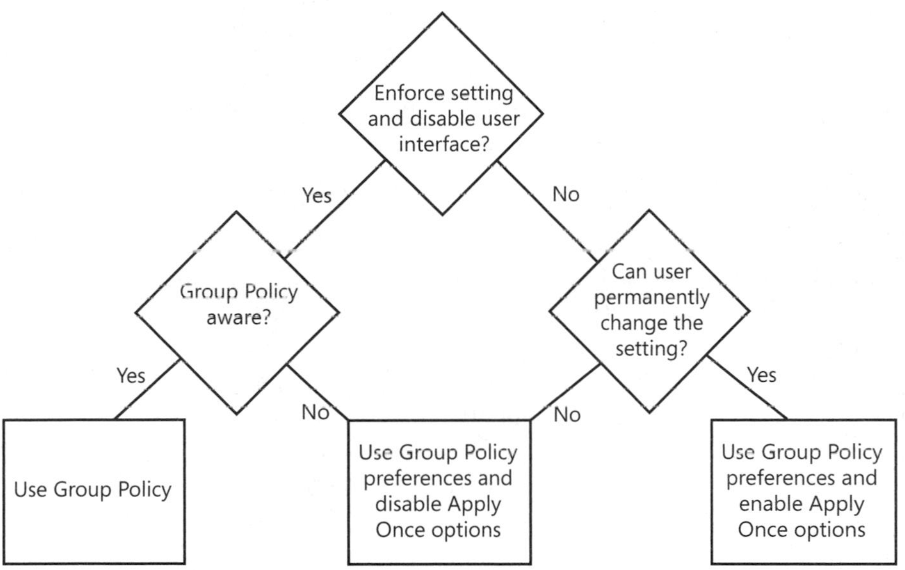

Figure 13-3 Choosing between Group Policy settings and Group Policy Preferences

Client-Side Extensions

You don't need to install any services to create GPOs that contain Group Policy Preferences. If you want to deploy preferences to client computers, the clients must have a Policy preferences client-side extension (CSE). You can download the CSE from *www.microsoft.com/downloads/*. The CSE supports the following Windows versions:

Windows XP with SP2

Windows Vista

Windows Server 2003 with SP1

Windows Server 2008 already includes the CSE.

To view Group Policy Preferences, start Group Policy Management from the Administrative Tools menu and follow these steps:

1. Navigate to the domain. Right-click Default Domain Controllers Policy and select Edit from the shortcut menu.
2. Under Computer Configuration, expand Preferences, expand Windows Settings, and then expand Control Panel Settings.
3. Under User Configuration, expand Windows Settings, and then expand Control Panel Settings.

As you can see in Figure 13-4, the Computer Configuration and User Configuration lists are very similar. However, even when the names are identical, the properties may differ. The following preferences do not overlap: Applications, Drive Maps, Internet Settings, Regional Options, and Start Menu under User Configuration; and Network Shares and Network Options under Computer Configuration.

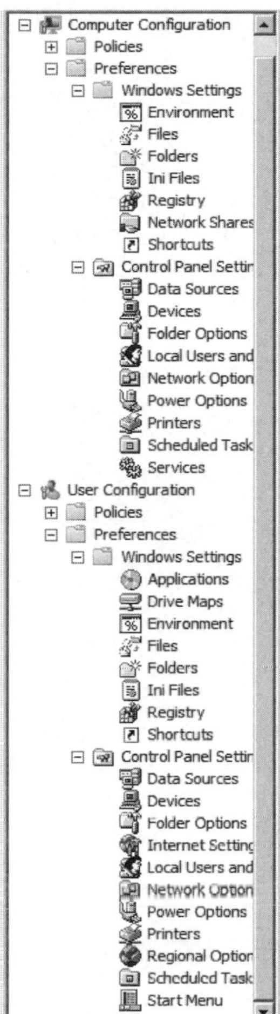

Figure 13-4 Group Policy Preferences extensions

Using Group Policy Preferences for Windows

Like Group Policy settings, preferences are almost infinitely configurable. In the next sections, we'll discuss a selection of the most commonly used extensions, beginning with the Windows settings.

Drive Maps

The Drive Maps setting allows you to create, update, and delete mapped drives and their properties. To create a mapped drive preference item, follow these steps:

1. Start Group Policy Management Console.

2. Right-click the GPO that will contain the new preference item, and then click Edit on the shortcut menu.
3. In the console tree, navigate to User Configuration, expand the Preferences folder, and then expand the Windows Settings folder. Right-click the Drive Maps node, point to New, and select Mapped Drive.
4. In the New Drive Properties dialog box, select one of the following actions for Group Policy to perform, as shown in Figure 13-5.
   - **Create** Creates a new mapped drive
   - **Replace** Deletes an existing mapped drive and creates a new one
   - **Update** Changes specific settings of an existing mapped drive
   - **Delete** Removes a mapped drive
5. Enter drive map settings, which are described in Table 13-2.
6. Click the Common tab and select the options you want. (For more information, see "Configuring Common Options" later in this chapter.)
7. Click OK. The new preference item appears in the details pane.

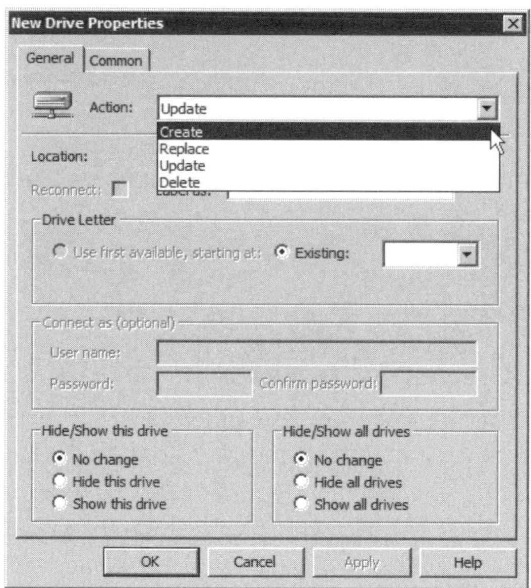

Figure 13-5 Creating a new mapped drive

Table 13-2 **Drive Map Settings**

Setting Name	Action	Description
Location	Create, Replace, or Update	To create or replace an existing mapped drive, enter a fully qualified UNC path. To modify an existing drive mapping, leave this field empty. Note that this field also accepts processing variables. Press F3 for a list of acceptable variables.
Reconnect	Create, Replace, or Update	Select this option to save the mapped drive in the user's settings and reconnect to it at subsequent logons.
Label As	Create, Replace, or Update	Provide a descriptive label. This field also accepts preference processing variables. Press F5 for a list.
Drive Letter	Create, Replace or Update	To assign the first available drive letter, select Use First Available Starting At and choose a drive letter. To assign a specific drive letter, select Use and then choose a drive letter.
Drive Letter	Update	To change an existing drive mapping, select Existing and then choose the drive letter.
Drive Letter	Delete	To delete all drive mappings, select Delete All, Starting At and then select the beginning drive letter. To delete a specific mapping, select Delete and then choose the drive letter.
Connect As	Create, Replace, or Update	To map a drive using credentials other than those of the currently logged on user, type the name and password to be used.
Hide/Show This Drive	Create, Replace, or Update	To prevent the drive from being displayed in Windows Explorer, select Hide This Drive. To allow it to be displayed, select Show This Drive. These settings take priority over the Hide/Show All Drives setting.

Environment

The Environment preference extension allows you to create new environment variables as well as modify existing ones. To create a new Environment Variable preference item, follow these steps:

1. Start Group Policy Management Console.
2. Right-click the GPO that will contain the new preference item, and then click Edit on the shortcut menu.
3. In the console tree under Computer Configuration or User Configuration, expand the Preferences folder, and then expand the Windows Settings folder.

4. Right-click the Environment node, point to New, and select Environment Variable.
5. In the New Environment Variable Properties dialog box, select an Action for Group Policy to perform.
6. Enter the environment variable settings for Group Policy to configure or remove. Table 13-3 describes these settings.
7. Click the Common tab and select the options you want. (For more information, see "Configuring Common Options" later in this chapter.)
8. Click OK.

Table 13-3 Environment Variable Settings

Setting Name	Description
User Variable	Under User Configuration, the variable will affect each user independently. Under Computer Configuration, the variable affects only the default user of the computer.
System Variable	The variable will affect all users of the computer.
Name	Enter a name for the variable. To select PATH, leave the name field blank.
PATH	Select this option to create or replace the value of the PATH variable. This option available only when System Variable is selected.
Value	If PATH is selected, type a semicolon-delimited list of folder paths. If Partial is selected, type one segment of the PATH variable omitting semicolons.
Partial	Available only when both System Variable and PATH are selected. If the chosen Action is Create, the specified Value will be added to the PATH variable. If Replace or Update is chosen, the specified part of the PATH variable will be replaced. If Delete is chosen, the specified segment will be removed from the existing PATH variable.

Files

With the Files preference extension you can copy, modify the attributes of, replace, or delete files. The extension supports wildcards in file paths and environment variables. Before configuring a file preference item, review the behavior of each type of action and setting shown in Table 13-4.

To create a new file preference item, follow these steps:

1. Start Group Policy Management Console.
2. Right-click the Group Policy object (GPO) that will contain the new preference item, and then click Edit on the shortcut menu.

3. In the console tree under Computer Configuration or User Configuration, expand the Preferences folder, and then expand the Windows Settings folder.
4. Right-click Files, point to New, and select File.
5. In the New Files Properties dialog box, select one of the following actions from the drop-down list:
   - **Create** Copies a file or multiple files from a source to a destination, and then configures the file attributes for computers or users.
   - **Delete** Removes a file or multiple files.
   - **Replace** Overwrites files at the destination location with replacement files. If the file does not exist at the destination, the Replace action copies the file from the source location to the destination.
   - **Update** Modifies attributes of an existing file.
6. Enter the file settings, which are described in Table 13-4.
7. Click the Common tab and select the options you want. (For more information, see "Configuring Common Options" later in this chapter.)
8. Click OK. The new preference item appears in the details pane.

Table 13-4 File Settings

Setting	Action	Description
Source File(s)	Create, Replace, or Update	Enter the location from which to copy the source file. The field can include variables. You can use a local or mapped drive or a fully qualified UNC path.
Destination File	Create, Replace, or Update *and* the Source File(s) field (includes wildcards)	Enter the location to which to copy files or the location of the files to be changed. You can use a local or mapped drive (from the perspective of the client) or a fully qualified UNC path.
Delete File(s)	Delete	Type the path to the file(s) from the perspective of the client. The field can include wildcards.
Suppress Errors On Individual File Actions	Replace, Update, or Delete	Select this option to allow multiple files to transfer during the replace, delete, or update operation even if one or more files fail to transfer.
Attributes	Create, Replace, or Update	Select attributes for the file(s) being transferred. If necessary to complete an operation, the Read Only attribute will be reset.

Folders

The Folders preference extension is similar to the Files extension. You can create, replace, update, delete, and even clean up folders on targeted computers. Like the Files preference extension, Folders supports environment variables but doesn't allow wildcards in folder paths.

Before configuring a Folder preference item, review the behavior of each type of action and setting, shown in Table 13-5.

To create a new Folder preference item, follow these steps:

1. Start Group Policy Management Console.
2. Right-click the GPO that will contain the new preference item, and then click Edit on the shortcut menu.
3. In the console tree under Computer Configuration or User Configuration, expand the Preferences folder, and then expand the Windows Settings folder.
4. Right-click Folders, point to New, and select Folder.
5. In the New Folder Properties dialog box, select one of the following actions from the drop-down list:
   - **Create** Creates a new folder for users or computers.
   - **Replace** Deletes the contents of an existing folder and overwrites settings associated with the folder. If the folder doesn't exist, Replace creates a new folder.
   - **Update** Modifies an existing folder.
   - **Delete** Removes a folder.
6. Enter the folder settings, which are described in Table 13-5.
7. Click the Common tab and select the options you want. (For more information, see Configuring Common Options, later in this chapter.)
8. Click OK. The new preference item appears in the details pane.

Table 13-5 Folder Settings

Setting	Action	Description
Path	Create, Replace, Update, or Delete	Enter a path to the folder from the client's perspective. Do not use quotes or a trailing slash. This field can include variables.
Attributes	Create, Replace, or Update	Select attributes for the folder.

Table 13-5 Folder Settings

Setting	Action	Description
Options	Replace or Delete	Delete This Folder (If Emptied): Select this option to delete the folder in the path if it is empty. Recursively Delete All Subfolders (If Emptied): If you select this option, the lowest level of folders (if empty) will be deleted, then parent folders, until reaching the folder shown in the Path field. This option takes effect after the option to Delete All Files In The Folder has been processed. Delete All Files In The Folder: Select this option to delete all files in this folder that are allowed to be deleted. If you also select Recursively Delete All Subfolders, all files that are allowed to be deleted within all subfolders are also deleted. Allow Deletion Of Read Only Files/Folders: Select this option to clear the read-only attribute of files and folders to be deleted. Ignore Errors For Files/Folders That Cannot Be Deleted: If you don't select this option, an error will be returned when the folder item tries to delete a folder that is not empty or for which the user doesn't have permission.

Ini Files

The Ini File preference allows you to add, replace, or delete sections or properties in configuration settings (.ini) or setup information (.inf) files. Each section in an .ini or .inf file is arranged in the following format:

```
[SectionName]
PropertyName1=PropertyValue1
PropertyName2=PropertyValue2
```

Before creating an Ini File preference item, review the behavior of each type of action and setting, shown in Table 13-6.

To create a new Ini File item, follow these steps:

1. Start Group Policy Management Console.
2. Right-click the GPO that will contain the new preference item, and then click Edit on the shortcut menu.
3. In the console tree under Computer Configuration or User Configuration, expand the Preferences folder, and then expand the Windows Settings folder.

4. Right-click Ini Files, point to New, and select Ini File.
5. In the Action drop-down list, choose one of the following:
   - **Create** Adds and configures a property for an .ini file or .inf file. If the file doesn't exist, it is created.
   - **Replace** Replaces a property in an .ini or .inf file. If the property doesn't exist, the Replace action creates it.
   - **Update** Has the same effect as Replace.
   - **Delete** Removes a section or a property of an .ini file or .inf file or removes the file completely.
6. Enter the configuration settings, which are described in Table 13-6.
7. Click the Common tab and select the options you want. (For more information, see "Configuring Common Options" later in this chapter.)
8. Click OK. The new preference item appears in the details pane.

Table 13-6 Ini and Inf Settings

Setting	Action	Description
File Path	All	Enter the path, from the client's perspective, to the .ini or .inf file. Do not use quotes. If the file or parent folders don't exist, they are created.
Section Name	All	Enter the name of the section to be configured. Leave this field blank to delete the entire file.
Property Name	All	Enter the name of the property to be configured. If you are deleting the entire section or the entire file, leave this field empty.
Property Value	Create, Replace, or Update	Enter a value for the property. You can use quotes, but they are typically removed when an application or operating system reads the value. If this field is left empty, the property has an empty value that is read as if the property doesn't exist.

Network Shares

The Network Shares preference extension provides a way to manage network shares on multiple, targeted computers. (See "Configuring a Targeting Item" later in this chapter.) This extension allows you to take the following actions:

- Create and configure a share.
- Replace a share and thereby modify its folder path.

- Delete a share.
- Modify share properties.

To create a Network Share preference item, follow these steps:

1. Start Group Policy Management Console.
2. Right-click the GPO that will contain the new preference item, and then click Edit on the shortcut menu.
3. In the console tree under Computer Configuration, expand the Preferences folder, and then expand the Windows Settings folder.
4. Right-click Network Shares, point to New, and select Network Share.
5. In the New Network Share Properties dialog box, select an Action from the drop-down list:
   - **Create** Create a new share.
   - **Replace** Deletes and replaces a share. If the share doesn't exist, Replace will create a new one.
   - **Update** Modifies a share. This setting updates only the settings you define. If the share doesn't exist, Update will create a new one.
   - **Delete** Removes a share from computers.
6. Enter network share settings for Group Policy to configure or remove. These settings are described in Table 13-7.
7. Click the Common tab and select the options you want. (For more information, see "Configuring Common Options," later in this chapter.)
8. Click OK. The new preference item appears in the details pane.

Table 13-7 Network Share Settings

Setting	Action	Description
Share Name	Create, Replace, Update, or Delete	Enter a name for the share. Press F3 for a list of the variables that can be included in this field. The Share Name field isn't available if you have chosen Update or Delete and are using Action Modifiers.
Folder Path	Create, Replace, Update, or Delete	Enter a path to an existing folder to which the share will point. Press F3 for a list of the variables that can be included in this field. The Folder Path field isn't available if you have chosen Update or Delete and are using Action Modifiers.

Table 13-7 Network Share Settings

Setting	Action	Description
Comment	Create, Replace, or Update	Enter text to be displayed in the Comment field of the share. If you're updating a share and leave this field empty, the existing comment will remain unchanged. Press F3 for a list of variables that are accepted in the field.
Action Modifiers	Update or Delete	Update/Delete All Regular Shares: Updates or deletes all shares except hidden shares (shares with names ending in $) and special shares (SYSVOL and NETLOGON). Update Or Delete All Hidden Non-Administrative Shares: Updates or deletes hidden shares except administrative drive letter shares, ADMIN$, FAX$, IPC$, and PRINT$. Update Or Delete All Administrative Drive Letter Shares: Updates or deletes all administrative shares (shares with names ending in $).
User Limit	Create, Replace, or Update	No Change: Leaves the allowed number unchanged when updating a share. If you are creating or replacing a share, this option will set the number of users to the maximum allowed. Maximum Allowed: Select this option to make the number of users unrestricted. Allow This Number Of Users: Select this option to configure a specific number of users allowed.
Access-based Enumeration	Create, Replace, or Update	No Change: Visibility of shares in a folder will remain unchanged. Enable: Folders in the share will be visible only to users with Read access. Disable: Folders in the share will be visible to all users.

Note For a share point to be generated, the folder to be shared must already exist on computers to which the GPO is applied. When a share is deleted, the share point leading to the folder is removed, but the folder and its contents are not deleted. See the section on the Folders preference extension earlier in this chapter to create or delete folders using Group Policy.

Registry

The Registry preference extension allows you to copy registry settings from one computer and apply them to other computers. You can also manage registry values and keys. To create and manage registry preference items, follow these steps:

1. Start Group Policy Management Console.
2. Right-click the GPO that will contain the new preference item, and then click Edit on the shortcut menu.
3. In the console tree under Computer Configuration or User Configuration, expand the Preferences folder, and then expand the Windows Settings folder.
4. Right-click Registry, point to New, and select Registry Item.
5. In the New Registry Properties dialog box, select an Action from the drop-down list:
   - **Create** Makes a new registry key or value for users or computers.
   - **Replace** Deletes a registry value or key and replaces it. Replace will overwrite all existing settings of the key or value. If the registry key or value doesn't exist, the Replace action creates a new one.
   - **Update** Changes the settings of an existing registry value or key. The Update action modifies only settings defined in the preference item. If the registry key or value doesn't exist, the Update action creates a new one.
   - **Delete** Deletes a registry value or key and all subkeys and values.
6. Enter Registry settings, which are described in Table 13-8.
7. Click OK. The new preference item appears in the details pane.

Table 13-8 Registry Settings

Setting	Action	Description
Key Path	All	Click Browse to navigate to the value or key to be acted upon. If you browse, the Hive, Key Path, and Default fields will be filled automatically. If you don't browse, enter the path without the hive name or a leading or following slash. Press F3 to see a list of variables that can be selected for this field.
Hive	All	Select a hive if you don't browse to the value or key.
Value Name	All	Select either Default to configure the default value or type the name of the value to configure. To configure only a key, leave this field blank. Press F3 to see a list of variables that can be selected for this field.
Value Type	Create, Replace, or Update	If you have entered a value name, select the type. If you're configuring a key, leave this field blank.
Value Data	Create, Replace, or Update	If you have entered a value type, type the data for the registry value.

Creating Multiple Registry Items

You can create multiple registry preference items and organize them into a folder that mimics the registry structure. To create multiple registry preferences, follow these steps:

1. Start Group Policy Management Console.
2. Right-click the GPO that will contain the new preference item, and then click Edit on the shortcut menu.
3. In the console tree under Computer Configuration or User Configuration, expand the Preferences folder, and then expand the Windows Settings folder.
4. Right-click Registry, point to New, and select Registry Wizard.
5. In the Registry Browser dialog box, select the source computer. Click Next.
6. Browse through the registry and select the check box for each key or value from which you want to create a Registry preference item, as shown in Figure 13-6. Select the check box for a key only if you want to create a Registry item for the key. If you want to create a Registry item for a value within a key, select the check box for the value.

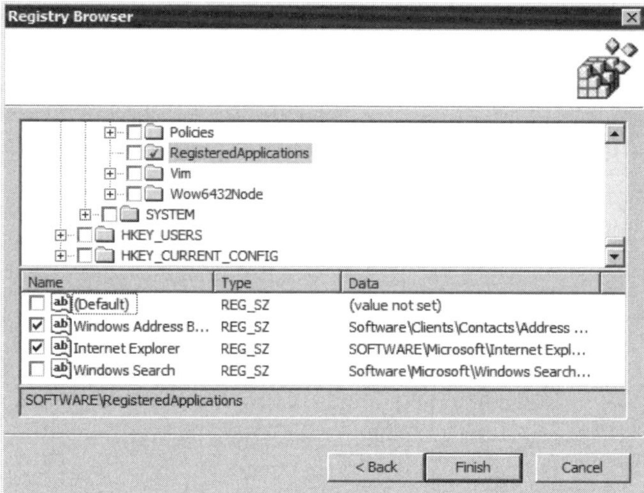

Figure 13-6 Selecting multiple registry items

7. Click Finish. The settings that you selected appear as preference items in the Registry Wizard Values collection.
8. In the console tree, right-click the Registry Wizard Values collection and click Rename. Enter a descriptive name.

You can modify the setting in a collection using the steps described earlier in the Registry section.

Shortcuts

Creating a Shortcut preference item allows you to make a shortcut to a file, folder, computer, printer, Web page–all the objects an ordinary shortcut can point to–and apply it through Group Policy. Shortcut preference items have many possible settings, so review them carefully.

To create a new Shortcut preference item, follow these steps:

1. Start Group Policy Management Console.
2. Right-click the GP that will contain the new preference item, and then click Edit on the shortcut menu.
3. In the console tree under Computer Configuration or User Configuration, expand the Preferences folder, and then expand the Windows Settings folder.

   Important If any path in the configuration contains a mapped drive, the Shortcut preference item must be under User Configuration. Likewise, be sure the drive letter exists before the Shortcut item is processed, and select Run In Logged On User's Security Context on the Common tab.

4. Right-click Shortcuts, point to New, and select Shortcut.
5. In the New Shortcut Properties dialog box, select an Action from the drop-down list:
   - **Create** Makes a new shortcut for computers or users.
   - **Replace** Deletes a shortcut and re-creates it. If the shortcut doesn't exist, Replace creates a new one.
   - **Update** Updates only the settings defined within the preference item. If the shortcut doesn't exist, Update creates a new one.
   - **Delete** Removes a shortcut for users or computers.
6. Enter the folder settings. See Table 13-9 for descriptions of these settings.
7. Click the Common tab and select the options you want. (For more information, see "Configuring Common Options" later in this chapter.)
8. Click OK. The new preference item appears in the details pane.

Table 13-9 Shortcut Settings

Setting	Action	Description
Name	All	Enter a name for the shortcut. If you are replacing, updating, or deleting a shortcut, the name must match the name of the existing shortcut. This field accepts preference processing variables. Press F3 to display a list of variables from which you can select.
Target Type	All	Select the type of target from the drop-down list.
Location	All	From the drop-down list, select the location for the shortcut item to appear. Any location other than All Users is relative to the logged-on user. To place a shortcut in a subfolder at the location, enter the path in the Name field followed by the display name. (For example, to place a shortcut with the display name References in the Tools subfolder on the Start menu, type Tools\References for the Name and select Start Menu for Location.)
Target Path	Create, Replace, or Update a targeted File System Object	Enter a local or UNC path or a drive letter to which the shortcut will point. This field accepts preference processing variables. Press F3 to display a list of variables from which you can select.
Target URL	Create, Replace, or Update a targeted URL	Enter the URL to which the shortcut will point. This field accepts preference processing variables. Press F3 to display a list of variables from which you can select.
Target Object	Create, Replace, or Update a targeted Shell Object	Click Browse and select the shell object to which the shortcut will point.
Arguments	Create, Replace, or Update targeted File System Object	Enter any arguments to use when opening the targeted object.
Start In	Create, Replace, or Update targeted File System Object	Enter a path for the folder that contains files required by the folder, or click Browse to navigate to the folder. Press F3 for a list of the variables that can be included in this field.
Shortcut Key	Create, Replace, or Update	Provide a keyboard shortcut. To remove a shortcut key, click the field and press the Delete key.
Run	Create, Replace, or Update targeted File System Object	From the drop-down list, choose the size of the window to open.

Table 13-9 **Shortcut Settings**

Setting	Action	Description
Comment	Create, Replace, or Update targeted File System Object or Shell Object	Type in the text for a tooltip that will display when the mouse pointer pauses on the shortcut. Press F3 for a list of the variables that can be included in this field.
Icon File Path and Icon Index	Create, Replace, or Update	To select an icon other than the default for the type, click the browse button and select an icon. Press F3 for a list of the variables that can be included in this field.

Configuring Common Options

All Group Policy preference items have a Common tab and many items share common options, including the following:

- **Stop Processing Items In This Extension If An Error Occurs** More than one item can be configured in each extension. If this option is selected, a failed preference item will stop the remaining preference items from processing.

> **Note** Preference items are processed from the bottom of the list, moving toward the top. If you select this option, items processed before the failing item will still be processed successfully. This option only stops preference items that follow the failed item.

- **Run In Logged-On User's Security Context (User Policy Option)** By default, user preferences are processed using the security context of the SYSTEM account. Select this option and the preference items are processed in the security context of the logged-on user. This lets the preference extension access resources as the user and not as the computer. This can make a difference when using mapped drives and other network resources.
- **Remove This Item When It Is No Longer Applied** By default, Group Policy doesn't remove preferences when the GPO is removed from the user or computer. When you select this option, the preference item is removed when the GPO is removed.
- **Apply Once And Do Not Re-Apply** The results of preference items are rewritten each time Group Policy refreshes, which is every 90 minutes by default. When you select this option, preferences will apply once for the computer, no matter how many users share the computer. When you select this option in user configuration, the item will be applied once on each computer the user logs on to.

- **Item-level Targeting** You can use item-level targeting to apply preference items to individual users and computers. You can include multiple preference items, each tailored for selected users or computers and each targeted to apply settings only to the relevant users or computers.

Using Group Policy Preferences for Control Panel

In addition to the Windows category, you can make the following preference settings under Control Panel.

Data Sources

You can use the Data Sources preference item to configure Open Database Connectivity (ODBC) data sources to store information for how users and computers can connect to a data provider.

To create a Data Source preference item, follow these steps:

1. Start Group Policy Management Console.
2. Right-click the GPO that will contain the new preference item, and then click Edit on the shortcut menu.
3. In the console tree under Computer Configuration or User Configuration, expand the Preferences folder, and then expand the Control Panel Settings folder.
4. Right-click Data Sources, point to New, and select Data Source.
5. In the New Data Source Properties dialog box, select an Action from the drop-down list:
   - **Create** Creates a new data source name for the user or computer. If the data source exists, don't change it.
   - **Replace** Removes and replaces a data source name. The Replace action overwrites all existing settings for the data source name. If the data source name doesn't exist, the Replace action creates a new one.
   - **Update** Modifies settings for an existing data source name. The only settings changed are those defined within the preference item. If the data source name doesn't exist, Update creates a new one.
   - **Delete** Removes an existing data source name.
6. Enter the settings for the data source item, as described in Table 13-10.
7. Click the Common tab and select the options you want. (For more information, see "Configuring Common Options" earlier in this chapter.)

8. Click OK. The new preference item appears in the details pane.

Table 13-10 **Data Source Settings**

Setting	Action	Description
User Data Source or System Data Source	All	Select User Data Source to make the item visible only to users receiving the preference item. Select System Data Source to make the data source available to all users of the computer.
Data Source Name (DSN)	All	Enter the name used to identify the data source. Click Browse to see a list of data sources names on the current computer. Press F3 to see a list of variables that can be selected for this field.
Driver	All	Type the name of the ODBC driver used to connect to the data provider. Click Browse to select from a list of ODBC drivers.
Description	Create, Replace, or Update	Type in the text used to describe the data source. Press F3 to see a list of variables that can be selected for this field.
User Name	Create, Replace, or Update	Enter the user name used to connect to the data source.
Password and Confirm Password	Create, Replace, or Update	Type the password to connect to the data provider.
Attributes	Create, Replace, or Update	Click Add to create new attributes. Click Remove or Change to remove or change attributes.

Devices

Use the Devices preference item to centralize the enabling or disabling of specific types of hardware for users or computers. You may configure an entire class of devices such as Ports (COM & LPT) or narrow the selection to a particular type of device such as Communications Port (COM2). To configure a Device preference item, follow these steps:

1. Start Group Policy Management Console.
2. Right-click the GPO that will contain the new preference item, and then click Edit on the shortcut menu.
3. In the console tree under Computer Configuration or User Configuration, expand the Preferences folder, and then expand the Control Panel Settings folder.
4. Right-click Devices, point to New, and select Device.

5. In the New Device Properties dialog box, select Use This Device (Enable) or Do Not Use This Device (Disable) from the Action drop-down list.
6. Enter the Device settings, which are described in Table 13-11.
7. Click the Common tab and select the options you want. (For more information, see "Configuring Common Options" earlier in this chapter.)
8. Click OK. The new preference item appears in the Details pane.

Table 13-11 Device Settings

Setting	Action	Description
Device Class	Enable or Disable	Click Browse to select the enabled or disabled device class plus the device type, if required.
Device Type	Enable or Disable	If a device type is selected, it will appear in this field.

Folder Options

The Folder Options preference extension under Control Panel allows you to configure Folder, File, and Open With preference items.

Creating a Windows XP Folder Options Item

Windows XP Folder Options items apply only to computers running Windows Server 2003 and Windows XP. To create a new Windows XP Folder Options item, follow these steps:

1. Start Group Policy Management Console.
2. Right-click the GPO that will contain the new preference item, and then click Edit on the shortcut menu.
3. In the console tree under User Configuration, expand the Preferences folder, and then expand the Control Panel Settings folder.
4. Right-click Folder Options, point to New, and select Folders Options (Windows XP).
5. In the New Folder Options (Windows XP) Properties dialog box, shown in Figure 13-7, select the folder options for Group Policy to construct.

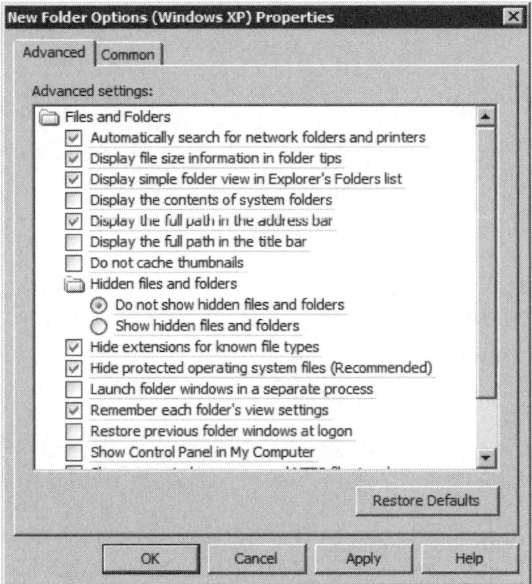

Figure 13-7 Selecting new folder options

6. Click the Common tab and select the options you want. (For more information, see "Configuring Common Options" earlier in this chapter.)
7. Click OK. The new preference item appears in the details pane.

Configuring a Windows Vista Folder Options Item

Windows Vista folder options apply only to computers running Windows Server 2008 and Windows Vista. To create a new Windows Vista Folder Options item, follow these steps:

1. Start Group Policy Management Console.
2. Right-click the Group Policy object (GPO) that will contain the new preference item, and then click Edit on the shortcut menu.
3. In the console tree under User Configuration, expand the Preferences folder, and then expand the Control Panel Settings folder.
4. Right-click Folder Options, point to New, and select Folders Options (Windows Vista).
5. In the New Folder Options (Windows Vista) Properties dialog box select the folder options for Group Policy to construct.
6. Click the Common tab and select the options you want. (For more information, see "Configuring Common Options" earlier in this chapter.)

7. Click OK. The new preference item appears in the details pane.

Configuring an Open With Item

An Open With preference item is a configured file association. To create an Open With preference item, follow these steps:

1. Start Group Policy Management Console.
2. Right-click the GPO that will contain the new preference item, and then click Edit on the shortcut menu.
3. In the console tree under User Configuration, expand the Preferences folder, and then expand the Control Panel Settings folder.
4. Right-click Folder Options, point to New, and select Open With.
5. In the New Open With Properties dialog box, select an action from the drop-down list:
   - ❑ **Create** Creates a new Open With association. If the file extension in the Open With item already exists in the user profile, the new association isn't created.
   - ❑ **Replace** Removes and re-creates an Open With association. The Replace action overwrites all existing settings in the Open With association. If the Open With association doesn't exist, Replace creates a new one.
   - ❑ **Update** Modifies an existing Open With association. Only the settings defined within the preference item are updated. If the Open With association doesn't exist, Update creates a new one.
   - ❑ **Delete** Removes an existing Open With association.
6. Enter the settings for the Open With association. Table 13-12 describes the available settings.
7. Click the Common tab and select the options you want. (For more information, see "Configuring Common Options" earlier in this chapter.)
8. Click OK. The new preference item appears in the details pane.

Table 13-12 Open With Settings

Setting	Action	Description
File Extension	All	Enter the file extension (without the period) to associate with the application specified. Press F3 for a list of variables that you can select for this field.

Table 13-12 **Open With Settings**

Setting	**Action**	**Description**
Associated Program	Create, Replace, or Update	Type the name of the application, including its path, to associate with the file extension.
Set As Default	Create, Replace, or Update	Select this option to make the association between the extension and the application the default.

Configuring a File Type Item

The File Type preference item allows you to manage and create file extensions associated with particular types of files. To create a File Type preference item, follow these steps:

1. Start Group Policy Management Console.
2. Right-click the GPO that will contain the new preference item, and then click Edit on the shortcut menu.
3. In the console tree under Computer Configuration, expand the Preferences folder, and then expand the Control Panel Settings folder.
4. Right-click Folder Options, point to New, and select File Type.
5. In the New File Type Properties dialog box, select an action from the drop-down list:
   - **Create** Creates a new file type association.
   - **Replace** Deletes and re-creates a file type association. The Replace action overwrites all settings of the existing file type association. If none exists, Replace creates a new one.
   - **Update** Modifies a file type association. Update changes only those settings defined within the preference item. If the file type association doesn't exist, Update creates a new one.
   - **Delete** Removes the specified file type association.
6. Enter the file type settings, which are described in Table 13-13.
7. Click the Common tab and select the options you want. (For more information, see "Configuring Common Options" earlier in this chapter.)

8. Click OK. The new preference item appears in the details pane.

Table 13-13 File Type Association Settings

Setting	Action	Description
File Extension	All	Enter the extension to associate with the application.
Associated Class	Create, Replace, or Update	Click the drop-down list and select the registered class to associate with the file type. Press F3 for a list of the variables that can be included in this field.
Configure Class Settings	Create, Replace, or Update	Select to configure advanced class settings. Icon File Path: To associate a particular icon with the file type, click Browse and navigate to the icon's location. The Icon Index field will be automatically filled. Actions: Click New to associate applications for this file type.

Internet Settings

The Internet Settings preference item allows you to configure Internet settings in different ways, including:

- Setting an initial configuration but allow users to make modifications
- Configuring some settings but allowing users to modify others

Creating an Internet Explorer 7 Item

A choice of actions is not available when making an Internet Explorer item because options can't be created, deleted, or replaced. They can only be updated.

To create a new Internet Explorer 7 preference item, follow these steps:

1. Start Group Policy Management Console.
2. Right-click the GPO that will contain the new preference item, and then click Edit on the shortcut menu.
3. In the console tree under User Configuration, expand the Preferences folder, and then expand the Control Panel Settings folder.
4. Right-click Internet Settings, point to New, and select Internet Explorer 7.
5. In the New Internet Explorer 7 Properties dialog box, shown in Figure 13-8, enter the options for Group Policy to configure.

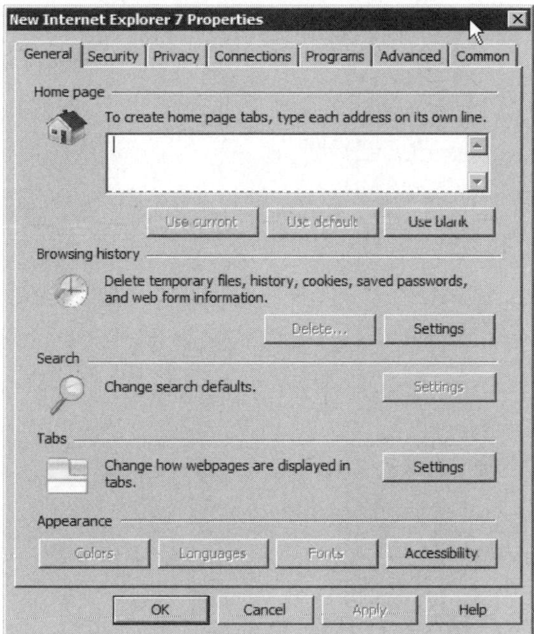

Figure 13-8 Configuring options for Internet Explorer 7

6. Click all tabs for the options available. Some settings cannot be set using a preference item and are unavailable. (For more information on the Common tab, see "Configuring Common Options" earlier in this chapter.)
7. Click OK. The new preference item appears in the details pane.

Creating an Internet Explorer 5 or 6 Item

A choice of actions is not available when making an Internet Explorer item because options can't be created, deleted, or replaced. They can only be updated.

To create a new Internet Explorer 5 or 6 preference item, follow these steps:

1. Start Group Policy Management Console.
2. Right-click the GPO that will contain the new preference item, and then click Edit on the shortcut menu.
3. In the console tree under User Configuration, expand the Preferences folder, and then expand the Control Panel Settings folder.
4. Right-click Internet Settings, point to New, and select Internet Explorer 5 And 6.
5. In the New Internet Explorer 5 And 6 Properties dialog box, as shown in Figure 13-9, enter the options for Group Policy to configure.

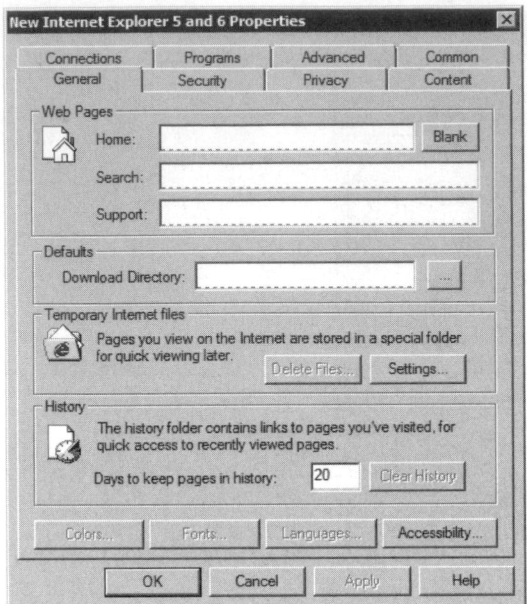

Figure 13-9 Configuring options for Internet Explorer 5 and 6

6. Click all tabs for the options available. Some settings cannot be set using a preference item and are unavailable. (For more information on the Common tab, see "Configuring Common Options" earlier in this chapter.)
7. Click OK. The new preference item appears in the details pane.

Local Users and Groups

Local Group preference items allow you to centrally create and manage local groups as well as change group memberships. Local User preference items include the ability to create and manage local users and change local user passwords.

Creating a Local User Item

To create a new Local User Preference item, follow these steps:

1. Start Group Policy Management Console.
2. Right-click the GPO that will contain the new preference item, and then click Edit on the shortcut menu.
3. In the console tree under Computer Configuration or User Configuration, expand the Preferences folder, and then expand the Control Panel Settings folder.
4. Right-click Local Users And Groups, point to New, and select Local User.

5. In the New Local User Properties dialog box, select an action from the drop-down list:
   - **Create** Creates a new local user on the local computer.
   - **Replace** Deletes and re-creates a local user with the same name on the local computer. Replace overwrites all the setting for the existing user. If the local user doesn't exist, Replace creates a new one. The Replace action will assign a new security identifier (SID) to the user, which may change the user's ability to access resources.
   - **Update** Renames a user or modifies user settings. Only the settings defined in the preference item will be affected. If the local user doesn't exist, Update creates a new one. The Update action does not change the user's SID.
   - **Delete** Removes a local user.
6. Enter the settings for the Local User preference item, which are described in Table 13-14.
7. Click the Common tab and select the options you want. (For more information, see "Configuring Common Options" earlier in this chapter.)
8. Click OK. The new preference item appears in the details pane.

Table 13-14 Local User Settings

Setting	Action	Description
User Name	All	Enter the name of the targeted user. If the user doesn't exist, a new user will be created. If the user exists, that user will be the target of the selected Action.
Rename To:	Update	Enter the new name for the local user.
Full Name	Create, Replace, or Update	Enter the full display name of the local user. Press F3 for a list of the variables that can be included in this field.
Description	Create, Replace, or Update	Enter any descriptive text needed for the local user. Press F3 for a list of the variables that can be included in this field.
Password and Confirm Password	Create, Replace, or Update	Type in the password. The password is encrypted when the preference item is saved. It is decrypted by the Local User client-side extension.

Table 13-14 Local User Settings

Setting	Action	Description
User Must Change Password At Next Logon, User Cannot Change Password, Password Never Expires	Create, Replace, or Update	Select the option you want for password handling.
Account Is Disabled	Create, Replace, or Update	Select this check box if the user account should be disabled.
Account Never Expires	Create, Replace, or Update	Use this setting if you don't want the account to expire. If the account has a specific lifespan, clear the check box and choose an expiration date from the Account Expires list.

Creating a Local Group Item

To create a new Local Group Preference item, follow these steps:

1. Start Group Policy Management Console.
2. Right-click the GPO that will contain the new preference item, and then click Edit on the shortcut menu.
3. In the console tree under Computer Configuration or User Configuration, expand the Preferences folder, and then expand the Control Panel Settings folder.
4. Right-click Local Users And Groups, point to New, and select Local Group.
5. In the New Local Group Properties dialog box, select an action from the drop-down list:
   - **Create** Creates a new local Group on the local computer.
   - **Replace** Deletes and re-creates a local Group with the same name on the local computer. Replace overwrites all the settings for the existing Group. If the local Group doesn't exist, Replace creates a new one. The Replace action will assign a new SID to the Group, which may change the Group's ability to access resources.
   - **Update** Renames a Group or modifies Group settings. Only the settings defined in the preference item will be affected. If the local Group doesn't exist, Update creates a new one. The Update action does not change the Group's SID.
   - **Delete** Removes a local Group.
6. Enter the settings for the Local Group preference item. Table 13-15 describes the available settings.

7. Click the Common tab and select the options you want. (For more information, see "Configuring Common Options" earlier in this chapter.)
8. Click OK. The new preference item appears in the details pane.

Table 13-15 **Local Group Settings**

Setting	Action	Description
Group Name	All	Enter the name of the local group. If the group doesn't exist, the preference item creates a new one.
Rename To: Update	Update	Enter the new name for the local group.
Description	Create, Replace, or Update	Enter any descriptive text needed for the local group. Press F3 for a list of the variables that can be included in this field.
Add The Current User	Create, Replace, or Update	Select to include the currently logged-on user as a member of the group. This option is available only when the preference item is created under User Configuration.
Remove The Current User	Create, Replace, or Update	Select to remove the currently logged-on user from membership in the group. This option is available only when the preference item is created under User Configuration.
Do Not Configure For The Current User	Create, Replace, or Update	Select to prevent the currently logged-on user from being added to or removed from the group.
Delete All Member Users	Create, Replace, or Update	Select to remove all user accounts from the group.
Delete All Member Groups	Create, Replace, or Update	Select to remove all group accounts from the local group.
Add	Create, Replace, or Update	Select to add users or groups to the members of the local group.
Remove	Create, Replace, or Update	Highlight a name in the members list and click Remove to delete the member from the member list.
Change	Create, Replace, or Update	Highlight a name in the members list and click Change to modify the member.

Network Options

The Network Options preference item includes configuration of virtual private network (VPN) connections and dial-up networking (DUN) connections.

Creating a New VPN Connection Item

To configure a new VPN connection item, follow these steps:

1. Start Group Policy Management Console.
2. Right-click the GPO that will contain the new preference item, and then click Edit on the shortcut menu.
3. In the console tree under Computer Configuration or User Configuration, expand the Preferences folder, and then expand the Control Panel folder.
4. Right-click Network Options, point to New, and then select VPN Connection.
5. In the New VPN Properties dialog box, select an action from the drop-down list:
   - **Create** Creates a new VPN connection.
   - **Replace** Deletes and re-creates a VPN connection. Replace overwrites all the existing settings of the existing connection. If the connection doesn't exist, Replace creates a new one.
   - **Update** Renames or changes an existing connection. Only settings within the preference item are updated; all other settings are unchanged. If the connection doesn't exist, Update creates a new one.
   - **Delete** Removes a connection.
6. Enter the VPN settings, which are described in Table 13-16.
7. Click the Options tab to select dialing and redialing settings.
8. Click the Security tab to set Typical or Advanced security settings for the VPN connection.
9. Click the Networking tab to select the type of VPN connection.
10. Click the Common tab and select the options you want. (For more information, see "Configuring Common Options" earlier in this chapter.)
11. Click OK. The new preference item appears in the details pane.

Table 13-16 VPN Options Settings

Setting	Action	Description
User Connection	All	Select this option to make the connection visible only to the applied user (or to delete a connection that is visible only to the applied user).

Table 13-16 **VPN Options Settings**

Setting	Action	Description
All Users Connection	All	Select this option to make the connection visible to all users on the computer (or to delete a connection visible to all users).
Connection Name	All	Enter connection name.
IP Address or Use DNS Name	Create, Replace, or Update	Type the IP address for the remote computer or select the Use DNS Name check box and type the fully qualified domain name of the remote computer.
Dial Another Connection First	Create, Replace, or Update	Enter the name of the dial-up network connection that is established prior to connecting to the VPN.
Show Icon In Notification Area When Connected	Create, Replace, or Update	Display an icon in the notification area while the connection is in use.

Creating a New DUN Connection Item

To create a new Dial-Up Networking Connection item, follow these steps:

1. Start Group Policy Management Console.
2. Right-click the GPO that will contain the new preference item, and then click Edit on the shortcut menu.
3. In the console tree under Computer Configuration or User Configuration, expand the Preferences folder, and then expand the Control Panel Settings folder.
4. Right-click Network Options, point to New, and then select DUN Connection.
5. In the New DUN Properties dialog box, select an action from the drop-down list:
   - **Create** Creates a new DUN connection.
   - **Replace** Deletes and re-creates a DUN connection. Replace overwrites all the existing settings of the existing connection. If the connection doesn't exist, Replace creates a new one.
   - **Update** Renames or changes an existing connection. Only settings within the preference item are updated; all other settings are unchanged. If the connection doesn't exist, Update creates a new one.
   - **Delete** Removes a connection.
6. Enter settings for the DUN connection. Table 13-17 describes the available settings.

7. Click the Common tab and select the options you want. (For more information, see "Configuring Common Options" earlier in this chapter.)
8. Click OK. The new preference item appears in the details pane.

Table 13-17 DUN Options Settings

Setting	Action	Description
User Connection	All	Select this option to make the connection visible only to the applied user (or to delete a connection that is visible only to the applied user).
All Users Connection	All	Select this option to make the connection visible to all users on the computer (or to delete a connection visible to all users).
Connection Name	All	Enter connection name.
Phone Number	Create, Replace, or Update	Type in the phone number the connection uses. Press F3 for a list of the variables that can be included in this field.

Power Options

The Power Options preference item configures how Windows Server 2003 and Windows XP respond to power events such as returning from standby, closing of portable computers, and using the sleep option. The Power Scheme item configures a group of power management settings grouped under a name.

Configuring a Windows XP Power Options Item

To configure a new Windows XP Power Options item, follow these steps:

1. Start Group Policy Management Console.
2. Right-click the GPO that will contain the new preference item, and then click Edit on the shortcut menu.
3. In the console tree under Computer Configuration or User Configuration, expand the Preferences folder, and then expand the Control Panel Settings folder.
4. Right-click Power Options, point to New, and then select Power Options (Windows XP).
5. In the New Power Options (Windows XP) Properties dialog box, select the settings you want to use for the preference item.

Table 13-18 **Local Printer Settings**

Setting	Action	Description
Printer Path	Create, Replace, or Update	Click Browse to select a fully qualified UNC path to a shared connection for the printer driver.
Set This Printer As The Default Printer	Create, Replace, or Update	Select this check box to make the local printer the default printer for the current user.
Location	Create, Replace, or Update	Enter a description of the printer's location. This appears in the printer's Location box. Press F3 to see a list of variables that can be selected for this field.
Comment	Create, Replace, or Update	Enter text that will appear in the printer's Comments box. Press F3 to see a list of variables that can be selected for this field.

Creating a Shared Printer Item

To create a new Shared Printer preference item, follow these steps:

1. Start Group Policy Management Console.
2. Right-click the GPO that will contain the new preference item, and then click Edit on the shortcut menu.
3. In the console tree under User Configuration, expand the Preferences folder, and then expand the Control Panel Settings folder.
4. Right-click Printers, point to New, and then select Shared Printer.
5. In the New Shared Printer Properties dialog box, select an action from the drop-down list:
   - **Create** Creates a new shared printer
   - **Replace** Deletes and re-creates the shared printer. Replace overwrites all settings associated with the printer. If the shared printer doesn't exist, Replace creates a new one.
   - **Update** Changes or renames a shared printer. Update changes only settings defined in the preference item. All other settings remain unchanged. If the shared printer doesn't exist, Update creates a new one.
   - **Delete** Removes a local printer. Delete doesn't remove the printer driver, just the printer.
6. Enter the local printer settings, which are described in Table 13-19.

7. Click the Common tab and select the options you want. (For more information, see "Configuring Common Options" earlier in this chapter.)
8. Click OK. The new preference item appears in the details pane.

Table 13-19 Shared Printer Settings

Setting	Action	Description
Share Path	All	Click Browse to choose a fully qualified UNC path of a shared printer.
Set This Printer As The Default Printer	Create, Replace, or Update	Select this option to make the printer the default printer for the current user.
Only If A Local Printer Is Not Present	Create, Replace, or Update	Check this box to avoid changing the default printer if a local printer is present. This setting is available only after you select Set This Printer As The Default Printer.
Delete All Shared Printer Connections	Delete	Delete all shared printer connections for the current user.
Local Port	All	To map the shared connection to a local port, select the port from the drop-down list. If you are deleting a preference item and a value is in the Local Port field, the shared printer connection associated with that local port will be deleted.
Reconnect	Create, Replace, or Update	Select to make the printer connection persistent.
Unmap All Local Ports	Delete	Select this option if you want to remove all shared connections from all local ports.

Note When processing shared printer preference items, the printer driver is always installed in the security context specified on the Common tab.

Creating a TCP/IP Printer Item

To configure a preference item for a local printer, follow these steps:

1. Start Group Policy Management Console.
2. Right-click the GPO that will contain the new preference item, and then click Edit on the shortcut menu.
3. In the console tree under Computer Configuration or User Configuration, expand the Preferences folder, and then expand the Control Panel Settings folder.
4. Right-click Printers, point to New, and then select TCP/IP Printer.

5. In the New TCP/IP Printer Properties dialog box, select an action from the drop-down list:
   - **Create** Creates a new TCP/IP printer connection.
   - **Replace** Deletes and re-creates the TCP/IP printer. Replace overwrites all settings associated with the printer connection. If the TCP/IP printer doesn't exist, Replace creates a new one.
   - **Update** Changes or renames a TCP/IP printer. Update changes only settings defined in the preference item. All other settings remain unchanged. If the TCP/IP printer doesn't exist, Update creates a new one.
   - **Delete** Removes a TCP/IP printer. Delete doesn't remove the printer driver or the port, just the printer connection.
6. Enter the TCP/IP printer settings, which are described in Table 13-20.
7. Click the Port Settings tab to set up port settings beyond the standard default settings.
8. Click the Common tab and select the options you want. (For more information, see "Configuring Common Options" earlier in this chapter.)
9. Click OK. The new preference item appears in the details pane.

Table 13-20 TCP/IP Printer Settings

Setting	Action	Description
IP Address or Use DNS Name	All	Type in the IP address of the printer or select the Use DNS Name check box and type in the fully qualified domain name of the printer.
Local Name	All	Enter the local name of the TCP/IP printer connection. If a printer connection with this name doesn't exist, the preference item creates a new one. Press F3 for a list of the variables that can be included in this field.
Printer Path	Create, Replace, or Update	Click Browse to choose a fully qualified UNC path of a shared printer connection. This is the installation source for the printer driver.
Set This Printer As The Default Printer	Create, Replace, or Update	Select this option to make the printer the default printer for the current user.
Only If A Local Printer Is Not Present	Create, Replace, or Update	Select this check box to avoid changing the default printer if a local printer is present. This setting is available only after you select Set This Printer As The Default Printer.

Table 13-20 TCP/IP Printer Settings

Setting	Action	Description
Delete All IP Printer Connections	Delete	Delete all TCP/IP printer connections for the current user.
Location	Create, Replace, or Update	Enter a description of the printer's location. This appears in the printer's Location box. Press F3 to see a list of variables that can be selected for this field.
Comment	Create, Replace, or Update	Enter text that will appear in the printer's Comments box. Press F3 to see a list of variables that can be selected for this field.

Regional Options

The Regional Options preference item configures the same values as in the Regional And Language Options in Control Panel. To create a new Regional Options preference item, follow these steps:

1. Start Group Policy Management Console.
2. Right-click the GPO that will contain the new preference item, and then click Edit on the shortcut menu.
3. In the console tree under User Configuration, expand the Preferences folder, and then expand the Control Panel Settings folder.
4. Right-click Regional Options, point to New, and then select Regional Options.
5. In the New Regional Options Properties dialog box, shown in Figure 13-10, select settings for Group Policy to configure. Click all tabs for the options available. Some settings cannot be set using a preference item and are unavailable. (For more information on the Common tab, see "Configuring Common Options" earlier in this chapter.)
6. Click OK. The new preference item appears in the details pane.

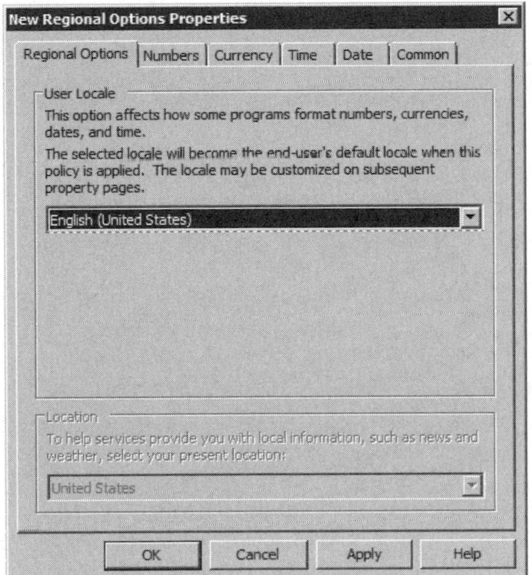

Figure 13-10 Configuring regional options

Note For more information, see the "Enable and Disable Preference Item Settings" sidebar later in this chapter.

Scheduled Tasks

Using the Schedules Tasks preference item, you can automate maintenance chores (virus scans, backups, disk cleanup, and so forth), refresh Group Policy and create a task to run immediately after the refresh (Windows XP), launch a process at user logon, and generally manage all sorts of scheduling tasks.

Configuring a New Scheduled Task

To create a new Scheduled Task, follow these steps:

1. Start Group Policy Management Console.
2. Right-click the GPO that will contain the new preference item, and then click Edit on the shortcut menu.
3. In the console tree under Computer Configuration or User Configuration, expand the Preferences folder, and then expand the Control Panel Settings folder.
4. Right-click Scheduled Tasks, point to New, and then select Scheduled Task.
5. In the New Task Properties dialog box, select an action from the drop-down list:

- **Create** Creates a new task for users or computers.
- **Replace** Deletes and re-creates scheduled tasks. Replace overwrites all settings associated with the task. If the scheduled task doesn't exist, Replace creates a new one.
- **Update** Changes settings of a scheduled task. Update changes only settings defined in the preference item. All other settings remain unchanged. If the scheduled task doesn't exist, Update creates a new one.
- **Delete** Removes a scheduled task.

6. Enter the task settings, which are described in Table 13-21.
7. Click all tabs for the options available. Some settings cannot be set using a preference item and are unavailable. (For more information on the Common tab, see "Configuring Common Options" earlier in this chapter.)
8. Click OK. The new preference item appears in the details pane.

Table 13-21 Scheduled Task Settings

Setting	Action	Description
Name	All	Enter a name for the scheduled task. This name will appear in the list of scheduled tasks in Control Panel. For all actions except Create, this name must match the name of the existing task.
Run	Create, Replace, or Update	Enter the name of the command to run or click Browse to navigate to the command.
Arguments	Create, Replace, or Update	Enter any needed command arguments.
Start In	Create, Replace, or Update	Enter the working directory for the command being launched.
Comments	Create, Replace, or Update	Enter a task description. The description is visible to users or computers where the item is applied.
Run As	Create, Replace, or Update	Configure the security context for the scheduled task, if it is to run in a security context other than the default. If the task is under User Configuration, the task runs by default in the security context of the logged-on user. If the task is under Computer Configuration, it's run by default in the security context of the SYSTEM account.
Enabled	Create, Replace, or Update	Select this check box to allow the task to run.

Configuring an Immediate Task (Windows XP) Item

Immediate Task preference items run immediately after the refresh of Group Policy and are then removed. You can configure Immediate Tasks for computers running Windows XP or Windows Server 2003.

> **Note** Immediate Task doesn't offer a choice of actions because these tasks are always newly created and then deleted after running.

To create an Immediate Task, follow these steps:

1. Start Group Policy Management Console.
2. Right-click the GPO that will contain the new preference item, and then click Edit on the shortcut menu.
3. In the console tree under Computer Configuration or User Configuration, expand the Preferences folder, and then expand the Control Panel Settings folder.
4. Right-click Scheduled Tasks, point to New, and then select Immediate Task (Windows XP).
5. In the New Immediate Task (Windows XP) Properties dialog box, enter the task settings, which are described in Table 13-22.
6. Click the Settings and Common tabs to enter additional settings. (For more information on the Common tab, see "Configuring Common Options" earlier in this chapter.)
7. Click OK. The new preference item appears in the details pane.

Table 13-22 Immediate Task Settings

Setting	Description
Name	Enter a name for the scheduled task. This name will appear in the list of immediate tasks in Control Panel.
Run	Enter the name of the command to run or click Browse to navigate to the command.
Arguments	Enter any arguments necessary to the command.
Start In	Enter the working directory for the command being launched.
Comments	Enter a description of the task. The description will be visible to users and computers.
Run As	Configure the security context for the task if it is to run in a security context other than the default. If the task is under User Configuration, the task runs by default in the security context of the logged-on user. If the task is under Computer Configuration, it's run by default in the security context of the SYSTEM account.

Services

You can configure existing services on computers using a Service preference item. To create a Service item, follow these steps:

1. Start Group Policy Management Console.
2. Right-click the GPO that will contain the new preference item, and then click Edit on the shortcut menu.
3. In the console tree under Computer Configuration, expand the Preferences folder, and then expand the Control Panel Settings folder.
4. Right-click Services, point to New, then select Service.
5. In the New Service Properties dialog box, select a service action from the Startup drop-down list:
   - **No Change** Do not modify the running status of the service.
   - **Automatic** The service starts during the boot and logon process.
   - **Manual** Service requires a manual start.
   - **Disabled** Service is disabled.
6. Enter the settings for the service, as described in Table 13-23.
7. Click the Recovery tab and select additional options, as described in Table 13-24.
8. Click the Common tab and select the options you want. (For more information, see "Configuring Common Options" earlier in this chapter.)
9. Click OK. The new preference item appears in the details pane.

Table 13-23 Service Settings (General Tab)

Setting	Description
Service Name	Click Browse to select a service from the list of installed services.
Service Action	Select the action for the named service.
Wait Timeout If Service Is Locked	If the service is locked or transitioning from one state to another, this option determines the amount of time the preference item will wait for availability.
Log On As No Change	The services logon credentials stay the same.
Log On As Local System Account	The services logon credentials will be set to the Local System account.

Table 13-23 Service Settings (General Tab)

Setting	Description
Allow Service To Interact With Desktop	This option is available after the Local System Account is selected. Select this check box if you want the service to be able to interact with the desktop.
Logon As: This Account	Click Browse and select the user name for the logon credentials.
Password and Confirm Password	Enter the password for the user account.

Table 13-24 Service Recovery Settings

Setting	Description
Select The Computer's Response If This Service Fails	No Change: Recovery action is unchanged. Take No Action: If the service fails, no action is taken. Restart The Service: If the service fails, the service is restarted. Restart The Computer: If the service fails, the computer is restarted.
Restart Fail Count After	Select the number of days for the fail count to restart. This setting available when at least one of the failure settings is set to Take No Action, Restart The Service, or Restart The Computer.
Restart Service After	Enter the number of minutes to wait before a failed service is restarted. This option is available only when Restart The Service is one of the failure responses.
Run Program	If one of the failure responses is set to Run A Program, click Browse and navigate to the application you want to run.
Append Fail Count To End Of Command Line	Select this check box if you want the fail count to be added to the command line.
Restart Computer Options	Click this button to select options for restarting the computer after the service fails.

Start Menu

Preference items for the Start Menu can be configured for Windows Vista and Windows XP. Start Menu items don't include a list of actions because Update is the only possible action.

Creating a Start Menu Item (Windows Vista)

To create a Start Menu item for Windows Vista, follow these steps:

1. Start Group Policy Management Console.

2. Right-click the GPO that will contain the new preference item, and then click Edit on the shortcut menu.
3. In the console tree under User Configuration, expand the Preferences folder, and then expand the Control Panel Settings folder.
4. Right-click Start Menu, point to New, and then select Start Menu (Windows Vista).
5. In the New Start Menu (Windows Vista) Properties dialog box, shown in Figure 13-11, select settings for Group Policy to configure. Click all tabs for the options available. Some settings cannot be set using a preference item and are unavailable. (For more information on the Common tab, see "Configuring Common Options" earlier in this chapter.)
6. Click OK. The new preference item appears in the details pane.

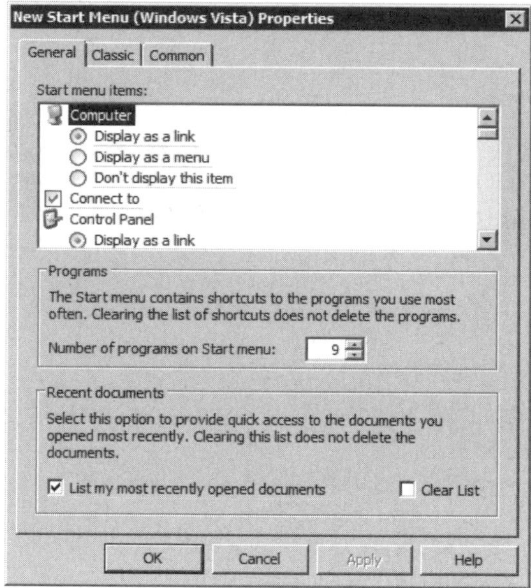

Figure 13-11 Selecting Start Menu settings for Windows Vista

Note For more information about the meaning of green and red markings in the selections, see the "Enable and Disable Preference Item Settings" sidebarlater in this chapter.

Creating a Start Menu Item (Windows XP)

To create a new Start Menu item for Windows XP, follow these steps:

1. Start Group Policy Management Console.

2. Right-click the GPO that will contain the new preference item, and then click Edit on the shortcut menu.
3. In the console tree under User Configuration, expand the Preferences folder, and then expand the Control Panel Settings folder.
4. Right-click Start Menu, point to New, and then select Start Menu (Windows XP).
5. In the New Start Menu (Windows XP) Properties dialog box, shown in Figure 13-12, select settings for Group Policy to configure. Click all tabs for the options available. Some settings cannot be set using a preference item and are unavailable. (For more information on the Common tab, see "Configuring Common Options" earlier in this chapter.)
6. Click OK. The new preference item appears in the details pane.

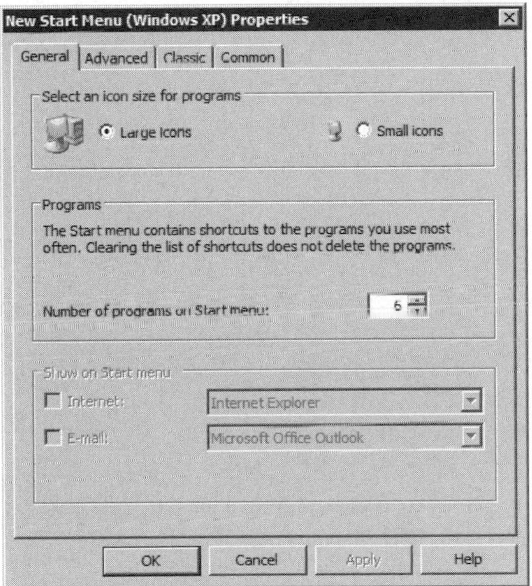

Figure 13-12 Creating a Start Menu preference item for Windows XP

Configuring a Targeting Item

To configure a preference item so that it targets only specific users or computers, follow these steps:

1. Start Group Policy Management Console.
2. In the console tree, right-click the GPO that should contain the new preference item, and select Edit from the shortcut menu.

3. In the console tree under Computer Configuration or User Configuration, expand the Preferences folder, and then browse to the preference extension.
4. Double-click the node for the preference extension, and then right-click the preference item and select Properties from the shortcut menu.
5. In the Properties dialog box, click the Common tab.
6. Select Item-level Targeting, and then click Targeting.
7. In the Targeting Editor dialog box, click New Item.
8. Click a type of targeting item, as shown in Figure 13-13, to apply to the preference item, and then configure settings for the targeting item.

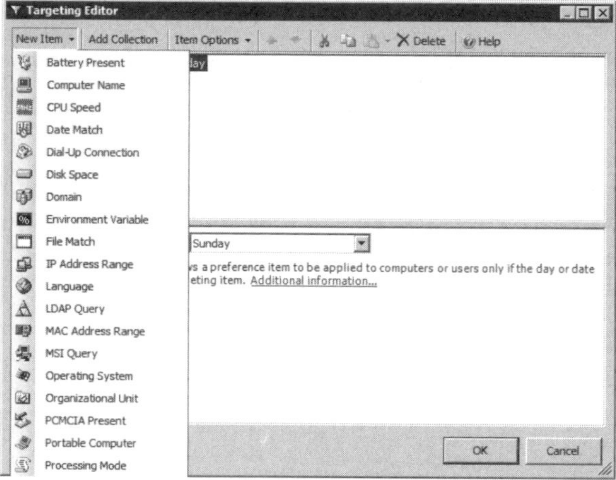

Figure 13-13 Selecting from the list of targeting items

Note To change the value of the targeting item to its opposite, click the Item Options menu and select Is Not from the drop-down list.

9. To configure multiple targeting items, click Item Options and select the logical operation for combining the preference item with the previous item.
10. Click OK twice to close the dialog boxes.

Note Text fields accept preference processing variables. Press F3 to display a list of variables from which you can select.

Enable and Disable Preference Item Settings

The underlining or circle of the setting indicates whether it is currently enabled or disabled:

1. A setting with a solid green underline or a green circle is enabled. The preference extension applies this setting's value to the user or computer.
2. A setting with a broken red underline or red circle with a slash is disabled. The preference extension does not apply this setting's value to the user or computer.

You can enable or disable these settings within a preference item by pressing the following function keys:

- **F5** Enable all settings on the current tab.
- **F6** Enable the currently selected setting.
- **F7** Disable the currently selected setting.
- **F8** Disable all settings on the current tab.

Delegating Permissions on GPOs

Not every network is of the size and complexity that requires delegation of permissions on GPOs. However, many networks *are* this complicated, so if you're considering handing off some of the responsibility for GPOs, keep the following issues in mind:

- If permission is set to inherit to all child containers, authority delegated at the domain level will affect all objects in the domain.
- Permissions granted at the OU level can affect just that OU or that OU plus its child OUs.
- Control delegated at the site level is likely to span domains and can influence objects in domains other than the domain where the GPO is located.
- Always assign control at the highest OU level possible.

Just about every chore connected with Group Policy can be delegated, including creating, editing, and managing GPOs. However, the right to edit, delete, or modify security is delegated separately from the right to link GPOs. And linking and editing GPOs are separate from permission to create GPOs.

Delegating Permission to Create

1. Open Group Policy Management Console and navigate to the domain where you want to grant permission. In the console tree, select Group Policy Objects.
2. Click the delegation tab, shown in Figure 13-14, and then click Add to identify the user or group you want to permit to create GPOs.

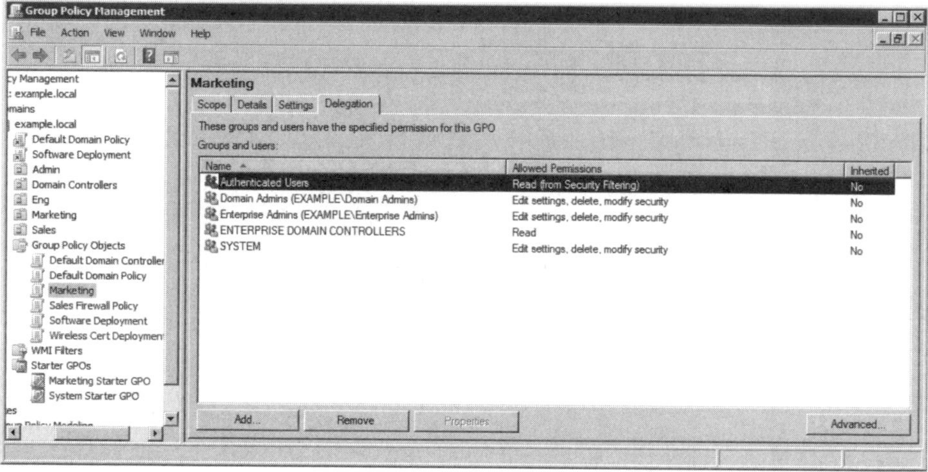

Figure 13-14 Delegation tab for a Group Policy Object

Delegating Permission to Link

1. Open Group Policy Management Console and navigate to the domain where you want to grant permission.
2. In the console tree, click the domain.
3. In the details pane, click the Delegation tab.
4. In the drop-down list, select Link GPOs and click Add to identify the user or group you want to give link permission.

Delegating Permission to Edit, Delete, or Modify Security

1. Open Group Policy Management Console, and navigate to the domain where you want to grant permission.
2. In the console tree, select the specific Group Policy Object.
3. In the details pane, click the Delegation tab.
4. Click the Add button to locate the user or group. In the Add Group Or User dialog box, select the range of permissions you want to delegate.

Disabling a Branch of a GPO

If a GPO has an entire node under User Configuration or Computer Configuration that's not configured, disable the node to avoid processing those settings. This speeds up startup and logon for all users subject to that GPO.

To disable a GPO node, follow these steps:

1. Open Group Policy Management Console.
2. In the console tree, expand Group Policy Objects.
3. Right-click the GPO that contains the user or computer settings you want to disable, point to GPO Status, and then choose one of the following options:
   - **User Configuration Settings Disabled** Select this option to disable user settings for the GPO.
   - **Computer Configuration Settings Disabled** Select this option to disable computer settings for the GPO.

Refreshing Group Policy

Policy changes are immediate, but they are not instantly propagated to clients. Client computers process a policy each time one of the following events happens:

- The computer starts.
- A user logs on.
- An application requests a refresh.
- A user requests a refresh.
- The Group Policy refresh interval has elapsed.

By default, client computers receive policy updates every 90 minutes, though to prevent multiple computers from refreshing at the same time, the actual refresh interval can vary from 90 to 120 minutes.

The value of shorter times between policy refreshes must be measured against the increase in network traffic generated as a result.

To change a Group Policy refresh interval, follow these steps:

1. Start Group Policy Management Console.
2. Right-click the GPO you want to edit and select Edit.

3. In the console tree, expand Computer Configuration, Policies, Administrative Templates, and then System, until you reach Group Policy.
4. In the details pane, double-click Group Policy Refresh Interval For Computers.
5. Click Enabled, specify the refresh interval, and then click OK.

Because policy can be set at several levels, when you click a policy object, you see both local policy and the policy in effect on the system. These might not be the same if the computer is inheriting settings from domain-level policies. If you make a policy setting and it isn't reflected in effective policy, a policy from the domain is overriding your setting. It's also possible that the policy change hasn't been refreshed since you made it. To force a policy refresh for the local computer, open a Command Window and type the following command:

```
gpupdate [/target:{computer | user}] /force
```

Use the *target* parameter if you want only computer settings or only user policy settings to be refreshed.

Backing Up a Group Policy Object

Regular backups of all GPOs should be part of your overall disaster planning strategy. To back up a GPO, follow these steps:

1. Open Group Policy Management Console.
2. In the console tree, navigate to Group Policy Objects in the domain that contains the GPO to be backed up.
3. To back up a single GPO, right-click the GPO and select Back Up from the shortcut menu. To back up all GPOs in the domain, right-click Group Policy Objects and select Back Up All.
4. In the Back Up Group Policy Object dialog box, type the path to the backup location and then click Back Up.
5. After the operation completes, click OK.

Restoring a Group Policy Object

To restore backed-up GPOs, follow these steps:

1. Open Group Policy Management Console.
2. In the console tree, navigate to Group Policy Objects in the domain that contains the GPO that you want to restore.

3. To restore a previous version of an existing GPO or to restore a deleted GPO, right-click Group Policy Objects and select Manage Backups.
4. In the Manage Backups dialog box, select the GPO to restore and click the Restore button.

When you have a lot of GPOs to sort through, select the box to display only the latest versions of the backed-up GPOs. If you're unsure which GPO to restore, highlight them one at a time and click View Settings.

Note A deleted GPO can't be restored if it has never been backed up, which is why you are wise to back up GPOs on a regular schedule. And don't wait for the schedule when you make major changes in a GPO. Back it up at once.

Using Group Policy for Folder Redirection

Folder Redirection is an extension to Group Policy that allows you to place folders that you choose on the network. For example, you might want to redirect users' Documents folders that can become quite large over time. This feature has real benefits, including:

- Users can log on to different computers and still have access to the redirected folders.
- If you use roaming profiles, only the network path to the redirected folders is part of the user profile, making logging on and off much faster.
- Folders on a network server can be backed up as part of routine maintenance without the users having to do anything extra.

Folders can be redirected to one location for everyone in the Active Directory container affected by the GPO. They can also be redirected to different locations according to security group membership.

Redirecting to One Location

By far, the most common form of redirection is to send everyone's Documents folder to a single location on a network server. The following steps show how to do this (you can substitute other Windows special folders in the steps to redirect them as well):

1. Create a shared folder on the server.

   Insert a dollar sign ($) at the end of the share name for the folder on the server to prevent the folder from appearing in the Network folder. It will also hide the folder from casual browsers.
2. Open the GPO linked to the Active Directory container containing the users whose folders are to be redirected.

3. In the console tree, click User Configuration, then click Policies, Windows Settings, and then click Folder Redirection.
4. Right-click Documents and choose Properties from the shortcut menu.
5. On the Target tab, select Basic–Redirect Everyone's Folder To The Same Location. Choose the Target folder location that coincides with the new shared folder on the server and provide a root path.
6. Click the Settings tab. The following settings are enabled by default:
   - **Grant The User Exclusive Rights To Documents** The user and the local system have exclusive rights to the folder. No administrative rights are enabled. If this setting is disabled, the permissions that exist on the folder in its present position remain.
   - **Move The Contents Of Documents To The New Location** The contents of the user's current Documents folder are sent to the new location. If this option is disabled, the user has a new, but empty, Documents folder at the new location.
   - **Policy Removal** The default is to leave the folder in the new location when the policy is removed. If you choose to redirect the folder back to the local user, see the "Removing Redirection" section later in this chapter.
7. Click OK when finished.

Redirecting by Group Membership

Special folders can also be redirected based on the user's membership in security groups. To do so, follow these steps:

1. Create the shared folders at the locations to which the folders will be redirected.
2. Open the GPO linked to the site, domain, domain controller, or OU containing the users whose folders are to be redirected.
3. In the console tree, click User Configuration, then click Policies, Windows Settings, then click Folder Redirection.
4. Right-click the special folder (in this case, Documents), and choose Properties from the shortcut menu.
5. In the drop-down list, select Advanced – Specific Locations For Various User Groups, and then click Add.
6. In the Specify Group And Location dialog box, type the security group and the location for the redirected folders. Always use a UNC path, even if the folders are to be on the local computer, so that roaming users will be able to see their folders.
7. Click OK. Add more groups and locations as needed.

8. Click the Settings tab. The following settings are enabled by default:
   - **Grant The User Exclusive Rights To My Documents** The user and the local system have exclusive rights to the folder. No administrative rights are enabled. If this setting is disabled, the permissions that exist on the folder in its present position remain.
   - **Move The Contents Of Documents To The New Location** The contents of the user's current Documents folder will be sent to the new location. If this option is disabled, the user will have a new, but empty, Documents folder at the new location.
   - **Policy Removal** The default is to leave the folder in the new location when the policy is removed. If you choose to redirect the folder back to the local user, see the "Removing Redirection" section later in the chapter.
9. Click OK when you're finished.

Removing Redirection

When folders have been redirected and later the policy changes, the effect on the folders depends on the combination of choices made on the Settings tab in the special folder's Properties dialog box. Table 13-25 shows the various combinations of settings and the outcome when the policy is changed. (Software policy settings are covered in Chapter 28.)

Table 13-25 Settings and Outcomes When Redirection Is Removed

Policy Removal Option	Move Contents of Folder to New Location	Outcome When Policy Is Removed
Redirect The Folder Back To The Local User Profile Location When Policy Is Removed.	Enabled	The folder returns to its user profile location, the contents of the folder are copied back to the original location, and the contents are not deleted from the redirected location.
Redirect The Folder Back To The Local User Profile Location When Policy Is Removed.	Disabled	The folder returns to its user profile location and the contents of the folder are not moved or copied back to the original location. Warning: This means the user cannot see the folder contents.
Leave The Folder In The New Location When Policy Is Removed.	Enabled or Disabled	The folder and its contents remain at the redirected location and the user has access to the contents at the redirected location.

Using Resultant Set of Policy (RSoP)

The Resultant Set of Policy (RSoP) tool gathers information on all existing policies to determine the policies in effect and the order in which they are applied.

RSoP has two modes: logging mode and planning mode. In planning mode, RSoP helps construct a "what if" scenario so that you can test the effect of a new policy or test policy precedence. In logging mode, RSoP can tell you what policies are being applied to a particular user and can help you discover policies that should be removed or repaired.

Running an RSoP Query

An RSoP query can be run on a site, a domain, a computer account, a user account, or an OU. Both planning mode and logging mode have options to assist in configuring your query.

Note To query a site, open Active Directory Sites And Services, right-click the site, select All Tasks, and then select Resultant Set Of Policy.

A Planning RSoP

The planning mode in RSoP simulates the effect of change on your system. If you're thinking of moving, adding, or deleting a group or making any changes to group policy, RSoP tells you what the result of proposed changes will look like. When you select Planning Mode as described in the previous section, the Resultant Set Of Policy Wizard starts, and leads you through the follow steps:

1. On the User And Computer Selection page of the Resultant Set Of Policy Wizard, use the Browse buttons to specify the user, computer, or container to be analyzed, and then click Next. The following simulation options are on the Advanced Simulation Options page:
   - **Slow Network Connection** Some policies do not apply when a dial-up or other slow connection is used. Choose this option to simulate a slow connection.
   - **Loopback Processing** If you're in a situation where you must modify the user policy based on the computer the user logs on to, loopback processing simulates the application of the GPOs to any user who logs on to a computer controlled by alternate user policy settings. You can choose to replace the user's usual policies or merge the new with the existing policies.
   - **Site** Specifies the site and physical location of the subnet to use. Use this setting to test startup or logon events on a different subnet.
2. After making your selections, click Next.
3. To simulate changes to the user or computer location, enter the new location and click Next.

4. In the list of Security groups, add or remove groups to simulate the result of policies based on changes in security group membership. Click Next.
5. On the next page, Computer Security Groups, you can simulate changes to the computer's security group memberships. Click Next.
6. On the WMI Filters For Users page, you can link Windows Management Instrumentation (WMI) filters to arrive at resulting policy based on whether the user meets the criteria specified in all or some WMI filters. Click Next.
7. On the WMI Filters For Computers page, you can link Windows Management Instrumentation (WMI) filters to arrive at resulting policy based on selected information such as installed software. Click Next.
8. The next page summarizes the selections made so far. Review it carefully. This wizard has a lot of steps, and one error can make the results useless.
9. Click Next. When the operation is complete, select Finish.

The RSoP will appear in a Microsoft Management Console, which you can examine, compare to other RSoP planning results, and save for future reference.

A Logging RSoP

In logging mode, RSoP reports on current policy settings as they apply to users and computers. Planning mode shows the administrator the outcome of a possible future change, but logging mode is all about what's going on now. A logging RSoP is what you need to discover which policies are applied to a particular user or computer or to investigate why certain policies are not working as expected.

In the Group Policy Management Console, right-click Group Policy Results to launch the Group Policy Results Wizard.

> **Note** To run RSoP on a remote computer, you must be a member of Domain Admins, be a member of Enterprise Admins, or have had the right to generate RSoP delegated to you. You must be a member of Enterprise Admins to cross domain boundaries in a forest.

Summary

This chapter covered details of Group Policy and Group Policy Objects, all in pursuit of organizing and centralizing security and other settings. In the next chapter, we address the common daily chores an administrator inherits, and how to simplify them where possible.

Part III
Administer the Network

Chapter 14

Managing Daily Operations

A network administrator's job consists of masses of details, and if you're going to cope, you must find ways to handle and track them. Windows Server 2008 supplies plenty of tools for doing this, including tools that allow you to delegate tasks to other users or groups, use scripts to automate tasks, and schedule tasks to run periodically.

Nevertheless, administering a network is still largely a process of planning and organization, and in that area there's no substitute for brain power. This chapter discusses some of the tools that can help in the daily business of network management.

User Account Control (UAC) for Administration

In the never-ending struggle to persuade administrators to not use administrative accounts all the time, Windows Server 2008 introduces User Account Control (UAC). UAC allows an administrator to log on as a non-administrator user and still do occasional administrative tasks without having to switch users, log off, or use the Run As command. UAC can also require administrators to expressly approve applications that will make system-wide changes before those applications are permitted to run, even in the administrator's user session. The primary goal of User Account Control is to reduce the system's exposure to attack.

UAC prompts are very common when first using Windows Server 2008 because many system-wide changes occur during initial configuration. The prompts diminish over time as fewer changes occur.

UAC appears in both Windows Server 2008 and Windows Vista, although the default configurations differ in three ways:

- The Admin Approval Mode (AAM), by default, is not enabled for the Built-in Administrator Account in either Windows Server 2008 or Windows Vista.

- The Built-in Administrator account is disabled by default in Windows Vista, the first user account created is placed in the local Administrators group, and AAM is enabled for that account.
- The Built-in Administrator account is enabled by default in Windows Server 2008 and AAM is disabled for this account.

The Admin Approval Mode (AAM)

The Admin Approval Mode (AAM) is a UAC configuration in which an administrator receives two separate access tokens when logging onto a Windows Server 2008 computer.

The principal difference between a standard user and an administrator in Windows Server 2008 is the level of access the user has over protected areas of the computer. Administrators can install drivers and services, turn the firewall off, set security policies, change the system state, and perform other tasks that standard users can't.

When AAM is enabled, a full access token and a second filtered access token are granted to the administrator during the logon process. The filtered access token is used to start Explorer.exe, the process that creates and owns the user's desktop. Because applications normally inherit their access tokens from the process that starts them, which in this case is Explorer.exe, they all run with the filtered access token as well. The full access token isn't used until the administrator attempts to perform an administrative task.

Just by the nature of how servers are used, administrators log on to a server much more often than to a client workstation. So AAM is disabled by default for the Built-In Administrator account in Windows Server 2008. AAM is *enabled* for other members of the local Administrators group. When a standard user logs on, only one user access token is created, which grants no more access privileges than an administrator's filtered access token.

UAC and Registry Virtualization

Because User Access Control is new to Windows Server 2008 and Windows Vista, some of your applications will be non-UAC compliant and may require an administrator's access token to run correctly. Left alone, these applications will fail silently or fail intermittently. For these applications, Windows Server 2008 includes file and registry virtualization to make sure that applications that are not UAC compliant are compatible with Windows Server 2008.

How It Works

When a noncompliant application attempts to write to a protected resource, UAC provides a virtualized view of the resource it is attempting to change, using a copy-on-write strategy. The virtualized copy is maintained under the user's profile. So a virtualized copy of the file is created for each user that runs the noncompliant application.

While this works effectively, it's not a long-term solution. Over time, developers will modify applications to meet the requirements of UAC.

Disabling Aspects of User Account Control

Needless to say, every time you disable some part of User Access Control, you are decreasing in some amount the security of your computers. However, there's also no point in pretending that everyone will leave every feature in place. In the next sections, we cover these operations, which we're sure you will approach with caution.

Disabling Admin Approval Mode

To disable the Admin Approval Mode, you must be logged on with an account that has administrative privileges, and then follow these steps:

1. Select Run from the Start menu.
2. In the Open box, type **secpol.msc** and then click OK.
3. If the User Account Control dialog box appears, confirm that the action it displays is what you want, and then click Continue.
4. From the Local Security Policy console tree, expand Local Policies, and then expand Security Options.
5. Scroll down and double-click User Account Control: Run All Administrators In Admin Approval Mode.
6. Select the Disabled option, and then click OK.
7. Close the Local Security Policy window.

Changing the Behavior of the Elevation Prompt

You can change how the elevation prompt behaves with the following procedures. First, for administrators, follow these steps:

1. Select Run from the Start menu.
2. In the Open box, type **secpol.msc** and then click OK.
3. If the User Account Control dialog box appears, confirm that the action it displays is what you want, and then click Continue.
4. From the Local Security Policy console tree, expand Local Policies, and then expand Security Options.

5. Scroll down to and double-click User Account Control: Behavior Of The Elevation Prompt For Administrators In Admin Approval Mode
6. From the drop-down menu, select one of the following settings:
   - **Elevate Without Prompting** Tasks requesting elevation will automatically run as elevated without prompting the administrator.
   - **Prompt For Credentials** This setting requires a user name and password before an application or task will run as elevated.
   - **Prompt For Consent** This is the default setting for administrators.
7. Click OK.
8. Close the Local Security Policy window.

To change the behavior of the elevation prompt for standard users, follow these steps:

1. Select Run from the Start menu.
2. In the Open box, type **secpol.msc** and then click OK.
3. If the User Account Control dialog box appears, confirm that the action it displays is what you want, and then click Continue.
4. From the Local Security Policy console tree, expand Local Policies, and then expand Security Options.
5. Scroll down to and double-click User Account Control: Behavior Of The Elevation Prompt For Standard Users.
6. From the drop-down menu, select one of the following settings:
   - **Automatically Deny Elevation Requests** Standard users will not be able to run programs requiring elevation, and will not be prompted.
   - **Prompt For Credentials** This setting requires user name and password input before an application or task will run as elevated.
   - **Prompt For Consent** This is the default setting for administrators.
7. Click OK.
8. Close the Local Security Policy window.

Disabling UAC Prompts to Install Applications

To disable UAC prompts to install applications, follow these steps:

1. Select Run from the Start menu.
2. In the Open box, type **secpol.msc** and then click OK.
3. If the User Account Control dialog box appears, confirm that the action it displays is what you want, and then click Continue.

4. From the Local Security Policy console tree, expand Local Policies, and then expand Security Options.
5. Scroll down and double-click User Account Control: Detect Application Installations And Prompt For Elevation.
6. Select the Disabled option, and then click OK.
7. Close the Local Security Settings window.

Configuring an Application to Always Run Elevated

To configure an application to always run elevated, follow these steps:

1. Right-click an application that is not likely to have been assigned an administrative token, such as a word-processing application.
2. Click Properties, and then click the Compatibility tab.
3. In the Privilege Level area, select Run This Program As An Administrator, as shown in Figure 14-1, and then click OK.

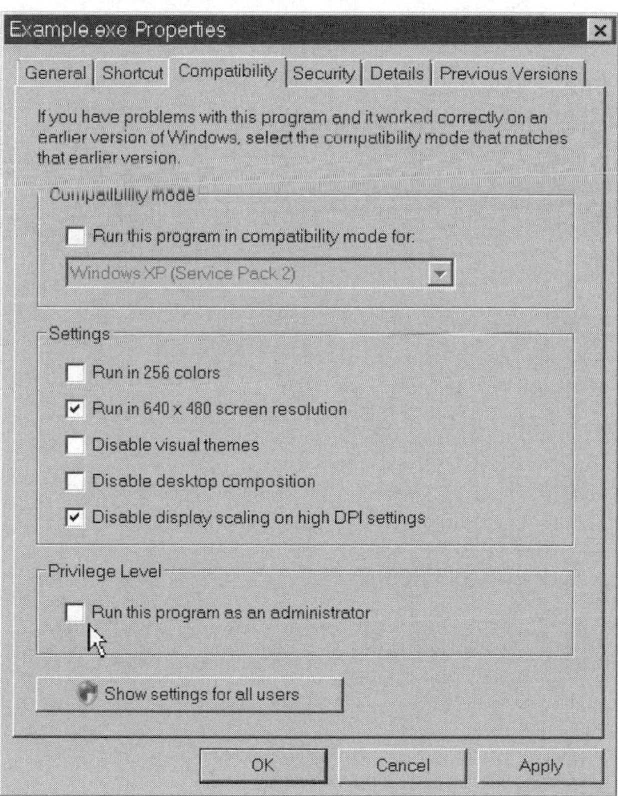

Figure 14-1 Configuring an application to run as administrator

Note If the Run This Program As An Administrator option is unavailable, several explanations are possible: The application is blocked from always running elevated; the application does not require administrative credentials to run; the application is part of the current version of Windows Vista; or you are not logged on to the computer as an administrator.

Turning Off UAC

To turn of UAC, you must be able to log on with or provide the credentials of a member of the local Administrators group.

Important Turning of UAC will expose your computer to increased risk. It is not a good idea to leave UAC disabled any longer than necessary.

To turn off UAC, follow these steps:

1. Open Control Panel.
2. Click User Accounts.
3. Under Make Changes To Your User Account, click Turn User Account Control On Or Off, as shown in Figure 14-2.

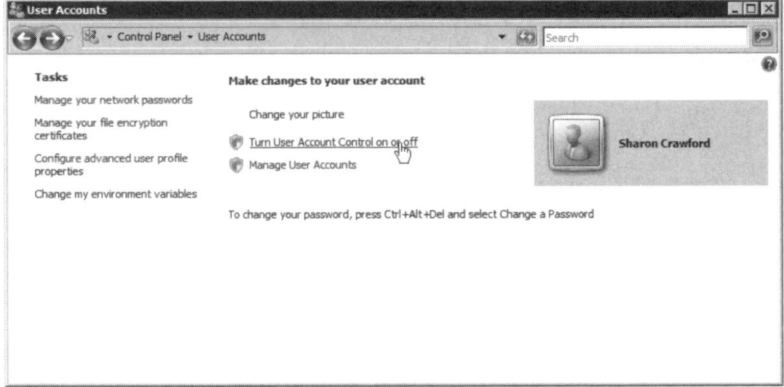

Figure 14-2 Navigating to User Account Control

4. On the Turn User Account Control On Or Off page, shown in Figure 14-3, clear the Use User Account Control (UAC) To Help Protect Your Computer check box and then click OK.

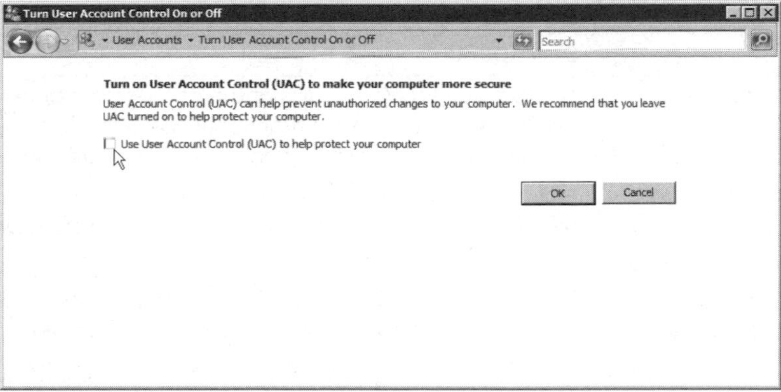

Figure 14-3 Clear the check box to disable UAC

5. You'll be prompted to restart Windows to apply the change. Click Restart Now or Restart Later.
6. Close User Accounts.

Using Microsoft Management Console 3.0

Microsoft Management Console (MMC) is the framework for displaying administrative tools that configure the hardware, software, and network components of Windows Server. These tools, called *snap-ins*, are created by Microsoft and other software vendors. Server Manager in Windows Server 2008 is an expanded instance of MMC. From a user's point of view, the most obvious change in MMC 3.0 is the Actions pane, which replaces the old taskpad views, although you can still create taskpad views. (For more details, see "Using the New Taskpad View Wizard" later in this chapter.)

Setting MMC 3.0 Console Options

When creating a custom MMC console, you can set the console to either author mode or one of three types of user mode. Table 14-1 describes the options.

Table 14-1 MMC Console Modes

Option	Description
Author mode	This mode has no restrictions. The user can access all parts of the console tree as well as change this console file at will. The completed console is usually saved in one of the user modes.

Table 14-1 MMC Console Modes

Option	Description
User mode/full access	The user can access all parts of the console tree but cannot make changes that affect functionality. Cosmetic changes, such as the arrangement of windows, are saved automatically.
User mode/limited access, multiple window	Provides access only to those parts of the tree that were visible when the console was saved. Users can create new windows, but can't close existing windows.
User mode/limited access, single window	Provides access only to those parts of the tree that were visible when the console was saved. Users can't create new windows.

Consoles are opened by default in author mode, if any of the following conditions apply:

- A console is opened at the command prompt with the */a* option.
- You open a console by right-clicking the saved file and selecting Author from the shortcut menu.
- MMC is already open when a snap-in console is opened.

Creating an MMC Console with Snap-Ins

Building your own tools with the MMC standard user interface is a straightforward process. The next few sections walk you through the creation of a new console and describe how to arrange its administrative components into separate windows.

> **Note** In the following steps, you should *not* maximize the console window or any other window in the MMC you are creating.

To create an MMC Console, follow these steps:

1. Click Start and select Run. In the Open text box, type **mmc /a** and then click OK. An empty MMC window opens, ready for you to add snap-ins.
2. From the File menu, select Add/Remove Snap-In. (The menu commands on the menu bar at the top of the MMC window apply to the entire console.)
3. The Add Or Remove Snap-In dialog box opens, as shown in Figure 14-4. Here you can choose which snap-ins to place in the console file and enable extensions. Click OK when finished.

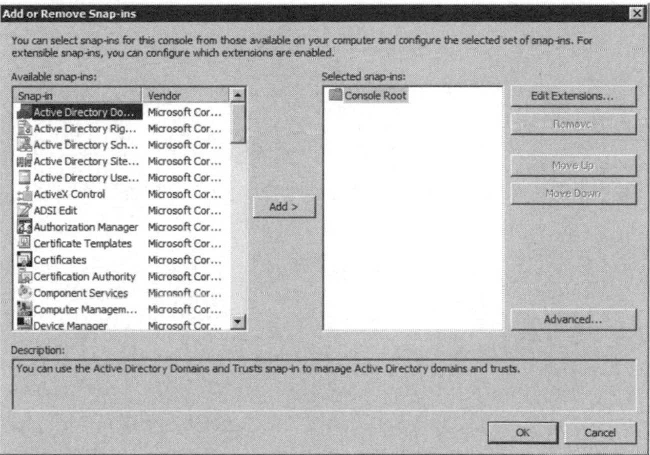

Figure 14-4 Choosing snap-ins for an MMC console

4. Click the File menu and select Options.
5. Enter a new name for the console.
6. Using the drop-down list, choose the mode for the saved console.
7. If the default mode for the console is one of the user modes, select the Do Not Save Changes To This Console check box. This will prevent users from editing the console. Select the Allow The User To Customize Views check box to enable users to access the Customize View dialog box.

Using the New Taskpad View Wizard

The New Taskpad View Wizard isn't new. In fact, it's an old way to create a customized taskpad view for a tree item in a console. To create a customized view, follow these steps:

1. Start an MMC console.
2. Select New Taskpad View from the Action menu to start the New Taskpad View Wizard. Click Next.
3. On the Taskpad Style page, select the styles you want for the Results pane and the task description. As you change selections, the display changes to show how that choice affects the display. Click Next.
4. On the Taskpad Reuse page, indicate whether the view you've selected will apply to this console only or to all tree items that are of the same type. Click Next.
5. On the Name And Description page, accept the default name or provide a new name for the taskpad. Click Next.

6. Click Finish and proceed to adding new tasks. The New Task Wizard starts. Click Next.
7. Select the type of command you want to use. Click Next.
8. Supply the specifics for the command you choose. Click Next.
9. On the Name And Description page, accept the default name or provide a name for the task. Click Next.
10. On the Task Icon page, select an icon for the task. Click Next and then Finish.

Distributing and Using Consoles

The default location for saved console files is the Administrative Tools folder. You can distribute console files in a variety of ways. You can copy a console file to a shared folder on the network, or you can mail it to another person by right-clicking the file, pointing to Send To, and selecting Mail Recipient. When you assign a console to be used by a particular person, be sure that the person's user profile includes permission to access the tools and services in the console. The user also has to have any administrative permissions necessary to use the system components administered by the console.

If you know the location of a console, you can open it using Windows Explorer by clicking it as you would any other file. You can also open it from the command line. For example, to open the DHCP management console from the command line, type **dhcpmgmt.msc**. (For consoles that are not on your path, you'll need to specify the path to the console.)

Using MMC for Remote Administration

MMC-based tools are admirably suited for remote administration. You can easily construct a console to administer a number of computers or a single computer. This section describes how to create a console that can be used to remotely administer another computer. The console in this example includes the Services snap-in, which manages system services, and the Event Viewer snap-in, which allows access to the various event logs. To create this remote administration console, follow these steps:

1. Click Start, and then select Run. In the Open text box, type **mmc** and then click OK.
2. From the File menu, select Add/Remove Snap-In.
3. In the Add Or Remove Snap-Ins dialog box, highlight Services and click Add.
4. In the Services dialog box, select the computer you want the snap-in to manage. Click Finish.
5. In the Add Or Remove Snap-Ins dialog box, highlight Event Viewer and click Add.

6. Again specify the computer you want to manage. Click OK.
7. In the Add Or Remove Snap-Ins dialog box, click OK.

Expand any of the snap-ins to view the information from the remote computer. Figure 14-5 shows details of the security log on the remote computer.

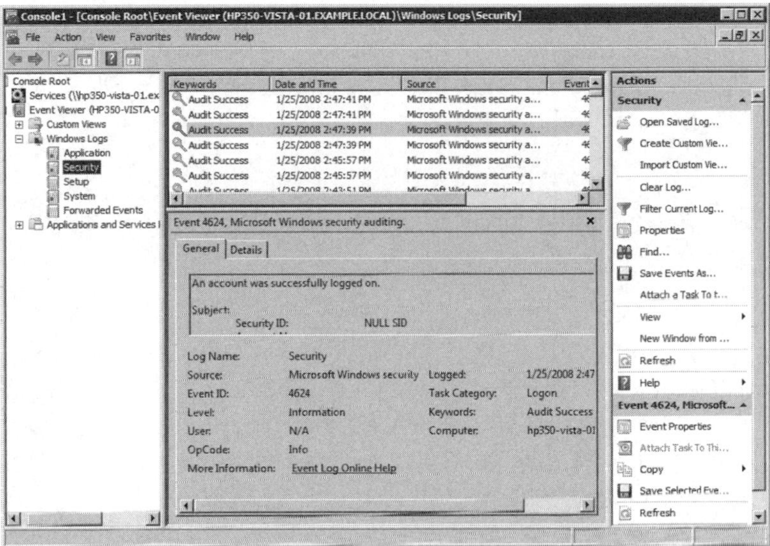

Figure 14-5 Viewing the security log on a remote computer

Setting Auditing Policy

Auditing certain computers, users, and operating system events is a necessary part of network administration. You choose what to audit and then review the event logs to track usage patterns, security problems, and network traffic trends. Beware of the impulse to audit everything, however. The more events you audit, the bigger the logs will be.

Reviewing huge event logs is a painful chore, and eventually no one looks at them anymore. These logs can take up enormous amounts of space. Therefore, it's critical to choose an auditing policy that protects your network without creating a large administrative burden. Also bear in mind that every audited event results in a small increase in performance overhead.

An auditing policy identifies the categories of security-related events that you want to audit. By default, all auditing categories are disabled when Windows Server 2008 is installed.

Each audit setting has three options:

- **Success** When the requested action succeeds, an audit entry is generated.
- **Failure** When the requested action fails, an audit entry is generated.
- **No Auditing** No audit entry is generated for the associated action.

Exposure

When no auditing is selected, establishing what occurred during a security incident can be quite difficult. However, if too many authorized activities generate events, the Security event log will collect masses of useless data. Overall computer performance will be affected if you configure too many audit settings.

Defenses

You need sensible Audit Policy settings for all computers in your organization so that unauthorized activity can be detected and tracked.

Likely Effect

If too few audit settings are configured on the computers in your organization when a security attack occurs, not enough information will be available for you to determine what happened. On the other hand, if audit settings are too strict, critically important entries in the Security log can be overwhelmed by all of the irrelevant entries, and computer performance may be negatively affected.

Auditing Categories

Policy settings for auditing fall into the categories described in the following sections. Some information can be garnered from every category but, depending on your situation, only a few categories will generate useful data. The use of subcategories is helpful to refine auditing.

Account Logon Events

Account logon events occur when a domain controller receives a logon request. A setting to log successes creates an entry when an account logon succeeds. Failure audits generate an audit entry when an account logon attempt fails, which is helpful for intrusion detection. If you log successful account logon audit events on a domain controller, workstation logon attempts do not generate logon audits. Only interactive and network logon attempts to the domain controller itself generate logon events on the domain controller.

This setting creates the potential for a denial of service attack if you enable the Audit: Shut Down System Immediately If Unable To Log Security Audits setting. An attacker could generate millions of logon failures and force the computer to shut down.

Account Logon Events has the following subcategories:

- Kerberos Service Ticket Operations
- Other Account Logon Events
- Kerberos Authentication Service
- Credential Validation

Account Management

This policy setting controls whether to audit each account management event–when a user account or group is created, modified, or deleted or a password is set or changed. A Success setting will record a log entry when any account management event succeeds. Failure audits generate an audit entry when any account management event fails.

Account Management has the following subcategories:

- User Account Management
- Computer Account Management
- Security Group Management
- Distribution Group Management
- Application Group Management
- Other Account Management Events

Directory Service Access

This setting determines whether to audit when a user accesses an AD DS (Active Directory Directory Services) object with a System Access Control List (SACL).If you enable this policy setting and configure SACLs on directory objects, many entries will be generated in the Security logs on domain controllers. Don't enable this policy unless you know what you plan to do with all those entries.

> **Note** To configure a SACL on an Active Directory object, right-click the object, select Properties, and then click the Security tab. This process is similar to Audit Object Access, except that it applies only to Active Directory objects and not to file system and registry objects.

Directory Service Access has the following subcategories:

- Directory Service Access
- Directory Service Changes
- Directory Service Replication
- Detailed Directory Service Replication

These subcategories are discussed in "Auditing Directory Service Events" later in this chapter.

Logon Events

This setting is activated when a user logs on or logs off the computer that records the event. A log entry is created when a logon event succeeds or fails on the computer. This setting also creates the possibility of a denial of service attack in the same way the Account Logon setting can.

Logon Events has the following subcategories:

- Logon
- Logoff
- Account Lockout
- IPsec Main Mode
- IPsec Quick Mode
- IPsec Extended Mode
- Special Logon
- Other Logon/Logoff Events
- Network Policy Server

Object Access

A Success setting generates a log entry when a user successfully accesses an object with an associated SACL. A Failure setting likewise generates a log entry when a user unsuccessfully attempts to audit an object with an associated SACL

If you configure the Audit Object Access policy setting and configure SACLs on objects, many entries will be generated in the Security logs on domain controllers. Enable this auditing only if you know what you plan to do with the large volume of entries.

Object Access has the following subcategories:

- File system
- Registry
- Kernel Object
- SAM
- Certification Services
- Application Generated
- Handle Manipulation

- File Share
- Filtering Platform Packet Drop
- Filtering Platform Connection
- Other Object Access Events

Policy Change

This policy setting determines whether to audit every change that affects user rights, trust policies, or audit policies. The Success setting will log a successful change to user rights assignment policies, audit policies, or trust policies. The Failure setting will log an unsuccessful change to user rights assignment policies, audit policies, or trust policies.

Subcategories of Policy Change are:

- Audit Policy Change
- Authentication Policy Change
- Authorization Policy Change
- MPSSVC Rule-Level Policy Change
- Filtering Platform Policy Change
- Other Policy Change Events

Privilege Use

This setting determines whether to audit when a user right is used to perform an action. Success records when the exercise of a user right is successful. Failure records when the exercise of a user right fails. This setting will also generate a large number of entries.

Audit events are not generated for use of the following user rights, even if success audits or failure audits are specified for this policy setting: bypass traverse checking, debug programs, create a token object, replace process level token, generate security audits, backup files and directories, restore files and directories.

Privilege Use has the following subcategories:

- Sensitive Privilege Use
- Non Sensitive Privilege Use
- Other Privilege Use Events

Process Tracking

This policy setting determines whether to audit when an application executes an action that is being tracked. Success generates a log entry when the process being tracked is successful. Failure generates an entry when the process being tracked fails. When enabled, this policy setting produces a large number of entries.

Process Tracking has the following subcategories:

- Process Termination
- DPAPI Activity
- RPC Events
- Process Creation

System Events

This policy setting determines whether to audit when a computer is rebooted or shut down or another event occurs that affects security. Success audits when an event executes successfully. Failure audits when an event fails. Because all system events are important and enabling Success and Failure options creates few additional log entries, this option should be enabled on all computers. System Events has the following subcategories:

- Security System Extension
- System Integrity
- IPsec Driver
- Other System Events
- Security State Change

To audit access to objects as part of your audit policy, you must enable either the Audit Directory Service Access category (for auditing objects on a domain controller) or the Audit Object Access category (for auditing objects on a member server or a client computer). After you've enabled the object access category, you can then specify what types of access you'd like to audit for each group or user.

Auditing Directory Service Events

In Windows 2000 Server and Windows Server 2003, one audit policy, Audit Directory Service Access, controlled whether auditing for directory service events was enabled or disabled. In Windows Server 2008, this policy is divided into four subcategories:

- Directory Service Access
- Directory Service Changes
- Directory Service Replication
- Detailed Directory Service Replication

Auditing changes to objects in AD DS is enabled with one of the new audit subcategories: Directory Service Changes. AD DS objects with SACLs configured to enable the objects to be audited can generate the following log entries:

- When an attribute is modified, AD DS logs the previous and current values of the attribute. If the attribute has more than one value, only the changed values are logged.
- When a new object is created, the values of existing attributes are logged. If the user adds attributes during the create operation, those new attribute values are logged. The values of system attributes assigned by default are not logged.
- If an object is moved within a domain, both old and new locations (distinguished name) are logged. When an object is moved to a different domain, a create event is generated on the domain controller in the target domain.
- If an object is undeleted, the location is logged. In addition, if the user adds, modifies, or deletes attributes while performing an undelete operation, the values of those attributes are logged.

Enabling Auditing of AD DS Objects

Enabling logging of objects in Active Directory is a two-step process. First, you open the Default Domain Controller Policy in Group Policy Object Editor and enable the Audit Directory Service Access global audit policy found under Computer Configuration\Policies\Windows Settings\Security Settings\Local Policies\Audit Policy.

Next, configure the SACL on the object or objects you want to audit. For example, to enable Success auditing for access by Authenticated Users to User objects stored within an organizational unit (OU), you do the following:

1. Open Active Directory Users And Computers, and make sure Advanced Features is selected from the View menu.
2. Right-click the OU you want to audit, and select Properties.
3. Click the Security tab, and then click Advanced to open the Advanced Security Settings dialog box.
4. Click the Auditing tab, and then click Add to open the Select User, Computer Or Group dialog box.
5. In the Enter The Object Name To Select box, type **Authenticated Users** and click OK. The Auditing Entry dialog box opens, as shown in Figure 14-6.

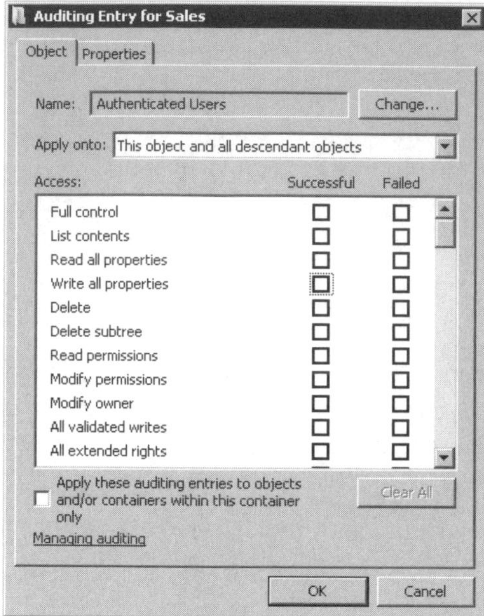

Figure 14-6 The Auditing Entry dialog box

6. In the Apply Onto list box, select how you want the auditing applied.
7. In the Access box, select the entries you wish to audit.
8. Click OK to return to Advanced Security Settings dialog box, which should now display the new SACL you configured, as shown in Figure 14-7.

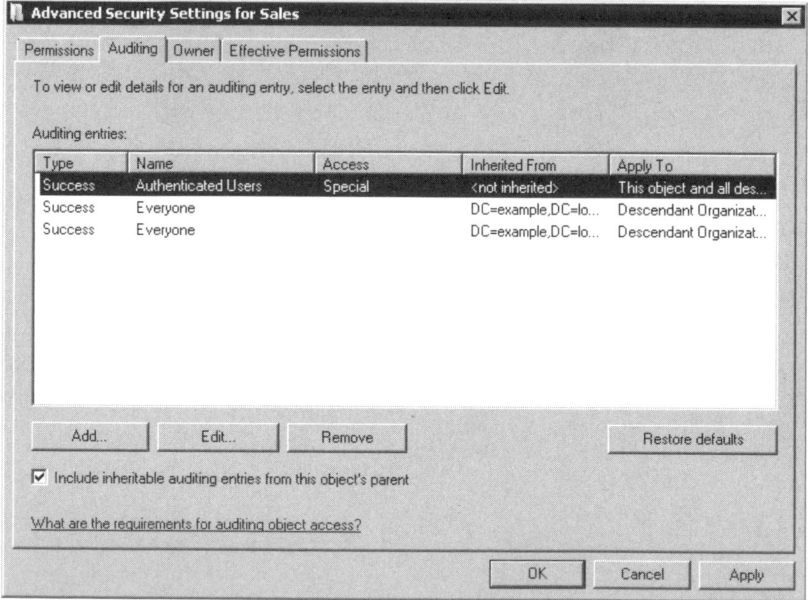

Figure 14-7 A newly added SACL

Now when you make a change to an account in the Sales OU–adding a telephone number, for example–the Event Viewer displays an entry with the Event ID 5136. The Event IDs for Directory Service Changes audit events are listed in Table 14-2.

Table 14-2 Event IDs for Directory Service Changes

ID	Type of event	Description
5136	Change	This event is logged when a successful modification is made to an attribute in an AD DS object.
5137	Create	This event is logged when a new object is created in the directory.
5138	Undelete	This event is logged when an object in the directory is undeleted.
5139	Move	This event is logged when an object is moved within the domain.

Note The Event ID 566 for a Directory Service Access audit in Windows Server 2003 has been changed to 4662 in Windows Server 2008.

Using Auditpol.exe

The subcategories for Audit Directory Service Access can't be viewed with the Local Group Policy Editor (GPedit.msc). You can only view them with the command line tool Auditpol.exe. To use auditpol.exe, right-click Command Prompt and select Run As Administrator

To view the subcategories, type the following at the command line and press Enter:

```
auditpol /get /category:"ds access"
```

The result, shown in Figure 14-8, shows the list of subcategories and their current settings.

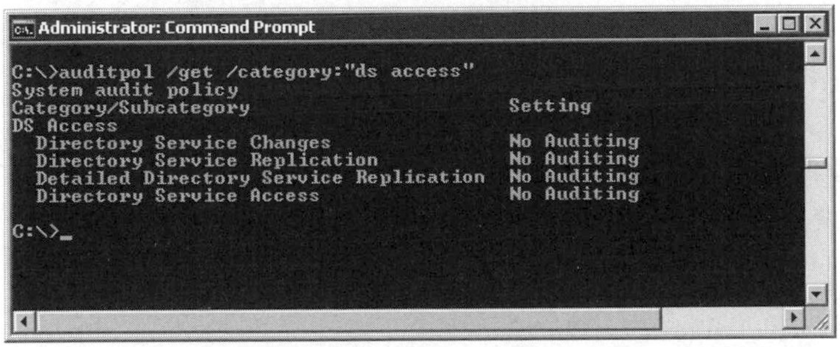

```
Administrator: Command Prompt
C:\>auditpol /get /category:"ds access"
System audit policy
Category/Subcategory                          Setting
DS Access
  Directory Service Changes                   No Auditing
  Directory Service Replication               No Auditing
  Detailed Directory Service Replication      No Auditing
  Directory Service Access                    No Auditing

C:\>_
```

Figure 14-8 Audit setting for AD DS subcategories

To view the entire audit policy, type the following at the command line and press Enter:

```
auditpol /get /category:*
```

To enable auditing on the subcategory Directory Service Changes, type the following at the command line and press Enter:

```
auditpol /set /subcategory:"directory service changes"
```

By default, auditing will be set to log successes. To log both successes and failures, type the following at the command line and press Enter:

```
auditpol /set /subcategory:"directory service changes" /success:enable /
failure:enable
```

To verify settings, type the following at the command line and press Enter:

```
auditpol /get /category:"ds access"
```

Figure 14-9 confirms that the subcategory is set to audit both success and unsuccessful changes.

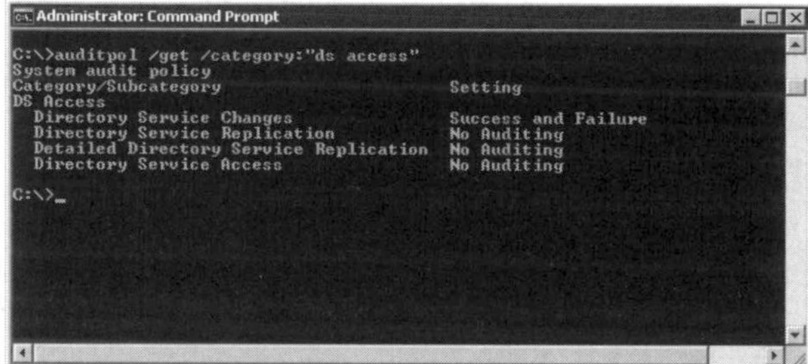

Figure 14-9 Confirming the setting to audit Directory Service Changes

---

Note You can use Auditpol.exe to view and set policy for all auditing categories and subcategories. Type **auditpol /?** at a command prompt to view parameters and syntax.

Setting Global Audit Policy

Enabling the global audit policy Audit Directory Service Access enables all of the directory service policy subcategories. To set this global audit policy in the Default Domain Controllers Group Policy, follow these steps:

1. Select Group Policy Management from the Administrative Tools menu.
2. Navigate to your domain and click Domain Controllers.
3. Right-click the Default Domain Controllers Policy and select Edit.

4. Navigate through Computer Configuration, Policies, Windows Settings, Security Settings, and Local Policies to reach Audit Policy.
5. In the results pane, right-click Audit Directory Service Access and select Properties.
6. On the Security Policy Setting tab, select Define These Policy Settings. Select Success, Failure, or both options. Click OK.

Enabling Auditing

The previous sections covered enabling AD DS objects. To enable auditing on other auditing categories, select Group Policy Management from the Administrative Tools menu and follow these steps:

1. Navigate to the domain where you want to enable auditing. Right-click the Default Domain Policy and select Edit from the shortcut menu.
2. In the console tree, expand Computer Configuration, Policies, Windows Settings, Security Settings, and Local Policies to reach Audit Policy, as shown in Figure 14-10.

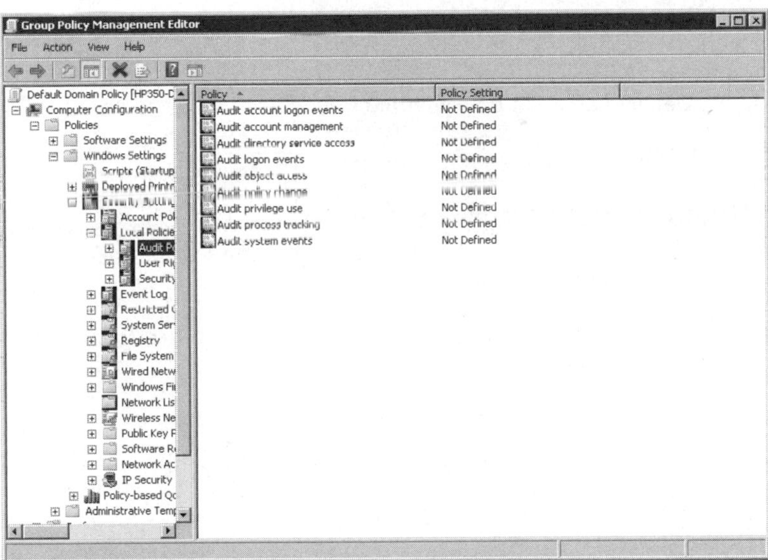

Figure 14-10 Categories of events for auditing

3. Right-click the event category you want to audit and choose Properties from the shortcut menu.
4. On the Security Policy Setting tab, shown in Figure 14-11, select the check box to define the setting and select the option to audit successful attempts, failed attempts, or both.

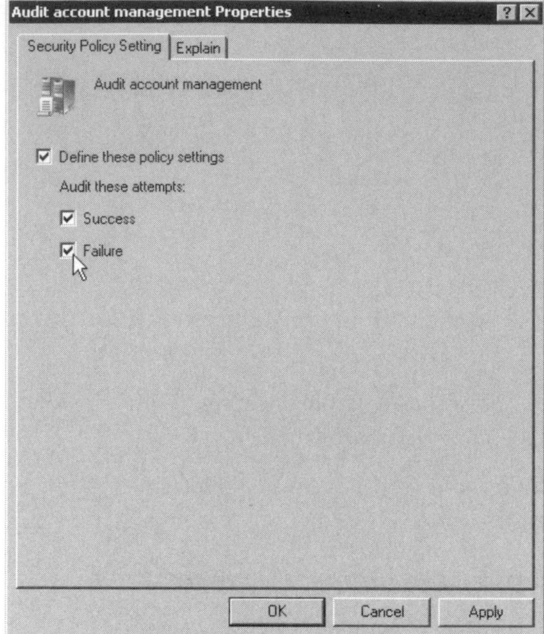

Figure 14-11 Defining an audit policy setting

5. Click OK when finished.

Auditing Settings for Objects

After you've turned on a policy setting for auditing an Active Directory object, you can create audit settings for objects by following these steps:

1. Right-click the object you want to audit and choose Properties from the shortcut menu. Click the Security tab.
2. Click Advanced, and then click the Auditing tab.
3. Click Add to set up auditing for a new group or user. Make your selection and click OK.
4. Select the events you want to audit, as shown in Figure 14-12. Table 14-3 lists the options and their definitions.

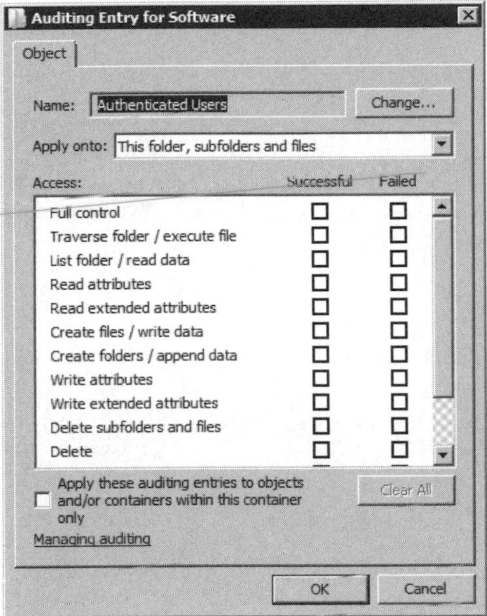

Figure 14-12 Selecting events to be audited

Table 14-3 Auditable File-System Events

Event	Activated when
Traverse Folder/Execute File	A folder is traversed (that is, someone passes through the folder on the way to a parent folder or a child folder) or an application is run.
List Folder/Read Data	A folder is opened or file contents are viewed.
Read Attributes	The attributes of a file or folder are viewed.
Read Extended Attributes	Extended attributes (defined and created by programs) of a file or folder are viewed.
Create Files/Write Data	A file is created inside a folder or a file is changed, overwriting existing information in the file.
Create Folders/Append Data	A folder is created inside the folder being audited or information is added to an existing file.
Write Attributes	A file or folder attribute is changed.
Write Extended Attributes	Extended attributes (defined and created by programs) of a file or folder are changed.
Delete Subfolders and Files	A file or subfolder is deleted.
Delete	A specific file is deleted.
Read Permissions	Permissions for a file or folder are viewed.
Change Permissions	Permissions for a file or folder are modified.
Take Ownership	Ownership of a file or folder changes.

Note By default, audit settings are inherited by child objects. The Auditing tab of the Access Control Settings dialog box includes a check box for allowing inheritable auditing entries. If you clear this check box, the audit settings for the object remain constant, even if the parent object's audit settings are changed. In addition, clearing this check box removes any audit settings that have already been inherited. The second check box on this tab—Replace All Existing Inheritable Audit Entries On All Descendants With Inheritable Auditing Entries From This Object—resets existing auditing and allows audit entries to be inherited from the parent object once again.

Using Event Viewer

The new Event Viewer shows two categories of event logs: Windows Logs and Applications And Services Logs.

Windows Logs

Windows Logs include the logs available in previous versions of Windows: the Application, Security, and System logs. Added in Windows Server 2008 are the Setup log and the ForwardedEvents log.

The Application log records events logged by programs. Program developers decide which events are recorded. For example, an error in the Exchange service that addresses e-mail messages through address lists will create an entry in the Application log.

The Security log records events that you have specified through audit settings.

The System log contains events logged by Windows system components. For example, a service that fails to start or a driver that doesn't load will generate an entry in the System log. The events logged are predetermined by Windows.

The Setup log records events related to application setup. The ForwardedEvents log stores events collected from remote computers. To collect events from remote computers, you must create an event subscription. Event subscriptions are covered in "Forwarding and Collecting Events" later in this chapter.

Applications And Services Logs

Applications And Services logs are a new category of event logs, and there are many, many new logs. Essentially, they all fall into one of four subtypes:

- *Analytic events* describe application operations and problems that can't be resolved through user intervention.
- *Admin events* show a problem and the solution, such as when an application driver fails. The event will show what happened and the steps necessary to fix the situation.

- *Operational events* are used to evaluate and diagnose a problem. For example, when users try to connect to a deleted printer an operational event will be logged.
- *Debug events* are used by developers troubleshooting program issues.

Note To see the full range of event logs, select Show Analytic And Debug Logs from the View menu.

Creating Custom Views

Filters have always been available in Event Viewer to select only certain events for viewing. Filters are essential in helping you to avoid being overwhelmed by the sheer volume of logged events. Custom Views are an extension of filters in that you can specify filtering rules, and then name and save the view. A custom view can then be reused without recreating the basic filter.

To create a custom view, open Event Viewer from the Administrative Tools menu and follow these steps:

1. Select Create Custom View from the Action menu.
2. In the Create Custom View dialog box, select how you want the events filtered.
3. To filter events based on when they were generated, select a time span in the Logged drop-down list. If none of the times suits your purposes, select Custom Range and specify the earliest date and time from which you want events and the latest date and time from which you want events. Click OK.
4. In Event level, select the check boxes next to the types of events that you want included in the custom view.
5. If you want events from specific logs, select By Log and choose the logs in the Event Logs drop-down list. To filter by event cause, select By Source and specify the sources in the Event Sources drop-down list.
6. In Includes/Excludes Event IDs, type the event IDs that you to display. Separate multiple event IDs by commas. To include a range of IDs, such as 1610 through 1620 inclusive, type **1610-1620**. If you want your filter to display events with all IDs except certain ones, type the IDs of those exceptions, preceded by a minus sign. For example, to include all IDs between 1610 and 1620 except 1612, type **1610-1620, -1612**.
7. In Task Category, open the drop-down list and select the check boxes next to the task categories to be included in the custom view.
8. In Keywords, open the drop-down list and select keywords you want to filter for.
9. In User, enter the names of the user accounts to include. Separate multiple user names by using a comma.

10. In Computers, enter the names of computers to be included. Enter multiple computers by separating them with a comma.
11. Click OK.
12. In the Save Filter To Custom View dialog box, enter a name and description for the custom view. Select a location for saving the custom view. Click OK.

The saved custom view will be listed under the Event Viewer's Custom Views in the console tree. To import, export, or copy a custom view, use the Event Viewer Action menu.

Forwarding and Collecting Events

Event Viewer lets you see events on a single remote computer, but obviously you sometimes need to examine a series of event logs on more than one computer. Windows Server 2008 and Windows Vista include the ability to collect copies of events from multiple remote computers and store them locally. To choose the events to collect, you create an event subscription. The subscription describes which events will be collected and where they'll be stored locally. You can view and manage these collected events like any other stored events.

Before you can create a subscription, you must enable event collecting on the computer that will be doing the collecting and on all the computers from which the events will be collected.

To configure computers in a domain to forward and collect events, log on to each computer using an account with administrative privileges and then follow these steps:

1. On each source computer, right-click Command Prompt and select Run As Administrator from the shortcut menu.
2. At the prompt, type **winrm quickconfig.** The command may return the following:

   ```
   WinRM is not set up to allow remote access to this machine for management.
   The following changes must be made:

   Set the WinRM service type to delayed auto start.
   Start the WinRM service.
   Create a WinRM listener on HTTP://* to accept WS-Man requests to any IP on this
      machine.
   Enable the WinRM firewall exception.

   Make these changes [y/n]?
   ```
   Type **y** and press Enter.
3. Add the computer account of the collector computer to the local Administrators group on each of the source computers.

4. On the collector computer, right-click Command Prompt and select Run As Administrator from the shortcut menu.
5. At the prompt, type **wecutil qc** and press Enter. The command may return the following message:

   ```
   The service startup mode will be changed to Delay-Start. Would you like to
   proceed?
   ( Y- yes or N- no)?
   ```

   Type **Y** and press Enter.

The source and collector computers are now configured to forward and collect events. The next step is to create a subscription to specify what to collect.

Creating Subscriptions

To create a subscription, follow these steps:

1. On the collector computer, run Event Viewer as an administrator.
2. Right-click Subscriptions in the console tree and select Create Subscription from the shortcut menu.

   > **Note** If the Windows Event Collector service isn't started, you'll be prompted to start it. You must be logged on as member of the Administrators group to start this service.

3. In the Subscription Properties dialog box, configure the new subscription by following these steps:
   - In the Subscription Name box, type in a name for the subscription.
   - In the Description box, provide a short description of the subscription.
   - Select a destination for the forwarded event from the drop-down list in Destination Log. By default, collected events are stored in the ForwardedEvents log.
   - In the Subscription Type And Source Computers pane, you can choose to have either the collector computer or the source computers initiate the subscription. For collector–initiated subscription, click Select Computers and add the source computers. For source computer–initiated subscription, click the Select Computer Group and add the source computers.
   - Click Select Events to open the Query Filter dialog box. Configure the filter.

- ❑ Click Advanced to open the Advanced Subscription Settings dialog box. Here you can specify either an event delivery optimization or specify the account used to manage the process of collecting events.

4. Click OK until all dialog boxes are closed.

The subscription will be added to the subscription pane and will display as Active. To change or delete a subscription, right-click the name in the subscription pane and choose an action from the shortcut menu.

Working with Events on a Remote Computer

To manage event logs on a remote computer, follow these steps:

1. Start Event Viewer.
2. Right-click the root node, as shown in Figure 14-13, and select Connect To Another Computer from the shortcut menu.

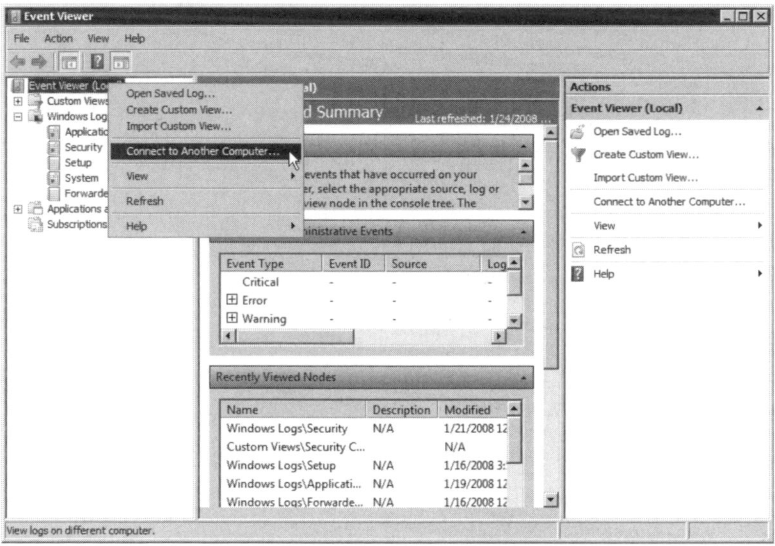

Figure 14-13 Connecting to events on another computer

3. In the Select Computer dialog box, enter the computer's name or click Browse to find it.
4. To connect as a different user, select the Connect As Another User check box and click Set User. Click OK.

Event Viewer will connect to the other computer and the Event Viewer for that computer will display.

Running a Task When a Given Event Occurs

Event Viewer is integrated with Task Scheduler, so you can right-click most events to start the process of scheduling a task to run when that event is logged in the future. To run a task when a particular event occurs, follow these steps:

1. Start Event Viewer.
2. In the console tree, navigate to the log that contains the event to be associated with a task.
3. Right-click the event and select Attach Task to This Event on the shortcut menu.
4. The Create Basic Task wizard starts. Supply a name and description for the operation you're configuring. Click Next.
5. Confirm that the event is correctly selected. Click Next.
6. Select an action for the task to perform. Click Next.
7. Provide the information needed to perform the task you selected. Click Next.
8. On the Summary page, review the selections and click Finish.

   The new task will be created and added to your Windows schedule.

Managing Event Logs

To manage an event log, you would normally open Event Viewer, right-click the log, and select Properties from the shortcut menu. Values are then updated in the Properties dialog box.

Setting the Maximum Log Size

Event logs are stored in files that have a maximum size set by default. To change the size, follow these steps:

1. Open Event Viewer.
2. Right-click the log you want to manage in the console tree and select Properties from the shortcut menu.
3. In the Log Properties dialog box, shown in Figure 14-14, you can type in a different log path and use the spin box to change the maximum log size.

Note The log size must be at least 1024 Kb and must be a multiple of 64 Kb. If you type in a value, it will be rounded to the nearest multiple of 64 Kb.

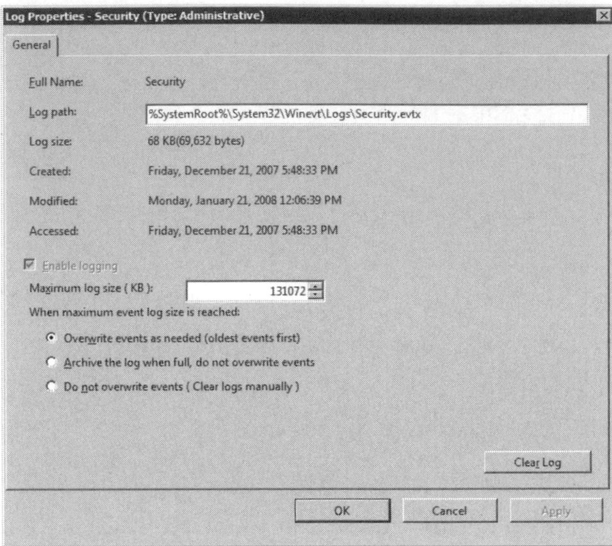

Figure 14-14 Setting log properties

4. Click OK when finished.

Setting the Retention Policy

Eventually, all log files will reach their maximum size limit. What happens to new events is determined by the retention policy you set. You have three options:

- **Override Events As Needed** This policy is the classic first-in-first-out rule. New events replace the oldest entries.
- **Archive The Log When Full, Do Not Overwrite Events** This option saves everything. When the log is full, it is automatically archived and new events continue to be stored. Everything is saved and no events are overwritten.
- **Do Not Overwrite Events** Choose this setting if you want to clear the log manually rather than automatically. This setting requires that you pay attention to the log. When it is full, it will not accept any new events.

To set a log retention policy, follow these steps:

1. Open Event Viewer.
2. Right-click the log you want to manage in the console tree and select Properties from the shortcut menu.
3. In the Log Properties dialog box, select an option under When Maximum Event Log Size Is Reached.
4. Click OK.

Saving Event Logs

If you need to save an event log, you can do so manually while including additional information that will make the saved log viewable by others. To export and save an event log, follow these steps:

1. Start Event Viewer.
2. In the console tree, right-click the log you want to save and select Save Events As from the shortcut menu.
3. In the Save As dialog box, navigate to the file location you want and enter a file name for the saved log. Click Save.
4. In the Display Information dialog box, select either No Display Information (the log will not be viewed on any other computer) or Display Information For These Languages (the saved log is intended to be viewed on other computers).

Note If you want the log to be viewed in additional languages, select Show All Available Languages and select the check boxes for the language information to be included.

Using Task Scheduler

It's true that you could—and still can—schedule tasks using the AT command, as described later in this chapter, but Task Scheduler provides a graphical interface and is much easier to use. Tasks can be scheduled to run repeatedly during off-hours. To start Task Scheduler, select Task Scheduler from the Administrative Tools menu.

Task Scheduler organizes the creation of tasks into two categories: Basic Tasks and Tasks. A basic task will start a program, send an e-mail, or display a message at a specific time or when a specific event occurs. Most of the scheduled tasks you'll configure will fall into this category.

Creating a Basic Task

To create a basic task, follow these steps:

1. Start Task Scheduler.
2. Select Create Basic Task from the Action pane. The Create Basic Task Wizard starts.
3. On the Create Basic Task page, provide a name and description for the task. Click Next.
4. On the Task Trigger page, select when you want the task to start. Click Next.
5. If you selected a time, specify the start time and any other information needed. If you selected When A Specific Event Is logged, provide the Log, Source, and Event ID. Click Next.

6. On the Action page, select the action you want the task to perform. Click Next.
7. Provide the information needed to perform the task you selected. Click Next.
8. On the Summary page, review the selections and click Finish.

The new task is created and listed in the Task Scheduler Library in the console pane.

Creating a More Complicated Task

Task Scheduler is capable of creating a very detailed and granular task. If this is the sort of task you need to create, follow these steps:

1. Start Task Scheduler.
2. Select Create Task in the Actions pane. The Create Task dialog box with five tabs starts.
3. On the General tab, enter a name for the task and configure any of the Security Options that apply.
4. On the Triggers tab, click New to create a trigger for the task.
5. On the Actions tab, click New to specify the action that will happen when the task starts.
6. On the Conditions tab, specify any conditions that must be true (along with the trigger events) for the task to run.
7. On the Settings tab, select additional options that can affect how the task is run.
8. Click OK when finished.

Note The History tab will show you the history of the task once it has run.

Using the AT command

You can also use the AT command to schedule tasks. By default, the AT command is run using the LocalSystem account, which requires administrative privileges.

The command structure for the AT command is as follows:

```
AT [\\computername] [id] [[/delete]| /delete [/yes]]
AT [\\computername] time [/interactive] [/every:date[,…] |
/next:date[,…]] command
```

You can use the following parameters with the AT command. Used without parameters, the AT command returns a list of scheduled commands.

- *\\computername* Specifies a remote computer. Without this parameter, the local computer is assumed.
- *id* Indicates the identification number, if one is assigned.
- */delete* Cancels a scheduled command. If no identification number is specified, all scheduled commands on the computer will be canceled.
- */yes* Forces a yes answer to all system queries when canceling all commands.
- *time* Specifies when the command is to run, expressed as hours:minutes in 24-hour notation.
- */interactive* Allows the task to interact with the desktop of the user logged on at the time the job is run.
- */every:date[,...]* Runs the command on the date specified. You can specify the date as one or more days of the week (M, T, W, Th, F, S, Su) or as one or more days of the month (numbers 1 through 31). Separate multiple dates with commas. If this parameter is omitted, the current day of the month is assumed.
- */next:date[,...]* Runs the command on the next occurrence of the specified day. If this parameter is omitted, the current day of the month is assumed.
- *command* Indicates the program, batch file, or command to be run. If a path is required, use the Uniform Naming Convention (UNC) path.

Keep the following additional facts in mind about the AT command:

- The AT command doesn't automatically load Cmd, the command interpreter. Therefore, if the command parameter doesn't point to an executable file, you must explicitly specify Cmd, followed by the */c* switch, at the beginning of the command.
- Commands scheduled using AT run as background processes, so no output is displayed. To redirect output to a file, use the redirection symbol (>). The redirection symbol must be preceded by the escape symbol (^), so a sample command would be *AT retrieve.bat ^>c:\daylog.txt*.
- If you have to use a drive letter to connect to a shared directory, include an AT command to disconnect the drive when the task is completed. Otherwise, the assigned drive letter will be neither available nor seen at the command prompt.

Note You can switch back and forth between the AT command and Task Scheduler, with some limitations. For example, if you schedule a task using AT and later modify that same task using Task Scheduler, the task is then "owned" by Task Scheduler and you can no longer access it using AT.

Delegating Tasks

Obviously, one of the simplest ways to lessen your administrative burden is to delegate tasks to others. The recipient of the delegated authority can have complete administrative control within the area chosen but not the sweeping administrative rights inherent in being a member of the Domain Admins group.

Assign control by organizational unit (OU) whenever possible, because assigning permissions at the object level quickly becomes too complicated to be worthwhile. Records of security assignments are critical, so keep track of all delegations. To delegate control, use the Delegation Of Control Wizard, which always assigns permissions at the OU level. To use the wizard, follow these steps:

1. Launch Active Directory Users And Computers from the Administrative Tools menu.
2. Expand the domain node, right-click the container for which you want to delegate control, and choose Delegate Control from the shortcut menu. This starts the Delegation Of Control Wizard. Click Next.
3. Click Add to select the user or group to which you want to grant control. Make your selection on the Select Users, Computers, Or Groups page. Click Next.
4. On the Tasks To Delegate page, shown in Figure 14-15, select the tasks that you want to delegate. Select from the common predefined tasks, or click Create A Custom Task To Delegate. Click Next.

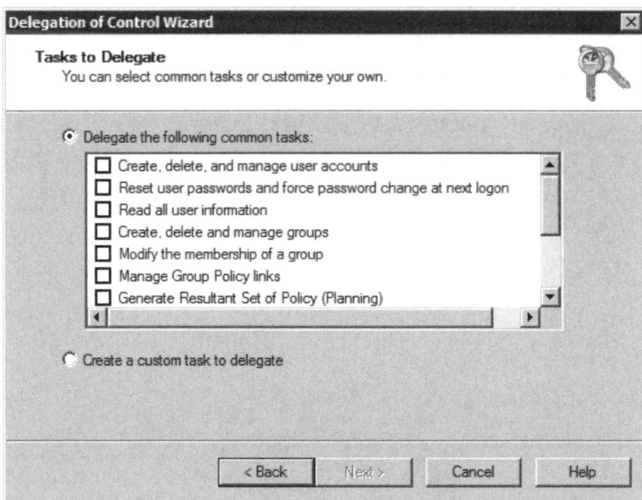

Figure 14-15 Selecting tasks to delegate

5. If you selected a predefined task, you're essentially finished. Review the summary and click Finished.
6. If you selected Create A Custom Task To Delegate, you're presented with more specific choices about what objects you're delegating control of and the specific permissions to be granted. After you make these choices, you'll see a summary of the delegation. Click Finished.

What Tasks to Delegate?

Common tasks to delegate include the following:

- Creating, deleting, and managing user accounts
- Resetting user passwords
- Creating, deleting, and managing groups
- Modifying group membership
- Joining computers to a domain
- Managing Group Policy links
- Generating Resultant Set of Policy

If you have inetOrgPerson accounts, you can delegate the creation and management of these accounts as well.

Summary

In this chapter we've covered a number of the day-to-day tasks administrators must deal with themselves or delegate to others. In the next chapter, we move on to scripts—the administrator's ultimate labor-saving device.

Chapter 15

Using Scripts for Consistent Administration

The Microsoft Windows scripting infrastructure has grown dramatically since the late 1990s, and Windows Server 2008 is the first server operating system with a powerful scripting language *and command shell* built in to the operating system—Windows PowerShell. All versions of Windows Server 2008 except Server Core versions have PowerShell available as a feature. In this chapter we're not going to pretend to try to teach you *how* to script—that's really the topic of a whole book. But we do intend to provide you some basic understanding of how PowerShell works and give you some concrete examples of how you can use PowerShell in your daily life as a Windows system administrator.

We believe strongly, even passionately, that using scripts to automate Windows Server 2008 administration is essential to building a consistent, efficient, and productive network infrastructure. The GUI has taken a huge step forward with the new Roles and Features Wizards, which help to ensure that the original addition of a Role or Feature is done a consistent and correct way, but ongoing administration is still very much a "click and change" process that is subject to the vagaries of exactly which click and change is made. By building and using scripts for daily administration, you ensure that changes are made the same way every time. If you need to change an administrative process, you only have to change the script, not retrain everyone in the new process.

In this chapter we provide a basic introduction to using PowerShell, including features and how to use them. This is followed by a section that provides practical examples across many areas of daily administration. Where appropriate, we've included the full script or command line in the body of the chapter, but in other cases we've chosen to show only a key element of a script, with the full script on the CD that accompanies the book.

Introducing Windows PowerShell

So what is Windows PowerShell anyway? PowerShell is Microsoft's next-generation scripting language and command shell. It can be used interactively, as your every day command shell, but it is also a full scripting language. By being interactive, PowerShell allows you to enter commands into a console and get immediate feedback. By being scriptable, PowerShell allows you to put all of your commands in a basic text file (with a .ps1 extension) and run them.

If you are starting to use PowerShell, but are coming from some other scripting language, you'll have a bit of a learning curve, as with any new language, before you can use all of PowerShell's incredible features.

Note Unless otherwise stated, all scripts and examples in this chapter apply to Windows PowerShell version 1.0 released in November 2006 and included with Windows Server 2008. A Community Technology Preview(CTP) for version 2 of PowerShell was released in November 2007, and it will likely be updated shortly after the release of Windows Server 2008. Version 1.0 scripts should run without modification in a version 2 environment.

PowerShell is available as a download for Windows XP, Windows Server 2003, and Windows Vista from *http://www.microsoft.com/windowsserver2003/technologies/management/powershell/download.mspx*, and is included in the box with Windows Server 2008 as an installable feature. See Chapter 7, "Configuring a New Installation," for details on how to enable the Windows PowerShell feature.

Late in 2007, Microsoft announced that Windows PowerShell would be in their Common Engineering Criteria (CEC) for 2009. The CEC basically outlines the criteria that Microsoft server products should meet.

More Info For more details on the CEC, check out the homepage at *http://www.microsoft.com/windowsserversystem/cer/allcriteria.mspx*.

Understanding Windows PowerShell

PowerShell is a completely new language, written from the ground up to manage and administer Microsoft Windows. It has inherited many things from its predecessors while introducing a whole new way of doing things in an interactive shell and language. The architects of Windows PowerShell had deep roots in UNIX and the shells and languages that are a part of everyday life to the UNIX administrator, but they knew that simply reworking the Korn Shell for Microsoft Windows wasn't going to be enough to really change how administrators, and developers, work with Windows. Windows is fundamentally object-oriented, and any language or shell that needs to work with Windows needs to work with objects.

For the most part—we will cover some exceptions a bit later—PowerShell can run DOS batch command files, Perl scripts, VBScript scripts, and even Korn Shell scripts if you have the Subsystem for UNIX Applications installed. Most of these languages use an interpreter to run their scripts, and PowerShell will allow these commands to run without interference. In a few places it is better to run from a DOS console window, and we'll show some examples later.

Under the Hood Server Products That Support PowerShell

Many of the latest server products that are shipping today from Microsoft use and support PowerShell. The most prominent example is Microsoft Exchange Server 2007. Exchange 2007 was built from the ground up on PowerShell. Every single thing you can do from the Exchange 2007 graphical interface—and more—you can do from PowerShell, using the Exchange Management Console (EMC). The EMC is an add-on that gets plugged into the PowerShell to provide the Exchange functionality.

Although Exchange 2007 was the first server product to be based on PowerShell, there are now several more. Some fully support PowerShell, while others have PowerShell extensions available. Some examples of these products include:

- Microsoft Operations Manager 2007
- Microsoft Data Protection Manager 2007
- Microsoft Virtual Machine Manager 2007
- Microsoft SQL Server 2008
- Microsoft Windows HPC Server 2008 (not yet shipping)

Basics

Let's start with some basics you'll need before you can actually use Windows PowerShell. In this section we'll cover:

- Security
- Terminology
- Case sensitivity
- The PowerShell console
- Customizing

Security

Consistent with Microsoft's direction on security, PowerShell is secure by default. The default installation of PowerShell has the following limitations:

- It cannot run any scripts. PowerShell can only be used interactively by opening the PowerShell console.
- Double-clicking a PowerShell script opens the script for editing in Notepad.
- There is no remote access to the PowerShell process.

More Info Several useful blog posts and articles are available from both the PowerShell team at Microsoft and community members on PowerShell security subjects. A very brief list includes:

- *http://www.windowsecurity.com/articles/PowerShell-Security.html* includes basic security concepts, and a useful link to a PowerShell Group Policy template.
- *http://blogs.msdn.com/powershell/archive/2006/08/03/687838.aspx* discusses a proof-of-concept PowerShell virus.
- *http://www.hanselman.com/blog/SigningPowerShellScripts.aspx* offers a detailed overview, including screenshots, on how to sign your own scripts.
- *http://blogs.msdn.com/powershell/archive/2007/05/06/running-scripts-downloaded-from-the-internet.aspx* discusses additional prompts and warnings that scripts downloaded from the Internet have.

Under the Hood The Next Version

In November 2007, PowerShell version 2 released to the public. This CTP has quite a few improvements, including the following major additions since version 1.0:

- **Remoting** Support for running scripts that manage a remote computer. While version 1.0 does have some limited functionality for dealing with remote systems using WMI, version 2 provides native remote capability.

- **Background jobs** Support for running scripts as background processes. This can be done in version 1 of PowerShell, but version 2 provides native support.

The PowerShell V2 CTP is a very early look at the next version. As with any CTP or Beta product, you should not use it on production computers. No official dates for a production release have been set, but we're excited to see the changes already in PowerShell v2.

Terminology

As with any programming or scripting language, PowerShell has some specialized terminology that is useful to understand first. We will use the following basic terms throughout this chapter:

- **Cmdlet** The most basic command in PowerShell is called a cmdlet (pronounced *command-let*). PowerShell comes with more than 100 built-in cmdlets. The output of a cmdlet is an object.
- **Provider** PowerShell provides access to certain types of data in a consistent format that resembles a file system.
- **Snap-in** A snap-in is a DLL typically written in either C# or VB.NET. The snap-in contains all of the extra functionality of PowerShell that a particular set of features use. Exchange 2007 uses a snap-in to provide the additional functionality used by Exchange. Snap-ins include cmdlets and might also include one or more providers.
- **Pipeline** Cmdlets can be strung together using the pipe ("|") character. The output objects from one cmdlet are piped into the next cmdlet. This is analogous to how UNIX commands work, except instead of passing text from one command to the next, we're passing objects. Powerful stuff.
- **Script block** A script block is a grouping of statements and commands into a single block of code. These are denoted by curly braces: { }.

Case Sensitivity

In general, PowerShell is not case sensitive. Case sensitivity becomes more important when actually comparing data, which we will cover later in this chapter.

The PowerShell Console

You can open the PowerShell console from the Start menu in the same way that you open other applications. And in Windows Server 2008 you can easily pin PowerShell to the front of the Start Menu by right-clicking the shortcut for it and selecting Pin To Start Menu from the menu. While you're at it, you can also select Add To Quick Launch to add a shortcut to your Taskbar Quick Launch Toolbar.

If you haven't already done so, you need to change the default execution policy for PowerShell to ensure that PowerShell can run scripts. To set or change the execution policy to RemoteSigned, use the following steps:

1. Click Start, right-click Windows PowerShell, and select Run As Administrator from the Action menu.
2. Select Continue at the User Account Control prompt to open PowerShell with administrative privileges.
3. At the PowerShell prompt, run following the command:

   ```
   Set-ExecutionPolicy RemoteSigned
   ```

> **Note** See Chapter 7 for full details on installing and initially configuring PowerShell, along with details on what the available execution policies mean.

Tab Completion

PowerShell supports tab completion of cmdlet names, paths, and filenames. Tab completion is useful for shortcuts and can be used in several scenarios. To see how tab completion works, try the following procedure:

1. Open a PowerShell Window.
2. Type **Write-** and then press Tab. Each time you press Tab, a different cmdlet is displayed as the tab completion cycles through the possible ways to complete the command. Press Enter when you arrive at the one you want.
3. Now, type **Get-Content** (including a space after you type **Get-Content** is critical) and press Tab. This time, tab completion will cycle through the filenames of the files in the current directory. When you get to the text file that you want the content of, press Enter.
4. Finally, try changing to the Program Files directory. It's always a nuisance to navigate at the command line where there are embedded spaces. Type **cd C:\Program** and press Tab. PowerShell's tab completion will add quotes automatically and expand C:\Program into 'C:\Program Files'. Nice.

Basic Customizing

Everyone likes their shells just a little different, and PowerShell gives you the ability to customize your shell. But it's important to know *where* to customize and some basics about customizing. First, the where–in the correct profile file. And then the most basic of customizations, the way your prompt looks.

Managing Profiles

By default, PowerShell automatically runs the four scripts shown in Table 15-1 on start-up. By customizing the appropriate script, you can control automatic customizations.

Table 15-1 Default Profile Scripts in Windows PowerShell

Full Profile Name	Purpose
InstallationDirectory\profile.ps1	Customizes *all* PowerShell sessions, including hosted sessions for applications
InstallationDirectory\Microsoft.PowerShell_profile.ps1	Customizes all PowerShell.exe sessions for all users
Documents\WindowsPowerShell\profile.ps1	Customizes all PowerShell sessions for the user
Documents\WindowsPowerShell\Microsoft.PowerShell_profile.ps1	Customizes the PowerShell.exe sessions for the user

To modify a profile, you can add commands exactly the way you would type them into the console, but you put the commands in the appropriate .ps1 file.

To make changes to your regular PowerShell sessions, open a PowerShell console and type the following:

```
notepad $profile
```

Note This file isn't created by default, so you'll likely get an error from Notepad when you type this. Click OK and the file will be created. If you prefer a different text editor, such as gvim (*http://www.vim.org*), you can simply substitute that for Notepad.

More Info See this MSDN article on profiles for more information: *http://msdn2.microsoft.com/en-us/library/bb613488(VS.85).aspx.*

Setting the Prompt

You can customize quite a few things regarding the PowerShell console. Two of the most common things users want to change are the prompt and the title bar:

```
1  PSH>(Get-host).ui.rawui.windowtitle="testing"
2  PSH>function prompt {"PSHv1>"}
```

To change the title bar, use the command in line 1. We don't discuss this command in any more detail in this chapter, but we do provide tools for getting more information from PowerShell that may help.

The prompt is set up as a function, and we will discuss functions later. To change the prompt, you use a command string like line 2. Enter the text you want to see as your prompt in brackets. Some of us have quite complicated prompts; others settle for simple ones. Charlie's prompt, for PowerShell windows that have a white background, is:

```
Function prompt {
Write-Host ("[") -nonewline -foregroundcolor red
Write-Host ($Hostname) -nonewline -foregroundcolor Magenta
Write-Host ("]") -nonewline -foregroundcolor Red
Write-Host ([string]$(Get-Location) +":") -foregroundcolor DarkGreen
Write-Host ("PS >" ) -nonewline -foregroundcolor DarkBlue
}
```

PowerShell as a Shell

Using PowerShell as your main shell is certainly the future for system administrators. In this section we'll show you some basics of using the PowerShell shell. Sadly, none of these are available when running Server Core, because PowerShell doesn't run on Server Core. For that, you'll have to live with the plain old CMD shell.

What Is an Interactive Shell?

We said that PowerShell is also an interactive shell. That means you can enter commands directly into the console and get immediate feedback. PowerShell is a fairly forgiving and smart shell, as such things go, and tries to help you.

Here's what happens when PowerShell decides a command is not completed:

```
PSH>"testing
>>
>>
>> "
>>
testing
```

Here's what happened: At the PowerShell prompt, enter **"testing** and press Enter a few times. PowerShell sees the leading double quote, and says "OK, I've got a string." Now it waits until it gets a closing double quote to know you're done. It puts >> in the next line to show that our command isn't finished. When we type in a second double quote, it closes out the string and lets us have one more chance to add to that string, and then prints the string back to the console.

This is the first time we have entered anything into the console. Let's point out a special character, the semicolon, and how multiple commands can be handled in PowerShell.

We want to write two strings to the console: testing, and More Testing. Figure 15-1 shows two ways to do it.

```
[hp350-ts-05]
PSH> "testing"
testing
PSH> "More Testing"
More Testing
PSH> "Testing" ; "More Testing"
Testing
More Testing
PSH> _
```

Figure 15-1 Using the semicolon to separate commands

The semicolon acts just the same as a new line: It separates the two commands.

Avoiding Errors

Several cmdlets that actually perform an action such as deleting a file support the *–whatif* parameter. Using the *–whatif* parameter lets you verify exactly what will happen *before* you do something irrevocable. A perfect example is showing what would happen if we tried to stop any PowerShell processes that were currently running:

```
PSH>Get-Process powershell|Stop-Process -whatif
What if: Performing operation "Stop-Process" on Target "powershell (5576)".
```

Here we've asked PowerShell to return an object that is the PowerShell process, and then stop the process. By including the *–whatif* parameter, PowerShell will output the action it would have taken, but doesn't actually complete it.

Running Cmd Commands

You can run all the regular DOS commands (actually, the commands available from the standard Cmd.exe shell) from PowerShell. A simple example is the *ipconfig* command:

```
PSH>ipconfig
Windows IP Configuration

Ethernet adapter Local Area Connection 3:
        Connection-specific DNS Suffix  . :
        IP Address. . . . . . . . . . . . : 192.168.20.1
        Subnet Mask . . . . . . . . . . . : 255.255.255.0
        Default Gateway . . . . . . . . . :
```

We mentioned previously that Server 2008 uses Windows Eventing 6.0 for certain logs. Wevtutil.exe is the utility to retrieve information from these logs from the command line.

Real World Repeating netsh Commands

Let's say you have a new server to set up, or even an existing one, and you need to add several virtual IPs to one of the interfaces. One option is to manually add every single IP address though the advanced settings of the TCP/IP properties of the card. Another option is to the use the network shell, or netsh, that has been provided since Windows 2000. But using the PowerShell console gives us ways to make netsh work smarter. For example:

```
1  PSH> netsh interface ip show config
2  <Output removed>
3  PSH> $ips="10.10.10.20","10.10.10.21"
4  PSH> $subnet="255.255.255.0"
5  PSH> $ips|foreach-object {netsh interface ip add address
     "Local Area Connection" $_ $subnet}
6  Ok.
7  Ok.
8  PSH> netsh interface ip show config
9  <Output removed>
```

In the preceding example, we show a very simple way to use netsh to add multiple virtual IPs to an interface. Line 1 shows how to get the current interface configuration. We have omitted the output as indicated. On line 3, we declare an array of values–in this case, the IP addresses we want to add. We will talk more about arrays later. On line 4, we set a variable named *subnet.*

Line 5 is where the work is done. We pass the array *$ips* that we created to *foreach-object* cmdlet, and then enclose a netsh command in curly braces. Lines 6 and 7 basically indicate that the two netsh commands were successful. Finally, we recheck the interface configuration to confirm that the IPs have been added.

The key is "$_" on line 5. It's a powerful construct in PowerShell, and we'll discuss it later, but here we're using it to insert the next value from the *$ips* array each time we iterate through the script.

User Credentials

The Get-Credential cmdlet is a useful cmdlet for getting credentials when a command will need them later. Typically, only cmdlets that are expected to connect to some kind of service will support Get-Credential. If you type **$creds=Get-Credentials** at the PowerShell command line, you'll get a standard Windows Credential Request window, as shown in Figure 15-2.

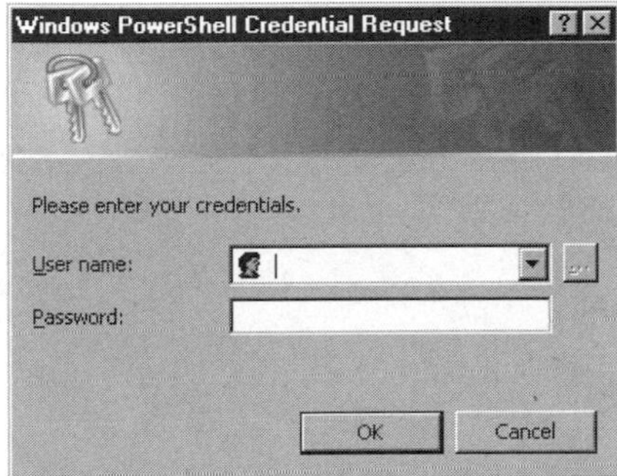

Figure 15-2 The Windows PowerShell Credential Request window

The result is stored in $creds as:

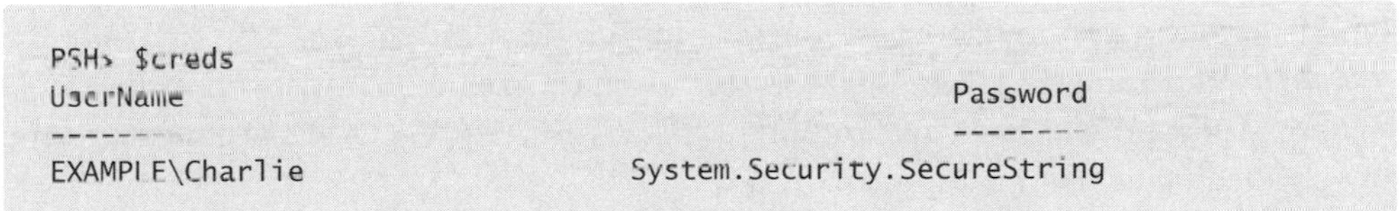

```
PSH> $creds
UserName                                          Password
--------                                          --------
EXAMPLE\Charlie                   System.Security.SecureString
```

> **Note** By default, Get-Credential will create a popup window. You can change this so that the credentials are requested directly from the console by changing the registry:
>
> ```
> PSH>New-Itemproperty hklm:\software\microsoft\powershell\1\shellids `
>    -name consoleprompting -propertytype string -value true
> ```
>
> Notice the backtick character (`). This is a line continuation character, and also the escape character.

Cmdlets

Cmdlets are the most basic of PowerShell commands. They have the form "Verb-Noun," as in Get-Help or Format-List. They are properly shown with initial caps, as we just wrote them, but they are actually not case sensitive. GET-HELP, Get-Help, and get-Help are all the same.

What Is a Cmdlet?

As we said, cmdlets are verb-noun pairs. The verb part is usually based on some kind of action like get, stop, start, new, remove, and so on, whereas the noun part varies greatly. Microsoft provides some standards regarding verb usage. The basic syntax of a cmdlet is:

```
Verb-Noun -parameter argument
```

A simple example of a cmdlet is Write-Output. It accepts parameters and arguments. So, at the PowerShell prompt we see:

```
1 PSH>Write-output -inputObject "testing"
2 testing
3 PSH>Write-Output "testing"
4 testing
5 PSH>write "testing"
6 testing
7 PSH>
```

This demonstrates several concepts. On line 1, the command is written out completely and provides the full command to write *testing* to the console. This is the full and proper way to use Write-Output, but it does seem a bit more than absolutely necessary and appropriate for writing a simple string to the console.

On line 3, we use an implied positional parameter. Even though we didn't include the *–inputObject* parameter, PowerShell was able to determine that because the string immediately follows the cmdlet declaration, it is meant to represent the argument to the unspecified *inputObject* parameter.

Finally, on line 5, we took advantage of an alias to Write-Output. Write is an alias for Write-Output, and PowerShell is able to do the mapping from one to the other. PowerShell comes with 101 aliases by default. Now, an example using Write-Host, which accepts the *–object* parameter, is this simple example with same result–printing out a string onto the console:

```
PSH>Write-Host -object "testing"
testing
PSH>Write-Host -o "testing"
Write-Host : Parameter cannot be processed because the parameter name 'o'
  is ambiguous. Possible matches include: -OutVariable -OutBuffer.
At line:1 char:11
+ Write-Host <<<<  -o "testing"
PSH>Write-Host -ob "testing"
Write-Host: Cannot bind parameter 'OutBuffer' Cannot convert value "testing"
to type "System.Int32". Error: "Input string was not in a correct format."
At line:1 char:15
+ Write-Host -ob  <<<< "testing"
PSH>Write-Host -obj "testing"
testing
```

When typing out parameters, you only need to use enough of the parameter to ensure uniqueness from the set of parameters that are supported by that cmdlet. On lines 3 and 8 in the previous example, we attempted to use a shorter version of the object parameter, but it was too short and considered ambiguous.

Line 13 shows that *-obj* was sufficient for PowerShell to know that we meant *-object*. Some cmdlet parameters are sufficiently unique with only a single letter.

Some Commonly Used Cmdlets

Here's a brief introduction to some of the more common of the more than 120 cmdlets included with Windows Server 2008. For more detailed information and examples, review the "Get-Help" section later in this chapter.

- **Add-Content** Writes content to a file. Example: write the string "testing" to the file testing.txt:

  ```
  Add-Content -object "testing" -filepath testing.txt
  ```

- **Copy-Item** Copies an item to a new one. Example: copy the file test.txt to test1.txt:

  ```
  Copy-Item test.txt test1.txt
  ```

- **Export-Csv** Writes objects to a CSV file. Example: write a list of all services to a CSV file:

  ```
  Get-Process|Export-Csv test.csv
  ```

- **ForEach-Object** Executes a scriptblock to each object in the pipeline. Examples are provided later in the chapter.
- **Format-Custom, Format-List, Format-Table, Format-Wide** Is appended at the end of a pipeline to format how objects are displayed. This cmdlet is discussed later in the chapter.
- **Get-Alias** Gets the entry for an alias. Takes an argument of an alias or wildcard for a list of matching aliases, or with no argument provides a complete list of aliases. Example:

  ```
  Get-Alias write
  ```

- **Get-Childitem** Gets the items and child items in one or more specified locations.
- **Get-Command** Gets information about a cmdlet. You can simply provide another cmdlet as an argument to Get-Command to get more information on that cmdlet or without any arguments; this cmdlet prints out a listing of all the commands on the system.
- **Get-Content** Gets the contents of a file. Example: get the contents of the file testing.txt:

  ```
  Get-Content testing.txt
  ```

- **Get-Credential** Gets a credential object, such as getting the user's user name and password and storing them in an object to be used with another cmdlet. Examples are provided later in this chapter.
- **Get-Eventlog** Administers Windows Event Logs. Examples are provided later in this chapter.
- **Get-Help** This is a built-in help cmdlet. You can simply provide another cmdlet as an argument to Get-Help to get more information on that cmdlet. Example: provide help for the Write-Host cmdlet:

```
Get-Help Write-Host
```

- **Get-Item** Gets an instance of an item. Example: get the details of the current directory:

```
Get-Item $pwd
```

- **Get-Itemproperty** Gets the property of an item.
- **Get-Location** Gets the current directory.
- **Get-Member** Is used to list all the supported properties and methods of an object. Examples are provided later in this chapter.
- **Get-Process** Gets the list of processes or a specific process. Example: get the details of the PowerShell process:

```
Get-Process powershell
```

- **Get-Service** Gets the list of services or a specific service. Example: get the details of the Event Log service:

```
Get-Service eventlog
```

- **Get-Variable** Gets a specific variable that has already been created.
- **Get-Wmiobject** Gets a specific WMI object. Examples are provided later in the chapter.
- **Group-Object** Groups objects together. A practical example is shown later in the chapter.
- **Import-Csv** Gets the contents of a CSV file while creating objects. Example: import the file file.csv:

```
Import-Csv file.csv
```

- **Invoke-Expression** Runs the specified command. Used to execute a command placed in a variable previously.
- **Measure-Object** Performs various calculations on objects.

- **Move-Item** Moves an item to a new one. Example: move the file file.txt to a new name:

  ```
  Move-Item file.txt new_name.txt
  ```

- **New-Alias** Creates a new alias. Example: create an alias *gevl* for the command Get-Eventlog:

  ```
  New-Alias gevl Get-Eventlog
  ```

- **New-Item** Creates a new item. Example: create a new empty file:

  ```
  New-Item -type file foo.txt
  ```

- **New-Itemproperty** Creates a new property of an item.
- **New-Object** Creates a new object. Examples of using New-Object are provided later in the chapter.
- **New-Variable** Creates a new variable. Example: create a new variable called *testing* and assign it the value of 0:

  ```
  New-Variable testing 0
  ```

- **Read-Host** Reads input from the console. An example is provided later in the chapter.
- **Remove-Item** Removes an item. Example: delete a file:

  ```
  Remove-Item file.txt
  ```

- **Select-Object** Allows only the selected properties to either be shown to the console or passed along the pipeline. Select-Object is discussed in more detail later in the chapter.
- **Select-String** Searches for a particular string. Example: search for *testing* in the file file.txt:

  ```
  Select-String test.txt -pattern testing
  ```

- **Set-Alias** Changes the current value of an existing alias.
- **Set-Content** Writes content to a specific file. Example: write the string "testing" to the file test.txt:

  ```
  Set-Content test.txt “testing”
  ```

- **Set-Item** Changes the value of an existing item.
- **Set-Itemproperty** Changes the value of a property of an item.
- **Set-Location** Changes the working directory. Example: change to the root of the C: drive:

  ```
  Set-Location c:\
  ```

- **Set-Variable** Changes the value of an existing variable.
- **Sort-Object** Sorts objects based on a particular property, either in ascending or descending order. A practical example is shown later in the chapter.
- **Start-Service** Starts a specific service. Example: start a service:

  ```
  Start-Service eventlog
  ```
- **Start-Transcript** Starts a log of the current session.
- **Stop-Process** Stops a specific process. Example: stop a PowerShell process:

  ```
  Stop-Process powershell
  ```
- **Stop-Service** Stops a specific service. Example: stop a service:

  ```
  Stop-Service eventlog
  ```
- **Stop-Transcript** Stops logging the current session.
- **Test-Path** Tests for the existence of an item. Examples are provided later in this chapter.
- **Where-Object** When several objects are passed along a pipeline, this cmdlet will basically allow only the selected objects to either be shown to the console or be passed along the pipeline. Where-Object is discussed later in the chapter.
- **Write-Host** Writes a string of text to the console. Examples are provided later in the chapter.

Windows Infrastructure

PowerShell is first and foremost a *Windows* language and shell, and as such it builds on—and is built on—the components and infrastructure of Windows. This includes the .NET Framework, Windows Management Instrumentation (WMI), Windows Remote Management (WinRM), and the Component Object Model (COM). Understanding some basics of these underpinnings will help you understand how PowerShell works and where PowerShell gets its power and flexibility.

The .NET Framework

In a traditional scripting environment, whether it be DOS, VBScript, Perl, or another scripting language, you mostly work with simple strings. PowerShell, however, relies on the .NET Framework for most of what it does: Where a traditional scripting language manipulates strings, PowerShell manipulates objects. The intent here is to introduce you to some of the basic concepts and terminology of the .NET Framework. First, some terms:

- **Namespace** *Namespaces* are the major categories used to split up the .NET Framework into related functions.
- **Class** A *class* defines what an object will look like and its characteristics. Think of it as a blueprint for objects that can be created from it. A namespace contains several classes.
- **Object** When we create a particular instance of a class, we have an *object*. This is an important concept to undestand in PowerShell if you really want use all of its power.
- **Members** *Members* are the features that a class provides. These are split into two categories: methods and properties. (There are also events, but we ignore those mostly.)
- **Methods** *Methods* are the things that an object can do. In PowerShell, these are the verbs.
- **Properties** *Properties* are what an object has, and the qualities that are specific to that object.
- **Constructor** A *constructor* is an argument that is passed when invoking a class. This is not always required, depending on the class being used.
- **Type** A *type* tells how to interpret the data provided. We include a listing of all the types that are supported later in this chapter (at least the most common ones).

Let's start with a simplistic example of what the .NET Framework provides to PowerShell by examining a simple string of text: "testing".

We'll manipulate this string the long way first, and then we'll use the New-Object cmdlet to do it the short way—by creating an instance of a class.

Let's start by creating a new instance of the System.String class, and passing "testing" as its constructor. This gets assigned to the variable *$mystring*.

```
PSH> $mystring=New-Object -typeName System.String -argumentList "testing"
```

Now, to make sure that we have a System.String object, we're going to use a quick little trick:

```
PSH> $mystring.gettype().FullName
System.String
```

Okay, that's one way to create a System.String object. The shorter way shows us how PowerShell does some of the work for us:

```
PSH> $mystring2="testing"
PSH> $mystring2|Get-Member
   TypeName: System.String
Name             MemberType          Definition
----             ----------          ----------
Clone            Method              System.Object Clone()
CompareTo        Method              System.Int32 CompareTo
  (Object value), System.Int32 CompareTo(String
Contains         Method              System.Boolean Contains(String value)
CopyTo           Method              System.Void CopyTo
  (Int32 sourceIndex, Char[] destination, Int32 dest
EndsWith         Method              System.Boolean EndsWith
  (String value), System.Boolean EndsWith(Strin
Equals           Method              System.Boolean Equals(Object
  obj), System.Boolean Equals(String valu
GetEnumerator    Method              System.CharEnumerator GetEnumerator()
GetHashCode      Method              System.Int32 GetHashCode()
GetType          Method              System.Type GetType()
GetTypeCode      Method              System.TypeCode GetTypeCode()
IndexOf          Method              System.Int32 IndexOf(Char
  value, Int32 startIndex, Int32 count), Sys
IndexOfAny       Method              System.Int32 IndexOfAny
  (Char[] anyOf, Int32 startIndex, Int32 count)
Insert           Method              System.String Insert
  (Int32 startIndex, String value)
```

The preceding code tells us that we still have a System.String object, as we requested. But it also tells us a great deal more, because Get-Member lists all of the methods and properties that an object provides.

Two of the methods that we can use with a System.String object are ToUpper and Replace:

```
PSH> $mystring
testing
PSH> $mystring.ToUpper()
TESTING
PSH> $mystring.Replace("ing","ed")
tested
```

What we did in the preceding example is use two methods provided by the System.String object. ToUpper changes all of our letters into uppercase, and the Replace method replaces a particular string with another.

Note To use a method, even if nothing is passed, you must add "()" to the end of the method name.

Note Different objects provide different methods. For example, the methods we have access to when dealing with a string are different from when we are dealing with an array. Looking at the methods of an object and looking up the information online can be very useful when attempting to become more efficient with PowerShell.

And now on to the properties of the System.String object. System.String only supports a single property, length:

```
PSH> $mystring.length
7
```

For a string, the length property is simply the number of characters contained in the object.

Another useful feature of the .NET Framework that PowerShell inherits is garbage collection. The .NET Framework is smart enough to recover memory efficiently. In scripts and other commands in this chapter, we don't use an exit routine to clear up variables and objects created: .NET takes care of this for us.

To provide a useful example, we are going to use a class from the .NET Framework to allow us to easily check whether an IP address is valid:

```
PSH>[system.net.ipaddress]::tryparse("155.0.0.0",[ref]$null)
True
PSH>[system.net.ipaddress]::tryparse("555.0.0.0",[ref]$null)
False
```

In the preceding example, we called a .NET Framework class along with one of its methods (one of its static methods, actually) to verify whether an IP address provided is a valid (True) or invalid (False) address. That was the whirlwind tour of the basics of the .NET Framework.

More Info A useful blog post on how to create your own custom objects in PowerShell can be found at: *http://www.bsonposh.com/modules/wordpress/?p=25.*

Note For an excellent example using the .NET Framework to create a complex graphical interface to retrieve WMI information, see the Marc van Orsouw (aka MoW) PowerShell Guy site: *http://thepowershellguy.com/blogs/posh/archive/tags/WMI+Explorer/default.aspx*.

Windows Management Instrumentation (WMI)

WMI is a feature of Windows operating systems that allows you to control and manage systems remotely. PowerShell uses the Get-Wmiobject cmdlet to retrieve WMI information from remote systems. The default namespace used by Get-Wmiobject is root/cimv2.

Throughout the chapter, we provide some WMI examples using the Get-Wmiobject and show some other methods to get this information. Here are a few interesting WMI classes to keep in mind:

- **Win32_DiskQuota** Retrieves information on disk quotas
- **Win32_PageFileUsage** Retrieves information on the page file usage
- **Win32_Printer** Retrieves information on the printers configured
- **Win32_PrintJob** Retrieves information on current print jobs
- **Win32_Process** Retrieves information on running processes
- **Win32_Processor** Retrieves information on the installed processors
- **Win32_QuickFixEngineering** Retrieves information about the hotfixes/updates that have been applied on the system
- **Win32_QuotaSetting** Retrieves the setting information for disk quotas
- **Win32_Service** Retrieves the service information
- **Win32_TimeZone** Retrieves the time zone information

Some of these classes may require using different authentication settings to access this information remotely. WinRM, which we discuss in the next section, provides a workaround for this.

Important A few preliminary steps are required before you can use WMI remotely on a newly installed Server 2008 system. Run the following netsh commands from the an elevated PowerShell or CMD prompt:

```
Netsh firewall set service RemoteAdmin
Netsh advfirewall set currentprofile settings remotemanagement enable
```

Note The next version of PowerShell will provide more support for using WMI. Some preliminary information can be found here: *http://www.microsoft.com/technet/scriptcenter/topics/winpsh/wmiin2.mspx.*

Real World Using WMI

A couple of examples of how useful WMI is are in order. In the first example, we demonstrate how to start a remote process—specifically, how to start a Microsoft security update installation. The update will apply itself, without requiring user intervention, and we can use a parameter to force the server to restart after the update is installed.

You can install a security update remotely in two ways. The first method assumes that you are logged on to a system as a Domain Administrator, and that the target system is in the same domain:

```
PSH>([WMICLASS]"\\<servername>\root\cimv2:win32_process").create
   ("cmd.exe /c `"c:\\WindowsServer2003-KB941644-x86-ENU.exe
   /quiet /norestart`" /q")
```

In the preceding example, we've used a UNC path to the WMI class on a remote system. The [WMICLASS] casts the string to the WMICLASS type. (More on casting later in this chapter.) The */quiet* and */norestart* flags tell the update installer to not ask for user input and not restart after the update.

Important The entire preceding command must be on one line.

But what if we're not in the same domain, or we aren't using a Domain Administrator account? No problem. In the following method, we use WMI to install a networked printer on a remote server:

```
1  PSH>$printer=\\print_server\printer
2  PSH>$creds=Get-Credential
3  PSH>$obj=gwmi -computer 10.10.10.10 -class meta_class
     -filter '__this is a "Win32_Printer"' -namespace
    'root\cimv2' -credential $creds
4  PSH>$obj.AddPrinterConnection($printer)
5  PSH>$obj.Put()
6  PSH>gwmi -computer 10.10.10.10 -class Win32_Printer
     -namespace 'root\cimv2' -credential $creds
```

Here's what we did, line by line:

1. Defines a variable ($printer) that represents the UNC path to the printer we want to add.
2. Gets a credential object and stores it in the variable $creds.
3. Uses Get-Wmiobject to get a remote instance of the Win32_Printer class.
4. Uses the AddPrinterConnection method with a reference to the network printer.
5. Applies the change back to the remote system.
6. Uses Get-Wmiobject again to verify that we created the remote printer.

Windows Remote Management (WinRM)

WMI is a great tool, but can be challenging to use across firewalls or where authentication is required. WinRM, however, uses the HTTP/HTTPS protocols, allowing it to pass through firewalls, and, since the commands actually run *on* the remote computer, remote authentication is more easily handled. The winrs (Windows Remote Shell) command uses WinRM to execute commands on a remote system.

Here is a simple example of using winrs is to run the ipconfig command remotely:

```
PSH>winrs `-r:http://servername `-u:Username ipconfig
```

Note Because we're running this in PowerShell, we need to add a backtick character (`) to escape the dashes. From a Cmd console, the backticks aren't required. This command will prompt you for the password associated with the user name specified.

Important Before you can use WinRM on Windows Server 2008 you need to do the following from an elevated prompt:

```
Winrm quickconfig
Winrm set winrm/config/client @{TrustedHosts="*"}
```

Note The first line sets up WinRM on the system, and the second designates all client systems as trusted. You can limit the systems that have access using this syntax: @{TrustedHosts="server1","server2"}.

More Info For more on WinRm, see: *http://www.microsoft.com/technet/script-center/newswire/winrm.mspx*. The following link is also an excellent overview of WinRM and example commands: *http://blogs.technet.com/otto/archive/2007/02/09/sample-vista-ws-man-winrm-commands.aspx*.

Note The next version of PowerShell will use WinRM to implement remote management in PowerShell.

Component Object Model (COM)

Although Microsoft is shifting toward providing .NET interfaces for all products, some products (Microsoft Office and Microsoft Internet Explorer, for example) still provide only a COM interface.

Using Internet Explorer, here's an example using PowerShell and Internet Explorer's COM interface:

```
1  $ie=New-Object -comobject internetexplorer.application
2  $ie.navigate2("about:blank")
3  while($ie.busy){sleep -m 50}
4  $ie.visible=$true
5  $ie.navigate2("http://www.microsoft.com")
```

Here's how it works, line by line:

1. Use the COM interface to Internet Explorer to create a COM object.
2. Open a blank page.
3. Wait for the Internet Explorer process we created to be idle.
4. Make the window visible
5. Open the Microsoft home page.

Note In some instances a COM interface may work perfectly fine in VBScript, for example, but may not exhibit the same behavior when called from PowerShell.

More Info Check out the following link for other cool things you can do with COM and PowerShell: *http://bartdesmet.net/blogs/bart/archive/2006/12/02/PowerShell-_2D00_-Ask-Merlin_3A00_-a-cool-demo-of-using-COM-objects.aspx.*

Creating Popup and Input Boxes

PowerShell can use two more COM interfaces: VBScript and Windows Scripting Host (WSH). First, here's a simple example using WSH:

```
PSH>$msgbox = New-Object -comobject wscript.shell
PSH>$return=$msgbox.popup("Do you like PowerShell?",0,"PowerShell window",1)
PSH>$return
```

First, instantiate the object as $msgbox. Then, pass the object to the *$return* variable with appropriate syntax, and finally execute it in line 3, as shown in Figure 15-3.

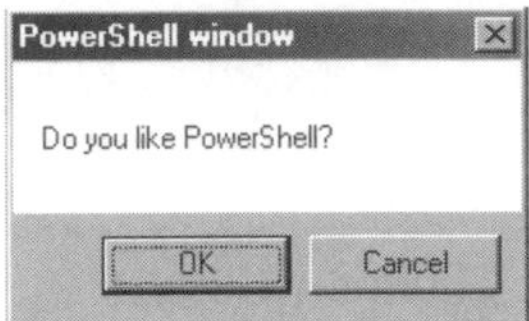

Figure 15-3 A popup box created using COM and WSH

Now, using VBScript, here's how to create a simple popup where the user can input text and have it returned to PowerShell:

```
1  PSH>$obj = New-Object -comobject MSScriptControl.ScriptControl
2  PSH>$obj.language = "vbscript"
3  PSH>$obj.addcode("function getInput() getInput = inputbox(
     `"Message box prompt`",`"Message Box Title`") end function" )
4  PSH>$return = $obj.eval("getInput")
5  PSH>$return
```

This time we instantiate a different kind of object on line 1, set our scripting language to VBScript on line 2, and then pass some specific VBScript code on line 3. Finally, we run the code on line 4, and also pass the results to the return variable, which is written to console on line 5. The result is shown in Figure 15-4.

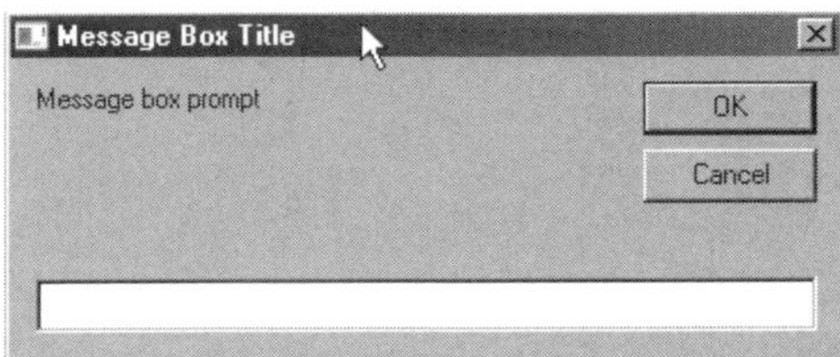

Figure 15-4 An input box created using COM and VBScript

Exploring PowerShell

PowerShell is highly discoverable. You can use PowerShell to learn more about PowerShell. For us, this is one of its most important strengths. Every day that we use PowerShell, we learn a little more about it, and find more ways to do what we need to do. Three critical cmdlets make this possible:

- **Get-Command** Lists the available commands, allowing you to look for a cmdlet that might do what you are trying to do. It accepts wildcards and other parameters. Its alias is *gcm*.

- **Get-Help** Provides built-in help on available cmdlets and other built-in features such as functions and operators. Its alias is *man*.
- **Get-Member** Provides detailed information on various features that cmdlets support. Its alias is *gm*.

Get-Command

Definitions are great, but examples are often more useful. With no arguments, the output will provide a listing of all the cmdlets on the system. Get-Command accepts various parameters, but, more important, it accepts wildcards. Let's say we want to administer a service, but we aren't sure what cmdlets are available. So, let's use PowerShell to help us find out, as shown in Figure 15-5.

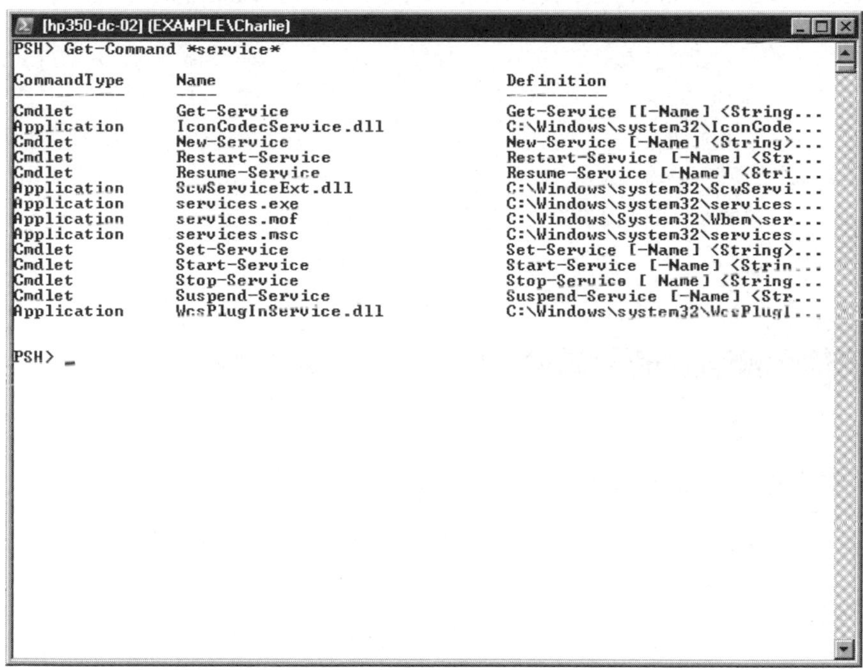

Figure 15-5 Using PowerShell Get-Command

Useful, but it gave us rather more than we wanted. All we really wanted was a list of cmdlets that had *service* in their names. OK, try this:

```
PSH> get-command -commandtype cmdlet *service* | format-table "Name"

Name
----
Get-Service
New-Service
ReStart-Service
Resume-Service
Set-Service
Start-Service
Stop-Service
Suspend-Service
```

That's a bit easier to read, and gives us only commands of type cmdlet. Two other useful parameters to Get-Command are *–verb* and *–noun*.

Get-Help

Get-Help is the PowerShell equivalent of the UNIX *man* command. And not only is *man* an alias for Get-Help, but the output looks very much the same. With no arguments, the output is help on the Get-Help command itself.

Use Get-Help with the full cmdlet name as an argument. So, for the Get-Service command we used in the previous example, we have the result shown in Figure 15-6.

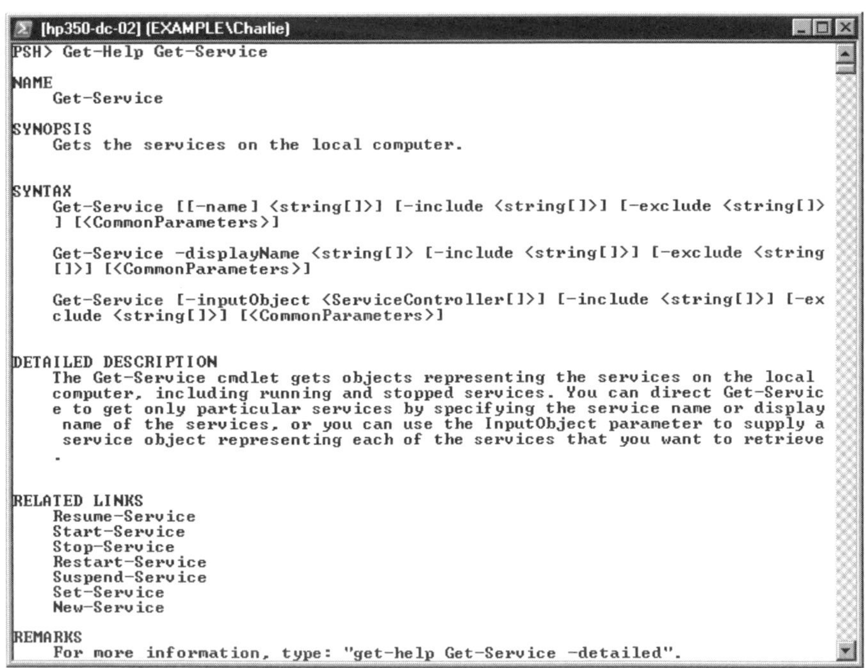

Figure 15-6 The results of Get-Help Get-Service

Short, and to the point, but a lot more useful than the help that most Cmd commands give you with a /? parameter, certainly. Plus, in the Remarks section, we see a hint that we can get a good deal more information using the *–detailed* or *-full* parameters. Finally, our favorite parameter is the *–examples* parameter. Using *–examples* gives you a very short description, but with a set of examples at the end that make it much more useful, as shown in Figure 15-7.

```
[hp350-dc-02] (EXAMPLE\Charlie)
PSH> Get-Help Get-Service -examples

NAME
    Get-Service

SYNOPSIS
    Gets the services on the local computer.

    -------------------------- EXAMPLE 1 --------------------------

    C:\PS>get-service


    This command retrieves all of the services on the system. It behaves as tho
    ugh you typed "get-service *". The default display shows the status, servic
    e name, and display name of each service.



    -------------------------- EXAMPLE 2 --------------------------

    C:\PS>get-service wmi*


    This command retrieves services with service names that begin with "WMI".



    -------------------------- EXAMPLE 3 --------------------------

    C:\PS>get-service -displayname *network*


    This command displays services with a display name that includes the word
    "network." This command lets you find network-related services even when th
    e service name does not include "Net," such as xmlprov, the Network Provisi
    oning Service.
```

Figure 15-7 Using the –examples parameter of Get-Help

> **Note** Another quick way to get a short listing of the parameters is to simply use *PSH>Get-Command Get-Service Select-Object definition Format-List.*

Finally, Get-Help provides more detailed information on general topics and concepts with the Get-Help about group of help files. To see a list of these, use Get-Help about_*. Invaluable for those of us still learning about PowerShell.

Get-Member

In the .NET Framework section, we briefly talked about the members of a class. We're going to continue using Get-Service as an example. When a cmdlet is piped to Get-Member, it will list the methods and properties associated with the class or type that the cmdlet produces, as shown in Figure 15-8.

```
[hp350-ts-05]
PSH> Get-Service|Get-Member -membertype property,method


   TypeName: System.ServiceProcess.ServiceController

Name                      MemberType Definition
----                      ---------- ----------
add_Disposed              Method     System.Void add_Disposed(EventHandler v...
Close                     Method     System.Void Close()
Continue                  Method     System.Void Continue()
CreateObjRef              Method     System.Runtime.Remoting.ObjRef CreateOb...
Dispose                   Method     System.Void Dispose()
Equals                    Method     System.Boolean Equals(Object obj)
ExecuteCommand            Method     System.Void ExecuteCommand(Int32 command)
GetHashCode               Method     System.Int32 GetHashCode()
GetLifetimeService        Method     System.Object GetLifetimeService()
GetType                   Method     System.Type GetType()
get_CanPauseAndContinue   Method     System.Boolean get_CanPauseAndContinue()
get_CanShutdown           Method     System.Boolean get_CanShutdown()
get_CanStop               Method     System.Boolean get_CanStop()
get_Container             Method     System.ComponentModel.IContainer get_Co...
get_DependentServices     Method     System.ServiceProcess.ServiceController...
get_DisplayName           Method     System.String get_DisplayName()
get_MachineName           Method     System.String get_MachineName()
get_ServiceHandle         Method     System.Runtime.InteropServices.SafeHand...
get_ServiceName           Method     System.String get_ServiceName()
get_ServicesDependedOn    Method     System.ServiceProcess.ServiceController...
get_ServiceType           Method     System.ServiceProcess.ServiceType get_S...
get_Site                  Method     System.ComponentModel.ISite get_Site()
get_Status                Method     System.ServiceProcess.ServiceController...
InitializeLifetimeService Method     System.Object InitializeLifetimeService()
Pause                     Method     System.Void Pause()
Refresh                   Method     System.Void Refresh()
remove_Disposed           Method     System.Void remove_Disposed(EventHandle...
set_DisplayName           Method     System.Void set_DisplayName(String value)
set_MachineName           Method     System.Void set_MachineName(String value)
set_ServiceName           Method     System.Void set_ServiceName(String value)
set_Site                  Method     System.Void set_Site(ISite value)
Start                     Method     System.Void Start(), System.Void Start(...
Stop                      Method     System.Void Stop()
```

Figure 15-8 Using Get-Member to get the properties and methods of a cmdlet

In this example, we piped Get-Service to Get-Member, and used the parameter *membertype* with the values property and method to limit it to just those two properties. The result is a listing of all the members we have access to. Of particular interest is the first line of text where we have the class or type of object we have. In this case, we are dealing with a System.ServiceProcess.ServiceController object. If you were to check the Microsoft online documentation on the .NET Framework, you'd see that all the methods and properties are enumerated and these should coincide with the output seen in the preceding example.

Data Display

We've said that objects are the output of cmdlets. Let's contrast the output from Get-Service when we look at the eventlog service, and compare that to when we use Get-Member to see the list of properties, as shown in Figure 15-9:

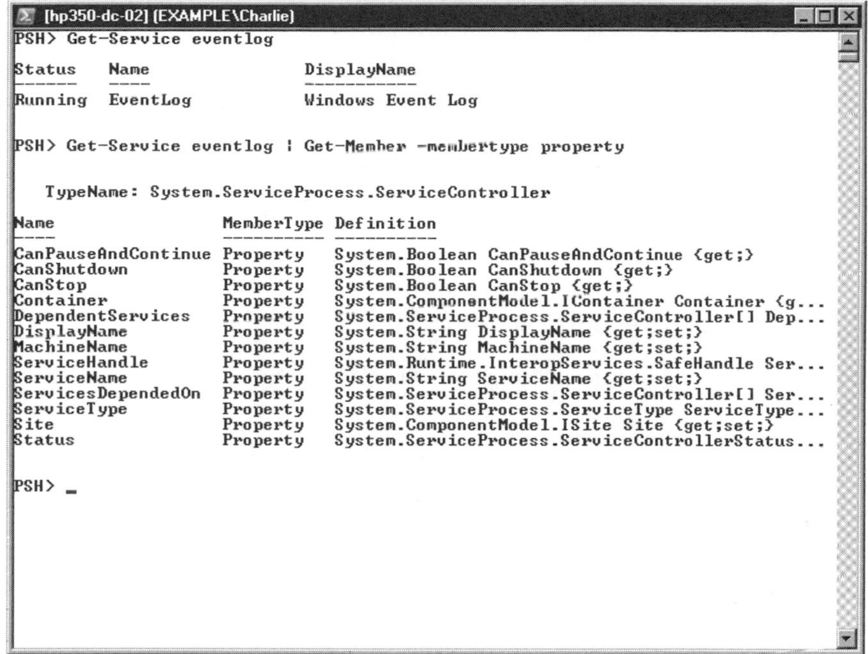
```
[hp350-dc-02] (EXAMPLE\Charlie)
PSH> Get-Service eventlog

Status   Name               DisplayName
------   ----               -----------
Running  EventLog           Windows Event Log

PSH> Get-Service eventlog | Get-Member -membertype property

   TypeName: System.ServiceProcess.ServiceController

Name                MemberType Definition
----                ---------- ----------
CanPauseAndContinue Property   System.Boolean CanPauseAndContinue {get;}
CanShutdown         Property   System.Boolean CanShutdown {get;}
CanStop             Property   System.Boolean CanStop {get;}
Container           Property   System.ComponentModel.IContainer Container {g...
DependentServices   Property   System.ServiceProcess.ServiceController[] Dep...
DisplayName         Property   System.String DisplayName {get;set;}
MachineName         Property   System.String MachineName {get;set;}
ServiceHandle       Property   System.Runtime.InteropServices.SafeHandle Ser...
ServiceName         Property   System.String ServiceName {get;set;}
ServicesDependedOn  Property   System.ServiceProcess.ServiceController[] Ser...
ServiceType         Property   System.ServiceProcess.ServiceType ServiceType...
Site                Property   System.ComponentModel.ISite Site {get;set;}
Status              Property   System.ServiceProcess.ServiceControllerStatus...

PSH> _
```

Figure 15-9 Using Get-Member to get a list of properties for a service

So when we first call Get-Service eventlog, only three properties (Status, Name, and DisplayName) are displayed in the console. However, when we pipe this to Get-Member and ask for all the properties of the object, we get many more properties listed. Why were there only three in our first listing?

PowerShell uses XML configuration files that control the formatting of objects based on their class. For the most part, the default properties are what most would want to see.

We can change how PowerShell displays the data by creating the appropriate XML files, but that is well beyond this scope of this chapter. Instead, we can simply use the Select-Object cmdlet to get us the properties we want to display:

```
PSH>Get-Service eventlog

Status   Name               DisplayName
------   ----               -----------
Running  Eventlog           Event Log


PSH>Get-Service eventlog|Select-Object status|Format-Table -autosize

 Status
 ------
Running
```

Note The Format-Table cmdlet is used to show the data in a more presentable format. Otherwise, the column would not be seen in current window.

Parameter Sets and Positional Parameters

Parameter sets are groups of parameters that must be used together, although some parameters in a parameter set might be optional.

```
PSH> Get-Command Get-Service|select parametersets|Format-List

 ParameterSets : {Default, DisplayName, InputObject}

PSH>
```

In the preceding output, three parameter sets are defined, and they are all separated by commas. Basically, the parameter sets indicate that, for example, I cannot use the Get-Service cmdlet, and define both the *Name* and *DisplayName* parameters together:

```
PSH> Get-Service -Name WinRM -DisplayName $display
Get-Service : Parameter set cannot be resolved using the specified named
parameters.
At line:1 char:12
+ Get-Service <<<<  -Name WinRM -DisplayName $display
```

From the preceding output, we see that PowerShell generates an error when we try to use parameters from different parameter sets together.

The previous example doesn't tell us, however, what the default parameter set is. In some cases, a default parameter set applies when only positional parameters are used (when the actual parameter name is dropped from the command and only the values are typed).

Let's look at positional parameters. Again we use the Get-Service cmdlet. To get a detailed listing of the parameters and their specific details, we use Get-Help Get-Service *–full*:

```
PARAMETERS
    -name <string[]>
        Specifies the service names of services to be retrieved.
        Wildcards are permitted. By default, Get-Service gets
        all of the services on the computer.

        Required?                    false
        Position?                    1
```

```
        Default value                *
        Accept pipeline input?       true (ByValue, ByPropertyName)
        Accept wildcard characters?  true

    -include <string[]>
        Retrieves only the specified services. The value of this
        parameter qualifies the Name parameter. Enter a name element
        or pattern, such as "s*". Wildcards are permitted.

        Required?                    false
        Position?                    named
        Default value
        Accept pipeline input?       false
        Accept wildcard characters?  true
```

The (partial) output tells us that both parameters are optional, allowing us to call Get-Service with no parameters. In addition, we also see that the *Name* parameter is the default parameter (and thus in position 1), while the *include* parameter must be named:

```
PSH>Get-Service Eventlog

Status   Name               DisplayName
------   ----               -----------
Running  Eventlog           Event Log


PSH>Get-Service ev*

Status   Name               DisplayName
------   ----               -----------
Running  Eventlog           Event Log
Running  EventSystem        COM+ Event System


PSH>Get-Service ev* -include eventl*

Status   Name               DisplayName
------   ----               -----------
Running  Eventlog           Event Log

PSH>Get-Service ev* -inc eventl*

Status   Name               DisplayName
------   ----               -----------
Running  Eventlog           Event Log
```

With no parameters, Eventlog is assumed to be the *Name* parameter because it is in position 1.

Loading a Snap-in

PowerShell extensions are provided via a snap-in. Some snap-ins are just a DLL file; others have a Windows Installer program.

Use the following steps if you're provided with only a DLL and not a full installer:

1. Create a permanent directory to place the DLL.
2. Copy the DLL to that new directory
3. Use the installutil.exe program from the .NET Framework to register the DLL. On Windows Server 2008, Installutil is located at %windir%\Microsoft.NET\Framework64\v2.0.50727 for 64bit DLLs, and in %windir%\\Microsoft.NET\Framework\v2.0.50727 for 32-bit DLLs. Using PowerShell, you can always find the location of the current .NET Framework.

   ```
   $framework=$([System.Runtime.InteropServices.
      RuntimeEnvironment]::GetRuntimeDirectory())
   ```

4. Use `Get-Pssnapin -registered` to get the assembly name.
5. Use `Add-Pssnapin` to load the assembly.
6. You can now use the feature(s) provided by the snap-in.
7. (Optional) Add the `Add-Pssnapin` command to your profile so that it loads automatically.

If an installer program is provided, usually only steps 4 through 7 are required.

Powershell Scripting Basics

Up to now, we've tried to give you an idea of how PowerShell works and some of its power when used as an interactive shell. In this section, we'll focus on some PowerShell scripting basics, including:

- Creating a .ps1 script
- Variables
- Scope
- Strings
- Here strings

- Wildcards and regular expressions
- Arrays
- Hashtables
- Operators
- Conditional statements
- Looping statements
- Exiting from scripts, functions, and loops
- Importing and exporting from and to files
- Flow control cmdlets
- Formatting cmdlets
- Using functions in a script
- Dot-sourcing
- Passing arguments to a script or function
- Param statement
- Using the pipeline with $_ and $input
- Adding comments to a script
- Handling errors
- Redirection operators
- Type accelerator
- Escaping characters

Creating a .ps1 Script

The interactive feature of the PowerShell console is very useful, but sometimes you need a script. We have a saying around here: "Do it once? Just do it. Do it twice? Write a script!" Windows PowerShell scripts use the .ps1 extension. We're going to start with a fairly simplistic example, and we'll build as we go.

We have the option of typing out the command in the console, but here we're going to use PowerShell to actually create a script, on the fly. Then we'll execute the script:

```
PSH>Write-Host "testing"
testing
PSH>Add-Content -path testing.ps1 -value "Write-Host `"testing`""
PSH>./testing.ps1
testing
PSH>
```

Here, we've first executed the Write-Host cmdlet, with the output you see on line 2. On line 3, we use the Add-Content cmdlet to create a PowerShell script in the current directory. Finally, on line 4, we execute that script.

Note If you haven't changed your default execution policy on this computer, you'll get an error when you try to execute the script on line 4. If you do, open a PowerShell window using Run As Administrator, and enter the following command: Set-ExecutionPolicy RemoteSigned

Real World Executing PowerShell Scripts

By default, .ps1 is not an automatically executed extension, and the current directory is not part of your execution path in PowerShell. Although we understand the security reasons for this, we frankly find it a bit annoying in the real world. You can do two things to make life easier. The first is to add .ps1 to your PATHEXT variable. To do this for a single session, just run this command in the session:

```
PSH> $ENV:PATHEXT="$ENV:PATHEXT;.PS1"
```

Add this to your profile, and it will be true for all sessions. We think that's a reasonable way to make life easier–you save having to add .ps1 every time you want to run a script, but the change is active only when you're actually in a PowerShell console. Now, instead of typing **myscript.ps1**, you'll only have to type **myscript** to execute the script.

The second change we think makes sense is adding the current directory to your path. The "." (dot) directory is the current directory, and it is *not* part of your execution path in a PowerShell console. There is a sound reason for this–adding it to your path is a potential security problem. But we think if you're smart, and you don't run As Administrator except when you actually *need* to, and you are moderately careful, and you only add the current directory at the *end* of your execution path, you have made your life simpler without creating a huge problem. To do this, enter the following command:

```
PSH> $ENV:PATH="$ENV:PATH;."
```

Again, this changes your path only for the current session. To change it for all your sessions, change it in your profile.

Do *not* make these changes without understanding the security implications, and do not make them in either of the all users profiles–only make them in your own profile.

The preceding method works great when the script we want to run doesn't contain any spaces in the filename. Where there is a space, we need to use the call operator, "&", to invoke the command, and we need to enclose the command in quotes:

```
PSH>Add-Content -path "testing 1.ps1" -value "Write-Host `"testing #2`""
PSH>dir testing*.ps1
Directory: Microsoft.PowerShell.Core\FileSystem::C:\Documents and
   Settings\Desktop\charlie
Mode                LastWriteTime     Length Name
----                -------------     ------ ----
-a---         1/26/2008  12:07 PM         25 testing 1.ps1
-a---          1/7/2008  10:33 PM         45 testing.ps1
PSH>./testing 1.ps1
The term './testing' is not recognized as a cmdlet, function, operable
   program, or script file. Verify the term and try again.
At line:1 char:6
+ ./testing <<<<  1.ps1
PSH>& "./testing 1.ps1"
testing #2
```

Comments

Comments are an essential part of any script. Although PowerShell is a reasonably easy-to-read language, comments make it far easier when it's six months down the road and you need to revise the script to understand what each element does, and why. If you get in the habit of commenting even trivial scripts, pretty soon it won't seem onerous or take any extra time–it becomes automatic. Comments are not extra work. They're an essential part of the script. This is especially true in an environment where more than one person will have to work with a script, or where common scripts and functions are shared. But even when you are just writing quick scripts for your own use, take the time to comment.

The comment character for PowerShell is the crosshatch character (#). It will be treated as the start of a comment wherever it appears, with everything after on the current line being a comment, unless the # is enclosed in quotes, or is escaped with a backtick:

```
PSH># Test comment
PSH>$d=Get-Date # Getting the current date
PSH>$d
02/02/2008 13:52:43
PSH>"$d " + "# Not a comment"
PSH>02/02/2008 13:52:43# Not a comment
```

The preceding example demonstrates the two basic ways of adding comments. PowerShell doesn't have a way to add multiline comments. You need to add the # character at the beginning of every full line of comments.

Variables

Variables are holding places for values, and those values can be simple strings, complex strings, numbers, and even .NET objects. And when we assign an object to a variable, all of the object's members remain.

A simple way to create a variable is to assign it a number of even a string. As we've seen, the assignment operator is a single equals sign (=).

```
PSH>$var_number=5
PSH>$var_string="testing"
```

Use Get-Member, as shown earlier in the chapter, to confirm what kind of objects we have.

Scope

Scope is a tricky concept. PowerShell has four named levels of scope:

- **Global** Available to the entire shell
- **Script** Available only to the current script
- **Local** Available only to the current scope and subscopes
- **Private** Available only to the current scope

Getting the scope wrong in a script can often lead to confusing and frustrating troubleshooting sessions. Scope applies to variables, functions, and filters. Let's look at scope as it applies to variables:

```
PSH>$a="My"
PSH>$a
My
PSH>function test {
>> $a="Test"
>> $a
>> }
>>
PSH>$a
My
PSH>test
Test
PSH>$a
My
PSH>
```

Here we assigned a value ("My") to the variable *$a* on line 1, and then created a function that also had a variable *$a*, but with the value "Test". The change to *$a* as part of the function only has scope within the function—it doesn't change the session value for *$a*—which is a global scope for the session:

```
PSH>function test1 {
>> $a
>> }
>>
PSH>test1
My
PSH>
```

Here, we've created another function with a variable *$a*, but we haven't assigned a value to it. The result is that *$a* inherits the value from the parent scope. For more on scope, see Get-Help About_Scope.

Strings

We talked about strings when we introduced the .NET Framework earlier. A string represents any kind of data. More often than not, a string is composed of non-numeric characters. But a number enclosed in double quotes is also a string:

```
PSH>"testing"
Testing
PSH>"255"
255
PSH> "255" | Get-Member gettype | ft typename
TypeName
--------
System.String
PSH> 255 | Get-Member gettype | ft typename
TypeName
--------
System.Int32
PSH>
```

If you enter a string into the PowerShell console, it is written back to the host.

Two useful things you can do with strings are adding strings and invoke-expression. In PowerShell, we can easily add, or concatenate, strings:

```
1   PSH>$var1="test"
2   PSH>$var2="ing"
3   PSH>$var1+$var2
4   testing
5   PSH>$var1
6   test
7   PSH>$var1+=$var2
8   PSH>$var1
9   testing
10  PSH>
```

On line 3, we use the addition operator to join two strings together. When PowerShell determines it is adding two strings together, it concatenates them. On line number 7, we used a shorthand for *$var1=$var1+$var2*.

We can execute strings as well, using Invoke-Expression.

```
PSH>$function=Read-Host "Enter function"
Enter function: Get-Process
PSH>$proc=Read-Host "Enter process"
Enter process: powershell
PSH>invoke-expression "$function $proc"
Handles  NPM(K)    PM(K)      WS(K) VM(M)   CPU(s)     Id ProcessName
-------  ------    -----      ----- -----   ------     -- -----------
   1792      11    62884       7080   193    40.19   5576 powershell
```

Here, we interactively created a string consisting of a cmdlet name and an argument and then we executed it.

Important Invoke-expression can be very dangerous to use. For example, consider what might have happened if you did this:

```
PSH>$function=Read-Host "Enter function"
Enter function: Get-Childitem c:\demo -force -recurse
PSH>$proc=Read-Host “Enter process”
Enter process: |ForEach-Object{Remove-Item $_ -recurse -whatif}
PSH>invoke-expression $function $proc
```

It's a good idea to avoid invoke-expression unless some kind of checking is being done on the variables being used.

Here Strings

A here string can span multiple lines:

```
1  PSH>$multi=@"
2  >> This is a test
3  >> of a here string.
4  >> "@
5  >>
6  PSH>$multi
7  This is a test
8  of a here string.
9  PSH>
```

Here strings are fussy. When you start the here string, you cannot leave a space or anything else after the quote on line number 1.

Wildcards and Regular Expressions

Wildcards are special characters that you can use in various places in PowerShell. You can use them when searching for cmdlets, you can use them as values passed to a parameter, and you can also use them when trying to search for strings.

The wildcard characters are:

- `*` Matches zero or more characters
- `?` Matches exactly one character.
- `[]` Matches the specified characters or a range.

Here are some quick examples:

```
PSH>Get-Command Get-servic?
CommandType     Name
-----------     ----
Cmdlet          Get-Service
PSH>Get-Command Get-servi*
CommandType     Name
-----------     ----
Cmdlet          Get-Service
PSH>Get-Command Get-servic[e]
CommandType     Name
-----------     ----
Cmdlet          Get-Service
PSH>Get-Command Get-servic[a-z]
CommandType     Name
-----------     ----
Cmdlet          Get-Service
```

Note We mentioned that Get-Help about_topic was a very useful way to get more help information from PowerShell. One thing that isn't currently available is an easy way to get some kind of summary of all of the about_ help topics. Here's a script that can help provide some of this information:

```
Get-Childitem C:\windows\system32\windowspowershell\v1.0\en-US
   about_* |` Foreach-object{
   " "
   [string]$help=gc $_.fullname
   $null=$help -match "^(?<BEGIN>.+?)SHORT DESCRIPTION(?<TXT>.+?)
   LONG ` DESCRIPTION(?<END>.+?)$"
   $_.name.replace(".help.txt","")
   $matches.TXT -replace "\s{2,}"," "
}
```

It does need a little bit of work on the formatting of the output, though.

Real World Valid E-mail Address?

Something that can be useful in a script is being able to verify whether a particular variable is a valid e-mail address. Exchange 2007 has .NET Framework classes that make this easier, but we work on a lot of computers that aren't Exchange 2007 servers. To validate a string as being a valid e-mail address, use a regular expression:

```
PSH>"some_user@domain.com" -match "([\w-\.]+)@((\[[0-9]{1,3}\.
  [0-9]{1,3}\.[0-9]{1,3}\.)|(([\w-]+\.)+))([a-zA-Z]{2,4}|
  [0-9]{1,3})(\]?)"
True
PSH>"some_user@@domain.com" -match "([\w-\.]+)@((\[[0-9]{1,3}\.
  [0-9]{1,3}\.[0-9]{1,3}\.)|(([\w-]+\.)+))([a-zA-Z]{2,4}|[0-9]
  {1,3})(\]?)"
False
```

This is a relatively complicated regular expression that tells us whether an e-mail address is valid. For an excellent reference on Regular Expressions, we recommend Jeffrey Friedl's *Mastering Regular Expressions, Third Edition* (O'Reilly, 2006).

More Info For more information, check out Get-Help about_wildcards and get_help about_regular_expressions.

Arrays

One way to look at an array is as a list of data:

```
PSH>$array="this","that"
PSH>$array
this
that
PSH>$array[0]
this
```

An array is simply a list of comma-separated values. Individual elements in the array are accessed with the [] syntax, starting from element 0.

A second way to define an array is with the @ operator:

```
1 PSH>$array1=@()
2 PSH>$array1=@("abc","123")
3 PSH>$array1
4 abc
5 123
6 PSH>
```

Line 1 initializes an array using the syntax @() and line 2 assigns values to the array.

When we read in a file using Get-Content, the results will be an array object. As a result, we can access lines that we have read in by using the [] operator, as we just mentioned:

```
PSH> Get-Alias | Format-Table -hide  > aliases.txt
PSH>$AliasArray = Get-Content aliases.txt
PSH>$AliasArray[30]
Alias           gsv                 Get-Service
PSH>
```

You can also update the elements in an array using the index of the specific element:

```
PSH>$array1[0]
abc
PSH>$array1[0]="xyz"
PSH>$array1[0]
xyz
PSH>
```

For more on arrays, see Get-Help About_Array.

Hashtables

Hashtables allow you to associate keys with values. You define a hashtable by using the syntax @{}.

```
1   PSH>$myhash=@{}
2   PSH>$myhash=@{key1="abc";key2="def"}
3   PSH>$myhash
4   Name                          Value
5   ----                          -----
6   key2                          def
7   key1                          abc
8   PSH>$myhash["key1"]
9   abc
10  PSH>$myhash["key3"]="ghi"
11  PSH>$myhash
12  Name                          Value
13  ----                          -----
14  key3                          ghi
15  key2                          def
16  key1                          abc
17  PSH>$myhash["key1"]="xyz"
18  PSH>$myhash
19  Name                          Value
20  ----                          -----
21  Key3                          ghi
22  key2                          def
23  key1                          xyz
```

Unlike arrays, which can't be extended, hashtables can be, as shown in line 10.

Operators

When you are working with scripts or even when working interactively with the shell, you will often use operators when dealing with data. There are several types of operators:

- **Arithmetic operators** +, -, *, /, % (See Get-Help About_Arithmetic_Operators for more information.)
- **Assignment operators** =, +=, -=, *=, /=, %= (See Get-Help About_Assignment_operators for more information.)
- **Comparison operators** -eq, -ne, -ge, -gt, -lt, -le, -like, -notlike, -match, -notmatch, -contains, -notcontains, -is, -isnot (See Get-Help About_Comparison_Operators for more information.)
- **Logical operators** -and, -or, -xor, and -not or ! (See Get-Help About_logical_Operator for more information.)

- **Binary operators** -band, -bor, -bxor, and -bnot (See Get-Help about_operator for more information.)
- **Other operators** See Get-Help about_operator for more information.

Functions

Functions allow us to break up a script into discrete modules, and to reuse those modules in another script when we need to perform the same action again. Not only is this a much more efficient use of programming resources, but it's also a good sound practice that makes debugging and troubleshooting scripts far easier than one continuous inline script:

```
1   PSH>function test-file {
2   >> if(Test-Path some.txt)
3   >> {
4   >> Write-Host "File exists"
5   >> }
6   >> else
7   >> {
8   >> Write-Host "File doesn't exist"
9   >> }
10  >> }
11  >>
12  PSH>
```

Let's say we are going to write a script, and we want to check for the existence of a particular file several times throughout the script. We could repeat lines 2 through 10 every time we wanted to check for the file. Instead, we create a function. Now to test for the file, all we need to do is invoke the function:

```
PSH>test-file
File doesn't exist
PSH>New-Item -type file -path some.txt
<Output removed>
PSH>test-file
File exists
PSH>
```

Functions can be used in scripts just as we did interactively.

Note Remember that you must declare your functions before you actually use them in your script.

Functions that you create can also be put directly into a pipeline, and can accept input from other cmdlets that are piping objects to it. We will cover this a bit later.

A filter is a different kind of function that doesn't wait for all the input it is going to receive before acting on it, but processes each input object as it receives it.

For more on functions and filters, see Get-Help About_Functions.

Conditional Statements

To handle conditional branching in your scripts, you use two basic constructs:

- if/elseif/else
- switch

Using the if/elseif/else, which has the following syntax, is very useful when testing conditions:

```
1  if(condition)
2  {statement block}
3  elseif(condition)
4  {statement block}
5  else
6  {statement block}
```

PowerShell tests the condition on line 1, and if the condition evaluates to true, the statement block on line number 2 is executed. (The statement block can contain multiple lines.) No further lines are evaluated or processed.

If line 1 tests false, the condition on line 3 is tested, and if it evaluates to true, the statement block on line 4 is executed. If the condition on line 3 evaluates to false, the statement block on line 5 is executed. You can have zero to many elseif statement blocks. (In the next sections we discuss all of the possibilities that you can use as conditions.)

The if/else form of the statement is simply an if/elseif/else with zero elseif conditions:

```
PSH>$var=5
PSH>if($var -eq 1){
>> Write-Host "var is 1"
>> }
>> elseif($var -eq 5){
>> Write-Host "var is 5"
>> }
>> else {
>> Write-Host "var isn't 1 or 5"
>> }
>>
var is 5
PSH>
```

PowerShell also has a switch statement with the following syntax that you can use when testing conditions:

```
1  switch -options (expression){
2  <value> {statement block}
3   or-
4  {expression} {statement block}
5  default {statement block}
6  }
```

First the expression on line number 1 is evaluated. Some options are supported, such as regex and wildcard. For more information, see Get-Help about_switch. Next we either have one or more lines like line number 2, like line number 4, or a mix of both.

PowerShell evaluates each line until it finds a match to the current value of the expression. When a match is found, the associated statement block is executed. If no match is found, the default statement block (shown on line number 5 in the preceding code) is executed:

```
PSH>$var
5
PSH>switch ($var) {
>> 1 {"Is one"}
>> 2 {"Is two"}
>> 3 {"Is three"}
>> 4 {"Is four"}
>> 5 {"Is five"}
>> default {"Not found"}
>> }
>>
Is five
PSH>
```

Note Any time you have to use more than one elseif statement, consider rewriting to use switch. It's cleaner, easier to read, and easier to debug.

Real World Calling Remote Desktops

While writing this book, we created and used a *lot* of different Windows Server 2008 computers, both physical and virtual. There was no way we wanted to have to sit down in front of that many different consoles, and we often needed to be able to view three or four different servers and clients at the same time to describe a process correctly. So, we created a single PowerShell script that we could call to connect to whatever computer we needed to connect to. We used Mklink to create hard links to the script, each with a different computer name. That single script now has 42 hard links to it, from core.ps1 to hp350-ts-05.ps1 to xpx64.ps1. The script is smart enough to know which name was used to call it, and it then uses a switch statement to execute the correct Mstsc.exe command to open a remote desktop session to the computer. Here's the script:

```
#  Simple shell wrapper to call mstsc and log in to a remote box.
#  Intent is to have this be a link that knows what name
#  it was called by...
#  ModHist: 19/07/07 -- more branching. Need to convert to switch...
#         : 28/10/07 -- changed to using switch
#         : 03/12/07 -- added $AdminSwitch check
#

$CallingScript = $myInvocation.mycommand.name
$FileRegEx = "(?<name>.*)(?<dot>\.)(?<extension>[pP][sS]1)"
$CallingScript -match $FileRegEx
$RDPTarget = $matches.name
if ($build -eq "6001") {
   $AdminSwitch = "/admin"
   } else {
   $AdminSwitch = "/console" }
switch ($matches.name) {
   whs           { mstsc $args $AdminSwitch /v:homesrv }
   head          { mstsc $args /v:hp380-clus-02 }
   homeserver    { mstsc $args $AdminSwitch /v:homesrv }
   home          { mstsc $args $AdminSwitch /v:homesrv }
   hp380         { mstsc $args /v:hp380-core-08.example.local }
   hp380-core-08 { mstsc $args /v:hp380-core-08.example.local }
   core08        { mstsc $args $AdminSwitch /v:hp380-core-08.example.local }
   core          { mstsc $args /v:hp350-core-04.example.local }
   dc            { mstsc $args /v:hp350-dc-02 }
   gw            { mstsc $args /v:hp350-gw-01 }
   sharon        { mstsc $args /v:sharon-pc }
   srv06         { mstsc $args /v:hp350-srv-06.example.local }
   test          { mstsc $args /v:hp350-test-11 }
   ts05          { mstsc $args /v:hp350-ts-05 }
   upg78         { mstsc $args /v:hp350-upg-78 }
   vista         { mstsc $args /v:hp350-vista-02.example.local }
   vista02       { mstsc $args /v:hp350-vista-02.example.local }
   srv03         { mstsc $args /v:hp380-srv-03.example.local }
   xp            { mstsc $args /v:hp350-xp-02.example.local }
   xpx64         { mstsc $args /v:hp350-xpx64-01 }
   ml350g5-7     { mstsc $args /v:192.168.50.7 }
   hp350         { mstsc $args $AdminSwitch /v:192.168.50.7 }
   vmhost        { mstsc $args /v:192.168.50.9 }
   default       { mstsc $args /v:$RDPTarget }
}
```

Nothing fancy here, just a simple switch statement. But it saves time and keystrokes. And that's what it's all about. Now, if we wanted fancy, we'd create a really smart script that could create the hard link, scan down the file, and insert a new line to call it in alphabetical order. One of these days...

Looping Statements

Looping statements are blocks of logic that run as long as a certain condition is true or until a particular condition is met. There are five basic looping statements:

- **For** Runs a statement block a set number of times based on conditions calculated as numerical values. (See Get-Help About_For for more information.)
- **Foreach** Runs a statement block a set number of times by iterating through a collection or list of items. (See Get-Help About_Foreach for more information.)
- **While** Runs a statement block as long as a condition is true. (See Get-Help About_While for more information.)
- **Do/while and do/until** Runs a statement block (the *do*) as long as (*while*) a condition is true, or as long as a condition is false (*until*).

For and foreach are used more often than others. The For statement has the following syntax:

```
For(<initialization>;<condition>;<increment>)
{ <statement block> }
```

The for loop starts typically with a variable set in the <initialization> element, such as $i=0. The loop runs a set number of times until the <condition> returns false, such as $i -lt 10. The <increment> element that sets the number of "jumps" before the <condition> element returns false. The increment statement can increment up or down, and can increment one or more units for each loop through the statement block:

```
PSH>$i=0
PSH>$i++
PSH>$i
1
PSH>$i+=2
PSH>$i
3
PSH>$i=0
PSH>$i--
PSH>$i
-1
PSH>$i-=2
PSH>$i -3
```

Any of these versions of incrementing can be used with a for loop.

In some situations you may need the for loop functionality, but you may need to skip values based on a certain condition. For more on looping statements see Get-Help About_For, Get-Help About_Foreach, and Get-Help About_While.

Importing and Exporting From and To Files

Several cmdlets get data into and out of files:

- **Add-Content, Get-Content, Set-Content** Used when dealing with plain text files.
- **Import-Csv, Export-Csv** Used when dealing with comma-separated values (CSV) files.
- **Import-Clixml, Export-Clixml** Used when dealing with XML-formatted files.
- **ConvertTo-HTML** Used to write data to an HTML-formatted file.

First, let's create a simple CSV file with the column headers server and IP:

```
PSH>Add-Content list.csv "server,ip"
PSH>Add-Content list.csv "server1,10.10.10.10"
PSH>Add-Content list.csv "server2,10.10.10.11"
PSH>Import-Csv list.csv
server                                                      ip
------                                                      --
server1                                                     10.10.10.10
server2                                                     10.10.10.11
```

A very helpful feature of Import-Csv is that it will create objects from the input data. We can use several cmdlets to handle the properties easily. For example, we might just want a listing of the server column. PowerShell sees the server column as a property:

```
PSH>Import-Csv list.csv|Select-Object server
server
------
server1
server2
```

Export-Csv is also useful. We can use it to create a CSV report that can be opened directly into Microsoft Office Excel:

```
PSH>Get-Process|Export-Csv proc.csv
PSH>Import-Csv proc.csv|Select-Object name,cpu -first 5
Name                                                        CPU
----                                                        ---
accelerometerST                                             0.203125
```

```
AcroRd32                                              86.609375
agent                                                 0.28125
AGRSMMSG                                              0.34375
alg                                                   0.109375
```

In the preceding example, we have written all of the output of the Get-Process cmdlet to the file proc.csv. When we then import it back in, we use the Select-Object cmdlet to get just two properties returned. Obviously, on your system the actual results will be different.

Note Not sure what properties you can get from the proc.csv we just created? Try this: *Import-Csv proc.csv | Get-Member*.

Flow Control

In addition to the looping statements covered in the previous sections, you can use two flow control cmdlets. These cmdlets are passed a scriptblock. There two such cmdlets:

- **ForEach-Object** Operates on each object as it passes through the pipeline
- **Where-Object** Selects objects from a list as it passes through the pipeline

It's useful to look at the differences between the foreach statement and the ForEach-Object. (To confuse you even further, the alias for the ForEach-Object cmdlet is foreach. But PowerShell handles it, choosing the right foreach.)

Let's contrast a foreach statement with the ForEach-Object cmdlet.

Using a foreach statement:

```
PSH>$computers=@("server1","server2")
PSH>foreach($computer in $computers){$computer}
server1
server2
```

Using ForEach-Object:

```
PSH>$computers=@("server1","server2")
PSH>$computers|foreach-object{$_}
server1
server2
```

In the previous example, we compare the syntax used with a foreach loop versus the ForEach-Object cmdlet.

Note The ForEach-Object cmdlet has another alias: %. Using the alias, this line in the preceding example

```
PSH>$computers|foreach-object{$_}
```

could also be represented as

```
PSH>$computers|%{$_}
```

Now, let's look at the Where-Object cmdlet. Going again with our foreach example, let's contrast its use with Where-Object.

Using a foreach loop:

```
PSH>$computers=@("server1","server2","desktop1","desktop2")
PSH>foreach($computer in $computers){$computer}
server1
server2
desktop1
desktop2
```

Using Where-Object:

```
PSH>$computers=@("server1","server2","desktop1","desktop2")
PSH>$computers|Where-Object{$_ -match "server"}
server1
server2
```

In the preceding example, we show an example of using Where-Object to select only certain objects based on matching the name. Using *–match* would allow us to use a regular expression here if we needed to match more complex names.

Note The Where-Object cmdlet has an alias: ?. Using the alias, this line

```
PSH>$computers| Where-Object{$_ -match "server"}
```

could also be represented as

```
PSH>$computers| ?{$_ -match "server"}
```

Formatting Cmdlets

On some occasions you may want to change the way data is displayed when you have determined that the default output just doesn't provide the information in the required manner. For these occasions, you can use one of the four formatting cmdlets:

- **Format-Custom** Formats the properties of the input objects based on a custom view
- **Format-List** Formats the properties of the input objects as a list
- **Format-Table** Formats the properties of the input objects as a table
- **Format-Wide** Formats the properties of the input objects in a summary view

To demonstrate formatting, let's use PowerShell to generate 100 random numbers between 1 and 10 (inclusive), manipulate them a bit, and finally pipe the output to Format-Table. The end result will look like a distribution of how many times each number occurred.

```
1   PSH>$rand=New-Object System.Random
2   PSH>1..100|%{$rand.next(1,10)}|group|select name,count|sort name
3   <Output removed>
4   PSH>1..100|%{$rand.next(1,10)}|group|select name,count|
      sort name|ft -autosize
      name,count,@{l="%";e={$_.count*1}},@{l="#";e={"#"*$_.count}}
5   Name Count  % #
6   ---- -----  - -
7   7  7 #######
8   12 12 ############
9   11 11 ###########
10  12 12 ############
11  16 16 ################
12  10 10 ##########
13  11 11 ###########
14  9  9 #########
15  12 12 ############
```

Let's look at what we've just done in detail:

- **Line 1** We used a class from the .NET Framework to produce a random number.
- **Line 2** We grouped the numbers together, selected just the two properties we were interested in, and then sorted the output.
- **Line 4** We used the same command as line 2, but we piped it to Format-Table. This cmdlet is used to create a table of the input. We used calculated properties to provide the values for the # of occurrences of the particular number, and then we used a little trick to print out a specific number of hash strings to match up with the number of occurrences of the particular number.

Note If you want a quick way to repeat strings, simply use something like this:

```
PSH>"testing"*10
testingtestingtestingtestingtestingtestingtestingtestingtestingtesting
```

More Info The following blog post on formatting is useful: *http://blogs.msdn.com/powershell/archive/2006/04/30/586973.aspx.*

Exiting from Scripts, Functions, and Loops

At times you will need to exit a script or loop without running to the end. PowerShell provides the *break* statement to exit from the current function, loop, or script. Each break statement exits one layer, so if you're in a while loop, and use break to leave the loop, the script will continue at the end of the while loop as if it had ended naturally. If you use break in a simple script, where it's not inside a loop or function, it will exit the script.

- *Continue* doesn't exit out of a loop–it just discontinues the *current* iteration of the loop, and starts on the next iteration of the looping statement from the start.
- *Return <value>* exits out of a script or function and allows you to return a specific value or output to the calling script or shell.
- *Exit <errorlevel>* will always exit all the way out of a script, whether called within a loop, a function, or at the outer level of the script. If called from the shell, however, it will exit the current shell, so this is not something you want to do interactively unless you're running in a nested shell for some reason and want to get back to the parent shell.

Dot-Sourcing

We talked briefly about scopes in PowerShell earlier in this chapter. One thing to note is how scripts and functions/filters work with scopes.

Here's a simple example using a script which contains a function. First, we create a file called "test_function.ps1" with a simple function in it:

```
function test-file {
if(Test-Path myfile.txt){
  Write-Host "File exists" }
else {
  Write-Host "File doesn't exist" }
}
```

Now, we execute the file, and then try to execute the function from the PowerShell prompt, but we get an error:

```
PSH>./test_function.ps1
PSH>test-file
The term 'test-file' is not recognized as a cmdlet, function, operable
program, or script file. Verify the term and try again.
At line:1 char:10
+ test-file <<<<
```

We get the error because the function test-file is out of scope at the shell level—it is available only within the script that created it. But now we "dot-source" the script, and see what happens:

```
PSH>. ./test_function.ps1
PSH>test-file
File exists
PSH>
```

We have now made the function "test-file" available outside the scope of the script that created it, by sourcing the script.

Note If you've spent any time in UNIX or Linux, this is the same method of sourcing a file that you're familiar with there.

Passing Arguments

Quite often, you may want to pass arguments to a script or function. PowerShell uses a "reserved" variable for this: *$args*. Actually, this is an array. You can pass multiple arguments to a script, and then later refer to each argument.

Let's rewrite our preceding test-file function to accept an argument, which is a lot more useful anyway:

```
PSH>function test-file {
>> $file=$args
>> if(Test-Path $file)
>> {
>> Write-Host "File exists"
>> }
>> else
>> {
>> Write-Host "File doesn't exist"
>> }
>> }
```

```
12  >>
13  PSH>test-file myfile.txt
14  File exists
15  PSH>test-file otherfile.txt
16  File doesn't exist
17  PSH>
```

From the preceding listing, we see that we only added line 2 to define a variable that contains the arguments passed to the function.

Finally, a quick demonstration to show when we have multiple arguments:

```
PSH>function show-args {
>> for($i=0;$i -lt $args.count;$i++){
>> Write-Host "arg $i is"$args[$i]
>> }
>> }
>>
PSH>show-args "me" "you" "me and you"
arg 0 is me
arg 1 is you
arg2  is me and you
PSH>
```

You can use *$args* for both scripts and functions. Consider the following script:

```
for($i=0;$i -lt $args.count;$i++){
  Write-Host "passed to script: arg $i is"$args[$i]
}
function echo_out {
  for($i=0;$i -lt $args.count;$i++){
    Write-Host "passed to function: arg $i is"$args[$i]
  }
}
echo_out "a" "b" "c"
```

Even though we use the same *$args* variable for the script and its function, *$args* has different values that don't interfere because of the difference in scope.

Param Statement

We can pass arguments to a script with *$args*, but what if we need to make sure we have a string or integer? We use the param keyword:

```
1   PSH>function test-args {
2   >> param([string]$one,[int]$two,[switch]$three)
3   >> Write-Host $one
4   >> Write-Host $two
5   >> Write-Host $three
6   >> }
7   >>
8   PSH>test-args you 1
9   you
10  1
11  False
12  PSH>test-args you 1 -three
13  you
14  1
15  True
16  PSH>test-args 1 2 3
17  1
18  2
19  False
20  PSH>test-args 1
21  1
22  0
23  False
24  PSH>test-args 1 you
25  <Error output truncated>
26  test-args : Cannot convert value "you" to type "System.Int32". Error:
"Input string wa…
27  At line:1 char:10
28  + test-args <<<<  1 you
29  PSH>test-args
30  0
31  False
```

What does this show us? Let's take a look:

- **Lines 1 through 6** We create a function to test the param statement. We expect a string for the first argument, and an integer for the second. The third parameter is either there or not, depending on whether the parameter name is specified.
- **Lines 8 through 11** The first two arguments are as expected, but there is no third argument, so the switch parameter returns false.
- **Lines 12 through 15** All three arguments are as expected, so we return True for the third.
- **Lines 16 through 19** Three arguments are here, but the last argument is not in the proper format, so the switch parameter returns false.

- **Lines 20 through 23** There is only a single argument, therefore the function returns a 0, and the last parameter is false.
- **Lines 24 through 28** Our two arguments are backward. The integer 1 gets automatically converted to a string, but a string can't be converted to an integer, causing an error.
- **Lines 29 through 31** No arguments here at all, but the first argument is returned as an empty string (*not* a null string, which is a different thing entirely), and the next two arguments are shown as a 0 and as false.

Note The param statement must be the first executable line in a script or function. Comments may precede it.

$_ and $input

Scripts and functions are useful by themselves, but the real strength of PowerShell is the pipeline. Let's take our Test-Path function again, but this time we'll build it so that it can participate in a pipeline, using two different methods. First, let's use the $_ :

```
PSH>$files="some.txt","other.txt"
PSH>function test-file {
>> if(Test-Path $_)
>> {
>> Write-Host "$_ exists"
>> }
>> else
>> {
>> Write-Host "$_ doesn't exist"
>> }
>> }
>>
PSH>$files|foreach-object{test-file}
some.txt doesn't exist
other.txt doesn't exist
PSH>New-Item -type file -path some.txt
<Output removed>
PSH>$files|foreach-object{test-file}
some.txt exists
other.txt doesn't exist
```

In PowerShell, $_ represents the objects in the pipeline. Using this special variable permits us to create a function, filter, or script that participates actively in a pipeline:

```
PSH>function test-files {
>> $files=$input
>> foreach($file in $files){
>> if(Test-Path $file)
>> {
>> Write-Host "$file exists"
>> }
>> else
>> {
>> Write-Host "$file doesn't exist"
>> }
>> }
>> }
>>
PSH>$files|test-files
some.txt exists
other.txt doesn't exist
PSH>
```

The other special pipeline variable is *$input*, which differs from $_ in that the *$input* enumerates the elements of the pipeline. *$input* is useful for handling data as a stream. As we see in the preceding example, when we use $input, we need to add logic so that we loop through all of the individual objects contained in $input.

Error Handling

PowerShell has a special variable named *$error* that automatically captures all errors in the current session. Because *$error* is an array, you can access a specific instance using the *[]* syntax. The most recent error is always *$error[0]*:

```
PSH>Get-Item testing.ps1
Directory: Microsoft.PowerShell.Core\FileSystem::C:\Documents and
Settings\Desktop\charlie
Mode                LastWriteTime     Length Name
----                -------------     ------ ----
-a---          1/7/2008  11:35 PM          0 testing.ps1
PSH>$error
PSH>Get-Item no_such_file.txt
Get-Item : Cannot find path 'C:\Documents and
Settings\Desktop\charlie\no_such_file.txt' because it does
not exist.
At line:1 char:9
+ Get-Item <<<<  no_such_file.txt
PSH>$error[0]
Get-Item : Cannot find path 'C:\Documents and
Settings\Desktop\charlie\no_such_file.txt' because it does
not exist.
At line:1 char:9
+ Get-Item <<<<  no_such_file.txt
PSH>
```

Note You'll see an empty $error variable as shown at the beginning of these steps only if this is a new session that hasn't had any errors in it. The $error array will continue to grow for the duration of the session, but its scope is only for that session.

Two common parameters that PowerShell recognizes are ErrorVariable and ErrorAction.

All PowerShell cmdlets support the ErrorVariable parameter. This lets us have errors go to a specific variable of our choice. They are still, however, added to the $error array:

```
PSH>Get-Item no_such_file.txt -errorvariable err
Get-Item : Cannot find path 'C:\Documents and
Settings\Desktop\charlie\no_such_file.txt' because it
does not exist.
At line:1 char:9
+ Get-Item <<<<  no_such_file.txt -errorvariable err
PSH>$err
Get-Item : Cannot find path 'C:\Documents and
Settings\Desktop\charlie\no_such_file.txt' because it
does not exist.
At line:1 char:9
+ Get-Item <<<<  no_such_file.txt -errorvariable err
```

Another common parameter for handling errors is the ErrorAction parameter. This parameter accepts three allowed values:

- **Continue** This is the default setting. Any errors are written to the $error variable and outputted to the screen. PowerShell will continue processing at the next line.
- **Silentlycontinue** When you use this parameter, any errors are written to the $error variable, but are not output to the screen. PowerShell will continue processing at the next line.
- **Stop** When you use this parameter, any errors are still written to the $error variable, but the error is output to the screen as an exception. PowerShell will stop processing at this point.

There is also an *$ErrorActionPreference* variable which accepts the same values as the ErrorAction parameter we just covered. Setting *$ErrorActionPreference* has an impact on every cmdlet run, so take the appropriate care and testing when using it.

Note Setting the ErrorAction parameter on a cmdlet is very different than setting the *$ErrorActionPreference* variable. Setting ErrorAction on a cmdlet applies the action to the cmdlet itself, whereas *$ErrorActionPreference* sets the value for the entire script or even session. You may want to set the variable temporarily in a script or directly in the console.

To set the variable up temporarily in a script, add the following lines at the top of your script:

```
$oldPreference=$ErrorActionPreference
$ErrorActionPreference="silentlycontinue"
```

Then add the following to the end of your script:

```
$ErrorActionPreference=$oldPreference
```

To set the variable up temporarily directly in the console, use the call operator and a script block. For example:

```
PSH> & {$ErrorActionPreference="silentlycontinue";your_commands}
```

Note At any point in time, if you want to clear the *$error* variable, simply invoke this in your PowerShell console:

```
PSH>$error.clear()
```

Hint: the () is required. Try it without.

Two other variables of interest: $? (pronounced *dollar hook*) is a Boolean value with the status of the last command. And *$lastExitCode* contains an integer that represents the error code of the last script or application that ran, with a zero denoting normal exit.

More Info Two other useful error-handling statements in PowerShell are Trap and Throw. For more on these, see *http://blogs.msdn.com/powershell/archive/2006/12/29/documenting-trap-and-throw.aspx*.

Note Sometimes simpler is better. In many cases, using extra Write-Host statements to see where a script is failing is all it takes to find the problem. And they're easy to add and easy to remove.

Redirection Operators

PowerShell supports the standard output redirection operators, (>) and (>>), but doesn't currently support input redirection (<), and doesn't support things like "1>&2", unfortunately. Heck, even Cmd supports that. For more information, see Get-Help About_Redirection.

Type Accelerators

Type accelerators, also known as *type shortcuts*, can simplify the amount of typing required when dealing with a specific type. Type accelerators can be useful when you need to force a variable to be of a certain type, or make sure it is a certain type. We have seen a few of them briefly in this chapter: [xml], [array], and [string].

Note Currently, there doesn't seem to be an online reference that lists all of the available types as well as explains their purpose. The following listing exists, but it may be incomplete: *http://blogs.msdn.com/powershell/archive/2006/07/12/663540.aspx*.

Escaping Characters

The escape character in PowerShell is the backtick (`). This is used in the same way as the backslash is used in UNIX–ignore any "specialness" about the character that follows. Here's an example of escaping the double-quote:

```
PSH>Write-Host "Your name is: "John"."
Your name is:  John.
PSH>Write-Host "Your name is: `"John`"."
Your name is: "John".
```

Windows PowerShell Examples

Enough about theory and the basics of PowerShell. What we really wanted out of this chapter, after all, were some real-world examples. So, let's take a look at some.

Typical File System Tasks

Two tasks a system administrator might need to do is search through a file system or directory for a particular file or for a particular string of text.

Let's provide an example of each of these tasks. First, search for a particular filename:

```
PSH>Get-Childitem . -recurse|foreach-object{if($_.name -match
   "some"){$_.fullname}}
C:\demo\SOME-1.TXT
C:\demo\SOME-22.TXT
C:\demo\some_other.txt
C:\demo\other\something.txt
```

Here we get all the items in the current directory, recursively, and pipe the results to ForEach-Object, which iterates a conditional match against the string "some". If the condition is true, the full path of the file is printed to the screen.

Note Get-Childitem supports *–include*, *-exclude*, and *–filter* parameter names for filtering out specific strings from the results.

How about getting a recursive listing of directories, starting from the current directory:

```
PSH>Get-Childitem . -rec|where{$_.psiscontainer}
    Directory: Microsoft.PowerShell.Core\FileSystem::C:\demo
Mode                LastWriteTime     Length Name
----                -------------     ------ ----
d----         1/15/2008   3:59 PM            other
```

The PSIsContainer property is true for directories.

Now, let's search for the string "test" in all files from the current directory and below:

```
PSH>Get-Childitem . -recurse|where{!$_.psiscontainer}|%{Select-String $_
   -pattern "test"}
some.txt:1:test
string.txt:1:testing
testing1.ps1:1:Write-Host "testing #2"
other\something.txt:1:test
```

Here we use the same Get-Childitem command to get all items recursively, use Where-Object to remove any objects that are directories–because they'll return an error if we try to search them for a string–and finally we pipe to % (an alias of ForEach-Object) to run Select-String on the object (file).

Testing Whether a File or Directory Exists

It's always good to test whether a path or directory exists before doing something that will not behave well if it doesn't. PowerShell provides the Test-Path cmdlet for us to use:

```
PSH>dir
    Directory: Microsoft.PowerShell.Core\FileSystem::C:\demo
Mode                LastWriteTime     Length Name
----                -------------     ------ ----
d----          1/4/2008   2:30 PM            test_directory
-a---          1/4/2008   2:30 PM          0 test_file.txt
```

```
PSH>Test-Path -type leaf test_file.txt
True
PSH>Test-Path -type container test_directory
True
PSH>Test-Path -type container test_file.txt
False
PSH>Test-Path -type leaf test_directory
False
PSH>
```

From the preceding output, we see that the Test-Path cmdlet returns a simple Boolean (true or false).

Windows Server Backup Cmdlets

For Windows Server 2008, with the demise of the venerable NTBackup, Microsoft has created some cmdlets to deal with backups.

More Info For more information and examples of the new backup cmdlets, see *http://richardsiddaway.spaces.live.com/blog/cns!43CFA46A74CF3E96!1006.entry*.

Examples of Managing Server Core

Unfortunately, we can't install PowerShell on Server Core. However, we can still use WMI and PowerShell together to do some Server Core administration. Here's a simple example of using WMI to get a list of services running on a remote Server Core computer (or any other remote computer):

```
PSH>$creds=Get-Credential
PSH>Get-Wmiobject -computer hp350-core-04.example.local
   -credential $creds Win32_Service
```

Server Core uses the Oclist.exe to list out the features and roles installed on a system. We can use WinRM to run Oclist from a remote system:

```
winrs `-r:http://hp350-core-04.example.local `-u:Administrator oclist
```

In the preceding example we use the Windows Remote Shell to execute the Oclist command from a remote system. We'll be prompted for Administrator's password.

Note PowerShell wants to interpret the dashes in this command line, so use the escape character to escape their special meaning. From a Cmd shell, this would not be necessary.

XML Support

PowerShell has the ability to deal with XML very well. We can use the new ServerManagerCmd.exe, from an elevated PowerShell prompt, to retrieve an XML formatted file of the server's current configuration:

```
PSH>servermanagercmd -query config.xml
PSH>$xml=[xml](Get-Content config.xml)
PSH>$xml

ServerManagerConfigurationQuery
-----------------------------------------------
ServerManagerConfigurationQuery

PSH>$xml.ServerManagerConfigurationQuery

Time     : 2008-02-02T16:25:40
Language : en-US
xmlns    : http://schemas.microsoft.com/sdm/Windows/ServerManager/
Configuration
           /2007/1
Role    : {AD-Certificate, Active Directory Domain Services, Active Directory
           Federation Services, ADLDS...}
Feature  : {NET-Framework, BitLocker, BITS, CMAK...}
```

Using the File Transfer Protocol (FTP)

FTP automation can be very useful. We can use the .NET Framework to enable FTP functionality from PowerShell.

Here's a sample function for getting a simple directory listing of a remote FTP server:

```
function ftplist{
param([string]$port=21,[string]$user,[string]$pass,[string]$ftpUri)
$ftp = [System.Net.FtpWebRequest]::create($ftpUri)
$ftp.Method = [System.Net.WebRequestMethods+Ftp]::ListDirectoryDetails
$ftp.Credentials = New-Object System.Net.NetworkCredential($user,$pass)
#Uncomment this line if you need to use passive mode for FTP transfers.
#$ftp.usePassive = $true
$response = $ftp.GetResponse()
$responseStream = $response.GetResponseStream()
$reader = New-Object System.IO.StreamReader($responseStream)
Write-Host $reader.ReadToEnd()
}
ftplist -port 21 -user "username" -pass "password" -ftpUri
  "ftp://some.ftp.server.com"
```

Downloading a File Using HTTP

PowerShell can easily download files from the Internet using the HTTP protocol. By simply using a class from the .NET Framework, we have access to a lot of functionality:

```
PSH>$client = New-Object System.Net.WebClient
PSH>$client|Get-Member d*
   TypeName: System.Net.WebClient
Name                MemberType Definition
----                ---------- ----------
Dispose             Method     System.Void Dispose()
DownloadData        Method     System.Byte[] DownloadData(String address),
DownloadDataAsync   Method     System.Void DownloadDataAsync(Uri address),
DownloadFile        Method     System.Void DownloadFile(String address, Str
DownloadFileAsync   Method     System.Void DownloadFileAsync(Uri address, S
DownloadString      Method     System.String DownloadString(String address)
DownloadStringAsync Method     System.Void DownloadStringAsync(Uri address)
PSH>$url = http://www.microsoft.com
PSH>$file = "$ENV:temp\microsoft.txt"
PSH>$client.DownloadFile($url,$file)
PSH>Test-Path ""$ENV:temp \microsoft.txt"
True
PSH>
```

In the preceding example we've used a .NET Framework class to create a quick and dirty Web client. It uses the Get-Member cmdlet to discover some of the members of the object created, and then points our *$url* variable at the home page of Microsoft. We then use the DownloadFile method to get the file and save it locally to the current user's temporary directory. Had we used the DownloadString method, the home page would have been streamed to the console.

Sending E-mail via SMTP

Here's a script that uses the .NET Framework to provide us with SMTP functionality from PowerShell:

```
function send-email {
param([string]$to,[string]$from,[string]$subject,[string]$body,[string]$file
  ,[string]$port,[string]$timeout,[string]$smtpserver)
    if ($smtpserver -eq "") {$smtpserver = "my.smtpserver.com"}
    $smtp = New-Object System.Net.Mail.SMTPclient($smtpserver)
    if ($port -ne "") {$smtp.port = $port}
    if ($timeout -ne "") {$smtp.timeout = $timeout}
    $message = New-Object
System.Net.Mail.MailMessage($from,$to,$subject,$body)
    if ($file -ne "") {
```

```
        $attach = New-Object System.Net.Mail.Attachment $file
        $message.attachments.add($attach)
    }
    $smtp.send($message)
}
send-email -to "user@example.com" -from "user@example.com" -subject
  "Test from PowerShell" -body "Testing" -smtpserver
  "smtp.example.com" -port 25 -file "C:\temp\test.txt"
```

Here we've defined a function (send-email), and then shown a simple example of how we can call the function with the appropriate arguments to be able to attach a particular file with the e-mail. Some of the particular details can also be coded directly into the script. For example, had we not passed a *–smtpserver* parameter when calling the function, the function would have automatically set the value to "my.smtpserver.com" in the example code.

Note You'll need to use real values for your smtp server name and other parameters to make this work. The values here are examples only, and won't work in your environment.

Compressing Files

David Aiken's MSDN blog has some useful file compression functions: *http://blogs.msdn.com/daiken/archive/2007/02/12/compress-files-with-windows-powershell-then-package-a-windows-vista-sidebar-gadget.aspx*. These functions take advantage of the Windows Scripting Host.

Dealing with Dates

Dealing with dates is something we all seem to have to do, and has often been awkward to handle in whatever scripting language we used. The Get-Date cmdlet, however, is both powerful and easy to use:

```
PSH>Get-Date|Get-Member

   TypeName: System.DateTime

Name                 MemberType     Definition
----                 ----------     ----------
…
AddDays              Method         System.DateTime AddDays(Double value)
AddHours             Method         System.DateTime AddHours(Double value)
AddMilliseconds      Method         System.DateTime AddMilliseconds(Double
                                      value)
```

```
AddMinutes          Method          System.DateTime AddMinutes(Double value)
AddMonths           Method          System.DateTime AddMonths(Int32 months)
AddSeconds          Method          System.DateTime AddSeconds(Double value)
...
Day                 Property        System.Int32 Day {get;}
DayOfWeek           Property        System.DayOfWeek DayOfWeek {get;}
DayOfYear           Property        System.Int32 DayOfYear {get;}
Hour                Property        System.Int32 Hour {get;}
...
Minute              Property        System.Int32 Minute {get;}
Month               Property        System.Int32 Month {get;}
Second              Property        System.Int32 Second {get;}
...
```

To get the current day of the week, use properties of Get-Date:

```
PSH> Get-Date
Saturday, February 02, 2008 5:13:42 PM

PSH> (Get-Date).day
2
PSH> (Get-Date).dayofweek
Saturday
PSH> (Get-Date).dayofyear
33
PSH>
```

It is very easy to use the properties associated with this object. In the preceding example we used three different properties to get the day of the week, day of the month (number of days since the month started), and day of the year (number of days since the year started).

Now, let's add or subtract a day by using one of the methods for Get-Date:

```
PSH>(Get-Date).adddays(1)

February-03-08 5:17:28 PM
PSH> (Get-Date).adddays(-1)
Friday, February 01, 2008 5:21:34 PM
PSH>
```

Real World More Examples Dealing with Dates

At times, the limitations of the Windows Task Scheduler are frustrating. However, running PowerShell from Task Scheduler lets us take advantage of the strengths of PowerShell to overcome some of those limitations. Let's see whether today is Patch Tuesday. If it is, we'll have more to do with this script, I'm sure.

```
Function patchday {
   $date=Get-Date
if(($date.dayofweek -match "Tuesday") `
  -and ($date.day -gt 7) `
  -and ($date.day -lt 15))
{"2nd Tuesday of the month"}
else
{"Not the 2nd Tuesday of the month"}
}
```

And we might want to know whether it's the last day of the month or year, to do special backups, so let's do that. The following functions will tell us if it's the last day of the month or the last day of the year:

```
function last_day_of_month {
  if((Get-Date).month -ne (Get-Date).adddays(1).month)
  {
  "Last day of month"
  }
}
function last_day_of_year {
  if((Get-Date).year -ne (Get-Date).adddays(1).year)
  {
    "Last day of year"
  }
}
```

Timer/Countdown

A way to get the elapsed time can be useful, so here's a quick stopwatch example:

```
PSH>$begin=Get-Date
PSH>Read-Host "Hit enter when ready to stop timer"
PSH>$end=Get-Date
PSH>$diff=$end-$begin
PSH>Write-Host "Elapsed time : "+$diff
Elapsed time :  +00:00:15.6557375
```

We can use New-TimeSpan to get the difference between two dates:

```
PSH>new-timespan $(Get-Date) $(Get-Date).adddays(-1)


Days              : -1
Hours             : 0
Minutes           : 0
Seconds           : 0
Milliseconds      : 0
Ticks             : -864000000000
TotalDays         : -1
TotalHours        : -24
TotalMinutes      : -1440
TotalSeconds      : -86400
TotalMilliseconds : -86400000
```

Here's a quick example of a countdown timer using New-TimeSpan:

```
PSH>$end=Get-Date -hour 11 -minute 00 -second 00
PSH>$end

Monday, January 14, 2008 11:00:00 AM

PSH>while($(Get-Date) -lt $end)
>> {(new-timespan $(Get-Date) $end).totalseconds;start-sleep -s 1}
>>
1109.7343684
1108.7343556
1107.7343428
1106.73433
1105.718692
```

Taking Input from the Console

Sometimes you need to be able to ask the user to enter something before a script continues. Here's a simplistic example you can build on that uses Read-Host:

```
function ask-user {
Read-Host "What's your name"
}
PSH>ask-user
What's your name: Wally
Wally
PSH>$user=ask-user
What's your name: Wally
PSH>$user
Wally
```

Important Whenever dealing with sensitive information, such as passwords, use the *–AsSecureString* parameter:

```
$secure_string=Read-Host "Enter your password" -AsSecureString
```

The resulting $secure_string will be a System.Security.SecureString object. Using *-AsSecureString* isn't a foolproof method of securing information such as passwords. Another user using the same account information that was used to create the secure string would have access to the password.

Storing Secure Information

One thing commonly required with automation is the need to store a password for use in scripts so that they have access to servers or services. Let's look at an example:

```
PSH>$credential=Get-Credential
PSH>$credential.Password|convertfrom-securestring|Set-Content secured.dat
```

Here, we've put credential object into the *$credential* variable. On the second line, we get the password property of the object we just created, pass it to the ConvertFrom-SecureString cmdlet, and write it out as an encrypted string to secured.dat.

To read back the encrypted string, we need two lines of code.

```
PSH>$pass=Get-Content secured.dat|convertto-securestring
PSH>$credential=New-Object system.management.automation.
  pscredential "Administrator",$pass
```

The first line retrieves the contents of the file we created containing the encrypted password, passes it to the ConvertTo-SecureString, and puts the result in the *$credential* variable. Now we can pass *$credential* to any cmdlet that supports the *–credential* parameter.

Note As previously mentioned, the file secured.dat would contain an encrypted string. However, in the event that the system is compromised, and access is obtained to the account that encrypted secured.dat, the contents of the file are compromised. If the data contains a password for a remote system, then the compromise of the local system can lead to the compromise of a remote system.

Checking Services and Processes

PowerShell provides several cmdlets to check services and processes:

```
PSH> Get-Command -type cmdlet *service*

PSH> Get-Command -type cmdlet *process*
```

There are cmdlets to do just about anything you need to do with a service. For processes, however, you can get a process, and you can stop (kill) it.

Under the Hood Working with Services

You can't get service startup configuration information directly from a PowerShell cmdlet. For that, you have to go back to WMI again:

```
PSH>Get-Wmiobject win32_service|Where-Object {$_.DisplayName -match "Event
Log"}

ExitCode  : 0
Name      : Eventlog
ProcessId : 636
StartMode : Auto
State     : Running
Status    : OK

PSH>
```

In the preceding output, the StartMode property is what indicates the startup configuration for this particular service.

Here's a query to get a list of autostart services that aren't currently running on a remote computer:

```
Get-Wmiobject -computer hp350-dc-02 win32_service|Where-Object
  {if($_.startmode -eq "Auto" -and $_.state -eq "Stopped")
  {$_.name}}
```

Let's build on this, creating a script, Check_Services.ps1. In it, we query a list of servers (servers.txt) to find which services aren't running that are set to automatically start:

```
$servers=Get-Content "servers.txt"
if(Test-Path "out.txt"){
  Remove-Item "out.txt"
}
[array]$list=@()

foreach($server in $servers){
  $list=$null
  Get-Wmiobject -computer $server win32_service|`
  Where-Object{if($_.startmode -eq "Auto" -and $_.state -eq
```

```
"Stopped"){$list+=$_.name+" "}}
  if($list -eq $null){
    $server+" All OK" | out-file -append "out.txt"
  }else{
    $server+" "+$list | out-file -append "out.txt"
  }
}
Get-Content "out.txt"
```

Here we're putting the pieces together a bit, and you can start to see the possibilities. We start by getting a list of servers and doing some cleanup to make sure that we don't read old information. From there, we loop through the list of servers, check the status, and send the results to our output file:

```
PSH>./check_services.ps1
Get-Wmiobject : The RPC server is unavailable. (Exception from HRESULT:
0x800706BA)
At C:\Documents and Settings\Desktop\charlie\check_services.ps1:11 char:16
+   Get-Wmiobject <<<< -computer $server win32_service|`
localhost Fax  MSIServer  SysmonLog  wscsvc
127.0.0.1 Fax  MSIServer  SysmonLog  wscsvc
hp350-ts-05 All OK
```

At this point, if our list of servers includes one that we can't connect to (hp350-ts-05 in this example), we'll get an error, but the script also reports that we're all OK. Not good.

We could approach this two ways: We could ping the system to make sure it's there, or we could set the *ErrorVariable* and *ErrorAction* parameters. Ping won't really tell us whether we have a WMI communication problem–it will only tell us that the server is present. So it's probably useful to try for a WMI connection, and if that fails, we can try a simple ping to see if the server is even up.

This gets pretty complicated, since we'll want to trap on a ping failure. This chapter is already very long, so we'll put the whole script, with full comments, on the CD and you can get it there.

Checking the Windows Event Log

One way that PowerShell shines is in how easy it makes analyzing events from the Windows Event Viewer. First, we suggest you review the help for the Get-Eventlog cmdlet using Get-Help Get-Eventlog or Get-Help Get-Eventlog –examples.

In its simplest form, we get a listing of all the event logs on the local system:

```
Get-Eventlog -list
```

Now get the last 10 events in the application event log:

```
Get-Eventlog -log application -newest 10
```

Now let's group all the matching events by the event ID of each event. PowerShell takes care of the calculations and formatting:

```
Get-Eventlog -log application -newest 10|Group-Object eventid
```

Now let's limit the display to get only the count and the name, and sort by count (and let's format it a bit more nicely):

```
Get-Eventlog -log application -newest 10|Group-Object eventid| Select-Object
count,name|Sort-Object count|Format-Table -autosize
```

Now let's change the display a bit by creating our own header for the event ID column. Using a *@{Expression=,Label=}* format is known as a *calculated property* and is available with a few other cmdlets also:

```
Get-Eventlog -log application -newest 10|Group-Object eventid| Select-Object
count,name|Format-Table -autosize
count,@{expression={$_.name};label="EventID"}
```

Here is an example of what the previous command will give as output:

```
PSH>Get-Eventlog -log application -newest 10|Group-Object eventid|
  Select-Object count,name|Format-Table -autosize count
,@{expression={$_.name};label="EventID"}

Count EventID
----- -------
    2 0
    1 518
    1 101
    1 103
    1 213
    1 224
    1 223
    1 221
    1 220
```

Here are some more examples:

- Getting the events that match a particular event ID:

  ```
  Get-Eventlog -log application -newest 100|Where-Object{$_.eventid -eq "0"}
  ```

- Getting the winlogon events that are all marked as an error:

```
Get-Eventlog -log application -newest 100|Where-Object{$_.entrytype -eq
"Error" -and $_.source -eq "Winlogon"}
```

- Getting the events that occurred between one and three days ago:

```
PSH>(Get-Date).adddays(-3)

Monday, January 07, 2008 10:39:56 PM


PSH>(Get-Date).adddays(-1)

Wednesday, January 09, 2008 10:39:58 PM


PSH>Get-Eventlog -log application|Where-Object{($_.timewritten -gt
(Get-Date).adddays(-3)) -and ($_.timewritten -lt (Get-Date).adddays(-
1))}
```

Getting Memory and CPU Information

One thing that is definitely useful is getting the CPU utilization on a server. Using WMI, you have access to a class that provides a lot of information on processors. In particular, the loadpercentage property will give you a current snapshot of CPU utilization:

```
PSH>Get-Wmiobject win32_processor|Select-Object loadpercentage
loadpercentage
--------------
13
```

We have retrieved the CPU utilization, which is very useful, but another useful value is the utilization of actual processes themselves.

Real World Using WMI Remotely

WMI also provides a Win32_PhysicalMemory class, giving you access to the actual physical memory configuration of a system, even remotely. We can determine the number of modules installed, their size and speed, and whether there are any spare slots:

```
PSH> PS > Get-Wmiobject win32_physicalmemory|Select-Object devicelocator,
   speed, capacity | Format-Table -autosize
devicelocator speed   capacity
------------- -----   --------
```

```
DIMM 1A         667 2147483648
DIMM 2B         667 2147483648
DIMM 3C         667 2147483648
DIMM 4D         667 2147483648
DIMM 5A         667 2147483648
DIMM 6B         667 2147483648
DIMM 7C         667 2147483648
DIMM 8D         667 2147483648
```

So, from the preceding example, we can quickly see that we have 8 memory modules, they're all the same speed, and they're 2 GB each. No spare slots, either. But here's an interesting anomaly—a virtual machine, running in a Hyper-V child partition of that same server:

```
devicelocator speed capacity
------------- ----- --------
DIMM1               16777216
DIMM2               16777216
DIMM2               16777216
DIMM2               16777216
```

From this, we see that the VM has 4 GB assigned to it, and the memory is apparently split between two of the underlying DIMMs on the physical computer.

Accessing Performance Counters

As we saw in a previous section, it is relatively easy, using WMI, to get a current snapshot of the total CPU utilization. In some cases, we may want to get the utilization of a specific process. The following sample shows how to get this directly from WMI. However, the results we obtained seemed inconsistent.

```
PSH>gwmi Win32_PerfFormattedData_PerfProc_Process|where{$_.name -eq
"powershell"}|select PercentPrivilegedTime,PercentUserTime
| ft -autosize
PercentPrivilegedTime PercentUserTime
--------------------- ---------------
                    0               0
```

There is another way to get performance data, and that is by using the System.Diagnostics.PerformanceCounter class from the .NET Framework:

```
$counter="Process","% Processor Time","powershell"
$obj=New-Object System.Diagnostics.PerformanceCounter $counter
[void]$obj.NextValue()
for($i=0;$i -lt 10;$i++){
start-sleep -s 1
$obj.NextValue()
}
```

Here we use the .NET Framework to access specific counters. Getting the *$counter* variable formatted properly is the only likely issue here. To get the proper *$counter*, you can simply open up the Performance Counter GUI to look for the values you might want.

Note If you need to monitor multiple instances of a process, for example, things could get a bit sticky. From the preceding example, to get the counter for the first PowerShell instance, we simply look for an instance named "powershell". If we had two or more PowerShell processes running, we would have to modify our preceding counter variable accordingly. For example, to watch the second PowerShell process (which would be the second process we started chronologically), we would have a counter variable defined like this:

```
$counter="Process","% Processor Time","powershell#1"
```

Real World Process Monitor

When you suspect that a process is using excess resources, you don't want to kill it without being sure that it really is the problem. So it's useful to check it several times. If you check the resources used at least ten times, and five samples show high resource usage, it's time to stop the process. And start looking for why.

```
$counter="Process","% Processor Time","powershell"
$obj=New-Object System.Diagnostics.PerformanceCounter $counter
[void]$obj.NextValue()
$j=0
for($i=0;$i -lt 10;$i++){
  start-sleep -s 1
  $value=$obj.NextValue()
  if($value -gt 50){
  $j++
  }
}
if($j -gt 5){
  Write-Host "Process exceeded 50 more than 5 times"
  Stop-Process -name powershell -whatif
}
```

Here we've set up a counter ($j) to keep track of how many times our process is over a utilization of 50. We increment it if and only if we're over 50. Then we check the value of $j, and if it's over 5, we write a message to the PowerShell console, and do a Stop-Process on the PowerShell process. We add the *whatif* parameter so that PowerShell writes what actions would have been taken to the screen rather than trying to kill itself.

Note If you had more than one PowerShell process, all of them would be stopped. This may not be the desired outcome.

Note There isn't a Start-Process cmdlet in a default PowerShell install. If this process is part of a Windows Service, the operating system will likely attempt to restart the service when it determines that the process has been killed. You should test this in a test environment before attempting to stop processes in production.

Checking Disk Space Usage

Keeping track of disk usage is something we all have to deal with. We can use the Win32_LogicalDisk WMI class to check either locally or remotely for disk information:

```
PSH>gwmi win32_logicaldisk|where {$_.DriveType -eq 3}
DeviceID     : C:
DriveType    : 3
ProviderName :
FreeSpace    : 11066040320
Size         : 80015491072
VolumeName   :
PSH>(gwmi win32_logicaldisk|where {$_.DriveType -eq 3}).freespace
11066023936
PSH>(gwmi win32_logicaldisk|where {$_.DriveType -eq 3}).freespace/1gb
10.306037902832
PSH>(gwmi win32_logicaldisk|where {$_.DriveType -eq 3}).size/1gb
74.5202331542969
```

A DriveType of 3 indicates a fixed disk, restricting our query to fixed hard disks only.

Note To get other values for other kinds of drive types, check out this MSDN document: *http://msdn2.microsoft.com/en-us/library/aa394173.aspx*.

The preceding information is helpful, but it leaves us having to actually do some extra calculations to get something more meaningful like disk space % used. Fortunately, PowerShell can automatically do these calculations for us:

```
PSH > gwmi win32_logicaldisk|where {$_.DriveType -eq 3}|
   Select-Object deviceid,@{e={[int]([long]$_.Freespace/[long]$_.Size*100)};
   n="%free"}| ft -autosize
deviceid %free
-------- -----
C:          79
D:          38
E:          32
F:          62
```

That command line is pretty long. We used calculated properties with the Select-Object cmdlet to get the % free value, and this time we ran it on our main server to get some more numbers for the table.

A small issue is illustrated with the preceding command. To work around this, we had to cast some of the values to a long. We also cast the calculation to an integer to drop all decimal places and gives us a rounded value.

Working with the Registry

PowerShell has a built-in provider for the following two registry hives:

- HKEY_LOCAL_MACHINE
- HKEY_CURRENT_USER

This allows us to navigate in the registry as thought it were a file system. Figure 15-10 shows an example using the PowerShell execution policy settings on a system:

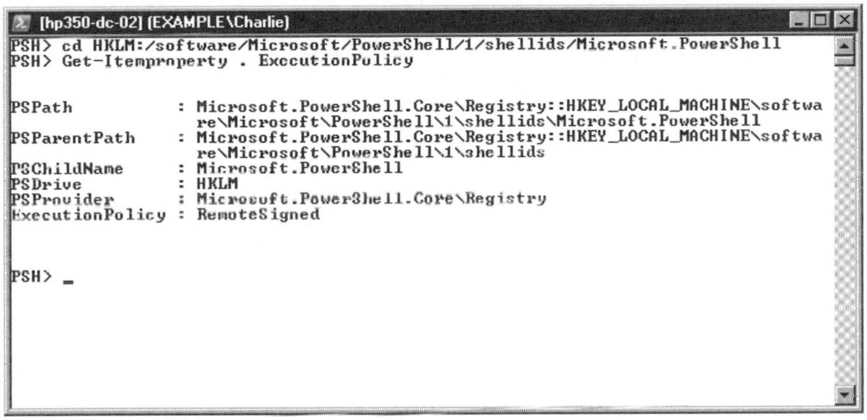

```
[hp350-dc-02] (EXAMPLE\Charlie)
PSH> cd HKLM:/software/Microsoft/PowerShell/1/shellids/Microsoft.PowerShell
PSH> Get-Itemproperty . ExecutionPolicy

PSPath          : Microsoft.PowerShell.Core\Registry::HKEY_LOCAL_MACHINE\softwa
                  re\Microsoft\PowerShell\1\shellids\Microsoft.PowerShell
PSParentPath    : Microsoft.PowerShell.Core\Registry::HKEY_LOCAL_MACHINE\softwa
                  re\Microsoft\PowerShell\1\shellids
PSChildName     : Microsoft.PowerShell
PSDrive         : HKLM
PSProvider      : Microsoft.PowerShell.Core\Registry
ExecutionPolicy : RemoteSigned


PSH> _
```

Figure 15-10 Using the Registry Provider

Note Shay Levi has been kind enough to provide us with a full set of registry functions to do just about anything with local and remote registries: *http://scriptolog.blogspot.com/2007/10/stand-alone-registry-functions-library.html*. These scripts show how PowerShell can use more of the .NET Framework for additional functionality.

Copying Files to Another Directory Recursively

Some things are just harder to do in PowerShell. One of those is copying files recursively from one folder into another. Oh, you can do it. But really, why bother? Good old Xcopy already does this, and does it well. And you can call it from PowerShell.

Rotating Logs

One common task—perhaps done weekly, monthly, or sometimes yearly—is rotating log files. For example, we may have the file application_log.txt, and might want to rename it to application_log1.txt to retain it for historical reasons, while clearing the current log for easier troubleshooting.

Here's an example that defines a variable (*$save*) at the beginning of the script controlling how many copies of the log file to retain before overwriting the old ones:

```
$save=4
if(!(Test-Path application_log.txt)){
  Write-Host "No such file"
break
}
for($i=$save;$i -ge 1;$i=$i--){
  if(Test-Path "application_log$i.txt"){
    Copy-Item -Force "application_log$i.txt" "application_log$($i+1).txt"
  }
}
Copy-Item -force application_log.txt application_log1.txt
Set-Content application_log.txt $null
```

Renaming Files

Regularly enough, you will find yourself needing to rename files from one pattern to another. In this simple example, we are going to take the file some.txt and rename it to someother.txt. One thing to remember is how everything in PowerShell is an object. We are going to do a little bit of discovering here:

```
PSH C:\demo> gci some.txt


    Directory: Microsoft.PowerShell.Core\FileSystem::C:\demo


Mode                LastWriteTime     Length Name
----                -------------     ------ ----
-a---         1/15/2008  10:20 PM          0 some.txt


PS C:\demo> (gci some.txt).name
some.txt
PS C:\demo> ((gci some.txt).name).gettype()

IsPublic IsSerial Name                                     BaseType
-------- -------- ----                                     --------
True     True     String                                   System.Object


PS C:\demo> ((gci some.txt).name).gettype().name
String
```

OK, so what we end up with for the name of the file is a string object. We already saw some of the methods we can use on a string object. In this case, we'll use the replace method, which replaces one string with another string:

```
PS C:\demo> gci some.txt|%{Move-Item $_.name
   $_.name.replace("some","someother")}
PS C:\demo> gci someother.txt


    Directory: Microsoft.PowerShell.Core\FileSystem::C:\demo


Mode                LastWriteTime     Length Name
----                -------------     ------ ----
-a---         1/15/2008  10:20 PM          0 someother.txt
```

Real World An Example of Renaming Files

For a more complicated–but very real-world–example, when writing this book, we created a bunch of screen captures. Early in the process, we had some screen captures that were using the wrong naming convention, and they needed changing. The files were named F12-1.bmp to F12-22.bmp. But they needed to be F12LH01.bmp to F12LH22.bmp. We also needed to make sure that only the files that that actually needed renaming were the ones that got renamed. So these were the requirements:

- If the number at the end is less than 10, we need to pad with a leading 0. In other words, 1 must become 01, but 22 would remain 22.
- We want to change the dash (-) to LH.

```
foreach($file in (gci . F12*.BMP){
  if($file.name -match '-\d{1}.BMP' ){
    mv $file.name $file.name.replace('-','LH0')
  }
  else{
    mv $file.name $file.name.replace('-','LH')
  }
}
```

Scheduling Tasks

The Scheduled Task user interface is fine if you want to work from the GUI, but if you want to run a PowerShell script at a regular interval, why not use PowerShell to create the tasks? You can, by using Schtasks.exe, which can be run from a PowerShell console.

Note WMI does have a Win32_ScheduledJob class, but it only has access to tasks created with the older AT command.

To schedule a PowerShell script, use schtasks with the /create command:

```
Schtasks /create /SC monthly /MO first /d Sun /TN PS1Task /TR "powershell.exe -
command '& {c:\demo\script.ps1}'"
```

This creates a monthly task that runs on the first Sunday of the month and runs the PowerShell script.ps1. You can see more details about using schtasks.exe by using the /? parameter.

Note One thing you might notice is a brief console window that opens when the PowerShell script runs. It is possible to hide this black console window using VBScript. For more information, see these two blog posts from Jeffrey Hicks: *http://blog.sapien.com/index.php/2006/12/20/schedule-hidden-powershell-tasks/* and *http://blog.sapien.com/index.php/2006/12/26/more-fun-with-scheduled-powershell/*.

Running Against Multiple Targets

Quite often as administrators, we need to run tasks against multiple computers. This is a problem with PowerShell v1, because there is no way to run a job in the background—it will block the console it is running in while it runs. The next version of PowerShell should allow background tasks, if the current CTP is any indication. However, Jim Truher from Microsoft, who was previously on the PowerShell team at Microsoft, posted a blog entry in 2007 that provides the required framework for creating background jobs: *http://jtruher.spaces.live.com/blog/cns!7143DA6E51A2628D!130.entry*

However, even without background jobs, we can still run a task against a list of computers by using some of the following possibilities:

- Use foreach, ForEach-Object, and Where-Object.
- Use Get-Content and a list of target computers in a text file:

```
PSH>Get-Content servers.txt|foreach-object{$_}
server1
server2
```

- Use Import-Csv and a list of computers saved from Office Excel to a CSV file:

```
PSH>Import-Csv servers.csv|Select-Object server|foreach-object{$_}

server
------
server1
server2
```

Creating XML-Formatted Data

As mentioned earlier, PowerShell has built-in support for XML. Two other useful cmdlets for dealing with XML are the Export-Clixml and Import-Clixml cmdlets.

An example of using XML-formatted data may be to pass information between systems/users. Once in an XML format, the data can easily be transferred, as shown in Figure 15-11:

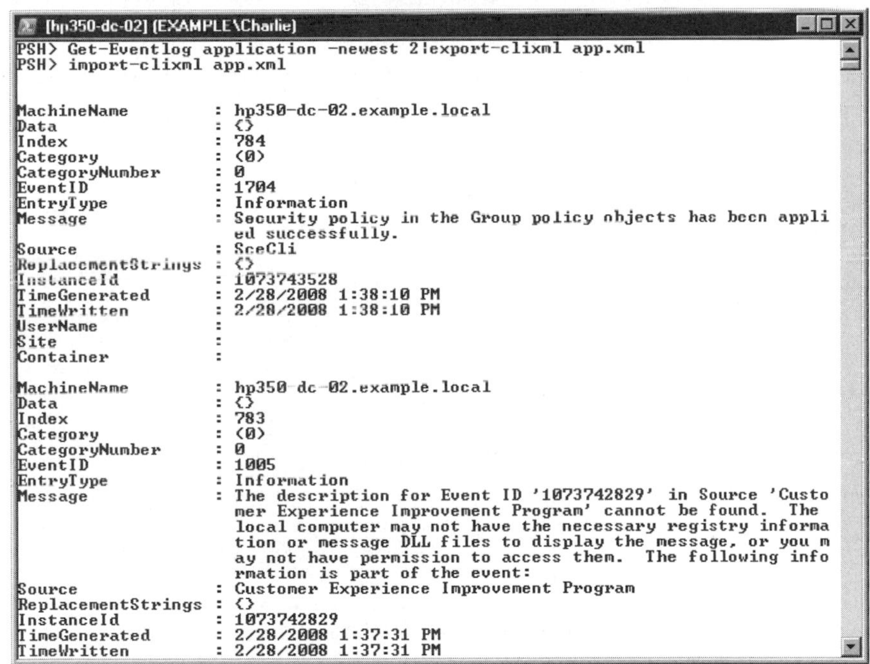

Figure 15-11 Using XML-formatted data to pass information

As Figure 15-11 shows, we first exported the two most recent events to an XML format, then imported the data back to view it. We also could have used Export-Csv and Import-Csv cmdlets in a similar fashion.

Checking Open Ports

When troubleshooting certain problems, it's helpful to connect to a TCP port, and even send commands to the port. (SMTP testing comes to mind.) You could enable and use the built-in telnet client in Windows Server 2008, but in many environments, telnet is explicitly disallowed for security reasons.

You can create an equivalent to using telnet by leveraging PowerShell, and the .NET Framework, though it is a bit complicated. OK, a lot complicated. Fortunately, Lee Holmes, one of the PowerShell developers, has some useful blog posts to help. See *http://www.leeholmes.com/blog/ReplacingTelnetexeNowRemovedFromVista.aspx* and *http://www.leeholmes.com/blog/ScriptingNetworkTCPConnectionsInPowerShell.aspx*.

Head, Tail, Touch, and Tee

If you've spent any time in a UNIX environment, there are some utilities that are hard to live without. Head, tail, touch, and tee are certainly ones we find it hard to live without.

Head and tail are typically used to get the beginning (head) or end (tail) of a data stream or text file without disturbing the file. You can use Select-Object to mimic the output of both head and tail:

```
PSH>Get-Content test1.txt
1111
2222
3333
PSH>Get-Content test1.txt|Select-Object -first 1
1111
PSH>Get-Content test1.txt|Select-Object -last 1
3333
PSH>Get-Process|Select-Object -last 1

Handles  NPM(K)    PM(K)      WS(K) VM(M)   CPU(s)     Id ProcessName
-------  ------    -----      ----- -----   ------     -- -----------
    117       6     1484        808    39     0.34   4000 Wuser32
```

Select-Object with *–first* or *–last* parameters gives us similar functionality to head and tail.

Tee is usually used as part of a set of piped commands. Tee takes output in the datastream and sends it to screen (standard output), while also passing the output along the pipe on to the next command in the pipeline.

In PowerShell, some cmdlets support the *–passthru* parameter, which can be used to mimic the functionality provided by tee, but PowerShell also has a Tee-Object cmdlet. Here's a simple example demonstrating Tee-Object:

```
PSH>notepad
PSH>Get-Process notepad

Handles  NPM(K)    PM(K)      WS(K) VM(M)   CPU(s)     Id ProcessName
-------  ------    -----      ----- -----   ------     -- -----------
     43       2     1000       3480    30     0.13   1116 notepad


PSH>Get-Process notepad|Stop-Process
PSH>notepad
PSH>Get-Process notepad|tee-object -filepath tee.txt|Stop-Process
PSH>Get-Content tee.txt

Handles  NPM(K)    PM(K)      WS(K) VM(M)   CPU(s)     Id ProcessName
-------  ------    -----      ----- -----   ------     -- -----------
     43       2     1000       3420    30     0.06   5544 notepad


PSH>
```

In the preceding example, we first start up a simple Notepad instance, and then do a Get-Process to get information on the process we just started. We can pipe the Get-Process command directly to Stop-Process to stop our Notepad process, but there's no indication on the screen of what we did. However, if we insert Tee-Object in the pipe, we can get output to a file (including the console screen), or to a variable to manipulate. Meanwhile, Tee-Object passes the input on to the next stage in the pipeline.

Now let's look for something similar to touch:

```
function touch ($file)
{
  if(Test-Path $file) {
   (Get-Childitem $file).set_LastWriteTime([datetime]::now)
  } else {
    New-Item $file -type "file"
  }
}

PSH>Get-Childitem touchtest.txt
    Directory: Microsoft.PowerShell.Core\FileSystem::C:\demo

Mode    LastWriteTime          Length Name
----    -------------          ------ ----
-a---   1/15/2008   3:59 PM        12 touchtest.txt
```

```
PSH>touch touchtest.txt
PSH>Get-Childitem touchtest.txt
    Directory: Microsoft.PowerShell.Core\FileSystem::C:\demo

Mode           LastWriteTime     Length Name
----           -------------     ------ ----
-a---   1/15/2008  10:20 PM          12 touchtest.txt


PSH>touch other.txt
    Directory: Microsoft.PowerShell.Core\FileSystem::C:\demo

Mode           LastWriteTime     Length Name
----           -------------     ------ ----
-a---   1/15/2008  10:21 PM           0 other.txt

PSH>
```

There we go. If the file exists, its last write time is updated to the current time; if the file doesn't exist, a new file is created. And if you want a bit more advanced version of touch, see Keith Hill's blog at: *http://keithhill.spaces.live.com/blog/cns!5A8D2641E0963A97!226.entry#permalinkcns!5A8D2641E0963A97!226*.

Summary

In this chapter, we've given you a taste of PowerShell, and how you can use it in your daily administrative tasks. PowerShell is quickly becoming the scripting language and shell of choice for system administrators, and we're really happy to see it. In the next chapter, we start our coverage of Directory Services, starting with how to install and configure them.

Chapter 16

Installing and Configuring Directory Services

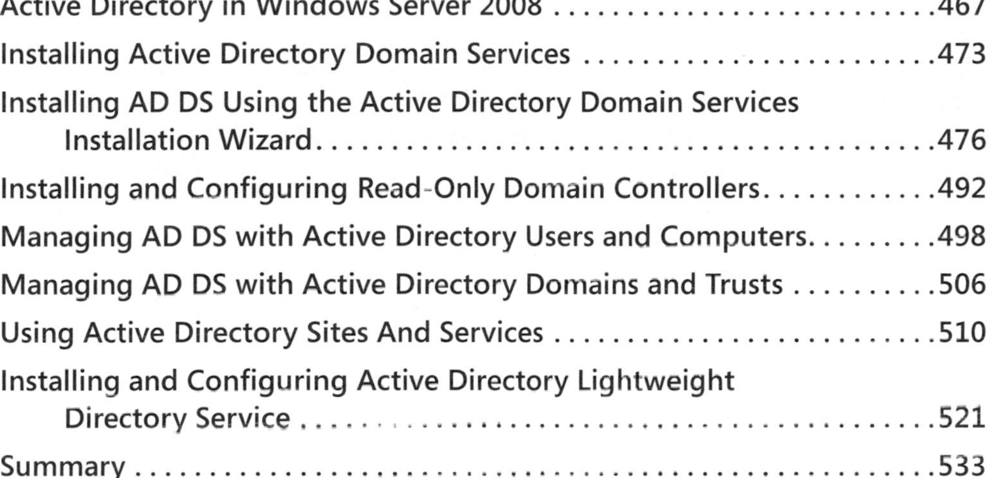

Installing and configuring Microsoft Active Directory is an important part of the Windows Server 2008 administration process, and familiarity with the various tools provided for this purpose is essential. This chapter describes Windows Server 2008 Active Directory components and then goes into detail on how to install and administer the core Active Directory components.

Active Directory in Windows Server 2008

In Windows Server 2008, the concept of Active Directory has been expanded from what it meant in Windows Server 2003 to include several additional components. Each of these components is installed as a server role in Windows Server 2008. At the core of Active Directory is Active Directory Domain Services (AD DS), which provides network authentication and authorization services for users in most organizations. The other Active Directory server roles extend the functionality provided by AD DS in a variety of ways to support application deployment, application sharing between organizations, and enhanced security.

Active Directory Domain Services

Active Directory Domain Services (AD DS) provides a secure directory service for the organization's users and resources. AD DS also provides the core user account management services for the other Active Directory server roles, each of which adds additional features in providing a secure network environment.

Note If you are familiar with previous versions of Active Directory in Windows 2000 or Windows Server 2003, AD DS is the equivalent of Active Directory directory service in these operating systems.

AD DS is a centralized directory for user and computer management and authentication. It provides authentication services for a Windows Server 2008 network. The directory contains user objects, group objects, computer objects, and service information. This allows the service to provide information about these objects as well as provide authentication and managing access to network resources.

You have already seen AD DS in action in several chapters in this book:

- Chapter 2, "Introducing Directory Services," provided an overview of AD DS components.
- Chapter 3, "Planning Namespace and Domains," provided guidance on planning AD DS deployments.
- Chapter 11, "Managing Users and Groups," described how to manage user and group accounts in AD DS.
- Chapter 13, "Group Policy," described how to manage Group Policy in AD DS.

Note This chapter includes additional detailed information on installing and configuring AD DS.

Active Directory Lightweight Directory Services

A second component included in Active Directory in Windows Server 2008 is Active Directory Lightweight Directory Service (AD LDS). AD LDS, known as Active Directory Application Mode (ADAM) when it was released with Windows Server 2003, is a Lightweight Directory Access Protocol (LDAP) directory service that can replace AD DS functionality in some scenarios or be deployed together with AD DS. AD LDS provides much of the same directory service functionality as AD DS, but it does not require the deployment of domains or domain controllers. AD LDS provides a much more flexible deployment model. For example, you can run multiple instances of AD LDS concurrently on a single computer with an independently managed schema for each AD LDS instance. You can also configure AD LDS replication so that the same instance of AD LDS is distributed across multiple computers.

AD LDS is designed to complement rather than replace AD DS. AD DS provides a network authentication and management directory, while AD LDS is designed to be used purely as a directory service for applications. AD LDS is designed to be deployed in the following scenarios:

- **Enterprise directory store** AD LDS can store application data in a local directory service either on the same computer as the application or on a different computer. One example of the type of application that could use AD LDS is an enterprise application that stores personalization data associated with corporate users who access a Web site. Storing this personalization data in AD DS would require AD DS schema changes. By using AD LDS to store application-specific data, and using user principals in AD DS for authentication and for controlling access to objects in AD LDS, you can prevent a proliferation of user IDs and passwords for end users every time a new directory-enabled application is introduced to the network.
- **Extranet authentication store** Many organizations deploy Web portal applications that require extranet access to corporate business applications but provide access for users who are outside the organization. These servers and portal applications require an authentication store to save authorization information for the users. AD LDS can provide this authentication store because it can host user objects that are not Windows security principals but can be authenticated with LDAP simple binds.
- **Directory consolidation solution** Enterprise organizations frequently have several directories deployed. User accounts may be located in multiple AD DS forests, domains, and OUs, or in several identity systems and other directories, such as human resource databases, SAP databases, and telephone directories. AD LDS can integrate with a metadirectory, which means that identities created in AD LDS can be synchronized with the metadirectory. AD LDS can also accept identity synchronization from the metadirectory.
- **Development environment for AD DS and AD LDS** Because AD LDS uses the same programming model and provides virtually the same administration experience as AD DS, developers can use AD LDS when staging and testing various AD DS–integrated applications. For example, if an application under development requires a different schema from the current AD DS schema, the application developer can use AD LDS to build the application and test a schema update process. The application can then be ported to AD DS after the application and schema update process have been thoroughly tested.

Active Directory Rights Management Services

The Active Directory Rights Management Services Roles (AD RMS) is used to augment an organization's existing security solution by providing an object-based, persistent-usage policy. AD RMS extends that security solution to include persistent-usage policies that can protect sensitive corporate data, such as word processing documents, customer data, e-mail messages, and financial data, even if that data is moved or sent outside the organization. The security restrictions for a specific file follow the document wherever it is moved, and are not assigned to the container in which the document is stored (unlike ACLs).

Using AD RMS, network users can restrict the ability to copy, print, or forward sensitive data. This enables you to send confidential e-mail messages: The recipient can open and read the message, and store it in either a network folder or a local folder. Recipients who receive rights-protected messages will not be able to cut, copy, or forward the message to other recipients. Confidential corporate communication remains confidential by restricting e-mail recipients from forwarding rights-protected communication. AD RMS also disables the ability to copy permissions-restricted data and then paste it into a non-restricted e-mail message or document. When a rights-protected document is open, AD RMS–aware screen capture utilities, such as Microsoft OneNote, cannot be used to capture the screen image, either in whole or in part.

An AD RMS system issues rights account certificates, which identify trusted entities (either users, groups, or services) that can publish rights-protected content. When trust has been established, users can assign usage rights and restrictions to the content they want to protect. These usage rights specify which users can access rights-protected content and what they can and cannot do with it. When the content is protected, a publishing license is created for the content. This license binds the specific usage rights to a given piece of content so that the content can be distributed. Figure 16-1 shows the process of how AD RMS works.

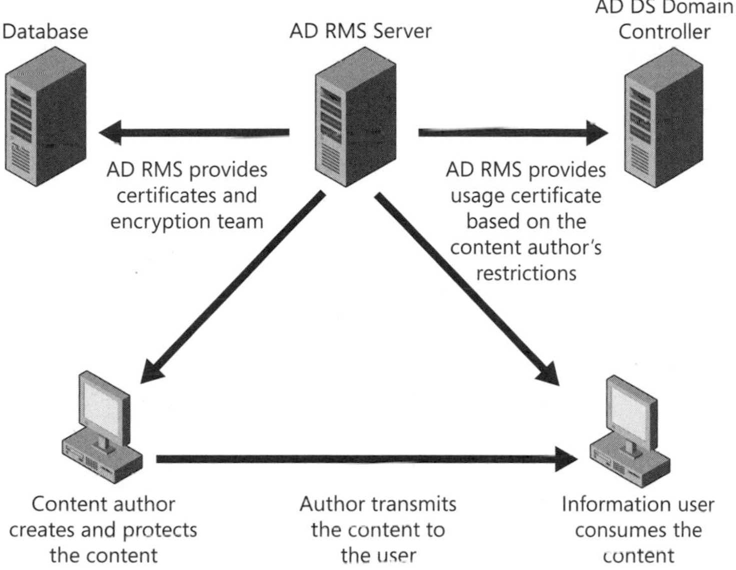

Figure 16-1 AD RMS is used to protect content from unauthorized access.

Users who have been granted a rights account certificate can access rights-protected content by using an AD RMS–enabled client application that allows users to view and work with rights-protected content. When users attempt to access rights-protected content, requests are sent to AD RMS to access, or *consume*, that content. When a user attempts to consume the protected content, the AD RMS licensing service on the AD RMS cluster issues a unique use license that reads, interprets, and applies the usage rights and conditions specified in the publishing licenses. The usage rights and conditions are persistent and automatically applied everywhere the content goes. In addition, AD RMS–enabled applications can use predefined usage-rights templates to help users efficiently apply a predefined set of usage policies, such as Confidential – Read-Only templates for e-mail messages.

The AD RMS–enabled client must have an AD RMS–enabled browser or application, such as Microsoft Office Word 2007, Microsoft Office Outlook 2007, or Microsoft Office PowerPoint 2007 in the 2007 Microsoft Office system. To create rights-protected content, the 2007 Office system Enterprise, Professional Plus, or Ultimate Edition is required. Windows Vista includes the AD RMS client by default, but other client operating systems must have the RMS client installed. The RMS client with Service Pack 2 (SP2) can be downloaded from the Microsoft Download Center; it works on versions of the client operating system earlier than Windows Vista and Windows Server 2008.

Note Designing and deploying an AD RMS infrastructure is quite complicated. For details on this process, see the Active Directory Rights Management Services Web site at *http://technet2.microsoft.com/windowsserver2008/en/library/909a3fa6-a7c5-4c86-9468-2b77b72c54841033.mspx?mfr=true.*

Active Directory Federation Services

Active Directory Federation Services (AD FS) is a server role in the Windows Server 2008 operating system that is used to extend the AD DS account authentication functionality beyond the boundary of an AD FS forest and across multiple platforms, including both Windows and non-Windows environments. AD FS is well-suited for Internet-facing applications or any environment where a single user account will need to access resources on different networks. In these scenarios, a user may be prompted for credentials whenever she tries to access an application that is using a different authentication source (for example, in another organization or in a different forest such as an perimeter network forest in the same organization).

When you implement AD FS, you can implement a federated trust between two different organizations or between two different forests. This federated trust enables users to use the security credentials from their own forest when accessing an application in an environment outside their forest. The federated trust is configured between *resource organizations* (organizations that own and manage resources and applications that are accessible from either the Internet or other third-party networks) and the *account organizations* (organizations that own and manage the user accounts that will then be granted access to the resources in the resource organizations). Figure 16-2 shows the components included in an AD FS deployment.

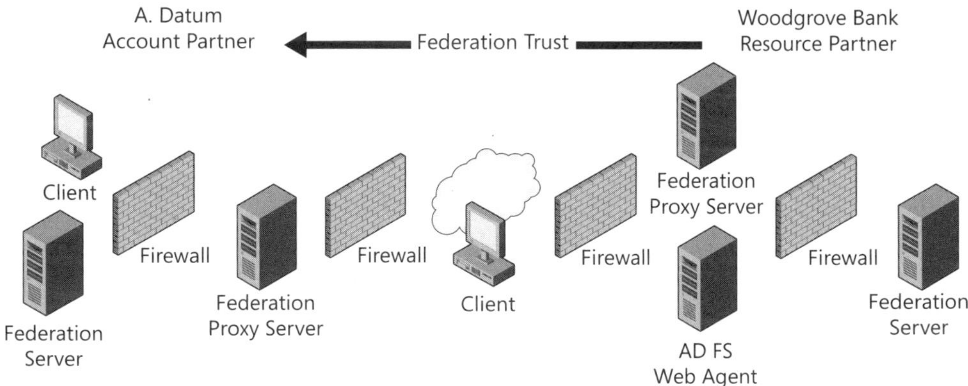

Figure 16-2 AD FS is used to provide secure single sign on access to applications.

In this scenario, AD FS offers a single sign on (SSO) access to resources in the resource organization to users who have been authenticated in the account organization. SSO enables a user to log on to the local network and receive a security token that will provide him with access to resources on different networks that have been configured to trust those accounts. Even within a single organization with separate networks and security boundaries, users will appreciate the convenience of having an SSO for accessing all appropriate network resources. AD FS is suitable both within large organizations with separate resource and account organizations, and is Internet-scalable to support access requests from users accessing resources with a Web browser.

Note Designing and deploying an AD RMS infrastructure is quite complicated. For details on this process, see the ADFS Design and Deployment Guide located at *http://www.microsoft.com/downloads/details.aspx?FamilyID=B92EA722-0C30-4EA6-BD45-7E5934B870CF&displaylang=en*. Although this guide is based on Windows Server 2003 R2, many of the same concepts and procedures apply to Windows Server 2008.

Active Directory Certificate Services

Active Directory Certificate Services (AD CS) is the Microsoft implementation of public key infrastructure (PKI). PKI deals with the components and processes for issuing and managing digital certificates that are used for encryption and authentication. It is not mandatory to implement AD CS as part of a Windows Server 2008 Active Directory structure. However, many organizations find it useful to deploy this service internally rather than relying on an external provider.

The digital certificates issued by AD CS can be used in many different ways to provide enhanced security. These options include Secure/Multipurpose Internet Mail Extensions (S/MIME), secure wireless networks, virtual private network (VPN), Internet Protocol security (IPsec), Encrypting File System (EFS), smart card logon, Secure Socket Layer/Transport Layer Security (SSL/TLS), and digital signatures.

Note Chapter 26, "Implementing Remote Access Strategies: SSTP, VPN, and Wireless," provides details on how to install and configure AD CS.

Installing Active Directory Domain Services

The process of installing Active Directory Domain Services (AD DS) on a server running Windows Server 2008 is straightforward. In most cases, you will use the Active Directory

Domain Services Installation Wizard. When AD DS is installed on a computer running Windows Server 2008, the computer becomes a domain controller. This process is also called *promotion*—a member server is promoted to domain controller. If the promoted server is the first domain controller in a new domain and forest, a pristine directory database is created, with just the default directory service objects. If the promoted server is an additional domain controller in an existing domain, the replication process is used to propagate to this new domain controller all of the directory service objects of this domain.

Prerequisites for Installing AD DS

Any server running Windows Server 2008 that meets the prerequisites described in the following section can host AD DS and become a domain controller. In fact, every new domain controller begins as a stand-alone server until the AD DS installation process is complete.

After AD DS is installed, the directory database is stored on the hard disk of the domain controller as the Ntds.dit file. During the installation of Windows Server 2008, the necessary packages are copied to the computer to install AD DS. Then, during installation of AD DS, the Ntds.dit database is created and copied either to a location identified during the installation process or to the default folder %systemroot%\NTDS.The installation process will also install all of the necessary tools and DLLs required to operate the directory service.

Hard Disk Space Requirements

The amount of hard disk space required to host AD DS will ultimately depend upon the number of objects in the domain, and in a multiple domain environment, whether the domain controller is configured as a global catalog (GC) server. To perform an installation of AD DS on a server running Windows Server 2008, the following minimum hard disk requirements should be met:

- 15 megabytes (MB) of available space required on the system install partition.
- 250 MB of available space for the AD DS database Ntds.dit.
- 50 MB of available space for the extensible storage engine (ESENT) transaction log files. ESENT is a transacted database system that uses log files to support rollback semantics to ensure that transactions are committed to the database.

In addition to the hard disk requirements, at least one logical drive must be formatted with the NTFS file system to support the installation of the SYSVOL folder.

Network Connectivity

Before you install AD DS, you need to configure the Internet Protocol (TCP/IP) settings on the Local Area Connection Properties sheet. To access this dialog box, right-click the Local Area Connection object in the Network Connections folder, select Manage Network Connections in the Network And Sharing Center in Control Panel, and then select Properties. On the Local Area Connection Properties dialog box, select Internet Protocol Version 4 (TCP/IPv4) and/or Internet Protocol Version 6 (TCP/IPv6) and then click the Properties button. On the Internet Protocol (TCP/IP) Properties dialog box, take the following actions:

- On the General tab, configure the computer with a static IP address.
- On the General tab, if the domain controller you are installing is *not* going to serve as a DNS server, configure the DNS server address with the IP address of the DNS server that is authoritative for the domain.
- For the IP v4 stack, on the Advanced TCP/IP Settings page, click Advanced on the General tab of the Internet Protocol Version 4 (TCP/IPv4) Properties dialog box, click the WINS tab, and configure the server with the IP address of the Windows Internet Naming Service (WINS) server that the domain controller will use.

Note Windows Server 2008 fully supports IPv6. If you are implementing IPv6 on your network, you should also configure a static IPv6 address on the network adapter. If you are not implementing IPv6, you should disable IPv6 on the domain controller network adapters.

DNS

AD DS requires DNS as its resource locator service. Client computers rely on DNS to locate the domain controllers so that they can authenticate themselves and the users who log on to the network as well as to query the directory to locate published resources. The DNS service must support service locator (SRV) resource records, and it is recommended that it also support dynamic updates. If DNS has not been previously installed on the network or if the Active Directory Domain Services Installation Wizard cannot detect an authoritative name server for the AD DS zone, the wizard will install and configure DNS at the same time as AD DS.

Note In Windows Server 2003, DNS server installation is offered if it is needed. In Windows Server 2008, DNS installation and configuration is automatic if it is needed. When you install DNS on the first domain controller in a new child domain in Windows Server 2008, a delegation for the new domain is created automatically in DNS. However, if you prefer to install and configure DNS manually, this is also possible.

Administrative Permissions

To install or remove AD DS, you must supply account credentials with administrative permissions. The type of account permissions you must have to install an AD DS domain depends on the installation scenario: installing a new Windows Server 2008 forest, installing a new Windows Server 2008 domain in an existing forest, or installing a new Windows Server 2008 domain controller in an existing domain. The Active Directory Domain Services Installation Wizard checks account permissions before installing the directory service. If you are not logged on with an account with administrative permissions, the wizard prompts you to provide the appropriate account credentials.

When you choose to create a new forest root domain, you must be logged on as a local administrator, but you are not required to provide network credentials. When you choose to create either a new tree-root domain or a new child domain in an existing tree, you must supply network credentials to install the domain. To create a new tree-root domain, you must provide account credentials from a member of the Enterprise Admins group. To install an additional domain controller in an existing domain, you must be a member of the Domain Admins global group.

Installing AD DS Using the Active Directory Domain Services Installation Wizard

The easiest way to promote a server to be a domain controller in Windows Server 2008 is to run the Active Directory Domain Services Installation Wizard. However, the AD DS server role must be installed on the computer before the Active Directory Domain Services Installation Wizard will run. To install the AD DS server role, either add the role in Server Manager or start the Active Directory Domain Services Installation Wizard by running dcpromo.exe. If you install the server role through Server Manager, you can start the wizard after the role is installed. If you run dcpromo.exe, the AD DS server role is installed and then the Active Directory Domain Services Installation Wizard starts.

The Active Directory Domain Services Installation Wizard can be started by typing **dcpromo.exe** in the Run dialog box or at the command prompt. Several command-line parameters are available for use with dcpromo.exe:

- The */adv* parameter is used to start the Active Directory Domain Services Installation Wizard in Advanced mode. In Windows Server 2008, the option to run Dcpromo in Advanced mode is now available from the Welcome page of the Active Directory Domain Services Installation Wizard.
- The */unattend:*[*unattendedfile*] parameter is used to perform an unattended installation of AD DS on either a full install of Windows Server 2008 or on a Server Core installation.

- The */CreateDCAccount* parameter is used to create a Read-Only Domain Controller (RODC) account.
- The */UseExistingAccount:Attach* parameter attaches the server to an RODC account.

> **Note** These options will be explained in more depth later in this chapter.

When you run dcpromo.exe, the Active Directory Domain Services Installation Wizard Welcome page appears. On the Welcome page, you can choose to run Dcpromo in Advanced mode, which includes additional wizard pages for all but the most common installation scenarios. As you progress through the installation wizard, you will need to make some key decisions, which are explained in the following sections.

Operating System Compatibility

The first screen in the installation wizard presents a warning about operating system compatibility (see Figure 16-3). Domain controllers running Windows Server 2008 provide additional security over previous versions of the Windows Server operating system, and the installation wizard provides information on how this security affects client logon. The default security policy for domain controllers running Windows Server 2008 requires two levels of domain controller communication security: Server Message Block (SMB) signing and encryption and signing of secure channel network traffic.

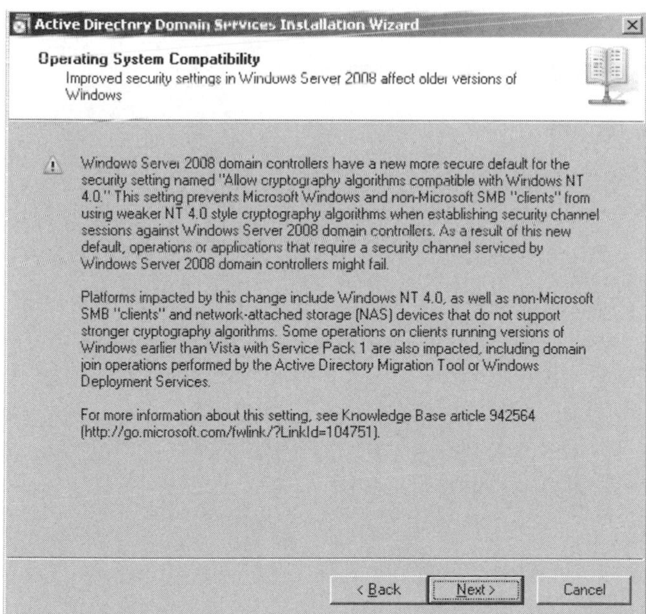

Figure 16-3 Windows Server 2008 domain controllers may not be compatible with older operating systems or applications.

These domain controller security features can present a problem for down-level client computers when logging on, as well as for some third-party applications. If you have down-level clients or applications that require reduced security, you should upgrade the operating systems and applications to newer versions. If that is not possible, you can decrease the security of domain controller security setting in the Default Domain Controller policy. Because this decreases the security of your network, changing this setting is not recommended.

Deployment Configuration

The first actual decision you must make in the installation process is to determine what type of domain controller you are creating. On the Choose A Deployment Configuration page of the wizard, you must select either to create a domain controller in an Existing Forest or to Create A New Domain In A New Forest, as illustrated in Figure 16-4. If you are creating a new domain, you must choose whether to create a root domain in a new forest, a child domain in an existing domain, or a new domain tree in an existing forest. To create either a child domain in an existing domain or a new domain tree in an existing forest, you must supply the appropriate network credentials to continue with the installation process. No network credentials are required to create a new forest root domain, but you must be a local administrator.

Note The option to install a new domain tree appears only if you run the Active Directory Domain Services Installation Wizard in Advanced mode.

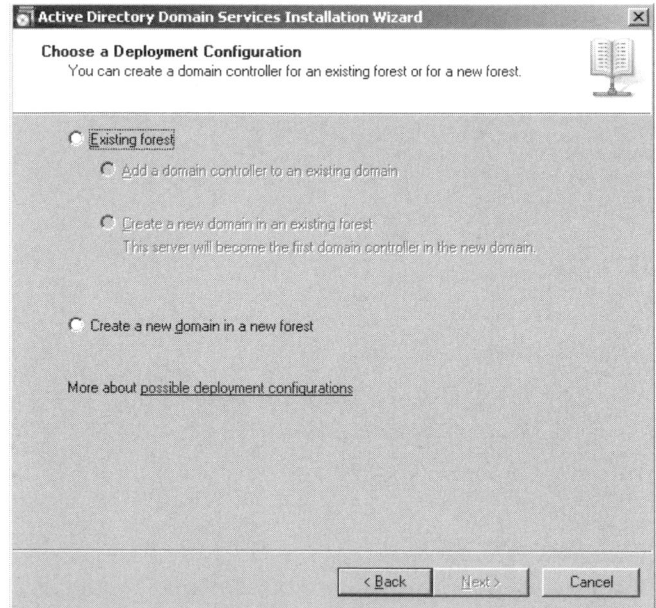

Figure 16-4 The Choose A Deployment Configuration page

Naming the Domain

When creating a new domain controller for a new forest, you must provide the fully qualified domain name (FQDN) of the new forest root domain. Figure 6-5 shows the Name The Forest Root Domain page of the wizard, which is the first stage of this process. The FQDN must contain a unique name for the new domain and, if you are creating a child domain, the parent domain must be included in the DNS name and the parent domain must be available. For example, if you are creating the new domain NA in the Adatum.com domain tree, you must provide the FQDN NA.Adatum.com.

When naming the domain, you can use the case-insensitive letters A through Z, numerals 0 through 9, and the hyphen (-). Each component (label) of the FQDN (the sections separated by the dot [.]) cannot be longer than 63 bytes.

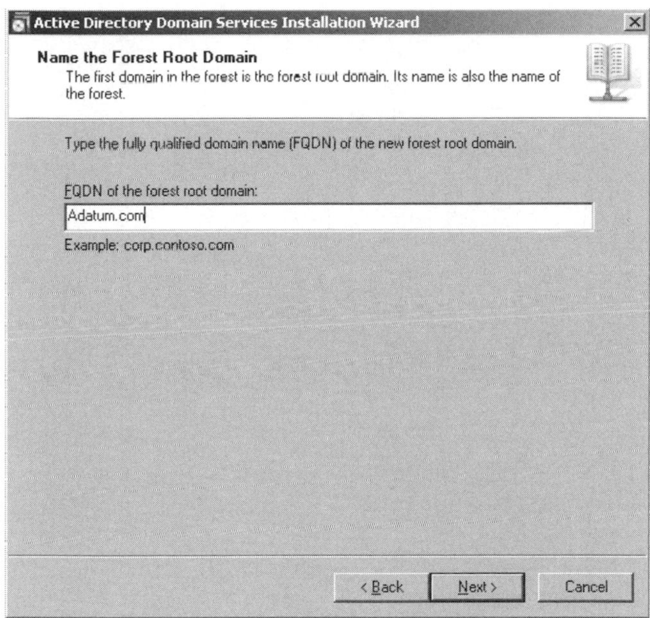

Figure 16-5 The Name The Forest Root Domain page

Best Practices It is recommended that you do not use single-label DNS names when naming your AD DS domain. DNS names that do not contain a suffix such as .com, .corp, .net, .org, or companyname are considered to be single-label DNS names. For example, *host* is a single-label DNS name. Most Internet registrars do not allow the registration of single-label DNS names. It is also recommended that you do not create DNS names that end with .local. For more information on this best practice, see the article "Information about configuring Windows for domains with single-label DNS names" at *http://support.microsoft.com/kb/300684*.

Setting the Windows Server 2008 Functional Levels

The next decisions that you need to make relate to the forest and domain functional levels, as shown in Figure 16-6. These settings determine the AD DS features that are enabled in a domain or in a forest and which version of Windows Server can be installed as domain controllers in the domain or forest. Forest and Domain Functional Levels are named after the Windows Server operating system that represents the features supported for that version of Active Directory: Windows 2000, Windows Server 2003, and Windows Server 2008. For information on the features and domain controller operating systems supported at each functional level, see Chapter 6, "Upgrading to Windows Server 2008."

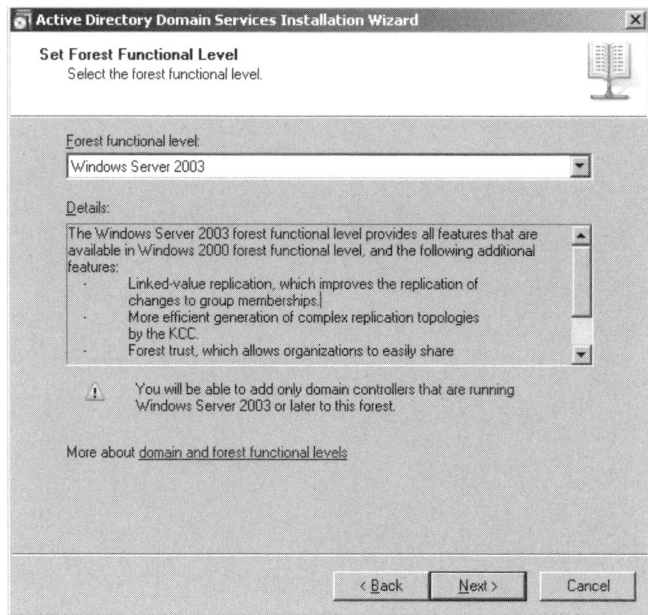

Figure 16-6 The Set Forest Functional Level page

When you are setting the forest functional level and domain functional level, in general, set them to the highest value that your environment can support. This way, you can use as many AD DS features as possible. However, if you may be adding Windows Server 2003 domain controllers to your environment, you should select the Windows Server 2003 functional level during Dcpromo. You can raise the functional level at a later time, after you have removed any Windows 2000 Server or Windows Server 2003 domain controllers from your environment.

Important You cannot go back to a lower functional level after raising the domain or forest functional level or setting the domain or forest functional level to Windows Server 2008 during Dcpromo.

Additional Domain Controller Options

Another choice you need to make in the installation wizard is what additional domain controller components will be installed on the domain controller. (See Figure 16-7.) You have three options: DNS, Global Catalog, and Read-Only Domain Controller (RODC).

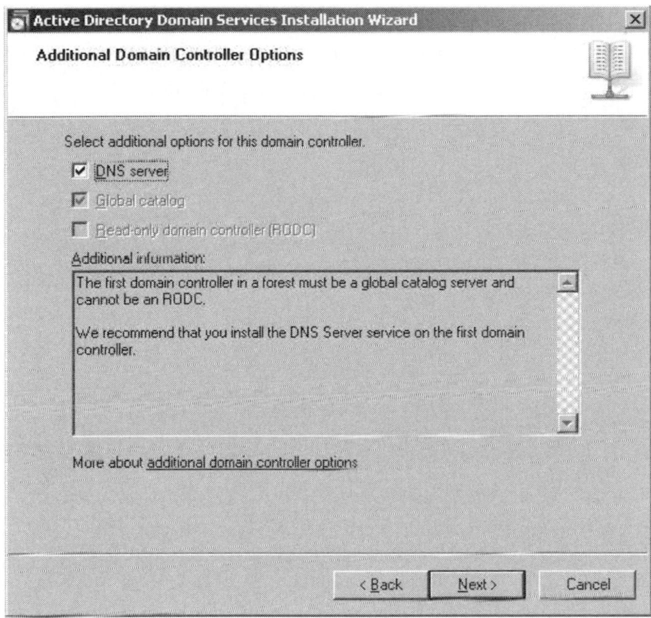

Figure 16-7 The Additional Domain Controller Options page

If the computer on which you are installing AD DS is not a DNS server, or if the Active Directory Domain Services Installation Wizard can not verify that a DNS server is properly configured for the new domain, the DNS Server service can be installed during the AD DS installation. If a DNS implementation is located on the network but is not configured properly, the Active Directory Domain Services Installation Wizard DNS Registration Failure dialog box provides a detailed report of the configuration error. At this point, you should make any necessary changes to the DNS configuration and retry the DNS diagnostic routine. If you select the default option to install and configure the DNS server, the DNS server and the DNS Server service will be installed during the installation of AD DS. The primary DNS zone will match the name of the new AD DS domain, and it will be configured to accept dynamic updates. The Preferred DNS Server setting (on the TCP/IP properties sheet) will be updated to point to the local DNS server using the loopback (127.0.0.1) address. Forwarders and root hints are also configured to ensure that the DNS server service is functioning properly.

Note When the DNS Server service is installed by the Active Directory Domain Services Installation Wizard, the DNS zone is created as an AD DS integrated zone.

If you are creating the first domain controller in a new forest, the domain controller must be configured as a global catalog server. As well, the first Windows Server 2008 domain controller in domain cannot be configured as an RODC. In the Dcpromo interface, the Global Catalog option is selected by default and cannot be cleared, and the RODC option is unavailable. These options become configurable when you are installing additional domain controllers in the domain.

Note If you have IPv6 enabled on one or more network adapters but have not configured a static IPv6 address for the network adapter, you will receive a static IP assignment warning message after you choose the additional domain controller options. You can proceed without assigning a static IP address.

File Locations

The Active Directory Domain Services Installation Wizard prompts you to select a location to store the AD DS database file (Ntds.dit), the AD DS log files, and the SYSVOL folder. You can either select the default locations or specify the locations for these folders.

The default location for both the directory database and the log files is the %systemroot%\NTDS folder. However, for best performance, you should configure AD DS to store the database file and the log files on separate physical hard disks. The SYSVOL shared folder default location is %systemroot%\sysvol. The only restriction on selecting the location for the shared SYSVOL folder is that it must be stored on an NTFS v5 volume. The SYSVOL folder stores all of the files that must be accessible to all clients across an AD DS domain . For example, logon scripts or Group Policy Objects must be accessible to all clients upon logging on to the domain, and they are stored in the SYSVOL folder.

Completing the Installation

The final pages of the Active Directory Domain Services Installation Wizard are straightforward. They include setting the Directory Services Restore Mode password and reviewing the Summary page.

The Directory Services Restore Mode (DSRM) password is used for authenticating to the registry-based security accounts manager (SAM) database when the domain controller is started in this special recovery mode. If you are creating the first domain controller in the forest, the password policy in effect on the local server is enforced for the DSRM Administrator password. For all other installations, the Active Directory Domain Services Installation Wizard enforces the password policy in effect on the domain controller that is used as the replication partner. This means that the DSRM password that you specify must meet the minimum password length, history, and complexity requirements for the domain that contains the installation partner. By default, a strong password that contains a combination of uppercase and lowercase letters, numbers, and symbols must be provided.

The Summary page reports all of the options that you selected during the Active Directory Domain Services Installation Wizard. You should review your selections on the Summary page before completing the installation wizard and installing AD DS, going back to previous pages if necessary. If you are satisfied with your selections, you can also click Export Settings on the Summary page to create an unattended file containing all of the options you selected in the Active Directory Domain Services Installation Wizard. You can use the unattended file for installing additional domain controllers when you initiate the install process using the command *Dcpromo /unattend:unattendfilename*.

When you click Next on the Summary page, Windows Server 2008 starts the process of installing and configuring AD DS on the server. If this is the first domain controller in a new domain, this process is relatively quick because only the default domain objects are created and the directory partitions are quickly created. If you are installing an additional domain controller for an existing domain, all of the directory partitions must be fully synchronized after the domain controller is created. To allow you to delay this full replication process until after the computer restarts, a Finish Replication Later button appears at the beginning of the initial replication process. While it is not recommended as a best practice, choosing this option enables the normal replication process to synchronize the directory partitions on this domain controller at a later time.

Note Because the initial replication of the directory partition data can be time-consuming, especially across slow network links, you can choose to install an additional domain controller from restored backup files. This feature is discussed in "Install from Media" later in this chapter.

Adding a Domain Controller to an Existing Domain

When you add a new domain controller to an existing domain, most of the steps in the Active Directory Domain Services Installation Wizard do not change. However, be aware of the following minor changes:

- You must provide credentials for a member of the Domain Admins group.
- You will be given a choice of which domain in the forest to install the domain controller.
- You will be given a choice of which site you want to place the domain controller. (See Figure 16-8.) On the Select A Site screen, you can choose to place the domain controller in a site that matches the domain controller's IP address, or choose another site. The second option is useful if you are building the domain controller in one office and shipping it to another office.

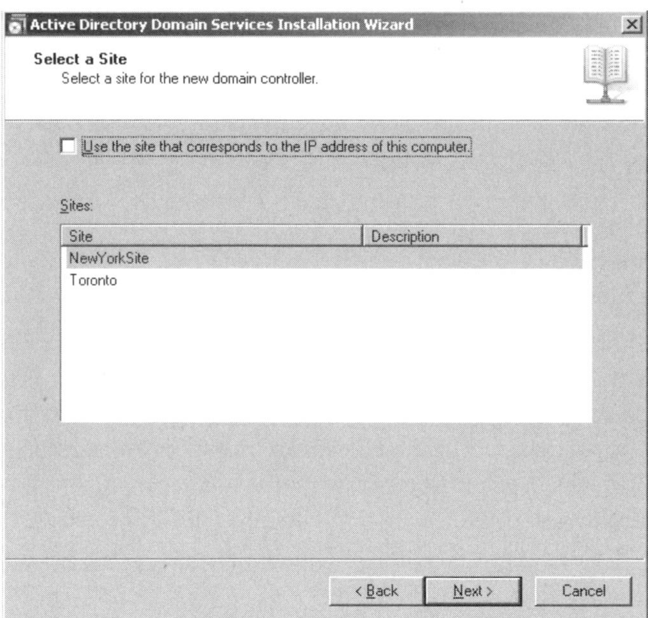

Figure 16-8 Choosing a site during AD DS installation

Verifying the Installation of AD DS

After you install AD DS, you should open Active Directory Users And Computers and verify that all of the Builtin security principals were created, such as the Administrator user account and the Domain Admins and Enterprise Admins security groups. You should also verify the creation of *special identities*, such as Authenticated Users and Interactive.

Special identities are commonly known as *groups*, but you cannot view their membership. Instead, users will automatically be joined to these groups as they log on or access particular resources. These special identities, however, are not displayed in Active Directory Users And Computers by default. To view these objects, select View and then select Advanced Features. This will display additional components in the tool that are not visible by default. For example, when you open the ForeignSecurityPrincipals container, you will find the objects *S-1-5-11* and *S-1-5-4*, which are *Authenticated Users SID* and *Interactive SID*, respectively. Double-click these objects to view their properties and default permissions.

In addition to the verification steps in ADUC, perform the following steps to verify the installation of AD DS:

- Check the Directory Service log in Event Viewer and resolve any errors.
- Ensure that the SYSVOL folder is accessible to clients.
- If you installed DNS during the installation of AD DS, verify that the service installed properly:
  1. Open DNS Manager.
  2. Click Start, click Server Manager, and then navigate to the DNS Server page.
  3. Navigate to the Forward Lookup Zones page to verify that the _msdcs.*forest_root_domain* and *forest_root_domain* zones were created.
  4. Expand the *forest_root_domain* node to verify that the DomainDnsZones and ForestDnsZones application directory partitions were created.
- Verify that AD DS replication is working properly using the Domain Controller Diagnostics tool, Dcdiag.exe:
  1. Open a Command Prompt window.
  2. Type the following command, and then press Enter:

     ```
     dcdiag /test:replications
     ```

  3. To verify that the proper permissions are set for replication, type the following command and then press Enter:

     ```
     dcdiag /test:netlogons
     ```

  4. The responses to the command should indicate that the connectivity and netlogons tests passed.

Advanced Options

Some of the Active Directory Domain Services Installation Wizard pages appear only if you select the Use Advanced Mode Installation check box on the Welcome page of the wizard or by running DCpromo with the */adv* switch. If you do not run the installation wizard in advanced mode, the wizard uses default options that apply to most configurations.

Use the advanced mode installation options when you must make the following choices during installation:

- **Install A New Domain With A Non-Contiguous Name Space In A Forest.** When you choose this option, you will be creating a new domain tree in the forest.
- **Use A Backup Of The AD DS Database As The Source For The AD DS Information On A New Domain Controller.** By installing from media, you can minimize replication of all directory data over the network.
- **Use A Specific Existing Domain Controller As The Replication Source For The New Domain Controller During Installation.** If you choose this option, the installation wizard lists all of the domain controllers that the wizard detected in the domain where you are adding a new domain controller. You can then choose which domain controller will be used as the initial replication source. You might choose this option if only one of the domain controllers has a fast network connection to the new domain controller that you are creating.
- **Modify The Default Domain NetBIOS Name.** By default, the NetBIOS name for the domain is the first 15 characters of the first part of the DNS domain name.
- **Define A Password-Replication Policy For A Read-Only Domain Controller (RODC).** By default, the RODC will not cache any passwords. You can modify this during installation by choosing an advanced installation or modify it after installation.

Install from Media

You can use the Install From Media (IFM) option to install an additional domain controller in an existing domain and use restored backup files to populate the AD DS database. This will minimize replication traffic during the installation, and is well suited for deployments with limited bandwidth to other replication partners (such as a branch office scenario).

You have two options for creating the install from media files. First, you can create the installation media by using the Windows Server Backup tool in Windows Server 2008. In this case, you need to use the Wbadmin command-line tool option to restore system state data to an alternate location.

Second, Windows Server 2008 includes an improved version of Ntdsutil.exe that you can also use to create the installation media. Using Ntdsutil.exe is recommended because Windows Server Backup can back up only the set of critical volumes, which occupies much more space than is required for AD DS installation data. Ntdsutil.exe can create four types of installation media—listed in Table 6-1—for both writeable domain controllers and RODCs.

Table 16-1 IFM Types

Parameter	Type of installation media
Create Full	Full (or writeable) domain controller without SYSVOL data
Create RODC	Read-only domain controller without SYSVOL data
Create Sysvol Full	Full (or writeable) domain controller with SYSVOL data
Create Sysvol RODC	Read-only domain controller with SYSVOL data

> **Note** For RODC installation media, *ntdsutil* removes any cached secrets, such as passwords.

To create installation media using Ntdsutil.exe, follow these steps:

1. Click Start, right-click Command Prompt, and then click Run As Administrator to open an elevated command prompt.
2. Type **ntdsutil** and then press Enter.
3. At the ntdsutil prompt, type **activate instance ntds** and then press Enter.
4. At the ntdsutil prompt, type **ifm** and then press Enter.
5. At the ifm prompt, type the command for the type of installation media that you want to create and then press Enter. For example, to create RODC installation media that does not include SYSVOL data, type the following command:

   ```
   Create rodc filepath
   ```

   Where *filepath* is the path to the folder where you want the installation media to be created. You can save the installation media to a local drive, shared network folder, or to any other type of removable media.

To populate the AD DS database when installing additional domain controllers, you will provide the location of the shared folder or removable media where you store the installation media on the Install From Media page in the Active Directory Domain Services Installation Wizard. During an unattended installation, you will use the */ReplicationSourcePath* parameter to point to the installation media.

Unattended Installation

In addition to the graphical user interface for installing AD DS, the installation process can be run in an unattended, or silent, mode by creating and using an unattended installation file. The unattended installation file passes values for all of the user-input fields that you would ordinarily complete when using the Active Directory Domain Services Installation Wizard. For any key that is not defined in the unattended file, either the default value will be used for that key or an error will be returned by Dcpromo indicating that the answer file is incomplete.

Note Unattended installations of AD DS will likely be much more frequent with Windows Server 2008 than for previous versions of Active Directory. This is because the only way you can install AD DS on a computer running Windows Server 2008 Server Core is to use a command line or unattended installation.

To perform an unattended installation of AD DS after the Windows Server 2008 operating system has been installed, create an answer file that contains all of the information necessary to install AD DS. To execute this unattended installation, at the command prompt or in the Run dialog box, type **dcpromo /unattend:unattendfile.** The unattended installation file is an ASCII text file that contains all of the information required to complete the pages of the Active Directory Domain Services Installation Wizard. For example, to create a new domain in a new tree in a new forest with the DNS Server service automatically configured, the contents of the unattended installation file would look like this:

```
[DCInstall]
InstallDNS=yes
NewDomain=forest
NewDomainDNSName=Adatum.com
DomainNetBiosName=Adatum
ReplicaOrNewDomain=domain
ForestLevel=3
DomainLevel=3
DatabasePath="C:\Windows\NTDS"
LogPath="C:\Windows\NTDS"
RebootOnCompletion=yes
SYSVOLPath="C:\Windows\SYSVOL"
SafeModeAdminPassword=Pa$$w0rd
```

Note For keys with no values set or omitted keys, the default value will be used. The required keys for the unattended installation file will change depending on the type of domain to be created (new or existing forest, new or existing tree). *ReplicationSourcePath* is an additional key that you can use for promoting a domain controller using a restore from backup media. To use this key, assign the value of the location of the restored backup files that will be used to populate the directory database for the first time. (This is the same as the path to the restored backup files that you select when using this feature through the Active Directory Domain Services Installation Wizard.)

For more information regarding keys and appropriate values, see the "Appendix of Unattended Installation Parameters" in the Step-by-Step Guide for Windows Server 2008 Active Directory Domain Services Installation and Removal at *http://technet2.microsoft.com/windowsserver2008/en/library/f349e1e7-c3ce-4850-9e50-d8886c866b521033.mspx?mfr=true.*

Uninstalling AD DS

AD DS is removed from a domain controller by using the same command that is used to install it—*Dcpromo.exe*. When you run this command on a computer that is already a domain controller, the Active Directory Domain Services Installation Wizard notifies you that it will uninstall AD DS if you choose to proceed. When you remove AD DS on a domain controller, the directory database is deleted, all of the services required for AD DS are stopped and removed, the local SAM database is created, and the computer is demoted to member server or stand-alone server.

To remove AD DS from a domain controller, type **dcpromo** at the command prompt or in the Run dialog box. Your first decision is to determine whether the domain controller is the last domain controller in the domain. Figure 16-9 shows the wizard page that prompts you for that decision.

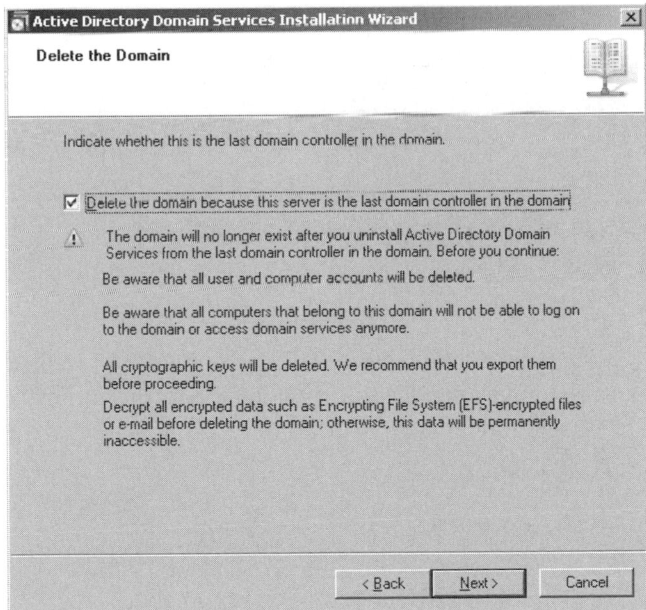

Figure 16-9 The option to remove the last domain controller

Next, the Active Directory Domain Services Installation Wizard displays a list of all of the application directory partitions found on the domain controller. If this is the last domain controller in the domain, this is the last source for this application data. You may want to back up or otherwise protect this data before continuing to use Active Directory Domain Services Installation Wizard, which will delete these directory partitions. If the domain controller from which you are removing AD DS is also a DNS server, and the default DNS zones are AD DS–integrated, at least two application directory partitions will be available for storing the zone data. Figure 16-10 shows an example of DNS application directory partitions found while uninstalling AD DS.

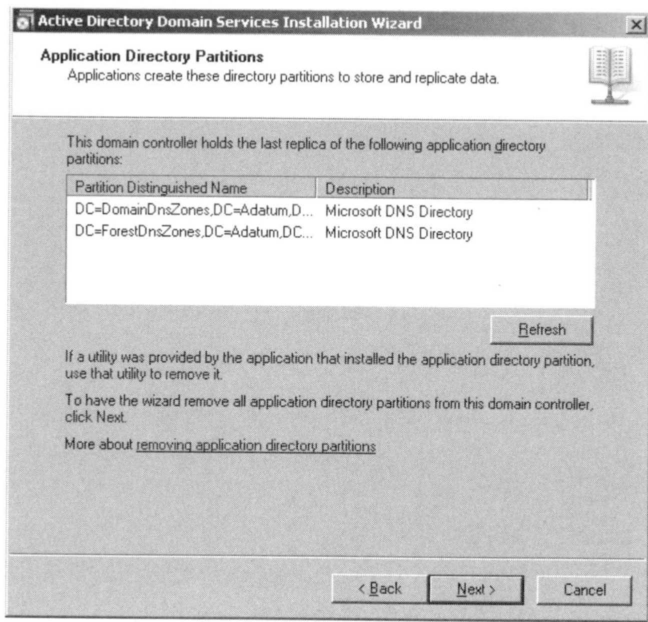

Figure 16-10 Removing the DNS application directory partitions

After you confirm the removal of the application directory partitions, you are prompted to enter a new password for the local Administrator account. Finally, review the Summary page and complete the removal of AD DS. You must restart the computer to complete the process.

Note You cannot uninstall the last domain controller in a parent domain if the domain still has child domains. When you start the AD DS removal process, Active Directory Domain Services Installation Wizard verifies that no child domains exist. Removal of AD DS is blocked if child domains are found.

Forced Removal of a Windows Server 2008 Domain Controller

One of the options in Windows Server 2008 is to forcefully remove a domain controller. This feature is specifically useful if the domain controller cannot connect to other domain controllers in the domain or forest. Normally, if the domain controller cannot connect to other domain controllers, it will not allow you to demote it.

You can forcefully remove a domain controller at the command line or by using an answer file. To force the removal a Windows Server 2008 domain controller using the graphical user interface, perform the following steps:

1. At a command prompt, type **dcpromo /forceremoval**, and then press Enter.
2. If the domain controller hosts any FSMO roles, or if it is a DNS server or a global catalog server, warning messages appear that explain how the forced removal will affect the rest of the environment. After you read each warning, click Yes.

   > **Note** To suppress the warnings in advance of the removal operation, type **/demotefsmo:yes** at the command line.

3. On the Welcome page of the Active Directory Domain Services Installation Wizard, click Next.
4. On the Force The Removal Of Active Directory Domain Services page, review the information about forcing the removal of AD DS and metadata cleanup requirements, and then click Next.
5. On the Administrator Password page, type and confirm a secure password for the local Administrator account, and then click Next.
6. On the Summary page, review your selections in the wizard. Click Back to make any necessary changes.
7. Click Next to remove AD DS.

You can select the Reboot On Completion check box to have the server restart automatically, or you can restart the server to complete the AD DS removal when you are prompted to do so.

> **More Info** Because the domain controller cannot contact other domain controllers during the operation, the AD DS forest metadata is not automatically updated as it is when a domain controller is removed normally. Instead, you must manually update the forest metadata after you remove the domain controller. For more information about performing metadata cleanup, see article 216498 in the Microsoft Knowledge Base (*http://go.microsoft.com/fwlink/?LinkId=80481*).

Installing and Configuring Read-Only Domain Controllers

One of the important new features in Windows Server 2008 is the option to use read-only domain controllers (RODCs). RODCs provide all of the functionality that clients require while providing additional security for domain controllers deployed in branch offices. When configuring RODCs, you can specify which user account passwords will be cached on the server and configure delegated administrative permissions for the domain controller. This lesson describes how to install and configure RODCs.

What Are Read-Only Domain Controllers?

An RODC is a new type of domain controller that Windows Server 2008 supports. An RODC hosts read-only partitions of the AD DS database. This means that no changes can ever be made to the database copy that the RODC stores, and all AD DS replication uses a one-way connection from a domain controller that has a writeable database copy to the RODC.

RODCs have the following characteristics:

- **Read-only AD DS database** The RODC holds the same AD DS objects and attributes that a writeable domain controller holds, with the exception of security-sensitive information such as user or computer passwords. However, changes cannot be made to the database that is stored on the RODC. Changes must be made on a writeable domain controller and then replicated back to the RODC.
- **RODC filtered attribute set** Only some attributes are replicated to the RODC. You can dynamically configure a set of attributes called the *RODC filtered attribute set* so that the attributes are not replicated to an RODC. Attributes that are defined in the RODC filtered attribute set are not allowed to replicate to any RODCs in the forest.
- **Unidirectional replication** Because no changes are written directly to the RODC, no changes originate at the RODC. Accordingly, writeable domain controllers that are replication partners do not have to pull changes from the RODC. This means that any changes or corruption that a malicious user might make at branch locations cannot replicate from the RODC to the rest of the forest. This also reduces the workload of bridgehead servers in the hub and the effort required to monitor replication.
- **Credential caching** Credential caching is the storage of user or computer credentials. By default, an RODC does not store user or computer credentials. The exceptions are the computer account of the RODC and a special krbtgt account that is unique to each RODC. You can configure credential caching on the RODC by modifying the Password Replication policy for the specific domain controller. For exam-

ple, if you want the RODC to cache the credentials for all users in the branch office who routinely log on in the office location, you can add all user and computer accounts for users in the branch office to the Password Replication policy. The next time the users log on to the domain controller, their passwords will be cached on the RODC. In this way, users will be able to log on to the domain controller even if the WAN connection to a writeable domain controller is unavailable.

- **Administrator role separation** You can delegate local administrative permissions for an RODC to any domain user without granting that user any user rights for the domain or other domain controllers. This permits a local branch user to install the RODC, log on to an RODC, and perform maintenance work on the server, such as upgrading a driver. However, the branch user cannot log on to any other domain controller or perform any other administrative task in the domain.
- **Read-only DNS** You can install the DNS Server service on an RODC. An RODC is able to replicate all application directory partitions that DNS uses, including ForestDNSZones and DomainDNSZones. If the DNS server is installed on an RODC, clients can query it for name resolution just like they would query any other DNS server. However, the DNS server on an RODC does not support client updates directly.

Why Use RODCs?

RODCs are designed primarily for branch office deployments where you cannot guarantee the RODC's physical security. By deploying an RODC in a branch office, you can provide users with a local domain controller to ensure that they can log on and have group policies applied even if the wide area network (WAN) link to the main office is not available. A local domain controller also ensures faster logon compared to logging on across a slow network connection.

You also can deploy RODCs in a scenario where a domain controller has other special administrative requirements. For example, a line-of-business (LOB) application may run successfully only if it is installed on a domain controller. Or the domain controller might be the only server in the branch office and may have to host server applications. In this scenario, users other than domain administrators may need to log on to the computer regularly. By deploying an RODC, you can provide those users with permission to log on and administer the domain controller, without granting them any administrative permissions in the domain.

Delegating RODC Installations and Administration

If you are a member of the Domain Admins group, you can install an RODC by running the Active Directory Domain Services Installation Wizard and choosing the option to configure a Read-Only Domain Controller on the Additional Domain Controller Options page. When you install an RODC, keep the following considerations in mind:

- Before installing an RODC in your forest, you have to prepare it by running adprep /rodcprep (available from the Windows Server 2008 installation media). This is required only if you are upgrading a Windows 2000 or 2003 Active Directory deployment to Windows Server 2008.
- The first domain controller installed in a new forest must be a global catalog server (GC) and cannot be an RODC.
- The RODC must replicate domain data from a writeable domain controller that runs Windows Server 2008.

However, you can also perform a staged installation of an RODC where you prepare the domain controller account for the installation of AD DS, and delegate the actual installation to a local administrator. You can delegate the installation of an RODC by performing a two-stage installation.

Staging the RODC Account

To stage the RODC account, right-click the Domain Controllers organizational unit in Active Directory Users And Computers, and then click Pre-create Read-Only Domain Controller Account. The Active Directory Domain Services Installation Wizard will begin and record all of the installation choices, including the RODC account name and the site in which it will be placed.

When you run the Active Directory Domain Services Installation Wizard to pre-create the RODC, the same options are presented as when you run the wizard on a physical server, with one additional page. The additional page (shown in Figure 16-11) enables you to specify which users or groups can complete the next stage of the RODC installation. By doing this, you can delegate the installation to users who are not members of the Domain Admins group. If you do not specify any delegate to complete the installation, only a member of the Domain Admins group or the Enterprise Admins group can complete the installation.

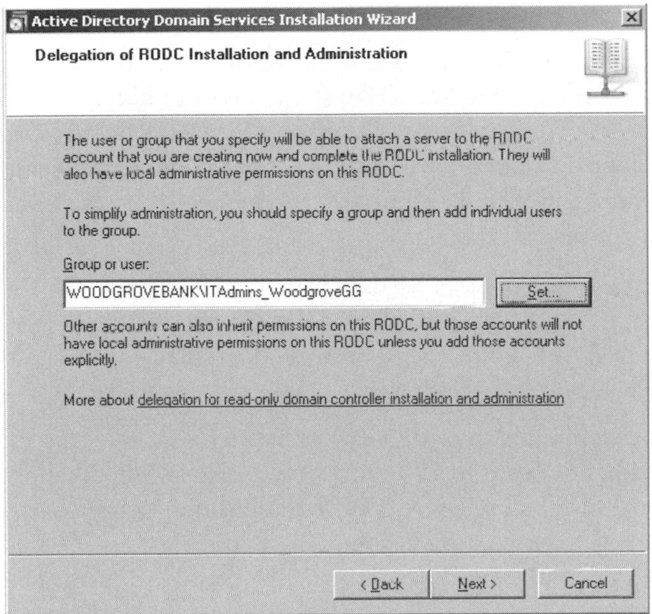

Figure 16-11 Configuring delegated administration while pre-creating the RODC account

> **Note** When you delegate the right to install the RODC to a user or group, that user or group also will have local administrator permissions on the RODC after installation.

Installing AD DS on the RODC

After the RODC account has been pre-created, you must ensure that the computer name where you are planning to install AD DS matches the staged computer account name and that the computer account has not been added to AD DS. Then start the Active Directory Domain Services Installation Wizard by typing **dcpromo /UseExistingAccount:Attach**. As part of the installation, the wizard automatically detects whether the name of the server matches the names of any RODC accounts that have been created in advance for the domain. When the wizard finds a matching account name, it prompts the user to use that account to complete the RODC installation. The wizard then installs AD DS on the server that will become the RODC and attaches the server to the domain account that was created for it previously.

Configuring Password Replication Policies

Another option that you will need to consider when deploying RODCs is credential caching. By default, no credentials other than the RODC computer account and a special krbtgt account are stored on the RODC. This means that the RODC must have an available connection to a writeable domain controller whenever a user or computer authenticates to the RODC. When the RODC receives the authentication request, it forwards the request to a writeable domain controller.

If you modify the Password Replication policy, passwords will be cached on the RODC after the next successful logon of a security principal identified in the policy. After the credentials are cached on the RODC, the RODC can directly service that user's logon requests until the credentials change or until the Password Replication policy changes.

When implementing a Password Replication policy, you must balance user convenience with security concerns. By default, no passwords are cached on the RODC. In addition, the policy explicitly denies credential caching for all domain administrative groups and the delegated local administrator. If you do not change the default, users will not be able to log on to the RODC if a connection to the Windows Server 2008 writeable domain controller is not available. If you enable password caching for all accounts, the impact of a security breach on the RODC is increased.

Real World If an RODC Is Compromised

If the security of an RODC is compromised, you should remove the RODC computer account from AD DS and reset the passwords for all user accounts that are cached on the server. When you delete the RODC account, you are given the opportunity to export a list of all accounts with cached credentials on the RODC. In addition, if the RODC is compromised, you should perform a security check on all workstations in the site to ensure that they have not been compromised as well.

When implementing a Password Replication policy, you have three high-level options:

- Accept the default configuration so that no credentials are cached on the server.
- Explicitly allow or deny caching of user or computer credentials from being cached on the server.
- Configure the RODC replication groups to configure credential caching. AD DS has two groups designed for RODCs to manage credential caching:

- The Allowed RODC Password Replication Group includes all accounts whose credentials can be cached on all RODCs in the domain. When you add a user or group to this list, their credentials will be cached on all RODCs in the domain. By default, this group does not have any members.
- The Denied RODC Password Replication Group includes all accounts whose credentials are explicitly denied from being cached on all RODCs in the domain. By default, this group contains all administrator accounts and all domain controller accounts. The Denied Password Replication Group takes precedence over the Allowed group, which means that if a user or computer is in both allowed and denied groups, the credentials are not allowed to be cached on the RODC.

To configure the Password Replication policy for an RODC, complete the following steps:

1. Right-click the RODC computer account properties in Active Directory Users And Computers and click Properties.
2. On the Password Replication Policy tab, click Add. You then have the option of configuring users' accounts so that their credentials will be cached on the RODC or not, as shown in Figure 16-12. Choose one of the options and click OK.

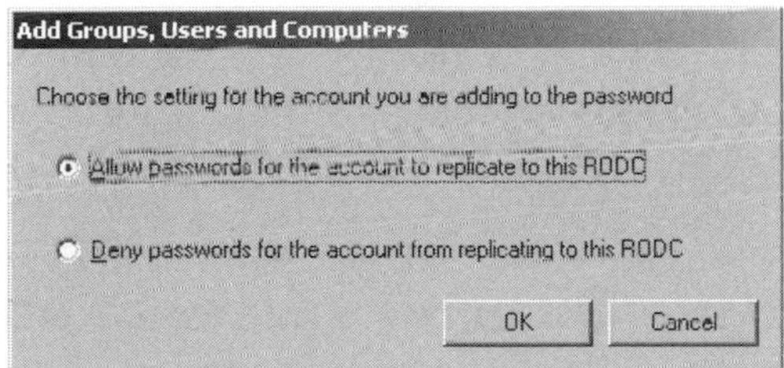

Figure 16-12 Configuring password replication options

3. In the Add Groups, Users And Computers dialog box, type the names of the users, groups, or computers, and then click OK.
4. You can also determine which user accounts have authenticated to the RODC and which passwords are stored on the RODC by clicking Advanced on the Passwords Replication Policy tab, shown in Figure 16-13. You can also use this dialog box to prepopulate the passwords for the specified accounts on the RODC.

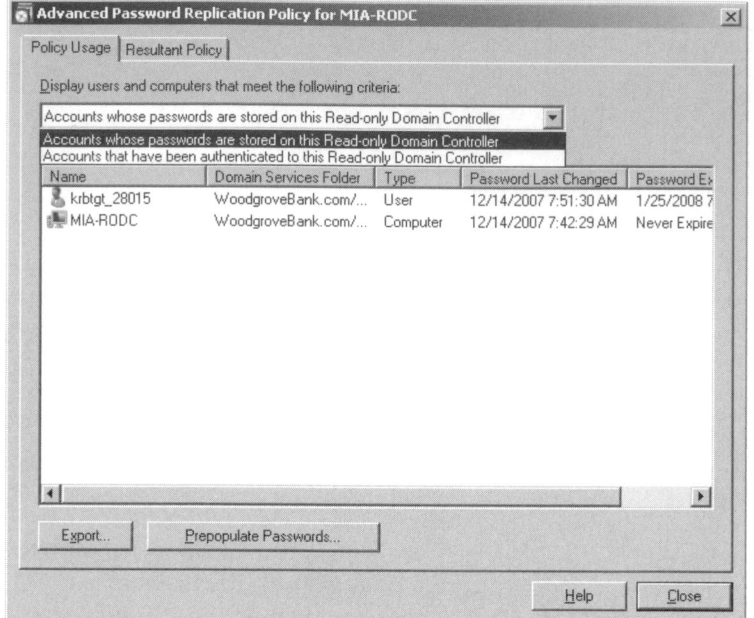

Figure 16-13 Determining which users have authenticated to an RODC

To configure the Password Replication policy by using Allowed RODC Password Replication Group or Denied RODC Password Replication Group, just add user accounts or group accounts to the appropriate built-in group.

Managing AD DS with Active Directory Users and Computers

The Active Directory Users And Computers snap-in is the primary tool for AD DS administrators, and it's the tool you use most often for day-to-day directory maintenance. Active Directory Users And Computers displays all the objects in a domain by using a Windows Explorer–style expandable tree display. Dialog boxes for each object provide access to the object's properties, which you can modify to update user information and account restrictions.

You also use Active Directory Users And Computers to create new objects and model the tree hierarchy by creating and populating container objects such as organizational units (OUs). The following sections examine some of the tasks administrators perform using Active Directory Users And Computers.

Note The most common tasks that administrators perform in Active Directory Users And Computers relate to creating and managing user and group accounts and organizational units. For information on how to perform those tasks, see Chapter 11.

Viewing AD DS Objects

The main Active Directory Users And Computers dialog box (Figure 16-14) contains many of the standard Microsoft Management Console (MMC) display elements. The console tree (on the left) lists an AD DS domain and the container objects within it in an expandable display. The result pane (on the right) displays the objects within the highlighted container. The console includes a specialized toolbar providing quick access to commonly used functions and a description bar that provides information about the console's status or the currently highlighted object. The program displays the actions you can perform on each object in the Action menu after you click the objects.

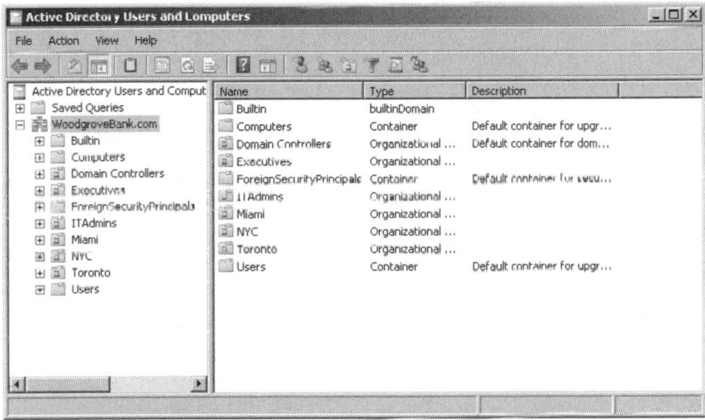

Figure 16-14 The main Active Directory Users And Computers dialog box

AD DS Object Types

The objects in the Active Directory Users And Computers dialog box represent both physical entities such as computers and users, and logical ones such as groups and organizational units. The object types that you can create in an AD DS domain are listed in Table 16-2.

Table 16-2 **Object Types You Can Create in an AD DS Domain**

Object Type	Function
Organizational Unit	Container object used to create logical groupings of computer, user, and group objects.
User	Represents a network user, and functions as a repository for identification and authentication data.
Computer	Represents a computer on the network, and provides the machine account needed for the system to log on to the domain.
Contact	Represents a user external to the domain for specific purposes such as e-mail delivery; doesn't provide the credentials needed to log on to the domain.
Group	Container object representing a logical grouping of users, computers, or other groups (or all three) that is independent of the AD DS tree structure. Groups can contain objects from different organizational units and domains.
Shared Folder	Provides AD DS–based network access to a shared folder on a Windows Server 2003 system.
Shared Printer	Provides AD DS–based network access to a shared printer on a Windows Server 2003 system.

By modifying the schema that controls the directory service structure, you can create new object types in AD DS and modify the attributes of existing types. For more information, see Chapter 17, "Managing Directory Services."

Normal Mode vs. Advanced Mode

By default, the Active Directory Users And Computers snap-in is displayed in normal mode. Only the objects that administrators use most often are visible. This also hides from view certain tabs in an object's Properties dialog box, including the Object tab and the Security tab that you use to set permissions for the object.

When you choose Advanced Features from the console's View menu, however, the display changes to include all the system objects in AD DS, which represent policies, DNS records, and other directory service elements, as well as the LostAndFound container, shown in Figure 16-15.

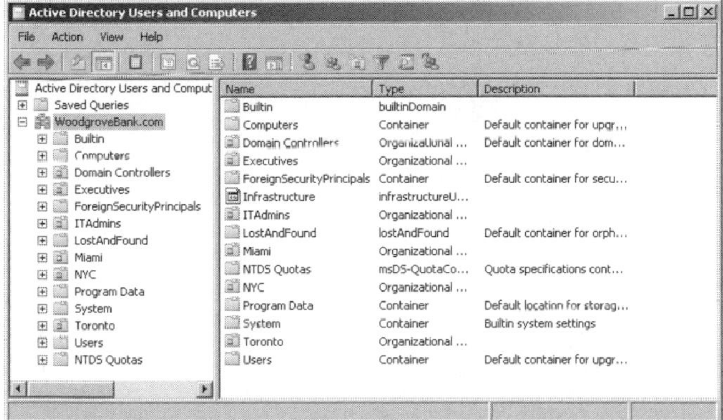

Figure 16-15 The Active Directory Users And Computers Advanced Features mode displaying all the system objects in the selected domain

From this interface, you can view information about the system objects and control access to them by modifying the associated permissions. Because access to these objects isn't required as frequently, you can suppress their appearance by leaving the console in normal mode. However, when you want to modify the permissions for standard objects such as organizational units, users, and groups, you must enable Advanced Features to see the Security tab in an object's Properties dialog box.

Changing the Domain

You can use the Active Directory Users And Computers snap-in to administer any domain where you have administrative permissions on the network. To change the currently displayed domain in the console, select the root or domain object in the console tree and choose Connect To Domain from the Action menu. This displays the Connect To Domain dialog box, where you can type the name of the domain or browse to another domain.

From the Action menu, you can also choose Connect To Domain Controller to access the selected domain by using a specific domain controller on the network. Unless your domain controllers are out of sync, the information should be the same on all the replicas, but sometimes you might want to select a domain controller at a different location to avoid a slow or expensive WAN connection.

Using Filters to Simplify the Display

When you begin to populate AD DS with new objects, it can rapidly grow to an unwieldy size. The sheer number of objects in the display can make locating the specific object you need difficult. To temporarily suppress the display of objects you don't need to see, you can apply a filter to the Active Directory Users And Computers snap-in based on object types or based on the contents of specific object attributes.

When you choose Filter Options from the View menu, the Filter Options dialog box appears, as shown in Figure 16-16. Here you can opt to display all object types, select specific object types to display, or build a custom filter based on object attributes.

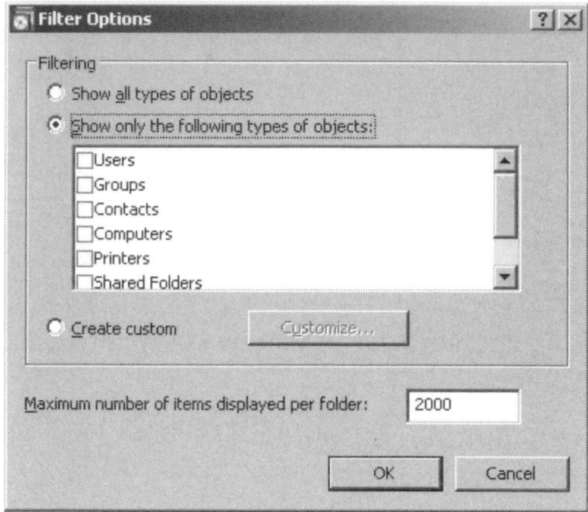

Figure 16-16 The Filter Options dialog box of Active Directory Users And Computers

When you select the Create Custom option and click Customize, you see a Find Custom Search dialog box like the one shown in Figure 16-17. In this dialog box, you can select an object type, choose an attribute of that object, and specify a full or partial value for that attribute.

For example, you can display only the user objects that have the value *Sales* in the *Department* attribute (as shown in the figure), or you can choose to display only the users that have a particular area code in the *Telephone Number* attribute. This enables you to quickly zero in on the objects you need to use without scrolling through an unnecessarily cluttered display.

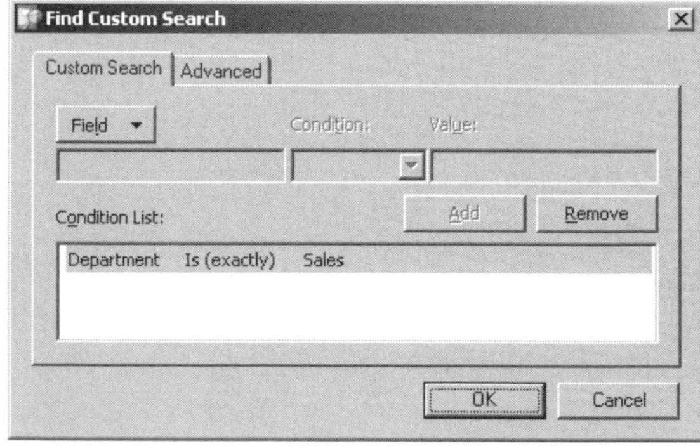

Figure 16-17 The Find Custom Search dialog box of Active Directory Users And Computers

Note You can also use the search functionality in Active Directory Users And Computers to locate specific objects. For more details, see Chapter 11.

Creating a Computer Object

In addition to container objects, group objects, and user objects, AD DS also has objects representing computers. To log on to a domain, a Windows Server 2008 computer must have an object representing it in the domain. When you promote a computer to become domain controller, or when you add a computer to the AD DS domain, Windows Server 2008 automatically creates a computer object. However, you can also create computer objects manually, just as you create any other object. This can be useful if you want to pre-stage computers' accounts for automatic operating system installation by using Windows Deployment Services (WDS).

To create a computer account in Active Directory Users and Computers, right-click the container where you want to create the account, choose New from the Action menu, and select Computer. In the New Object– Computer dialog box, supply the Computer Name and NetBIOS names for the new computer object. You can also specify the particular user or group that is authorized to join the computer to the domain and whether this account is for a pre–Windows 2000 computer, or whether this account should be for a backup domain controller.

Note The Active Directory Users And Computers snap-in creates objects one at a time, but sometimes administrators have to create a great many objects, and this tool becomes impractical. For more information about creating objects en masse, see Chapter 15, "Using Scripts for Consistent Administration."

Configuring Computer Objects

You can also manage existing computer accounts by configuring the following nine properties: General, Operating System, Member Of, Delegation, Location, Managed By, Object, Security, and Dial-in. Almost all the tabs have the same purpose as those in other objects. The four that are unique to the computer object are Operating System, Location, Delegation, and Dial-in.

The Operating System tab identifies the operating system running on the computer, the version, and the currently installed service pack. These fields are not editable; they are blank when you manually create a computer object and are filled in when the computer joins a domain. The Location tab enables you to specify which locations are served by the site in the directory setup, the Delegation tab allows you to set a computer as trusted for delegation, and the Dial-in tab allows you to set the Dial-in policy for this computer account.

Using Remote Computer Management

Active Directory Users And Computers provides administrative access to remote computers represented by objects in AD DS. When you click a computer object and choose Manage from the Action menu, the console opens the MMC Computer Management snap-in with that computer as its focus. With this capability, you can read the remote system's event logs, manipulate its services, and perform many of the other tasks provided by the Computer Management snap-in.

Publishing a Shared Folder

Shared folder objects enable you to publish shared network directories in AD DS, allowing users to access them directly by browsing in the network for the object. This eliminates the need for users to know the exact location of the shared folder. Creating a shared folder object doesn't actually create the share; you must do this manually on the Sharing tab of the drive or folder's Properties dialog box in the Windows Explorer window or the Computer window.

To create a shared folder object, click a container object in Active Directory Users And Computers, choose New from the Action menu, and then select Shared Folder. In the Create New Object dialog box, specify a name for the new object and type the UNC pathname to the share. After you create the object, you can configure it using the tabs in the object's Properties dialog box.

Publishing a Printer

Creating a printer object enables users to access the printer through AD DS in much the same way that they can access shared folders. You create a printer object just as you do a shared folder object, by selecting a container and choosing New\Printer from the Action menu and specifying the UNC path to the shared printer. The console then creates the object, combining the name of the host system and the share to form the object name. For more information about printer administration, see Chapter 10, "Managing Printers."

Real World Limitations with Publishing Shared Folders and Printers

When you publish a shared folder or printer in AD DS, you simplify the process for users in the domain to locate and connect to the object. For example, when you publish a shared folder, you can configure key words that enable users to locate the shared folder by searching for the key words. When you publish a shared printer, you can configure properties on the printer object that describe printer functionality such as two-sided or color printing. Users can then locate a printer based on these properties.

However, because the AD DS object is not actually linked to the shared folder or printer, the published objects are not automatically updated if you change the shared folder or printer. For example, if you move a shared folder to another server, or rename a computer object, the AD DS object is not automatically updated. When users try to connect to the moved object by connecting to the AD DS object, they will receive an error message.

Similarly, the permissions you set on the Security tab of the shared folder's Properties dialog box don't control access to the shared folder itself, only to the shared folder object. To access the folder using AD DS, a user must have permission to access both the share and the object. The same is true for a printer object.

Moving, Renaming, and Deleting Objects

After you create objects in AD DS, you can use Active Directory Users And Computers to reconfigure your domain at any time by moving objects to different containers, renaming them, and deleting them. The Action menu for nearly every AD DS object contains a Move command that opens a dialog box in which you can browse for a container where you want to place the object. You can also select several objects by holding down the Ctrl key while clicking them and moving them all to the same container. Or simply use the drag-and-drop feature to move objects around as you want.

Moving a container object to a new location modifies some attributes of the object but does not modify others. For example, if User X is a member of Group Y and you move User X to a new OU, User X remains a member of Group Y. However, any Group Policy objects that were assigned to User X based on the original location will no longer apply. When you rename an object using the Rename command on the Action menu, all the references to that object throughout AD DS change to reflect the new name. When you delete a container object, all the objects in the container are deleted as well.

Important Moving users or groups between OUs can change the way Group Policy objects are applied to the accounts. When you perform this action, Active Directory Users And Computers displays a warning to this effect.

Managing AD DS with Active Directory Domains and Trusts

Windows Server 2008 Active Directory Domains And Trusts is an MMC snap-in you can use to view a tree display containing all the domains in your forest. With this snap-in, you can manage the trust relationships between the domains, change the domain mode, and configure the user principal name (UPN) suffixes for the forest.

Launching Active Directory Domains And Trusts

Windows Server 2008 adds the Active Directory Domains And Trusts Manager snap-in to the Start menu by default, so after logging on using an account with administrative privileges, you can run the utility by selecting Active Directory Domains And Trusts from Administrative Tools in the Start menu's Programs group. The MMC snap-in file is called Domain.msc, so you can also launch the manager from the Run dialog box by executing that filename.

When the Active Directory Domains And Trusts console loads, the console tree (on the left side of the screen shown in Figure 16-18) displays all the domains in the forest in expandable tree fashion, stemming from a root labeled Active Directory Domains And Trusts. The result pane (on the right) displays the children of the currently selected domain or, if you select the root, the root domains of all the trees in the forest. The functions provided by Active Directory Domains and Trusts are accessible from the Action menus produced by clicking a domain name or the root object, as well as within the Properties dialog box for a domain.

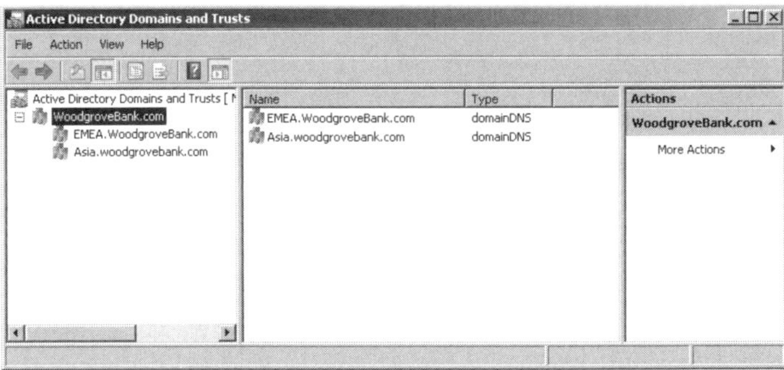

Figure 16-18 The Active Directory Domains And Trusts snap-in

Note One of the tasks that you can perform with Active Directory Domains And Trusts is to raise the domain and forest functional levels. For an explanation of the functional level options available in Windows Server 2008 and a description of how to raise the functional levels, see Chapter 6.

Managing Domain Trust Relationships

The trust relationship between domains is managed in the Trusts tab of a domain's Properties dialog box, shown in Figure 16-19. When you establish a trust relationship between two domains, users in one domain can access resources located in another trusted domain. An Active Directory domain tree is a collection of domains that share not only the same schema, configuration, and namespace, but are also connected by trust relationships.

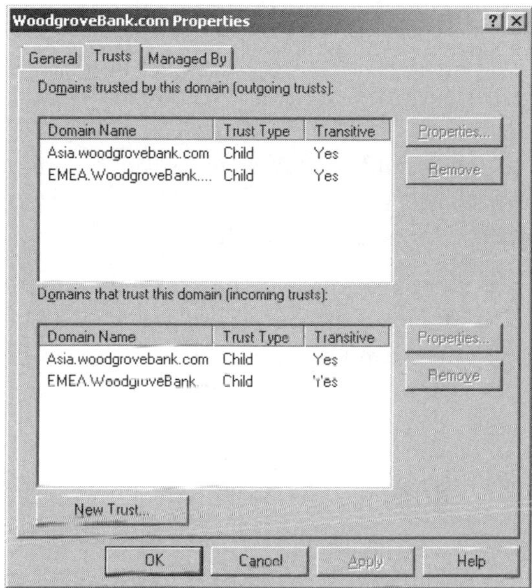

Figure 16-19 The Trusts tab of the Properties dialog box for a domain

Windows Server 2008 supports the following types of trust relationships:

- **Transitive two-way trusts** All domains in a forest maintain transitive, two-way trust relationships with every other domain in that forest. Within a forest, the trusts are set up as either parent-child trusts or as tree root trusts. An example of a parent-child trust is the trust between the NA.WoodgroveBank.com domain and the WoodgroveBank.com domain. A *tree root trust* is the trust between two trees in the forest—for example, between WoodgroveBank.com and TreyResearch.com. However, all of the trusts between domains in a forest are also *transitive*. The transitive nature of the trust means that all the domains in the forest trust each other. If the WoodgroveBank.com domain trusts the NA.WoodgroveBank.com domain, and the EMEA.WoodgroveBank.com domain trusts the WoodgroveBank.com domain, transitivity means that the EMEA.WoodgroveBank.com domain also trusts the NA.WoodgroveBank.com domain.

- **Shortcut trusts** In addition to the automatic, two-way transitive trusts that are created when a new child domain is created, shortcut trusts can be created between domains in the forest. Shortcut trusts are used to optimize performance when accessing resources between domains that are connected through transitive trusts. A shortcut trust is desirable when there is frequent resource access between domains that are remotely connected through the domain tree or forest. For example, if users in the Research.EMEA.WoodgroveBank.com domain have a frequent need to access a shared resource in the Sales.NA.WoodgroveBank.com domain, you could configure a shortcut trust between the two domains.
- **Forest trusts** A forest trust is a two-way transitive trust between two separate forests. With a forest trust, security principals in one forest can be given access to resources in any domain in a completely different forest. Also, users can log on to any domain in either forest using the same UPN. If you want to configure a forest trust, both forests must be at the Windows Server 2003 forest functional level.
- **External trusts** An external trust is a trust relationship that can be created between AD DS domains that are in different forests or between an AD DS domain and a Windows NT 4.0 or earlier domain. You can use external trusts to provide access to resources in a domain outside of the forest that is not already joined by a forest trust or to create a direct trust between two domains that are joined by a forest trust. An external trust is different from a forest trust in that the external trust is configured between any two domains in either forest, not just between the forest root domains. In addition, external trusts are not transitive.
- **Realm trusts** A realm trust is configured between a Windows Server 2008 domain or forest and a non-Windows implementation of a Kerberos v5 realm. Kerberos security is based on an open standard, and several other implementations of Kerberos-based network security systems are available. You can create realm trusts between any Kerberos realms that support the Kerberos v5 standard. Realm trusts can be either one-way or two-way, and they can also be configured to be transitive or non-transitive.

AD DS automatically creates trust relationships in all the domains in a tree and between all trees in a forest. To provide access to users from a domain in another forest or to grant the users in your domain access to another forest, you can manually establish trust relationships. To establish a trust relationship with another domain, you specify the name of the domain in the Add Trusted Domain dialog box and supply a password. To complete the process, an administrator of the other domain must specify the name of your domain in the Add Trusting Domain dialog box and furnish the same password. Both domains must approve before the systems can establish the trust relationship.

Note If you know the user credentials of a Domain Admin group member (in the case of a shortcut or external trust) or an Enterprise Admin group member (in the case of a forest trust), you can configure and verify both sides of the trust at the same time.

Specifying the Domain Manager

The third tab in a domain's Properties dialog box identifies the individual who is the designated manager for the domain. This tab provides contact information about the manager derived from the associated user account in AD DS. You can change the manager by clicking Change and selecting another user account from the AD DS display shown. The information is informative, but doesn't actually *do* anything.

Configuring User Principal Name Suffixes for a Forest

A UPN is a simplified name users can supply when logging on to AD DS. The name uses the standard e-mail address format consisting of a user name prefix and a domain name suffix, separated by an at sign (@), as defined in RFC 822 (for example, user@WoodgroveBank.com). UPNs provide network users with a unified logon name format that insulates them from the AD DS domain hierarchy and the need to specify the complex Lightweight Directory Access Protocol (LDAP) name for their user objects when logging on.

By default, the suffix of the UPN for users in a particular forest is the name of the first domain created in the first tree of that forest, also called the *forest DNS name*. Using Active Directory Domains And Trusts Manager, you can specify additional UPN suffixes that users can employ in place of the forest DNS name when logging on. To do this, select the root object in the console tree of the main Active Directory Domains And Trusts display (that is, the object labeled *Active Directory Domains And Trusts*), and choose Properties from the Action menu, as shown in Figure 16-20. On the UPN Suffixes tab, type the new UPN suffix, then click Add to specify additional suffixes. These suffixes apply to the entire forest and are available to any user in any domain of any tree in that forest.

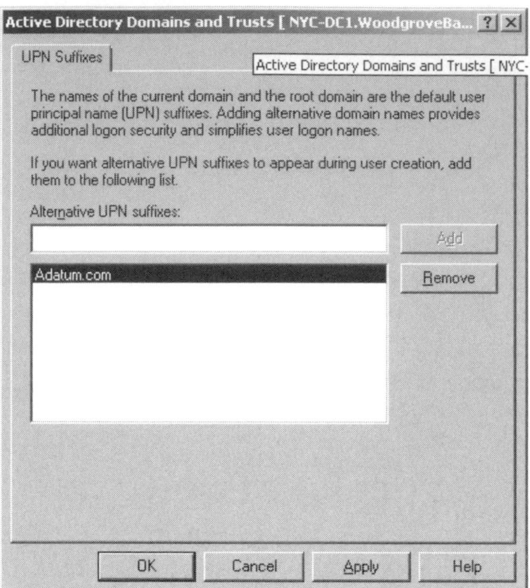

Figure 16-20 Configuring additional UPNs

Using Active Directory Sites And Services

Active Directory Sites And Services is a snap-in for the Microsoft Management Console (MMC) that administrators use to create and manage the sites that make up a Microsoft Windows Server 2008 forest as well as to establish links between sites. A *site*, in AD DS terminology, is defined as a group of computers on one or more Internet Protocol subnets that are well connected. *Well connected* means that the systems share a network transport that provides low-cost, high-speed communication between the computers, and it typically refers to systems in a single location that are connected by local area networks (LANs). Systems that aren't well connected are those that use relatively slow, expensive communication.

When you design trees and forests for AD DS installation, the boundaries between forests, trees, domains, and organizational units (OUs) are often motivated by political or administrative considerations. For example, AD DS for a large corporation might consist of separate trees corresponding to corporate divisions, domains for individual departments, and OUs for workgroups. Sites, on the other hand, are always based on geographical locations and the types of connections between those locations.

For example, an organization may have two divisions, each of which has its own Fast Ethernet LAN running at 100 Mbps. If the two divisions are located in separate buildings on the same campus, they might have a high-speed fiber-optic connection between the two LANs, also running at 100 Mbps. In this case, because all the computers in the two divisions are equally well connected, they can be said to form a single site. If, on the other hand, the two divisions are located in separate cities and are connected by a T1 line operating at only 1.544 Mbps, the divisions would form two separate sites because all the computers on the network aren't equally well connected.

Sites don't appear as objects in the AD DS namespace; they're completely separate from the hierarchy of forests, trees, and domains. A site can contain objects from different domains, and you can split a domain's objects among different sites. The primary reason for creating sites is to be able to manage any network traffic that must use slow network connections. Sites are used to control network traffic within the Windows Server 2008 network in three different ways:

- **Replication** One of the most important ways that sites are used to optimize network traffic is in the management of replication traffic between domain controllers. For example, within a site, any change made to the directory will be replicated within a few minutes. You can manage the replication schedule between sites so that the replication traffic will occur less frequently or during non-working hours. By default, replication traffic between sites is compressed to conserve bandwidth, while replication traffic within a site is not compressed.
- **Authentication** When a user logs on to a Windows Server 2008 domain from a Windows 2000, Windows XP Professional, or Windows Vista client, the client computer will always try to connect a domain controller in the same site as the client. Every domain controller registers site-specific service locator (SRV) records—when the client computer tries to locate a domain controller, it will always query the DNS servers for these site records. This means that the client logon traffic will remain within the site.
- **Site-aware network services** The third way that sites can preserve network bandwidth is by limiting client connections to site-aware applications and services on the site. For example, by using Distributed File System (DFS), you can create multiple replicas of a folder in different sites on the network. Because DFS is designed to be aware of the site configuration, a client computer always tries to access a DFS replica in its own site before crossing a WAN link to access the information in another site. Exchange Server 2007 also uses the AD DS site configuration to define the message routing topology within the organization. Messages sent between Exchange Servers in the same site will always be sent directly from the source Exchange Server to the destination Exchange Server even if the message needs to be sent to several servers in the same site. Only single copies of messages are sent between Exchange Servers in different sites, even if the messages are intended for users on several different Exchange Servers in the destination site.

Every computer on a Windows Server 2008 network will be assigned to a site. When AD DS is installed in a Windows Server 2008 environment, a default site is created, and all computers in the forest will be assigned to that site unless additional sites are created. When additional sites are created, the sites are linked to IP subnets. When a server running Windows Server 2008 is promoted to become a domain controller, the domain controller is automatically assigned to a site that corresponds to the computer's IP address. If necessary, you can also move domain controllers between sites using the Active Directory Sites And Services administrative tool.

Client computers determine their sites the first time they start up and log on to the domain. Because the client computer does not know which site it belongs to, it will connect to any domain controller in the domain. As part of this initial logon process, the domain controller will inform the client which site it belongs to, and the client will cache that information for the next logon.

AD DS Sites Overview

When you create the first Windows Server 2008 domain controller on your network, the Active Directory Domain Services Installation Wizard creates the default first site and names it Default-First-Site-Name. You can supply a more descriptive name for this site if you want or leave it as is. If all the AD DS domains on your network are located on the same LAN, you don't need any other sites. As you promote each server on the network to a domain controller, AD DS adds it to the site and automatically configures the replication topology between the servers.

If you will have servers at remote locations, however, you can create additional sites using Active Directory Sites And Services. By creating subnet objects and associating them with specific sites, you give AD DS the information it needs to automatically add each server that is subsequently promoted to a domain controller to the appropriate site, based on the subnet where the computer is located. If you move a server to a new location at a different site, however, you must also manually move the server object to the new site object. Thus, if you plan to install and configure a domain controller at the office and then ship it to a remote location, you have to use Active Directory Sites And Services to move the server object to the appropriate site.

Subnet Objects

AD DS uses subnet objects to define the boundaries of a site. Each subnet object consists of a network address and a subnet mask used by some or all of the computers in a site. You can associate a site with multiple subnet objects so that if your network has multiple subnets in a single location, you can include all of them in a single site.

Server Objects

Server objects are always children of site objects and are created by the Installation Wizard whenever it promotes a server to a domain controller. Don't confuse an AD DS server object with the computer object that the wizard also creates during the promotion process. The two, although linked, are completely separate objects with different purposes. You can manually create server objects in the Sites And Services snap-in, but this shouldn't be necessary.

When AD DS installation includes two or more sites, the Installation Wizard uses the subnets associated with the site objects to suggest a site that is appropriate for the server object. If no site is associated with the subnet used by a new domain controller, you can choose the site where the domain controller will be created. Afterward, you have to create the site where the server belongs and move the server to it.

Understanding AD DS Replication

Replication is the process of copying AD DS data between domain controllers to ensure that they all have the same information. The Windows Server 2008 uses a *multi-master replication* model for AD DS replication. This means that administrators can modify AD DS by writing to any domain controller (except RODCs). All the domain controllers with a writeable copy of the AD DS data periodically replicate the modifications to all the other domain controllers. The schedule and topology for these replication events differ depending on whether the domain controllers are at the same or different sites. The following sections examine these two replication scenarios.

Intrasite Replication

Replication between domain controllers in the same site is known as *intrasite replication* and is completely automatic and self-regulating. A component known as the *knowledge consistency checker* (KCC), which runs on each domain controller, creates connections between the domain controllers in the site. Because all the domain controllers in the site are assumed to be well connected, the replication process is designed to keep *latency* (the delay between directory writes and their propagation to the other domain controllers) to a minimum, even at the expense of network bandwidth. Within a site, the domain controller where a change is made to AD DS waits only 15 seconds before replicating the changes to its direct replication partners. The 15-second wait occurs so that if multiple updates are committed to the database, they can all be replicated at the same time.

The KCC dynamically creates connection objects in AD DS. When KCC creates the replication topology, it creates a series of connection objects that are stored in the configuration directory partition of AD DS. The connection objects are direct logical connections between domain controllers that are used to replicate directory information. KCC tries to create a replication topology that is both efficient and fault-tolerant. When communication between domain controllers in the same site is disrupted, the KCC will create new connections to ensure continued replication. Administrators can create additional connection objects, which can improve communication between controllers and reduce latency further by decreasing the maximum number of hops allowed, but this approach also increases the system resources used by the replication process, including processor cycles, disk accesses, and network bandwidth. As a general rule, the replication topology within a site requires no administrative maintenance.

Intersite Replication

When you create multiple sites in AD DS, the domain controllers assume that the network connections between the sites are slower than those within a site, more expensive, or both. As a result, the domain controllers use *intersite replication* to attempt to minimize the replication traffic between sites and also to provide administrators with a much more flexible replication topology.

When you have domain controllers in multiple sites, AD DS still creates a default replication topology automatically during the installation process. However, distinct differences exist between the default replication patterns for intrasite and intersite topologies, including:

- **Number of connections** The KCC still automatically creates connections between domain controllers in different sites, but it creates fewer of them. Replication connections are created only between bridgehead domain controllers in each site.
- **Replication schedule** Replication activities within a site are triggered by changes to the AD DS database on a domain controller. Replication between sites takes place at scheduled times and intervals—the default is every 180 minutes across each site link. Administrators can customize the schedule to take advantage of time periods when traffic is low and bandwidth is less expensive.
- **Compression** Domain controllers transmit replication data uncompressed within a site, thus saving the processor cycles needed to decompress the data at the destination. Traffic between sites is always transmitted in compressed form to conserve bandwidth.

One of the primary functions of the Active Directory Sites And Services snap-in is to configure the replication pattern between sites. To do this, you create site link and site link bridge objects that specify how and when replication data should be transmitted between sites. The following sections examine the functions of Active Directory Sites And Services and how you use it to create a customized domain controller replication topology for your network.

Launching Active Directory Sites And Services

The Sites And Services tool is a standard snap-in for the MMC application, which you launch by selecting Active Directory Sites And Services from the Administrative Tools folder in the Start menu's Programs group. The snap-in module is called Dssite.msc; you can also launch Sites and Services by executing that filename from the command line or the Run dialog box.

Viewing Replication Objects

The Active Directory Sites And Services interface uses the same console tree and result panes as many of the other AD DS administration tools. The Sites container in the console tree contains the *Default-First-Site-Name* object automatically created by the AD DS installation, and two other containers called the Inter-Site Transports container and the Subnets container. When you create additional sites, they appear as separate objects in the Sites container. Administrator-created objects appear in the containers under Sites, subnet objects appear in the Subnets container, and site link and site link bridge objects appear in the Inter-Site Transports container.

Creating Site Objects

Creating additional site objects in AD DS is simply a matter of right-clicking the Sites container and choosing New Site from the shortcut menu. When the New Object – Site dialog box appears (as shown in Figure 16-21), you supply a name for the site object and select a site link it should use to define the transport mechanism for the site. The Active Directory Domain Services Installation Wizard creates the *DEFAULTIPSITELINK* object during the installation process, so this object is always available if you haven't yet created any other site links. After the site object is created, you can move server objects into it and associate them with the subnets on which they're located.

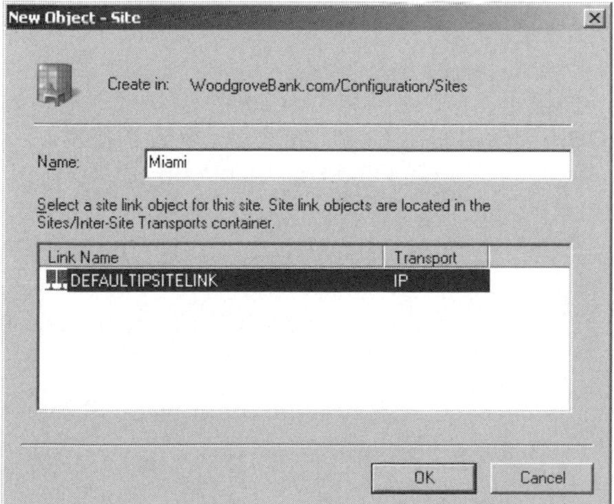

Figure 16-21 The New Object – Site dialog box

Each site object in Active Directory Sites And Services has a Servers container holding objects representing the servers in the site and an *NTDS Site Settings* object. The site object's Properties dialog box enables you to specify a description for the site and its location, as well as containing the standard Object, Security, and Attribute Editor tabs found in the dialog boxes of so many AD DS objects.

In the Properties dialog box for the *NTDS Site Settings* object, you can set the schedule for replication and enable or disable the Universal Group Membership caching, as shown in Figure 16-22. In the *NTDS Settings* object for an individual server, you can manually configure replication if necessary.

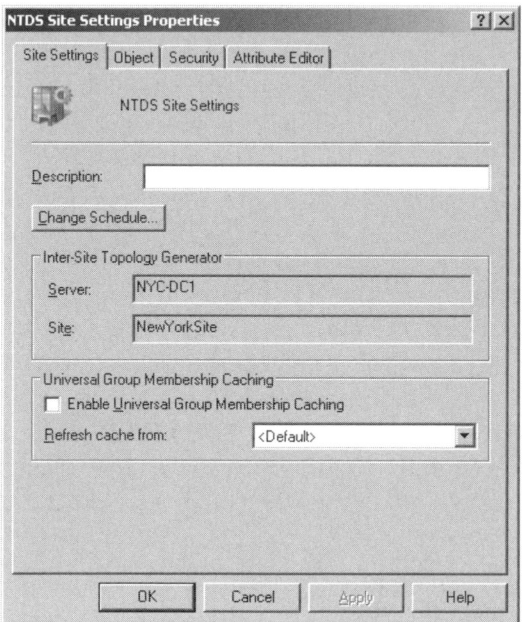

Figure 16-22 The NTDS Site Settings Properties dialog box

Creating Server and Connection Objects

Server objects are created during the installation of AD DS on each domain controller in the site associated with the subnet on which the server is located. Each server object contains an *NTDS Settings* object, which in turn displays the objects that represent that server's connections to other domain controllers on the network. All connections, whether created automatically by the KCC or manually by an administrator, appear as objects associated with a server.

The KCC automatically creates connection objects that ensure the continued replication of AD DS data to all the functioning domain controllers in each domain. Normally, the only reason you manually create connection objects is to customize your network's replication topology. If, for example, you want replication activities to occur only at specific times, you can create a connection object and configure when receiving domain controllers will check for updates on sending domain controllers. You can also create connection objects to decrease the number of hops between specific domain controllers.

The major difference between manually created connection objects and those created by the KCC is that the manual objects remain in place until you remove them manually; the KCC doesn't remove them no matter how the replication topology changes. Connection objects created by the KCC, however, are removed automatically as the replication topology changes. To create a connection object, follow these steps:

1. Right-click a server's *NTDS Settings* object in the Sites And Services console tree and choose New Connection from the shortcut menu. This displays the Find Active Directory Domain Controllers dialog box.
2. Select the domain controller you want to create a connection to and click OK to open the New Object Connection dialog box.
3. Supply a name for the new connection, and click OK. The program adds a connection object to the details pane.

Creating Subnet Objects

If you are implementing additional sites in your organization, you should also create objects representing the IP subnets on the network and associate them with specific site objects in the Subnets container. When you promote the first server to a domain controller, the Active Directory Domain Services Installation Wizard creates a site and places the server object in that site. If you create additional sites, subnet objects are used to ensure that each subsequent domain controller you install is placed in the appropriate site. During the promotion process, the wizard identifies the subnet on which the server resides and searches AD DS for a corresponding subnet object. When the wizard finds the subnet object, it reads its properties to determine the site with which that subnet is associated, and it creates the new server object in that site.

To create a subnet object, follow these steps:

1. Right-click the Subnets container in the console tree of the Active Directory Sites And Services snap-in and choose New Subnet from the shortcut menu.
2. In the New Object – Subnet dialog box (shown in Figure 16-23), specify the subnet's network address and number of masked bits.

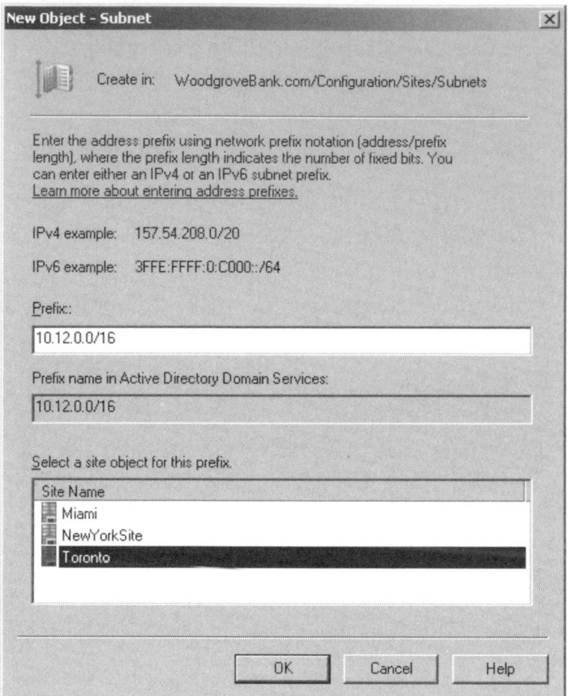

Figure 16-23 The New Object – Subnet dialog box

3. Select the site with which that subnet is to be associated, and click OK.

Any servers on that subnet that you promote to domain controllers are automatically added to this site. You can associate multiple subnets with a single site to support a network of almost any size.

Note The network address is the portion of the IP address that identifies the network on which a computer resides. The number of bits masked refers to how many of each IP address's 32 bits the system uses to identify the network. The design of the network and the IP addresses you use for workstations determine the value for this number. For example, if your organization has a class B network address (which uses 16 bits to identify the network) and uses a further 8 bits to identify subnets, the result is a total of 24 out of 32 bits that are devoted to the network address. The value for the subnet object's name field is therefore something like 172.16.2.0/24.

Creating Site Link Objects

The Inter-Site Transports container is where you create the site link and site link bridge objects that dictate how replication traffic is to be transmitted between sites. Two containers within Inter-Site Transports represent the two transport protocols supported by AD DS: IP and Simple Mail Transfer Protocol (SMTP).

A site link object is used by AD DS to differentiate replication settings between sites. AD DS creates a default site link object called *DEFAULTIPSITELINK* when you promote the first server to a domain controller. If all your sites are linked using technologies with exactly the same speed, you don't need to create additional site links. When you have different technologies connecting sites, however, you create multiple site link objects to have different replication settings for each one.

The site link costs define the path that replication traffic will take through the network. When KCC is creating the routing topology, it uses the accumulated costs for all site links to calculate the optimal routing. For example, your organization may have three locations: New York, Miami, and Toronto. If you have fast WAN connections between New York and Miami, and between New York and Toronto, and slow WAN connection between Miami and Toronto, you may want to have all replication traffic between Miami and Toronto pass through New York. You can do this by configuring a site for each location and then configuring separate site links between each of the sites. If the cumulative cost of the site links between Miami and New York and the site link between New York and Toronto is less than that of the site link between Miami and Toronto, all replication traffic between Miami and Toronto will be sent through New York. Only if the connection through New York is not available will replication traffic be sent directly between Miami and Toronto.

When creating a site link object, you select two or more sites that are connected by the transport mechanism and specify a cost value for the link. The cost value enables you to assign priorities to the various WAN connections based on their relative speeds.

To create a site link object, follow these steps:

1. Right-click either the IP or SMTP transport in the console tree of Sites And Services and choose New Site Link from the shortcut menu.
2. In the New Object – Site Link dialog box, specify a name for the object and select the sites that the link connects. If you choose multiple sites, the replication schedule and availability for replication between all of the sites will be identical.
3. Click OK.

Important You can only use SMTP site links to replicate AD DS data between domain controllers in different domains in the same forest, not between domain controllers in the same domain. To implement SMTP site links, you must also implement a PKI solution to enable encryption of all SMTP traffic sent between domain controllers.

Configuring Site Links

To configure a site link, right-click the new link object, and select Properties to configure its properties. The Site Link Properties dialog box for a site link object (shown in Figure 16-24) contains the standard tabs, as well as a General tab where you can provide a description of the object and specify the sites connected by the link. You can add new sites to the link as needed after creating the object.

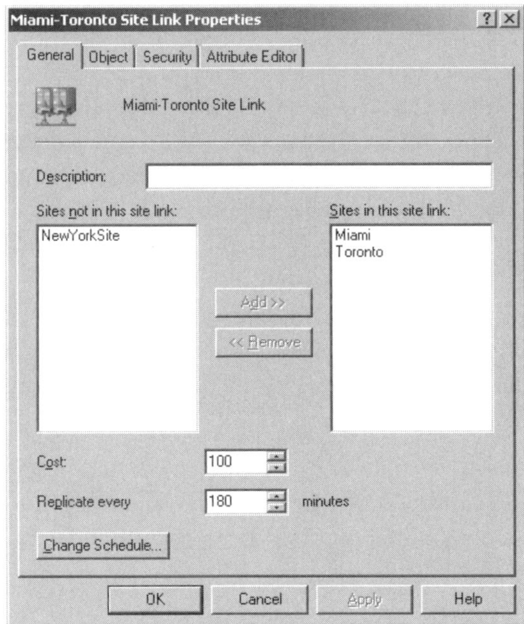

Figure 16-24 The General tab of the Site Link Properties dialog box

The General tab also contains fields with which to specify the cost for the link (from 1 to 32,767) and the interval between replication events (from 15 to 10,080 minutes). Click Change Schedule to specify the time periods that replication is or is not permitted. If you want to limit replication activities to non-peak traffic hours, for example, you can specify that replication events not occur between 9:00 A.M. and 5:00 P.M. The KCC observes the site link object's scheduling limitations when it dynamically creates connections between domain controllers.

Creating Site Link Bridge Objects

By default, all site links in a Windows Server 2008 forest are transitive. In Windows Server 2008 AD DS, all site links are considered transitive by default. This means that you can create connection objects between domain controllers that are not in adjacent sites. For example, you could implement site links between Toronto and New York, and between New York and Miami. Because of the transitive nature of the site links, this means that domain controllers in Toronto can also replicate directly with domain controllers in Miami.

In some cases, you might want to turn off the transitive nature of site links by turning off site link bridging and manually configuring site link bridges. When you configure site link bridges, you define which site links should be seen as transitive and which site links should not. Turning off the transitive nature of site links can be useful when you do not have a fully routed network—that is, if all segments of the network are not available at all times (for example, if you have a dial-up or scheduled-demand dial connection to one network location). You can also use site link bridges to configure replication in situations where a company has several sites connected to a fast backbone with several smaller sites connecting to each larger center using slow network connections. In such cases, you could use site link bridges to manage the flow of replication traffic more efficiently.

The first step in configuring site link bridging is to disable the default transitive nature of the site links. To turn off the transitive site links, expand the Inter-Site Transport container in Active Directory Sites and Services, right-click IP, click Properties, and then clear the Bridge All Site Links option on the General tab of the IP Properties dialog box.

Important The site link bridging setting affects all site links using the transport protocol where you disable site link bridging. This means that all site link bridging is disabled, and you will now have to configure site link bridges for all site links if you want transitive site connections.

The procedure for creating a site link bridge object is virtually identical to that of creating a site link object, except that you select two or more site links instead of sites. You don't need to specify a routing cost for a site link bridge because AD DS automatically computes it by adding the routing costs of all the bridge's sites. Thus, a site link bridge object containing two sites with routing costs of 3 and 4 has a routing cost of 7.

Installing and Configuring Active Directory Lightweight Directory Service

AD LDS is implemented in Windows Server 2008 as a server role. To install the server role, use Server Manager to add the role. To install the server role on a Windows Server 2008 computer running Server Core, run the *start /w ocsetup DirectoryServices-ADAM-ServerCore* command. During the role installation, you do not need to make any installation decisions other than choosing to install the role. To install AD LDS, your user account must be a member of the local Administrators group.

AD LDS Overview

AD LDS is designed specifically to provide directory services for directory-enabled applications. A directory-enabled application uses a directory rather than (or in addition to) a database, flat file, or other data storage structure to hold its data. The application may be storing configuration or application data in the directory or it may be using the directory for authentication. AD LDS provides this functionality.

AD LDS Features

To provide the features required by directory-enabled application, AD LDS includes the following features:

- **The same architecture and the same code base as AD DS** AD LDS provides a hierarchical data store, a directory service component, and interfaces that clients can use to communicate with the directory service. This means that developers and administrators who are used to working with AD DS will be able to transfer those skills to AD LDS.
- **Support for multiple AD LDS instances on one computer** An AD LDS instance refers to a single running copy of the AD LDS directory service. Multiple instances of AD LDS can run simultaneously on the same computer. Each instance of the AD LDS directory service has a separate directory data store, a unique service name, a unique service description and a unique port for clients to be able to access the instance. Each instance also has a single schema, so by deploying multiple instances, you can support multiple directories with different schemas on one server.
- **Support for multiple application directory partitions** Application directory partitions hold the data that your applications use. You can create an application directory partition during AD LDS setup or any time after installation. You can store multiple application directory partitions in a single instance, or distribute copies of application directory partitions across multiple instances.
- **Support for extensible schemas** AD LDS includes several options for configuring the schema in each AD LDS instance. In addition, you can modify the schema for each instance to support application requirements.
- **Support for directory replication** AD LDS supports replication of directory information between AD LDS instances installed on multiple computers. In this way, you can provide high availability or provide access to the directory information in geographically dispersed locations.

Configuring Instances and Application Partitions

After installing the AD LDS server role, you use the Active Directory Lightweight Directory Services Setup Wizard to create AD LDS service instances. Multiple instances of AD LDS can run simultaneously on the same computer. Each instance of the AD LDS directory service has a separate directory data store, a unique service name, and a unique service description that is assigned during installation. When you run the wizard, you also have the option of creating an application directory partition.

To create a new AD LDS instance by using the Active Directory Lightweight Directory Services Setup Wizard, complete the following steps:

1. Start the Active Directory Lightweight Directory Services Setup Wizard. You can start the wizard from the Administrative Tools menu or from Server Manager.
2. On the Welcome page, click Next.
3. On the Setup Options page, you have a choice of creating a new instance or creating a replica of an existing instance, as shown in Figure 16-25. Click A Unique Instance, and then click Next.

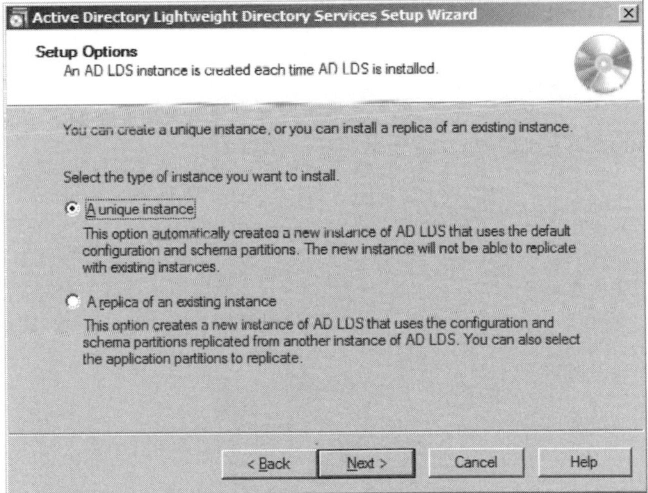

Figure 16-25 Creating an AD LDS instance

4. On the Instance Name page, provide a name for the AD LDS instance that you are installing. The name that you choose must meet the following requirements:
   - It must be different from other AD LDS instances running on the same computer.
   - It must be no longer than 44 characters.

- It must use characters only from the ranges of *a* through *z*, *A* through *Z*, or *0* through *9*.
- The name *ntds* cannot be used.

5. On the Ports page, specify the communications ports that the AD LDS instance uses to communicate. AD LDS can communicate using both LDAP and Secure Sockets Layer (SSL).

> **Note** If you install AD LDS on a computer where either of the default ports is in use, the Active Directory Lightweight Directory Services Setup Wizard automatically locates the first available port, starting at 50000. If you install AD LDS on a AD DS domain controller, you cannot use ports 389 and 636—or ports 3268 and 3269 on global catalog servers—because these ports are used for AD DS domain controller and global catalog lookups.

6. On the Application Directory Partition page, you can create an application directory partition during the AD LDS installation, as shown in Figure 16-26. If you do not install an application directory partition now, you must create an application directory partition manually after installation. When you create the application partition, you must provide a fully qualified partition name.

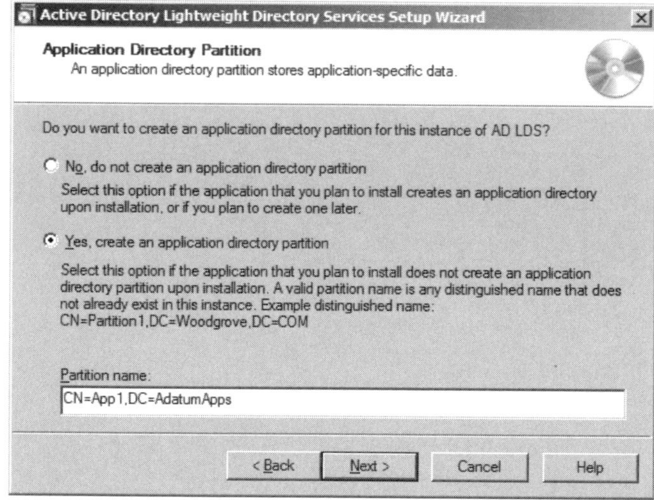

Figure 16-26 Creating an application directory partition when creating an AD LDS instance

7. On the File Locations page, you can view and change the installation directories for AD LDS data and recovery (log) files. By default, AD LDS data and recovery files are installed in %ProgramFiles%\Microsoft ADAM*instancename*\data, where *instancename* represents the AD LDS instance name that you specified on the Instance Name page.

8. On the Service Account Selection page, select an account to be used as the service account for AD LDS. The account that you select determines the security context in which the AD LDS instance runs. The Active Directory Lightweight Directory Services Setup Wizard defaults to the Network Service account.

> **Note** If you are installing AD LDS on a computer that is a member of a Windows Server 2000 or later domain, you can use the Network Service account even if you plan to implement replication. If you are deploying AD LDS on a computer that is a member of a workgroup or you want to enable replication between AD LDS computers in different untrusted domains, you will need to use the identical user account on all computers as the AD LDS service account.

9. On the AD LDS Administrators page, select a user or group to become the default administrator for the AD LDS instance. The user or group that you select will have full administrative control of the AD LDS instance. By default, the Active Directory Lightweight Directory Services Setup Wizard specifies the currently logged-on user. You can change this selection to any local or domain account or group on your network.
10. On the Importing LDIF Files page, you can import schema .ldf files into the AD LDS instance, as shown in Figure 16-27.

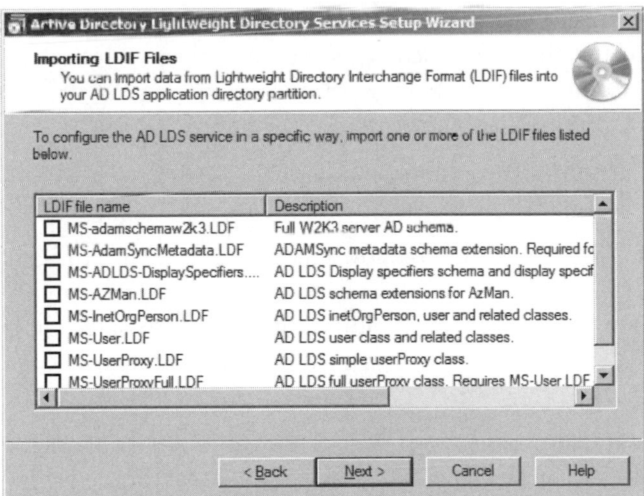

Figure 16-27 By adding .ldf files, you modify the AD LDS schema.

11. On the Ready To Install page, review your installation selections. After you click Next, the Active Directory Lightweight Directory Services Setup Wizard copies files and sets up AD LDS on your computer.

Note If an error occurs in the Active Directory Lightweight Directory Services Setup Wizard before the Summary page, you can review the error message that appears. In addition, you can view the adamsetup.log file and the adamsetup_loader.log files in the %windir\debug folder for information on why the installation failed.

Note To remove an AD LDS instance, access the Programs And Features console in Control Panel. All AD LDS instances are listed as installed programs, and you can uninstall the instance just like you would uninstall any other program.

Managing AD LDS

In most cases, after you install an AD LDS instance, you will install the application that will use the instance. (In fact, the application may install AD LDS and configure the instance for you.) However, you can also manage AD LDS instances by using the administration tools provided with AD LDS.

Using the ADSI Edit Tool

ADSI Edit is an MMC snap-in for general administration of AD LDS. It is installed as part of the AD LDS and AD DS server roles. To use ADSI Edit to administer an AD LDS instance, you must first connect to the instance. When you open ADSI Edit for the first time, it is not connected to any directory. To connect to a directory, on the Action menu, click Connect To. On the Connection Settings screen, shown in Figure 16-28, you must provide the following information:

- **A name for this connection** If you choose one of the well-known naming contexts, this name is filled in for you.
- **A connection point** This can be a well-known naming context like the configuration or schema partitions, the RootDSE object, or the Default naming context (which only applies to AD DS domains or application directory partitions). If you want to connect to a application directory partition, you must enter the distinguished name of the application directory partition.
- **The server to which you are connecting** If you are using a port other than the standard LDAP ports, you must also provide the port number for the connection.

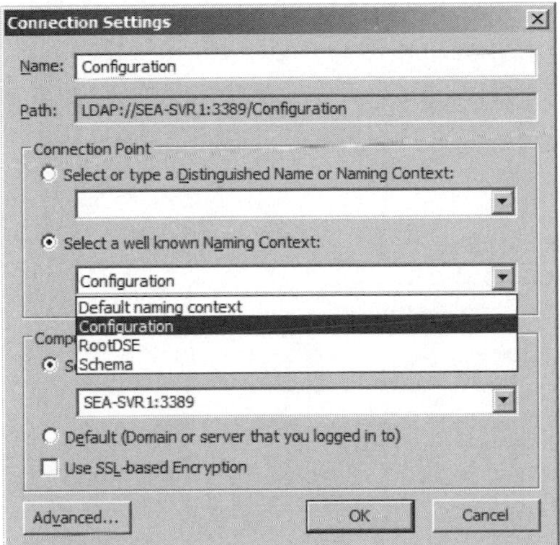

Figure 16-28 Connecting to an AD LDS instance by using ADSI Edit

Using the Ldp.exe Tool

Ldp.exe is a tool that you can use to administer any LDAP directory service. To use Ldp.exe to administer an AD LDS instance, you must connect and bind to the instance and then display the hierarchy (tree) of a distinguished name of the instance.

1. To connect to an instance using LDP, open a Command Prompt window, type **LDP.exe** and press Enter.
2. On the Connection menu, click Connect. Provide the server name and the port used for the AD LDS instance and choose whether to use SSL.
3. After connecting to the instance, you need to provide your credentials by binding to the instance. On the Connection menu, click Bind.
   - To bind using the credentials that you logged on with, click Bind As Currently Logged-On User.
   - To bind using a domain user account, click Bind With Credentials. Then type the user name, password, and domain name (or the computer name if you are using a local workstation account) of the account that you are using.
   - To bind using just a user name and password, click Simple Bind and then type the user name and password of the account that you are using.
   - To bind using an advanced method (NTLM, Distributed Password Authentication (DPA), Negotiate, or Digest), select Advanced (DIGEST). Then click Advanced, and in the Bind Options dialog box, select the desired method. Set other options as needed.

4. After you have been authenticated, on the View menu, click Tree. Type or select the distinguished name for the directory partition that you want to connect to.
5. To view information about the objects in the directory partition, click the object in the left pane. Detailed information about the object is displayed in the right pane, as shown in Figure 16-29.

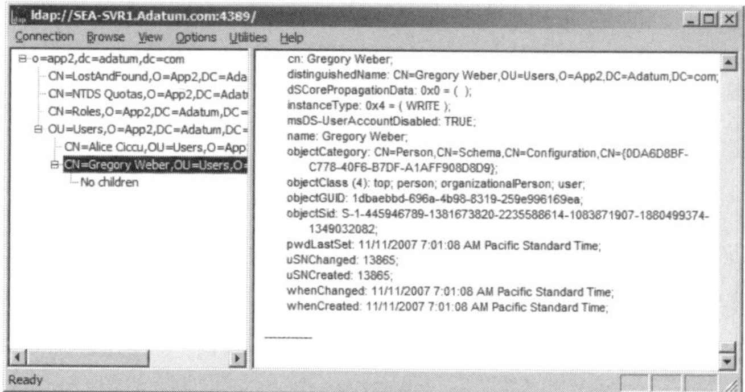

Figure 16-29 View details of all objects in AD LDS with Ldp.exe

6. To edit the object, right-click the object and select one of the options for modifying the object or adding child objects.

Note For details on how to use ADSI Edit and LDP.exe to manage AD LDS objects such as OUs and user and group accounts, see the "Working with Authentication and Access Control" article in the AD LDS online help, or see the "Step-by-Step Guide for Getting Started with Active Directory Lightweight Directory Services" article at *http://technet2.microsoft.com/windowsserver2008/en/library/141900a7-445c-4bd3-9ce3-5ff53d70d10a1033.mspx?mfr=true*.

Using the Dsdbutil Tool

Dsdbutil is a directory service management tool that provides much of the same functionality as Ntdsutil does for AD DS. With Dsdbutil, you can do the following:

- Back up and perform authoritative restores of AD LDS data
- Move the AD LDS data files
- Change the AD LDS service account and port numbers
- List all of the AD LDS instances running on a server

To use Dsdbutil, start the utility from a command prompt. Then connect to a specific instance by typing **Activate Instance instancename**. To see all of the commands available in Dsdbutil, type **Help**. Like Ntdsutil, Dsdbutil also provides context-sensitive help, so typing **Help** at any command prompt will display all of the options available in that context.

Note If you add the MS-ADLDS-DisplaySpecifiers.ldf file, you can use the Active Directory Sites And Services snap-in to manage AD LDS sites. To connect to an AD LDS instance, you must provide the server name and port number.

Configuring Access Control

In AD LDS, each directory object has an access control list (ACL) that determines which users have access to that object. By default, ACLs are assigned only at the top of each directory partition. All objects in a given directory partition inherit these ACLs. If your application required specific permissions to be assigned at different levels in the directory structure, you can use tools such as Dsacls and LDP.exe to view and assign permissions.

Dsacls is a command-line tool that you can use to view and modify permissions in a directory such as AD LDS. Dsacls uses the following syntax:

```
dsacls object [/a] [/d {user | group}:permissions [...]] [/g {user |
group}:permissions [...]] [/i:{p | s | t}] [/n]
[/p:{y | n}] [/r {user | group} [...]] [/s [/t]]
```

Dsacls uses permissions bits in the command to configure permissions on the object. For example, dsacls provides the generic permissions: GR (Generic Read), GE (Generic Execute), GW (Generic Write), and GA (Generic All).

More Info For detailed information on how to use Dsacls to manage permissions in a directory, including details on the permission bit settings, see the knowledge base article "How to Use Dsacls.exe in Windows Server 2003 and Windows 2000", located at *http://support.microsoft.com/kb/281146*. You can also type **dsacls /?** at the command line.

Table 16-3 describes some sample Dsacls commands.

Table 16-3 Sample Dsacls Commands

Command	Explanation
dsacls \\SEA-SVR1:4389\O=App2, DC=Adatum,DC=com	Displays the permissions assigned to the references application partition
dsacls \\SEA-SVR1:4389\O=App2, DC=Adatum,DC=com /G "CN=Gregory Weber, OU=Users,O=App2, DC=Adatum,DC=com ":SD	Grants the user *Gregory Weber* the special Delete permission on the object CN=APP1
dsacls "\\SEA-SVR1:4389\O=App2, DC=Adatum,DC=com" /D "CN=Alice Ciccu, OU=Users,O=App2, DC=Adatum, DC=com ":SDDCDT	Denies the Delete, Delete Child, and Delete Tree permissions on the O=App2 object for Alice Ciccu

You can also use LDP.exe to configure permissions on AD LDS objects. To configure permissions using LDP, complete the following steps:

1. Open Ldp.exe, and then connect and bind to an AD LDS instance.
2. On the View menu, click Tree View and then select the directory partition that you are connecting to.
3. Right-click the directory partition object for which you want to modify the permissions, click Advanced, and then click Security Descriptor. The Security Descriptor dialog box displays all access control entries (ACEs) and their assigned access rights over the selected directory partition object.
4. Click anywhere in the discretionary access control list (DACL), and then click Add ACE. Figure 16-30 shows the ACE – Access Control Entry dialog box. Type the distinguished name of the user account and select the appropriate permissions. You can also choose to allow or deny permissions and configure permission inheritance.

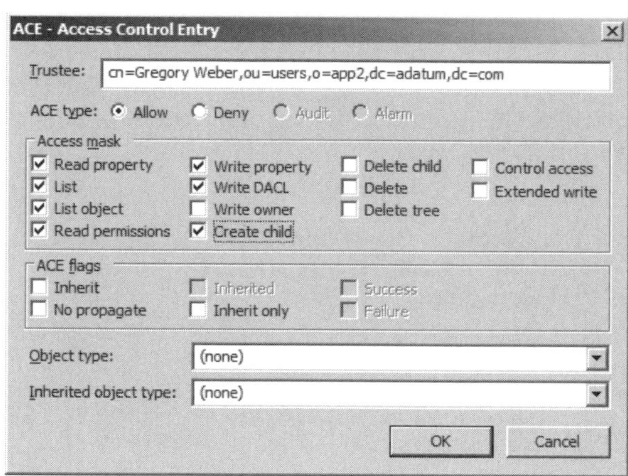

Figure 16-30 Configuring permissions by using LDP.exe

Configuring Replication

Like AD DS, AD LDS uses replication to provide redundancy, geographic distribution, and load balancing for AD LDS instances.

Creating AD LDS Replicas

To configure AD LDS replication, you start by creating additional replicas of the AD LDS instance. The replica can be configured only when you create the instance. All AD LDS instances in a configuration set replicate a common configuration directory partition and a common schema directory partition, plus any number of application directory partitions.

To create an AD LDS instance and join it to an existing configuration set, use the Active Directory Lightweight Directory Services Wizard to create a replica AD LDS instance. You need to know the DNS name of the server running an AD LDS instance that belongs to the configuration set, as well as the LDAP port that was specified when the instance was created. You can also supply the distinguished names of specific application directory partitions that you want to copy from the configuration set to the AD LDS instance that you are creating.

To create a replica AD LDS instance by using the Active Directory Lightweight Directory Services Setup Wizard, complete the following steps:

1. Start the Active Directory Lightweight Directory Services Setup Wizard. On the Welcome page, click Next.
2. On the Setup Options page (shown previously in Figure 16-25), click A Replica Of An Existing Instance.
3. On the Instance Name page, configure an instance name. AD LDS instance names have to be unique on a given computer. Also, the instance name can (but does not need to) match the instance name of other replicas.
4. On the Ports page, configure the port numbers for the instance. These port numbers define the ports clients will use to connect to the server, so it is recommended but not required that you use the same ports as the existing instance.
5. On the Joining A Configuration Set page, provide the host name or DNS name of the computer where the first AD LDS instance is installed. Then type the LDAP port number in use by the first AD LDS instance. This port number must match the port number configured on the existing instance.
6. On the Administrative Credentials For The Configuration Set page, click the account that is used as the AD LDS administrator for your first AD LDS instance.
7. On the Copy Application Directory Partition page, select the application directory partitions that you want to replicate to the new AD LDS instance.
8. Accept the default values on the remaining Active Directory Lightweight Directory Services Set Wizard pages by clicking Next on each page, and then click Finish on the Completing The Active Directory Application Mode Setup Wizard page.

Configuring AD DS and AD LDS Synchronization

One of the most common ways to integrate AD DS and AD LDS is to use AD DS user accounts when configuring authorization in AD LDS. To implement this level of integration, you do not need to perform any additional steps beyond installing AD LDS on a computer that is either part of the same AD DS domain as the user accounts or in a trusted domain. When installed on a domain member, the AD DS users accounts can be directly assigned to ACLs in AD LDS or added to AD LDS groups that are assigned to ACLs.

Another option for integrating AD DS and AD LDS is to configure synchronization from AD DS to AD LDS. This option can significantly decrease the administrative effort required to administer the AD DS instance. For example, if you are deploying AD LDS in a perimeter network, you may not want to install AD LDS on a server that is a member of an internal domain. However, you may still want to use internal user accounts to assign permissions to the AD LDS data, or the application using AD LDS may require the internal accounts. By configuring synchronization from AD DS to AD LDS, you can automate the process of creating the user accounts in the AD LDS instance.

To implement Adamsync synchronization, complete these steps:

1. To add the .ldf files to the schema, open a command prompt, switch to the %windir%\ADAM directory, and then use the following command:

   ```
   ldifde -i -u -f ldf_filename -s server:port -b user_name domain password
   -j . -c "cn=Configuration,dc=X" #configurationNamingContext
   ```

   In this command, replace *ldf_filename* with *MS-adamschemaw2k3.ldf* (to import the Windows Server 2003 schema) or *MS-adamschemaw2k8.ldf* (to import the Windows Server 2008 schema).

2. To add the <MS-AdamSyncMetadata.ldf file, use the following command.

   ```
   ldifde -i -s server:port -c CN=Configuration,DC=X #ConfigurationNamingContext
   -f MS-AdamSyncMetadata.ldf
   ```

3. Open the MS-AdamSyncConf.xml file located in the %windir%\Adam directory with Notepad. Make the following changes to the contents of the configuration file:

   - Replace the value of *<source-ad-name>* with the name of the source AD DS domain controller.
   - Replace the value of *<source-ad-partition>* with the distinguished name of the source domain.
   - Replace the value of *<source-ad-account>* with the name of an account in the Domain Admins group of the source domain.
   - Replace the value of *<account-domain>* with the fully qualified Domain Name System (DNS) name of the source domain.
   - Replace the value of *<target-dn>* with the name of the partition of the target AD LDS instance. This value must use a partition name and cannot use a container inside the partition.

- Replace the value of <*base-dn*> with the base distinguished name of the container in the source AD DS domain from which you want to import users. For example, if you want to import only users from a specific OU, change this value to something like *"OU=NYC,DC=Adatum,DC=com."*

4. Save the file with an .xml extension, using a different filename.

> **Note** You can modify other settings in the file to define which attributes are replicated to AD LDS. For a complete description of the file syntax, see "Adamsync Configuration File XML Reference" located at *http://technet2.microsoft.com/windowsserver/en/library/d4b6dbdc-eb53-4229-9118-b7d80c9125671033.mspx?mfr=true.*

5. The next step is to prepare the AD LDS instances for replication by installing the Adamsync instance. To do this, at the command prompt, type the following command, where *xml_file* is the name of the file that you created in the previous step:

   ```
   adamsync /install server:port .\xml_file
   ```

   If this file is not in the %windir%\Adam directory, you must provide the full path to the file.

6. After running the adamsync /install command, type the following command, where *xml_file* is the name of the file that you used in the previous step:

   ```
   adamsync /delete .\xml_file
   ```

   This command deletes the configuration file from the adam instance. This is required if the user needs to update the .xml file or restart the sync process.

7. After you prepare the AD LDS instance for synchronization, you can initiate synchronization from the specified AD DS forest to the AD LDS instance. To do this, type the following command, where *configuration_dn* is the root of the application directory partition to which you are synchronizing the data:

   ```
   adamsync /sync server:port configuration_dn /log Adamsynclog.txt
   ```

Summary

This chapter has covered the basic tools and techniques for installing and administering Active Directory in Windows Server 2008. Active Directory Users And Computers, in particular, is a tool that administrators use frequently to perform day-to-day maintenance tasks. Other tools that you will use on occasion are Active Directory Domains And Trusts and Active Directory Sites And Services. This chapter also covered some of the tasks in administering AD LDS. In the next chapter, we'll cover the ongoing maintenance tasks of an Active Directory deployment.

Chapter 17
Managing Active Directory

After completing your deployment and initial configuration of your Active Directory environment, you will find that your work load is much reduced. When Active Directory is properly deployed, it is very stable and requires little daily maintenance. However, you need to perform some tasks regularly. These tasks include managing the AD DS database and domain controller roles and ensuring that you have a consistent disaster recovery process in place.

Maintaining the AD DS Database

One of the important components of managing AD DS is maintaining the AD DS database. Under normal circumstances, you will rarely manage the AD DS database directly because regular automatic database management will maintain the health of your database in all but exceptional situations. These automatic processes include an online defragmentation of the AD DS database as well as a garbage collection process to clean up deleted items. For those rare occasions when you do need to directly manage the AD DS database, Windows Server 2008 provides the Ntdsutil tool.

AD DS Data Storage

The AD DS database is stored in a file called Ntds.dit, which is located in the %systemroot%\NTDS folder by default. The contents of this folder are shown in Figure 17-1. This folder also contains the following files:

- **Edb.chk** This file is a checkpoint file that indicates which transactions from the log files have been written to the AD DS database.
- **Edb.log** This file is the current transaction log. This log file is a fixed-length file exactly 10 megabytes (MB) in size.
- **Edbxxxxx.log** After AD DS has been running for a while, you might have one or more log files whose *xxxxx filename* portion is a value that is incremented in hexadecimal numbers. These log files are previous log files; whenever the current log file is filled up, the current log file is renamed to the next previous log file and a new Edb.log file is created. The old log files are automatically deleted as the changes in the log files are made to the AD DS database. Each of these log files is also 10 MB in size.
- **Edbtmp.log** This log is a temporary log that is used as the current log file (Edb.log) fills up. A new file named Edbtemp.log is created to store any transactions, and the Edb.log file is renamed to the next previous log file. Then the Edbtmp.log file is renamed to Edb.log. Because use of this filename is transient, it is typically not visible.
- **Edbres00001.jrs and edbres00002.jrs** These files are reserved log files that are used only when the hard disk that contains the log files runs out of space. If the current log file fills up and the server cannot create a new log file because no hard disk space is left, the server will flush any AD DS transactions currently in memory to the two reserved log files and then shut down AD DS. Each of these log files is also 10 MB in size.
- **Temp.edb** This is a temporary file used during database maintenance and to store information about transactions that are currently in progress.

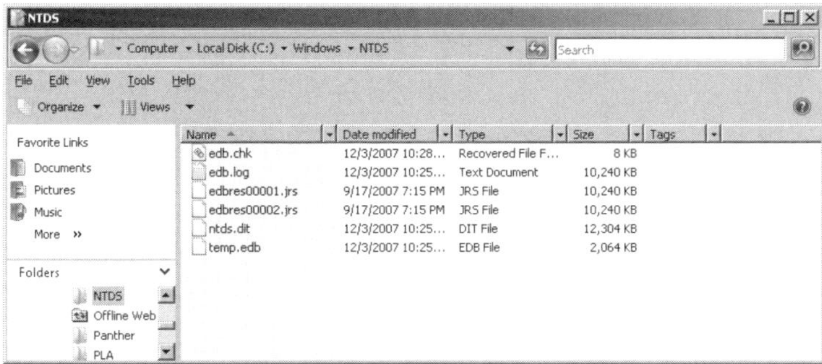

Figure 17-1 AD DS files located in %systemroot%\NTDS

Garbage Collection

One of the automatic processes used to maintain the AD DS database is garbage collection. Garbage collection is a process that runs on every domain controller every 12 hours. During the garbage collection process, free space within the AD DS database is reclaimed.

The garbage collection process starts by first removing tombstones from the database. *Tombstones* are the remains of objects that have been deleted from AD DS. When an object such as a user account is deleted, the object is not immediately deleted. Rather, the *isDeleted* attribute on the object is set to *true*, the object is marked as a tombstone, and most of the attributes for the object are removed from the object. This tombstone is then replicated to other domain controllers in the domain. Each domain controller maintains a copy of the tombstoned object until the tombstone lifetime expires. By default, the tombstone lifetime is set to 180 days. The next time the garbage collection process runs after the tombstone has expired, the object is deleted from the database.

Online Defragmentation

The final step in the garbage collection process is an online defragmentation of the AD DS database. This online defragmentation frees up space within the database and rearranges the storage of AD DS objects within the database to improve the efficiency of the database.

During normal operation, the database system for AD DS is optimized to be able to make changes to the AD DS database as quickly as possible. When an object is deleted from AD DS, the database page where the object is stored is loaded into the computer memory and the object is deleted from the page. As objects are added to AD DS, they are written to database pages without consideration for optimizing the storage of that information for later retrieval. After several hours of committing changes to the database as fast as possible, the storage of the data in the database might not be optimized. For example, the database might contain empty pages where objects have been deleted, there might be many pages with some deleted items, or AD DS objects that should logically be stored together might be stored on many different pages throughout the database.

The online defragmentation process cleans up the database and returns the database to a more optimized state. One of the limitations of the online defragmentation process is that it does not shrink the size of the AD DS database. If you have deleted a large number of objects from AD DS, the online defragmentation process might create many empty pages in the database as it moves objects around in the database. However, the online defragmentation process cannot remove these empty pages from the database. To remove these pages, you must use an offline defragmentation process.

The online defragmentation process runs every 12 hours as part of the garbage collection process. When the online defragmentation process is complete, an event is written into the Directory Service log indicating that the process has completed successfully. Figure 17-2 shows an example of this event log message.

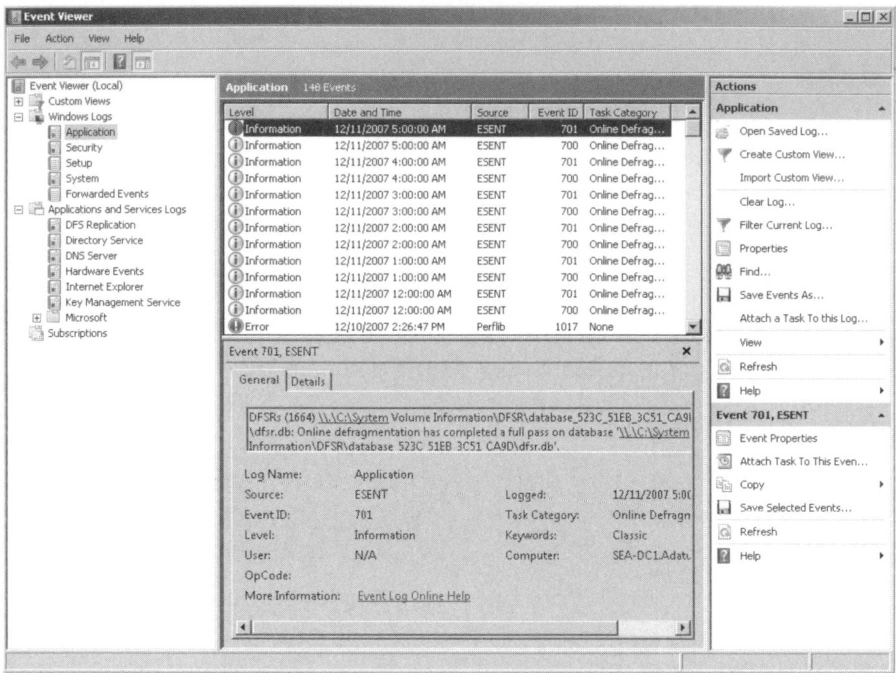

Figure 17-2 A Directory Service log message indicating a successful online defragmentation

Restartable Active Directory Domain Services

Unlike previous versions of Active Directory, AD DS in Windows Server 2008 can be stopped and restarted while the computer is booted up. In previous versions, if an administrator wanted to start a domain controller without loading AD DS, the server had to be rebooted into Active Directory Restore Mode. This would start the server as a stand-alone server, without AD DS. You then could perform offline maintenance tasks, such as an offline defragmentation or moving the database and log files. With Windows Server 2008, the directory service can be taken offline while the computer is running, with minimal disruption to other services.

The three possible states for AD DS on domain controller running Windows Server 2008 are listed in Table 17-1.

Table 17-1 Possible AD DS States

State	Description
AD DS Started	In this state, AD DS is started. For clients and other services running on the server, a Windows Server 2008 domain controller running in this state is the same as a domain controller running Windows 2000 Server or Windows Server 2003.
AD DS Stopped	In this state, AD DS is stopped. Although this mode is unique, the server has some characteristics of both a domain controller in Directory Services Restore Mode and a domain-joined member server. As with DSRM, the AD DS database (Ntds.dit) on the local domain controller is offline. Another domain controller can be contacted for logon if one is available. If no other domain controller can be contacted, you can use the DSRM password to log on to the local domain controller.
Directory Services Restore Mode	In this mode, the AD DS services are offline and the administrator must log on to the computer using the DSRM password. Domain policies are not applied to the server.

By stopping the AD DS service, you can perform some database administrative tasks These include:

- Performing an offline defragmentation
- Moving the AD DS database or log files

> **Important** You cannot restore the AD DS database while the AD DS service is stopped. To do this, you must still boot into Directory Services Restore Mode.

To stop the AD DS service, start the Services management console from the Administrative Tools folder. Then right-click Active Directory Domain Services and click Stop. Note that stopping the AD DS also will stop the following dependent services:

- Kerberos Key Distribution Center (KDC)
- Intersite Messaging
- File Replication Service (FRS)
- DNS Server

Offline Defragmentation of the AD DS Database

As mentioned previously, the online defragmentation process does not shrink the size of the AD DS database. Under normal circumstances, this is not a problem because the database pages that are cleaned up during the online defragmentation are just reused as new objects are added to AD DS. However, in some cases, you might want to use offline defragmentation to shrink the overall size of the database. For example, if you remove the global catalog from a domain controller, you should run an offline defragmentation on the database to clean up the space used in the database to store the global catalog information. This need for an offline defragmentation is especially true in a multiple-domain environment where the global catalog can become very large. You might also want to use offline defragmentation if you have removed a large number of objects from the AD DS domain.

To run offline defragmentation, perform the following steps:

1. Back up the AD DS information on the domain controller. This process is described later in this chapter.
2. Open the Services console and stop the Active Directory Domain Services service and all related services as prompted (or type **net stop ntds** at a command prompt).
3. Open a command prompt and type **ntdsutil**.
4. At the Ntdsutil prompt, type **activate instance NTDS**.
5. At the Ntdsutil prompt, type **files**.
6. At the File Maintenance prompt, type **info**. This option displays current information about the path and size of the AD DS database and its log files.
7. Type **compact to** drive:\directory. Select a drive and directory that have enough space to store the entire database. If the directory path name contains any spaces, the path must be enclosed by quotation marks.
8. The offline defragmentation process creates a new database named Ntds.dit in the path you specified. As the database is copied to the new location, it is defragmented.
9. When the defragmentation is done, type **quit** twice to return to the command prompt.
10. Copy the defragmented Ntds.dit file over the old Ntds.dit file in the AD DS database path and delete the old log files.
11. Restart the Active Directory Domain Services service.

Note If you are defragmenting the database because you have deleted a large number of objects from AD DS, you must repeat this procedure on all domain controllers.

Moving Database and Transaction Log Locations

The Ntdsutil tool can also be used to move the AD DS database and transaction logs. For example, if the transaction logs and the database are all on the same hard disk, you might want to move one of the components to a different hard disk. If the hard disk containing the database file fills up, you will have to move the database.

To move the database and transaction log to new locations with the server in Directory Services Restore Mode (or with the Active Directory Domain Services service stopped), perform the following steps:

1. Open a command prompt and type **ntdsutil**.
2. From the Ntdsutil prompt, type **activate instance NTDS**.
3. From the Ntdsutil prompt, type **files**.
4. To see where the files are currently located, at the Ntdsutil prompt, type **info**. This command lists the file locations for the database and all logs.
5. To move the database file, at the file maintenance prompt, type **move db to** directory, where *directory* is the destination location for the files. This command moves the database to the specified location and reconfigures the registry to access the file in the correct location.
6. To move the transaction logs, at the file maintenance prompt, type **move logs to** directory.
7. Reboot the server or restart the AD DS service.

Backing Up AD DS

The process for backing up AD DS in Windows Server 2008 is different from the process used in Windows Server 2003 and Windows 2000 Server. Windows Server Backup and Wbadmin.exe replace the previous Backup utility Ntbackup.exe. The new backup utility has the following changes:

- Windows Server Backup and Wbadmin.exe are not installed by default. You must install the Windows Server Backup and the Command-line Tools features to use these utilities. When you install the command-line tools, the Windows Powershell feature is also installed.

- Only full volumes can be backed up. Windows Server Backup has no option to back up only system state data, which includes AD DS. With Windows Server Backup, you must back up all critical volumes to back up system state data.

> **Note** You can back up just the system state information on a domain controller by using the Wbadmin.exe command-line tool. As a general practice, however, you should back up all system volumes as part of your regular backup process.

- Backups are performed only to disk or DVD. Windows Server Backup does not perform backups to tape. If you want to perform backups to tape, you must use a third-party backup solution. You can store backups on a local disk, external disk, remote share, or DVD.

System state data is a collection of configuration data on a server. This data is tightly integrated and must be backed up and restored as a single unit. In Windows Server 2008, when using Windows Server Backup, you must back up critical volumes containing system state data. In Windows Server Backup, the option Enable System Recovery is used to automatically select all critical volumes, as shown in Figure 17-3.

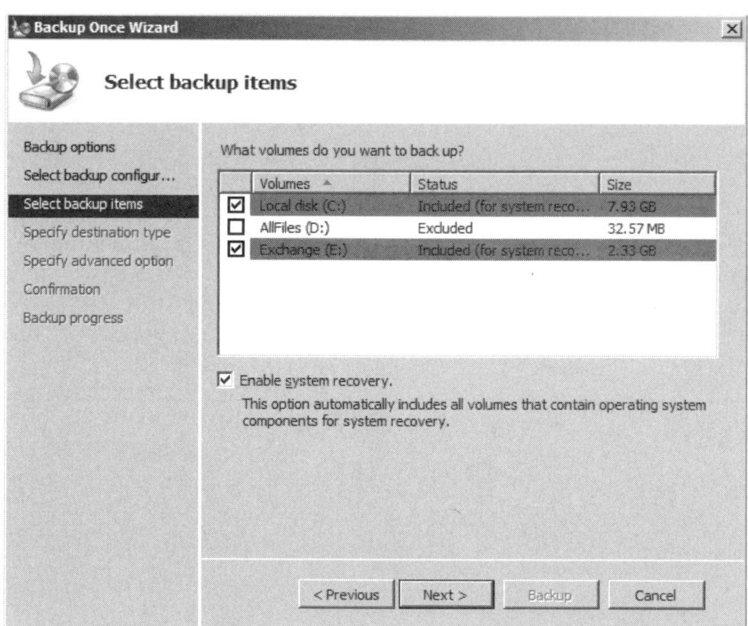

Figure 17-3 Using Windows Server Backup to back up critical volumes

The critical volumes for a server vary depending on the roles installed on a server. The system volume hosts the boot files, such as the Boot Configuration Data (BCD) store and Bootmgr, and is a critical volume. The boot volume with the Windows operating system is also a critical volume. Volumes hosting the following additional data are also critical volumes:

- SYSVOL directory
- AD DS database and log files
- Registry
- COM+ Class Registration database
- Active Directory Certificate Services database
- Cluster service information
- System files that are under Windows Resource Protection

Note Members of the Administrators and Backup Operators groups have the necessary rights to perform a manual backup. Only members of the Administrators group have the necessary right to perform a scheduled backup and this right cannot be delegated.

The Need for Backups

The primary method for backing up AD DS is replication to a second domain controller. If one domain controller in a domain fails, other domain controllers have the same information and make that information available to clients for logon or other queries. There should always be at least two domain controllers per domain for this purpose.

Even though domain information is replicated between domain controllers, a domain controller should still be backed up regularly. You may need to restore an existing domain controller or AD DS in the following situations:

- **Applications are configured to use a specific domain controller** Some applications are configured to use a specific domain controller to access AD DS. In such a case, restoring a domain controller avoids the need to reconfigure the application.
- **All domain controllers for a domain are lost** In the event of a major disaster such as a building fire, all domain controllers for a domain may be lost. In such a case, AD DS must be restored from backup.
- **Objects are deleted** If an AD DS object is deleted by accident, you can restore the deleted objects from backup. Depending on the number of objects, this may be much faster than recreating the objects.

Real World Preparing for a Disaster

The first steps in disaster recovery must take place long before the disaster strikes. In fact, if you haven't done the proper planning for a potential disaster, a problem such as a hardware component failure on a domain controller might turn into a real catastrophe rather than just a minor inconvenience.

Planning for disaster includes considering all the elements that make up the normal network infrastructure, as well as some AD DS–specific planning. The following procedures are critical:

- Develop a consistent backup and restore regimen for the domain controllers.
- Test your backup plan before you deploy AD DS and frequently after you deploy.
- Test changes to AD DS in a lab environment. This minimizes the risk that major updates to AD DS, such as schema changes, will cause problems in the production environment.
- Deploy Active Directory domain controllers with hardware redundancy. Most servers can be ordered with some level of hardware redundancy at little additional cost. For example, a server with dual power supplies, redundant network cards, and a hardware-based redundant hard disk system should be standard equipment for the domain controllers.
- In all but the smallest networks, you should deploy at least two domain controllers. AD DS uses circular logging for its log files, and this default cannot be modified. This circular logging means that with a single domain controller, you might lose AD DS data if the domain controller crashes and you have to restore from backup. Even in a small company, multiple domain controllers are critical. If you want all the users to use one domain controller most of the time, you can modify the DNS records by adjusting the priority for each domain controller. The second domain controller can then serve another function and be used for backup only when the first domain controller fails.

Backup Frequency

A backup is valid only for the length of the tombstone lifetime configured in AD DS. You cannot restore an AD DS backup that is older than the tombstone lifetime. Although the tombstone lifetime places a hard limit on the frequency of backups, you should back up the domain controllers much more frequently than the tombstone lifetime. Many issues in addition to the tombstone problem need to be considered if you are trying to restore the domain controller from a backup that is more than a couple of days old. Because the restore of AD DS includes all the information on critical volumes, that information will be restored to a previous state. If the server has the Active Directory Certificate Services role installed, any certificates that you issued since the backup will not be included in the Active Directory Certificate Services database. If you have updated drivers or installed any new applications, they might not work because the registry has been rolled back to a previous state. Almost all companies use a backup regimen in which at least some servers are backed up every night. The domain controllers should be part of the nightly backup.

Performing an AD DS Backup with Windows Server Backup

To perform an AD DS backup using Windows Server Backup, complete the following steps:

1. In the tree pane of the Server Manager window, expand Storage, and then click Windows Server Backup. You can also open Windows Server Backup from the Administrative Tools menu.
2. In the Actions pane of the Windows Server Backup result pane, click Backup Once to start the Backup Once Wizard. You can also choose to schedule a regular backup.
3. On the Backup Options page of the Backup Once Wizard, click Next.
4. On the Select Backup Configuration page, you can either perform a full server backup or a custom backup, which will enable you to exclude some volumes from the backup. Click Custom and click Next.
5. On the Select Backup Items page, click Next. By default, on a domain controller all of critical volumes will be selected. See Figure 17-3.
6. On the Specify Destination Type page, you can choose the location for the backup files. You can choose a local drive or remote shared folder if you are performing an on demand backup. Click Next.
7. On the Select Backup Destination page, select the location where you want store the backup file, and then click Next.
8. On the Specify Advanced Option page, you can choose to perform a VSS copy backup or a VSS full backup. Click Next.
9. On the Confirmation page, click Backup.

You can also use the Wbadmin command-line tool to back up AD DS. By using this tool, you can back up and restore just the system state data on a domain controller. To back up only the system state data, use the following command, where *Driveletter*: is the drive where you want to store the backup files:

```
WBAdmin Start Systemstatebackup -backuptarget:Driveletter:
```

Restoring AD DS

You might need to restore AD DS for two reasons: The first reason is if your database is unusable–perhaps because one of your domain controllers has experienced a hard disk failure or because the database has been corrupted to the point where it cannot be loaded. The second reason is if human error has created a problem with the directory information. For example, if someone has deleted an OU containing several hundred user and group accounts, you will want to restore the information rather than reenter all the information.

If you are restoring AD DS because the database on one of your domain controllers is not usable, you have two options. The first option is to not restore AD DS to the failed server at all, but rather to create another domain controller by promoting another server running Windows Server 2008 to become a domain controller. This way, you are restoring the domain controller functionality rather than restoring AD DS on a specific domain controller. The second recovery option is to repair the server that failed and then restore the AD DS database on that server. In this case, you will perform a nonauthoritative restore. A *nonauthoritative restore* restores the AD DS database on the domain controller, and then all the changes made to AD DS since the backup are replicated to the restored domain controller.

If you are restoring AD DS because someone deleted a large number of objects in the directory, you have only one way to restore the information. You will restore the AD DS database on one of the domain controllers using a backup that contains the deleted objects. Then you will perform an authoritative restore. During the authoritative restore, the restored data is marked so that it is replicated to all other domain controllers, overwriting the deletion of the information.

Removing Domain Controllers from AD DS with Ntdsutil

If you do choose to restore AD DS functionality by creating a new domain controller, you still need to remove the old domain controller from the directory and from DNS. If you are planning to use the failed domain controller's name for the restored domain controller, you need to clean up the directory by using Ntdsutil before installing AD DS on the new domain controller. If you are using a different name for the new domain controller, you can clean up the directory after installation.

To clean up the failed domain controller information in AD DS, complete the following steps:

1. Open a command prompt.
2. Type **ntdsutil** and press Enter.

3. At the Ntdsutil prompt, type **metadata cleanup** and press Enter.
4. At the Metadata Cleanup prompt, type **connections** and press Enter. This command is used to connect to a current domain controller to make changes to AD DS.
5. At the Server Connections prompt, type **connect to server servername**, where *servername* is the name of an available domain controller, and press Enter. If you are logged on with an account that has administrative rights in AD DS, you will be connected to that domain controller. If you do not have administrative rights, you can use the **set creds** domain username password command to enter the credentials of a user with domain-level permissions.
6. At the Server Connections prompt, type **quit** and press Enter. This returns you to the Metadata Cleanup prompt.
7. At the Metadata Cleanup prompt, type **select operation target** and press Enter. This command is used to select the domain, site, and domain controller so that you can remove the domain controller.
8. At the Select Operations Target prompt, type **list domains** and press Enter. All the domains in the forest are listed with a number assigned to each.
9. At the Select Operations Target prompt, type **select domain** number, where *number* is the domain containing the failed domain controller, and press Enter.
10. At the Select Operations Target prompt, type **list sites** and press Enter. All the sites in the forest are listed with a number assigned to each.
11. At the Select Operations Target prompt, type **select site** number, where *number* is the site containing the failed domain controller, and press Enter.
12. At the Select Operations Target prompt, type **list servers in site** and press Enter.
13. At the Select Operations Target prompt, type **select server** number, where *number* is the failed domain controller, and press Enter.
14. Type **quit** and press Enter. This returns you to the Metadata Cleanup prompt.
15. Type **remove selected server** and press Enter.
16. Click **Yes** to confirm removal of the server.
17. Type **quit** at each prompt to exit Ntdsutil.

Note This process with Ntdsutil is also used when you have forced the removal of AD DS from a server by using *Dcpromo /forceremoval*. This command demotes a domain controller without cleaning up AD DS metadata. When AD DS becomes unusable for some reason, this can be an alternative to completely rebuilding a server.

In addition to cleaning up the directory object using Ntdsutil, you should clean up the DNS records for the failed domain controller. Remove all DNS records from DNS, including all domain controller records, global catalog server records, and primary domain controller (PDC) emulator records. (The last two will exist only if the domain controller was configured with these roles.) If you do not clean up the DNS records, clients will continue to receive the DNS information and try to connect to the domain controller. This can result in slower connections to AD DS as clients fail over to use alternate domain controllers.

Performing a Nonauthoritative Restore of AD DS

A nonauthoritative restore of AD DS is performed in two situations. When the AD DS database on a server becomes corrupted, performing a nonauthoritative restore of AD DS recreates the database and allows it to function. When you perform a full recovery of a domain controller, you also use a nonauthoritative restore of AD DS. A full recovery of a domain controller is required if the only domain controller in a domain fails. You can also perform a full recovery of a domain controller when you want the identity of a failed domain controller kept the same.

If you have made any changes to AD DS since the backup, the backup tape will not contain those changes. However, the other domain controllers in the domain will have the most recent information. If you are rebuilding the domain controller because the server failed, the domain controller should get the changes from its replication partners after the restore is complete.

To perform a nonauthoritative restore of AD DS, boot into Directory Services Restore Mode (DSRM), restore the system state from the critical volumes by using Wbadmin.exe, and then reboot Windows Server 2008 normally. After the domain controller reboots, it will connect to its replication partners and begin updating its own database to reflect any domain information modified since the backup.

DSRM is a version of safe mode for domain controllers where AD DS is stopped. To log on to DSRM, you must use the DSRM Administrator account that is created during the installation of AD DS. This is a local Administrator account created during the installation of AD DS on the domain controller. The password is set during installation and is not the same as the domain Administrator password.

Note In Windows Server 2003 and Windows Server 2008, Ntdsutil is used to reset the DSRM Administrator account password. At the Set Dsrm Password context, use the command *reset password of server server*, where *server* is the name of the domain controller on which you want to reset the DSRM Administrator account password. You can use *null* to represent the local server.

To perform a nonauthoritative restore of AD DS, complete these steps:

1. Repair the failed domain controller. At this point the server is functional with the exception of AD DS.
2. Restart the server and press F8 to open the Advanced Boot Options menu. See Figure 17-4.

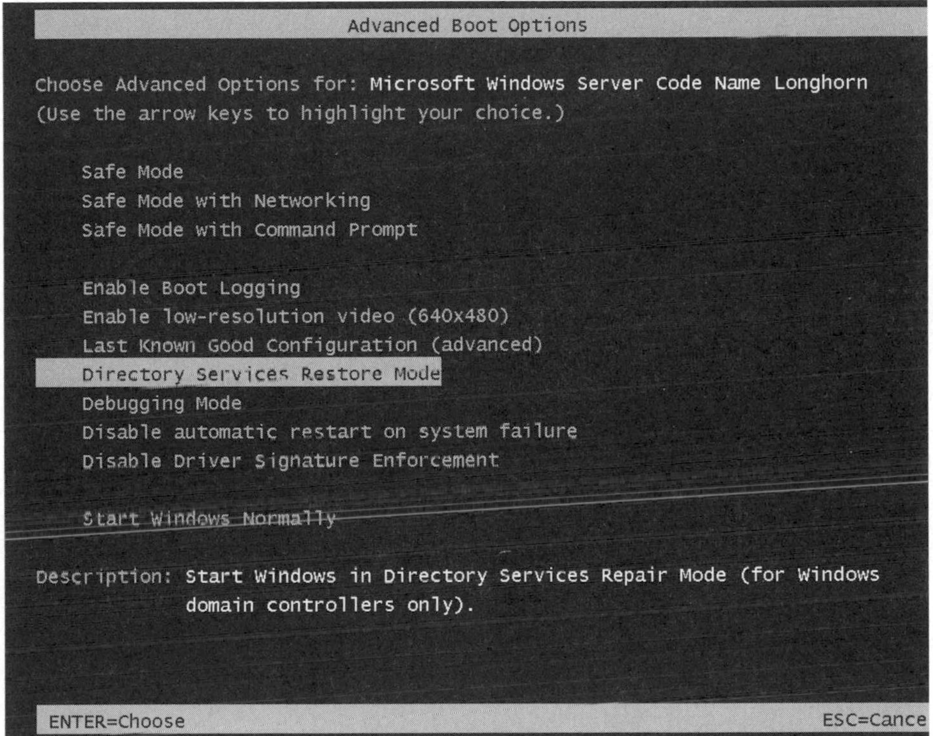

Figure 17-4 The Advanced Boot Options menu with DSRM

3. Select Directory Services Restore Mode.

> **Note** As an alternative to using the Advanced Boot Options menu, you can use *bcdedit /set safeboot dsrepair* to set the default start option as Directory Services Restore Mode (DSRM). After the installation is complete, use *bcdedit /deletevalue safeboot* and reboot to start Windows normally.

4. Log on as the DSRM Administrator account. To log on as this user, enter **.\Administrator** as the user name.
5. Open a command prompt.

6. Type **wbadmin get versions –backuptarget:*backuplocation***, where *backuplocation* is the drive letter or UNC path storing the backup, and press Enter. This lists the backups stored in the location.
7. Take note of the version identifier of the backup you wish to restore. This identifier is the time at which the backup was taken.
8. Type **wbadmin start systemstaterecovery –version:*identifier* –backuptarget:*backuplocation***, where *identifier* is the version identifier noted in step 7 and *backuplocation* is the drive letter or UNC path storing the backup, and press Enter. Figure 17-5 shows a system state restore using Wbadmin.

```
Administrator: Command Prompt - wbadmin start sysstaterecovery -version:11/16/2007-20:38 -bac...

C:\Users\Administrator.SEA-DC1>wbadmin get versions -backuptarget:E:
wbadmin 1.0 - Backup command-line tool
(C) Copyright 2004 Microsoft Corp.

Backup time: 11/16/2007 2:38 PM
Backup target: Fixed Disk labeled BackupVolume(E:)
Version identifier: 11/16/2007-20:38


C:\Users\Administrator.SEA-DC1>wbadmin start sysstaterecovery -version:11/16/200
7-20:38 -backuptarget:E:
wbadmin 1.0 - Backup command-line tool
(C) Copyright 2004 Microsoft Corp.

Do you want to start the system state recovery operation?
[Y] Yes [N] No y

Starting System State Restore [12/3/2007 11:29 AM]
Processing files to restore (This may take a few minutes)...
Processed (28) files
Processed (320) files
Processed (886) files
```

Figure 17-5 System state restore using Wbadmin.exe

9. Type **Y** and press Enter to begin the system state restore.
10. After the restore is complete, restart the domain controller.

Performing an Authoritative Restore of AD DS

An authoritative restore is required in situations where you need to recover objects that have been deleted from AD DS. For example, if someone has just deleted an OU that contains several hundred users, you do not want the domain controller to simply reboot after performing the restore and then begin replication with other domain controllers. If you do, the domain controller will receive the information that the OU has been deleted from its replication partners, and by the time you open the Active Directory Users And Computers administrative tool, the OU will be deleted again.

In this scenario, you must use an authoritative restore to ensure that the restoration of the OU is replicated to the other domain controllers. When you perform an authoritative restore, you restore a backup copy of the AD DS that was made before the data was deleted and then force that data to be replicated to all the other domain controllers. Forced replication is done by manipulating the update sequence number (USN) for the restored information. By default, when you perform an authoritative restore, the USN on the restored objects is incremented by 100,000 so that the restored object becomes the authoritative copy for the entire domain.

The basic process for performing an authoritative restore of AD DS is the same as a non-authoritative restore except for one step. After the restore of AD DS is complete in DSRM, you use Ntdsutil to specify which objects are authoritative, as shown in Figure 17-6. You can specify single objects or a subtree in the domain.

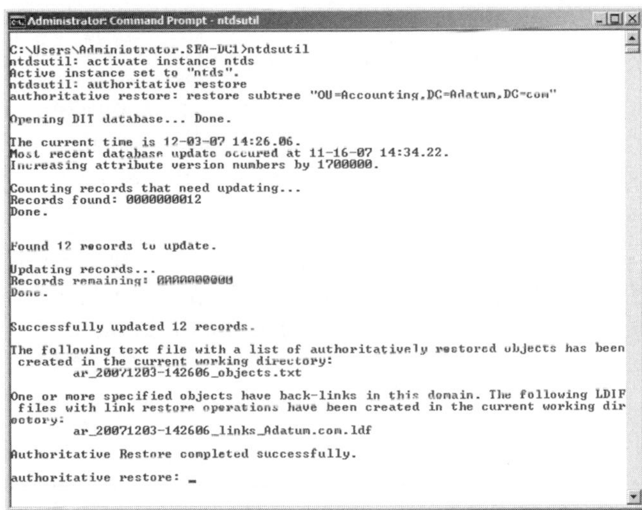

Figure 17-6 Using Ntdsutil to specify authoritative objects after a restore

To perform an authoritative restore, complete these steps:

1. Restart the server and press F8 to enter the Advanced Boot Options menu.
2. Select Directory Service Restore Mode.
3. Log on as the DSRM Administrator account. To log on as this user, enter **.\Administrator** as the user name.
4. Open a command prompt.

5. Type **wbadmin get versions -backuptarget:*backuplocation***, where *backuplocation* is the drive letter or UNC path storing the backup, and press Enter. This lists the backups stored in the location.
6. Take note of the version identifier of the backup you wish to restore. This identifier is the time at which the backup was taken.
7. Type **wbadmin start systemstaterecovery -version:*identifier* -backuptarget:*backuplocation***, where *identifier* is the version identifier noted in step 6 and *backuplocation* is the drive letter or UNC path storing the backup, and press Enter.
8. Type **Y** and press Enter to begin the system state restore.
9. After the restore is complete, type **ntdsutil** and press Enter.
10. At the Ntdsutil prompt, type **activate instance ntds** and press Enter.
11. At the Ntdsutil prompt, type **authoritative restore** and press Enter.
12. To restore a single object: At the Authoritative Restore prompt, type **restore object "DN"**, where *DN* is the distinguished name of the object to be authoritatively restored. The restore process specifies the location of an LDIF file for repairing backlinked objects if any are restored.
13. To restore a hierarchy of OUs: At the Authoritative Restore prompt, type **restore subtree "DN"**, where *DN* is the distinguished name of the OU that begins the hierarchy to be authoritatively restored. The restore process specifies the location of an LDIF file for repairing backlinked objects if any are restored.
14. Exit Ntdsutil and reboot the server.

Managing the AD DS Schema

The *schema* is the blueprint of AD DS, dictating what kinds of objects can exist in the database and what the attributes of those objects are. To customize AD DS for use on a network, you can modify the schema to create new object types, add new attributes to existing object types, and modify the type of information installed on an attribute. To do this, use the MMC snap-in called Active Directory Schema.

Modifying the schema is a task that the average administrator never has to perform. At most, you change the schema occasionally or perhaps only once. Modifying the schema is subject to the same cautions as modifying a Windows Server 2008 system's registry, except on a larger scale. Just as improper registry modifications can adversely affect a single system, improper schema modifications can have a devastating effect on the entire network.

Real World Making Schema Changes

The two most common scenarios for modifying the AD DS schema are when you upgrade the forest from a previous version of Active Directory to a newer version, and when you install a directory-enabled application. Newer versions of Active Directory invariably include new features, and many of these features require new objects or attributes in AD DS. This means that the first step in upgrading a Windows Server 2003 Active Directory forest to Windows Server 2008 AD DS is to run either Adprep or Forestprep. This utility makes the schema changes required to install Windows Server 2008 domain controllers.

The second common scenario for modifying the AD DS schema is when you install directory-enabled applications such as Exchange Server 2007. Exchange Server 2007 requires several hundred new objects in AD DS, so you must extend the schema before installing and Exchange Server. To prepare the AD DS forest for Exchange Server 2007, you need to run Exchange Server setup with the */prepareAD* parameter.

In both of these cases, the AD DS schema changes are included in .ldf files. During the schema update process, these files are imported into the AD DS schema using the LDIFDE utility. As a best practice, you should emulate this process when making schema changes. Rather than manually editing the schema, create and thoroughly test an .ldf file that contains your schema changes. Then, use the LDFIDE utility to import the .ldf file into AD DS.

Requirements for Modifying the AD DS schema

Because modifying the AD DS schema isn't something to do casually, you can modify the schema on only one domain controller in the forest, and you can only modify the schema if your user account is a member of the Schema Admins group.

Because of the importance of the schema in an AD DS environment, the schema changes can be made on only one domain controller in the forest. This domain controller is the Schema Operations Master. By default, the first domain controller deployed in a forest is the schema master. To make schema changes, you must be logged on to the Schema Operations Master, or you must be able to access the domain over the network.

To modify the schema, you must be logged on to a server or workstation in the Windows Server 2008 domain using an account that is a member of the Schema Admins group. This is a built-in group created during AD DS installation that grants its members permission to write to the schema object. The Administrator account in the forest root domain is automatically made a member of the Schema Administrators group, but members of the Domain Admins group are not automatically part of the Schema Admins group. Users who aren't members of this group can also modify the schema if an administrator has granted them the appropriate permissions to the schema object.

Important It is critical that you strictly limit the members of the Schema Admins group. Don't automatically add new administrators to the group, and don't routinely log on with an account that is a member of the Schema Admins group.

Launching Active Directory Schema

Because of its infrequent use and potential dangers, the Active Directory Schema snap-in is not added to the Administrative Tools on a domain controller by default. To use the snap-in you must first register the schmgmt.dll and then add the snap-in to an MMC. To launch Active Directory Schema, complete these steps:

1. To register the dll, open a command prompt, type **Regsvr32 schmmgmt.dll**, and then press Enter.
2. To add the Active Directory Schema to an MMC, click Start and select Run. Type **mmc** and press Enter.
3. On the File menu of the blank MMC console, click Add/Remove Snap-In.
4. Click Active Directory Schema from the list of snap-ins provided, click Add, and then click OK. When the snap-in is loaded, you can save the console screen to a file to provide easy access to the snap-in in the future. When the view pane opens, you see two containers in the console tree, which hold the object classes and the attributes that make up those classes, shown in Figure 17-7. Selecting either of these two containers displays AD DS's classes or attributes in the result pane.

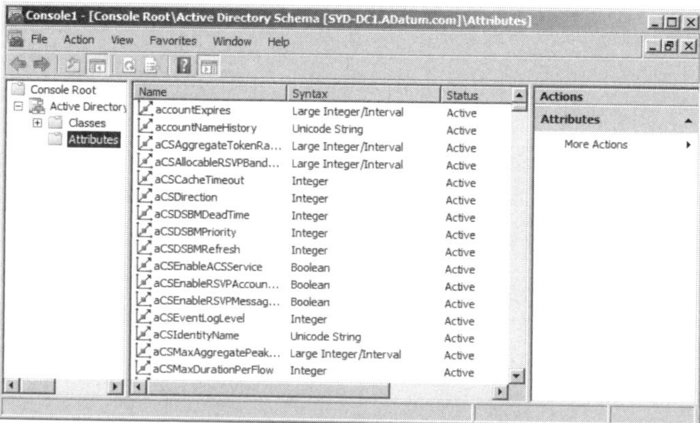

Figure 17-7 Schema Manager object classes and attributes stored in AD DS

Before changing the schema, be sure that the schema snap-in is connected to the domain controller that is currently functioning as the Schema Master (that is, the one domain controller to which write access to the schema is permitted). To connect to the schema operations master, right-click the Active Directory Schema object in the console tree and click Connect To Schema Operations Master from the shortcut menu.

Modifying the Schema

The process of modifying the AD DS schema involves creating or modifying the classes and attribute object types displayed in Schema Manager. *Classes* are essentially collections of attributes that either form an AD DS object type by themselves or contribute certain attributes to another object type. The latter instance is known as an *auxiliary class*. To add attributes to an existing object type, the best method is to create a new class containing the new attributes and add it to the object type as an auxiliary. This method is more manageable and less dangerous than modifying the class representing the object type itself.

Third-party software products might supply their own schema modifications that create entirely new object types, but adding attributes to an existing object type is the most common form of schema modification manually performed by administrators—for example, adding attributes to the user object type that enable you to store additional information about the user in AD DS. This relatively easy process consists of the following steps, which are examined in more detail in the following sections:

- Creating new attribute objects corresponding to the information fields you want to add to the object
- Creating a new class object to be used as an auxiliary to the existing object type
- Adding the newly created attributes to the new auxiliary class
- Adding the auxiliary class to the existing object class

Creating Attributes

Creating an attribute is a matter of supplying a name by which the attribute will be identified and specifying the type of data that will be stored there. The data can be text or numerical, and you can apply constraints that limit the data to a particular length or value type. For example, to add an attribute to hold the user's Employee Hire Date, you specify that the attribute's data should be in Generalized Time. To create an attribute object, follow these steps:

1. Right-click the Attributes container in the Active Directory Schema console tree and click Create Attribute from the shortcut menu. This first produces a warning that creating an object permanently modifies the AD DS, and then it produces the Create New Attribute dialog box shown in Figure 17-8.

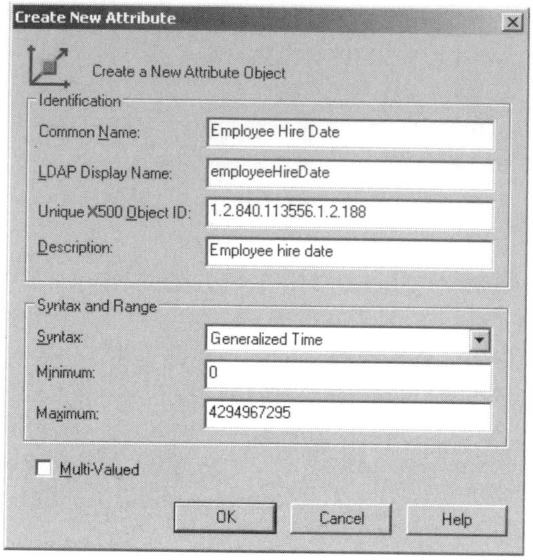

Figure 17-8 The Create New Attribute dialog box

2. In the Identification area, specify the name for the new object. The Common Name field should contain the name by which the attribute will be listed in standard dialog boxes, and the LDAP Display Name field should contain the name by which it is known in the LDAP directory hierarchy. (LDAP stands for Lightweight Directory Access Protocol.) Often these two names are the same. The Unique X.500 Object ID field must contain a numerical string that uniquely identifies the attribute object in the X.500 namespace. Standards organizations such as the International Telecommunications Union issue Object IDs (OIDs) to ensure that they have unique values. In the Description box, fill in a description of the object and its function.

> **More Info** You can obtain Object Identifiers either directly from an ISO Name Registration authority or from Microsoft. If you intend to extend the AD DS schema and want to apply for the Certified For Windows logo, you must register the OID with Microsoft. For more information about obtaining an OID from an ISO Name Registration Authority, see *http://msdn2.microsoft.com/en-us/library/ms677621.aspx*. To obtain a base OID directly from Microsoft, see *http://msdn2.microsoft.com/en-us/library/ms677620(VS.85).aspx*.

3. In the Syntax And Range area, define the nature of the data to be stored in the attribute. The Syntax field provides more than a dozen options that define the types of information that can be stored in an attribute. The Minimum and Maximum fields enable you to define a range of possible values. You can also specify whether the attribute should be able to have multiple values.

4. Click OK, and the the new attribute object is created.

You can also configure the new (or any other) attribute object by opening the Properties dialog box from its shortcut menu, shown in Figure 17-9. From this window, you can specify a description for the object, modify its range of possible values, and enable any of the following options:

- Deactivate this attribute
- Index this attribute in Active Directory
- Ambiguous Name Resolution (ANR)
- Replicate this attribute to the Global Catalog (GC)
- Attribute is copied when duplicating a user
- Index this attribute for containerized searches in Active Directory

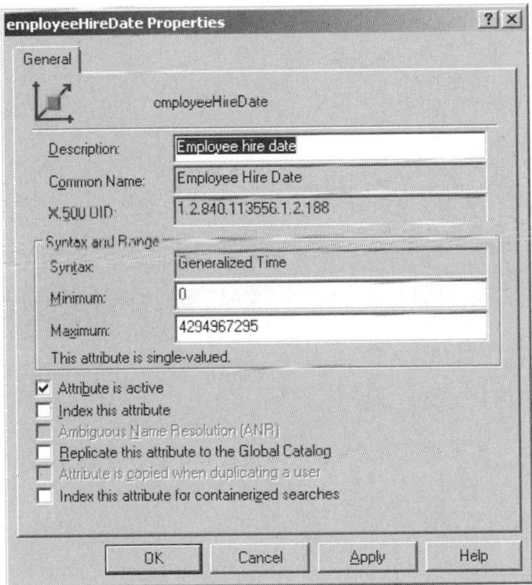

Figure 17-9 The Properties dialog box of an attribute object

Important Although you can deactivate changes that you make to the schema, you can never remove new classes or attributes that you create in the schema. You should make changes to the schema only after careful planning and thorough testing in test forest. Ensure that your schema changes are compatible with current and future applications that require schema changes.

Creating Object Classes

Attribute objects by themselves are useless until they belong to an object class. You can add the attribute objects you created to an existing class, but creating a new class object for them is generally more practical. To create a class object, right-click the Classes container in the Active Directory Schema snap-in and choose Create Class from the shortcut menu. This displays the Create New Schema Class dialog box shown in Figure 17-10.

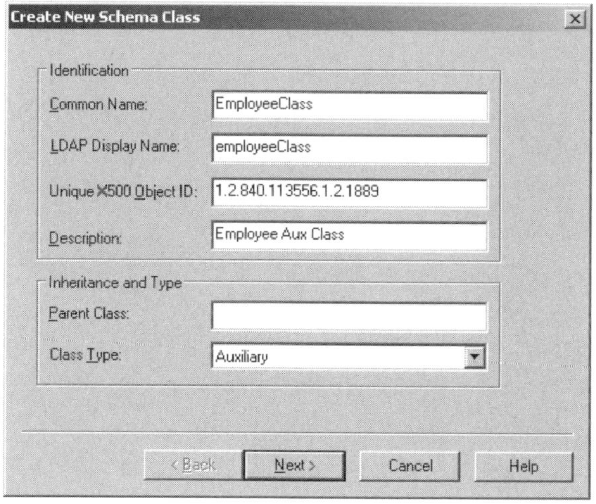

Figure 17-10 The Create New Schema Class dialog box

As with an attribute object, you must first specify a Common Name, an LDAP Display Name, and a Unique X.500 Object ID. Then, in the Inheritance And Type area, specify the Parent Class for the new object (that is, the class from which the new object should be derived), and choose one of the following three class types:

- **Structural class** The typical directory objects you work with in programs such as Active Directory Users And Computers. A structural class object can have either an abstract class or another structural class as its parent object.
- **Abstract class** Objects from which structural class objects are derived. You can also specify an existing abstract class as the parent of a new abstract class object.
- **Auxiliary class** Collections of attributes you can add to either an abstract or structural class object to augment its capabilities. New auxiliary class objects can be derived only from abstract classes.

To hold your new attributes, create an auxiliary class type.

Adding Attributes to a Class

After you create the attribute objects and the class object to contain them, you must add the attributes to the class. You do this by opening the Properties dialog box for the newly created class object. The dialog box for a class object has four tabs, including the standard Default Security tab. On the General tab, supply a description for the object and specify whether the object class should show while browsing. You can also disable the object by deselecting the Class Is Active check box.

In the Attributes tab (shown in Figure 17-11), add your newly created attribute objects to the class by clicking Add for either the Mandatory or Optional list and then selecting the objects by name. When an attribute is mandatory, you must supply a value for the attribute when creating a new object of that class. If, for example, you create an *EmployeeHireDate* attribute, add it to your auxiliary class as a mandatory attribute, and then add the auxiliary class to the user class; the next time a new user object is created, an Employee ID Number will be required for the user. Values for optional attributes aren't required.

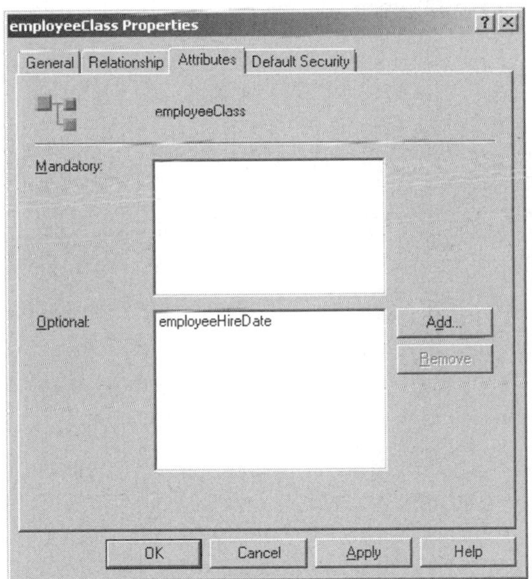

Figure 17-11 The Attributes tab of the Properties dialog box

Adding an Auxiliary Class to a Structural Class

An auxiliary class object can't store attribute information until you add the auxiliary class object to a structural class object, such as a user or computer. To do this, open the structural class object's Properties dialog box and select the Relationship tab, shown in Figure 17-12.

On this tab, click Add Class for the Auxiliary Classes list, and select the class object you just created. This causes AD DS to add the attributes in the auxiliary class to the structural class. In the Possible Superior list, specify which other object classes can contain the current object class. For example, the user object class has the organizational unit object class in its Possible Superior list, which enables the creation of new users in OUs. The opposite is not true, however; you can't create an OU beneath a user, so the user object isn't a possible superior of the OU object.

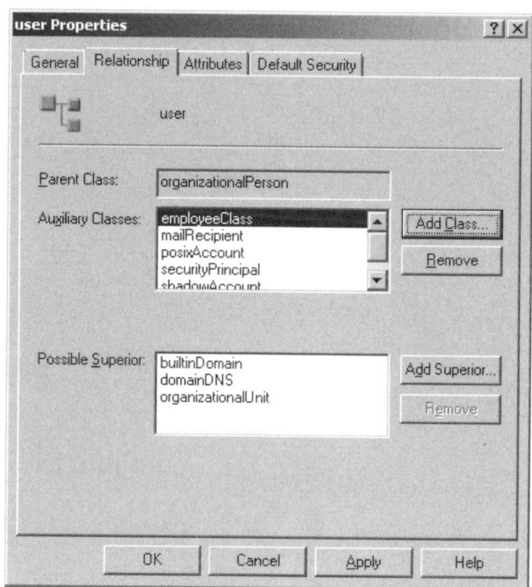

Figure 17-12 The Relationship tab of the Properties dialog box

---

Note Adding a new attribute to the schema does not mean that the attribute will automatically be accessible from any of the administrative tools. The administrative tools such as Active Directory Users And Computers show only some of the attributes for each class and do not show any attributes you add. If you want the new attribute to appear in an administrative tool, you must either modify the existing tool or create your own. For information on how to modify and create administrative tools, see the "Extending the User Interface for Directory Objects" article at *http://msdn2.microsoft.com/en-us/library/ms676902.aspx*. ADSIEdit will display new attributes because the list of available attributes on an object are dynamically loaded from the schema.

Managing Operations Master Roles

AD DS is designed as a multimaster replication system. This requires that all domain controllers other than RODCs have Write permissions for the directory database. This system works well for most directory operations, but for certain directory operations a single authoritative server is required. The domain controllers that perform specific roles are known as *operations masters*, and each has a flexible single-master operations (FSMO, pronounced *fizz-mo*) role. The domain controllers that hold operations master roles are designated to perform specific tasks to ensure consistency and to eliminate the potential for conflicting entries in the AD DS database. AD DS has the following five operations master roles:

- Schema master
- Domain naming master
- RID master
- PDC emulator
- Infrastructure master

The first two roles, schema master and domain naming master, are per-forest roles. This means that there is only one schema master and only one domain naming master for every forest. The other three roles are per-domain roles; there is one of these operations master roles for each domain in the forest. When you install AD DS and create the first domain controller in the forest, it will possess all five of these roles. Similarly, as you add domains to the forest, the first domain controller in each new domain will also acquire the per-domain operations master roles. As you add domain controllers to a domain, you can transfer these roles to other domain controllers.

Schema Master

As described earlier, the schema master is the only domain controller that has Write permissions to the directory schema. To make any change to the schema, the administrator (who must be a member of the schema admins security group) must be connected to the schema master. If a modification to the schema is attempted on a domain controller other than the schema master, it will fail. After a change has been made, schema updates are replicated to all other domain controllers in the forest.

Domain Naming Master

The domain naming master is the domain controller that manages the addition and removal of all directory partitions in the forest hierarchy. The domain controller that has the domain naming master role must be available when you do the following:

- **Add or remove domains** When you create or remove a child domain or new domain tree, the installation wizard contacts the domain naming master and requests the addition or deletion. The domain naming master is responsible for ensuring that domain names are unique. If the domain naming master is unavailable, you cannot add domains or remove them from the forest.
- **Add or remove application directory partitions** Application directory partitions are special partitions that can be created on domain controllers running Windows Server 2003 or Windows Server 2008 to provide storage for dynamic application data. If the domain controller hosting the domain naming operations master role is not available, you cannot add or remove application directory partitions from the forest.
- **Add or remove cross-reference objects** When a new forest is created, the schema, configuration, and domain directory partitions are created on the first domain controller in the forest. A cross-reference object is created for each directory partition in the Partitions container in the configuration directory partition (*CN=partitions,CN=configuration,DC=forestRootDomain*). As new domains or application directory partitions are created, an associated cross-reference object is also created in the Partitions container. If the domain naming master is unavailable, you cannot add or remove cross-reference objects.
- **Validate domain rename instructions** When you use the domain rename tool, Rendom.exe, to rename an AD DS domain, the tool must be able to access the domain naming operations master. When you run the tool, the XML-encoded script containing the domain rename instructions is written to the msDS-*Update-Script* attribute on the Partitions container object (*CN=partitions,CN=configuration,DC=ForestRootDomain*) in the configuration directory partition. In addition, the new DNS name of each domain being renamed is also written by Rendom.exe to the *msDS-DnsRootAlias* attribute on the cross-reference object (class *crossRef*) corresponding to that domain. Both of these objects are stored in the Partitions container, and the container can only be updated on the domain controller holding the domain naming operations master role for the forest.

RID Master

The RID master is a per-domain operations master role. It is used to manage the RID pool to create new security principals throughout the domain, such as users, groups, and computers. Each security principal is issued a unique security identifier (SID) which includes a domain identifier, which is the same for all SIDs in the domain, and a relative identifier (RID), which is unique for each security principal. Because security principals can be created on any domain controller with a writeable copy of the directory, the RID master is used to ensure that two domain controllers do not issue the same RID. The RID master issues a block of RIDs, called the *RID pool*, to every domain controller in the domain. When the number of available RIDs in the RID pool on any domain controller begins to run low (below about 100), a request is made for another block of RIDs from the RID master. When this happens, the RID master issues a pool of about another 500 RIDs to the domain controller.

If the RID master is unavailable for a period of time, the process of creating new accounts on specific domain controllers may be interrupted. The mechanism for requesting a new block of RIDs is designed so that this should not happen, because the request is made before all of the available RIDs in the RID pool are exhausted. However, if the RID master is offline and the requesting domain controller depletes the remainder of its RIDs, account creation will fail. To re-enable account creation, either the RID master role holder must be brought back online or the role must be transferred to another domain controller in the domain.

PDC Emulator

The PDC emulator role operates as a primary domain controller (PDC) for pre-Windows 2000 operating systems. Windows NT member servers and client computers must be able to communicate with a PDC to process password changes. In addition to providing services for older clients, the PDC emulator also plays an important role in replicating passwords.

Note In Windows 2000 and Windows 2003 Active Directory, one of the important roles for the PDC Emulator is to act as the PDC for down-level (Microsoft Windows NT versions 4 or 3.51) backup domain controllers (BDCs). Because Windows Server 2008 does not support coexistence with pre-Windows 2000 domain controllers, this functionality is no longer relevant.

Even if no Windows NT member servers or client computers exist in the domain, the PDC emulator has a role in maintaining password updates. All password changes made on other domain controllers in the domain are sent to the PDC emulator using urgent replication. If a user authentication fails on a domain controller other than the PDC emulator, authentication is retried on the PDC emulator. If the PDC emulator has accepted a recent password change for the account, authentication will succeed. When a user successfully authenticates on a domain controller where the previous attempt failed, the domain controller notifies PDC emulator of the successful authentication. This resets the lockout counter at the PDC emulator in case another client attempts to validate the same account by using a different domain controller. The PDC emulator has the following functions:

- Acts as the root time server for the domain.

- Acts as the Group Policy originator. All GPO changes are initially made to the PDC emulator, and then replicated to the rest of the domain controllers.
- Acts as the password change and account lockout originator to ensure consistency across the domain.

Infrastructure Master

The infrastructure master is responsible for updating the cross-domain group-to-user references. This operations master role ensures that changes made to object names (changes to the common name attribute, *cn*) are reflected in the group membership information for groups located on a different domain. The infrastructure master maintains an up-to-date list of these references, and it then replicates this information to all other domain controllers in the domain. If the infrastructure master is unavailable, the cross-domain group-to-user references will be out of date.

Transferring Operations Master Roles

You can move operations master roles between domain controllers either to better optimize domain controller performance or to substitute a domain controller if a role holder has become unavailable. The process for doing this will depend on the role being transferred. Table 17-2 lists the tools used to transfer the five operations master roles.

Table 17-2 Tools for Managing the Operations Master Roles

Operations master role	Administration tool
Schema master	Active Directory Schema
Domain naming master	Active Directory Domains And Trusts
RID master, PDC emulator, and infrastructure master	Active Directory Users And Computers

To transfer the role of PDC emulator, follow these steps:

1. Launch Active Directory Users And Computers from the Administrative Tools folder.
2. Right-click the domain node and choose Change Domain Controller from the shortcut menu.
3. Select the domain controller you want to assign the role of PDC emulator. Click OK.
4. Right-click the domain node and choose Operations Masters from the shortcut menu. Click the PDC tab to see the current focus (the controller that will become the PDC emulator) and the controller that is the current operations master. (See Figure 17-13.)

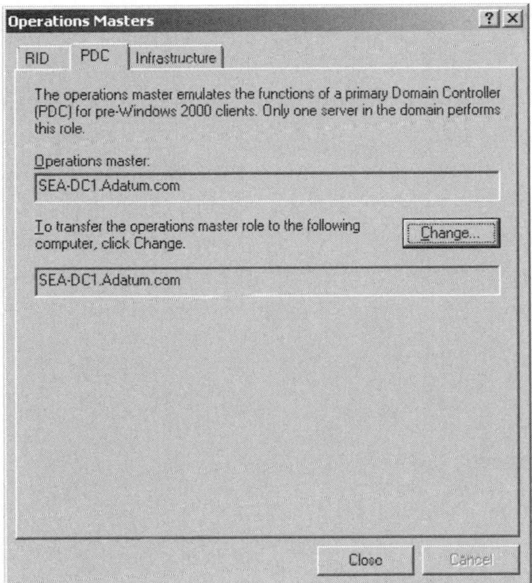

Figure 17-13 Changing the PDC emulator operations master

5. Click Change and then click OK.

To transfer an operations master role, there must be connectivity to both the current and proposed role holder domain controllers. In the event of server failure, the current role holder may not be available to complete a role transfer. In this case, the role can be seized. Seizing operations master roles is not a preferred option and should be done only if absolutely necessary. You should only seize an operations master role if it is indicated that the domain controller hosting this role will be unavailable for an extended period.

Note You can move the operation master roles to any other domain controller in the domain. The only restriction on operation master placement is that you should not install the infrastructure master role on a domain controller that is also a global catalog server if the forest contains multiple domains, unless every domain controller in the domain is also a global catalog server. By default, the first domain controller in a forest is both a global catalog server and holds the infrastructure master role. When you install the second domain controller in the domain and that domain controller is not a global catalog server, the Active Directory Domain Services Installation Wizard prompts you to move the infrastructure master to the new domain controller during the AD DS installation.

Seizing Operations Master Roles

In some cases, you might decide that rebuilding the failed domain controller will take longer than your network can operate without that operations master. Or you might decide that you do not want to restore that domain controller at all, but would rather create a new domain controller and transfer the operations master role to the new domain controller. Transferring the operations master role is easy if both domain controllers are online because the domain controllers can ensure that they have completed replication before the role is transferred. However, if the operations master has failed and you need to move the role to another domain controller, you will need to seize the role.

To seize operations master roles by using Ntdsutil, complete the following steps:

1. Open a command prompt.
2. At the command prompt, type **ntdsutil** and press Enter.
3. At the Ntdsutil prompt, type **roles** and press Enter.
4. At the Fsmo Maintenance prompt, type **connections** and press Enter.
5. At the Server Connections prompt, type **connect to server** ServerName, where *ServerName* is the name of the server that you want to place the operations master role on, and press Enter.
6. At the Server Connection prompt, type **quit** and press Enter.
7. At the Fsmo Maintenance prompt, type **seize** role, where *role* is the operations master role you want to seize, and press Enter. The valid values for role are *schema master, domain naming master, infrastructure master, RID master*, and *PDC*.
8. Accept the warning. The server will first try to perform a normal transfer of the specified operations master role. When that fails because the domain controller cannot be contacted, the role will be seized.
9. Use the **quit** command to exit Ntdsutil.

Note You can also use Active Directory Users And Computers to seize the PDC Emulator and Infrastructure Master operations roles.

Important Before seizing the domain naming master, you must completely disconnect the controller holding the domain naming master role from the network. Seizing the domain naming master role is a radical step, and you should not do it unless the original domain naming master is permanently out of service. Before you can bring the original domain naming master back online, you must first reformat its boot disk and reinstall Windows Server 2008.

Auditing AD DS

In most organizations, AD DS provides a central authentication and authorization directory service. Most, if not all, network applications may depend on AD DS to enable user access or to prevent unauthorized users from accessing the application. These means that any changes made to AD DS can have far-reaching consequences on your network. To ensure that only authorized users can make these changes, you need to configure all administrative accounts with the minimal permissions needed to perform required tasks. A second component to managing changes made to AD DS is to audit changes made on the domain controllers. By auditing changes made on domain controllers, you can identify who is responsible for directory changes and when the changes were made.

Configuring the Audit Policy

Windows Server 2008 introduces some important changes to auditing on domain controllers. In Windows 2000 Server and Windows Server 2003, you had one audit policy option, Audit directory service access, that controlled whether auditing for directory service events was enabled or disabled. In Windows Server 2008, this policy is divided into four subcategories:

- Directory Service Access
- Directory Service Changes
- Directory Service Replication
- Detailed Directory Service Replication

These subcategories are not visible through Group Policy Management Editor. To view and configure the subcategories, use the Auditpol.exe command-line tool. To view the current directory service access audit settings, type **Auditpol /get /category:"ds access"**. Figure 17-14 displays the output from the command with the default settings.

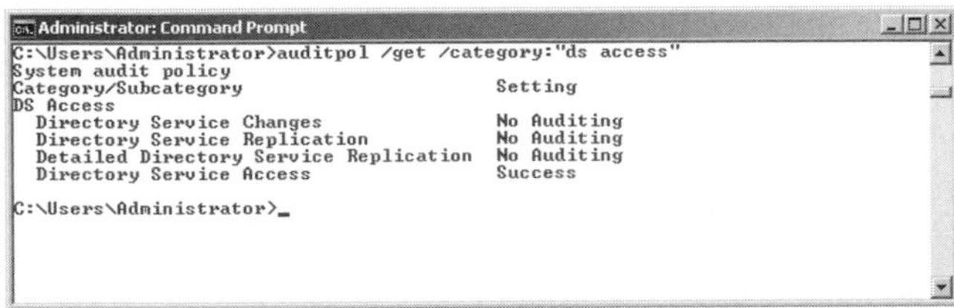

Figure 17-14 Displaying the directory service audit policies

From a security auditing perspective, the most important new feature is the Directory Service Changes subcategory. This new subcategory adds the following functionality:

- When you change an attribute on an object, AD DS logs the previous and current values of the attribute. If the attribute has more than one value, only the values that change as a result of the modify operation are logged.
- When you create a new object, values of the attributes that are populated at the time of creation are logged. If the user adds attributes during the create operation, those new attribute values are logged. In most cases, AD DS assigns default values to attributes (such as *samAccountName*). The values of such system attributes are not logged.
- If an object is moved, the previous and new location (distinguished name) is logged for moves within the domain. When an object is moved to a different domain, a create event is generated on the domain controller in the target domain.
- If an object is undeleted, the location where the object is moved to is logged. In addition, if the user adds, modifies, or deletes attributes while performing an undelete operation, the values of those attributes are logged.

By default, the Audit directory service access audit category is not enabled in the Default Domain Controllers OU, but the Directory Service Access subcategory is enabled. This audit policy logs when administrators access objects in AD DS, but the changes to those objects are not logged. To enable the Directory Services Changes auditing, you can choose to enable the Audit directory service access option in the Default Domain Controllers Policy audit policy. When you enable this option, all subcategories are also enabled. (See Figure 17-15.)

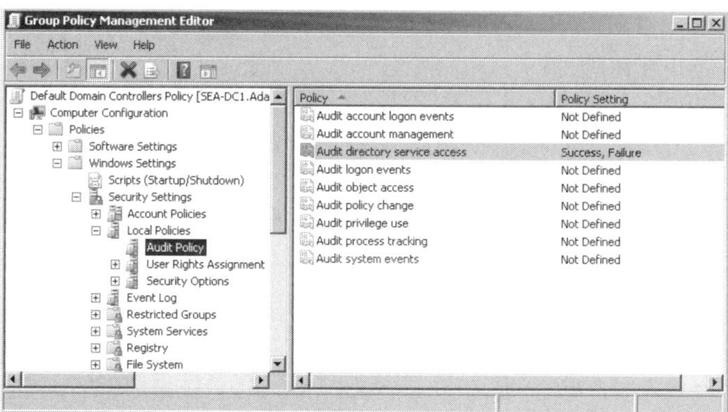

Figure 17-15 Configuring directory service auditing

To enable just the Directory Service Changes subcategory, you must use the Auditpol.exe command-line tool and run the following command:

```
auditpol /set /subcategory:"directory service changes" /success:enable
```

Windows Server 2008 also introduces subcategories under the other audit categories. The categories, subcategories, and default settings for AD DS specific audit settings are listed in Table 17-3. To view these audit settings, use the **Auditpol /get /category:*** command.

Table 17-3 Configuring Domain Controller Audit Policy Settings

Category	Subcategory	Default setting
Audit logon events	Logon	Success and Failure
Audit logon events	Logoff	Success
	Account Lockout	Success
Audit logon events	IPsec Main Mode, IPsec Extended Mode, IPsec Quick Mode	No Auditing
Audit logon events	Special Logon	Success
Audit logon events	Other Logon/Logoff events	No Auditing
Audit logon events	Network Policy Server	Success and Failure
Audit policy change	Audit Policy Change	Success
Audit policy change	Authentication Policy Change	Success
Audit policy change	Authorization Policy Change, MPSSVC Rule-Level Policy Change, Filtering Platform Policy Change, Other Policy Change Events	No Auditing
Audit account management	User Account Management	Success
Audit account management	Computer Account Management	Success
Audit account management	Security Group Management	Success
Audit account management	Distribution Group Management, Application Group Management, Other Account Management Events	No Auditing
Audit account logon events	Kerberos Service Ticket Operations	Success
Audit account logon events	Other Account Logon Events	No Auditing
Audit account logon events	Kerberos Authentication Service	Success
Audit account logon events	Credential Validation	Success

In most cases, if the goal of your audit policy is to audit administrator activity in AD DS, you should accept the default domain controller audit settings. If you are using the audit policy for other purposes, such as intrusion detection, you may want to also audit the failure of events such as logon events or account management events. By default, if you enable auditing for any of the categories, auditing will also be enabled for all subcategories.

Enabling Auditing of AD DS Changes

Configuring the audit policy is only the first step in enabling AD DS auditing. After configuring the audit policy, you must configure the System Access Control List (SACL) on each object to enable auditing. To audit changes to objects in AD DS, enable auditing for the Domain Controllers OU in Active Directory Users And Computers.

To enable auditing on the Domain Controllers OU, complete the following steps:

1. Open Active Directory Users And Computers.
2. Click the View menu and then click Advanced Features.
3. Right-click the Domain Controllers OU, and then click Properties.
4. In the Properties dialog box, click the Security tab, click Advanced, and click the Auditing tab, shown in Figure 17-16.

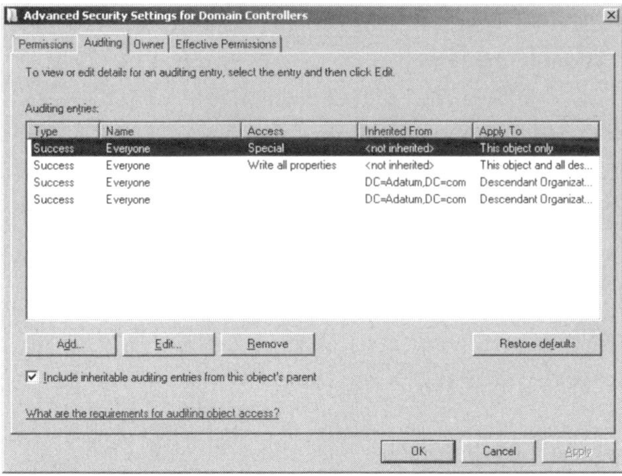

Figure 17-16 Configuring auditing for the Domain Controllers OU

5. Click Add, and in the Select User, Computer, Or Group dialog box, type **Everyone** and then click OK. By choosing Everyone, you can audit all changes made by anyone to AD DS.

6. In the Auditing Entry for Domain Controllers dialog box (see Figure 17-17), select the check box to audit both Successful and Failed Write All Properties, and then click OK twice.

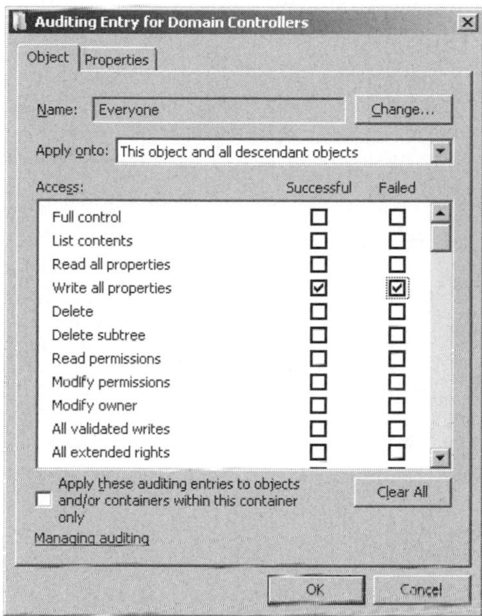

Figure 17-17 Auditing all changes made to AD DS

After you enable Directory Service Changes auditing, all changes made to AD DS are displayed in the Security Event log, as shown in Figure 17-18.

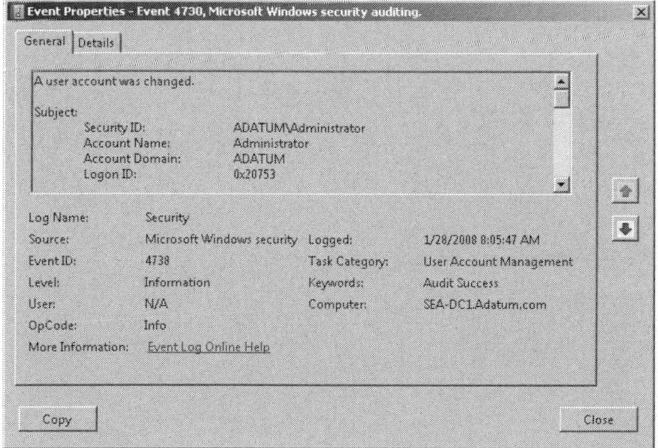

Figure 17-18 Changes to AD DS are shown in the Security Event log

Summary

AD DS is an essential part of the Windows Server 2008 enterprise network infrastructure, and maintaining it is a important part of the network administrator's job. Although AD DS does not require a great deal of maintenance after it is deployed, you do need to spend time creating a backup and recovery plan and understand the procedures for performing tasks such as managing operation master roles and configuring auditing.

In the next chapter, we cover the basics of setting up and administering your TCP/IP infrastructure.

Chapter 18

Administering TCP/IP

The core underlying networking protocol of the modern network is Transmission Control Protocol/Internet Protocol (TCP/IP). The key thing to remember about TCP/IP is that it *isn't a single entity*. TCP and IP are both protocols, but they are only two of the protocols included in TCP/IP. TCP/IP is really an entire suite of protocols, each with its own specialized area of importance and use.

The predominant version of TCP/IP, used by virtually all networks around the world, is version 4, known as IPv4. IPv4 is based on a 32-bit address space, limiting the maximum number of potential unique addresses to 4,294,967,296 (2^{32}). While this seems like a lot, the reality is that the available number of IPv4 addresses is rapidly running out. The widespread adoption of Network Address Translation (NAT) devices has improved the situation, but the time for a larger address space is upon us. The next version of TCP/IP is version 6, known as IPv6. IPv6 is based on a 128-bit address space, a number of addresses so large that if you had a penny for every million addresses in the IPv6 address space, you could personally pay off the combined North American national debt and still be the richest person on the planet by several orders of magnitude.

Virtually all TCP/IP-based networks need to use three basic network features:

- Dynamic Host Configuration Protocol (DHCP) to dynamically provide clients with IP addresses and configuration information
- Domain Name System (DNS) to translate IP addresses into friendly names that are easier to deal with and vice versa
- Windows Internet Naming Service (WINS) to translate NetBIOS names and IP addresses for clients that still use NetBIOS

Although Active Directory and Windows clients will work with non-Windows DHCP and DNS servers, such as those available for UNIX systems, Active Directory works best with the DHCP and DNS servers that are part of Windows Server. If you are running Berkeley Internet Name Domain (BIND) DNS servers on UNIX or Linux, they should be running BIND version 8.2.2 patch 7 or later, and ideally should be running BIND version 9.

WINS servers shouldn't still be required on a modern network. All of us who have lived with WINS wish it would go away. But the reality is that it's still used and still required for some applications. We were really hoping that Windows Server 2008 would finally drive a stake through the heart of WINS and completely deprecate it. But it's still here–you can even run it as a role on Server Core. And these days you can even use Linux for your WINS server.

This chapter shows you how to install and manage DHCP, DNS, and WINS servers running Windows Server 2008.

Using DHCP

If you've ever managed more than a very small number of computers on a network, you've probably used DHCP. DHCP can provide both an IP address and all the essential configuration information that any client on the network needs to connect and communicate with other computers, both on the network and outside on the Internet. By providing a central location for address management and disbursement, the DHCP service of Windows Server 2008 makes it easy to configure and manage your TCP/IP network.

The DHCP server provided with Windows Server 2008 is truly excellent–it works predictably, reliably, and properly. The following sections describe how to use it.

Designing DHCP Networks

It's important that you design the deployment of DHCP servers in a way that fits the network. Small, nonrouted networks can use a single DHCP server. If you have a larger network, consider the subnets and routers in use, and also split the address space between two servers or host your DHCP service on a cluster to improve fault tolerance. Use the following checklist as part of your planning:

- Draw a map of the network showing each physical and logical subnet and the routers joining the subnets.
- If the network uses routers to subnet the network, determine whether the routers support forwarding DHCP broadcasts. (Most newer routers do, although this option usually needs to be turned on.)
- Plan to section the IP address range between two DHCP servers to provide fault tolerance. (DHCP servers can't communicate with each other, so they can't share the

same addresses.) Give 80 percent of the addresses to one server, and 20 percent to the other server. (This is called the 80/20 rule.) If one server goes down, clients can still receive IP addresses from the other server. Alternatively, you can set up a DHCP server cluster to handle 100 percent of the addresses.

- If the link between the subnets is fast and reliable and the routers in between can be configured to forward DHCP broadcasts (or if you add a DHCP relay agent), you can place the second DHCP server on a different physical subnet. Otherwise, deploy a pair of DHCP servers to each physical subnet.
- Deploy DHCP servers on hardware with good I/O subsystems. DHCP servers frequently access the disk drives, and a fast storage subsystem means better DHCP performance.

Note Another method of protecting against DHCP server failure is to have a hot backup. To do this, set up a DHCP server identical to the primary DHCP server, except with its own scope, that encompasses 20 percent of the address space (or possibly less). Don't activate this server. (It could be serving other roles that you don't want to slow down except in the case of an emergency.) If the primary DHCP server goes down, manually bring the backup server online by activating its scope. However, splitting the address range between two live servers or using a DHCP server cluster is a superior solution because it provides automatic fault tolerance—no manual intervention is required.

DHCP Security Considerations

Although DHCP servers aren't high-value targets for hackers, a number of vulnerabilities are nonetheless inherent to DHCP servers. Because the number of IP addresses in a scope is limited, an unauthorized user can launch a denial-of-service (DoS) attack on the network by acquiring a large number of IP addresses from the DHCP server. A DoS attack on the DNS server can also be initiated by performing a large number of DNS dynamic updates via DHCP. Similarly, a user with physical access to the network can easily use a non-Microsoft DHCP server to set up a rogue DHCP server that provides improper IP addresses to other clients.

A final DHCP security vulnerability is that any user that obtains an IP address from the DHCP server will probably also obtain the addresses for company DNS and WINS servers. A hacker can then obtain further information about the network configuration from these servers–or attack them.

To minimize these risks, limit physical access to your network. If a hacker can plug into your network, her job is immensely easier than trying to break through a firewall. The use of 802.1x across the entire physical network to control access can significantly reduce the risk. Also make sure to maintain and regularly review DHCP audit logs (stored by default in the %windir%\System32\Dhcp folder).

Plan the IP Address Range and Exclusions

Besides determining how to place the DHCP servers into the network structure, you also need to plan the IP address ranges you'll use, as well as which IP addresses to reserve or exclude from this pool of addresses. Use the following list to help plan the IP address ranges to use and exclude:

- Determine the range of IP addresses that the DHCP server will manage. Most likely, this will be a private address range such as 10.x.x.x or 192.168.x.x, or a site-local addresses such as FEC0::/10.
- Make a list of any IP addresses to exclude to support hosts with static IP addresses. Only DHCP servers and hosts that don't work as DHCP clients *need* static IP addresses, but DNS servers are a good choice for a static IP address as well.

> **Note** Consider switching all hosts with statically assigned IP addresses to DHCP assigned addresses. Servers that need unchanging addresses should get client reservations for the servers in DHCP. (Lease reservations are covered later in this chapter.) This allows the servers to use an unchanging address and yet still have all TCP/IP options configured automatically through DHCP. It also makes it easier to track and manage IP addresses, and it will make your life much easier if your company ever needs to change its addressing, as might happen after a merger. The fewer static addresses, the better.

- Make a list of servers that need to have unchanging IP addresses, such as DNS and WINS servers, and then decide whether you can use a DHCP reservation or whether bona fide static addresses are needed.

If the DHCP server will be using Internet-registered IP addresses (which it probably won't), register the IP addresses with the Internet service provider (ISP).

Adding the DHCP Server Role

You can add the DHCP Server Role to any Windows Server 2008 with a fixed IP address. If you're only adding a DHCP scope for IPv4 addresses, you *can* use a fixed IPv4 address and an automatically generated link-local IPv6 address, but Windows Server 2008 will complain. And we think that complaint is valid–you really should be using fixed IPv4 and IPv6 addresses on DHCP servers.

To add the DHCP Role to a Windows Server 2008 computer, follow these steps:

1. Open Server Manager if it isn't already open.
2. Select Roles in the left-hand pane and then select Add Roles from the Action menu to open the Add Roles Wizard.
3. Click Next to open the Select Server Roles page of the Add Roles Wizard, as shown in Figure 18-1.

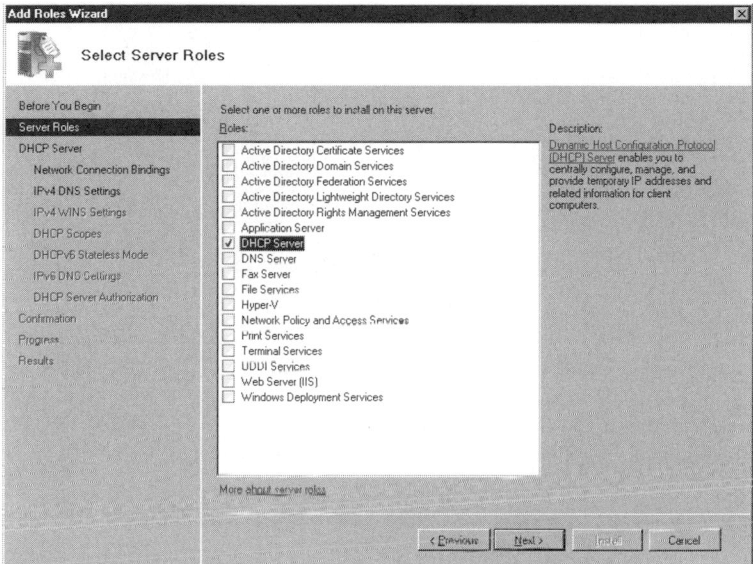

Figure 18-1 The Select Server Roles page of the Add Roles Wizard

4. Select DHCP Server and click Next. On the DHCP Server page, read the Things To Note carefully, and click the links under Additional Information if you want to see additional help on a topic.
5. Click Next to open the Select Network Connection Bindings page of the Add Roles Wizard, as shown in Figure 18-2. Select only those network connections that you want the DHCP server to use.

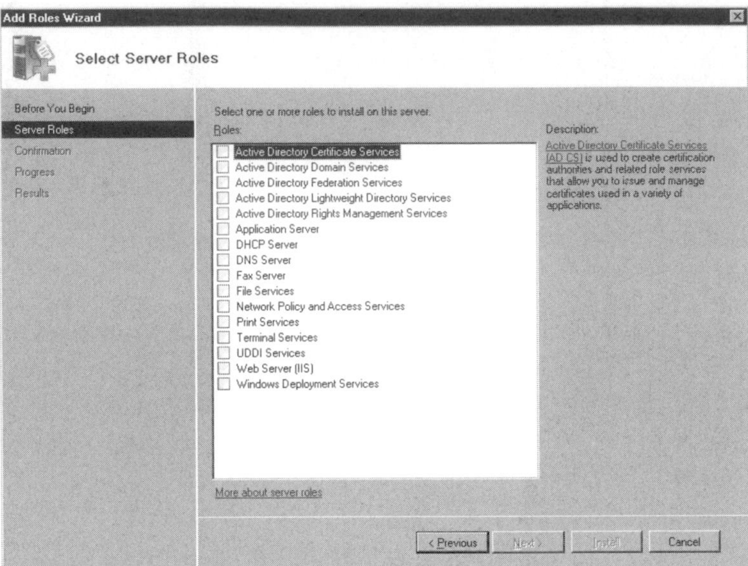

Figure 18-2 The Select Network Connection Bindings page of the Add Roles Wizard

6. Click Next to open the Specify IPv4 DNS Server Settings page. Specify at least the domain name and the DNS server IPv4 address, as shown in Figure 18-3.

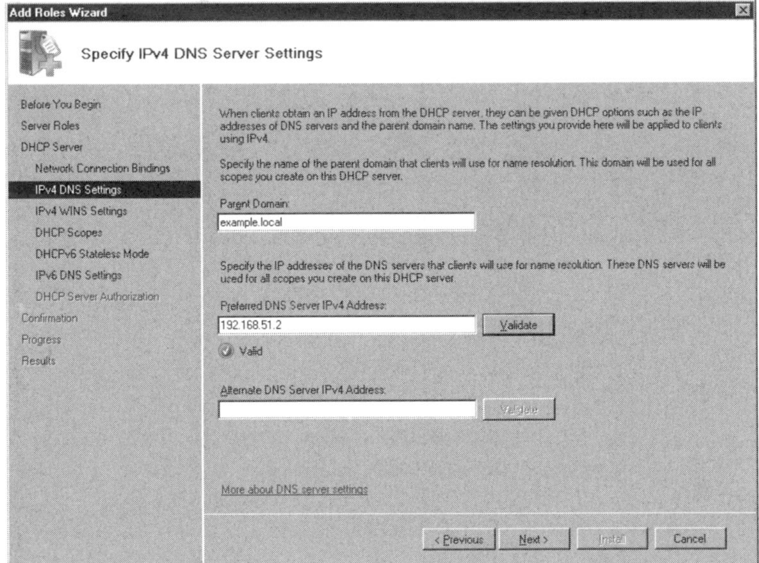

Figure 18-3 The Specify IPv4 DNS Server Settings page of the Add Roles Wizard

7. Click Next to open the Specify IPv4 WINS Server Settings page. If you need to support legacy clients or applications that are dependent on WINS, select WINS Is Required For Applications On This Network and specify the IPv4 address of the WINS server. Otherwise, accept the default of WINS Is Not Required For Applications On This Network.
8. Click Next to open the Add Or Edit DHCP Scopes page, shown in Figure 18-4.

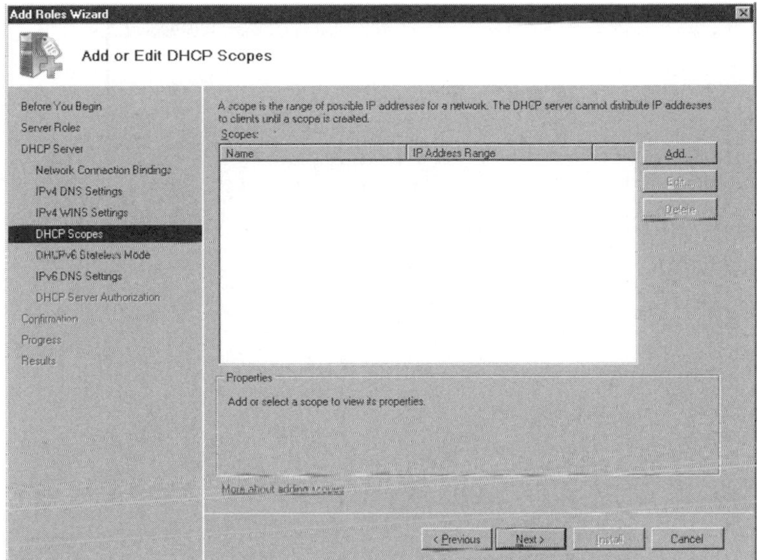

Figure 18-4 The Add Or Edit DHCP Scopes page of the Add Roles Wizard

9. Click Add to open the Add Scope dialog box shown in Figure 18-5.

Add Scope

A scope is a range of possible IP addresses for a network. The DHCP server cannot distribute IP addresses to clients until a scope is created.

Scope Name: 51v4
Starting IP Address: 192.168.51.200
Ending IP Address: 192.168.51.250
Subnet Mask: 255.255.255.0
Default Gateway (optional): 192.168.51.2
Subnet Type: Wired (lease duration will be 6 days)

Activate this scope

OK Cancel

Figure 18-5 The Add Scope dialog box

10. Specify at least a scope name, starting and ending IP addresses, and a subnet mask. Also specify the subnet type (wired or wireless).
11. Click OK to return to the Add Or Edit DHCP Scopes page. Add additional scopes now, if appropriate.
12. Click Next to open the Configure DHCPv6 Stateless Mode page, shown in Figure 18-6.

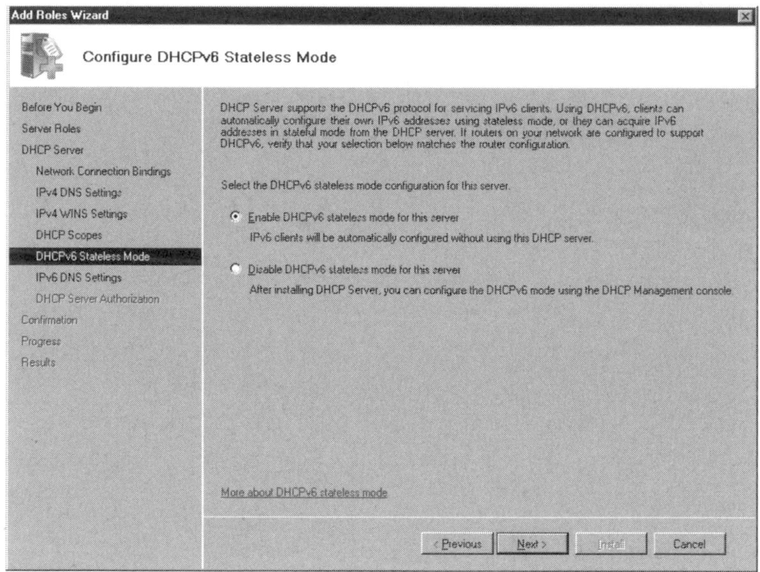

Figure 18-6 The Configure DHCPv6 Stateless Mode page

13. Select Enable DHCPv6 Stateless Mode For This Server if you want IPv6 clients to auto-configure themselves. (This is the default.) Or choose Disable DHCPv6 Stateless Mode For This Server if you will be configuring DHCP options and scope for the network.
14. Click Next to open the Specify IPv6 DNS Settings page. (Skip this step if you disabled Stateless DHCPv6 mode.) Enter the parent domain and at least a preferred DNS server IPv6 address. Click Validate to verify the DNS Server address, as shown in Figure 18-7.

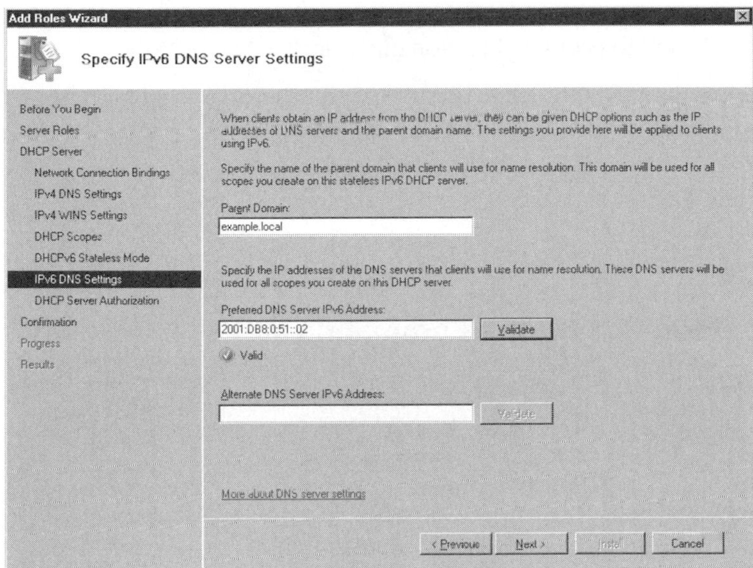

Figure 18-7 The Specify IPv6 DNS Settings page

15. Click Next to open the Authorize DHCP Server page, shown in Figure 18-8. You can choose to use your current credentials (the default), specify alternate credentials, or skip authorization. If you skip authorization, the DHCP Server will not function until you authorize it.

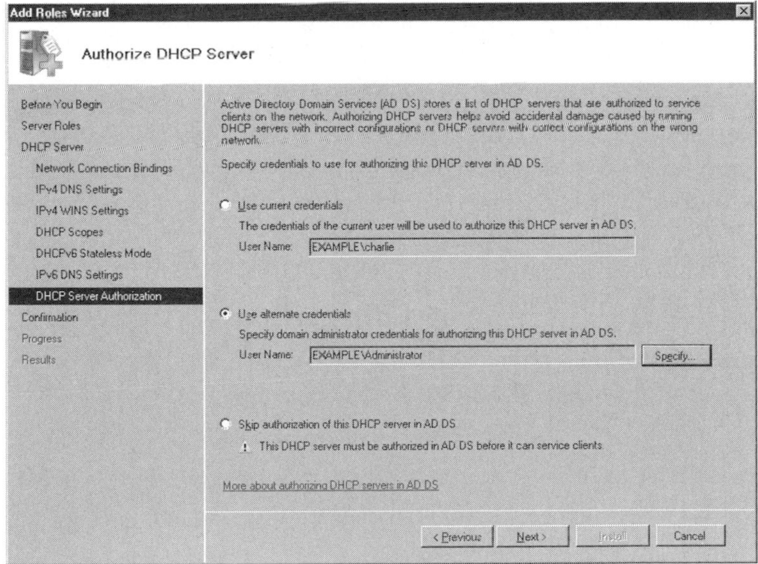

Figure 18-8 The Authorize DHCP Server page

16. Click Next to open the Confirm Installation Selections page. If everything is as you expect, click Install to begin installation of the DHCP Server Role.
17. When the installation completes, the Installation Results page will open. If there were no errors, the page will display the message Installation Successful. If a reboot is required (as often happens when you install more than one role at a time), you'll see a Pending Restart message. Close the Add Roles Wizard and restart the server if requested.

Under the Hood Using the Command Line

To add the DHCP Server Role using the command line, follow these steps:

1. Open an elevated Command Window by right-clicking the Command Prompt shortcut on the Start Menu and selecting Run As Administrator.
2. Type **Servermanagercmd /?** to see a list of command-line options for the command. Use **Servermanagercmd -query** to see all the possible roles or features, with the installed ones highlighted. The shorter version of the role or feature name in brackets ([]) is the exact parameter that must be used with the *-install* switch at the command line to install the role or feature.
3. To install the DHCP Server Role use the following command:

```
ServerManagerCmd -install DHCP
```

4. There should be no need to reboot the server, so do not specify the *-restart* command-line parameter.

Creating a New Scope

If you used the graphical Server Manager console to install the DHCP Server Role, an initial scope (range of IP addresses managed by the server) and options are configured as part of the installation. If you used the command line to install the DHCP Server Role, you'll need to create an initial scope, set the global server options and the scope specific options, and then authorize the server.

Real World DHCP Options

You can configure DHCP options in a Windows Server 2008 DHCP server at three levels:

- **Server options** These options apply to all clients of the DHCP server you're managing. Because of this, use server options sparingly–specify server options only for parameters common across all scopes on the server.
- **Scope options** These are the most commonly used type of options–they apply to all clients within a scope and override any server options set on the DHCP server.
- **Client options** These options are specified for individual clients. This is useful if specific computers need special options. Client options override all other options, and are set for reservations.

Creating a New IPv4 DHCP Scope

To create a new IPv4 scope, follow these steps:

1. Open the DHCP Console if it isn't already open.
2. Connect to the server you want to add a scope to. Expand the server name in the left-hand pane.
3. Right-click IPv4 and select New Scope to open the New Scope Wizard.
4. Click Next to open the Scope Name page of the New Scope Wizard, shown in Figure 18-9.

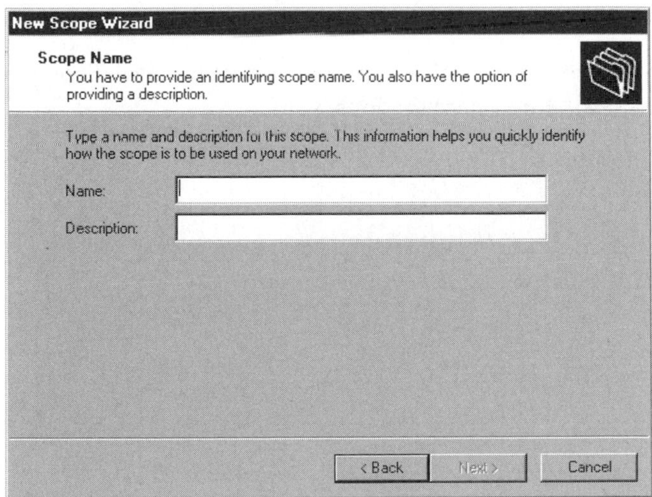

Figure 18-9 The Scope Name page of the New Scope Wizard.

5. Enter a name in the Name field, and optionally enter a description for the new scope. Click Next to open the IP Address Range page of the New Scope Wizard, shown in Figure 18-10, and fill in the fields to define the address range of the scope.

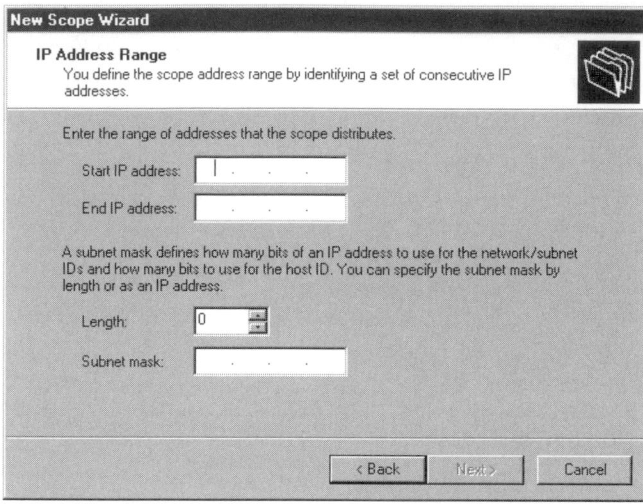

Figure 18-10 The IP Address Range page of the New Scope Wizard

6. Click Next to open the Add Exclusions page of the New Scope Wizard. Enter any address ranges you want to exclude from the scope and click Add to exclude them. (You can exclude single IP addresses by entering the IP address in the Start IP Address field and leaving the End IP Address field blank.)

7. Click Next to open the Lease Duration page. The default is eight days, which is appropriate for most wired networks, but too long for a wireless network. For a wireless network, one day is the most we'd choose.

8. Click Next to open the Configure DHCP Options page of the New Scope Wizard. Select Yes, I Want To Configure These Options Now.

9. Click Next to open the Router (Default Gateway) page of the New Scope Wizard, shown in Figure 18-11.

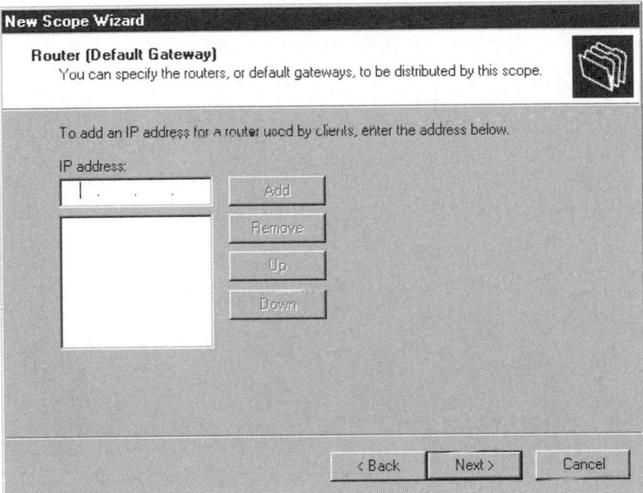

Figure 18-11 The Router (Default Gateway) page of the New Scope Wizard

10. Enter the IP address of the default gateway for this IP address range and click Add. If this is a nonrouted, internal-only IP address range, leave this field blank.

11. Click Next to open the Domain Name And DNS Servers page of the New Scope Wizard. Enter local domain name in the Parent Domain field. Enter the IP address of the primary DNS server. You can also enter it by name in the Server Name field and click Resolve, as shown in Figure 18-12.

Figure 18-12 The Domain Name And DNS Servers page of the New Scope Wizard

12. Click Add to add the IP address of the primary DNS server for this DHCP scope. You can add additional DNS servers as appropriate to your environment.
13. Click Next to open the WINS Servers page. If you use WINS servers in your environment, add them the same way you added DNS servers.
14. Click Next to open the Activate Scope page of the New Scope Wizard. The DHCP scope will not be available and the DHCP server will not answer DHCP requests for this scope until the scope is activated.
15. Click Next and then click Finish to create the DHCP scope and activate it (if that was your selection in the previous step).

Real World Scopes, Superscopes, and Multicast Scopes

A *scope* is simply the range of possible IP addresses on a network. To add more clients to a network where the scope is exhausted, you can add another scope as long as the scope doesn't overlap with an existing scope. An excellent source of information about the complex subject of choosing subnet masks and other TCP/IP issues is *Microsoft Windows Server 2003 TCP/IP Protocols and Services Technical Reference* by Thomas Lee and Joseph Davies (Microsoft Press, 2003).

When you create multiple scopes, it's important to understand that clients from one logical subnet aren't able to obtain IP addresses from a different scope than the one they currently belong to, because the other scope is in a different logical subnet. If this is the behavior you want, great. However, if you want clients to be able to use addresses from other scopes, use a superscope.

A *superscope* is a collection of scopes grouped together into a single administrative whole. You might want to use superscopes for three primary reasons:

- One scope is running out of IP addresses.
- You need to renumber the IP network, and therefore move clients from one set of addresses to another.
- You want to use two DHCP servers on the same subnet for redundancy.

When you create a superscope, you enable clients to obtain or renew leases from any scope within the superscope, even if they contain addresses from a different logical subnet.

A *multicast scope* is simply a scope of multicast addresses (class D addresses) that are then shared by many computers (members of the multicast group).

Creating a New IPv6 DHCP Scope

To create a new IPv6 scope, follow these steps:

1. Open the DHCP Console if it isn't already open.
2. Connect to the server you want to add a scope to. Expand the server name in the left-hand pane.
3. Right-click IPv6, and select New Scope to open the New Scope Wizard.
4. Click Next to open the Scope Name page of the New Scope Wizard. Enter a name in the Name field, and optionally enter a description for the new scope.
5. Click Next to open the Scope Prefix page of the New Scope Wizard, as shown in Figure 18-13. Enter a 64-bit prefix for the scope and set the preference for the scope.

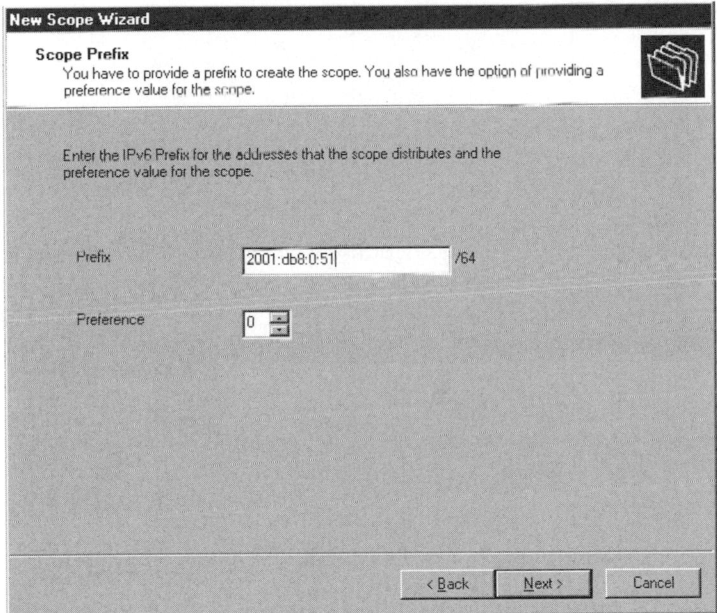

Figure 18-13 The Scope Prefix page of the New Scope Wizard

6. Click Next to open the Add Exclusions page of the New Scope Wizard, as shown in Figure 18-14. Enter a starting and ending IPv6 address to exclude from the DHCP scope and click Add. (You can exclude single IPv6 addresses by entering the IP address in the Start IPv6 Address field and leaving the End IPv6 Address field blank.)

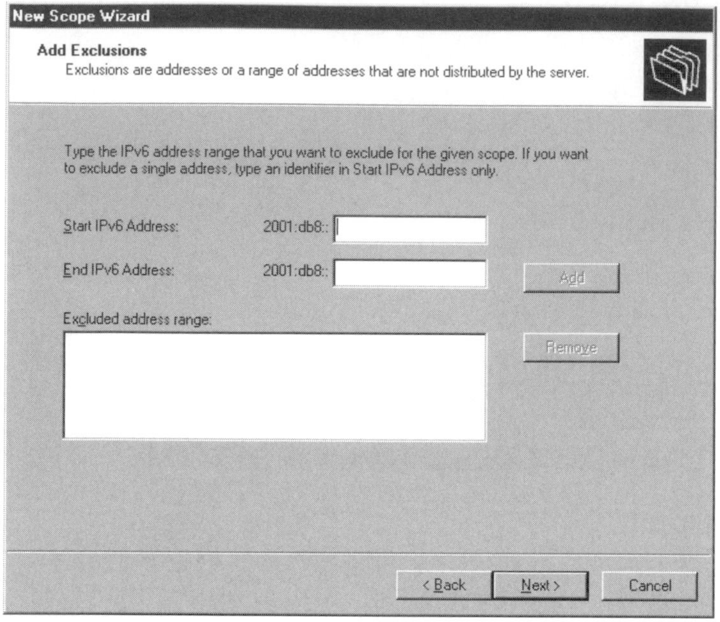

Figure 18-14 The Add Exclusions page of the New Scope Wizard

7. Click Next to open the Scope Lease page of the New Scope Wizard, as shown in Figure 18-15.

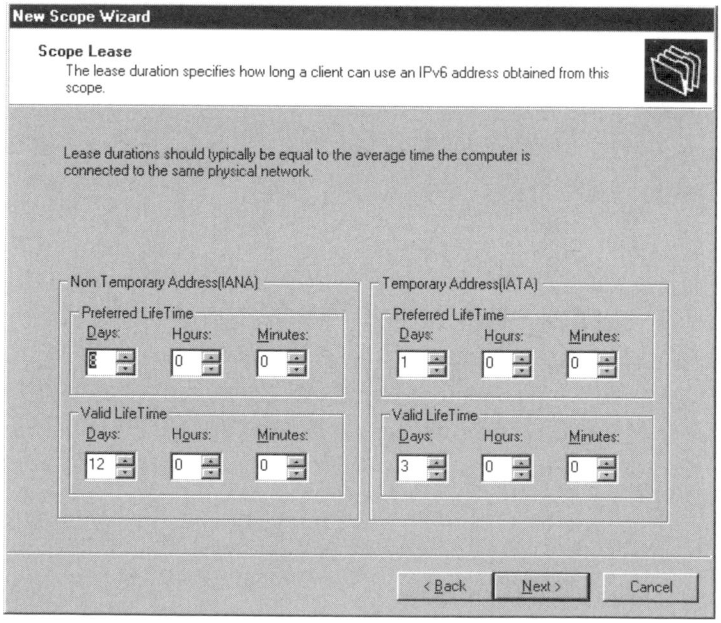

Figure 18-15 The Scope Lease page of the New Scope Wizard

8. Set the scope durations. IPv6 DHCP addresses have a preferred life time and a valid life time. The defaults are generally a good choice, though you can adjust them if you need to.
9. Click Next to open the Completing The New Scope Wizard page. Select Yes in the Activate Scope Now section to have the scope activated, or No to create the scope but not activate it.
10. Click Finish to complete the wizard and activate the scope (if that was your selection in the previous step).

Real World Setting Lease Durations

Use longer leases for networks without redundant DHCP servers to permit more time to recover an offline DHCP server before clients lose their leases, or to minimize network traffic at the expense of less frequent address turnover. You can also use longer leases if scope addresses are plentiful (at least 20 percent available), the network is stable, and computers are rarely moved.

In contrast, scopes that support dial-up clients or mobile clients such as laptops or personal digital assistants (PDAs) can have shorter leases and therefore function well with fewer addresses.

If you're planning a major network change, change the scope lease duration to be quite short. This will allow you to make the changes you need to the DHCP Scope properties and have them rapidly deployed to all clients. After the network change is made, don't forget to set the DHCP back to a more reasonable duration to minimize the amount of network traffic and resource utilization on the DHCP server.

Authorizing the DHCP Server and Activating Scopes

Normally, when you add the DHCP Server Role, or when you add a scope to an existing DHCP server, you will authorize the server and activate the scope at the time of creation. However, if you're managing a Server Core DHCP server, or have added the DHCP server from the command line using ServerManagerCmd.exe, the server won't have been authorized during the installation if it was installed on a non-domain controller. And when you create a new scope, you have an option to *not* activate the scope during creation.

Windows Server 2008 requires a DHCP server to be authorized before it can be used to reduce the occurrence of unauthorized (rogue) servers. In most cases, rogue servers are innocently installed by well-meaning folks who are trying to solve a problem, but they can also be a potential security issue it they are set up to hand out false IP addresses to clients as an attack vector. Although rogue DHCP servers that use UNIX or hardware-based DHCP servers can still be set up, Windows Server–based DHCP servers can't be used in a Windows Server 2008 domain without authorization.

To authorize the DHCP server after installing the service, select the server in the DHCP console and then choose Authorize from the Action menu. To manage the list of authorized servers, right-click DHCP at the root of the console tree and choose Manage Authorized Servers from the shortcut menu.

To activate a scope, right-click the scope in the console tree and then choose Activate from the shortcut menu. Don't activate a scope until you finish selecting all the options you want. When you activate a scope, the Activate command on the menu changes to Deactivate.

Under the Hood Scope Deactivation

When you deactivate a scope, the assumption is that those addresses are not being used by the network and the DHCP server will not accept those addresses as valid. Any existing clients will be unable to renew their addresses, and when they try, they'll cause DHCP negative acknowledgement messages to be sent from the server to the client. This is the correct method if your intent is to never use those addresses as part of a DHCP scope again, and you should deactivate a scope prior to deleting it. But if what you want to do is temporarily stop handing out addresses in a particular scope, the preferred method is to add an exclusion that covers the entire address range of the scope. This way, any existing addresses already given out are retained by the clients and are considered valid. When you're ready to re-enable the scope, you simply remove the exclusion.

Adding Address Reservations

Reservations are used to provide a consistent and unchanging IP address to servers and other hosts that need to be at a predictable IP address. The only servers that can't use a reservation are DHCP servers—they must be at a fixed IP address. Using reservations instead of static addresses guarantees that a server has a consistent IP address, while giving you the ability to easily change settings as required, and to recover the IP address in the future if the server is decommissioned or moved.

To add an address reservation to a scope, right-click the Reservations folder under the desired scope, and choose New Reservation from the shortcut menu. Walk through the wizard and add the new reservation. You'll need to know the MAC address for the DHCP client you want a reservation for, and the IP address you want to assign to it.

Important When reserving an address for a client, make the reservation on all DHCP servers that potentially service that client. You can create reservations outside the address range of the scope on the server. This allows you to use the same set of reservations even when you're using multiple servers.

Under the Hood **Finding the MAC Address**

Before you can add a reservation to DHCP, you need to know the MAC address of the DHCP client you want to make a reservation for. While you could read the MAC address off the network device (somewhere on the device is a sticker with the address), that's hardly easy in most cases. So, how to easily get the MAC address? Well, two ways we know are by using the `getmac` command (only available on Windows Server 2003 and Windows Server 2008), and by using the `ipconfig` command.

To obtain the MAC address using the `ipconfig` command, go to the client computer (or make a remote desktop connection) and type **`ipconfig /all`** at the command prompt. The MAC address is listed as the physical address. Using `ipconfig /all` doesn't require elevation.

To obtain the MAC address using the `getmac` command, from a command prompt, type:

```
getmac /s computer /v
```

where *computer* is the IP address, host name, or DNS name of the remote computer you want the MAC address for. You'll want to use the `/v` (verbose) parameter when getting the MAC address for a computer with more than one network card, as shown in Figure 18-16.

```
[hp350-srv-06] (EXAMPLE\Charlie)
[hp350-srv-06]C:\Users\Charlie:
PS > getmac /s 192.168.51.20 /v

Connection Name Network Adapter Physical Address    Transport Name
=============== =============== =================== ==========================================================
50 Network      Marvell Yukon 8 00-11-2F-F6-3D-E1   \Device\Tcpip_{AE5A266B-B492-4733-98D8-C39977A67ABE}
51Network       Intel(R) PRO/10 00-04-23-C8-F6-96   \Device\Tcpip_{29AC91D5-242F-4A25-8DCD-5A3BA228A26F}
0 Network       Intel(R) PRO/10 00-04-23-C8-F6-97   \Device\Tcpip_{6778D570-C5D7-4EC0-BD13-05BA7E2641E0}
Bluetooth Netwo Bluetooth Devic 00-50-F2-E4-2C-DF   Media disconnected
[hp350-srv-06]C:\Users\Charlie:
PS > _
```

Figure 18-16 Using the getmac command to find the MAC address of a remote client computer.

Finally, you can obtain the MAC address of any current DHCP client by looking at the current DHCP lease for the client–the MAC address is shown in the Unique ID column.

Using Multiple DHCP Servers for Redundancy

Computers don't lose network connectivity immediately when a DHCP server goes down, but new computers, returning laptops, or little-used systems that haven't recently logged on might not be able to obtain network access until a DHCP server is available.

To ensure that a DHCP server will continue to be available even if the primary DHCP server is down, configure multiple DHCP servers. The traditional solution is to set up two or more servers with a split scope across the servers. Another solution is to use a Windows Server 2008 Failover Cluster as your DHCP server. Failover clustering is covered in Chapter 21, "Using Clusters."

Splitting the Address Space Between Two Servers

To employ two DHCP servers for load balancing and redundancy, follow these steps:

1. Create identical scopes on each server for all valid IP addresses that the DHCP servers you're setting up will manage. This might mean creating a single scope (if you have a single subnet), or multiple scopes encompassing a number of subnets.
2. Set up exclusions so that the primary DHCP server handles 80 percent of the address pool and the secondary server handles the other 20 percent of the addresses. Thus, each server excludes the addresses available on the other server so that no address appears in both servers' address pools.
3. Create an IPv4 superscope on both servers that contains all valid scopes for the physical subnet. To do so, select the appropriate DHCP server from the console tree, choose the New Superscope command from the Action menu, name the superscope, and then select the member scopes to include.

Note You can delete a superscope without affecting the member scopes by selecting the superscope and pressing Delete. However, *deactivating* a superscope deactivates all member scopes as well.

Note If you have a routed network with DHCP relay agents or routers that forward DHCP broadcasts between the physical subnets, you can use DHCP servers on other subnets as secondary servers. However, unless the DHCP server has at least one scope with available addresses from the client's own subnet, the client cannot obtain or renew an IP address lease. To make sure this doesn't happen, create two superscopes on each server, one for each logical subnet. Thus, each server owns 80 percent of the address pool for its local subnet, and 20 percent of the address pool for the other DHCP server's local subnet.

Setting Up a DHCP Server Cluster

Although splitting the address space between two DHCP servers is an adequate way to provide redundancy and load balancing, an even more powerful solution is to set up the DHCP service to run on a Windows Server 2008 Failover Cluster. The members of the cluster equally share the DHCP service workload, and if one of the servers fails, the other servers continue to provide addresses to clients as if nothing had happened. Instead of an address space split between servers, each server in the cluster has access to the complete address space. See Chapter 21 for details on how to set up and configure Windows Server 2008 clustering.

Enabling Server-Based Conflict Detection

The Windows Server 2008 DHCP server provides the ability to enable server-based conflict detection for IPv4 addresses, which is a technique that pings an IP address before leasing it to a client to ensure that it's not already in use by a static IP client. This was a really useful option in the days when most of the DHCP clients on the network were Windows 9x and Windows NT. But it's an essentially useless option for any Windows servers or clients from Windows 2000 or later. Windows Server 2008, Windows Server 2003, Windows Vista, Windows XP, and Windows 2000 clients all automatically verify that the IP address offered by the DHCP server is available before accepting it, so conflict detection is useful only for earlier versions of Windows or for non-Windows clients that don't do auto-conflict detection. Unless you have clients that fit this description, leave this option disabled.

To enable server-based conflict detection, right-click the IPv4 server icon in the left-hand pane of the DHCP console and choose Properties from the shortcut menu. Click the Advanced tab, and then set the number in the Conflict Detection Attempts field to 1.

Setting Up a DHCP Relay Agent

If you have a routed network, deploy DHCP servers on both sides of routers to maximize reliability and minimize bandwidth usage. However, in some cases you will want to allow DHCP to work across a router; for example, if the routed network is very reliable and fast–as might be the case with a partitioned local network–you might want to simply allow clients to cross the router to reach a DHCP server.

You can configure most routers manufactured in the last several years to pass DHCP broadcasts, but if the router doesn't support forwarding DHCP broadcasts, you can set up a server running Windows Server 2008 with the Routing And Remote Access Services Role Service enabled as a DHCP relay agent by following these steps:

1. Launch Routing And Remote Access from the Administrative Tools folder on the Programs menu.
2. Select the IPv4 or IPv6 icon in the left-hand pane, right-click General, and then select New Routing Protocol from the shortcut menu.

3. Select DHCP Relay Agent (or DHCPv6 Relay Agent) and then click OK to add a DHCP or DHCPv6 Relay Agent object, as shown in Figure 18-17.

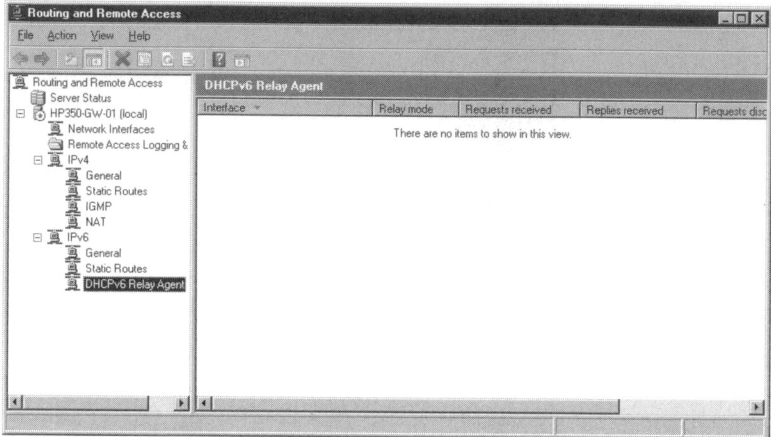

Figure 18-17 The newly added DHCPv6 Relay Agent in the Routing And Remote Access console

4. Right-click the DHCP Relay Agent (or DHCPv6 Relay Agent) and select New Interface from the shortcut menu.
5. Select the network adapter connected to the network *whose DHCP client requests need to be forwarded*, and then click OK to open the DHCP Relay Properties of the connection, as shown in Figure 18-18.

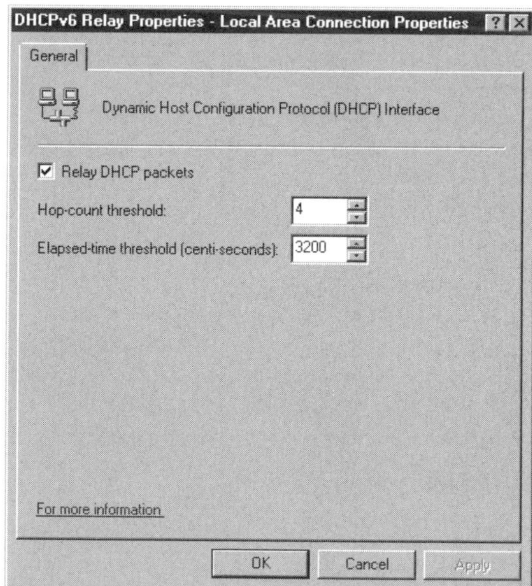

Figure 18-18 The DHCPv6 Relay Properties of a Local Area Connection

6. Set the Hop-Count Threshold and Elapsed-Time Threshold (centi-seconds) for IPv6, or Hop-Count Threshold and Boot Threshold (Seconds) for IPv4. The default values are a good starting point.
7. Right-click the DHCP Relay object again, and choose Properties from the shortcut menu.
8. For IPv4, type the address of a DHCP server you want to forward DHCP requests to, and then click Add. For IPv6, click the Servers tab and then enter a server address to forward to.

DHCP Command-Line Administration

The DHCP server in Windows Server 2008 provides full command-line administration capabilities with the rather unfriendly but powerful `netsh` command. To use these capabilities, follow these steps:

1. Open a Command Prompt window or PowerShell window with elevated privileges.
2. Type **netsh** at the command prompt. The prompt changes to netsh>.
3. Type **dhcp**. The prompt changes to netsh dhcp>.
4. Type **server** followed by the server name or IP address to connect to the desired DHCP server—for example, **server \\hp350-dc-02** or **server 192.168.51.2**. (If no server name or address is specified, the local computer is assumed.)
5. Type **list** to view a list of the available commands. To obtain help with a particular command, type the command name followed by /?.

Using DNS Server

Modern TCP/IP networks use DNS for name resolution, and DNS is a requirement for Active Directory. Active Directory supports the DNS server included with Windows 2008 Server, Windows Server 2003, and Windows 2000 Server, either stand-alone or integrated directly into Active Directory, and it also supports BIND version 8.2.2 or later. However, if you use BIND, you really should update to the latest version 9.x to avoid potential security issues with older versions. (As of this writing, BIND is at 9.4.2 with 9.5 in beta.)

To install the DNS Server Role in Windows Server 2008, follow these steps:

1. Open Server Manager if it isn't already open.
2. Select Roles in the left-hand pane and then select Add Roles from the Action menu to open the Add Roles Wizard.

3. Click Next to open the Select Server Roles page of the Add Roles Wizard. Select DNS Server.
4. Click Next and then click Install to begin the installation. In most cases a reboot will not be required.
5. Click Close when the installation completes.

You manage the DNS Server Role from within Server Manager by using the DNS Server console, or by directly launching the stand-alone DNS Server console. You can launch the stand-alone console from the Administrative Tools section of the Start menu, or by typing **dnsmgmt.msc** at a command prompt.

Setting Up a DNS Server

Both large and small networks have similar DNS requirements, although many small networks will usually function well without reverse lookup zones. If your internal domain name is different from your public, Internet domain name (that is, internally you use *example.local* or *example.lan*, but externally you use *example.com*), you must configure an internal DNS server to support your internal network.

If your DNS domain name is the same on your local network as it is on the Internet (that is, *example.com* is your Active Directory domain name as well as your Internet domain name), you could, theoretically, have only external DNS records, but this is a really bad idea because it exposes your internal network topology and names to the world. In this case, it is better to maintain an internal DNS server that supports your internal network, while the publicly visible DNS server or servers for your domain should only have records for publicly visible servers.

Real World The Need (or Lack Thereof) for Secondary DNS Servers

Because of the pivotal role DNS plays in any TCP/IP-based network, it's vital that it be reliable. Small networks can often make do with a single DNS server, but medium and large networks must have fault-tolerant DNS service.

One way of providing DNS redundancy is to set up secondary DNS servers using standard zone files to provide redundancy if the primary DNS server (of which there can be only one) doesn't respond to client queries. Secondary DNS servers can also be useful in reducing network traffic if placed in a location where the zone is heavily queried.

Another approach is to add another Active Directory–integrated DNS server. Because Active Directory uses a full multiple-master model, all DNS servers using

Active Directory–integrated zones can be primary servers—no secondary zones are required.

If you are going to use standard primary and secondary DNS servers, set up secondary DNS servers for both forward and reverse lookup zones. Fewer secondary servers are required for reverse lookup zones because of their infrequent use.

The Configure A DNS Server Wizard makes it easy to set up a DNS server. To use the wizard, follow these steps:

1. Open the DNS Manager and select the DNS server you want to configure. (Choose the Connect To Server command from the Action menu if the server isn't displayed in the console tree.)
2. Select Configure A DNS Server from the Action menu.
3. Click Next to open the Select Configuration Action page of the Configure A DNS Server Wizard and then select Create Forward And Reverse Lookup Zones (Recommended For Large Networks), as shown in Figure 18-19.

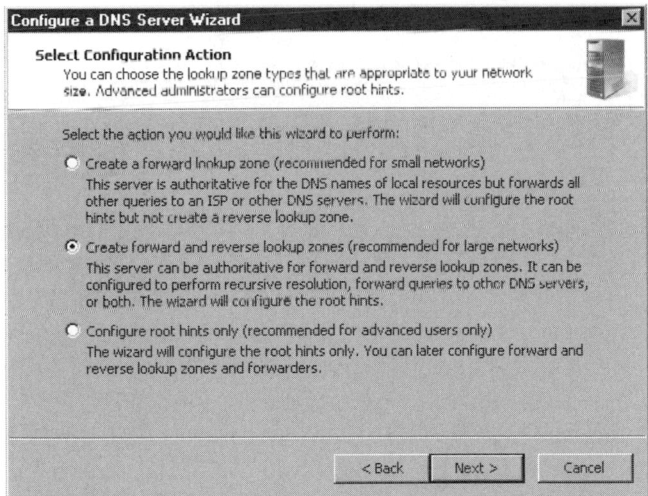

Figure 18-19 The Select Configuration Action page of the Configure A DNS Server Wizard

4. Click Next to open the Forward Lookup Zone page. Select Yes, Create A Forward Lookup Zone Now (Recommended).
5. Click Next to open the Zone Type page, as shown in Figure 18-20. Select one of the three options for zone type:

- **Primary Zone** Use this option if the DNS server is to be authoritative for the zone you want to create. Only authoritative servers can update the DNS database.
- **Secondary Zone** Use this zone if the DNS server is hosted on UNIX servers. You should also use it if this server is to have read-only privileges in the zone with all data obtained from the primary DNS server.
- **Stub Zone** Use this type of zone to create a pseudo-zone that allows the server to directly query DNS servers from a specific zone without having to locate the zone's DNS servers by querying the root servers or Internet DNS servers.

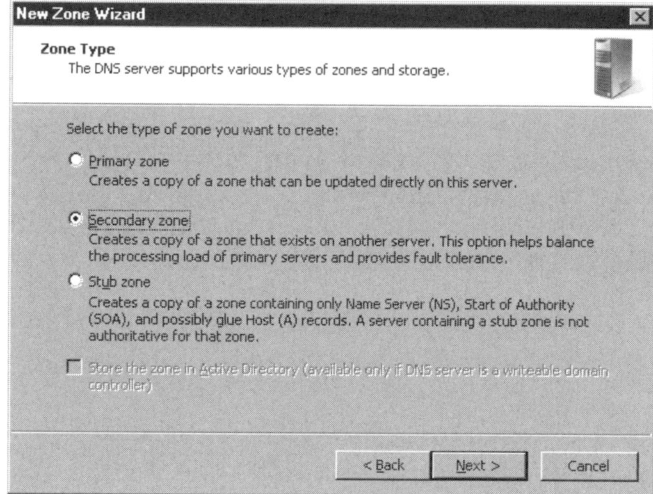

Figure 18-20 The Zone Type page of the Configure A DNS Server Wizard

6. If you're creating a zone on a domain controller, and you choose Primary Zone, also select Store The Zone In Active Directory (Available Only If The DNS Server Is A Writeable Domain Controller). This will replicate the zone across all domain controllers. (Read-Only domain controllers have only secondary DNS zones.) Click Next to open the Active Directory Zone Replication Scope page, shown in Figure 18-21, and select one of the following options.

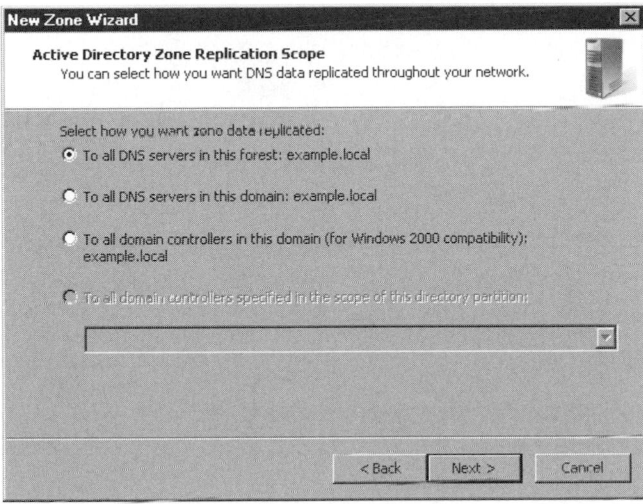

Figure 18-21 The Active Directory Zone Replication Scope page of the Configure A DNS Server Wizard

- **To All DNS Servers In This Forest: <forestname>** Use this option to enable replication of the DNS records across all domain controllers and DNS servers in the entire forest.
- **To All DNS Servers In This Domain: <domainname>** Use this option to enable replication of the DNS records across all domain controllers and DNS servers in the entire domain.
- **To All Domain Controllers In This Domain (For Windows 2000 Compatibility): <domainname>** Use this option when you still have Windows 2000 domain controllers in your domain.

7. Click Next to open the Zone Name page. Enter the full name for the DNS zone, as shown in Figure 18-22.

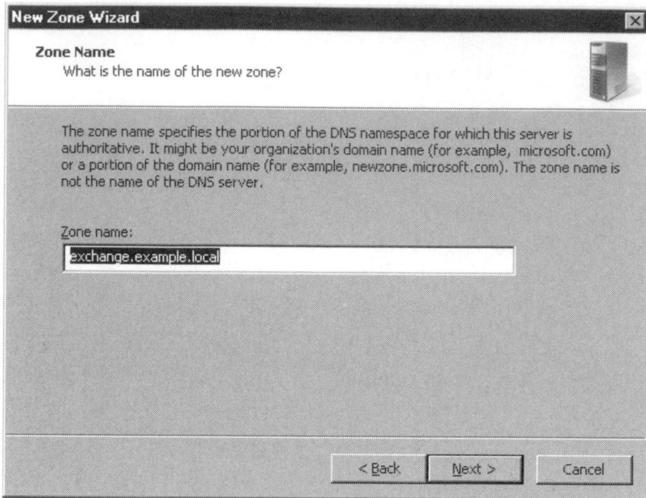

Figure 18-22 The Zone Name page of the Configure A DNS Server Wizard

8. Click Next. If this is a primary zone, you'll see the Dynamic Update page. Choose from the following options:
   - **Allow Only Secure Dynamic Updates (Recommended For Active Directory)** This is the default for Active Directory–integrated zones (and is available only for Active Directory–integrated zones), and it provides the best security.
   - **Allow Both Nonsecure And Secure Dynamic Updates** This is the recommended setting for standard zones.
   - **Do Not Allow Dynamic Updates** All changes must be manually made. This is only appropriate for essentially static environments using fixed IP addresses or DHCP reservations for all computers in the zone.
9. If this is a secondary zone, you'll see the Master DNS Servers page. Type in the IP address or DNS name of an authoritative DNS server for this zone.
10. Click Next to open the Reverse Lookup Zone page. Select Yes, Create A Reverse Lookup Zone Now.
11. Click Next to open the Zone Type page. Select one of the following three options for zone type:
    - **Primary Zone** Use this option if the DNS server is to be authoritative for the zone you want to create. Only authoritative servers can update the DNS database.

- **Secondary Zone** Use this zone if the DNS server is hosted on UNIX servers. Also use it if this server is to have read-only privileges in the zone with all data obtained from the primary DNS server.
- **Stub Zone** Use this type of zone to create a pseudo-zone that allows the server to directly query DNS servers from a specific zone without having to locate the zone's DNS servers by querying the root servers or Internet DNS servers.

12. If you're creating a zone on a domain controller, and you choose Primary Zone, also select Store The Zone In Active Directory (Available Only If The DNS Server Is A Writeable Domain Controller). This will replicate the zone across all domain controllers. (Read-Only domain controllers have only secondary DNS zones.) Click Next to open the Active Directory Zone Replication Scope page. (Skip this step for a secondary zone.)
    - **To All DNS Servers In This Forest: <forestname>** Use this option to enable replication of the DNS records across all domain controllers and DNS servers in the entire forest.
    - **To All DNS Servers In This Domain: <domainname>** Use this option to enable replication of the DNS records across all domain controllers and DNS servers in the entire domain.
    - **To All Domain Controllers In This Domain (For Windows 2000 Compatibility): <domainname>** Use this option when you still have Windows 2000 domain controllers in your domain.
13. Click Next to open the Reverse Lookup Zone Name page. Select IPv4 Reverse Lookup Zone or IPv6 Reverse Lookup Zone.
14. Click Next to open the Reverse Lookup Zone Name page. Enter the IPv6 address prefix for an IPv6 address, or the network ID for an IPv4 address.
15. Click Next. If this is a primary zone, you'll see the Dynamic Update page. Choose from the following options:
    - **Allow Only Secure Dynamic Updates (Recommended For Active Directory)** This is the default for Active Directory–integrated zones (and is available only for Active Directory–integrated zones), and it provides the best security.
    - **Allow Both Nonsecure And Secure Dynamic Updates** This is the recommended setting for standard zones.

- **Do Not Allow Dynamic Updates** All changes must be manually made. This is only appropriate for essentially static environments using fixed IP addresses or DHCP reservations for all computers in the zone.

16. If this is a secondary zone, you'll see the Master DNS Servers page. Type in the IP address or DNS name of an authoritative DNS server for this zone.
17. Click Next to open the Forwarders page. Here you choose (or don't) to forward queries to other DNS servers. See the Real World sidebar on DNS poisoning attacks to help make your decision.
18. Click Next and then click Finish to create the DNS zones.

Real World DNS Poisoning Attacks

The standard setup for most DNS servers that supported only internal network clients was to set up your DNS server as a primary zone and then configure it to forward all other requests to your ISP's designated DNS servers. This resulted in fast and private support for internal name resolution, while providing the fastest resolution of names outside your private network and reducing overall traffic for your ISP and the Internet as a whole. Unfortunately, this exposes your network to DNS poisoning attacks such as the widespread cache corruption attack that affects all versions of BIND before version 9. If some malicious program manages to subvert the DNS servers maintained by your ISP because your ISP hasn't gotten around to updating them, your DNS server would pass that problem on to your internal clients.

The problem is especially a concern if your ISP is somewhat slow to apply updates to its DNS servers, which seems to be the case for many ISPs, both large and small. BIND is the most common DNS server software used by ISPs, and several vulnerabilities have been identified against BIND, especially versions before BIND 9. Updates to correct these vulnerabilities are available, but if your ISP is slow to apply the update, you could be exposed.

If you don't specify a server to forward to, your DNS server will use root hints to directly resolve the address. This might be somewhat slower, and it certainly increases the overall traffic on the Internet, but if the root servers are poisoned, we're all in trouble. If you trust your ISP to maintain its servers adequately, continue to forward to their servers. Personally, we've stopped doing so.

Creating Subdomains and Delegating Authority

In most large network environments, you need to create subdomains and delegate their management to other DNS zones hosted by other DNS servers. Doing so eliminates the undesirable situation of having a large namespace hosted in a single zone by a single server. Thus, you might have a zone containing the root domain *example.local* as well as the subdomain *exchange.example.local*. However, you might have the subdomain *eng.example.local* and its subdomains delegated to a separate zone managed by another DNS server, as shown in Figure 18-23.

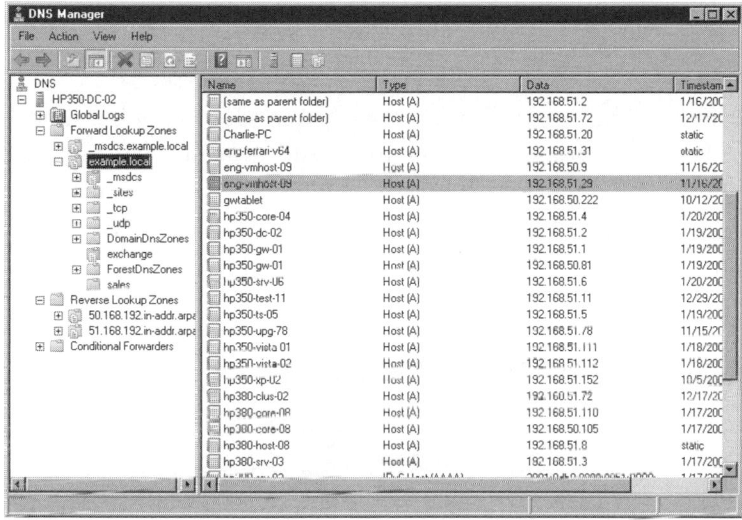

Figure 18-23 A domain tree with zones identified

Important Be sure you have a host record created for the DNS server in the forward lookup zone and a pointer record for the DNS server in the reverse lookup zone. DNS might not automatically create these (especially the pointer record), so double-check them—otherwise, the server might not work.

Note Zones must have a contiguous namespace, so it isn't possible to combine subdomains from different branches of the namespace and place them in a single zone. Create separate zones for each noncontiguous part of the domain.

To create a new subdomain in an existing zone and then delegate authority over the domain to another DNS server, perform the following steps:

1. Select the domain in which you want to create a new subdomain, and then choose New Domain from the Action menu.
2. Type the name of the subdomain in the dialog box that appears, and then click OK. This name must not be fully qualified. For example, if you were creating the subdomain *eng.example.com* under the domain *example.com*, type only **eng** in this dialog box.

> **Note** Subdomains don't have to be delegated to a different DNS server. Subdomains can even be created in new zone files and still be managed by the same server. This is useful if you want to host the domains on the same computer yet manage them differently.

3. To delegate authority over the subdomain, select the parent domain of the subdomain, choose New Delegation from the Action menu, and then click Next to start the New Delegation Wizard.
4. Type the name for the subdomain you want to delegate, as shown in Figure 18-24. Check that the fully qualified name of the subdomain displayed is correct and then click Next.

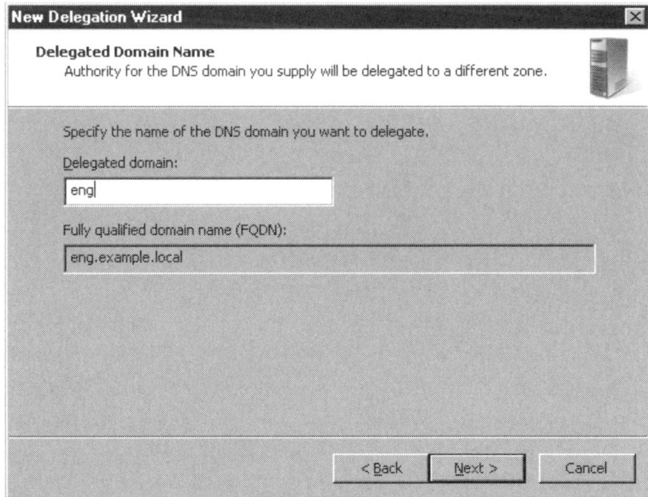

Figure 18-24 Delegating a subdomain

5. Click Add to specify the servers to which you want to delegate the subdomain.
6. Type the name of the server to which you want to delegate authority and then click Resolve, as shown in Figure 18-25. Alternatively, type the IP address or addresses for the server directly into the IP Addresses Of This NS Record box, clicking Add after typing each one. Click OK when you're done.

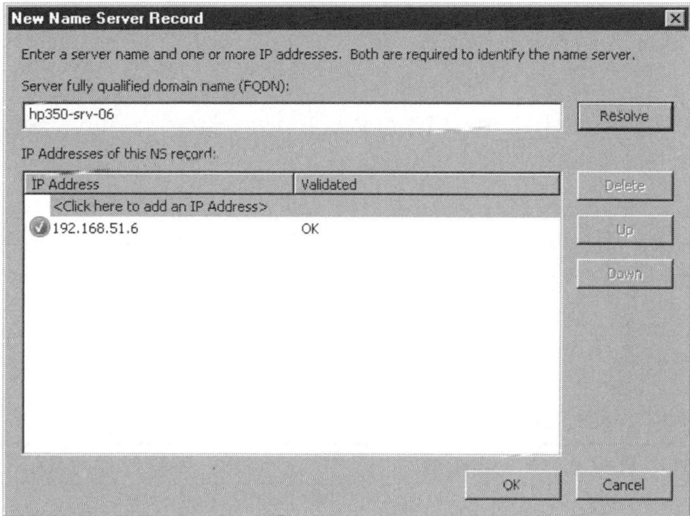

Figure 18-25 The New Name Server Record page of the New Delegation Wizard

7. Add any other DNS servers that will host the delegated subdomain. Click Next to continue.

> **Note** When you delegate control over a subdomain to multiple DNS servers, Windows automatically monitors the round-trip times to the servers and selects the closest (fastest) one.

8. Review the summary window and click Finish to complete the delegation process.

Adding Resource Records

After creating zones and subdomains, add resource records for the domain server and any other servers with static IP addresses or IP reservations (DHCP servers, WINS servers, routers, and so on). The steps that follow are for adding new host records (A), but the process to add new pointer records (PTR), Alias (CNAME) records, mail exchangers (MX), or other resource records is similar. (Note that the DNS server doesn't work properly without a host record and a pointer record, which might not be created automatically for you.)

1. Select the zone and domain or subdomain to which the host belongs, and then choose New Host from the Action menu. Alternatively, choose New Alias, New Mail Exchanger, or another type of record from the Action menu. Table 18-1 lists the records supported by Windows Server 2008 DNS server.

2. In the Name box, type the host name (and *only* the host name–the name must not contain any periods), or leave the Name box blank to use the name of the parent domain. Type the host's IP address.
3. Select the Create Associated Pointer (PTR) Record to create a resource record for the host in the reverse lookup zone.
4. If you want to allow any authenticated user to update the resource record you're creating, select the Allow Any Authenticated User To Update DNS Records With The Same Owner Name check box.
5. Click Add Host, and then fill out the fields for any additional host records you want to create, or click Done.

Table 18-1 Supported DNS Record Types

Record Type	Common Name	Function	RFC
A	Address record	Maps a fully qualified domain name (FQDN) to a 32-bit IPv4 address	
AAAA	IPv6 Host	Maps an FQDN to a 128-bit IPv6 address	1886
AFSDB	Andrews file system (AFS) or distributed computing environment (DCE) record	Maps a DNS domain name to a server subtype that is either an AFS version 3 volume or an authenticated name server (NS) using DCE or network computing architecture (NCA)	1183
ATMA	Asynchronous Transfer Mode (ATM) address	Maps a host name to an ATM address	"ATM Name System Specification Version 1.0"
CNAME	Canonical name or alias record	Maps a virtual domain name (alias) to a real domain name	1035
HINFO	Host information record	Specifies the CPU and operating system type for the host	1700
ISDN	ISDN information record	Maps an FQDN to an ISDN telephone number	1183
KEY	Public key resource record	Contains a public key for a DNS zone	2535
MB	Mailbox name record	Maps a domain mail server name to the actual host name of the mail server	1035

Table 18-1 **Supported DNS Record Types**

Record Type	Common Name	Function	RFC
MG	Mail group record	Maps a domain mailing group to the actual mailbox (MB) resource records of its members	1035
MINFO	Mailbox information record	Specifies a mailbox for the person who maintains the mailbox or list, and can also specify a mailbox for related errors	1035
MR	Mailbox renamed record	Maps an old mailbox name to a new mailbox name for forwarding purposes	1035
MX	Mail exchange record	Provides routing information to reach a given mailbox	974
NS	Name server record	Specifies that the name server listed has a zone starting with the owner name	1035
NXT	Next record	Specifies the nonexistence of the specified name	2035
OPT	Option resource record	Specifies optional data with a DNS request or reply	2671
PTR	Pointer resource record	Points to another DNS resource record—most often used in reverse lookup to point to the A record	1035
RP	Responsible person information record	Provides information about the person responsible for a server	1183
RT	Route-through record	Provides routing information for hosts lacking a direct WAN address	1183
SIG	Signature resource record	Digitally signs a host name	2535
SOA	Start of authority	Specifies the beginning of a zone, and indicates the authoritative server	1034
SRV	Service locator record	Provides a way of locating multiple servers providing similar TCP/IP services	2052

Table 18-1 Supported DNS Record Types

Record Type	Common Name	Function	RFC
TXT	Text record	Maps a DNS name to a string of descriptive text	1035
WKS	Well-known services record	Describes the most popular TCP/IP services supported by a protocol on a specific IP address	1035
X25	X.25 information	Maps a DNS address to a public switched data network (PSDN) address number	1083

Configuring Zone Transfers

Because the DNS service is so important to a modern TCP/IP-based network, and because it's essential to the operation of Active Directory, always configure multiple DNS servers in each zone to provide fault tolerance.

Windows Server 2008 supports several ways of achieving zone transfers between DNS servers managing a zone. If the DNS servers are using Active Directory to store their zone data, Active Directory handles the zone replication, allowing for a full multimaster model in which all servers are peers and any can make changes to the DNS database. Additionally, zone transfers are incremental so that only changed records are synchronized.

Windows Server 2008 also supports RFC 1995–compliant incremental zone transfers when using standard zone files. This incremental zone transfer method permits a secondary DNS server to pull only the zone changes that it needs to synchronize its copy of the zone data with the primary server's. If the serial number of the primary DNS server's zone file matches that of the secondary DNS server's serial number, no changes were made, so no zone transfer need take place.

Incremental zone transfers occur only if both servers support this feature. When performing zone transfers with DNS servers that don't support this feature, a full zone transfer occurs. In a full zone transfer, the entire contents of the zone file are pulled from the primary DNS server by the secondary server.

Real World Controlling Zone Transfers

The default configuration for Active Directory–integrated DNS is to not allow zone transfers to any computer that isn't a domain controller. This means that if you set up a secondary DNS server in a zone, you should first create a Name Server resource record for the secondary server, as described previously in the section

"Adding Resource Records." Then configure the properties of the zone to perform zone transfers only to servers listed in the Name Servers tab of the zone properties, as shown in Figure 18-26. This will ensure that a rogue DNS server can't download records from your server.

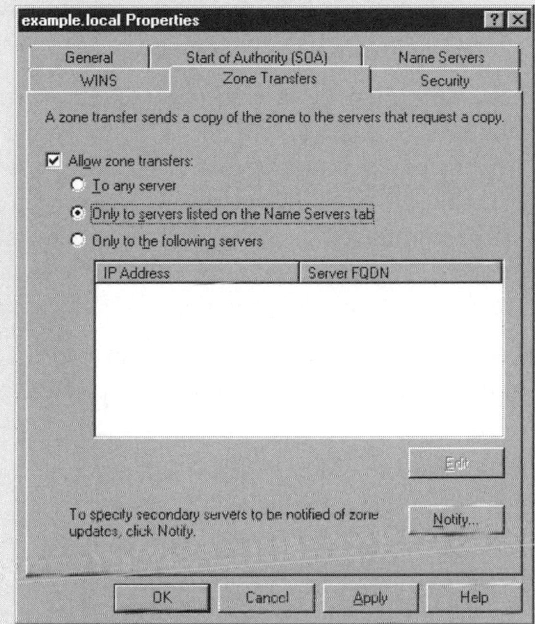

Figure 18-26 The Zone Transfers tab of the Zone Properties dialog box

Interoperating with Other DNS Servers

Windows Server 2008 DNS servers perform fast zone transfers with data compression and multiple resource records sent in each message when transferring zones to other Windows DNS servers. This zone transfer method works with all Windows DNS servers, and BIND DNS servers version 4.9.4 or later.

Although you can use Windows Server 2008 DNS servers and Active Directory in conjunction with BIND servers later than version 4.9.4, there are serious compatibility and security issues for all older versions of BIND. You should upgrade BIND to the latest version for maximum security, and in all cases you should be using version 8.4.4 or later. For the current state of BIND versions and vulnerabilities, see *http://www.isc.org/index.pl?/sw/bind/bind-security.php*.

Setting Up a Forwarder

No name server is able to answer the queries of all clients; for example, sometimes clients request a DNS name that isn't in a zone managed by the DNS server—let's say *example.microsoft.com*. The DNS server goes to the Internet to the top level of the DNS domain tree. The top-level DNS servers then provide the address of the DNS server for the first level (.com). This server in turn provides the address of the *microsoft.com* DNS server, which then provides the address of the *example.microsoft.com* DNS server.

This process is called *recursion*, and it takes time and a number of trips out to the Internet by the DNS server. In a network with multiple DNS servers and domains, it can be advantageous to have DNS servers forward their unresolved queries to another DNS server. This server then either replies with the desired record from its own DNS zone or from its cache of previous queries, or hunts down the unresolved query and reports back to the DNS server that forwarded the request, meanwhile adding the result into its cache so that the next query will be quicker. This can reduce WAN link usage in two ways:

- If the server is authoritative for the zone containing the requested DNS record, the DNS server can reply directly without having to hunt for the appropriate DNS server.
- If the server isn't hosting the zone with the requested record, it still might be able to answer the query from its cache of recent DNS queries.

Important See the "Real World: DNS Poisoning Attacks" sidebar earlier in this chapter before deciding whether to enable forwarders. You should understand the serious security implications involved before taking this step.

To configure the DNS server to forward unresolved queries to another DNS server, follow these steps:

1. Open the dnsmgmt.msc console.
2. In the console tree, select the DNS server on which you want to enable forwarding, choose Properties from the Action menu, and then click the Forwarders tab as shown in Figure 18-27.

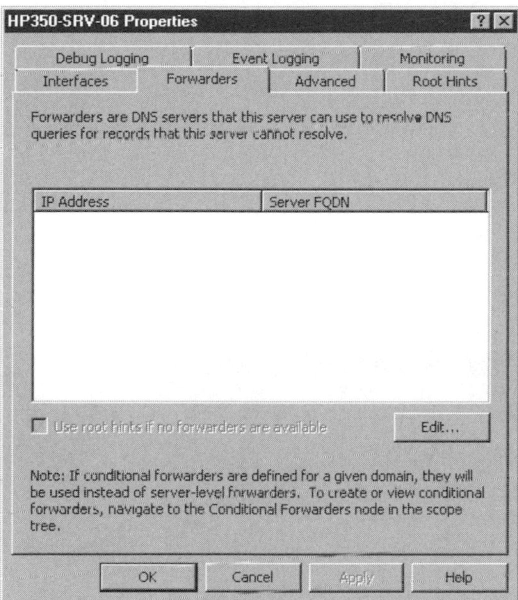

Figure 18-27 The Forwarders tab of the DNS Server Properties dialog box

3. Click Edit to open the Edit Forwarders dialog box.
4. Type one or more IP addresses or DNS names into the IP Addresses Of Forwarding Servers box. If the address or name is successfully resolved, and the DNS server responds, a green check mark will indicate that the address has been validated, as shown in Figure 18-28.

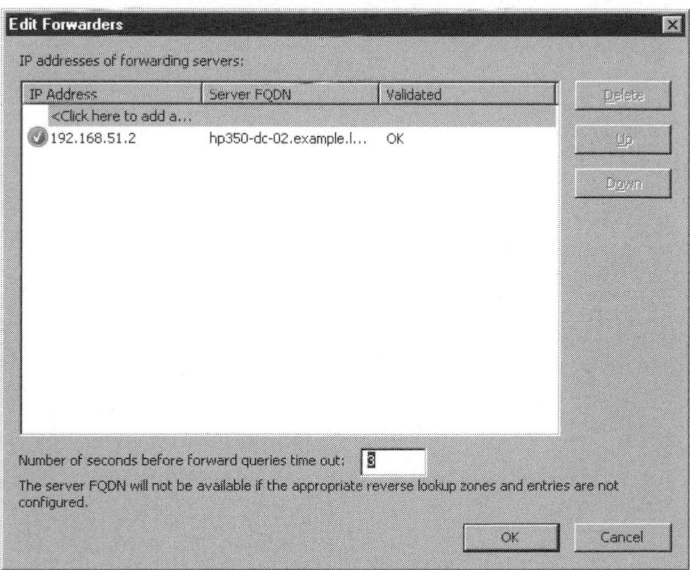

Figure 18-28 The Edit Forwarders dialog box

5. Adjust the Number Of Seconds Before Forward Queries Time Out value if the default of 3 seconds isn't appropriate and click OK to return to the Forwarders tab of the DNS Server Properties dialog box.
6. Click OK to close the DNS Server Properties dialog box and enable forwarding.

To enable forwarding queries for a specific domain to a specific DNS server (conditional forwarding) follow these steps:

1. In DNS Manager, right-click Conditional Forwarders and select New Conditional Forwarder to open the New Conditional Forwarder dialog box shown in Figure 18-29.

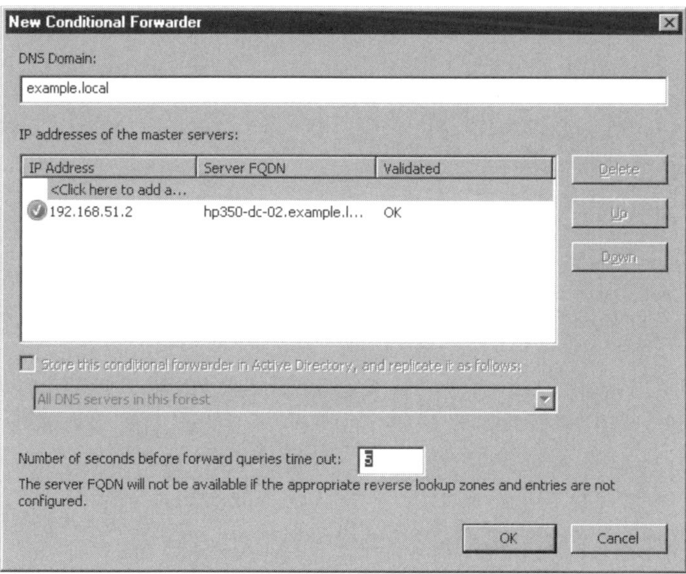

Figure 18-29 The New Conditional Forwarder dialog box

2. Type the name of the DNS domain you want to set up a conditional forwarder for in the DNS Domain field.
3. Type an IP address or DNS name into the IP Addresses Of The Master Servers field. The resolved IP address should be that of an authoritative server for the DNS domain you're setting up conditional forwarding for.
4. If this DNS server is an Active Directory server, you can choose to store any conditional forwarders in Active Directory, and have them replicated to other DNS servers. You have the following choices:
    - **All DNS Servers In This Forest** Will replicate to all other Active Directory–integrated DNS servers in the forest that are Windows Server 2003 or later.

- **All DNS Servers In This Domain** Will replicate to all other Active Directory–integrated DNS servers in the current domain that are Windows Server 2003 or later.
- **All DNS Servers In This Domain (For Windows 2000 Compatibility)** Will replicate to all DNS Servers in the domain and supports Windows 2000 DNS servers as well.

5. Click OK to close the dialog box and implement the changes.

Setting Up a WINS Server

The Windows Internet Naming Service (WINS) used to be an essential part of any large network. And those of us who've had to administer and manage it over the years keep hoping that the *next* version of Windows will make WINS go away. Sadly, it's still around, and some applications still require it or some other form of NetBIOS to IP address name resolution. WINS provides the functional equivalent of a DNS server, except that it is for the NetBIOS namespace. WINS servers resolve NetBIOS names into IP addresses by using the WINS dynamic database to call up the appropriate name records. If all your systems are Windows 2000 or later, they can function without WINS, although you may still have server applications that require it.

If your network currently uses WINS, the chances are you should keep it in place and functioning. If you're creating a new network, you might be able to get away without WINS, but be prepared to add the feature if something you're running requires it. One example we know of that still requires WINS is Microsoft Exchange 2003. In larger Exchange environments, or those with clustered Exchange 2003 servers, WINS is required, according to Microsoft Knowledge base Article 837391 (*http://support.microsoft.com/kb/837391*). As far as we've been able to determine, Microsoft Exchange 2007 does not require WINS.

If you need to add a WINS server, use the Add Feature functionality of Server Manager, as described in Chapter 8, "Installing Server Roles and Features." And Server Core computers can also be WINS servers, should that be required. But we actually hope and expect that WINS is finally, slowly, going away.

For more than you ever really wanted to know about WINS, start with the Help And Support Center on Windows Server 2008, or see the WINS Technical Reference on the Microsoft TechNet site at: *http://technet2.microsoft.com/WindowsServer/en/library/01b8e158-4587-4269-917a-5ad38c2537021033.mspx?mfr=true*.

Summary

DHCP and DNS are essential on any modern network, and Windows Server 2008 includes both a DHCP Server Role and a DNS Server Role. The biggest change in these two servers is full, native support for IPv6. WINS continues to be available as an installable feature on Windows Server 2008, but is finally no longer essential on many networks.

In the next chapter we move from essential networking to essential storage as we cover implementing and configuring disk management for Windows Server 2008.

Chapter 19

Implementing Disk Management

Servers are used for many functions and have many reasons for existence, but the single most pervasive function of most servers is storage. And you can't store anything if you don't have something to store it on. For servers, that something is primarily hard disks. Rather than cover all topics related to storage in a single chapter, we've split it up a bit. Both for reasons of length (our editors have this irrational fear of 100+ pages chapters) and also to group topics together rationally.

In this chapter, we'll start by defining some terms that we'll use throughout our discussions of storage. Once we've got that basic ground covered, we'll move on to the physical aspects of storage—the disk subsystem and how you manage and administer it. This includes disks, partitions, and volumes, along with logical drives. And we'll cover special features of the NTFS file system, including encryption and quotas. Throughout this chapter, we'll cover both the graphical way to do things and the command-line way.

In Chapter 20, "Managing Storage," we'll shift gears and talk about storage from a logical perspective, with full coverage of the Storage Resource Manager, and we'll also cover Storage Area Networks (SANs)—a way to centralize and abstract storage for a group of servers.

The hard disk management functions of Windows Server 2008 build on earlier versions of Windows Server to make hard disk management flexible and easy for administrators while hiding the complexities from end users. One important—and long overdue—new feature is the ability to grow or shrink partitions dynamically without losing data.

Understanding Disk Terminology

Before going into the details of managing disks and storage, let's review some definitions:

- **Physical drive** The actual hard disk itself, including the case, electronics, platters, and all that stuff. This is not terribly important to the disk administrator.
- **Partition** A portion of the hard disk. In many cases, this is the entire hard disk space, but it needn't be.
- **Allocation unit** The smallest unit of managed disk space on a hard disk or logical volume. It's also called a *cluster*.
- **Primary partition** A portion of the hard disk that's been marked as a potentially bootable logical drive by an operating system. MS-DOS can support only a single primary partition, but Windows Server 2008 can support multiple ones. There can be only four primary partitions on any hard disk.
- **Extended partition** A nonbootable portion of the hard disk that can be subdivided into logical drives. There can be only a single extended partition per hard disk, but it can be divided into multiple logical drives.
- **Extended volume** Similar to, and sometimes synonymous with, a spanned volume. This is any dynamic volume that has been extended to make it larger than its original size. When an extended volume uses portions of more than one physical disk, it is more properly referred to as a *spanned volume*.
- **Logical drive** A section or partition of a hard disk that acts as a single unit. An extended partition can be divided, for example, into multiple logical drives.
- **Logical volume** Another name for a logical drive.
- **Basic disk** A traditional disk drive that is divided into one or more partitions, with a logical drive in the primary partition, if present, and one or more logical drives in any extended partitions. Basic disks do not support the more advanced functions of Disk Management, but they can be converted to dynamic disks in many cases.
- **Dynamic disk** A managed hard disk that can be used to create various volumes.
- **Volume** A unit of disk space composed of one or more sections of one or more disks. Prior versions of Windows Server used volume only when referring to dynamic disks, but Windows Server 2008 uses it to mean partitions as well.
- **Simple volume** Used interchangeably with partition in Windows Server 2008, earlier versions of Windows used simple volume only when referring to a dynamic disk. A portion of a single disk, a simple volume can be assigned either a single drive letter or no drive letter and can be attached (mounted) on zero or more mount points.

- **RAID (redundant array of independent [formerly "inexpensive"] disks)** The use of multiple hard disks in an array to provide for larger volume size, fault tolerance, and increased performance. RAID comes in different levels, such as RAID-0, RAID-1, RAID-5, and so forth. Higher numbers don't necessarily indicate greater performance or fault tolerance, just different methods of doing the job.
- **Spanned volume** A collection of portions of hard disks combined into a single addressable unit. A spanned volume is formatted like a single drive and can have a drive letter assigned to it, but it will span multiple physical drives. A spanned volume–occasionally referred to as an *extended volume*–provides no fault tolerance and increases your exposure to failure, but does permit you to make more efficient use of the available hard disk space.
- **Striped volume** Like a spanned volume, a striped volume combines multiple hard disk portions into a single entity. A striped volume uses special formatting to write to each of the portions equally in a stripe to increase performance. A striped volume provides no fault tolerance and actually increases your exposure to failure, but it is faster than either a spanned volume or a single drive. A stripe set is often referred to as *RAID-0*, although this is a misnomer because plain striping includes no redundancy.
- **Mirror volume** A pair of dynamic volumes that contain identical data and appear to the world as a single entity. Disk mirroring can use two drives on the same hard disk controller or use separate controllers, in which case it is sometimes referred to as *duplexing*. In case of failure on the part of either drive, the other hard disk can be split off so that it continues to provide complete access to the data stored on the drive, providing a high degree of fault tolerance. This technique is called *RAID-1*.
- **RAID-5 volume** Like a striped volume, a RAID-5 volume combines portions of multiple hard disks into a single entity with data written across all portions equally. However, it also writes parity information for each stripe onto a different portion, providing the ability to recover in the case of a single drive failure. A RAID-5 volume provides excellent throughput for read operations, but it is substantially slower than all other available options for write operations.
- **SLED (single large expensive disk)** Now rarely used, this strategy is the opposite of the RAID strategy. Rather than using several inexpensive hard disks and providing fault tolerance through redundancy, you buy the best hard disk you can and bet your entire network on it. If this doesn't sound like a good idea to you, you're right. It's not.
- **JBOD** Just a bunch of disks. The hardware equivalent of a spanned volume, this has all the failings of any spanning scheme. The failure of any one disk will result in catastrophic data failure.

More Info Additional RAID levels are supported by many hardware manufacturers of RAID controllers. These include RAID 0+1, RAID 10, RAID 6, and RAID 50. For more details on various RAID levels, see the manufacturer of your RAID controller or *http://en.wikipedia.org/wiki/RAID#Standard_RAID_levels*.

Real World Disk Technologies for the Server

The first time we wrote a chapter about disk management, basically three possible technologies were available: Modified Field Modification (MFM), Pulse Frequency Modulation (PFM), and Small Computer System (or Serial) Interface (SCSI). Unless you were a total geek (and had oodles of money), your systems used either MFM or PFM, and RAID wasn't even an option. Over time, SCSI became the only real choice for the vast majority of servers and even became mainstream on high-end workstations. Servers at the high end might use fiber, but SCSI had the vast majority of the server disk market. SCSI has changed over the years to support faster speeds, more disks, and greater ease of configuration and use, but is finally reaching its limits as a parallel interface.

Integrated Device Electronics (IDE), later called Advanced Technology Attachment (ATA), became the standard on the personal computer. However, IDE never made a serious inroad into the server market because, while fast for single tasks, it lacked the inherent multitasking support and bus mastering that a server disk interface technology required, and no real hardware RAID solutions supported it.

Recently, the introduction of Serial ATA (SATA) technology has made serious inroads into the lower end of the server marketplace. With SATA RAID controllers built into many motherboards, and stand-alone SATA RAID boards that support 8 or more SATA drives and have substantial battery-backed RAM cache onboard, many low- to mid-range servers are finding that SATA RAID solutions provide a cost-effective alternative to SCSI. While most SATA RAID controllers lack the ability to hot-swap a failed drive, and don't have the performance potential of SCSI or Serially Attached SCSI (SAS), they are still quite attractive alternatives where cost is a primary factor. SATA also makes sense as secondary or "near-line" storage for a server.

The new kid on the block, however, is SAS. This is the most interesting addition to the server storage equation in quite a while. Using the same thin cables and connectors as SATA, with none of the configuration nuisance of traditional SCSI, SAS is definitely the way to go. When combined with new 2.5-inch drives, the ability to put a really large amount of very fast storage in a small space has taken a significant step forward. SAS drives interoperate with SATA drives to combine the two technologies on the same controller. SAS disk controllers can control SATA drives as well, though the reverse is not true.

With the main bottleneck for servers continuing to be I/O in general, and especially disk I/O, there will continue to be pressure to find new and faster methods to access disk-based storage. SAS, combined with 2.5-inch drives, enables fast and flexible storage arrays in remarkably smaller spaces. Because 64-bit servers are the only real option, and because of the enormous datasets supported on 64-bit Windows Server 2008, the need for fast and easily expandable disk storage keeps increasing. Windows virtualization technology and the move to greater virtualization in the data center also drive the need for faster disk and I/O subsystems.

Overview of Disk Management

While solid state and hybrid disks are starting to find their way into laptops and even some desktops, conventional hard disk storage continues to be the long-term storage method of choice for modern computers, from the mainframe to the desktop. In Windows Server 2008, you must first initialize this conventional hard disk storage and organize it into volumes, drives, and partitions before you can use it.

Under the Hood RAID

RAID (redundant array of independent disks) is a term used to describe a technique that has gone from an esoteric high-end solution to a normal procedure on most servers. Fifteen years ago, RAID was mostly unheard of, although the original paper defining RAID was written in 1988. In the past, most server systems relied on expensive, higher-quality hard disks—backed up frequently. Backups are still crucial, but now you can use one form or another of RAID to provide substantial protection from hard disk failure. Moreover, this protection costs much less than those big server drives did.

You can implement RAID at a software or hardware level. When implemented at the hardware level, the hardware vendor provides an interface to administer the arrays and the drivers to support the various operating systems it might need to work with. Processing for the RAID array is handled by a separate processor built into the RAID controller, offloading the work from the computer's CPU. Additionally, many hardware RAID controllers include a substantial dedicated RAM cache, often with a battery backup. The combination of a separate, dedicated processor and a separate, dedicated cache provides a substantial performance advantage over software RAID. Additionally, most server-class hardware RAID controllers offer additional RAID levels when compared to software RAID, providing redundancy advantages such as multiple disk failure protection. Hardware RAID is generally substantially more expensive than the software RAID built into Windows Server 2008, though many manufacturers today include basic hardware RAID capabilities on the motherboard.

Windows Server 2008 includes an excellent and flexible implementation of RAID levels 0, 1, and 5 in software. It doesn't cover all the possibilities by any means, but it is certainly sufficient for some purposes. However, most serious servers should be using hardware RAID.

The primary GUI for managing disks in Windows Server 2008 is the Disk Management console, Diskmgmt.msc, shown in Figure 19-1, which can be run stand-alone or as part of Server Manager. The primary command-line tool for managing disks is DiskPart.exe.

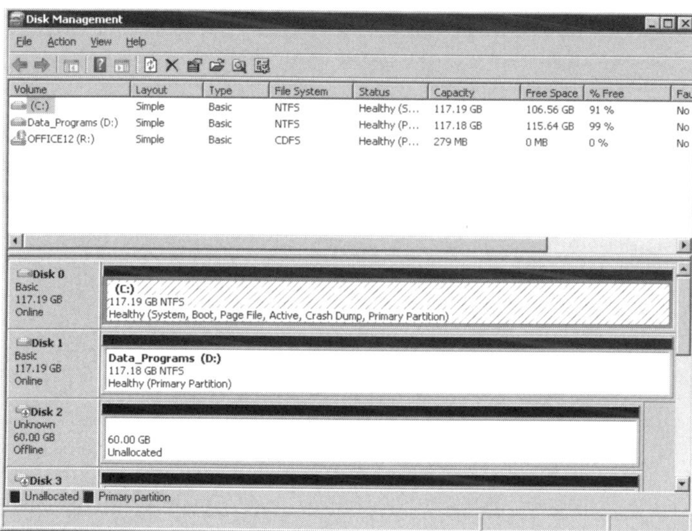

Figure 19-1 The Disk Management console

To open Disk Management, you can start it stand-alone by running Diskmgmt.msc from a command line, or by typing it into the Run dialog box on the Start menu. Disk Management is also part of the Server Manager console, in the Storage section, as shown in Figure 19-2.

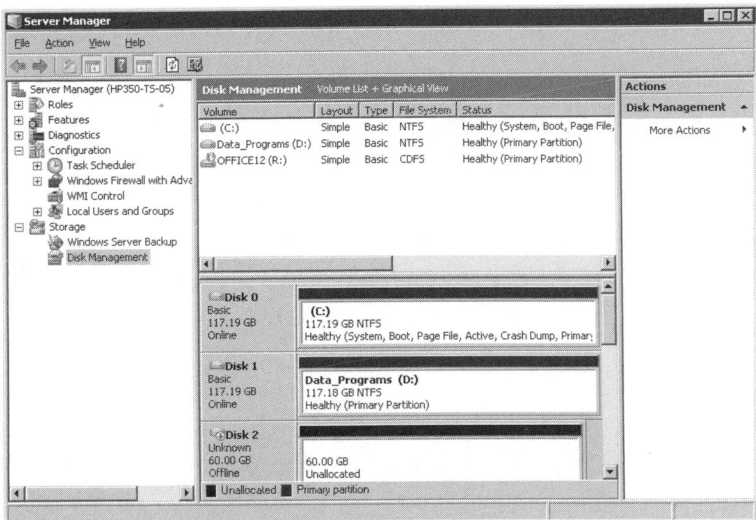

Figure 19-2 The Server Manager console

Real World Hardware RAID

Although Disk Management provides an adequate software RAID solution, hardware RAID is widely available, from either the original server vendor or from third parties, and it provides substantial advantages over software RAID. Hardware RAID solutions range from a simple, motherboard-integrated RAID controller to fully integrated, stand-alone subsystems. Features and cost vary, but all claim to provide superior performance and reliability over a simple software RAID solution such as that included in Windows Server 2008. In general, they do, with the notable exception of some basic motherboard-integrated solutions offered on consumer-level motherboards for SATA drives. Even if circumstances force you to use what is an essentially desktop system, avoid using the built-in RAID on the motherboard, except as a simple SATA controller. Acceptable, uncached, stand-alone RAID controllers are reasonably priced and will provide far better performance and reliability. If your budget is so limited that even that is too much, use Windows Server 2008's built-in software RAID.

Some advantages that a good hardware RAID controller offers can include the following:

- Hot-swap and hot-spare drives, allowing for virtually instantaneous replacement of failed drives
- Integrated disk caching for improved disk performance

- A separate, dedicated system that handles all processing, for improved overall performance
- Increased flexibility and additional RAID levels, such as RAID 1+0 or RAID 0+1, combinations of striping (RAID-0) and mirroring (RAID-1) that provide for fast read and write disk access with full redundancy

Not all stand-alone hardware RAID systems provide all these features, but all have the potential to improve the overall reliability and performance of your hard disk subsystem. They belong on any server that isn't completely fungible.

Remote Management

The Disk Management console in Windows Server 2008 lets you manage not only the local hard disks but also drives on other computers running any version of Windows 2000, Windows XP, Windows Server 2003, Windows Vista, or Windows Server 2008, allowing an administrator to manage disk tasks and space allocations from a workstation without having to sit at the computer that is being administered. This capability is a boon for remote site management and also simplifies management of Windows Server 2008 Core.

For details on how to create custom management consoles that connect to remote computers, see Chapter 14, "Managing Daily Operations."

Dynamic Disks

Dynamic disks were introduced in Windows 2000 Server. By converting a disk to a dynamic disk, you give Disk Management the ability to manage it in new ways, *without requiring a reboot* in most cases. You can extend a disk volume, span a volume across multiple physical disks, stripe the volume for improved performance, mirror it, or add it to a RAID-5 array—all from the Disk Management console and all without a reboot, after the disk is converted to a dynamic disk. When combined with the new remote management functionality, dynamic disks give the system administrator powerful tools for managing the type and configuration of hard disk storage across the enterprise.

Real World Dynamic versus Basic Disks

We used to be big fans of dynamic disks. They provided increased flexibility and functionality in a way that was pretty transparent. And they were a huge step forward when they were introduced in Windows 2000. At the time, RAID controllers were both more expensive and less functional, and many servers didn't have hardware RAID on them. That's simply not the case anymore.

If using dynamic disks increases your options, isn't that a good thing? Well, yes. But. And it's a big but. A dynamic disk complicates the disaster recovery process, and we dislike anything that creates potential issues in a disaster recovery scenario. We definitely don't think dynamic disks are appropriate for a system disk. And we just have a hard time seeing where the upside is given the functionality that your RAID controller or SAN array management application provides.

If you do find a need that can't be solved any other way, then by all means use dynamic disks. There's no apparent performance cost, and you use the same tools to manage both dynamic disks in Windows Server 2008 and basic disks. But avoid converting your system disk to dynamic. And make sure your disaster recovery procedures are updated appropriately.

Command Line

Windows Server 2008 includes a full command-line interface for disks. The primary command-line tool is DiskPart.exe. This command line utility is scriptable or it can be used interactively. Additional functionality is available using Fsutil.exe and Mountvol.exe. As we go through the steps to manage disks in this chapter, we'll provide the equivalent command lines and a few basic scripts that you can use as the starting point for building your own command-line tools.

The one task that doesn't appear to have a command-line solution is initializing a new disk. As far as we've been able to tell, you need to use Disk Management to initialize new disks before they can be used.

Adding a New Disk

Adding a new disk to a Windows Server 2008 server is straightforward. First, obviously, you need to physically install and connect the drive. If you have a hot-swappable backplane and array, you don't even have to shut the system down to accomplish this task. If you're using conventional drives, however, you need to shut down and power off the system.

After you install the drive and power up the system again, Windows Server 2008 automatically recognizes the new hardware and makes it available. If the disk is a basic disk that is already partitioned and formatted, you can use it without initializing, but it will initially appear "offline" in Disk Management. If it's a brand-new disk that has never been partitioned or formatted, you need to initialize it first. And if it's a dynamic disk or disks, but from another computer, you need to import it before it's available. If the disk has never been used before, you're prompted by the Initialize And Convert Disk Wizard.

Note If you're adding a drive to your server that uses a different technology than existing drives, or simply a different controller, it might require a new driver before the system recognizes the disk.

Setting a Disk Online

To set an offline disk to online, follow these steps:

1. Open Disk Management.
2. Right-click the disk you want to bring online, and select Online from the Action menu, as shown in Figure 9-3.

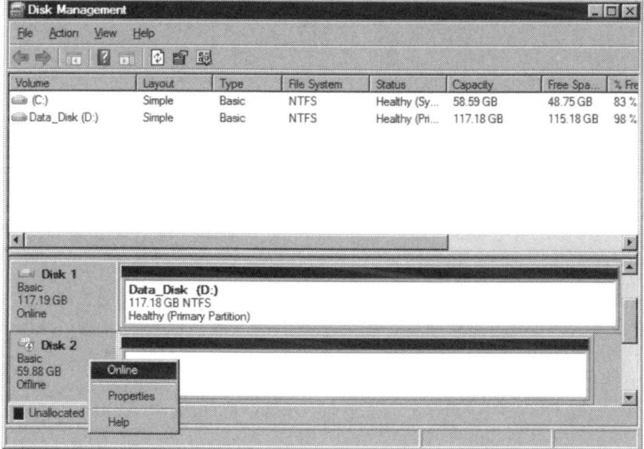

Figure 19-3 Bringing a disk online using Disk Management

The command-line equivalent is shown in Figure 19-4.

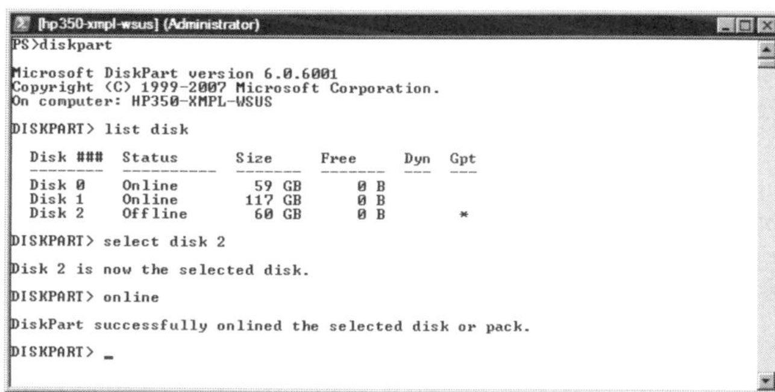

Figure 19-4 Bringing a disk online using the command line

Initializing a New Disk

When you install a brand-new disk that has never been formatted or used by Windows, you need to initialize it. It might initially be shown as offline. If so, you need to first set the disk online, and then initialize it. If the new disk is online, the Initialize Disk dialog box will automatically display when you start Disk Management, as shown in Figure 19-5.

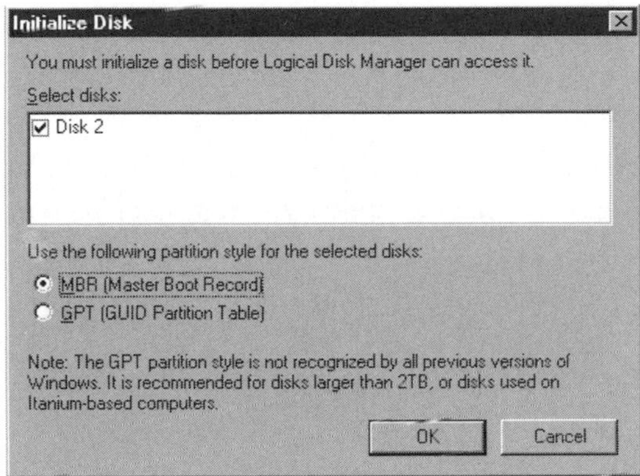

Figure 19-5 The Initialize Disk dialog box

When you initialize the disk, you can choose whether to use Master Boot Record (MBR) or GUID Partition Table (GPT) as the partition style. For any disk larger than 2TB, GPT is recommended. We're still using MBR for all our disks, except for the one huge SAN volume we have, but we're leaning toward changing that for all new disks.

Partitions and Volumes

In Windows Server 2008 the distinction between volumes and partitions is somewhat murky. When using Disk Management, a regular partition on a basic disk is called a *simple volume*, even though technically a simple volume requires that the disk be a dynamic disk.

As long as you use only simple volumes or partitions, you can easily convert between a basic disk (and partition) and a dynamic disk (and a volume). Once you use a feature that is supported only on dynamic disks, however, changing back to a basic disk will mean data loss. Any operation that would require conversion to a dynamic disk will give you fair warning, as shown in Figure 19-6.

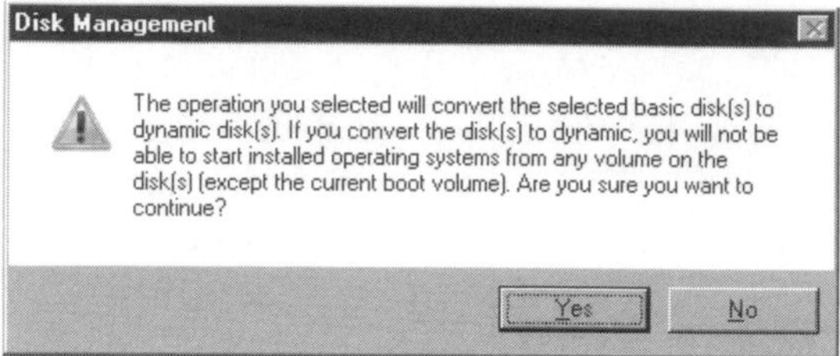

Figure 19-6 Disk Management will warn you before any operation that would cause a conversion to dynamic disks.

When using Disk Management, the conversion to dynamic disks as required happens automatically. When using DiskPart, however, you need to explicitly specify each step of the process.

Creating a Volume or Partition

You can create a new volume or partition on any disk that has empty space. If the disk is dynamic, a volume is created. If the disk is a basic disk, a primary partition is created. If the empty space is part of an extended partition, a new logical drive will be created. All of them called a simple volume, but each one a different structure.

> **Note** You can no longer create an extended partition in Disk Manager. If you need to create an extended partition, you need to use DiskPart.exe. But there's really no longer any need for extended partitions.

To create a new volume or partition, follow these steps:

1. In Disk Management, right-click the unallocated disk and select the type of volume to create, as shown in Figure 19-7. Click Next.

Figure 19-7 Creating a volume

Depending on the number of available unallocated volumes, you see one or more options for the type of volume, including the following:

- New Simple Volume
- New Spanned Volume
- New Striped Volume

- ❑ New Mirrored Volume
- ❑ New RAID-5 Volume

2. Select the type you want to create. The New Volume Wizard for that specific type of volume will open. Figure 19-8 shows the New RAID-5 Volume Wizard.

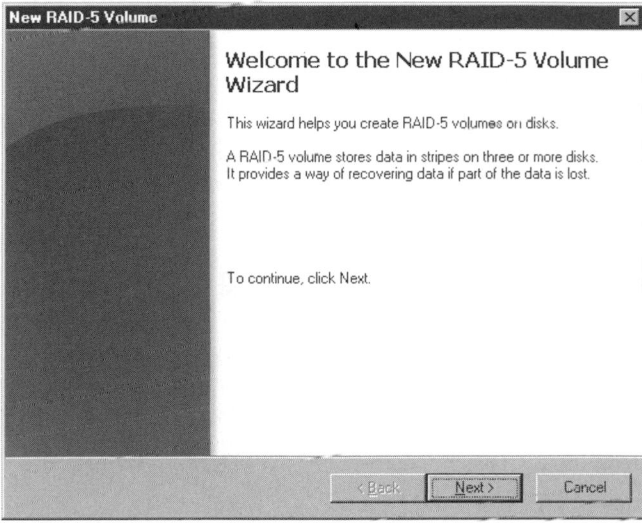

Figure 19-8 The New RAID-5 Volume Wizard

3. Select the disks to use for the new volume. The choices available and the selections you need to make depend on the type of volume you're creating and the number of available unallocated disks. Figure 19-9 shows a RAID-5 volume being created.

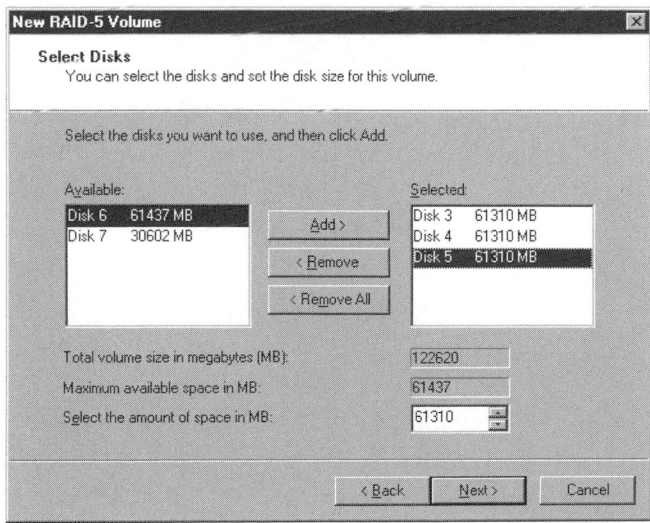

Figure 19-9 Select the disks that will be part of this volume.

4. On the same page, adjust the size of the new volume. By default, the new volume will use the maximum available space from each of the selected disks. For spanned volumes, this will be the sum of the free space on the selected disks; for other types of volumes, it will be the number of disks multiplied by the available space on the smallest of the selected disks. Click Next.
5. Select either a drive letter or a mount point for the new volume, as shown in Figure 19-10, or opt not to assign a drive letter or path at this time. With Windows Server 2008, you can "mount" a volume on an empty subdirectory, minimizing the number of drive letters and reducing the complexity of the storage that is displayed to the user. If you want to take advantage of this feature, click Browse to locate the directory where you will mount the new volume. Click Next. (See the Real World sidebar "Mounted Volumes" for more about this subject.)

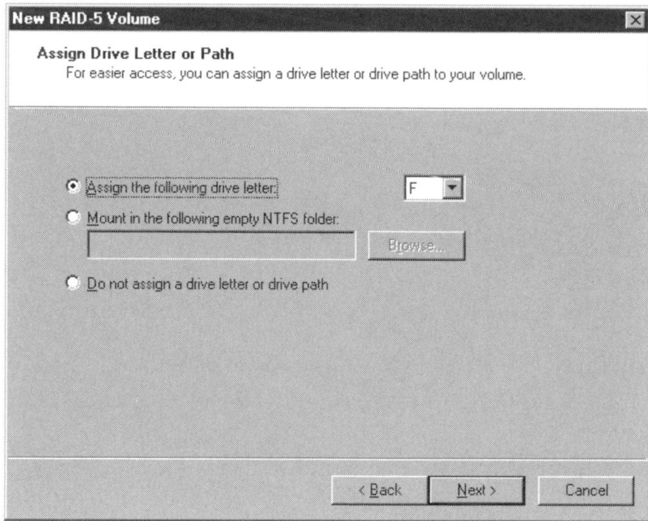

Figure 19-10 Select a drive letter or mount point for the new volume.

6. Select the formatting options you want (shown in Figure 19-11). Even when mounting the volume rather than creating a new drive, you can choose your format type without regard to the underlying format of the mount point. Click Next.

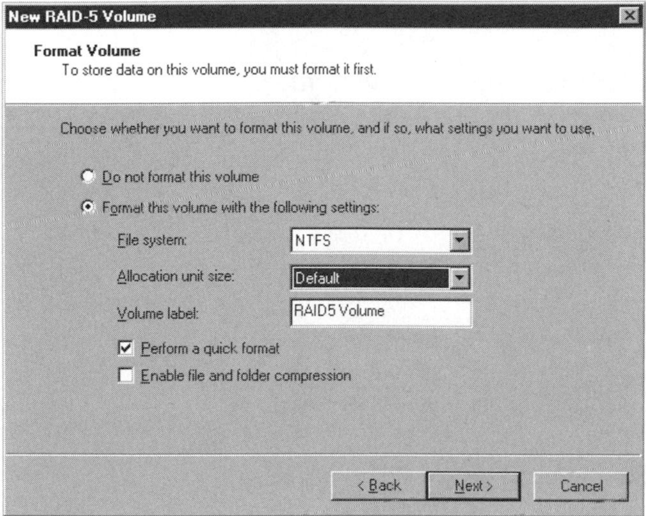

Figure 19-11 Set the formatting options for the new volume.

7. On the confirmation page, if all the options are correct, click Finish to create and format the volume. If the type you've selected requires that the disks be converted to dynamic disks, you'll see a confirmation message from Disk Management, as shown in Figure 19-12.

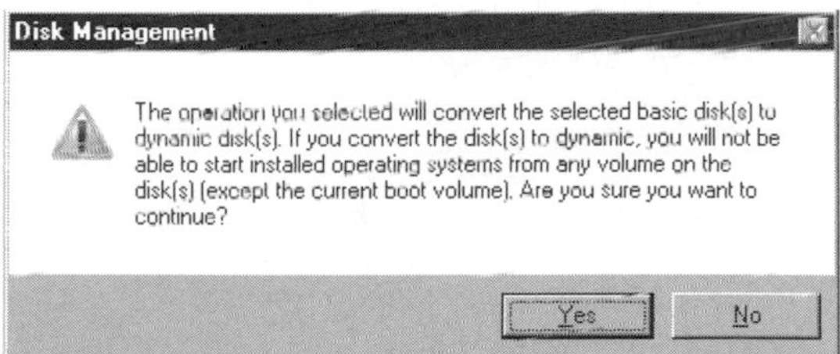

Figure 19-12 Before converting disks to dynamic, you must confirm the change.

8. Once the volume is created, it's displayed in Disk Management, as shown in Figure 19-13.

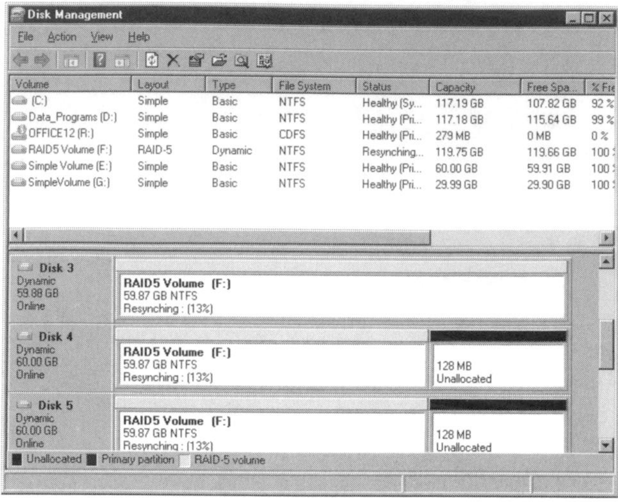

Figure 19-13 The new RAID-5 volume being created

You could use the following script to perform the same RAID-5 volume creation using DiskPart.exe:

```
REM Filename: RAID5Vol.txt
REM
REM This is a DiskPart.exe Script. Run from the command line
REM or from another script, using the syntax:
REM
REM    diskpart /s RAID5Vol.txt > logfile.log
REM
REM to run this script and dump the results out to a log file.
REM
REM This script creates a RAID5 Volume combining disks 3,4 and 5,
REM and then formats it and assigns the next available drive letter to it.

REM First, list out our disks. Not required for scripting, but useful
REM to show the overall environment if we need to troubleshoot problems
list disk

REM Create the volume (No SIZE parameter, so the maximum size for the
REM selected disks will be used.)
create volume RAID disk=3,4,5

REM Format the new volume.
Format fs=NTFS label="RAID 5 Volume" quick

REM Assign without parameters will choose the next available HD letter.
Assign
```

Real World Mounted Volumes

Windows Server 2008 borrows a concept from the UNIX world by adding the ability to mount a volume or partition on a subfolder of an existing drive letter. A mounted volume can also have a drive letter associated with it—although it does not need to—and it can be mounted at more than one point, giving multiple entry points into the same storage.

A volume must be mounted on an empty subfolder of an existing NTFS volume or drive. FAT and FAT32 drives do not support mounted volumes. You can, however, mount a FAT or FAT32 volume at any mount point. (But really, it's time to let go of FAT as a file system for hard disks!) You can mount only a single volume at a given mount point, but you can then mount further volumes on top of an existing mounted volume, with the same rules and restrictions as any other mount. The properties of a drive do not show all the available disk space for that drive, because they do not reflect any volumes mounted on the drive.

You can use mounted volumes to provide a mix of redundant and nonredundant storage in a logical structure that meets the business needs of the enterprise while hiding the complexities of the physical structure from the users. Unfortunately, mounted volumes are not handled correctly by Network File System (NFS) shares and should be avoided in environments where Server for NFS is used.

Creating Extended Partitions and Logical Drives

If you have extended partitions on your disks for some reason, you can create logical drives on the partition using DiskPart.exe. However, you no longer have a graphical way to create an extended partition or a logical drive, nor any real need to do so. With Windows Server 2008 providing full support for GPT disks, the old limit of a maximum of four partitions on a disk is gone—GPT disks in Windows Server 2008 support 128 partitions. If you have any existing MBR disks that include an extended partition, either because you moved a disk from another computer to your Windows Server 2008 computer or because you upgraded to Windows Server 2008 from an earlier version, we suggest you remove the existing extended partition and convert the disk to GPT.

Converting a Disk to a Dynamic Disk

Unlike earlier versions of Windows Server, with Windows Server 2008 you generally have no need to directly convert a disk to a dynamic disk. Operations that require conversion to a dynamic disk will perform the conversion as part of the operation. And deleting a volume that required dynamic disks causes the disks to convert back to basic disks in most cases. There are a few cases where the automatic conversion doesn't happen if you're using DiskPart.exe to manipulate the disk, but all the operations you perform in Disk Management do automatic conversions. For those few situations in DiskPart where explicit conversion is necessary, use the following commands:

```
DISKPART> select disk <n>
DISKPART> convert BASIC
```

Where <*n*> is the disk number you want to convert, and where BASIC can be replaced by DYNAMIC depending on which conversion you need to do.

Conversions can only occur when there are no structures on the disk that are not supported in the target disk type.

Converting a Disk to a GPT Disk

One of the important new features of Windows Server 2008 disk management is full support for GPT disks. GPT disk support was initially only available in 64-bit Itanium versions of Windows Server, but with the release of Windows Server 2003 Service Pack 1 and the initial version of x64 Windows Server 2003, GPT support was added for all versions of Windows Server 2003. In Windows Server 2008, this support is fully integrated.

You can convert a disk between MBR and GPT as long as the disk is completely empty. Unfortunately, once you've created any partitions or volumes on the disk, you can no longer convert between the two types.

To convert a disk to GPT, follow these steps:

1. In Disk Management, delete any existing volumes or partitions.

   Note Deleting a volume or partition will delete any data on the volume or partition. It will not destroy the data, however, so that it might be possible to recover the data.

2. Right-click the empty disk and select Convert To GPT Disk, as shown in Figure 19-14.

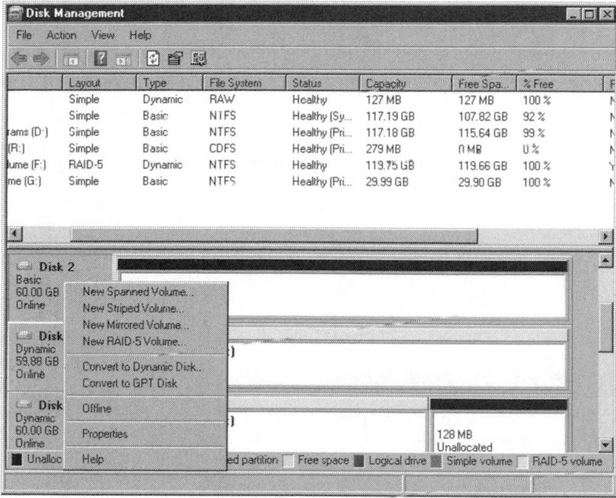

Figure 19-14 Converting from an MBR disk to a GPT disk

3. To do the same operation from DiskPart, type the following command:

```
DISKPART> select disk <n>
DISKPART> convert GPT
```

Where <*n*> is the disk to be converted. That's all there is to it.

Changing the Size of a Volume

Windows Server 2008 allows you to change the size of an existing volume without losing data. You can extend the volume, either by using additional free space on the existing disk, or by spanning onto another disk that has free space. This capability is essentially unchanged from earlier versions of Windows Server. New to Windows Server 2008, however, is the ability to shrink a volume without having to use a third-party product or lose data.

When you extend or shrink a volume, only a simple volume or a spanned volume can be modified: You cannot extend or shrink striped, mirrored, or RAID-5 volumes without deleting the volume and recreating it.

Important Once you extend a volume across multiple disks, you normally cannot shrink it back down onto a single disk without deleting the volume entirely and recreating it. This means you *will* lose data, so consider carefully before you decide to extend a volume across multiple disks.

Extending a Volume

You can add space to a volume without having to back up, reboot, and restore your files if the volume is a simple volume or a spanned volume. To extend a volume, follow these steps:

1. In Disk Management, right-click the volume you want to extend. Choose Extend Volume from the menu to open the Extend Volume Wizard. Click Next.
2. Highlight one or more disks from the list of disks that are available and have unallocated space, as shown in Figure 19-15. Click Add to add the selected disk or disks, and indicate the amount of space you want to add. Click Next.

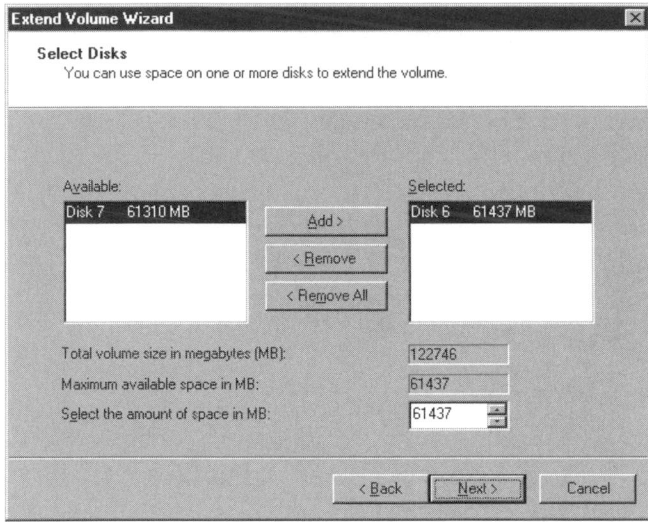

Figure 19-15 Selecting the disks to use to extend the volume

3. The Extend Volume Wizard displays a final confirmation page before extending the volume. Click Finish to extend the volume, or click Cancel if you change your mind. If you need to convert any of the disks to dynamic before extending, you'll get another confirmation prompt.
4. To perform the same steps from the DiskPart command line, use the commands shown in Figure 19-16.

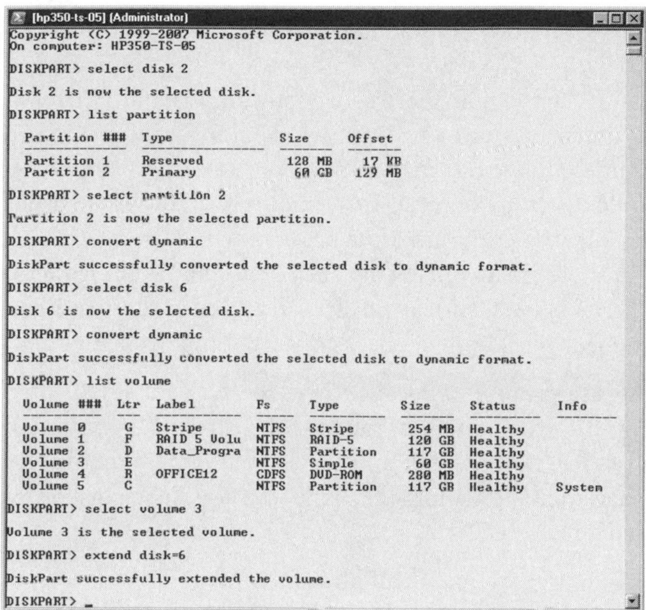

[hp350-ts-05] (Administrator)
Copyright (C) 1999-2007 Microsoft Corporation.
On computer: HP350-TS-05
DISKPART> select disk 2
Disk 2 is now the selected disk.
DISKPART> list partition
Partition ### Type Size Offset
Partition 1 Reserved 128 MB 17 KB
Partition 2 Primary 60 GB 129 MB
DISKPART> select partition 2
Partition 2 is now the selected partition.
DISKPART> convert dynamic
DiskPart successfully converted the selected disk to dynamic format.
DISKPART> select disk 6
Disk 6 is now the selected disk.
DISKPART> convert dynamic
DiskPart successfully converted the selected disk to dynamic format.
DISKPART> list volume
Volume ### Ltr Label Fs Type Size Status Info
Volume 0 G Stripe NTFS Stripe 254 MB Healthy
Volume 1 F RAID 5 Volu NTFS RAID-5 120 GB Healthy
Volume 2 D Data_Progra NTFS Partition 117 GB Healthy
Volume 3 E NTFS Simple 60 GB Healthy
Volume 4 R OFFICE12 CDFS DVD-ROM 280 MB Healthy
Volume 5 C NTFS Partition 117 GB Healthy System
DISKPART> select volume 3
Volume 3 is the selected volume.
DISKPART> extend disk=6
DiskPart successfully extended the volume.
DISKPART> _

Figure 19-16 Extending a disk using the DiskPart command-line tool

As you can see from the figure, using the command line to extend a volume is quite a few more steps than using Disk Management. Given that we hardly ever extend a volume (see the RealWorld sidebar), it's probably just as well to use Disk Management for this particular task. We're firm believers in using the command line whenever possible, but sometimes it just doesn't make sense.

Note A spanned (extended) volume is actually less reliable than a simple disk. Unlike a mirror or RAID-5 volume, which both have built-in redundancy, a spanned or striped volume will be broken and all data lost if any disk in the volume fails.

Real World Extending—Administrator's Friend or Foe?

Most administrators have wished at some point that they could simply increase the users' home directory space on the fly. Without having to bring the system offline for several hours while the entire volume is backed up and reformatted to add the additional hard disks, the backup is restored, and the share points are re-created. Fun? Hardly. Risky? Certainly. And definitely a job that means coming in on the weekend or staying late at night–in other words, something to be avoided if at all possible.

All this makes Windows Server 2008's ability to create additional space on a volume without the need to back up the volume, reformat the disks, and re-create the volume a seductive feature. However, if you're using conventional hard disks without hardware RAID, you might want to think twice before jumping in. Only spanned or striped volumes allow you to add additional storage on the fly, and, because neither is redundant, using them exposes your users to the risks of a failed drive. Yes, you have a backup, but even under the best of circumstances, you'll lose some data if you need to restore a backup. Further, using spanned volumes actually increases your risk of a hard-disk failure. If any disk used as part of the spanned volume fails, the entire volume is toast and will need to be restored from backup.

Why, then, would anyone use spanning? Because they have hardware RAID to provide the redundancy. This combination offers the best of both worlds–redundancy provided by the hardware RAID controller and flexibility to expand volumes as needed, using Disk Management. Yet another compelling argument for hardware RAID, in case you needed any more.

Shrinking a Volume

While most of the time we're concerned with increasing the size of a volume on the server, there can be occasions when it might be convenient to shrink a volume. For example, if you are using a single large RAID array for multiple volumes, and one of the volumes has empty space while another volume on the same array is running out of space, it would be handy to be able to shrink the volume that has extra space and then extend the one that is running out of room. In the past, the only way you could do this was to back up the volume you wanted to shrink, delete it, extend the volume that needed growing, recreate the volume you deleted, and restore the backup. Possible, certainly. But both risky and highly disruptive to your users. The other alternative was to use a third-party product, such as Acronis Disk Director Server (*http://www.acronis.com/enterprise/products/diskdirector/*).

Now, in Windows Server 2008, you can use Disk Management to shrink a volume without having to delete it and recreate it. While not quite as flexible as products like Acronis Disk Director, this new capability is all that most system administrators will need. To shrink a volume, follow these steps:

1. In Disk Management, right-click the volume you want to shrink. Choose Shrink Volume from the menu to open the Shrink dialog box shown in Figure 19-17.

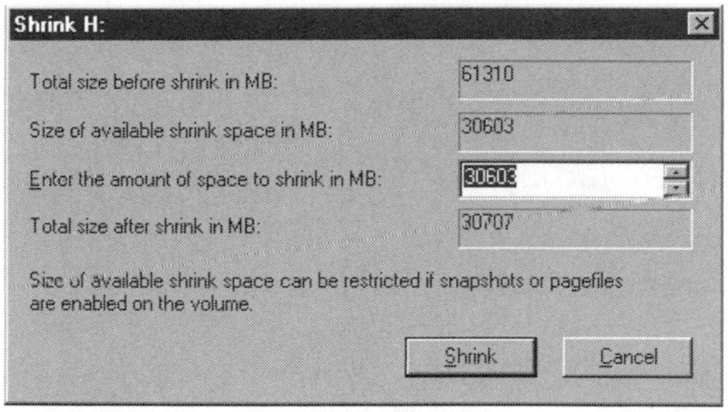

Figure 19-17 Shrinking a volume

2. Select the amount of space to shrink the volume by, and click Shrink.
3. From the command line, the syntax of the DiskPart command is:

```
SHRINK [DESIRED=<N>] [MINIMUM=<N>] [NOWAIT] [NOERR]
SHRINK QUERYMAX [NOERR]
```

   where SHRINK by itself will shrink the selected volume the maximum amount possible.

Note Shrinking a volume is one place where DiskPart is well behaved. If you select a partition on a basic disk and attempt to shrink it, DiskPart doesn't require you to first convert the disk to dynamic before you can shrink the volume.

Adding a Mirror to a Volume

When your data is mission critical and you want to make sure that no matter what happens to one of your hard disks the data is protected and always available, consider mirroring the data onto a second drive. Windows Server 2008 can mirror a dynamic disk onto a second dynamic disk so that the failure of either disk does not result in loss of data. To mirror a volume, you can either select a mirrored volume when you create the volume (as described in the "Creating a Volume or Partition" section earlier in this chapter) or add a mirror to an existing volume. To add a mirror to an existing volume, follow these steps:

1. In the Disk Management console, right-click the volume you want to mirror. If a potential mirror is available, the shortcut menu lists the Add Mirror command, as shown in Figure 19-18.

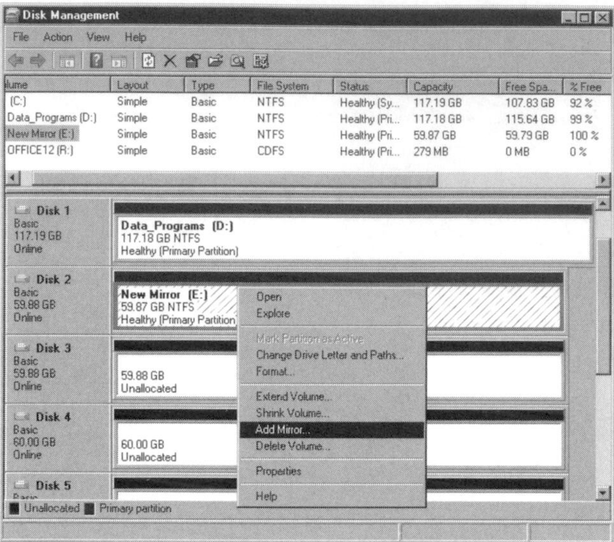

Figure 19-18 The action menu for Disk 2 includes the Add Mirror command

2. Choose Add Mirror to display the Add Mirror dialog box (shown in Figure 19-19), where you can select the disk to be used for the mirror.

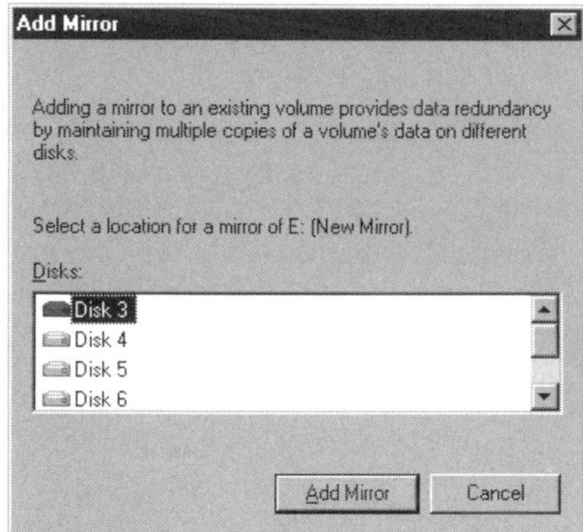

Figure 19-19 The Add Mirror dialog box

3. Highlight the disk that will be the mirror and click Add Mirror. You'll be prompted that this action will convert the disks to dynamic. Click Yes. The mirror is created immediately and starts duplicating the data from the original disk to the second half of the mirror, as shown in Figure 19-20. This process is called *regeneration* or *resynching*. (The process of regeneration is also used to distribute data across the disks when a RAID-5 volume is created.)

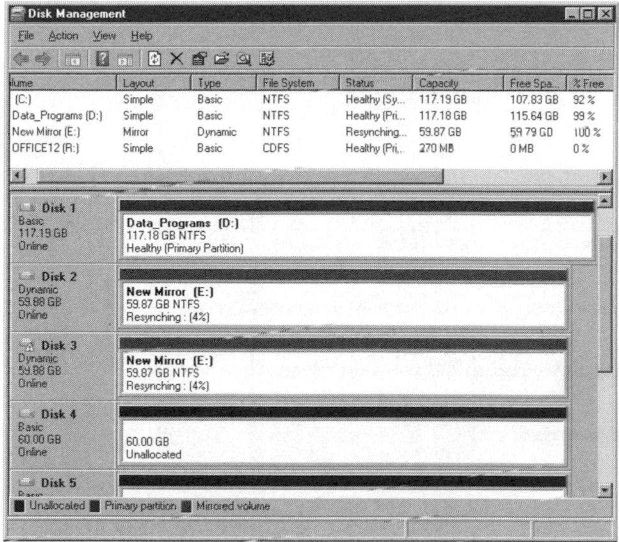

Figure 19-20 A newly created mirrored disk in the process of regeneration

4. Mirroring can also be done from the DiskPart command line. First select the disk and then use the ADD command, which has the following syntax:

```
ADD DISK=<N> [ALIGN=<N>] [WAIT] [NOERR]
```

where DISK is the disk that will be added to make the mirror, and ALIGN is used to align with a specific hardware RAID Logical Unit Number (LUN) alignment boundary.

Best Practices Regeneration is both CPU-intensive and disk-intensive. When possible, create mirrors during slack times or during normally scheduled downtime. Balance this goal, however, with the equally important goal of providing redundancy and failure protection as expeditiously as possible.

Best Practices To improve your overall data security and reliability, mirror your volumes onto disks that use separate controllers whenever possible. This process is known as *duplexing*, and it eliminates the disk controller as a single point of failure for the mirror while actually speeding up both reading and writing to the mirror, because the controller and bus are no longer potential bottlenecks.

Drive Failure in a Mirrored Volume

If one of the disks in a mirrored volume fails, you continue to have full access to all your data without loss. If a disk in the mirror set fails, the failed disk is marked missing and offline, and the mirror is unavailable, as shown in Figure 19-21. An alert is sent to the alert log.

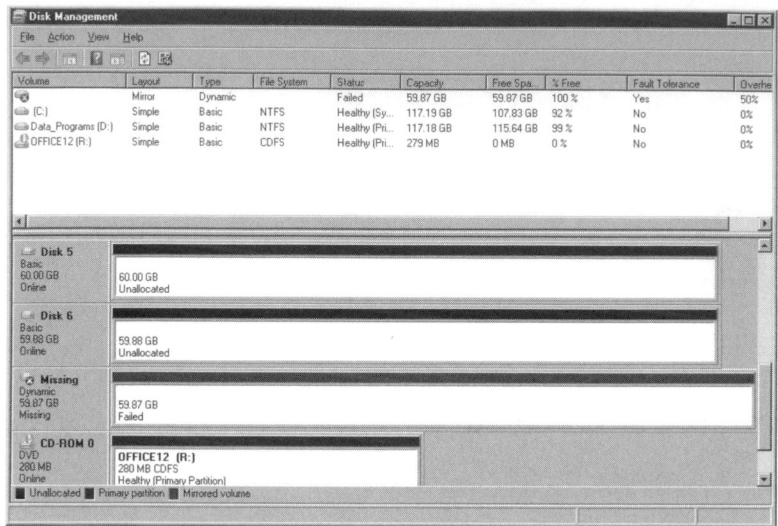

Figure 19-21 Failed disk in mirror shown as missing and offline

Once the mirror is unavailable, you need to remove, or "break," the mirror, bringing the good disk back online and available. Once the problem disk has been replaced, you can rebuild the mirror by following the steps in the section "Adding a Mirror to a Volume" earlier in the chapter.

To remove the mirror, follow these steps:

1. In Disk Management, right-click either disk and select Remove Mirror from the action menu, as shown in Figure 19-22.

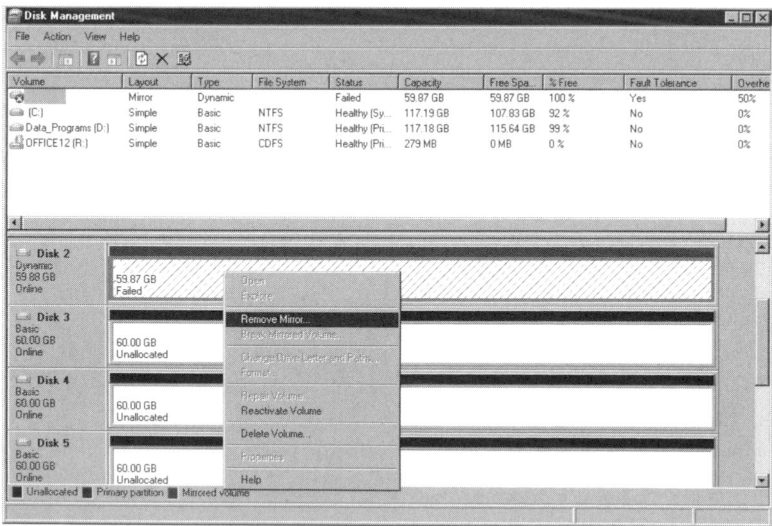

Figure 19-22 Breaking the mirror of a failed mirror pair

2. In the Remove Mirror dialog box, select the failed disk and click Remove Mirror.

After you replace the failed disk or correct the problem and reactivate the failed disk, the mirror automatically starts regenerating if you didn't have to remove the mirror. If you can solve the problem without powering down the system, you can regenerate the mirror on the fly. To reactivate the failed disk, follow these steps:

1. Right-click the icon for the failed disk on the left side of the Disk Management console.
2. Choose Reactivate Disk. Windows Server 2008 warns you about running chkdsk on any affected volumes, brings the disk back online, and starts regenerating the failed mirror.

Real World Removing a Mirror

We all know that every system administrator is always fully aware of the ongoing requirements of her servers, and never runs out of disk space without plenty of warning. Oh, wait, this is a Real World sidebar. OK, reality check, then. If you have the luxury of huge budgets and large, flexible, highly redundant Storage Area Networks, you probably haven't been caught short on disk space. But if you're running a more ordinary network where budgets interfere and resources are constrained, we strongly suspect you've certainly had times when you were scrambling to clean up disks to make sure you didn't run out of room for a critical process. Certainly we have. If you have a mirrored volume, you can get yourself out of trouble pretty quickly. But at a significant risk in the long run.

Just remove the mirror from the mirrored volume. When you remove a mirror, the data on one of the disks is untouched, but the other disk becomes unallocated space. You can then use the unallocated space to extend the volume that is short.

Of course, you will have lost all redundancy and protection for the data, so you need to take steps to restore the mirror as soon as possible. Plus the volume you've extended is now more susceptible to failure, since it has an extra disk included in it. Until you can buy more disks, you'll want modify your backup schedule for the affected disks. And don't put off buying the new disks–you're at serious risk until you get your system back to where it should be.

Setting Disk Quotas

Windows Server 2008 supports two mutually exclusive methods for setting quotas on the amount of file system resources a user can use–disk quotas or directory quotas. Disk quotas were introduced in Windows 2000, and are applied to specific users and limit the amount of disk space that user can use on a particular volume. Directory quotas are applied to all users and limit the amount of disk space that users can use in a particular folder and its subfolders. Directory quotas were introduced in Windows Server 2003 R2 with the new File Server Resource Manager, and they are covered in detail in Chapter 20.

Enabling Quotas on a Disk

By default, disk quotas are disabled in Windows Server 2008. You can enable disk quotas on any volume that has been assigned a drive letter. To enable quotas on a volume, follow these steps:

1. In Windows Explorer, right-click a drive letter and open the properties of that drive.
2. Click the Quota tab, shown in Figure 19-23, and then click Show Quota Settings.

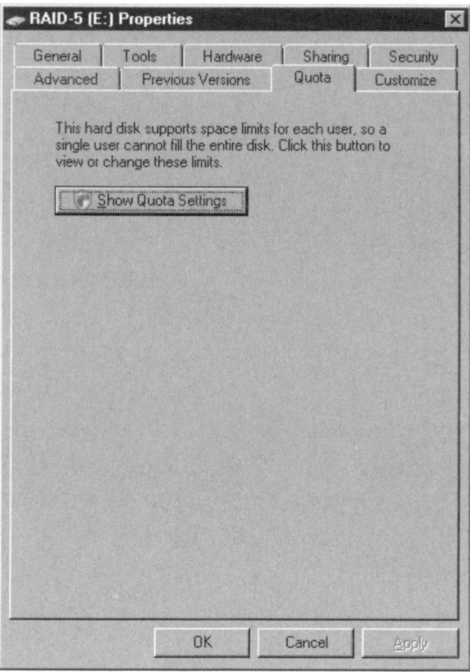

Figure 19-23 The Quota tab of a drive's properties

3. Select the Enable Quota Management check box to enable quotas for the disk, as shown in Figure 19-24.

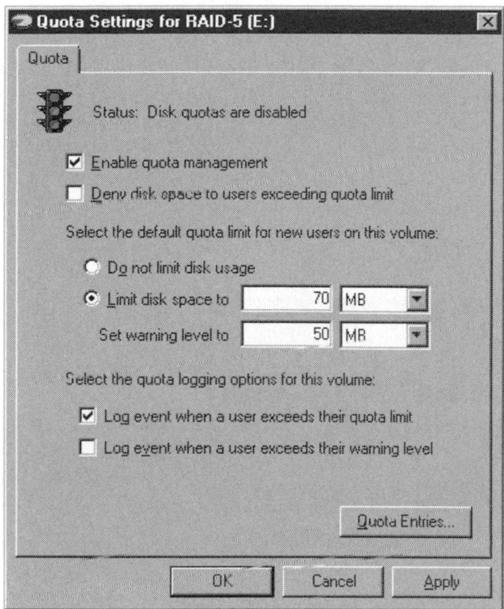

Figure 19-24 The Quota Settings dialog box for a disk

4. To enable hard quotas that can't be exceeded, select the Deny Disk Space To Users Exceeding Quota Limit check box.
5. Set the limits and warning level, as shown in Figure 19-24. You can also enable logging on this page.
6. Click OK to enable the quotas. You'll be prompted one last time to confirm, as shown in Figure 19-25. Click OK and the quotas will be enabled.

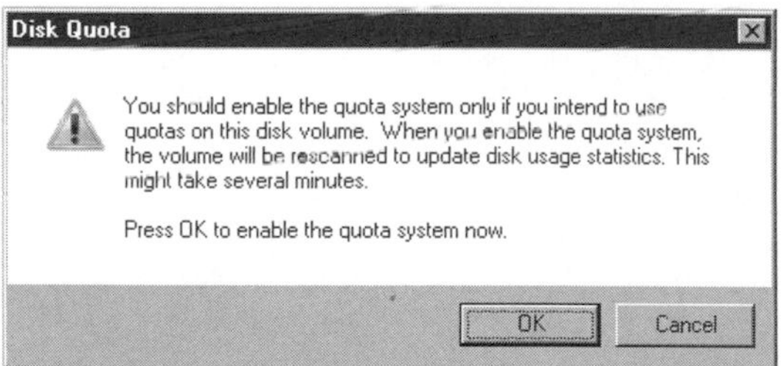

Figure 19-25 The Disk Quota confirmation message

Setting Per-User Quotas

You can set quota limits on individual users, or you can have limits apply equally to all non-administrative users. Unfortunately, you can't set limits on groups of users. And any users who already own files on the disk will have their quotas initially disabled. New users will have the default quotas for the disk applied as you would expect when they first save a file on the disk.

To set the quotas for individual users, follow these steps:

1. In Windows Explorer, right-click a drive letter and open the properties of that drive.
2. Click the Quota tab, and then click Show Quota Settings to bring up the Quota Settings dialog box for that disk.
3. Click Quota Entries to open the Quota Entries dialog box for the disk, as shown in Figure 19-26.

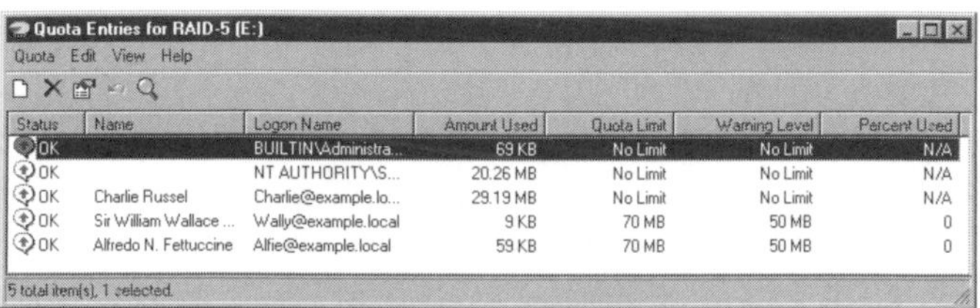

Figure 19-26 The Quota Entries dialog box for a disk

4. To modify the quota for a user already listed, select the user and then click Properties to open the quota settings for that user, as shown in Figure 19-27. Set the quota for the user and click OK to return to the Quota Entries dialog box.

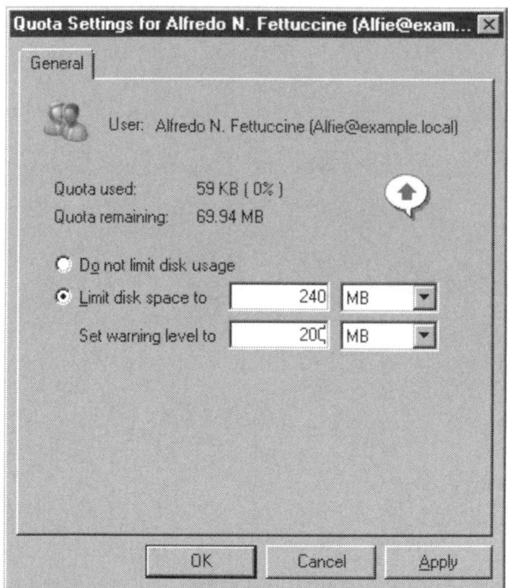

Figure 19-27 The Quota Settings dialog box for an individual user

5. To create a quota for a user who doesn't have one yet, and who needs a quota different from the default for the disk, click New Quota Entry.

6. Select the user or users to apply the new quota to, and click OK to bring up the Add New Quota Entry dialog box, as shown in Figure 19-28.

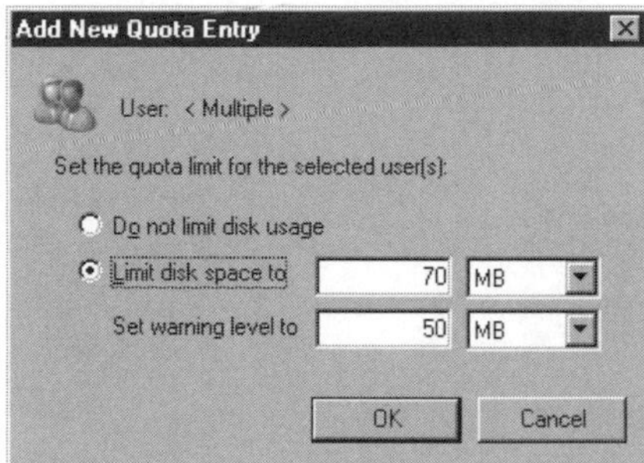

Figure 19-28 The Add New Quota Entry dialog box

7. Click OK to add the new entry and return to the Quota Entries dialog box. Close the Quota Entries dialog box, click OK in the Quota Settings dialog box, and then click OK in the Properties dialog box for the drive.

8. To manage quotas from the command line, you need to use Fsutil.exe. Even for a determined command-line type, it's pretty lame. Stick to the GUI, and use import and export whenever possible.

Importing and Exporting Quotas

Managing disk quotas is a potentially tedious job if you try to use fine-grained control of individual quotas. The best solution is to use a single, general quota that is correct for almost all users, and then do only limited exceptions to that quota for very specialized cases. If you do have complicated quotas, however, and you need to transfer them to another server or another volume, you can export a set of quotas and then import them to another volume.

To export the quotas on a volume, follow these steps:

1. Open the Quota Settings page for the volume you want to export the quotas from.
2. Click Quota Entries to open the Quota Entries dialog box.
3. Highlight the quotas you want to export.
4. Choose Export from the Quota menu. Type in a name and location for the export file and click Save.

To import a quota file to a volume, follow these steps:

1. Open the Quota Settings page for the volume you want to import the quotas to.

2. Click Quota Entries to open the Quota Entries dialog box.
3. Choose Import from the Quota menu. Type in a name and location for the import file and click Open.
4. If there are conflicting quotas, you'll be prompted to replace the existing quotas, as shown in Figure 19-29.

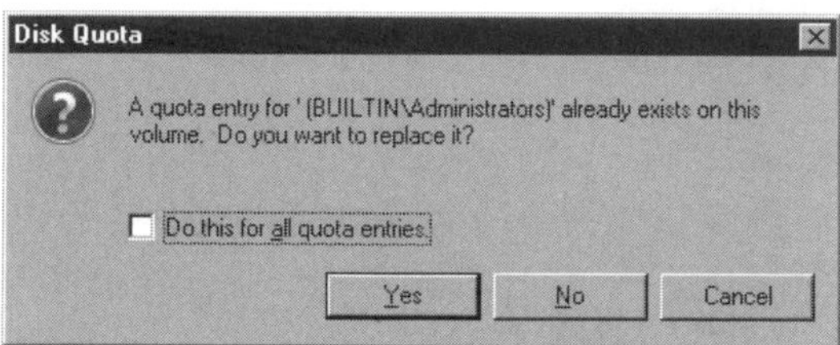

Figure 19-29 Importing quotas can cause an existing quota to be replaced.

5. Choose to replace a quota by clicking Yes or to not keep the existing one by clicking No. You can have the action repeated for any further conflicts by selecting the Do This For All Quota Entries check box.

Real World Just Say No to Disk Quotas

Disk quotas, which were originally introduced in Windows 2000, were a big step forward and gave the Windows system administrator a new and valuable tool to limit the spiraling growth of storage requirements on the server. But like many Microsoft version 1.0 implementations, it wasn't a perfect solution. It's difficult to manage quotas effectively without creating too many exceptions to easily keep track of. You can apply quotas only on a per-drive letter level, and they don't affect mounted volumes at all. And quotas are indiscriminant–they treat document files the same way they treat .MP3 files.

Quotas also arrived too late to the scene. Just about the time disk quotas were introduced, the hard disk industry started a round of massive growth in hard drive size. At the same time, the price of even enterprise-class hard drives came down dramatically.

Finally, with the introduction of the File Server Resource Manager, we now have folder-level quotas and file-type filtering. If you need quotas, we recommend that you use these.

Enabling File Encryption

With the introduction of Windows 2000, Microsoft added the ability to encrypt individual files or entire subdirectories stored on an NTFS volume in a totally transparent way. To their creator, encrypted files look exactly like regular files—no changes to applications are required to use them. However, to anyone except the creator/encryptor, the files are unavailable. Even if someone did manage to gain access to them, they would be gibberish because they're stored in encrypted form.

Encryption is simply an advanced attribute of the file, like compression. However, a file cannot be both compressed and encrypted at the same time—the attributes are mutually exclusive. Encrypted files are available only to the encryptor, but they can be recovered by the domain or machine recovery agent if necessary. You can back up encrypted files by normal backup procedures if the backup program is Windows Server 2008–aware. Files remain encrypted when backed up, and restored files retain their encryption.

Under normal circumstances, no user except the actual creator of an encrypted file has access to the file. Even a change of ownership does not remove the encryption. This prevents sensitive data—such as payroll information, annual reviews, and so on—from being accessed by the wrong users, even ones with administrative rights.

> **Note** Encryption is available only on NTFS. If you copy the file to a floppy disk or to any other file system, the file is no longer encrypted. This means that if you have a USB key drive, for example, that is formatted with FAT, or if you use NFS file systems, copying the file there will remove the encryption.

When you encrypt a folder, all new files created in that folder are encrypted from that point forward. You can also elect to encrypt the current contents when you perform the encryption. However, be warned that if you choose to encrypt the contents of a folder when it already contains files or subfolders, those files and subfolders are encrypted *for the user performing the encryption only*. This means that even files owned by another user are encrypted and available for your use only—the owner of the files will no longer be able to access them.

When new files are created in an encrypted folder, the files are encrypted for use by the creator of the file, not the user who first enabled encryption on the folder. Unencrypted files in an encrypted folder can be used by all users who have security rights to use files in that folder, and the encryption status of the file does not change unless the filename itself is changed. Users can read, modify, and save the file without converting it to an encrypted file, but any change in the name of the file triggers an encryption, and the encryption makes the file available only to the person who triggers the encryption.

Important If you use EFS, it is *essential* that you back up EFS certificates and designate a Recovery Agent to protect against *irreversible* data loss. EFS certificates and recovery agents are covered in Chapter 23, "Implementing Security."

To encrypt a file or folder, follow these steps:

1. In Windows Explorer, right-click the folder or files you want to encrypt, and choose Properties from the shortcut menu.
2. Click Advanced on the General tab to open the Advanced Attributes dialog box shown in Figure 19-30.

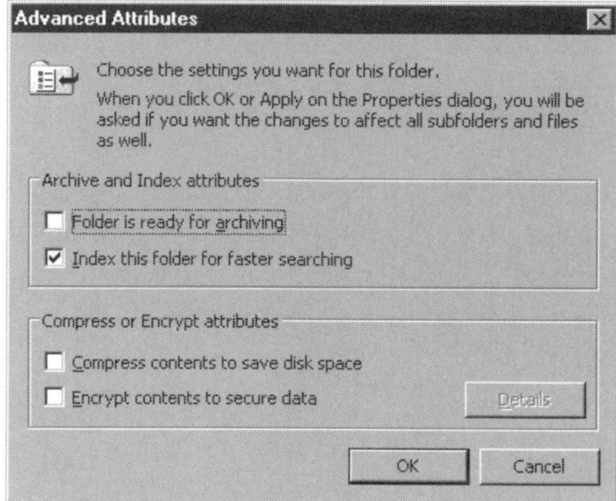

Figure 19-30 The Advanced Attributes dialog box

3. Select the Encrypt Contents To Secure Data check box and click OK to return to the main Properties window for the folder or file. Click OK or Apply to enable the encryption. If any files or subfolders are already in the folder, you're presented with the dialog box shown in Figure 19-31.

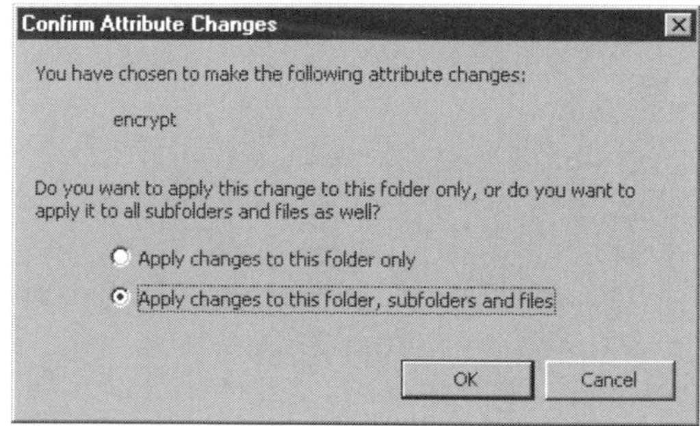

Figure 19-31 Choosing whether to encrypt the files already in a folder or just new files

4. If you choose Apply Changes To This Folder Only, all the current files and subfolders in the folder remain unencrypted, but any new files and folders are encrypted by the creator as they are created. If you choose Apply Changes To This Folder, Subfolders, And Files, all the files and folders below this folder are encrypted so that only you can use them, regardless of the original creator or owner of the file.
5. Click OK and the encryption occurs.

Real World The Limitations of EFS

The EFS capabilities of Windows Server 2008 provide a useful way to encrypt folders and files to prevent unauthorized access. However, EFS has limitations, and you need to manage it carefully to not create issues.

Once an EFS folder is created, any files created in the folder will always be encrypted *by the creator of the file*. This is not always what you intend. If you have a publicly available folder that has encryption on it, you need to carefully manage who has access to that folder using NTFS file permissions, share permissions, or other methods of preventing unauthorized access.

Another problem is that anyone who has access to your system drive *can* break EFS encryption. This shouldn't be a big problem on a well-secured server, but it's still a concern. The solution is to enable BitLocker on your server. BitLocker was introduced with Windows Vista as a solution for the mobile laptop, but it has very real possibilities for the enterprise trying to fully secure its environment. For more on BitLocker, see Chapter 23.

Summary

Windows Server 2008 provides the system administrator with a richer set of disk management tools than any previous version of Windows. Disk Management is now smarter, with automatic, seamless conversion between basic and dynamic disks. The full support for GPT disks eliminates the need for extended partitions, and gives Windows Server 2008 the ability to support really *large* disks. And the ability to shrink or extend a volume without taking it offline gives the system administrator much greater flexibility.

In the next chapter, we'll cover the many aspects of storage, including Storage Area Networks, the Storage Resource Manager, and removable and remote storage.

Chapter 20

Managing Storage

The need for storage has increased dramatically in recent years, putting ever-increasing stress on the system administrator, whose job it is to provide adequate storage at a reasonable cost. Fortunately, the cost of hard disk space has plummeted while the capacity of drives has increased. With the increase in the availability of Storage Area Networks (SANs) and Network Attached Storage (NAS), system administrators can now centralize and rationalize storage more effectively across the network, helping to eliminate much of the waste associated with local storage.

The temptation to manage storage requirements by simply buying more disks has its appeal, but this leads to backup and archival complications, and can end up making it even more difficult to manage the storage of your network.

In this chapter, we'll cover the tools in Windows Server 2008 that help manage storage on the network, including File Server Resource Manager (FSRM), the Storage Manager For SANs (SMS), and the Distributed File System (DFS).

More Info For information about shared folders, see Chapter 12, "Managing File Resources," and for information about disk management, see Chapter 19, "Implementing Disk Management."

Using File Server Resource Manager

The File Server Resource Manager is installed as a role service of the File Services Role. FSRM is made up of three tools:

- Storage Reports Management
- Quota Management
- File Screening Management

These tools allow administrators of Windows Server 2008 file servers to keep track of storage growth and usage, as well as create hard or soft policies limiting the amount and type of files that users can save in specific folders.

Installation and Initial Configuration of FSRM

Installation and initial configuration of FSRM follows the familiar Add Role Service path. Most of the global options and configuration take place during the initial installation–a big improvement over the installation of FSRM in Windows Server 2003 R2!

To install the FSRM role service, follow these steps:

Note These steps assume that the File Service role is already installed. If it hasn't yet been installed, then install it now.

1. Open Server Manager and highlight the File Services role.
2. Select File Server Resource Manager from the Role Services list, as shown in Figure 20-1.

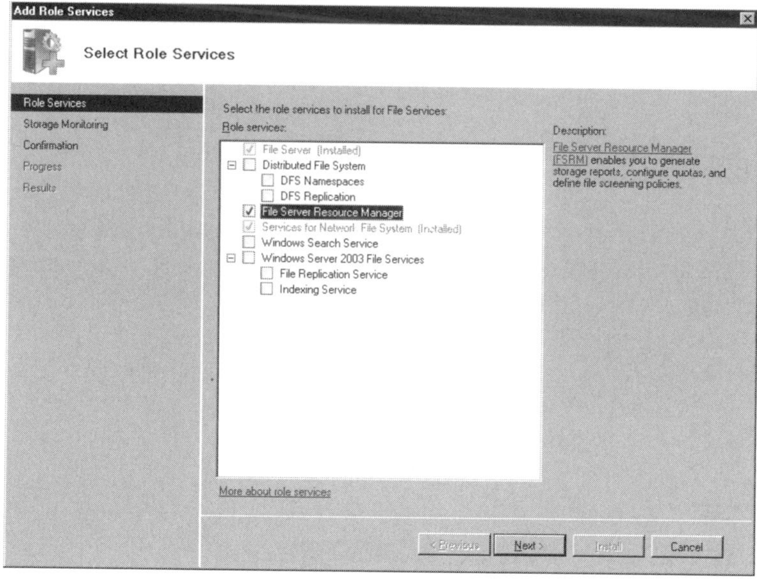

Figure 20-1 The Select Role Services page of the Add Role Services dialog box for the File Services role

3. Click Next, and select the volumes to monitor the storage on, as shown in Figure 20-2.

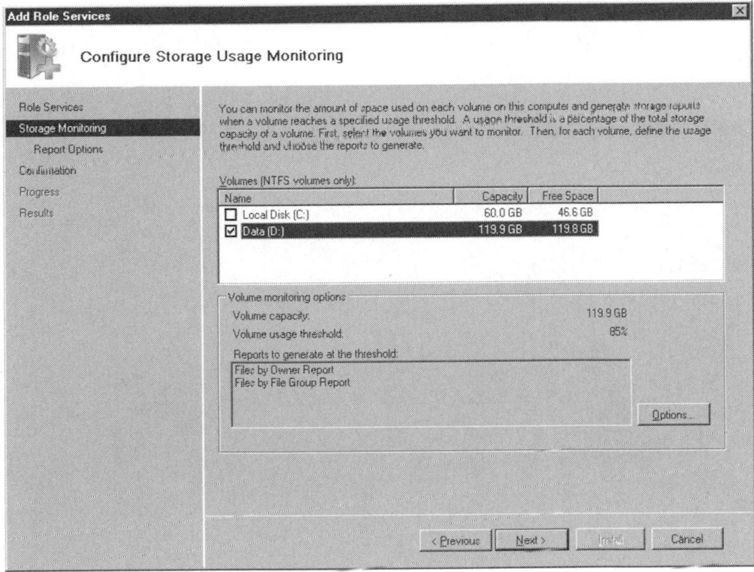

Figure 20-2 The Configure Storage Usage Monitoring page of the Add Role Services dialog box for the File Services role

4. The default usage threshold before alerts begin is 85 percent of total capacity of the volume being monitored, and the default reports created are Files By Owner and Files By File Group. Click Options to change these defaults, as shown in Figure 20-3. Click OK to return to the Configure Storage Usage Monitoring page.

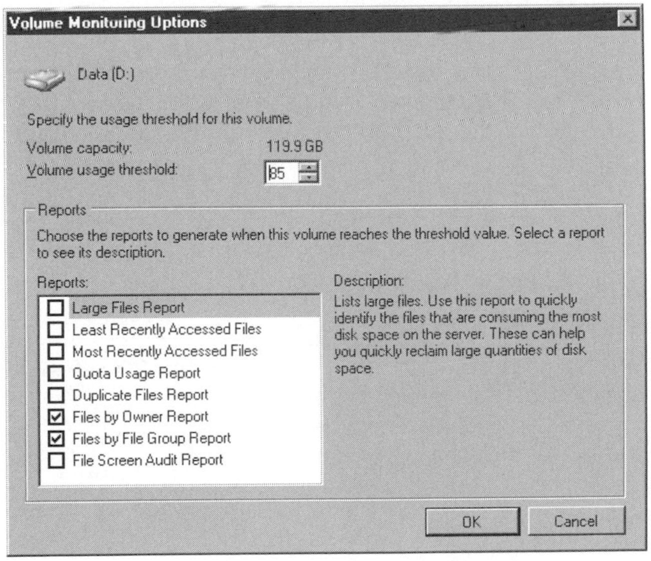

Figure 20-3 The Volume Monitoring Options page

5. Click Next to open the Set Report Options page, as shown in Figure 20-4. On this page you can specify where reports are stored, and have them automatically e-mailed to one or more addresses.

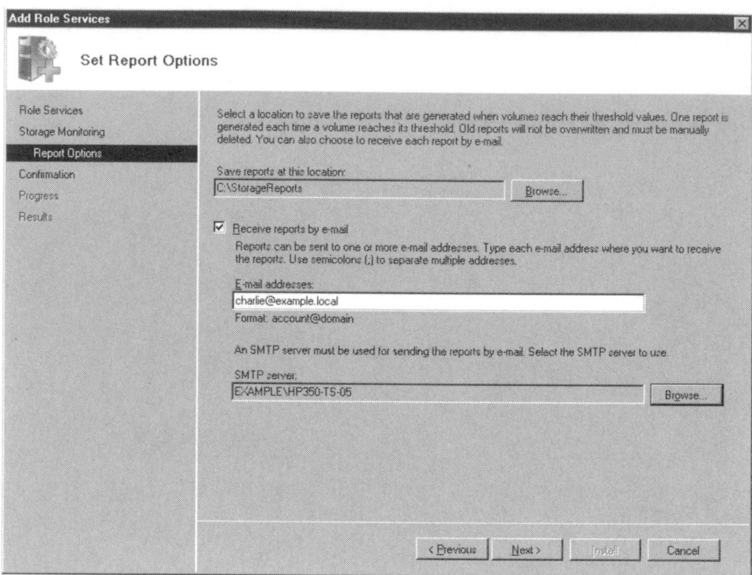

Figure 20-4 The Set Report Options page of the Add Role Services dialog box for the File Services role

6. Click Next to bring up the confirmation page, then click Install to begin installing FSRM. Click Close when the wizard is finished.

Note You can always print, e-mail, or save a complete installation report from any of the Add Role Services or Add Features dialog boxes by clicking on the Print, E-Mail Or Save The Installation Report link on the Installation Results page of the wizard.

Note Windows stores File Server Resource Manager global settings in the %WINDIR%\system32\srm\defaults\SrmGlobalSettings.xml file.

Note As with other role management consoles in Windows Server 2008, the File Server Resource Manager console can be used in stand-alone mode, or as part of the Server Manager console. Our preference is generally to use the stand-alone consoles, but the functionality is the same regardless of how you use the console.

Scheduling Storage Reports

FSRM supports reporting in Dynamic Hypertext Markup Language (DHTML), HTML, Extended Markup Language (XML), Comma-Separated Values (CSV) text, or plain text, making it easy to view reports or process them using scripts, Microsoft Excel, or other applications.

File Server Resource Manager includes the following default storage reports (more can be defined and added):

- Duplicate files
- File screening audit
- Files by file group
- Files by owner
- Large files
- Least recently accessed files
- Most recently accessed files
- Quota usage

To schedule a storage report, follow these steps:

1. In the File Server Resource Manager, click Storage Reports Management.
2. Choose Schedule A New Report Task from the actions menu. The Storage Reports Task Properties dialog box appears, as shown in Figure 20-5.

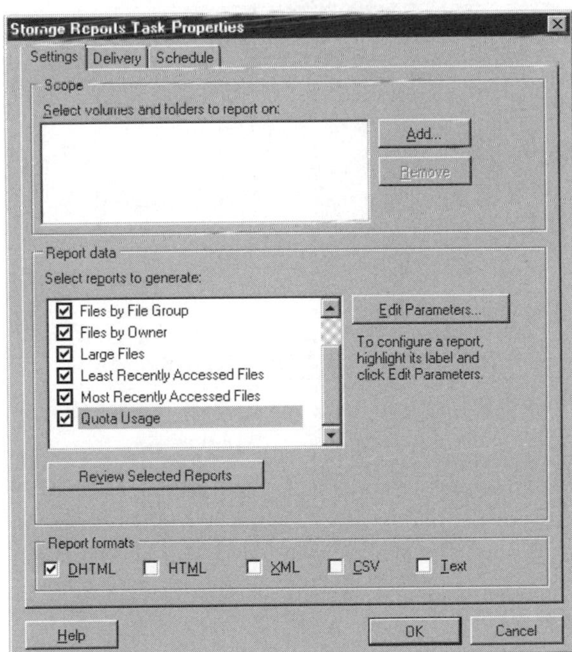

Figure 20-5 The Storage Reports Task Properties dialog box

3. In the Scope section of the dialog box, click Add to select the local folders that you want to monitor.
4. In the Report Data section of the dialog box, select the reports that you want to generate.

   To view the settings for all selected reports, click Review Selected Reports. To adjust the settings for a report, select the report and then click Edit Parameters.
5. In the Report Formats section of the dialog box, select the formats in which you want to generate the reports.
6. Click the Delivery tab, select the Send Reports To The Following Administrators check box, and type the e-mail addresses of the administrators who should receive the storage reports, separating each address with a semicolon.
7. Click the Schedule tab, and then click Create Schedule. The Schedule dialog box appears, which you can use to schedule the storage reports.
8. After you finish creating the scheduled report task, click OK in the Storage Reports Task Properties dialog box. The new scheduled report task appears in the File Server Resource Manager console, as shown in Figure 20-6.

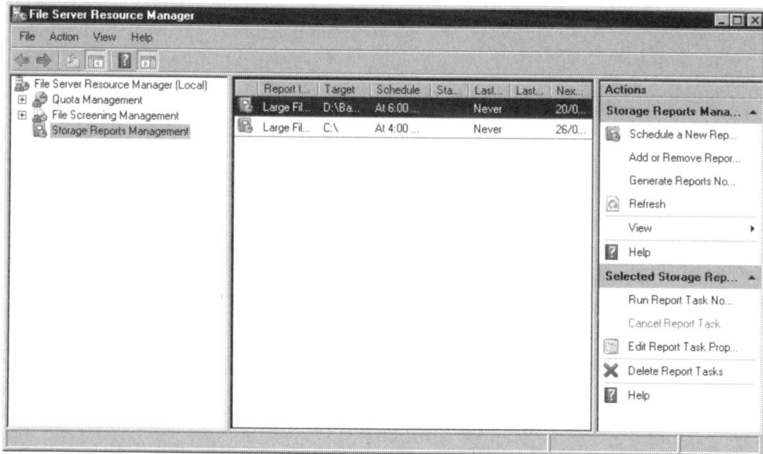

Figure 20-6 The Storage Reports Management node in the File Server Management console

9. To run the scheduled report immediately, right-click it and choose Run Report Task Now. The Generate Storage Reports dialog box appears, asking whether you want to view the reports immediately, or whether File Server Resource Manager should generate the reports in the background for viewing later from the report storage folder.

10. To schedule a storage report from a command prompt, use the **Schtasks /Create** command to create a task in the Scheduled Tasks folder for the report and then use the **Storrept Reports Add** command to create the report. For example, open an elevated command prompt window and then type the following commands:

```
Schtasks /Create /S Srv1 /SC Monthly /MO First /D Sun /TN "Monthly Large Files
   Storage Report" /TR "C:\Windows\System32\Storrept.exe Reports Generate /
   Scheduled /Task:"MonthlyFiles"" /RU ""
Storrept Reports Add /Add-Report:LargeFiles /Task:"Monthly Large Files
   Storage Report" /Scope:"E:\Projects|E:\Legal" /Name:"Monthly LargeFiles
   Storage Report" /Format:DHTML /Remote:Srv1
```

Note When viewing a storage report in DHTML format, you can sort the listing by columns as long as Internet Explorer can display active content. (You might need to use the Information Bar in Internet Explorer to allow blocked content.)

Under the Hood Storage Reports, Snapshots, and Performance

To create a storage report, Windows creates a Scheduled Task in the Task Scheduler library that uses the Volume Shadow Copy Service to take a snapshot of the specified storage volumes, and then creates the storage report from this snapshot using XML style sheets stored in the %WINDIR%\system32\srm\xslt folder. This process minimizes the performance impact on the server, but does degrade file server performance temporarily.

Schedule your storage reports during slack times to minimize the impact on users and combine reports whenever possible. Because all storage reports in a storage report task use the same snapshot, you can minimize the performance impact on a server by consolidating your reports to minimize the number of snapshots required.

Using Directory Quotas

One way to slow the growth of storage on a network is to limit the amount of disk space each user can utilize on a server. There are two ways of doing this in Windows Server 2008–disk quotas and directory quotas. Disk quotas allow you to create storage limits on each volume for individual users and are covered in Chapter 19.

Directory quotas allow you to manage storage at a folder level. You can create quota templates and auto quotas that Windows automatically applies to subfolders and newly created folders. Directory quotas, unlike disk quotas, look at the actual amount of disk space used by a file and also provide powerful notification capabilities.

Note Directory quotas apply to all users as a group, unlike disk quotas which you can apply differentially to individual users. Both directory quotas and disk quotas apply only to a single server.

Directory quotas and disk quotas can use either hard limits, which prevent users from exceeding their quotas, or soft limits, which merely serve as a warning and notification method.

Directory Quota Types

The following list describes the three types of directory quotas.

- **Quotas** Sets the total amount of disk space that a folder *and all subfolders* can consume. For example, if you create a quota that limits the \Users folder to 10 GB, the total contents of this folder and all subfolders cannot exceed 10 GB in size. If one user uses 9 GB of file space, all the other users combined are limited to 1 GB.
- **Auto Quotas** Sets the amount of disk space that the first level subfolders (children) of a folder can consume. For example, if you create an auto quota for the \Users folder and set the limit at 2 GB, each first level of subfolder (e.g. \Users\Charlie; \Users\Wally) is limited to 2 GB in size. An auto quota does not set a limit on the contents of the parent folder, only the subfolders (children).
- **Quota Templates** Standardizes and centralizes quota and auto quota settings. When you change the settings of a quota template, you can automatically apply the changes to all quotas that use the quota template you change.

Note Directory quotas work only on fixed NTFS volumes; you cannot use directory quotas on removable drives or FAT volumes.

Creating Quotas and Auto Quotas

To create a quota or auto quotas, follow these steps. To create a quota template, see the "Creating and Editing Quota Templates" section of this chapter.

1. In the File Server Resource Manager, expand Quota Management.
2. Right-click Quotas in the console tree and choose Create Quota.
3. The Create Quota dialog box appears, as shown in Figure 20-7.

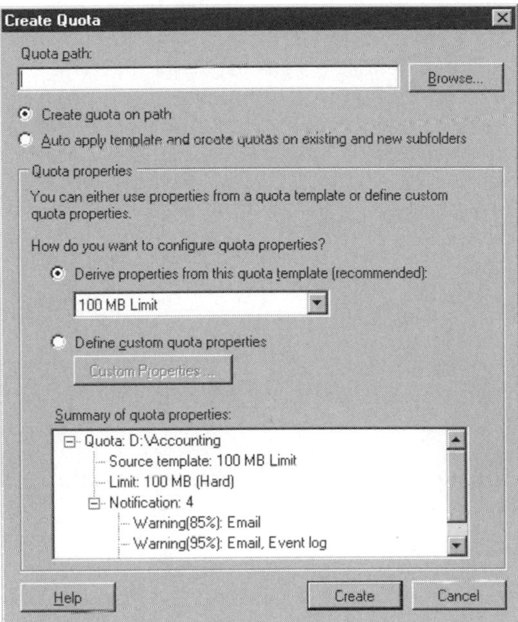

Figure 20-7 The Create Quota dialog box

4. Click Browse, select the folder to which you want to apply a quota, and then click OK.
5. To create a quota that limits the size of a folder, including all subfolders, select the Create Quota On Path option. To create an auto quota, which limits the size of subfolders individually (useful for setting quotas on the \Users folder), select the Auto Apply Template And Create Quotas On Existing And New Subfolders option.
6. Select the quota template you want to apply, or choose Define Custom Quota Properties and click Custom Properties to create a custom quota. (You cannot create custom quotas for auto quotas.) Click Create when you are finished.
7. If you chose to create a custom quota, the Save Custom Properties As A Template dialog box appears. Use this dialog box to save the custom quota as a quota template, or choose Save The Custom Quota Without Creating A Template.
8. To create a directory auto quota from a command prompt, use the `Dirquota Quota Add` command. For example, open a command prompt window and then type the following command:

```
Dirquota AutoQuota Add /Path:E:\Users /SourceTemplate:"200 MB Limit Reports
   To User" /Remote:Srv1
```

Note Use quota templates instead of custom quotas. Using a quota template allows you to make changes to the template that applies to all quotas that are derived from the template. For example, to change the administrator e-mail address for all quotas on a server, edit the appropriate quota templates and then apply these changes to all quotas. This eliminates the need to manually update each quota individually.

Viewing and Managing Quotas

Click Quotas in the File Server Resource Manager console tree (shown in Figure 20-8) to view or manage existing quotas:

1. To filter the display by quota type or path, click the Filter hyperlink and then use the Quota Filter dialog box.
2. To disable a quota, select the quota or quotas, right-click the quota, and then choose Disable Quotas. To enable a disabled quota, right-click it and choose Enable Quota.
3. To reset the peak usage data for a quota, select the quota or quotas, right-click the quota, and choose Reset Peak Usage.

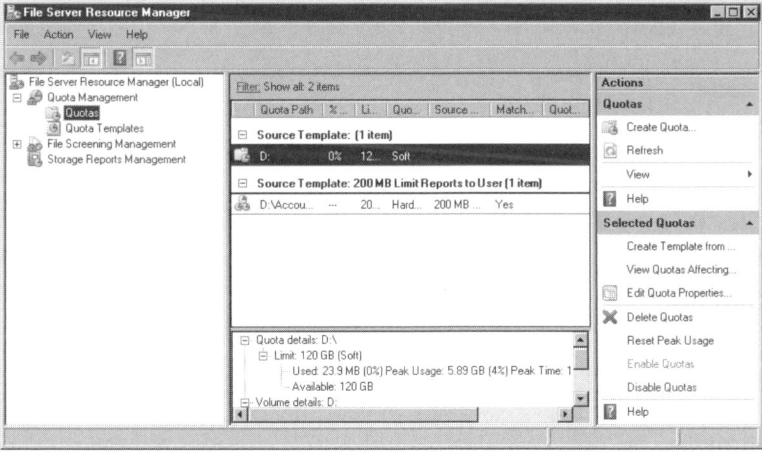

Figure 20-8 The quotas pane of the File Server Resource Management console

Creating and Editing Quota Templates

Quota templates enable you to quickly apply standardized quota settings, as well as simultaneously update all quotas that make use of a template–when you edit a quota template, Windows gives you the option to update all quotas based on the template. To create or edit a quota template, follow these steps:

1. In the File Server Resource Manager console, right-click Quota Templates and choose Create Quota Template, or right-click an existing quota template and choose Edit Template Properties. To create a quota template based on an existing quota, right-click the quota and choose Create Quota From Template.
2. To base the template on an existing template, in the Create Quota Template dialog box choose a template from the Copy Properties From Quota Template box and then click Copy, as shown in Figure 20-9.

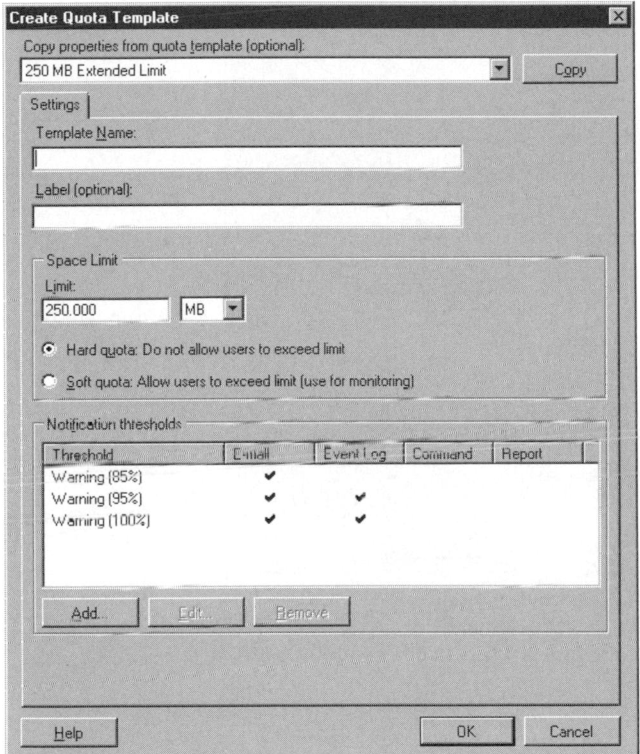

Figure 20-9 The Create Quota Template dialog box

3. Type a name and label for the template in the Template Name and Label boxes.
4. In the Limit box, type the maximum amount of disk space each user can utilize in the specified folder.
5. Choose Hard Quota to prevent users from exceeding the limit you specify, or Soft Quota to use the quota only for monitoring.

6. In the Notification Thresholds section of the dialog box, click Add to create a new notification, or select an existing notification and then click Edit to open the properties for the threshold, as shown in Figure 20-10.

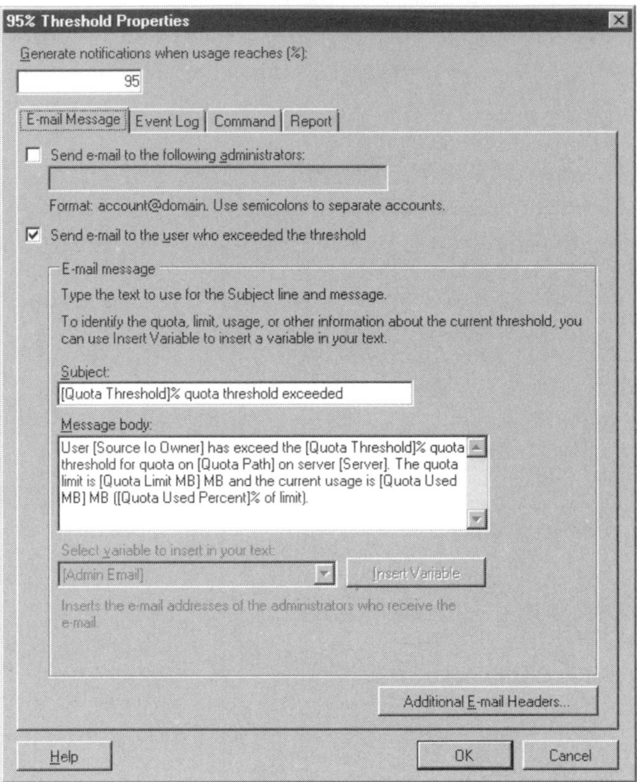

Figure 20-10 The properties of a quota notification threshold

7. In the Generate Notifications When Usage Reaches box, specify when to notify users.

   A typical configuration is to use three notification thresholds, which are often set at 85%, 95%, and 100%.

8. Specify what actions to take when a user exceeds the threshold you specify, and click OK when you are finished.

   - Use the E-mail Message tab to send an e-mail notification to users who exceed the threshold. (You can also choose to send the notification to an administrator.) Use the E-mail Message section of the tab to customize the message that Windows generates.

   - Use the Event Log tab to record a log entry on the server when a user exceeds the threshold.

- Use the Command tab to run a command or script when a user exceeds the threshold.
- Use the Report tab to generate a storage report when a user exceeds the threshold. See the "Scheduling Storage Reports" section of this chapter for more information about storage reports.

Note To insert additional variables in an e-mail message or event log entry, select the variable from the list and click Insert Variable.

9. Click OK when you are finished. If you are editing an existing template, the Update Quotas Derived From Template dialog box appears. Choose one of the following options and then click OK:
   - **Apply Template Only To Derived Quotas That Match The Original Template** Updates quotas based on the quota template only if you have not customized them
   - **Apply Template To All Derived Quotas** Updates all quotas based on the quota template
   - **Do Not Apply Template to Derived Quotas** Does not update any quotas based on the template
10. To create a quota template from a command prompt, use the `Dirquota Template Add` command. For example, open a command prompt window and then type the following command:

```
Dirquota Template Add /Template:"500 MB Limit Reports to User" /Limit:"500 MB"
   /SourceTemplate:"200 MB Limit Reports To User" /Remote:Srv1
```

Note To import or export quotas from one file server to another, use the `dirquota template export` and `dirquota template import` commands. For example, to export all templates, type dirquota template export c:\quoatatemplates.xml. To import only a template named 1 GB limit, type **dirquota template import /template:"1 GB limit" /file:c:\templates.xml**.

Screening Files

Administrators who use storage reports for the first time are often surprised, and occasionally outraged, over how many audio and video files they find on file servers. In addition to the massive amounts of disk space that audio and video files can consume, companies may be legally liable if users obtained these files illegally or share them with coworkers.

To help administrators control what type of files users can save on a file share, Windows Server 2008 includes File Screening Management as part of the File Server Resource Manager console. With File Screening Management, administrators can block users from saving files with certain file extensions to a specific file share, as discussed in the following sections.

Controlling Audio and Video Files on Company Servers

If you are serious about blocking users from saving personal audio and video files on public file shares, or you want to protect the organization from any legal liability from users' MP3 collections, you need two things:

- **An acceptable use policy that clearly states what users may and may not place on file shares** This policy should state that users may not save illegally obtained files of any type on company file servers, including audio and video files for which the users do not own a license. You might also want to state that users may only save legally obtained audio and video files to their home directory (on which you create a directory quota, limiting users to a reasonable amount of disk space).
- **A file screen that implements this policy** The best way to get people to follow a company policy is to make it hard for them to violate the policy. A file screen makes it difficult for an average user to violate an acceptable-use policy concerning audio and video files, and reduces legal liability by demonstrating that the organization is taking active steps to prevent its employees from violating its written policy.

Because file screens use a filename mask to block files, not a content mask, users can still save MP3 files by changing the file extension of the file to something that isn't blocked. However, if you have a clear and unambiguous acceptable-use policy, and a file screen for that policy in place, the discussion with any employee who violates the policy has changed dramatically. Ignorance as a defense is out–there has been a clear and deliberate violation of company policy *and* a knowing attempt to hide that violation.

Creating File Screens

To create a file screen, follow these steps:

1. In the File Server Resource Manager console, click File Screening Management node.

2. Click the File Screens container, right-click File Screens in the console tree, and choose Create File Screen. The Create File Screen dialog box appears, as shown in Figure 20-11.

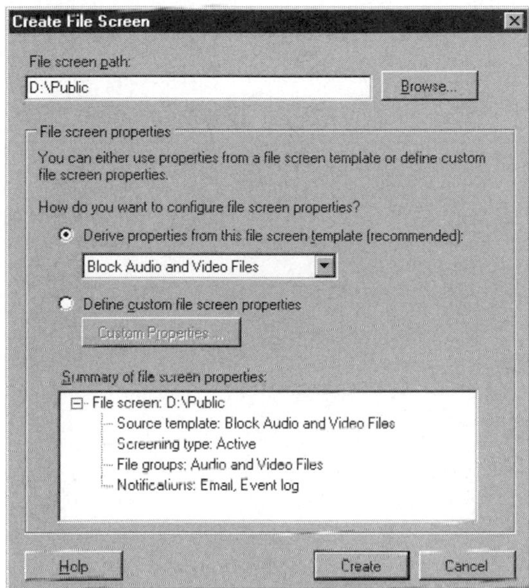

Figure 20-11 The Create File Screen dialog box

3. Click Browse, select the folder to which you want to apply the file screen, and then click OK.

4. Select the file screen template you want to apply, or choose Define Custom File Screen Properties and then click Custom Properties to create a custom file screen. Click OK when you are finished.

5. If you chose to create a custom file screen, the Save Custom Properties As A Template dialog box appears. Use this dialog box to save the custom file screen as a file screen template, or choose Save The Custom File Screen Without Creating A Template.

6. To create a file screen from a command prompt, use the `Filescrn Screen Add` command. For example, open a command prompt window and then type the following command:

```
Filescrn Screen Add /Path:D:\Public /SourceTemplate:"Block Audio and Video
  Files"
```

Creating Exceptions

To create an exception to a file screen, follow these steps:

1. Click the File Screens container, right-click File Screens in the console tree, and choose Create File Screen Exception. The Create File Screen Exception dialog box appears, as shown in Figure 20-12.

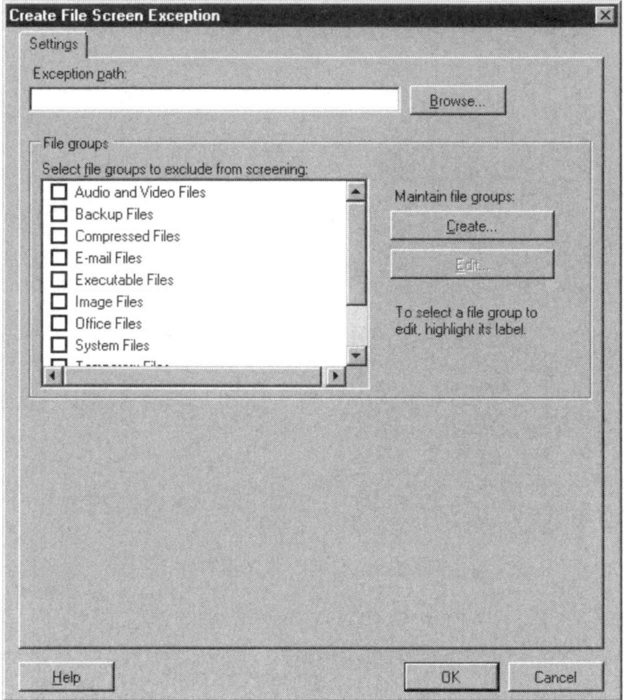

Figure 20-12 The Create File Screen Exception dialog box

2. Click Browse, select the folder to which you want to apply the file screen exception, and then click OK. The folder you select cannot already contain a file screen, but it can be a subfolder of a folder that contains a file screen.

3. Select the groups that you want to allow, excluding them from any file screens applied to parent folders. Click OK when you are finished to return to the File Server Resource Manager console.

4. To create a file screen exception from a command prompt, use the `Filescrn Exception Add` command. For example, open a command prompt window and then type the following command:

```
Filescrn Exception Add /Path:"D:\Public\Company Videos  /Add-Filegroup:"WMV
   Files"
```

Creating and Editing File Screen Templates

To create or edit a file screen template, follow these steps:

1. In the File Server Resource Manager console, right-click File Screen Templates and choose Create File Screen Template, or right-click an existing template and choose Edit Template Properties. To create a file screen template based on an existing file screen, right-click the file screen and choose Create A Template From File Screen.
2. To base the template on an existing template, in the Create File Screen Template dialog box, choose a template from the Copy Properties From Template box, as shown in Figure 20-13. Click Copy.

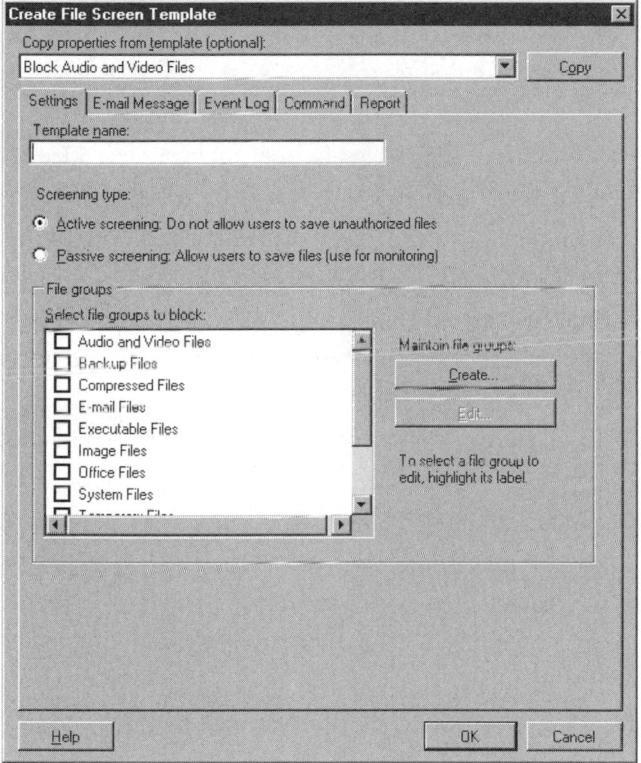

Figure 20-13 The Create File Screen Template dialog box

3. Type a name and label for the template in the Template Name box.
4. Choose Active Screening to prevent users from saving files of the type you specify, or Passive Screening to use the file screen only for monitoring.
5. Select the file group or groups that you want to block. To create a new file group, click Create; to edit an existing file group, select the group and then click Edit.

6. Specify what actions to take when a user saves a screened file type, and click OK when you are finished.
   - Use the E-mail Message tab to send an e-mail notification to the user who saved a screened file type. (You can also choose to send the notification to an administrator.) Use the E-mail Message section of the tab to customize the message that Windows generates.
   - Use the Event Log tab to record a log entry on the server when a user saves a screened file type.
   - Use the Command tab to run a command or script when a user saves a screened file type.
   - Use the Report tab to generate a storage report when a user saves a screened file type. See the "Scheduling Storage Reports" section of this chapter for more information about storage reports.

   To insert additional variables in an e-mail message or event log entry, select the variable from the list and click Insert Variable.
7. If you are editing an existing template, the Update File Screens Derived From Template dialog box appears. Choose one of the following options and then click OK.
   - **Apply Template Only To Derived File Screens That Match The Original Template** Updates file screens based on the quota template only if you have not customized them
   - **Apply Template To All Derived File Screens** Updates all file screens based on the quota template
   - **Do Not Apply Template to Derived File Screens** Does not update any file screens based on the template
8. To create a file screen template from a command prompt, use the `Filescrn Template Add` command. For example, open a command prompt window and then type the following command:

   ```
   Filescrn Template Add /Template:"Monitor Image Files" /Type:Passive
     /Add-Filegroup:"Image Files"
   ```

Working with File Groups

A file group is a group of files with a common set of characteristics in their filenames. For example, the Audio and Video file group includes audio files (with .mp3, .wma and .aac file extensions), and video files (with .wmv, .mpeg, and .mov file extensions). Storage reports use file groups when reporting on the types of files present on a file share, while file screening uses file groups to control which files to block. To create or edit a file group, follow these steps:

1. In the File Server Resource Manager console, click File Screening Management.
2. Click the File Groups container and choose Create File Group from the Actions menu. The Create File Group Properties dialog box appears, as shown in Figure 20-14.

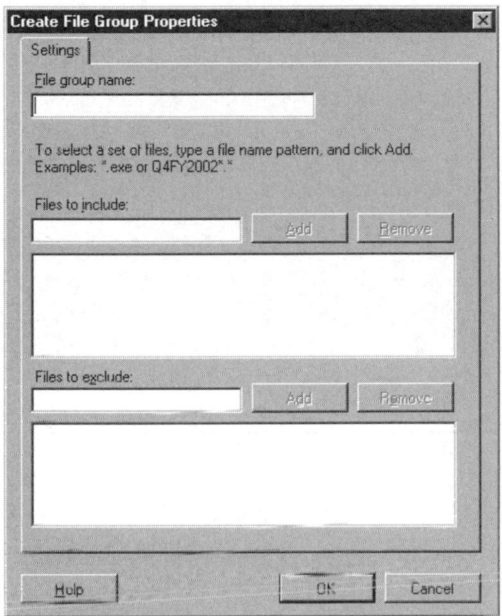

Figure 20-14 The Create File Group Properties dialog box

3. Type a name for the file group in the File Group Name box.
4. Type the filename criteria to include in the file group in the Files To Include box, using asterisks (*) as wildcards, and then click Add. For example, type *.xml, or financial*.*.
5. To exclude files from the file group, type the filename criteria to exclude from the file group in the Files To Exclude box, Click OK when you are finished.
6. To create a file group from a command prompt, use the `Filescrn Filegroup Add` command. For example, open a command prompt window and then type the following command:

```
Filescrn Filegroup Add /Filegroup:"Financial files" /Members:"*.qif | *.mny |
   *.m12 | *.mbf"
```

Under the Hood File Groups

File screening isn't just for file extensions. It's actually based on pattern matching against the entire filename to define the file group. This means you can have a file group that matches all MP3 files by creating a file group that matches "*.mp3". But you could also have a file group that matched all Company Policy files by matching "POL*.PDF" if all your company policies are stored in files that start with "POL" and are Adobe PDF files. Or, if monthly financial reports are consistently stored as MMMYYYY.XLS, you could create a file group that matched all 2008 financials by using "???2008.XLS" as your pattern.

The normal tendency with File Groups is to think only of the file's extension. But by using the entire filename in the pattern match, you can use file groups more creatively, and also do enhanced reporting based on the file groups.

Overview of SAN Manager

The Storage Manager For SANs console in Windows Server 2008 lets small and mid-sized organizations with sophisticated storage needs take advantage of low-cost Storage Area Network (SAN) hardware, without using complicated third-party SAN management software that often requires extensive training and a dedicated SAN administrator. It also enables you to administer SAN subsystems from different vendors from the same management computer, using the same tool (Storage Manager For SANs).

Large enterprises with basic SAN requirements can also benefit from Storage Manager For SANs. However, it does not provide the same capabilities as enterprise-level SAN management software. For example, Storage Managing for SANs does not provide any built-in notification capabilities–you would need to use System Center Operations Manager to provide the notification capability that is part of an enterprise-level SAN management package.

More Info SANs are complicated and their implementation varies greatly from manufacturer to manufacturer. Consult the manufacturer of the SAN subsystem for information about what network topologies and methods of SAN discovery the SAN subsystem supports. For more information about Microsoft support for iSCSI, or to download the Microsoft iSCSI Initiator or iSNS Server, see the Microsoft Web site at *http://www.microsoft.com/WindowsServer2003/technologies/storage/iscsi/default.mspx*.

Advantages and Disadvantages of SANs

SANs are often proposed as the solution to storage woes, but they aren't without their own issues. However, they do offer the following advantages:

- **Better utilization of storage resources** Because a SAN centralizes storage, you reduce the amount of unused disk space scattered across multiple servers in small, unusable chunks. For example, instead of 10 servers with 40 GB of free disk space, a SAN centralizes the storage resources into a single 400 GB chunk of free space, which you can allocate to servers as their needs grow. If a server stops hosting an application and no longer requires the associated disk space, you can allocate it to other servers.

  Many SANS offer "thin provisioning"–space is allocated and made available, but not actually used until needed, allowing a simplified management and updating experience.
- **Greater reliability** Storage on a SAN subsystem usually is fault tolerant, with redundant hard disks, disk controllers, network or Fibre Channel adapters, and power supplies.
- **Faster performance** SANs use large numbers of high-performance hard disks with various hardware RAID levels, and often communicate with servers over high-performance connections such as Fibre Channel. Multiple servers use the storage resources, allowing you to scale out to service more requests than a single server or Network Attached Storage (NAS) device. In addition, SAN subsystems communicate with servers using low-level data blocks with lower communication overhead than the high-level Server Message Block/Common Internet File System (SMB/CIFS) protocol used by NAS appliances and normal file servers. Centralized storage also makes centralized backup easier and faster because backups use the same high-performance storage network (or sometimes a dedicated network for backups).

However, SANs also have a number of drawbacks when compared to traditional direct-attached storage or NAS devices such as Windows Storage Server appliances. The most relevant drawbacks are:

- **Cost and complexity** SAN subsystems are usually more expensive than NAS devices and direct-attached storage, and are more complex than NAS devices that are designed to be very simple and easy to use, and direct-attached storage, which has very few settings to configure.

- **Inability of SANs to share a single folder with multiple servers** SANs must allocate storage exclusively to a server or server cluster, unlike NAS devices that can share a folder with any number of clients and servers.

New SAN and NAS devices blur the differences between the technologies, and make it possible to choose hybrid approaches, such as NAS appliances that can connect to iSCSI SAN subsystems, and SAN subsystems that can function either as a SAN subsystem or as direct-attached storage.

Concepts and Terminology

To manage a SAN, it is helpful to understand the basics of how SANs work, as well as the terminology Storage Manager For SANs uses to describe various components of a SAN.

At a basic level, a SAN consists of the following components (shown in Figure 20-15):

- **SAN subsystem** A specialized server or server appliance that hosts a large number of hot-swappable hard disks for use on the storage network. The hard disks and hard disk controller(s) in the SAN subsystem usually use Fibre Channel, SAS, or SATA connections.
- **Storage network switch** A Fibre Channel or Gigabit Ethernet switch (when using the iSCSI protocol) that connects to the SAN subsystem and any hosts that directly access storage on the SAN subsystem.
- **Hosts** Servers or server clusters that utilize storage on the SAN subsystem. Storage assigned to the host appears as a normal hard drive in Windows. Hosts are connected to the storage network switch via a Host Bus Adapter (HBA) or a Gigabit Ethernet network card (when using iSCSI), and to the LAN switch via an Ethernet network card.
- **Management computer** A server running Windows Server 2008 that is connected to the SAN subsystem for management purposes. This could be a host server or another server on the storage network.
- **LAN switch** Connects computers to the organization's internal network, where other servers and client computers are located.

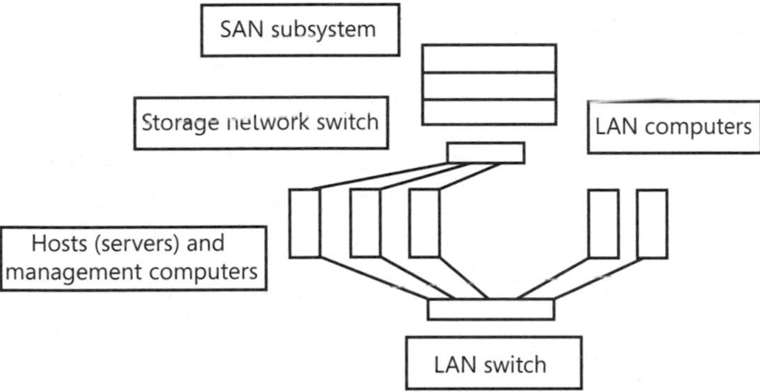

Figure 20-15 An example of a simple SAN

The SAN subsystem contains numerous hard drives that Storage Manager For SANs can segment and then allocate to hosts. A portion of a SAN that the SAN subsystem makes available to hosts and management servers is called a *Logical Unit* (LU). Hosts cannot directly access a LU—first you must use Storage Manager For SANs (or the SAN subsystem's management software) to assign an address to the LU—the Logical Unit Number (LUN). After you create a LUN, you can use Storage Manager For SANs to assign it to a server, where it appears as a normal hard drive. As with a real hard disk, only one server or server cluster can safely access a LUN at a time. To meet this requirement, you must assign the LUN to a server (when using Fibre Channel to communicate with the SAN subsystem), or to a target (when using iSCSI).

A *target* is group of one or more LUNs that you create on an iSCSI subsystem using Storage Manager For SANs or other iSCSI management software. To access a LUN on an iSCSI SAN, the host server or server cluster must log on to the target using an iSCSI initiator (driver). The initiator connects to the target using one or more IP addresses and port numbers. The combination of an IP address and port number is called a *portal*.

Note Windows cannot boot from an iSCSI LUN unless you use an iSCSI HBA that supports this functionality.

iSCSI Network Considerations

To maximize the security and performance of a SAN subsystem that utilizes the iSCSI protocol, do the following:

- Use a dedicated network that is physically separate from other networks and do not bridge it with other networks. Also limit who has physical access to ports on this network, the SAN subsystem, and servers on the storage network.

- If you cannot ensure physical security for the storage network, create Virtual Local Area Networks (VLANs) with your Ethernet switch, or at the very least, use a separate subnet for the storage network.
- Implement mutual Challenge Handshake Authentication Protocol (CHAP) authentication on all storage networks and Internet Protocol security (IPsec) encryption on any storage network that does not have adequate physical security for the sensitivity of the data on the SAN. When using IPsec, use network interface cards or HBAs with TCP Offload Engines (TOE) on the host servers to reduce processor utilization.
- Ensure that all devices on the storage network support Gigabit or 10 Gigabit Ethernet connections and Ethernet Jumbo Frames.
- Use an Ethernet switch designed for enterprise networks instead of small business or home users.
- Configure all NICs to use the highest possible Maximum Transmission Unit (MTU).
- When using iSCSI with a server cluster, use a minimum of three NICs per node. Connect each NIC to a physically separate network:
  - **SAN** Connect this NIC to the storage network. To add redundancy, use two NICs or iSCSI HBAs to connect to the storage network.
  - **Private/Cluster** Connect this NIC to a switch that connects to the other nodes in the cluster and nothing else.
  - **Corporate** Connect this NIC to the company's internal network.

Installing Storage Manager For SANs

Before you can use Storage Manager For SANs, you must perform the following steps:

1. Follow the instructions provided with the SAN subsystem to physically install the hardware and configure it to work on the appropriate network (preferably a dedicated storage network with limited physical access).
2. Setup the host server(s). This process includes the following tasks:
   - Installing Multipath IO (MPIO) software on the host if using MPIO with multiple Fibre Channel HBAs, or a storage array that uses multiple ports. Only install MPIO if your hardware supports it.

- ❑ Installing iSCSI initiator software on the host if using an iSCSI SAN. To use MPIO with iSCSI, select the Microsoft MPIO Multipathing Support For iSCSI option when installing the Microsoft iSCSI Initiator.
- ❑ Setting up the clustering service if using the host in a server cluster (see Chapter 21, "Using Clusters," for information about clustering).

Important You must install MPIO software on a host before you enable MPIO support for that host in Storage Manager For SANs. Failure to do so causes irreversible corruption of the volume.

3. Follow the instructions included with the SAN hardware to install the VDS hardware provider (provided by the SAN subsystem hardware manufacturer) on the computer on which you want to manage the SAN.

   Host computers that access the SAN do not need Storage Manager For SANs or VDS hardware providers.
4. Install Storage Manager For SANs on a computer running Windows Server 2008 or Windows Server 2003 R2 SP2. On Windows Server 2008, install by adding the Storage Manager For SANs feature from within Server Manager.

Using the Storage Manager For SANs Console

To use the Storage Manager For SANs console, open the Server Manager console or open the Storage Manager For SANs console (SANMMC.msc) from the Administrative Tools folder.

The Storage Manager For SANs console, shown in Figure 20-16, consists of three nodes, as discussed here and in the sections that follow:

- **LUN Management** This node is where you can perform all management tasks, such as managing server connections, iSCSI targets, creating LUNs, and assigning them to servers.
- **Subsystems** This node lists all SAN subsystems detected by the Storage Manager For SANs console.
- **Drives** This node lists all hard disks in all SAN subsystems, and allows you to blink drive lights or beep drive speakers (if supported by the SAN subsystem hardware).

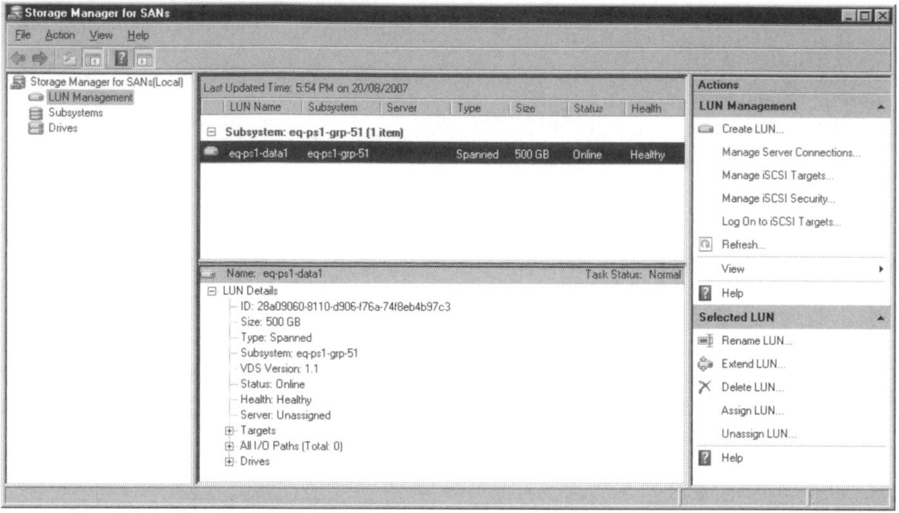

Figure 20-16 The Storage Manager For SANs console

Managing Server Connections

Before you can create and manage LUNs, you need to configure Storage Manager For SANs with connections to the appropriate SAN host computers. By default, Storage Manager For SANs connects to the local computer, but you can configure it to connect to any other computer. This allows you to run Storage Manager For SANs remotely for convenience. To configure Storage Manager For SANs to connect to a server, follow these steps:

1. In the Storage Manager For SANs console on the SAN administration computer, select LUN Management, then choose Manage Server Connections from the Actions menu. The Manage Server Connections dialog box appears as shown in Figure 20-17.

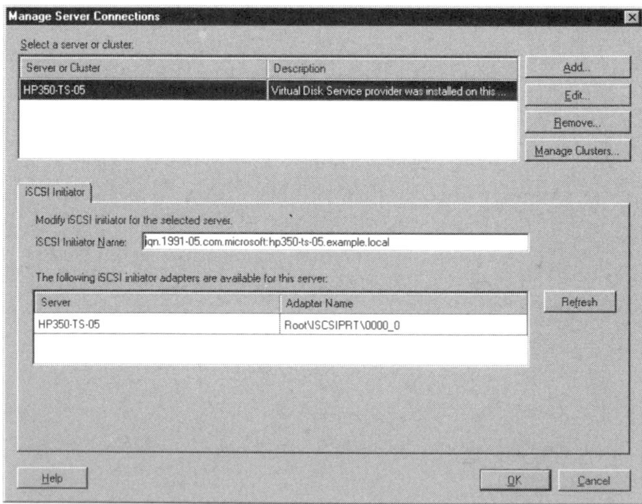

Figure 20-17 The Manage Server Connections dialog box

2. To add a server, click Add. In the Configure Server dialog box, type the server name and a description, and then click OK.
3. To add a server cluster, add all servers in the cluster, click Manage Clusters, and then click Add in the Manage Clusters dialog box. In the Add New Cluster dialog box, type a name for the cluster, select the servers in the cluster, and then click OK.

> **Important** Create the server cluster before adding it to Storage Manager For SANs—Storage Manager For SANs cannot create clusters. If you add servers to a cluster in Storage Manager for SANs that do not have the clustering service properly installed and configured, you will irretrievably corrupt the volume.

4. Select a server and then use the Fibre Channel or iSCSI tabs to view and enable ports on the server.
   - **Fibre Channel** Windows automatically detects Fibre Channel HBA ports on servers running Windows Server 2008 and lists them on the Fibre Channel tab if the server is on the same physical network as the management computer. To add a Fibre Channel port manually, click Add, type the World Wide Name (WWN) of the port and a description in the Add Port dialog box, and then click OK.
   - **iSCSI** Windows lists any iSCSI initiators it detects on the iSCSI tab. If the iSCSI initiator does not appear, click Refresh Adapters. If Windows cannot find the iSCSI initiator name, locate the name by running the Microsoft iSCSI Initiator Control Panel tool on the host computer, typing the name in the iSCSI Initiator Name box, and then clicking Refresh.
5. Select the check box next to each port you want to enable for communication with a LUN. Click OK when you are finished.
6. To manage server connections from a command prompt, use the *Diskraid* command. For example, open the command prompt window and then type the following commands:

```
Diskraid
List Subsystem
Select Subsystem 0
List HbaPort
Select HBAPort 0
Detail HBAPort
```

> **Important** Do not enable multiple Fibre Channel ports for communication with a LUN unless you install and configure MPIO software that is compatible with the HBAs. In addition, do not enable multiple iSCSI initiator adapters unless you also enable MPIO support in the iSCSI initiator. Enabling MPIO before properly configuring the HBAs or iSCSI initiator can cause irretrievable corruption of the LUN.

Managing iSCSI Targets

If the SAN subsystem is an iSCSI device, follow these steps to manage iSCSI targets before creating a LUN:

1. In Storage Manager For SANs, select LUN Management and then select Manage iSCSI Targets from the Actions menu. The Manage iSCSI Targets dialog box, shown in Figure 20-18, appears, listing the storage subsystem and any targets you have already added to the management console.

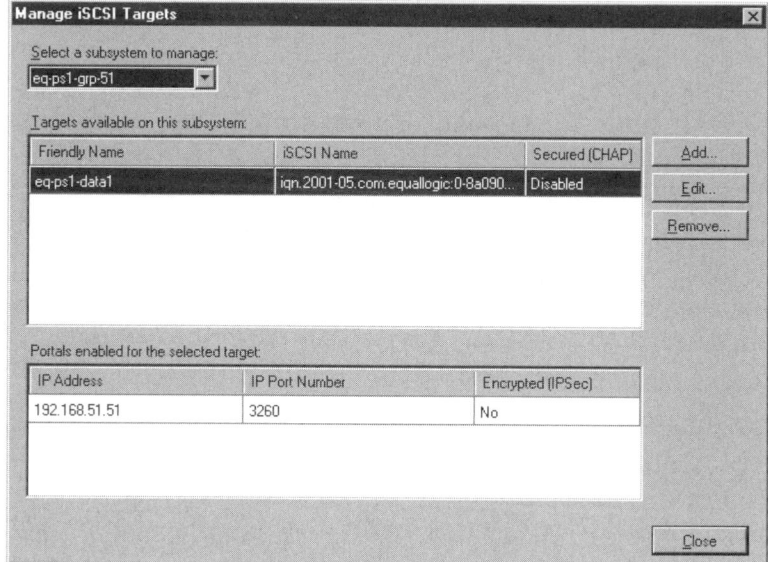

Figure 20-18 The Manage iSCSI Targets dialog box

2. Select a subsystem from the Select a Subsystem box and then click Create Target to add a target, or select an existing target and click Modify Target to change the target's settings.
3. In the Create Target dialog box, type a descriptive name for the target, and then select the portals to enable with this target. Click OK when you are finished.
4. To perform this procedure from a command prompt, use the **Diskraid** command. For example, open the Command Prompt window and then type the following commands:

```
Diskraid
Select Subsystem 0
Create Target Name="SQL Data"
```

Under the Hood DiskRAID

The command-line tool for managing SANs is Diskraid.exe. For any administrator who has spent any time in DiskPart, this tool will feel quite comfortable, and you can script it in the same way: by creating a text file with the commands you want to run in Diskraid, and then running them with the /s switch from the command line. The syntax for Diskraid is:

```
Usage:  DISKRAID [/? | [/s <script>] [/v]]
   Launches the DiskRAID application.
   /?            specifies that DiskRAID should display this usage text.
   /s <script>   specifies that DiskRAID should execute commands from the
                 script file at the location specified.
   /v            specifies that DiskRAID should run in verbose mode, printing
                 out additional information about each command being executed.
```

Managing iSCSI Security

Although a physically separate storage network provides the best performance and security, it is not always practical. In addition, even a physically separate network is not necessarily secure, and it is a best security practice to enable two-way authentication (where the host authenticates with the SAN hardware and SAN hardware authenticates with the host) and IPsec encryption on all iSCSI targets and hosts that contain important data. To configure iSCSI authentication and encryption, follow these steps:

1. In Storage Manager For SANs, select LUN Management and then choose Manage iSCSI Security from the Actions menu to bring up the Manage iSCSI Security dialog box, shown in Figure 20-19.

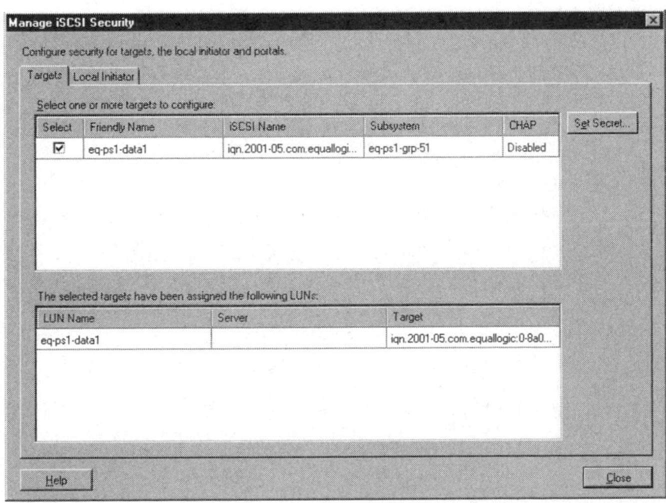

Figure 20-19 The Manage iSCSI Security dialog box

2. On the Targets tab, configure one-way CHAP authentication with the appropriate target or targets.
3. On the Local Initiator tab, configure CHAP authentication for the iSCSI initiator (which is the second part of mutual CHAP authentication).
4. On the Portals tab (if present), set IPsec keys for portals, thereby enabling encryption on the portals.
5. To manage iSCSI security from a command prompt, use the `Diskraid` command. For example, open the Command Prompt window and then type the following commands:

```
Diskraid
Select Subsystem 1
Select target 1
CHAP Target Set Secret="password"
CHAP Target Remember Secret="password"
   Initiator=iqn.1991-05.com.microsoft:srv1.example.local
CHAP Initiator Set Secret="password"
CHAP Initiator Remember Secret="password"
   Initiator= iqn.1991-05.com.microsoft:srv1.example.local
```

Important Use strong secrets and IPSec keys that comply with the password policies of your administrator accounts, and do not leave these passwords in locations that are not secure—such as on sticky notes in the datacenter.

Logging In to iSCSI Targets

Before you can create a LUN on an iSCSI target, the iSCSI initiator must log in to the target. You only need to do this once; afterward the iSCSI initiator will log in automatically.

1. In Storage Manager For SANs, select LUN Management and then select Login To iSCSI Targets from the Actions menu. The Login To Target dialog box appears.
2. Select the targets that you want to log in to, and then select the authentication method used on the targets from the following:
   - Login with no CHAP authentication
   - Login with one-way CHAP authentication (target secret only)
   - Login with mutual CHAP authentication (target with initiator secrets)
3. Click Login.
4. To log in to an iSCSI target from a command prompt, use the `Diskraid` command. For example, open the Command Prompt window and then type the following commands:

```
Diskraid
Select Subsystem 1
Select Target 1 Create TPGroup
Login Target Iadapter=0
```

Creating and Deploying Logical Units (LUNs)

To give a server or server cluster storage resources on a SAN, you must first create a LUN and assign it to the server or cluster. A LUN that you assign to a server or cluster appears on the server just like a normal hard drive. Follow these steps to create and deploy a LUN:

Note The following steps are for an iSCSI SAN. If you're using a Fibre Channel SAN, your steps will be slightly different.

1. Click the Subsystems node in the Storage Manager For SANs console and verify that Storage Manager For SANs lists the storage subsystem on which you want to create a LUN, as shown in Figure 20-20.

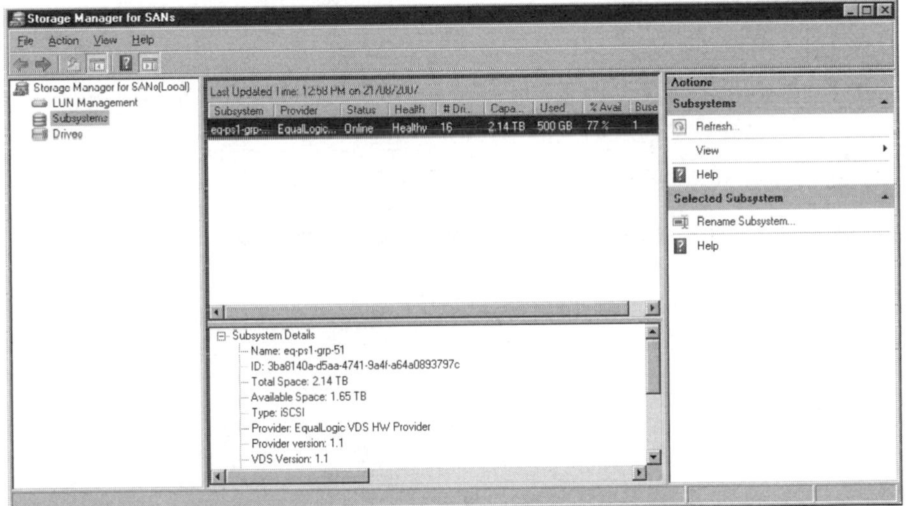

Figure 20-20 The Subsystems node of Storage Manager For SANs

2. Select LUN Management and then select Create LUN from the Actions menu. The Provision Storage Wizard appears, as shown in Figure 20-21.

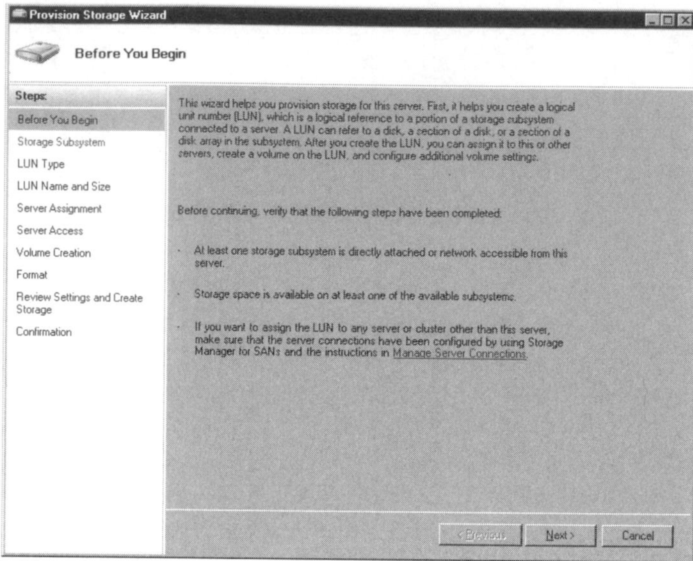

Figure 20-21 The Before You Begin page of the Provision Storage Wizard

3. Read the Before You Begin page carefully. Make sure you're ready to proceed, and then click Next to bring up the Storage Subsystem page. Select the subsystem you want to create the LUN on.

4. Click Next to bring up the LUN Type page, as shown in Figure 20-22.

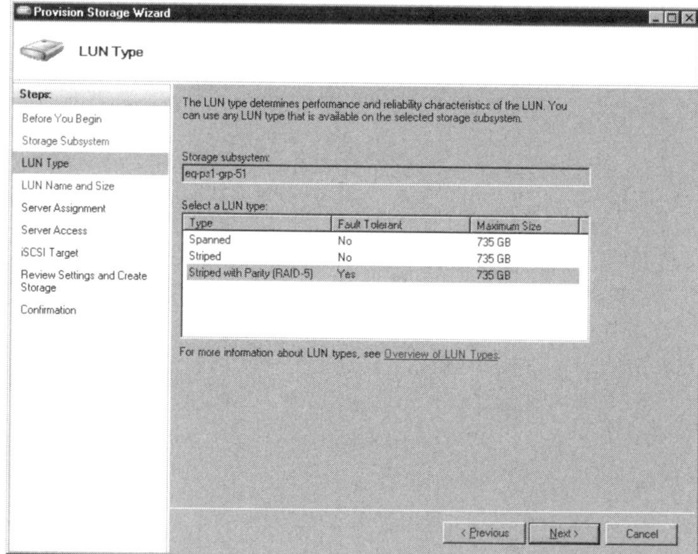

Figure 20-22 The LUN Type page of the Provision Storage Wizard

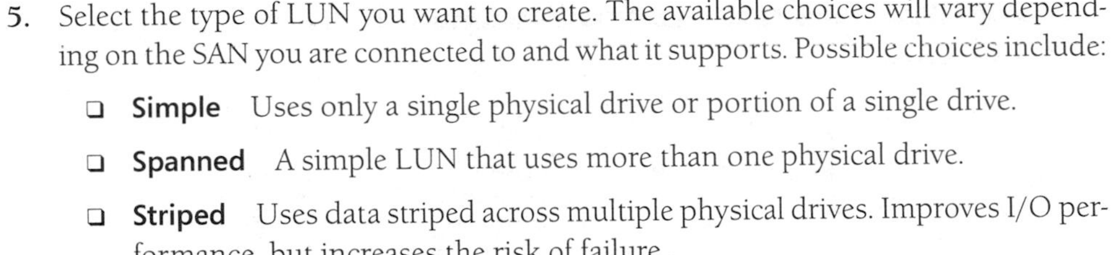

5. Select the type of LUN you want to create. The available choices will vary depending on the SAN you are connected to and what it supports. Possible choices include:
   - **Simple** Uses only a single physical drive or portion of a single drive.
   - **Spanned** A simple LUN that uses more than one physical drive.
   - **Striped** Uses data striped across multiple physical drives. Improves I/O performance, but increases the risk of failure.
   - **Mirrored** Uses two physical drives. The second drive has an exact duplicate of the data on the first drive. Provides full redundancy in case of failure of either drive.
   - **Striped With Parity (RAID-5)** Uses data striped across multiple physical drives, with parity information spread across the drives as well, providing fault tolerance in the event of failure of any one disk.

   Note The LUN types in the Provision Storage Wizard list correspond roughly to the Redundant Array of Independent Disks (RAID) level used by the SAN subsystem. However, the actual implementation depends on the hardware. For example, some SAN subsystems use RAID 1+0 (10) for the Striped With Parity setting, while others use the more standard RAID 5. Consult the hardware manufacturer for details on the RAID levels that the SAN subsystem supports.

6. Click Next to move to the LUN Name And Size page of the Provision Storage Wizard, shown in Figure 20-23. Type a name for the LUN (if the SAN subsystem supports LUN naming), and the size for the LUN. Click Next.

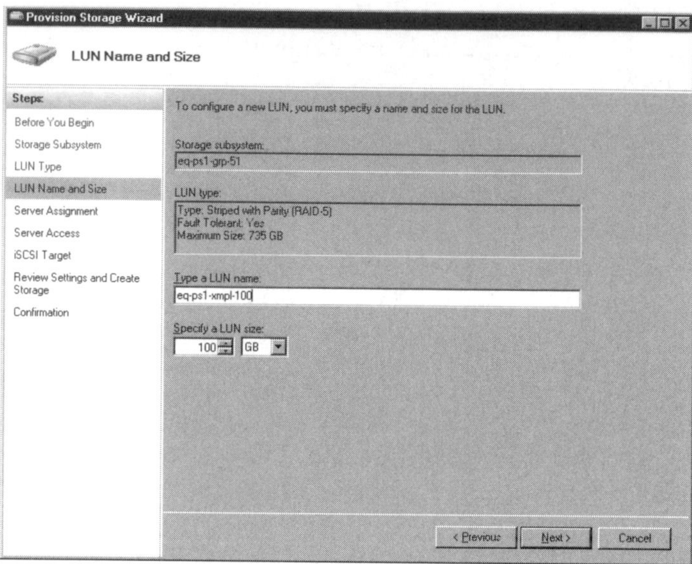

Figure 20-23 The LUN Name And Size page of the Provision Storage Wizard

7. On the Server Assignment page, choose This Server Only, Other Server Or Cluster, or Not Assign LUN Now. You must assign the LUN to a server, cluster, or iSCSI target before you can create a volume on it or access it from the server or server cluster. Click Next.

8. On the Server Access page, specify the server or cluster to assign the LUN to. Click Next.

9. On the iSCSI Target page, shown in Figure 20-24, you can assign the LUN now, or choose to assign it later. Click Next.

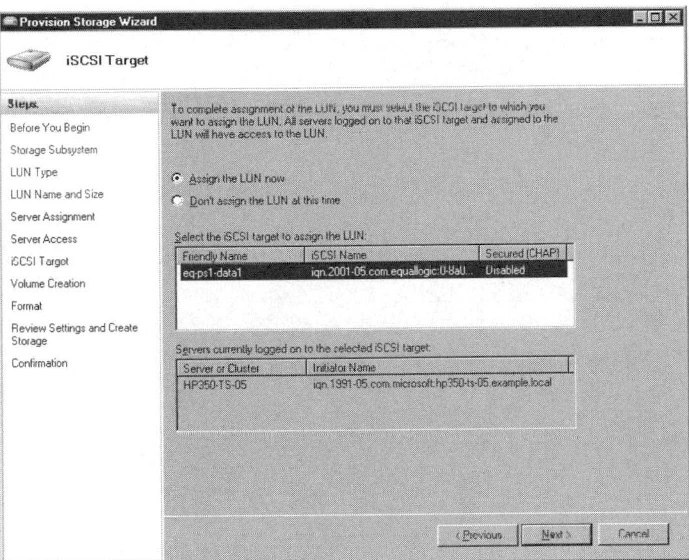

Figure 20-24 The iSCSI Target page of the Provision Storage Wizard

10. On the Volume Creation page, shown in Figure 20-25, you can create a volume and assign a drive letter or mount on an existing NTFS folder. The Provision Storage Wizard cannot create volumes on remote servers, so you won't have this option if you're creating a LUN that's assigned to a remote server. Use the Disk Management snap-in or Diskpart.exe command-line tool to create a volume on a remote server. Click Next.

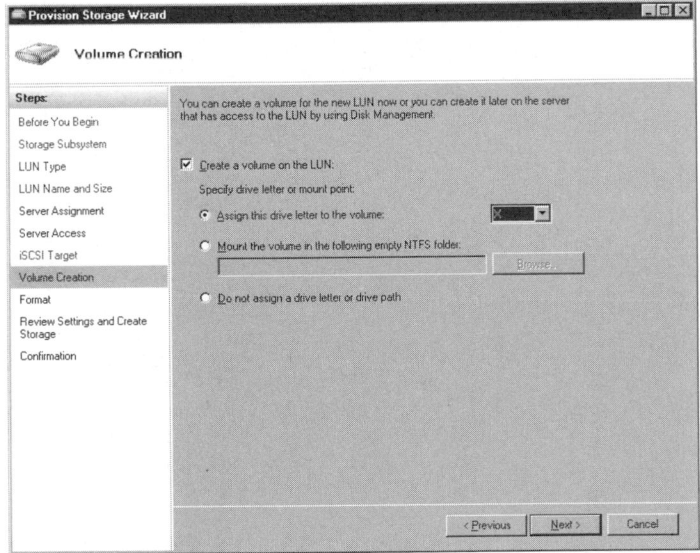

Figure 20-25 The Volume Creation page of the Provision Storage Wizard

11. On the Format page, shown in Figure 20-26, you can specify the formatting options. Only NTFS is supported. Click Next.

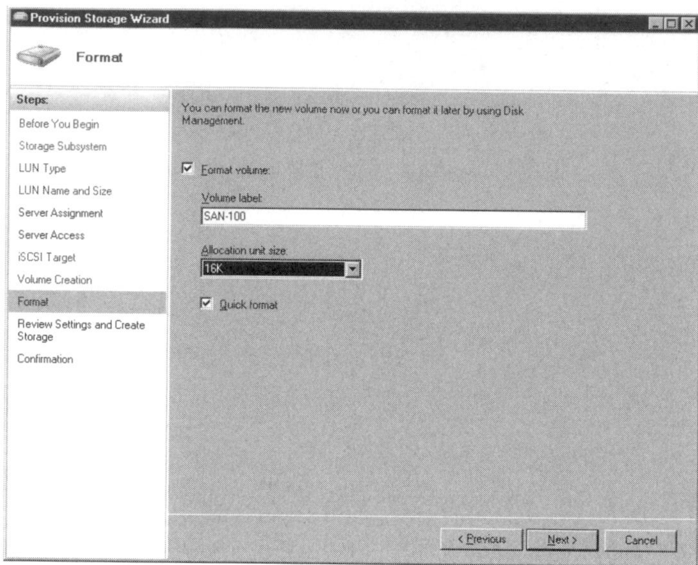

Figure 20-26 The Format page of the Provision Storage Wizard

12. The Review Settings And Create Storage page displays all your settings, as shown in Figure 20-27. If the settings are correct, click Create to actually create the LUN. Storage Manager For SANs creates the LUN, assigns it to the server or target you specify, and formats the volume (if you chose to format it on the Format page).

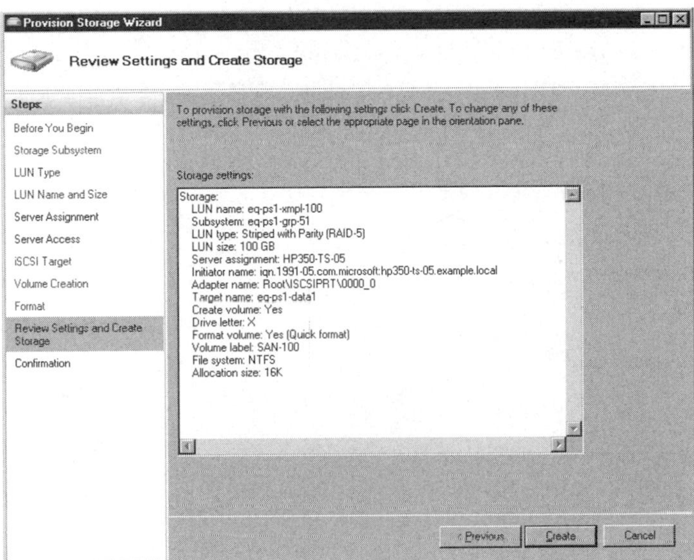

Figure 20-27 The Review Settings And Create Storage page of the Provision Storage Wizard

13. If you did not assign the LUN to a server in the wizard, do so now by right-clicking the LUN in the Storage Manager For SANs console and choosing Assign LUN. Then, in the Assign LUN To Server dialog box, select the server to which you want to assign the LUN. To unassign a LUN, right-click it and choose Unassign LUN.

14. To create a LUN and assign it to a server or an iSCSI target from a command prompt, use the **Diskraid** command. For example, open the Command Prompt window and type the following commands:

```
Diskraid
Select Subsystem 0
Create LUN RAID Size=10GB
Associate Targets 1
```

Note It is a good idea to do a full format of new volumes on LUNs. Although slower than a quick format, it scans the LUN for bad sectors and excludes them from the volume, decreasing the likelihood of volume corruption.

Extending a LUN

As long as you have available storage space on the SAN, you can increase (extend) the size of an existing LUN. If the SAN subsystem runs low on available disk space, simply add more hard disks.

To extend a LUN, right-click the LUN you want to extend, choose Extend LUN, and then specify a new LUN size in the Extend LUN dialog box, shown in Figure 20-28. After extending a LUN on a remote server, you must use Disk Management or Diskpart.exe to extend the file system.

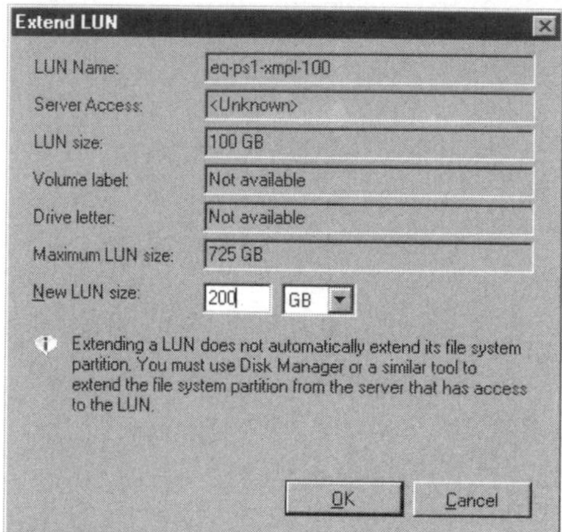

Figure 20-28 The Extend LUN dialog box

Extending a LUN remotely will force the LUN (and its file system) offline, as shown in Figure 20-29.

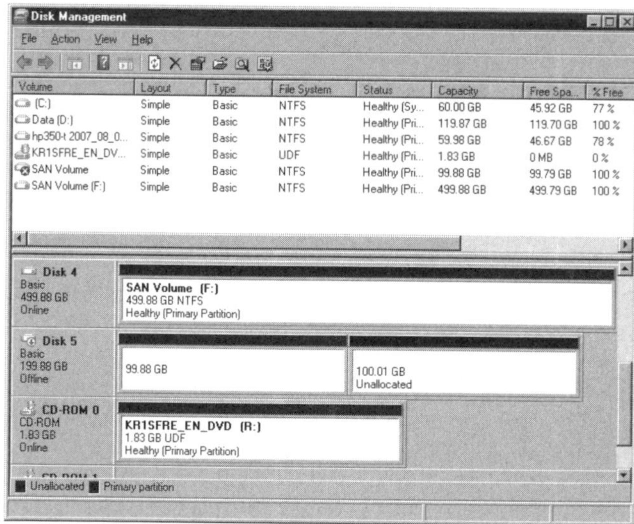

Figure 20-29 Disk Management showing the disk on the extended LUN offline

To extend the file system using Disk Management, select the disk, right-click, and select Online. Then, right-click the volume and select Extend Volume. To do the same using the command line, follow the sequence shown in Figure 20-30.

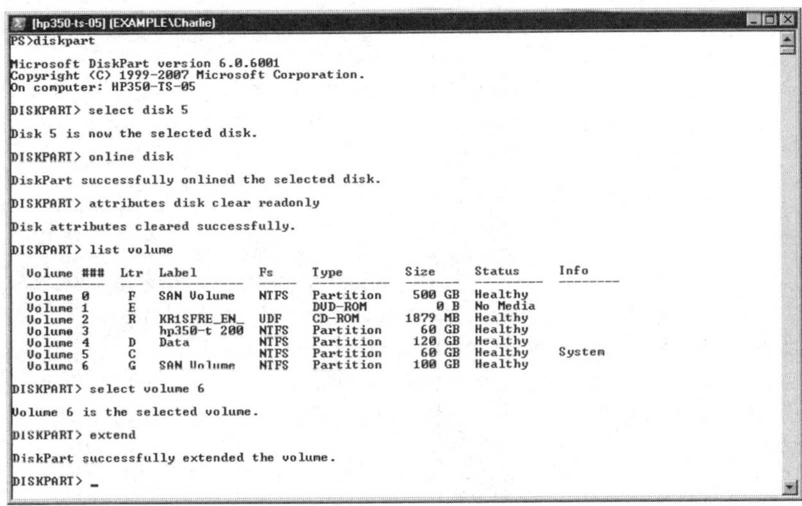

Figure 20-30 DiskPart sequence to bring the disk on an extended LUN online and extend the volume to fill the new space

Removable Storage

If you need to manage removable storage (tapes and writeable optical media), you can add the Removable Storage feature of Windows Server 2008. Removable storage has been deemphasized in Windows Server 2008, and you can no longer use it for backups or other functions, though third-party backup applications can still use tape.

Concepts and Terminology

Removable Storage has its own language, specific to removable devices, so a quick glossary will help keep us all on the same page.

Removable Devices and Libraries

Removable storage collectively refers to removable storage devices and their associated media (tapes or disks) as libraries. Before you purchase a removable storage library to use with Removable Storage, check the Windows Server Catalog Web site at *http://www.microsoft.com/windows/catalog/server* to make sure Windows Server 2008 fully supports the device. Also check to make sure the program you plan to use the device with supports the class of device.

When you connect a removable storage device to the system, Windows tries to recognize and configure it. When you launch Removable Storage, it performs its own device configuration and attempts to configure all removable storage devices connected to the system.

Important If you plan to use a robotic media library with Removable Storage and want the library to be automatically configured (trust us, you do), make sure that all drives in the library are connected to the same SCSI (or similar) bus as the drives' associated media changer, and that no other devices reside on this SCSI bus. Also make sure that the library supports drive-element address reporting.

Media Pools

All removable media belong to a *media pool*, which is a group of media that all have the same properties. Media are available for use by applications only if they belong to the appropriate media pool. Two types of media pools exist: system pools and application pools. All media that are not reserved for use by an application reside in one of the three system media pools. See Table 20-1 for a description of the three system media pools.

Note The *free media pool* is where applications look when they need media and no media exists with space available in the application's pool. Therefore, try to keep some media in the free media pool so that applications can draw from it as necessary.

Table 20-1 The Three System Media Pools

System Media Pool	Purpose
Free	To hold empty (blank but formatted) media available to all applications.
Import	To hold newly added media to the system that has a recognizable format but has never been used in the system before. You can move the media to the free media pool if you want to erase the media; you can move the media to an application pool to use in a particular application.
Unrecognized	To hold unrecognized media until they can be moved into the free pool or an application pool by a user or an application.

An *application media pool* is any media pool that applications create to hold their own media. Applications can create multiple media pools, or multiple applications can share the same media pool, although most applications require media to be in their own application pool.

Removable Storage Media Identification

Removable Storage keeps track of all media that you insert into the removable storage libraries in one of two ways: by using on-media identifiers or by using barcodes. *On-media identifiers* are small data stamps that Removable Storage imprints on the media the first time you insert them. The identifier has two parts: a label type and a label ID. The label type identifies the format used on the media, and the label ID uniquely identifies the tape or disk. Removable Storage uses these two identifiers to determine which media pool to place new media in and to keep track of all the media in the system. Table 20-2 shows how Removable Storage deals with recognized and unrecognized labels.

Table 20-2 Removable Storage and Media Identifiers

	Label Type Recognized	Label Type Unrecognized
Label ID Recognized	Media placed in appropriate media pool and database updated to show media is online	N/A
Label ID Unrecognized	Media placed in import media pool	Media placed in unrecognized media pool

If you have a robotic library that has a barcode reader, you can use it to quickly keep track of all media that goes with the library. Removable Storage can use either the on-media identifier or the barcode to identify the media, although using the barcode is often much faster than using on-media identifiers because you do not have to mount each piece of media to keep track of it.

Removable Storage handles media with file systems on them (such as CD-ROMs and Zip disks) a little differently than other types of media. The label type for these media is usually the format type (NTFS, FAT, or CDFS), and the label ID is the volume serial number. Additionally, in the case of CD-ROM and DVD media, Removable Storage permits multiple media with the same label ID (such as a CD-ROM tower with multiple copies of the same disc), as the media can function interchangeably.

Media States

Removable Storage uses *media states* to figure out the current status of a piece of media, both in terms of the physical state of the media–whether it is being used or sitting idle–and in terms of the media's availability for additional data (for example, whether the media is full, formatted incorrectly, or reserved by a single program). Removable Storage refers to these two types of media states as physical states and side states.

Note Libraries and drives also have their own states, but they are self-explanatory and less important than media states.

Physical States

Physical states describe the actual physical availability of the media–is the media in the drive, and if so, is it ready to be used? Removable Storage recognizes the following five physical states:

- **Idle** The media is in the library or shelved offline in a changer.
- **In-use** The media is currently in the process of being mounted or dismounted.
- **Loaded** The media is mounted and available for read/write operations.
- **Mounted** The media is mounted but not yet available for read/write operations.
- **Unloaded** The media has been dismounted and can be removed from the drive.

Side States

A *side* is the location, the physical side of the disk or tape, where information is located. Side states in Removable Storage indicate media use; physical states report media readiness.

Removable Storage uses side states in part to determine which media pool to place the media into. Media pools can only hold media in the same state as the pool–for example, the import pool can contain sides that are currently in only the Imported state, the unrecognized pool can contain sides only in the Unrecognized state, and so on. The nine side states that Removable Storage uses are as follows:

- **Allocated** An application has reserved the side.
- **Available** The side is currently available for use by applications.
- **Completed** The side is in use but full, so it is unavailable for further write operations.
- **Decommissioned** The side is no longer available for use because it has reached its allocation maximum.
- **Imported** The side label type is recognized, but the label ID hasn't yet been cataloged into a media pool by this computer's Removable Storage tool.
- **Incompatible** The formatting of the side is incompatible with the library. Remove the media.
- **Reserved** The side is unavailable to all applications except the application that allocated the opposite side. Applies only to dual-sided media where one side has already been allocated.
- **Unprepared** The side has been placed in the free media pool but doesn't yet have a free media label. This state is temporary and changes to the available side state, barring a problem.

- **Unrecognized** Removable Storage cannot recognize the side's label type and ID.

Use and Management

The Removable Storage console is not integrated into Server Manager. You can only use it stand-alone (NTmsmgr.msc) or as part of Computer Management.

Managing Libraries

The tasks involved with managing libraries are all physically oriented: configuring libraries added to the system, enabling and disabling libraries, changing the available media types, working with robotic libraries, and cleaning libraries.

Inventorying Libraries

Removable Storage automatically creates an inventory of the media as you insert them into the library (actually, each time a library door is accessed). To change the way Removable Storage updates the media inventory for robotic storage libraries, or to force Removable Storage to recheck the inventory, follow these steps:

1. To inventory the robotic storage library, right-click the library in the Libraries folder of Removable Storage and choose Inventory from the shortcut menu. Removable Storage inventories the library according to the default method specified for the library.
2. To change the default method of inventorying for a library, right-click the library in the Libraries folder of Removable Storage and choose Properties from the shortcut menu. Then choose an option from the Inventory Method drop-down list box, described in Table 20-3.
3. Clear the Perform Full Inventory On Mount Failure check box if you don't want Removable Storage to conduct a full inventory every time the library fails to mount a tape or disk.
4. To inventory a library from the command line, use the `RSM Inventory` command. For example, type: **RSM Inventory /LF"Archive Python 06408-xxx SCSI Sequential Device" /AFast**.

Note Run the `RSM View` command to obtain the friendly name or GUID to use with other commands. For example, to view the friendly name and GUID for all libraries in the server, type **RSM View /TLibrary /GUIDDisplay**. Enclose friendly names that contain spaces within quotes when using them in commands, and make sure the quotes are strict ACSI quotes, not Microsoft Word "smart quotes."

Table 20-3 **Library Inventory Methods**

Inventory Method	Description
None	No automatic inventory is performed.
Fast	Performs a quick inventory by checking which slots have had media swapped.
Full	Mounts each media in the library and reads the media's on-media identifier. Can be slow on libraries with a lot of media.

Setting Door and Inject/Eject Port Timeouts

All libraries have at least one inject/eject port that is used for inserting and removing media from the library, and robotic libraries also often have a door that can be opened to directly access media in a particular drive. To set the amount of time allowed before Removable Storage times out the port or door, thereby preventing further operations with it, follow these steps:

1. Right-click the library you want to configure, and then choose Properties from the shortcut menu.
2. Click the Components tab, and then type a timeout period in minutes for the library door (if available) and inject/eject ports.

> **Note** To open a library door, right-click the library and then choose Door Access from the shortcut menu. When prompted, you can open the door and access the media (you have until the door timeout period expires). However, whenever you open the library door, Removable Storage needs to perform a full inventory unless you use a barcode reader. Therefore, it is preferable to use the inject/eject port in most circumstances.

Enabling and Disabling Individual Drives in a Library

If you have a storage library with multiple drives, you can disable or enable individual drives as needed by following these steps:

1. Select the library containing the drive you want to configure, and then double-click Drives.
2. Right-click the drive you want to enable or disable, and then choose Properties from the shortcut menu.
3. Clear the Enable Drive check box on the General tab to disable the drive.

> **Note** To enable or disable a removable storage library (making the library unavailable for use by applications), right-click the library you want to enable or disable, choose Properties, and then select or clear the Enable Library check box.

Cleaning Libraries

Most removable storage libraries need to be cleaned—maybe once a week or more depending on their use and the type of drive. Because of this ongoing need, Removable Storage makes it easy to clean the drives and keep track of when you last did so.

1. To clean a robotic library, right-click the library you want to clean and choose Cleaner Management from the shortcut menu. Then use the Cleaner Management Wizard to clean the drive.
2. To clean a stand-alone library, manually insert the cleaning tape and clean the drive as instructed by the drive manufacturer or the tape manufacturer. When you are finished, right-click the drive you cleaned in the pane on the right and choose Mark As Clean from the shortcut menu.

Managing Media Pools

Handling media pools is the most important task you perform with Removable Storage. Applications draw from either the free media pool or one or more application media pools when they require media.

Note To move a piece of media from one media pool to another, drag the media from its current location to the media pool in which you want to store it.

Managing Physical Media

Physical media—tapes or disks—are the reason storage libraries and media pools exist. Actually dealing with the physical media is pretty easy, and the kind of tasks involved include inserting and ejecting media, mounting and dismounting media, enabling and disabling media, and moving media between media pools. This is simple stuff, but a quick review might be useful.

Injecting and Ejecting Media

Use Removable Storage to handle injecting and ejecting media into robotic storage libraries instead of using the device's physical buttons or ports. Injecting (inserting) and ejecting media in stand-alone drives is simple: to inject, place the media in the drive; to eject, press the eject button.

To inject media from a storage library, right-click the library and choose Inject from the shortcut menu. To eject a tape or disk from the storage library, right-click the media you want to eject, and then choose Eject from the shortcut menu.

Mounting and Dismounting Media

When you insert a piece of media in a library, the media is in the Idle state and cannot be immediately accessed by an application. To use a piece of media, Windows must first mount the media, which puts it in the Loaded state. Most applications automatically mount the media as needed; however, you can also manually mount media. To do so, right-click the media and then choose Mount from the shortcut menu.

To eject a piece of media, the media must be idle. Normally if an application is finished accessing the media, the media returns to the Idle state; however, if the media is currently in the Loaded state and you need to eject the media immediately, you have to manually dismount the media before you eject it. To dismount the media, right-click the media and then choose Dismount from the shortcut menu.

Note To make a particular piece of media unavailable for use, eject it and store it somewhere. To keep the media in the library and prevent applications from using it, right-click the media in Removable Storage, choose Properties, and then clear the Enable Media check box.

Using the Work Queue

The work queue is a list of all activities that have been performed in Removable Storage and acts in much the same way as the Windows event log does, except that the work queue lists actions that need to be performed as well as completed actions. To view the work queue or the operator requests list, select Work Queue from the console tree in the Removable Storage MMC snap-in. From the list of actions in the Work Queue, you have additional options on individual actions:

- To view any additional information about an action, such as additional error messages on failed actions, right-click the action and choose Properties from the shortcut menu.
- To cancel a pending action, right-click the action and choose Cancel Action from the shortcut menu.
- To adjust the priority of a pending action, right-click the pending action and choose Reorder Mounts. Removable Storage displays the Change Mount Order dialog box.
- To move the request to the beginning of the queue, select Move To The Front Of The Queue.
- To move the request to the end of the queue, select Move To The End Of The Queue.
- To specify exactly which place in the queue the request should be, select Make It Number and then select the number in the queue that you want the request to be.

Working with Operator Requests

Operator requests occur when an action requires direct operator intervention, such as the insertion of offline media or the need for a new cleaning cartridge. When an operator request occurs, the system displays a message indicating that a specific action is required. Perform the action and click OK to resolve the request.

- To refuse the request or manually mark the request as completed, select Operator Requests in the Removable Storage console tree, right-click the pending operation, and choose Refuse from the shortcut menu to cancel the request, or choose Complete after fulfilling the request.
- To modify how long Removable Storage keeps old operator requests, right-click Operator Requests in the console tree, choose Properties from the shortcut menu, and then use the Operator Requests Properties dialog box to change these settings.
- To change how Removable Storage notifies you when an operator request is due, right-click the Removable Storage root in the console tree, choose Properties, and then set the values for the Display Operator Request Dialogs and Use Status Area Icon For Notifying About Mounts check boxes.

Summary

Windows Server 2008 provides a number of new and improved features that help you manage storage, including the storage reports, quotas, and file screens of File Server Resource Manager; and the Storage Manager For SANs console, which makes it far easier to manage simple SANs. Windows Server 2008 also continues to support Removable Storage as a feature, essentially unchanged from earlier versions of Windows Server. The next chapter covers failover clustering in Windows Server 2008.

Chapter 21

Using Clusters

Windows Server 2008 supports two high-availability clustering technologies: Network Load Balancing (NLB) clusters and Failover clusters. Microsoft does not support combining these clustering technologies. This chapter describes the two types of clustering supported by Windows Server 2008, their place in the enterprise, and their configuration and requirements. Finally, we'll take a brief look at a new Microsoft clustering technology that is designed to support high-performance computing (HPC)–Microsoft HPC Server 2008.

What Is a Cluster?

A *cluster* is a group of two or more computers functioning together to provide a common set of applications or services with a single apparent identity to clients. The computers are physically connected by a network and usually share storage such as iSCSI, Serial Attached SCSI, or Fibre Channel. The clustering software provides a virtual identity to clients while managing the cluster resources and load internally.

Windows Clustering provides the following benefits:

- **High availability** When a clustered application or computer in the cluster fails, the cluster responds by restarting the application if possible or by moving the failed application from the failed server to another computer in the cluster.

- **Scalability** For cluster-aware applications, adding more computers to the cluster adds more capabilities.
- **Manageability** Administrators can move applications, services, and data from computer to computer within the cluster, allowing them to manually balance loads and to offload computers scheduled for maintenance.

Network Load Balancing Clusters

NLB gives TCP/IP-based services and applications high availability and scalability by combining up to 32 servers running Windows Server 2008 in a single cluster. By combining NLB with round-robin DNS, NLB clustering can scale well beyond 32 servers. Client requests for applications and services provided by the cluster are distributed across the available servers in the cluster in a way that is transparent to the client. NLB clusters are supported in all versions of Windows Server 2008.

If a server fails or is taken offline, the cluster is automatically reconfigured and the client connections are redistributed across the remaining servers. If additional servers are added to the cluster, they are automatically recognized and the load is reconfigured and distributed.

Failover Clusters

Failover clusters are manually configured to distribute the workload among the servers in a cluster, with each server running its own workload. Like other types of clusters, Failover clusters are scalable and highly available. In the event of a failure, applications and services that can be restarted, such as print queues and file services, are restarted automatically. Ownership of shared resources passes to the remaining servers. When the failed server becomes available again, the workload can be automatically rebalanced.

Windows Server 2008 supports Failover clusters only in the Enterprise and Datacenter versions. There are four basic types of Failover clusters supported by Windows Server 2008: single node clusters, single quorum device clusters, MNS clusters, and hybrid clusters, as shown in Figure 21-1.

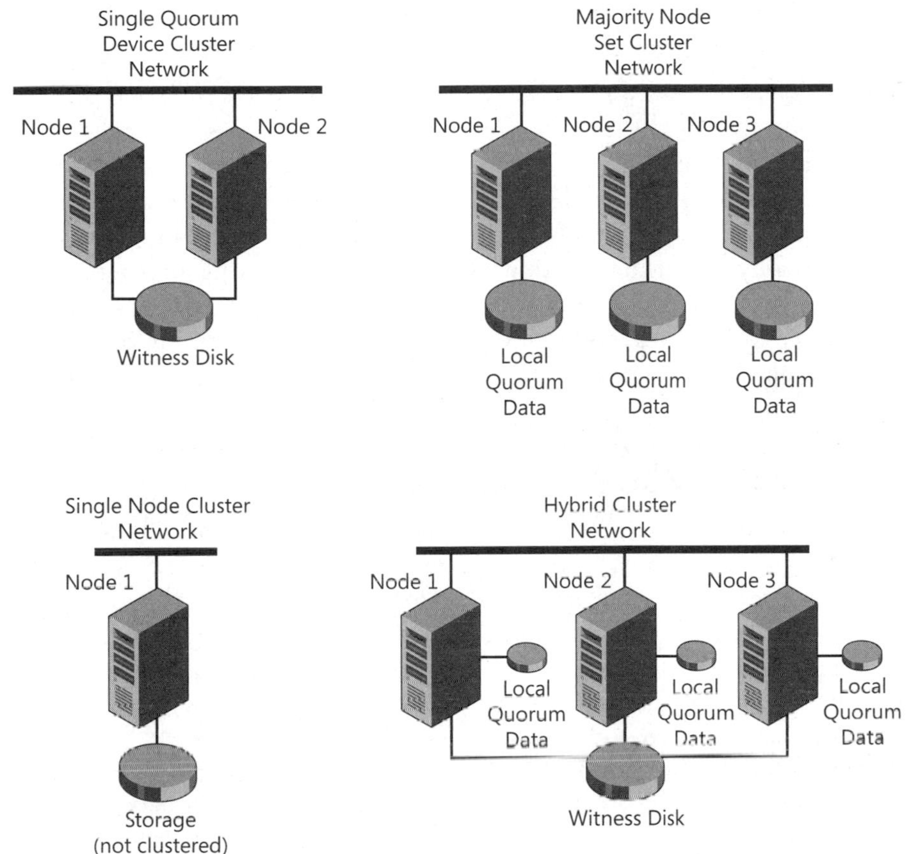

Figure 21-1 Windows Server 2008 supports four different Failover cluster models.

New Failover Cluster Features

There are several changes to Failover clusters in Windows Server 2008. The changes include a unique new way Microsoft determines supportability of Failover clusters, new setup processes, operational changes, and infrastructure improvements. The list is quite long, but some of the key new features include:

- **Cluster Validation Tool** The new Validate Tool in Failover clusters performs tests to determine whether your system, storage, and network configuration is suitable for a cluster. This replaces the old concept of vendors assembling, configuring, and testing Failover cluster configurations and publishing the results as a cluster-compliant solution.

- **Cluster Setup** The new setup process includes tests to ensure that all Failover cluster components have the proper number and type of resources. It also includes a new scriptable interface to enable administrators to script installation processes for multiple Failover clusters.
- **Cluster Infrastructure** A new Failover type called a Hybrid cluster combines Majority Node Set and Single Quorum cluster concepts to reduce complexity and single points of failure. Administrators can also add new disk resources to application on the fly to provide additional capacity without taking a resource offline. Disks that are more than 2 terabytes in size are now supported by using GUID Partition Table (GPT) disks. And Failover clusters now have built-in support for IPV6-based clusters.

Windows Server 2008 Core

Windows Server 2008 introduces a new concept called Server Core (See Chapter 9, "Installing and Configuring Server Core," for more information) that enables administrators to deploy servers with a smaller installation footprint, reduce complexity, and lower TCO. A primary advantage of Server Core is the reduction in managing updates, maintenance, and configuration of the Windows GUI. Server Core is an ideal operating configuration for both NLB and Failover clusters. Because this mode reduces the complexity of the install, the maintenance requirements of Server Core–based servers are reduced. This translates to less downtime for maintenance and updates. In addition, it also improves the overall reliability of the cluster by reducing the possibility of errant applications, services, and drivers.

Real World Clustering Server Core

Unless your cluster applications specifically require components offered only by a full install, you should carefully and thoroughly consider using Server Core for your clusters. After all, you're considering clustering your applications because they are important to your business, so you should maximize the uptime of your cluster.

By choosing to cluster Server Core, you reduce the complexity, reduce the maintenance requirements, reduce the attack surface, and reduce the update requirements. All of these things can interfere with uptime. So if your goal is maximized uptime, choosing Server Core for your clustered workloads that can use it just makes sense.

Cluster Scenarios

In deciding whether and how to implement clustering, you first need to understand what problem is being solved and how best to solve it using the available technologies. Then you can make a business case for the particular solution or combination of solutions that best solves the particular problem. This section describes various scenarios and the type of clustering appropriate for each.

Web Server

An intranet or Internet Web server is a prime candidate for an NLB cluster. By enabling an NLB cluster across multiple servers, you provide your Web site with both redundancy and increased capacity. If a server fails, the load is distributed transparently among the remaining servers.

Each Web server in the cluster runs its own IIS service and uses a local copy of the Web site. This type of clustering is called *shared nothing* clustering–there are no shared disks and no shared applications or data, with the possible exception of a common back-end database. NLB clusters are an appropriate and relatively inexpensive way to achieve both redundancy and high availability for your Web site, whether it's internal or external. Clients that need access to Web pages are distributed among the servers in the cluster according to the load at each server. What makes this work is that most Web pages change infrequently, allowing manual updates of all Web servers with the same information when you need to make changes.

Terminal Services

Starting with Windows Server 2003, Terminal Services supports clustering using NLB clusters and the new Session Broker to distribute Terminal Services sessions across a farm of servers running Terminal Services. This allows for high availability and load balancing, and presents a single face to Remote Desktop clients. If you have large numbers of Terminal Services users, Windows Server 2008 using NLB clustering for Terminal Services gives them additional flexibility, redundancy, and improved user experience. For more information about Terminal Services Session Broker, see *http://technet2.microsoft.com/windowsserver2008/en/library/f9fe9c74-77f5-4bba-a6b9-433d823bbfbd1033.mspx?mfr=true.*

Mission-Critical Applications and Services

If your business absolutely, positively can't be run without a certain application or set of applications, you need a highly reliable server to make sure that the application is always available. A Failover cluster is a good solution in this scenario, providing both high availability and scalability. With a Failover cluster, you organize your critical applications into groups that contain all the needed resources to operate. All the resources for each group are self-contained on the server, but if any server in the cluster fails, the others pick up the services and applications from the failed server, allowing for nearly continuous availability of critical services and applications. You can control the failover and fallback actions for each group of clustered resources.

Failover clusters require a substantially greater investment in hardware and planning than NLB clusters. Three types of Failover clusters are defined based on the method they use to manage and track the configuration of the cluster. The traditional method uses a quorum disk—now called a Witness Disk—to determine which server is in control of the cluster and to ensure that all the cluster computers can communicate changes to each other. Majority node set (MNS) clustering does not use a Witness Disk resource but instead replicates data across the cluster to local disks. MNS clustering was originally designed for geographically diverse clusters and requires specialized support from original equipment manufacturers (OEMs) and independent software vendors (ISVs). For a TechNet support webcast on MNS clustering, see *http://support.microsoft.com/kb/838612*. This is a Windows Server 2003 webcast, but still has value for understanding MNS clustering in Windows Server 2008. Windows Server 2008 introduces a third type of Failover cluster that is a hybrid of the two previous types. In the event that a Witness disk is unavailable, the cluster will continue to run as long as the remaining nodes are able to communicate with each other.

Requirements and Planning

Before you attempt to implement any form of clustering, you need to clearly understand the business reason for doing so. You also need to be aware of the costs and benefits of the implementation, as well as the resource requirements for a successful implementation. Treat the implementation of a Windows Server 2008 cluster as you would any other major project. Clearly state the business case for the cluster, and obtain a commitment from all levels before you expend substantial resources on the project.

Identifying and Addressing Goals

The first step in planning your cluster is to identify your goals for the implementation and the needs that using clusters will meet. This sounds obvious, but it is actually the part of the process that is most often overlooked. The implementation of any technology should always be first and foremost a business decision, not a technology decision. Creating and maintaining clusters is not a trivial task, and it requires both technological and financial resources. You'll have a hard time selling your project if you haven't clearly identified one or more needs that it will meet.

In identifying the needs to be met and the goals of your project, you need to be as objective as possible. Always keep in mind that what you might view as "cool" technology can look remarkably like scary, unproven gobbledygook to those in the organization who are less technically savvy than you are. This doesn't mean that those individuals won't support your project, but it does mean that you need to make the case for the project on a level that they can understand and identify with.

Start by clearly identifying the business goals that you're trying to accomplish. State the general goals, but provide enough detail to make the success of the project clearly measurable. Identify the specific gains you expect and how those gains will be measured. Be sure to clearly indicate how the needs you've identified are currently being met. This step is critical because it lets you point out both the costs of your suggested method and the risks associated with it.

Identifying a Solution

Once you know the business needs you're trying to meet, you can identify some solutions. If you've clearly laid out your goals and objectives for the project, the technology that achieves those goals will be driven by those needs, not the other way around. This is also the time to use your best political judgment. You need to identify not only the best way to meet the business needs, but also how much you can realistically sell and implement in a single shot. If you think that ultimately you will need a fully integrated, three-tiered, multiple-cluster solution, you might want to build your plan around a phased approach that allows you to distribute the risks and costs over a broader period.

In addition, if you're proposing a clustering solution to the problem, spend some time and energy identifying methodologies that might be considered alternatives to clustering and clearly laying out the strengths and weaknesses of those alternatives. This effort will short-circuit objections and diversions as you build support for your project.

Identifying and Addressing Risks

As you plan your schedule, be sure to identify the risks at each step of the process and plan solid fallback positions if problems arise. Selling the project is also much easier if it's clear that you've actually thought about the risks. For example, if your goal is to replace an existing manual methodology, have you left yourself a way to fall back to it if there are problems? Or are the two mutually incompatible? If you're replacing an existing client/server application with a clustered, Web-based, distributed, *n*-tiered application, have you drawn a clear roadmap for how you will make the transition from one to the other? What are the risks of that transition?

Spend some time identifying failure points in your project. If you're building a Failover cluster to provide 24-hour, 7-day access to your Microsoft Exchange messaging, have you identified redundant network connections to the cluster? It does little good to create a highly available server if the network connection to it is questionable.

Making Checklists

Take the time to identify all the possible pieces of your cluster implementation ahead of time. Use this time to build a checklist of steps that you need to take and the dependencies at each point. At each major step, identify the hardware, software, knowledge, and resources required, and create a checklist of the prerequisites for that step. Use the checklists in the Windows Help for Cluster Administrator as a starting point, but build onto them with specific details that concern your implementation and your environment. The time you spend planning your clustering implementation will easily be saved in the actual installation and implementation, and it greatly reduces your risks of failure.

Network Load Balancing Clusters

NLB provides a highly available and scalable solution for TCP/IP-based network applications such as a Web server or an FTP server. By combining the resources of two or more servers into a single cluster, NLB can provide for redundancy of information and resources while servicing far more clients than a single server alone could handle.

NLB Concepts

NLB is a Windows Server 2008 networking driver. It acts independently of the TCP/IP networking stack and is transparent to that stack. The NLB driver (Nlb.sys) sits between the TCP/IP stack and the network card drivers, with the Windows Load Balancing Service (Nlb.exe)–the necessary NLB control program–running on top, alongside the actual server application. (See Figure 21-2.)

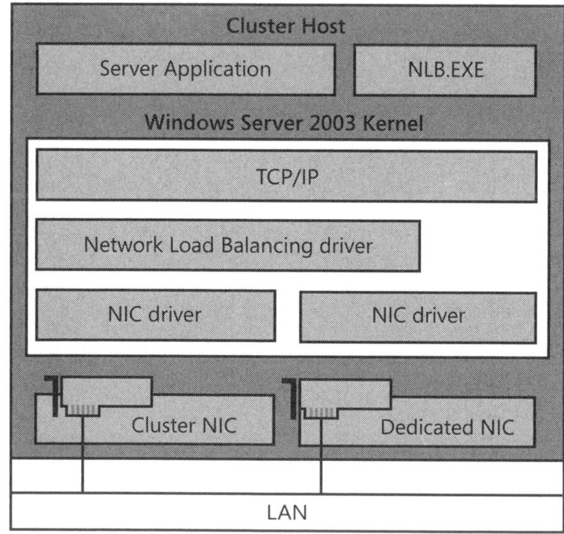

Figure 21-2 NLB as a network driver

Optimally, each server participating in an NLB cluster should have two network interface cards (NICs), although this is not an absolute requirement. Communication and management are materially improved with two NICs, especially in unicast mode. (Unicast mode, as opposed to multicast mode, allows each NIC to present only a single address to the network.) Overall network throughput is also improved, as the second network adapter is used to handle host-to-host traffic within the cluster. NLB clustering is not a place to try to cut costs on network cards. Server-grade NICs will provide full network throughput while minimizing the load on the servers.

NLB supports up to 32 computers per cluster. Each server application can be balanced across the entire cluster or can be primarily hosted by a single computer in the cluster, with another computer in the cluster providing directed failover redundancy. For fully distributed applications, the failure of any single host causes the load currently being serviced by that host to be transferred to the remaining hosts. When the failed server comes back online, the load among the other hosts is redistributed to include the restored server. While NLB clustering does not provide the failover protection appropriate for databases, it does provide for high availability and scalability of TCP/IP-based applications.

Choosing an NLB Cluster Model

A host in an NLB cluster can use one of the following four models, each with its own merits and drawbacks:

- Single network adapter in unicast mode
- Single network adapter in multicast mode
- Multiple network adapters in unicast mode
- Multiple network adapters in multicast mode

The choice of model for a given host and cluster varies depending on the circumstances, requirements, and limitations imposed on the design of the cluster. The sections that follow provide details on each of the models.

Note NLB in Windows Server 2008 does not support a mixed unicast mode and multicast mode environment. All hosts in the cluster must be either multicast or unicast. Some hosts, however, can have a single adapter, whereas others have multiple adapters. In addition, NetBIOS cannot be supported in a single-adapter-only configuration.

Single Network Adapter in Unicast Mode

A single network adapter running in unicast mode is in some ways the easiest type of host to set up, and with only a single adapter, it is cheaper than a host with multiple network adapters. It does, however, impose significant limitations:

- Overall network performance is reduced.
- Ordinary communication among cluster hosts is disabled.
- NetBIOS support is not available within the cluster.

Single Network Adapter in Multicast Mode

Using multicast mode in clusters in which one or more hosts have a single network adapter means that normal communications are possible between hosts within the cluster. This capability overcomes one of the most awkward limitations of the single adapter in unicast mode. However, this mode still has the following significant disadvantages:

- Overall network performance is reduced.
- Some routers do not support multicast media access control (MAC) addresses.
- NetBIOS support is not available within the cluster.

Multiple Network Adapters in Unicast Mode

Using multiple network adapters in unicast mode is generally the preferred configuration. It does impose the cost of a second network adapter per host, but given the relatively low cost of network adapters, including the per-port cost of hubs, this is a relatively minor price to pay for the resulting advantages:

- No limitations are imposed on ordinary network communications among cluster hosts.
- Ordinary NetBIOS support is available through the first configured adapter.
- No bottlenecks occur as a result of a single network adapter.
- The model works with all routers.

Multiple Network Adapters in Multicast Mode

If you are forced by circumstances to use some hosts within a cluster that have only a single network adapter, and you must be able to maintain normal network communications among the hosts in the cluster, you must run all the hosts in multicast mode, even those with multiple adapters. You can't run some hosts in unicast mode and some in multicast mode. This limitation could cause a problem with some routers, but otherwise it is a viable solution.

Creating an NLB Cluster

Creating an NLB cluster requires using Server Manager, shown in Figure 21-3, to add the Network Load Balancing feature. This new manager simplifies the creation and management of Windows Server features, bringing all the pieces into a single management interface.

New NLB Cluster

To create a new NLB cluster, follow these steps:

1. Open Windows Server 2008 Server Manager from the Administrative Tools folder, as shown in Figure 21-3.

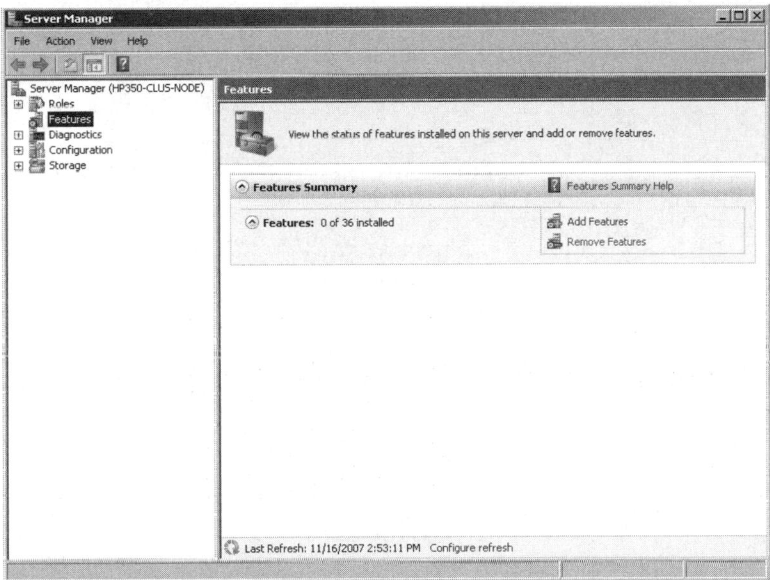

Figure 21-3 Server Manager main screen

2. Select Features in the left pane and click Add Features in the right pane.
3. Select Network Load Balancing in the left pane and click Next, as shown in Figure 21-4.

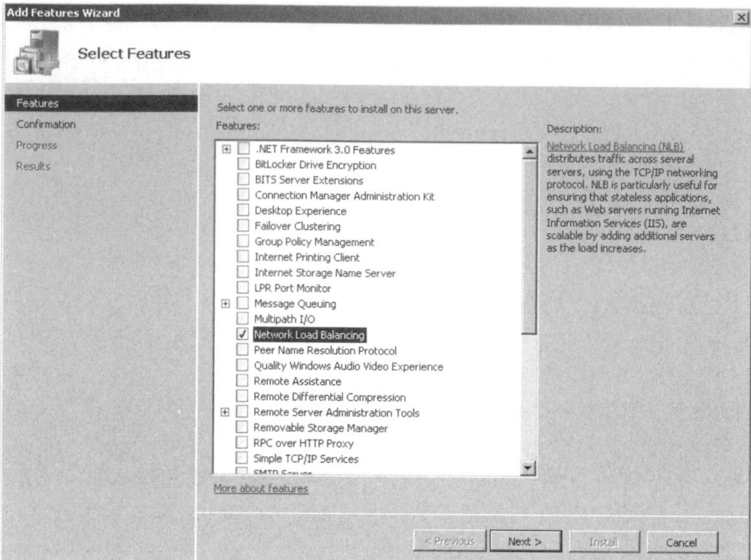

Figure 21-4 Select Network Load Balancing.

4. The install process will prompt you to confirm that the server might need to be restarted when the install is completed. Click Install to continue, as shown in Figure 21-5.

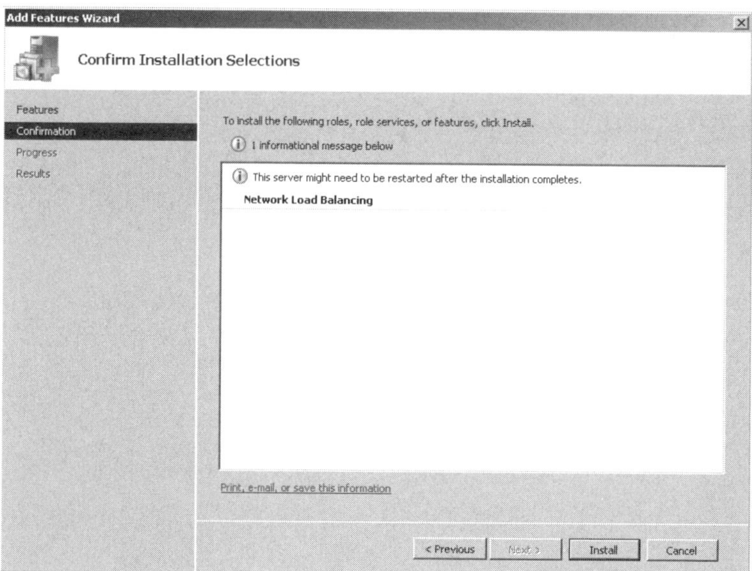

Figure 21-5 Initiating the installation process of an NLB cluster

5. Open the Network Load Balancing Manager from the Administrative Tools folder.
6. Right-click Network Load Balancing Clusters in the left pane and select New Cluster, as shown in Figure 21-6.

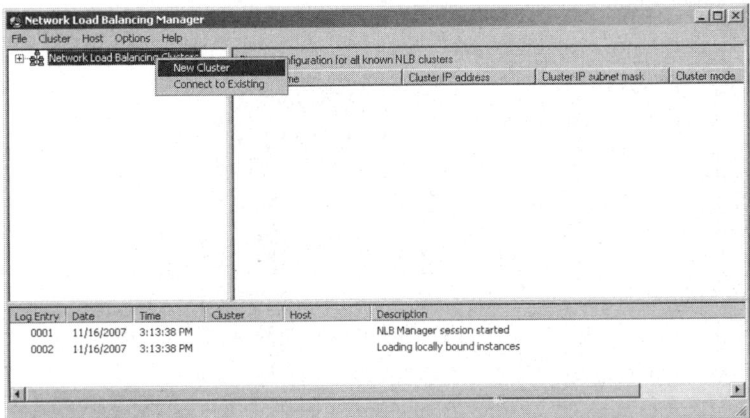

Figure 21-6 Select New Cluster to create a new NLB cluster.

7. On the New Cluster: Connect page, shown in Figure 21-7, you are required to specify one of the servers that will be part of the NLB cluster. If you are running the NLB Manager on the server itself, you can use the name **localhost** to indicate the local computer. You will also need to specify which network interface to use when configuring the NLB. Highlight the interface that will host the public traffic of the cluster (as opposed to private, node-to-node traffic).

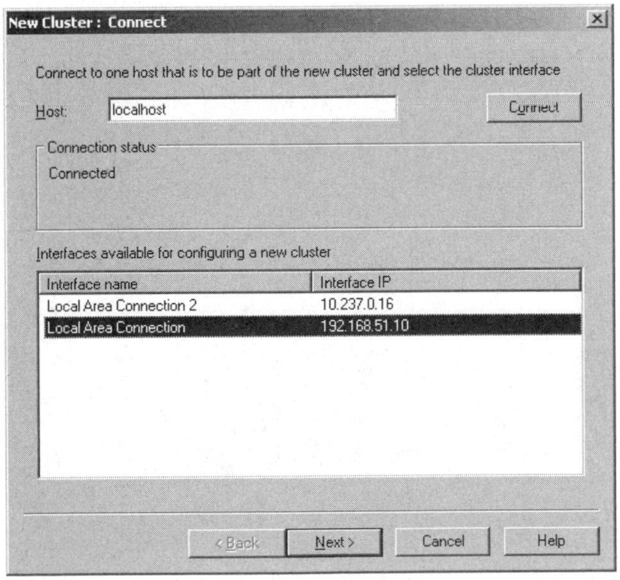

Figure 21-7 The Connect page of the New NLB Cluster Wizard

8. Click Next to bring up the Host Parameters page, shown in Figure 21-8. Here you set the priority for this host of the cluster and the dedicated IP address that will be used to connect to this specific server (as opposed to the cluster as a whole). This IP address must be a fixed IP address, not a DHCP address. Finally, set the initial state of this host when Windows is started.

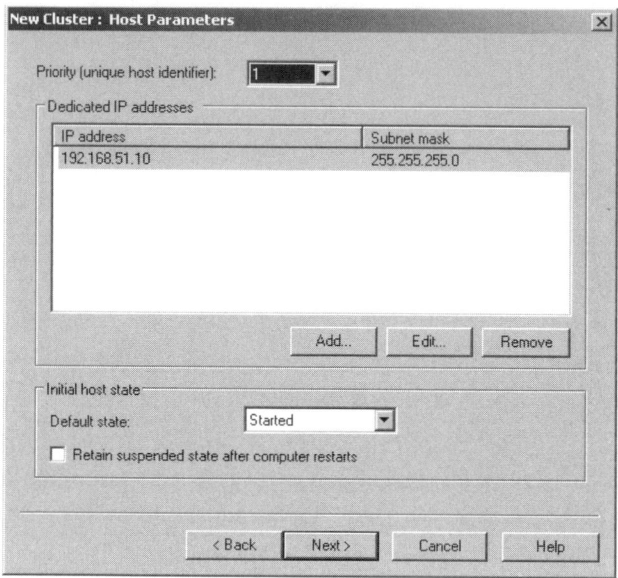

Figure 21-8 The Host Parameters page of the New NLB Cluster Wizard

9. Click Next to bring up the Cluster IP Addresses page, shown in Figure 21-9. Click Add to add IP address information for the cluster.

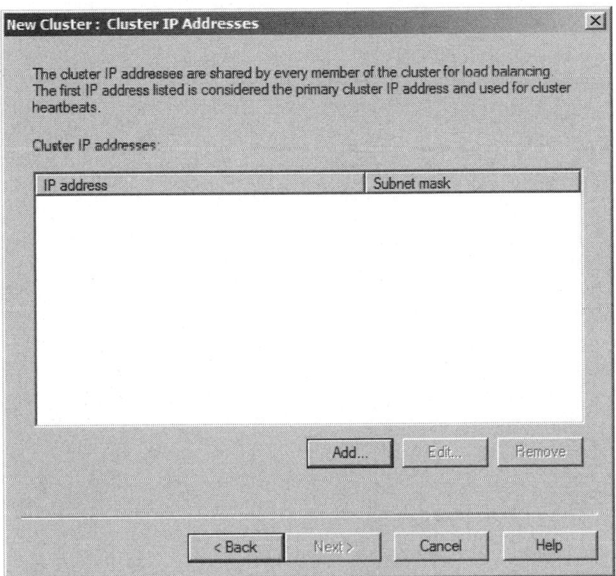

Figure 21-9 The Cluster IP Addresses page of the New NLB Cluster Wizard

10. On the Add IP Address page, shown in Figure 21-10, you need to enter the IP address information for the NLB cluster you are creating. This includes the IP address the cluster will use for clients to connect to it. You can add both IPv4 and IPv6 address information on this page.

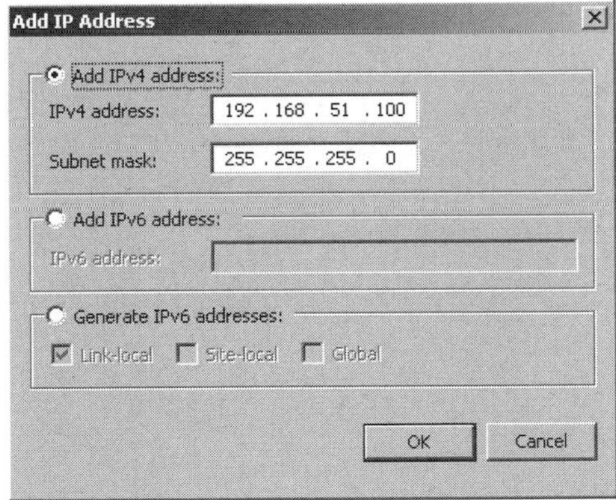

Figure 21-10 Adding IP address information in the New NLB Cluster Wizard

11. Click Next to bring up the Cluster Parameters page, shown in Figure 21-11. You need to enter a Fully Qualified Domain Name (FQDN) for each IP address you configured on the previous page. The Internet name is the name that will be registered in DNS and will be the name that the cluster will be known by.

12. Select whether the cluster will be unicast or multicast and then click Next.

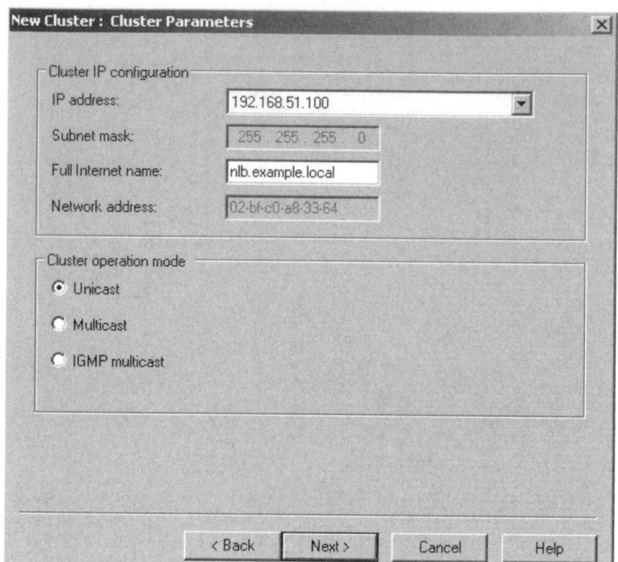

Figure 21-11 The Cluster Parameters page

13. You can enter port rules on the next page, or wait to configure these after you get the cluster up and running. Port rules can be used to control the behavior of various types of TCP/IP traffic. Windows Server 2008 allows you to configure different port rules for different IP addresses. Click Finish after you have configured any rules you want to configure and to start up the NLB service and configure the server into the new cluster.

Adding a Node to an NLB Cluster

To add another node to an existing NLB cluster, follow these steps:

1. On the new node, open Windows Server 2008 Server Manager from the Administrative Tools folder (shown previously in Figure 21-3).
2. Select Features in the left pane and click Add Features in the right pane.
3. Select Network Load Balancing in the left pane and click Next (shown previously in Figure 21-4).
4. The install process will prompt you to confirm that the server might need to be restarted when the install is completed. Click Install to continue (shown previously in Figure 21-5).

5. On a node that is already a member of the NLB cluster, open the Network Load Balancing Manager from the Administrative Tools folder.
6. Right-click the cluster you want to add a node to in the left pane, and select Add Host To Cluster, as shown in Figure 21-12.

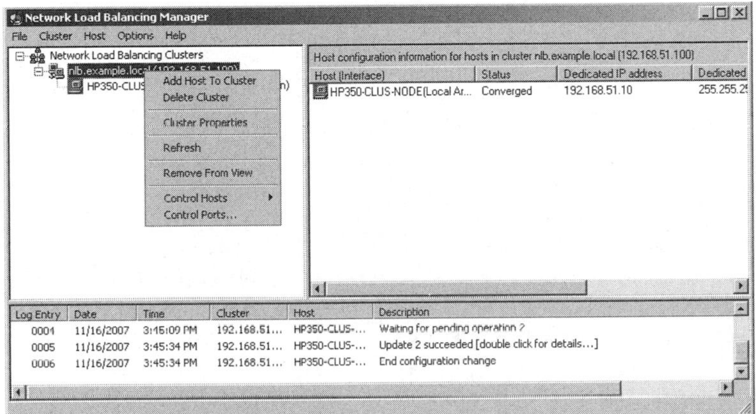

Figure 21-12 Adding a host to an existing cluster

7. Enter the name or IP address of the host that will be joined to the cluster on the Connect page (shown previously in Figure 21-7). Click Connect to connect to the server and bring up a list of network interfaces available. Select the interface that will host the public traffic of the cluster (as opposed to private, node-to-node traffic).
8. Click Next to bring up the Host Parameters page, shown earlier in Figure 21-8. Here you set the priority for this host of the cluster and the dedicated IP address that will be used to connect to this specific server (as opposed to the cluster as a whole). This IP address must be a fixed IP address, not a DHCP address. Finally, set the initial state of this host when Windows is started.
9. Click Next to bring up the Firewall port rules. You can configure these now or at a later point.
10. Click Finish to start the NLB service on the new node and configure the server into the existing cluster. When the node is up and part of the cluster, it shows a status of Converged in the NLB Manager, as shown in Figure 21-13.

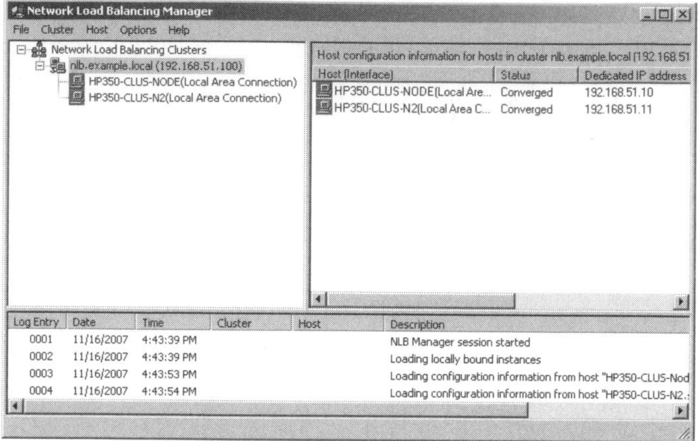

Figure 21-13 The NLB Manager shows the new node added with a status of Converged.

Removing a Host from an NLB Cluster

To remove a host from an NLB cluster, follow these steps:

1. Open the Network Load Balancing Manager from the Administrative Tools folder.
2. Connect to the cluster you want to remove a node from by right-clicking Network Load Balancing Clusters in the left pane and selecting Connect To Existing.
3. Right-click the node you want to remove in the left pane, and select Delete Host.

Planning the Capacity of an NLB Cluster

In general, an NLB cluster should contain as many hosts as needed to handle the client load for the applications being run in the cluster. The exception to this is a case in which the sole function of the cluster is to provide failover tolerance for a critical TCP/IP application—that is, when a single server can handle the load and the second server is there simply for fault tolerance.

The maximum number of hosts in a given cluster is 32. If your application requires more than 32 hosts, you can set up multiple clusters, using round-robin DNS to distribute the load among the clusters. The effective limitation, however, is likely to be the network saturation point. If you do run multiple clusters in a subnet, you should host each on its own network switch to minimize the network bottleneck.

Although fewer and more powerful servers might look cost-effective for a given application, you should consider how the failure of a server will affect the application and the remaining servers. If the remaining servers can't handle the resulting load, you could potentially have a cascading failure, bringing down the entire application. Always provide sufficient server capacity within the cluster to handle the expected load when a single server is down. Also consider ways to limit the load to the application after a failure.

When determining the expected cluster capacity, you also need to consider the application being clustered and the type of load it imposes on the cluster. Plan your servers according to where the limitation and stress will be greatest. Web serving and FTP applications are input/output (I/O)-intensive, whereas Terminal Services can be very CPU-intensive, depending on the types of applications your user community uses.

Providing Fault Tolerance

Although NLB clusters provide overall fault tolerance for your TCP/IP application, they are not a complete solution for all possible failures. Because they are shared nothing clusters, there is always some data lag between servers. For fully fault-tolerant, high-availability clustering that can run any application, you should probably use Failover clustering, which provides the greatest level of fault tolerance.

One thing you can do to improve the overall fault tolerance of the cluster is to make the hard disks fault tolerant, whether physically attached to the server or as Network-Attached Storage (NAS). Both hardware and software RAID solutions are viable options for improving the fault tolerance of an NLB cluster. For more on RAID and fault tolerance in general, see Chapter 19, "Disk Management," and Chapter 35, "Planning Fault Tolerance and Avoidance."

Optimizing an NLB Cluster

Optimizing an NLB cluster calls for clearly understanding where the bottleneck in your clustered application is likely to be. An application such as a Web front end that is essentially a file server, for example, tends to be a heavy user of both disk I/O and network bandwidth, and such an application can be a RAM hog if you're going to do effective caching. Terminal Services, on the other hand, can put a heavy load on the CPU, and to a somewhat lesser extent, on RAM, depending on your user community. Focus your optimization efforts on the bottleneck and you'll get the most gain for your effort.

One area that can be a problem is running an NLB cluster in a switched environment without planning your network load carefully. If each of the servers in your cluster is connected to a different switched port, you can easily end up flooding your switched ports because every client request to the cluster passes through all switched ports to which a member of the cluster is attached. Running in multicast mode can exacerbate the problem. If you're running in a switched environment, you should follow these guidelines:

- Use a top-quality hub to connect the servers in the cluster to one another, and uplink the hub to a single switched port. If you do use switches, separate each cluster onto its own VLAN.

- Use unicast mode. If you enabled multicast mode during setup, change it. (You'll need to change this on all servers in the cluster.) It is possible to use multicast mode, but this requires enabling Internet Group Multicast Protocol (IGMP) support, introduced in Windows Server 2003. Given the other limitations of multicast mode, unicast is preferred.

Failover Clusters

A Failover cluster is a group of independent nodes that work together as a single system. They either share a common cluster database–or contain a local copy that is identical to the other nodes–that enables recovery in the event of the failure of any node. A traditional Failover cluster uses a common resource–generally a disk on a shared SCSI bus or Fibre Channel–that is available to all nodes in the cluster. Each server node in the cluster must be able to access the disk, and each node in the cluster must be able to communicate at all times with the other nodes in the cluster.

Windows Server 2008 supports Failover clusters only on computers running Enterprise Edition or Datacenter Edition. Both editions support up to eight node clusters, and can be configured in four different models: single node clusters, single quorum device clusters, MNS clusters, and hybrid clusters, which combines single quorum and MNS clusters. We focus on hybrid Failover clusters in this chapter because this is the new default implementation in Windows Server 2008. Single node Failover clusters are primarily used for creating virtual servers and for proof of concept and development of cluster-aware applications. MNS Failover clusters require at least three nodes to properly operate and five to be in an optimal configuration. Hybrid clusters combine single quorum and majority node sets.

Failover Cluster Concepts

To understand and implement Failover clusters, it is important to understand several new concepts and their ramifications, as well as specialized meanings for certain terms.

Validated Cluster Configuration

Windows Server 2008 introduces the concept of validated cluster configuration. This concept is based on the idea that before a cluster can be installed and supported by Microsoft, it first must pass a series of hardware and cluster configuration tests. If you do not run the validation or your configuration does not pass the test, you won't be prevented from running a Failover cluster, but Microsoft may offer limited or no support for your cluster. Considering the importance of the application you are clustering, you would be wise to ensure that your configuration is validated and supported. Prior to Windows Server 2008, this validation was performed by manufacturers and the results posted in the Cluster section of the Windows Server Catalog. This method was often out of date, placed the burden on manufacturers to update, and offered customers limited options for upgrading and changing cluster components.

Networks (Interconnects)

A cluster has two distinct types of networks: the *private network* (sometimes referred to as a *heartbeat*), which is used to maintain communications between nodes in the cluster, and the *public network,* which clients of the cluster use to connect to the services of the cluster. Each of these networks can share the same network card and physical network cabling, but it is a good practice to keep them separate. This gives you an alternate path for interconnection between the nodes of the cluster. Because the interconnect between the nodes of a cluster is a potential single point of failure, it should always be redundant. The cluster service can use all available networks, both private and public, to maintain communications between nodes.

Real World Always Have at Least Two Interconnects

If you have only a single method of communication in a cluster, the failure of that interconnect has a 50 percent chance (in a two-node cluster) of causing the entire cluster to become unavailable to its clients—hardly why you opted for a highly available technology like clustering. Here's what happens when the nodes of a cluster can no longer communicate: When the communication fails, each node recognizes that it is no longer able to talk to the other nodes of the cluster and decides that the other nodes in the cluster have failed. Each node therefore attempts to take over the functions of the cluster by itself. The nodes are "partitioned," and as each node attempts to enable itself to take over the functions of the entire cluster, it starts by trying to gain control of the Witness Disk (discussed in the "Types of Resources" section later in the chapter) and, therefore, the shared disk on which the Witness Disk resides. Because only one node is able to gain control of the Witness Disk, the other nodes are automatically shut down while the single node attempts to maintain the processes of the cluster. However, because any given node has an equal chance of gaining control of the Witness Disk resource, there's a 50 percent chance in a two-node cluster that the node with a failed network card wins, leaving all the services of the cluster unavailable.

Nodes

A *node* is a member of a Failover cluster. It must be running Windows Server 2008, Enterprise Edition or Windows Server 2008, Datacenter Edition, and Failover clustering. It must also be running TCP/IP, be connected to the shared cluster storage device, and have at least one network interconnect that connects to the other nodes in the cluster and is accessible to client computers.

Services and Applications

Services and applications are groups of resources that are required to make the application available on the Failover cluster. Each group contains one or more resources. Should any of the resources within the group fail, all group resources fail over together according to the failover policy defined for the group. A service or application can run on only one node at a time. All resources within the group run on the same node. If a resource within the group fails and must be moved to an alternate node, all other resources in that group must be moved as well. When the cause of failure on the originating node is resolved, the group falls back to its original location, based on the failback policy for the group.

Resources

Any physical or logical entity that can be brought online or offline can be a Failover cluster resource. It must be able to be owned by only one node at a time and will be managed as part of the cluster. The *Witness Disk resource* is a special resource that serves as the repository of the configuration data of the cluster and the recovery logs that allow recovery of the cluster in the event of a failure. The Witness Disk resource must be able to be controlled by a single node, it must provide physical storage for the recovery logs and cluster database, and it must use the NTFS file system. The only resource type supported for a Witness Disk resource in single quorum device clustering is the Physical Disk resource as shipped with Windows Server 2008 (which, along with other resource types, is described in the next section).

Types of Resources

Windows Server 2008 Enterprise Edition includes several resource types. The sections that follow examine some of the most common resource types and the role they play in a Failover cluster, including the following:

- Client Access Point
- File Server
- Dynamic Host Configuration Protocol (DHCP)
- Windows Internet Naming Service (WINS)
- Print Spooler
- IP Address
- IPv6 Address

- IPv6 Tunnel Address
- iSNSClusRes
- NFS Share
- Generic Application
- Generic Script
- Generic Service
- Volume Shadow Copy Service Task
- Cluster Disk

Client Access Point

The Client Access Point resource type is a combination of an IP address and a network name. The Client Access Point will provide a network name for a service or application that will be used by client computers to connect to its service. When a failover occurs, another node in the cluster will assume the IP address and thus receive any communications sent to the network name registered in DNS.

File Server

You can use a Failover cluster to provide a high-availability file server. A Failover cluster file server resource type lets you create different shared file systems:

- As standard file shares with only the top-level folder visible as a share name.
- As shared subfolders, where the top-level folder and each of its immediate subfolders are shared with separate names. This approach makes it extremely easy to manage users' home directories, for example.
- As a stand-alone Distributed File System (DFS) root. You cannot, however, use a cluster server file server resource as part of a fault-tolerant DFS root.

DHCP and WINS

The DHCP service provides IP addresses and various other TCP/IP settings to clients, and WINS provides dynamic resolution of NetBIOS names to IP addresses. Both resource types can be run as a resource of the cluster, providing for high availability of these critical services to network clients. For failover to work correctly, the DHCP and WINS databases must reside on the shared cluster storage.

Print Spooler

The print spooler resource type lets you cluster print services, making them fault tolerant and saving a tremendous number of help desk calls when the print server fails. It also eliminates the problem of people simply clicking Print over and over when there's a problem, resulting in a long and repetitious print queue.

To be clustered, a printer must be connected to the server through the network. Obviously, you can't connect the printer to a local port such as a parallel or Universal Serial Bus (USB) port directly attached to one of the nodes of the cluster. The client can address the printer either by name or by IP address, just as it would a non-clustered printer on the network.

In the event of a failover, all jobs that are currently spooled to the printer are restarted. Jobs that are in the process of spooling from the client are discarded.

Internet Protocol Address

The Internet protocol address resource type is used to manage the IP addresses of a service or application. Windows Server 2008 supports both IPv4 and IPv6 IP addresses for both the cluster itself and any service or application it is hosting. IP addresses can be added individually to a service or application to provide multiple network addresses. When creating the initial IP address for a service or application you should use a Client Access Point, described earlier.

iSNSClusRes

The iSNSClusRes resource type is designed to facilitate the automated discovery, management, and configuration of iSCSI and Fibre Channel devices on a TCP/IP network. iSNS provides intelligent storage discovery and management services comparable to those found in Fibre Channel networks, allowing a commodity IP network to function in a similar capacity as a storage area network. iSNS also facilitates a seamless integration of IP and Fibre Channel networks because of its ability to emulate Fibre Channel fabric services, and manage both iSCSI and Fibre Channel devices.

NFS Share

The NFS Share resource type enables you to share files and folders with clients other than Windows-based clients, such as UNIX and Linux. UNIX uses the Network File System (NFS) protocol to share files and folders on the network. The NFS Share includes full support for NFS v3. You can also use an NFS share to make interoperability and migration in a mixed environment easier.

Generic Application

The generic application resource type allows you to manage regular, cluster-unaware applications in the cluster. A cluster-unaware application that is to be used in a cluster must, at a minimum, be able to do the following:

- Store its data in a configurable location
- Use TCP/IP to connect to clients
- Have clients that can reconnect in the event of an intermittent network failure

When you install a generic, cluster-unaware application, you have two choices: You can install it onto the shared cluster storage or you can install it individually on each node of the cluster. The first method is certainly easier because you install the application only once for the whole cluster. However, if you use this method you won't be able to perform a rolling upgrade of the application, because it appears only once. (A *rolling upgrade* is an upgrade of the application in which the workload is moved to one server while the application on the other server is upgraded and then the roles are reversed to upgrade the first server.)

To give yourself the ability to perform rolling upgrades on the application, you need to install a copy onto each node of the cluster. You need to place it in the same folder and path on each node. This method uses more disk space than installing onto the shared cluster storage, but it permits you to perform rolling upgrades, upgrading each node of the cluster separately.

Generic Script

Similar to the generic application resource, the generic script resource type is used to manage operating system scripts as a cluster resource. The generic script resource type provides limited functionality.

Generic Service

Finally, Failover clusters support one additional type of resource—the generic service resource. This is the most basic resource type, but it does allow you to manage your Windows Server 2008 services as a cluster resource.

Volume Shadow Copy Service Task

The volume shadow copy service task resource type allows you to create jobs in the Scheduled Task folder that will be run against whatever node is currently hosting a particular resource group, allowing the task to fail over with the resource. As shipped, this resource type is used only to support shadow copies of shared folders in a Failover cluster.

Cluster Disk

The cluster disk resource type is used to manage a shared cluster storage device. Applications and services that depend on disk storage for files and programs should use a cluster disk as opposed to a local physical disk. A cluster disk has the same drive letter on all cluster nodes.

Defining Failover and Failback

Windows Server 2008 Failover clusters allow you to define the failover and failback (sometimes referred to as *fallback*) policies for each group or virtual server. This ability enables you to tune the exact behavior of each application or group of applications to balance the need for high availability against the overall resources available to the cluster in a failure situation. Also, when the failed node becomes available again, your failback policy determines whether the failed resource is immediately returned to the restored node, maintained at the failed-over node, or migrated back to the restored node at some predetermined point in the future. These options allow you to plan for the disruption caused when a shift in node ownership occurs, limiting the impact by timing it for off-hours.

Configuring a Failover Cluster

When planning your Failover cluster, you'll need to think ahead to what your goal is for the cluster and what you can reasonably expect from it. Failover clusters provide for extremely high availability and resource load balancing, but you need to make sure your hardware, applications, and policies are appropriate.

High Availability with Load Balancing

The most common cluster configuration is static load balancing, also known as *Active/Active clustering*. In this scenario, the cluster is configured so that some applications or resources are normally hosted on one node, whereas others are normally hosted on another node. If one node fails, the applications or resources on the failed node fail over to another node, providing high availability of your resources in the event of failure and balancing the load across the cluster during normal operation. The limitation of this configuration is that in the event of a failure, your applications will all attempt to run on fewer nodes, and you need to implement procedures either to limit the load by reducing performance or availability, or to not provide some less critical services during a failure. Another possibility for managing the reduced load-carrying capacity during a failure scenario is to have "at risk" users and applications that can be shut off or "shed" during periods of reduced capacity, much like power companies do during peak load periods when capacity is exceeded.

It's important to quickly take steps to manage load during periods of failure when you configure your cluster for static load balancing. Failure to shed load can lead to catastrophic failure, or such extreme slowdown as to simulate it, and then no one will have access to the cluster's resources and applications.

Maximum Availability Without Load Balancing

The cluster configuration with the highest availability and reliability for critical applications is to run one node of the cluster as a hot spare, also known as *Active/Passive clustering*. This scenario requires that the hot spare node be sufficiently powerful to run the entire load of any other node in the cluster. You then configure all the applications and resources to run on the other nodes, with the one node sitting idle. In the event of failure on one of the primary nodes, the applications fail over to the idle node and continue with full capability. After the primary node is back online, it can continue as the new hot spare, or you can force the applications back to the primary node, depending on the needs of your environment.

This scenario provides full and complete fault tolerance in the event of the failure of one of the nodes, but it has the greatest hardware cost. It also does not provide for full and complete fault tolerance in the event of multiple node failures—that would take essentially one hot spare for each primary node. Use this clustering configuration only where your applications or resources are critical and you can afford the extra hardware expense far more than any limits to the load in case of a failure.

Partial Failover (Load Shedding)

Another cluster configuration is called *load shedding* or *partial failover*. In this configuration, critical applications and resources are designed to fail over to the other nodes in the cluster in the event of a failure, but noncritical applications and resources are unavailable until the cluster is back to full functionality. The critical resources and applications are thus protected in a failure situation, but noncritical ones simply run as though they were on a stand-alone server.

In this configuration, you might—depending on capacity and load conditions—have to configure the noncritical applications and resources on all nodes to be unavailable in the event of a failure on other nodes. This allows you to maintain a high level of performance and availability for your most critical applications while shedding the load from less critical applications and services when necessary. This strategy can be very effective when you must, for example, service certain critical applications or users under any and all circumstances but can allow other applications and users with a lower priority to temporarily fail

Virtual Server Only

You can create a Failover cluster that has only a single node, which allows you to take advantage of the virtual server concept to simplify the management and look of the resources on your network. For example, the File Share resource lets you create automatic subdirectory shares of your primary share and control their visibility, a perfect way to handle users' home directories. Having a single node doesn't give you any additional protection against failure or any additional load balancing over that provided by simply running a single stand-alone server, but it allows you to easily manage groups of resources as a virtual server.

This scenario is an effective way to stage an implementation. You create the initial virtual server, putting your most important resources on it in a limited fashion. Then, when you're ready, you add another node to the Failover cluster and define your failover and failback policies, giving you a high-availability environment with minimal disruption to your user community. In this scenario, you can space hardware purchases over a longer period while providing services in a controlled test environment.

Planning the Capacity of a Failover Cluster

Capacity planning for a Failover cluster can be a complicated process. You need to thoroughly understand the applications that will be running on your cluster and make some hard decisions about exactly which applications you can live without and which ones must be maintained under all circumstances. You'll also need a clear understanding of the interdependencies of the resources and applications you'll be supporting.

The first step is to quantify your groups or virtual servers. Applications and resources that are in the same group will fail over together onto the same server. This means you'll need to plan out which applications are dependent on each other and will need to function together. Make a comprehensive list of all applications in your environment, and then determine which ones need to fail over and which ones can be allowed to simply fail but still should be run on a virtual server.

Next, determine the dependencies of the applications and the resources they need to function. This allows you to group dependent applications and resources in the same group or virtual server. Keep in mind that a resource can't span groups, so if multiple applications depend on a resource, such as a Web server, they must all reside in the same group or on the same virtual server as the Web server and thus share the same failover and failback policies.

A useful mechanism for getting a handle on your dependencies is to list all your applications and resources and draw a dependency tree for each major application or resource. This helps you visualize not only the resources that your application is directly dependent on, but also the second-hand and third-hand dependencies that might not be obvious at first glance. For example, a cluster that is used as a high-availability file server uses the File Share resource. And it makes perfect sense that this File Share resource is dependent on the Physical Disk resource. It's also dependent on the Network Name resource. However, the Network Name resource is dependent on the IP Address resource. Thus, although the File Share resource isn't directly dependent on the IP Address resource, when you draw the dependency tree you will see that they all need to reside in the same group or on the same virtual server. Figure 21-14 illustrates this dependency tree.

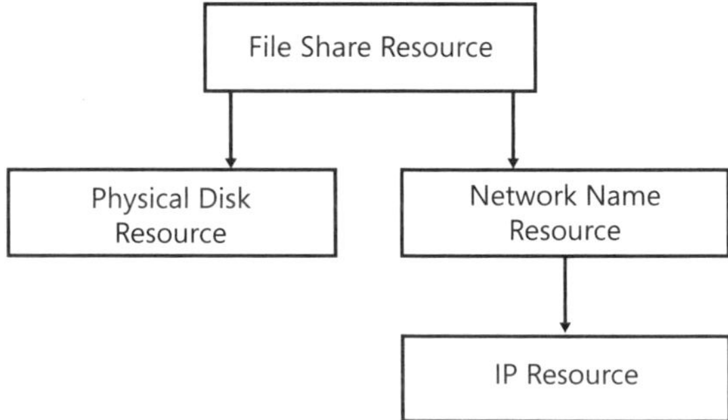

Figure 21-14 The dependency tree for a File Share resource.

Finally, as you're determining your cluster capacity, you need to plan for the effect of a failover. Each server must have sufficient capacity to handle the additional load imposed on it when a node fails and it is required to run the applications or resources owned by the failed node.

The disk capacity for the shared cluster storage must be sufficient to handle all the applications that will be running in the cluster and to provide the storage that the cluster itself requires for the quorum resource. Be sure to provide enough RAM and CPU capacity on each node of the cluster so that the failure of one node won't overload the other node to the point that it also fails. This possibility can also be managed to some extent by determining your real service requirements for different applications and user communities and reducing the performance or capacity of those that are less essential during a failure. However, such planned load shedding might not be sufficient and frequently takes a significant amount of time to accomplish, so give yourself some margin to handle that initial surge during failover.

Creating a Failover Cluster

Once you've thoroughly researched and planned your implementation of Failover clusters, you're ready to actually create the cluster. The mechanism to create and manage Failover clusters is the Cluster Administrator application, part of the Administrative Tools folder.

New Failover Cluster

To create a new Failover cluster, follow these steps:

> **Note** The following three steps must be performed on all nodes that will be part of the Failover cluster.

1. Open Windows Server 2008 Server Manager from the Administrative Tools folder, as shown previously in Figure 21-3.
2. Select Features in the left pane and click Add Features in the right pane.
3. Select Failover Clustering in the left pane and click Next, as shown in Figure 21-15.

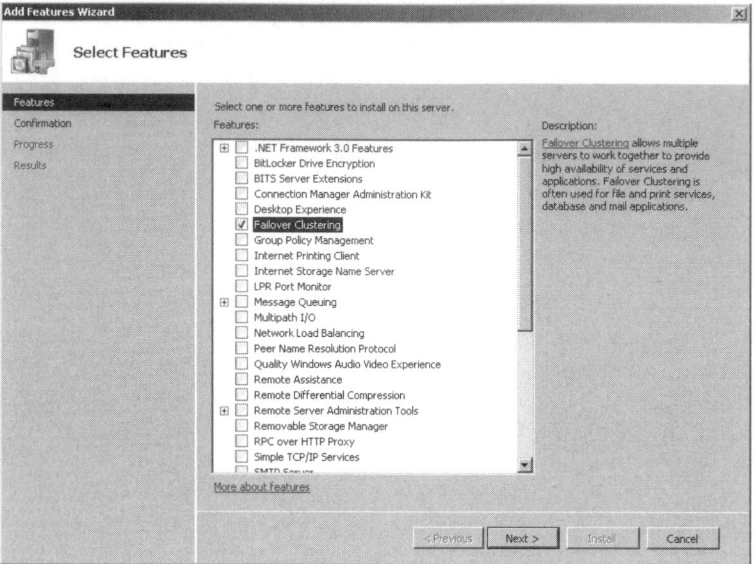

Figure 21-15 Select Failover Clustering.

4. Open Failover Cluster Management from the Administrative Tools folder. In the center pane, click Validate A Configuration from the Management section, as shown in Figure 21-16.

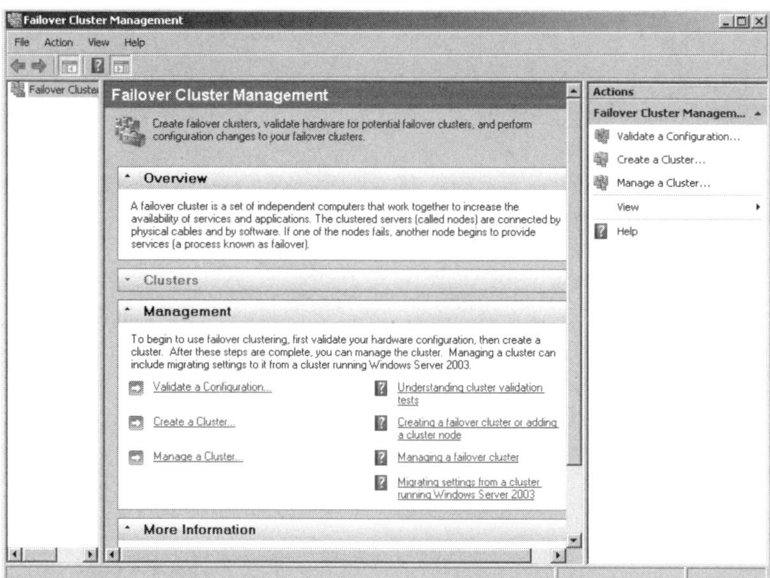

Figure 21-16 The Failover Cluster Management Window

5. On the first screen of the Validate A Configuration Wizard, shown in Figure 21-17, you need to enter the network name of each node. You should select all of the nodes that are available to ensure that your testing validation is as accurate as possible.

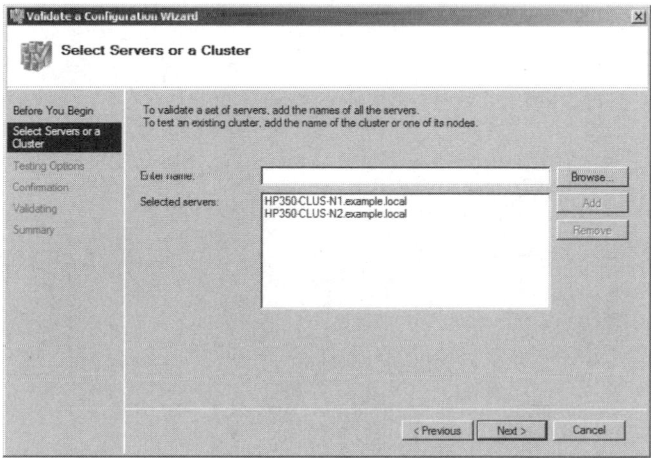

Figure 21-17 Enter the network names of all nodes to be validated.

6. Click Next to show the Testing Options page, shown in Figure 21-18. It is recommended that you run all tests to ensure that you fully test your configuration. If you are running the validation process of failing a previous validation, you can run only the tests that were not successful earlier.

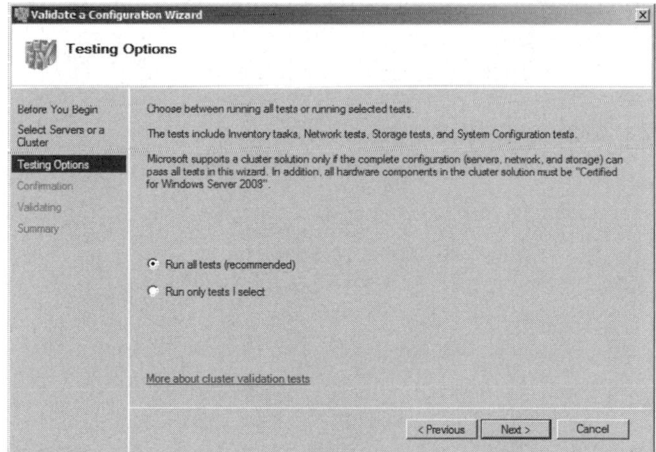

Figure 21-18 Select which validation tests to perform.

7. Click Next to verify the tests to be performed. Once the tests are completed, the Summary page will indicate whether the tests were successful and whether the configuration is suitable to use as a Failover cluster, shown in Figure 21-19.

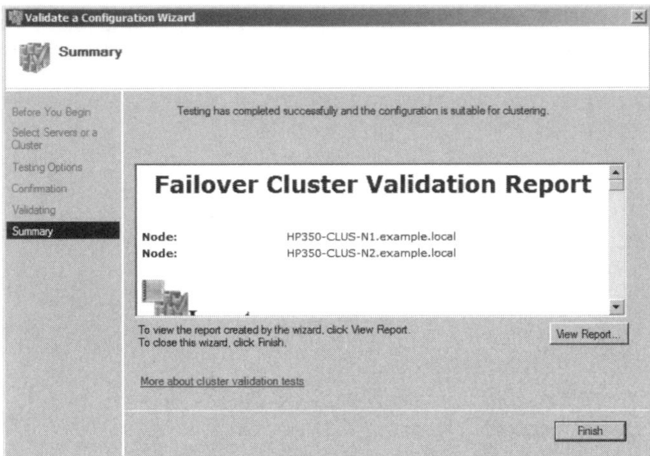

Figure 21-19 Completion of the cluster validation process

8. Click Finish to end the Validate A Configuration Wizard. If errors were reported, fix the problems indicated and run the wizard again. If the validation was successful, click Create A Cluster in the Failover Cluster Management window, shown previously in Figure 21-16.

9. Once the Create Cluster Wizard starts, you need to enter the names of the nodes that will be used to form the cluster, shown in Figure 21-20. These should be the same nodes you entered previously during the validation process.

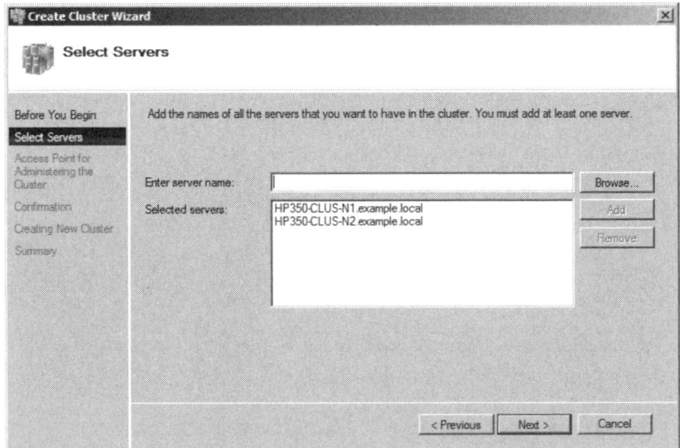

Figure 21-20 Enter the nodes to be used to form the Failover cluster.

10. Click Next to proceed to the Access Point For Administering The Cluster page, shown in Figure 21-21. On this page you need to enter the cluster name and IP address that will be used to identify and administer the cluster once it is created. The cluster name and IP address will be the virtual name registered in DNS and will be used to connect and manage the cluster itself. This information is usually different than the name and IP address that will be used by clients to connect to clustered applications.

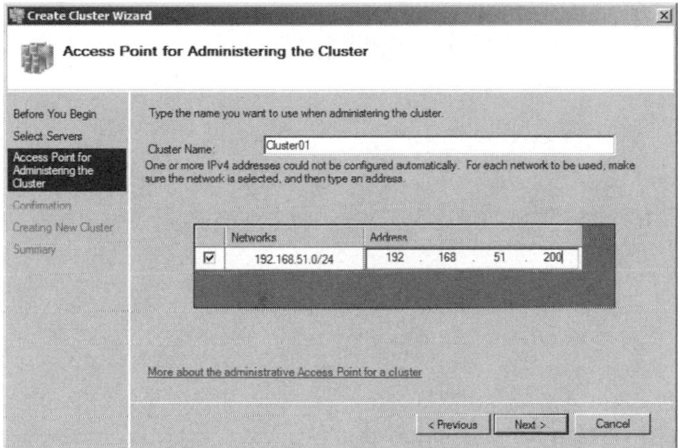

Figure 21-21 Enter the name and IP address for the new cluster.

11. Click Next to validate the settings and proceed to the Confirmation page, shown in Figure 21-22. Ensure that all the information is accurate for the creation of the cluster. If not, click Previous to go back and change the settings. Otherwise, click Next to proceed to the cluster creation page.

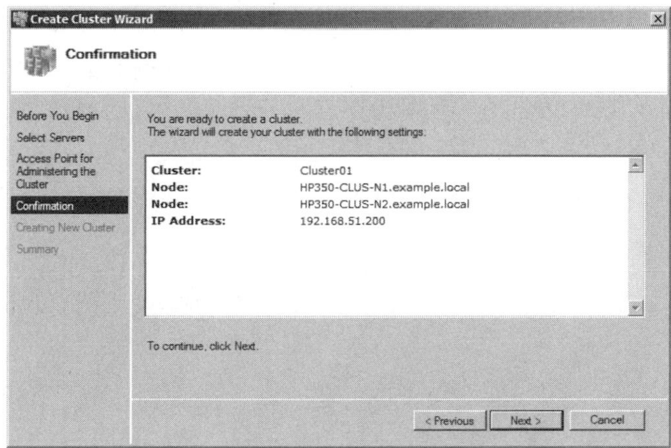

Figure 21-22 Verify the cluster creation properties.

12. At the completion of the cluster creation process, the Summary page will show you the results, shown in Figure 21-23. If there were no errors, your cluster was successfully formed. If there were any errors, click the View Report button to get details. Click Finish to exit the wizard.

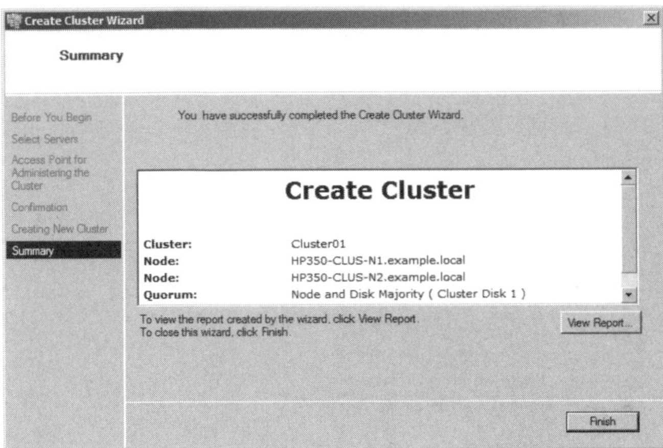

Figure 21-23 Summary information on the creation of the cluster

Creating a Clustered Resource

Once you have your cluster created, you can take advantage of the management capabilities of Failover Cluster Management to create cluster services and applications. In the following steps, we walk through the creation of a File Share cluster resource in a virtual server called HOME. Referring to Figure 21-14, you'll see the list of dependencies and resources required for a File Share.

New File Server

To create a new Clustered File Server, follow these steps:

1. Open Failover Cluster Management from the Administrative tools folder, and connect to the cluster where you will be creating the service.
2. Select your Failover cluster listed in the left pane and then click Configure A Service Or Application in the center pane in the Configure section, shown in Figure 21-24.

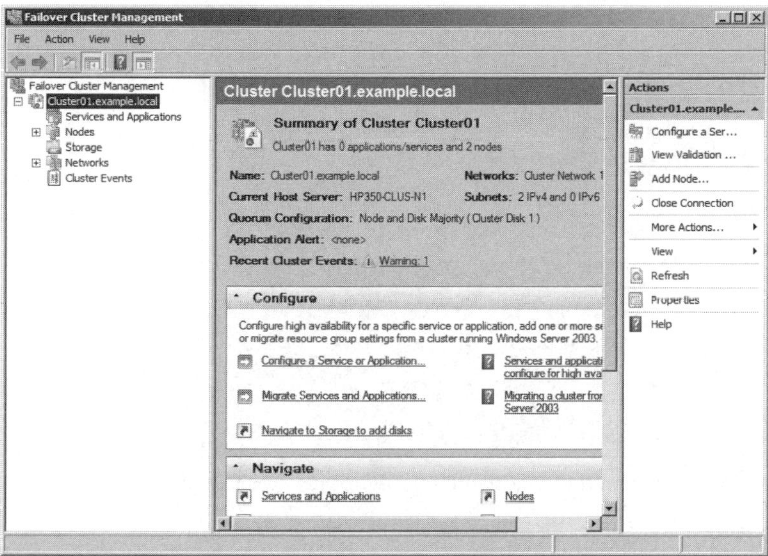

Figure 21-24 Click Configure A Service Or Application.

3. Select File Server on the Select Service Or Application page, shown in Figure 21-25. Click Next.

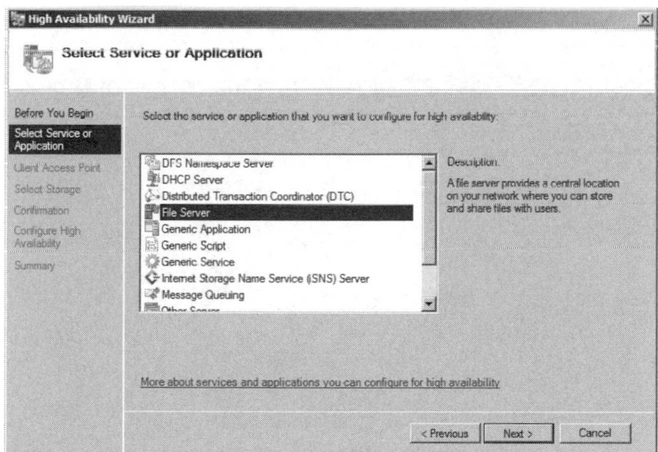

Figure 21-25 Select File Server.

4. Enter the network name that clients will use to connect to the file server. You also need to specify the IP address that will be registered in DNS for this name, shown in Figure 21-26.

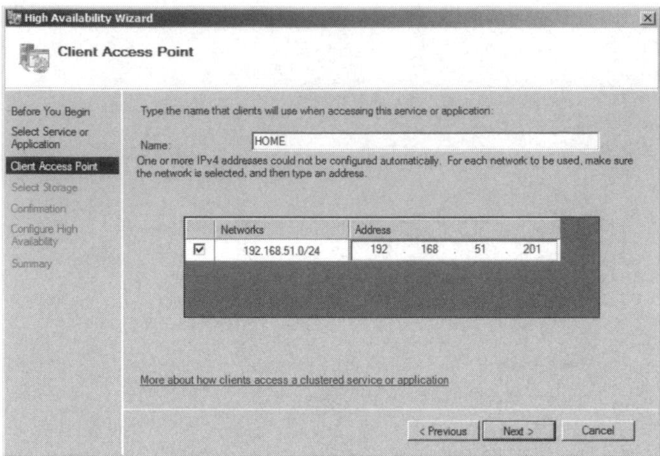

Figure 21-26 Enter the network name and IP address for the file server.

5. Click Next to proceed to the Select Storage page, shown in Figure 21-27. You need to select which of your storage devices will be associated with this file server. Only storage devices accessible by all nodes in the cluster will be listed. Local storage devices are not usable.

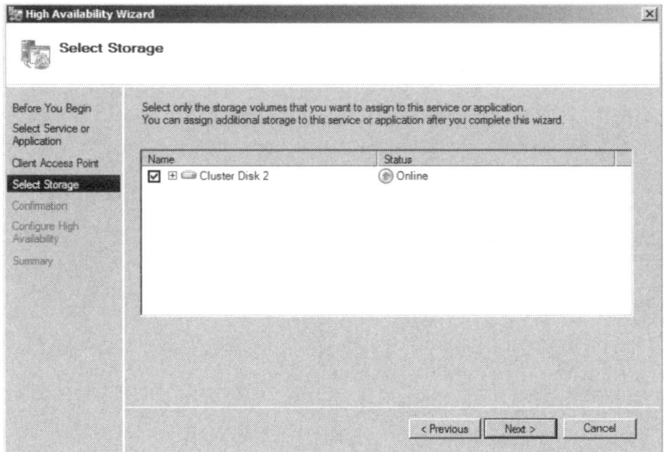

Figure 21-27 Select storage devices to use with the file server.

6. Click Next to confirm your settings and to create the File Server. Once completed, the Summary page will display the results, shown in Figure 21-28. Click Finish to close the wizard.

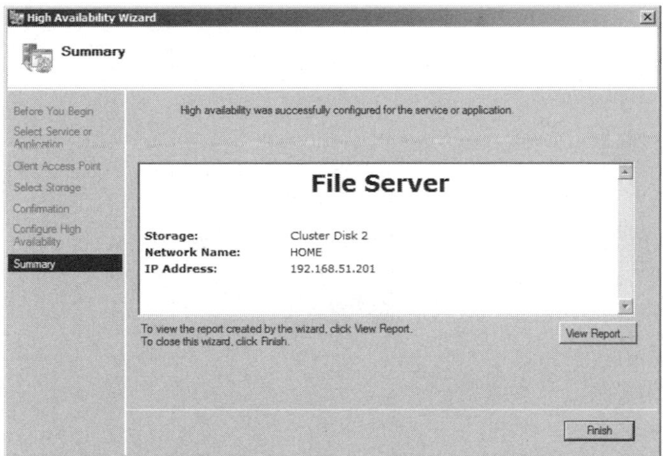

Figure 21-28 File Server creation status page

New File Share

To create a new File Share resource, continue with the following steps:

1. Right-click the File Server created in the previous steps and select Add A Shared Folder to start the Shared Folder Wizard, shown in Figure 21-29.

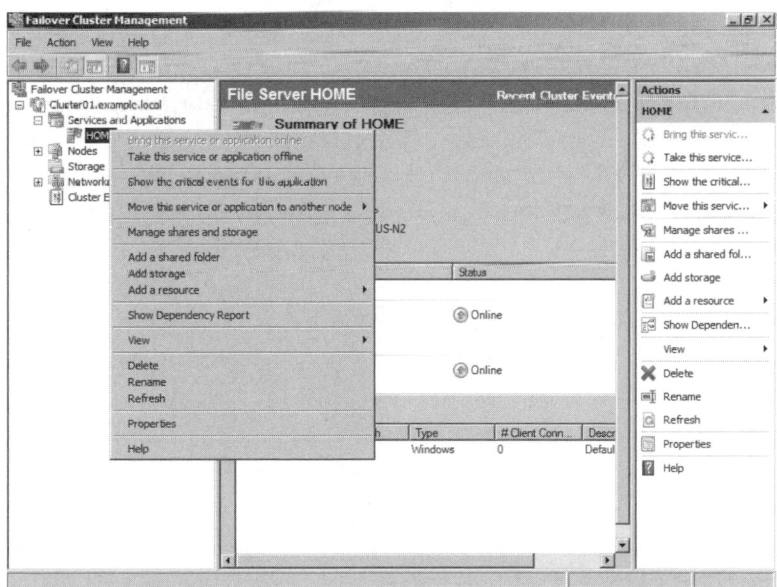

Figure 21-29 Right-click Add A Shared Folder to create a new file share.

2. On the Shared Folder Location page of the wizard, shown in Figure 21-30, enter the location on the disk that contains the folder you want to share. The folder must exist on a disk resource that is part of the File Server.

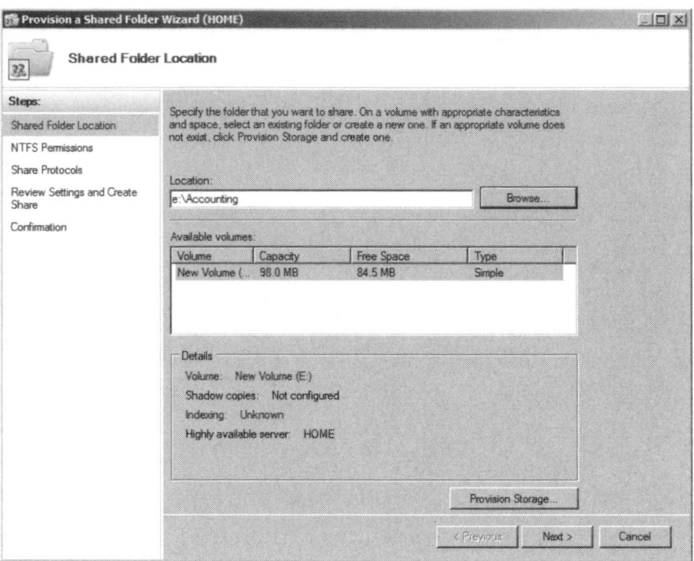

Figure 21-30 Specify the location of the folder you want to share.

3. Click Next to open the NTFS Permissions page, shown in Figure 21-31. If you want to use the existing NTFS permission in place on the folder and files, use the default setting and leave the permissions as they are. If you want to change the permission, select Yes, Change NTFS Permissions and click Edit Permissions. This has the same effect as editing the NTFS permissions directly using Windows Explorer.

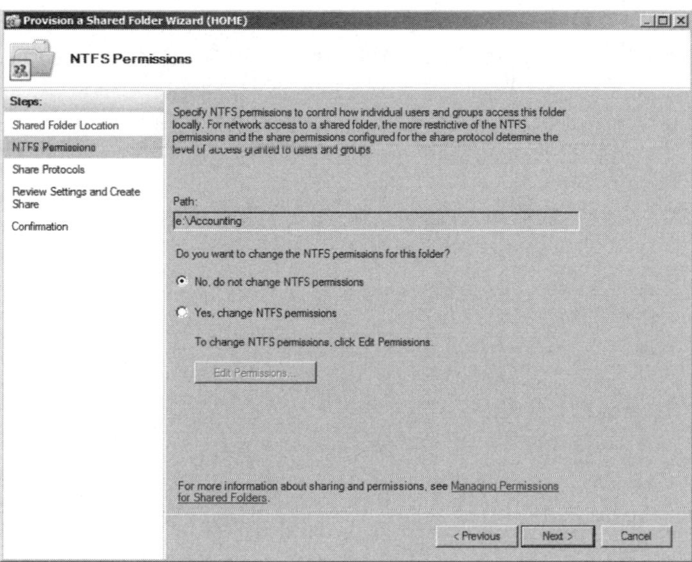

Figure 21-31 Determine whether you want to change the NTFS permissions of the shared folder.

4. Click Next to proceed to the Share Protocols page, shown in Figure 21-32. Specify the name of the share. If you have Network File System (NFS) installed for UNIX-based clients, you can specify the NFS name to use to share the folder as well. Click Next.

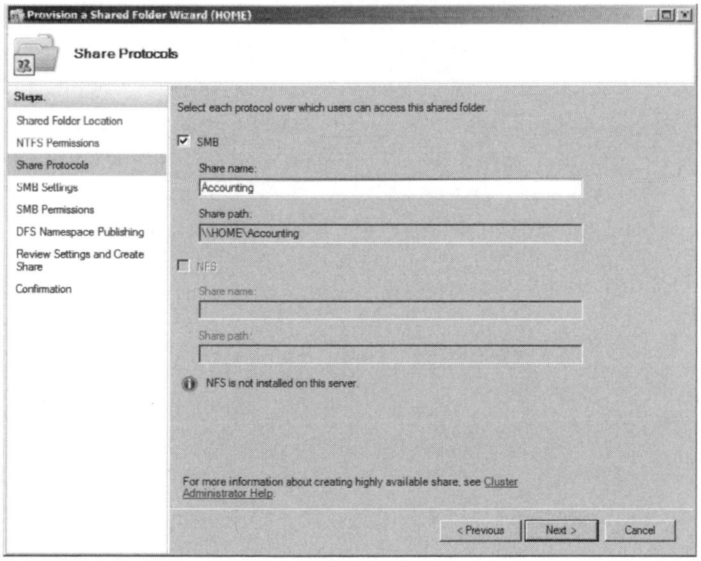

Figure 21-32 Configure the share name of the folder.

5. On the SMB Settings page, shown in Figure 21-33, you can enter a description for your file share, as well as configuring the maximum number of users that can connect to the share at one time, whether the files can be synced and used offline by clients, and whether Access-based enumeration can be used. Set these options by clicking the Advanced button. Click Next to proceed.

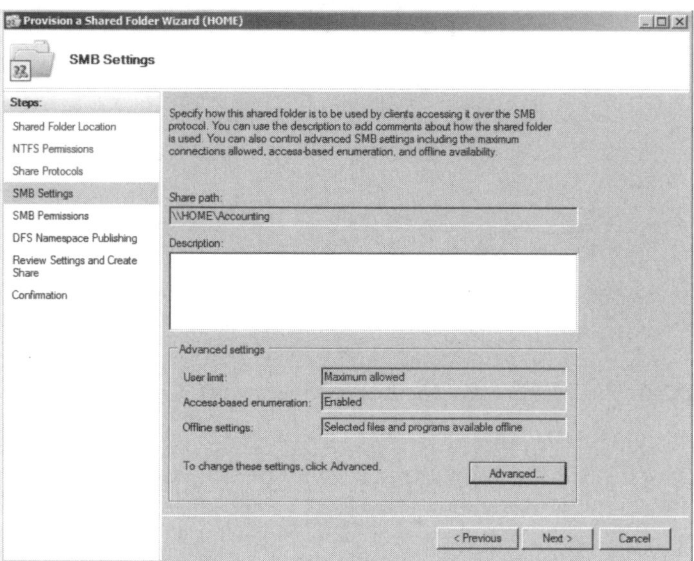

Figure 21-33 Configure the SMB file share settings.

6. The SMB Permissions page, shown in Figure 21-34, enables you to set the permissions for the file share itself. Remember that file share permissions act as a filter to NTFS permissions. If a user has full NTFS permissions, but the file share grants only Read-Only, the user has Read-Only. You can use one of the predefined groups of permissions or you can use a custom set of permissions.

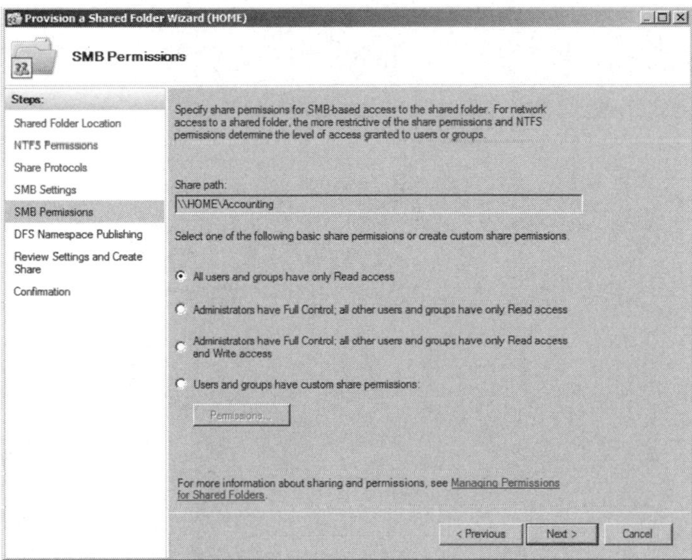

Figure 21-34 Configure the share permissions for the new shared folder.

7. Click Next to proceed to the DFS Namespace Publishing page, shown in Figure 21-35. If you are using a DFS namespace, you can publish this new shared folder into the DFS.

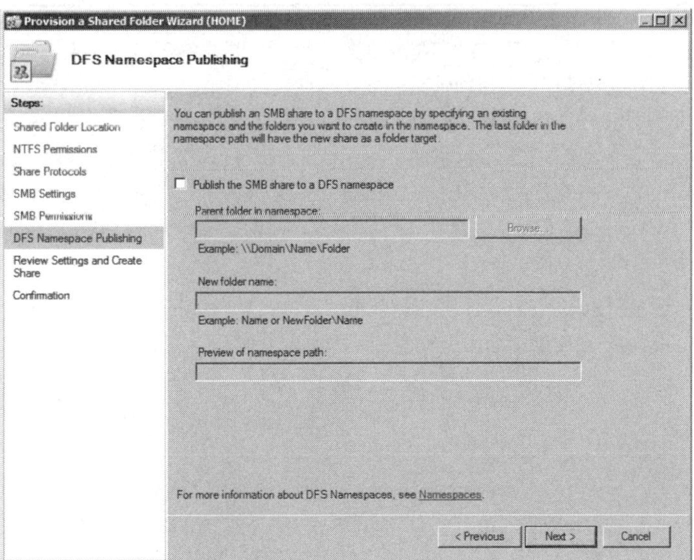

Figure 21-35 Configure DFS namespace publishing if applicable.

8. Click Next to confirm the settings and to initiate the creation process. Click Close after the wizard successfully creates the shared folder, shown in Figure 21-36.

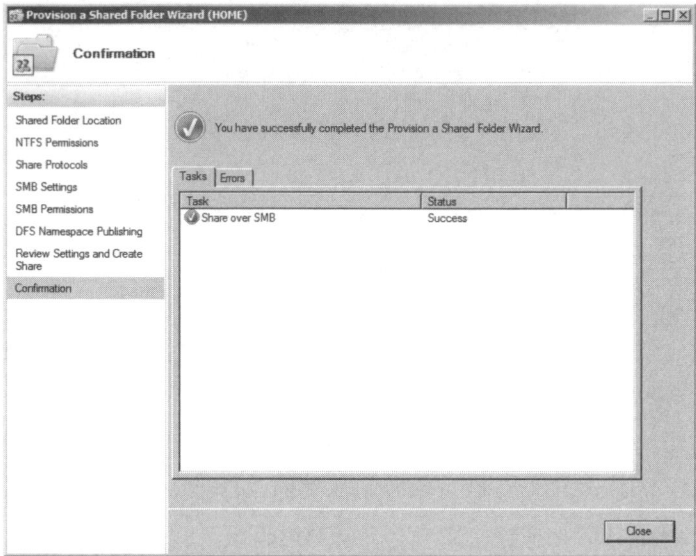

Figure 21-36 The successful creation of a shared folder

HPC Clusters

An additional type of clustering is high-performance computing (HPC) clusters, also called *compute clusters*. Unlike NLB or Failover clusters, HPC clusters are not designed to provide high-availability for critical applications, but rather to distribute highly parallel and complex computing tasks across multiple nodes. Windows HPC Server 2008, and its predecessor Windows Compute Cluster Server (CCS), enable super-computer functionality from the desktop to the enterprise.

Windows HPC Server is a combination of Windows Server 2008 and a package of interfaces, management tools, and utilities known as the Microsoft HPC Pack 2008. The HPC Pack is available separately and can be installed on any x64 version of Windows Server 2008.

Note Windows HPC Server 2008 is supported *only* on x64 versions of Windows Server 2008. It is not available on 32-bit Windows Server or on Itanium 64-bit editions.

Windows HPC Server supports configurations that have one, two, or three NICs per node, with the preferred configuration being a head node with a public (internal network LAN) interface, a private intra-cluster communications interface, and a high-speed Message Passing Interface (MPI). Each node in the cluster would have at least a private communications interface, and the MPI interface.

New to Windows HPC Server 2008 is support for configurations that combine HPC clustering of the compute nodes with Failover clustering of the head node, greatly increasing the redundancy and availability of Windows HPC Server 2008. Figure 21-37 shows the topology of an HPC cluster using Windows HPC Server 2008.

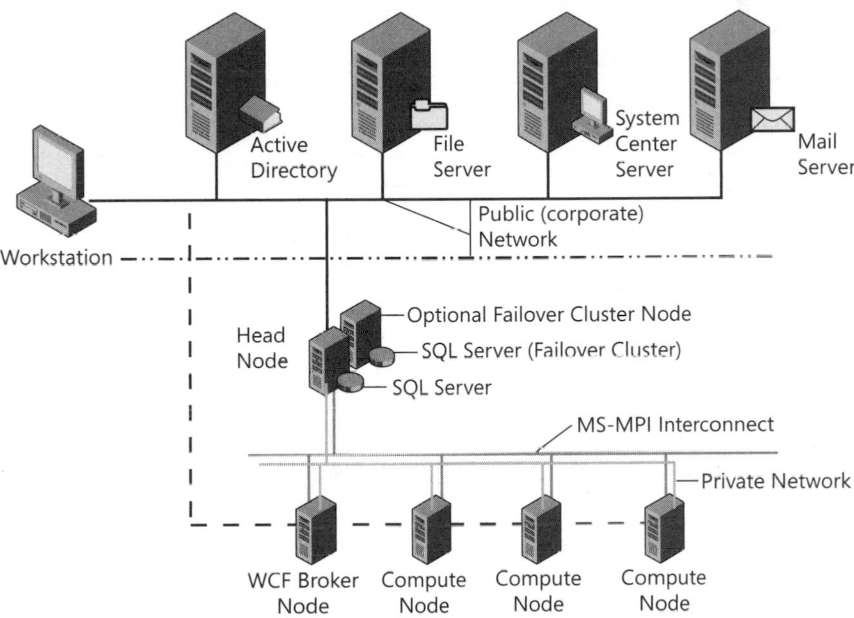

Figure 21-37 Windows HPC Server 2008 topology

Windows HPC Server 2008 includes Windows Deployment Services (WDS) that allows the easy setup and deployment of nodes on demand. After the head node is created and configured, individual nodes are simply connected to the network and powered up. WDS deploys Windows Server 2008 HPC to the new node and configures it to be part of the cluster.

Windows HPC Server 2008 includes a Node Template Generation Wizard that guides the administrator through creating a template for compute node configuration. Where advanced configuration is needed, a Template Editor provides additional capabilities, including configuring the template for automatic application deployment. The Windows HPC Server 2008 Template Generation Wizard includes support for injecting drivers into images.

The HPC Job Scheduler supports interactive Service-Oriented Architecture (SOA) workloads. SOA workloads run on Windows Communication Foundation (WCF) Hosts, and communicate with the submitting systems through WCF Brokers. You can add more WCF Brokers as necessary for additional scalability.

HPC also includes the Microsoft Message Passing Interface (MS MPI), a highly compatible implementation of the Argonne National Labs MPICH2 specification. Because the MS MPI implementation is completely compatible with MPICH2 at the API level, existing HPC applications that use MPICH2 will easily migrate to Windows HPC Server 2008.

> **More Info** For additional information on HPC, including details of MPI, migration of existing parallel applications, and parallel debugging, see *http://www.microsoft.com/downloads/details.aspx?FamilyId=7A4544F0-81F2-4778-8A59-35C43BA49875&%20displaylang=en&displaylang=en*.

Summary

Windows Server 2008, Enterprise Edition provides two high-availability clustering models: Network Load Balancing clusters and Failover clusters. Clusters provide a highly available and scalable environment. Network Load Balancing clusters use standard hardware to distribute TCP/IP applications across a cluster. Failover clusters use specialized shared disk resources to provide failover and static load balancing for a variety of applications. Windows HPC Server 2008 clusters support high-performance computing and highly parallel computing tasks. In the next part of the book we'll focus on security and on building a secure network using Windows Server 2008.

Part IV
Secure the Network

Chapter 22

Planning Security

In the old days, IT professionals–if they thought about security at all–tended to think of it in terms of software or hardware they could bolt on to their networks and not think about again, with the expectation that this was all that was required to completely protect their network from the dangers of an online world.

Well, that's simply not good enough anymore. Regardless of what some vendors may say otherwise, security is not a product–it's a process, and one that requires us to think strategically about how we use technical solutions to meet the objectives of our corporate security policy. This allows us to proactively address the risks to the information assets in our business, and make security decisions appropriate for the organization.

Security is about risk mitigation–not risk avoidance. We make security decisions based on our assessment of the acceptable risk for our environment. Acceptable risk is defined differently for each organization, meaning that the appropriate solution is different for each organization as well.

In this chapter, we cover the principles and practices of information security to help you make better security decisions. We help you balance the costs of implementing security with the positive returns in doing so. And finally, we focus on how to develop a higher security mindset to make appropriate decisions regarding which technical safeguards available in Windows Server 2008 should be used and when.

The Fundamental Principles of Security

Any security program has multiple objectives that it attempts to achieve to protect information. The three key security characteristics that make up the CIA triad, shown in Figure 22-1, are confidentiality, integrity, and availability. Together, these fundamental principles should be part of all security decisions.

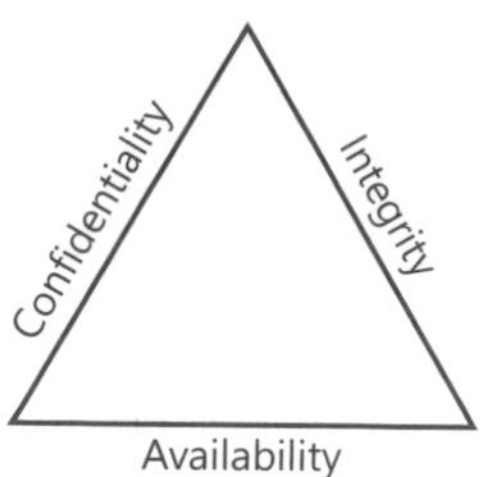

Figure 22-1 The CIA triad

Note The CIA triad is also referred to as the Security Functionality Triangle in some texts.

The level of security required to meet the objectives of these principles differs from business to business. However, no matter what the security goal may be, the technical safeguards you choose are an attempt to address one or more of these principles. Equally, risks, threats, and vulnerabilities are measured by their capability to compromise one or more principles in the CIA triad.

Confidentiality

Let's start with a definition: *Confidentiality is the assurance that information will stay private.*

Some information is public—a company's public Web site, for example. Some information should be extremely private—such as a company's human resource records or a patient's medical records. And most information falls somewhere in between. A secure system enforces an appropriate level of secrecy to ensure that no form of unauthorized information disclosure occurs—either when data is being processed or at rest.

How is confidentiality compromised? Some common attack vectors include network monitoring, shoulder surfing, account/password theft, and social engineering. This last one is the most often overlooked—and yet the hardest to protect against.

Users can accidentally (or on purpose) disclose sensitive information by not protecting the information as it's being processed. They can forget to encrypt it before sending it across an unsecure channel such as the network or even the Internet, or may forget to store it securely on disk when not in use. They may fall prey to social engineering, or even disclose information for personal gain.

The use of encrypted storage and transmission, along with strict access control and data classification, are methods to achieve appropriate confidentiality.

Windows Server 2008 has many features that support confidentiality, including the following:

- Rights Management Services
- Virtual private networking with PPTP and L2TP
- IPSec
- Authentication protocols including Kerberos, Secure Socket Layer (SSL), NT LAN Manager (NTLM), and Microsoft Challenge Handshake Protocol v2 (MSCHAP2)
- Certificate Services
- Discretionary Access Control Lists (DACL)
- Encrypting File System (EFS)
- BitLocker

Integrity

Integrity is the assurance that data stays in an unaltered state to maintain the accuracy and reliability of information. Integrity includes two important concepts:

- *Source integrity* is the assurance that the sender is who he claims to be.
- *Data integrity* is the assurance that the information received has not been altered during transmission.

Integrity safeguards protect against the potential interference or contamination of information by attackers. Integrity attacks can alter information during transmission (or before reception), or they can appear to come from a trusted source when they are not. Phishing attacks, for example, redirect users to a Web site that appears *in all respects* to be a trusted site, but is actually run by the attacker.

Windows Server 2008 has many features to ensure integrity, such as the following:

- PKCS#7 digitally signed messages
- Rights Management Services
- Certificate Services
- IPSec
- Internet Explorer 7

Availability

Availability is the assurance that data can be reliably accessed by authorized users in a reasonable amount of time. This requires that a data request be completed in a *consistent* and *predictable* manner with an *acceptable* level of performance. Any request for data that fails must recover from disruption quickly to minimize productivity loss while ensuring that security is maintained at all times. When possible, you should avoid single point of failures in an effort to maintain reliable access to information.

A weak implementation of this portion of CIA can negatively impact both productivity and availability. A Denial of Service (DoS) attack can disrupt business services and prevent real employees or customers from accessing resources. For example, an attack that attempts to gain remote access can trigger account lockouts caused by password policy enforcement, making it impossible for valid users to log on. Such an attack can even cause the entire IT infrastructure to grind to a halt on systems that rely heavily on internetworking across the Internet.

Windows Server 2008 includes several features that help protect and support availability while protecting against DoS attacks, including:

- Host-based firewall services for both ingress and egress filtering
- Individualized and grouped password lockout policies through Password Setting Objects (PSO)
- Virtual Private Networking with PPTP and L2TP
- Terminal Services

The Eight Rules of Security

When people think about security, they typically think of firewalls and antivirus software. After all, isn't that what security vendors have told us is the way to secure our systems? Well, the vendors are wrong. Each year the Computer Security Institute (CSI) releases a security survey in conjunction with the FBI Computer Crime Unit on the impact of security on businesses and the trends that they continue to see. The most recent study (*www.gocsi.com*) showed that 98 percent of the businesses that reported security breaches in the past year had firewalls in place; 97 percent stated that they also had antivirus software deployed.

What this shows is that security is not achieved by a single product. No single technology can be bolted on to indemnify you from all risk. Security is a process that requires consideration of the information assets you are trying to protect, enforced by appropriate technical safeguards that will reduce risk to acceptable levels for the organization.

When we think about process, it's easy to envision flurries of paperwork and documentation that no one will ever read. But it really doesn't have to be that way. As Kevin Day first proposed in his book *Inside the Security Mind: Making the Tough Decisions*, you can follow eight simple rules to considerably increase your security effectiveness when it comes to the security process:

- Rule of Least Privilege
- Rule of Change Management
- Rule of Trust
- Rule of the Weakest Link
- Rule of Separation
- Rule of the Three-Fold Process
- Rule of Preventative Action
- Rule of Immediate and Proper Response

Each of these rules plays an important role in helping you define your security best practices.

Rule of Least Privilege

Only give sufficient privilege to accomplish the task at hand. A person, place, or thing (a "subject") should only have sufficient access to an object to do the job.

A proper policy of least privilege will allow a subject to completely do its tasks without incident. It is only when the subject goes *against* policy that barriers arise. This is a subtle but important distinction. If you make the safeguards too stringent or complex, people will try to circumvent them so they can get their jobs done. Yet if you apply the safeguards correctly, people will rarely even know unless they try to do something they are not supposed to do.

Rule of Change Management

When you make a new change to your IT infrastructure, you expose your business to new risk. With a clear and concise change management policy that is universally enforced, all changes are examined for their impact on security before they're implemented. This also ensures that you're aware of all changes in your environment, simplifying troubleshooting in the event that a change causes problems.

Rule of Trust

You need to understand the implications of extending trust to anyone or anything within your organization. Always apply the rule of least privilege. What happens if you need to lay off a system administrator, for example? What about the key person in Human Resources? If she left, would (or could) she take a full set of employee records? Almost 80 percent of all security breaches are *internal* to the network. The internal threat is a significant one, and one you need to address with the rule of trust.

Rule of the Weakest Link

The old analogy still stands: You are only as strong as your weakest link. Think about it for a second. If you spend $25,000 on that new wiz-bang security device, but allow anyone inside or outside your organization to directly access your server, how effective is that device? Let's look at a more practical example. If you spend $10,000 on a new solid oak front door for your home, and $5,000 for a solid metal back door, but have a sliding glass door onto your patio, your entire home security is only as strong as the glass in that patio door. The same principle should be applied when detecting the weakest link in your security safeguards.

Rule of Separation

Keep critical business assets isolated and segregated to minimize the risks to those critical assets. By isolating critical business resources and services to their own computers, while using the rule of least privilege, you significantly reduce the attack surface of those resources. Even where you're using fewer servers by leveraging Windows Server Virtualization, you can still apply this rule effectively. The more people or applications that need to access a given resource, the greater the risk. Separating services to different hosts, and providing access only as required, significantly reduces the risk and strengthens the overall security of the services.

Rule of the Three-Fold Process

Security is not just about technology implementation. (Too bad, since we're just like most system administrators—we love an excuse to install fancy new stuff.) It's critical to follow through the entire security management life cycle. This includes implementation, monitoring, and maintenance to effectively safeguard your resources. You should know what is being monitored and logged, know when something is wrong, and know how to respond to it. You need to keep up to date with what is happening in your environment and what your overall security posture is at all times.

Rule of Preventative Action

Effective defense requires proactively assessing the security in your environment. To be aware of new security risks that are in the wild, you need to keep current with security tracking mailing lists, RSS feeds, and so forth. Regularly test your defenses by using vulnerability assessment tools before an attacker does. Maintain a strong three-fold process and keep your systems up to date with the latest security patches.

Rule of Immediate and Proper Response

Even though you hope and expect to never suffer a serious security breach, you should have an Incidence Response Plan in place so that you know and understand exactly what to do in the event of a problem. All too often when an organization responds poorly to an intrusion, they do more harm than the attacker did. A rational, well-thought-out response plan can make all the difference. You need to react quickly, document everything, and, above all, *stay calm*. Ensure that you have a very clear and well-understood Standard Escalation Procedure in place so that the issue can be reported quickly to the right people to mobilize the correct resources. Be discreet (yelling "the sky is falling" is never productive) and follow your plan.

The Higher Security Mindset

History tends to be a good educator when it comes to computer security. In the Windows world we have seen all too many examples of poorly designed software that was compromised because it wasn't sufficiently resilient to attack. In many of those cases, poor IT administration contributed to the problem and led to chaos on the network.

Real World Slammer

On January 23, 2003, a small piece of malicious code in the form of a worm began to propagate across the Internet. In less than ten minutes it had infected more than 75,000 systems, and ended up causing serious denial of service across the Internet for sometime afterward as systems continued to be infected. The entire Internet was seriously slowed down as key routers failed under the burden of extremely high bombardment traffic from infected servers. The name of this hostile worm? SQL Slammer.

The Vulnerability

The buffer overflow vulnerability that Slammer targeted existed in both SQL Server and MSDE 2000, allowing it to infect both desktops and servers. The vulnerability was well known, and an update had been released a full six months *before* the worm launched. Microsoft released Security Bulletin MS02-039 on July 24, 2002, with an update to SQL Server (and MSDE) and guidance on deployment.

The attack pattern included a single UDP packet to port 1434, a SQL Server Resolution Service that doesn't need to be accessed by the general public. Once infected, the compromised host would then rapidly propagate to other servers in the exact same manner.

The Security Breakdown

No one single failure of the eight rules of security was the cause of the massive disruption that Slammer produced. It took the combination of four failures across thousands of computers to make Slammer so effective. A single packet to a service port that shouldn't have been open was accepted by untrusted hosts for a service (SQL Server) that didn't need to accept it. A simple firewall rule on the SQL Server host restricting communications to the resolution service would have defended against this attack from unprivileged hosts. Once infected, the propagation of Slammer would have been significantly slowed if simple access control had been used at both the host and edge firewall. A server running SQL has no need to send unsolicited UDP packets to other resolution servers on the Internet. And, finally, if the Rule of Preventative Action had been followed, the SQL Server and MSDE instances would have been fully updated and not susceptible to the bad packet.

Much of the 20/20 hindsight looking back at Slammer has focused on the last part of the failure: patch management by administrators. And certainly, that's part of the problem. But a system designed with proper security from the outset would not have been affected by Slammer *even if no update were available at all*. By applying the Rule of Least Privilege alongside the Rule of Preventative Action and the Rule of Separation, SQL Slammer attacks to your network would simply be dropped, no matter whether they originated from an external or internal host.

When we talk about having a higher security mindset, we mean that instead of being reactive to threats to our networks, we need to think strategically while applying appropriate technical safeguards. By using the eight rules of security and the technology that supports them, we can defend against the unknown more effectively.

If you plan for individual things to fail by building resilient systems that implement a strategic, defense-in-depth design, you reduce the likelihood that an attack will cause serious and irreparable damage. If you understand which assets need protecting and what you need to do to protect them, you mitigate the risk to acceptable levels for those assets.

How do you develop and implement a higher security mindset? You need to take five key actions to improve your overall security design:

- Think in terms of zones.
- Create chokepoints.
- Layer your security.
- Understand relational security.
- Divide responsibility.

Think in Terms of Zones

The concept of security zones isn't new or unusual. We see it in things like Internet Explorer to segregate different trust levels within the browser, for example. Zoning can be much more than that, however. It is a process in which you isolate different *subjects* (people, places, or things that are trying to gain access) from *objects* (people, places, or things the subject is trying to gain access to). The concept of zoning can apply to anything–as long as each zone treats security differently.

A zone is a group of resources that have a similar security profile. They have similar risks, trust levels, exposures, and/or security needs. For example, a public Web server has a different trust and exposure level than an intranet Web site and should therefore be in a different zone. Though you can have as many different zones as appropriate for your environment, the most common scenario has three zones:

- The trusted (internal) zone
- The semi-trusted (perimeter network) zone
- The untrusted (external) zone

These three zones can apply to almost anything, including network-based services, secure software development, and even physical security access systems.

The trick is separating zones in such a way that we can maintain higher levels of security by protecting resources from zones of lesser security controls. The separation mechanism between zones could be as simple as a firewall, a piece of managed code, or a locked door. The goal is to have some degree of control over what happens between the zones. And to have logical communication mechanisms that allow zones to communicate safely where appropriate. Let's look at a possible scenario to demonstrate how zones work and can help.

Contoso Pharmaceuticals is a major supplier of llama pain medicines to veterinarians and breeders worldwide. The shipping department wants to give customers the ability to track orders, but the information on ordering and order status resides on the company's internal SQL Server computer. The IT team needs to design a system that will allow customers to get the information *without* exposing the company's private and sensitive data to unnecessary risk.

What steps could be used to accomplish this request? One scenario would be the following:

1. Determine the trust levels of all subjects and objects, and then determine which zone they belong to. The objects (order data) are located in a SQL database stored in the internal trusted zone. The subjects (customers) are located in the untrusted external zone.

2. Determine the direction in which communication initiation will occur. Ideally, higher levels of trust should initiate the connection to zones of less trust. However, because the customers will be establishing the connection via a Web browser, this is not possible. Because Contoso Pharmaceuticals doesn't want customers to have direct access to the corporate network, they'll use a Web server in a semi-trusted zone, such as the company's Internet perimeter network.
3. Determine the privileges the customers (*subjects*) really need to the data (*objects*). In this scenario, they only need real-time *read* access to orders that belong to them. The SQL database administrator can reduce privileges to enforce only limited access to this information by utilizing the built-in security of Microsoft SQL Server.
   a. Create stored procedures and views that will only return the specific information necessary to provide a customer's order status.
   b. Create a restricted database user account with only enough privileges to log on and execute the stored procedures and views. The Web server can then use this reduced privilege account to log on to SQL Server and get access to the needed information.
4. Open up the appropriate ports on the firewall to allow the IP address of the Web server to communicate with the SQL Server computer.
5. Document the security decisions made here for future access and reference.

In this simple example, you can reduce the attack surface of the information into distinct areas by looking at the access in terms of zones. You ensure that your customers have sufficient privilege to get the information they need without having access to the entire trusted database. Even if the Web server can be successfully compromised, it has no effect on the underlying information stored in the SQL Server computer. While an attacker who managed to compromise the public Web server might be able to get information on the status of shipping orders, the attacker has no avenue to further attack the trusted zone.

Create Chokepoints

The concept of deploying chokepoints in security has deep roots in the history of humankind. In medieval times, kings would force their attackers through tight doors and drawbridges in an effort to pour down fiery oil on them. These chokepoints were also easier to guard, limiting the ability of serfs and assassins to get close to royalty when they least expected it.

In information security, chokepoints make it easy for you to focus your protections and monitoring more effectively. You can limit access and reduce the attack surface of the system, making it easier to control and more cost effective to manage.

Chokepoints are a critical component of a higher security mindset because they greatly reduce the possible attack surface. They do, however, present a single point of failure: if all your critical information flows through a single NIC or router, you want to be sure that NIC or router is redundant and can be repaired or replaced without significant downtime. The two basic types of chokepoints are network chokepoints and application chokepoints.

Network Chokepoints

A network chokepoint is a network path through which all traffic must pass to get to a critical resource. This can take the form of a router or firewall, for example, that controls access to (and from) the Internet. Network chokepoints are the more common type of chokepoint, and the type most associated with network security.

The two key practices for network chokepoints are to ensure first that the chokepoint is monitored and filtered to identify attacks, and second that the chokepoint really *is* a chokepoint and hasn't been compromised by a back door or alternate access point. It does you little good to install a top-notch firewall on your network if you also have unsecured direct dial-in modems.

Application Chokepoints

The second type of chokepoint is the application chokepoint. Application chokepoints allow users to access applications and services in a centralized fashion. Instead of having to manage safeguards individually across different systems and services, we can consolidate them at a single point where they can be filtered and monitored.

In Windows Server 2008, Active Directory acts as an application chokepoint. Each workstation and server is part of a domain that controls authentication, authorization, auditing, and other aspects of security, as are users and groups in the domain. By centralizing authentication, authorization, and auditing in Active Directory, we can easily monitor across all systems.

Windows Server 2008 Terminal Services is another form of application chokepoint. By centralizing key applications onto the server, we can more easily control access to them, and monitor that access.

Layer Your Security

Absolute security is a myth. The belief that a single technology can protect you against all threats is, frankly, ludicrous. Worse, reliance on a single technology or solution can be disastrous. If a single vulnerability in the system can be exploited, you are compromised. And even the best systems can have unsuspected vulnerabilities or be compromised by misconfiguration. Many (perhaps most) security breaches can be traced to the misconfiguration of an otherwise safe system.

Defense in depth—the layering of multiple security solutions and technologies—gives you additional protection even if a key layer of your security fails. We live in a coastal climate, and the wise person here wears layers of clothes in the winter. A rain jacket over a sweater over a wool shirt over a silk t-shirt provides multiple layers of protection against wind, rain, and cold. Security works much the same way.

A defense-in-depth strategy has three tiers: the internal, middle, and external layers. The *internal layer* is direct security on an asset you are trying to protect. Examples include a host-based firewall, an ACL on a file, or the application of object auditing on the protected resource to ensure that you know when someone has accessed it.

The second tier is the *middle layer*. This is the layer people most often think about when they talk about security, and where most of the money is spent. We include firewalls, intrusion-detection sensors, and even VPN endpoint servers in this tier.

The final tier is the *external layer*, and it's the front line of defense. The Internet-facing router on your network, for example, that protects the firewall against Denial of Service attacks.

When applied together, these three tiers provide a more effective defense in depth. The external layer helps screen out obviously bad data such as Denial of Service floods against services. The middle layer includes the primary firewall that controls access at the network layer. And the internal layer includes the host-based firewall that lets you make informed decisions about which services are allowed to and from the host based on authenticated users and processes.

Any one of these layers might fail. The external layer might not be configured correctly, allowing normally unacceptable data through when it shouldn't. Or the safeguard in the middle layer might have a vulnerability that could be attacked, leaving the final defense to be the internal layer.

Windows Server 2008 includes multiple features that together build a defense in depth:

- ACLs for file, registry, and native processes
- Host-based firewall
- IP address restrictions in service such as IIS
- Windows authentication
- Audit Object Access Policies in Active Directory

Understand Relational Security

When you look at your information assets and consider the implications of applying security safeguards to protect them, you should consider the various chains and relationships. The asset–whether device, file, disk, server, or entire network–has a series of relationships with the applications that access or consume it; the computers and network that the application uses to communicate with it; and the people who run the applications from those computers over those networks. By understanding those relationships and how they interact, you can more effectively and transparently protect the asset without interfering with appropriate and necessary access.

Because of the interdependencies in relational security, actions or security decisions at any layer of the relationships can potentially interfere with necessary and appropriate use of the asset, just as it can cause inadvertent and unintended vulnerabilities or attack vectors. If your attempt to protect your asset prevents users from doing their jobs, you haven't improved security–you've effectively propagated your own Denial of Service attack. Inappropriate or poorly implemented security safeguards can do more harm than good when they affect productivity. At the same time, if you don't provide adequate and appropriate security, you can expose the asset to unnecessary risk.

Let's take the case of a business-critical server that isn't directly connected to the Internet or any outside networks. If we have a firewall between the server and the Internet, and we don't forward traffic to the server, the server should be completely safe against external intruders, correct? Unfortunately, that simply isn't true. It isn't that easy, we're afraid. It's still possible to attack the server if there is any chain of relationships that would allow an attacker to indirectly access the server by some other means.

What happens if an employee telecommutes from home using a VPN connection to the network and accesses assets on that server? By following the chain of relationships, you can see that an attacker could breach the system by first attacking the employee's host over the Internet and then piggybacking the VPN tunnel. Therefore, when thinking about threats to this server, we have to consider the fact that it *is* connected to the Internet, even if this connection is indirect.

Under the Hood Back Doors

By following the relational security chains, you can often find vulnerabilities you didn't originally expect. Hackers know this and traverse these chains in hopes of finding weak or nonexistent safeguards that can be easily attacked. When you hear that a hacker broke in through a "back door," it means that they did exactly this: They traversed a chain of relationships from a less secured and theoretically noncritical system to the system they ultimately compromised. And it's a lot more common than you might think.

Real World SQL Slammer, Again

SQL Slammer was able to compromise a United States Nuclear Power facility in January of 2003. Even though the plant had a firewall that was not compromised, Slammer succeeded by penetrating the unsecured network of an external contractor and then moved on through a dedicated (and unsecured) T1 line, bridging that network to the Nuclear Power facility network.

Investigators later found that there wasn't one line connecting the nuclear facility to external networks, but lines to *multiple* other networks that completely bypassed the plant's firewall, which was programmed to block the port that SQL Slammer used to propagate.

By following the relational security trail and looking for the weakest links, worms, viruses, and other malicious code can find their way into even supposedly secure networks if the designers of these networks don't understand and protect against this kind of attack.

The potential risks of relational security failures are serious: From the unavailability of major bank ATM systems to hospitals that are forced to take patients off medical monitoring systems, the weaknesses in insecure systems have the ability to affect more secure systems. This is known as *vulnerability inheritance.*

Vulnerability inheritance is arguably the most important security relationship between two objects, but it is often the most neglected. The level of vulnerability of one object directly impacts the security of another that shares a relationship. A remotely mounted drive between a secure system and an unsecure system reduces the security effectiveness of the secure one. A seemingly secure file simply isn't secure if the host it is stored on is not. If the secure system is in any way accessible by the vulnerable system, the secure system can inherit those vulnerabilities.

What makes this an even greater concern is that many systems have multiple paths of entry. Many of these entry points are often overlooked, including such things as removable media (CD, USB, and so on) and dial-up connections.

Real World Found USB Keys?

In June of 2006, a security professional was asked to audit the security effectiveness of a credit union. He placed 20 USB keys in various locations around the employee parking lot and the outside smoking area of the bank. Of those 20 keys, 15 were found by employees of the credit union, and every one of them was plugged into computers inside the bank's corporate network as people tried to see what was on the key.

Each key that was plugged in included a Trojan that automatically ran and inserted itself onto the computer that the key was plugged in to–giving that security professional access to the system on behalf of the unknowing participant. What would have happened if the keys had hostile code designed to traverse the network and exploit a back door, giving hackers access? How likely is it that your employees have the same curiosity?

Hackers are skilled at ferreting out unprotected entry points. They look for the weakest links in the system, and focus on ways to take advantage of those links to compromise the system. You need to think of *all* entry points, not just the traditional ones. And you need to understand how systems relate to each other so that you can provide appropriate safeguards against all entry points–direct and indirect–to your information assets.

Windows Server 2008 includes Network Access Protection (NAP), a technology designed to help address relational security issues. NAP is a policy enforcement platform that works with Windows Vista and Windows XP SP3 or later. It allows clients entering the domain to be forced to comply with system health requirements. With NAP, you can create customized health policies to validate computer health before allowing access to the network. If client computers require updates, you can automatically update the computer before allowing it access to network resources. Or you can confine noncompliant computers to a restricted network until they become compliant. This gives you stronger assurance that hosts on your network meet a security baseline before they are allowed to connect.

Divide Responsibility

No one person in the business should have absolute authority over all information assets. All too often, all responsibility and power is simply abdicated to the IT department, with little or no thought of the consequences, or any concern about exactly who has what authority. Or worse, that responsibility and power is outsourced to external consultants a continent away.

No one person should be completely trusted and have complete control. And everyone (including IT administrators) should be subject to the same degree of security enforcement within the organization, based on their roles and responsibilities. The CEO or CIO may want access to everything, but does he really need it? The Rule of Least Privilege should prevail. The whole point of the Rule of Trust is to ensure that in the worst case scenario, the business can still function. An irate administrative employee may quickly become a business's worst enemy. And even though you have legal recourse should an attack from a current or former employee occur, by then it's already too late. Your business has suffered, and likely your reputation as well.

Divided responsibility isn't just about people. Whenever possible, you should separate responsibility of services and technical safeguards that protect information assets. If you only have one server that is protecting everything in the business, what happens when it fails? You *need* to know the answer to that simple question. Technical safeguards are not unbreakable. Systems will fail. At the very minimum, you need secondary systems monitoring the primary ones to enable a quick reaction in the event of a failure.

The new Windows Event Log allows you to subscribe to filters that monitor your systems' state and ensure that they operate as expected. Security events can quickly be cataloged, prioritized, and reviewed.

You can use the fine-grained group controls for administrative users in Active Directory to limit a user's permissions and policies and control the systems that user can administer. Enabling audit policies allows you to keep an audit trail of changes. Those changes should directly correspond to the expected changes out of your change management process.

By following standard management practices for IT systems, you can easily divide responsibility without interfering with business productivity into the following three key areas:

Staff redundancy

At least two people should have the knowledge, authority, and privilege to accomplish all administrative and security tasks. They should audit each other in a manner that ensures that the other can take over primary responsibilities when needed.

Monitor everyone

Yes, everyone. All technical safeguards should be globally enforced on everyone equally. This includes administrators and senior executives in the business. It is a good idea to have someone independent of normal IT responsibilities be responsible for monitoring IT administrators. The person or persons responsible don't have to be IT experts, but they do have to have a clear understanding of what is and isn't appropriate access.

No one is above security enforcement

When it comes to enforcement, there should be no exceptions. Security policies should be enforced universally and equally. This requires a clear and unambiguous acceptable use and security standards policy that is applied at all levels of the company. It can't happen, however, if you don't have full buy-in from senior management.

The one simple rule we'd suggest is *trust, but verify*. Trust your IT staff to manage your systems. That is, after all, their job function. But always have checks and balances in the system and verify that what they should be doing is allowed. And only what they should be doing. Any administrator who thinks that she shouldn't be subject to the same rules and responsibilities as others is probably someone you don't want in the organization. Always assume that something could go wrong and plan for it.

Summary

This chapter has covered the basic tenets of good security planning. Security is about risk mitigation and not risk avoidance. It is a process, and not a product. And it requires a higher level of thinking than simply trying to install technology in an effort to bolt on security after the fact.

When making security decisions we should always consider how they impact confidentiality, integrity, and availability of the information assets we are trying to protect. We need to understand how security decisions in one area will affect relationships on other systems, people, and processes. Combining the eight rules of security with the discipline of a higher security mindset, we can make more informed decisions that are more effective in protecting our information.

The next chapter will continue where this one leaves off, and show you how to implement the technical safeguards available in Windows Server 2008 to meet required security objectives.

Chapter 23

Implementing Security

If you look back on the history of major security events, many have shaped the way Microsoft engineers software. Two stand out as pivotal:

- The Code Red/Nimba worm
- The MS Blaster worm

In this chapter, we'll cover the security features of Windows Server 2008 that would have prevented these two attacks, and show you how to implement security to help protect your network from the next attack. As you implement security on your network, however, it's essential to remember that securing a network is not an event or an action–it's a goal. A goal that requires an ongoing process of investigation, research, and implementation to achieve.

More Info For an in-depth analysis of the security features of Windows Server 2008, *Windows Server 2008 Security Resource Kit* (Microsoft Press, 2008) would be an excellent addition to your Server 2008 library.

Introduction

The Code Red/Nimba worm was an attack that exploited a security vulnerability in IIS 5. What made it devastating was that *every* Windows 2000 computer automatically enabled IIS 5 as part of the normal installation. Microsoft learned an important lesson from this and now enables only the exact and specific services that are required for the server's role in Windows Server 2008.

One of the reasons that the MS Blaster worm was so devastating was that even on a Windows XP computer with the firewall enabled, the computer could become infected in the time between booting up and the automatic enabling of the Windows Firewall stack. In Windows Server 2008, external network connections are disabled until after the firewall is up and running.

Secure at Installation

One of the first things to notice about a freshly built Windows Server 2008 computer is the number of services running. As with Windows Server 2003, only services that are critical for the base installation process are enabled by default. Table 23-1 show the default running services on a fresh Windows Server 2008 Enterprise installation.

Table 23-1 Default Services in Windows Server 2008

Service Name	Startup Type	Log On As
Application Experience	Automatic	Local System
Application Information	Manual	Local System
Background Intelligent Transfer Service	Started (Delayed start)	Local System
Base Filtering Engine	Automatic	Local Service
COM + Event System	Automatic	Local Service
Cryptographic Services	Automatic	Network Service
DCOM Server Process Launcher	Automatic	Local System
Desktop Windows Manager Session	Automatic	Local System
DHCP Client	Automatic	Local Service
Diagnostic Policy Service	Automatic	Local Service
Diagnostic System Host	Manual	Local System
Distributed Link Tracking Client	Automatic	Local System
Distributed Transaction Coordinator	Automatic (delayed start)	Network Service
DNS Client	Automatic	Network Service
Function Discovery Provider Host	Manual	Local Service

Table 23-1 **Default Services in Windows Server 2008**

Service Name	Startup Type	Log On As
Function Discovery Resource Publication	Automatic	Local Service
Group Policy Client	Automatic	Local System
IKE and AuthIP IPsec Keying Modules	Automatic	Local System
IP Helper	Automatic	Local System
IPSec Policy Agent	Automatic	Network Service
KtmRM for Distributed Transaction Coordinator	Automatic (Delayed start)	Network Service
Network Connections	Manual	Local System
Network List Service	Automatic	Local Service
Network Location Awareness	Automatic	Network Service
Network Store Interface Service	Automatic	Local Service
Plug and Play	Automatic	Local System
Print Spooler	Automatic	Local System
Remote Access Connection Manager	Manual	Local System
Remote Procedure Call (RPC)	Automatic	Network Service
Remote Registry	Automatic	Local Service
Secondary Logon	Automatic	Local System
Secure Socket Tunneling Protocol Service	Manual	Local Service
Security Accounts manager	Automatic	Local System
Server	Automatic	Local System
Shell Hardware Detection	Automatic	Local System
SL UI Notification Service	Manual	Local Service
Software Licensing	Automatic	Network Service
System Event Notification Service	Automatic	Local System
Task Scheduler	Automatic	Local System
TCP/IP NetBIOS Helper	Automatic	Local Service
Telephony	Manual	Network Service
Terminal Services	Automatic	Network Service

Table 23-1 Default Services in Windows Server 2008

Service Name	Startup Type	Log On As
User Profile Service	Automatic	Local System
Windows Error Reporting Service	Automatic	Local System
Windows Event Log	Automatic	Local Service
Windows Firewall	Automatic	Local Service
Windows Management Instrumentation	Automatic	Local System
Windows Modules Installer	Manual	Local System
Windows Remote Management (WS-Management)	Automatic (Delayed start)	Network Service
Windows Time	Automatic	Local Service
Windows Update	Automatic (Delayed start)	Local System
Workstation	Automatic	Local Service

An important change in Windows Server 2008 is that some services have a delayed start. This is to ensure that they are in place in the stack in the proper order.

System Account Roles

Each of the default running services is logged in with one of three accounts:

- **Local System** Services running as Local System have the rights similar to a domain account when used for services on domain controllers. Local System is a powerful account that can provide full access to the computer. The actual name of the account is NT Authority\System.
- **Local Service** Local Service account is a built-in account with reduced privileges. It is similar to an authenticated local user account. Using this account versus Local System helps safeguard the computer from attacks or compromises.
- **Network Service** The Network Service Account is similar to authenticated user account. This service accesses network resources using the credentials of the computer account the same way that the Local System service does.

The choice of account for each service is just sufficient to enable it to function. No unnecessary privileges are granted to the account that aren't required for the service to function correctly.

For each of these account roles, changing the default could prevent services from running correctly. To maintain a Microsoft-supported state, you should only modify services if the Microsoft Specialized Security-Limited Functionality guidelines described in the sidebar "High Security Level" indicate that the changed state is supported under that guidance.

Under the Hood High Security Level

The High Security level is also known as the Specialized Security-Limited Functionality level. It is appropriate for extremely hostile environments that have a significant risk of attack. The Specialized Security-Limited Functionality level is for guarding the most valuable assets, including government systems or systems designed to meet government regulations and requirements. This level of security is described and covered under Microsoft Knowledge Base article 885409 (*http://support.microsoft.com/kb/885409*). This level is not appropriate for the majority of Windows systems. The High Security level is really appropriate only for systems in which a compromise could result in the loss of extremely valuable information or lots of money—or where lives are at stake.

Where you do decide to implement Specialized Security-Limited Functionality, it is essential to follow the Microsoft guidance to ensure that both security and acceptable functionality are maintained. Remember that even when you use the official Microsoft security guidelines, Specialized Security-Limited Functionality settings *will* break line-of-business applications that have not been designed to function on a hardened system. If you adjust or deviate from the default settings or the Specialized Security-Limited Functionality settings as provided in the Microsoft Security guides, you will need to test your system and possibly be unsupported by Microsoft Customer Support Services.

For example, some services that were run as Local System in Windows Server 2003 are run as Local Service in Windows Server 2008. The Com+ Event System services was adjusted as was the Cryptographic Service which was changed to run as Network Service.

Server Core

An alternative to adjusting the running default services you see above is to consider deploying Windows Server 2008 Server Core. Server Core is exactly what it says: The core functions of a server operating system. No Internet Explorer, no media player, no managed code of any sort. Just the essentials. When you install Server Core, you are literally welcomed to the desktop with a blinking c:\ prompt. Server Core is covered at length in Chapter 9, "Installing and Configuring Server Core," but when compared to the default services in a full installation of Windows Server 2008 Enterprise, shown earlier in Table 23-1, the services installed and enabled on Server Core are more limited, as shown in Table 23-2.

Table 23-2 **Service Settings in Windows Server 2008 Server Core**

Service Name	Startup Type	Log On As
AeLookupSvc - Application Experience	Automatic	Local System
BFE - Base Filtering Engine	Automatic	Local Service
BITS - Background Intelligent Transfer Service	Started (Delayed start)	Local System
CryptSvc - Cryptographic Services	Automatic	Network Service
DcomLaunch - DCOM Server Process Launcher	Automatic	Local System
Dhcp - DHCP Client	Automatic	Local Service
Dnscache - DNS Client	Automatic	Network Service
DPS - Diagnostic Policy Service	Automatic	Local Service
EventLog - Windows Event Log	Automatic	Local Service
EventSystem - COM + Event System	Automatic	Local Service
Gpsvc - Group Policy Client	Automatic	Local System
IKEEXT - IKE and AuthIP IPsec Keying Modules	Automatic	Local System
Iphlpsvc - IP Helper	Automatic	Local System
KtmRm - KtmRM for Distributed Transaction Coordinator	Automatic (Delayed start)	Network Service
LanmanServer - Server	Automatic	Local System
LanmanWorkstation - Workstation	Automatic	Local Service
Lmhosts - TCP/IP NetBIOS Helper	Automatic	Local Service
MpsSvc - Windows Firewall	Automatic	Local Service
MSDTC - Distributed Transaction Coordinator	Automatic (delayed start)	Network Service
Netprofm - Network List Service	Automatic	Local Service
NlaSvc - Network Location Awareness	Automatic	Network Service

Table 23-2 **Service Settings in Windows Server 2008 Server Core**

Service Name	Startup Type	Log On As
Nsi - Network Store Interface Service	Automatic	Local Service
PlugPlay - Plug and Play	Automatic	Local System
Policyagent - IPSec Policy Agent	Automatic	Network Service
ProfSvc - User Profile Service	Automatic	Local System
RemoteRegistry - Remote Registry	Automatic	Local Service
RpcSs - Remote Procedure Call (RPC)	Automatic	Network Service
SamSs - Security Accounts manager	Automatic	Local System
Schedule - Task Scheduler	Automatic	Local System
Seclogon - Secondary Logon	Automatic	Local System
SENS - System Event Notification Service	Automatic	Local System
Slsvc - Software Licensing	Automatic	Network Service
TermService - Terminal Services	Automatic	Network Service
W32Time - Windows Time	Automatic	Local Service
WdiSystemHost - Diagnostic System Host	Manual	Local System
Winmgmt - Windows Management Instrumentation	Automatic	Local System
WinRM - Windows Remote Management (WS-Management)	Automatic (Delayed start)	Network Service
Wuauserv - Windows Update	Automatic (Delayed start)	Local System

Server core has only 32 running services as its default, and has a much smaller footprint. If your application will run on Server Core, choose that option before trying to shut off services in a full Windows Server 2008 installation. You'll have fewer problems and a clear and unambiguous supported environment.

Roles and Features Wizards

New to Windows Server 2008 are the concepts of Roles and Features, and the wizards to enable them. The wizards install Roles (or Features) with the appropriate settings, startup types, and service logons, as well as setting the Windows Firewall correctly and installing and configuring any dependencies. The Add Roles Wizard is shown in Figure 23-1.

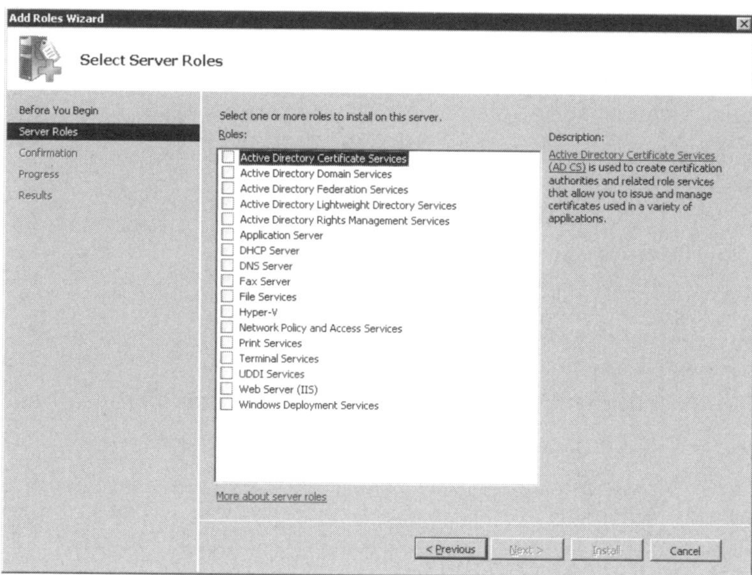

Figure 23-1 The Add Roles Wizard

The available Server Roles that are installed by the Add Roles Wizard are shown in Table 23-3.

Table 23-3 Windows Server 2008 Enterprise Roles

Server Role
Active Directory Certificate Services
Active Directory Domain Services
Active Directory Federation Services
Active Directory Lightweight Directory Services
Active Directory Rights Management Services
Application Server
DHCP Server
DNS Server

Table 23-3 Windows Server 2008 Enterprise Roles

Server Role
Fax Server
File Services
Hyper-V
Network Policy and Access Services
Print Services
Terminal Services
UDDI Services
Web Services (IIS)
Windows Deployment Services
Windows SharePoint Services

Features are additional items that you can add to the server. By controlling the installation and enablement of features (as with Roles), Microsoft is able to ensure that the appropriate settings are installed and configured and any necessary dependencies are also installed. The features that can be installed are listed in Table 23-4.

Table 23-4 Windows Server 2008 Enterprise Features

Server Feature
.NET Framework 3.0 Features
BitLocker Drive Encryption
BITS Server Extensions
Connection Manager Administration Kit
Desktop Experience
Failover Clustering
Group Policy Management
Internet Printing Client
Internet Storage Name Server
LPR Port Monitor
Message Queuing
Multipath I/O
Network Load Balancing
Peer Name Resolution Protocol
Quality Windows Audio Video Experience
Remote Assistance
Remote Differential Compression

Table 23-4 Windows Server 2008 Enterprise Features

Server Feature
Remote Server Administration Tools
Removable Storage Manager
RPC over HTTP Proxy
Simple TCP/IP Services
SMTP Server
SNMP Services
Storage Manager for SANs
Subsystem for UNIX-based Applications
Telnet Client
Windows Internal Database
Windows PowerShell
Windows Process Activation Service
Windows System Resource Manager
WINS Server
Wireless LAN Service

Real World Roles and Features Wizards

When we first saw the new wizards that are used for installing Roles and Features in Windows Server 2008, we frankly didn't like them. We especially didn't like that we had no choice about using them. We thought this was a totally unwarranted intrusion into the realm of the system administrator and was all about dumbing down Windows Server. We even went so far as to have some fairly passionate arguments with some of the people at Microsoft who were responsible for them. Well, not only did we lose the argument, but we now have to admit we were wrong. Microsoft made the right decision about roles and features in Windows Server 2008. It's not that system administrators couldn't get it right–many could. But doing a good job of installing a role or feature–without installing any unnecessary components or missing critical ones, and then setting the security properly on the installed components–is not a trivial task, and to have it all automated is a very good thing. It gets done right and gets done the same way, every time.

Microsoft has also provided a command-line tool to install Roles and Features: *servermanagercmd.exe*. Not our favorite command-line tool, but it does the job. And you can use an XML file to automate it.

For more on Server Roles and Features, see Chapter 8, "Installing Server Roles and Features."

Securing the Startup: BitLocker

BitLocker is a new security feature first introduced with Windows Vista and now available for Windows Server 2008. BitLocker is best known for its ability to encrypt the disk, but it also provides the ability to lock the normal startup process until you supply a personal identification number (PIN) or a removable USB Flash drive that contains the startup key.

Note Using BitLocker and especially using a PIN or a USB Flash drive for startup can slow the startup process and can require someone to physically be at the server to start it.

Important Always maintain security for the USB Flash drive that you use for BitLocker. If it gets into the wrong hands, the security of the server is compromised.

Setting Up BitLocker

BitLocker has the following minimum requirements:

- A computer that meets the minimum requirements for Windows Server 2008.
- One of the following:

  A Trusted Platform Module (TPM) microchip, version 1.2 or later

  A Trusted Computing Group (TCG)–compliant BIOS

  A USB 2.0 slot
- At least two NTFS drive volumes. The active volume must be at least 1.5 gigabytes (GB), and the second volume will contain the operating system files and has the same space requirements as the Windows partition of any Windows Server 2008 computer.

The BIOS on the server should be set to boot first from the hard drive, and must be configured to permit reading *and writing* to the USB ports if you're using a USB Flash drive scenario.

Setting Up the Volumes

Before you can install BitLocker, you need to configure the necessary volumes. BitLocker requires that the system (boot) volume be separate from the volume that contains Windows Server 2008. The system volume must be at least 1.5 GB and it is not subject to file system growth, so you won't need (or want) to make it any larger than absolutely necessary.

You can set up the BitLocker partitions by opening a command prompt during the initial installation of Windows Server 2008 and using Diskpart.exe to set up the volumes. Figure 23-2 shows the Diskpart commands required.

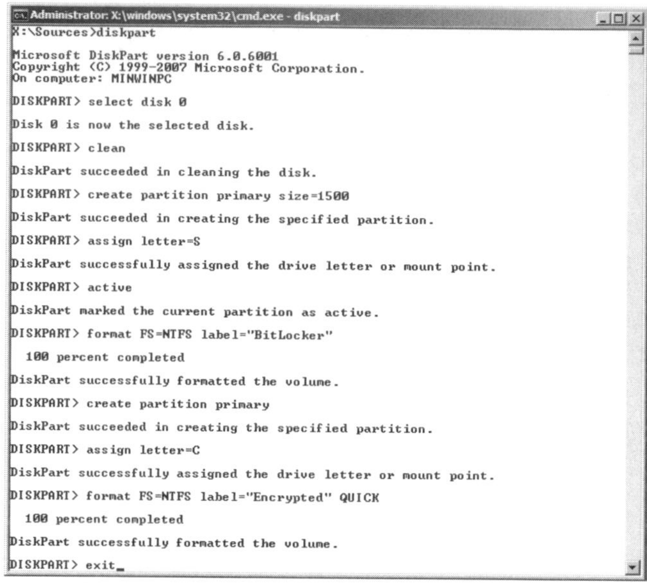

Figure 23-2 The Diskpart.exe commands to prepare the Windows Server 2008 volumes for BitLocker

To open a command prompt during the initial installation, use the following steps:

1. Boot from the Windows Server 2008 DVD.
2. On the first page of the Install Windows Wizard, choose language, time and currency, and keyboard options.
3. Click Next to open the Install Now page. Select Repair Your Computer.
4. With no operating system selected, click Next.
5. Select Command Prompt to open the Command Prompt window.
6. Type **Diskpart** to open the command-line disk partitioning utility.
7. At the Diskpart> prompt, run the following commands:

```
DISKPART> select disk 0
DISKPART> clean
DISKPART> create partition primary size=1500
DISKPART> assign letter=s
DISKPART> active
DISKPART> format FS=NTFS label="BitLocker"
```

```
DISKPART> create partition primary
DISKPART> assign letter=C
DISKPART> format FS=NTFS label="Encrypted" QUICK
DISKPART>  exit
```

8. At the command prompt, type **Exit** to return to the System Recovery Options page.
9. Press Alt+F4 to close the System Recovery Options page and continue installing Windows Server 2008.
10. On the Where Do You Want To Install Windows page of the Install Windows Wizard, shown in Figure 23-3, select the partition labeled Encrypted as the target for Windows Server 2008.

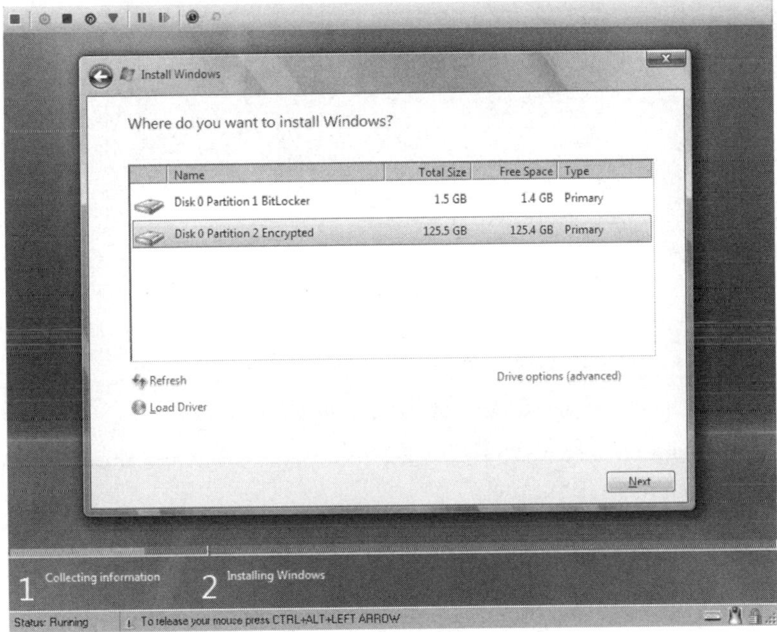

Figure 23-3 The Where Do You Want To Install Windows page of the Install Windows Wizard

11. Click Next and continue installing Windows Server 2008.

Installing the BitLocker Feature

Once the installation of Windows Server 2008 completes, follow the initial configuration steps of the Initial Configuration Tasks Wizard as described in detail in Chapter 7, "Configuring a New Installation." Add the BitLocker feature by following these steps:

1. Click Add Features.
2. Click Next on the initial page.

3. On the Select Features page, shown in Figure 23-4, select BitLocker Drive Encryption.

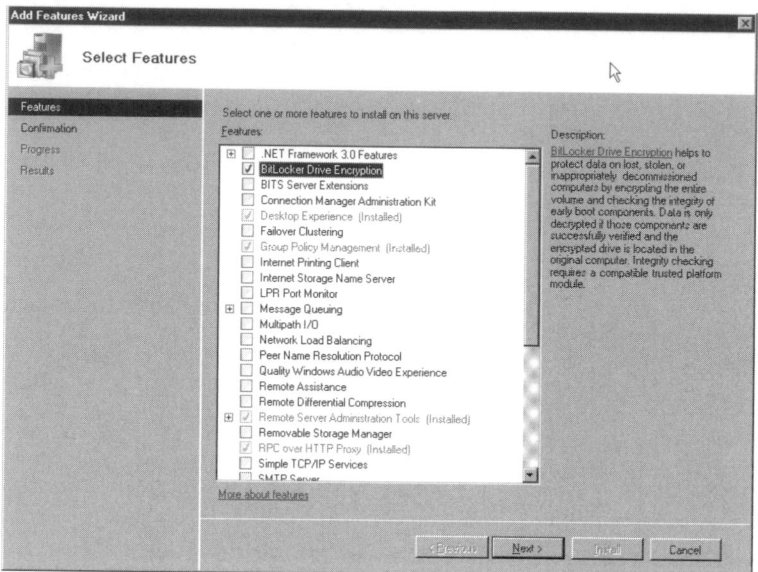

Figure 23-4 Select BitLocker Drive Encryption on the Select Features page of the Add Features Wizard.

4. Click Next and then click Install to begin the installation.
5. When prompted, choose Yes to reboot the server.
6. Log back on to the server with the same account you used to add the BitLocker feature. The installation will complete.
7. Click Close to close the Add Features Wizard.

Note The command line to install the BitLocker feature is `Servermanagercmd -install BitLocker.`

Enabling BitLocker Encryption

Installing the BitLocker feature doesn't actually encrypt your drive. To enable BitLocker encryption of your Windows drive, use the following steps:

1. Open BitLocker Drive Encyption from the Control Panel.
2. Click Turn On BitLocker. You will get a warning that it may impact performance, as shown in Figure 23-5.

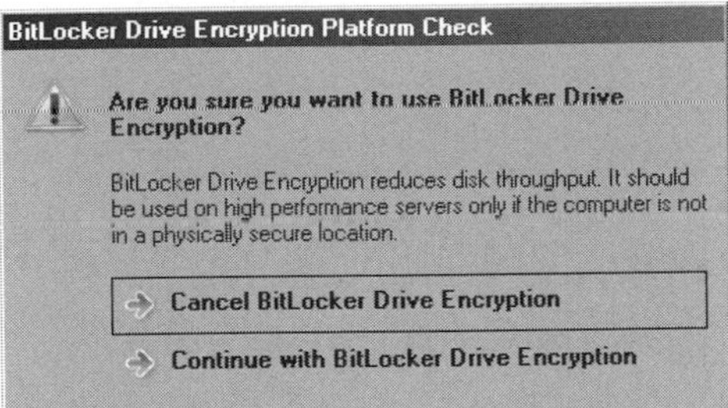

Figure 23-5 The BitLocker Drive Encryption Platform Check

3. Click Continue With Bitlocker Drive Encryption.
4. If your TPM is not initialized, you will see the Initialize TPM Security Hardware Wizard. Restart the system when prompted.
5. On the Save The Recovery Password page, you can choose to save the password onto a USB Flash drive or on shared folder, or you can choose to print it. We think you should choose all three options.
6. On the Encrypt The Selected Disk Volume page, select Run Bitlocker System Check and click Continue. Restart when prompted.
7. Log on to the server with the same account you enabled BitLocker encryption with. The encryption will begin. This is a slow process for large hard drives and seriously impacts server performance, so plan accordingly. An indicator in the system tray shows the progress of the encryption, as shown in Figure 23-6.

Figure 23-6 BitLocker encryption progress

Under the Hood BitLocker with No TPM

Most servers shipped today do not have a TPM, making it impossible to use BitLocker in its normal TPM-based mode. But there is a workaround: You can use a USB key during startup for BitLocker. But to use BitLocker without a TPM, you need to make a change to the local Group Policy on the server. Use the following steps to change the local Group Policy:

1. Open the Group Policy Editor (gpedit.msc).

2. Navigate to Local Computer Policy/Administrative Templates/Windows Components/BitLocker Drive Encryption.
3. Double-click Control Panel Settings: Enable Advanced Setup Options Policy.
4. Select Enable, and then select Allow BitLocker Without A Compatible TPM.
5. Exit from Group Policy Editor and reboot the server.

Now, when you enable BitLocker, you'll first get the BitLocker Drive Encryption Platform Check, shown earlier in Figure 23-5, as with normal BitLocker, but when you click Continue With Bitlocker Drive Encryption, you'll see the Set BitLocker Startup Preferences page shown in Figure 23-7.

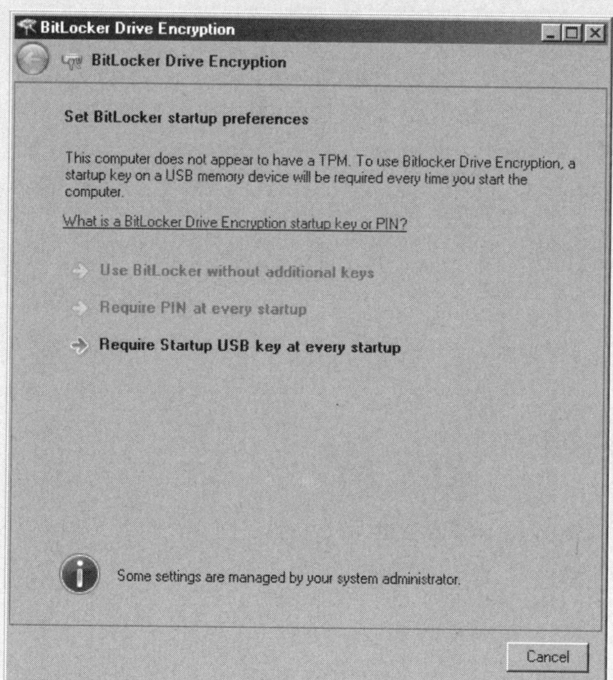

Figure 23-7 The Set BitLocker Startup Preferences page of the BitLocker Drive Encryption Wizard

Click Require Startup USB Key At Every Startup. On the Save Your Startup Key page, select the USB Flash drive that will hold the startup key. Continue with the rest of the initialization and configuration of BitLocker just as if you had a TPM.

Our hope is that there will be TPM-enabled servers available as part of the standard OEM server offerings, but at this point they are few and far between. Some servers and server motherboards built around Intel 5400 chipsets have built-in TPM modules, and at least one major OEM is shipping servers with a built-in TPM module.

Encrypting Server Data Volumes

To increase the security of remote servers, you can configure BitLocker encryption on server data volumes. You need to be logged on as administrator, BitLocker must be installed, and you must have a USB drive to save the password.

If you have not already done so, enable BitLocker as described in "Enabling BitLocker Encryption" earlier in the chapter, and then follow these steps to encrupt a data volume:

1. Open an elevated command prompt and run the following command:

   ```
   manage-bde -on D: -rp -rk U:\
   ```

   D: is the data volume you want to encrypt and *-rp* generates a recovery password and stores the recovery key on U:\ . The data volume will need to be unlocked after each restart.

2. To enable automatic unlocking of data volumes, run the following command:

   ```
   manage-bde -autounlock -enable <volume>:
   ```

   <volume>: is the drive letter you want to unlock automatically.

3. From now on, this USB Flash drive must be present in the server for startup.

This system now provides additional security for places where physical security may be an issue. Consider using BitLocker in branch office locations as needed. Requiring that a USB flash drive be entered each time the system boots may make rebooting of remote computers an issue, so consider this option carefully in your deployment needs.

Recovery with BitLocker

With every deployment, you also need to plan recovery techniques. BitLocker is no different. At startup, the server is locked if the boot files have been modified or the TPM chip isn't present (or, where using a USB Flash drive without a TPM module, the USB drive wasn't present when the computer was turned on). To recover access to data, you will need to either provide the USB key with the recovery password, or be prepared to type in the recovery password by hand. When BitLocker has locked the computer, and the TPM or USB Startup key isn't present at power on, the BitLocker Drive Encryption Recovery Console will open. You can insert the USB Flash drive with the recovery password, or press Enter to type in the password.

Securing the Accounts

Two important steps you can take to improve the overall security of your server are disabling the default Administrator account and enabling strong password policies. Many attacks on servers (and workstations) are simple password dictionary attacks. By disabling the well-known Administrator account, you force those attackers to first find an administrative account to attack; by enforcing strong password policies, you make a pure dictionary attack more difficult.

Disabling the Administrator Account

Disabling the built-in Administrator account (also known as the 500 account because of the last three digits of its GUID) and building a new Administrator account is one method of "security by obfuscation." It is an often recommended security solution, but one that you'll need to decide the value of.

If you do want to disable the built-in Administrator account, you'll need to set up an alternative local Administrator account. Even in a domain environment, it's a good idea to have a local administrative account that allows access to the server even when networking to the domain is down for some reason. Just make sure you choose a seriously strong password (or pass phrase) for the account. The default for Windows Server 2008 is to require a strong password, but we think the definition of strong password is still too weak. If you don't have some form of two-factor authentication in place on your servers, a pass phrase of 15 to 20 or more characters is closer to what we think should be used.

Note A strong password is required in Windows Server 2008. The password policy has been preenabled on the server.

Real World Internet Explorer Enhanced Security Configuration

First introduced in Windows Server 2003, the default configuration on a Windows Server is for Internet Explorer to run in a restricted, more secure mode that disables many of the potential attack vectors against a Web browser. In Windows Server 2008 this is known as Internet Explorer Enhanced Security Configuration (IE ESC), and includes settings that block the use of scripts and also prevent the downloading of files. The default configuration on a Windows Server 2008 installation is to have IE ESC enabled for all administrators and users. This is highly annoying if you're trying to download a file to fix a problem on the server, and there's a certain temptation to disable IE ESC. Resist the temptation. There are almost no reasons be using Internet Explorer on a server anyway—browsing the Web is something that should be done from your own workstation, not from the server. And while it's easy enough to disable IE ESC, by doing so you are exposing your network to unnecessary risk. Worse, you'll have a really hard time justifying why you did it if a problem does arise.

Password Policies on Standalone Servers

Windows Server 2008 defaults to a local security policy of Password Must Meet Complexity Requirements. This setting requires that passwords must meet the following requirements:

1. Not contain the user's name or parts of the full name that exceed two consecutive characters
2. Be at least six characters in length
3. Contain characters from three of the following four categories:
   a. Roman uppercase characters of A through Z
   b. Roman lowercase characters of a through z
   c. Base 10 digits of 0 through 9
   d. Non-alphabetical characters (such as !, $, #, % and so on)

Frankly, we think six characters, no matter how complex, is simply not sufficient on a server.

Password Policies in Domains

New in Windows Server 2008 are Fine-Grained Password Policies. In the past, password policies were set per domain, so if you wanted a stronger password for administrative accounts than for user accounts, you had few native options available. Windows Server 2008, however, has granular password policies that allow different password requirements by global security group or user. You can set these policies from the command line, or using third-party graphical tools. You can find available, free, third-party tools at the following links:

- *http://www.specopssoft.com/wiki/index.php/SpecopsPasswordPolicybasic/SpecopsPasswordPolicybasic/*
- *http://blogs.chrisse.se/blogs/chrisse/pages/fine-grain-password-policy-tool.aspx*
- *http://www.joeware.net/freetools/tools/psomgr/index.htm*
- *http://www.powergui.org/entry.jspa?externalID=882&categoryID=46*

Important Fine-Grained Password Policies are supported only at the Windows Server 2008 native domain functional level, which requires that all domain controllers in the domain be running Windows Server 2008.

Start by deciding what your policy should be. What should your administrator's password policies be? Your users'? Your service accounts'? Can you use your existing OU definitions? While a Password Setting Object (PSO) can't be applied to an OU directly, you can create a "shadow group" of a global security group that is mapped to an OU.

Only Domain Administrators can set and create PSOs. Policies can only be set to user objects and global security groups.

To set and create a PSO, log on with Domain Administrator rights and perform the following steps:

1. Click Start, click Run, and type **adsiedit.msc**.
2. Click OK.
3. If this is the first time you have connected to the domain, right-click ADSI Edit and click Connect To.
4. Type in the fully qualified domain name of the domain in the Name section of the domain in which you want to create the PSO and click OK.
5. Double-click the domain name.
6. Double-click DC=(domain name).
7. Double-click CN=System.
8. Click CN=Password settings container.
9. Right-click CN=Password Settings container, click New, and then click Object to open the Create Object dialog box shown in Figure 23-8.

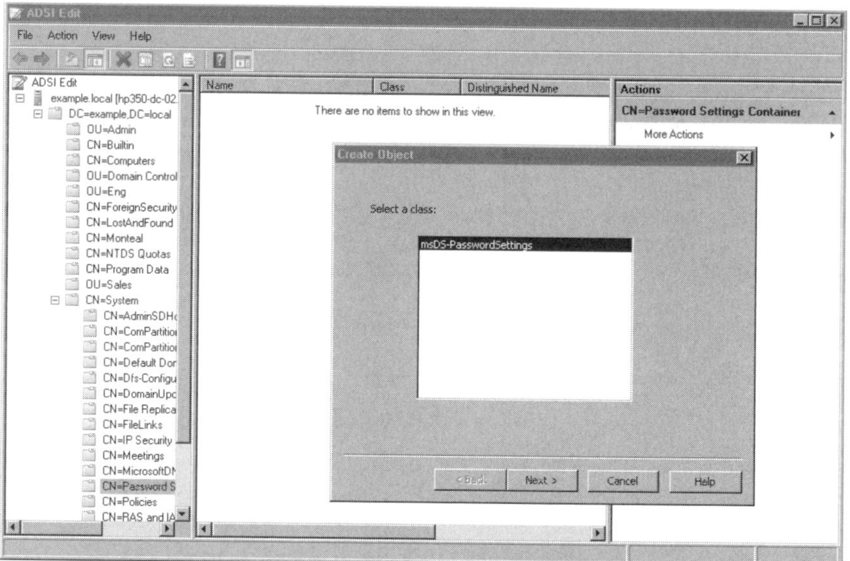

Figure 23-8 The Create Object dialog box in the CN=Password Settings container of ADSIEdit

10. Select msDS-PasswordSettings and click Next.

11. Enter a name for your new PSO in the Value field and click Next.
12. Fill out the attributes for each section as shown in Table 23-5, clicking Next as required.

Table 23-5 PSO Attributes

Attribute Name	Description	Acceptable Value Range	Example Value
msDS-PasswordSettingsPrecedence	Password settings precedence	Greater than 0	10
msDS-PasswordReversibleEncryption-Enabled	Password reversible encryption status	FALSE / TRUE (Recommended: FALSE)	FALSE
msDS-PasswordHistoryLength	Number of prior pass-words to remember for user accounts	0 through 1024	12
msDS-PasswordComplexityEnabled	Password complexity status	FALSE / TRUE (Recommended: TRUE)	TRUE
msDS-MinimumPasswordLength	Minimum password length	0 through 255	12
msDS-MinimumPasswordAge	Minimum time until password can be changed again	(None) 00:00:00:00 through msDS-MaximumPass-wordAge value	1:00:00:00 (1 day)
msDS-MaximumPasswordAge	Maximum time until password must be changed	(Never) msDS-MinimumPass-wordAge value through (Never msDS-MaximumPass-wordAge cannot be set to zero)	42:00:00:00 (42 days)
msDS-LockoutThreshold	Number of failed pass-word attempts before account is locked out	0 through 65535	10
msDS-LockoutObservationWindow	Length of time to count failed password attempts before lockout	(None) 00:00:00:01 through msDS-LockoutDura-tion value	0:00:30:00 (30 minutes)
msDS-LockoutDuration	Length of time to lock out account before reenabling	(None) (Never) msDS-LockoutObser-vationWindow value through (Never)	0:00:10:00 (10 minutes)

Table 23-5 PSO Attributes

Attribute Name	Description	Acceptable Value Range	Example Value
msDS-PSOAppliesTo	Links to objects that this password setting object applies to (forward link)	0 or more DNs of users or global security groups	"CN=u1,CN=Users,DC=DC1,DC=contoso, DC=com"

13. On the last screen of the wizard, click More Attributes.
14. In the Select Which Property To View list, select Optional Or Both.
15. In the Select A Property To View list, select msDS-PSOAppliesTo.
16. In the Edit Attribute box, add the fully distinguished name of the user or global security groups that the PSO should apply to and click Add.
17. Repeat the previous step to add additional users or global security groups. Click OK when you've added all the users or groups this policy will apply to.
18. Click Finish.

You can also use the Ldifde command as a scriptable alternative.

More Info For more information on setting fine-grained passwords, see the TechNet article: *http://technet2.microsoft.com/windowsserver2008/en/library/2199dcf7-68fd-4315-87cc-ade35f8978ea1033.mspx?mfr=true.*

Real World Two-Factor Authentication

If your network contains sensitive information–and whose doesn't these days–you might want to consider two-factor authentication (TFA) for all administrative accounts. TFA requires two methods to uniquely identify individuals attempting to authenticate to a Windows Server 2008 computer. The first method is the user name and password of the user, and the second is something else, such as a biometric reader, smart card, or one-time password. We like one-time password tokens–they're easy to implement, relatively inexpensive, and more reliable than most biometric solutions.

Third-party one-time password token providers include AuthAnvil (*http://www.authanvil.com*), Cryptocard (*http://www.cryptocard.com*), and RSA SecureID (*http://www.rsa.com/node.aspx?id=1156*). We personally use and recommend AuthAnvil.

Windows Server 2008 Firewall

Windows Firewall in Windows Server 2008 is the same basic firewall included in Windows Vista and adds many new features and capabilities when compared to Windows Firewall included in Windows Server 2003 SP1. New features include outbound filtering; filtering based on SIDs; a better management UI; configuration for local, remote, local port, remote port, and protocol; and tight integration with IPsec. It has three profiles: a domain profile, a private profile for servers that aren't domain members but are on secured networks, and a public profile for servers that reside on publicly accessible networks. And, finally, per-user rules are now supported.

An important change in Windows Server 2008 is that Windows Firewall is on by default. All of the wizards in Windows Server 2008 that are used to add Roles and Features will automatically set the necessary Windows Firewall rule(s) to ensure proper functionality while still securing the server.

Windows Server 2003 SP1 had a built-in firewall, but most of the wizards used to configure the server were not designed to configure the firewall, and most environments had Windows Firewall disabled on servers, relying on an external firewall to protect the network. In Windows Server 2008, the expectation is that Windows Firewall will remain enabled. When Windows Server 2008 is installed, the core networking firewall policy is enabled, as shown in Figure 23-9.

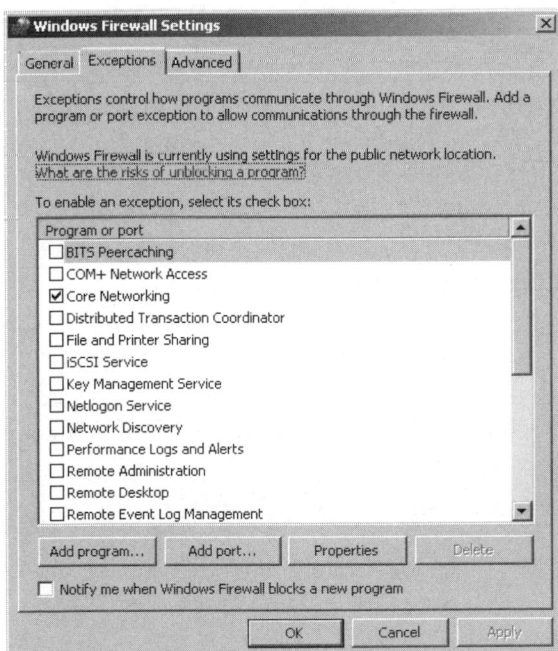

Figure 23-9 Default Windows Firewall settings

The Windows Server 2008 Windows Firewall allows more granular control over the configuration and settings than previous versions. To open the Windows Firewall with Advanced Security console, shown in Figure 23-10, type *wf.msc* at the command prompt, or click Windows Firewall With Advanced Security in the Administrative Tools folder.

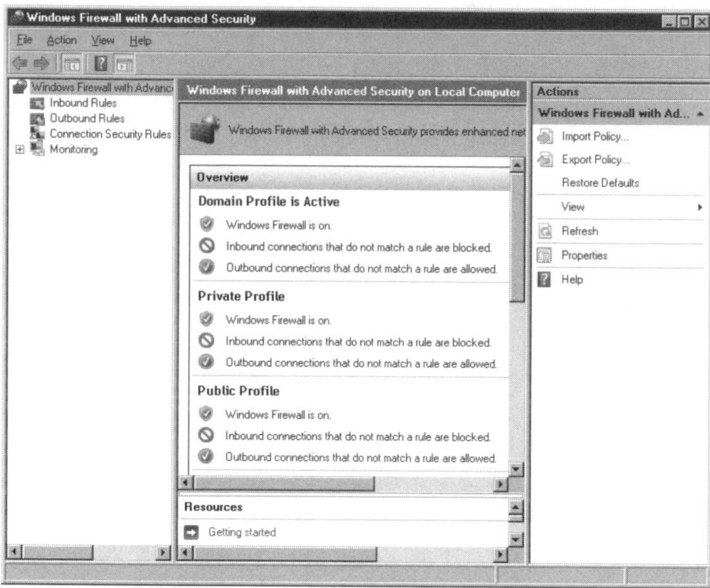

Figure 23-10 The Windows Firewall With Advanced Security console

Windows Firewall has three profiles: Domain Profile, Private Profile, and Public Profile. Each profile can have different inbound and outbound rules as needed. To build a specific rule, click Inbound Rules or Outbound Rules and then click New Rule. You can set custom rules for programs or for ports. If the server is a member of a domain, it's a good idea to set the firewall rules using Group Policy.

Setting Firewall Policies Using Group Policy

Use Group Policy ensure a consistent application of Windows Firewall Policies across the domain. Using normal Group Policy rules as discussed in Chapter 13, "Group Policy," set up a Group Policy to manage a group of systems. You can use WMI filters to separate client and server computers as described in the UnderThe Hood sidebar, or you can use OUs to assign GPOs to groups of computers.

Under the Hood Using a WMI Filter to Set a Group Policy for Windows Vista Workstations

It can be useful to have a group policy that applies only to Windows Vista computers, for example, or only to Windows Server 2008 computers. You could create separate OUs for each, but that can be awkward and not always an ideal solution. By using a WMI filter to build the Group Policy, you can limit it to the type and version of operating system desired.

To create a new WMI Filter, open the GPMC and select WMI Filters in the domain where you want to create the filter, as shown in Figure 23-11. Then use the following steps to create a new filter.

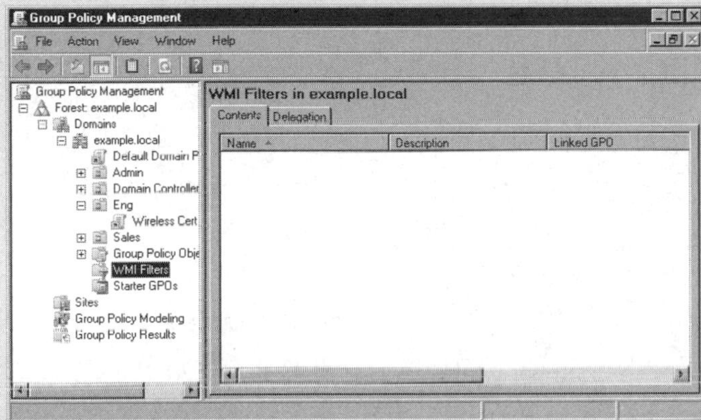

Figure 23-11 Group Policy Management WMI Filters

Create a New WMI Filter

1. Select New from the Action menu to open the New WMI Filter dialog box shown in Figure 23-12.

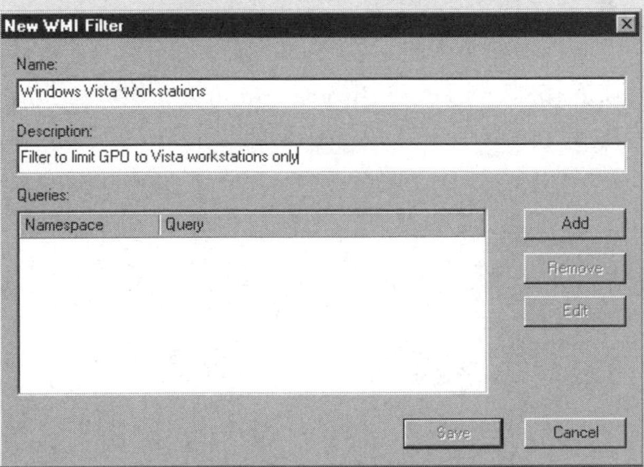

Figure 23-12 The New WMI Filter dialog box

2. Fill in the Name and Description fields.
3. Click Add to open the WMI Query dialog box. The default Namespace is root\CIMv2, which is correct.
4. Type the following into the Query field, as shown in Figure 23-13:

```
Select * from WIN32_OperatingSystem where Version>6.0 and ProductType=1
```

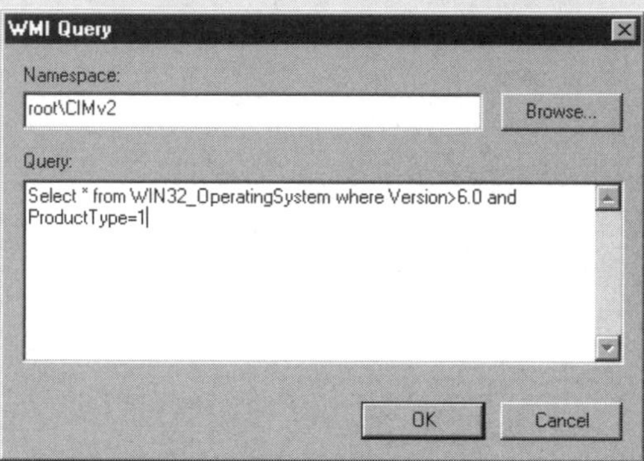

Figure 23-13 The WMI Query dialog box

5. Click OK to return to the New WMI Filter dialog box, and then click Save.

After you build the filter, you can link the filter to a GPO so that the GPO will only apply to Windows Vista computers.

Firewall Rule Basics

When you build Windows Firewall rules, you have three possible actions for a connection that matches the rule:

- Allow the connection.
- Only allow a connection that is secured through the use of IPsec (authenticated bypass).
- Explicitly block the connection.

The order of precedence for Windows Firewall rules is:

- Authenticated bypass
- Block connection
- Allow connection
- Default profile behavior

Thus if you have a Block rule and an Allow rule, and your connection meets both criteria, the Block rule will always win. By being as specific as possible with your rules, you have less likelihood of conflict and more direct control. Using a port rule is much more general than using an application rule, and should be avoided whenever possible.

Rule Definitions

Building rule definitions is the process of building up a combination of conditions and specific access types into a rule that either allows or disallows a connection. Rules can be defined for the following:

- **Programs** Specific applications that are either allowed or disallowed by the rule
- **Ports** General allow or disallow of a protocol through a port
- **Predefined** Preconfigured and well known services and programs
- **Custom** Can combine programs, ports, and specific interfaces into a custom rule

Rules can allow or disallow traffic to or from programs, system services, computers, or users. Rules can use the following protocol values:

- Any
- IANA IP protocol numbers
- TCP
- UDP
- ICMPv4
- ICMPv6
- Other possible protocol values include IGMP, HOPOPT, GRE, IPv6-NoNxt, IPV6-Opts, VRRP, PGM, L2TP, IPv6-Route, and IPv6-Frag.

Rules for local ports (UDP or TCP) can include:

- All Ports
- Specific Ports (comma-separated list)
- Dynamic RPC
- RPC Endpoint Mapper
- Edge Traversal

Rules for Remote Ports (TCP and UDP) can include:

- All ports
- Specific Ports (comma-separated list)

Rules for ICMP traffic (ICMPv4 and ICMPv6) can include:

- All ICMP types
- Specific types of ICMP traffic

Rules can be for a Local IP address scope of the following:

- Specific IPv4 or v6 addresss or list of addresses
- Range of IPv4 or v6 addresses or list of ranges
- Entire IPv4 or v6 subnet or list of subnets

Rules can be for a Remote IP address scope of the following:

- Specific IPv4 or v6 address or list of addresses
- Range of IPv4 or v6 addresses or list of ranges
- Entire IPv4 or v6 subnet or list of subnets
- Predefined set of computers (localsubnet, default gateway, DNS servers, WINS servers, DNS servers, or a list of such items)

Rules can specify the following types of interface type:

- All interface types
- Local area network
- Remote access
- Wireless

Rules can include the following program types:

- All programs
- System (a special keyword that restricts traffic to the system process)
- Specific path and .exe name to an executable

Rules for services can:

- Apply to all programs and services.
- Apply to services only.
- Apply to a specified service.

There are three predefined, special local ports:

- Dynamic RPC is used by applications and services that receive dynamic RPC traffic over TCP. (Does not include traffic over Named Pipes.)

- RPC Endpoint Mapper is used only with the RPCSS service and allows traffic to the endpoint mapper.
- Edge Traversal is used only with the iphlpsvc (Teredo) service and allows the traffic to be decapsulated by the Teredo service on a dynamic port.

Additional rules can be set to allow only secure connections. For secure connections, you can specify the following:

- The connection must require encryption.
- Allow connections only from specified computers in Active Directory.
- Allow connections only from specified users or security groups in Active Directory.

Important Whenever possible, resist the temptation to create specific Windows Firewall rules for specific computers or users. While it is technically possible, it can quickly become a management and documentation nightmare. Using security groups or OUs to control firewalls is flexible, easy to maintain, and can be easily documented.

Creating a Firewall Policy

You can create policies based on specific rules or on rule sets. To demonstrate how this works, let's create a typical Windows Firewall policy that covers a typical set of functionality. In this policy we'll use five of the predefined rule sets: Core Networking, File And Printer Sharing, Remote Assistance, Remote Desktop, and Windows Management Instrumentation.

Use the following steps to create this policy:

1. Open the Group Policy Management Console.
2. Select the Domain or OU for the policy and then select Create A GPO In This Domain And Link It Here to open the New GPO dialog box.
3. Type a descriptive name for the new GPO and click OK.
4. Right-click the new policy and select Edit from the Action menu to open the Group Policy Management Editor console.
5. Navigate to Computer Configuration, Policies, Windows Settings, Security Settings, Windows Firewall with Advanced Security and then Windows Firewall with Advanced Security – LDAP, as shown in Figure 23-14.

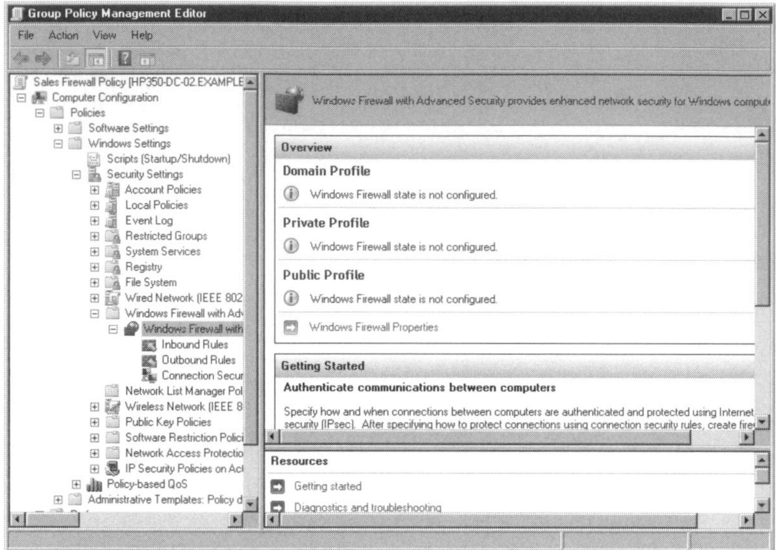

Figure 23-14 Group Policy Management Editor

6. Right-click Inbound Rules and select New Rule from the Action menu to open the New Inbound Rule Wizard shown in Figure 23-15.

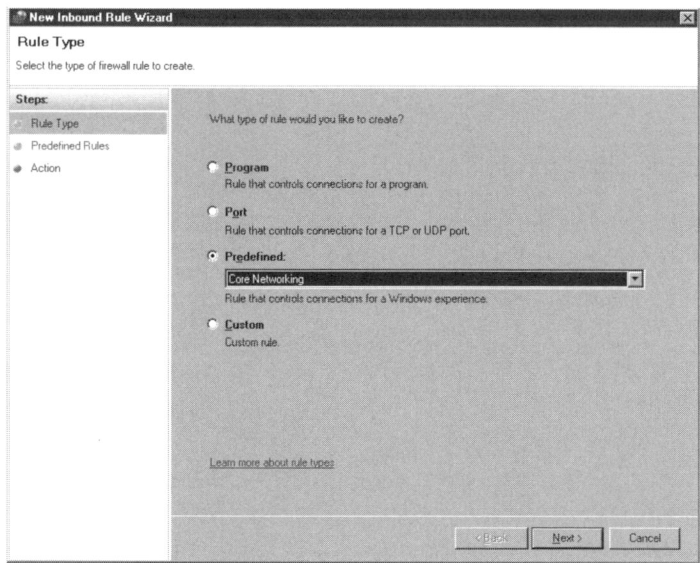

Figure 23-15 The Rule Type page of the New Inbound Rule Wizard

7. Select Predefined and then select Core Networking from the drop-down list.

8. Click Next to open the Predefined Rules page of the New Inbound Rule Wizard.
9. You can clear any of the predefined rules that are part of the Core Networking rule set or you can leave them all selected.
10. Click Next to open the Action page of the New Inbound Rule Wizard.
11. Select Allow The Connection and click Finish to create the rule and return to Group Policy Management Editor, as shown in Figure 23-16.

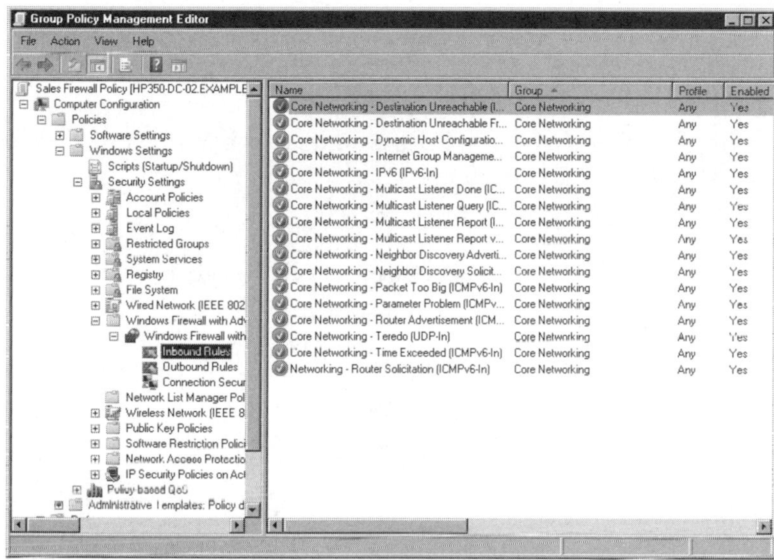

Figure 23-16 Group Policy Management Editor

12. Repeat steps 6 through 11 for each of the remaing rule sets: File And Printer Sharing, Remote Assistance, Remote Desktop, and Windows Management Instrumentation.

Windows Firewall Via Command Line

Windows Fireall can be managed from the command line using the *netsh* commands. Start by opening an elevated command prompt and then typing *netsh* to open the netsh prompt shown in Figure 23-17.

```
Administrator: Command Prompt - netsh

Commands in this context:
?              - Displays a list of commands.
consec         - Changes to the `netsh advfirewall consec' context.
dump           - Displays a configuration script.
export         - Exports the current policy to a file.
firewall       - Changes to the `netsh advfirewall firewall' context.
help           - Displays a list of commands.
import         - Imports a policy file into the current policy store.
monitor        - Changes to the `netsh advfirewall monitor' context.
reset          - Resets the policy to the default out-of-box policy.
set            - Sets the per-profile or global settings.
show           - Displays profile or global properties.

The following sub-contexts are available:
 consec firewall monitor

To view help for a command, type the command, followed by a space, and then
 type ?.

netsh advfirewall>_
```

Figure 23-17 The netsh advfirewall context

In addition to all the commands that are inherited from netsh as a whole, the advfirewall context has the following specific commands:

- **?** Help
- **consec** Change to the consec subcontext to set rules for IPsec rules.
- **dump** Lists the current configuration as a script.
- **export** Saves the current policy to a file.
- **firewall** Changes to the firewall subcontext.
- **help** Lists the available commands. The same as ?.
- **import** Imports a policy from a file.
- **monitor** Changes to the monitor subcontext.
- **reset** Restores the out-of-box default policy.
- **set** Changes settings for specific profiles or globally.
- **show** Shows the current settings for specific policies or globally.

Real World Netsh Command Line

One of our least favorite command-line utilities is netsh. It has a hopelessly painful interface and fussiness. But it's the only game in town for managing the firewall and networking settings on Windows Server Core from the command line. And it is scriptable, if only painfully so. When we're trying to create a netsh script, we've learned to use netsh interactively until we get it exactly right. Then we can take that exact command, put it at the end of the context, and create a single command line for the command. So, for example, to use netsh interactively to allow a server to respond to ping requests, you'd type the following interactively in netsh:

```
netsh> firewall
netsh firewall>set icmpsetting ?
set icmpsetting
      [ type = ] 2-5|8-9|11-13|17|ALL
      [ [ mode = ] ENABLE|DISABLE
        [ profile = ] CURRENT|DOMAIN|STANDARD|ALL
  Sets firewall ICMP configuration.
  Parameters:
  type - ICMP type.
      2    - Allow outbound packet too big.
      3    - Allow outbound destination unreachable.
      4    - Allow outbound source quench.
      5    - Allow redirect.
      8    - Allow inbound echo request.
      9    - Allow inbound router request.
      11   - Allow outbound time exceeded.
      12   - Allow outbound parameter problem.
      13   - Allow inbound timestamp request.
      17   - Allow inbound mask request.
      ALL  - All types.
  mode - ICMP mode (optional).
      ENABLE  - Allow through firewall (default).
      DISABLE - Do not allow through firewall.
  profile - Configuration profile (optional).
     CURRENT  - Applies to the active profile. Active profile can be domain,
                 standard (i.e. private), or public. (default).
      DOMAIN   - Applies to the domain profile.
      STANDARD - Applies to the standard (i.e. private) profile.
      ALL      - Applies to the domain and standard (i.e. private) profile.
                 Does not apply to the public profile.
  Examples:
      set icmpsetting 8
      set icmpsetting 8 ENABLE
      set icmpsetting type=ALL mode=DISABLE
netsh firewall>set icmpsetting 8 enable
Ok.
```

Once you have the command correct, it becomes a single line:

```
.netsh firewall set icmpsetting 8 enable
```

Additional Security Changes

Additional security changes in Windows Server 2008 include groups, auditing, changes to default authentication protocols, and more—which all adds up to a more secure server.

New Groups

Windows Server 2008 adds several new default security groups, enabling better control of which users are allowed to do what functions. Table 23-6 shows the new groups in Windows Server 2008.

Table 23-6 New Groups in Windows Server 2008

Name of Group	New duty or role or changes from 2003
Cryptographic Operators	Members are authorized to perform cryptographic operations.
Certificate Service DCOM Access	Members of this group are allowed to connect to Certification Authorities in the enterprise.
Event Log Readers	Members of this group can read event logs from the local computer.
IIS_IURS	A built-in group used by Internet Information Services. In Windows 2003, this was the IIS_WPG or IIS Worker Process Group. In Windows Server 2003, this group included IWAM_Server, Network Service, Service, and System. In Windows Server 2008, this includes just the IUSER account.
Performance Log users	Members of this group may schedule logging of performance counters, enable trace providers, and collect event traces both locally and via remote access to this computer. During setup, this group has no members—unlike Windows 2003, which includes Network Service as a default member.
Performance Monitor Users	Members of this group can access performance counter data locally and remotely. During setup, this group has no members, unlike Windows 2003, which includes the Administrator as a default member.

Auditing

There are new auditable items, including Registry value change events, Active Directory change events, improved operation-based audit, and User Account Control Audit events. Improved IPsec audit events include support for AuthIP, RPC call events, Share Access audit events, Share Management events, Cryptographic function audit events, NAP audit events, and IAS (RADIUS) audit events. A new Event Viewer is easier to use, has better filtering, and more finely grained control of views and actions. It even allows event forwarding, allowing you to build a central event server. For more on the new Event Viewer, see Chapter 14, "Managing Daily Operations."

LanMan Hashes and Authentication Level

For many years the easiest way to crack passwords on a Windows network was merely to use any number of freely available password-cracking tools on the inside of your network, such as Cain and Able, that looked at the internal LanMan hash values. In Windows Server 2008, LAN Manager hash values have been disabled by default. The setting Network Security: Do Not Store LAN Manager Hash Value On Next Password Change is enabled by default. If you adjust this default policy to support older clients, you will be lowering the security of your network dramatically.

The other important change to the default local security policy is that the LAN Manager Authentication Level is set to NTLMv2 only, as shown in Figure 23-18.

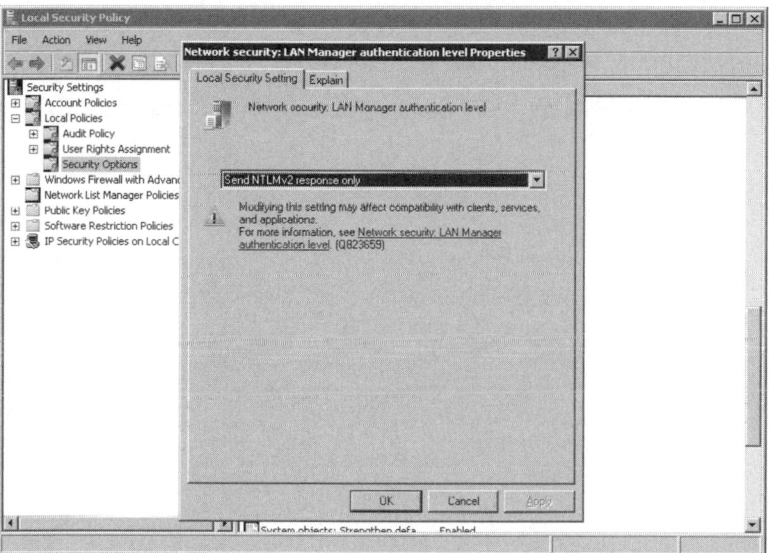

Figure 23-18 LAN Manager Authentication setting in Windows Server 2008

SMBv2

Windows Server 2008 and Windows Vista will be the first combination of server and workstation that will natively support SMBv2. The rebuilt TCP/IP stack has been simplified, but new APIs have been added. Instead of the 80 commands in SMBv1, SMBv2 has only 16. SMBv2 uses implicit sequence numbers for hashing, and it supports SHA-256 signatures, instead of the MD-5 in SMBv1 for improved security.

Read Only Domain Controllers

Last but not least, the Read Only Domain Controller (RODC) provides additional security for branch and remote offices while still providing full functionality. For more information on RODCs, review the information in Chapter 17, "Manage Active Directory."

Summary

With the deployment of Windows Server 2008 and Windows Vista clients side by side, many new security settings will increase the security and resiliency of a modern network. BitLocker, Server Core, and Read Only Domain Controllers add to the network administrator's tool kit to deploy secure networks. Combined with appropriate handling of Administrator Accounts, passwords, and the ability to set granular password policies in a single domain, the administrator has additional protection and resiliency for the network.

In the next chapter we highlight another major improvement to Windows Security: Network Access Protection.

Chapter 24

Administering Network Access Protection

Network Access Protection (NAP) is one of the most anticipated parts of Windows Server 2008. It promises to finally bring an affordable means to ensure the health of the network to the masses.

Why the Need for NAP?

In the history of security events at Microsoft, arguably no event drove home the lesson of managed and unmanaged computers and their impact on a network harder than the MSBlaster virus. All that was needed to take down an entire network was for one unmanaged home PC infected by the virus to attach remotely back into the corporate network, and suddenly any computer that had not been updated was fair game.

The use of internal host-based firewalls was rare indeed at that time, and still is for many organizations. Corporate policies regarding the health of remote personal computers were probably nonexistent. Corporate networks–even those with host-based firewalls–were battered by MSBlaster because the infection levels were so high and the firewall stack came up after the TCP/IP connection was made. Windows XP SP2 and Windows Vista changed the manner in which the firewall service protects the TCP/IP stack. But companies needed more help to protect, defend, and remediate infected computers. They needed a way to identify noncompliant workstations and servers and bring them into health compliance.

While Windows Server 2003 provides Network Access Quarantine Control (NAQ), very few companies outside of Microsoft have been able to deploy NAQ dependably. In addition, it was limited in use. But don't confuse NAP and NAQ–they are different from one another. NAP is more flexible and has a greater ability to check the health of the attached systems to the network. In addition to Microsoft, several vendors came to the marketplace with health policy solutions. The first such solution in the Microsoft family was Network Access Quarantine control, released with Windows Server 2003. Windows Server 2008 brings a new solution called Network Access Protection.

> **Important** Network Access Quarantine control provides protection only for remote access connections. Network Access Protection adds protection from and for Virtual Private Network (VPN) connections, Dynamic Host Configuration Protocol (DHCP) configuration, and Internet Protocol Security (IPsec)–based communication.

When designing your network for deployment of NAP, it's probably wiser to think of it less as a security solution and more as a compliance solution. Depending on the needs of your network, NAP can be a solution that reports on the health of the network or enforces a standard of health on the network. NAP helps control both managed and unmanaged computers on your system and forces those computers that need management into a domain profile. For anyone who needed a reason to move computers from workgroups into domains, this feature of Windows 2008 is it.

Real World The Risk of Mobile Systems

The highest risk to a network (and the reason so many network administrators have so little hair) comes from portable computers and other mobile devices. More and more of these devices are sold every day, and users expect to be able to connect remotely into the network from every corner coffee shop. If you work in any number of regulated industries mandated by ISO 27002, Sarbanes-Oxley, HIPAA, or other security-based regulations, your networks may need a means to first check the status of roaming computers and ensure that they meet the firm's security standards *before* they communicate on the domain. NAP is designed to check the health status of the desktops and portable computers. If a computer doesn't pass the necessary health benchmark, it is moved into a quarantine location, remediated back to good health, and then permitted onto the network with full access. The process is actually quite logical and reasonable. Only the issues of equipment age, network topology, and other typical network design matters are potential roadblocks to deployment.

Review the detailed documentation on the various Microsoft Web sites and set up a test network. Once you see the possibilities of health enforcement–even if you don't use a strictly Microsoft solution to ensure the health of your network–an administrator should review other options. Your internal network is beginning to be as risky and infected as the external network, and the more you can do to proactively keep it clean the closer you are to ensuring that the network can meet compliance and regulatory guidelines for your industry.

More Info This chapter is designed to begin and help you with the planning process for NAP. For a full discussion and details on deployment, see *Windows Server 2008 Network and Network Access Protection* by Joseph Davies and Tony Northrup with the Microsoft Networking Team (Microsoft Press, 2008).

Planning the Deployment

One step in the deployment of Network Access Protection cannot and should not be stinted: Planning the deployment. This step is essential for a successful implementation. Do you have the necessary network clients, servers, and switches to make a NAP deployment successful? Have you defined a policy for what is and isn't a healthy computer? Can you restrict access, or will you merely use NAP as a means to report health status? Can you successfully identify and organize unsupported platforms so that they can be isolated and separated? Is your staff proficient in Active Directory and Group Policy to set groups and policies?

NAP Shopping List

First, inventory the network and determine network health polices before a deployment–even before you deploy a test network. On the server side, you must have Windows Server 2008 for the Network Policy Server, but you can use Windows 2003 servers for various roles, including certificate servers used in IPsec deployments. On the client side, the NAP solution can control and manage both Windows Vista and Windows XP. Windows XP Service Pack 3 will have NAP included natively. Plans with partners are in the works to include Windows 2000, Linux, and possibly Macintosh operating systems in the future. Whether you use a strictly Microsoft solution or a hybrid between Cisco and other third-party vendors, the first step in deployment is determining which method is appropriate for the environment. Table 24-1 summarizes the pros and cons of each method.

Table 24-1 Pros and Cons of Each Deployment

Type	Enforcement quality	Advantages	Disadvantages
IPsec (Internet Protocol Security)	Best	Strongest enforcement. Can do additional server/ domain isolation as a result.	To enable full enforcement, workstation must be compliant to obtain network access; otherwise, use as reporting server. Compliance policy needs to be carefully crafted.
IEEE 802.1X–authenticated network connections	Better	Can be used in VLANs deployments Used in wireless.	Need to ensure that switches and access points support 802.1x.
Remove Access VPN connections	Better	The use of NAP with VPN will assist in keeping the network healthy.	With Windows 2008, businesses may be moving away from VPN as the remote access of choice.
Dynamic Hose Configuration Protocol (DHCP)	Acceptable	Minimal costs. Single server needed for the policy enforcement server. Can be used with older servers.	Clients can change IP settings to Static and bypass enforcement. DHCP has to be supplied by the Windows 2008 server.

You can use one or a combination of all of these methods of communication as an enforcement method, but this does add complexity to the deployment. When deciding your deployment strategy, keep this in mind: The more complex the deployment, the harder it will be to troubleshoot.

Servers Needed for NAP

It is easiest to deploy NAP using only Windows Server 2008 computers, but you can include Windows 2003 servers. For a more global deployment, it's obviously wiser to have some redundancy and distribution, but the number of NAP health servers needed is actually very lightweight considering what NAP is doing. If you have all Windows Vista and Windows Server 2008 computers, you have the choice of IPsec, which gives you increased ability to harden the server and improve client isolation. Keep in mind that NAP is not a perfect security solution. It is a platform to check the health of the clients. Although you can deploy a NAP solution without a remediation policy, the most successful deployments will be designed with both enforcement and remediation. Always begin your deployment in reporting mode to best get an understanding of the health condition of your network. At minimum, you'll need the following hardware to begin to test deployment of NAP:

- One domain controller (can be Windows Server 2003), with DNS and Certificate services installed for an enterprise root CA.
- One member server running the Network Policy and Access Services role, which provides the Network Policy Server (NPS), Routing And Remote Access, Health Registration Authority (HRA) and Host Credential Authorization Protocol (HCAP), and the role of Active Directory Certificate Services.
- Windows Vista or Windows XP SP3 workstations.
- Domain-joined computers.
- Additional testing computers can include:
  - Linux computers with a third-party supplicant from Avenda.
  - Third-party supplicants that enable OEM-specific features or other architectures such as Macintosh.
- The last element in the list actually offers additional benefits because domain-joined workstations are now able to participate in Group Policy settings and Windows Software Update Services–mandated patching. In large deployments you will want to review the best practices for PKI deployment to ensure that clients in remote links will be able to contact the certificate servers and the policy enforcement. As shown in Figure 24-1, the number of servers to add NAP to a network is amazingly small.

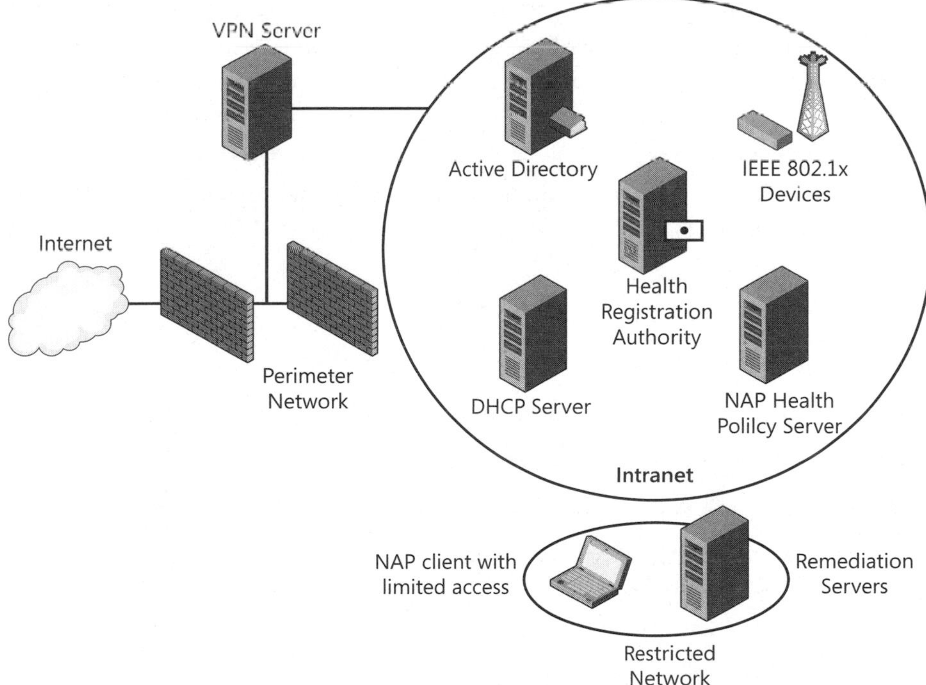

Figure 24-1 Network Access Policy components

Benefits of NAP

One interesting side effect of NAP that a business may not anticipate is the additional freed-up bandwidth. If a workstation has been infected and is spewing out phishing and spams unknowingly before implementing NAP and afterward it is forced into remediation and cleaned up, suddenly that bandwidth is freed for other needs.

Employee reallocation also occurs when the person who was running around putting out fires on desktops is free to be more proactive and less reactive. Thus when costing out the solution and proposing it to management, don't forget to include as a potential cost savings the fact that your costs should be moved from putting out fires to planning a healthier network.

Determining the Health Policy

Before any deployment of NAP can begin, inventory the workstation and server health requirements and determine how draconian your enforcement of those policies should be. Remember, however, that NAP isn't just about enforcement, it is also about remediation. The key to a successful deployment is that your solution not only includes the enforcement deemed appropriate for your environment, but also the ability to move the client from non-compliance to compliance. Before you install and test NAP, it is important that you understand and make decisions about the settings that you will report on and enforce. A solid understanding of Microsoft security update ranking is essential to properly set NAP policies.

Policies Checked

The policies that are checked and remediated are the Windows Security Health Agent and Windows Security Health Validator and include the following checks and ability to enforce compliance:

- Firewall software is installed and enabled.
- Antivirus is installed and running.
- Antivirus updates are installed (up to date).
- Antispyware is installed and running.
- Antispyware updates are installed (up to date).
- Microsoft update services are enabled.

If a Windows Software Update Services server is in the network, NAP can be used to check whether security updates are installed based on the WSUS settings, as shown in Figure 24-2.

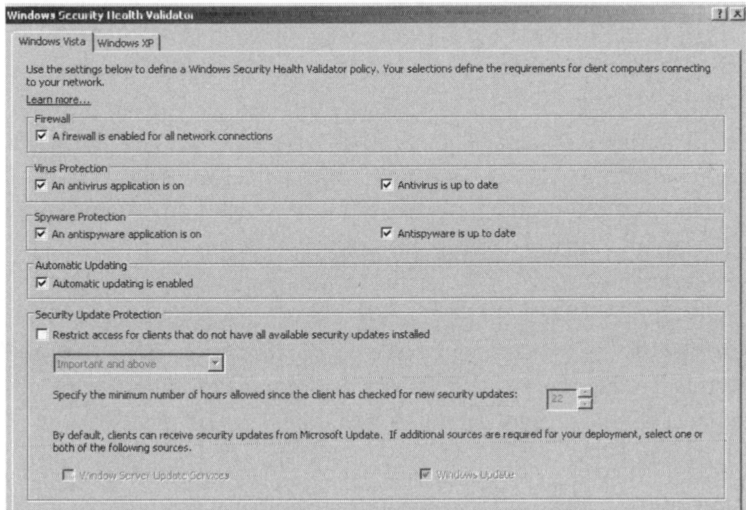

Figure 24-2 Security Health Validators

Of all the policies shown in Figure 24-2, the most difficult one to determine is the setting for the Security Update protection. The policy can be set to compare the workstation with that of a WSUS server and limit access or ensure health status on the following levels:

- **Critical Only** Will not restrict access for clients if they meet what the Microsoft Security Response Center (MSRC) Bulletin Severity Rating system defines as critical only patches. Critical patches are defined by the MSRC as "A vulnerability whose exploitation could allow the propagation of an Internet worm without user action." In addition, the policy can be adjusted to allow the workstations time to check in with the WSUS server for updates.
- **Important And Above** Will not restrict access for clients if they meet the MSRC's guidelines for important and critical security updates. Important is defined as "A vulnerability whose exploitation could result in the compromise of the confidentiality, integrity, or availability of users data, or the integrity or availability of processing resources."
- **Moderate And Above** Will not restrict access for clients if they meet the MSRC's guidelines for moderate, important, and critical security updates. Moderate is defined by the MSRC as "Exploitability is mitigated to a significant degree by factors such as default configuration, auditing, or difficulty of exploitation."

- **All** Will not restrict access for clients if they meet the MSRC's guidelines for low, moderate, important, and critical security updates. Low severity rating is defined as "A vulnerability whose exploitation is extremely difficult, or whose impact is minimal."

You can then define the minimum number of hours allowed between security updates. The default minimum value is 22 hours. You can chose to auto-remediate for security patches only if you have a WSUS server in the network. But choose these selections carefully and determine whether the manner in which you choose to patch your network matches up with an acceptable NAP Windows Security Health Validator (WSHV) setting. If your network policy means that you do not patch within a certain a certain timeframe, you may need to be selective in your use of NAP enforcement and only use NAP as a reporting tool. In fact, when deploying NAP, you would be wise to proceed in stages and first enforce only those items for which you know you have an appropriate policy set. You can later deploy the remainder of the policies, which are harder to enforce. Take the time to understand these security update rankings and how your organization deploys security updates. Meet with your Patch Management division to discuss their security update strategies before setting these policies.

This basic SHA can be augmented with additional separate System Health Agents such as third-party antivirus and System Center Configuration Manager (SCCM). The SHA for SCCM ensures that software updates managed by SCCM are deployed on the client computers.

Enforcement Levels

NAP enforcement settings provide a way to ensure compliance after you've determined the health policies that you will allow on your network. If the workstation matches the policy you have set, the workstation will have full network access. If the computer does not match the policy, you can place it in a quarantine location, separating it from the rest of the network until it is compliant with the policy. Also, you can allow full network access but only for a limited time. Based on your business needs and goals, some groups might have full enforcement of the policies and some groups may be allowed to be out of compliance. In a large organization, you may not be able to deploy all security patches across all groups at the same time, but may have antivirus and antispyware software automatically deployed. Therefore, look to your written security polices for client access guidance when setting enforcement. Confer with your patch management team regarding their ability to deploy patches and how they "zone" the network when deploying NAP in your network.

Third-party vendors with right of entry to your network should not be immune from these access polices. Their network health impacts your network health. Thus getting signed agreements and SLAs among vendors and consultants on your network will ensure that they understand the new policies you have set for network access.

Determining Exemptions

A key element to successful deployment is determining which computers are allowed to bypass requirements for a health certificate regardless of their health state. Depending on your network and perhaps even your management, you may exclude key computers. Begin by setting up NAP in deferred enforcement mode so that clients report their status but access isn't restricted. Monitor to determine whether it's necessary to move from reporting to true enforcement. You may find that the knowledge of health is enough and enforcement would be too extreme for your environment.

Note In Microsoft's own deployment of NAP, they began with "deferred enforcement," notifying the user of their system health but not restricting access to the domain. Auto-remediation was included in the client deployments. Lab deployments, global locations, and Windows Server 2008 domains were deployed in reporting mode.

Real World **Domain Deployment Tips**

Here are some key deployment tips when deploying NAP:

Placement of the NAP server

Typically when deploying a NAP solution you want to separate the Remediation Server roles from the Enforcement Server roles to isolate and clean the computers before they connect to the network. In a domain, Network Policy Server (NPS) should be installed on a domain controller to minimize NPS authentication and authorization response times and minimize network traffic. When using universal principal names (UPNs) on Windows Server 2008 or 2003 domains, NPS uses the global catalog to authenticate users. Therefore the NPS computer should also be a global catalog server or a server that is on the same subnet to minimize this time factor.

Minimizing network traffic

To minimize network NAP traffic with remote RADIUS server groups, disable NAS notification forwarding for individual servers in each remote RADIUS server group. In the Internet Authentication Service console, click Connection Request Processing and then click Connection Request Policies. Double-click on Use Windows Authentication For All Users, and click on Edit Profile. Click on the Accounting tab and ensure that Record accounting information on the servers in the following remote RADIUS server group is deselected. Next, in the Remote RADIUS Server group, double-click on the Group name set in the server. Click on the RADIUS server you need to ensure is not forwarding unnecessary traffic and click on properties. Click on the Authentication/Accounting tab and clear the Forward Network Access Server Start And Stop Notifications To This Server check box.

In Windows 2008, on the Network Policy Server console, under RADIUS Clients And Servers, select Remote RADIUS Servers Groups, and right click on the RADIUS Server group. Click on the Authentication/Accounting tab, and clear the Forward Network Access Server Start And Stop Notifications To This Server check box and click OK.

Create separate groups

When using remote access policies to restrict access for all but certain groups, don't put all users directly into a universal group. Always create separate groups that are members of the universal group and then add users to those groups.

Use UPN

To provide scalability for organizations with a large number of domains, use User Principal Names (UPNs).

Installing NPS on Member Servers

When installing NAP on a member server, increase the number of concurrent authentications between the NPS server and the domain controller. The registry key to adjust is located at: HKEY_LOCAL_MACHINE\SYSTEM\CurrentControlSet\Services\Netlogon\Parameters.

Add a new value named MaxConcurrentApi and assign it a value from 2 through 5. If the value is too high, your NPS server might place an excessive load on your domain controller. If this is an issue, install NPS as a RADIUS server on all of your domain controllers. Then configure two or more NPS proxies to forward the authentication requests between the access servers and the RADIUS servers. Next, configure your access servers to use the NPS proxies as RADIUS servers.

Testing IPsec NAP Enforcement

Now that we have planned out our test deployment, it's time to test our deployment *before* deploying it in production.

To use NAP IPsec enforcement, you must have a root certificate authority to deploy certificates on all computers participating. Even servers that are not NAP clients will need long-lived NAP exception certificates.

More Info From virtual labs to step-by-step white papers, Microsoft has a number of resources to help in the deployment of NAP at *http://technet.microsoft.com/en-us/network/bb545879.aspx*.

Setting Up a Certificate Server

If Microsoft Certificate Services is not deployed, you need to choose the server that will be the certificate server. To exempt any server or client from the health check, ensure that you set up an Active Directory group that will allow selected computers to be exempted from the policy.

To set up a certificate server, follow these steps:

1. Install a Windows 2003 or 2008 server operating system and perform the steps necessary to make it a domain controller or additional domain controller in your network. In Windows 2008, install Active Directory Domain Services role first.
    a. Click Start, then on Server Manager, click Roles, click Add Roles, and then click Active Directory Domain Services. Remember that you cannot add the DNS role at the time.
    b. Click Next. The introduction to Active Directory Domain Services will launch.
    c. Click Next again and then click Install. The wizard will need to close to launch the dcpromo.exe part of the domain install.
    d. Launch dcpromo.exe and click Next. You will be informed of a new setting in Windows 2008 that may impact when a domain controller services older Windows and non-Windows clients. (More information on this can be found in Knowledge Base article 942564 *http://support.microsoft.com/default.aspx?scid=kb;en-us;942564*.)
    e. Click Next and choose to set up new domain/forest or enter an existing one.
    f. Click Next and enter the domain name you will use as the fully qualified domain name (FQDN). The system will verify if the domain is in use. Choose a forest and domain functional level of Windows 2003 or 2008. (If you can, try to choose a functional level of 2008 for the granular password capability.) Ensure that the DNS server check box is enabled if this is the first domain controller you are installing for this forest and click Next. The system will warn you that it needs to create an authoritative parent zone. Click Yes to continue.
    g. Choose the location where you will place the AD database, log files, and sysvol folders, and then click Next.

   h. Enter the DSRM Administrator account password and click Next. Review the settings in the summary screen and click Next. Reboot the system after the dcpromo wizard completes.

2. For Windows 2003, you will use the Add/Remove Windows Components. Click Start, go to the control panel, and click the Add/Remove Windows Components dialog box. In the Windows Components Wizard dialog box, select Certificate Services.
3. For Windows 2008, click Start, choose Server Manager, choose the Add Roles Wizard, and select Active Directory Certificate Services.
4. Click Next to begin the installation wizard and ensure Certification Authority is selected.
5. Install Certificate Services on this server. Keep in mind that any server where a CA is installed cannot have its domain or computer name changed.
6. Select Enterprise Root CA, click Next, and select Root CA.
7. Choose to create a new private key and click Next.
8. Choose the cryptographic service and hash algorithm as per your firm's PKI policy. Click Next.
9. Enter a common name for the CA such as **Root CA** or another descriptive term.
10. Choose the validity period of the certificate and click Next.
11. Choose the location of the database and log file location and click Next.
12. Click Install and the necessary dependent services will be installed.
13. Ensure that the roles have installed and the wizard reports back that no errors have been found.

Confirm that the root CA does not require administrator approval by checking the following setting:

1. Click Start, click Administrative Tools, and then click Certification Authority.
2. In the tree view, click the Root CA you just built, right-click and select on Properties.
3. On the Policy Module tab, click Properties.
4. Confirm that Follow The Settings In The Certificate Template, If Applicable. Otherwise, Automatically Issue The Certificate is checked.
5. Close the console.

Next you set up an exemption group by following these steps:

1. Create a new security group in your Active Directory Users And Computers called **IPsec NAP Exemption**. Leave the group type as Global And Security and click OK.
2. Next, click Start, click Run, and then type **certtmpl.msc**. In the right-hand pane, scroll to the bottom and find the Workstation Authentication template. Right-click and select Duplicate Template to make a duplicate of the Workstation Authentication Certificate as it already has been configured with a client authentication application. Right-click the Workstation Authentication Certificate and make a copy. Choose the default of Windows 2003 Server, but consider the Windows Server 2008 if your network can support it.
3. Name the duplicated template **System Health Authentication**.
4. Ensure that the certificate is published by selecting Publish Certificate In Active Directory on the General tab.
5. Now click the Extensions tab of the template, click Application Policies, and click Edit.
6. Click Add, select System Health Authentication, and click OK.
7. Click Edit to review that under Object Identifier on the Extensions tab, it has the value of **1.3.6.1.4.1.311.47.1.1**. Click Cancel and then click OK.
8. Click the Security tab, then click Add to add the IPsec NAP Exemption security group you created earlier. Click Find, then click Find Now, scroll down in the resulting window to find the security group that was built earlier, and select Allow to enable autoenrollment of the certificate. Click OK to close the template and close the console.

Under the Hood 1.3.6.1.4.1.311.47.1.1

So where does this particular Object Identifier come from? Microsoft's reserved Object Identifier (OID) is 1.3.6.1.4.1.311, assigned by the Internet Assigned Numbers Authority (IANA). 47 represents an Enterprise Network and 1.1 signifies a version 1 certificate. In this case it is being used in cryptography and more specifically for the health certificate assigned to the clients.

You can read the details in Knowledge Base article 287547 at *http://support.microsoft.com/kb/287547/en-us*.

It's important for a successful deployment to identify those servers, printers, devices, and non-Microsoft platforms that you cannot obtain third-party supplicants for *before* you start the deployment. This allows you to exclude them from the health checks that NAP will be running.

The next step is to publish the templates, which you can do by following these steps:

1. Click Start, then click Run. In the run box, type **certsrv.msc**, and click Enter,
2. Open the Root CA that you previously built. Expand the window on the left to show Certificate Templates.
3. Right-click Certificate Templates, click New, and then click Certificate Templates To Issue.
4. Scroll down, click System Health Authentication, and then click OK.
5. Close the Certification Authority console.

Next, we will set the Root CA so that the certificates are issued automatically by following these steps:

1. Click Start, select All Programs, select Administrative Tools, and launch the Group Policy Management Console.
2. Expand the console until you see the domain name.
3. Click the plus sign next to the domain name to see the category Default Domain Policy.
4. Right-click Default Domain Policy, and then click Edit.
5. Select Computer Configuration, Policies, Windows Settings, Security Settings, Public Key Policies and expand the settings.
6. In the Details pane, select Certificate Services Client-Auto-Enrollment properties.
7. Your certificate should be selected for Enroll Certificates automatically. To confirm this, select the Ensure That The Certificate Is Selected for Enroll Certificates Automatically by setting Configuration Model to Enabled and selecting the Renew Expired Certificates, Update Pending Certificates And Remove Revoked Certificates and Update Certificates That Use Certificate Templates check boxes.

The resulting screen should look like Figure 24-3.

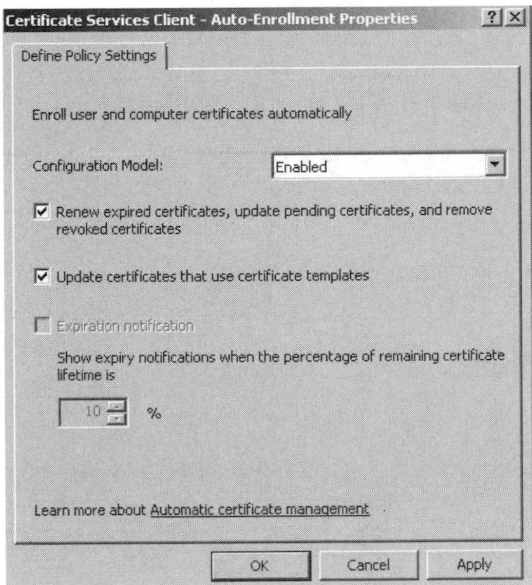

Figure 24-3 Auto-enrollment properties for Certificate Services Client

Setting Up the NAP Server

The next step is to set up the actual server that will be the Network Policy Server and the reporting or enforcement server. To install the NAP server, follow these steps:

1. Install Windows Server 2008 on a server and join it to the domain, ensuring that you are logging onto this server with domain administrator credentials.
2. Because you need to ensure that the NAP server itself will not be restricted, you need to ensure that the NAP server gets its health certificate immediately.
3. On the Domain controller server, Click Start, select All Programs, select Administrative Tools, and click Active Directory Users And Computers.
4. Click the domain name in the console and double-click the IPsec NAP Exemption group you previously set up.
5. On the Members tab of this group, click Add, select Object Types, and then select the Computers check box. Click OK.
6. In the Enter The Object Names To Select (examples) box, type the name of the NAP server (and any other computer, printer, or group you want exempted) so that these computers will be exempted.
7. At a command prompt, type **gpupdate /force** (or your favorite Group Policy refresh command) to refresh the Group Policy.

Next you need to add the actual NAP role to your NAP server. To do so, follow these steps on the server you designated to be the NAP server:

1. Launch the Windows Server 2008 Server Add Roles Wizard to add the needed role to the server.
2. On the Select Server Roles page, select both Active Directory Certificate Services and Network Policy And Access Services to add these roles to the NAP server.
3. The additional needed services will be automatically installed by the Install Wizard. Figure 24-4 shows how easy it is to add these roles to a Windows 2008 server.

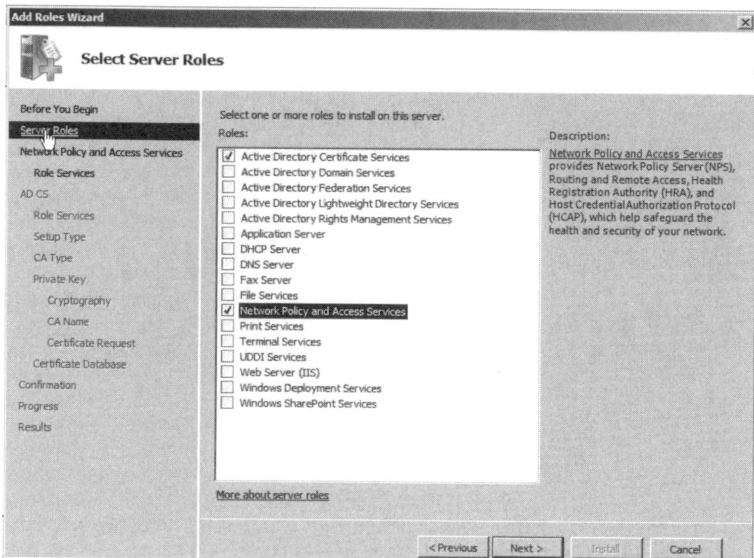

Figure 24-4 Installing the proper role

To add the Health Registration Authority role to the Windows Server 2008, follow these steps:

1. On the Select Role Services To Install For Network Policy And Access Services page, select Health Registration Authority. Confirm that you really want to add the necessary roles and services and click Add Required Role Services, which will add all of the necessary dependent services to the ADCS and NAP services you have chosen. Click Next.
2. When prompted to select a certificate server, choose Select A Certificate Server Later Using The HRA Console, and Click Next.

Note For a normal install in a domain, merely choose the default of "yes" and continue. For a more flexible set up to allow computers to be enrolled with health certificates in a workgroup environment, choose No, Allow Anonymous Requests For Health Certificates at this step. This will set the permissions accordingly. Your domain needs may make this the preferred manner of deployment.

3. In the setup here, you will choose No, Allow Anonymous Requests For Health Certificates and click Next.
4. Select Choose A Certificate For SSL Encryption Later and click Next. (SSL is recommended but not required.)
5. Confirm that the Certification Authority role is selected and click Next.
6. For this example, because we are installing the CA server role on the same server as the NAP and Health Registration Authority, ensure that on the Select Role Services page, you choose Certification Authority as a Stand-Alone CA and click Next.
7. On the Specify CA Type page, select Subordinate CA and click Next.

Next you set the options for cryptographic services. The options for a cryptographic service provider and hash algorithm demonstrate that you can choose different versions based on the needs of your firm.

1. Click to create a new private key.
2. For purposes of your testing, select the default private key and cryptographic settings for the next step. The defaults shown in Figure 24-5 should be fine for most organizations.

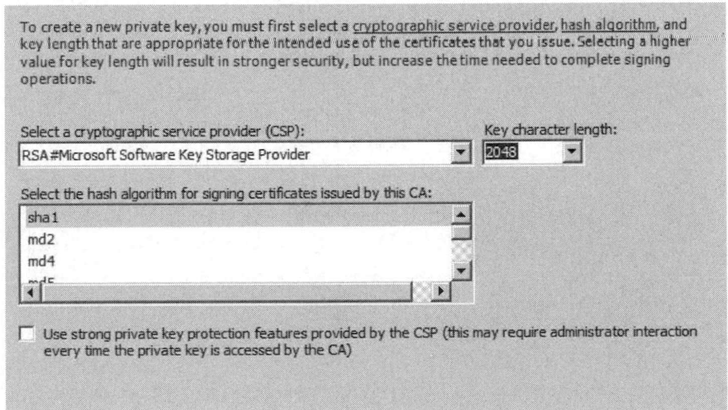

Figure 24-5 Selecting the cryptographic service providers

3. On the Configure CA Name page, select a common name for this CA that indicates its role as a SubCA by indicating that in its title, such as **Example.com-NAP-SubCA**. Click Next to continue.
4. On the Request Certificate From A Parent CA screen, ensure that the option Send A Certificate Request To A Parent CA is selected and click Browse
5. In the Select Certification Authority window, click the Root CA that you previously built and click OK. Click Next.
6. Determine where the database for the certificate will be located as well as the Web server. Click Next, click Next again, and then confirm that the necessary IIS roles have been selected and click Next.
7. A confirmation screen will appear. Click Install.

Confirm that the installation is successful.

Installing the Group Policy Management Console

To configure policies on the server for IPsec health enforcement, use the Group Policy Management Console to edit Group Policy. On a Windows Server 2008 NAP server, install the Group Policy Management Console (GPMC) by choosing this feature in the Add Features Wizard. You'll use the GPMC to edit Group Policy to configure the IPsec policies for health enforcement using the following steps:

1. Open the Server Manager if it isn't already open.
2. Click Features and then select Add Features from the Action menu to open the Add Features Wizard.
3. Select Group Policy Management and click Next.
4. Click Install to begin the installation and ensure that the console installs correctly.

Now that the GPMC is installed, use the following steps to configure the subordinate CA to automatically issue certificates upon request:

1. Click Start. In the Start Search box, type **certsrv.msc** to launch the console.
2. In the Certification Authority console, choose the SubCA certificate you built previously, right-click and then choose Properties from the shortcut menu. Click the Policy Module tab and then click Properties.
3. Ensure that the Follow The Settings In The Certificate Template, If Applicable, Otherwise, Automatically Issue The Certificate check box is selected.
4. To restart the Active Directory Certificate Services, select the SubCA, right-click and select All Tasks from the shortcut menu, then click Stop Service.

5. Click the SubCA, right-click and select All Tasks from the shortcut menu, and then click Start Service to restart it.

When the HRA is installed on a server that is not the issuing CA, specific permissions must be given to the HRA computer name. If the HRA and CA are located on the same server, assign the permissions to the Network Service by following these steps:

1. Click Start. In the Start Search box, type **certsrv.msc** to launch the console.
2. In the Certificate Authority Console tree, right-click the SubCA, and then click Properties in the shortcut menu.
3. On the Security tab, click Add and then type Network Service in the Enter The Object Names To Select (Examples) box and click OK If prompted, enter domain administrator credentials.
4. In the Group window, click Network Service and select Issue and Manage Certificates. Select the Manage CA and Request Certificate check boxes and click OK.
5. If this HRA service was not installed on the server issuing the certificates, instead of allowing the Network Service those permissions, you would specifically select the HRA Machine name to have these permissions. On the Security tab, click Add and add the specific Machine Name that holds the HRA role in the Enter The Object Names To Select (Examples) check box.
6. As before, select the Issue And Manage Certificates, Manage CA, and then Request Certificate check boxes and click OK.

You must configure the Health Registration Authority Server with a Certificate Authority to issue health certificates. You can select a stand-alone CA or enterprise CA by following these steps:

1. Launch the MMC snap in by typing **mmc.exe** in the Search box.
2. In the Microsoft Management Console, click File and then click Add/Remove Snap-in. Choose the Health Registration Authority snap-in.
3. Choose the local computer (the one on which this console is running) and click OK.
4. Click OK to launch the console.
5. In the Health Registration Authority (Local Computer) console, expand the items below by clicking the plus sign (+).
6. Right-click Certificate Authority and select Add Certificate Authority from the shortcut menu, and then browse to choose the SubCA you previously built. You should see the original Root CA and the Sub CA. Choose the Sub CA and click OK.

7. Right-click Certificate Authority and select Properties from the shortcut menu. Verify that Use Standalone Certification Authority is checked, and click OK. If you have chosen to use Enterprise CA, it must be changed and matched up to the Enterprise Authority CA you have selected.

Configuring the NAP Health Policy Server

For this step, you need sufficient lab time to determine the policies that will work with your organization. And even after sufficient lab testing, preparing test production deployments is a good idea. Most firms are looking for NAP deployments for clients and in particular for portable computers and can't deploy NAP to servers.

The NAP Health Policy Wizard sets up System Health Validators that allow you to choose antivirus, antispyware, firewall, and update status. You can add third-party validators as well.

1. Click Start and in the Search box type **nps.msc** and then press Enter.
2. Under standard configuration, click Configure NAP.
3. Select the connection method. In this case we are using IPsec With Health Registration Authority (HRA). Edit the policy name if so desired and click Next.
4. In the case of a NAP Health Policy Server that has HRA installed locally, click Next, otherwise select Specify NAP Enforcement Servers Running HRA and choose the remote HRS servers that will be RADIUS clients.
5. If the NAP Health Policy Server is installed separate from the HRA server, set up RADIUS clients and specify the remote servers.
6. If you had RADIUS clients, in the Configure Groups page, configure the appropriate computer groups as needed based on your deployment.
7. On the Define NAP Health Policy page, select the Windows Security Health Validator and Enable Auto-Remediation Of Client Computers check boxes and click Next.
8. On the Completing NAP Enforcement Policy And RADIUS Client Configuration page, click Finish.

When you deploy NAP, the best solution will not only check the health of the client but also offer auto-remediation options. Thus choosing Windows Security Health Validator and Enable Auto-Remediation Of Client Computers ensures that your policy will be effective. By default, the Windows SHV is configured to require a firewall, virus protection, spyware protection, and automatic updating.

To tailor your System Health Validator selections, follow these steps:

1. Click Start, key **nps.msc** in the Search box, and then press Enter.
2. In the Details pane, click Configure System Health Validators under Network Access Protection node.
3. Under Name, double-click the Windows Security Health Validator.
4. In the Properties dialog box, click Configure.
5. Based on the policies you previously decided on, choose the policies that you plan to report and/or enforce on. This is where your planning and discussion time with your Patch Management team will be key. Choose only those items you plan to track with your policies. Determine if you will monitor Firewall, Virus protection, Spyware and/or check for updating policies.

Client Settings for NAP

Now that we have set up the server, it's time to focus on the settings for the workstations. The first step is to change the group policy to expose the Security Center on workstations. By default, the Security Center reporting in a domain is turned off when joined to a domain. To enable this, follow these steps:

1. Launch the Group Policy Management Console by going to the local computer you are testing and clicking Start, typing **gpedit.msc**, and finding the Local Computer Policy section.
2. In a domain setting you will need to go to your Group Policy server, launch GPMC.msc, and define a new Group Policy for the Organizational Unit you are deploying NAP to.
3. In the Computer Configuration/Administrative Templates/Windows Components/Security Center, click Turn On Security Center (Domain PCs Only), and set it to Enabled.

Enable IPsec Enforcement

To enable IPsec enforcement on NAP client computers, you need to ensure that the IPsec enforcement client is enabled on all NAP client computers. To do so, follow these steps:

1. Click Start, and in the Search box launch the NAP client configuration by typing **napclcfg.msc**.
2. Select the NAP Client Configuration Console and then select Enforcement Clients.
3. In the Detail pane on the right, right-click IPsec Relying Party and select Enable, as shown in Figure 24-6. Click OK.

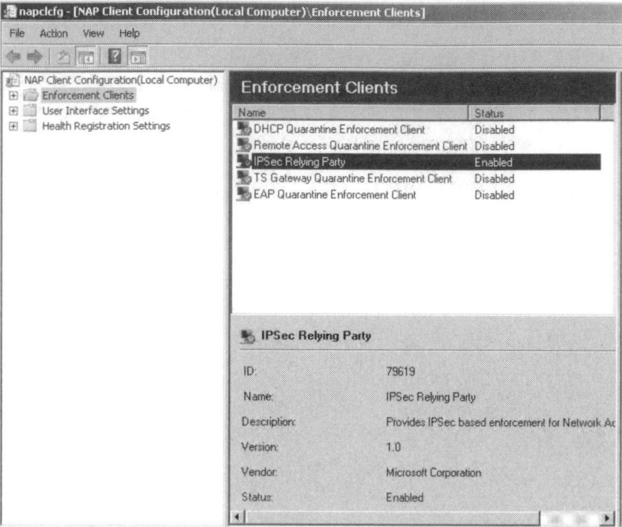

Figure 24-6 Choosing the enforcement

We now need to configure a Web address that allows the IPSec NAP client computers to obtain their health certificates.

1. Click Start and launch the NAP client configuration by typing **napclcfg.msc** in the Search box.
2. Double-click the Health Registration Settings, and expand the selections underneath. Click Trusted Service Groups, right-click, and select New from the shortcut menu to build a new group.
3. In our example we're using the name Trusted HRA Servers. Enter the phrase **Trusted HRA Servers** in the Group Name box and click Next.
4. Because we're not using an SSL-secured Web site for our HRA URL, we will clear the Require Server Verification (Https) For All Servers In This Group check box.
5. Under the URLs of the health registration authority that you want the client to trust, type in your HRA Web site. In our example we're using **http://nap1.example.com/domainhra/hcsrvext.dll** for the Web site that we will use for domain-authenticated requests for health certificates. Because this is the first Web site in the list, client computers will use this trusted server first to attempt to obtain a health certificate.
6. For non-domain client computers, add the Web site **http://nap1.example.com/nondomainhra/hcsrvext.dll**. Because this is the second server in the list, client

computers will look to this server after the first server fails to provide a certificate. Click Finish.

7. Confirm that your trusted server groups are listed as Available URLs as shown in Figure 24-7.

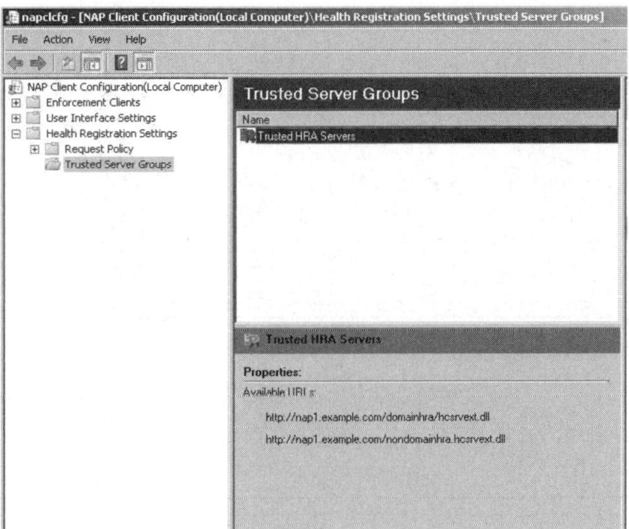

Figure 24-7 Setting up trusted server groups

Steps on the Workstations

On each workstation, the Network Access Protection Agent is set with a default startup type of Manual. To change this so that the NAP agent will automatically start on Windows XP SP3 and Windows Vista computers, launch the Group Policy Management Console on the Domain Controller and follow these steps:

1. Click Start and type **GPMC.msc** in the Search box.

2. Build a new OU-connected Group Policy (entering your group policy structure according to your firm's OU needs on the server) and browse to Computer Configuration, Windows Settings, System Services. Find the Network Access Protection Agent and set the service startup to Automatic. Figure 24-8 documents the location in the Security Settings, System Services where this policy can be found.

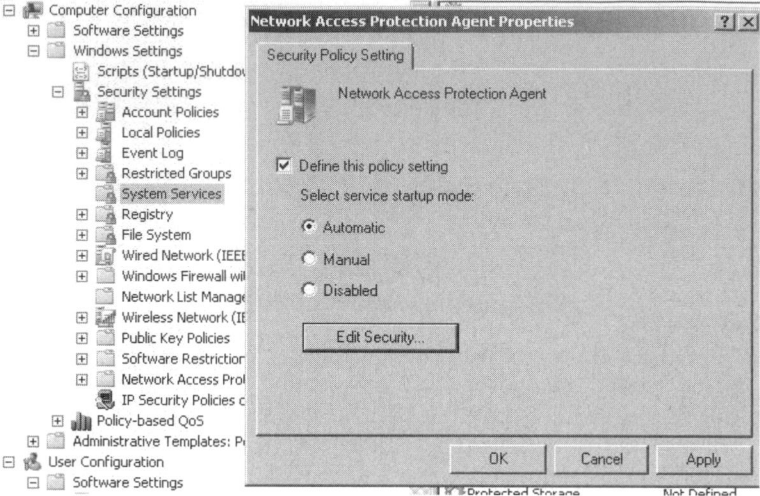

Figure 24-8 Enabling the service to be automatic

3. Set up the Group Policy to apply to Windows Vista and Windows XP SP3 clients to enable the Network Access Protection Agent on those operating systems by building WMI filters to limit the policies to these workstations.

Under the Hood WMI filters

If you want to build selected group policies that only impact certain workstations, remember you can always build WMI filters for additional filtering. To build WMI filters, follow these steps:

1. Click Start and type **gpmc.msc** in the Search box.
2. In the Group Policy Management Console, under Domains, on the WMI Filter node, right-click and then click New.
3. On the New WMI Filter page that launches, name the WMI filter.
4. Enter an appropriate description in the Description box.
5. Enter the necessary Namespace and Query commands as needed to filter for Windows XP and Windows Vista as listed below in step 7and click Save.
6. You can now add these WMI filters to the bottom section of any policy you create that will further granularly deploy the policy to computers that match the filter.
7. The section of the GPO called WMI Filtering can be easily used to link to a specific WMI filter that you design.

For Windows XP SP3 the WMI filter is as follows:

*Namespace: root\CIMv2 Query: Select * from WIN32_OperatingSystem where ServicePackMajorVersion>=3 and Version='5.1.2600' For Windows Vista the WMI filter is as follows:*

*Namespace: root\CIMv2 Query: Select * from WIN32_OperatingSystem where Version>6.0 and ProductType=1*

Creating Boundaries for IPsec

To use IPsec, you must set domain isolation policies in Active Directory. Create the necessary OUs for the secure health enforcement as deemed by your planned policies. You will need at least one IPsec policy for boundary computers. In our example, we'll create several OUs, but in your deployment the OUs need to be tailored to your organizational needs. In versions of workstations prior to Windows Vista, the application of IPsec was clunky at best. In Windows Vista, you use the Windows Firewall with Advanced Security Group Policy extension to create the needed IPsec policy.

Begin first by defining the OUs that will create one group that allows compliant NAP clients and another group that will be a boundary group that will prefer inbound connections from computers with health certificates. To do so, follow these steps:

1. In Active Directory on your domain controller, click Start, click Administrative Tools, and then click Active Directory Users And Computers.
2. Click your domain name and then click New, and then click Organizational Unit.
3. In the Name box, type **IP Secure** and click OK.
4. Repeat this process for the second (or additional OUs) called **IPsec Boundary**.
5. Leave the check box in Protect Container From Accidental Deletion.

In the Group Policy MMC, once you have created the necessary OUs per your design and planning for your domain, you can use the Window Firewall with Advanced Group Policies to create the IPsec policies. This firewall policy ability is brand-new in Windows Server 2008 and greatly decreases the complexity of preparing IPsec policy rules. We will be preparing these rules on our Domain Controller servers by following these steps:

1. Click Start and type **gpme.msc** in the Search box.
2. Browse for a Group Policy Object and click IPSecure.yourdomain.com (the Secure IPsec OU name you created in the prior step).
3. Choose the Create New Group Policy Object to the right of IP Secure.yourdomain.com, enter the phrase **Secure Policy**, and click OK.

4. The normal Group Policy Management Editor console will open. From here browse to the Computer Configuration\Windows Settings\Security Settings\Windows Firewall with Advanced Security\Windows Firewall with Advanced Security – LDAP setting in the Group Policy console. Right-click Windows Firewall With Advanced Security – LDAP and go to the properties of the Firewall Settings. On the Domain Profile tab, choose the following settings:
   - Firewall State: On (recommended)
   - Inbound Connections: Block (default)
   - Outbound Connections: Allow (default)
5. On the Private Profile and Public Profile tabs in the same firewall settings, use the same settings that were on the Domain profile. They should match what is shown in Figure 24-9. If you want to tailor these firewall ports and further restrict outbound connections, you can choose to do so based on the profile chosen.

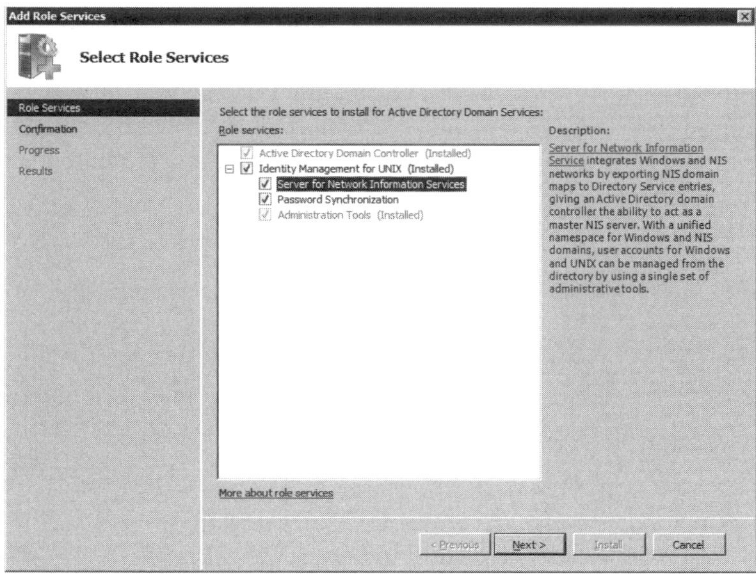

Figure 24-9 Building the IPsec and firewall rules

Next, follow these steps to build a Connection Security Rule for the firewall setting you are building. The rule will set in place certain authentication requirements.

1. In the same Group Policy console where you were previously, under Windows Firewall With Advanced Security – LDAP, click Connection Security Rules.
2. On the right-hand side of the screen, right-click, and then click New Rule in the shortcut menu. Choose Isolation as the Rule Type.
3. For the rule's Requirements, select Require Authentication For Inbound Connections And Request Authentication For Outbound Connections. (This requires

inbound—but not outbound—connections to be authenticated.) This will be the policy that we will use for isolating the servers.

4. Because the authentication will be certificate-based, choose Computer Certificate on the Authentication Method page, select Only Accept Health Certificates, and browse to the generated Root Certificate Authority that was prepared. Ensure that domain, public, and private profiles will be covered by this authentication rule.
5. Name the rule **Secure Rule** and finish the wizard.

> **Note** Take the time at this point to set up whatever additional firewall policies your workstations may need for full functionality at this time, but only enable the minimum required ports.

For a boundary group policy rule, set up the same basic firewall profiles as you did in the preceding steps. but this time build a New Isolation rule:

1. Click Start. In the Search box, type **gpme.msc** and press Enter to launch the Group Policy editor.
2. Browse for a Group Policy Object and double-click IPBoundary.yourdomain.com or whatever you named the rule previously.
3. Click Create New Group Policy Object, type **Boundary Policy**, and then click OK.
4. The Group Policy Management Editor will open. Open the Boundary Policy [computer.domain.com] Policy\Computer Configuration\Windows Settings\Security Settings\Windows Firewall with Advanced Security\Windows Firewall with Advanced Security – LDAP setting in the group policy console. Right-click Windows Firewall With Advanced Security – LDAP and go to the the Firewall Settings dialog box.
5. On the Domain Profile tab, choose the following settings:
   - Firewall State: On (recommended)
   - Inbound Connections: Block (default)
   - Outbound Connections: Allow (default)
6. Choose these same settings for the Private and Public Profile tabs in the firewall and click OK.
7. In the Group Policy Management Editor console tree, under Windows Firewall with Advanced Security – LDAP, right-click Connection Security Rules and choose New Rule from the shortcut menu.
8. The New Connection Security Rule Wizard will start. On the Rule Type page, verify that Isolation is selected and click Next.

9. The Requirements page should be set to ensure that Request Authentication For Inbound And Outbound Connections is selected. Click Next.
10. On the Authentication Method page, select Computer Certificate and select the Only Accept Health Certificates box.
11. Click Browse to find your Root CA, as shown in Figure 24-10. Click OK and then click Next.

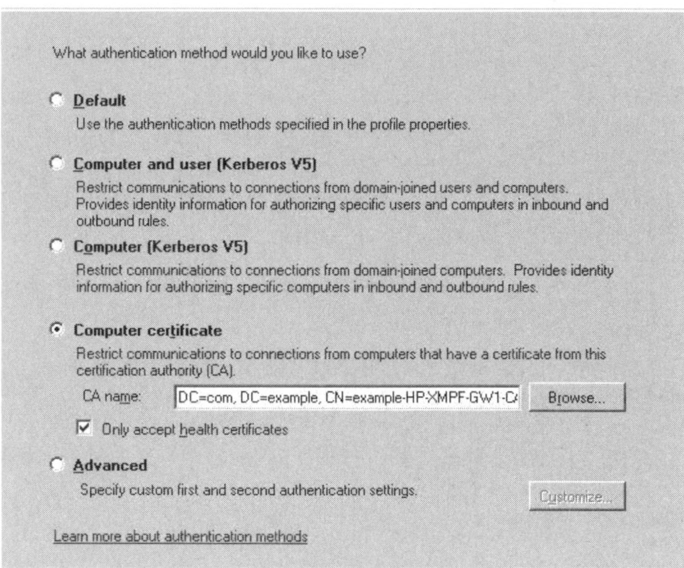

Figure 24-10 Choosing the enforcement

12. On the Profile page, confirm that the Private, Public, and Domain check boxes are selected and click Next.
13. On the Name page, name this connection rule **Boundary Rule** and then click Finish.

Begin your NAP deployment with a small test deployment group and place computers into these OUs as you determine for your rollout plans. Move some of your systems into the various OUs by following these steps:

1. On your domain controller, click Start, then click Administrative Tools, and then click Active Directory Users And Computers.
2. Open your domain name and click Computers.
3. Right-click each workstation, click Move, and move the workstations in your test deployment into OUs.

Choose edge computers to be in the boundary group representing those computers that would prefer but not require inbound connections from healthy computers and move your test computers that you will require healthy inbound connections into the IP Secure OU.

IEEE 802.1x Enforcement in NAP

Another deployment method, 802.1x, requires 802.1x systems to supply the health state before connecting. If you deploy using 802.1x enforcement, the key to a successful deployment is ensuring that all switches or access points are capable of 802.1x. The components include:

- Supplicant: the client authenticating
- Pass-through authenticator: RADIUS server
- Authenticator: 802.1x access point

Using this method, the enforcement policy instructs an access point to limit a system to a restricted network. This can either be VLAN or IP packet filters. The process of client authentication is relatively straightforward and is shown in Figure 24-11.

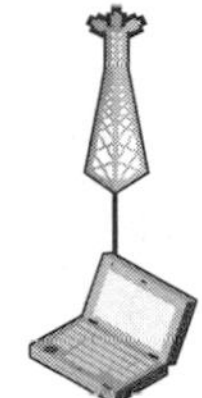

The 802.1x authentication is initiated.

Client uses PEAP and a configured PEAP authentication method for user or computer authentication to the network.

Health certificate of the EAPHost NAP EC is sent to the NPS Server using PEAP-TLV message.

Health certificate is obtained. It contains the validated health state of the 802.1X client.

A PEAP-TLV message is sent from the NPS Server to the 802.1X client. It contains the Statement of Health Response (SoHR).

A RADIUS Access-Accept message is sent from the NPS Server to the 802.1X access point. It contains the SoHR.

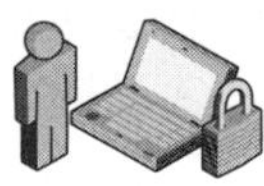

The NAP client will have unlimited access. The Health Certificate is valid as the RADIUS Access-Accept message does not include a limited access profile.

Figure 24-11 The 802.1X process

Configuring IEEE 802xz Enforcement

Similar to the earlier NAP deployment method, the hardware requirements for deployment are lightweight with one exception: hardware. You must ensure that your switches and access points support 802.1X.

Real World Hardware Shopping List for 802.1X Enforcement

If 802.1x is your chosen deployment methodology, supported hardware becomes a bigger issue. Most modern switches should support NAP. However, the specific list of switches that Microsoft used in their test labs consisted of the following:

- Enterasys Networks model 2G4072-52
- D-Link model DES-3828
- Nortel Networks model 5520-24T-PWR
- ProCurve Networking/HP model 3500yl-24G-PWR
- Foundry Networks model FGS624P
- Extreme Networks model X450-24t
- Aruba Networks model 800
- Cisco Systems model 3560
- Alaxala Networks model AX2400S/AX3600S
- Meru Networks model AP200/MC1000

You may wish to check the switches you plan to use in deployment with either the vendor or the Microsoft NAP forum located at *http://forums.microsoft.com/TechNet/ShowForum.aspx?ForumID=576&SiteID=17* for more information.

Configuring 802.1X Enforcement

To configure and install 802.1X switches that can authenticate on your NAP enabled network, first determine the authentication method you want to use. Choosing EAP-TLS or PEAP-ELS, with and without smart cards, depends on what your vendors and hardware can support. As with IPsec, you need to set up a certificate authority, or in the case of PEAP-MS-CHAP v2 only, you can purchase server certificates instead of setting up your own CA Server.

More Info Information on how to obtain and install a VeriSign WLAN server certificate for PEAP-MS-CHAP v2 wireless authentication is available at *http://www.microsoft.com/downloads/details.aspx?FamilyID=1971d43c-d2d9-408d-bd97-139afc60996b&DisplayLang=en*.

If you decide to use EAP-TLS or PEAP-TLS without smart cards, be sure to auto-enroll user certificates and computer certificates to domain member client computers. You might need to deploy both types of certificates to these roles. Although you could configure 802.1X wireless clients prior to Windows Vista with Group Policy, configuring wired 802.1X in XP was impossible and actually introduced some risks to the business. So Windows Vista is the preferred platform for wired deployments.

Follow these steps to configure the switches as RADIUS clients in NPS and create a user group in Active Directory that contains the users in the network that are allowed to access the network through these switches:

1. Click Start. In the Search box, type **nps.msc** and press Enter.
2. Click RADIUS Clients And Servers\RADIUS Clients and then right-click New RADIUS Client from the shortcut menu.
3. In the Friendly Name box, enter a descriptive name for the switch.
4. Enter the IP or DNS address and optionally choose to verify the IP address.
5. Choose RADIUS Standard for the bulk of RADIUS clients. If you have a specific vendor, the list is quite lengthy and includes vendors such as 3Com, ACC, ADC Kentrox, Ascend Communications, BBN, BinTec Communications, Cabletron, Cisco, Digi International, EICON, Gandalf, Intel, Lantronix, Livingston Enterprises, Proteon, Shiva Corporation, Telebit, U.S. Robotics, Xylogics, Microsoft, Redback Networks, and Nortel Networks.
6. In the Shared Secret box, determine (based on your network deployment properties) whether you use a manually generated secret or allow for a generated shared secret. Note that not all RADIUS clients support the long generated shared secret, so you may need to edit this.
7. Select Access-Request Messages Must Contain The Message-Authenticator Attribute.
8. If the RADIUS client is a NPS proxy server or a VPN Server with Routing and Remote Access Service installed, select RADIUS Client Is NAP-Capable; otherwise, leave the box cleared.

9. Ensure that on your compliant switch you have entered in the exact same shared secret.

Of course, always test your deployment in a test lab before beginning your production 802.1X deployment.

The Politics of Deployment

When deploying your first test of Network Access Protection, don't begin by enforcement as your first setting. Instead, change default policies in the NAP enforcement to merely report the health or lack of health of the system. Restricting access shouldn't be the goal in your first deployments. Instead, focus on compliance with your policy.

When you have a noncompliant computer, set policy to block access of that system to your network. The noncompliance message explains to the end user that he is not "healthy" enough to connect to the network and allows him to try again. Figure 24-12 shows the notification of noncompliance; Figure 24-13 shows that a client is compliant.

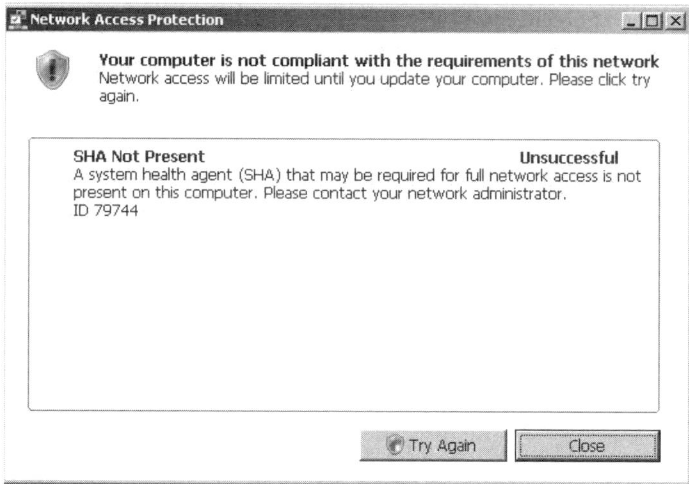

Figure 24-12 Notification of noncompliance on the client

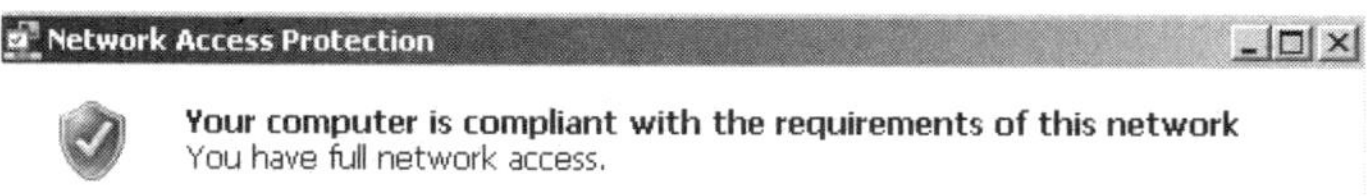

Figure 24-13 Notification of compliance

In NAP enforcement, your optional settings for enforcing Network Access Protection for the policy you set up (whether for IPsec, 802.1X, VPN, Terminal Server Gateway, or DHCP) can be granularly set and changed depending on your needs for enforcement. For noncompliant workstations, you can choose the first enforcement option that allows full network access for clients when the connection request they are making matches the policy. Allow Full Network Access is commonly referred to as "reporting mode" because it merely allows the administrator to get feedback and reports on network health and compliance with the policies. To enable this reporting mode, perform the following steps on the NAP server:

1. Click Start, type **nps.msc** in the Search box, and launch the Network Policy Server console.
2. Click Policies and then click on Configure Network Policies. In this example, we have NAP IPsec With HRA Compliant Properties and NAP IPsec With HRA Noncompliant Properties.
3. Double-click NAP IPsec with HRA Compliant (or the policy you have set up) and on the Overview tab, review the settings. You will generally find that the policy is enabled and that the type of Network Access Server is a Health Registration Authority.
4. On the Settings tab, review the settings on the NAP Enforcement option. You can choose the setting Allow Full Network Access. This first Enforcement selection is called reporting mode and is the recommended first deployment methodology.

The second enforcement option allows the workstation access for a limited amount of time. Similar to Internet access policies, you can set a time and date for enforcement:

1. Click Start, type **nps.msc** in the Search box, and launch the Network Policy Server console.
2. Click Policies and then click Network Policies.
3. Double-click NAP IPsec with HRA Compliant (or the policy you have set up).
4. Click the Settings tab, and then click NAP Enforcement.
5. Click Allow Full Network Access For A Limited Time and choose a time and a date for full network enforcement.

The third enforcement option allows a network administrator to allow limited access of the workstation:

1. Click Start, type **nps.msc** in the Search box, and launch the Network Policy Server console.
2. Click Policies and then click Network Policies.
3. Double-click NAP IPsec With HRA Compliant (or the policy you have set up).
4. Click the Settings tab, and then click NAP Enforcement.
5. Select Allow Limited Access for full enforcement of noncompliance.

Finally, you can set options to allow only certain servers or a Web site for remediation. If you plan a self-server sort of remediation kiosk, you could limit the workstation to a Web page with links for information on obtaining network health. Or you could ensure that you have several health remediation servers that the workstation can check with to get cleaned up. You can also choose to use both means for cleaning up the workstation:

1. Click Start, type **NPS.msc** in the Search box, and launch the Network Policy Server console.
2. Click Policies and then click Network Policies.
3. Double-click NAP IPsec With HRA Compliant (or the policy you have set up).
4. Click the Settings tab, and then click NAP Enforcement.
5. In the Remediation Server Group and Troubleshooting URL box, choose Configure and specify a group of servers that the unhealthy workstation can connect to (such as your antivirus deployment servers) or a troubleshooting Web site that gives users instructions on how to bring the computer and devices into compliance.

Last, check Enable Auto-Remediation Of Client Computers so that the NAP clients can automatically update and fix their noncompliant health state, thus making the deployment as painless as possible for everyone. The goal is to encourage compliance, not block access:

1. Click Start, type **NPS.msc** in the Search box, and launch the Network Policy Server console.
2. Click Policies and then click Network Policies.
3. Double-click NAP IPsec With HRA Compliant (or the policy you have set up).
4. Click the Settings tab, and then click NAP Enforcement.
5. On the bottom of that screen, you'll see the box labeled Enable Auto-Remediation Of Client Computers. It's highly recommended that this be the default policy for your NAP deployments.

You can even ensure that compliant and noncompliant computers get to key critical resources (perhaps one printer in the office) by placing key critical access servers in the remediation server group allowing noncompliant printers to have access to them.

Summary

Planning for NAP is key to a successful deployment. Set up a test lab with virtual servers to see the technology in action. Go slowly in your use of enforcement–use NAP as a reporting mechanism initially. This will give you the foundation you need to discover and uncover information regarding the health of your network.

In the next chapter, we move on to Patch Management: the essential process of obtaining, assessing, and deploying software updates.

Chapter 25

Patch Management

Patches—everyone hates them, but they are an inescapable part of the everyday computing world. I hated them and complained about them when I was a UNIX system administrator some 20 years ago. And I still hate them now, even though the overall process of obtaining, testing, and applying them has improved substantially. I doubt that anything we can say will make you like patches any better than we do, but in this chapter we'll try to cover the basics to make the process of patch management as straightforward and manageable as possible.

Real World Terminology

The first rule of patches is that Microsoft doesn't like that word. It uses several different terms, each with a slightly different meaning, but the reality is that to the rest of the world, they're still called patches. We call them patches, the magazines and newspapers call them patches, even most Microsoft employees call them patches, unless they're giving a formal presentation. So throughout this chapter, that's what we'll call them. But Microsoft does have official terminology, and we should all be clear on what it is:

- **Critical Update** A generally available fix for a critical but non-security-related bug. A critical update has an accompanying Knowledge Base (KB) article.
- **Security Update** A generally available fix for a security vulnerability. Security updates have an accompanying Knowledge Base article and a Security Bulletin.

- **Software Update** A broad term that covers Service Packs, hotfixes, update rollups, security updates, feature packs, and so on. A software update has an accompanying Knowledge Base article.
- **Service Pack** A generally available collection of fixes and feature enhancements. Service packs are cumulative and contain all currently available updates, update rollups, security updates, critical updates, and hotfixes, and they might contain fixes for problems that were found internally and have not been otherwise released. Service packs also sometimes add new features (Microsoft Windows XP SP2, for example).
- **Hotfix** A narrowly available fix for a specific issue. Hotfixes are generally available only through Microsoft Product Support Services and cannot be redistributed. Hotfixes have not had as thorough a test cycle as updates, update rollups, or service packs.
- **Update** A generally available fix for a specific, nonsecurity, and noncritical problem. An update has an accompanying Knowledge Base article.
- **Update Rollup** A generally available, tested collection of hotfixes, security updates, critical updates, and updates that are packaged together. An update rollup has an accompanying Knowledge Base article.

You see? All sorts of terms and terminology and not one of them is a patch. For complete, up-to-date details on Microsoft update terminology, see *http://support.microsoft.com/kb/824684/*.

Why It's Important

In the old days, when your network wasn't connected to the Internet, when system administrators were the only people who installed software, and when users had only a green screen terminal, deciding when to apply a patch was a fairly straightforward decision. If you were having a specific problem and you wanted a bit of overtime on the weekend, you came in and applied a patch. If no one was complaining and you didn't want to work on the weekend, you threw the tape (patches always came on tapes in those days) in the drawer and waited until you had to come in on the weekend for some other maintenance, or until users started complaining about a problem that seemed related. Or you simply never got around to it at all.

Even in the more recent past it was possible to have a more considered and gradual approach to applying patches. When a vulnerability was identified, it often took months before any real risk threatened your network.

Today, that approach simply won't work, as Code Red, Nimda, Slammer, and others have all too clearly demonstrated. Within hours, or at most days, of the release of a critical security update, sample exploit code will almost certainly be posted on the Internet telling anyone and everyone how to exploit the vulnerability. If you ignore critical security updates, you place your entire network—and the data stored on it—at risk.

Applying patches is only one part of a defense-in-depth strategy to protect your network, but it's a critical part. Don't neglect it.

Real World Patch Tuesday

In the old days, patches, especially security updates, were released whenever a new vulnerability was identified and corrected. When that happened only a few times a year, it wasn't a big problem, and system administrators dealt with updates as they came out. In most cases, you could just wait till the Service Pack came out and deal with a whole bunch at once. But as more and more security updates and critical updates were released on an almost daily basis, it became increasingly difficult to properly test and identify all the patches necessary for your system. The whole process became a serious impediment to productivity.

In direct response to many, many complaints, Microsoft has moved to a monthly update release process. Unless there is a compelling and immediate need for a critical security update to be released off-cycle, Microsoft releases all security updates once a month, on the second Tuesday of the month. This change has greatly simplified the planning and deployment of patches.

The Patching Cycle

There are, or should be, four basic phases in the ongoing cycle of maintaining a well-patched and up-to-date network:

- Assess
- Identify
- Evaluate and plan
- Deploy

Each of these phases is essential to the successful management of patches on your network. Depending on the size and complexity of your network, you might combine phases and even bypass them on occasion. However, it's good to have an understanding of the phases and to think through the steps involved in each one, even if you're combining them.

Assess

The *assess* phase of patch management is all about understanding what your environment is, where and how it is vulnerable and can be attacked, and what resources and procedures are in place to ameliorate those vulnerabilities.

When a patch is released, you can't make an informed decision about whether you need to install that patch unless you first know what software is present in your environment and which of your critical business assets must absolutely, positively be protected. So the first step to an overall patch management process is to figure out what software is running in your environment. All of it, hopefully. Whether you build a big spreadsheet, have a fully relational database, or use an enterprise tool such as System Center Configuration Manager, you need to get your software environment audited and documented. If you don't know what you have, you don't know what patches you need. It's just that simple.

Identify your critical business assets. Is there confidential data that you couldn't function without? Are there critical systems that must be available at all times? Are there individuals whose productivity is mission-critical? All of these are business assets that you should factor into your overall patch-management strategy.

The next part of the assessment phase is to understand what security threats and vulnerabilities you currently have. Do you have legacy Windows NT 4 systems that are no longer supported? Does your network have Windows 95 or Windows 98 computers? Are you running old versions of software programs that can't be easily updated or replaced? Do you have public-facing Web servers that are not behind your firewall? What are your security policies, and how are they enforced? These and many, many more questions need to be asked. And answered.

Finally, you need to assess your patching infrastructure and resources. How do you deploy software and patches? Who is responsible for identifying, testing, and deploying patches? What resources do they have to help with that? How rapidly can you respond to a critical vulnerability that affects your systems? What steps can you take to improve your response time?

Identify

The *identify* phase is about finding out what software updates or patches are available, and how critical it is that they be deployed in your environment.

You need to do the following:

- Discover the patch.
- Decide whether it's relevant to your environment.
- Download the patch.
- Identify the patch's criticality.

There are many ways to discover patches, but for Microsoft products one of the best ways is to sign up for e-mail alerts. If you do this, Microsoft will send you notifications of security updates before they are actually released. The signup page is at: *http://www.microsoft.com/technet/security/bulletin/notify.mspx*. You can choose how you receive alerts, and what level of detail the alerts contain to suit your needs.

Note The preceding link provides alerts only for security-related patches.

Whatever method you use to discover patches, it's important that you have a way to trust the source of the patch information. All Microsoft security update alerts are signed with a publicly available PGP key, for example. And it *shouldn't* be necessary to say this, but just in case: *Microsoft will never send a security update as an attachment to an e-mail!* Never.

Once you know about a patch, you need to decide whether it's relevant to your environment. If all your client machines are running Windows XP Professional SP2 or Windows Vista (and they should be!), a patch that applies only to Windows 2000 isn't really relevant to your environment. However, if the patch is a critical security update for Microsoft Office 2007, and you run that in your environment, you'll need to apply it.

When you determine that a patch is relevant to your environment, you need to obtain the patch *from a known and trusted source*. For a Microsoft patch, this means downloading it directly from Microsoft–either automatically, using Windows Server Update Services (WSUS) or another tool, or directly by going to Windows Update or to the relevant Knowledge Base article for the patch. If you go the KB article, cut and paste the link to the download page directly into your browser. Do *not* click the link in an e-mail to get your patch. Even when you have verified that the e-mail is really from Microsoft and is a legitimate e-mail, you still shouldn't click the links in it. Get into the habit of always using cut and paste. When you use cut and paste to put a link into your browser, you greatly reduce the likelihood of a *phishing* attack–that is, being unknowingly redirected to a site that looks *exactly* like the site you expected to go to, but is actually a site designed to steal information from you or download unwanted spyware onto your computer.

Note Most e-mail clients today have the ability to force all e-mail to display as plain text. This is a *good thing*, because it prevents unscrupulous people from hiding the real destination of a link. The giveaway for detecting a bogus link will usually be that it's a link to an IP address, not the actual DNS domain name—or if it is a DNS name, it's not exactly the one you think it is. If you make the change to only reading e-mail in plain text, your e-mail won't be as pretty, but you'll give yourself an additional layer of protection from phishing attacks.

To enable plain text e-mail handling in Outlook 2003, select Options from the Tools menu. Click the Preferences tab, then click E-Mail Options. Select the Read All Standard Mail In Plain Text, and Read All Digitally Signed Mail In Plain Text check boxes. Click OK and restart Outlook.

After you've downloaded the patch and read the associated Knowledge Base article, you are in a position to determine just how critical the patch is in your environment. Is this a patch that you need to deploy immediately, with limited testing, or even with no testing? Or are there ameliorating factors that allow the patch to be deployed as part of a regular patching schedule after full testing?

Evaluate and Plan

The *evaluate and plan* phase of patch management flows naturally out of the identify phase, and in many ways is an extension of it. In this phase, you determine how to respond to the software update you've downloaded. Is it critical, or even necessary? How should it be deployed? And to whom? Should interim countermeasures be employed that will minimize your exposure to the vulnerability? What priority does the patch have?

The initial determination of need, suitability, and priority is made during the identify phase, but in the evaluate and plan phase, you should take a closer look at the patch. What priority is the patch? If it affects a critical business asset, and there's no easy or appropriate countermeasure except the patch, it will have a higher priority for testing and deployment than if you can implement a simple countermeasure until the patch can be deployed. If the patch targets critical business assets, it's going to have a higher priority than if the only computers affected are several old Windows 98 machines that aren't running any critical business applications and aren't allowed to connect to the Internet.

Once you've identified the priority of the patch, you need to plan the actual deployment. Which computers need to have the patch deployed to them? Do any constraints or issues interfere with the deployment? Who needs to be notified, and what steps need to be taken so that the deployment minimizes the disruption to the environment? If this is an emergency release, will it go through a staged deployment, or is every affected computer going to have the patch deployed as soon as possible?

Deploy

The *deployment* phase of patch management is in many ways the easiest. You've done all your preparatory work, now all you need to do is the actual deployment.

First and foremost, *communicate*. Let everyone who will be affected know that you will be deploying a patch, and what application or area of the operating system it affects. If you know that the deployment will cause changes in behavior, tell your users *before* the deployment. You will have far fewer support calls if you've warned people that a certain behavior is expected than if you surprise them.

Depending on what the priority of the patch is and how many computers it affects, you should test your deployment on a subset of the computers or on your test network. If no problems are reported, you can extend the deployment to additional users.

Repeat

The four phases of patch management are circular: when you've finished the last phase–deployment–it's time to start the first phase–assessment–all over again. You should, at the very least, verify that the patch has been successfully deployed to the affected computers. Update your software map and database so that you know which computers have had the patch applied. If the vulnerability required you to make other changes in addition to, or instead of, a patch, make sure that those nonpatch countermeasures have been successfully deployed as well. Verify that the patch hasn't caused issues for your end users that were missed during the testing of the patch.

Deployment Testing

Sometimes a patch is so critical and such an emergency that you simply have to deploy it immediately and hope that it doesn't cause too many other problems. We hope that doesn't happen to you too often, and it shouldn't if you have a good defense-in-depth approach to protecting your network. But when it does, do the deployment–you might have some issues on some computers, but the risks of serious problems from the vulnerability are a good deal more serious.

For all the rest of your patch deployments, however, it's basic good practice to test the deployment before you roll it out to all the computers on your network. We like to use a three-stage deployment approach, though there are excellent arguments for adding additional stages into the process. We use the following three deployment stages:

- Test Network
- Beta Users
- Full

Test Network Deployment

In an ideal IT world, we would have a test network that included all the hardware and software configurations of all our client and server computers. We could then test-deploy patches, software updates, and new software applications to this test network before we deployed them in the production network. We'd also have a dedicated team to actually *use* all our applications and configurations to ensure that there weren't incompatibilities that only daily use would identify.

Well, in the real world, most of us don't have the luxury of that kind of setup, unfortunately. But by using virtualization technologies, such as Windows Hyper-V (discussed in Chapter 29, "Virtualization") and VMWare Workstation 6, we can do a very good job of emulating a full test network on one or two servers.

At this point, you might be asking why we are recommending both Windows Virtualization and VMWare Workstation 6. Don't they perform much the same functions? And aren't they competing products? Well, yes, they perform very similar functions, though with a completely different interface; and yes, they are competing. But each has strengths and weaknesses, and can do some things a good deal better than the other. We like Windows Virtualization, and it has the distinct advantage of being built into Windows Server 2008, simplifying training, licensing, and support. But not all your servers will instantly be running Windows Server 2008, and besides, Windows Virtualization won't be available until after Windows Server 2008 is released, and has very specific hardware requirements. You could use Microsoft Virtual Server 2005 R2 SP1, and we do in some situations. But it won't virtualize 64-bit guests, which creates a significant problem. With x64 playing an increasingly significant role in our environment, we use VMWare Workstation 6 to test x64 patches. VMWare Workstation 6 fully supports x64 guests, giving us much more flexibility to test patches on all our environments before we actually deploy them.

Beta User Deployment

Once you've tested the deployment of a patch or software update on your test network, you should test the deployment in a controlled release to a dedicated group of users before deploying across the entire enterprise. No matter how much testing you do in a test lab, you can never completely replicate what real users will do. It's much easier to find a problem and address it when you're dealing with a limited beta deployment than dealing with a full scale, enterprise-wide deployment that has problems.

For your beta-user deployments, you should build a dedicated team of real users from across the company for your beta team. They should cover as broad a range of user types and configurations as possible, but all need to be willing and able to both identify and deal with problems that the patch or software update might cause, while communicating clearly exactly what the problem is.

Building a beta team is just like building any other team–you need to make them part of the process, give them ownership of the process, and reward them for being on the team. Rewards can, and should, be simple and appropriate. Public recognition of their efforts and their importance to the protection of your network assets is often the most compelling and appropriate reward.

Full Deployment

The final phase of patch deployment is to roll it out to the entire organization. Even though you've tested it thoroughly, and your beta testers have also tested it thoroughly, the possibility remains that there will be problems when you deploy the update across the entire enterprise. Be prepared for an extra support load on the days immediately following a major deployment. And make sure you communicate completely with your user community. They should know that they're going to be getting a new software update *and* be warned about specific problems if they develop.

Obtaining Updates

Microsoft has three basic methods for updating client and server computers: automatic updates from the Windows (or Microsoft) Update site, Windows Server Update Services (WSUS), and System Center Configuration Manager (SCCM).

Automatic Updates

Automatic updates, using either Windows Update or Microsoft Update sites, is not a great option for most enterprise environments. It takes control of which updates are applied–and when–out of the hands of the system administrators and makes it difficult to know who has what patch applied.

For a small business, with fewer than 20 clients, automatic updates from Windows Update or Microsoft Update is probably an appropriate solution. Even here, though, we'd recommend setting your clients to automatically download updates but not install them. That will allow you to have one or two people test the release before you tell everyone else to go ahead and install it.

Windows Server Update Services

Windows Server Update Services (WSUS) has been through several name changes, along with the accompanying acronym changes, but the name seems to have finally settled down and the software is now officially released–which is a good thing. WSUS is Microsoft's free software update tool, and it's quite a useful tool. It doesn't have the features and capabilities of SCCM, but most of us don't actually need SCCM, and the costs of implementing SCCM are significant.

Installation

You can install WSUS on the 32-bit and x64 editions of Windows Server 2003 SP1, with the exception of Windows Server 2003 Web Edition, and on the 32-bit and x64 editions of Windows Server 2008, with the exception of Windows Server 2008 Web Edition, or any version of Windows Server 2008 Core. WSUSv3 requires at least Internet Information Server 6, Microsoft Management Console 3.0 (MMCv3), and .NET Framework 2.0 installed prior to installation of WSUS. If SQL Server 2005 SP1 is not already installed, the Windows Internal Database will be installed as part of the installation of WSUS.

Prerequisites

You need to download the necessary files before you begin the installation of WSUS. If your server is not already running Windows Server 2003 SP1 or later, you must first upgrade to at least SP1. Additionally, if you're missing any of the following, you'll need to download them and install prior to attempting to install WSUS v3:

- .NET Framework 2.0, which is available at: *http://go.microsoft.com/fwlink/?LinkId=47358*
- MMCv3, which is available at: *http://www.microsoft.com/downloads/details.aspx?familyid=4C84F80B-908D-4B5D-8AA8-27B962566D9F&displaylang=en*
- Microsoft Report Viewer, which is available at: *http://www.microsoft.com/downloads/details.aspx?FamilyID=e7d661ba-dc95-4eb3-8916-3e31340ddc2c&DisplayLang=en*

In all cases, you must download WSUS itself. You can download WSUS v3 at: *http://www.microsoft.com/downloads/details.aspx?FamilyId=E4A868D7-A820-46A0-B4DB-ED6AA4A336D9&displaylang=en.*

Once you have downloaded the necessary software, you can begin installing the prerequisites:

- Install IIS6 on your Windows Server 2003 WSUS server if it isn't already installed. You can install IIS6 using Add/Remove Programs, Add/Remove Windows Components.
- Install the Application Server Role on your Windows Server 2008 Server if it isn't already installed. Include the Web Server (IIS) Support role service, at a minimum, and add support for IIS 6 Management Compatibility as a Role Service of the Web Server (IIS).
- Install .NET Framework 2.0. If you're running Windows Server 2008, you don't need to install this.
- Install the Microsoft Report Viewer.
- On Windows Server 2008, install the Windows Internal Database Feature if you're not using an existing SQL Server 2005 SP1 database for storage. WSUSv3 isn't able to add this feature directly during the installation on Windows Server 2008.

If any of the prerequisite steps requires a reboot, you need to do that reboot before starting the WSUS installation.

To install Windows Server Update Services, perform the following steps:

1. Complete the prerequisite installations described previously.

2. Navigate to the location where you downloaded WSUS. Double-click WSUS3Setupx86.exe or WSUS3Setupx64.exe as appropriate for the version of Windows Server you're using to begin the installation, and then open the Microsoft Windows Server Update Services 3.0 Setup Wizard.
3. Click Next to open the Installation Mode Selection dialog box. Select Full Server Installation Including Administration Console.
4. Click Next to open the License Agreement dialog box. As usual, you can either agree to the license or cancel the installation.
5. Click Next to open the Select Update Source dialog box, which is shown in Figure 25-1.

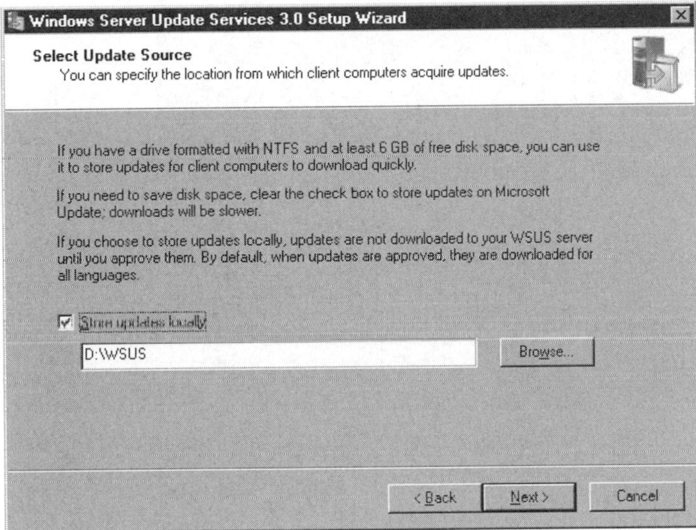

Figure 25-1 The Select Update Source dialog box of the Microsoft Windows Server Update Services 3.0 Setup Wizard

6. Select Store Updates Locally, and enter a location on an NTFS formatted volume. You can also choose to download updates directly from Microsoft, which will slow down updating clients but save on hard drive space.
7. Click Next to open the Database Options dialog box. By default, WSUSv3 uses the Windows Internal Database to store updates. If an existing SQL Server 2005 installation is present or available on the network, you can choose to use the existing database server.
8. Click Next. The Windows Server Update Services 3.0 Setup Wizard will attempt to connect to the database instance you've selected, as shown in Figure 25-2.

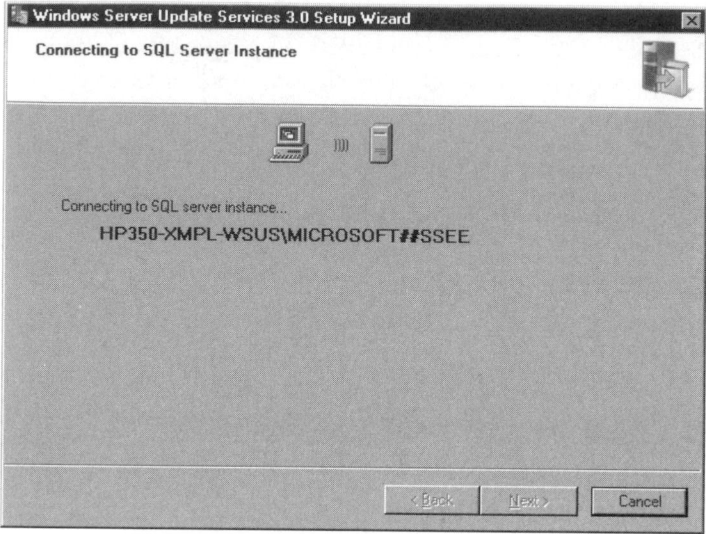

Figure 25-2 The Connecting to SQL Server Instance dialog box of the Microsoft Windows Server Update Services 3.0 Setup Wizard

9. Click Next to open the Web Site Selection dialog box. You can choose to use the IIS Default Web site, or create a special WSUS site.
10. Click Next twice and the actual installation will begin.

Basic Configuration

The basic configuration of WSUS requires you to configure and deal with quite a few things right at the beginning, but then the process should be straightforward. The steps to initial configuration are as follows:

- **Configure networking and proxy settings** WSUS needs to be configured to work with your proxy and firewall server or servers.
- **Configure language and products settings** WSUS downloads a list of languages and products available and needs to be configured for the languages, products, and type of update your network uses.

> **Note** By selecting "All Products" and "All Classifications," any new products or classifications will be automatically selected as they become available.

- **Configure synchronization** You can configure WSUS to automatically synchronize with Microsoft Update up to 24 times a day, or you can have it synchronize manually.

- **Synchronize the WSUS server with Microsoft Update** WSUS downloads the complete list of Critical and Security updates from Microsoft Update for the kinds of client computers on your network. Or you can configure WSUS to use another WSUS server instead of connecting directly to Microsoft Update.
- **Create computer groups** WSUS creates two new groups by default (All Computers and Unassigned Computers), but you'll likely want additional groups, such as Test and Beta groups, to manage the deployment process.
- **Approve and deploy updates** WSUS defaults to automatic approval of critical security updates, but you can change the settings and control details of approval. Software isn't actually downloaded and deployed until approved.

More Info For more information about WSUS, see *http://www.microsoft.com/technet/windowsserver/wsus/default.mspx*.

Systems Center Configuration Manager

Microsoft SCCM is far more than just a patch-management application, it is an entire network and infrastructure management solution. It has the ability to inventory your network; manage network devices; and deploy applications, operating systems, and patches across a diverse enterprise environment. It also has comprehensive reporting and asset-management features.

The setup and deployment costs for SCCM are significant, but the payback for complex environments will be worth it in the long run. If you're managing 50 desktops, don't bother. But if you're managing 500 or more desktops, SCCM is worth investigating.

More Info For more information on SCCM, see *http://www.microsoft.com/smserver/default.mspx*.

Third-Party Products

Patch management continues to be a major source of pain for users and system administrators. And where there is pain, there are those who see an opportunity to help reduce the pain while making a profit. The products that can help manage patches on your Microsoft network range from the fairly simple, which deal only with Microsoft patches, to complete infrastructure management and deployment programs, which can handle extremely complex environments.

Of all the products we've seen, the one we like the best is unquestionably Shavlik's NetChk Protect available at: *http://www.shavlik.com/netchk-protect.aspx*. The original release of Microsoft Baseline Security Analyzer used code written by Shavlik to scan for vulnerabilities. Shavlik NetChk Protect can scan client computers across the network, with or without an agent on the client, and then automatically deploy patches to each computer. It has the ability to handle both Microsoft products and some common third-party products such as Real Audio, WinZip, Adobe Acrobat, and Firefox/Mozilla.

The biggest strength of NetChk Protect, in our opinion, is its deployment engine. From a single central console, you can easily deploy patches and even full service packs to targeted groups of computers, setting the time for the actual deployment and scheduling a reboot if appropriate. Click the button, and the patches are downloaded to the client computers and the actual installation will happen automatically without further intervention.

NetChk Protect scales well from small networks up to quite large ones. You can easily create test networks for beta deployments, and then follow through with the final enterprise deployment with the assurance that the exact same set of parameters and patches will be deployed as on the test network.

Summary

In this chapter we've looked at some of the concepts of patch management, as well as the Microsoft solutions to help you manage and deploy patches and software updates. We also took a quick look at a third-party solution to patch management, Shavlik's NetChk Protect. In the next chapter, we'll cover using Microsoft Certificate Services to manage and deploy certificates on your network.

Chapter 26

Implementing Remote Access Strategies: SSTP, VPN, and Wireless

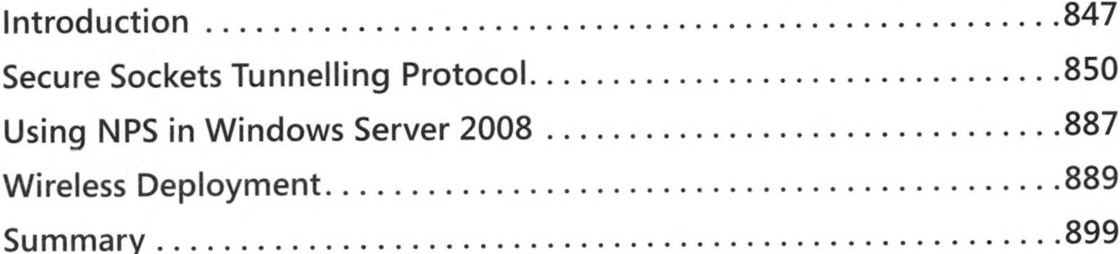

In the old days, remote access meant dialing up to a bank of modems and connecting to your network that way, but in the modern world, remote access has come to mean many different things–Virtual Private Networks (VPNs), Secure Sockets Tunnelling Protocol (SSTP), and wireless connectivity.

Introduction

It's the rare business that does not have a need for remote computing. More and more firms have mobile workers and have to plan for their remote needs. Whether your needs are wireless deployment on the shop floor or ensuring that remote workers can log on from a hotel or remote coffee shop that has a wireless access point, your users need a secure way to connect to network resources. And that means you need a remote access strategy and policy. Arguably the biggest change in remote access is the addition of the Terminal Server Gateway, which is discussed in Chapter 30, "Deploying Terminal Services." But Windows Server 2008 also includes new ways of doing the more familiar remote access strategies, including an updated Remote Authentication Dial-In User Service (RADIUS) server called Network Policy Server.

Network Policy Server

Windows Server 2003 and earlier versions of Windows Server included a RADIUS server—the Internet Authentication Service (IAS)—but in Windows Server 2008, IAS has a new name and expanded functionality. The Network Policy Server Role (NPS) combines the RADIUS server and proxy as well as providing a centralized management tool to deploy and manage Virtual Private Network servers, wireless access points, dial-up servers, and 802.1X deployments, with secure remote access using Protected Extensible Authentication Protocol (PEAP)-MS-CHAP v2 for wireless connections. The following capabilities are included in the Network Policy server:

- **RADIUS server** Authentication, authorization, and accounting for wireless, switches, remote access dial-up, and VPN connections. This includes connections to computers running Terminal Server Gateway. RADIUS clients, including wireless access points and VPN servers, connect to the server.
- **RADIUS proxy** NPS can act as a RADIUS proxy server, forwarding connections to other RADIUS servers.
- **IEEE 802.11 wireless** Wireless access points can use the NPS RADIUS server to process connection requests for wireless clients, providing an 802.1X authentication infrastructure to support WPA2 wireless security.
- **IEEE 802.3 wired** 802.1X-compliant switches can use the NPS RADIUS server to process connection requests for IEEE 802.3 wired clients. As in IEEE 802.11 wireless, you can use the power of the Network Access Policy server to maintain the health and enforce compliance with network policies.
- **SSTP Remote Access** Windows Vista SP1 clients can use the NPS server to enable SSTP VPNs. Firewalls that block Point to Point Tunnelling Protocol (PPTP) and Layer 2 Tunneling Protocol (L2TP) VPNs allow SSTP VPNs.
- **Network Access Policy Server** The Network Access Policy server (discussed in Chapter 24, "Administering Network Access Protection") evaluates the health of clients and controls access to the network based on the health of those.

Planning for NPS

As with any technology solution, begin first by planning and testing. Virtualization, either in the form of Microsoft Virtual Server or Windows Server Virtualization, is an excellent tool for testing a new remote access deployment to ensure that the solution meets your needs and your expectations. Although VPN and wireless are not new, the enforcement and reporting ability of NAP—along with the new capabilities of SSTP VPNs—make thorough testing and validation important before deploying to real users.

Remote access enables portability, flexibility, and increased productivity, but it also increases potential risks to an organization. While all connections, including wired connections, have risks, remote connectivity brings unique risks, especially when using wireless technologies. With wireless, the underlying communication backbone is over the air, which means all network traffic can be captured. That doesn't mean that wireless can't be secure, but it does mean that you need to take the time and care to ensure that you've addressed the risks. Adding security after the solution is deployed is never successful. Deciding early on the tradeoffs between usability, performance, and risk is wise. Until Windows Server 2008 and Windows Vista, deploying IPsec was cumbersome at best. Now the ability to set policies is built into the advanced firewall capabilities.

Real World Wireless Policies

Not protecting your wireless communications can have catastrophic consequences. Recently, retailer TJ Maxx was the victim of an attack on their network through a poorly secured wireless connection. The result was that more than 45 million credit card and debit card users who had shopped at any of TJ Maxx's locations had their card information stolen and resold. Not only are there direct costs for TJ Maxx, but there are also ongoing indirect costs resulting from the damage to customer confidence and trust.

Your wireless connection policies need to be clearly defined and standardized to protect your organization. Wireless connections should use the best available encryption technologies (currently WPA2), and you should consider an independent audit of your wireless security infrastructure if your network includes *any* sensitive customer or employee data.

Start with the Policies

Your remote access policies need to match your organization's technical requirements. Some things to consider include:

- Where existing policies are in place, staff might need training on the new methods and processes used by Windows Vista.
- Periodically audit the remote network for rogue access points, unauthorized wireless, or any other noncompliant technology.
- Audits should align with the policies of the organization as well as relevant regulatory bodies.
- Include regular updating of policies to align with changing security regulations.

- Include regular updating of policies to take advantage of the latest technologies for wireless security. Wire Equivalent Privacy (WEP) is completely unacceptable for encryption, as the TJ Maxx case demonstrates all too well.
- Include regular and clearly defined reevaluations of remote deployments to ensure that they still comply with your security plan as well as meet the changing regulatory needs and technologies that are important to ongoing remote security.

A well designed and implemented remote network can provide the same level of confidentiality, integrity, availability, and access control as a local, wired network.

More Info A useful discussion of wireless security issues and concerns from an overall planning perspective can be found at *http://csrc.nist.gov/publications/nistpubs/800-48/NIST_SP_800-48.pdf.*

Define the Support

A key element in providing seamless and transparent mobility while ensuring appropriate security and privacy is to define the technologies that your firm will support. Standardizing specific client access devices, access points, wireless bridges, and base stations simplifies managing the infrastructure. You may wish to consider standardizing the following technologies:

- Bluetooth devices
- Ultra-Wideband IEE 802.15.3
- IEEE 802.11 a/b/g/n
- IEEE 802.11i/WGA2

Secure Sockets Tunnelling Protocol

Although Network Access Protection (covered in Chapter 24) is one of the new technologies in Windows Server 2008, it's not the only new thing in networking technologies. While Citrix, Cisco, and other vendors have had the ability to tunnel VPN connections over a standard Secure Sockets Layer (SSL) Web port of 443, earlier versions of Windows Server were not able to do this. In Windows Server 2008, Secure Socket Tunneling Protocol (SSTP) enables VPN access over SSL, a port that isn't usually blocked by hotels and other public access locations. In addition, it has integration with Network Access Protection (NAP) and supports native IPv6 traffic. SSTP is integrated into Routing And Remote Access and minimizes network utilization while enabling load balancing through the use of a single HTTP over SSL connection.

The SSTP Process

When a client that has a SSTP configuration for VPN configured, the following steps take place in the session:

1. The SSTP client establishes a TCP connection with the SSTP server. This is a dynamically allocated TCP port on the client, and port 443 (TCP) on the server, as shown in Figure 26-1.

Figure 26-1 The SSTP client establishes the connection.

2. The SSTP client sends an SSL Client Hello message. This indicates that the client wishes to start an SSL session with the SSTP server.
3. The SSTP server sends its computer certificate to the SSTP client, as shown in Figure 26-2.

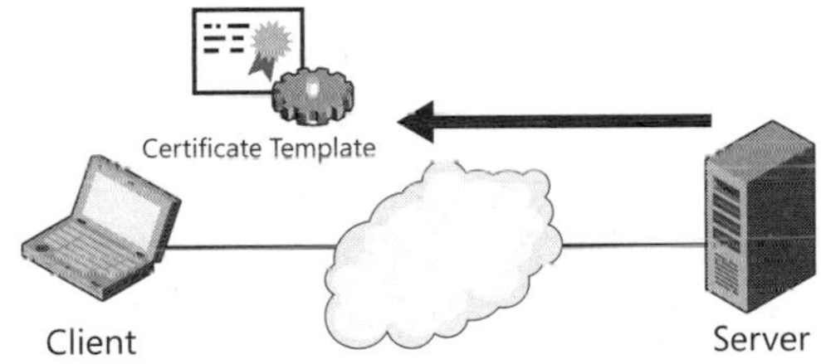

Figure 26-2 The server sends the certificate to the client.

4. The SSTP client validates the certificate. It then determines the encryption method for the Secure Socket Layer session, generates an SSL session key, and then encrypts it with the public key of the SSTP servers' certificate.
5. The SSTP client sends the encrypted form of the SSL session key to the SSTP server.
6. The SSTP server decrypts the encrypted SSL session key. It uses the private key of its computer certificate. At this point, all future communication between the SSTP client and server are encrypted with the negotiated encryption method and SSL session key.
7. The SSTP client sends an HTTP over SSL request message to the SSTP server.
8. The SSTP client negotiates an SSTP tunnel with the SSTP server.

9. The SSTP client now negotiates a PPP connection with the SSTP server. At this point of the negotiation, the negotiation includes authenticating the user's credentials with a PPP authentication method and configuring IPv4 or IPv6 traffic.
10. The SSTP client begins sending IPv4 or IPv6 packets over the PPP link, as shown in Figure 26-3.

Figure 26-3 The client and server have negotiated a secure session over port 443.

Configuring SSTP

When you are deploying SSTP in an actual network, you must determine the appropriate number of servers needed for proper load balancing for remote access. All edge servers supporting SSTP must be running Windows Server 2008 and be domain joined, and the domain must be at the Server 2008 Domain Functional Level.

Note Always begin any project by setting up a test network configuration. Virtual Server or Windows is a perfect way to test your deployment plans.

Installing Prerequisites For SSTP

The server providing SSTP functionality must meet the following criteria:

- Be a Windows Server 2008 computer
- Be joined to a domain with at least one Windows Server 2008 domain controller
- Have a minimum of two NICs

You then install Active Directory Certificate Services and Application Server roles on the server. The Application Server role enables IIS, allowing you to provide Web enrollment of a computer certificate. Because SSTP uses an encrypted SSL connection, these services are required to build the SSL certificate that will be sent to the VPN client during the handshake phase.

Important If you haven't yet added a Windows Server 2008 domain controller to your Active Directory domain, you need to do that first. See Chapter 8, "Installing Server Roles and Features," for details on how to install the AD DS server role.

Configure the Active Directory Certificate Services role on a Windows Server 2008 computer by following these steps:

1. Configure the server with static IP addresses appropriate to your domain. One connection is to the internal LAN; the other is external to the LAN. Depending on your edge configuration, the SSTP server can be on the edge of your network, or, more typically, behind one or more layers of firewall.
2. If the server is not yet a member of the domain, you need to join it to the domain. A restart is required after joining the domain.
3. After the system reboots, from Server Manager, highlight Roles in the left pane and select Add Roles from the Action menu to open the Add Roles Wizard.
4. Click Next and then select Active Directory Certificate Services on the Select Server Roles page, as shown in Figure 26-4.

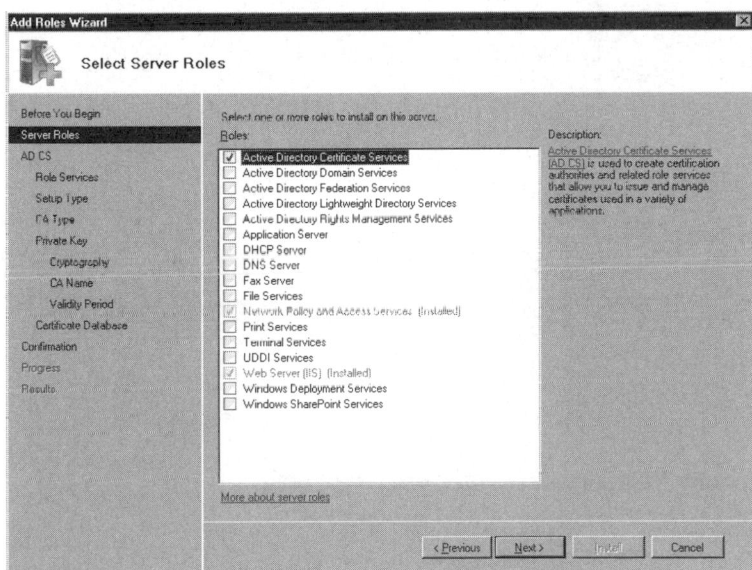

Figure 26-4 Select Active Directory Certificate Services

5. Click Next twice to open the Select Role Services page, as shown in Figure 26-5.

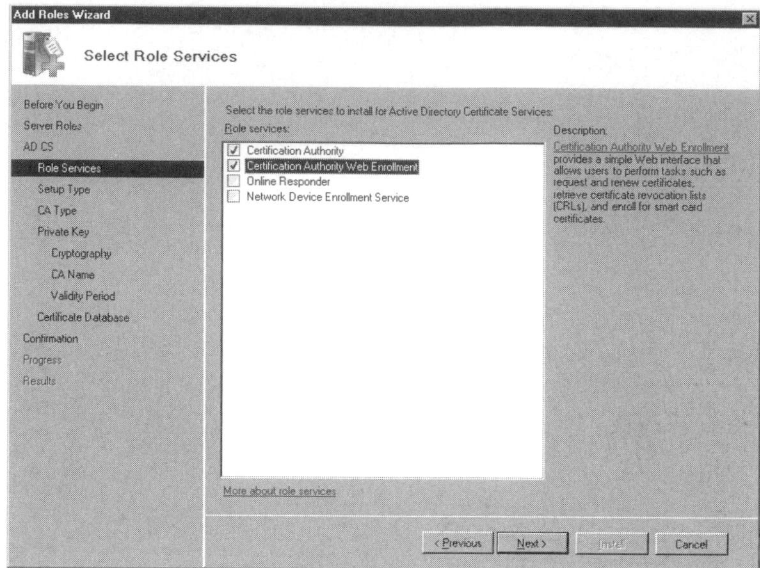

Figure 26-5 Select Certification Authority and Certification Authority Web Enrollment Role Services

6. Select the Certification Authority and Certification Authority Web Enrollment role services. This will open the Add Role Services And Features Required For Certification Authority Web Enrollment confirmation dialog box shown in Figure 26-6.

> **Note** If the Application Server role is already installed, the list of required services will be much shorter or might completely skip this step if all the required services are already installed.

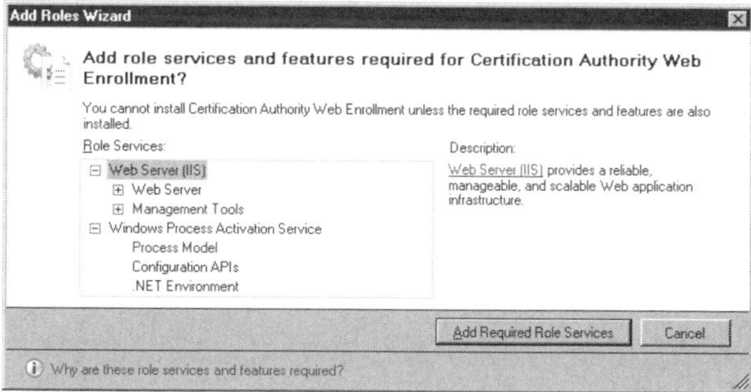

Figure 26-6 The confirmation message before adding all the required role services for Web Enrollment of certificates

7. Review the list of services that will be added and then click Add Required Role Services.

Note An optional step can be to install the Network Device Enrollment Service that allows you to issue and manage certificates for devices without user accounts on your network. To do this, when you select Certificate Authority Web Enrollment, also select Network Device Enrollment Service.

---

8. Click Next to bring up the Specify Setup Type page. Select Enterprise or Standalone CA deployment based on your needs. If in doubt here, review the Under the Hood "Certification Authority Types" sidebar, click the More About The Differences Between Enterprise Or Standalone Setup, or choose Standalone CA.
9. Click Next to bring up the Specify CA Type page shown in Figure 26-7. If this is your first deployment, choose Root CA.

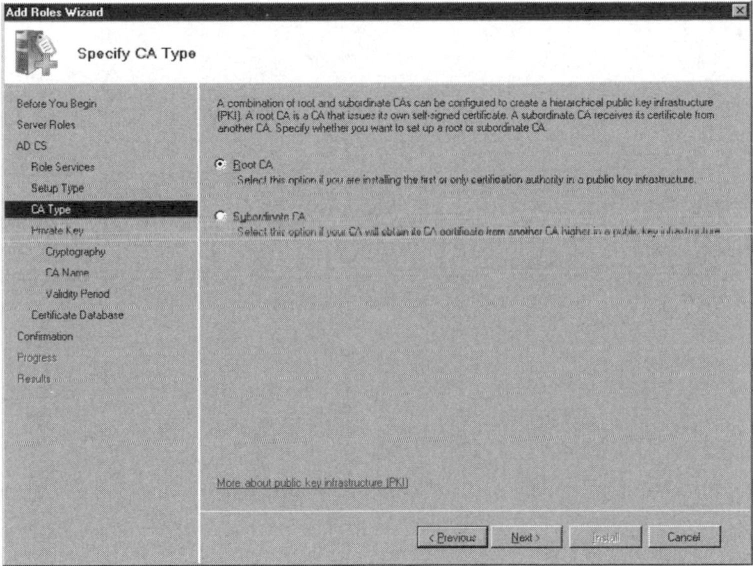

Figure 26-7 The Specify CA Type page of the Add Active Directory Certificate Services Role Wizard

10. Click Next. Choose Create A New Private Key unless you are redeploying.
11. Click Next to bring up the Configure Cryptography For CA page shown in Figure 26-8. Choose the appropriate cryptographic strength based on the needs and policies of your organization. The default is RSA#Microsoft Software Key Storage Provider with a key character length of 2048. If in doubt, this is a good choice. Also

choose a hash algorithm. Generally, accept the default value of sha1 unless you have a known need for a different hash algorithm.

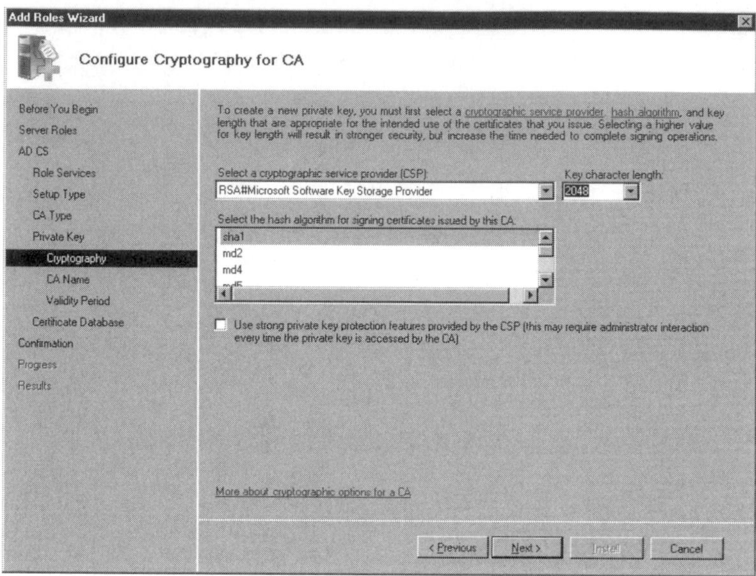

Figure 26-8 The Configure Cryptography For CA page of the Add Active Directory Certificate Services Role Wizard

---

More Info For more information on setting up a Windows Server–based PKI infrastructure, review the guidance in *Windows Server 2008 PKI and Certificate Security* (Microsoft Press, 2008).

12. Click Next to open the Configure CA Name page. The default selection is generally a good choice unless you have a known specific need to change it.
13. Click Next. Specify the length of time the certificate will be valid. The default is 5 years.
14. Click Next to specify the location of the Certificate Database. Don't change this location without a good reason.
15. Click Next to install the necessary Web Server role if Web Services are not already running on the server.
16. Click Next to open the Select Role Services dialog box for the Web Server role. The default selections shown in Figure 26-9 will provide the necessary services for the Active Directory Certificate Service role.

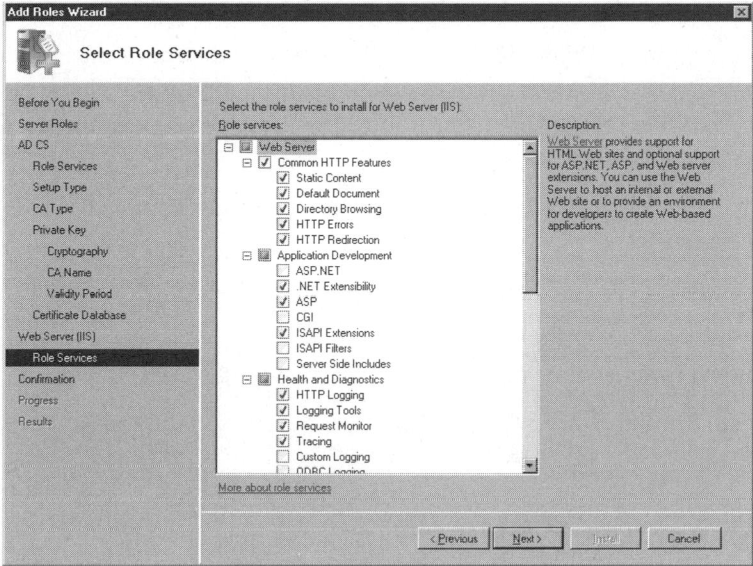

Figure 26-9 The Select Role Services page for the Web Server role installation

17. Click Next to open the Confirm Installation Selections page. This will include a warning that you can't change the name or the domain of the server once the installation completes.
18. Click Install to begin the installation. Click Close when the installation completes.

Under the Hood **Certificate Authority Types**

When choosing a certificate authority, you are faced with the option of Enterprise or Standalone. Generally speaking, you would normally think to pick Enterprise if you are deploying certificates for a domain. An Enterprise CA is integrated with Active Directory. Deployment can be done silently to workstations. Standalone CA certificate deployments, on the other hand, need administrator intervention. They must be requested and then approved. The advantage they have, however, is that they don't just offer up certifications for domain use, but can be used when non-domain-joined clients need to request a certificate to connect to the domain. Thus when one needs a secure certificate for remote needs, intranets, or other deployments where Web and Internet use is a must, Standalone is the preferred method.

Installing the Server Authentication Certificate

Before you can configure SSTP, you need to install a Server Authentication certificate on the gateway server. To install this certificate, you'll need to temporarily change the settings for Internet Explorer on the server. Once you've installed the certificate, you should revert the settings to match.

1. Click Start, right-click Internet Explorer, and select Run As Administrator to open Internet Explorer.
2. Select Tools from the Tools menu and choose Internet Options, then click the Security tab.
3. With the Local Intranet zone highlighted, click Custom Level.
4. Select Prompt For Initialize And Script ActiveX Controls Not Marked Safe, as shown in Figure 26-10.

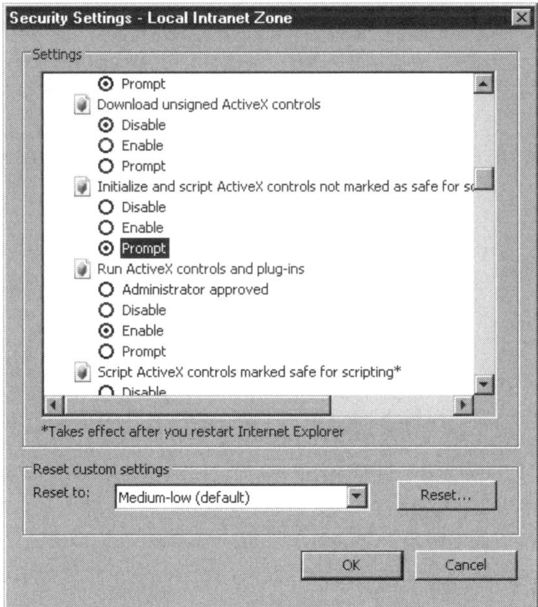

Figure 26-10 Security Settings for the Intranet Zone

5. Click OK, click Yes, and click OK again.
6. In Internet Explorer, navigate to http://localhost/certsrv to bring up the page shown in Figure 26-11.

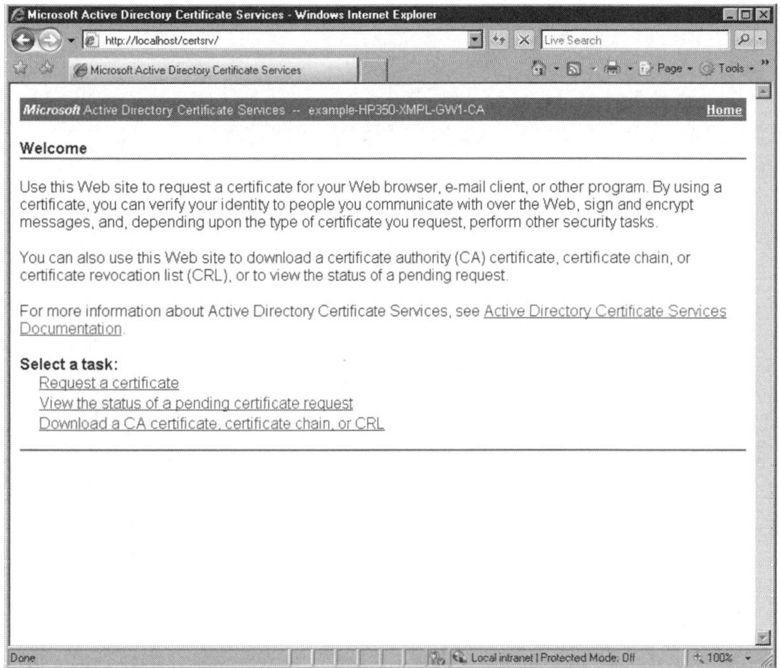

Figure 26-11 The Microsoft Active Directory Certificate Services page for requesting a certificate

7. Click Request A Certificate, and then click Advanced Certificate Request.
8. Click Create And Submit A Request To This CA.
9. Click Yes to allow the resulting ActiveX control.
10. Fill in the Identifying Information fields. The Name field must match the publicly resolvable DNS name of your VPN gateway server, such as remote.example.com for our example network.

> **Note** The Identifying Information fields must match your environment, especially the Name field. The DNS name for SSTP connection settings must match the Certificate Subject name. The screen shot for Figure 26-12 is only appropriate for our example network. Yours will be different.

11. Choose Server Authentication Certificate in the Type Of Certificate Needed drop-down list, as shown in Figure 26-12.

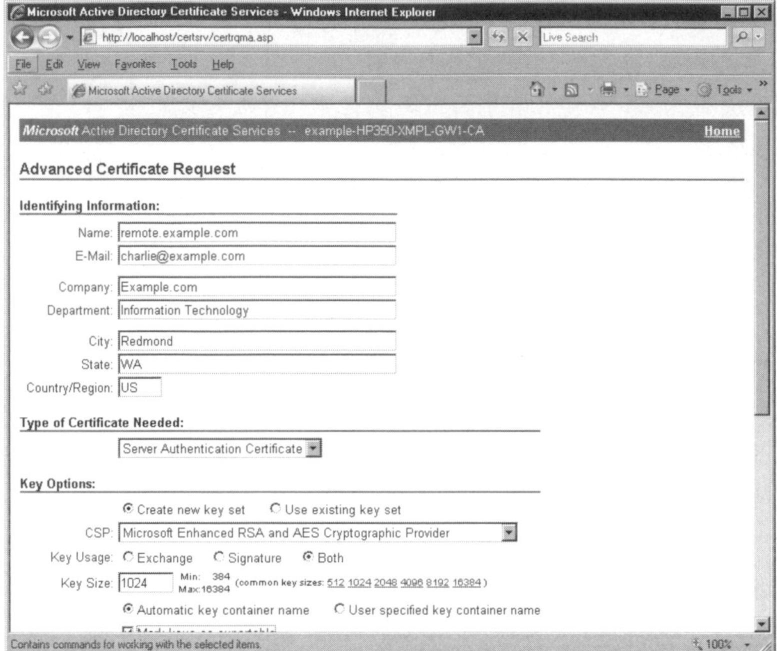

Figure 26-12 The Advanced Certificate Request form for a Server Authentication Certificate

12. In the Key Options sections, review the settings. Take the defaults unless you have a compelling reason to change them. The default is a CSP of Microsoft Enhanced RSA and AES Cryptographic.
13. Select Both as the default for Key Usage.
14. Choose the key size according to your needs. The default is 1024.
15. Select Mark Keys As Exportable.
16. Click Submit, and then click Yes on the Web Access Confirmation page.
17. The server certificate is now pending, as shown in Figure 26-13.

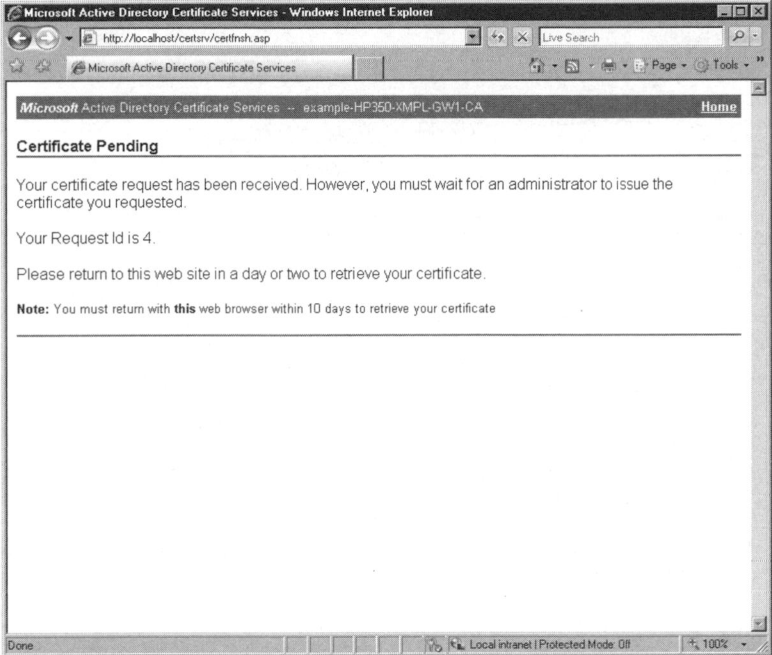

Figure 26-13 The Certificate request is now in pending mode.

Follow these steps to issue and install the Server Authentication Certificate:

1. In Server Manager, open Roles, expand Active Directory Certificate Services, and then select the certificate authority you created in the preceding steps, as shown in Figure 26-14. Or open the Certificate Authority directly by running `certsrv.msc`.

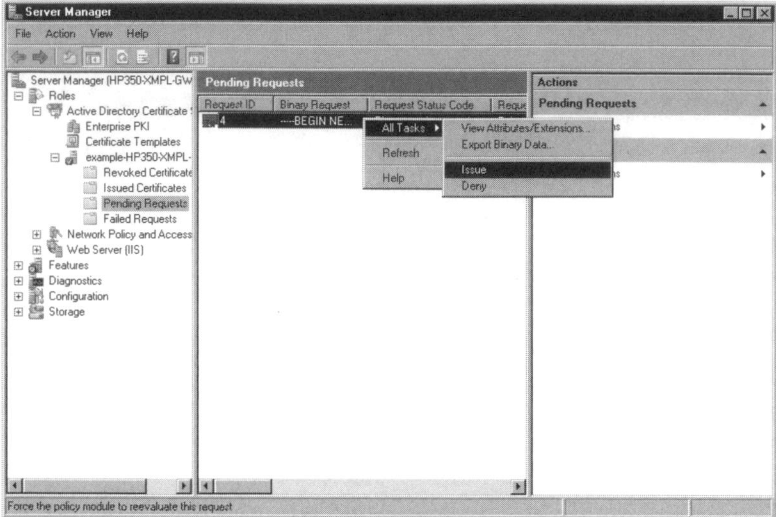

Figure 26-14 The Certificate Authority console of the Active Directory Certificate Services role in Server Manager

2. Select Pending Requests to see the pending certificate request.
3. Select the pending Server Authentication Certificate request. Right-click and then select Issue from the All Tasks menu.
4. Verify that the certificate is now in the Issued Certificates folder.
5. To view that the certificate has been issued on the server, log on to http://localhost/certsrv with Internet Explorer 7 (running as administrator) and click View The Status Of A Pending Certificate Request.
6. On the View The Status Of A Pending Certificate Request page, you should see a link for the certificate you requested, as shown in Figure 26-15.

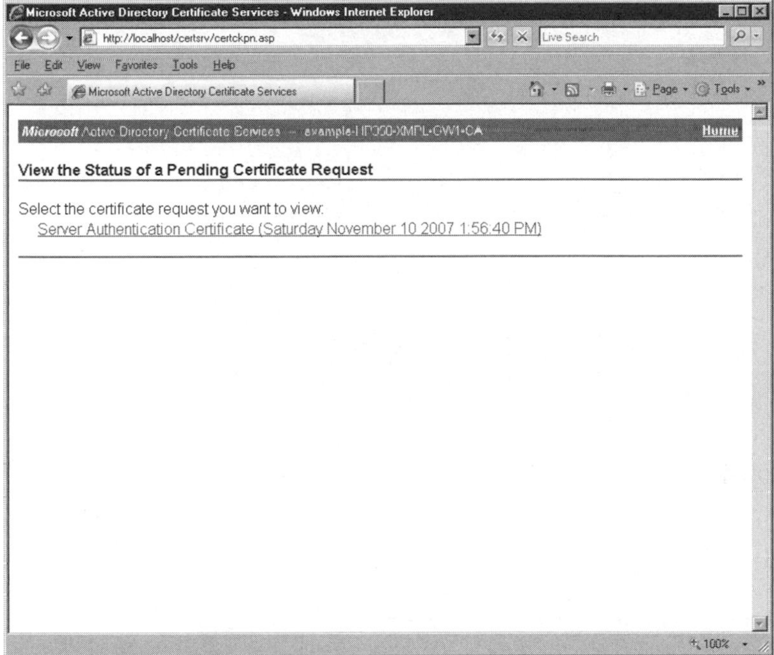

Figure 26-15 The View Status Of A Pending Certificate Request page

7. Click the link for the Server Authentication Certificate you requested and click Yes on the ActiveX warning.
8. Click Install This Certificate.
9. Click Yes in the Web Access Confirmation dialog box to confirm the installation.

Important Don't forget to change the security settings for Internet Explorer 7 back to their default state.

Moving the Certificate

After the certificate has been issued, the next step is move it to the default store location in the personal certificate store by following these steps:

1. Open a blank MMC console by typing **MMC** at a command prompt.
2. Click Add/Remove Snap-In from the File menu to open the Add Or Remove Snap-ins dialog box shown in Figure 26-16.

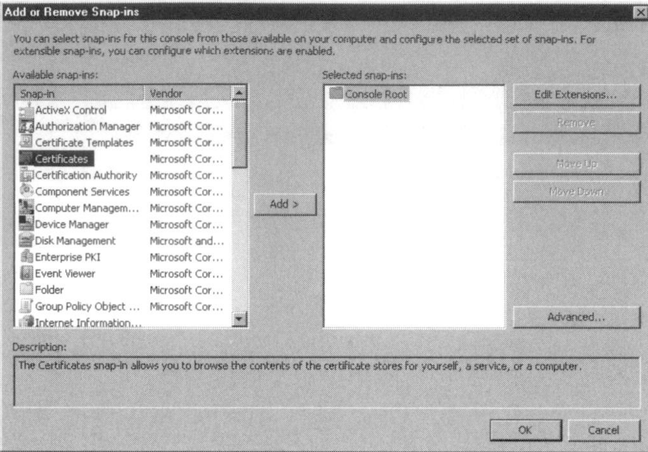

Figure 26-16 The Add Or Remove Snap-In dialog box

3. Select Certificates and click Add. Select Computer Account from the Certificates Snap-in dialog box, as shown in Figure 26-17.

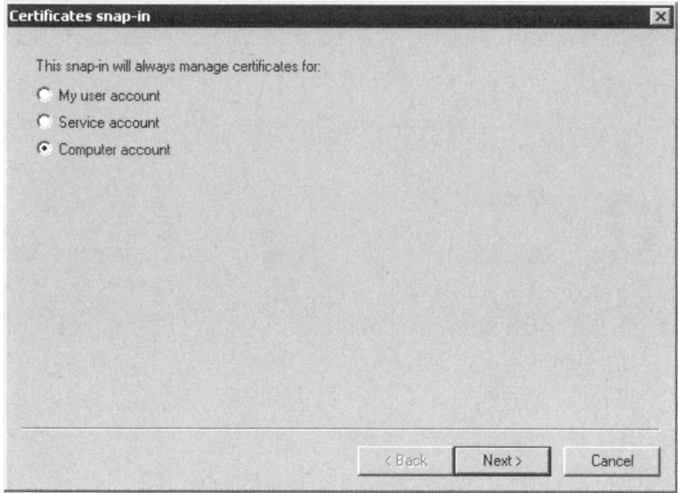

Figure 26-17 The Certificates Snap-In dialog box

4. Select Local Computer (The Computer This Console Is Running On) in the Select Computer dialog box and then click Finish.
5. Select Certificates and click Add. Select My User Account from the Certificates Snap-In dialog box.
6. Click Finish then click OK.
7. Expand the Certificates-Current User in the left pane, expand the Personal folder, and then select Certificates. Figure 26-18 shows the requested and issued certificate in the center pane.

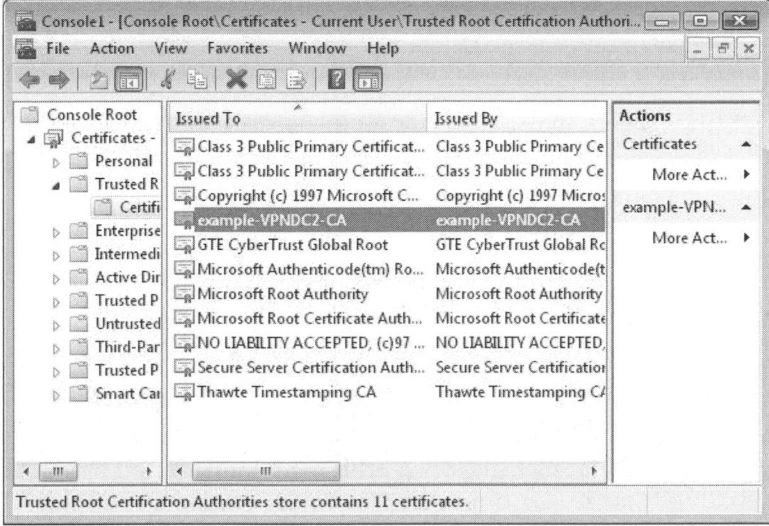

Figure 26-18 The Current User Personal Certificate including the certificate just requested

8. Right-click the certificate and select Export from the All Tasks menu. Click Next on the Welcome To The Certificate Export Wizard page.
9. Select Yes, Export The Private Key, and click Next to open the Export File Format page, shown in Figure 26-19.

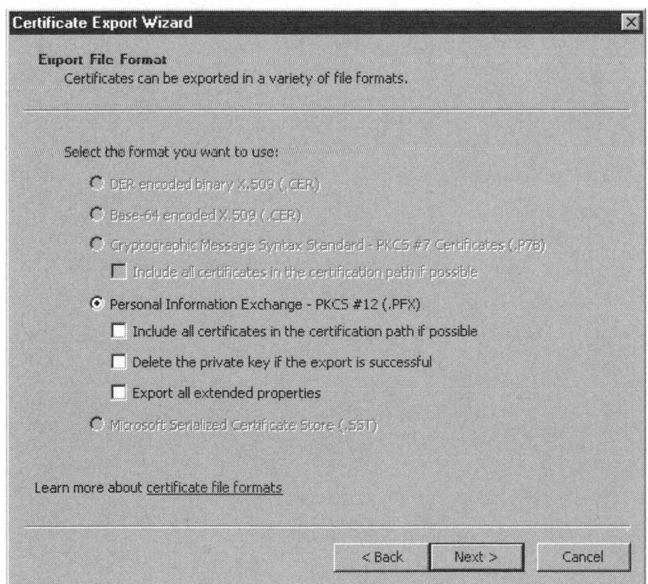

Figure 26-19 The Export File Format page of the Certificate Export Wizard

Important Certificates created with Windows Server 2008 must have the key marked as exportable for the certificate to be portable.

If it is your firm's policy to delete the local private key if the export is successful, choose that option.

10. Select Delete The Private Key If The Export Is Successful if your organization's PKI policy requires it.
11. Click Next to open the Password page. Enter a password to protect the key in transit and confirm that password.
12. Click Next to open the File To Export page. Click Browse and browse to a location where you can easily retrieve the exported key. Enter a filename and click Save to return to the File To Export page.
13. Click Next to open the Completing The Certificate Export Wizard page. Click Finish to actually export the certificate and click OK to acknowledge that it was exported.
14. Expand the Certificates (Local Computer) in the left pane, expand the Personal folder, and then select Certificates.
15. Right-click Certificates and select Import from the All Tasks menu to open the Certificate Import Wizard.
16. Click Next on the Welcome To The Certificate Import Wizard page to open the File To Import page shown in Figure 26-20.

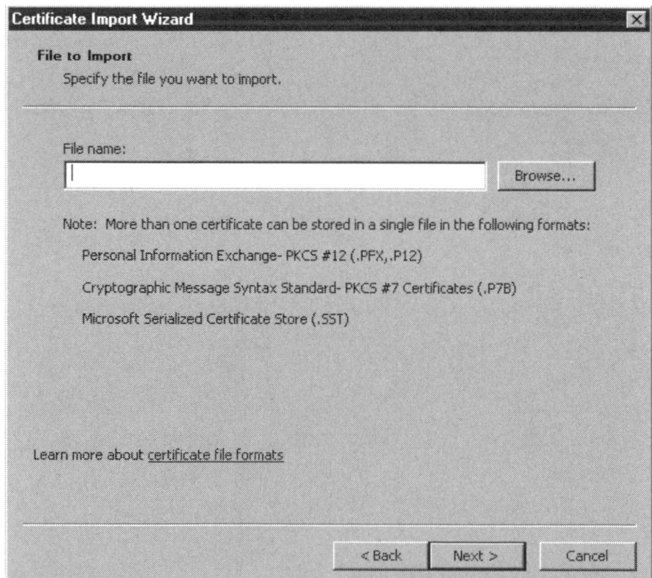

Figure 26-20 The File To Import page of the Certificate Import Wizard

17. Browse to the location where you saved the exported certificate. Change the File Type to Personal Information Exchange (*.pfx, *.pf12), select the certificate, and click Open to return to the File To Import page.
18. Click Next to open the Password page shown in Figure 26-21.

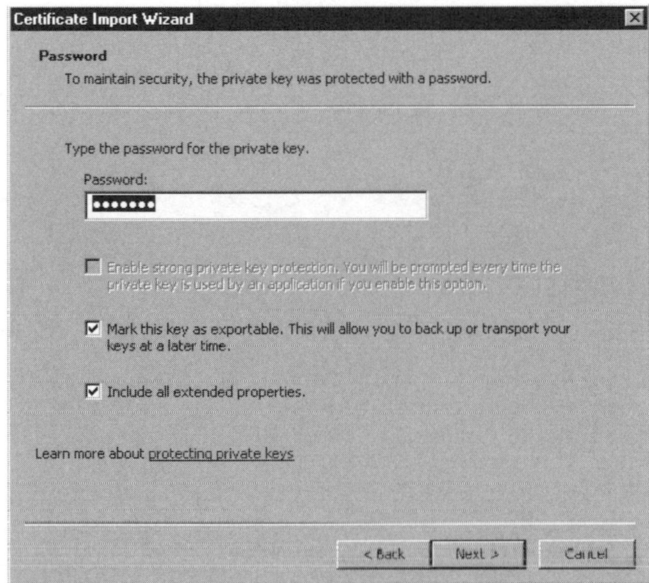

Figure 26-21 The Password page of the Certificate Import Wizard

19. Enter the password you protected the export with and select Mark This Key As Exportable.
20. Click Next to open the Certificate Store page. Select Place All Certificates In The Following Store and browse to Personal if it isn't already selected, as shown in Figure 26-22.

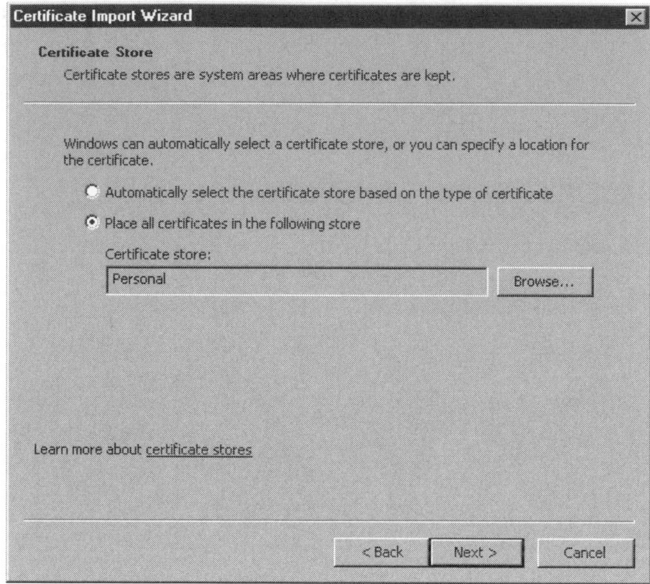

Figure 26-22 The Certificate Store page of the Certificate Import Wizard

21. Click Next and then click Finish to import the certificate. Click OK to acknowledge that the import was successful.

Note A good fundamental understanding of PKI and public certificates will be helpful in the Windows Server 2008 era.

Important Don't forget to change the security settings for Internet Explorer 7 back to their default state.

Installing Routing And Remote Access

Routing And Remote Access (RRAS) is a role service of the Network Policy And Access Services role. It can act both as a routing service–providing a gateway for computers on the local network to access the Internet–and as a Remote Access Service, allowing selected remote computers onto the local network. To add the RRAS role service, follow these steps to install the Network Policy And Access Services role (if it isn't already installed):

1. In Server Manager, launch the Add Roles Wizard by selecting Add Roles from the Action menu.

2. Click Next and select Network Policy And Access Services from the Select Server Roles page of the Add Roles Wizard.
3. Click Next to open an informational page on Network Policy And Access Services. Use the links on this page for additional information on the various aspects of Network Policy And Access Services.
4. Click Next to open the Select Role Services page. Select Routing And Remote Access Services, as shown in Figure 26-23.

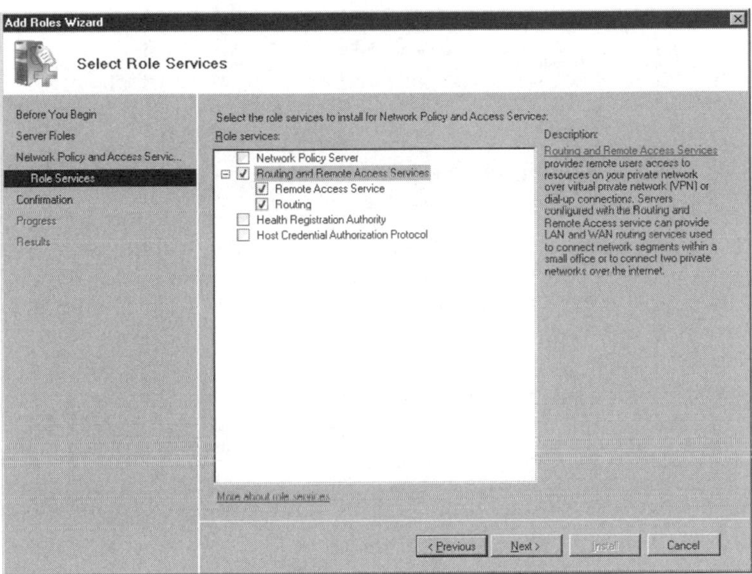

Figure 26-23 Selecting Routing And Remote Access Services on the Select Role Services page

5. Click Next open the Confirm Installation Selections page. This page includes a warning that a reboot might be required. It wasn't required on our test network.
6. Click Install to begin the installation and click Close when the installation is complete.

Configuring Routing And Remote Access

Once the RRAS role service is installed, follow these steps to configure it. The RRAS initial configuration is controlled by the Configure And Enable Routing And Remote Access Wizard.

1. Open the Routing And Remote Access console (rrasmgmt.msc), as shown in Figure 26-24, or navigate to Routing And Remote Access in the left pane of Server Manager.

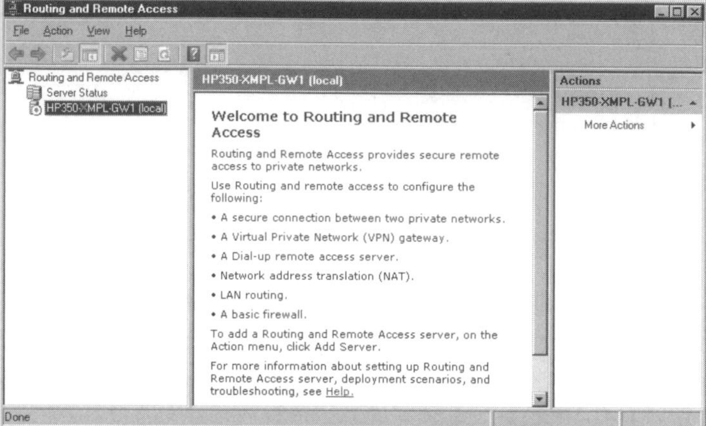

Figure 26-24 The Routing And Remote Access console

Note The view we've chosen to show here is with the Action pane visible as the right-hand pane. If your view of the Routing And Remote Access console doesn't display the Action pane, you can change the view by selecting Customize from the View menu.

2. Select the server in the left pane and select Configure And Enable Routing And Remote Access from the Action menu to open the Routing And Remote Access Server Setup Wizard.
3. Click Next to open the Configuration page of the Routing And Remote Access Server Setup Wizard, as shown in Figure 26-25.

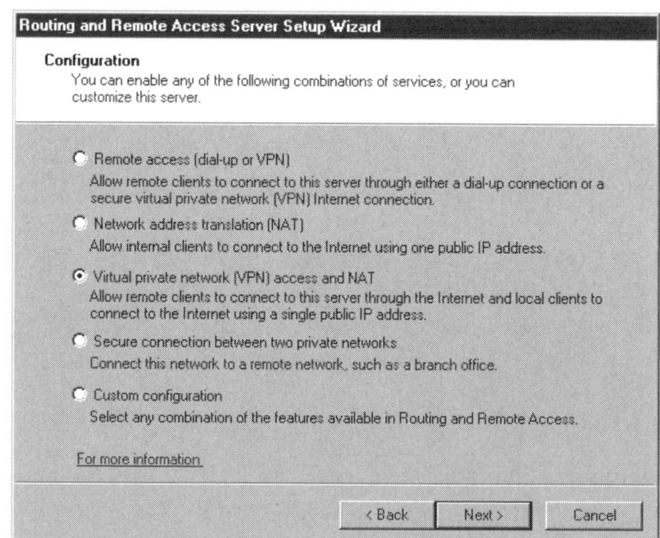

Figure 26-25 The Configuration page of the Routing And Remote Access Server Setup Wizard

4. Choose the type of configuration this RRAS server will have from the five choices shown:
   - **Remote Access (Dial-up Or VPN)** Enables remote client access using either direct dial-up or a VPN.
   - **Network Address Translation (NAT)** Enables network clients to connect to the Internet with all clients sharing a single visible IP address.
   - **Virtual Private Network (VPN) Access And NAT** Combines the first two options to enable the server to be a general-purpose gateway server.
   - **Secure Connection Between Two Private Networks** Enables one end of a secure VPN tunnel between two private networks, such as between a head office and a branch office.
   - **Custom Configuraton** Lets you choose any combination of specific features available.

   Important You can't easily run this initial configuration wizard again, so it's important that you choose all the options you're planning to need on this server. For this example, we've chosen the VPN plus NAT combination, but if your choice is different you'll see different screens in the wizard.

5. Select Virtual Private Network (VPN) Access And NAT and click Next to open the VPN Connection page shown in Figure 26-26.

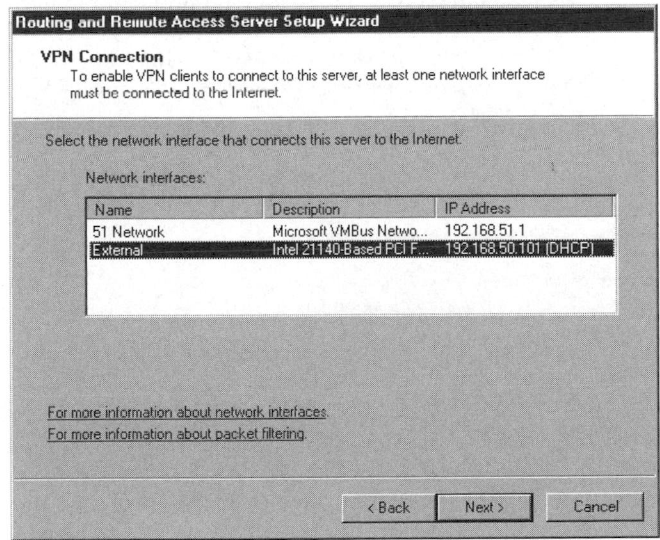

Figure 26-26 The VPN Connection page of the Routing And Remote Access Server Setup Wizard

6. Select the network interface that connects your server to the Internet (External in our case).
7. Click Next to open the IP Address Assignment page shown in Figure 26-27. Select Automatically if your network has a DHCP server available to provide network addresses for VPN clients. Select From A Specified Range Of Addresses if you want the VPN Server to assign addresses from a pool of addresses you set up.

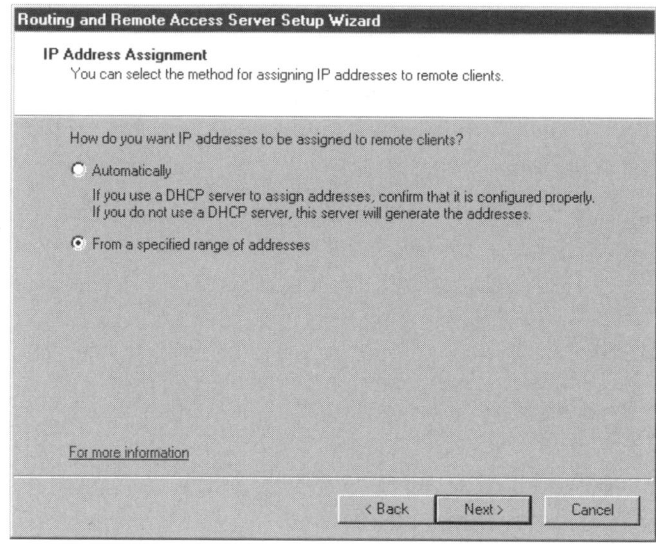

Figure 26-27 The IP Address Assignment page of the Routing And Remote Access Server Setup Wizard

8. If you selected From A Specified Range Of Addresses, follow these additional steps:
   a. Click Next to open the Address Range Assignment page.
   b. Click New to open the New IPv4 Address Range page shown in Figure 26-28.

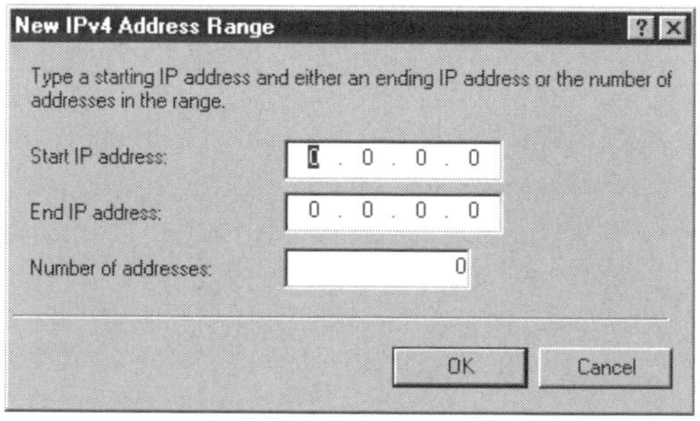

Figure 26-28 The New IPv4 Address Range page of the Routing And Remote Access Server Setup Wizard

c. Enter a starting and stopping address in the range used by your network and click OK to return to the Address Range Assignment page. You can add additional ranges by clicking New again.

9. Click Next to open the Managing Multiple Remote Access Servers page shown in Figure 26-29.

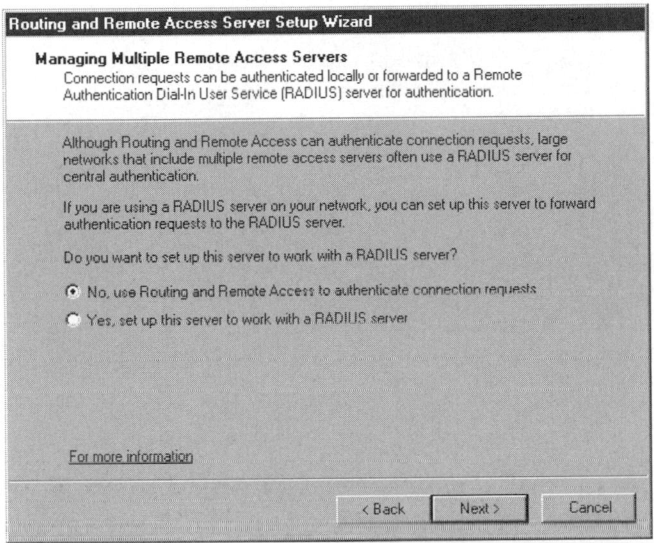

Figure 26-29 The Managing Multiple Remote Access Servers of the Routing And Remote Access Server Setup Wizard

10. If your network doesn't use a RADIUS server, select No, Use Routing And Remote Access To Authenticate Connection Requests and skip to step 12.

11. Select Yes, Set Up This Server To Work With A RADIUS Server.

12. Click Next to open the RADIUS Server Selection page, shown in Figure 26-30.

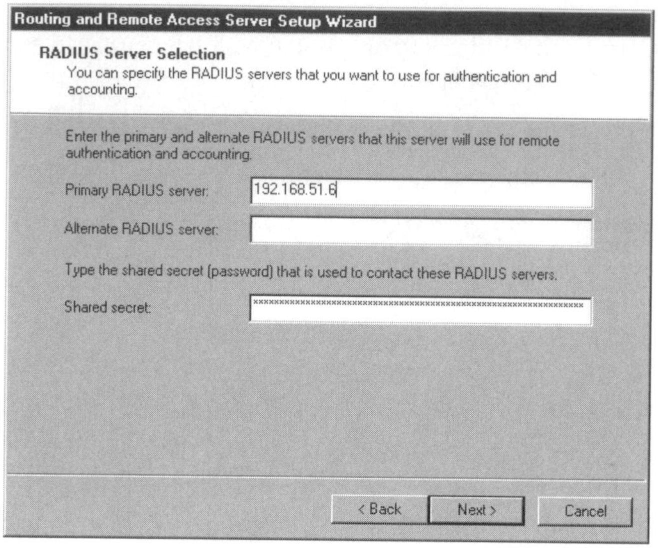

Figure 26-30 The RADIUS Server Selection page of the Routing And Remote Access Server Setup Wizard

a. Enter the DNS name or IP address of your primary RADIUS server.

b. Optionally, enter a DNS name or IP address for a secondary RADIUS server if your network uses multiple RADIUS servers.

c. Enter the shared secret that your RADIUS server has for this computer.

13. Click Next to open the confirmation page, and then click Finish to configure your RRAS server.

14. If you're using your network's DHCP server to provide addresses, you'll see the warning in Figure 26-31. Click OK and the configuration will finish and open the Routing And Remote Access console.

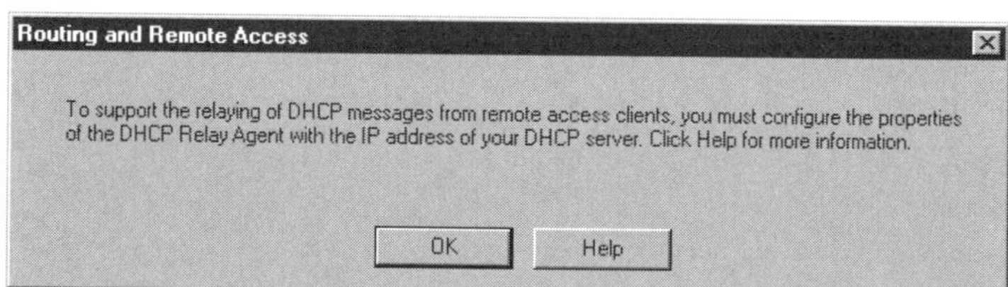

Figure 26-31 The Routing And Remote Access warning about configuring DHCP Relay Agent

To configure RRAS for use with an internal DHCP server, you need to configure the DHCP Relay Agent by following these steps:

1. Open the Routing And Remote Access console if it isn't already open.

2. In the left-hand pane, navigate to the server name and then open the IPv4 section.
3. Select DHCP Relay Agent and then click Properties on the Action menu to open the DHCP Relay Agent Properties dialog box shown in Figure 26-32.

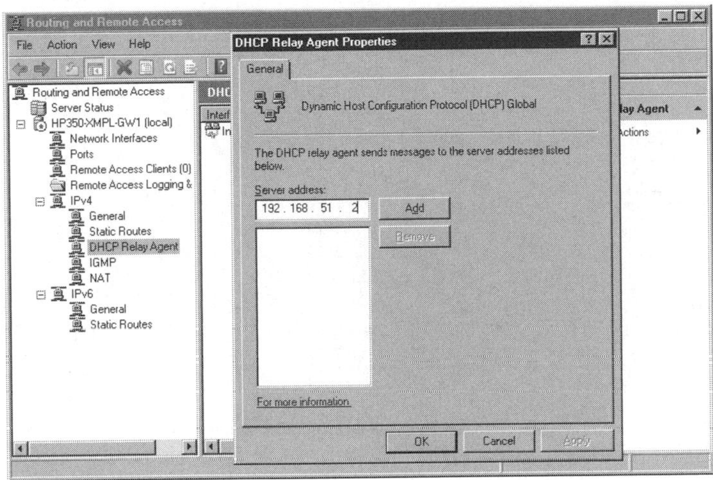

Figure 26-32 The DHCP Relay Agent Properties dialog box

4. Enter the address of your DHCP server and click Add. Repeat if you use multiple DHCP servers.
5. Click OK to complete the DHCP Relay Agent configuration.

That completes the basic configuration of the RRAS settings needed for the SSTP VPN server.

Under the Hood IP Packet Filtering

Routing And Remote Access supports IP packet filtering if you are not configuring the server to support both NAT and VPNs. This allows you to specify what traffic is allowed into and out of the router. The default configuration when packet filtering is enabled uses a basic set of Inbound Deny rules, as detailed in Table 26-1.

Deny rules are designed to exclude *all* traffic except traffic you explicitly allow. This requires you to clearly understand the traffic your network uses and explicitly enable those ports or types of traffic, but we think Deny rules are a far better and more secure method of filtering than Allow rules, which allow everything unless it is explicitly disallowed.

To configure IP packet filtering, follow these steps:

1. Open the Routing and Remote Access console if it isn't already open.

2. In the left-hand pane under the server name, open the IPv4 or IPv6 section and select General.
3. In the Details pane, select the external interface and click Properties on the Action menu to open the Properties page for the interface (see Figure 26-33.)

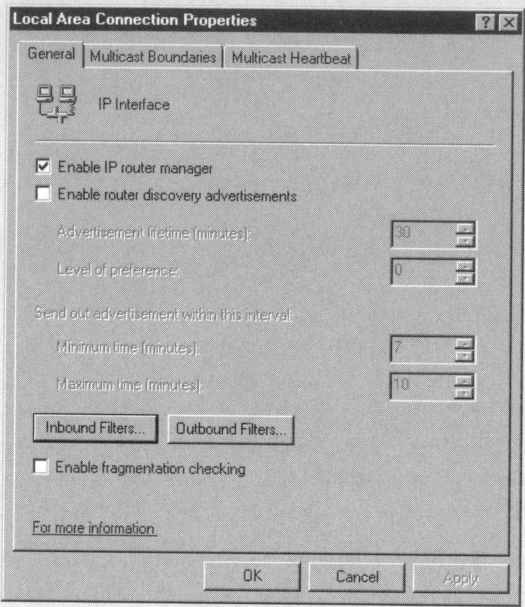

Figure 26-33 The General tab of the public interface's Properties page

4. Click Inbound Filters to open the Inbound Filters dialog box shown in Figure 26-34 or Outbound Filters to open the Outbound Filters dialog box. Both behave the same.

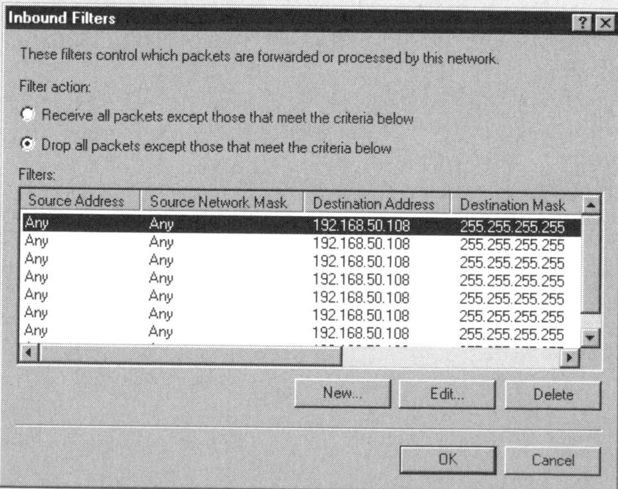

Figure 26-34 The Inbound Filters dialog box

5. Select Drop All Packets Except Those That Meet The Criteria Below.
6. Select a rule and click Edit to change one of the default rules, or click New to add a new rule. You can also delete a rule here.
7. Once you've configured the both Inbound and Outbound filters, click OK to return to the RRAS console.

Table 26-1 Default Packet Filters

Protocol	Port	Used for
47	Any	VPN connectivity - Generic Routing Encapsulation (GRE)
50	Any	Encapsulating Security Payload (ESP) for firewalls that use NAT transversal
TCP	1723	PPTP
UDP	500	Internet Protocol Security (IPsec)
UDP	1701	L2TP
UDP	4500	IPsec with network address translation (NAT)
TCP	443	SSTP (HTTP over SSL)

Configuring SSTP-based Connection Clients

The key to deploying SSTP connections is deployment of the Root CA certificate of the VPN computers computer certificate. Using Web enrollment gives you the greatest flexibility and allows you to enable SSTP VPNs for clients that don't ever directly connect to the internal network. In our example, we'll assume that you have a publicly resolvable Web address that you have set up with appropriate permissions to allow your authenticated user to browse to the site and obtain the Web enrollment certificate.

Note The minimum client requirement for SSTP VPNs is Windows Vista Service Pack 1 or Windows Server 2008. If you're running Windows XP or earlier clients to connect to a Windows Server 2008 RRAS server, use standard Point-to-Point Tunneling Protocol (PPTP) or Layer 2 Tunneling Protocol (L2TP).

To configure Windows Vista SP1 clients to connect with an SSTP VPN, follow these steps:

1. On the Windows Vista client, start Internet Explorer as an administrator.
2. Navigate to the publicly facing Web enrollment site as shown in Figure 26-35.

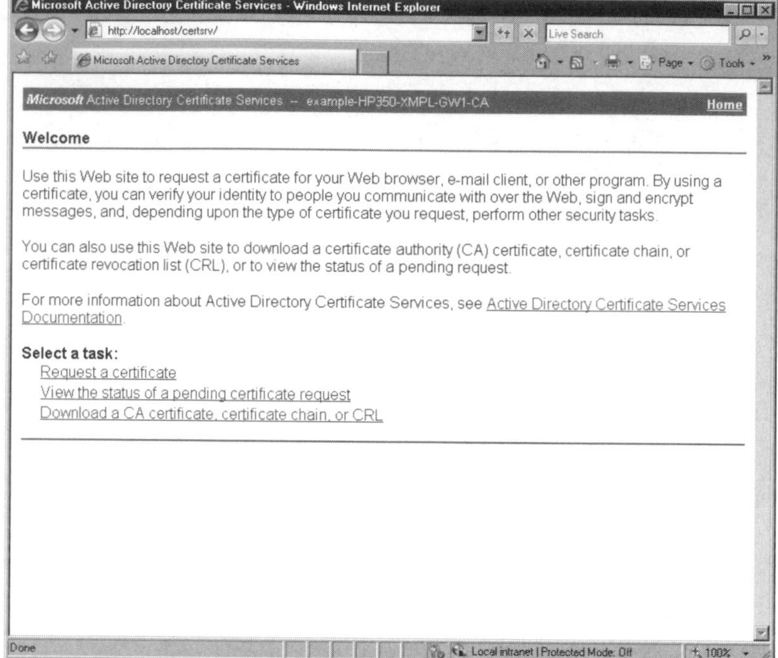

Figure 26-35 Installing the Active Directory Certificate on the client

3. Click Download A CA Certificate, Certificate Chain, Or CRL.
4. Close the warning and allow the add-on to run, and then click Run to allow the ActiveX control to run as shown in Figure 26-36.

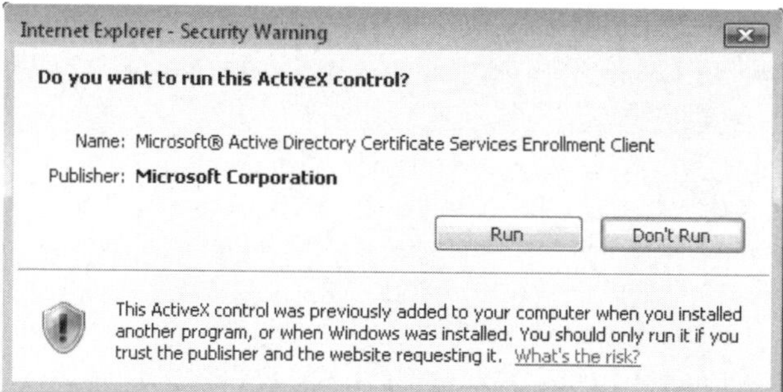

Figure 26-36 Approving the Internet Explorer add-on in the browser

5. Click Download CA Certificate and in the file download box that appears, click Open to install the certificate as shown in Figure 26-37.

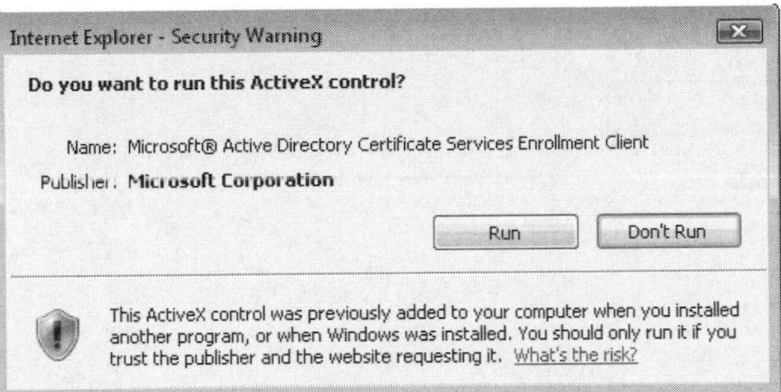

Figure 26-37 ActiveX Warning for Certificate Services Enrollment

6. Click Install Certificate as shown in Figure 26-38.

Figure 26-38 Installing the certificate

7. Click Next to start the Certificate Import Wizard and select Place All Certificates In The Following Store.
8. Browse to the Trusted Root Certification Authorities as shown in Figure 26-39 and click OK.

Figure 26-39 Installing the certificate in the trusted root location

9. Click Next and then click Finish to open the Security Warning dialog box shown in Figure 26-40. (This warning will only show if you're using self-published Certificates as we have been in this example.)

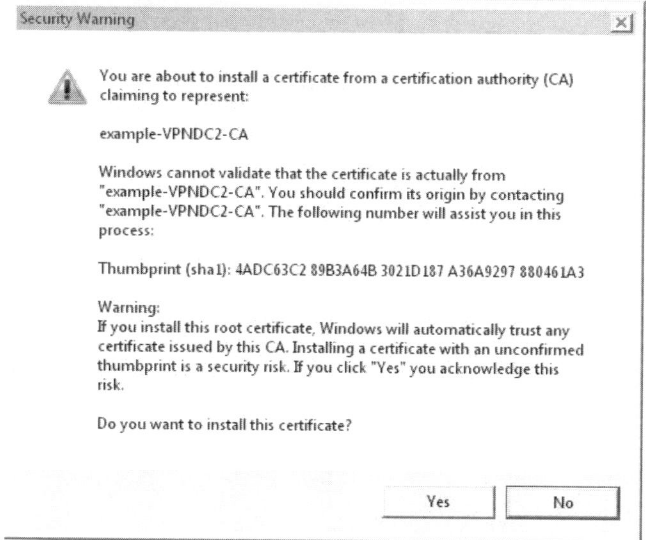

Figure 26-40 Confirming the installation of a self-signed Certificate in the Trusted Root store

To confirm that the trusted root certificate has been placed properly, follow these steps:

1. Create a new, blank MMC by typing **MMC** from the Run dialog box or the command line.
2. Select Add/Remove Snap-In from the File menu.

3. Select Certificates and click Add. Select My User Account and click Finish.
4. Click OK to launch the Certificates console.
5. Expand Certificates in the left pane, and then expand Trusted Root Certication Authorities.
6. Select Certificates to see the actual trusted root certificates that are installed. You should see the Certificate you installed, as shown in Figure 26-41.

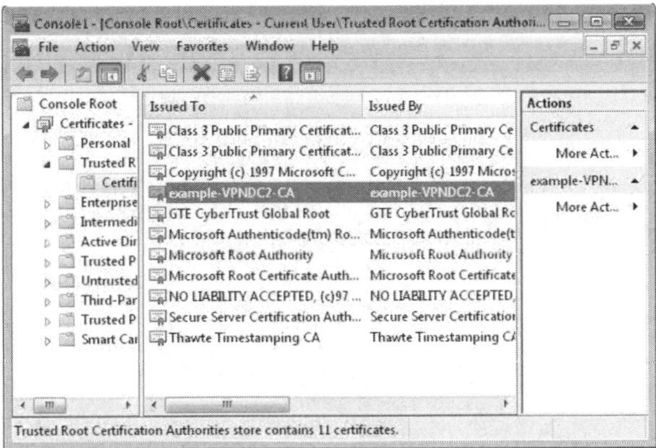

Figure 26-41 Verifying that the Certificate has been installed as a Trusted Root Certificate

Making the SSTP Connection

Now that the server and the client have both been set up, it's time to set up the VPN connection back to the server. On the client, perform the following steps to confirm the setup:

1. Click Connect To on the Start menu and then click Set Up A Connection Or Network because you have not set up a VPN connection before.
2. Select Connect To A Workplace and click Next to launch the Connect To A Workplace Wizard, shown in Figure 26-42.

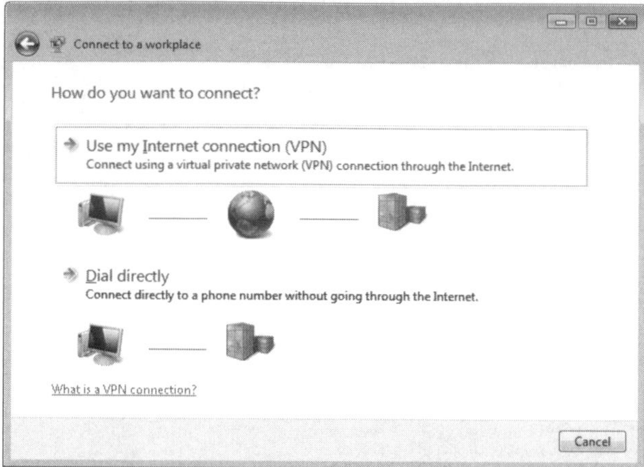

Figure 26-42 The Connect To A Workplace Wizard

3. Select Use My Internet Connection (VPN) to open the Type The Internet Address To Connect To page shown in Figure 26-43.

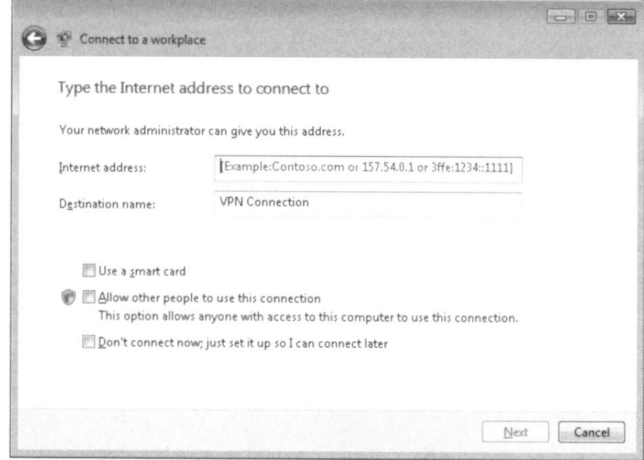

Figure 26-43 The Type The Internet Address To Connect To page of the Connect To A Workplace Wizard

4. Enter a DNS name or IP address in the Internet Address field and give the VPN connection a meaningful name in the Destination Name field.
5. If this is a shared computer and you expect other users to be able to use the connection, select Allow Other People To Use This Connection.

Note Allowing others to share a connection has security implications, but does simplify connecting from multiple accounts.

6. Click Next and enter a user name, password, and domain to use for this connection. If you're sharing the connection, you should not choose to remember the password. Click Create to finish creating the connection.
7. Open the Network And Sharing Center and click Manage Nework Connections.
8. Right-click the VPN connection you just built and select Properties from the Action menu.
9. Click the Networking tab to open the dialog box shown in Figure 26-44.

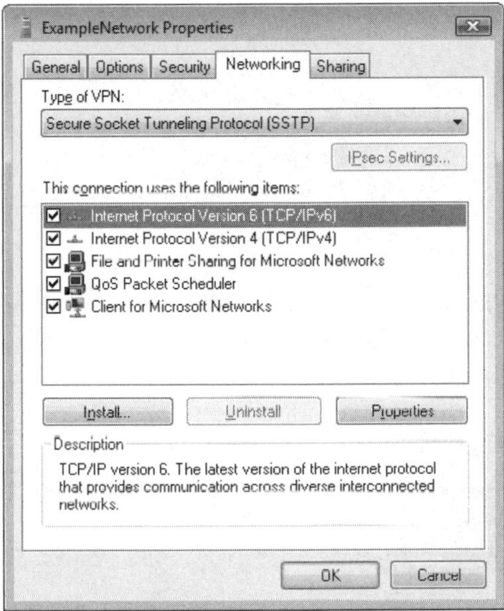

Figure 26-44 The Networking tab of the VPN Network Properties dialog box

10. Select Secure Socket Tunneling Protocol (SSTP) from the Type Of VPN drop-down list and click OK to close the Properties dialog box.

Note The SSTP VPN option is available only with a Windows Vista SP1 or later client.

Troubleshooting Connections

When connecting to SSTP VPN connections–as with any remote connection technology–when you first set things up you might see error messages, including the following:

0x800704C9

Error 0x800704C9 can occur if the remote access is disabled on the server, no SSTP ports are free on the server, or the server is not listening on the appropriate port number. Use the following commands on the server to confirm that the remote access and the SSTP services are running in a command prompt:

```
Sc query remoteaccess
```

and

```
Sc query sstpsvc
```

This should return a response that the services are running, as shown in Figure 26-45.

```
Command Prompt
C:\Users\Charlie>sc query remoteaccess

SERVICE_NAME: remoteaccess
        TYPE               : 20  WIN32_SHARE_PROCESS
        STATE              : 4  RUNNING
                                (STOPPABLE, PAUSABLE, ACCEPTS_SHUTDOWN)
        WIN32_EXIT_CODE    : 0  (0x0)
        SERVICE_EXIT_CODE  : 0  (0x0)
        CHECKPOINT         : 0x0
        WAIT_HINT          : 0x0

C:\Users\Charlie>sc query sstpsvc

SERVICE_NAME: sstpsvc
        TYPE               : 20  WIN32_SHARE_PROCESS
        STATE              : 4  RUNNING
                                (STOPPABLE, NOT_PAUSABLE, IGNORES_SHUTDOWN)
        WIN32_EXIT_CODE    : 0  (0x0)
        SERVICE_EXIT_CODE  : 0  (0x0)
        CHECKPOINT         : 0x0
        WAIT_HINT          : 0x0

C:\Users\Charlie>_
```

Figure 26-45 Running state of remote services

Start the services if needed and ensure that the RRAS server has the needed ports configured by opening up the RRAS console and navigating to the Ports section. Right-click Ports and select Properties, as shown in Figure 26-46.

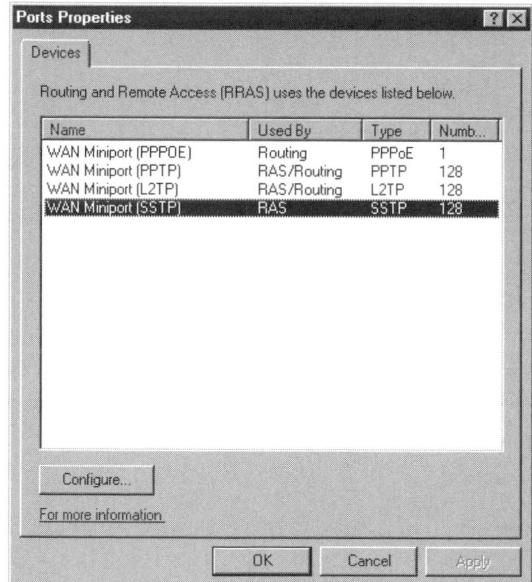

Figure 26-46 Confirming the SSTP ports

You can also use the *netstat –aon* command to confirm that the server is listening on a correct port.

0x80070040

If the SSTP VPN client fails to connect and gives you an error message 0x80070040, the server authentication certificate is probably not installed on the RRAS server. To correct this, follow these steps:

1. Open a blank MMC console by typing **mmc** at a command prompt.
2. Select Add/Remove Snap-In from the File menu.
3. Select Certificates and click Add. Select Computer Account, click Finish, and then click OK to create a Certificates console.
4. Select Personal, and then select Certificates to confirm that the server authentication certificate is installed.

0x800B0101

If the SSTP VPN client fails to connect and gives you the error message 0x800B0101, you probably have an expired certificate. To correct this, follow these steps:

1. Open a blank MMC console by typing **mmc** at a command prompt.
2. Select Add/Remove Snap-In from the File menu. Select Certificates and click Add.
3. Select Computer Account, click Finish, and then click OK to create a Certificates console.
4. Select Personal and then select Certificates to confirm that the server authentication certificate is installed. Verify that the Certificate hasn't expired. If it has, renew the Certificate.

0x800B0109

If the SSTP VPN client fails to connect with an error message of 0x800B0109, the appropriate trusted root CA certificate server is probably not installed on the client side. Review the client installation instructions to confirm that the certificate is installed in the trusted root location.

0x800B010F

If the SSTP VPN client fails to connect with an error message of 0x800B010F, the destination host name in the VPN connection might not match the SSL certificate The name of the certificate must match the connection address the client connects to. If you are using IP addresses instead of DNS names, your certificate must use the IP address.

0x80092013

If the SSTP VPN client fails to connect with an error message of 0x80092013, the client is failing the certificate revocation check. Ensure that the CRL check servers on the server side are available and publicly exposed on the Internet (published appropriately) as the CRL check is done by the client during the SSL connection establishment.

809

An error message of 809 is a generic connection failure message. The issue can be one of many things, including:

1. There might be a blocking firewall between the client and the server.
2. The proxy server settings on the client might be incorrect.
3. The SSTP or RRAS service on the server might be stopped.
4. The SSTP service might not be listening on port 443.
5. Confirm that the server certificate is connected to http.sys using *netsh http show sslcert*. You should see a certificate results similar to Figure 26-47.

```
Administrator: Command Prompt

C:\Users\Administrator>netsh http show sslcert

SSL Certificate bindings:
-------------------------

    IP:port                 : 0.0.0.0:443
    Certificate Hash        : 59093a07ba4600585e4e96c20cb3de4f069d9a7b
    Application ID          : {ba195980-cd49-458b-9e23-c84ee0adcd75}
    Certificate Store Name  : MY
    Verify Client Certificate Revocation    : Enabled
    Verify Revocation Using Cached Client Certificate Only    : Disabled
    Usage Check    : Enabled
    Revocation Freshness Time : 0
    URL Retrieval Timeout   : 0
    Ctl Identifier          :
    Ctl Store Name          :
    DS Mapper Usage    : Disabled
    Negotiate Client Certificate    : Disabled

    IP:port                 : [::]:443
    Certificate Hash        : 59093a07ba4600585e4e96c20cb3de4f069d9a7b
    Application ID          : {ba195980-cd49-458b-9e23-c84ee0adcd75}
    Certificate Store Name  : MY
    Verify Client Certificate Revocation    : Enabled
    Verify Revocation Using Cached Client Certificate Only    : Disabled
    Usage Check    : Enabled
    Revocation Freshness Time : 0
    URL Retrieval Timeout   : 0
    Ctl Identifier          :
    Ctl Store Name          :
    DS Mapper Usage    : Disabled
    Negotiate Client Certificate    : Disabled


C:\Users\Administrator>_
```

Figure 26-47 Confirming the SSL certificate

6. Confirm that the server certificate is present in the Local Computer, Personal store.
7. Verify that RRAS Inbound and Outbound filters are not blocking SSTP connections by following these steps:
   a. In the Routing and Remote Access console, select IPv4.
   b. Select the public interface and verify that the Inbound and Outbound filters are allowing port 443.
   c. Repeat for IPv6.
8. Verify that the Windows Firewall on the client isn't blocking SSTP connections.
9. Ensure that no third-party firewall on either the client or the server is blocking the connection.

Using NPS in Windows Server 2008

Network Policy Server is the new implementation of Routing And Remote Access services from previous versions of Windows Server. As before, you can authorize remote access by user or by group to better suit your remote needs.

The server allows you to set configuration policies that are processed locally on the server or forwarded to remote RADIUS servers. It also allows you to set a policy of who is allowed to connect to the network and the circumstances of connection. Finally, it sets the required health policies as described in Chapter 24.

Configuring Remote Access Per User

You can enable remote access on a per-user basis by following these steps:

1. Open Active Directory Users And Computers and navigate to the user account you want to enable remote access for.
2. Open the Properties of the user account and click the Dial-in tab.
3. Select the access control desired from these choices: Allow Access, Deny Access, or Control Access Through NPS Network Policy.
4. Click OK.

Configuring Remote Access in the NPS Network Policy

First configure the type of remote access authentication policy allowed. If you have only installed RRAS role service and not the NPS role service, follow these steps to set remote access:

1. Open the Routing And Remote Access console.
2. In the left pane, right-click the server, select Properties from the Action menu, and then click the Security tab.
3. Set the remote access Authentication Providers.

If you have installed the Network Policy Server role service, you use NPS to configure authentication and accounting providers by following these steps:

1. Open the Network Policy Server console.
2. Expand Policies in the left pane, then expand Network Policies.
3. Click Network Policies and then click New.
4. Enter the policy name and the type of network access server you are setting up. In our case, we'll set up a Remote Access Server (VPN-Dial up). Click Next.

5. We will now add a condition for connectivity. Click Add and scroll down to see the various types of rule conditions: Windows Groups, Machine Groups, User Groups, Location Groups, HCAP User groups, Day And Time Restrictions, A Group That Meets A Statement Of Health (used for NAP), Service class, Health policies, NAP-Capable Computers, Matching An Operating System, Authentication Type, and so on.
6. Choose Windows Groups and click Add Groups in the resulting Group Selection window.
7. The normal Active Directory Group window will launch and you can then choose the group of remote access users from your Active Directory structure. Click Next to continue the Wizard.
8. Choose Access Granted for remote access if the client matches the policy and click Next.
9. Configure the authentication method based on your firm's deployment needs.

> **Note** Designing a public key infrastructure is best done *before* you begin your remote access deployment. Thus we recommend that you review the needs for authentication and determine the authentication method during the planning stages of your network. The decision to be deploying Smart Cards, Protected EAP (PEAP), Secured Password (EAP-MSCHAP v2), or MS-CHAP-v2 should be done before this step.

10. Choose the appropriate authentication based on your firm's needs, as shown in Figure 26-48.

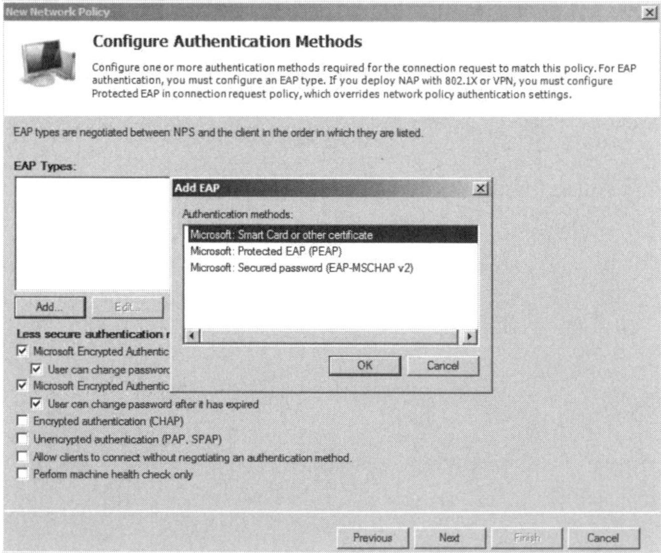

Figure 26-48 Adjusting the authentication

11. Configure Constraints such as time-outs and day and time restrictions as required.
12. On the Configure Settings page, choose the RADIUS attributes and any NAP rules that you will enforce with this connection. Click Next.
13. Confirm that the policy meets your company's needs and click Finish.

You can set up a basic policy and then copy the template to reuse for additional deployments.

Wireless Deployment

The minimum requirements for properly and securely deploying protected wireless connections are actually quite simple:

- Windows Vista, Windows XP, Windows Server 2003, or Windows Server 2008 for the wireless client operating system. All of these have built-in support for IEEE 802.11 wireless access and IEEE 802.1x authentication.
- At least two Remote Authentication Dial-In User Service (RADIUS) servers for authentication. The Network Policy Server role service of the Network Policy and Access Service role is a good choice for a RADIUS server to provide full functionality.
- Active Directory Domain Services for user account authentication and authorization.

Note Placing the NPS server on a domain controller will optimize authentication and authoritization and response times.

Just as in our SSTP deployment, the key for a successful 802.1x deployment is to plan for and deploy certificates to the workstations. For EAP-TLS or PEAP-TLS a certificate instrastructure, or public key infrastructure (PKI), is required to issue certificates. Computer (or machine) certificates, User certificates, and Root CA certificates are required.

Securing Your Certificates

Planning the deployment and security of your PKI infrastructure should involve the physical security of your signing keys. Secure it with a Hardware Security Module and keep it in a secure locations such as a lockbox or vault to minimize the potential for private key insecurity. Ensure that you have policies for handling and access to this private key and audit access accordingly. In larger institutions, plan to keep the Root CA offline to better protect the issuing authority.

The basic assumptions we are making in this section are:

- You have policies in place for security and handling of your PKI, or you're using Windows Server 2008 Enterprise Server or Datacenter server for Autoenrollment Certificates.
- Your domain is at the Windows Server 2003 domain functional level or greater.
- Your gateway servers are domain joined.
- Your wireless access points support 802.1x (802.11i).
- You have deployed one or more servers with the Network Policy Server role service installed.

Prerequisites

Before we can configure wireless security policies, we need to add the Active Directory Certificate Services role and the Network Policy Server and Access role.

Active Directory Certificate Services

Add the Active Directory Certificate Services role, as described in "Installing Prerequisites For SSTP" earlier in the chapter, selecting the Certification Authority and Certification Authority Web Enrollment role services. Create an Enterprise CA rather than a Standalone CA for maximum flexibility and ease of deploying certificates.

Network Policy Server Role Service

Add the Network Policy Server role service of the Network Policy And Access Service role by following these steps:

1. Open Server Manager if it isn't already open, and select Add Roles from the Action menu.
2. Click Next if you see the Before You Begin page.
3. Select Network Policy And Access Services and click Next twice.
4. Choose Network Policy Server and the Routing And Remote Access Services. If deploying NAP (see Chapter 24), also choose Health Registration Authority.
5. Click Next and then click Install. Click Close when the installation is complete.

Configure Certificates for PEAP

The next step is to set up a computer certificate on the NPS server for server side PEAP authentication. Use the following steps:

1. Open a blank MMC console by typing **mmc** at a command prompt.
2. Select Add/Remove Snap-In from the File menu. Select Certificates and click Add.
3. Select Computer Account, click Finish, and then click OK to create a Certificates console.

4. Select Personal, and then select Certificates in the left pane.
5. On the left, click Certificates (Local Computer), click Personal, right-click Certificates, and then select Request New Certificate from the All Tasks menu, as shown in Figure 26-49.

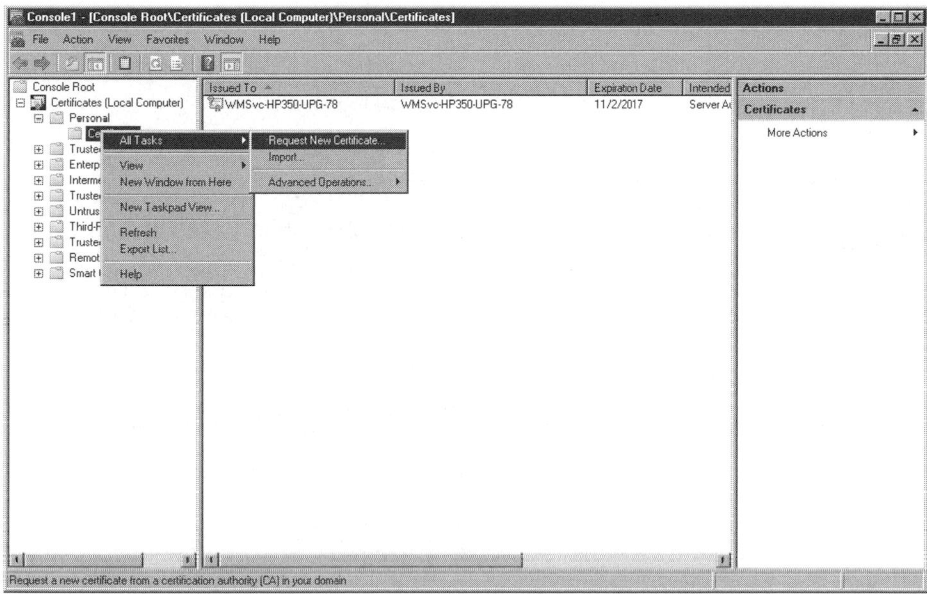

Figure 26-49 Requesting the certificate

6. Click Next on the Before You Begin page to open the Certificate Enrollment page, as shown in Figure 26-50.

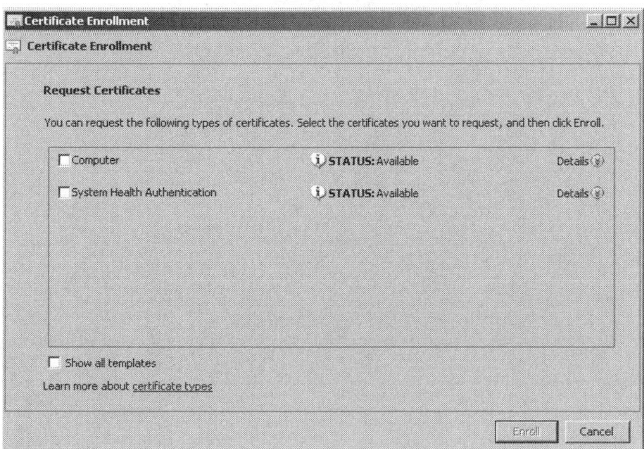

Figure 26-50 Choosing the computer template

7. Select Computer (or select both Computer and System Health Authentication if you are also deploying NAP) and then click Enroll.
8. Confirm that the resulting screen shows that the certificate is available. Click Next and then click Finish.

Adding RADIUS Clients to the Network

We can now add 802.1x switches–wired or wireless–to the network as RADIUS clients. Client computers are not RADIUS clients for 802.1x–the switches are the clients. Follow these steps to enable RADIUS:

1. Click Start, click Run, type **Nps.msc**, and press Enter.
2. On the Getting Started page, select RADIUS Server For 802.1X Wireless Clients Or Wired Connections from the drop-down list.
3. Click Configure 802.1X to open the Select 802.1x Connections Type Wizard shown in Figure 26-51.

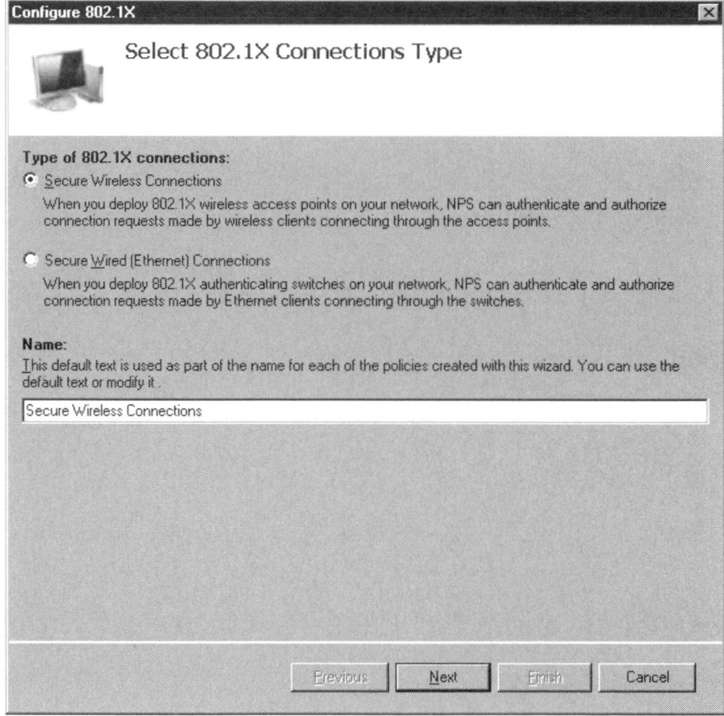

Figure 26-51 The Select 802.1x Connections Type Wizard

4. Select Secure Wireless Connections and enter a name for the policy or keep the default name. Click Next to open the Specify 802.1x Switches page.
5. Click Add to enter authenticating switches and wireless access points, as shown in Figure 26-52. Enter a friendly name and an address (IP or DNS) for the device. Select Manual or Generate for the shared secret.

> **Note** The generated shared secret is 64 characters long, which is longer than some devices can accept. If your device can't accept a shared secret that long, use a manual secret, or edit the generated one to shorten it.

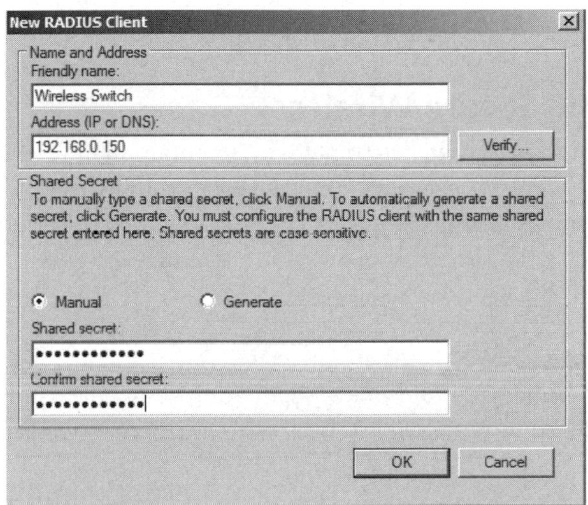

Figure 26-52 Adding a switch as a RADIUS client

6. Click OK, click Next, and select an EAP type. The choices are Smart Card Or Other Certificate, Microsoft Protected EAP (PEAP), or Secured Password (EAP-MSCHAP v2). Click Next to open the Specify User Groups page.
7. Click Add to add a domain user group or groups. Click Next when you're finished.
8. If you plan to have your RADIUS clients support VLANs, click Configure to configure your VLAN settings now or click Next to configure VLAN settings later.
9. Click Finish.

Configuring the Access Points

Once the server has been configured with computer certificates and the wireless policy, configure your access points accordingly. The exact procedure will depend on the make and model of wireless access point being deployed. The following are the general steps required:

1. Create a fixed IP address for the access point using DHCP reservations.
2. Disable the DHCP service of the access point.
3. Set the SSID for the access point.
4. Configure the access point to use the IP address of the NPS server as its primary RADIUS server, specifying a destination port of 1812.
5. Enter the shared secret that you used when setting up the RADIUS client 802.1X access point.
6. Enable WPA2 Encryption and enable 802.1X authentication.

Configuring Clients to Use Secure Wireless

Wireless clients must first be connected to the wired network to obtain their certificates, which are deployed using Group Policy. Giving wireless clients the ability to access the wireless network securely involves connecting them first to the wired network to obtained their certificates. Ensure that the client workstation is joined to the domain where they will recevie the certificate via Group Policy.

Group Policy Deployment of Certificates

Group Policy is used to deploy certificates. Build a new policy–don't edit an existing one. Use the following steps to create a new Group Policy to deploy a wireless certificate:

1. Open the Group Policy Management Console (GPMC).
2. Navigate to Domains and then to the name of the domain where you're creating a policy.
3. Select Group Policy Objects and then select New from the Action menu.
4. Enter a name for the GPO and click OK.
5. Link the new GPO by dragging it to the appropriate OU or container.
6. Select the GPO you created and choose Edit from the Action menu.
7. Navigate to Computer Configuration, Policies, Windows Settings, Security Settings, and then to Public Key Policies.
8. Select Automatic Certificate Request Settings, select New, and then select Automatic Certificate Request from the Action menu to open the Automatic Certificate Request Setup Wizard. Click Next.

9. On the Certificate Template page shown in Figure 26-53, choose Computer, click Next, and then click Finish.

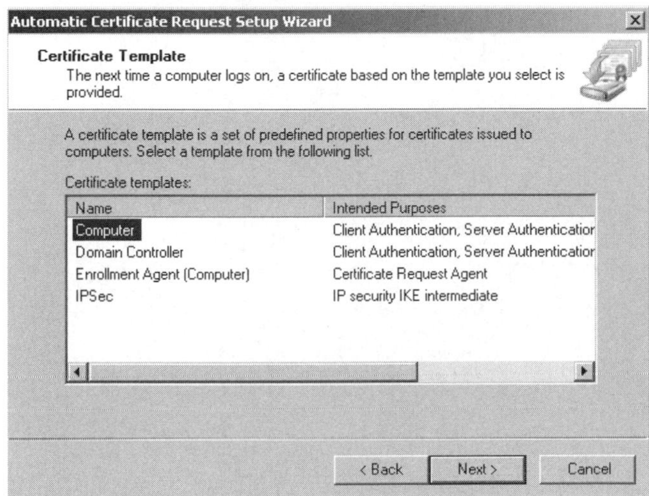

Figure 26-53 Choosing the computer certificate

10. Open a blank MMC console by typing **mmc** at a command prompt.
11. Select Add/Remove Snap-In from the File menu. Select Certificates and then click Add.
12. Select Computer Account, click Finish, and then click OK to create a Certificates console.
13. Select Personal, and then select Certificates from the left pane.
14. Right-click the personal computer certificate that was generated earlier and select Export from the All Tasks menu to open the Certificate Export Wizard. Click Next.
15. Select No, Do Not Export The Private Key and click Next.
16. Leave the default file format and click Next. Enter a filename and location (or use the Browse button) and click Next.
17. Click Next and then click Finish to complete the export.
18. Go back to the Group Policy Management console and right-click the Trusted Root Certificate Authorities. Select Import from the Action menu. Click Next to launch the Certificate Import Wizard.
19. Browse to the certificate that was just exported, select it, and then click Open to import the file, as shown in Figure 26-54.

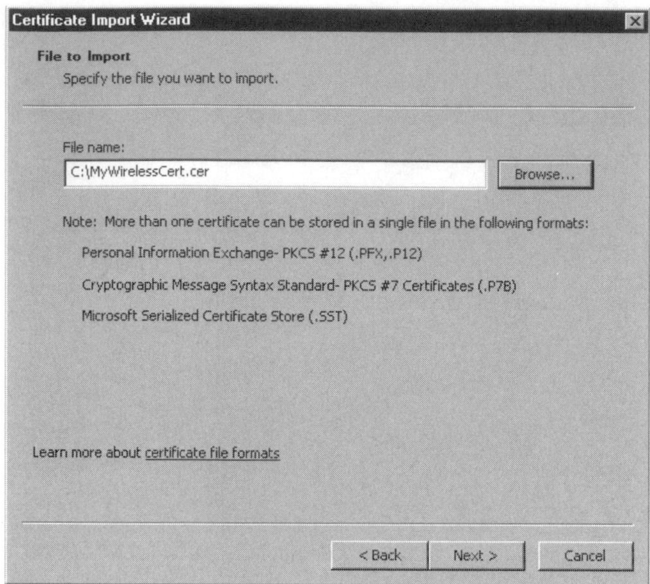

Figure 26-54 The File To Import page of the Certificate Import Wizard

20. Click Next and then click Next again on the Certificate Store page. Click Finish.
21. In the Group Policy Management Editor console, verify that the certificate appears in the Trusted Root Certificate Authorities container.
22. Navigate to Computer Configuration, Policies, Windows Settings, Security Settings and then to Wireless (IEE 802.11) Policies. Right-click and select Create A New Windows Vista Policy or Create A New Windows XP Policy from the Action menu.
23. Enter a name and description for the policy in the Properties dialog box.
24. For Windows Vista, click Add on the General tab and select Infrastructure. Enter the SSID of your preferred network in the Network Name(s) (SSID) field.
25. For Windows Vista, click the Security tab and Select WPA-2 Enterprise for Authentication, AES for Encryption, Microsoft Protected EAP (PEAP) for a network authentication method and Computer Authentication for an Authentication Mode, as shown in Figure 26-55. Click OK and click OK again.

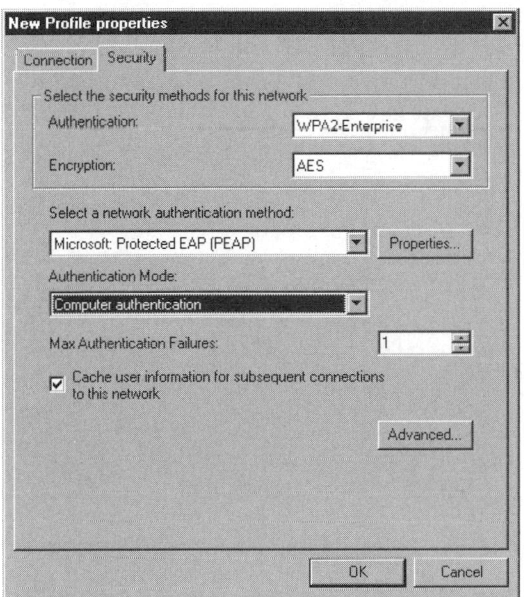

Figure 26-55 Creating a new Windows Vista Wireless Policy

26. For Windows XP, click the Preferred Network tab, click Add, and then select Infrastructure. Enter the SSID of your preferred network in the Network Name(s) (SSID) field.

27. For Windows XP, select WPA2 for Authentication and AES for Encryption. Click the IEEE 802.1x tab, select Microsoft Protected EAP (PEAP) for an EAP Type, and select Computer Only for an Authentication Mode. Click OK and click OK again.

The Workstation Settings

Finally, you need to configure your workstations to connect to the wireless access points in a secure manner. Follow these steps for Windows XP:

1. Start the Network Connections control panel application by typing **ncpa.cpl** at a command prompt or in the Run dialog box.

2. Right-click your wireless connection and select Properties from the Action menu. Click the Wireless Networks tab and select the secure wireless network from the list of preferred networks. Click Properties.

3. Select WPA2 for the Network Authentication type and AES for the Data Encryption type.

4. Click the Authentication tab and click to enable IEEE 802.1X authentication. Select Protected EAP (PEAP) from the EAP Type drop-down list and then click Properties.

5. Click Protected EAP properties. In the dialog box, ensure that Validate Server Certificate and Enable Fast Reconnect are selected. If you have deployed NAP, Enable Quarantine Checks should also be selected.

For Windows Vista clients, follow these steps:

1. Open the Network And Sharing Center in the Control Panel.
2. Select Manage Wireless Networks from the Tasks pane.
3. Right-click the wireless network you want to configure and select Properties from the Action menu. Click the Security tab, as shown in Figure 26-56.

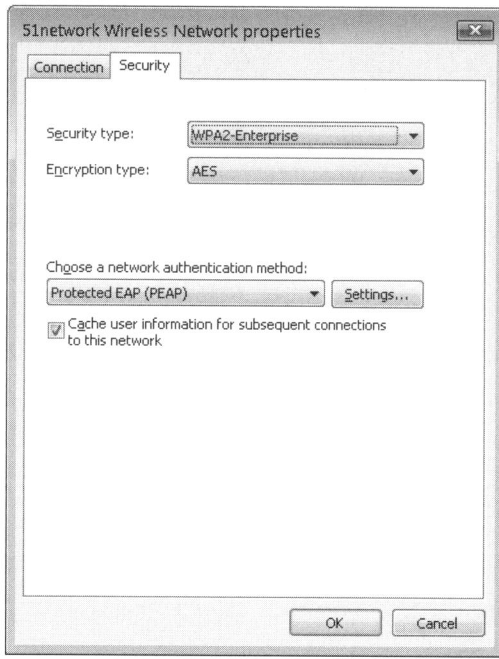

Figure 26-56 The Security tab of the Wireless Network Properties dialog box

4. Select WPA2-Enterprise for a security type and AES for an encryption type. Select Protected EAP (PEAP) from the Choose A Network Authentication Method drop-down list.
5. Click Settings and ensure that Validate Server Certificate and Enable Fast Reconnect are selected. If you have deployed NAP, Enable Quarantine Checks should also be selected. Click OK and then click OK again.

Now test your settings to ensure that you have secure protected wireless for your domain clients.

Summary

Secure and dependable remote and wireless access is a critical business need today. Planning for the needed authentication, deployment, and accountability is critical to a successful implementation. Secure and dependable remote access is built into Windows Server 2008, especially with the new SSTP VPN capabilities. All the necessary services and tools to build a secure WPA2-Enterprise wireless connection environment are included in Windows Server 2008.

In the next chapter we move from the securing of wireless and remote connections to the interoperability of Windows Server 2008 with UNIX and Linux computers.

Part V
Use Support Services and Features

Chapter 27

Interoperability

Enterprise computing inevitably means interacting with other environments and operating systems. That can mean interoperating with, and integrating with, existing UNIX and Linux networks; connecting to and working with Novell networks; or supporting Macintosh clients that need full access to the resources of the Microsoft Windows network.

In this chapter, we'll focus on UNIX and Linux interoperability. Windows Server 2003 R2 greatly enhanced the interoperability of Windows Server with UNIX and Linux, and Windows Server 2008 extends that even further. Beginning with Windows Server 2003 R2, the Subsystem for UNIX Applications (SUA) gives Windows the ability to compile and run UNIX applications natively on Windows Server, while the inclusion of native support for the Network File System greatly enhances the ability of Windows Server 2008 to seamlessly interoperate with UNIX and Linux computers.

General UNIX Interoperability

Frequently, Windows Server 2008 networks need to connect to and work with UNIX or Linux in one or another of their various incarnations. Windows Server 2008 has the components to allow UNIX and Windows Server 2008 to work nearly seamlessly together, so the system administrators of both environments can provide users with full access to the resources of the other environment almost transparently.

This chapter assumes you have at least a passing familiarity with UNIX or Linux, and that's why you're trying to interoperate. We start by examining permissions and security issues because they are related to many of the other subjects in this chapter. Next come basic connectivity and file systems, followed by a look at the changes and improvements introduced with Window Server 2003 R2 and now fully integrated into Windows Server 2008. Finally, we cover the differences between the Windows Server 2008 cmd.exe shell and the new Subsystem for UNIX Applications (SUA) shells.

Permissions and Security Concepts

One of the most important and pervasive differences between Windows Server 2008 and UNIX is the manner in which they handle permissions and security. These differences are subtle and frequently lead the unwary to make false assumptions. Because Chapter 22, "Planning Security" and Chapter 23, "Implementing Security" have already explained in great detail how Windows Server 2008 handles security, we'll spare you further details here, but if you're going to coexist with UNIX servers, you need to understand how UNIX handles security to avoid problems. Let's look at a UNIX file listing first, and then examine symbolic links, privilege levels, and permissions.

A UNIX File Listing

A UNIX file listing might look something like this:

```
-rwxr-x--x  2 charlie    dba          2579 Aug 30 15:49 resize
```

This listing tells you virtually all you need to know about the security and permissions of the file you're looking at. Start at the left of the line and work your way across to see what's here and what it means–and how it compares to Windows Server 2008.

The first dash (-) tells you this listing is *not* a directory. If it were a directory, a "d" would be in that place instead. UNIX treats a directory as simply another file, although a special one, and the permissions have a slightly different meaning when referring to a directory as opposed to a file. We'll cover directory permissions shortly, but let's stay with regular files for now.

The next three characters correspond to the permissions of the file owner, who can be someone other than the original creator because UNIX allows a user to "give" a file to another user. The "r" indicates that the owner has the right to read the file; the "w" means she or he can write to it, delete it, or otherwise modify it; and the "x" allows the owner to execute the program.

Real World UNIX-Executable Programs

In Windows Server 2008, the operating system decides whether a program is executable based on the filename. If the filename has an extension of .com, .exe, .bat, .cmd, or any other extension included in %PATHEXT% ($ENV:pathext if you use PowerShell as your command-line shell), it can be executed, assuming the user has the appropriate permissions. In UNIX, no association exists between the extension and whether the file is executable. In fact, most UNIX files have no extension at all. The only determinant of whether a file is executable is the permission of the file. So, although it might be the convention in a particular system to always name shell scripts (the UNIX equivalent of a batch file) with a name that ends in .sh or .ksh, this has no actual meaning. The file must be given the execute permission before it can be executed directly.

The fifth, sixth, and seventh characters correspond to the permissions of members of the same group as the owner of the file. The "r" indicates that members of the group can read the file (or perform actions that leave it unchanged, such as copying it); the dash indicates that they do *not* have permission to write to it, delete it, or otherwise modify it; and the "x" gives them the ability to execute the program.

Finally, the last three characters of the first group correspond to the permissions of the rest of the world. The initial dash indicates that these users don't have the right to read the file, or in any way look at the contents, nor do they have permission to copy the file. The second dash indicates that they don't have permission to change, modify, or delete the file, and finally, the last "x" indicates that they can execute the file if executing doesn't actually require a read.

Under the Hood Permissions

UNIX has only three basic permissions: Read, Write, and Execute.

- **Read** The right to read a file or list its contents. The right to make a copy of the file. For directories, the right to list the contents of the directory.
- **Write** The right to alter the contents of a file. For a directory, the right to create files and subdirectories. If you have Write permission on a directory, you have the right to delete files in the directory even if you don't have Write permission on the file–if you also have either Read or Execute permission on the directory.
- **Execute** The right to execute the file. Even the owner of a file needs this permission to execute it. For a directory, the right to change into the directory or to execute files within the directory. Having this right on a directory does not, however, give you permission to list the contents of the directory, so you might be able to execute a file without being able to see that it is there.

The next character, the number 2, indicates that there are two hard links to the file. A *hard link* gives the exact same file another name. Only a single actual file is still stored on the hard disk, but two directory entries point to the file. There are no practical limits to the number of hard links that can exist to a single file, but all links to the file must exist on the same file system. Windows Server 2008 supports hard links on the NTFS file system.

The next two groups in the listing are the owner of the file, "charlie," and the group for the file, "dba." These are normally user and group names, but they could also be a number if either the owner or group of the file doesn't actually have an account on the system.

Next is the size of the file (2579 bytes in this case), the date and time when the file was created or last updated, and the name of the file–actually, the directory entry for the file that corresponds to this hard link to the file. Note that no link has any precedence over any other. No significance is attached to which name comes first; all are treated equally. Deleting one link does not delete the file–just that reference to it. Any other versions of the file remain.

Symbolic Links

UNIX supports both hard links and symbolic links. *Symbolic links* are vaguely analogous to Windows shortcuts but with several important differences. The most important difference is that in UNIX, when you access the symbolic link, you actually access the file it points to, not the link itself. For example, if you edit a symbolic link to a text file, you're actually editing the original text file. With a Windows Server 2008 shortcut, you can use the shortcut only to start an executable file or to open a folder. New in Windows Server 2008 is direct support for symbolic links. *Finally.* Unfortunately, the Windows Server 2008 symbolic links aren't usable by the SUA subsystem, nor are the SUA subsystem version of symbolic links usable by the Windows subsystem.

Under the Hood Mklink

The command that supports creating a link in Windows Server 2008 is the `mklink` command. `Mklink` can create both symbolic links (new to Windows Server 2008 and Windows Vista), and hard links, and can create links for both directories and files. The syntax for `mklink` is:

```
MKLINK [[/D] | [/H] | [/J]] Link Target

        /D      Creates a directory symbolic link.  Default is a file
                symbolic link.
        /H      Creates a hard link instead of a symbolic link.
        /J      Creates a Directory Junction.
        Link    specifies the new symbolic link name.
        Target  specifies the path (relative or absolute) that the new link
                   refers to.
```

Hard links made with `mklink` are fully supported by the SUA subsystem. But symbolic links created with mklink are not: For symbolic links in the SUA subsystem you must use the SUA `ln -s` command.

A symbolic link differs from a hard link in that the actual file has precedence over any of the symbolic links to it. In fact, the listing for a symbolic link to the earlier resize file makes it immediately clear that this is a symbolic link, not a hard link:

```
lrwxrwxrwx  1 charlie   dba  2579 Aug 30 15:49 resize -> /u/cpr/resize
```

As you can see, the listing not only begins with the letter "l" in the first position, but it also actually shows where the link is pointing. You'll notice that the two filenames are identical. Although this isn't a requirement, it is the most common use of symbolic links–to make a file appear as if it were in one place when it actually resides elsewhere.

Another feature of a symbolic link that distinguishes it from a hard link is that it can point across to a different file system or even a different computer. You can have a symbolic link that points to a file that resides on a completely different computer.

Note If you copy a file on top of a symbolic link, the link is broken. Your new file actually replaces the link with the file. The original file still exists, however, which makes the duplication of files confusing at best.

Privilege Levels

Traditionally, UNIX divides the world into only three types of users: the owner of a file, a member of the same group as the owner, and the rest of the world. These three privilege levels are called owner, group, and other. So far, so good. This sounds a lot like Windows Server 2008, right? A big difference is in the second privilege level: group.

On UNIX systems with traditional security, a user is active only in a single group at a time. When that user creates a file, the file has permissions for the group based strictly on the current group of the file creator. This situation can have interesting and subtle complications when compared to the Windows Server 2008 methodology. If a user's primary logon is to one of the standard groups, things generally behave as you expect. However, when a user belongs to a specialized group with limited membership and creates files while that group is the active group, the ability of users outside the group to access the file could be constrained.

A user who isn't an active member of the group that owns a file and who isn't the actual owner of the file is in the other privilege level. This arrangement is essentially the same as the Windows Server 2008 Everyone group. A user in the other category has no permission to access the file except what every other user has. It's important to understand that UNIX lacks the equivalent of "Authenticated User" in the Windows Server 2008 world—so the other group aligns with the Windows Everyone group, not the Authenticated User.

Real World The UNIX Super User

In discussions of UNIX security, keep in mind one overriding principle: The *root* user (sometimes called the *super* user) has access to everything. In the Windows Server 2008 world, you can easily set a file or directory so that even users with administrative privileges don't have access without changing the ownership of the file, but in the UNIX world that restriction doesn't exist. Not only that, but the super user can even change identities to have the same identity as you without knowing your password. This ability to change user identities (impersonate) without knowing the user's password is not available from within the SUA subsystem. Even when running as an administrator, you must know the password for the account you want to impersonate.

Basic Connectivity

Now that you understand the differences between the security models of Windows Server 2008 and UNIX, let's look at how they are compatible. For one thing, with no additional add-ons, Windows Server 2008 coexists reasonably well with UNIX servers. The default networking protocol for both operating systems is the same—TCP/IP. They can easily share DNS, DHCP, and other services. FTP and Telnet can handle simple connectivity between Windows Server 2008 and UNIX.

File Transfer Protocol

All versions of Windows Server 2008 include a simple FTP command-line client and can handle FTP from within Microsoft Windows Explorer or Internet Explorer to a limited extent. The character-mode client provides no frills but should feel quite comfortable to the UNIX user—and it works without quirks, though it lacks some of the sophistication that a UNIX user would expect. Those who want a more graphical, friendly FTP client have a variety to choose from, including shareware and some that are pure freeware. A personal favorite is WS_FTP Pro from Ipswitch (*http://www.ipswitch.com*). Windows Server 2008 also includes full-featured FTP server capability as part of its Internet Information Services (IIS) component. With both an FTP server and a client natively available, you can easily copy files between the UNIX and Windows Server 2008 computers on your network.

Telnet

All versions of Windows Server 2008 come with the character-mode Telnet client that debuted in Services for UNIX (SFU). The semi-graphical Telnet client that had been around since Microsoft Windows 3 is well and thoroughly gone, and is not missed! The new client is faster, has better terminal emulations, and is actually quite decent for most uses. It supports American National Standards Institute (ANSI) features–including color, VT52, VT100, and VTNT (a special emulation that can be useful when running character-mode Windows Server 2008 applications such as Edit). If one of these modes doesn't meet your need for terminal emulation, excellent third-party commercial Telnet clients are available.

Note Edit.com, that legacy from the DOS days, is not available on any 64-bit version of Windows. If you want a text editor that works well with ASCII text files, complete with syntax highlighting and a graphical or pure text mode version, we recommend Vim/GVim (*http://www.vim.org*). It even understands UNIX files and can read and write them without problems.

Real World Secure Shell (SSH)

Telnet and FTP, although great and useful protocols, have an inherent security risk, as they transmit information, including passwords, across the network in plain text without encryption. This can be acceptable in many situations where the internal network is thoroughly protected from outside intrusion and internal users are all trusted, but it poses unacceptable risks in other situations. One solution–and the de facto standard in the UNIX world–is the SSH protocol, a secure, encrypted protocol that supports a Telnet-like character mode logon feature, an FTP-like file transfer protocol, and additional features.

Both commercial and open-source versions of SSH are available. Of the commercial versions, Reflection for Secure IT is FIPS-certified, and it supports virtually all UNIX operating systems, as well as Windows Server 2008. OpenSSH is an excellent Open Source implementation of the SSH protocol and is widely available in both compiled forms and as source code.

Windows Server 2008 even has two built-in Telnet daemons, or servers. The first, which operates as a Windows service and is part of the Win32 subsystem, uses the Windows character mode shell (Cmd.exe) for client sessions. The second is the *telnetd* daemon of the SUA subsystem. It must be enabled by editing the /etc/inetd.conf file. Only one telnet server can be running at any given time, so do not enable telnetd unless you first disable the Win32 telnet service.

Important Telnet is an inherently insecure protocol that passes information—including logon name and password—unencrypted on the network.

File Systems

Windows Server 2008 network file sharing supports both Server Message Block (SMB), the native Microsoft networking mechanism, and the UNIX-originated Network File System (NFS). To allow Windows Server 2008 and UNIX to share a common file system, you need to add SMB to your UNIX systems or NFS to your Windows systems.

Until the original release of SFU, only third-party NFS solutions were available for Windows systems that needed to be able to share file resources with UNIX systems, and most of these solutions were expensive and problematic. The biggest issue was their inability to keep up with Microsoft Windows service packs, which seemed to break these NFS solutions more often than not. In addition, these solutions often had significant performance problems. The Client for NFS, Server for NFS, and Gateway for NFS included with SFU were the first Microsoft shipped solutions, and now, in Windows Server 2008, Services for Network File System provides full NFS client and server functionality.

Several powerful, SMB-based UNIX and Linux solutions address the problem of sharing file resources between Windows and UNIX by adding support for SMB to UNIX, rather than NFS to Windows. These SMB solutions vary in cost from free to expensive, and they support native Windows networking at either the workgroup or domain level. The underlying problem for all of these SMB solutions, however, is trying to work effectively with Active Directory. Samba, the clear favorite among the available solutions, provides limited support for Active Directory in version 3 of Samba, and is actively developing version 4 to ensure full support for Active Directory.

The Network File System

Originally, NFS was designed to run as a broadcast protocol using User Datagram Protocol (UDP). This protocol created substantial performance and network traffic issues for those intending to implement large amounts of NFS networking and made it difficult to share file systems across routed boundaries. Eventually, the NFS standard changed to support TCP for NFS networking, and virtually all modern clients and servers support this mechanism. However, some older NFS implementations still in use don't support TCP, so Windows Server 2008 Client for NFS supports UDP, TCP, or both. The default is TCP only.

Server Message Block

The biggest issue that the SMB-on-UNIX crowd has to deal with is the changing Windows Server 2008 security model. Two mechanisms are used for handling security with the SMB-on-UNIX solutions—workgroup-level security and limited Active Directory authentication.

Workgroup security suffers from all the same problems as workgroups in the enterprise environment: It becomes more difficult to manage as the number of users and computers increases, and it has limited options for actually managing security. However, workgroup security has a definite place in the smaller environment, where it's easy to understand and simple to set up. Plus, there's a nice cost advantage—a widely available and well-implemented freeware SMB server called Samba is available on virtually all UNIX and Linux platforms. Version 3 of Samba supports direct authentication against Active Directory. Other commercial workgroup SMB servers are also available that run on a variety of platforms. They tend to be more Windows-like and easier to set up and administer than Samba, which shows its open-source heritage.

Windows NT 4 domain SMB servers are also still available from a number of UNIX vendors. All of these (except Samba) are based on AT&T's initial port to UNIX of Microsoft Advanced Server technology. Each is limited to running on the platform for which it was designed, and each has slight differences because the port from AT&T required tweaking in most cases. All of these UNIX SMB servers can be either primary domain controllers or backup domain controllers in a Windows NT domain, and some can even be a simple member server, but all have problems dealing with the Active Directory–based security model in Windows Server 2008. Because these servers are based on the Windows NT 4 security model, you'll be forced to stay in mixed mode.

Real World Avoid UNIX SMB Domain Servers

We honestly never expected to get to the point of actively discouraging the use of the AT&T ported UNIX SMB domain servers. After all, we even wrote a book about one of them many years ago. But the reality is that they are a dead end. The agreement that allowed for their creation ended with the introduction of Active Directory in Microsoft Windows 2000 Server, and they are simply too far out of date to be a desirable solution. If you've still got legacy servers running Advanced Services for UNIX, it's time to retire them. If you still have a need for serving up SMB from your UNIX servers, use Samba. It's well supported, gets regular updates and security fixes, and just plain works better.

Printing

Windows Server 2008 includes native support for TCP/IP printing protocols. When installing or configuring a printer, you can add a TCP/IP printer port as described in Chapter 10, "Managing Printers." In addition, you can add support for the UNIX lpr/lpd protocol, allowing Windows Server 2008 to function as a remote print server for UNIX clients.

To add remote print services for UNIX, follow these steps:

1. Open Server Manager.
2. Select Add Features from the Action menu.
3. Select LPR Port Monitor on the Select Features page of the Add Features Wizard, as shown in Figure 27-1.

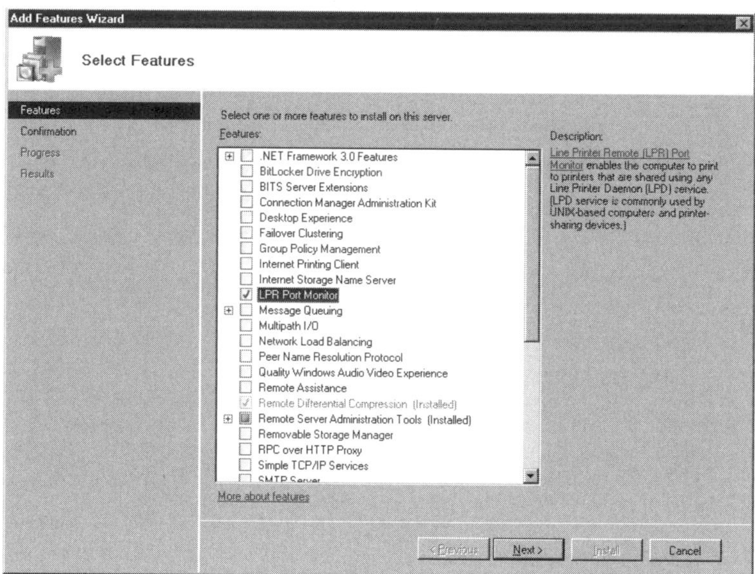

Figure 27-1 The Select Features page of the Add Features Wizard

4. Click Next and then click Install to add the service. Click Close when the wizard completes.

Network File System

Windows Server 2008 includes the Services for Network File System (Services for NFS) as a Role Service of the File Server role.

If your Active Directory is not at least at the Windows Server 2003 domain functional level, you must install Server for NFS Authentication on every domain controller in the domain, and on every domain controller of any domain whose accounts might need access to NFS resources on this domain.

To install Services for Network File System, follow these steps:

1. Open Server Manager.
2. If the File Server Role is not installed, click Roles in the Console Tree pane, and select Add Role from the Action menu. Include the Services for Network File System role service, as shown in Figure 27-2.

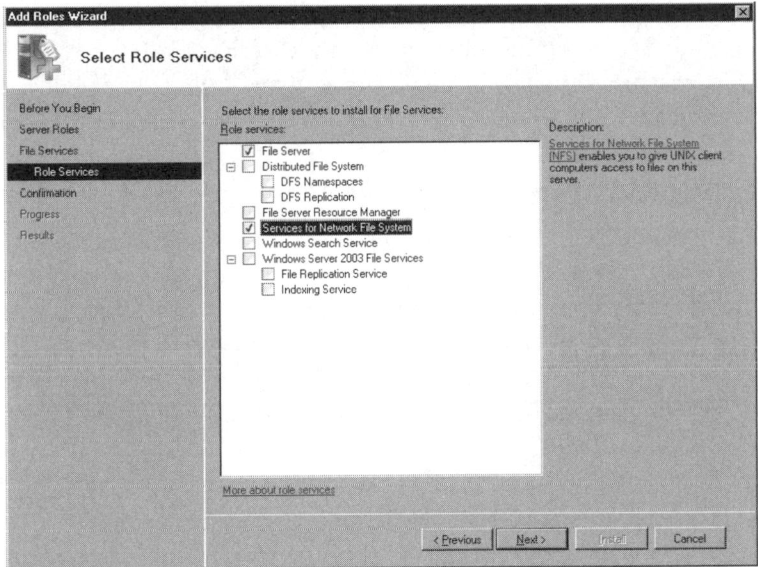

Figure 27-2 The Select Role Services page of the Add Roles Wizard

3. If the File Server Role is already installed, highlight the role in the Console Tree pane, and select Add Role Service from the Action menu. Select the Services for Network File System role service.
4. Click Next, and then click Install to install the services. Click Close when the wizard has completed the installation.

Real World Services for Network File Systems vs. Microsoft Services for UNIX

How is Services for Network File Systems different from the NFS included in Microsoft Services for UNIX? Good question. The first and most obvious answer is that Services for Network File Systems is supported on both 32-bit and 64-bit servers. This is a major advancement over SFU, which supports only 32-bit Windows.

Services for Network File Systems also has significant performance and usability enhancements when compared with earlier versions of NFS from Microsoft. The new NFS Management console is a definite improvement. And the ability to use Active Directory lookups directly, instead of User Name Mapping, is a definite plus. The overall speed of NFS is significantly improved with a new file filter in Services for Network File Systems, though NFS is still slower than SMB in almost all cases.

Legacy User Name Mapping

If you need to support older NFS clients or servers, or you have to maintain your Active Directory at a level lower than the Server 2003 functional level, you should install User Name Mapping (UNM) on your network. UNM is not part of Windows Server 2008, but is included in Windows Server 2003 R2, and was part of Microsoft Services for UNIX version 3.5. You need to install only one User Name Mapping server on the local subnet. Ideally, User Name Mapping should be installed on a domain controller to limit network traffic, but you can install it on any Windows 2000 or later computer in the domain.

Note SFU is supported only on 32-bit versions of Windows. If you need to install UNM on a computer running a 64-bit version of Windows, you'll need to be running Windows Server 2003 R2 x64 Edition.

Configuring User Name Mapping

Even when a user has exactly the same logon name in UNIX and Windows Server 2008, it isn't actually the same user. The UNIX system uses a combination of user identity (UID) and group identity (GID) to identify a user. This UID/GID pair could be repeated across multiple systems—nothing about it is unique. Windows Server 2008 uses a globally unique Security Identifier (SID) to identify the user—even if a user is deleted from the system and then re-created with exactly the same name, the SID will be different. The User Name Mapping service was originally introduced by Services for UNIX to handle mapping between the UNIX UID/GID and the Windows Server 2008 SID. While largely supplanted by Windows Server 2008's Identity Management for UNIX (an AD DS role service), UNM can still be used by Windows Server 2008 Services for Network File System, but is not included as part of it. The latest versions are those that shipped in Windows Server 2003 R2 and SFU 3.5.

When a UNIX user requests access to a Windows resource, or when a Windows user requests access to a UNIX resource, UNM is called to map the UNIX user to the Windows user or vice-versa. Note, however, that UNM doesn't actually *do* the authentication–that is performed by Active Directory in the case of Windows Server 2008, or the UNIX authentication mechanism on a UNIX system, as appropriate. Services for Network File System does not include UNM, but it can leverage an existing User Name Mapping already up and running on your network. Only a single UNM is required for most networks.

Note You can map multiple Windows users to a single UNIX user, but you cannot map multiple UNIX users to a single Windows user.

Note You can also use the command-line tool mapadmin.exe to manage User Name Mapping. Type **mapadmin /?** for syntax details or **man mapadmin** from the SUA shell for additional help.

To enable other computers to connect to the User Name Mapping service on a server, you must edit the .maphosts file. This file is in the %SFUDIR%\Mapper directory on SFU servers and in %windir%\msnfs in Windows Server 2003 R2 servers. If the file is not present, no computers can connect to the User Name Mapping server. If the file is present, but empty, only the local computer can connect to the User Name Mapping server. Entries in .maphosts explicitly allow or disallow connection by remote computers. Table 27-1 gives the syntax and meaning of entries in the .maphosts file.

Table 27-1 Entries in .maphosts

Entry	Result
host	The host or hosts that resolve to *host* are permitted access to the User Name Mapping server. An explicit IP address can also be entered.
host -	The host or hosts that resolve to *host* are prohibited from access to the User Name Mapping server. An explicit IP address can also be used.
+	All hosts can connect to the User Name Mapping server, unless explicitly excluded by a prior entry. All entries after this are ignored.
-	All hosts are prohibited from connecting to the User Name Mapping server unless explicitly granted access by a prior entry. All entries after this are ignored.
#	This begins a comment line.

Additional instructions for the syntax required are included as comments in the file as shipped with both SFU and Windows Server 2003 R2. If you choose to use UNM, you should initially configure it to enable all computers to access UNM. Once you have confirmed that everything is working as desired, you can then restrict access to only those computers that need access, including the UNIX computers that will need to connect to UNM.

Server For NFS

Windows Server 2008 can act as a file server for UNIX and other clients that use NFS. The primary interface to manage the settings of Server for NFS is the Services for Network File Systems console, Nfsmgmt.msc. The command-line management tool is Nfsadmin.exe. You can also edit some of the settings for NFS from Server Manager on a computer that has the NFS Role Service installed using the Microsoft Services for NFS Configuration Guide.

To open the Microsoft Services for NFS Configuration Guide, shown in Figure 27-3, follow these steps:

1. Open Server Manager.
2. Expand Roles, File Services in the left-hand pane, and highlight Share And Storage Management.
3. Select Edit NFS Configuration from the Action menu.

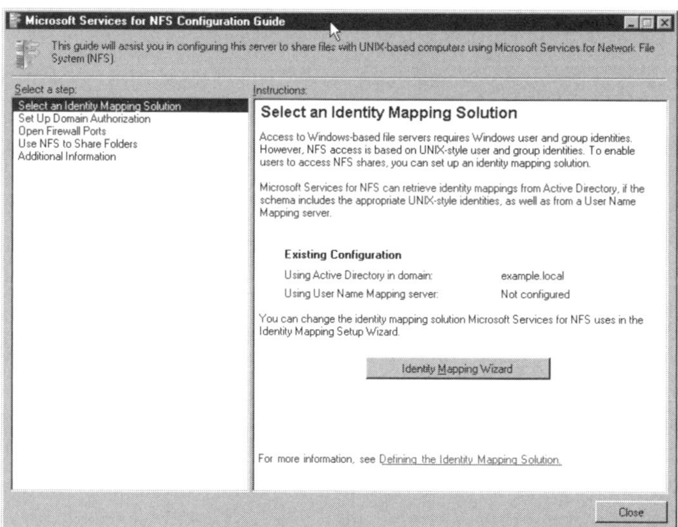

Figure 27-3 The Microsoft Services for NFS Configuration Guide

The configuration guide is a new wizard designed to eliminate some of the problems users have had creating a working NFS configuration. It has four basic sections:

- **Select An Identity Mapping Solution** Lets you choose between Active Directory user mapping or a User Name Mapping server.
- **Set Up Domain Authorization** Describes the steps to ensure that domain authentication works correctly, depending on the domain functional level.
- **Open Firewall Ports** Describes the need for opening firewall ports. These are done automatically for Windows Firewall Service, but need to be done manually if you're using a third-party firewall.
- **Use NFS To Share Folders** Contains a button to open the Provision A Shared Folder Wizard.

Creating an NFS Share

Server for NFS enables you to share (or *export*, to use the UNIX terminology) a folder or file system. Sharing is simple from the command line, from Windows Explorer, or from Server Manager.

Real World NFS Doesn't Support Multilevel Exports

The NFS protocol doesn't support sharing the subdirectory of an already shared resource, so you need to ensure that you share from as far up the tree as necessary, because you won't be able to then share another folder within that directory structure. The one exception to this is that each drive letter is shared as the top of a file system.

To share a directory with NFS, follow these steps:

1. Open Server Manager.
2. Open Roles, File Services in the left-hand pane, and highlight Share And Storage Management as shown in Figure 27-4.

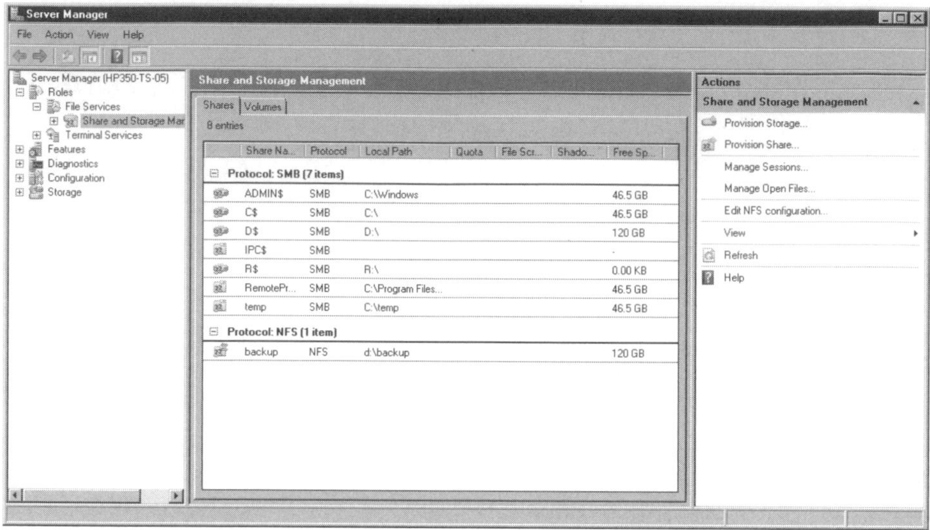

Figure 27-4 The Share And Storage Management View in Server Manager

3. Click Provision Share on the action menu to open the Provision A Shared Folder Wizard, shown in Figure 27-5.

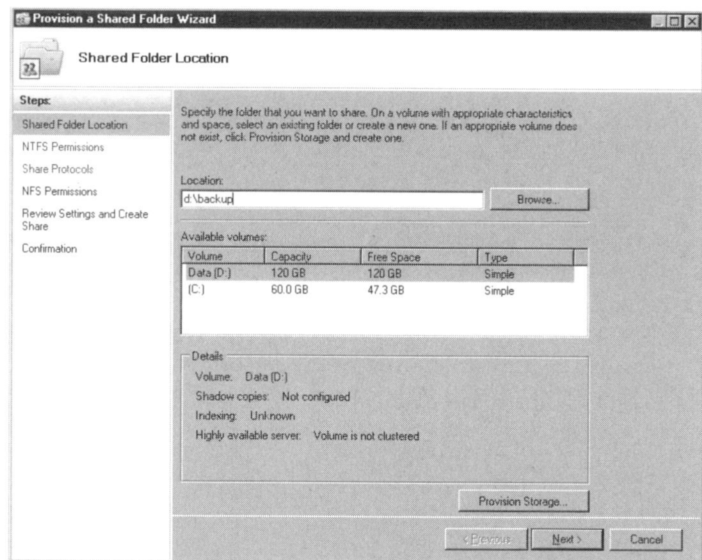

Figure 27-5 The Shared Folder Location page of the Provision A Shared Folder Wizard

4. Select a folder to share and click Next.

5. On the NTFS Permissions page, you can change the NTFS permissions on the folder, or leave them as they are. Click Next when you've made any changes necessary.
6. Choose the NFS protocol to use for sharing, as shown in Figure 27-6.

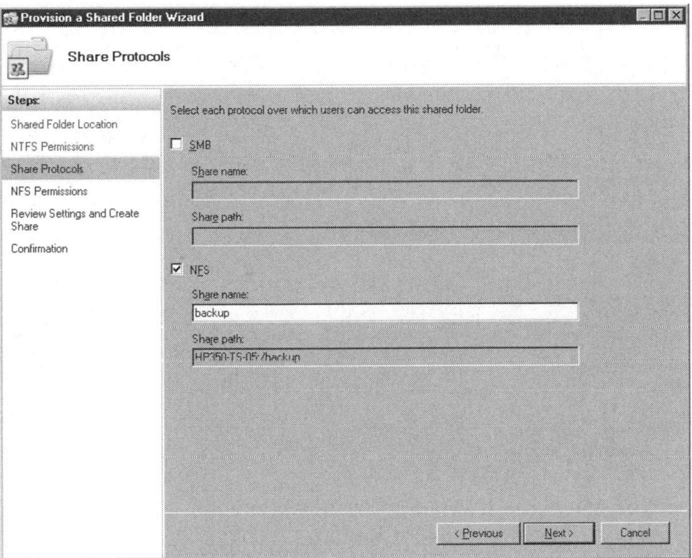

Figure 27-6 The Share Protocols page of the Provision A Shared Folder Wizard

7. Click Next. Specify the NFS share permissions, as shown in Figure 27-7.

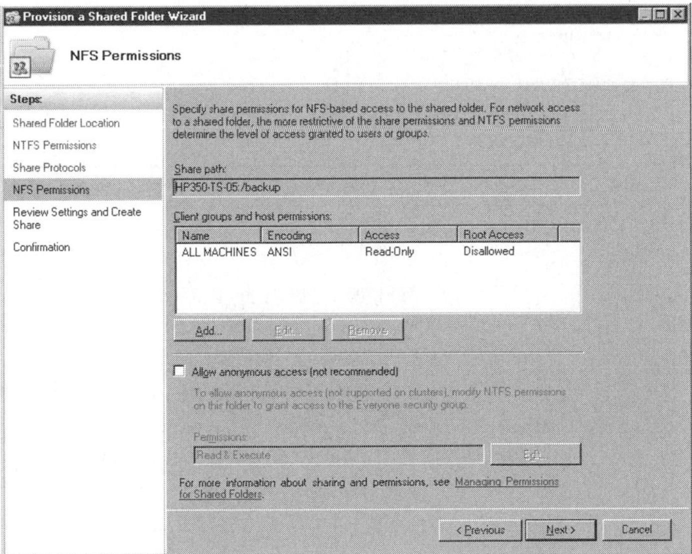

Figure 27-7 The NFS Permissions page of the Provision A Shared Folder Wizard

8. The default share permissions are Read-Only for all computers with no root access and no anonymous access. Add specific permissions, by computer or group of computers, by clicking Add, or edit the defaults by highlighting the default permissions and clicking Edit.
9. Click Next. If you've selected Allow Anonymous Access, you'll get the warning message shown in Figure 27-8. Enabling anonymous access changes how unauthenticated users are treated by Windows security. You should only do this if it is absolutely necessary to provide anonymous access to NFS shares. And you should *never, ever* enable anonymous access on a domain controller.

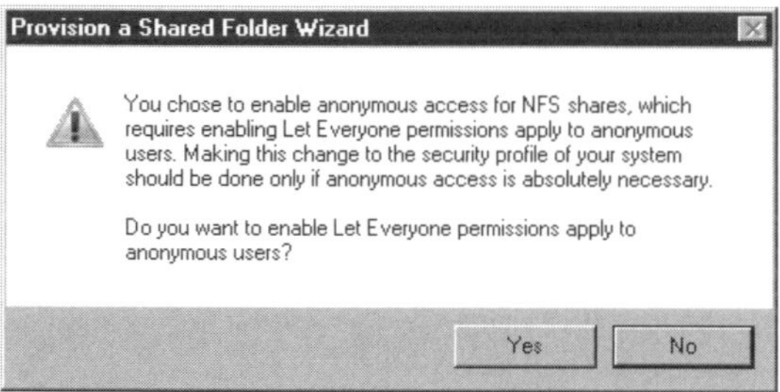

Figure 27-8 The Provision A Shared Folder Wizard warning about anonymous access.

10. Click Create. The share will be created with the options you've set. Click Close to close the wizard.
11. The command line to share the same backup directory shown in Figure 27-7 with default options would be

```
nfsshare backup=D:\backup
```

Table 27-2 shows the properties you can set on an NFS share.

Table 27-2 Properties of NFS Sharing

Property	Default	Options
Share name	The shortest name of the directory	
Encoding	ANSI	ANSI, Big5, EUC-JP, EUC-KR, EUC-TW, GB2312-80, KSC5601, ShiftJIS.
Allow anonymous access	No	Requires a security change to how all unauthenticated users are treated.
Permissions	All Machines	Read-only, ANSI, Root Access Denied. Click Add to add additional computers with specific permissions levels.

Table 27-2 Properties of NFS Sharing

Property	Default	Options
Type of access	Read-only	No Access, Read-only (includes Execute), Read/Write.
Allow root access	No root access	Allow or Deny Root Access.
Encoding	ANSI	ANSI, Big5, EUC-JP, EUC-KR, EUC-TW, GB2312-80, KSC5601, ShiftJIS.

Configuring Server for NFS

You can configure several options in Server for NFS, including the protocols and NFS version to use, filename handling, locking options, and auditing. Table 27-3 describes the options available. To set these options, open the Services for Network File Systems console, right-click Server For NFS, and select Properties from the Action menu.

Table 27-3 Server for NFS Properties

Setting	Page	Options
Enable NFS v3 Support	Server Settings	Enabled by default. When not selected, only NFSv2 support is available.
Transport Protocols	Server Settings	TCP, UDP, TCP+UDP. Default is TCP+UDP.
Authentication Cache Renewal	Server Settings	Renewal period set in seconds or don't renew at all.
Translate File Names	Filename Handling	Disabled by default. You can specify a character translation table.
Create Files That Have Names Beginning With . As Hidden Files	Filename Handling	When checked, files that begin with a period (.) are marked hidden.
Enable Case-Sensitive Filename Support In Server For NFS	Filename Handling	Enabled by default. When enabled, filenames are case sensitive for NFS clients.
Waiting Period	Locking	45 seconds is the default period to wait for clients to reclaim locks after connectivity is interrupted.
Existing File Locks	Locking	Any existing locks are shown and can be forced to release.
Mount And Unmount Requests	Activity Logging	Disabled by default. When enabled, all mount and unmount requests are logged to the event log whether successful or not.

Table 27-3 Server for NFS Properties

Setting	Page	Options
Lock And Unlock Requests	Activity Logging	Disabled by default. When enabled, all locks and unlocks are logged to the event log.
Read And Write Requests	Activity Logging	Disabled by default. When enabled, all read and write requests are logged to the event log.
Create And Delete Requests	Activity Logging	Disabled by default. When enabled, all create and delete file requests are logged to the event log.

Note Enabling NFS event logging will have a serious impact on overall NFS performance and can rapidly fill the event log. Logging should be enabled only for sufficient time to troubleshoot an issue and then disabled.

Connecting to an NFS Share

Services for Network File System includes an NFS client that enables Windows Server 2008 computers to connect to a shared (exported) NFS file system on a remote UNIX computer. To use the command line to connect to an NFS export on a remote server, follow these steps:

1. Open a command window or SUA shell.
2. Type the following:

   ```
   net use drive: servername:/export
   ```

   where *drive:* is the drive letter to use, *servername* is the name of the NFS server, and *export* is the NFS share name on the NFS server.
3. You can also use the UNIX mount command, which provides additional options for how the NFS export is mounted. Type **mount -?** for full syntax or **man mount** from a SUA shell for additional help details on the mount command.

You can use any of the following to connect to an NFS export. They will all have the same result.

```
net use * servername:/export
net use * \\servername\export
mount servername:/export *
mount \\servername\export *
```

Note When specifying an NFS resource, use the **server:/export** syntax, instead of **\\server\export**, for faster connection setup.

Configuring Client for NFS

You can configure several options in Client for NFS, including the protocols to use, the default mount type, buffer size, and default file permissions. You can set any of these options manually for a specific mount by using the mount command with the appropriate options. Table 27-4 describes the options available. To set these options, open the Services for NFS Management console, right-click Client For NFS, and select Properties from the Action menu.

Table 27-4 Client for NFS Settings

Setting	Page	Options
Transport Protocol	Client Settings	TCP, UDP, TCP+UDP. Default is TCP+UDP.
Use Soft Mounts	Client Settings	Number of times to retry a connection. Default is 1 attempt.
Use Hard Mounts	Client Settings	When enabled, will use hard mounts. Disabled by default.
Interval Between Retries	Client Settings	Default is 0.8 seconds, and applies to both hard and soft mounts.
Use Reserved Ports	Client Settings	Enabled by default.
Owner	File Permissions	Default file permissions for new files. Read(r), Write(w), and Execute(x) are true by default.
Group	File Permissions	Default file permissions for new files. Read(r) and Execute(x) are true by default.
Others	File Permissions	Default file permissions for new files. Read(r) and Execute(x) are true by default.

Microsoft Identity Management for UNIX

Windows Server 2008 includes integrated UNIX identity management directly as part of Active Directory. Microsoft Identity Management for UNIX includes support for Network Information Systems (NIS) with Server for NIS, password synchronization, and Active Directory UNIX UID and GID lookup. The UNIX identity management components extend the identity management components that have been part of Services for UNIX and bring them into Windows as a part of the operating system. Server for NIS acts as a master NIS server for your existing UNIX NIS domain, integrating into and extending the Active Directory schema to support both standard and nonstandard mappings.

The normal way to use Microsoft Identity Management for UNIX is to install Server for NIS and use NIS to manage the UNIX identity authentication and verification. You can, however, directly edit the UNIX attributes of the AD DS user and group objects to set the UID Number and GID Number.

Installing Microsoft Identity Management for UNIX

The default installation of Microsoft Identity Management for UNIX will install Server for NIS, Password Synchronization, and the Administration tools. If you don't need to install Server for NIS or the password synchronization portions, just clear them during the install. To install Microsoft Identity Management for UNIX, follow these steps:

1. Open Server Manager.
2. Highlight the Active Directory Domain Services in the Console Tree pane.
3. Select Add Role Service from the Action Menu.
4. Select Identity Management For UNIX, as shown in Figure 27-9.

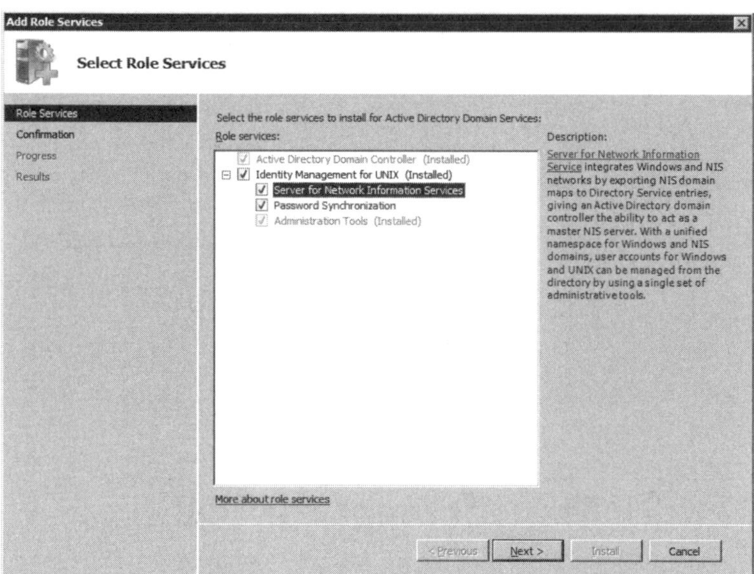

Figure 27-9 The Select Role Services page of the Add Role Services Wizard for the AD DS role

5. Click Next, and then click Install to install the services.
6. A reboot is required to complete the installation, as shown in Figure 27-10. Click Close, and then click Yes to restart now, or No to postpone the restart. If you post-

pone a restart, you cannot add or remove any additional roles, role services, or features until the pending restart is complete.

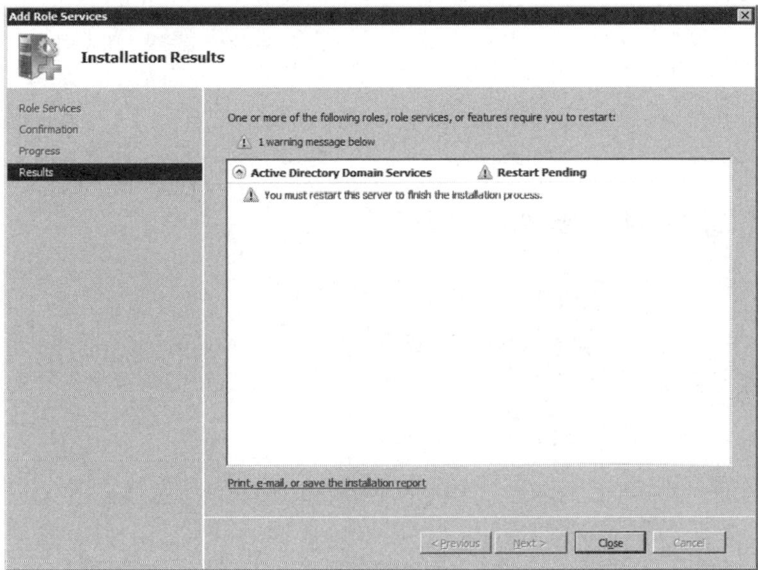

Figure 27-10 The Installation Results page showing a pending restart

7. When the server restarts and you log back in, the installation will resume automatically. Click Close when it finishes.
8. Before you can actually use Identity Management for UNIX and Server for NIS, you need to run niscnfg.exe, which is in the %windir%\idmu\setup folder. This will create the default NIS Domain, as shown in Figure 27-11.

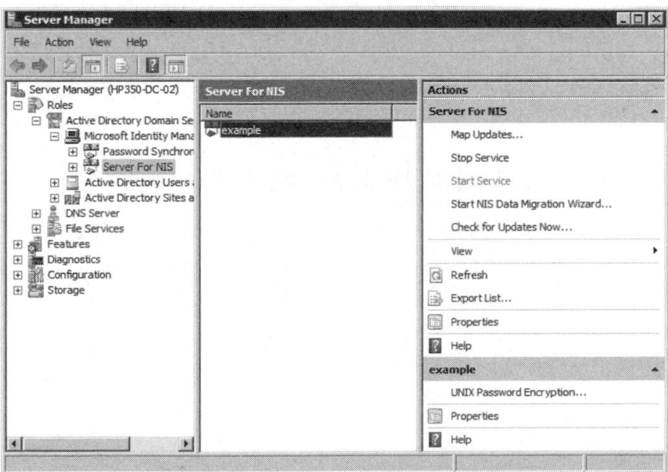

Figure 27-11 Running niscnfg.exe creates the default NIS Domain

The default NIS Domain will be based on your NetBIOS name. In Figure 27-11 niscnfg.exe chose a default NIS Domain of "example." Yours will be different.

9. Alternatively, if you have an existing NIS domain that you are migrating to Server for NIS, open the NIS Migration tool by selecting Start NIS Data Migration Wizard from the Action menu of Server for NIS.

10. Open the properties page for a user or group in Active Directory Users And Computers, and you'll now see a new tab: UNIX Attributes, as shown in Figure 27-12.

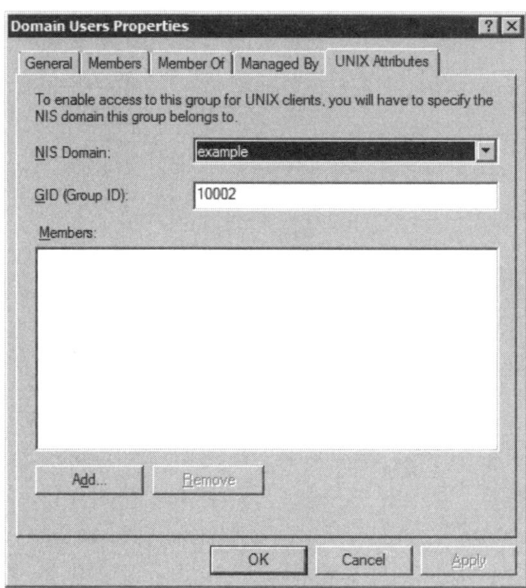

Figure 27-12 The UNIX Attributes page of Domain Users Properties

If you are manually configuring UNIX UID and GID values, instead of migrating from an existing NIS domain, you must assign GID values to the appropriate security groups first, then assign UID and GID values for individual users.

Under the Hood Setting UNIX Attributes Manually

Whether you script the creation of UNIX Attributes or enter them interactively using ADSI Edit, as shown in Figure 27-13, you can set the values without installing Server for NIS.

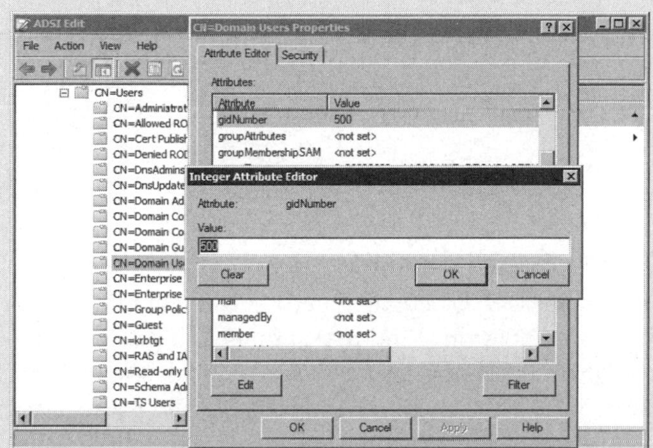

Figure 27-13 Using ADSIEdit to set UNIX attributes manually

You need to set the following attributes for a user:

- *gidNumber*

  This is the primary GID value of the UNIX user, or the GID of the UNIX group.

- *loginShell*

  This is the login shell of the UNIX user.

- *msSFU30Name*

  This is a legacy value used by Services for UNIX Server for NIS. It corresponds to the login name of the UNIX user, or the group name of the UNIX group.

- *msSFU30NisDomain*

  This is a legacy value used by Services for UNIX Server for NIS. It corresponds to the NIS Domain name of the UNIX user or UNIX group.

- *uid*

  This is the login name (account name) of the UNIX user. The value is case-sensitive.

- *uidNumber*

  This is the UID value of the UNIX user.

- *unixHomeDirectory*

  This is the path to the user's home directory.
- *unixUserPassword*

  This is the encrypted UNIX password of the user.

Subsystem for UNIX-based Applications

First introduced as part of Services for UNIX v3.0, the Interix subsystem provided a full UNIX application execution environment on Windows running as a native Windows subsystem. The Subsystem for UNIX-based Applications (SUA) extends the Interix subsystem to support 64-bit processors and brings it into the core operating system beginning with the release of Windows Server 2003 R2.

SUA is a full-featured, POSIX-compliant, UNIX application environment with more than 2000 UNIX APIs. The SUA shells and applications run as a full subsystem on the Windows kernel and support standard UNIX shell programs and applications.

SUA gives the UNIX programmer or user a familiar environment, with a single-rooted file system that supports typical file locations such as /etc, /usr/bin, and /usr/local/bin. SUA supports symbolic and hard links that are transparent to the UNIX user. SUA can also support full-case sensitivity and SUID behavior if required.

The Subsystem for UNIX-Based Applications Architecture

The SUA architecture, shown in Figure 27-14, provides a highly compatible environment for UNIX applications. SUA supports both multiprocess and multithreaded applications. Applications can use *fork* to spawn new processes, but note that fork is not supported across the SUA/Win32 boundary. SUA also supports POSIX threads that use the pthread APIs.

Note While SUA ships on the Windows Server 2008 DVD, the SUA SDK, applications, and shells are available only as a separate download from *http://go.microsoft.com/fwlink/?LinkId=59121*

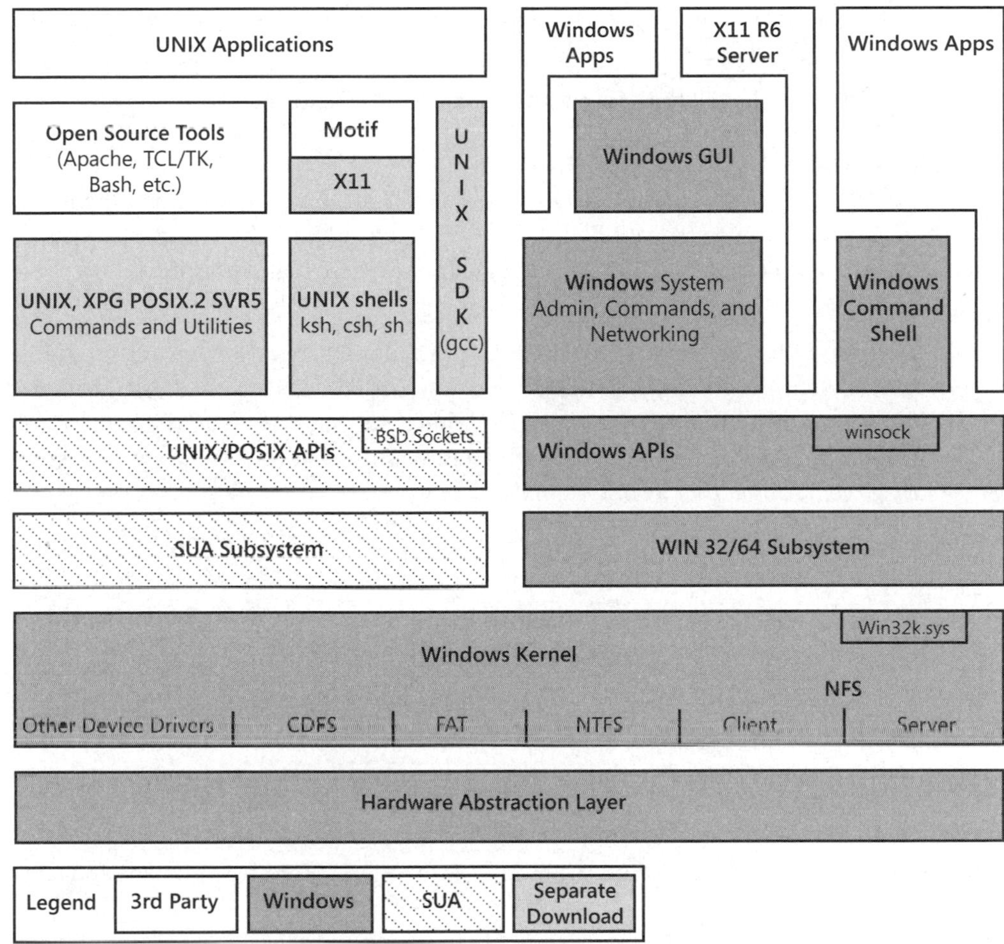

Figure 27-14 The Subsystem for UNIX-based Applications Architecture

Installing the Subsystem for UNIX-Based Applications

The installation of SUA only installs the actual subsystem. You'll need to download and install the shells and SDK to make it fully useful. These are available only as a separate download. To install SUA, follow these steps:

1. Open Server Manager.
2. Highlight Features in the Console Tree pane.
3. Select Add Feature from the Action menu.

4. Select Subsystem For UNIX-Based Applications on the Select Features page of the wizard, and click Next.
5. Click Install to install the service, and then click Close to complete the wizard.

Installing the SUA SDK and Utilities

The SUA SDK and utilities are not installed by default; you have to download them separately. They also have a separate EULA. Unfortunately, SUA isn't very useful without them, so you'll want to download them. To install the SUA SDK and utilities, follow these steps:

1. From the Subsystem For UNIX-Based Applications section of the All Programs menu, select Download Utilities For Subsystem For UNIX-Based Applications. This will take you to the download page, where you can download the correct utilities and SDK for your processor architecture and version of Windows. Or go to *http://go.microsoft.com/fwlink/?LinkId=59121*.
2. After you've downloaded the utilities and SDK (a 197-MB download!), you will need to install them on the server.
3. Navigate to the location where you saved the download, and open the self-extracting ZIP file. Select a location to extract the files to, or accept the default.
4. After the files are extracted, the installation wizard should automatically start. If it does not, run the Setup.exe application in the extraction location.
5. Click Next on the Welcome screen, enter a user and organization name on the Customer Information page, and click Next again.
6. Read and accept the EULA on the License And Support Information page and click Next.
7. Select Custom Installation and click Next.
8. On the Selecting Components page, shown in Figure 27-15, adjust the default components installed. The default is to not include the GNU utilities and SDK for legal reasons, but most environments will want them. Select Next. If you added any of the GNU SDK, you'll see the GNU SDK page, which informs about the GNU LGPL license. Click Next.

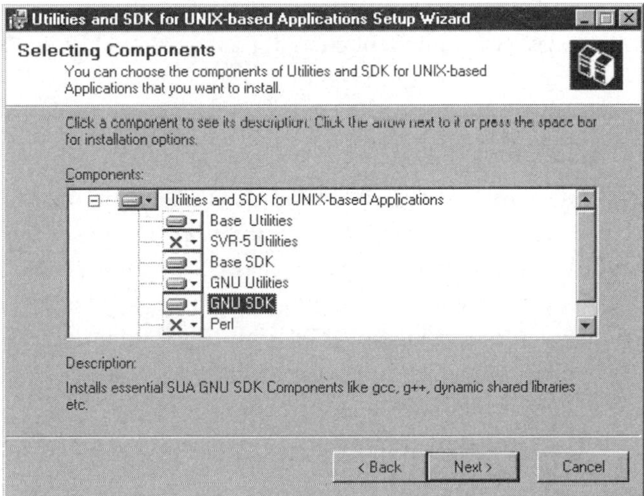

Figure 27-15 The Selecting Components page of the SUA installer

9. On the Security Settings page, shown in Figure 27-16, adjust the setuid, SuToRoot, and case-sensitivity settings. Each of these settings has security implications, and you should read the Install.htm file located in the same directory as the setup.exe program. In general, normal UNIX behavior requires that all three settings be selected.

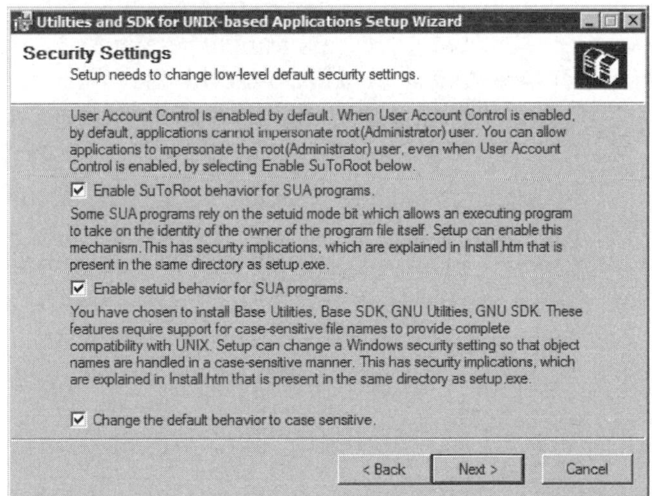

Figure 27-16 The Security Settings page of the SUA installer

10. Click Next, click Install, and then click Finish when the installation completes. You'll need to reboot the server to finalize the installation.

Macintosh Interoperability

Despite periodic predictions of its demise, the Apple Macintosh remains popular in some environments, and the increased capabilities and interoperability of the latest versions of Mac OS X have made it easier to support mixed environments. If your Mac clients are running Mac OS X 10.1 or later, you have little or no need for the legacy File Server for Macintosh (FSM) or the Print Server for Macintosh (PSM), which are no longer available on Windows Server 2008. The last supported version of FSM and PSM is Windows Server 2003 R2. If you need to support legacy Macintosh clients that can't be upgraded to at least OS X 10.1, you should consider running Windows Server 2003 to support them. If your Macintosh clients are running a version of Mac OS earlier than Mac OS X, you need to use FSM and PSM for full interoperability. FSM and PSM are *not* supported on 64-bit versions of Windows Server 2003.

Summary

Windows Server 2008 includes a full suite of UNIX interoperability tools and protocols as a part of the operating system. This includes the Subsystem for UNIX-Based Applications that gives UNIX and Linux application developers a highly compatible and high-performance subsystem to compile and run UNIX applications on Windows natively. Also included are full Services for Network File Systems to provide file system compatibility across platforms, and an integrated suite of UNIX identity management components.

In the next chapter, we'll look at deploying Windows Terminal Services on your network to provide centralized application and processing.

Chapter 28

Managing Software

Managing software on client computers can be a tedious task. Fortunately, Windows Server 2008 integrates several technologies that can make managing computers, and the software on them, more efficient. You can use Group Policy to deploy applications automatically. You can use Software Restriction Policies to block unauthorized programs and scripts. Finally, you can use Windows Deployment Services (WDS) to boot client and server computers from a network connection and easily install Windows. Although these features are not as powerful as those provided by dedicated management programs such as Microsoft System Center Configuration Manager (ConfigManager), they are easy to use and provide a basic set of management capabilities.

Note Because the Group Policy Software Installation extension, Software Restriction Policies, and Windows Deployment Services all use Group Policy, it is important to understand Group Policy before using these tools. See Chapter 13, "Group Policy," for more information about Group Policy.

Using the Group Policy Software Installation Extension

The Group Policy Software Installation extension enables you to deploy applications to computers in the domain or forest using Group Policy and includes the capability to do the following:

- Publish applications so that users can view and install programs from the network
- Assign applications to users or computers so that the applications are installed automatically when users need them or on the next restart or logon
- Target applications to different groups using Group Policy
- View installation status using Group Policy Results

To deploy an application, create or edit the appropriate Group Policy Object (GPO) and add the application's Windows Installer package to either the user or computer policy, depending on whether you want it to apply to users or computers. The next time the user logs on or the computer restarts, Windows applies the relevant policy to the user or computer depending on the package settings you specify in the GPO. Table 28-1 lists the GPO settings for installation actions.

Windows Installer handles the automatic installation or removal of all programs, as well as any upgrades or repairs.

Table 28-1 GPO Settings Needed for Specific Actions

Action	Setting required
Automatically install the application	Install This Application At Logon
Add the application to a list of installable programs in Programs And Features	Publish
Add a shortcut to the application in the Start menu and install it on first use	Assign The Application (Note: Do not use the Install This Application At Logon setting.)

Under the Hood IntelliMirror

IntelliMirror is a name you don't hear much about any more, but the technologies that enabled IntelliMirror are still very much in evidence and are now mature enough that they actually work. The idea behind IntelliMirror was to allows users' data, settings, and applications to follow them to whatever computer they happened to log on to, any where on the network. The components of IntelliMirror are as follows:

- **User Data Management** Allows users to access their documents and data from any computer on or off the network (in the case of synchronized laptops). This is done by redirecting the Documents folder to a network share and then using the offline folders feature to ensure the ability to access the data when offline. For information about folder redirection, see Chapter 13.

- **User Settings Management** Also known as *roaming profiles*, this feature allows users to log on to any computer on the network as if it were their own computer, with all their application and Windows settings intact.
- **Software Installation and Maintenance** Allows administrators to deploy applications automatically to users using Group Policy.
- **Windows Deployment Services (WDS)** Allows users to start a computer with no functioning operating system from the network, log on, and then select an approved operating system that Windows installs automatically. WDS is the replacement for Remote Installation Service (RIS).

Finding the Right Mix of Services

Take a look at the following details of the technologies to determine the best mix of services for your type of network:

- **Windows Deployment Services (WDS)** WDS permits a computer without an operating system have one automatically deployed to it. You can combine WDS with other technologies to deploy fully provisioned client or server computers from bare metal.
- **Group Policy** Group Policy allows users to access their data, settings, and applications from any computer on the network running at least Windows 2000. Group Policy distributes data, software, and settings using a *pull* approach, meaning that the client requests data from Active Directory as needed. This approach works best when connectivity between the client and the nearest domain controller or software distribution server is at LAN speeds.
- **System Center Configuration Manager (ConfigManager)** System Center Configuration Manager manages the deployment of software and operating systems on complex networks and networks with sophisticated software management requirements. System Center Configuration Manager controls the deployment schedule, and it provides software inventorying and license tracking, as well as planning and diagnostic tools. System Center Configuration Manager can push software and software updates to clients using almost any version of Windows. It can also push software to distribution points from which Group Policy either installs the software or allows users to do so. System Center Configuration Manager includes rich reporting and inventory capabilities, and flexible deployment templates. System Center Configuration Manager requires a significant investment of resources to install and configure on a complex network, so it is appropriate only for networks with sophisticated software deployment and management needs.

- **Microsoft System Center Essentials 2007** Essentials 2007 provides a combination of management, software and update deployment, and monitoring tools designed for networks of fewer than 500 computers. Essentials 2007 includes monitoring and troubleshooting of Windows computers and hardware devices, update management for both Windows and non-Windows applications, software deployment of both .msi and .exe applications, hardware and software inventory capabilities, and rich reporting capabilities.
- **Windows Server Update Services (WSUS)** WSUS provides a complete software updates solution to ensure that all Microsoft software on your network is fully updated. It does not, unfortunately, update non-Microsoft software.
- **System Center Operations Manager (Operations Manager)** Operations Manager provides an overarching management layer to Microsoft servers and server applications, allowing you to monitor the network and determine what tasks need to be done.

Windows Installer Packages

A native Windows Installer (.WMI) package created by the software manufacturer for use with Group Policy is usually the best option for deploying software. Deployment is relatively simple and requires no user intervention, and .WMI packages can repair themselves if a key file is inadvertently deleted or corrupted. You can also create transform files for some packages. For example, you can create a transform file to customize a Microsoft Office installation so that only Microsoft Office Word and Microsoft Office Outlook are installed rather than the entire suite.

Zap Files

The easiest way to deploy applications that are not natively authored for Windows Installer is to create a .zap file. A .zap file is a text file that points to the 32-bit or 64-bit setup program for the application and can optionally run automated setup scripts. (Microsoft Windows Small Business Server 2003 uses a similar approach to application deployment.)

Although .zap files are simple and easy to create, .zap files cannot do the following:

- Assign applications to particular users or computers, though you can use a .zap file to publish applications
- Install applications with elevated privileges (Windows Installer gives higher privileges to installation programs so that a local administrator account isn't needed to install software.)
- Install applications automatically on first use

- Perform partial installations of applications, with advanced features installed when needed
- Perform a complete rollback of an unsuccessful installation or enable applications to repair themselves

Despite these limitations, most users find that using .zap files to deploy earlier applications is more reliable than repackaging applications, because .zap files make use of the original installation program. (It's unlikely that you can write a better setup routine than the original, especially without access to more in-depth information about the program.)

Deciding Whether to Publish or Assign Applications

An application published in Active Directory becomes available from Add/Remove Programs (and Programs and Features in Windows Vista and Windows Server 2008) for the users to whom the Group Policy Object (GPO) applies. (As described earlier, applications are published to users, not computers.) An *assigned* application, on the other hand, can be assigned to either users or computers and is installed without any action on the user's part. Assigned applications appear on the Start menu and are installed on first use, unless you specify that they should be fully installed at the next logon.

Assign essential applications to users or computers so that these applications are always available, and publish optional programs to make it easy for users to find applications when they need them. Do not assign or publish an application to both computers and users. Table 28-2 summarizes the differences between publishing and assigning applications.

Table 28-2 Differences Between Publishing and Assigning Deployed Applications

	Published applications	Applications assigned to users	Applications assigned to computers
When, after deployment, is the software available for installation?	Immediately, or after replication to the nearest DC	After the next logon*	After the next reboot*.
How is the software installed?	Through Programs And Features in Control Panel	Automatically on first use, or after the next logon event (Icons are present on the Start menu or the desktop.)	The software is automatically installed on reboot*.
Is the software installed when a file associated with the application is opened?	Yes	Yes	The software is already installed.

Table 28-2 Differences Between Publishing and Assigning Deployed Applications

	Published applications	Applications assigned to users	Applications assigned to computers
Can the user remove the software?	Yes, by using Programs And Features (Reinstallation is also supported.)	Yes, although the software becomes available again after the next logon event	No, although software repairs are permitted. Local administrators can uninstall software.
What package types are supported?	Windows Installer packages and .zap files	Windows Installer packages	Windows Installer packages.

Note By default, Windows XP and Windows Vista clients process Group Policy asynchronously as a background refresh during startup and logon, which shortens startup times but requires two restarts to install assigned software to computers and users at logon. For more information, see the "Windows XP Takes Two Restarts or Logons to Install Assigned Applications" sidebar in the "Setting Software Installation Options" section of this chapter.

Updating Applications Deployed via Group Policy

The Group Policy Software Installation extension does not explicitly support updating applications. To update Microsoft applications, use Windows Server Update Services (WSUS). To update applications that WSUS does not support, use a third-party patch management application—such as Shavlik's NetChk Protect, available at *http://www.shavlik.com/netchk-protect.aspx*—that supports the necessary applications, deploy the updates via login scripts, or instruct users to install the software updates from a network share (assuming that the users are local administrators).

There are two other noteworthy methods of updating applications using Group Policy. The simplest method is to update the administrative installation or setup files in the software distribution point, and then redeploy the application (as discussed later in this chapter). However, this method can cause the client computers to become out of sync if users use the Install On Demand or Detect And Repair features before reinstalling the application. When using this method, promptly update Group Policy for all affected users and computers so that the application is reinstalled before it can get out of sync. Be prepared for a surge in network traffic as the computers reinstall the application from the network. When a client computer is out of sync with the software distribution point, Windows might prompt users for an installation CD and refuse to install the updated version. To resolve this condition, try logging off or restarting the computer, or use a local administrator account to uninstall the application and then reinstall it using Group Policy. You can also use the Install This Application At Logon setting when assigning applications to users.

Another way to update applications using Group Policy is to make a copy of the administrative install or folder in the software distribution point containing the setup files. Update this copy and then add the updated application to the GPO as an upgrade to the existing application. This enables existing clients to continue to access the original installation files until Windows applies the GPO and upgrades the application. When using this method, copy the original GPO and use the copy for testing and pilot deployment. (Make sure that the copy has a lower link order than the original so that Windows applies the copy instead of the original.) After you verify that the upgrade works properly, disable the original GPO (and eventually delete it).

Whichever method you use to update applications, test the method thoroughly in a lab before implementing it on a production network, and perform pilot deployments of updates or staged rollouts to mitigate risk.

Setting Up the Group Policy Software Installation Extension

Before deploying software using Group Policy, create a shared folder or DFS folder to store the setup files, and create a GPO for application deployment, as discussed in this section.

Creating a Software Distribution Point

To deploy applications using Group Policy, first create a software distribution point on the network that contains the setup files for the applications. (Make sure you have appropriate licenses for the applications.) The best way to do this is to create a folder structure in DFS. This allows you to alter the location of the software distribution point without breaking application deployment, add multiple folder targets for load balancing, and set up WAN-friendly replication, as discussed in Chapter 20, "Managing Storage."

To create a software distribution point, use the following steps:

1. Design and create a DFS or shared folder structure for software.

   Create a DFS folder that contains other DFS folders that categorize software. The second (or third) level of DFS folders usually contains DFS folders with folder targets that store the actual installation files. For example, the DFS folder that contains the 2007 Microsoft Office system setup files might be *\\example.local\Software\Productivity\Microsoft Office 2007*, with the *\\Srv2\Software\Productivity\Microsoft Office 2007* folder target.

2. Set the following NTFS permissions on the software distribution folder. (Set the share permissions to Everyone = Full Control to prevent conflicting file and share permissions.)
   - Authenticated Users = Read and Execute
   - Domain Computers = Read and Execute
   - Administrators = Full Control

   Important Permissions that are incorrectly set are among the most common causes of problems when deploying software via Group Policy, so verify that file and share permissions are set properly on the software distribution folder.

3. Copy the application setup files to the software distribution point, or use an administrative setup command to install the setup files to the software distribution point. Consult the software manufacturer for specific instructions and recommendations.

   Note To publish the software distribution folder in Active Directory so that users can find the folder when searching Active Directory for shared folders, right-click the appropriate container in the Active Directory Users And Computers console, choose New, select Shared Folder, and then type the path of the DFS folder or shared folder in the Network Path box.

Creating a GPO for Application Deployment

Before adding or administering deployed applications, create a new GPO for the applications by following these steps:

1. Install the Group Policy Management Console, if necessary, and then open the Group Policy Management Console from the Administrative Tools folder on the Start menu.
2. Right-click the domain, site, or organizational unit (OU) where you want to create the GPO, and select Create A GPO In This Domain, And Link It Here, as shown in Figure 28-1.

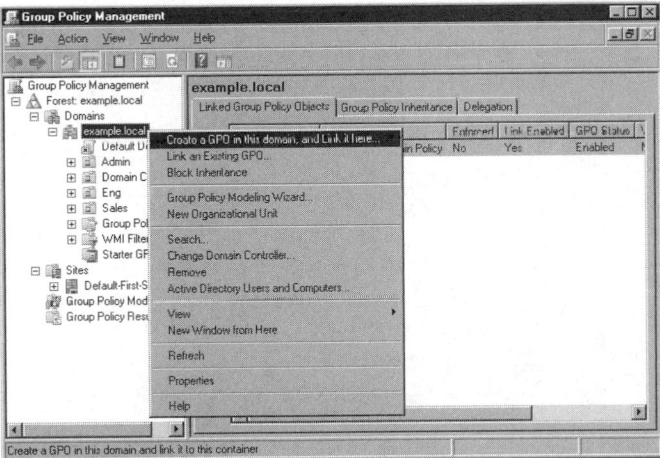

Figure 28-1 Creating a new GPO and linking it in Group Policy Management Console

3. In the New GPO dialog box, enter a name for the GPO, as shown in Figure 28-2, and click OK.

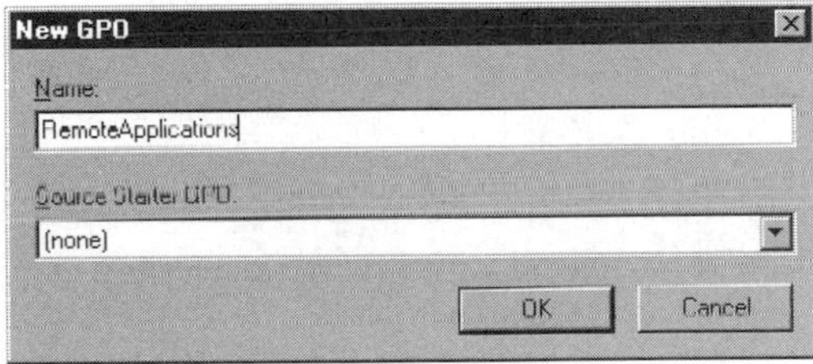

Figure 28-2 New GPO dialog box

4. Navigate to the new GPO in the left pane of the GPMC, and use the Security Filtering section to assign it to the group of users or computers you want to have the GPO apply to, as shown in Figure 28-3.

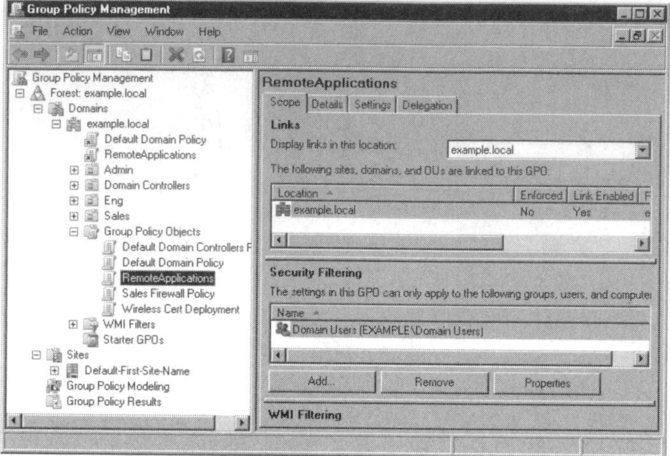

Figure 28-3 Setting the Security Filtering for the new GPO

Note Do not unlink or delete a GPO immediately after using it to uninstall applications. Windows applies the policy when users log on or restart their computers, so if you unlink or delete the GPO before these events occur, Windows does not uninstall the applications.

Real World Planning Ahead

Use the following list to help plan software deployment via Group Policy:

- To deploy applications to certain groups, create multiple GPOs and use the Security tab in Active Directory Users and Computers to apply each GPO only to the appropriate group. Or change the security settings for individual programs within a GPO so that only the appropriate groups have access to the applications (as discussed later in this chapter).
- Assign GPOs as high up in the Active Directory tree as possible. If all users in a domain need Office Word and Microsoft Office Excel, put those applications in a GPO that applies to that domain, not in a separate policy for each OU.
- Test software deployment in a lab, and use OUs to pilot software deployment in a production network. For example, create a GPO and test it in a single OU. If the GPO functions properly, unlink it from the OU and link it to the appropriate domain. (Do not assign or publish the same applications to the same users or computers in multiple GPOs.)
- Modify quotas to allow users enough disk space to install applications, and leave room for the temporary files created during software installations.

- Enable Group Policy Results, formerly known as Resultant Set Of Policies (RSoP), on Windows XP Service Pack 2 clients by enabling the Windows Firewall: Allow Remote Administration Exception Group Policy setting. This enables you to remotely check which GPOs Windows has processed on clients.

Configuring the Group Policy Software Installation Extension

A number of options control how Group Policy deploys and manages software packages. These options determine how packages are added to the GPO, the amount of control users have over an installation, and the default application for a given file extension, as well as which categories you can use for grouping applications. The following sections cover these options in detail.

Note Software Installation settings for applications deployed to users are not shared with applications that are deployed to computers. Each type of deployment maintains its own set of applications and settings.

Setting Software Installation Options

To change the default settings for the Group Policy Software Installation extension, first open the Software Installation Properties dialog box by performing the following steps:

1. Open the GPMC if it isn't already open.
2. Select the GPO you created for application deployment, as shown earlier in Figure 28-3, and select Edit from the Action menu to open the Group Policy Management Editor, as shown in Figure 28-4.

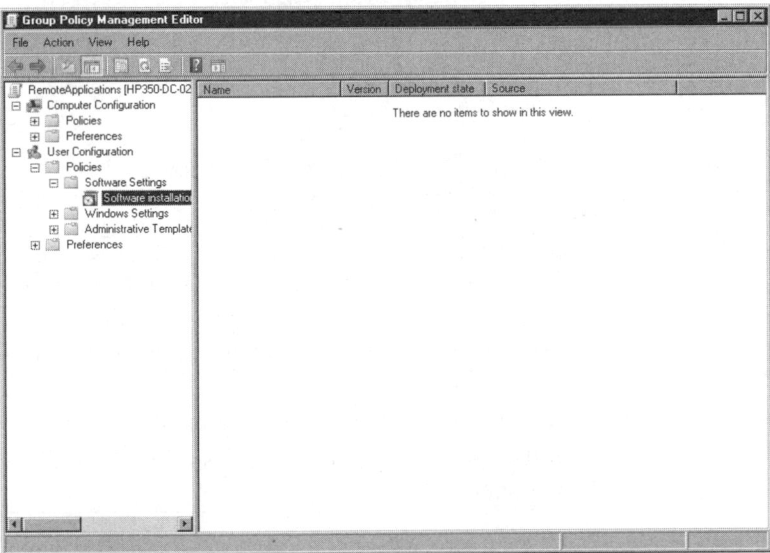

Figure 28-4 The Group Policy Management Editor

3. Right-click the Software Installation container, and then choose Properties to open the Software Installation Properties dialog box shown in Figure 28-5.

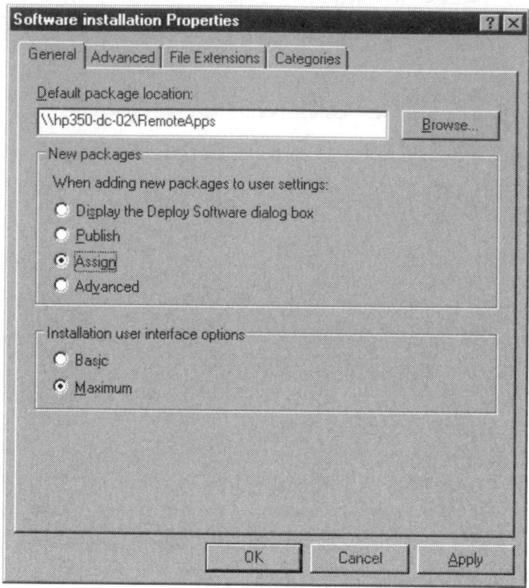

Figure 28-5 The Software Installation Properties dialog box

4. On the General tab, set the following default properties for software installation packages:

   - **Default Package Location** Specify the default location for software packages under this GPO. This location must be a UNC path, and cannot be a reference to a local drive.
   - **New Packages** Specify the default behavior for new packages under this GPO. Table 28-3 shows the choices.

Table 28-3 Default Behavior Options When Adding New Packages

Option	What it does
Display The Deploy Software Dialog Box	Displays a dialog box asking whether to publish (User Configuration only) or assign the application, or whether to customize the configuration
Publish (User Configuration only)	Automatically publishes the application, using the default settings
Assign	Automatically assigns the application, using the default settings
Advanced	Displays the application's advanced properties, allowing a customized configuration

- **Installation User Interface Options** Choose Basic for limited visibility to the user of the installation process; select Maximum to full visibility during installation.

5. Click the Advanced tab of the Software Installation Properties dialog box to set additional options for the software packages under this GPO:

   - To uninstall applications automatically when the GPO no longer applies to the user or computer, select the Uninstall The Applications When They Fall Out Of The Scope Of Management check box.
   - To add OLE information as part of the application deployment, select the Include OLE Information When Deploying Applications check box.
   - To allow standard .MSI applications to be deployed to 64-bit computers, select the Make 32-Bit X86 Windows Installer Applications Available To Win64 Machines check box. (This is the default behavior.)
   - To allow legacy 32-bit applications (ZAP files) to be deployed to 64-bit computers, select the Make 32-Bit X86 Down-level (ZAP) Applications Available To Win64 Machines check box

   Important Selecting the Uninstall The Applications When They Fall Out Of The Scope Of Management check box can lead to a user inappropriately losing an important application. For example, if a GPO is applied by site and a laptop user travels to a branch office, the user might lose software if the branch office's GPOs do not include the same software applications. To avoid this, be careful when choosing this option, especially when applying Group Policy by site. In general, assigning applications through GPOs by site is not recommended.

6. Click the File Extensions tab of the Software Installation Properties dialog box to set additional options for the software packages under this GPO:

   - To change which application Windows installs to open files of a given format, select a file extension from the Select File Extension drop-down list, select the default application for the extension, and then click Up to move it to the top of the list. This list will be empty when you first create and configure a new GPO, because Windows lists only the file extensions associated with packages already present in the GPO.
   - To set up a list of software categories, thereby making it easier for users to find the applications they want, click the Categories tab, click Add, and type the category name. Categories apply to the entire domain, not just the current GPO.

Real World Windows XP Takes Two Restarts or Logons to Install Assigned Applications

By default, Windows XP clients use the Fast Logon Optimization feature to process Group Policy asynchronously during startup and logon, which shortens startup times. However, because this means that Windows processes Group Policy in the same way as a background refresh, Windows requires two restarts to install assigned software to computers, or two logons to fully install or remove assigned packages assigned to users.

To apply a Group Policy to a computer or user without two restarts or logons, open a Command Prompt window, type **Gpupdate**, and then log off or restart the computer. To force Windows XP and Windows Vista clients to always process Group Policy synchronously like Windows 2000 clients, open the appropriate GPO; select Computer Configuration, Policies, Administrative Templates, System; and then select Logon. Then enable the Always Wait For The Network At Computer Startup And Logon policy. For more information, see Microsoft Knowledge Base Article 305293 at *http://support.microsoft.com/kb/305293/*.

Changing Software Installation Behavior over Slow Links

Group Policy by default considers all connections slower than 500 Kbps (kilobits per second) to be slow links. When Windows detects a slow link, it disables logon and startup scripts, software installation, folder redirection, and disk quotas. To change the connection speed Windows considers slow, use the following procedure:

1. Open the GPMC if it isn't already open.
2. Select the GPO you created for application deployment and select Edit from the Action menu to open the Group Policy Management Editor.
3. Select Computer Configuration or User Configuration, select Policies, Administrative Templates, select System, and then select Group Policy.
4. In the details pane, double-click the Group Policy Slow Link Detection policy setting to open the Group Policy Slow Link Detection Properties dialog box shown in Figure 28-6.

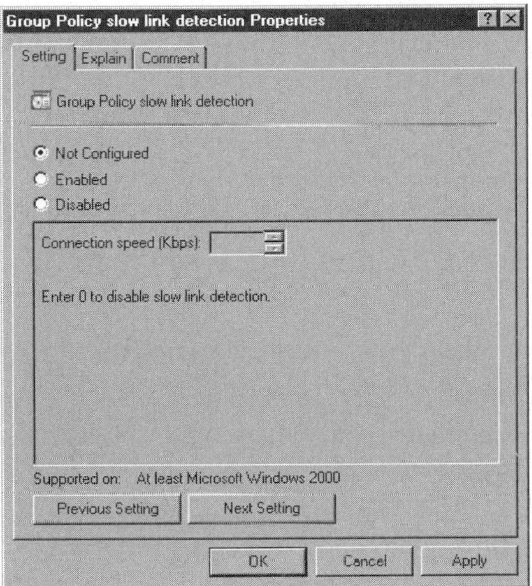

Figure 28-6 The Group Policy Slow Link Detection Properties dialog box

5. Choose the Enabled option and then type the connection speed to define as slow. Type **0** to disable slow link detection, forcing Group Policy to consider every connection a LAN connection.

Working with Packages

After you create the GPO and the general software installation options, you can start working with software packages—the setup files for a software application. The following sections help you add packages to the GPO, change their properties, upgrade and modify packages, and remove obsolete packages.

Adding a Package to a Group Policy

Before Group Policy can assign or publish applications that you copy to the software distribution point discussed earlier in this chapter, you must add the installation packages to the GPO. To add a package to a GPO, follow these steps:

Note You must apply any modifications (transforms) to a package when adding the package—you cannot add transforms to deployed packages.

1. Install the application to the software distribution point using an administrative setup command or by manually copying the setup files, as discussed in "Creating a Software Distribution Point" earlier in this chapter.
2. Open the GPMC if it isn't already open.
3. Select the GPO you created for application deployment and select Edit from the Action menu to open the Group Policy Management Editor.
4. Select either User Configuration or Computer Configuration, and then select Policies, Software Settings.
5. Right-click Software Installation, choose New, and then choose Package.
6. Select either Windows Installer Package(*.msi) or from the drop-down list of file types, depending on the type of application you want to deploy. (Note that you can deploy .zap files only to users, not computers.)
7. Navigate to the software distribution point you created and select the package, as shown in Figure 28-7. Do not use a local file path.

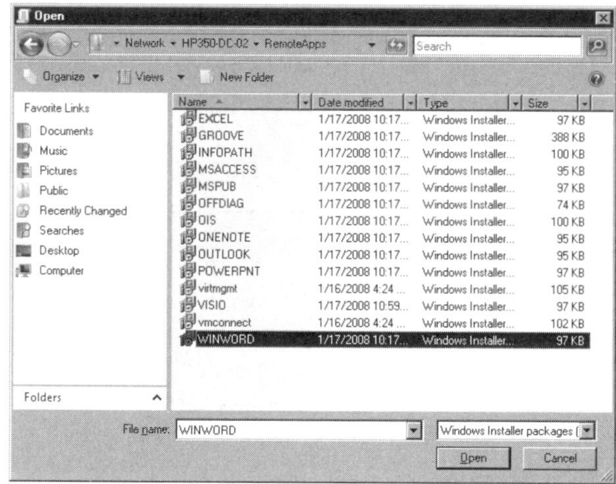

Figure 28-7 Selecting the software distribution package to add to a GPO

Note You can use Group Policy to assign Windows operating system upgrades to computers or publish a Windows upgrade to users. To do so, first verify that each computer in the GPO has sufficient disk space and is compatible with the version of Windows you want to deploy. Then copy the entire Windows CD-ROM to the software distribution point and add the Winnt32.msi package to the appropriate GPO, just like any other piece of software. After adding the package, modify the package or GPO security settings so that the upgrade applies only to the appropriate computers or users.

8. Click Open to open the Deploy Software dialog box, shown in Figure 28-8, and choose from the following options for how to deploy the package. When you have made your selections, click OK.
   - Select Published to publish the application in Active Directory with the default settings (available only with User Configuration).
   - Select Assigned to assign the application with the default properties.
   - Select Advanced to modify how Windows deploys the application. (The next section describes the deployment options.)

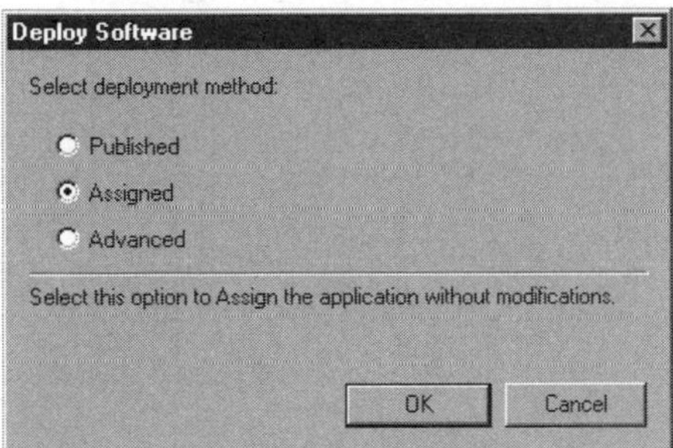

Figure 28-8 The Deploy Software dialog box

> **Note** Windows deploys packages after the second logon or restart for Windows XP clients, after the first logon or restart for Windows 2000 clients, and after the first logon or restart if you enable the Always Wait For The Network At Computer Startup And Logon policy. For more information, see the "Windows XP Takes Two Restarts or Logons to Install Assigned Applications" sidebar earlier in this chapter.

Under the Hood Creating .zap Files for Earlier Applications

To publish an application that does not provide a Windows Installer package (a setup file containing the .MSI file extension), you can repackage the application or you can create a .zap file.

A .zap file is a text file that points to the setup program for an earlier application. To create a .zap file, type the following text, replacing the file and computer names as necessary:

```
[Application]
FriendlyName="Your Application's Name"
SetupCommand="\\servername\sharename\foldername\setup.exe"
```

Many installers permit you to record or create installation scripts, which you can then use to automatically install the program after setup is launched by the .zap file. To do this for a program that uses InstallShield to install, use the following procedure:

1. Run the program's setup followed by the */r* parameter (for example, Setup.exe /r).
2. Step through the setup. Each choice is recorded in the installation script.
3. When the setup finishes, locate the Setup.iss file that is created in the %windir% folder, and copy it to the subfolder of the distribution folder where the application is stored.
4. Use the following setup command in the .zap file to launch the installation file using the newly created setup script: Setup /R /F1:"C:\Temp*Setup.iss*", replacing Setup.iss with the filename for the setup script.

For more information about using .zap files, see Microsoft Knowledge Base Article at 231747 *http://support.microsoft.com/kb/231747/*. For more information about scripting program installations, go to the support Web site for the installer program (InstallShield, Wyse, and so on), and perform a search for "silent install."

Changing Application Properties

After you add a software package to a GPO, you can change the package's application category, deployment type (assign or publish), or security settings.

To do so, double-click the software package in the Software Installation node of the Group Policy Object Editor console. The Properties dialog box appears, as described in the following list:

- To change the name of the package and support information, click the General tab.
- To assign the application or publish it, use the Deployment Type area of the Deployment tab (shown in Figure 28-9).

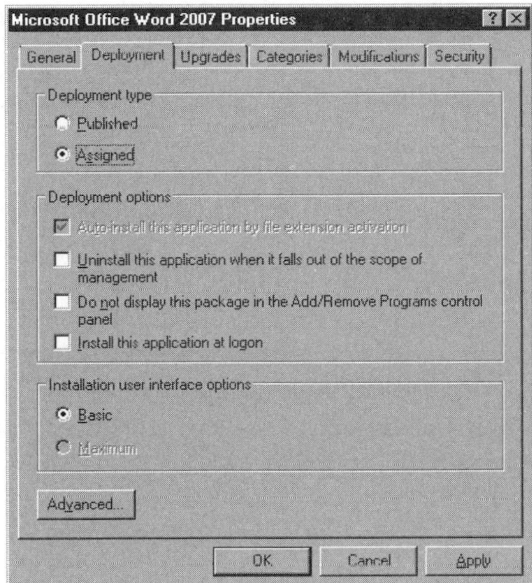

Figure 28-9 The Deployment tab of a software package's Properties dialog box

- To automatically install the application when a user opens a file associated with the program, select the Auto-Install This Application By File Extension Activation check box on the Deployment tab.
- To prevent users from installing or uninstalling the application from Add/Remove Programs, select the Do Not Display This Package In The Add/Remove Programs Control Panel check box on the Deployment tab.
- To completely install the application the first time users log on after the application is assigned to them, select the Install This Application At Logon check box on the Deployment tab. This option allows clients with intermittent network connectivity (such as laptop users) to get the whole application when they log on rather than the first time they launch the program, which might occur when they're offline.
- To show users a limited amount of information about the installation progress, select Basic in the Installation User Interface Options section of the Deployment tab. To display all screens and messages to the user, select Maximum.
- To make a 32-bit application available on 64-bit versions of Windows, uninstall previous installations of the product, or force Group Policy to ignore language settings when deploying the package, click Advanced on the Deployment tab.

- To assign the application to a category, click the Categories tab, select a category, and click Select. You can assign an application to more than one category.
- To allow only certain groups or users access to the program, click the Security tab.

Applying Package Upgrades

You can use Group Policy to automatically upgrade software packages. For example, when you get a new version of an application, publish it as both an upgrade and a full installation (for those without an earlier version of the application) so that users can upgrade to it if they want. Later, assign the application to users, and require them to either upgrade or install the new version in parallel with the old version (if you make that option available). You can also prevent new installations of the old version. After all users are accustomed to the new version, remove the old software package and uninstall it from users' systems to complete the transition.

Use the following procedure to install upgrades. See the "Removing and Redeploying Packages" section later in this chapter for information about how to complete the process and remove obsolete packages.

Note You can apply a transform to the upgrade package—for example, to allow Microsoft Outlook 2003 users to upgrade to Microsoft Office Outlook 2007 without installing the rest of the 2007 Office system. To do this, see the next section, "Applying Package Modifications."

1. Open the GPMC if it isn't already open.
2. Select the GPO you created for application deployment and select Edit from the Action menu to open the Group Policy Management Editor.
3. Select either User Configuration or Computer Configuration, and then select Software Settings.
4. Right-click Software Installation, choose New, and then choose Package.
5. After adding the upgrade package (if necessary), right-click the upgrade package (*not* the older version), and choose Properties from the shortcut menu.
6. Click the Upgrades tab and then click Add (unless the older application was automatically detected and listed here).
7. In the Add Upgrade Package dialog box (shown in Figure 28-10) select the package to upgrade from the list of packages provided, and choose whether to uninstall the existing package before installing the new package (which might discard user's settings). Click OK when you are finished.

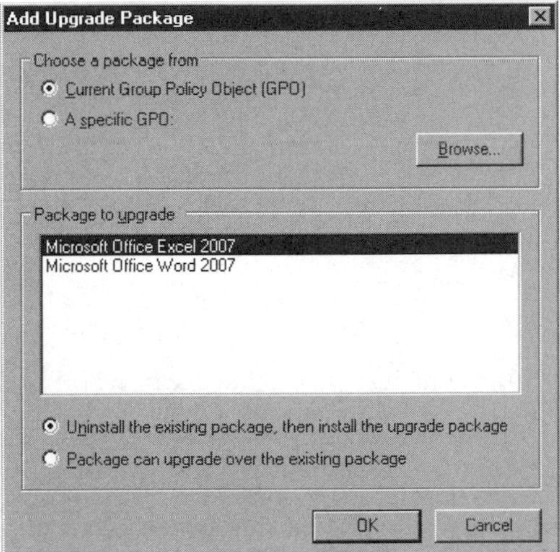

Figure 28-10 The Add Upgrade Package dialog box

> **Note** Select the Uninstall The Existing Package, Then Install The Upgrade Package option when a real upgrade is not possible (in the case of upgrading to a different application) or desirable (when the upgrade process works poorly). Also select this option when upgrading a repackaged application.

8. Select the Package Can Upgrade Over The Existing Package check box to require users to upgrade to the new package. (Otherwise, users have a choice to not upgrade.)
9. Click OK. Windows applies the upgrade package after the next logon or restart (or after the second logon or restart for Windows XP clients, as described earlier in the "Windows XP Takes Two Restarts or Logons to Install Assigned Applications" sidebar).

Applying Package Modifications

Package modifications, also called *transforms*, customize an installation package without completely re-authoring it. For example, instead of offering Microsoft Office only in its complete configuration, you can deploy a package with only Office Word and Office Outlook.

Because transforms are merely a way to modify a package for deployment, not a mechanism for allowing a single package to present multiple options to users and administrators, you still need to add the package multiple times—once for each transform configuration available to users. For example, to deploy Office in its entirety, first deploy the standard Office .MSI package. Then deploy transforms of this installation to allow users to quickly select a customized installation of Office.

To add a transform, first create the transform (this process varies by program), and then follow these steps:

1. Open the GPMC if it isn't already open.
2. Select the appropriate GPO, and then select Edit from the Action menu to open the Group Policy Management Editor.
3. Select either User Configuration or Computer Configuration, and then select Software Settings.
4. Right-click Software Installation, choose New, and then choose Package.
5. Navigate to the software distribution point for the package you want to deploy, select the package, and click Open. Do not use a local file path.
6. Choose the Advanced option in the Deploy Software dialog box, and then click OK.

   If the Deploy Software dialog box does not appear, select the Display The Deploy Software Dialog Box option in the Software Installation Properties window, as described in the "Setting Software Installation Options" section of this chapter.
7. Click the Modifications tab and then click Add.
8. Use the Open dialog box to select the Windows Installer transform package to add.
9. On the Modifications tab, add or remove any additional transforms and place them in the proper order, using the Move Up and Move Down buttons, as shown in Figure 28-11. Windows applies the transform at the bottom of the list last, and therefore this transform takes precedence over earlier transforms because it can overwrite files written by earlier transforms.

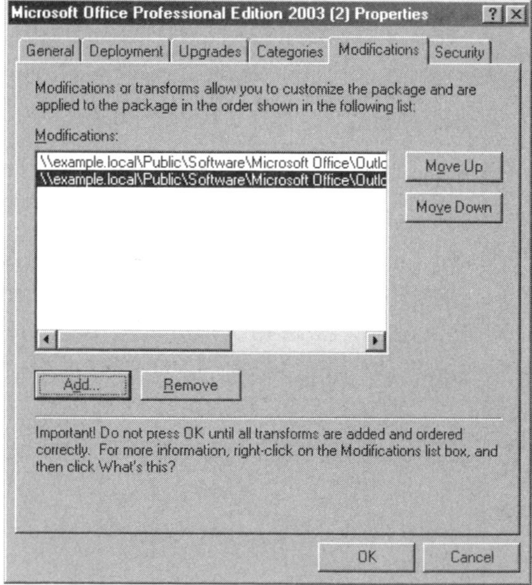

Figure 28-11 Placing transforms in the correct order

10. Review all tabs of the Properties dialog box to ensure that the settings are correct, and then click OK when you are finished.

Removing and Redeploying Packages

When an application outlives its usefulness in your company, it is time to remove it from all systems—or at least to stop deploying it on new systems. At times, you might also want to reinstall an application on all clients, such as after adding a software update. Follow these steps to perform these tasks:

1. Open the GPMC if it isn't already open.
2. Select the appropriate GPO, and then select Edit from the Action menu to open the Group Policy Management Editor.
3. Select either User Configuration or Computer Configuration, and then select Software Settings.
4. Right-click the application you want to remove or redeploy, and choose All Tasks from the shortcut menu.
5. To redeploy the application, reinstalling it on all systems that already installed it, choose Redeploy Application. To remove the application, choose Remove from the submenu.
6. In the Remove Software dialog box, shown in Figure 28-12, choose the first option to remove the software immediately from all computers. Choose the second option if you want to prevent new installations of the software while allowing existing users to continue using it and to perform repairs.

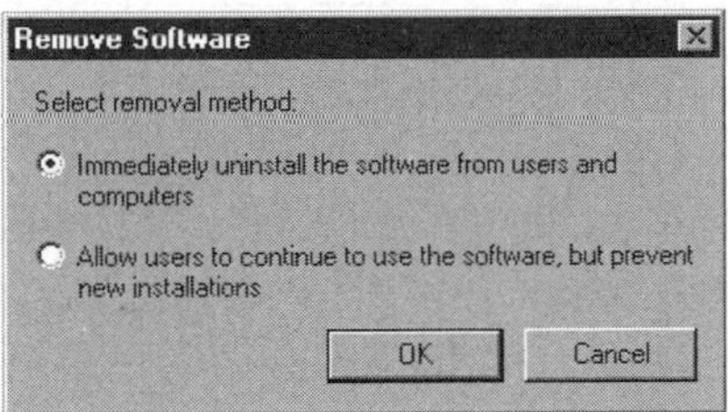

Figure 28-12 The Remove Software dialog box

Using Software Restriction Policies

You can use software restriction policies in two ways:

- To prevent users from running specific applications. This corresponds to the default policy of Unrestricted and is useful for typical users and computers.

- To lock down systems so that users can run only applications that you specifically allow. This corresponds to the default policy of Disallowed and is useful for low-security user accounts, Terminal Servers, and public kiosks.

Software restriction policies are not a substitute for antivirus programs or firewalls. Imprudently used, software restriction policies can add significantly to the workload of administrators and Help desk personnel *and* seriously irritate end users. So employ software restriction policies only when the increased security or reliability benefit outweighs the added administrative burden, and when extensive testing indicates that the policies do not adversely affect users.

How Software Restriction Policies Work

Software restriction policies provide two security levels for programs–unrestricted, which allows programs to run, and disallowed, which blocks programs from executing. Use the following types of rules to control which programs to allow or disallow:

- **Hash rules** Identify software by the unique characteristics of files, translated into an algorithmic hash. This is useful for identifying a specific version of a program because each version has a unique hash, even if a user renames or moves it.
- **Certificate rules** Identify software by its digital signature. This is useful for scripts you digitally sign. (You can block all scripts that do not contain an approved digital signature.)
- **Path rules** Identify software by file path or registry location. This is useful for controlling programs, scripts, and viruses that are always located in a specific location or named a certain name.
- **Network zone rules** Identify Windows Installer (.MSI) packages downloaded from various locations. This is useful for controlling from which Network zones (Trusted Sites, Intranet, and so on) users can download and install programs.
- **Default rule** Applies to all software not identified by a rule. Usually this is set to Unrestricted, but you can set it to Disallowed to block all unidentified software from running (though this can partially cripple a system if you don't create rules for *every* program needed by users and Windows itself).

Because a software restriction policy usually has multiple rules, Windows processes rules in the order listed in the preceding list. (When conflicting rules apply to the same program, the more specific rule wins.) Windows downloads software restriction policies with other Group Policy Objects during Windows startup or user logon, and it checks software restriction policies each time a user starts a program.

Note Software restriction policies do not apply to programs that use the common language runtime (the .NET Framework) because they are controlled separately using the Code Access Security Policy. Software restriction policies also do not apply to drivers, programs run by the SYSTEM account, and Microsoft Office macros.

Creating Software Restriction Policies

To create a software restriction policy, use the following steps:

1. Create and open a new GPO for the software restriction policy. (This makes it easy to disable.) To apply the policy to only a single computer, open the computer's Local Security Policy instead.

   Note Do not modify the default domain policy—leave it unchanged so that you have a pristine GPO to fall back on. Also, avoid linking a GPO containing software restriction policies to a different domain from which it resides—doing so can lead to poor program start times.

2. Right-click the new GPO and select Edit to open the Group Policy Management Editor. In the console tree, select User Configuration or Computer Configuration, and then Policies, Windows Settings, followed by Security Settings, and finally Software Restriction Policies as shown in Figure 28-13.

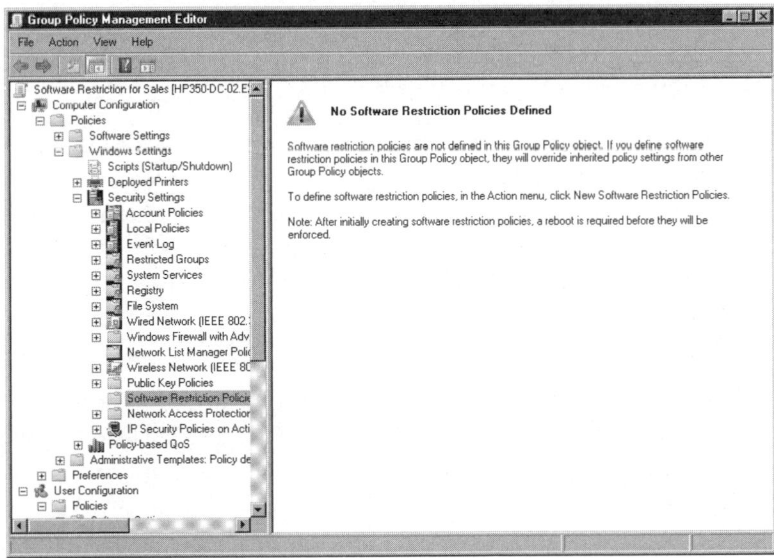

Figure 28-13 The Software Restriction Policies container

3. Select New Software Restriction Policies from the Action menu.
4. Specify the default rule by selecting the Security Levels container, right-clicking the appropriate security level, and choosing Set As Default from the shortcut menu.

Important If you set the default security level to Disallowed, you should create path rules to allow all locations from which Windows runs logon scripts, and you should not delete the default path rules or change them to Disallowed. Doing so can inadvertently prevent users from logging on by blocking the execution of key Windows programs. When using the Disallowed security level, set the Apply Group Policy permission of the GPO to Deny for the Domain Admins group, pay attention to any application dependencies, and test the policy extensively in a lab. The Disallowed setting increases your workload, because every new program and many updates require changes to the software restriction policy. If you inadvertently lock yourself out, restart the computer in Safe Mode, log on as a local Administrator and then change or disable the software restriction policy.

5. Create rules to identify software. To do so, right-click the Additional Rules container and then choose one of the following options:
   - **New Certificate Rule** Select the certificate to require or block.
   - **New Hash Rule** Select the file to allow or block.
   - **New Network Zone Rule** Select the Internet Zone from which you want to permit or block program installation.
   - **New Path Rule** Select or type the path to allow or block. Use the existing registry path rules as a guide for creating path rules that reference registry keys.
6. Double-click the Enforcement item in the Software Restriction Policies container to specify how to enforce the policies. Select the All Software Files Except Libraries option to reduce the risk of inadvertently blocking key files and to reduce the performance impact of the policy. Select the All Users Except Local Administrators option to allow local administrators to get around software restriction policies. (Local administrators can defeat software restriction policies anyway with a small amount of effort.)
7. Double-click the Designated File Types item to control which file types are included in the software restriction policies. Most of the essential types are listed, though you can add PowerShell (.ps1) or another file type to the list, depending on what is in use on the network.
8. Double-click the Trusted Publishers item to control whether End Users, Local Computer Administrators, or Enterprise Administrators are allowed to determine which certificates are trusted when opening ActiveX controls or other digitally signed programs.

Note When blocking access to system utilities, make sure to create a path rule that blocks the System File Protection cache folder (%SystemRoot%\System32\DLL-Cache) where Windows stores backup copies of system utilities.

Windows Deployment Services

Windows Deployment Services (WDS) is a Windows Server 2008 Server Role that enables users to boot a bare-metal, functioning, or nonfunctioning computer from the network and install Windows in a small number of simple steps. You can use WDS with the IntelliMirror technologies (User Settings Management, User Data Management, and Software Installation) to install Windows and then automatically add a user's personalized work environment–complete with the user's computer settings, software applications, and data.

We covered WDS in Chapter 5, "Getting Started," for deploying Windows Server 2008 computers, and the steps and requirements for Windows Vista deployments are essentially the same, so we're not going to repeat ourselves here. For deploying complete desktops, complete with applications and user settings, the best solution we know is the Microsoft Solution Accelerator for Business Desktop Deployment (BDD), available at *http://www.microsoft.com/bdd*.

The 2007 version of BDD provides you with a complete set of tools and practices to perform the following tasks:

- Create an inventory of hardware and software
- Create a test lab
- Manage application compatibility
- Automatically image and deploy desktops
- Manage the security of the desktop

Summary

Windows Server 2008 provides several useful tools for managing software. You can use the Software Installation component of Group Policy to deploy applications to computers on the network. The Software Restriction Policies component of Group Policy makes it possible to control which applications and scripts users can execute. Finally, WDS makes it easy to perform automated clean installations of Windows over the network, reducing the time it takes to set up new computers for employees or reuse old computers.

The next chapter describes the new Hyper-V virtualization capabilities of Windows Server 2008.

Chapter 29

Working with Windows Virtualization

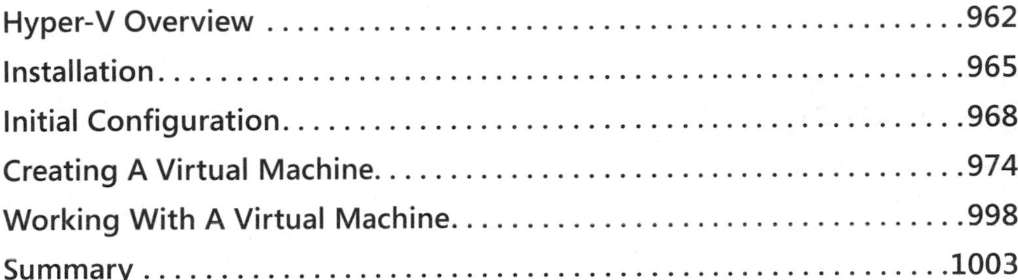

When we wrote the first edition of the *Windows Server 2003 Administrator's Companion*, virtualization was a tiny fraction of the market, and Microsoft had little or no interest in it, at least officially. By the time that *Windows Server 2003 Administrator's Companion, 2nd Edition*, came out, we added a chapter on virtualization: Microsoft had bought two products that were fully supported virtualization solutions: Virtual Server and Virtual PC. And now? It's a whole new world, with everyone not just talking about virtualization, but actively using it or planning to use it. And with Windows Server 2008, virtualization is built into the operating system at the most basic level with the new Hyper-V Server Role.

Real World What's Different?

Why has virtualization suddenly become such a compelling scenario? What has changed? We think that two very important changes are driving the move to virtualize: official support from Microsoft, and the wide availability of x64 hardware.

Official support means that if you have an issue with Windows or any of the Microsoft server applications–with the exception of Internet Security and Acceleration (ISA) server–and you're running in a virtualized environment, you're still supported, and Microsoft support won't say, "Sorry, we don't support you on Virtual Server." This is an important concern for anyone using virtualization in a production environment.

The wide availability of x64 hardware is also driving the move to virtualization. The biggest limiting factor for running virtualization on 32-bit Windows is the RAM limitation. By moving to x64 Windows Server, especially Windows Server 2008 with native Hyper-V, running many server workloads on a single physical server is easy. For example, while writing this book, we've been using an HP ML350G5 server with 16 gigabytes (GB) of RAM and two dual-core processors. That lets us easily run five or six Windows Server 2008 virtual machines and several Windows Vista and Windows XP virtual machines as well.

Hyper-V Overview

Windows Server 2008 includes built-in virtualization with the Hyper-V Server Role. Hyper-V is hypervisor-based native virtualization that uses the hardware virtualization capabilities of the latest Intel and AMD processors to provide a robust, fast, and resource-conserving virtual environment.

Because Hyper-V is built in to Windows Server 2008, it runs more efficiently and natively. A server running Hyper-V has multiple *partitions*, each running natively on the underlying hardware. The first partition is known as the *parent partition*, and acts as the hardware and operating system control partition for all the other partitions where virtualized operating systems run. The other partitions are *child partitions*, each with its own operating system, running directly on the hypervisor layer, as shown in Figure 29-1.

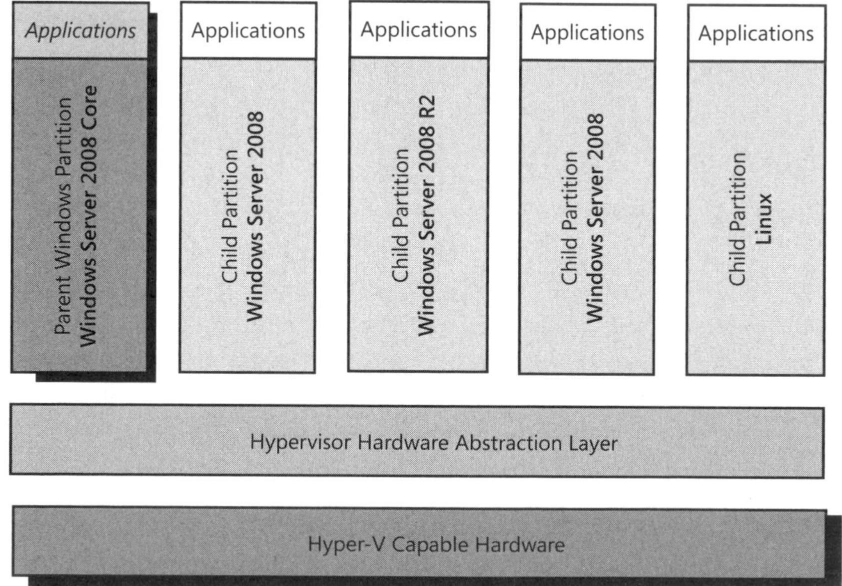

Figure 29-1 Windows Server 2008 Hyper-V Architecture

Windows Server 2003 supported using Microsoft Virtual Server 2005 R2 as a virtualization solution. Virtual Server is not a hypervisor-based virtualization: It is designed to run on top of an existing operating system–the *host* operating system–and provide an emulated hardware environment for *guest* operating systems, as shown in Figure 29-2.

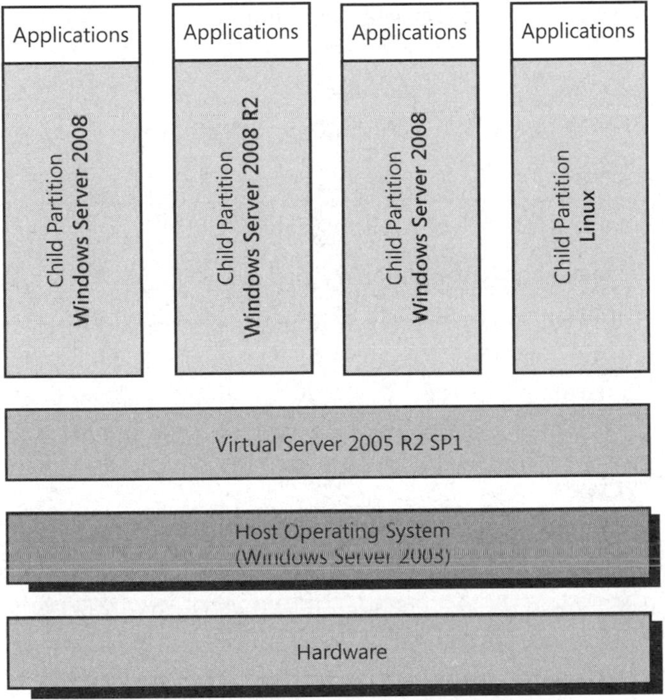

Figure 29-2 Microsoft Virtual Server Architecture

Hyper-V runs on x64 versions of full Windows Server 2008 and Server Core. In most cases, Server Core should be the preferred parent partition for a server that will be used for virtualization. This limits the resource footprint of the parent partition, and also makes it easier to protect, because the number of services and attack vectors is fewer on Server Core.

Scenarios

One of the key scenarios for Windows Server 2008 Hyper-V, as for any virtualization solution, is server consolidation. The reality is that many servers are under-utilized, and yet for reasons as diverse as politics and the need to run a legacy operating system, they need to be on their own servers. Maintaining old servers is expensive, and attempting to run older operating systems on modern hardware is often a problem. And the more servers you have, the more overhead you have, and the bigger your electric bill, and the bigger your hardware space requirements, and so on. By consolidating server workloads onto virtualized servers, you simplify maintenance, simplify the space and hardware requirements, and also simplify the disaster recovery requirements.

Another key scenario is for building test environments. We couldn't do what we do—writing about a wide variety of applications, operating systems, and enterprise environments—if we didn't have virtualization, or a much, much bigger hardware budget. Enterprises can also benefit, however, because virtualization gives you the ability to build a test environment that you can duplicate as often as needed, allowing you to test different deployment scenarios against a known and consistent baseline.

Requirements

The requirements for enabling the Hyper-V role on Windows Server 2008 are:

- x64 version of Windows Server 2008
- Hardware virtualization support (Intel-VT or AMD-V–enabled CPUs)
- Hardware Data Execution Protection (DEP)–enabled (Intel XD bit or AMD NX bit)

In addition to the requirements for the parent partition of Windows Server 2008, each child partition requires approximately 75 MB of RAM and the hard disk space used by the operating system in the child partition.

Real World I/O Subsystem

Any virtualization solution puts a *lot* of stress on the hardware of the I/O subsystem, especially the disk subsystem. Each virtual hard disk is a file, and with multiple operating systems each writing to files independently and concurrently, a lot of I/O traffic is writing to the parent partition's file system. As a result, a weak or slow I/O subsystem will quickly become the bottleneck limiting the overall performance of the virtual machines.

Also, unlike many applications, virtualization tends to be *write-intensive,* making it essential that you plan your RAID subsystem accordingly. RAID5 is a much less appealing alternative as a base RAID choice for the parent operating system. You also do not want to run software RAID on the parent Windows Server 2008.

Any RAID subsystem works better the more disks it has. A RAID 0+1 array that has four 400-GB disks has 800 GB of disk space available, but it is not as fast as a RAID 0+1 array of eight 200-GB disks, which provides the same 800 GB of disk space. By adding extra disks, the writing and reading from the array is distributed across more disks, putting less load on each individual disk.

The same stresses apply to the networking portion of the I/O subsystem that apply to the disk portion. Because many virtual machines can connect through a single physical NIC, you'll want to specify fast and resource-sparing network cards for your Hyper-V server. Here's a clue: a $20 GigE network card is not going to provide the same satisfactory experience as a quality, server-class network card connected to either the PCI-X or PCIe busses.

If you're building or specifying a server for Hyper-V (or *any* virtualization product), don't skimp on the I/O subsystem. A fast RAID controller with a large cache and a *wide* array with as many disks as you can manage is an important performance choice. And be especially aware of redundancy. If your Hyper-V server fails because you've had two disks in a RAID5 array fail, not only do you have one server down, but also every virtual machine running on that server.

Installation

Installing Hyper-V on Windows Server 2008 is just like installing any other server role. Use the Server Manager, or the command-line version, ServerManagerCmd.exe, on full Windows Server 2008. Or use OCSetup.exe on Server Core.

Installing On Windows Server Core

To install the Hyper-V role on Server Core, first complete the normal installation and configuration of Windows Server 2008 Server Core, as described in Chapter 9, "Installing and Configuring Server Core." Make sure that you enable remote administration, because you have no way to directly manage or create virtual machines on Server Core—the Hyper-V Management Console won't run on Server Core.

When you've completed the base operating system configuration, use the following commands to add the Hyper-V role:

```
bcdedit /set hypervisorlaunchtype auto
start /w ocsetup Microsoft-Hyper-V
```

You'll need to reboot the server after these commands have been run.

Note The bcdedit command shown previously is not strictly required, but if you don't run it, you need to do two reboots before Hyper-V is fully operational.

Installing on Windows Server 2008

To install the Hyper-V role on full Windows Server 2008, first complete the normal installation and configuration of Windows Server 2008, as described in Chapter 7, "Configuring a New Installation." When initial configuration has completed, you can install the Hyper-V role using the following steps:

1. Open the Server Manager console if it isn't open already.
2. Select Add Roles from the Action menu to open the Before You Begin page of the Add Roles Wizard.
3. Read the advice on the Before You Begin page. It's actually good advice and a useful reminder. If you've read the page, understand all its implications, and don't ever want to see the page again, select the Skip This Page By Default check box. We leave it unchecked, personally.

> **Note** If you've already run the Add Roles Wizard, and selected Skip This Page By Default, you won't see the Before You Begin page of the Add Roles Wizard.

4. Click Next to open the Select Server Roles page of the Add Roles Wizard.
5. Select Hyper-V from the list of roles.
6. Click Next to open the Hyper-V page, as shown in Figure 29-3.This page describes the Hyper-V role and includes a Things To Note section that includes cautions and advisories specific to the Hyper-V role. The page also has a link to several Additional Information pages with up-to-date information on Hyper-V.

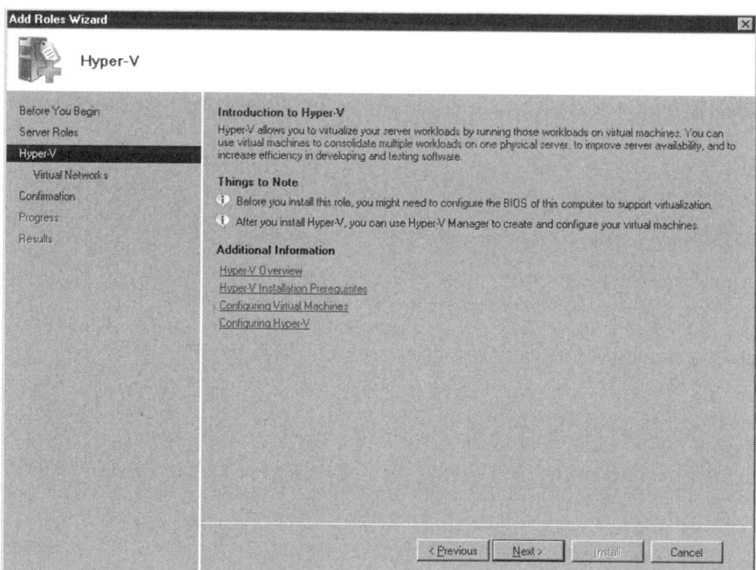

Figure 29-3 The Hyper-V page of the Add Roles Wizard

7. Once you've read the Things To Note, click Next to open the Create Virtual Networks page shown in Figure 29-4.

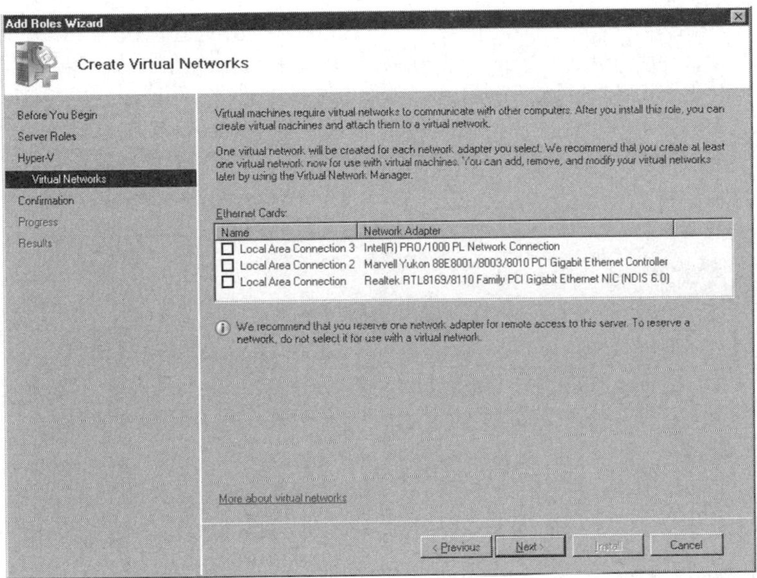

Figure 29-4 The Create Virtual Networks page of the Add Roles Wizard

8. Select the Ethernet Cards you want to create Virtual Networks for. The general rule is to leave one network card not used for virtual networks to ensure that you maintain full remote connectivity to the server. If you select all the network cards available, you'll see the warning shown in Figure 29-5.

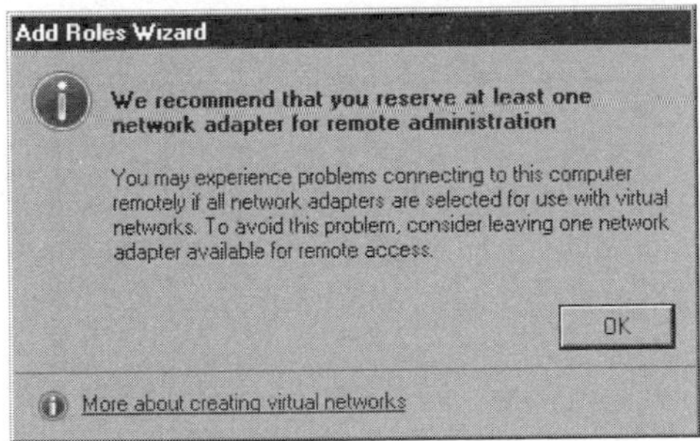

Figure 29-5 The Add Roles Wizard warning if all network cards are selected

9. When the Add Roles Wizard has all the information necessary to proceed, it will open the Confirm Installation Selections page. If everything looks correct, click Install to begin the installation.

10. When the installation completes, you'll see the Installation Results page. The Hyper-V installation will require a reboot. Click Close to complete the wizard. Click Yes to reboot now.
11. After the server reboots, log back on with the same account that you used to add the Hyper-V role. The Resume Configuration Wizard will open, and when the configuration is complete, you'll see the final Installation Results page, as shown in Figure 29-6.

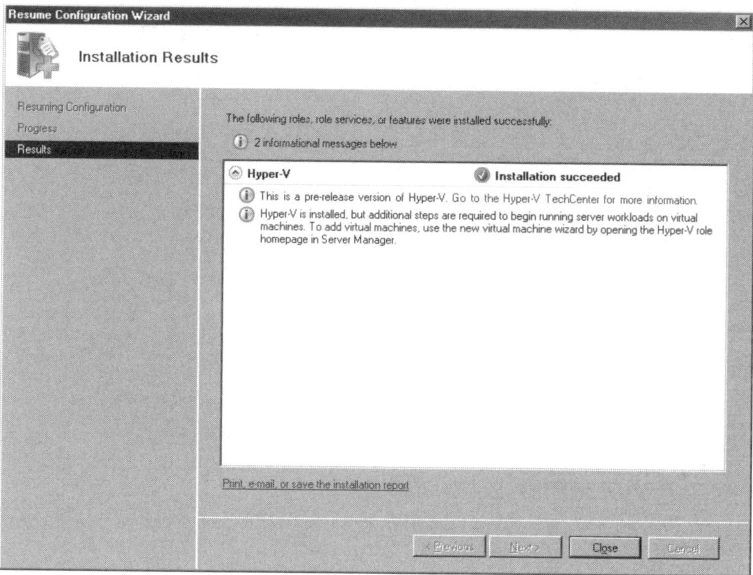

Figure 29-6 The Installation Results page of the Resume Configuration Wizard

12. Click Close to exit the wizard.

Initial Configuration

After you've installed the Hyper-V role, you need to actually configure Hyper-V and then start adding virtual machines. The management tool for Hyper-V is the Hyper-V Manager console. Like other management consoles in Windows Server 2008, it integrates into the Server Manager console. You can use it there, or run it as a stand-alone. We prefer stand-alone, frankly. Open Administrative Tools and select Hyper-V Manager from the list to run the Hyper-V Manager console as a stand-alone.

Note You could run the Hyper-V Manager console by starting it from the command line, but unlike other Windows Server 2008 management consoles, it's not in %windir%\system32. It is actually in %ProgramFiles%\Hyper-V, which isn't on your path. The command line for this is:

"%ProgramFiles%\Hyper-V\virtmgmt.msc" (quotes required).

The first time that you run the Hyper-V Manager console, the first thing you'll see is the Hyper-V EULA. Why we have to sign off on Hyper-V separately is something only the Microsoft lawyers can fathom, but select the I Have Read And Agreed To This EULA box, and click Accept. It's not like you have a choice if you want to open the Hyper-V Manager console, as shown in Figure 29-7.

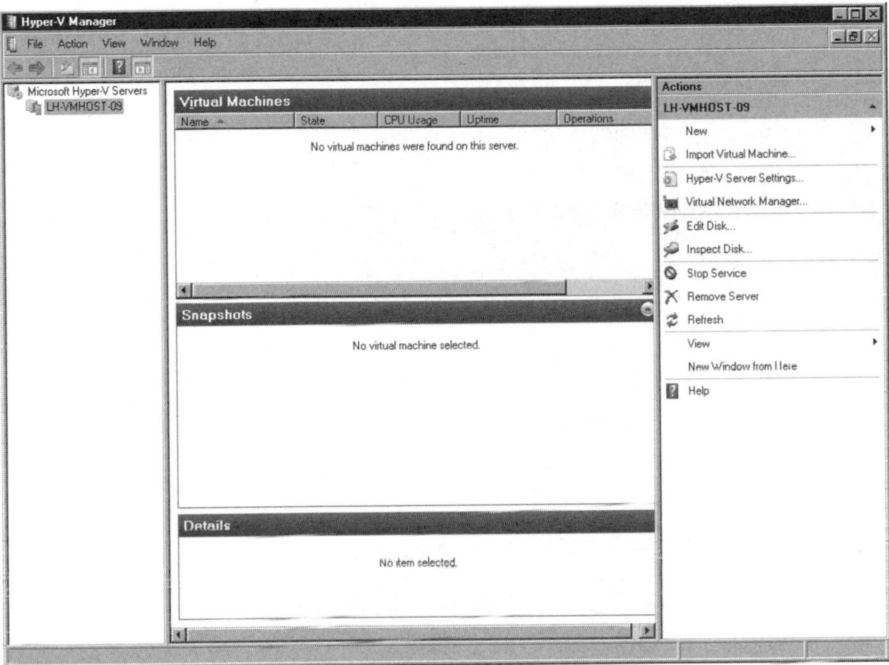

Figure 29-7 The Hyper-V Manager console

Configuring Networks

The first step after installing Hyper-V is to configure your networks. Step 7 in the Add Roles Wizard (described previously in the "Installing on Windows Server 2008" section) creates the network and attaches it to the network cards you selected, but that makes the new networks available only as a private network connection, which isn't terribly useful if you need to connect your virtual machines to the outside world, or another network.

Hyper-V supports three kinds of virtual networks:

- **External** An external network is a virtual network switch that binds to the physical network adapter, providing access to resources outside the virtual network. An external network can be assigned to a VLAN.
- **Internal** An internal network is a virtual network switch that allows virtual machines on the server to connect to each other, and to the parent partition. An internal network can be assigned to a VLAN.

- **Private** A private network is a virtual network switch that allows virtual machines to connect to each other, but provides no connection between the virtual machines and the physical computer.

Setting Network Type

To set your networks to be External networks, allowing them to connect through the physical network adapter to outside the physical computer, use the following steps:

1. Open the Hyper-V Manager console if it isn't already open.
2. Select the Hyper-V computer in the left-hand pane, and then click Virtual Network Manager in the Actions pane to open the Virtual Network Manager, shown in Figure 29-8.

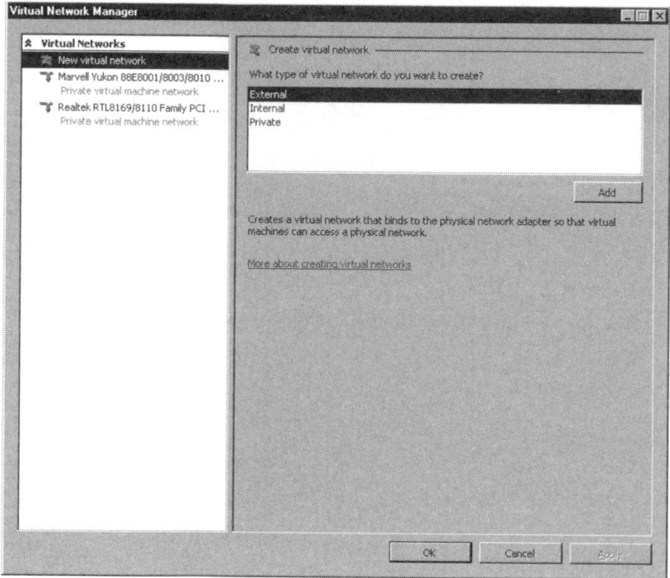

Figure 29-8 The Virtual Network Manager

3. Select the Virtual Network you want to make an External network. Edit the name to provide a more meaningful description, and add any notes you want to add.
4. Select External, and select the physical network adapter you want to connect this virtual network to from the drop-down list, as shown in Figure 29-9.

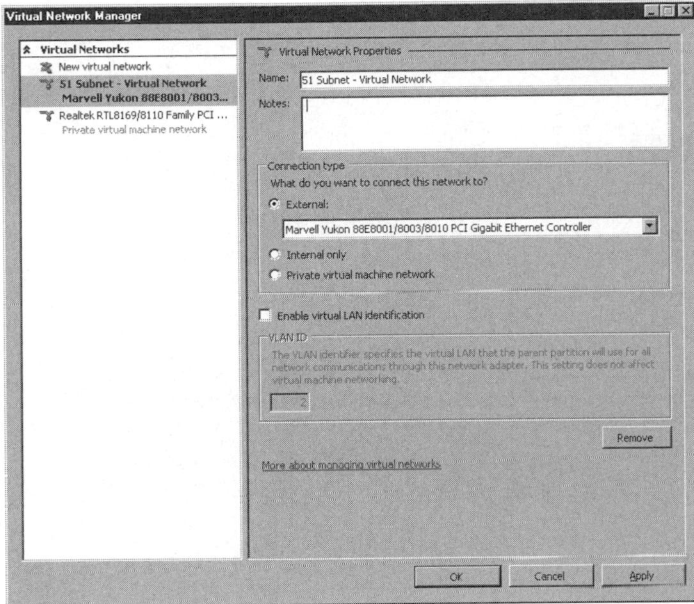

Figure 29-9 Attaching a virtual network to an physical adapter to create an External Network

5. Click OK to close the Virtual Network Manager and apply your changes.

Adding a Virtual Network

You can add additional virtual networks to your Hyper-V server. These can be private, internal, or external networks, as described earlier. To create additional virtual networks, follow these steps:

1. Open the Hyper-V Manager console if it isn't already open.
2. Select the Hyper-V computer in the left-hand pane, and then click Virtual Network Manager in the Actions pane to open the Virtual Network Manager.
3. Select New Virtual Network in the left-hand pane, and select the type of virtual network you want to create in the right-hand pane of the Virtual Network Manager.
4. Click Add, and the New Virtual Network pane replaces the Create Virtual Network pane on the right of the Virtual Network Manager, as shown in Figure 29-10.

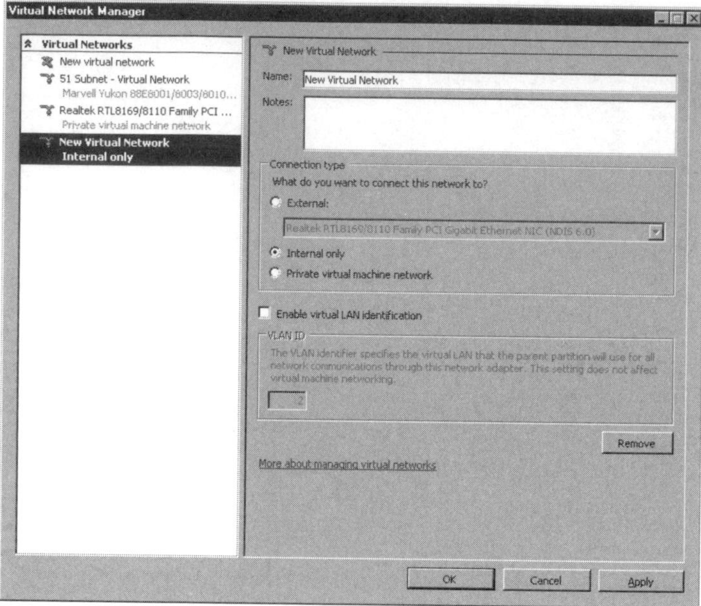

Figure 29-10 The New Virtual Network pane of the Virtual Network Manager

5. Enter a descriptive name for the new virtual network, and any notes. Select the type of virtual network, and click OK to add the network.

Server Settings

The next step in configuring your Hyper-V server is to set the overall server settings and the user-specific settings. General server settings include the default location for hard disks and the default location for virtual machines. User-specific settings include keyboard settings and saved credentials.

To set the server settings for a Hyper-V server, use the following steps:

1. Open the Hyper-V Manager console if it isn't already open.
2. Select the Hyper-V computer in the left-hand pane, and then click Hyper-V Server Settings in the Actions pane to open the Hyper-V Settings dialog box, shown in Figure 29-11.

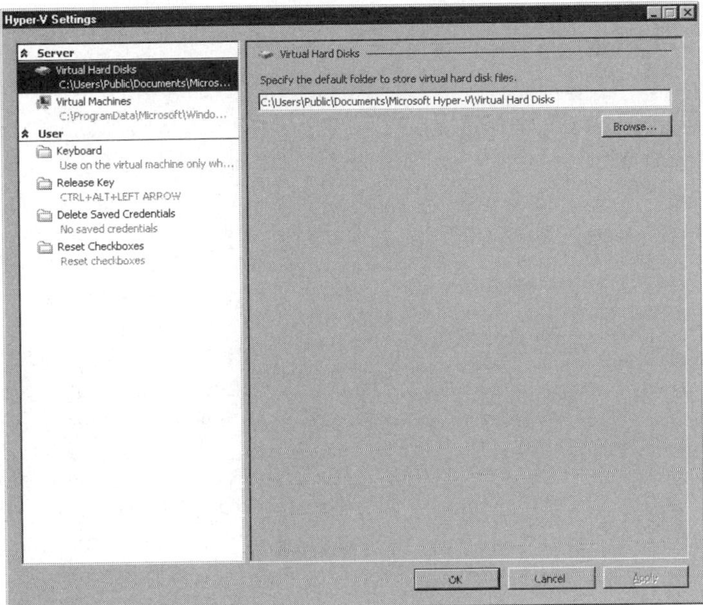

Figure 29-11 The Hyper-V Settings dialog box

3. Select Virtual Hard Disks in the left pane, and enter the root path to use as a default for storing the VHD files used by virtual machines. You can change the actual path of any specific VHD later—this just sets the default location.
4. Select Virtual Machines in the left pane, and set the default path for storing virtual machine snapshot files.
5. Select Keyboard in the left pane, and specify how special Windows key combinations (such as Alt+Tab and Ctrl+Esc) are used.
6. Select Release Key and set the default key combination to release a captured mouse when connecting to a virtual machine that doesn't have Integration Components installed.
7. Select Delete Saved Credentials or Reset Checkboxes to remove any saved credentials on the server or to reset all the Don't Ask Me Again check boxes on the server.
8. Click OK to change the settings and return to the main Hyper-V Manager.

Real World Default Locations

The default locations that Microsoft has chosen for VHD files and snapshot files frankly just don't make any sense at all. The default for VHD files is C:\Users\Public\Documents\Microsoft Hyper-V\Virtual Hard Disks–on the system drive of the parent partition! That's just wrong. Your VHD files are going to take up hundreds of gigabytes of space, possibly terabytes of space. Not what you want on the system drive of your parent partition.

The default for snapshots is equally bad: C:\ProgramData\Microsoft\Windows\Hyper-V. Still on the system drive of the parent partition, and again these are files that are going to take up a lot of space. Plus putting these files on the system drive is a bad decision for performance.

We suggest creating one or more disk volumes specifically for storing VHDs and snapshots. This makes backups easier, allows you to store your VHDs on your fastest array, and just makes good sense. Even if you had to completely rebuild the server, having your VHDs and snapshot files on separate volumes allows you to greatly simplify the recovery process.

Creating A Virtual Machine

OK, enough of that getting ready stuff and basic configuration. The real reason we're running Hyper-V is to actually create and use virtual machines (VMs), so let's get down to it. You can make a VM in several different ways, but they all start with the Hyper-V Manager console.

Note The next version of System Center Virtual Machine Manager will support Hyper-V, including the creation of VMs. We can't wait!

The basic steps for creating a VM are:

- Create a new VM, giving it a name and location.
- Assign RAM to the VM.
- Connect to a network.
- Assign or create a Virtual Disk.
- Specify where the operating system will be loaded from.

The New Virtual Machine Wizard handles all these basic steps, but it is pretty limited and for many situations won't be sufficient. You'll need to actually configure the VM further before you can begin installing or actually using an operating system. We'll start by walking through the steps for creating a VM, and then show you how to change that basic VM to be bit more useful and flexible.

Creating a Basic VM

To create a new VM, follow these steps:

1. Open the Hyper-V Manager console if it isn't already open.
2. Select the Hyper-V computer in the left-hand pane, click New, and then click Virtual Machine from the Actions menu to open the New Virtual Machine Wizard.
3. If you haven't disabled the Before You Begin page, you can read the description of what's going to happen, or click More About Creating Virtual Machines link to open the Help pages on creating a VM. Select the Do Not Show This Page Again check box so that you don't have to see this again.
4. Click Next to open the Specify Name And Location page, shown in Figure 29-12.

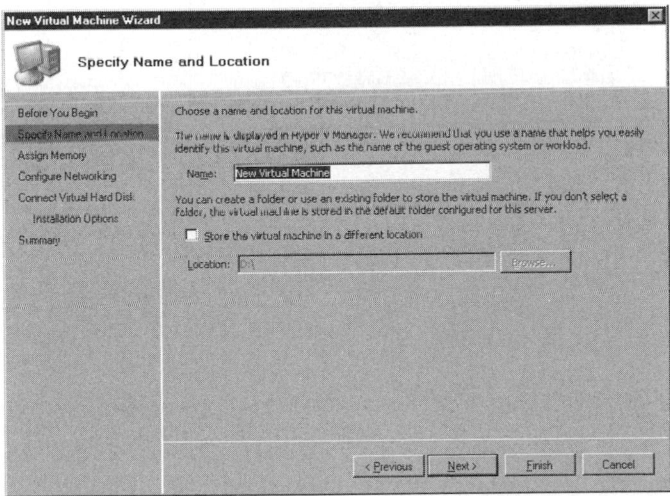

Figure 29-12 The Specify Name and Location page of the New Virtual Machine Wizard

5. Enter a name for the VM and select the Store The Virtual Machine In A Different Location check box. By selecting this box, all the files for this VM will be stored in a directory with the same name as the VM, immediately below that shown in the Location field.

Note For this first VM, with a name of hp350-test-12 and a default location of D:\, the result will be a new directory of D:\hp350-test-12 with the files and subdirectories of the VM stored in it.

6. Click Next to open the Assign Memory page. Specify the amount of memory that will be assigned to the new VM. You should specify the same amount of memory that you would specify for the RAM of the physical computer that this VM is replacing.
7. Click Next to open the Configure Networking page, shown in Figure 29-13. Choose the network that the VM will be connected to from the drop-down list, or leave it not connected if you'll be specifying the networking later.

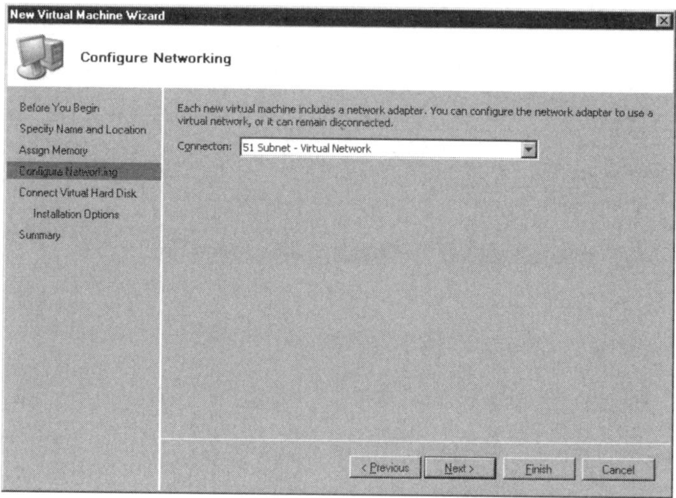

Figure 29-13 The Configure Networking page of the New Virtual Machine Wizard

8. Click Next to open the Connect Virtual Hard Disk page, shown in Figure 29-14.

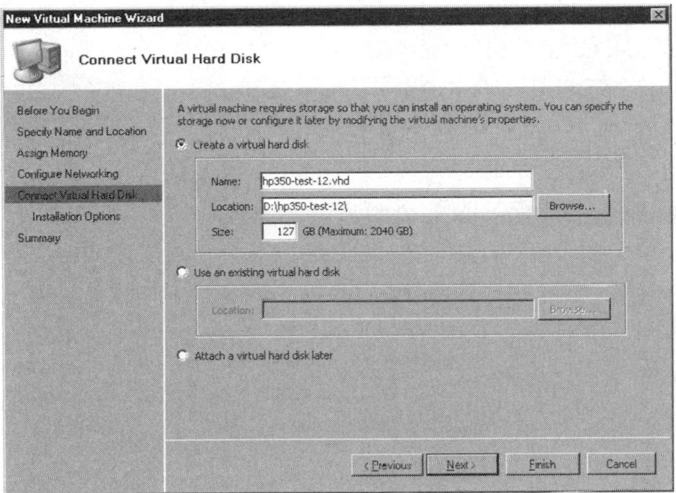

Figure 29-14 The Connect Virtual Hard Disk page of the New Virtual Machine Wizard

9. Select Create A Virtual Disk to create a new, automatically expanding virtual disk with a nominal size of 127 GB. Accept the default location and name, or modify as appropriate for your environment. If you think you'll need a system disk larger than 127 GB, change the Size field.

> **Important** The maximum size of an IDE VHD in Hyper-V is 2 terabytes (2,040 GB, actually). But a dynamically expanding virtual hard disk doesn't take up any more room on your physical hard disk or array than it actually needs to. As you expand your use of the VM, the size of the disk will continue to grow. See "Disks and Controllers" later in this chapter for a full discussion of disk types and strategies.

10. Click Next to open the Installation Options page, as shown in Figure 29-15. The choices are:

    - **Install An Operating System Later** This option requires you to configure how your operating system will be installed manually before starting the VM.
    - **Install An Operating System From A Boot CD/DVD-ROM** This option allows you to connect to the physical computer's CD or DVD drive, or to mount an ISO file stored on the physical computer's hard disk as if it were a physical CD/DVD drive.
    - **Install An Operating System From A Boot Floppy Disk** This option allows you to connect to a virtual floppy disk (.vfd) file as if it were a physical floppy drive.

- **Install An Operating System From A Network-Based Installation Server**
  This option changes the BIOS setting for the VM to enable a network boot from a PXE server, and also changes the network card for the VM to be an emulated Legacy Network Adapter instead of the default synthetic network adapter. If you're deploying using a WDS server, choose this option.

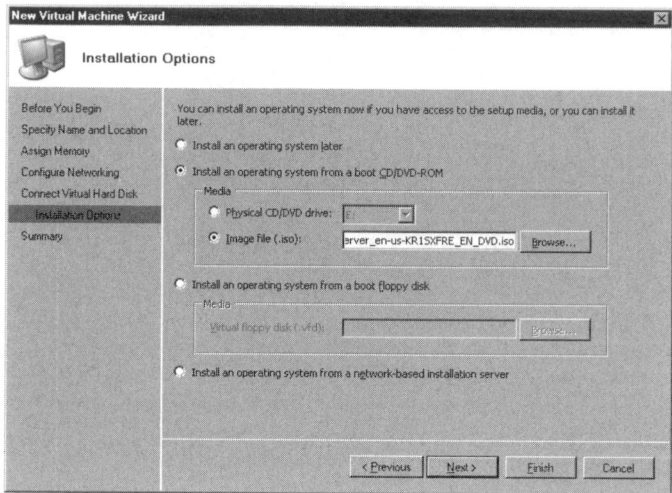

Figure 29-15 The Installation Options page of the New Virtual Machine Wizard

11. Click Next to open the Completing the New Virtual Machine Wizard summary page, or click Finish to skip the last step. On this last page, you can choose to automatically start the new VM as soon as you close the wizard, but we think that's a bad option. Just skip it—you should probably adjust the settings for the new VM before you start it anyway.

Machine Settings

After you've created a VM, you'll probably want to make some changes to the machine settings that the New Virtual Machine Wizard has configured. To adjust the settings of a VM, select the virtual machine in the center Virtual Machines pane of Hyper-V Manager, and click Settings from the Action menu to open the Settings dialog box for the VM, as shown in Figure 29-16.

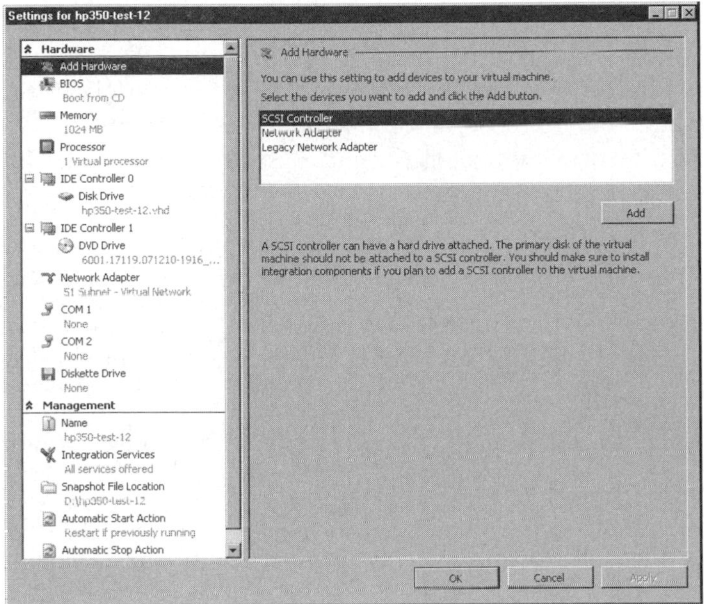

Figure 29-16 The Settings dialog box for the hp350-test-12 VM

The settings page of a VM allows you to control the virtual hardware that is available to a VM. The settings that can be changed on a virtual machine include:

- **Add Hardware** Add a SCSI Controller, Network Adapter, or Legacy Network Adapter.
- **BIOS** Change the boot order and Numlock state.
- **Memory** Set the amount of memory assigned to the VM. Each VM is limited to 64 GB of memory.
- **Processor** Set the number of logical processors assigned to the VM. This is limited to the number of logical processors available on the host computer, or four logical processors, whichever is fewer. Hyper-V is limited to a maximum of 16 logical processors per host computer in the initial release.

> **Note** Windows Server 2003 client operating systems are limited to one logical processor per machine.

> **Note** Running Windows NT 4 in a virtual machine requires limiting the processor functionality.

- **IDE Controllers 0, 1** Set the drives connected to each IDE controller. Both Hard Disk and DVD Drive types are supported on IDE controllers.
- **SCSI Controller(s)** Set the drives connected to the synthetic SCSI controller. Each SCSI controller is assigned to SCSI ID7, and can support up to six virtual SCSI drives. You cannot use SCSI drives as boot drives, and SCSI drives are not available until Integration Components are installed.
- **Network Adapters** Set the network, Mac type, and VLAN connections of the synthetic network adapters. Each VM is limited to a maximum of eight network adapters.
- **Legacy Network Adapters** Set the network, Mac type, and VLAN connections of the Legacy Network Adapters. Each VM is limited to a maximum of four Legacy Network Adapters.
- **COM 1, COM 2** Set the named pipe used to communicate with the physical host computer.
- **Diskette Drive** Set the virtual floppy drive (.vfd) that is connected to the virtual floppy drive. No pass-through to the physical floppy drive on the host (parent) computer is supported.

Adding Hardware

To add hardware to a VM, follow these steps:

1. Open the Hyper-V Manager console if it isn't already open. Select the virtual machine you want to add hardware to. For most changes the machine must be stopped (*not* paused).
2. Click Settings on the Action menu to open the Settings page for the VM.
3. With Add Hardware highlighted in the left pane, click the hardware you want to add:
    - **SCSI Controller** Select SCSI controller and click Add to add a synthetic SCSI controller. The right-hand pane changes to the SCSI Controller page, as shown in Figure 29-17.

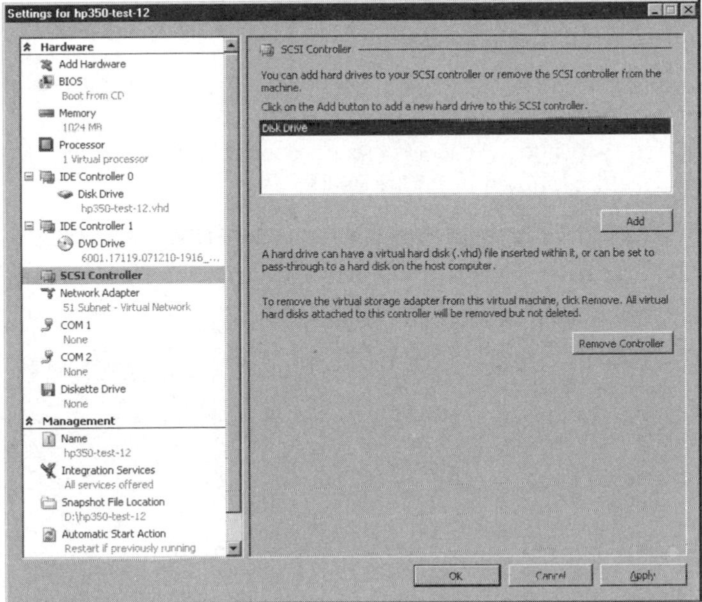

Figure 29-17 The SCSI Controller page of the Virtual Machine Settings Wizard

a. Select Disk Drive and click Add to open the Disk Drive page, as shown in Figure 29-18.

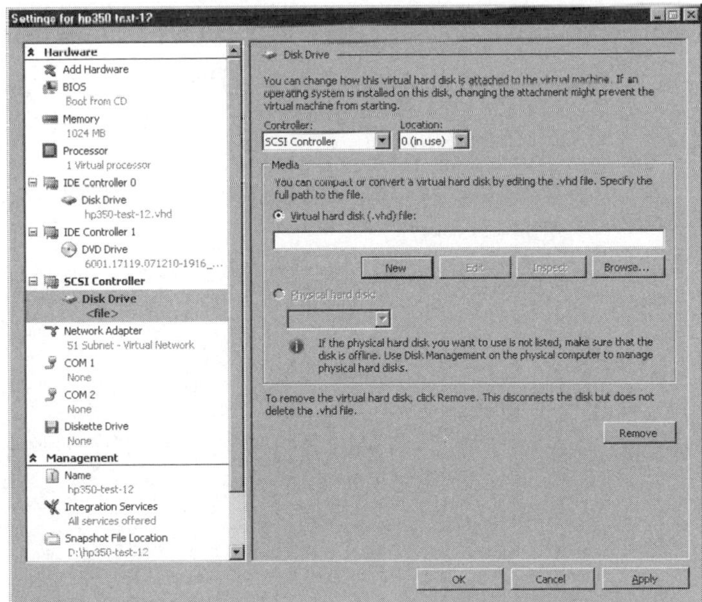

Figure 29-18 The Disk Drive page of the Virtual Machine Settings Wizard

b. Click New to open the New Virtual Hard Disk Wizard. (Click Browse to reuse an existing .vhd file.)

c. Click Do Not Show This Page Again and then click Next if the Before You Begin page opens.

d. On the Choose Disk Type page, choose the type of virtual hard disk to create, as shown in Figure 29-19.

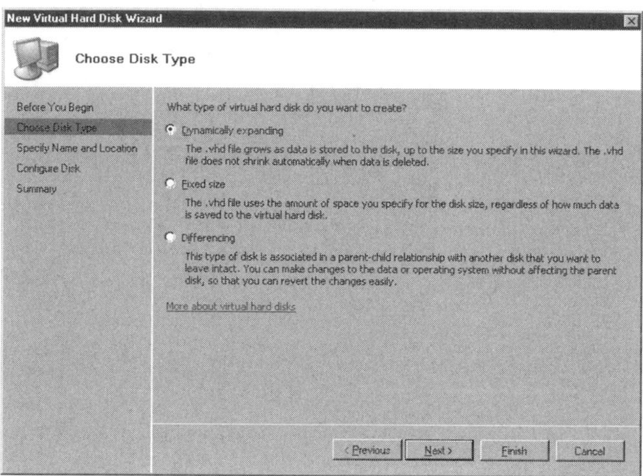

Figure 29-19 The Choose Disk Type page of the Virtual Hard Disk Wizard

e. Click Next to open the Specify Name And Location page. Enter a name and browse to the location to store the .vhd file.

f. Click Next to open the Configure Disk page. The page for a dynamically expanding or fixed size disk is shown in Figure 29-20. For a differencing disk, you'll have a page to specify the parent disk.

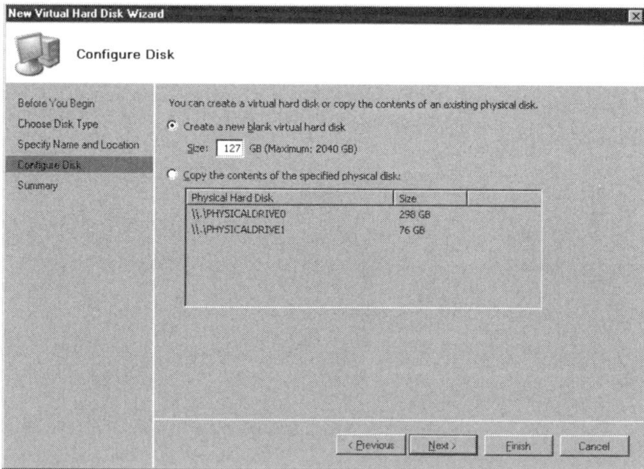

Figure 29-20 The Configure Disk page for a dynamically expanding disk

g. Specify the size of the disk, or specify a physical disk to copy, click Next, and then click Finish to create the virtual hard disk and return to the Disk Drive page of the Settings dialog box. If you specified a fixed size disk, this may take some time to complete.

h. Click Apply to actually add the disk to the VM. To continue adding hardware, click Add Hardware to return to the Add Hardware page, or Click OK to exit the Settings dialog if you are done.

- **Network Adapter** Highlight Network Adapter and click Add to open the Network Adapter page, as shown in Figure 29-21.

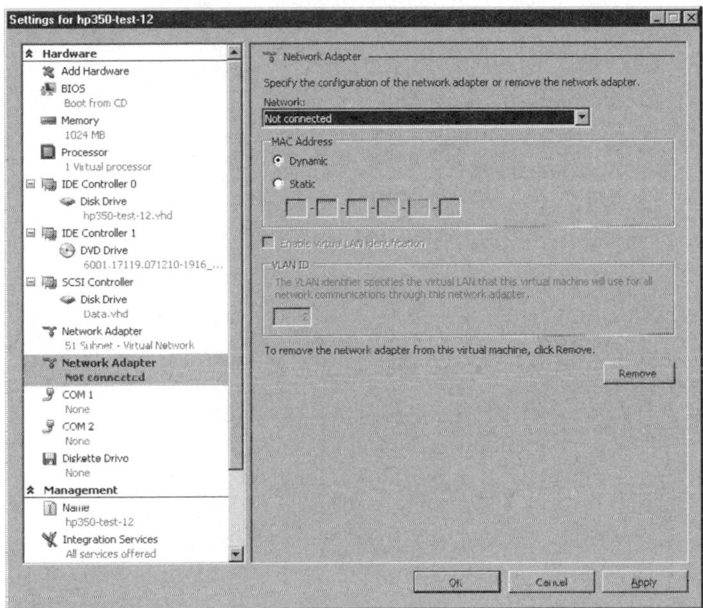

Figure 29-21 The Network Adapter page of the Virtual Machine Settings dialog

a. Select the Network to connect the new adapter to from the drop-down list.

b. Specify a dynamic or fixed MAC address. Avoid fixed MAC addresses unless you have a clear understanding of why you're choosing one.

c. Click Enable Virtual LAN Identification and specify a VLAN ID if this virtual machine is part of a VLAN.

d. Click Apply to apply the changes and enable the new adapter. To continue adding hardware, click Add Hardware to return to the Add Hardware page, or click OK to exit the Settings dialog box if you are done.

- **Legacy Network Adapter** Highlight Legacy Network Adapter and click Add to open the Legacy Network Adapter page.
  a. Choose the network to connect the new adapter to from the drop-down list.
  b. Specify a dynamic or fixed MAC address. Avoid fixed MAC addresses unless you have a clear understanding of why you're choosing one.
  c. Click Enable Virtual LAN Identification and specify a VLAN ID if this virtual machine is part of a VLAN.

4. Click Apply to apply the changes and enable the new adapter. To continue adding hardware, click Add Hardware to return to the Add Hardware page, or click OK to exit the Settings dialog box if you are done.
5. When you've completed adding hardware to your VM, click OK to close the Settings page for the VM.

Real World Legacy Network Adapters

The networking in Windows Server 2008 and Hyper-V uses a new, synthetic network adapter that is fast and has a low resource overhead. But the only drivers for it are those in the Integration Components. If your guest operating system doesn't have supported integration services, you have no choice but to choose the legacy network adapter.

The legacy network adapter is recognized by virtual machine operating systems as an Intel 21140-based PCI Fast Ethernet Adapter. It's a 10/100 emulated adapter and most operating systems will have a built-in driver for it. (A noticeable exception is Windows XP Professional x64 Edition.) You should use the legacy network adapter only when you really need to, however, because it has a substantially higher resource overhead and isn't as fast.

One place you *must* use the legacy adapter is when installing an operating system from the network. There is no support available for the new synthetic adapter until after the operating system is installed.

Memory and CPU

Hyper-V supports a maximum of 4 processors and 64 GB of RAM per VM. On host machines with fewer than four processors, you'll be limited to the number of logical processors on the host itself. And you need to be careful to not over-specify the RAM for VMs on a physical computer. You need to leave at least 500 MB of RAM for the host partition, plus a bit (fewer than 100 MB) per running VM.

You can change the amount of RAM assigned to a VM, or change the number of CPUs assigned to it, but only when the VM is fully shut down. (Just paused won't do.) You can also set the CPU resources that the VM reserves for itself, and set the relative weight of resource usage.

To change the memory or CPU for a VM, follow these steps:

1. Open the Hyper-V Manager console if it isn't already open. Select the Virtual Machine you want to add hardware to.
2. If the VM is running, select Connect from the Action menu and log on to the machine to shut it down. If Integration Services are installed on the VM, you can right-click the VM in Hyper-V Manager and select Shutdown from the menu.
3. Click Settings on the Action menu to open the Settings dialog box for the VM.
4. Click Memory in the left hand pane of the Settings dialog box and enter the amount of RAM to make available to the VM in the Memory pane on the right.
5. Click Processor in the left pane to open Virtual Processor pane on the right, as shown in Figure 29-22.

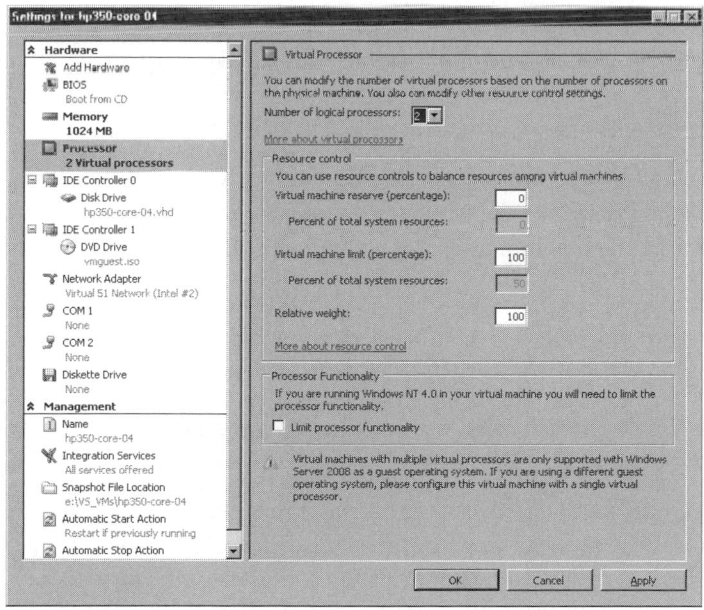

Figure 29-22 The Virtual Processor page of the Virtual Machine Settings dialog box

6. Choose the number of logical processors from the drop-down list. Only Windows Server 2008 virtual machines support more than one logical processor.
7. Adjust the Resource Control settings to reserve a percentage of the available processor resources for this VM, or to set the relative weight of the VM.
8. If this is a Windows NT 4 VM, or another older operating system, select Limit Processor Functionality.
9. Click OK when you've completed your changes to return to the Hyper-V Manager console. Or click Apply to save the changes but remain in the Settings dialog box to make further changes.

Disks and Controllers

Hyper-V uses a pair of synthetic IDE controllers for hard disks and DVD drives by default. You must use an IDE for the boot hard disk–the synthetic SCSI controller won't have drivers available in the operating system until after the Integration Services are installed.

If you're familiar with the IDE controller in Virtual Server 2005, you'll know that it was slow and only supported hard disks up to 127 GB. We quickly learned to use Virtual Server's SCSI controller and floppy disk to load the drivers during installation, greatly speeding up the process. But that workaround is no longer necessary. The new IDE controller in Hyper-V has full LBA-48 support, and it's much faster than the old Virtual Server one.

Before you can add additional disks and connect them to a SCSI controller, you'll need to add the SCSI controller. By default, a new VM doesn't include a SCSI controller. When you add the controller, you can also add one or more disks to the controller.

When you add a disk, you have a choice between a dynamically expanding disk, a fixed-size disk, or a differencing disk. See the RealWorld sidebar for our take on the choices. For new fixed or dynamically expanding disk, you have the choice of creating an empty disk or copying the contents of an existing physical disk into it.

Real World Choosing Disk Types

Hyper-V supports three virtual disk types: dynamically expanding disks, fixed-sized disks, and differencing disks.

Dynamically expanding disks are created with a maximum size, and this is the size that the operating system of the virtual machine sees. But the actual .vhd file of the disk only takes up as much space on your physical hard disk or array as absolutely required for the current contents of the virtual machine drive. As the VM requires more storage space, Hyper-V automatically grows the .vhd file. This is a very efficient use of hard disk space, allowing you to only add space as absolutely required. But it does mean a slight performance hit every time the disk needs to grow, and more important, the .vhd file tends to become somewhat fragmented over time, also impacting performance. Nonetheless, we almost always use this type of disk for our VMs.

A fixed-size disk is also a .vhd file, but instead of growing only as big as it needs to when it needs to, it is created at the full size on disk as it needs to be. It takes a significant time to create the .vhd file, but it will be created as a contiguous file (or as contiguous as the underlying fragmentation of your physical disk or array allows).

A differencing disk is an interesting disk type. It is like a dynamic disk in that it only gets as large as it needs to. But a differencing disk is a great way to combine the disk space requirements of multiple virtual machines. You create the original "base" VM, and then mark the disks as read-only. You can actually delete the VM that created the base disks. Now you create one or more VMs that are on the same operating system and you create them with differencing disk(s). The differencing disk points to the original base .vhd file, and the only thing that is saved to the differencing disk is any change from the base VM. This allows multiple VMs to share the same base, simplifying deployment of different versions of the same base system.

The biggest disadvantage of differencing disks is speed. As more VMs point back to the original .vhd files, the access to that .vhd can be slowed. And if anything causes a change to the original .vhd, all the VMs that point to it can be lost. Over time, the size advantage of differencing disks is also reduced as updates and service packs are applied to the differenced VMs. But for a test environment, differencing disks can be a great speed and resource saver.

To add a hard disk to a virtual machine, follow these steps:

1. Open the Hyper-V Manager console if it isn't already open. Select the Virtual Machine you want to add a virtual hard disk to. For most changes the machine must be stopped (*not* paused).
2. Click Settings on the Action menu to open the Settings page for the VM.
3. Highlight the controller you want to use for the new hard disk in the left pane, and click Add in the right pane.
4. Click New to open the New Virtual Hard Disk Wizard. (Click Browse to reuse an existing .vhd file.)

5. Click Do Not Show This Page Again and then click Next if the Before You Begin page opens.
6. On the Choose Disk Type page, choose the type of virtual hard disk to create.
7. Click Next to open the Specify Name And Location page. Enter a name and browse to the location to store the .vhd file.
8. Click Next to open the Configure Disk page. The page for a dynamically expanding or fixed size disk lets you specify the size of the new disks. For a differencing disk, you can specify the parent disk location and file name, as shown in Figure 29-23.

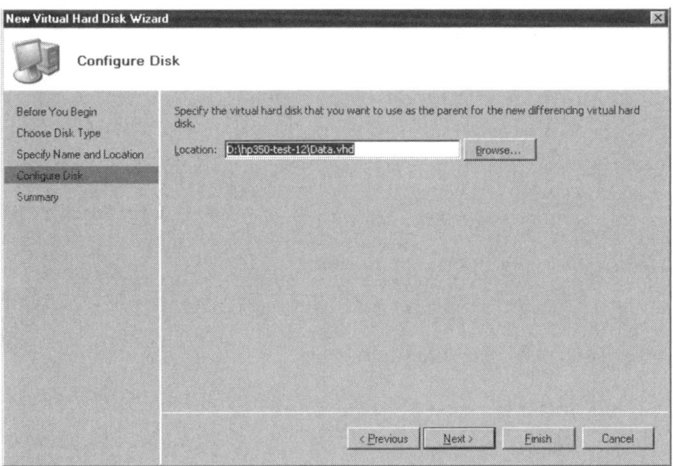

Figure 29-23 The Configure Disk page for a differencing disk

9. Click Finish to create the disk and return to the Virtual Machine Settings dialog box. Click OK to add the disk and close the Settings dialog box.

Creating a Differencing Disk

Creating a differencing virtual hard disk is a slightly different procedure than creating a regular disk. You need to first mark the original disk as read-only and make sure that no VMs are still pointing to it and trying to make changes to the disk.

Real World All Parent Disks Together

Because the parent disks for differencing disks need to all be read-only, we like to put them all together in a single directory. Or our main HP ML350 server, where most of our virtual machines are, we created a folder on the fastest disk array called BaseDisks and we put any differencing disk parents in that directory. Having the disks all together in one location makes it much easier to keep track of them, plus we're able to ensure that they're on the fastest array, because the I/O load on a parent disk is always a potential bottleneck.

One special consideration: If you're using differencing disks for the actual operating system disks, you need to sysprep the parent disk before you make it read-only. Otherwise you can run into issues with duplicate SIDs on the network.

To change an existing virtual disk to a parent disk, and create a new differencing disk connecting to the parent, follow these steps:

1. Log on to the VM where the proposed parent disk is currently running and shut down the VM.
2. When the VM is fully shut down, open Windows Explorer and move the .vhd file that will be the parent disk to your preferred location for parent disks. If the file needs renaming to match your standard naming conventions, do so now.
3. Right-click the parent disk .vhd and select Properties from the menu. Select Read-Only, as shown in Figure 29-24, and click OK to close the Properties dialog box for the file.

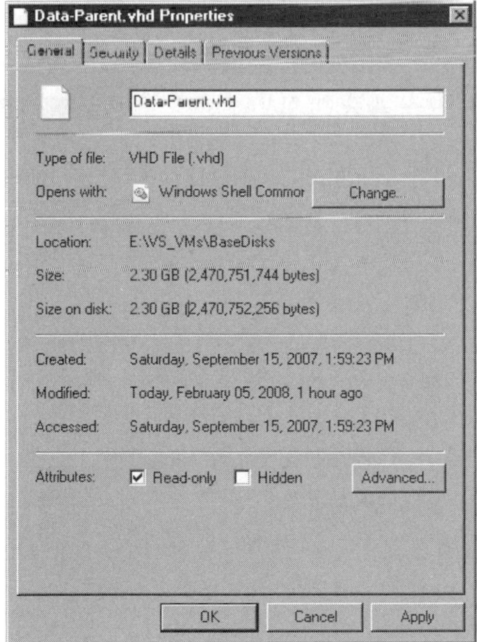

Figure 29-24 The Properties dialog box of a .vhd file

4. Open the Hyper-V Manager console if it isn't already open.

5. Select New and then select Hard Disk from the Actions pane to open the New Virtual Hard Disk Wizard.
6. If you see the Before You Begin page, click Do Not Show This Page Again and then click Next to open the Choose Disk Type page.
7. Select Differencing and click Next to open the Specify Name And Location page of the New Virtual Hard Disk Wizard, as shown in Figure 29-25.

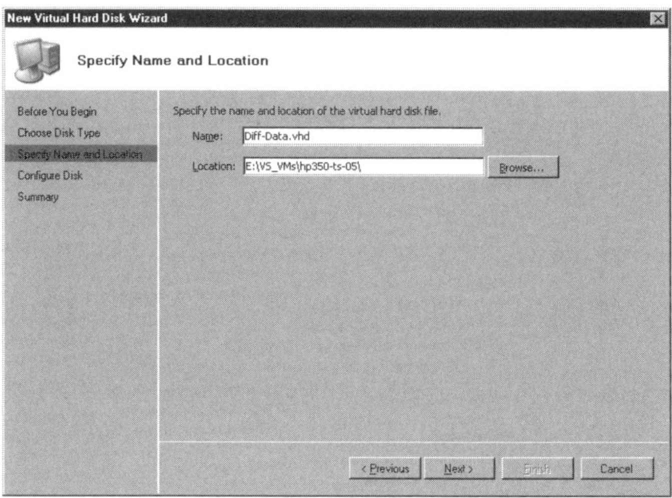

Figure 29-25 The Specify Name And Location page of the New Virtual Hard Disk Wizard

8. Specify a name for the new virtual hard disk file. This name should identify that this is a differencing disk to prevent confusion.
9. Specify the location for the new .vhd file. You can type the location in, or use the Browse button to navigate to the directory.
10. Click Next to open the Configure Disk page of the New Virtual Hard Disk Wizard. Specify the location of the .vhd file that will be the parent for the new differencing disk. Use the Browse button to navigate to the file, or type the full filename and path into the Location field, as shown in Figure 29-26.

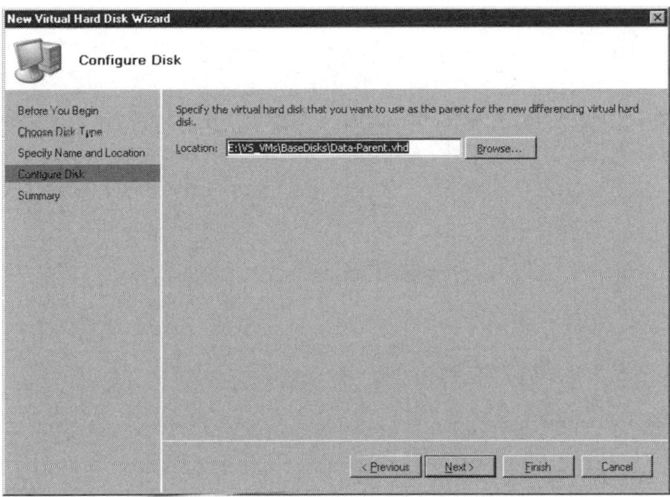

Figure 29-26 The Configure Disk page of the New Virtual Hard Disk Wizard

11. Click Next to open the Completing The New Virtual Hard Disk Wizard page, and if the Description looks correct, click Finish to create the disk and return to the Hyper-V Manager console.
12. Select the VM that you want to add the new VHD to. If the machine state is Off, you can add a new disk to it. Otherwise, you'll need to shut down the operating system in the VM completely.
13. Click Settings to open the virtual machine Settings dialog box. Select the controller you want to add a virtual hard disk to, and click Add.
14. In the Disk Drive pane of the Settings dialog box, use the Browse button to navigate to the differencing disk you created, and click Open.
15. Click OK to add the disk and return to the Hyper-V Manager console.

Network Adapters

When you create a new virtual machine, it will automatically include a single network adapter. Unless you choose to install the operating system from the network, VM will add one of the synthetic network adapters that are new to Hyper-V. These work great unless you are running an operating system that doesn't have Integration Services available for it. If that's the case, you'll need to change this adapter to a legacy network adapter. You can't directly change the adapter type–you'll need to delete the existing one and add a legacy adapter, following the steps under "Adding Hardware" earlier in the chapter.

COM and Floppy

Hyper-V automatically configures a pair of virtual COM ports (COM1 and COM2) and a virtual floppy disk drive for each virtual machine. But it doesn't actually connect them to anything. To connect a COM port to the host computer, you need to use named pipes. For floppy disks, you need to create a virtual floppy disk file (.vfd). A .vfd file is an image of a floppy disk. Hyper-V does not have a way to connect directly to any existing floppy drive on the server.

To connect a COM port to a named pipe, follow these steps:

1. Open the Hyper-V Manager console if it isn't already open.
2. Select the VM you want to connect a COM port on.
3. Click Settings from the Action menu.
4. Click the virtual COM port you want to connect in the left pane of the Settings dialog box. In the COM pane on the right side of the dialog box, enter a name for the named pipe, as shown in Figure 29-27.

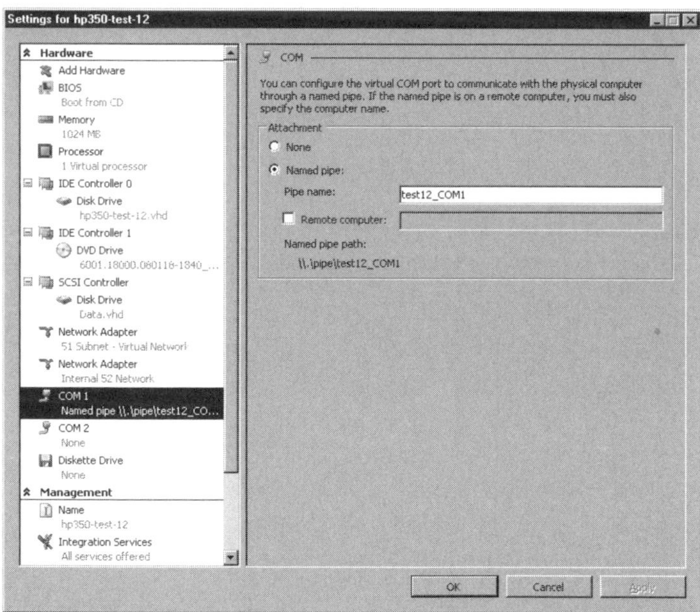

Figure 29-27 The COM page of the Virtual Machine Settings page

5. Click OK to close the Settings dialog box and connect the COM port.

Note You don't need to stop a virtual machine to connect a COM port, or to change the connection to a different named pipe.

To create and add a virtual floppy disk, follow these steps:

1. Open the Hyper-V Manager console if it isn't already open.
2. Click New, and then click Floppy Disk from the Action menu to open the Save As dialog box shown in Figure 29-28.

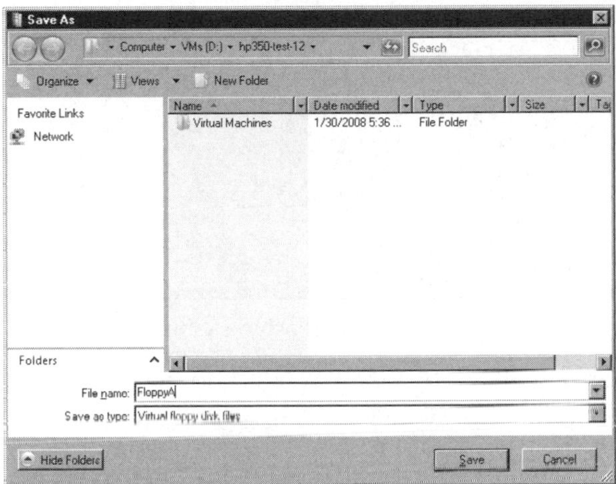

Figure 29-28 The Save As dialog box used to create a .vfd file

3. Type a name for the new .vfd file and click Save to create it and return to the Hyper-V Manager console.
4. Select the VM that you want to connect to the new virtual floppy disk. Click Settings to open the virtual machine Settings dialog box.
5. Click Diskette Drive in the left pane to display the Floppy Drive page in the right pane.
6. Select Virtual Floppy Disk (.vfd) File as shown in Figure 29-29 and type in the full path and name to the .vfd file you created in step 3, or use the Browse button to locate and select it.

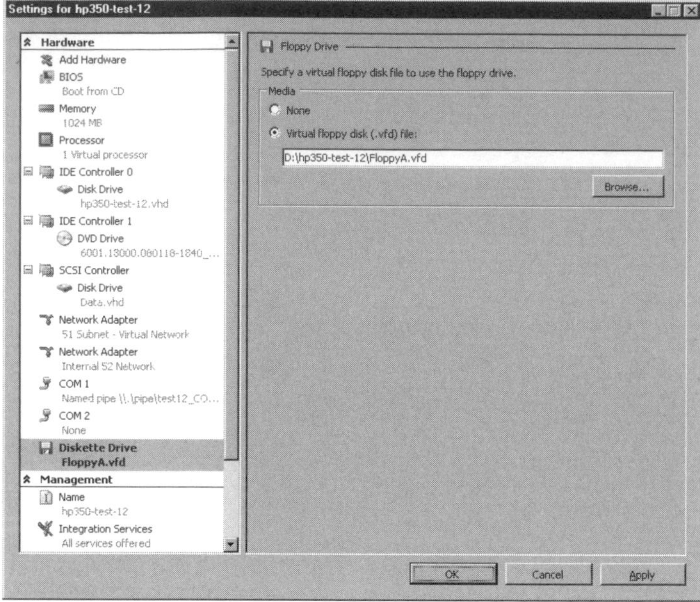

Figure 29-29 The Floppy Drive page of the Virtual Machine Settings dialog box

7. Click OK to connect to the virtual floppy disk and return to the Hyper-V Manager console.

Management Settings

You can configure several management settings on a per-virtual machine basis. When you open the Settings dialog box for a virtual machine, in the Management section in the lower half of the left pane you have the following settings:

- **Name** Allows you to change the name of the virtual machine and add notes on the change to the VM. If you use VM-specific directories, however, it will not change the directory names, causing some potential confusion.
- **Integration Services** The Integration Services page of the Settings dialog box lets you enable or disable various integration services, as shown in Figure 29-30. By default, all are enabled. (We really have a hard time thinking of a scenario where you would want to disable any of these, but if you need to, you can.)

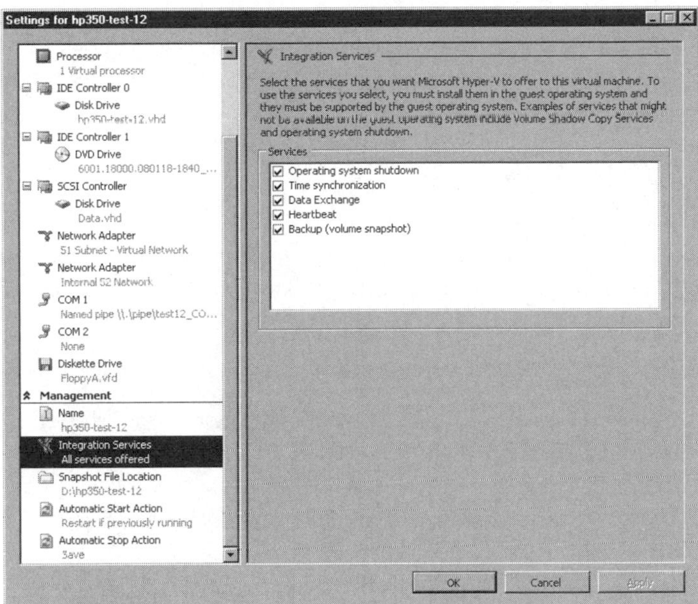

Figure 29-30 The Integration Services page of the Virtual Machine Settings dialog box

- **Snapshot File Location** The location used to store snapshot files. By default these will be in the same location as .vhd files for the virtual machine.
- **Automatic Start Action** Lets you set the VM autostart options. You can set the VM to never autostart, autostart only if it was running when the Hyper-V service last stopped, or always automatically start the VM. You can also specify a startup delay to allow the staged automatic startup of several VMs to reduce disk thrashing and processor contention.
- **Automatic Stop Action** Lets you set the VM autostop options. You can set a VM to save the current VM state, turn off the VM, or shut down the guest operating system before the physical computer shuts down.

Important Selecting Turn Off The Virtual Machine as a stop action is the VM equivalent of pulling the plug without warning on a physical computer. If this doesn't sound like a good idea, we agree.

Note Guest shutdown is only a valid option for VMs that have Integration Services installed.

Installing Integration Services

By default, all Integration Services are installed on virtual machines that are running Windows Server 2008 operating systems. You don't need to do anything to install them. On Windows Server 2003 child operating systems, you need to install the Integration Services by following these steps:

1. Open the Hyper-V Manager console if it isn't already open.
2. Start the virtual machine on which you want to install Integration Services and connect to it by right-clicking the VM in the console and selecting Connect from the menu.
3. Log on to the VM with an administrative account.
4. Select Insert Integration Services Setup Disk from the Action menu of the Virtual Machine Connection, as shown in Figure 29-31.

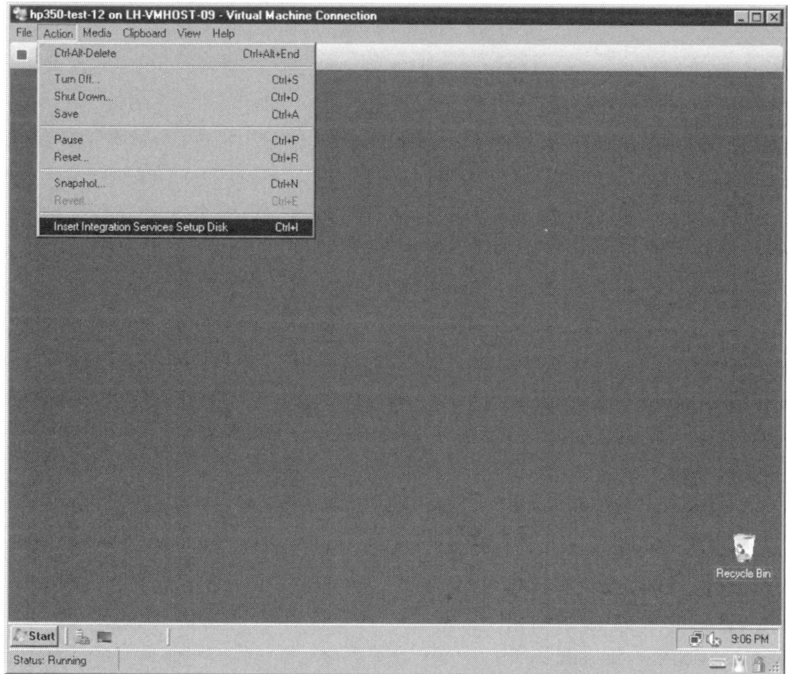

Figure 29-31 The Insert Integration Services Setup Disk menu option of the Virtual Machine Connection

5. When the AutoPlay dialog box opens, as shown in Figure 29-32, select Install Microsoft Hyper-V Integration Components and install the components.

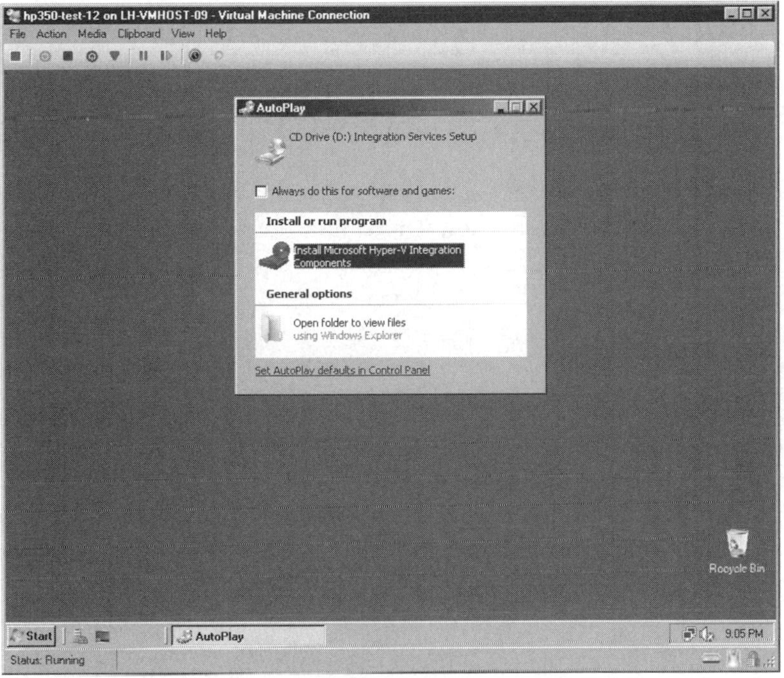

Figure 29-32 AutoPlay of Integration Components

6. If the AutoPlay dialog box doesn't appear, use Windows Explorer on the virtual machine to navigate to the D:\Support\Amd64 folder (for x64 VMs) or the D:\Support\x86 folder for 32-bit VMs (assuming D: is your CD/DVD drive letter on the VM), and double-click Setup.exe.

Real World Foreign Virtual Machines

Any virtual machine that was created in a virtualization solution that is *not* Hyper-V is a "foreign" VM to Hyper-V. That being said, moving a VM from Virtual Server or Virtual PC is a fairly easy process. The one thing that can cause problems is the VMAdditions that can be installed on these VMs. You should uninstall the VMAdditions before attempting to run the foreign VM in Hyper-V.

The easiest way to uninstall the VMAdditions is to start the VM in Virtual Server or Virtual PC and run the uninstallation from there before attempting to move the VM to your Hyper-V server.

Working With A Virtual Machine

Working with a Hyper-V Virtual Machine is almost identical to working with a physical computer. You should do virtually everything you need to do from the client operating system, just as you would on a physical computer. You can connect to the client operating system using Remote Desktop when that is a supported option, and you can always connect using the Virtual Machine Connection. This connection is to the virtual machine the same as the physical keyboard, mouse, and monitor of a physical computer. However, some actions need to be performed from the parent partition, either from the Hyper-V console or the from the menu bar of the Virtual Machine Connection.

Starting, Stopping, Saving, Snapshotting

To start a virtual machine, you need to either set the virtual machine to automatically start, as described earlier under "Management Settings," or use the Hyper-V Manager console to start the VM. Right-click the VM in the console and select Start from the menu. If you have the Virtual Machine Connection for that VM open, you can select Start from the Action menu.

To stop a VM, you should shut down the operating system in the virtual machine. You can initiate this from the Hyper-V Manager console, or the Virtual Machine Connection Action menu, if Integration Services are installed in the VM. You can also stop a VM by selecting Turn Off from the shortcut menu for the VM in the console, but this can cause corruption issues for the virtual machine's operating system, and is not recommended when other alternatives are available.

You can save a VM from the Hyper-V Manager console, or the Virtual Machine Connection for that VM, by selecting Save from the Action menu. This will save the current state of the VM to disk and is similar to hibernating a physical computer. It does release memory and resources back to the parent partition.

Pausing a VM is similar to putting a physical computer into sleep mode. It's not actively doing anything, but it also doesn't release any of the VM's resources back to the parent partition.

Snapshots are one of the ways that virtual machines are more useful and flexible than any physical computer. Snapshots allow you to take a "picture" of a running virtual machine at an exact moment in time and save it. You can revert back to that snapshot later, starting up the virtual machine at that exact configuration. This is *extremely* useful for building test machines, because it lets you try a new configuration or software application without the risk of having to either rebuild the computer if something really bad happens, or wasting time trying to get back to where you were before the change if the change didn't work.

Snapshots

Snapshots can be a powerful tool, giving you the ability to try something with the calm assurance that you can recover completely if it doesn't work. And snapshots happen in seconds. Just select the VM in the Hyper-V Manager console, right-click, and select Snapshot from the menu. The VM can be running or not–it doesn't matter.

After you create a snapshot, the virtual machine returns to its running state. You can rename the snapshot, check the settings that applied at the time of the snapshot, delete it, or even delete an entire snapshot subtree. All these actions are available from the Actions pane of the Hyper-V Manager console, or from the Action menu of the Virtual Machine Connection. You can also revert a virtual machine to its previous snapshot, or select another snapshot in the tree and apply it.

As you can see, this is powerful stuff, and the possibilities are something you'll just have to work with a bit to begin to understand.

To create a snapshot, follow these steps:

1. Open Hyper-V Manager console if it isn't already open.
2. Select the virtual machine you want to take a snapshot of and select Snapshot from the Actions pane on the right.
3. By default, the snapshot will be named with a date and time. We find it useful to change the name to include a description of the state the VM was in when the snapshot was taken. To change the name, right-click the snapshot in the middle section of the middle pane of the Hyper-V Manager console and select Rename from the menu.

To change a VM's running state to that of an earlier snapshot, you have two choices. You can revert the running VM to the most recent snapshot, or you can choose from any of the snapshots for a VM and apply that snapshot. To revert a VM, select it in the Hyper-V Manager console and click Revert in the Actions pane. To apply an earlier snapshot, first select the virtual machine in the Hyper-V Manager console, right-click the particular snapshot you want to apply in the Snapshots section of the middle pane, and then choose Apply from the menu.

Clipboard

The Hyper-V Virtual Machine Connection supports a limited ability to pass the contents of your clipboard between the parent partition and the running virtual machine. Only text can be passed, but this allows you to "replay" the text as keystrokes into the VM. To use this capability, you need to copy text to your clipboard on the parent partition using Ctrl+C or any other method. Then, in the child partition, prepare the location you want to type the text into, and select Type Clipboard Text from the Clipboard menu of the Virtual Machine Connection. The text is typed into the child partition at the cursor, one character at a time.

The other feature of the Hyper-V Virtual Machine Connection Clipboard menu is a screen capture utility. A pretty limited one, frankly, but it works if what you need to do is capture the entire screen of the child computer. To capture the screen, just select Capture Screen from Virtual Machine Connection Clipboard menu. This puts the screen into your clipboard, and from there you can paste into Microsoft Paint or any other graphics program.

Real World Screen Capture Utilities

The ability to capture screens is essential for any documentation task, and often important for troubleshooting as well. Having an exact picture of the situation at a specific point in time just makes everything clearer, in our experience. The screen capture utility in Hyper-V is, frankly, pretty limited. And it's difficult to get screen shots of individual windows or buttons because the keystrokes are usually captured from the parent partition, not the child. Our solution is to use a small utility called HyperSnap, which is much smarter at screen shots than anything we could do with the built-in facilities of Windows. You can download HyperSnap from *http://www.hyperionics.com*. Other good screen capture utilities are out there, but we've been using HyperSnap for more than 13 years now, and it does an excellent job. We can capture exactly what we want and save it in any format we can imagine. Plus if we do need to manipulate an image for some reason, HyperSnap gives us the ability to do that, too. We load a copy of HyperSnap into every test machine we run, using Group Policy to deploy it. And when we needed screen shots for Server Core? Hyperionics did a custom version for us that worked where nothing else had.

Export/Import

A new ability in Hyper-V is the ability to export a virtual machine, and then import it into another Hyper-V parent partition. This gives you flexibility in where your virtual machines are located, and simplifies backup and recovery scenarios as well.

To export a virtual machine and import it into another Hyper-V computer, follow these steps:

1. Open the Hyper-V Manager console on the source computer, if it isn't already open.
2. If the VM that you want to export is running, shut it down or save it. The only two states that are supported for an export are Off and Saved.

3. Right-click the VM and select Export from the menu to open the Export Virtual Machine dialog box shown in Figure 29-33.

Figure 29-33 The Export Virtual Machine dialog box

4. Type in the path to save the export, or use the Browse button. You can save to a network share or save locally.
5. Select the Don't Export Virtual Machine State Data check box if you don't want to save any saved state data. Then click Export to begin exporting the VM.
6. When the export completes, open the Hyper-V Manager console on the target Hyper-V computer.
7. Click Import Virtual Machine on the Actions pane to open the Import Virtual Machine dialog box shown in Figure 29-34.

Import Virtual Machine
Import Path
Reuse old virtual machine IDs.
Import
Cancel
After import, the files under this import folder will be used by the imported virtual machine. This folder can not be imported again.

Figure 29-34 The Import Virtual Machine dialog box

8. Type in the Import Path to open the import, or use the Browse button. The import should be on a local drive, because the VM will run from the import location.
9. Select the Reuse Old Virtual Machine IDs check box if you have completely removed the old VM and won't be running it again.
10. Click Import and the VM is imported into the Hyper-V Manager console. You can adjust the Settings as appropriate for the VM's new location, and then click Start to start the VM.

Note One setting you'll almost certainly have to redo for an imported VM is the networking. In most cases you can expect to have to add new network adapters to the imported VM.

Real World Hyper-V Alternatives

There are several alternatives to Hyper-V for virtualization, and the options are still increasing. The market leader is still certainly VMWare, with an entire suite of products ranging from the free to the quite expensive. Two additional products from Microsoft are also available: Virtual Server 2005 R2 and Virtual PC 2007. Beyond these two, you can also find Xen, VirtualIron, and VirtualBox, to name a few. We've used most of the available alternatives to Hyper-V, and we present them here for completeness. But we now use Hyper-V as our preferred solution and don't expect that to change.

Virtual Server and Virtual PC

Virtual Server and Virtual PC, two very different products from Microsoft, share the basic file format (.vhd) with Hyper-V, but are otherwise very different. Virtual PC is a workstation-class product, designed to run on Windows XP or Windows Vista, though you can run it on Windows Server. Virtual Server is a server-class product, designed to run on Windows Server products in production environments. You can run it on Windows XP or Windows Vista, but it is not supported in that environment.

Both products use the same basic method of virtualization–emulation. They create an emulated virtual environment where operating systems can run as guests. As an emulated environment, a speed penalty is inherent in the additional overhead required.

A more important limitation is that both products only support 32-bit guests. They have no support for running 64-bit Windows as a guest operating system.

Both Virtual Server 2005 R2 and Virtual PC 2007 are free products, and both can run on 32-bit and x64 versions of Windows.

VMWare

VMWare (*http://www.vmware.com*) has an entire suite of virtualization products, including workstation-class, server-class, and enterprise-class products, along with management products and free products. VMWare ESX Server is the VMWare hypervisor product that most directly compares to Hyper-V. It is expensive, and uses a parent partition that is based on a Linux kernel. But it does have some features that aren't available in Hyper-V. Yet.

VMWare Server is the VMWare server-class product that most closely compares to Virtual Server. It is free, and has limited snapshot capability (something not really available for Virtual Server without the use of an add-on such as System Center Virtual Machine Manager). It offers a wider virtualized hardware array to the guest operating system, including USB and sound, but in our use,, we found it less stable than either Hyper-V or Virtual Server.

VMWare Workstation is an interesting product. It is not free, but it is reasonably priced. It supports both x64 hosts and guests, and also has a broader range of supported virtual hardware, including audio support, generic SCSI support, and USB 2.0 support. VMWare Workstation also supports multiple snapshots, giving you the ability to recover to a known good point or test multiple scenarios.

Others

Xen (*http://www.xensource.com*) is now owned by Citrix, and has a full range of products from the workstation-class Citrix XenServer Express Edition to the enterprise-class Citrix XenServer Enterprise Edition. All are hypervisor-based and use an Open Source kernel for the parent partition. Xen uses the same .vhd file format as Microsoft products.

VirtualIron (*http://www.virtualiron.com*) is an enterprise-class virtualization product that is hypervisor-based, requires x64 hardware, and supports live migration of VMs.

VirtualBox (*http://www.virtualbox.org*) is an Open Source project. The current version of Virtual Box is a workstation-class product that is fast and flexible. VirtualBox is actively being developed and worked on, and looks like an interesting product we expect to see more of in the future.

Summary

Virtualization is a rapidly expanding area in the server world, as solutions mature and needs expand. The built-in hardware support at the CPU level for virtualization provides very fast and powerful capabilities. Hyper-V is Microsoft's hypervisor-based virtualization solution and is new to Windows Server 2008. The current version is only a beta, but is expected to be released in the second half of 2008.

In the next chapter we talk about another Windows Server 2008 technology that increases your flexibility: Terminal Services.

Chapter 30

Deploying Terminal Services

Microsoft Windows Terminal Services was introduced for Microsoft Windows NT 4 Server with the separate Terminal Server Edition. However, starting with Windows 2000, and continuing in Windows Server 2008, it is a fully integrated part of *all* Windows servers, at least in the Remote Desktop for Administration mode, equivalent to what was called Remote Administration Mode in Windows 2000 Server and Windows 2003 Server. It's also a part of Windows XP Professional and most editions of Windows Vista in a single-user mode, where it is called Remote Desktop. You can use Windows Terminal Services as a mechanism to manage and control your servers from anywhere in the enterprise, or you can take advantage of its application server ability to vastly simplify deployment and maintenance of a wide range of applications to a diverse user population.

Note Although both the client and server portion of Windows Terminal Services are sometimes referred to as Remote Desktop, in this chapter we'll use Windows Terminal Services whenever we're referring to the server portion, or the combination of the server portion and the client portion. We'll stick to referring to the client alone as Remote Desktop to help keep everything straight.

This chapter covers Windows Terminal Services concepts, requirements, and installation procedures. It also covers four main applications that are used to administer Terminal Services servers and clients: Terminal Services Manager, Terminal Services Configuration, Terminal Services Gateway Manager, and Terminal Services RemoteApp Manager.

All the major features from 2003 Terminal Services have carried over to Windows Server 2008 with numerous new features. Terminal Services RemoteApp, one of the new features, will be familiar to Citrix administrators. RemoteApp programs behave as if they are running on the end user's local computer. If a user is running more than one RemoteApp on the same Terminal Server, the Terminal Services session will be shared between the RemoteApps. Thankfully there are numerous ways you can publish RemoteApps to end users.

One method of publishing RemoteApps is to create an .rdp file that can be exported to the end user's desktop. Citrix administrators will recognize that this method is very similar to using ICA files to publish applications on Citrix farms.

A more elegant method is to create an MSI package that can be deployed with a software distribution software package such as System Center Configuration Manager (SCCM) or through Group Policy. The added benefit is that the MSI package can be configured to add Start menu items to the end user's computer and to associate file extensions with the RemoteApp.

If deploying RDP or MSI files is not optimal for your environment, you can take advantage of another new feature of Windows 2008 Terminal Services, Terminal Services Web Access. This feature makes RemoteApps available to user from a Web browser, either from an intranet or the Internet.

Terminal Services Session Broker is a new feature that provides an alternative to Network Load Balancing for Terminal Servers, and replaces the Windows 2003 Terminal Services Session Directory. With the Terminal Services Session Broker, new sessions are distributed to the least-loaded server within the farm. Users can reconnect to an existing session without having to know specific information about the server where the session was established, much like the Terminal Services Session Broker in Windows 2003. This configuration can also provide fault tolerance: If one of the farm servers is unavailable, the user will connect to the next least-loaded server in the farm. TS Session Broker Load Balancing sets a limit of 16 for the maximum number of pending logon requests to a particular Terminal Server, which helps prevent a single server from becoming overwhelmed with new logon requests.

The TS Session Broker Load Balancing feature also enables you to assign a relative weight value to each server. By assigning a relative weight value, you can help to distribute the load between more powerful and less powerful servers in the farm.

One of the most exciting additions to Windows Server 2008 Terminal Services is the Terminal Services Easy Print feature. Printers can now be supported without the need to install print drivers on the Terminal Server. When users want to print from a TS RemoteApp program or desktop session, they will see the full printer properties dialog box from the local client and have access to all the printer functionality. IT administrators can use Group Policy to limit the number of printers redirected to just the default printer, thereby reducing overhead and improving scalability.

TS Gateway, much like Citrix's Secure Access Gateway, tunnels traffic over HTTPS to help form a secure, encrypted connection between remote users on the Internet and the remote computers on which their productivity applications run, even if their use is located behind a network address translation (NAT) Traversal-based router.

TS Gateway eliminates the need to configure Virtual Private Network (VPN) connections, enabling remote users to connect to the corporate network through the Internet, while providing a comprehensive security configuration model that enables them to control access to specific resources on the network. The TS Gateway Management snap-in console provides a single, one-stop tool that enables you to configure policies to define conditions that must be met for users to connect to resources on the network.

If Network Policy Server (NPS) is deployed in your organization, you can configure TS Gateway policies and then use NPS to store, manage, and validate those policies. NPS is the Microsoft implementation of a Remote Authentication Dial-In User Service (RADIUS) server, previously called Internet Authorization Service (IAS) in Windows 2000 and Windows 2003.

Concepts

Windows Terminal Services is a new concept for many system administrators who expect systems to be essentially single-user. Terminal Services brings true multiuser capability to Windows. UNIX systems have traditionally been primarily multiuser, with a single large server that serves many terminals.

Each user who connects to a Windows Server 2008 server using Remote Desktop or a RemoteApp is actually using the resources of the server itself, not the particular workstation at which she is seated. The user's experience doesn't depend on the speed of the workstation; rather the user's workstation is actually sharing the processor, RAM, and hard disks of the server itself.

Each user gets her Windows Terminal Services session, and each session is completely isolated from other sessions on the same server. An errant program in one session can cause that session's user to have a problem, but other users are unaffected.

Each user who connects to a Windows Server 2008 server using Remote Desktop is actually functioning as a terminal on that server. Windows Terminal Services supports a wide variety of computers as terminals–from diskless display stations running Windows CE entirely in memory to Windows 95 and Windows 98 workstations to Windows Server

2008 servers. The terminal is responsible solely for the console functions—that is, the keyboard, mouse, and actual display. All else resides on and is part of the server, although the disks, printers, and serial ports of your local workstation can be connected to the remote session.

Important Because Windows 95 and Windows 98 are no longer supported operating systems, and because versions of Windows prior to Windows XP SP2 will not be able to install the latest version of the Remote Desktop Client software, it is *strongly* recommended that all client workstations be updated to at least Windows XP SP2 or later to take full advantage of the features of Windows Server 2008 Terminal Services, and to protect the security of the network.

Remote Access

Terminal Services provides an ideal solution for the mobile user who needs to be able to run network-intensive or processor-intensive applications even over a dial-up connection. Because the local computer is responsible only for the actual console, the responsiveness and bandwidth requirements are substantially better compared to trying to run applications across a dial-up line. The actual bandwidth used for Windows Terminal Services can be tuned by enabling or disabling certain graphics features to improve responsiveness over a slow connection.

Central Management

Because all applications in a Windows Terminal Services session are running on the server, management of sessions and applications is greatly simplified. Any changes to applications or settings only need to be made once, on the server, and these changes are seen by all future Windows Terminal Services sessions.

In addition, Windows Terminal Services allows an administrator to view what is happening in a user's session, or even to directly control it. Help desk personnel can actually see exactly what the user is seeing without leaving their desks. If the user is configured accordingly, the Help desk person can share control of the session, walking the user through a difficult problem.

When configured in the default Remote Desktop for Administration mode, Windows Terminal Services gives system administrators a powerful management tool. In this mode, administrators can log on directly to the computer from their desktops to perform normal system maintenance without having to sit at the server console. This is a powerful addition to the administrator's repertoire, enabling direct control of all servers without administrators leaving their desktop. Every system administrator will probably enable the Remote Desktop for Administration mode of all their servers. The overhead on the server is minimal compared to the benefits.

Requirements

Windows Terminal Services is installed on all Windows Server 2008 computers. It requires no additional space for the operating system. However, the real requirements are substantial for a computer that will be used with Windows Terminal Services in application server mode. Because each user will be executing her programs on the server itself, you need to determine exactly how your users work and what their real requirements are. Each installation will be different, but what follows are some guidelines to help you size your server appropriately.

RAM

Each session on the Windows Terminal Services server uses a minimum of approximately 20 MB of RAM just to log on. Add to this any RAM required to run the programs that each session launches. A typical user running Microsoft Office Outlook, Microsoft Office Word, and Microsoft Office Excel while connecting to the Internet uses approximately 40 MB of RAM, or approximately 20 MB beyond what the session itself requires. However, a power user can easily use twice that amount, and developers or other extreme users can go even farther.

CPU

Predicting exactly how much CPU power will be required per user is difficult, because each user has a different mix of applications and expectations. A dual-core, dual-processor server running an x64 version Windows Server 2008 with sufficient RAM present to avoid swapping can realistically host somewhere between 200 and 300 users. The same server, running 32-bit Windows Server 2008, can probably support no more than 50 to 75 users, realistically. The limiting factor in 32-bit Windows Server is usually *not* the CPU, or even the RAM, but the actual virtual memory address space available to the operating system. Most 32-bit Windows Terminal Services servers run out of system page table entries (PTEs) before they become processor-bound.

Windows Terminal Services is one area where the release of Microsoft Windows Server 2003 x64 Edition provided a dramatic gain, and that gain has been extended with the x64 versions of Windows Server 2008. An x64 architecture server, with 4 physical processors *and a well-designed I/O subsystem,* can support more than 400 concurrent users. The limiting factor for most real-world x64 servers is usually the I/O subsystem. Supporting hundreds of concurrent users requires a very well-thought-out disk array.

These numbers are our best estimates for reasonable expectations at this time; however, they are contingent on many factors. As with all estimates of this sort, you should test and verify them against your own mix of users and applications with the most up-to-date tools available from the Microsoft Web site.

Network Utilization

Typical network utilization depends on the type of client and level of graphics being transmitted (for example, an 800 × 600 connection takes a lot less bandwidth to support than a 1600 × 1200 connection), but the average bandwidth per user should work out to somewhere between 2 and 6 Kbps. The Remote Desktop client allows the end user to tailor the session to match the bandwidth available, significantly improving the end-user experience over limited-bandwidth connections.

Capacity Planning

The figures just mentioned should give you some starting points to plan the Terminal Services implementation, but the ultimate capacity the implementation will require depends on *your* situation and scenario. Use these figures only as a starting point for your own planning. Create a test environment that mimics the ultimate implementation on a smaller scale with real users and real applications to gather your own data.

More Info A useful, if somewhat dated, guide to capacity planning for Terminal Services is "Terminal Services Scaling and Performance on x64-Based Versions of Windows Server 2003," a white paper available at *http://www.microsoft.com/downloads/details.aspx?familyid=9B1A8518-D693-4BBB-9AF8-B91BBC0D2D55&displaylang=en*. This paper does not, unfortunately, cover Windows Server 2008 versions.

Some factors that play a major role in the requirements of the Terminal Services implementation are as follows:

- Which applications do your users run? Do they use a single, dedicated application or a wide variety of essentially standard applications?
- Are your users primarily performing a single, routine task, or are they knowledge workers using the computer as a primary tool?
- Are your users all connected using a LAN, or are they a mix of WAN, LAN, and mobile users?

Real World Planning for Maximum Capacity

Microsoft Windows Server 2008 is available in three different architectures: 32-bit x86, 64-bit x64, and 64-bit ia64 (Itanium). Both the traditional 32-bit x86 architecture and the new 64-bit x64 architecture are useful servers for supporting Windows Terminal Services clients. For smaller workloads of fewer than 50 concurrent users, either architecture will do a good job supporting the users, though we have a strong preference even in this space for x64 architecture servers. Their ability to handle RAM better, and a faster, wider access to their I/O subsystems, make x64 the architecture of choice for Terminal Services. For any deployment that is projected to go beyond 50 users, we strongly suggest using x64 architecture processors and one of the x64 versions of Windows Server 2008.

The limiting factor in supporting large numbers of concurrent Windows Terminal Services users is usually the I/O subsystem on x64 versions of Windows Server 2008. On 32-bit Windows Server 2008, the limiting factor is often the virtual memory address space available to Windows, which is limited to 2 GB in 32-bit versions of Windows. For x64 versions of Windows, the virtual memory address space for the operating system itself is 8 Terabytes (TB).

A well-designed redundant array of independent disks (RAID) for Windows Terminal Services should be composed of as many disks as possible. More but smaller disks are far better than a few larger disks because they distribute the I/O load across the whole array. Fibre Channel will usually support greater total I/O than Small Computer System Interface (SCSI), though a well-designed SCSI array is also a good choice, and the new Serial Attached SCSI (SAS), combined with 2.5-inch drives provides a high-density array in a significantly smaller footprint.

Another important consideration is the total RAM available. You should test your deployment under as close to real workload conditions as possible to determine the RAM used per user. To maximize the number of users that a server can support, allocate somewhat more RAM per user than the minimum required–additional RAM will allow Windows to allocate additional memory to cache, which will improve the overall I/O throughput.

Installation

If you're going to use Windows Terminal Services for Remote Administration only, you don't need to install it at all–it's already there. All you need to do is enable remote connections, and that's covered next. If you're going to be using Windows Terminal Services as an application and Terminal Server for multiple clients, however, you need to enable the Terminal Services role on the server.

To add the Terminal Services role to your Windows Server 2008 computer, use the following steps:

1. From the Server Manager console, select Add Role from the Action menu.

Note For these steps, we add the Terminal Server Role Service, the TS Gateway Role Service, and the TS Web Access Role Service. In a normal installation these role services would likely be on at least two different servers, and often three different servers, but this allows us to show all the configuration steps for all three in one set of steps. You should skip over configuration steps that don't apply to your installation.

2. If the Before You Begin page opens, click Next.
3. On the Select Server Roles page, shown in Figure 30-1, select Terminal Services and click Next.

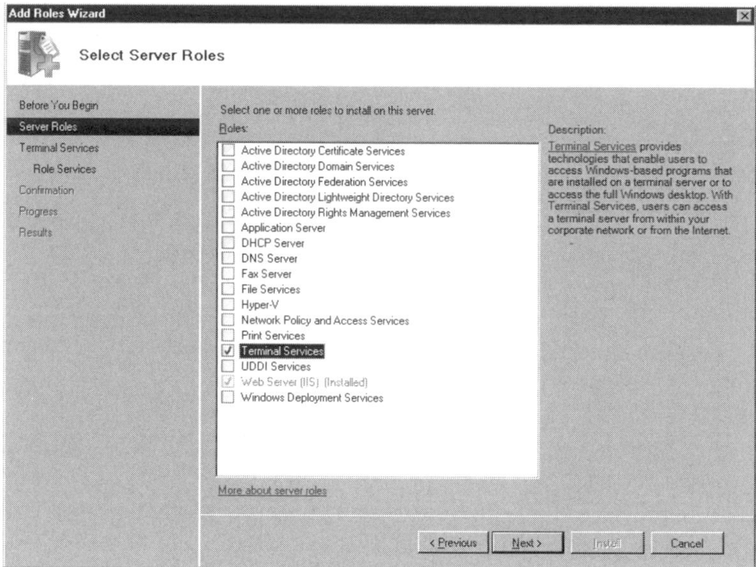

Figure 30-1 The Select Server Role page of the Add Roles Wizard

4. On the Terminal Services page, read the Things To Note, and click Overview Of Terminal Services if you want to read additional help on the subject.
5. Click Next to open the Select Role Services page, as shown in Figure 30-2.

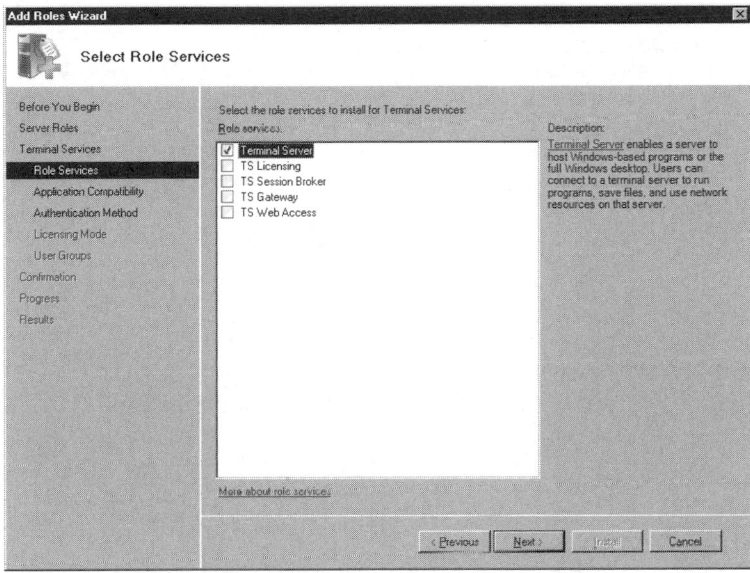

Figure 30-2 The Select Role Services page of the Add Roles Wizard for a Terminal Services addition

6. If you click TS Gateway, you'll be prompted to add the required additional role services and features, as shown in Figure 30-3. Click Add Required Role Services.

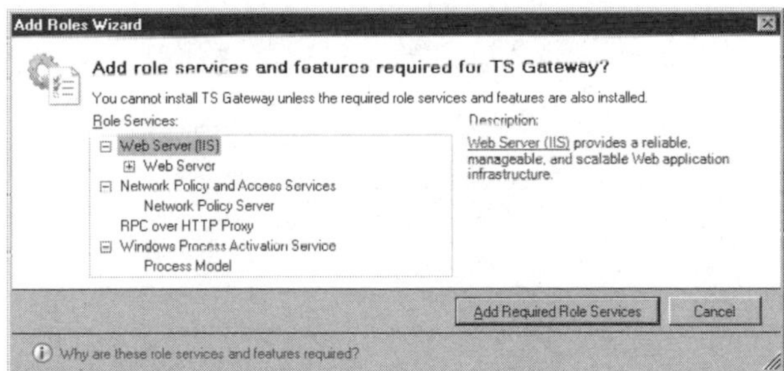

Figure 30-3 The Add Role Services And Features Required For TS Gateway page

7. If you click TS Web Access, you'll see the Add Role Services And Features Required For TS Web Access page shown in Figure 30-4. Click Add Required Role Services.

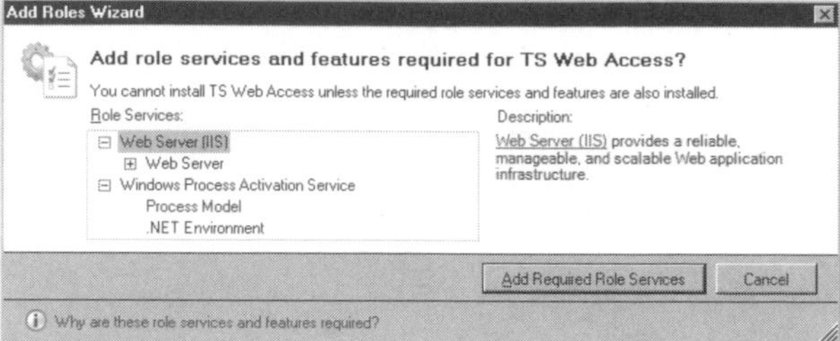

Figure 30-4 The Add Role Services And Features Required For TS Web Access page

8. Click Next to open the Uninstall And Reinstall Applications For Compatibility page, which warns you that adding the Terminal Server role to a server after applications are already installed can create compatibility issues and may require reinstallation of the application.
9. Click Next to open the Specify Authentication Method For Terminal Server page shown in Figure 30-5. If you have client computers that are not running at least Windows XP SP2, with the updated RDP client installed, you must select Do Not Require Network Level Authentication. If all your clients are running Windows Vista or Windows XP SP2, you should select Require Network Level Authentication.

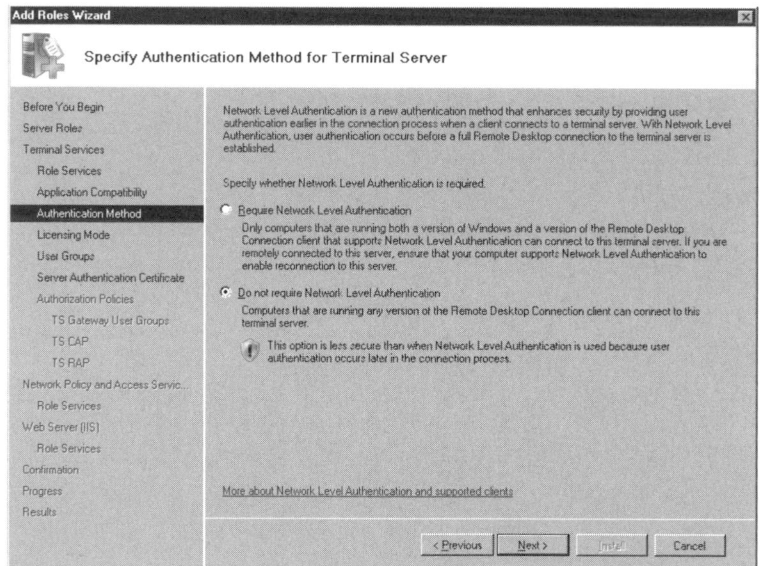

Figure 30-5 The Specify Authentication Method For Terminal Server page

10. Click Next to open the Specify Licensing Mode page. You can choose from three options:

- ❑ **Configure Later** Gives you up to 120 days to configure and install a Terminal Services license server and select licensing mode
- ❑ **Per Device** Requires a TS Per Device Client Access License (CAL) for each device that connects to the server
- ❑ **Per User** Requires a TS Per User CAL for each user that connects to the server

11. Click Next to open the Select User Groups Allowed To Access This Terminal Server page, shown in Figure 30-6.

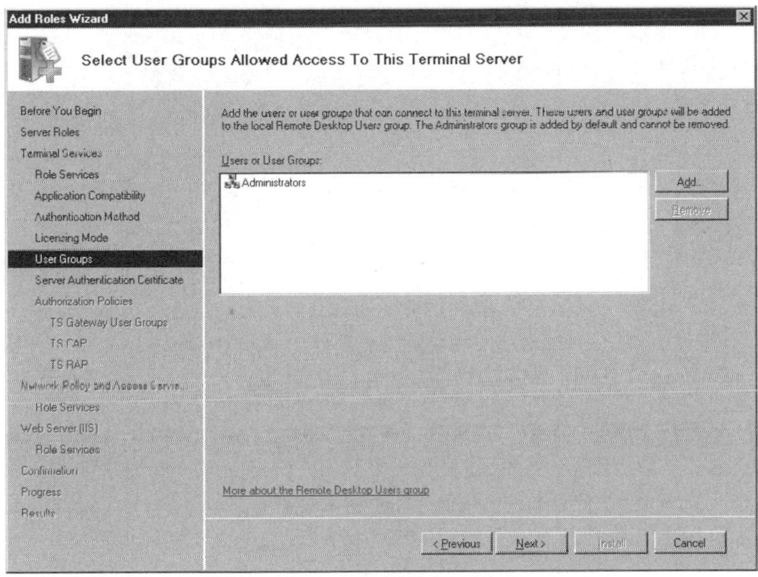

Figure 30-6 The Select User Groups Allowed To Access This Terminal Server page

12. By default, only Administrators are added to the local Remote Desktop Users group. This group controls which users are allowed to connect to the Terminal Server. If you want to allow additional users, add the necessary user groups to the local Remote Desktop Users group. Click Add to open the familiar Select Users, Computers, Or Groups dialog box and add the groups you want.
13. Click Next to open the Choose A Server Authentication Certificate For SSL Encryption page, as shown in Figure 30-7.

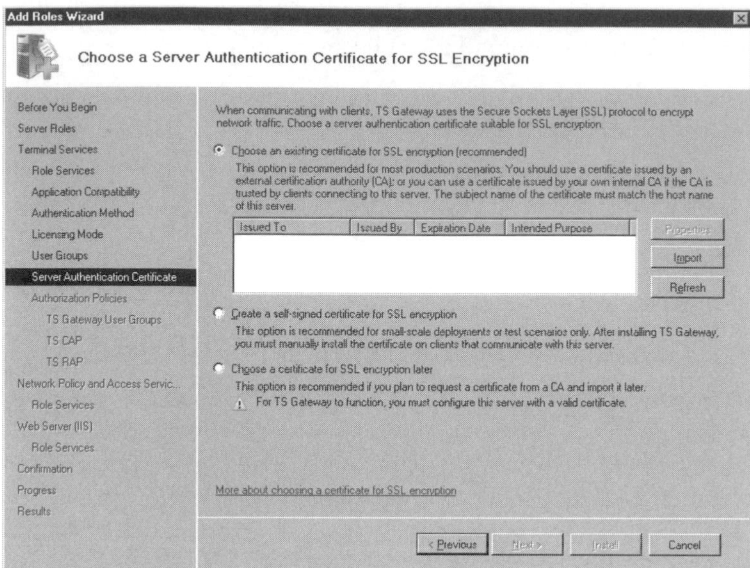

Figure 30-7 The Choose A Server Authentication Certificate For SSL Encryption page

14. For most large production environments, a certificate signed by an external authority is recommended. However, for small-scale deployments, you can choose the Create A Self-Signed Certificate For SSL Encryption option.

15. Click Next to open the Create Authorization Policies For TS Gateway page. You can choose to create the policies now, or later. Do it now. Until you have created the Terminal Services connection authorization policy (TS CAP) and Terminal Services resource authorization policy (TS RAP), users won't be able to connect through the TS Gateway.

16. Click Next to open the Select User Groups That Can Connect Through TS Gateway page. The default is the local Administrators group. Click Add to add additional user groups that will be added to the TS CAP and TS RAP.

17. Click Next to open the Create A TS CAP For TS Gateway page, shown in Figure 30-8.

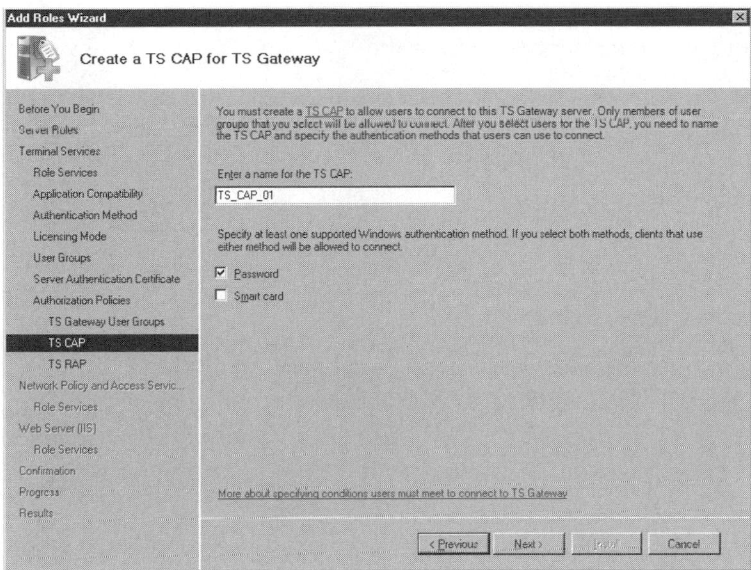

Figure 30-8 The Create A TS CAP For TS Gateway page

18. Enter a name for the policy, and select the authentication methods that will be allowed. If you select multiple methods, any one of them will be sufficient.
19. Click Next to open the Create A TS RAP For TS Gateway page shown in Figure 30-9.

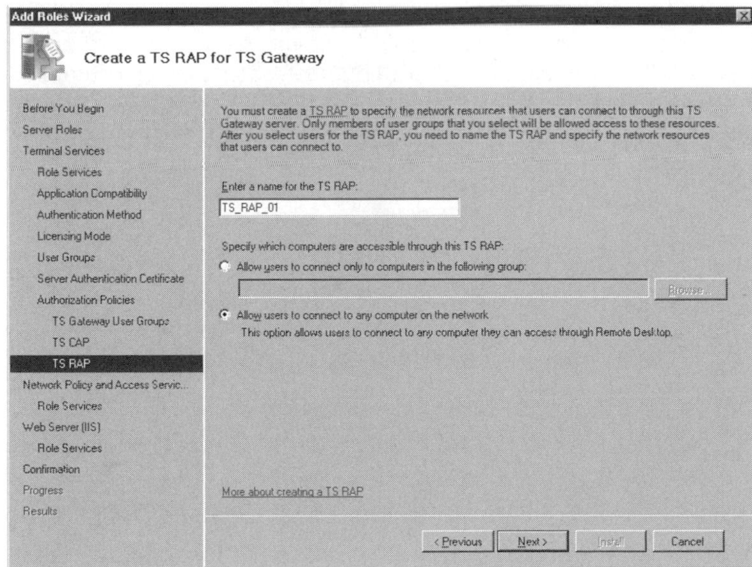

Figure 30-9 The Create A TS RAP For TS Gateway page

20. You can specify groups of computers that users can access, or you can allow them to connect to any computer on the network.
21. Click Next to open the Network Policy And Access Services page. This page includes Things To Note About NPS, and also includes additional information links for several topics that you might want to review before configuring NPS.
22. Click Next to open the Select Role Services page for NPS. By default, only the Network Policy Server role service is selected, because this is the minimum required to support the TS Gateway role. You can select additional role services if you expect this TS Gateway server to have additional roles.
23. Click Next to open the Web Server (IIS) page of the Add Roles Wizard. This page includes Things To Note About The Web Server role, including a link to Windows System Resource Manager (WSRM) , and also includes additional information links for several topics that you might want to review before configuring Web Server (IIS).
24. Click Next to open the Select Role Services page for the Web Server (IIS) role, as shown in Figure 30-10. This will have all of the role services required for the roles installed on this server, *and only those role services.* Don't change anything here unless you really, really understand the reasons and the consequences.

Important We've said this at several points during the book, but it's worth repeating. The new Add Roles and Add Features Wizards are a *lot* smarter than any previous configuration wizards we've seen from Microsoft, and they should be the only way you add or remove roles, role services, and features. They can be run multiple times as you add or remove roles, role services, and features and each time they are run, they will only add or remove the necessary settings for what you've enabled or removed. So resist the temptation to add something you think you might need later.

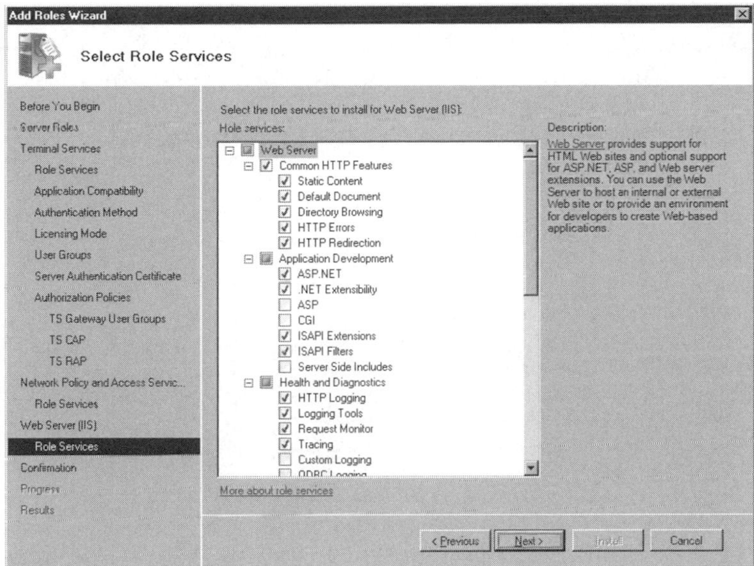

Figure 30-10 The Select Role Services page for the Web Server (IIS) role

25. Click Next to open the Confirm Installation Selections page. It will have at least one warning, about the possible need to reinstall applications, as shown in Figure 30-11.

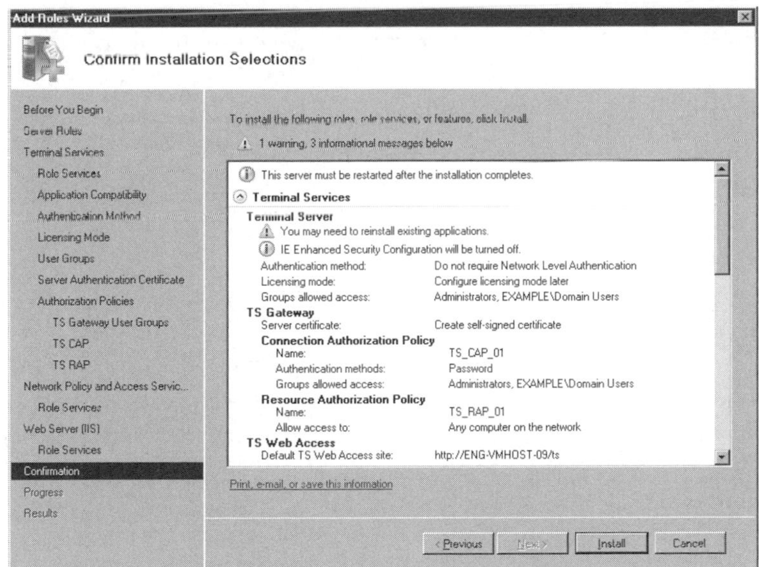

Figure 30-11 The Confirm Installation Selections page of the Add Roles Wizard

26. Click Install to begin the installation of the roles and role services you've selected. You'll almost certainly need to reboot when it finishes, as shown on the Installation Results page of Figure 30-12. Click Close and then Yes to restart the server.

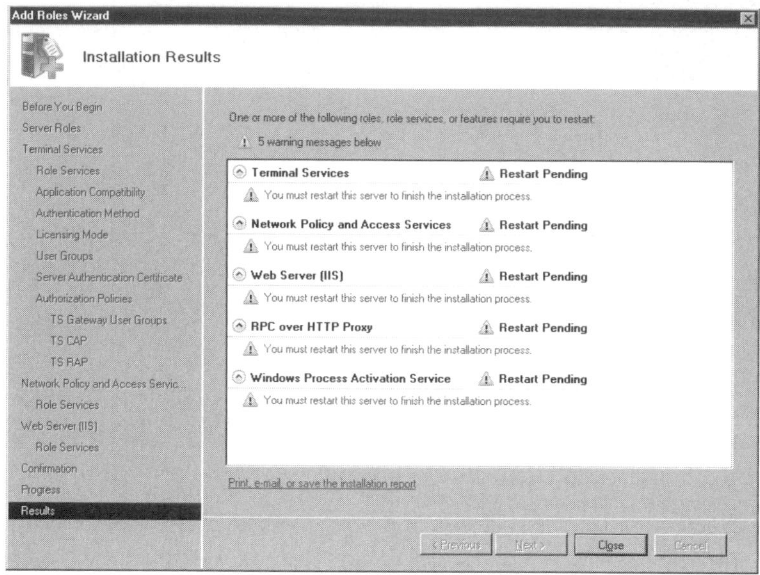

Figure 30-12 The Installation Results page of the Add Roles Wizard

27. When the server reboots, log back on with the same account that you used to add the Terminal Services Role to allow the installation and configuration to fully complete. The Installation Results page will open with the installation results of each of the roles and role services installed. Click Close, and Terminal Services is fully installed and ready to be used.

Improving the User Experience

While Terminal Services is fully installed at this point, you can take several additional steps to improve the overall end-user experience. By default, there is no audio on a Windows Server 2008 computer, and the default graphics level is set to a 16-bit maximum. You can change these and other settings to give Remote Desktop users a fuller experience, but the tradeoff is that they will use substantially more resources on the server.

To enable the full Desktop Experience, you can add the feature using the Add Features Wizard, following these steps:

1. Open the Server Manager console if it isn't already open.

2. Select Add Features from the Action menu to open the Add Features menu. Select Desktop Experience as shown in Figure 30-13.

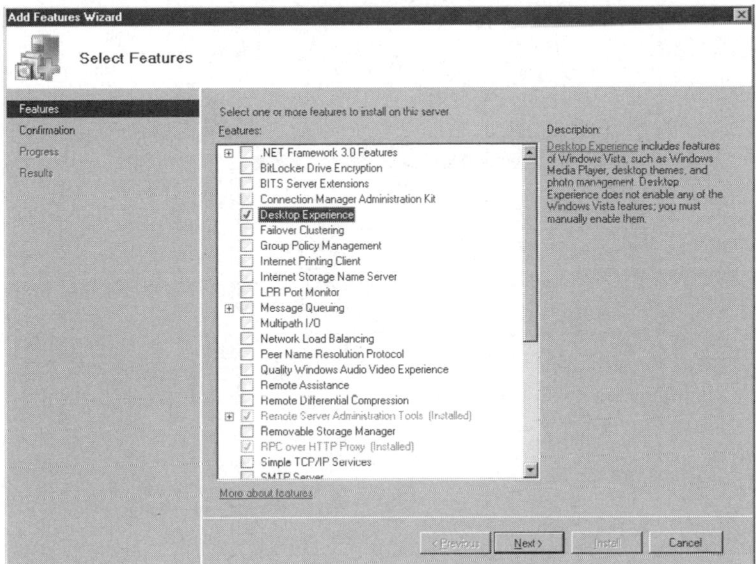

Figure 30-13 The Select Features page of the Add Features Wizard

3. Click Next, and then click Install.
4. Click Close and then click Yes to restart the server.
5. When the server reboots, log back on with the same account that you used to add the Desktop Experience feature to allow the installation and configuration to fully complete. The Installation Results page will open with the installation results of any features installed. Click Close and the Desktop Experience is fully installed.

To Enable 32-bit color and audio for RDP sessions, use the following steps:

1. Open the Server Manager console if it isn't already open.
2. Navigate to Roles, then Terminal Services, and then select Terminal Services Configuration in the leftmost pane of Server Manager.
3. Select RDP-Tcp in the center Connections pane, as shown in Figure 30-14.

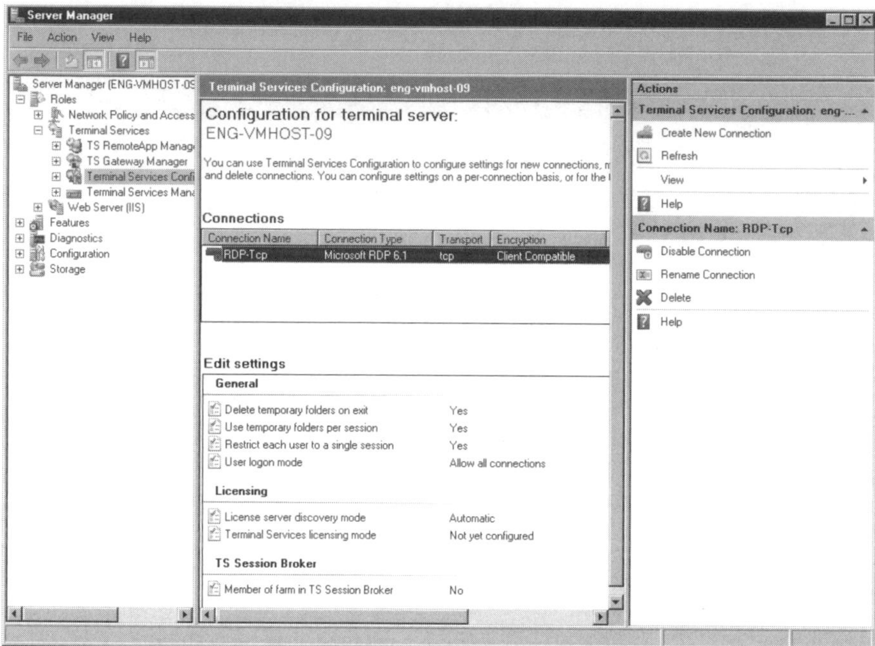

Figure 30-14 The Terminal Services Configuration pane of Server Manager

4. Right-click the RDP-Tcp connection and select Properties to open the RDP-Tcp Properties dialog box.

5. Click the Client Settings tab, as shown in Figure 30-15.

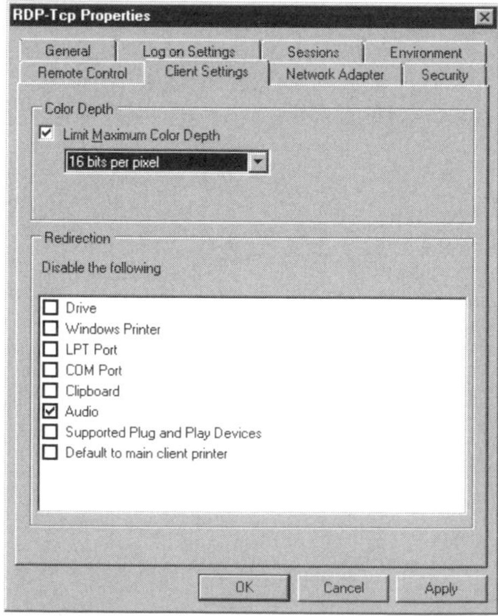

Figure 30-15 The Client Settings tab of the RDP-Tcp Properties dialog box

6. Select a maximum color depth of 32 Bits Per Pixel from the Limit Maximum Color Depth drop-down list to enable 32-bit color.
7. Clear the check box for Audio in the Disable The Following section.
8. Click OK to close the Properties dialog box. If there are current user sessions, you'll see the warning shown in Figure 30-16.

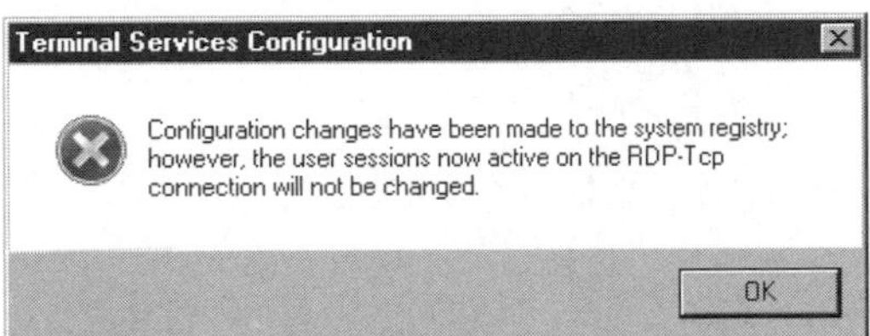

Figure 30-16 The current sessions warning for a Terminal Services configuration change

9. By default, the Audio service is disabled on Windows Server 2008. You need to enable it before RDP clients will get audio.
10. Click Services on the Administrative Tools menu, and then scroll down to Windows Audio service.
11. Right-click the service and then select Properties, change the Startup Type to Automatic, and then click Start to start the service.
12. Click OK and then close the Services console.

Enabling Remote Desktop for Administration Mode

Windows Server 2008 automatically installs all that is necessary for Windows Terminal Services Remote Desktop for Administration mode as part of all installations, but before it can be used, it must be enabled. To enable Remote Desktop for Administration mode, follow these steps:

1. From a command prompt, type **oobe** and press Enter to open the Initial Configuration Tasks Wizard.
2. Click Enable Remote Desktop to open the System Properties dialog box with the Remote tab in selected, as shown in Figure 30-17.

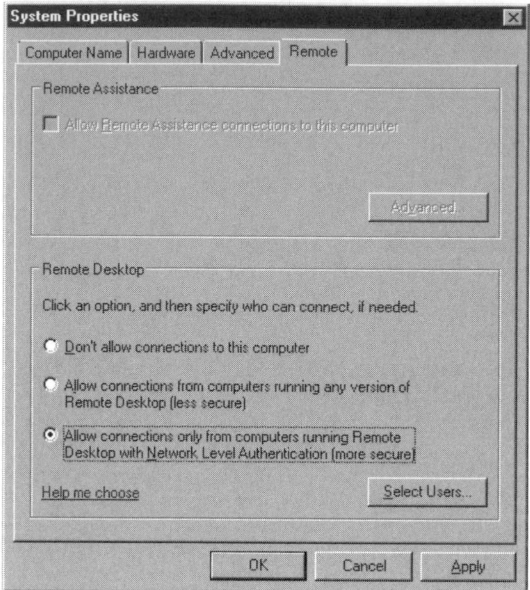

Figure 30-17 The Remote tab of the System Properties dialog box

3. Select Allow Connections Only From Computers Running Remote Desktop With Network Level Authentication (More Secure) if all your Administrator's clients that need to connect to this server have the latest version of the RDP client installed.
4. Click OK to save the settings and close the dialog box.

Installing Programs

Installing programs with Remote Desktop for Administration mode enabled is no different from installing on a server without Terminal Services. No special steps are required, and no changes to the installation process or special compatibility scripts to support applications are required.

Application server mode, however, requires special consideration when installing many programs. When you activate application server mode, Windows Server 2008 knows it must be prepared to deal with multiple users accessing the same application running simultaneously in separate memory spaces without interference or crossover. Certified for Windows programs handle the situation correctly, but if you're installing a noncertified program, carefully follow the required steps to ensure that the application is installed correctly and that it will function correctly as a multiuser application.

Most applications install without problems in application server mode, though some might require special compatibility scripts. Consult the documentation for the given application. Any application that meets the rigorous "Certified for Windows" Server 2008 logo requirements must run successfully in Windows Terminal Services.

Install Mode vs. Execute Mode

Windows Server 2008, when configured as a Terminal Services application server, has two separate and distinct modes of operation–Install mode and Execute mode. To install an application that doesn't meet the Certified for Windows logo requirements on a server, you must be in install mode or the application will not be installed correctly.

Windows Server 2008 is usually smart enough to recognize when you are running an installation program and automatically sets the necessary mode. However, if you're installing an older application that isn't Certified for Windows, especially if it doesn't use Setup.exe or Install.exe as its installation program, manually switch the server to install mode before running the installation by using the Change command.

The Change Command

The Change command was introduced in Windows NT 4 Terminal Server Edition and is still available in Windows Server 2008. The Change command allows you to change between user modes (install and execute), reassign port mappings for Terminal Services sessions, and enable or disable logon events to Terminal Services. The three basic commands, and their options for the Change command, are as follows:

- **Change User** Initiates change between install or execute mode when running as an application server and has the following options:
  - **Install** Installs new applications on the server for multiuser access
  - **Execute** Allows programs to be executed in multiuser mode (the default value on startup)
  - **Query** Displays the current user mode
- **Change Port** Changes the port assignments of COM port mappings for MS-DOS compatibility and has the following options:
  - **portx=porty** Maps port X to port Y
  - **/D portx** Deletes the current mapping for port X
  - **/Query** Displays the current port mappings
- **Change Logon** Enables or disables logon sessions and has the following options:
  - **/Enable** Allows users to log on from Terminal Services sessions
  - **/Disable** Prohibits users from initiating logon sessions (current sessions aren't disconnected or terminated)

- **/Drain** Disables new logon sessions, but allows current sessions to reconnect if disconnected
- **/Drainuntilrestart** Disables new logon sessions until the next reboot of the server, but allows current sessions to reconnect if disconnected
- **/Query** Displays the current logon status

Using the Change Command to Install an Application

You can also install new applications into Windows Terminal Services using the Change command. This is especially useful for scripting installations that will be installed on multiple Terminal Servers in an identical configuration. To install a new application using the Change command, follow these steps:

1. Disable new logons to the server by typing **change logon /disable**.
2. Find out which users are currently logged on to the server and what their session IDs are by typing **query session**.
3. Warn the users that they need to log off their current session using the Msg command below, A broadcast warning to all users would have the following form as shown in Figure 30-18:

   ```
   msg * "message text"
   ```

   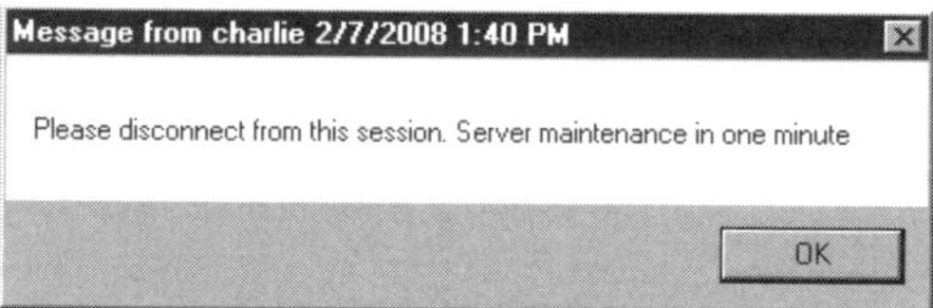

   Figure 30-18 A typical msg command displayed on the user's Terminal Server session

4. Reset sessions of users that are currently logged on to the server with the command **reset session** <sessionID>.
5. Change to install mode with the command **change user /install**.
6. Run the application's setup or installation program.
7. Change back to execute mode by typing **change user /execute**.
8. Re-enable logons to the server with **change logon /enable**.

As you can see, using the Change command, along with other command-line utilities included with Windows Server 2008, enables you to easily script the installation of a program to Windows Terminal Services. In large organizations where multiple Terminal Servers are being used, especially where Session Broker is used to support large user populations, using command-line utilities allows the administrator to limit the disruption to the network as new applications are installed and made available, and easily ensures that applications are installed uniformly across the enterprise, simplifying support and training.

Administration

Windows Terminal Services can be centrally administered and configured across a domain from a single console. The five main applications used to administer Terminal Services servers and clients are as follows:

- **Terminal Services Manager** Monitors and controls the connections to all Terminal Services servers on the network
- **Terminal Services Configuration** Runs only locally on each Terminal Server; a management console that lets you modify the configuration of the local Terminal Services server
- **TS RemoteApp Manager** A management console that lets you manage what applications are available as remote apps, and how they are deployed
- **TS Gateway Manager** A management console that lets you manage what applications are available as on the TS Gateway
- **Terminal Services Licensing Manager** Manages Client Access Licenses for Terminal Services across the domain or workgroup

Terminal Services Manager

Terminal Services Manager (Tsadmin.exe) is the main mechanism for managing the various connections to the servers. A typical Terminal Services Manager window is shown in Figure 30-19. From here, you can see not only the available Terminal Servers on the network, but also who is connected to them, which sessions are active, which protocols are being used, and so on.

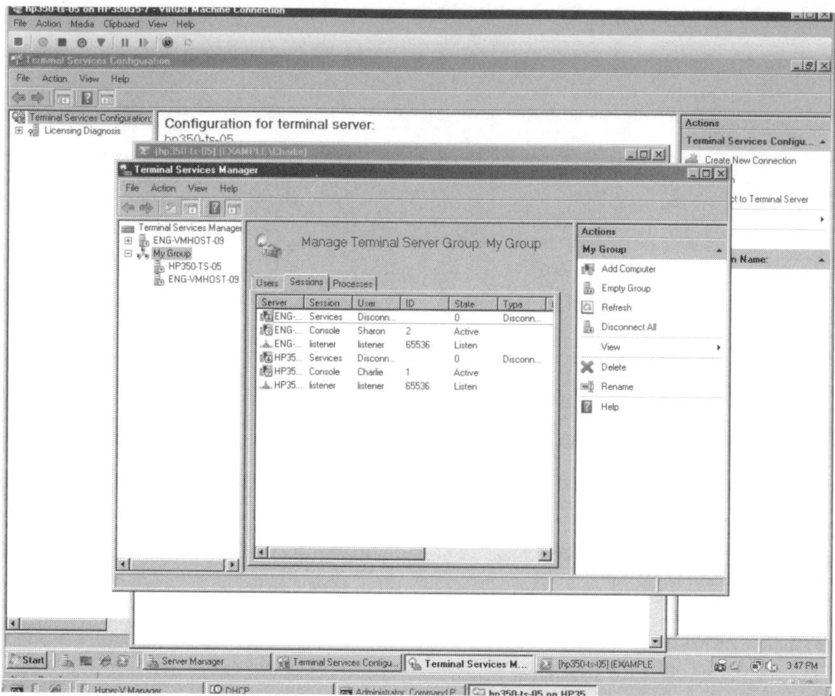

Figure 30-19 A typical Terminal Services Manager window

Overview

By default, Terminal Services Manager shows the local computer, and any additional servers added to My Group. The icons for the current active connection, server, and domain are shown in a different color (green, by default). With Terminal Services Manager, you can view and manage the users, sessions, and processes by network, domain, server, or connection, giving you a comprehensive look at the critical information for your Terminal Services deployment.

My Group

The Terminal Services Manager includes a default group called My Group to which you can add computers running Terminal Services. You can manage and view the status, users, sessions, and processes from multiple computers by adding them to My Group, as shown in Figure 30-20. Computers in My Group can be running the full Terminal Services Role (formerly Application Mode), or be a regular server with Remote Desktop enabled.

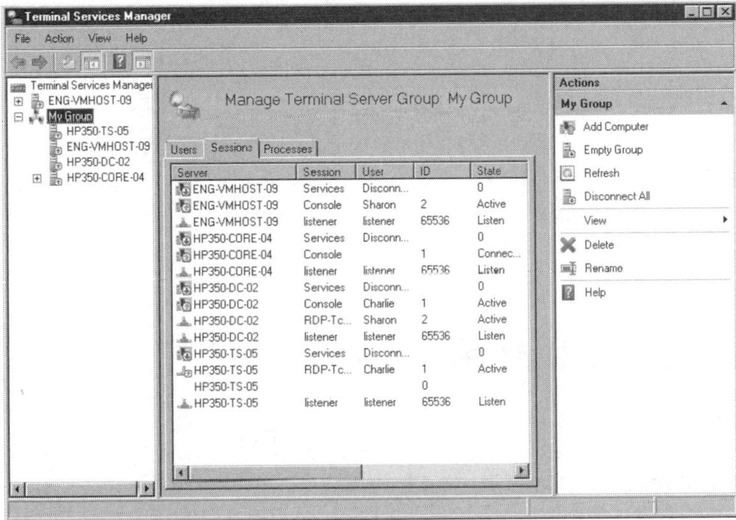

Figure 30-20 The default My Group in Terminal Services Manager

You can also add additional groups to Terminal Services Manager. To add a group, right-click Terminal Services Manager in the left pane, and select New Group from the menu. Type a name for the group into the Create Group dialog box and click OK.

To add a computer to a group, follow these steps.

1. Open the Terminal Services Manager console if it isn't already open.
2. Select the group you want to add a computer to in the left pane.
3. Click Add Computer on the Actions pane to open the Select Computer dialog box shown in Figure 30-21.

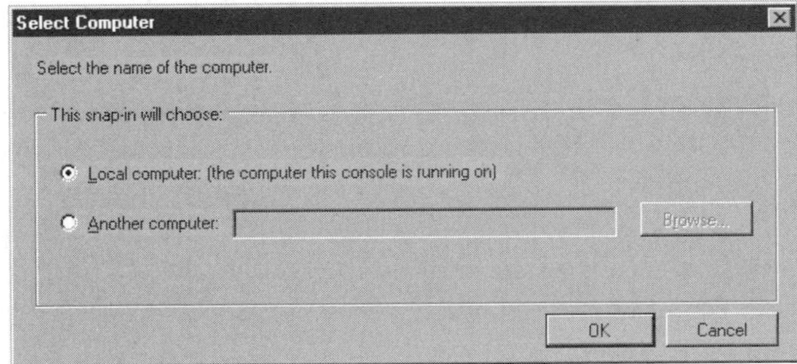

Figure 30-21 The Select Computer dialog box

4. Select Another Computer and type in the name or IP address of the computer or click Browse to locate the computer in Active Directory.
5. Click OK and the computer is added to the group.
6. To add a computer to another group, right-click the computer in any current group and select Add To Group from the menu.
7. In the Terminal Services Manager dialog box shown in Figure 30-22, select the Group to add the computer to, and click OK. Or if you want to create a new group, click Create Group.

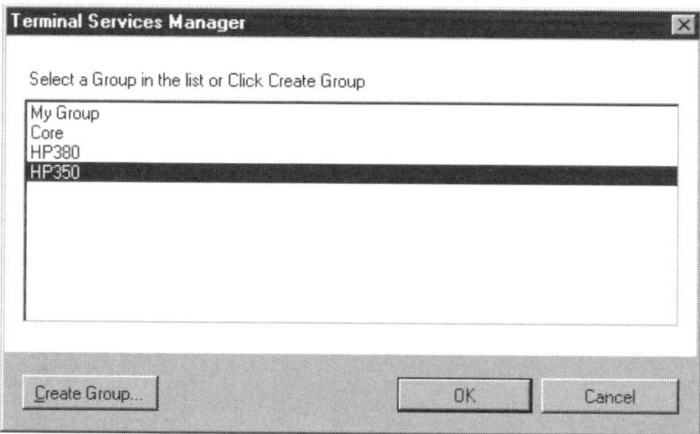

Figure 30-22 The Remote Desktop Disconnected message box

Making Connections

To manage the processes, sessions, and users connected to a given server, you need to first connect to that server using Terminal Services Manager. To connect to a server, right-click the server's icon in the left pane of Terminal Services Manager and choose Connect. If this is a server you regularly connect to, add it to My Group or one of your other groups.

Managing Connections

Terminal Services Manager lets you view and manage each of the connections to the Terminal Servers. From any session that has sufficient permissions, you can forcibly disconnect a session, reset a session entirely, log off a session, view the status of the connection, manage users' sessions, send a message to the display of a connection, use remote control to take control of a session on the connection, and connect to any other session. You can also use Terminal Services Manager to see a variety of information about the processes and status of the connections to a server and even to kill a hung process.

Disconnecting Sessions

When a session is disconnected, all the programs of that session continue to run, but the input and output from the session are no longer transmitted to the remote terminal. Disconnecting a session leaves user programs and data in their normal state, protecting them from loss of data. Disconnecting a session doesn't release memory or other resources from the server, and the session continues to be counted as a licensed session.

Any user can disconnect his own session, or an administrator with the Full Control privilege can disconnect a session. To disconnect a session using Terminal Services Manager, right-click the session in either pane of Terminal Services Manager and choose Disconnect from the shortcut menu. Click OK to confirm that this is what you really meant to do, and the session is disconnected.

You can disconnect multiple sessions on multiple servers as well. Simply select the sessions in the right pane of Terminal Services Manager and right-click. Choose Disconnect from the menu, click OK in response to the prompt, and the sessions are disconnected. The console where the sessions are being displayed receives a message like that shown in Figure 30-23. When you click OK, the message box disappears.

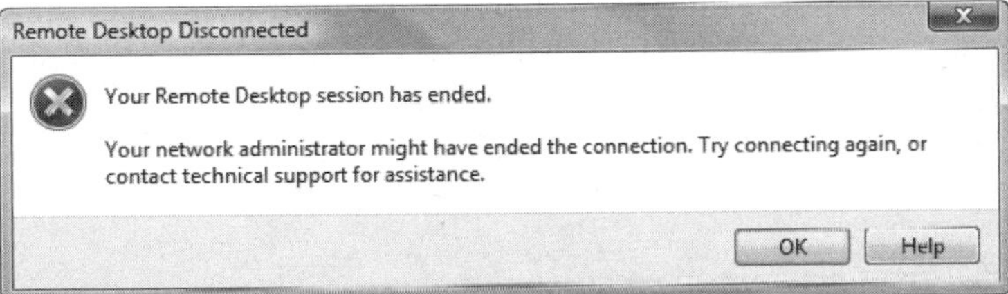

Figure 30-23 The Remote Desktop Disconnected message box

Real World **Using Disconnect to Manage Your Sessions from Multiple Locations**

Disconnecting from a Terminal Services session has many advantages for the mobile user who might need to connect from a different location or who wants to be able to work in relatively short bursts as time permits. When you disconnect from a session, everything continues to run, just as if you were connected. So when you reconnect to the same server, the session is restored exactly as you left it. You can then easily return to a project or document exactly where you left off. However, because the session continues to run, it continues to use resources on the server, so reserve disconnect for mobile users. Encourage regular users located on high-quality connections to log off their sessions to free the resources for others.

Resetting Sessions

You can reset a session if the session is your own or if you have the Full Control privilege for sessions. When you reset a session, all work in that session is lost, programs stop running, and memory is freed. To reset a session, right-click the session and choose Reset from the menu. You get a warning message. Click OK and the session is reset.

You can reset multiple sessions by selecting them in the right pane of Terminal Services Manager, right-clicking them, and selecting Reset. You must have the Full Control privilege for each of these sessions, or they must be your own.

You can also use the command line to reset sessions. To find out what sessions are active, type

```
query session
```

This will list all the sessions on the current server, including their session ID. To disconnect a session, type

```
reset session <ID>
```

The reset session command also accepts the session name as an argument instead of session ID, and lets you specify the server as well. The query session can provide more detailed information about the session parameters—type **query session /?** for full syntax.

> **Important** Resetting a session can result in data loss for the user of that session. Reset a session only when the session has stopped responding or has otherwise malfunctioned.

Logging Off a Session

You can log off your own session or log off a user's session if you have the Full Control privilege. Right-click the session in the right pane of Terminal Services Manager, and select Log Off from the shortcut menu, shown in Figure 30-24. You'll get a warning that the user's session will be logged off. If you click OK, the session is logged off. Logging off a session frees up any resources used by that session, returning them for use by other connections.

Figure 30-24 The shortcut menu for the Users tab of Terminal Services Manager

> **Important** Logging off a session can result in data loss for users of that session. Always warn users by sending them a message before logging off their session.

Viewing Processes and Other Information About a Session

You can view the active processes in a session and a variety of other information about the session, including which client the session is coming from, the security level, the session resolution, and so forth. To view the active processes in a session, highlight the computer in the left pane of Terminal Services Manager and click the Processes tab in the right pane, as shown in Figure 30-25.

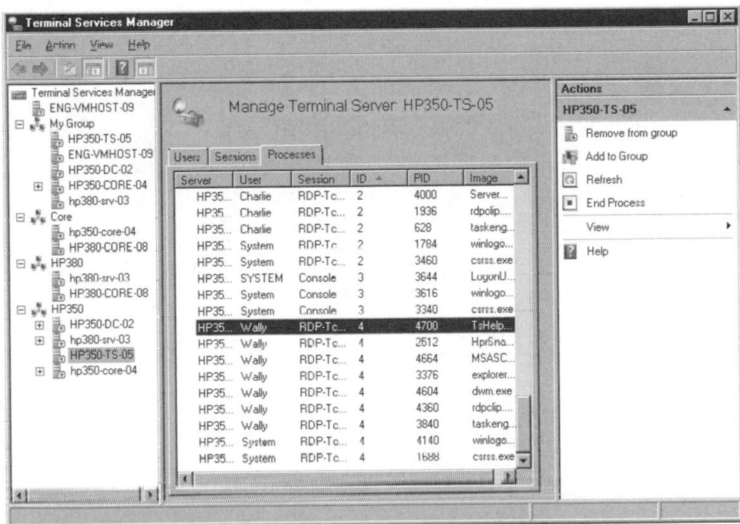

Figure 30-25 The Processes tab of Terminal Services Manager

Managing User Sessions

You can use Terminal Services Manager to view and manage the user sessions on a particular server or across an entire group of servers. To view all the users across the entire group, highlight the group name in the left pane of Terminal Services Manager and click the Users tab in the center pane. You can select any entry in the center pane and send a message to the user's session, disconnect the session, or take control of the user's session for troubleshooting or training.

Sending a Message to a Session

You can use Terminal Services Manager to send a message to a particular session. To send a message to all the sessions on a particular server, just highlight all the sessions and send a message to all of them at once. To send a message to one or more sessions or users, follow these steps:

1. Select the sessions or users in the middle pane of Terminal Services Manager.
2. Choose Send Message from the rightmost Actions pane to open the dialog box shown in Figure 30-26.

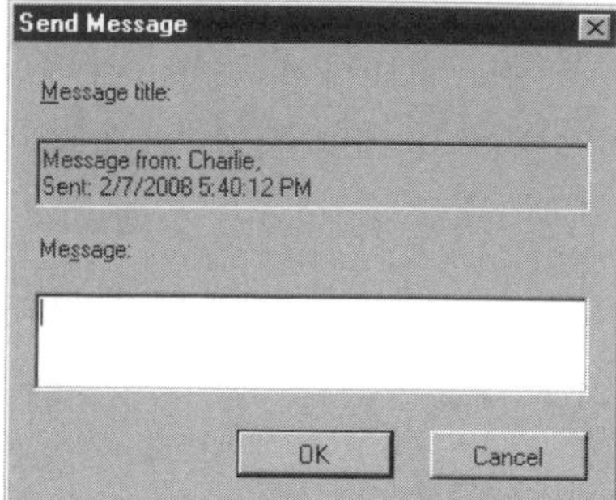

Figure 30-26 The Send Message dialog box

3. Type the message you want to send. Press Ctrl+Enter to start a new line.
4. Click OK to send the message.

You can also use the command-line Msg command to send a message to a particular session or to all the users on a particular server. The Msg command has additional options and functionality over the graphical Terminal Services Manager messaging. The syntax for the Msg command is as follows:

```
msg {username|sessionname|sessionid|@filename|*}
[/SERVER:servername] [/TIME:seconds] [/V] [/W] [message text]
```

The options for the Msg command are as follows:

- **username** Sends the message to a particular user on the server.
- **sessionname** Sends a message to a particular session, identified by the session name.
- **sessionid** Sends a message to a particular session identified by session ID.
- **@filename** Sends a message to a list of user names, session names, or session IDs contained in the file.
- ***** Sends a message to all users connected to the server.
- **/SERVER:***servername* Specifies the server to which the session or user is connected. The default is the current server.
- **/TIME:***seconds* Specifies the number of seconds to wait for the recipients to acknowledge the message. If the message isn't acknowledged in the time specified, it goes away. The default time is 60 seconds if no /TIME option overrides the default.
- **/V** Displays information back to the command line about the actions being performed on the server.

- **/W** Waits for a response from the user before returning control to the command line. If no response is received before the message times out, control is returned when it times out.
- **message text** Specifies the message to send. If none is specified, the text is accepted from STDIN or you are prompted for the text.

Controlling a Session

If you have appropriate permission (Full Control), you can connect to another user's session and remotely control it. The keyboard, mouse, and display are the same for both your session and the user's session. This gives you the ability to easily troubleshoot a user's session or train the user by walking her through the steps of a particular task. Input for the session comes equally from your session and the user's. If the user or protocol settings are set to view only the session, not directly control it, you see only what the user does on her screen, but you aren't able to interact with it using your mouse or keyboard.

By default, when you connect to a user's session using remote control, the user is notified that you are connecting and is asked to confirm the permission. This notification can be turned off on a per-user basis by modifying the user's account in Active Directory. You can also configure this notification on a per-protocol basis for a given server using Terminal Services Configuration. To take control of a user's session, follow these steps:

1. Right-click the session or user in the center pane of Terminal Services Manager.
2. Choose Remote Control to open the dialog box shown in Figure 30-27. Select an appropriate hot key that will terminate the remote session. The default is Ctrl+*, where the asterisk symbol (*) is from the numeric keypad.

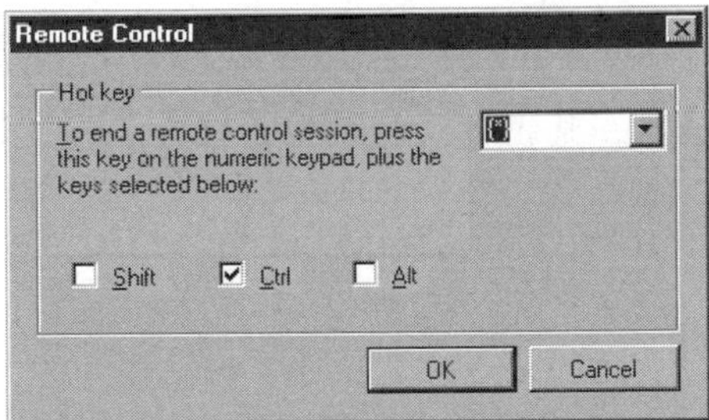

Figure 30-27 The Remote Control dialog box

3. The dialog box shown in Figure 30-28 appears to the user, requesting permission to allow you to connect.

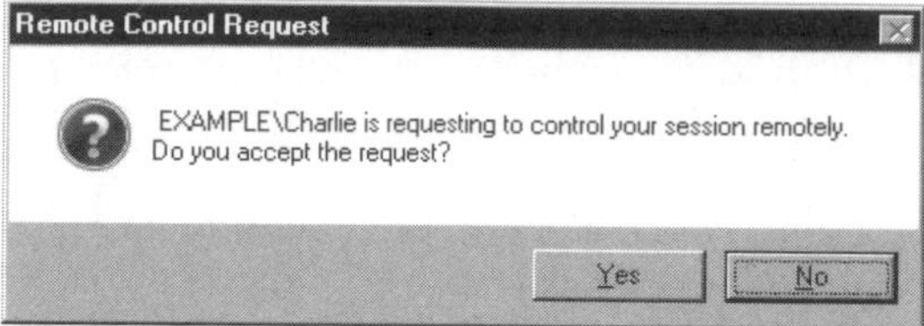

Figure 30-28 The Remote Control Request dialog box

You can also use the Shadow command to take control of a user's session. The Shadow command has the following syntax:

```
shadow {sessionname|sessionid} [/SERVER:servername] [/V]
```

In this syntax, *sessionname* and *sessionid* identify the particular session you want to take control of, and the server defaults to the current server if */SERVER* isn't specified. The */V* (verbose) option gives additional information about the actions being performed.

Connecting to a Session

You can connect to another session on the server you are on if you have the appropriate permission and the other session is either in an active or a disconnected state. You can always connect to a session that is logged on with the same user account as your current logon name, or you can connect to another user's session if you have Full Control or User Access permission. You are prompted for the user's password.

This ability to connect to another session can be a useful tool for both administrators and users. Get home and realize you forgot to finish off that important memo? Log on remotely and connect to your working session at the office and pick up right where you left off. To connect to a session, follow these steps:

1. Right-click the session or user in the center pane of Terminal Services Manager.
2. Choose Connect to connect to the session. If the session is that of a different user than the current user, you're prompted for the target session user's password. If the session is one of your own, you're switched to that session and your current session is disconnected.

Session Status

You can see a wealth of information about a particular session. To get information about the status of a session, right-click the session in the middle pane of the Terminal Services Manager and select Status to see the session status shown in Figure 30-29.

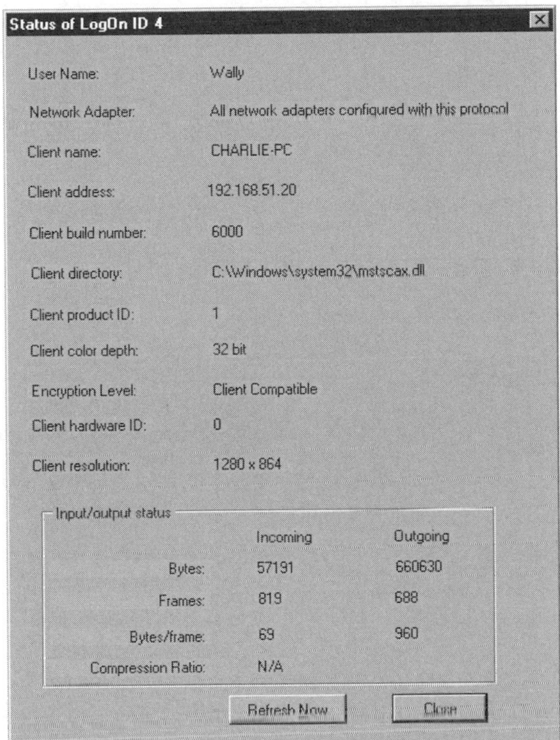

Figure 30-29 The Status of a Terminal Services session

Terminal Services Configuration

Use the Terminal Services Configuration console to change the settings for all connections to a particular server. (See Figure 30-30.)

From here, you can change any of the following settings:

- **Delete Temporary Folders On Exit** When enabled, automatically deletes any temporary folders created on the server when the user logs off. Default is true (Yes).
- **Use Temporary Folders Per Session** When enabled, each session gets its own set of temporary folders. Default is true (Yes).
- **Restrict Each User To One Session** When enabled, the default users are limited to a single session on the Terminal Server to conserve resources. Default is true (Yes).
- **User Logon Mode**
  - Allow All Connections (default) – normal operation.
  - Allow Reconnections, But Prevent New Logons (draining).
  - Allow Reconnections, But Prevent New Logons Until The Server Is Restarted.

- **Member of Farm in TS Session Broker** Disabled by default. When enabled, it allows Session Broker to manage the sessions in a cluster. (Present only on Windows Server 2008 Enterprise Edition or Datacenter Edition.)
- **License Server Discovery Mode** Choose between Automatic or specify specific license server(s).
- **Terminal Server Licensing Mode** Choose between Per Device and Per User.

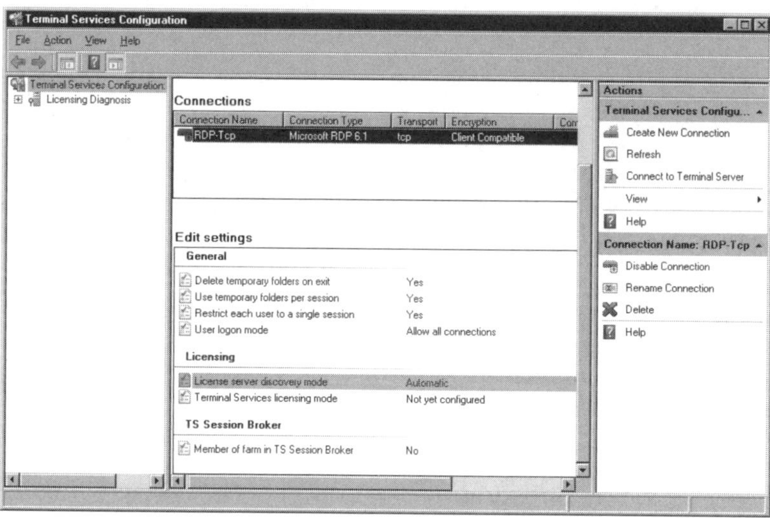

Figure 30-30 The Terminal Services Configuration console

Connection Properties

You can change the properties of the connections from Terminal Services Configuration. By default, the only connection protocol installed is Microsoft Remote Data Protocol (RDP) 6.1. Other protocols are available from third parties, including the Independent Computing Architecture (ICA) protocol used by Citrix MetaFrame. All protocols can be configured from this point.

RDP allows you to configure a wide variety of settings for each server (listed in Table 30-1). Most of these settings are normally controlled by the client, or you can set the server to override the client settings. To set properties for the RDP connections, double-click the RDP-Tcp entry under Connection to open the dialog box shown in Figure 30-31.

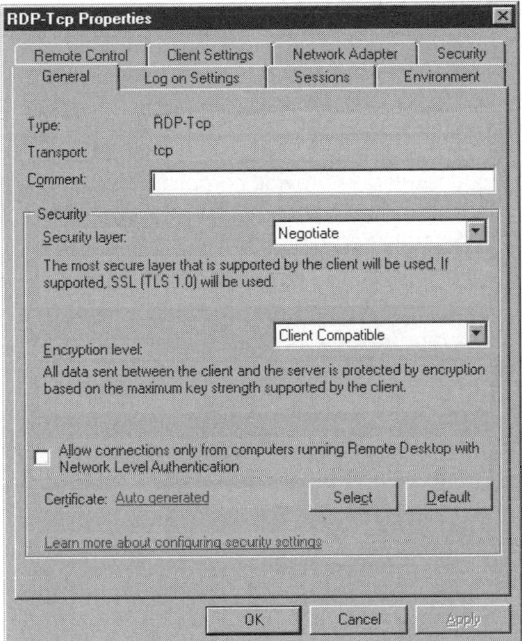

Figure 30-31 The RDP-Tcp Properties dialog box

Table 30-1 Terminal Services Configuration Settings for RDP

Tab	Property	Setting	Meaning
General	Security Layer	Negotiate	Uses maximum security the client will support.
		RDP Security Layer	Uses RDP encryption for communication between client and server.
		SSL(TLS 1.0)	Uses TLS 1.0 for server authentication and encryption between client and server.
	Encryption Level	Low	Data from client to server is encrypted using the standard encryption key.
		Client Compatible	Data is encrypted using the maximum key strength supported by the client in both directions (default setting).
		High	Data is encrypted in both directions using the maximum key length supported. Clients that do not support this level of encryption are not allowed to connect.

Table 30-1 **Terminal Services Configuration Settings for RDP**

Tab	Property	Setting	Meaning
		FIPS Compliant	Encrypts data in both directions using Federal Information Processing Standard (FIPS) encryption algorithms. This encryption is designed to provide compliance with FIPS 140-1 (1994) and FIPS 140-2 (2001) for Security Requirements for Cryptographic Modules.
	Allow Connections Only From Computers With Network Level Authentication	False	When selected (true), only RDP clients that support Network Level Authentication are allowed to connect.
Log On Settings	Use Client-Provided Log On Information	True	Client determines the logon security user.
	Always Use The Following Log On Information	False	Logon information for all clients uses this same logon information.
	Always Prompt For Password	False	Client can use embedded password. Security Tip: Domain Controllers should have this box selected to always force a remote session to enter a password.
Sessions	Override User Settings: (disconnected, active, and idle sessions)	False	User settings control termination of disconnected sessions, active session limit, and idle session limit.
		True	The server controls session limits.
	Override User Settings: (session limit action)	False	User settings control session limit behavior.
		True	Server settings control session limit behavior—disconnect or end the session.
	Override User Settings (reconnection)	False	User settings control reconnection.
		True	Server settings control reconnection.
Environment	Initial Program	Disabled	Forces clients to connect to the desktop.

Table 30-1 **Terminal Services Configuration Settings for RDP**

Tab	Property	Setting	Meaning
		False	Client specifies initial program. (This is the default.)
		True	All clients are forced to run the program specified.
Remote Control	Use Remote Control With Default User Settings	True	Settings for remote control are set as part of the user's account data.
	Do Not Allow Remote Control	False	When true, all remote control to sessions on the server is disabled.
	Use Remote Control With The Following Settings	False	When true, you override remote control settings for all users connecting to the server.
Client Settings	Limit Maximum Color Depth	True	When True, you can choose the maximum color depth used by clients. Default value is 16 bit.
	Drive Mapping	True (not selected)	Client drives are mapped to the user session.
	Windows Printer Mapping	True (not selected)	Clients can map Windows printers, and mappings are remembered.
	LPT Port Mapping	True (not selected)	Automatic mapping of client LPT ports is enabled.
	COM Port Mapping	True (not selected)	Clients can map printers to COM ports.
	Clipboard Mapping	True (not selected)	Clients can map clipboard.
	Audio Mapping	False (selected)	Clients can't map audio.
	Supported Plug And Play Devices	False	Clients can map PnP devices
	Default To Main Client Printer	False	When selected, default the printer is the default printer on the client
Network Adapter	Network Adapter	All	All available network adapters can be used to connect to Terminal Services.
	Unlimited Connections	True	There is no limit to the number of connections permitted.
	Maximum Connections	True	The maximum number of connections permitted using this adapter.

Table 30-1 Terminal Services Configuration Settings for RDP

Tab	Property	Setting	Meaning
Security	Full Control	Administrators /SYSTEM	Administrators and SYSTEM have Full Control privilege.
	User Access	Remote Desktop Users	Query, Logon, and Connect privileges.

Terminal Services Licensing

Windows Server 2008 requires that at least one Windows Terminal Services license server be installed and running on any network that uses application server mode. If a license server is not installed within 120 days, all Windows Terminal Services connections will be disabled. Windows Terminal Services requires a separate Terminal Server Client Access License (CAL) for each user or device in addition to any Windows Server CALs you might need. The Terminal Server Licensing server does not track per-user license usage, but it does enable you to install per-user licenses.

Installing Terminal Server Licensing

In small deployments, installing the Terminal Server Licensing service on the same server that is running Terminal Services is a reasonable choice, but in larger deployments, the Terminal Server License Server should be on a different server from Terminal Services.

To Install Terminal Services

To install Terminal Services, follow these steps:

1. Open Server Manager if it isn't already open.
2. If Terminal Services Role is installed, select Roles and then select Terminal Services in the leftmost pane, and then select Add Role Services from the Action menu.
3. If Terminal Services Role is not installed, select Add Roles from the Action menu.
4. On the Select Role Services page, select TS Licensing.
5. Click Next to open the TS Licensing Configuration page, shown in Figure 30-32. Select whether this license server will service only the current domain, or the entire forest.

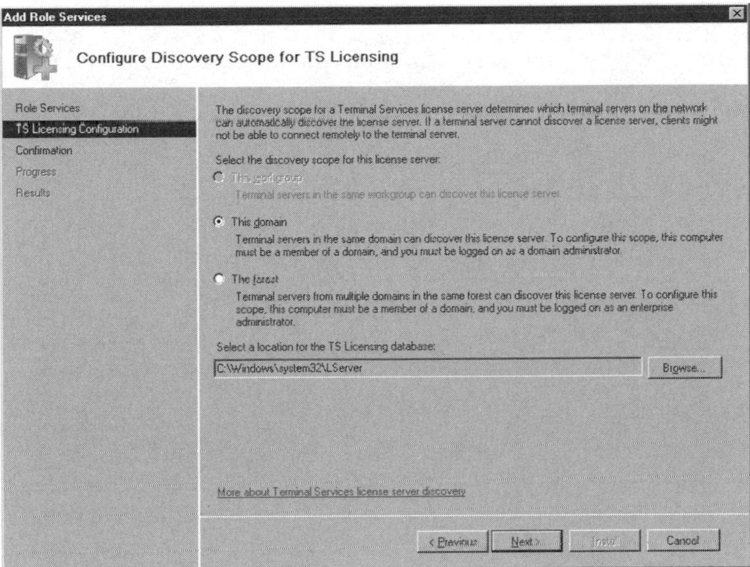

Figure 30-32 The Configure Discovery Scope for TS Licensing page of the Add Role Services Wizard

6. Click Next to open the Confirm Installation Selections page. If everything looks correct, click Install to begin the installation.
7. Click Close when the installation completes.

To Activate the License Server

1. Open the Terminal Services Licensing Manager (licmgr.exe).
2. If a license server is found, TS Licensing Manager will connect to it automatically. If it doesn't find one, you'll see the message shown in Figure 30-33 and you'll have to manually connect.

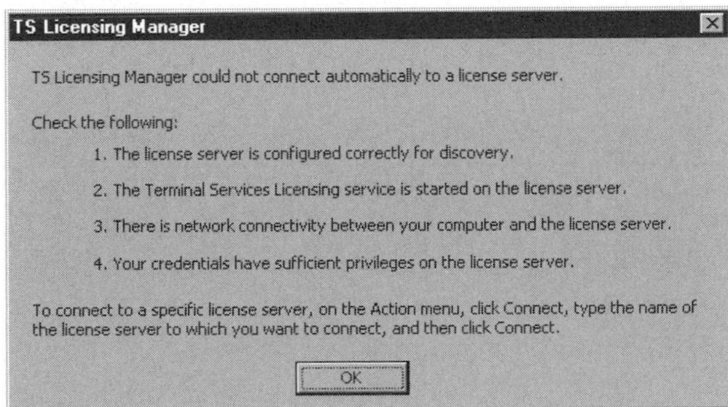

Figure 30-33 Terminal Server Licensing—No Server Found

3. Right-click All Servers in the leftmost pane, and select Connect.
4. Type the name of the new Terminal Server Licensing Server and click OK.
5. Right-click the server in the rightmost pane, and select Activate Server.
6. The Terminal Server License Server Activation Wizard opens. Click Next to open the Connection Method page.
7. Select a connection method from the drop-down list. The choices are Automatic Connection, Web Browser, or Telephone. Automatic Connection requires an Internet connection from the server you are activating. Web Browser also requires an Internet connection, but it can be run from any workstation. Click Next.
8. If you've chosen Automatic, the connection will be made, and then the first Company Information is displayed. Fill in all the fields on this page because they are required. Click Next.
9. The second page of company information is displayed. All information on this page is optional–fill it in only if you want to. Click Next, and if your connection is good, your server will activate, and you'll be presented with the completion page. You can continue to add Client Access Licenses by selecting the Start Terminal Server Licensing Wizard Now check box. Click Next or click Finish.

To Install Windows Terminal Server Client Access Licenses

1. Open the Terminal Server Licensing Wizard if it isn't already open.
2. Right-click the server you want to add licenses to.
3. Select Install Licenses to open the Install Licenses Wizard.
4. Click Next and fill in the license code. Click Next again, and the activation will complete.

Note Additional steps are required for either Web browser or telephone methods. If you need to reactivate your server and reinstall licenses, you will be required to use the telephone method.

RemoteApps

If there is one single thing in Windows Server 2008 that we think is "cool," it has to be Terminal Services RemoteApps. Instead of having users connect to a remote Terminal Server, open a full desktop, and then run the applications they need, TS RemoteApps allows users to run remote applications just as if they were running them locally, without opening up a desktop. The actual behavior is just like a regular application: When it needs to open an additional window—such as when you go to save a file—it automatically opens up a new window on your local workstation that has just the File Save dialog box in it.

Applications can be published as .rdp files or as .msi files, allowing deployment through Group Policy. When you install applications with an .msi file, you can even set them to take over the default extension of the application on the user's workstation, enabling automatic launch.

Note Before enabling RemoteApps on your network, you should consider changing the default configuration of your Terminal Server(s) to allow each user multiple connections. TS RemoteApp will work with users restricted to a single session, but they'll only be able to open one remote application at a time.

TS RemoteApp Manager

The TS RemoteApp Manager console (remoteprograms.msc), shown in Figure 30-34, is used to manage remote applications. From here, you can define the various settings that will control what applications are available, who can connect to them, and how they're distributed and published.

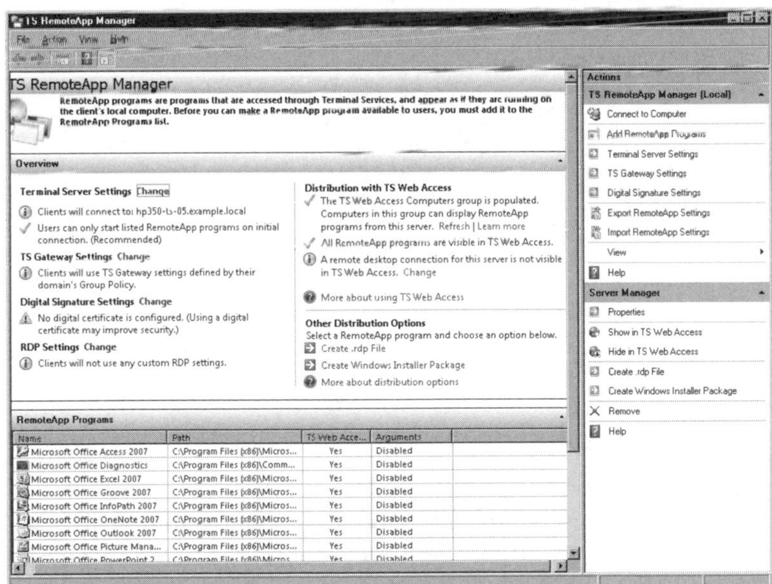

Figure 30-34 TS RemoteApp Manager

TS Gateway Settings

To change the settings for how TS Gateway makes RemoteApps available, follow these steps:

1. Open TS RemoteApp Manager if it isn't already open.
2. In the Overview section of TS RemoteApp Manager, click Change next to TS Gateway Settings to open the RemoteApp Deployment Settings dialog box, shown in Figure 30-35 with the TS Gateway tab in front.

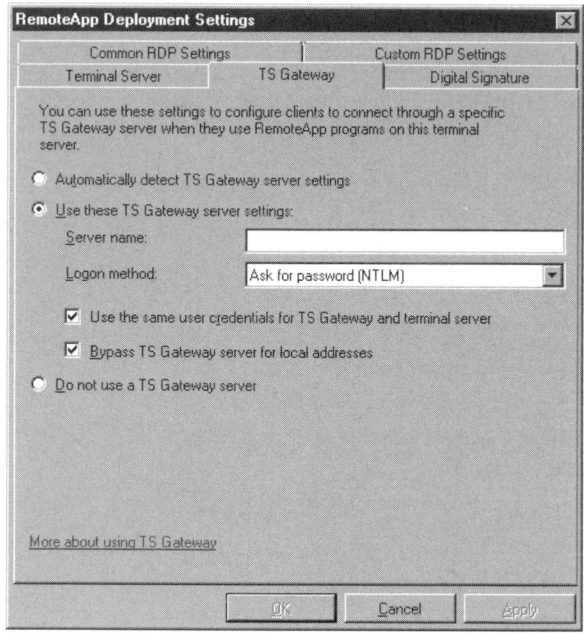

Figure 30-35 The TS Gateway tab of the RemoteApp Deployment Settings dialog box

3. Select the TS Gateway server settings appropriate for your environment. The choices include:
   - **Automatically Detect TS Gateway Server Settings** Will automatically locate and connect with TS Gateway servers on the network using the settings provided by the TS Gateway.
   - **Use These TS Gateway Server Settings** Manually configure the TS Gateway server name and logon method. Includes options to use the same credentials for the Gateway and the Terminal Server, and to bypass the Gateway for local addresses.

- **Do Not Use A TS Gateway Server** Disable publishing RemoteApps from this server through a TS Gateway.

4. Click OK to close the RemoteApp Deployment Settings dialog box and apply the changes.

Distributing RemoteApps with TS Web Access

You can configure RemoteApps to be available through TS Web Access. You need to populate the local TS Web Access Computers group with the TS Web Access computers that are allowed to provide applications running on this Terminal Services computer to users via TS Web Access. You can also control which applications are published via TS Web Access and configure a Remote Desktop connection directly to the server. To configure the necessary settings and enable TS Web Access distribution of RemoteApps, follow these steps:

1. Open the Server Manager if it isn't already open.
2. Expand Configuration in the leftmost pane, and then expand Local Users And Groups. Select Groups, as shown in Figure 30-36.

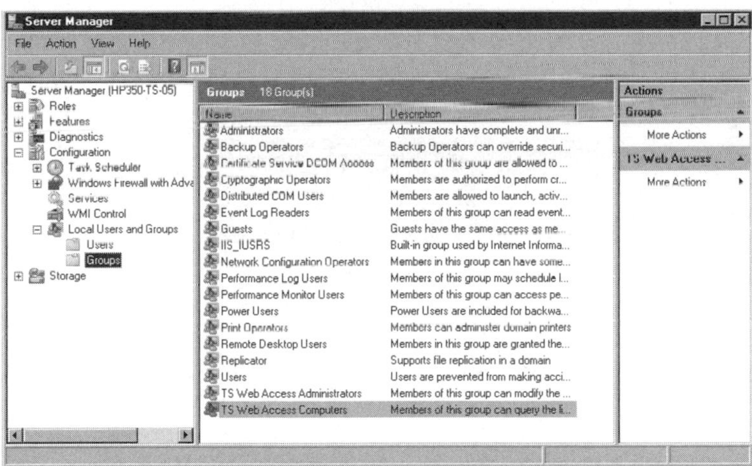

Figure 30-36 Local Users And Groups in Server Manager

3. Double-click the TS Web Access Computers group in the Results pane to open the TS Web Access Computers Properties dialog box shown in Figure 30-37.

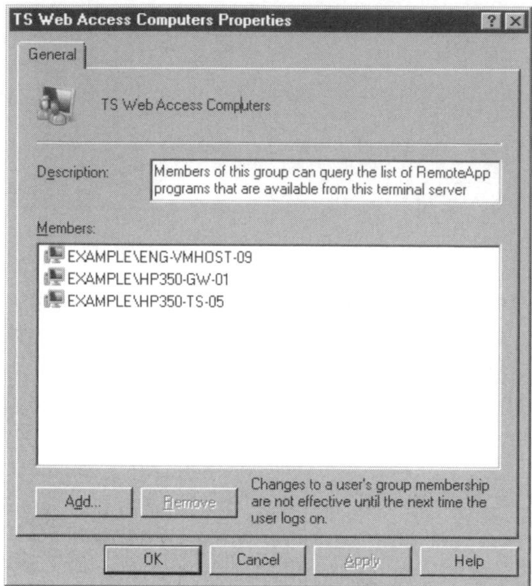

Figure 30-37 The TS Web Access Computers Properties dialog box

4. Click Add to open the Select Users, Computers, Or Groups dialog box. Click Object Types to open the Object Types dialog box, shown in Figure 30-38.

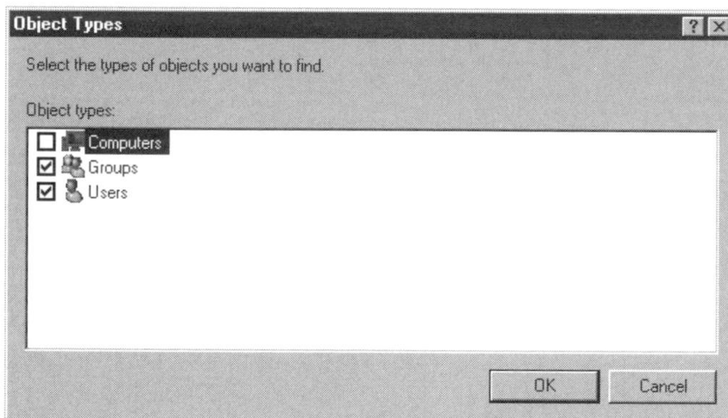

Figure 30-38 The Object Types dialog box

5. Select Computers and click OK to return to the Select Users, Computers, Or Groups dialog box as shown in Figure 30-39.

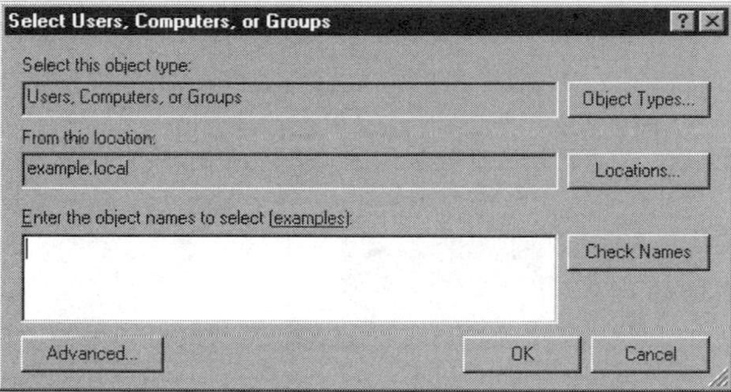

Figure 30-39 The Select Users, Computers, Or Groups dialog box

6. Enter the names of the TS Web Access computers that will be able to connect to this server. Separate multiple names with semicolons. Click Check Names to verify that the computer names are recognized, and then click OK to close the dialog box and return to the TS Web Access Computers Properties dialog box. The names of the TS Web Access computers should be listed in the Members pane.
7. Click OK to return to Server Manager.
8. Open TS RemoteApp Manager or navigate to it in the Roles section of Server Manager.
9. In the Overview section of the TS RemoteApp Manager, under Distribution With TS Web Access, click Change next to A Remote Desktop Connection For This Server Is Not Visible to open the RemoteApp Deployment Settings dialog box, with the Terminal Server Tab selected, as shown in Figure 30-40.

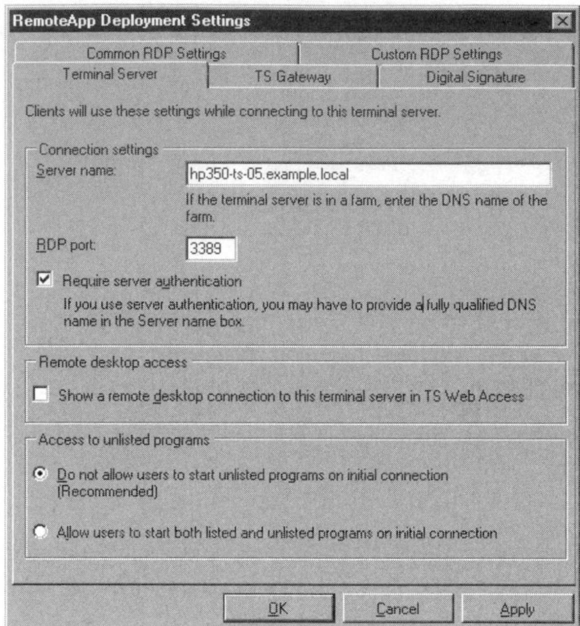

Figure 30-40 The Terminal Server tab of the RemoteApp Deployment Settings dialog box

10. Select the Show A Remote Desktop Connection To This Terminal Server In TS Web Access check box. Also configure any special settings for this Terminal Server, including a special RDP port, if necessary. Ensure that the Require Server Authentication box is selected.
11. To ensure that users can only open programs that you have explicitly enabled, select Do Not Allow Users To Start Unlisted Programs On Initial Connection (Recommended).
12. Click OK to close the dialog box and enable the changes.

Adding RemoteApps

Setting up TS Web Access and your Terminal Gateway settings is useful only if we actually have some RemoteApps defined for users to use. When you create a RemoteApp, you can set how it is distributed and available. You can make it available only through TS Web Access, or choose to create an .rdp file or a Windows Installer Package (.msi) file for it. Windows installer packages can be distributed using Group Policy.

To add or create a RemoteApp program, follow these steps:

1. Open the TS RemoteApp Manager if it isn't already open.
2. Click Add RemoteApp Programs in the Actions pane to open the RemoteApp Wizard.
3. Click Next to open the Choose Programs To Add To The RemoteApps Programs List page of the RemoteApp Wizard, as shown in 30-41.

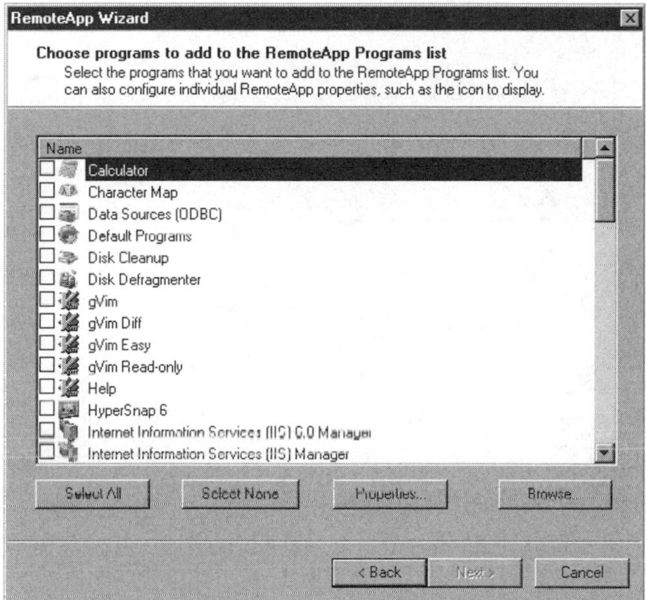

Figure 30-41 The Choose Programs To Add To The RemoteApp Programs List page of the RemoteApp Wizard

4. Select one or more programs to add to the RemoteApps programs list. You can add any programs you see in the list, or use the Browse button to locate the program's executable.
5. To change the run properties of the application you are adding, select it from the list of programs, and click the Properties button to open the Properties dialog box for the program, as shown in Figure 30-42 for our editor of choice, GVim.

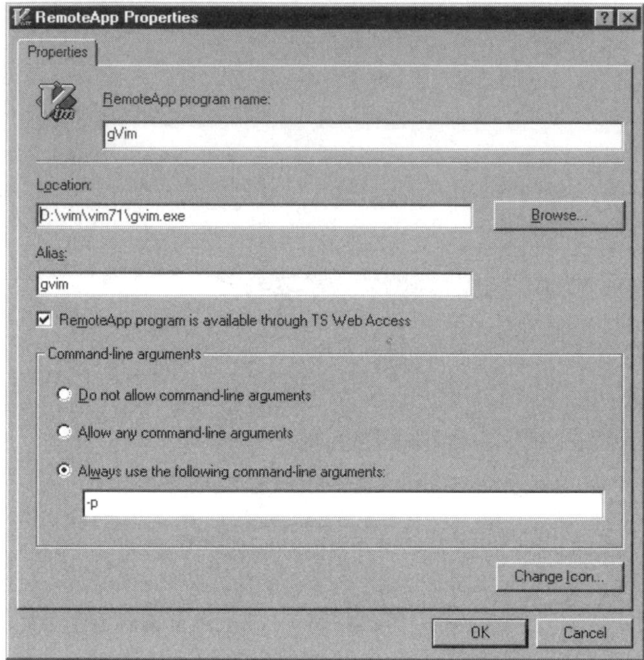

Figure 30-42 The RemoteApps Properties dialog box for the GVim editor

6. Change any application-specific properties that you want to change, and then click OK to close the Properties dialog box for the application.
7. Click Next and then click Finish to add the program to the list of available RemoteApps.

Deploying RemoteApps

The programs in the RemoteApps Programs list of TS RemoteApps Manager are available to be distributed and used in any one of three different ways:

- You can add a program to TS Web Access.
- You can create an .rdp file.
- You can create a Windows Installer Package.

Adding or Removing a Program from TS Web Access

By default, if you have TS Web Access enabled and configured, new RemoteApp programs are automatically enabled for TS Web Access. You can change this easily by right-clicking the application in the RemoteApp Programs pane to show the shortcut menu shown in Figure 30-43. Select Show In TS Web Access to make the application visible in TS Web Access, or Hide In TS Web Access to hide it from the Web portal. You can also change the properties of the application, including its name in TS Web Access, by selecting Properties from the menu.

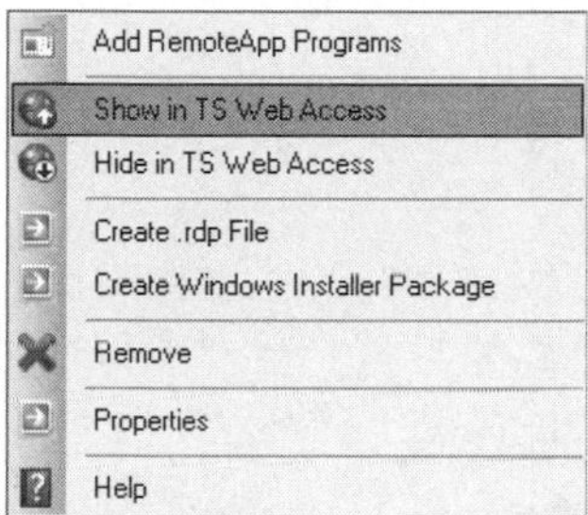

Figure 30-43 The reight-click menu for RemoteApp Programs

Creating .rdp and .msi Files

You can easily deploy remote applications to specific computers on your network by creating .rdp or .msi files. Personally, we prefer using .msi files, because they can be pushed out using Group Policy, and you can control additional settings with them. Create a file share to save the files to, and users can install the files to their computer.

To create a Windows Installer Package (.MSI) file, follow these steps:

1. Open the TS RemoteApp Manager if it isn't already open.
2. Select the application you want to create a package for in the RemoteApp Programs pane.
3. Click Create Windows Installer Package in the Actions pane to open the RemoteApp Wizard.
4. Click Next to open the Specific Package Settings page, shown in Figure 30-44.

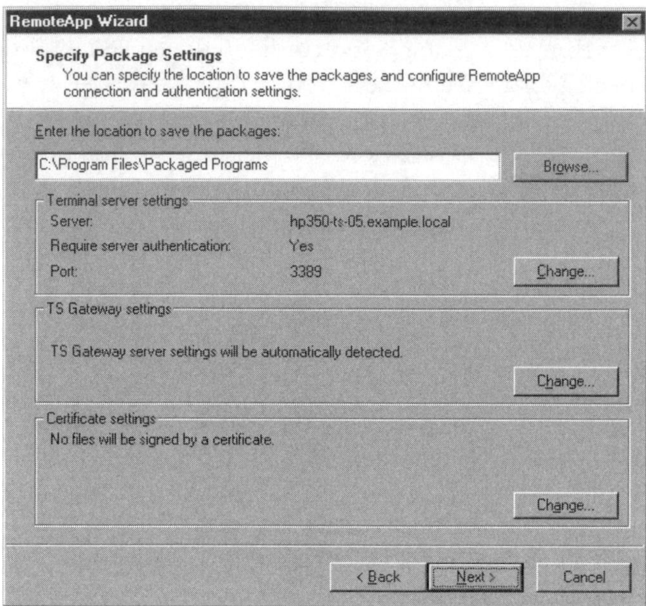

Figure 30-44 The Specific Package Settings page of the RemoteApp Wizard

5. Enter a location to save the package to. The default is C:\Program Files\Packaged Programs, but we think a shared folder makes more sense.
6. Change any TS Gateway, Terminal Server, or Certificate settings that need to be different for this application.
7. Click Next to open the Configure Distribution Package page shown in Figure 30-45.

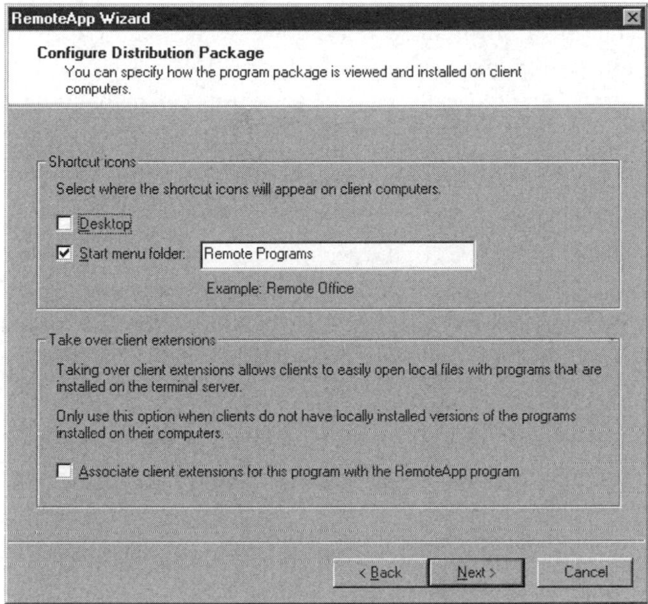

Figure 30-45 The Configure Distribution Package page of the RemoteApp Wizard

8. The default is to add the program to the Start menu folder Remote Programs. If this folder doesn't already exist, it will be created as part of the installation. You can also choose to have the RemoteApp program automatically added to the user's desktop. And you can have the remote application take over all the client extensions it would normally take over for the user's computer.

9. Click Next and then click Finish to create the Windows Installer Package.

Real World RemoteApps Rock

OK, you've probably figured out by now that we think the new RemoteApps capability is one of the best new things in Windows Server 2008. We think the TS Web Access is a nice touch, and a good way to make specialized applications available to a broad range of users without having to give everyone a copy, or do any special configuration on their desktops. And the new TS Gateway is huge as well. We've used something very similar on Windows Small Business Server 2003 called Remote Web Workplace, and we couldn't live without it. Just as with TS Gateway, it gives us easy and fast access to our work desktop whenever we need it, even while we're on the road.

The best of the improvements in Terminal Services, however, is RemoteApps. Now you can centralize all your critical applications onto Terminal Servers, and deploy them directly to users with Group Policy. Because RemoteApps can actually capture the extensions associated with application and connect them to the remote program, the end-user experience is almost completely transparent.

When Windows 2000 Server made Terminal Server Remote Administration mode available on every single server, we said that it was *the* reason to migrate to Windows 2000, and time has proven that feature to be absolutely indispensible. Well, we think two features in Windows Server 2008 are just as important: Hyper-V and TS RemoteApps.

TS Web Access

New to Windows Server 2008 is the TS Web Access method of connecting to your Terminal Services resources. If you install TS Web Access, as described earlier in the chapter, Windows Server 2008 creates a Web page at *https://<servername>/ts*. This Web page will be dynamically populated with the RemoteApps that are available, as shown in Figure 30-46

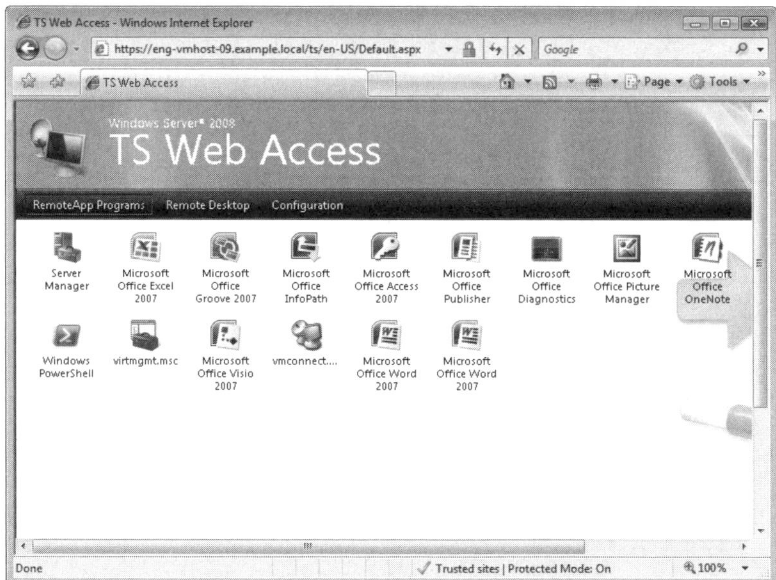

Figure 30-46 The TS Web Access page

To use TS Web Access, you'll need to install the ActiveX control for it. This control requires the latest version of Terminal Services Client, version 6.1, which is included in Windows Vista SP1 and Windows XP SP3.

Remote Desktop Web Connection

The TS Web Access page also acts as a gateway to Terminal Servers inside your domain. When you click the Remote Desktop bar at the top of the TS Web Access home page, it opens the Terminal Services Remote Desktop Web Connection page. From here, you can connect directly to any computer on your network that is running Terminal Services, including both servers and clients. The options you can set for Remote Desktop connections are shown in Figure 30-47.

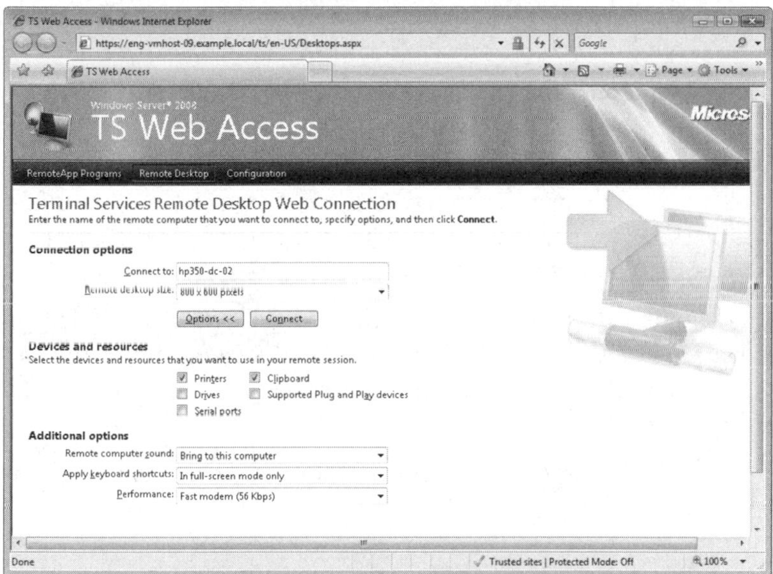

Figure 30-47 The TS Web Access Terminal Services Remote Desktop Web Connection options

When you click Connect, you'll likely be prompted with the warning shown in Figure 30-48, and then with a standard credentials prompt. Provide the credentials you want to connect with and click OK.

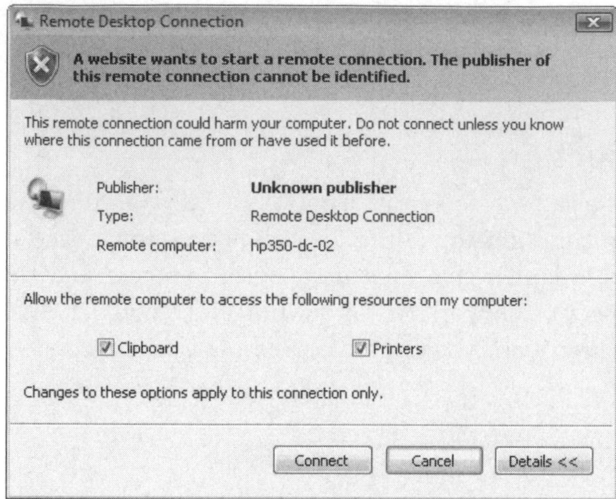

Figure 30-48 Remote Desktop Connection Publisher warning

TS Web Access RemoteApp Programs

Although connecting to your desktop or a server on the network is a useful tool, an equally useful and important tool is the access TS Web Access provides to the RemoteApps published on your network, as shown earlier in Figure 30-46.

When you click a RemoteApp program in TS Web Access, you will be prompted with an Unknown Publisher warning unless you've fully implemented signing and certificates across your network. You can select which local resources the remote application can connect to, as shown in Figure 30-48.

Click OK, and you'll then have to provide credentials to connect to the remote server, as shown in Figure 30-49.

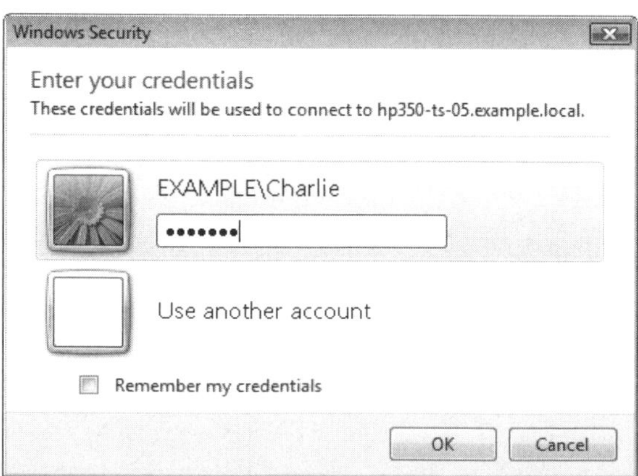

Figure 30-49 Credentials dialog box for connecting to a RemoteApp from TS Web Access

We already thought RemoteApps was one of the coolest new things in Windows Server 2008, but when combined with TS Gateway and TS Web Apps, it really gives you an incredible flexibility for making applications available to your users.

Summary

Windows Server 2008 Terminal Services is an important addition to *all* versions of Windows Server 2008 Server. It provides a way to centralize management and application deployment across the entire enterprise. The new TS Gateway, TS Web Access, and especially TS RemoteApps features make Terminal Services one of the most compelling changes to Windows Server 2008. The next chapter covers the new version of Internet Information Services, IIS7.

Chapter 31

Internet Information Services

Internet Information Services (IIS) 7.0 has changed in numerous ways since preceding versions. While many of these changes may seem superficial at first glance, some fundamental changes to the architecture of the Web server role in Windows Server 2008 are important for you to understand. You can customize IIS 7.0 by adding and removing modules to meet the unique requirements of your organization. For example, there are modules for compressing data when fulfilling client requests and there are different modules for caching various kinds of data managed by the Web server.

IIS 7.0 has several core components that these modules plug into. For example, Windows Process Activation Service (WAS) and World Wide Web Publishing Service (WWW service) are services, while HTTP.sys is a protocol listener. In IIS 7.0, request processing for both IIS and ASP.NET are combined into a single pipeline, eliminating code duplication found in earlier versions and simplying administration.

These architectural improvements facilitate numerous expanded capabilities, such as more robust security; improved diagnostic and troubleshooting tools; simplified application deployment; more refined delegation of administration; and better tools for server, site, and application administration. This chapter focuses on how to install, configure, and troubleshoot the various features available in IIS 7.0 rather than how to use them to develop custom Web applications.

Architecture

IIS 7.0 is made up of components and modules. The following components are key:

- Protocol listeners
- World Wide Web (WWW) Publishing Service
- Winodws Process Activation Service (WAS)

We'll cover the following key modules in this section:

- HTTP
- Application Development
- Health And Diagnostics
- Security
- Performance

More Info The architecture of IIS 7.0 could easily be the subject of an entire book by itself. For a thorough examination of the architecture of IIS 7.0 see *http://technet2.microsoft.com/windowsserver/en/library/05d86f78-4c24-4ecb-aae0-9b4b0e2d52801033.mspx.*

Components

IIS 7.0 consists of components that provide key functionality for various applications and server roles available in Windows Server 2008 as well as providing a extensible platform for hosting third-party applications. IIS 7.0 also includes several protocol listeners that receive incoming processing requests and outgoing responses.

Protocol Listeners

IIS 7.0 includes four default protocol listeners that listen for client requests: HTTP.sys, NET.PIPE, NET.MSMQ, and NET.TCP. HTTP.sys was originally part of IIS 6.0, but in the new version of IIS, this listener processes both standard Hypertext Transfer Protocol (HTTP) and Secure Socket Layer (SSL) protected requests. HTTP.sys is a kernel-mode device driver that includes request pre-processing, security filtering, caching, and request queuing. The other three protocol listeners support the communication infrastructure for the Windows Server 2008 service-oriented framework known as Indigo.

Another fundamental change in IIS 7.0 is how requests are processed. The IIS and ASP.NET pipelines are now integrated, which means that all file types can now use the capabilities of managed code. In other words, Uniform Resource Locator (URL) authorization is now available for static files and all other file types. This change also eliminates feature duplication between IIS and ASP.NET, and finally, administration is easier because all of the modules are managed in a single location.

World Wide Web Publishing Service

The functionality previously provided by the World Wide Web Publishing Service (WWW service) is now divided between two components: Windows Process Activation Service (WAS) and the WWW service. In IIS 7.0 the WWW service is the listener adapter for HTTP.sys. This service configures HTTP.sys and notifies WAS when requests are queued. The WWW service also collects data from the HTTP-specific performance counters.

Windows Process Activation Service (WAS)

In IIS 7.0, WAS enables support for protocols beyond HTTP and Secure HTTP (HTTPS). In fact, if your site doesn't require HTTP or HTTPS, you do not need to install the WWW service. WAS manages worker processes and application pools. The same configuration and process models apply to both HTTP and non-HTTP sites. When WAS starts, it sends configuration information to listener adapters on the server, such as the WWW service. The listener adapters moderate communication between WAS and the protocol listeners such as HTTP.

> **Note** With IIS 7.0 you can now run applications with discrete protocols in the same application pool because WAS manages the process for all of the protocols. This means that you no longer need to run an application in multiple sites if you want to publish it with multiple protocols.

Modules

When installing IIS 7.0, you customize your deployment by selecting which features to install. Each feature includes one or more modules, and each module is a dynamic-link library (DLL). When you use the Add Roles Wizard for installation, the features are organized into several categories: Common HTTP Features, Application Development, Health And Diagnostics, Security, and Performance. By default, the Internet Information Services (IIS) Manager console organizes the features by areas such as ASP.NET and IIS. To view them by category, as shown in Figure 31-1, follow these steps:

1. Open Internet Information Services (IIS) Manager.
2. Click the Group By drop-down list visible near the top of the middle pane.
3. Select Category.

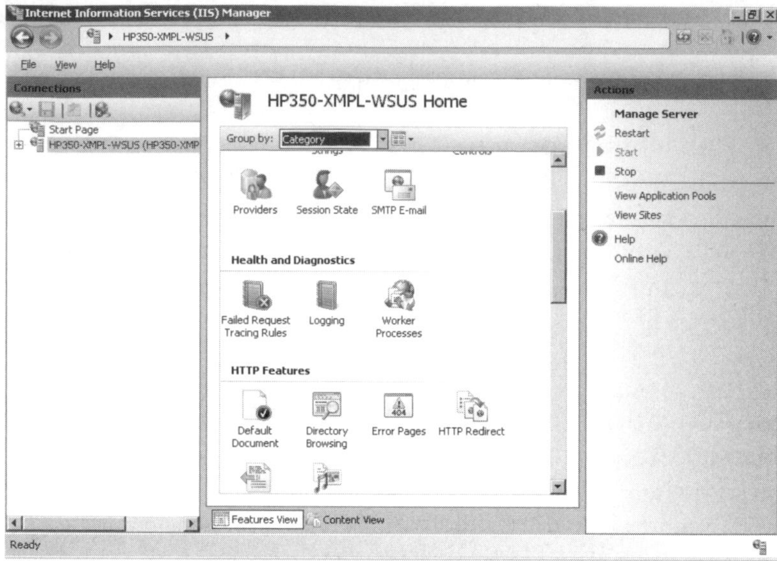

Figure 31-1 Category view displayed in Internet Information Services (IIS) Manager

This architecture allows you to install only the modules required by the sites hosted on your IIS server. Removing unnecessary modules improves security by reducing the overall attack surface and improves performance by reducing the amount of memory used by IIS.

HTTP Modules

HTTP modules process HTTP data in the request-processing pipeline. This includes the CustomErrorModule for sending both default and customized error messages to clients, the StaticFileModule that services static content, and the ProtocolSupport Module responsible for protocol-related procedures such as setting response headers.

Application Development Modules

Application development modules handle many of the requests for dynamic content and provide developers with access to the site with compatible content-development tools. For example, the CgiModule executes Common Gateway Interface (CGI) requests, the IsapiModule hosts Internet Server Application Programming Interface (ISAPI) Dlls, and the ServerSideIncludeModule processes code that uses server-side includes.

Health and Diagnostics Modules

Health and diagnostics modules follow and report request-processing events and provide logging capabilities. Examples include the FailedRequestsTracingModule that tracks failed requests and the HttpLoggingModule that sends information to the HTTP listener for logging.

Security Modules

Security modules provide support for each of the authentication schemes available in IIS 7.0 as well as scanning of requests for malicious data. The RequestFilteringModule executes URLScanning for allowed verbs, file extensions, unacceptable character sequences, and so on. Each form of authentication has separate modules, such as BasicAuthModule, which provides basic authentication capabilities, and WindowsAuthModule, which handles NTLM-integrated authentication.

Performance Modules

Performance modules support response compression and server-side caching. For example, HTTPCacheModule enables kernel mode and user mode caching within the HTTP listener and UriCacheModule provides caching of URL information.

Installing IIS

You have two methods for installing IIS 7.0 on Windows Server 2008: You can use the Server Roles Wizard, or you can use Windows Package Manager from a command prompt. The first method is fairly easy because the wizard walks you through the process, and descriptions of each feature are visible. Windows Package Manager is advantageous if you need to automate the installation process using a script, and it's the only way to install IIS on a server running Windows Server Core.

To determine which specific features to include, you should have a detailed discussion with the teams involved in administering the server, sites, and applications as well as the teams that are designing, implementing, and managing the content and applications that will be hosted on the server. Precisely who should be involved in such a discussion will vary from one organization to another–the point is that you won't know what you need to install and what you can omit if you don't understand how the server is going to be used.

Installing Using the Server Roles Wizard

After reading this far into this book you must be well-acquainted with the Server Roles Wizard. To start the wizard and add the IIS role, follow these steps:

1. Open Server Manager.
2. In Roles Summary, click Add Roles.
3. Use the Add Roles Wizard to add the Web Server role.
4. On the Select Role Services page of the wizard, specify which services, components, and features of IIS you wish to include, as shown in Figure 31-2.

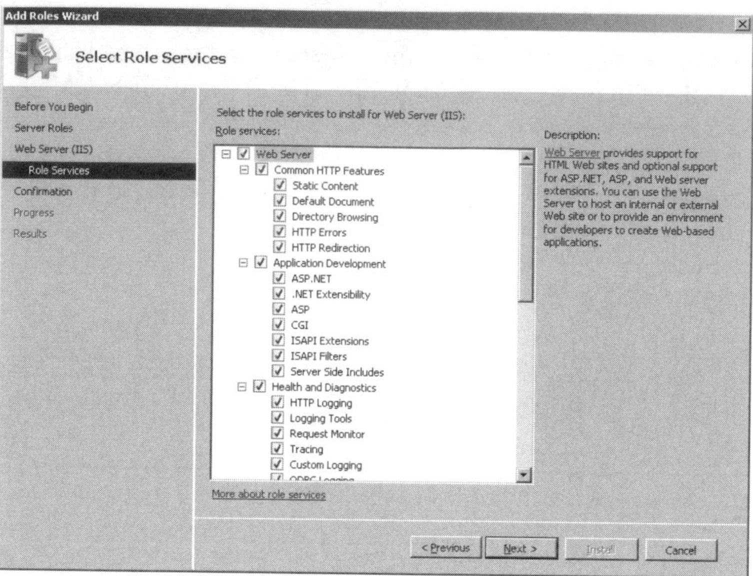

Figure 31-2 The Select Role Services page of the Add Roles Wizard

5. Step through the wizard and wait for the installation to complete.

Installing Using Windows Package Manager

Windows Package Manager provides the ability to install server roles and Windows features from a command prompt. The executable is named Pkgmgr.exe and it's located in %systemroot%\System32. You can view Windows Package Manager help by following these steps:

1. Open a command prompt from the Start menu.
2. Type **pkgmgr /h** at the command prompt.

To install only the core Web Server role, follow these steps:

1. Open a command prompt from the Start menu.
2. Type the following at the command prompt:

```
start /w pkgmgr /iu:IIS-WebServerRole
```

You can specify additional features by appending a semicolon to the example above and adding desired item separated by semicolons. For example, from the command prompt, the following command installs the core role with the ability to server static Web content:

```
start /w pkgmgr /iu:IIS-WebServerRole;IIS-WebServer;IIS-CommonHttpFeatures;IIS-
StaticContent
```

Table 31-1 presents all of the optional components available when you use Windows Package Manager and the more user-friendly name that corresponds to it when you use the Select Role Services page in the Add Roles Wizard and the Select Features page in the Add Features Wizard. All of the items that start with IIS- are part of the Web Server roles. The last four items that start with WAS- are part of the Windows Process Activation Service that is installed with the Add Features Wizard. Some of these components may be installed automatically depending upon the options you select when installing the Web Server role. The name of each item is self-explanatory: It is clear which item corresponds to its equivalent in the Add Roles Wizard and the Add Features Wizard.

Table 31-1 Features Available When Installing IIS With Package Manager

IIS-WebServer	IIS-CommonHttpFeatures	IIS-StaticContent
IIS-DefaultDocument	IIS-DirectoryBrowsing	IIS-HttpErrors
IIS-HttpRedirect	IIS-ApplicationDevelopment	IIS-ASPNET
IIS-NetFxExtensibility	IIS-ASP	IIS-CGI
IIS-ISAPIExtensions	IIS-ISAPIFilter	IIS-ServerSideIncludes
IIS-HealthAndDiagnostics	IIS-HttpLogging	IIS-LoggingLibraries
IIS-RequestMonitor	IIS-HttpTracing	IIS-CustomLogging
IIS-ODBCLogging	IIS-Security	IIS-BasicAuthentication
IIS-WindowsAuthentication	IIS-DigestAuthentication	IIS-ClientCertificateMapping-Authentication
IIS-IISCertificateMapping-Authentication	IIS-URLAuthorization	IIS-RequestFiltering
IIS-IPSecurity	IIS-Performance	IIS-HttpCompressionStatic
IIS-HttpCompressionDynamic	IIS-WebServerManagement-Tools	IIS-ManagementConsole
IIS-ManagementScriptingTools	IIS-ManagementService	IIS-IIS6ManagementCompatibility
IIS-Metabase	IIS-WMICompatibility	IIS-LegacyScripts
IIS-LegacySnapIn	IIS-FTPPublishingService	IIS-FTPServer
IIS-FTPManagement	WAS-WindowsActivationSer-vice	WAS-ProcessModel

Important The following features are not available as installation options on Server Core: IIS-ASPNET, IIS-NetFxExtensibility, IIS-ManagementConsole, IIS-ManagementService, IIS-LegacySnapIn, IIS-FTPManagement, WAS-NetFxEnvironment, and WAS-ConfigurationAPI.

Administration Tools

This section introduces the tools and methods you can use to manage your IIS servers. Three basic methods are available: the graphical user interface using Internet Information server (IIS) Manager, a command console using AppCmd.exe, or Windows Management Interface (WMI). For many people responsible for managing servers, sites, and applications, Internet Information server (IIS) Manager is the first choice because it is comprehensive yet approachable because of its fine design, which makes all tasks only a few mouse clicks away without overwhelming the user with a complex and cluttered interface. For others, AppCmd and WMI may hold great appeal because all management tasks can be performed from a command prompt, which facilitates the use of custom management scripts for creating, managing, and monitoring sites and applications. This section also provides a few examples of the tools in action. Subsequent sections offer greater detail on how to perform administrative tasks.

Internet Information Server (IIS) Manager

Internet Information Server (IIS) Manager (IIS Manager) in IIS 7.0 is significantly different from earlier versions. Although you can use it to perform the same tasks that you did in the past, you can also use IIS Manager to manage ASP.NET and the new features. Within this tool you can view health and diagnostic information; manage both local and remote servers, sites, and applications; and delegate administrative duties. To open IIS Manager, follow these steps:

1. Click Start.
2. Select Administrative Tools.
3. Click Internet Information Server (IIS) Manager.

Note If you're a fast typist, you can save mouse clicks and time by typing the name of the application you want to run after you open the Start menu. For example, to open IIS Manager without ever touching your mouse, press the Windows key on your keyboard, type **`inetmgr`**, and press Enter. The text will be entered in the Search box and IIS Manager will open. You can use this method to open other applications in Windows Server 2008 and Windows Vista. You can also find the name of the executable file for applications by viewing its properties from its Start menu shortcut.

The following major elements, shown in Figure 31-3, are viewable in the IIS Manager user interface:

- **Navigation Toolbar** Visible at the top of the window, it includes buttons for moving backwards, stopping the current action, and opening Help.
- **Connection Manager and Tree** The left-hand pane includes buttons for connecting to Web servers, sites, and applications. When you are connected, the tree appears in the lower section of this pane.
- **Workspace** This is the central pane. Its appearance changes depending upon the context. When you select Features View, you can configure features for the objects that are visible. When you select Content View, you can navigate the live content for the selected object.
- **Actions Pane** The right-hand pane displays different buttons and commands depending upon what objects are selected in the other panes.

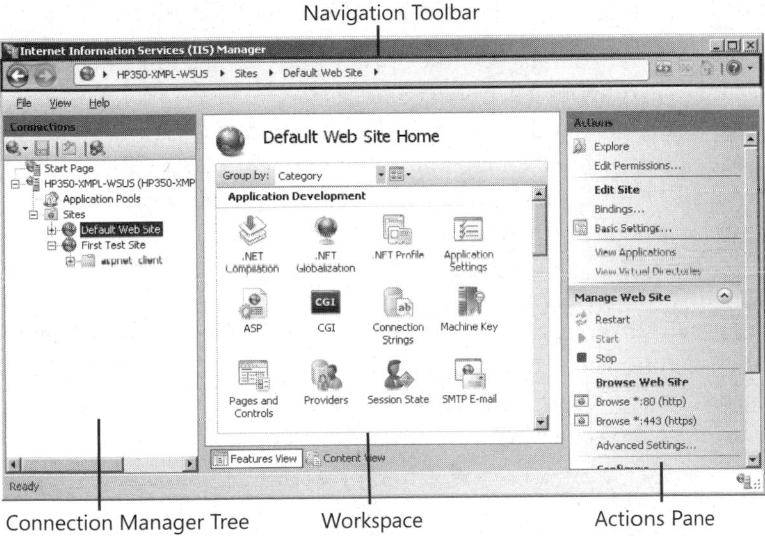

Figure 31-3 Elements visible in Internet Information Services (IIS) Manager

Connecting To Servers, Sites, and Applications

You can remotely manage Web servers, sites, and applications using IIS Manager, even if the remote server is running Server Core rather than a full installation of Windows Server 2008. You can also delegate specific site or application features, and authorized users can use IIS Manager to remotely manage their sites and applications. To remotely manage IIS 7.0 servers, follow these steps:

1. Open IIS Manager.

2. Expand Create New Connection from the toolbar at the top of the Connections pane.
3. Click Connect To A Server to open the Connect To Server Wizard.
4. On the Specify Server Connection Details page, type the name of the remote server in the Server Name box. The default port number is 80. If you need to use a different port number, append a colon and the port number to the server name, such as **hp350-xmpl-gw1:8888**.
5. Click Next. If your current credentials cannot be used to connect to the server, you will be prompted to specify new ones.
6. Click Next.
7. You can enter a descriptive name for the connection on the Specify A Connection Name page. Click Finish to complete establishing the connection.

Adding connections to sites is very similar: On the Specify Site Connection Details page enter the server name and port number if necessary as described in step 4 in the previous procedure, and then type the name of the site in the Site Name box on the Specify Site Connection Details page of the Connection To Site Wizard. To connect to applications, you need to specify the server name, site name, and the application name on the Specify Application Connection Details page of the Connection To Application Wizard.

Starting and Stopping the Server

You can stop and start a Web server by clicking appropriate buttons in the Actions pane. You can also do this from a command prompt. To stop the Web server, type **net stop WAS** and press Enter. To also stop the World Wide Web Publishing Service (W3SVC), type **Y** and press Enter. To start the Web server, type **net start W3SVC** .

Viewing Contents of a Site

In IIS 7.0 you can use the Content View in IIS Manager to view the content of the sites, application, or directory currently selected in the tree. This ability is useful when troubleshooting. You can navigate to the problematic Web page in Content View and then change to Features View to configure logging and tracing for that page. You switch between the two views using the Content View and Features View buttons visible at the bottom of the Workspace pane.

You have to use Content View to locate and configure settings for specific files because this is the only way you can view individual files in IIS Manager.

AppCmd.exe

AppCmd.exe is the new command-line tool for managing key features of IIS 7.0 from a command console. This tool can query and configure objects on your Web server and generate results in XML or plain text. This means that you can create custom management scripts to automate tasks such as provisioning new Web sites, monitoring worker processes, and recycling application pools. AppCmd is also the only way to locally manage IIS 7.0 when it is installed on Windows Server 2008 Server Core.

Note The folder where AppCmd.exe is located is not included in the PATH by default. You will need to use the following full path for the tool when executing it: %systemroot%\system32\inetsrv\AppCmd.exe. However, if you append this folder to your current path folder, you no longer need to specify the folder location when using AppCmd.exe.

Getting Started with AppCmd

Only users with administrative privileges are able to launch AppCmd; additionally, you must start it with elevated privileges to be able to make global configuration changes, such as settings stored in Machine.config, the root Web.config file, and in ApplicationHost.config. To start AppCmd, follow these steps:

1. Click Start.
2. Right-click Command Prompt and select Run As Administrator.
3. Type **cd \%systemroot%\system32\inetsrv** at the command prompt.
4. Type **appcmd** and press Enter.

AppCmd is a powerful and versatile tool, which also means that numerous options are available. Remembering the correct syntax or the options available for different object classes can be a challenge. Therefore, you will probably find the built-in help information to be useful. To see general help information, at the command prompt, type **appcmd /?** and press Enter. You can view help information about specific object classes by specifying the object when viewing help. For example, typing **appcmd app /?** will display information about working with applications. You can also see detailed information on how to use a particular command with a specific class of object by specifying the command and object when viewing help. Typing **appcmd delete app /?** displays information about deleting applications.

Working with Objects, Commands, and Attributes

When you use AppCmd you work with objects using commands to view or change attributes. Object classes include sites, apps, and servers. Some of the commands available are list, create, and delete. Different parameters may be applicable to different object classes, such as paths, URLs, output format, and default document. The general syntax of the tool is:

appcmd <*command*> <*object*> <*ID*> [/*parameter:value*]

Where *command* is the command to process, *object* is the object class, *ID* is the name of the object, *parameter* is the name of the parameter to process, and *value* is the value to assign to the parameter. For certain commands, you may not need a parameter or value.

Configuring Settings

The following examples of AppCmd in action will help you get started. The next section provides additional examples. To create a new site you need to specify a name and ID number; normally you'll also specify the bindings and the path for the root virtual directory. For example, to create a new site named First Test Site, assign it to ID 2, and bind it to the domain www.example.com on TCP port 8080 with the virtual directory pointing to c:\inetpub\firsttestsite, you would type the following:

```
appcmd add site /name:"First Test Site" /id:2 /bindings:http/www.example.com:8080:
/physicalpath:"c:\inetpub\firsttestsite"
```

To start this new site you would type the following:

```
appcmd start site "First Test Site"
```

To stop the site you would type the following:

```
appcmd start site "First Test Site"
```

To view a list of stopped sites you would type the following:

```
appcmd list site /state:stopped
```

You can change the properties on existing objects using the *set* command. If you want to trace failed requests using the default number and location for the log files, you would type the following:

```
appcmd set site "first test site" /tracefailedrequestslogging.enabled:true
```

This section has presented a taste of what you can do with AppCmd. You will see more examples in the section called "Administrative Tasks."

Note Some excellent resources are available online for learning more about AppCmd, including the Appcmd.exe section of the IIS 7.0 Operations Guide at *http://technet2.microsoft.com/windowsserver2008/en/library/d0de9475-0439-4ec1-8337-2bcedacd15c71033.mspx?mfr=true*, and "Getting Started with AppCmd.exe" by Mike Volodarsky at *http://www.iis.net/articles/view.aspx/IIS7/Use-IIS7-Administration-Tools/Using-the-Command-Line/Getting-Started-with-AppCmd-exe*.

Windows Management Instrumentation (WMI)

Like earlier versions, IIS 7.0 uses Windows Management Instrumentation (WMI) to build administrative scripts. By using the IIS 7.0 WMI provider namespace, WebAdministration, you can script tasks for managing sites, applications, and other objects. You can add or remove modules and configure features such as SSL bindings, MIME Maps, and HTTP errors. You can also use WMI to monitor and diagnose sites by utilizing the new features exposed by the Control API (RSCA) and Runtime Status.

More Info For more on using WMI to manage IIS 7.0 further, see the IIS WMI Provider Reference at *http://msdn2.microsoft.com/en-us/library/aa347459.aspx* and the IIS 7.0 Web Administration Reference at *http://msdn2.microsoft.com/en-us/library/ms691259.aspx*.

Administrative Tasks

You manage objects at four different levels in IIS 7.0: servers, sites, applications, and virtual directories. You install servers where you create new sites; within those sites you build applications that use one or more virtual directories. This section builds on the information you have learned earlier in this chapter by providing additional examples and more complex scenarios. The focus is on using the graphical user interface provided by IIS Manager. However, you will also see additional examples of using AppCmd to manage sites, applications, virtual directories, and servers.

Managing Servers

You can configure a large number of settings at the server level, including default documents, custom error responses, and logging. Many of the things you configure at the server level can also be adjusted for individual sites, applications, and virtual directories. To save space, the sections in this chapter that focus on sites, applications, and virtual directories will not repeat information on settings already discussed earlier. For example, you can configure some of the ASP settings at any of these four levels; however, they are only discussed in this section.

You can see icons for each of these features in IIS Manager in the Workspace pane. To configure a category, navigate the appropriate level in the Connection Manager Tree and then double-click the desired category icon. To configure these settings with AppCmd, use the *set* command with the *config* option with the desired object name and parameters. For example, the following command will enable default documents for the entire server:

```
appcmd set site -section:defaultDocument /enabled:true
```

To see a complete list of options, type the following command:

```
appcmd set site /?
```

If no object name is specified, AppCmd applies the change at the server level.

Configuring HTTP Settings

HTTP settings allow you to customize what visitors experience when they visit a site on your server. This category of settings includes default document behavior; allowing or disabling directory browsing; and configuring error responses, HTTP redirection, HTTP response headers, and MIME types. You can configure each of these categories at the server, site, application, and directory level.

Default Documents

Enabling default documents allows visitors to access content on your Web site without having to know the full path to a specific document. For example, a user might enter **http://www.example.com** in her browser instead of **http://www.example.com/index.html**. When you double-click the Default Documents icon in IIS Manager, you will see the current list of default documents in the Workspace pane; they are listed in order of priority. If a folder contains more than one document with a name on the default document list, the document with the highest priority will be sent to clients. The Action pane contains commands for adding, removing, and reordering. A command for disabling default documents is also available; clicking this command will completely disable the feature. Visitors will receive an HTTP 404 error when they navigate to a directory that has no default document or where the feature is disabled.

Directory Browsing

This feature is disabled by default. When the feature is enabled, visitors will view a page that lists the contents of the directory if they haven't specified a directory name in their request and no default document is configured for it. To configure directory browsing, double-click the Directory Browsing icon in IIS manager. You can use the check boxes in the Workspace pane to specify what information will be sent to visitors if you've enabled browsing. A command to enable or disable browsing is available in the Actions pane.

Important Directory browsing is disabled by default for a very good reason: security. Enabling this feature means than visitors can view all of the files in directories where no default document exists or where default documents are disabled, which means malicious users may view content that you didn't intend to expose. Never enable directory browsing at the server or site level—you should only enable it at the directory level.

Error Pages

Custom error pages, also known as error responses, allow users to see more descriptive responses when the server is unable to fulfill their requests. You need to weight the usefulness of this capability against security. Sending too much information may allow malicious users to determine details of your server and application configuration that they should not have access to. When you double-click the Error Pages icon in IIS Manager, you will see the current list of error pages in the Workspace pane, along with commands for adding error pages and editing the settings for the feature. If you select a specific error page in the list, you will also see commands for editing and changing the status code of that page. You can change the kind of information the server sends to users when errors are encountered by using the Edit Feature Settings command.

Important You cannot customize several error types. Errors with the following status codes cannot be modified: 400, 403.9, 411, 414, 500, 500.11, 500.14, 500.15, 501, 503, and 505.

HTTP Redirect

Redirection is a great feature when you have moved content to a different directory, site, or server. It is also useful when you are changing the directory structure for a site. When you configure redirection for a server, site, application, or directory, Web browsers will automatically navigate to the URL you have specified in the HTTP redirect. When you double-click the HTTP Redirect icon in IIS Manager, you will see the current configuration. If you enable redirection, you need to specify a URL. You also have the option of specifying whether to use relative or exact destinations, whether to redirect requests for subdirectories, and to specify a status code to send to clients. Using an exact destination is suitable when a site is still under construction or if it is down for maintenance.

HTTP Response Headers

IIS responses to client requests include an HTTP header. These headers include information about the requests page, such as the type of content, the date, and the HTTP version. You can configure custom headers to send additional information to clients, such as the names of the authors who wrote the content or the language used in the content. When you double-click the HTTP Response Headers icon in IIS Manager, you will see the current list of response headers in the Workspace pane along with commands to add headers and modify the common headers. Modifying the common headers allows you to enable or disable HTTP keep-alives and content expiration. When you select a response header, the Edit command appears in the Actions pane. Click this command to modify the selected response header.

MIME Types

Multipurpose Internet Mail Extensions (MIME) types, also known as Internet media types and Content-types, are file format identifiers. These identifiers were originally developed for e-mail sent through the Simple Mail Transport Protocol (SMTP), but they are now used for other protocols, including HTTP. IIS uses a default list of MIME types to determine what content to serve. A request for a MIME type that is not defined on the server will cause a 404.3 error to be sent to the client. When you double-click the MIME Types icon in IIS Manager, you will see the list of currently configured MIME types in the Workspace pane along with a command to add additional MIME types in the Actions pane. If you select a MIME type from the list, you will also see commands for editing and removing your selection. You define a MIME type by specifying the filename extension, such as .doc or .docs, and the MIME type, such as application/msword or application/vnd.openxmlformats-officedocument.wordprocessingml.document. The client's browser will use this information to determine what to do with the content, such as render it in the browser or open it using Microsoft Office Word.

Note To reduce the attack surface of your IIS server, you should enable only the MIME types that are actually needed for the applications running on it

Shared Configuration

You can configure IIS to use a configuration stored at a remote location by double-clicking the Shared Configuration icon in the Workspace pane of IIS Manager. When you enable this feature, specify the physical path to the configuration and optionally provide credentials different from those that you used to log on with. Additionally, you can use the Export Configuration command in the Actions pane to export the currently selected server's configuration.

Configuring Web Application Development Settings

IIS 7.0 supports a variety of technologies for developing and hosting dynamic content, including the .NET Framework, Active Server Pages (ASP), Common Gateway Interface (CGI), and Internet Server API (ISAPI). All of the application development features discussed in this section can be configured at the server, site, application, and directory level. When you click the desired icon in IIS Manager, you will see commands to stop, start, and restart the component in the Actions pane. When you double-click the icon, you will see a list of the settings in the Workspace pane along with commands to apply or cancel changes in the Actions pane.

.NET Compilation

When the response to a user request includes application code, IIS first compiles that code into one or more assemblies that have the .dll filename extension. When you double-click the .NET Compilation icon in IIS Manager, you can specify how ASP.NET code is compiled. The .NET Compilation settings are organized into three categories: batch settings, behavior settings, and general settings. Batch settings include the maximum file size that can be batched and the time-out period for batch completion; behavior settings include settings such as enabling the compilation of debug binaries; and the general settings including the default programming language.

.NET Globalization

In the context of application development, globalization is the process for localizing the application for various languages and cultures. This enables translating, storing, retrieving, and presenting application content for various locales. You can configure several globalization settings, such as the default culture for processing requests and the encoding used for processing requests and responses, by double-clicking the .NET Globalization icon in IIS Manager.

.NET Trust Levels

Trust levels define the permissions in the ASP.NET code access (CAS) policy. Applications with full trust can access all resource types and execute privileged operations. The default value for this setting is Full Trust. You can specify one of four lower levels of trust by selecting either High, Medium, Low, or Minimal from the drop-down list after double-clicking the .NET Trust Levels icon in IIS Manager.

Application Settings

Use this feature to store name/value pairs that can be used by applications running on the server. Adding these values at a higher level will cause them to be inherited by its child levels.

ASP

One-way IIS 7.0 supports server-side scripting via Active Server Pages (ASP). When IIS is processing a response that includes an ASP script, the script is executed on the server to generate the HTML Web page that is sent to the client. ASP scripts can also include HTML content and calls to COM components that can provide additional capabilities such as database connectivity. When you double-click the ASP icon in IIS Manager, you will see the settings are grouped into three categories in the Workspace pane:

- Behavior settings, which include the code page or default character set used by the application.
- Compilation settings, which include debugging settings and the default scripting language.
- Services settings, which include enabling or disabling session state persistence for the application.

CGI

The Common Gateway Interface (CGI) is an older technology for server-side scripting and application execution that is supported by IIS 7.0. You can configure settings such as the time-out value and user impersonation by double-clicking the CGI icon in IIS Manager.

Database Connection Strings

A connection string includes the information needed to communicate to a specific database. You specify database connection strings by double-clicking the Connection Strings icon in IIS Manager. You can add new connection strings or modify or delete existing ones. The string consists of a name for the string and either information for connecting to a Microsoft SQL Server database or a custom database. You need to specify the name of the database server, the name of the database, and credentials for connecting to that database.

Machine Key

This feature is used to specify encryption and hashing settings for applications–not to be confused with SSL and TLS settings covered in the "Configuring Security" section later in this chapter. You can use machine keys to protect forms authentication cookie data, page-level view status data, and other types of data. You can configure the encryption and decryption methods; whether to use pre-generated or runtime-generated keys; and whether to generate unique keys for each application by double-clicking the Machine Key icon in IIS Manager.

Important You should specify the same validation and decryption keys for all servers that are part of a Web farm; otherwise, forms authentication will fail.

Pages and Controls

Developers can add extra elements and custom controls to ASP.NET Web content that ASP.NET processes when the page is requested. You can configure settings for this feature by double-clicking the Pages And Controls icon in IIS Manager. Adjustable settings include whether to enable output buffering, whether pages are compiled or interpreted, and whether session state is enabled.

Providers

A provider is a code module that provides an interface between ASP.NET services and databases or other data stores. You can define default providers for applications. Three types of provider are available: .NET Roles for the role management service, .NET Users for the membership service, and .NET Profile for the profile service. Defining new providers works a little differently than other features because you specify the type of provider you want to add before you open the Add Provider dialog box. Follow these steps to define a new provider:

1. Open IIS Manager and navigate to the location you want to manage.

2. Double-click Providers in the Workspace pane.
3. On the Providers page, select the features you want to manage (roles, users, or profile) using the drop-down list near the top as shown in Figure 31-4.

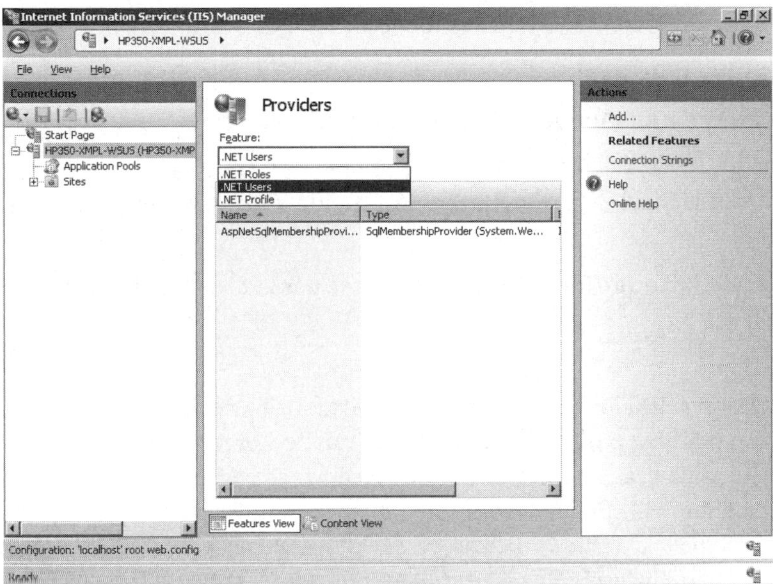

Figure 31-4 The drop-down list of features on the Providers page in IIS Manager

4. Click Add in the Actions pane. The Add Provider dialog box appears.
5. Select a provider type from the Type drop-down list.
6. Specify a name, connection string, and configure the other desired settings for the provider. The connection string here is identical to the section string discussed earlier in the "Database Connection Strings" section. Refer to that section for more information on how to configure the connection string.
7. Click OK when finished.

You can also add providers using AppCmd. However, doing so requires providing all of the information in a single command, as follows:

```
Appcmd set config /commit:MACHINE /section:featuretype
/
+"providers.[name='name',type='type',connectionStringName='connectionname',applic
ationName='appname',enablePasswordReset='True|False',enablePasswordRetrieval='Tru
e|False',requiresQuestionAndAnswer='True|False',requiresUniqueEmail='True|False',
storePasswordInSecureFormat='True|False']"
```

featuretype is the one of the three features: role manager, membership, or profile; *name* is the name to assign to the new provider; *type* is the provider type; *connectionname* is the name of the string to use to connect to the database; and *appname* is the virtual path of the application. The remaining parameters are only necessary when creating a user provider. Each is set to either True or False. The remaining parameters and their meanings are:

- **enablePasswordReset** Allows users to reset their passwords.
- **enablePasswordRetrieval** Allows users to recover forgotten passwords.
- **requiresQuestionAndAnswer** Requires users to create a question that they must answer correctly to recover their passwords.
- **requiresUniqueEmail** Requires users to provide a unique e-mail address when registering a new account.
- **storePasswordInSecureFormat** Encrypts user passwords when storing them in the database.

Session State

Configuring session state allows IIS and your applications to track what pages users visit and what they do on those pages. The session state can be stored as client cookies, as part of the URLs used to navigate the site, or on the IIS server as part of the in-process session state. This last option will consume additional memory on the server and all of the session state data will be lost if the worker process recycles. When you double-click the Session State icon in IIS Manager, you will see a page in the Workspace pane that allows you to disable session state, to use in-process session state, to define a custom configuration (for connecting to data sources other than SQL Server), to use a state server, or to use a SQL Server. These last two options mean that session state is stored outside of the worker process, which saves memory on the IIS Server. You can also specify whether to use cookies, and if so what type and the length of the time-out.

SMTP E-Mail

In IIS 7.0 the SMTP e-mail feature is not provided as a Web server extension; the development team may have made this decision to emphasize the fact that the SMTP e-mail feature is not designed to serve as an SMTP server for your entire organization but rather as something to be used by your IIS-based applications running on the same server. If you want to send e-mail from your ASP.NET applications using the System.Net.Mail API, you have to configure this feature. When you double-click the SMTP E-Mail icon in IIS Manager, you can specify what e-mail address will be used as the sender; then you can specify whether to deliver e-mail to a specific SMTP server or to store it in a pickup directory where another application or user can deliver e-mails as batches.

Optimizing Performance

IIS 7.0 has two features designed to help improve performance. *HTTP compression* reduces the amount of bandwidth consumed when sending responses to clients. *Caching output* allows the server to send content in the cache to clients more quickly because it does not need to be read from disk.

Compression

To configure compression of responses, double-click the Compression icon in IIS Manager. You can enable the compression of either static content, dynamic content, or both. You can also specify where static content is stored, how much space can be used for storing compressed content, and the minimum file size for compression. Compressing dynamic content can impact CPU performance because IIS does not cache compressed versions of dynamic content. You should enable compressing of dynamic content only when performance is constrained by network bandwidth rather than CPU usage.

Output Caching

When you enable output caching, IIS retains a copies of outbound pages that have been processed in memory. Subsequent requests for those pages can be processed more quickly because IIS can send them directly from memory rather than having to reprocess them. The impact on performance is particularly beneficial when data is coming from an external source such as a database or file server. Double-clicking the Output Caching icon in IIS Manager allows you to see the list of caching rules. You can configure settings that affect all of the caching rules by clicking the Edit Feature Settings command in the Actions pane. You can add new cache rules by clicking Add in the Actions pane. Doing so causes the Add Cache Rule dialog box to appear. You can specify what kinds of files to cache, whether to enable user-mode or kernel-mode caching, and other settings from this dialog box.

Monitoring

IIS 7.0 provides better diagnosis and troubleshooting capabilities than previous versions. Using trace rules, you can now track requests through the entire request and response cycle. You can also access real-time state information about in-process requests, sites, application domains, application pools, and worker processes.

Failed Request Tracing Rules

You can configure this feature at either the site or server level. To enable tracing of failed requests, navigate to the desired location and double-click the Failed Request Tracing Rules icon in IIS Manager. A request trace is recorded in XML format when either an error status code is generated or the time taken exceeds a specified duration. Gathering this information allows you to troubleshoot problems without necessarily needing to replicate them. When you add a new rule, the Add Failed Request Tacing Rule wizard is launched. On the first page you specify what kind of content to trace; on the second page you list what status codes should be traced, the amount of time for processing a request before a trace is generated, and the severity level of events for logging. On the last page you define what providers to trace, how verbose the entries should be, and what functional areas of each provider to trace.

Logging

IIS logging is separate from the operating system's event logs; it gathers detailed information about requests and responses to and from the server. This information can be very valuable for analyzing usage patterns, site popularity, and for tracking attempts to compromise the server by submitting malformed requests. You can configure this feature at the server, site, application, and directory level. When you double-click the Logging icon in IIS Manager, you will see the Logging page. On this page you specify whether to collect one log per server or per site, what format to use, where to store logs, and how IIS will roll over to new logs. You can also enable or disable logging from the Actions pane when the Logging page is visible.

Monitoring Worker Processes

You can view information about worker processes and the requests they are currently processing. You can use this feature at the server level. When you double-click the Worker Processes icon in IIS Manager you'll see a list of application pools, each with its process ID, memory usage, and CPU usage. Double-clicking one of the pools causes the Requests page to appear, where you can view the current requests in that pool. This is powerful information for troubleshooting applications. You can see which applications are running in a pool that is having performance issues and see which requests are taking an unusually long time within that pool. Developers can use this data to optimize their code by identifying the requests that seem to process slowly.

Configuring Request Processing

You modify the way requests are processed by configuring the application pools, modules, handler mappings, and ISAPI filters installed on the server. You can add new capabilities to your server by installing these types of components; you can reduce the attack surface by removing unneeded ones.

More Info The following three sites are excellent sources of further information on request processing:

- The IIS.net Web site: *http://www.iis.net/*.
- The IIS 7.0: Web Server Resources page on Microsoft TechNet: *http://technet2.microsoft.com/windowsserver2008/en/library/46b26381-2780-438a-b7fd-4da653f2c61f1033.mspx?mfr=true*.
- The Windows Server 2008 Web Server page: *http://technet2.microsoft.com/windowsserver2008/en/servermanager/webserver.mspx*.

ISAPI Filters

Internet Server Application Programming Interface (ISAPI) filters are programs that provide additional features to IIS. In IIS 7, modules replace ISAPI filters, but you can still use ISAPI filters if they are required by your applications. To see the currently installed filters and to add new ones, double-click the ISAPI Filters icon in IIS Manager. You can add filters at the server and site levels—the filters process all incoming requests sent to that level.

Application Pools

You use application pools to isolate applications, which allows you to improve security, performance, and availability by keeping applications in one pool from impacting those in other pools. For example, if an attacker compromises an application in one pool, he won't be able to use that successful attack to exploit applications in other pools. Application pools can run in either integrated mode or class mode. Integrated mode applications are able to access the integrated request-processing pipelines of IIS and ASP.NET. Classic mode applications are handled like applications in IIS 6.0: Their requests for managed code are processed in Aspnet_isapi.dll.

You can manage application pools only at the server level. You can view and manage application pools by clicking the Application Pools icon in the Connection Manager Tree in IIS Manager. Select a pool in the Workspace pane to see a list of possible commands in the Actions pane. You can add new pools; configure default settings for new pools; start, stop, and recycle pools; change settings for existing pools; and view applications for each pool. When you choose to view applications, you can move them to different pools.

When you create a new pool you only have to specify a Name, the .NET Framework Version, and the Managed Pipeline Mode. These are the settings you can modify by clicking the Basic Settings command in the Action pane. You can modify the conditions under which the pool is recycled by clicking the Recycling command. You rename pools with the Rename command. The Advanced Settings command opens a dialog box with dozens of settings organized into six sections. The General settings are displayed when you click the Basic Settings command. The CPU settings limit processer usage and allow you to force a pool to use a specific CPU. The Process Model settings define what account the pool uses, idle time-out, and other worker process settings. The Process Orphaning settings cause unresponsive worker process to be abandoned rather than terminate, which can be useful when debugging. The Rapid-Fail Protection settings define the conditions under which the application pool is terminated. The Recycling settings are the same as those visible when you click the Recycling command described previously.

Modules

IIS 7.0 supports both native and managed modules. Native modules, also called *unmanaged* modules because they do not use the ASP.NET model, are DLLs that support specific features. For example, the CertificateMappingAuthenticationModule is provided by the authcert.dll and enables the certificate mapping feature in IIS. Managed modules are

.NET assemblies created using the ASP.NET model. You can manage modules at both the site level and server level. Navigate to the desired location and click the Modules icon in the Workspace pane of IIS Manager. The list of modules appear in the Workspace pane; commands to add, edit, lock, and remove modules are displayed in the Actions pane. Note that you can add global modules only at the server level.

Handler Mappings

Handlers are similar to modules in that they respond to client requests, they are implemented in either native or managed code, and they can be configured at either the site level or server level. Handlers for each type of content hosted by a site must be available. For example, there is a handler for ASP pages and another handler for CGI requests.

Managing Sites

Sites are containers for Web applications. Clients access them through one or more unique bindings. A binding is defined as the combination of IP address, port, and (optionally) host headers. From the client's perspective, the binding corresponds to the Uniform Resource Locator (URL) they click or enter in the Web browser. For example, if the First Test Site is bound to the IP address 192.168.131.6, TCP port 8080, with the host name www.example.com, the client would specify *http://www.example.com:8080* for the URL to view content on the site. Of course, the client would also need to be able to access the properly configured Domain Name System (DNS) record for the domain name: www.example.com with the IP address of 192.168.131.6.

Viewing the Sites on a Server

IIS Manager displays a list of all sites on the server. By selecting a site you can view important information about its status and configuration or select commands to view and edit more advanced settings, such as logging configuration, permissions, physical path, and bindings.

IIS Manager

To see all of the sites hosted on your Web server, click Sites in the tree in the Connections pane. To view information about a site or to modify the site, select it from the tree and then click the desired command in the Actions pane.

Adding a Site

During installation a default Web site is created that points to the \Inetpub\Wwwroot physical directory on the system volume of your Web server. You can use this default site to publish content or create additional sites for hosting content. Information about all of the sites hosted on the server are stored in the ApplicationHost.config file.

IIS Manager

To add a new site to your Web server using IIS Manager, follow these steps:

1. In the Connections pane, right-click the Sites node in the tree.
2. Click Add Web Site.
3. The Add Web Site dialog box appears, as shown in Figure 31-5.

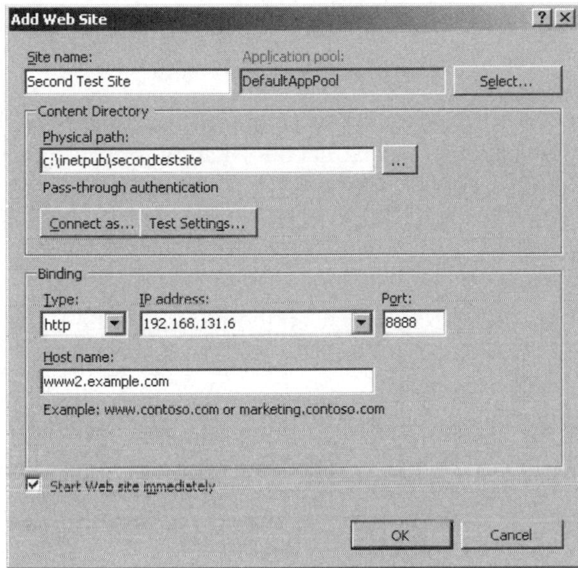

Figure 31-5 The Add Web Site dialog box

4. Enter a name for the site in the Site Name box in the Add Web Site dialog box.
5. If you want to specify an application pool other than the default, click Select. Select an application pool in the Select Application Pool dialog box from the Application Pool list. Click OK.
6. Type the physical path of the site in the Physical Path text box or click browse to navigate to the folder.
7. If the physical path you entered in step 6 is a remote share, click Connect As to specify credentials that can access that location or select the Application User (Pass-Thru Authentication) option.
8. Select the protocol from the Type list.
9. If you want to change the default value (All Unassigned) for the IP address, type an IP address in the IP Address box.

10. If you want to change the default value (80) for the port, type a port number in the Port box.
11. You can leave the Host Name box blank, but if you want to specify a host header for the site, enter it in this box.
12. If you do not want the site to be available immediately, clear the Start Web Site Immediately check box.
13. Click OK.

Adding a Binding to a Site

Sites can have more than one binding. For example, you might want to bind both HTTP and HTTPS to the same site so that customers' personal information is protected by SSL or TLS when they are making purchases.

IIS Manager

To add bindings using IIS Manager, follow these steps:

1. Open IIS Manager and navigate to the site you want to manage.
2. In the Actions pane, click Bindings.
3. Click Add in the Site Bindings dialog box.
4. Specify the binding information in the Add Site Binding dialog box and click OK.

AppCmd

To add a binding using AppCmd, type the following command:

```
appcmd set site /site.name:name /
+bindings.[protocol='protocol',bindingInformation='binding']
```

name is the name of the site, *protocol* is the protocol to use, and *binding* is the combination of the IP address, port, and host header for the new binding. The IP address, port, and host header are separated by colons in this string. For example, to add a binding for HTTPS on port 443, type the following:

```
appcmd set site /site.name: :"Default Web Site" /
+bindings.[protocol='https',bindingInformation='*:443:']
```

Configuring a Site's Application Pool

You may want to modify an application pool to improve performance, or you may want to establish a separate application pool for a site that currently shares its pool with other sites.

IIS Manager

To change an application pool for a site using IIS Manager, follow these steps:

1. Open IIS Manager and navigate to the site you want to manage.
2. Click Basic Settings in the Actions pane.
3. In the Edit Site dialog box, click Select to open the Select Application Pool dialog box.
4. Select an application pool from the drop-down list and click OK, as shown in Figure 31-6.

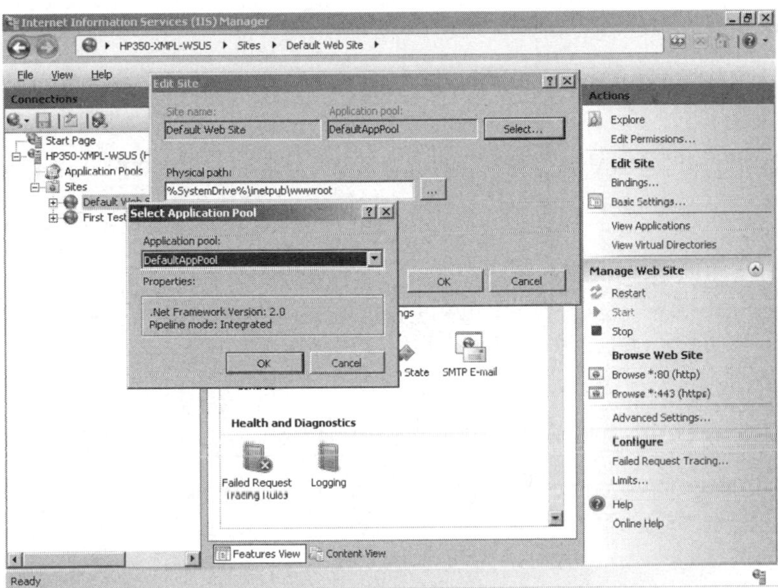

Figure 31-6 The Select Application Pool dialog box

5. Click OK again to close the Edit Site dialog box.

AppCmd

To change the application pool for a site by using AppCmd, type the following command:

```
appcmd set site /site.name:name /[path='path'].applicationPool:apppool
```

name is the name of the site, *path* is the path of the application to add to the pool, and *apppool* is the name of application pool to use.

To Configure Host Headers

For a client to connect to a Web site, that client needs to specify a unique combination IP address and TCP port. Ports 80 and 443 are the default ports. Sites that use nonstandard ports are likely to confuse users; therefore, each site typically has a unique IP address. However, a limited pool of addresses is available. Host headers allow you to bind more than one Web site to the same IP address and TCP port. Servers that support host headers examine incoming client requests. If more than one site on the server uses the IP address specified in the request, the server compares the host name present in the header of the request with the list of sites it hosts and sends the request to the appropriate site for processing.

IIS Manager

To add bindings using IIS Manager, follow these steps:

1. Open IIS Manager and navigate to the site you want to manage.
2. Click Bindings in the Actions pane.
3. Select the binding you want to modify and click Edit, or click Add to configure a new binding.
4. Enter the host header in the Host Name box, such as **www.example.com**.
5. Click OK.

Stopping or Starting a Site

When adding or modifying content, you might want to temporarily stop a site, or you may want to restart a site for performance or troubleshooting reasons.

IIS Manager

To stop and start a site using IIS Manager, follow these steps:

1. Open IIS Manager and navigate to the site you want to manage.
2. In the Actions pane, click either the Start or Stop command under Manage Web Site.

Configuring Security

Security in IIS 7.0 is significantly better than previous versions both in terms of a reduced attack surface and manageability. For example, URLScan is now a core component in IIS 7.0 and URL authorization is now supported in native code. New accounts and groups are used for anonymous access so that it is now possible to create custom anonymous accounts without disabling the built-in account. The old IIS_WPG group is replaced with IIS_IUSRS, and an account named IUSRS replaces the old IUSR_*%machinename%* account. This means that you can use the same account to define access control lists (ACLs) across multiple servers, thereby significantly reducing the burden of maintaining permissions across Web farms.

IPv4 Address and Domain Restrictions

One way to restrict which users can view the content on your Web servers is to configure restrictions based on IPv4 addresses and domain names. You can limit access by changing the default restriction to deny all clients and then create rules to grant access based on IP address or domain name. Conversely, you can leave the default restriction to allow all clients and then create rules to block traffic from specific domain names or IP addresses that you want to keep from accessing your server. For example, if you are concerned that malicious traffic is continuously received from a specific subnet, you could create a deny rule to block that range of addresses. Note that you must define the rules by domain name to affect IPv6 traffic. To configure the default behavior for address and domain restrictions, follow these steps:

1. Open IIS Manager and navigate to the site you want to manage.
2. Double-click IPv4 Address And Domain Restrictions.
3. In the Actions pane, click Edit Feature Settings.
4. Select either Allow or Deny from the Access For Unspecified Clients drop-down list.
5. If you want to be able to specify domain names in your rules, you need to enable the Enable Domain Name Restrictions option; however, this means that the server will perform a reverse DNS lookup on every connection. This is a time-consuming process that will significantly impact server performance.
6. Click OK.

To create deny or allow rules, follow these steps:

1. Open IIS Manager and navigate to the site you want to manage.
2. Double-click IPv4 Address And Domain Restrictions.
3. In the Actions pane, click either Add Allow Entry or Add Deny Entry.
4. In the dialog box that appears, select the appropriate radio button.
5. If you are creating a rule for a single host, you can enter its address in the Specific IPv4 Address text box.
6. If you are creating a rule for a range of IP addresses, enter the subnet in the IPv4 Address Range text box and the subnet mask in the Mask text box.
7. If you are creating a rule for a domain name, you can enter the domain name in the Domain Name text box.

Authentication

You can ensure that only authorized users are able to access content on your Web servers by configuring authentication. By default, all users are granted access because Anonymous Authentication is enabled. You can choose to continue to allow anonymous access to all or part of your content or combine restrictive permissions with one of the other authentication methods available in IIS 7.0. To view and manage the available methods, navigate to the desired level in IIS Manager and double-click Authentication. IIS 7.0 supports three classes of authentication: challenge-based authentication such as integrated Windows authentication; client certificate authentication; and login redirection such as forms authentication. To enable each method, you must select it in the Workspace pane and then click Enable in the Actions pane. To configure a method, select it and then click Edit in the Actions pane. You must provide different kinds of information when configuring each type, as detailed in the following list:

- **Anonymous Authentication** You must provide credentials for a specific user or choose to use the identity specified for the application pool, which is the Network Service account by default.
- **ASP.NET Impersonation** Use this method when you want to run your ASP.NET application with something other than the default security context. You can specify either the user authenticated by IIS or an arbitrary account.
- **Basic Authentication** This method is very insecure because the passwords are sent across the network in an unencrypted format. If you must use this method, you should mitigate this risk by using Secure Sockets Layer (SSL) encryption or Transport Layer Security (TLS) to protect the traffic. You also need to disable anonymous authentication. Optionally, you can specify the default domain or realm. Note that your internal Active Directory domain name could be exposed to external users if you specify it in the Realm text box.
- **Digest Authentication** Previously known as Advanced Digest authentication, this method uses an Active Directory domain controller to authenticate users. To use this method, you must disable anonymous authentication. You have the option to specify a realm that IIS should use for authentication.
- **Forms Authentication** This method uses client-side redirection to send users to an HTML form, where they enter their user names and passwords. After the credentials are validated, they are redirected to the page they requested. As with Basic Authentication, you should protect this traffic by requiring SSL or TLS for all pages in the application. You can specify the logon URL, time-out, and various cookie settings when using Forms Authentication.
- **Windows Authentication** This method forces clients to authenticate using NTLM or Kerberos. It is most appropriate in intranet scenarios because you can ensure that the client computers and servers are in the same domain using browsers that support integrated Windows authentication.
- **Client Certificate Mapping Authentication** Use this method when you want to allow users to automatically log on with client certificates. You can enable Active Directory Client Certificate Authentication only at the server level using IIS Manager. To configure one-to-one or many-to-one mapping, you must either edit the configuration files directly or use WMI, as described in "Configure Client Certifi-

cate Mapping Authentication" at the following site: *http://technet2.microsoft.com/windowsserver2008/en/library/db6ef395-f372-4ec5-9968-0531274c27af1033.mspx?mfr=true.*

Authorization Rules

By using authorization rules you can allow or prevent access for specific roles, groups, or account names. You can also define what actions a client request is allowed by specifying a list of HTTP verbs such as GET or POST. To configure authorization rules using IIS Manager, navigate to the site you want to manage and double-click Authorization Rules in the Workspace pane.

ISAPI and CGI Restrictions

You can allow or block requests for dynamic content, such as CGI files (.exe) or ISAPI extensions (.dll). These restrictions can be applied only at the server level. Double-click ISAPI And CGI Restrictions in IIS Manager to view the list of rules. To modify or delete an existing rule, select Edit or Remove in the Actions pane. To add a new rule, click Add in the Actions pane, specify the path to the executable, and optionally provide a description. The default action for a new rule is to block the executable. To allow the executable, click Allow Extension Path To Execute in the Add ISAPI Or CGI Restriction dialog box.

Request Filters

This is a feature that used to be part of URLScan, which was a separate download. You use this request filters to restrict the types of HTTP requests that your server will process. You cannot use IIS Manager to configure this type of filter—you must use AppCmd or WMI. Dozens of options are available for configuring global request filters, file name extension filters, request limits, and filtering by verbs. You can see more information online in "Configure Request Filters in IIS 7.0" at *http://technet2.microsoft.com/windowsserver2008/en/library/7b4d4d2b-780f-47d5-bc6c-514c65754c521033.mspx?mfr=true*. You can also view AppCmd's help information for this feature by entering the following at a command prompt:

```
appcmd set config /section:requestfiltering /?
```

Server Certificates and SSL

Server certificates make it possible for your IIS server to prove its identity to clients. You can enable SSL encryption at the site, application, and directory levels, but to do so you must first install the appropriate certificates at the server level. You can acquire server certificates in several ways. One way is to create a self-signed certificate on the IIS server; however, this method is appropriate only for development and testing—you should use one of the other methods for all of your production servers. You can also generate a domain server certificate if your windows domain has a Certificate Authority (CA) server; however, this approach is appropriate only for intranet sites because external users will not have your internal CA on their list of trusted CAs. You can also purchase certificates from a public CA. This type of certificate is suitable for any IIS Server, including those exposed to the Internet.

Configuring Server Certificates

To view and manage certificates in IIS Manager, navigate to the desired server and double-click Server Certificates in the Workspace pane. You can view, export, and remove an existing certificate by selecting the certificate in the Workspace pane and clicking the desired command in the Actions pane. You can also add the different types of certificates described previously by clicking the appropriate command in the Actions pane. Creating self-signed certificates is simple—you merely need to provide a name for the certificate. Importing is also straightforward: Select the certificate file and enter its password. When requesting certificates from a public CA and when creating domain certificates, you must provide more information, as shown in Figure 31-7. Its critical that the common name matches the URL for your Web site; otherwise, visitors to your Web site will see warning messages in their browsers that might cause them to leave your site. The other information you provide should be accurate, and it is important that you select a cryptographic service provider and bit length suitable for your situation. The longer the bit length, the more secure the SSL encrypted traffic will be and the greater the impact on performance. If you are generating a request for a public CA, you will also be prompted to specify a filename. You send this file to the CA where you are purchasing the certificate. If you are generating a request for a domain certificate, you must specify the address of the domain CA.

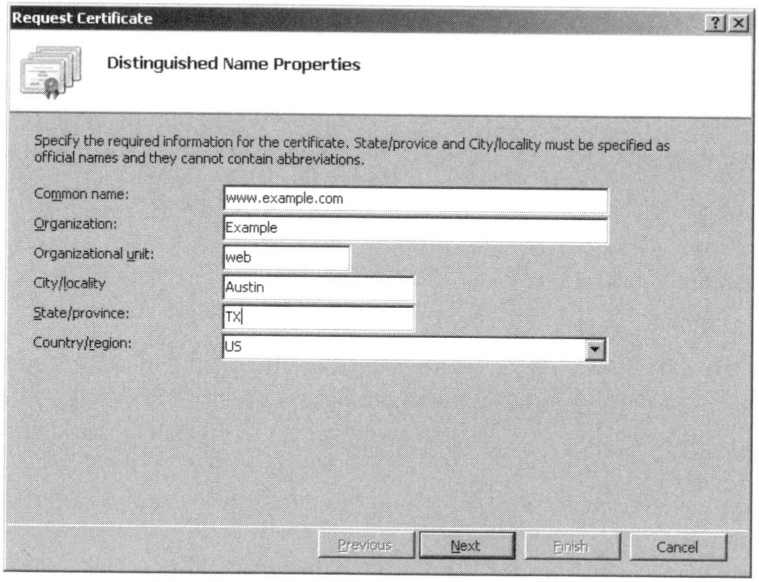

Figure 31-7 The Request Certificate dialog box

SSL

SSL encryption protects the traffic exchanged between the client and IIS server. When enabled, clients access your site by using URLs that start with https://. To enable or configure SSL, navigate to the desired level in IIS Manager and double-click SSL Settings in the Workspace pane. You can choose to Require SSL; to Require 128-bit SSL; and whether to Ignore, Accept, or Require client certificates.

Managing Web Applications

In IIS 7.0, applications are programs that send content or services to clients using protocols such as HTTP and HTTPS. Each site has one or more applications; the application's path becomes part of the site's URL. Each application belongs to an application pool. The pooling of applications isolates them from applications running in other pools so that problems with one pool will not affect applications that belong to other pools. You manage application pools at the server level by selecting Application Pools in the Connection Manager Tree pane as described previously in the "Application Pools" section. You manage applications at the site and folder levels. To add an application. follow these steps:

1. Open IIS Manager and navigate to the site or folder you want to manage.
2. Right-click the location desired location in the Connection Manager Tree pane and select Add Application to view the Add Application dialog box, as shown in Figure 31-8.

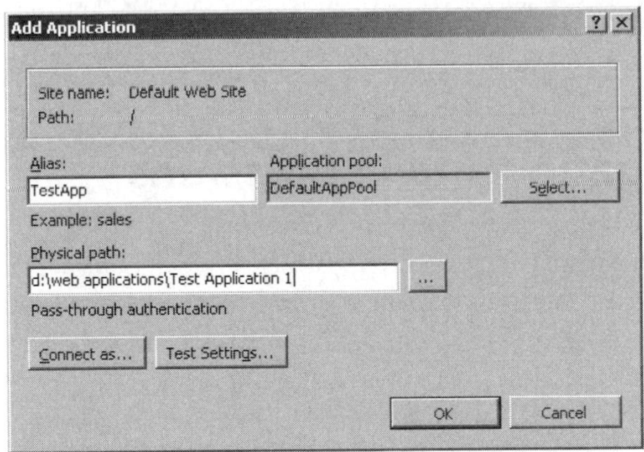

Figure 31-8 The Add Application dialog box

3. Enter a value for the application's URL in the Alias box.
4. Click Select if you want to select a different application pool.

5. Type the physical path of the application's folder in the Physical Path box, or click the browse button (...) to navigate the file system.
6. You can provide credentials for a different account or use pass-through authentication by clicking Connect As.
7. Click OK.

You can manage an application in IIS Manager by selecting it in the Connection Manager Tree pane and using the desired commands in the Actions pane. You can also right-click the application in the Connection Manager Tree pane to remove the application. Note that when you select Edit Permissions, you are editing the NTFS ACL.

Managing Virtual Directories

Virtual directories are similar to applications in that they have names that appear in IIS and in the URLs that clients submit. Virtual directories can point to physical directories located anywhere on the IIS server or on separate file servers.

The two types of directories are physical and virtual. A physical directory is a directory that is located in the physical file system of a computer, and it can contain files and additional directories. A virtual directory is a directory name that you specify in IIS and map to a physical directory on a local or remote server. You can use virtual directories to include content in your application without having to move or copy files to the application's directory. The procedures to add, remove, and change permissions on virtual directories in IIS Manager are virtually identical to those used for applications as described in the previous section. The main difference is that you don't specify an application pool.

Understanding Delegation and Permissions

IIS 7.0 has five levels of administration: server, site, application, directory, and file. You can delegate different abilities at each level–generally speaking, you can delegate the ability to manage features at the server, site, application, and directory levels; you can delegate the ability to view and manage content at the site, application, directory, and file levels. Complete security over feature delegation involves configuring delegation at the desired level and setting appropriate permissions on the corresponding config files. These files are Machine.config (server-level configuration), Root Web.config (site-level configuration), and ApplicationHost.config (application-level configuration). Delegating content management involves setting suitable NTFS permissions on the corresponding files and folders.

Using feature delegation, you can specify which features of a site or application to delegate to IIS Manager users and Windows users or groups. This means that you can delegate control of some features without having to give complete access to the server. For example, you might want to give content developers the ability to manage the features used by the sites and applications they create. You should then configure remote management so that the users who have been granted feature delegation can configure their sites and applications without needing to log on to the console of the IIS server. Remote administration is discussed in detail in the "Remote Administration" section later in the chapter.

Delegating Site and Application Management

You can use the Feature Delegation feature in IIS Manager or AppCmd to delegate features. Although this section provides details on how to use IIS Manager, it is important to note the difference in terminology used by each tool. IIS Manager calls this process *Feature Delegation*; AppCmd refers to it as *configuration locking* and *configuration unlocking*. For example, to unlock the Error Pages feature for a Web site you would enter the following at a command prompt:

```
appcmd unlock config "website" -section:httpErrors
```

website is the name of the Web site. To unlock a feature for all sites, you would omit the Web site name. However, if you want to unlock a feature for all sites except one, you actually have to perform two commands. First you unlock the feature for all sites, and then you re-lock the feature for the exception, as in the following example:

```
appcmd unlock config -section:httpLogging
appcmd lock config "Default Web Site" -section: httpLogging
```

You can explore the IIS schema file (%windire%\system32\inesrv\config\schema\IIS_schema.xml) to find all of the available configuration settings. The rest of this section will refer to locking and unlocking features because conceptually that is what you do with the Feature Delegation feature. Feature Delegation combines with the IIS Manager Permissions and IIS Manager Users features to enable non-administrative users to view and configure delegated features for their sites and applications.

Note Although you can configure Feature Delegation at various levels, you can access this feature only at the server level in IIS Manager. That is, you need to navigate to the desired server and then double-click Feature Delegation in the Workspace pane.

Configuring Delegation for a Server

When you configure Feature Delegation, you impact everything below that level. This means that settings at the server level impact all sites and applications on the server, and settings at the site level impact all applications on that site. Before you make changes at the server level, be certain you understand how the changes will affect delegation at the lower levels. This caution is especially important if you've previously customized delegation at the site or application level.

After you open the Feature Delegation feature, you can select a feature and click commands in the Actions pane to change its delegation. Each feature can be set to the values in the following list:

- **Read/Write** This option unlocks the feature's related configuration section(s) in the server-level configuration file. Configuring a feature to be Read/Write enables non-administrative users to see and configure that feature.
- **Read Only** This option locks the feature's related configuration section(s) in the server-level configuration files. Configuring a feature to be Read Only prevents non-administrative users from configuring that feature; however, they can view its configuration.
- **Not Delegated** This option locks the feature's related configuration section(s) in the server-level configuration files. Configuring a feature to be Not Delegated prevents non-administrative users from either seeing or configuring that feature.
- **Reset to Inherited** When you select this option, the feature inherits the delegation state from its parent.
- **Configuration Read/Write** This option unlocks the feature's related configuration section(s) in the server-level configuration file. This option is available only for features that have configuration in both a configuration file and a database, such as .NET Users and .NET Roles.
- **Configuration Read Only** This option locks the feature's related configuration section(s) in the server-level configuration file. This option is available only for features that have configuration in both a configuration file and a database, such as .NET Users and .NET Roles.
- **Reset All Delegation** Resets the delegation state of all features to the states set at the parent level. At the server-level, this option sets delegation to what is specified in the overrideModeDefault in the server-level configuration file.
- **Custom Site Delegation** This option opens the Custom Site Delegation feature page, where you can configure custom delegation for a single site.

Delegating a Site

To configure site-level delegation, you have to first open Feature Delegation at the server level and then click Custom Site Delegation in the Actions pane. This opens the Custom Site Delegation page; use the Sites drop-down list to select the site to manage. Then configure delegation as desired. The same commands are available at this level as at the server level with the exception of Custom Site Delegation. Delegation at this level will affect all applications located on the site.

You can copy the delegation from the currently selected site to other sites by clicking Copy in the Workspace pane. The Copy Delegation dialog box will appear, showing the list of the sites. Click each site to select or deselect it. When you click OK, the selected sites will be reconfigured to match the delegation settings from the original.

Configuring Permissions to View and Manage Content

Visitors to your Web sites require appropriate permissions to view the content and use the applications within each site. Users who need to manage the content and applications also need correct permissions to do so. You can define permissions using Windows user accounts and groups; you can also create IIS Manager accounts and grant permissions to them. As noted earlier, you can also use IIS Manager accounts with feature delegation.

Configuring IIS Manager Accounts

You can create non-Windows user accounts with the IIS Manager Users feature. These IIS user accounts can be used to connect to sites and applications to which they have been given permission. To add users, navigate to the desired server, double-click IIS Manage Users in the workspace pane, and click the Add User command in the Actions pane. To disable, remove, or change the password for an account, select the account and click the desired command in the Actions pane. These non-Windows accounts can be granted permissions to view or manage content and to manage features, as described later in this section.

Note If you want to use IIS Manager accounts, you also need to reconfigure the Management Service to accept both Windows credentials and IIS Manager credentials, as described in the section "Remote Administration" later in the chapter.

IIS Manager Permissions

This feature can be configured only at the site level. Navigate to the desired site and double-click IIS Manager Permissions in the Workspace pane to access it. To allow a user or group of users to access a site, click the Allow User command in the Actions pane. Click the desired radio button for adding Windows or IIS Manager accounts. To add a domain account, type the name in the form *domainname\name*. You can also click Select to search the respective account databases. To remove a user's or group's access, select it from the list in the Workspace pane and click Deny User. Users on this list have the ability to manage and view IIS features delegated for that site.

Note Searching for Windows groups using the Select button requires an additional step. By default, the Select User Or Group dialog box will have only the User object type enabled. Click Object Types to add the Groups object type to your search.

NTFS Permissions

The NTFS permissions on the files and folders for sites and applications determine who can view the content and who can change it. These permissions are distinct from the IIS Manager Permissions–configuring them for sites is analogous to configuring permissions for files and folders on file servers. Grant users and groups the minimum permissions necessary for them to access the content; in other words, give content developers full control but give Web site visitors read and execute permissions. You can edit NTFS permissions by navigating to the desired folder in Windows Explorer, or you can navigate to the desired location in IIS Manager and then select Edit Permissions in the Actions pane.

Understanding the Configuration Store

IIS stores configuration information for the server and the sites located on the server in several files. This section provides a brief description of each configuration file. As mentioned earlier, it is important that the NTFS permissions on these files correspond to your plans for delegation. In other words, you should ensure that users who you want to delegate site management have permissions to read and write to the config files for that site. The configuration files are:

- **applicationHost.config** This file, which stores global settings, contains the primary configuration information. It is located in the %systemroot%\System32\inetsrv\config directory. This file replaces the metabase.xmlfile used in IIS 6.0.
- **redirection.config** This file contains settings for redirecting a Web server to configuration files on another computer. It is located in the %systemroot%\System32\inetsrv\config directory.
- **administration.config** This file contains configuration information for the Management Service. It is located in the %systemroot%\System32\inetsrv\config directory.
- **machine.config** This file contains settings needed for all .NET Framework features. It is located in %systemroot%\microsoft.net\framework\v2.0.50727\config\.
- **web.config** You can change the ASP.NET configuration settings for a single application if you create a Web.config file in the root folder of the application. When you do this, the settings in the Web.config file override the settings in the Machine.config file.

You can use other kinds of configuration files in IIS 7.0. For example, depending on which features are installed, several others may be available in %systemroot%\microsoft.net\framework\v2.0.50727\config\. If you want to take advantage of all of the capabilities that this architecture offers, read more about it at IIS.net in "Deep

Dive into IIS7 Configuration" online at: *http://www.iis.net/articles/view.aspx/IIS7/Use-IIS7-Administration-Tools/Using-XML-Configuration/Deep-Dive-into-IIS7-Configuration.*

Using Shared Configuration

Enabling shared configuration allows you to store the configuration and encryption keys for multiple servers in a single location. This is particularly useful in Web farm scenarios where you want all of the servers hosting the same content to have the same settings and encryption keys. To enable shared configuration, follow these steps:

1. Open IIS Manager and navigate to the server you want to manage.
2. Double-click Management Service and then click Stop in the Actions pane.
3. Click the Back button in the toolbar.
4. Double-click Shared Configuration.
5. Select Enable Shared Configuration.
6. Specify the location for the configuration in the Physical Path box.
7. Provide credentials for an account that has access to this location.
8. Click Apply in the Actions pane.
9. Enter the password that was used when the encryption keys were exported in the Enter Encryption Key password box in the Encryption Keys Password dialog box.
10. Click OK.
11. Reselect the server in IIS Manager.
12. Double-click Management Service and then click Start in the Actions pane to restart the management service.

Remote Administration

As described earlier in this chapter, it is possible to manage Web servers, delegated sites and applications remotely with IIS Manager using the Management Service. Note that the Management Service itself can be configured only by administrators who are logged on locally. To enable this capability, you must install the Management Service Role Service: Select the local server in the Connection Manager Tree, double-click Management Service, and then click Enable Remote Connections in the Workspace pane. After you've enabled this capability, you can configure what type of credentials to accept, what IP addresses and port to bind to, what SSL certificate to use for protecting connections, and where to log remote administration requests. You also have the option to configure IPv4 address restrictions. What if you're running IIS on Server Core? You edit the registry using a .reg file. Copy the following text into a text file, save the file as EnableRemote.reg, and then execute it on the Server Core system:

```
// Code Block
REGEDIT4
[HKEY_LOCAL_MACHINE\Software\Microsoft\WebManagement\Server]
"EnableRemoteManagement"=dword:00000001
```

Note After enabling remote management and starting the Management Service, you have to stop it before you can change the configuration.

Another option for managing Server Core is to use Remote Desktop to connect to the system running Server Core. You can also enable Remote Desktop for Server Core by executing the following script on the system:

```
Cscript %systemroot%\system32\SCRegEdit.wsf /ar 0
```

Installing and Managing the FTP Publishing Service

IIS 7.0 includes support for the version of File Transfer Protocol (FTP) included with Windows Server 2003, but it is not installed by default. Installation through Server Manager is straightforward. Managing the legacy version of FTP is identical to managing it on Windows Server 2003; with IIS 6.0, open Internet Information Services (IIS) 6.0 Manager from the Administrative Tools folder. However, a new version of the FTP Publishing Service, known as FTP7, is available for download:

- 32-bit installation package: *http://go.microsoft.com/fwlink/?LinkId=87847*
- 64-bit installation package: *http://go.microsoft.com/fwlink/?LinkId=89114*

Important You cannot use both versions of the FTP Publishing Service simultaneously. If you have already installed the legacy version, you will be prompted to remove it when you try to install the IIS 7.0 version. You may also be prompted to restart your server after removing the legacy version. Do not install the old version after installing FTP7.

This new version has many additional capabilities and is fully integrated with IIS 7.0. It is strongly recommended that you use this version rather than the legacy version. After you have installed the updated FTP Publishing Service, you will be able to take advantage of the new features such as FTP over SSL, UTF8, IPv6, multiple FTP sites on the same IP address, improved logging, and new supportability features.

You can add support for FTP to an existing site by navigating to the site in IIS Manager and clicking Add FTP Publishing in the Actions pane. The Binding And SSL Settings page of the Add FTP Site Publishing Wizard appears, as shown in Figure 31-9.

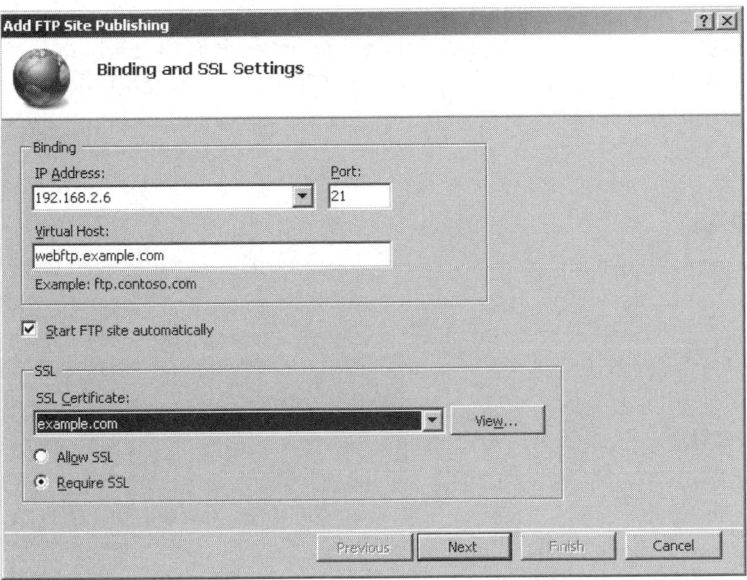

Figure 31-9 The Binding And SSL Settings page of the Add FTP Site Publishing Wizard

On this page you specify the binding information, enable or disable SSL, and configure SSL. When you click Next, the Authentication And Authorization Information page appears, as shown in Figure 31-10. On this page, you define who has access to the FTP site and what the level of access is. Remember that you can further refine what FTP users can do by configuring the NTFS permissions on the physical directories.

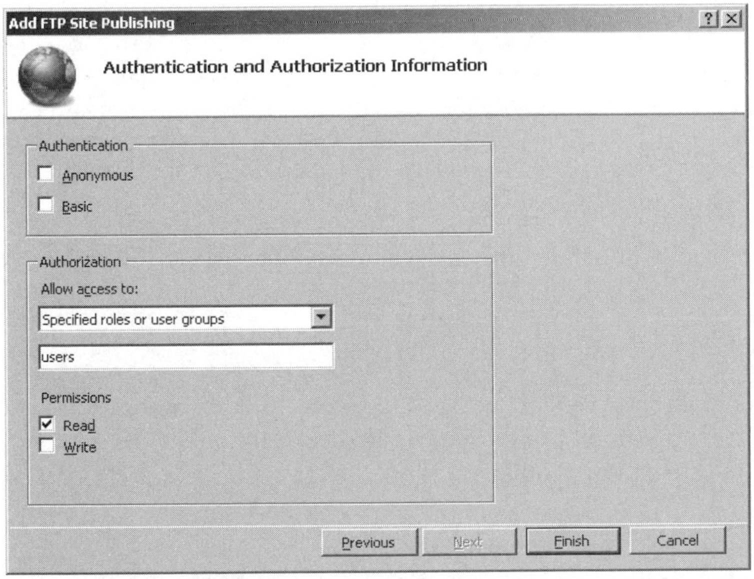

Figure 31-10 The Authentication And Authorization Information page of the Add FTP Site Publishing Wizard

After installing FTP7 you will see many new FTP features in the Workspace pane of IIS Manager when you select a server or site. Many of these features work similarly to their Web server counterparts, including FTP Authentication, FTP Authorization Rules, FTP IPv4 Address And Domain Restrictions, and FTP Logging. To avoid redundancy, these features are not covered here. However, the other features do merit additional attention.

FTP Current Sessions

This feature displays a list of all current sessions to the selected site, including each user's name, IP address, session start time, current command being executed, the last command, the start time of the command, how many bytes have been sent and received, and the session ID. The only action available is to disconnect the currently selected user.

FTP Directory Browsing

Use this feature to customize the users' experience when they browse directories. Directories can be displayed in MS-DOS or UNIX style and you can choose whether to display additional information such as how many bytes are available for storage.

FTP Firewall Support

This feature lets you configure the server to accept passive connections from an external firewall. You specify the data port range and the IP address of the firewall.

FTP Messages

Use this feature to configure custom a welcome message, exit message, and message for when a user is denied a connection because no additional connections are available. You can also replace the default banner with your own. Some administrators do this to make it more difficult for remote users to fingerprint the server. Note, however, that changing the banner only makes it slightly harder for a remote user to identify the brand and version of the FTP server.

FTP SSL Settings

Use this feature to reconfigure the SSL settings that you specified when you originally created the FTP site.

FTP User Isolation

This feature prevents users from accessing the FTP home directories of other users. You can specify what folder their session begins in and whether or not users are restricted from accessing the home directories of others.

More Info For more information on installing and troubleshooting FTP7, see *http://www.iis.net/articles/view.aspx/IIS7/Managing-IIS7/Using-FTP-Server-in-IIS7/Installing-and-Troubleshooting-FTP7*.

Active Directory Federation Services (AD FS)

Active Directory Federation Services (AD FS) is server role in Windows Server 2008 for providing browser-based clients with "one-prompt" access to protected applications, even when the accounts and applications are located on different networks. Normally when a user accesses secure Web sites hosted outside of her own organization, she has to provide secondary credentials—that is, she has to provide a user name and password discrete from the one she used to log onto her personal computer. This situation quickly becomes burdensome when users have to remember passwords for the networks of multiple business partners, vendors, and customers.

AD FS helps to alleviate this challenge by enabling organizations to establish trust relationships with the directory services system running at other organizations. This type of solution, also known as single sign-on (SSO), allows the systems at one organization to recognize the users of another organization without having to prompt them for credentials. For example, you might use AD FS to build a trust with the company that supplies your firm with office supplies. By doing so, employees at your firm will be automatically recognized when they navigate to the Web site of the office supply company, for example. They can create orders, specify purchase orders, and choose a delivery method without having to type in their user names and passwords. This type of solution also reduces administrative burden because the trusting organization no longer has to create and manage user accounts for visitors from the other organization; they merely have to manage trust relationship and map groups from the other organization to groups within their own Active Directory domain.

More Info More information on deploying and managing AD FS can be found at:

- "Active Directory Federation Services Overview": *http://technet2.microsoft.com/windowsserver2008/en/library/ff50a7ff-156b-4589-a77c-38dda91571d31033.mspx?mfr=true*.
- Active Directory Federation Services page: *http://technet2.microsoft.com/windowsserver2008/en/servermanager/activedirectoryfederationservices.mspx*.
- Step-by-Step Guide for AD FS in Windows Server 2008: *http://technet2.microsoft.com/windowsserver2008/en/library/a018ccfe-acb2-41f9-9f0a-102b80a3398c1033.mspx*.

Summary

This chapter provided you with an overview of managing IIS 7.0 and showed you how to use the graphical IIS Manager tool to perform management tasks. It also introduced you to the new command-line tool AppCmd, which you can use to create management scripts.

The next section of the book covers the tuning, maintenance, and repair of Windows Server 2008, beginning with Windows reliability and performance monitoring.

Part VI

Tune, Maintain, and Repair

Chapter 32

Windows Reliability And Performance Monitor

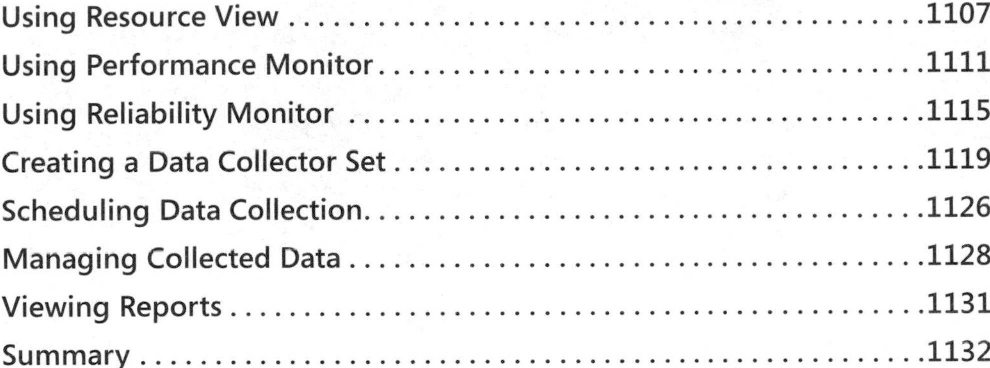

Monitoring and analyzing software and hardware performance are tasks that usually rank around number 23 on the administrator's to-do list. The purpose of this chapter is to persuade you to improve that ranking by even a few points. The Windows Reliability And Performance Monitor is a simple tool that can help you track server loads, locate persistent errors, customize the data you want to collect in logs, define limits for alerts and automatic actions, generate reports, and view past performance data.

Three tools make up the Windows Reliability And Performance Monitor: Resource View, Performance Monitor, and Reliability Monitor.

To open the Windows Reliability And Performance Monitor, click Start, type **perfmon** in the Start Search box, and press Enter. Or you can select Windows Reliability And Performance Monitor from the Administrative Tools menu.

Using Resource View

The Resource View screen is the home page for the Windows Reliability And Performance Monitor. On this screen, four scrolling graphs allow real-time monitoring of CPU, disk, network, and memory usage. Figure 32-1 shows the Resource View home page.

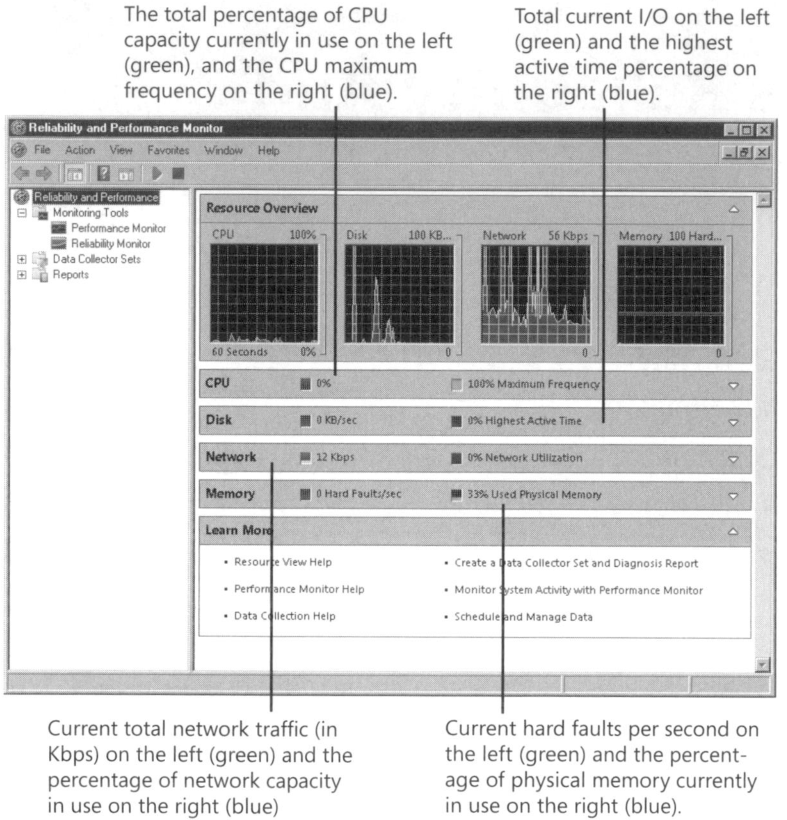

Figure 32-1 Resource View home page in Windows Reliability And Performance Monitor

If Resource View doesn't show real time, click the green Start button in the toolbar.

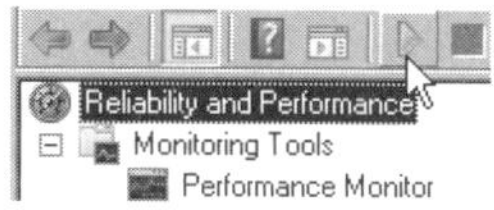

The four sections below the graphs contain details about each resource. Click the graph or click the section to display the detail, as shown in Figure 32-2.

Note Click a row and the highlight will remain on that row even when the application's position changes in the display.

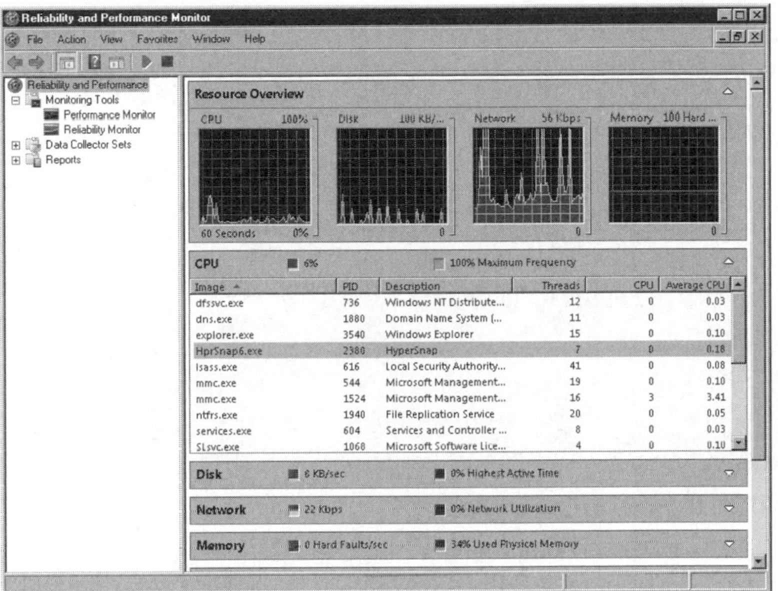

Figure 32-2 Displaying the detail of CPU usage

> **Note** Choose Take Control of the Session if the following message displays: "The Windows Kernel Trace provider is already in use by another trace session. Taking control of it may cause the current owner to stop functioning properly."

Click the column header in the detail view to sort by ascending order. Click a second time to sort in descending order.

The following sections describe the information in each detail view.

CPU Details

- **Image** The application using the CPU
- **PID** The process identification for the application instance
- **Description** Name of the application
- **Threads** Number of active threads in this instance
- **CPU** Number of currently active cycles for this instance
- **Average CPU** Average CPU load over the past 60 seconds, expressed as a percentage of the total capacity of the CPU

Disk Details

- **Image** The application using the disk
- **PID** The process identification for the application instance.
- **File** The file being read or written
- **Read** The current speed (in bytes per minute) at which the file is being read
- **Write** The current speed (in bytes per minute) at which the file is being written
- **I/O Priority** The priority of the IO task
- **Response Time** Disk activity response time in milliseconds

Network Details

- **Image** The application using the network resource
- **PID** Process ID of the application instance
- **Address** The network address with which the local computer is exchanging information. This can be an IP address, a computer name, or a fully qualified domain name
- **Send** Amount of data (in bytes per minute) that is being sent from the local computer to the network address
- **Receive** The amount of data (in bytes per minute) that the application is receiving from the network address
- **Total** The total bandwidth (in bytes per minute) of the data being sent and received

Memory Details

- **Image** Application using memory resource
- **PID** Process ID of the application instance
- **Hard faults/min.** Number of hard faults per minute being caused by the application instance

---

> **Note** A hard fault (also called a *page fault*) is not an error. It happens when a page at the address referenced is no longer in physical memory and has been swapped out or placed on a hard drive. However, an application that causes a high number of hard faults will be slow to respond because it constantly has to read from a hard drive rather than from memory.

- **Working set (KB)** Amount of memory (in kilobytes) currently used by the application instance
- **Shareable (KB)** Amount of the working set memory (in kilobytes) that may be available for other use
- **Private** Amount of the working set memory (in kilobytes) dedicated to the process

Using Performance Monitor

Performance Monitor is a simple tool to help you visualize what is happening on your network and on individual computers. Like Resource View, it can display events in real time, but it can also preserve data in logs for later viewing.

Insufficient memory or processing power can cause bottlenecks that severely limit performance. Unbalanced network loads and slow disk-access times can also prevent the network from operating optimally. Bottlenecks occur when one resource interferes with another resource's functioning. For example, if one application monopolizes the system processor to the exclusion of all other operations, there is a bottleneck at the processor.

Bottlenecks can occur in Windows subsystems or at any element of the network, for many reasons, including:

- Insufficient resources are available.
- A program or client monopolizes a resource.
- A program, device, or service fails.
- Software is incorrectly installed or configured.
- The system is incorrectly configured for the workload.

Performance Monitor helps you identify bottlenecks so they can be eliminated.

To start Performance Monitor, click Start and type **perfmon** in the Start Search box. In the navigation tree, expand Monitoring Tools, and then click Performance Monitor.

The initial screen (shown in Figure 32-3) shows one counter–the percentage of processor time in use.

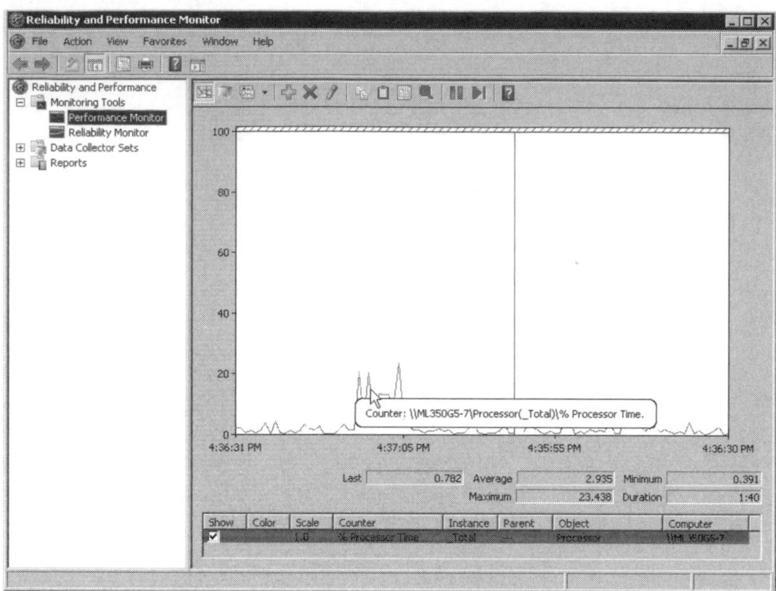

Figure 32-3 Performance Monitor showing the percentage of processor time in use

---

Note Move your mouse pointer to any position on the line to get the exact reading at that location.

Adding Counters in Performance Monitor

You can display any number of counters on the Performance Monitor. Simply right-click inside the Performance Monitor display and select Add Counters. This opens the Add Counters screen, as shown in Figure 32-4.

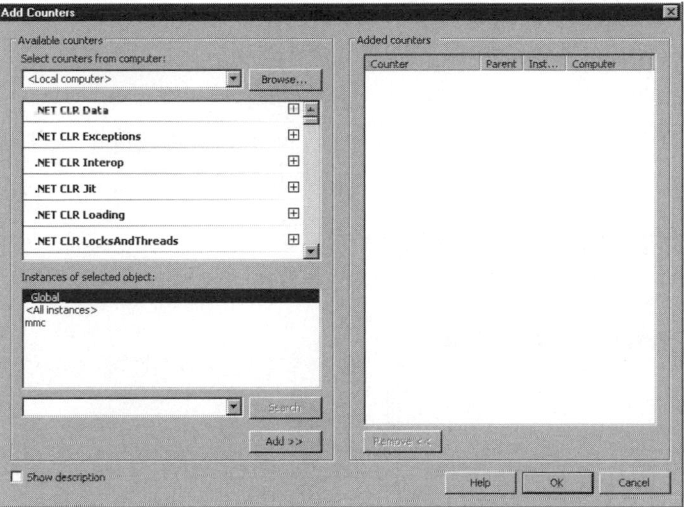

Figure 32-4 Available counters for Performance Monitor

To add a counter, follow these steps:

1. Select a computer from the drop-down list or click Browse to find other computers. If only the local computer is available and you want to connect to another computer, see "Connecting to a Remote Computer Using Performance Monitor" later in this chapter.
2. Available counters are listed below the computer selection box. You can add all the counters in a group or click the plus sign to select individual counters.

> **Note** Select the Show Description check box in the lower left of the window for information on what the selected counters actually count.

3. When you click a group or an individual counter, the current instances display in the Instances Of Selected Object window. Select a particular instance or All Instances. To search for a particular instance, type the process name in the drop-down box below the Instances Of Selected Object dialog box, and click Search.

> **Note** If your search produces no returns, highlight another group to clear the search. The search function is offered only if multiple instances are available.

4. Click Add to put the counter in the Added Counters list.
5. Click OK when you're finished.

Changing the Performance Monitor Display

If you are using multiple counters, the Performance Monitor screen can be difficult to decipher. To change the display, follow these steps:

1. Right-click the Performance Monitor display and select Properties to open the Performance Monitor Properties window, as shown in Figure 32-5.

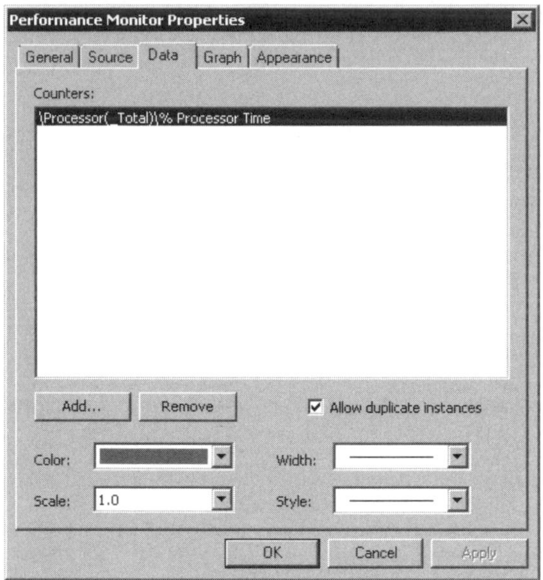

Figure 32-5 Changing the Performance Monitor display

2. Click the Data tab to select how you want the counters to display. Change the color, width, or style of the counter lines.
3. Change other display elements on the General, Graph, and Appearance tabs.
4. Click the Source tab to change the data source from Current Activity to a specified log file. For more on using performance logs, see "Managing Collected Data" later in this chapter.

Note Membership in the local Performance Log Users or Administrators group or equivalent is the minimum required to complete this procedure.

Saving the Performance Monitor Display

The current display of Performance Monitor can be saved as an image or as a Web page.

To save the display as an image, follow these steps:

1. Right-click the Performance Monitor display and select Save Image As.

2. Select a location and type in a name for the saved image. The image will se saved as a .gif file.
3. Click Save.

To save the Performance Monitor display as a Web page, follow these steps:

1. Right-click the Performance Monitor display and select Save Settings As.
2. Select a location and type in a name for the saved display. The display will be saved as an .html file.
3. Click Save.

Connecting to a Remote Computer Using Performance Monitor

To connect to a remote computer using Performance Monitor, follow these steps:

1. Open Performance Monitor.
2. In the navigation pane, right-click Reliability And Performance and then click Connect To Another Computer.
3. In the Select Computer dialog box, type the name of the computer you want to monitor or click Browse to select it from a list.

Note To view performance counters from a remote computer, the Performance Logs And Alerts firewall exception must be enabled on the remote computer. In addition, members of the Performance Log Users group must also be members of the Event Log Readers group on the remote computer.

Using Reliability Monitor

Reliability Monitor provides a System Stability Index that reflects whether unexpected problems are reducing system reliability. A graph of the Stability Index over time quickly identifies dates when problems began to occur. The accompanying System Stability Report presents details to help you locate and fix the root cause of reduced reliability. Looking at changes to the system (operating system updates or adding and removing software) along with failures (application, operating system, or hardware failures), you can develop a method for dealing with the problems.

To open Reliability Monitor, select Reliability And Performance Monitor from the Administrative Tools menu. Alternatively, click Start, click the Start Search box, type **perfmon**, and press Enter. In the navigation tree, expand Monitoring Tools and click Reliability Monitor.

How Reliability Monitor Collects Data

Reliability Monitor uses data collected by the RACAgent scheduled task, which runs by default after the operating system is installed. If this task is disabled, you must enable it manually. To enable the RACAgent scheduled task or to check on its status, follow these steps:

1. Click Start, click in the Start Search box, type **taskschd.msc**, and then press Enter.
2. In the navigation pane, expand Task Scheduler Library, expand Microsoft, expand Windows, and click RAC.
3. Right-click RAC, click View, and click Show Hidden Tasks.
4. Right-click RACAgent in the Console pane and select Enable.

Viewing Reliability Monitor on a Remote Computer

Information about the location of Reliability Monitor files is stored in the registry. Therefore, remote registry access is required to open data on a remote computer. To enable Remote Registry Service, follow these steps:

1. On the computer where you want to access Reliability Monitor data, click Start, type **services.msc** in the Start Search box, and press Enter.
2. In the Services list, right-click Remote Registry and select Start from the action menu, shown in Figure 32-6.

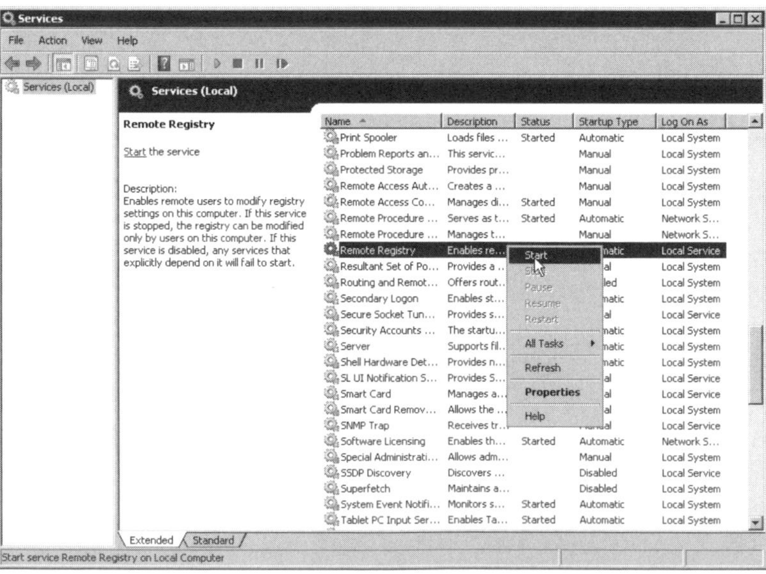

Figure 32-6 Enabling the Remote Registry service

Note You must be a member of the local Administrators group (or its equivalent) to perform the previous procedure.

Interpreting the System Stability Index

Reliability Monitor maintains up to a year of history for system stability and reliability events. The System Stability Chart (Figure 32-7) displays a rolling graph organized by date.

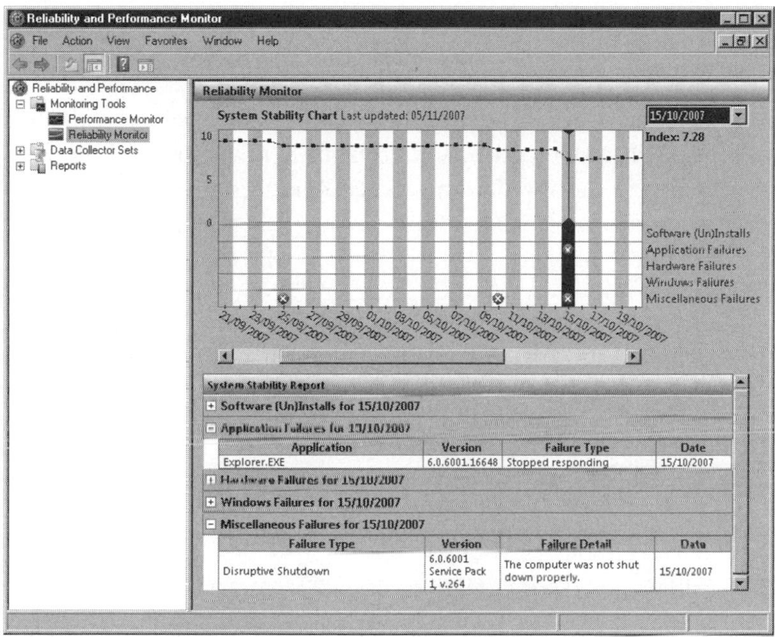

Figure 32-7 A sample System Stability Chart

The System Stability Index (SSI) generates a daily number from 1 (very unstable) to 10 (very stable). This is a weighted measurement derived over time. Recent failures are more heavily weighted than past failures. So once a problem has been resolved, the SSI number will rise. On days when there is not enough data to calculate a reliable System Stability Index, the graph line will be dotted. Days that the computer is turned off will not be calculated in the SSI.

In the lower half of the window, the System Stability Report uses the following five categories to track events that either affect the stability score or record software installation and removal. Click a date column in the chart and the events from that date will display in the report.

Software Installs and Uninstalls

Installations and removals are tracked in this category, which includes applications drivers, Windows updates, and parts of the operating system. The data display shows the following information:

- **Software** The name of the application, update, driver, or operating system
- **Version** The version number of the software
- **Activity** Install or uninstall
- **Activity Status** Success or failure of the activity
- **Date** Date of the activity

An application that repeatedly fails to install or uninstall might need to be updated. If it's a Microsoft application, use Windows Update and Problem Reports And Solutions in Control Panel to find solutions. If the application is not a Microsoft product, search the manufacturer's Web site for updates.

Application Failures

This category lists applications that have failed or stopped working. Non-responding applications that are terminated are also included. The data display shows the following information:

- **Application** The executable program name of the application
- **Version** The version number of the application
- **Failure Type** Whether the application stopped working or stopped responding
- **Date** Date of the failure

Applications that fail or stop responding might need updates. If it's a Microsoft application, use Windows Update and Problem Reports And Solutions in Control Panel to find solutions. If the application is not a Microsoft product, search the manufacturer's Web site for updates.

Hardware Failures

Memory and disk failures are in this category. The data display shows the following information:

- **Component type** Where the failure occurred
- **Device** Device that failed
- **Failure type** The type of failure that occurred
- **Date** Date of the failure

Repeated hardware failures can sometimes be resolved with software or firmware updates. Before replacing a piece of hardware, contact the manufacturer for troubleshooting instructions and advice.

Windows Failures

Operating system and boot failures are in this category. The data display shows the following information:

- **Failure type** Boot failure or operating system crash
- **Version** Version of operating system and service pack
- **Failure Detail** Shows the stop code in the event of an operating system crash. shows the reason code in the event of boot failure
- **Date** Date of the failure

Repeated operating system and boot failures can sometimes be resolved by reinstalling the operating system. Sometimes a boot failure can be caused by a hardware incompatibility. Use Windows Update and Problem Reports And Solutions in Control Panel to find solutions. Search the Windows Knowledge Base (*http://support.microsoft.com*) for more information.

Miscellaneous Failures

This category includes failures that are not included in the previous categories but nevertheless affect system stability. Usually these will be unexpected operating system shutdowns. The data display shows the following information:

- **Failure type** Indicates what happened
- **Version** Version of the operating system and service pack
- **Failure detail** Describes the nature of the failure
- **Date** Date of the failure

Creating a Data Collector Set

Data Collector sets are a new method of monitoring and reporting in Reliability And Performance Monitor. You can collect only information that's useful to you, and you can create individual Data Collector sets that can be viewed alone or combined with other Data Collector sets in Performance Monitor. Data Collector sets can be configured to generate alerts when thresholds are reached, or you can associate them with scheduling rules to data collection at specific times.

Enabling Performance Log Users

For members of the Performance Log Users group to launch data logging or modify Data Collector sets, the group must first be assigned the Log On As A Batch Job user right. To assign this user right, use the Local Security Policy snap-in in Microsoft Management Console (MMC). To complete this procedure you must be a member of the Local Performance Log Users group or Administrators group.

To assign the Log On As A Batch Job user right to the Performance Log Users group, follow these steps:

1. Click Start type **secpol.msc** in the Search box, and press Enter to open Local Security Policy.
2. In the navigation pane, expand Local Policies and click User Rights Assignment.
3. In the console pane, right-click Log On As A Batch Job and click Properties.
4. On the Properties page, click Add User Or Group.
5. In the Select Users Or Groups dialog box, click Object Types. In the Object Types dialog box, select Groups and click OK.
6. Type Performance Log Users in the Select Users Or Groups dialog box and then click Check Names. Click OK.
7. On the Properties page, click OK to finish.

Data Collector sets can contain performance counters, event trace data, and system configuration data (registry keys). To see the types of Data Collector sets, open Reliability And Performance Monitor. In the navigation tree, expand Data Collector Sets.

Building a Data Collector Set from a Template

Reliability And Performance Monitor includes several templates that concentrate on general system diagnosis information or collect performance data specific to server roles or applications. You can import templates created on other computers and export Data Collector sets that you create to use on other computers.

To create a Data Collector Set from a template, follow these steps:

Note To complete this procedure you must be a member of the Local Performance Log Users group or the Administrators group.

1. Click Start, type **perfmon** in the Start Search box, and then press Enter.
2. In the navigation pane, expand Data Collector Sets, right-click User Defined, point to New, and click Data Collector Set. The Create New Data Collector Set Wizard starts.
3. Enter a name for your Data Collector set. Select Create From A Template and click Next.
4. From the Template Data Collector Set menu, select the template you want to use to create your Data Collector set. A description of the data collected appears as you highlight each template (Figure 32-8).

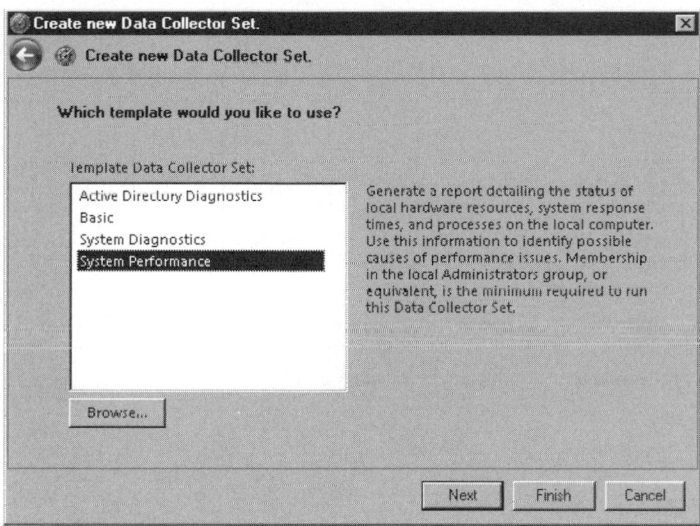

Figure 32-8 Highlight a template to read a description of the data it will collect

5. The Root Directory will contain data collected by the Data Collector set. If you want to store your Data Collector Set data in a location other than the default, click Browse or enter the directory name.
6. Click Next to choose a custom location for the Data Collector set or to define more options. Click Finish to save the current settings and exit.

Note If you type in a directory name, do not enter a backslash (\) at the end of the directory name.

7. Click Next to define a user for the Data Collector Set to Run As, or click Finish to save the current settings and exit.

8. When you click Next, you can also configure the Data Collector set to run as a specific user. Click Change to enter the user name and password for a different user than the default listed or click Finish to save the current settings and exit
9. Click Finish.

To start collecting data and storing it in the location specified in step 6, right-click the Data Collector set in the navigation pane and select Start (Figure 32-9).

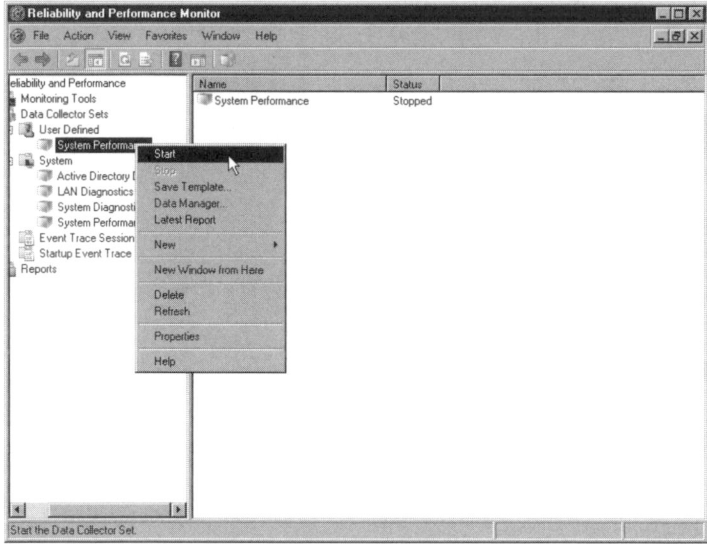

Figure 32-9 Starting a Data Collector set

To view the properties of the Data Collector set or make changes, right-click the name and select Properties. For more information about the properties of the Data Collector set, see "Managing Collected Data" later in this chapter.

Importing Templates

Data Collector set templates are stored as XML files and you can import them directly from a local hard drive or from a network drive.

To import a Data Collector Set template, run the Create New Data Collector Set Wizard and click Browse when asked which template you'd like to use. Browse to the location of the XML file you want to use, select it, and click OK.

Exporting Templates

To export a Data Collector set for use on other computers, open Reliability And Performance Monitor, expand Data Collector Sets, right-click the Data Collector set you want to export, and click Save Template. Select a directory in which to store the XML file and click Save.

Creating a Data Collector Set from Performance Monitor

To use the counters in a Performance Monitor display to create a Data Collector set, follow these steps:

> **Note** To complete this procedure you must be a member of the Local Performance Log Users group or the Administrators group.

1. Start Performance Monitor and add counters to create a custom view you want to save as a Data Collector set.
2. Right-click Performance Monitor in the navigation pane, point to New, and click Data Collector Set. The Create New Data Collector Set Wizard starts. The Data Collector set you create will contain all of the data collectors selected in the current Performance Monitor view.
3. Enter a name for the Data Collector set and click Next.
4. The Root Directory will contain data collected by the Data Collector set. If you want to store your Data Collector set data in a location other than the default, click Browse to navigate to the location or enter the directory name.

   > **Note** If you type in a directory name, do not enter a backslash (\) at the end of the directory name.

5. After clicking Next, you can configure the Data Collector set to run as a specific user. Click Change to enter a user name and password.

   > **Note** If you are a member of the Performance Log Users group, any Data Collector sets that you create must run under your own credentials.

6. Click Finish.

To start collecting data and storing it in the location specified in step 4, right-click the Data Collector set in the navigation pane and select Start.

Constructing a Data Collector Set Manually

You can create a customized Data Collector set made up of performance counters, configuration data, or data from trace providers. To make such a Data Collector set, follow these steps:

> **Note** To complete this procedure you must be a member of the Local Performance Log Users group or the Administrators group.

1. Open Windows Reliability And Performance Monitor.
2. In the navigation pane, expand Data Collector Sets, right-click User Defined, point to New, and click Data Collector Set.
3. Enter a name for your Data Collector set. Select Create Manually and click Next.
4. Select Create Data Logs. Select the check boxes next to the Data Collector types you want to use and click Next.
   - *Performance Counters* generates metric data about the system's performance.
   - *Event Trace Data* provides information about activities and system events.
   - *System Configuration Information* records the state of–and changes to–registry keys.
5. Depending on the Data Collector types you selected, you will be presented with dialog boxes to add Data Collectors to your Data Collector set.
   - Click Add to open the Add Counters dialog box. When you are finished adding performance counters, click Next to continue configuration or click Finish to exit and save the current configuration.
   - You can install event trace providers with the operating system or as part of a non-Microsoft application. Click Add to select from a list of available Event Trace Providers, as shown in Figure 32-10. You can select multiple providers by holding down the Ctrl key and highlighting. When you are finished adding event trace providers, click Next to continue configuration or click Finish to exit and save the current configuration.

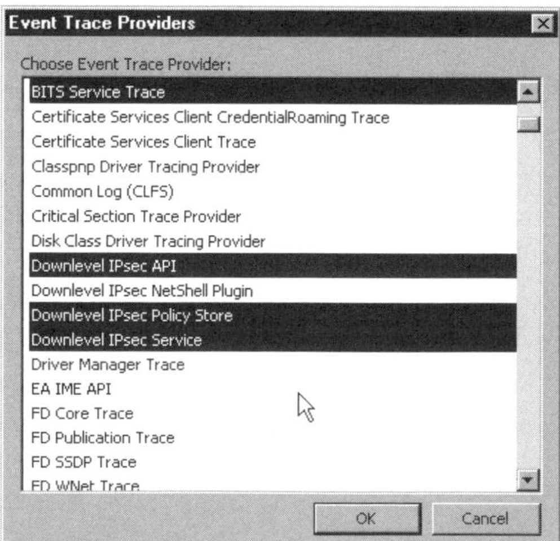

Figure 32-10 Selecting trace providers for a Data Collector set

6. To record system configuration data, enter the Registry keys you want to track. You must know the exact key.
7. When you've finished adding Registry keys, click Next to continue configuration or click Finish to exit and save the current configuration.
8. The Root Directory will contain data collected by the Data Collector set. If you want to store your Data Collector set data in a location other than the default, click Browse to navigate to the location or type the directory name.

> **Note** If you type in a directory name, do not enter a backslash (\) at the end of the directory name.

9. After clicking Next, you can configure the Data Collector set to run as a specific user. Click Change to enter the user name and password for a user other than the default listed.

> **Note** If you are a member of the Performance Log Users group, any Data Collector sets that you create must run under your own credentials.

10. Click Finish.

Creating a Data Collector Set to Monitor Performance Counters

Another type of Data Collector set that you can create will monitor performance counters and send out alerts when the counters exceed or fall below thresholds you set.

> **Note** To complete this procedure you must be a member of the Local Performance Log Users group or the Administrators group.

First create the data set and then configure the alerts by following these steps:

1. Open Reliability And Performance Monitor. In the navigation pane, expand Data Collector Sets, right-click User Defined, point to New, and click Data Collector Set.
2. Enter a name for your Data Collector set. Select the option to Create Manually and click Next.
3. Select the Performance Counter Alert option and click Next.
4. Click Add to open the Add Counters dialog box. When you are finished adding counters, click OK.

5. Highlight the counter you'd like to monitor. From the Alert When drop-down list, choose whether to alert when the performance counter value is above or below the limit. In the Limit box, enter the threshold value.
6. When you've finished defining alerts, click Next to continue configuration or click Finish to exit and save the current configuration.
7. After clicking Next, you can configure the Data Collector set to run as a specific user. Click Change to enter a user name and password.

Note If you are a member of the Performance Log Users group, any Data Collector sets that you create must run under your own credentials.

Scheduling Data Collection

Data collection can be scheduled and log data managed using Data Collector Sets. You can store the reports after log data has been deleted so that you can still have performance statistics without storing masses of individual counter values.

Note To complete this procedure you must be a member of the Local Performance Log Users group or the Administrators group.

To schedule when a Data Collection set starts, follow these steps:

1. After you create a Data Collection set, right-click the name of the Data Collector set name in the navigation pane and select Properties.
2. Click the Schedule tab.
3. Click Add to create a start date, time, or day for data collection, as shown in Figure 32-11. If you are configuring a new Data Collector set, be sure that the start date is after the current date and time.

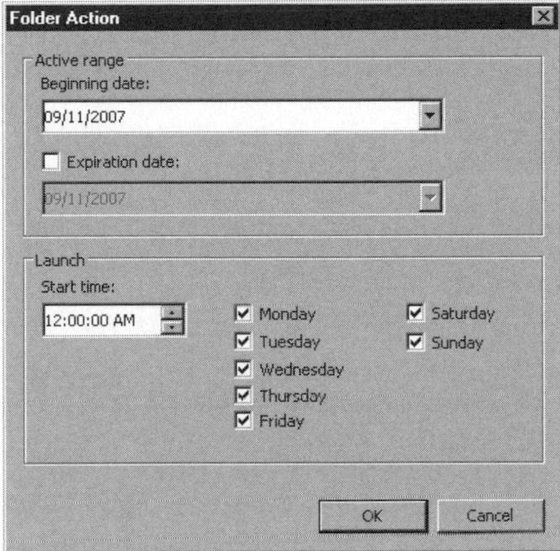

Figure 32-11 Scheduling the start date and time for a Data Collector set

4. If you don't want to collect new data after a specific date, select the Expiration Date box and supply the date.

5. Click OK when finished.

Note Specifying an expiration date will prevent new instances of data collection from starting after the expiration date.

To schedule when a Data Collection set stops, follow these steps:

1. After you create a Data Collection set, right-click the name of the Data Collector set name in the navigation pane and select Properties.

2. Click the Stop Condition tab.

3. To stop collecting data after a specified time, select Overall Duration and choose the number and units of time.

   Note If your aim is to collect data indefinitely, don't select Overall Duration.

4. In the Limits section, you can select When A Limit Is Reached, Restart The Data Collector Set to break the data collection into separate, more manageable logs.

   - Select Duration to configure a time period for data collection to write to a single log file.
   - Select Maximum Size to restart the Data Collector set or to stop collecting data when the log file reaches the limit.

Note If both limit types are selected, the collection of data will stop or restart when the first limit is reached. If you configure Overall Duration, those settings will override limits.

5. If you have set an overall duration, you can select Stop When All Data Collectors Have Finished so that all the counters can finish recording the most recent values before the entire Data Collector set is stopped.
6. Click OK to finish.

Managing Collected Data

Data Collector sets create log files and optional report files. Data Manager allows you to configure how log data, reports, and compressed data are stored for each Data Collector set.

Note To complete this procedure you must be a member of the Local Performance Log Users group or the Administrators group.

To configure Data Manager for a Data Collector Set, follow these steps:

1. Open Windows Reliability And Performance Monitor, expand Data Collector Sets, and expand User Defined.
2. Right-click the name of the Data Collector set that you want to configure and select Data Manager from the shortcut menu.
3. On the Data Manager tab, you can accept the default values or make changes according to your data retention policy. Table 32-1 describes each option.
   - Select Minimum Free Disk or Maximum Folders and previous data will be deleted when the limit is reached according to the Resource Policy you choose (Delete Largest or Delete Oldest).
   - Select Apply Policy Before The Data Collector Set Starts and previous data will be deleted before the data collector set creates its next log file.
   - Select Maximum Root Path Size and previous data will be deleted when the root log folder size limit is reached.
4. Click the Actions tab. You can accept the default values or make changes. To make changes, use the Add, Edit, or Delete buttons. Table 32-2 describes each option.
5. Click OK to finish.

Table 32-1 Data Manager Options

Options	Definition
Minimum Free Disk	Amount of free disk space that must be available on the drive where log data is stored. When the limit is reached, previous data will be deleted based on your Resource Policy.
Maximum Folders	Number of subfolders allowed in the data directory. When the limit is reached, previous data will be deleted according to your Resource Policy.
Resource Policy	Specifies whether the largest or the oldest log file or directory will be deleted when limits are reached.
Maximum Root Path Size	Maximum size of the Data Collector set data directory, including all subfolders. When selected, this maximum path size overrides the Minimum Free Disk and Maximum Folders limits. When the limit of the Maximum Root Path Size is reached, previous data will be deleted according to your Resource Policy.

Table 32-2 Actions Properties

Option	Definition
Age	The age of the data file in days or weeks. If the value is set to zero, the age is not considered.
Size	The size, in megabytes, of the log data folder. If the value is set to zero, the size is not considered.
Cab	A cabinet file. Cab files are archives that are created from raw log data that can be extracted later.
Data	Raw data log created by the Data Collector set. To save disk space, the data log can be deleted after a cab file is created.
Report	Report file generated from the log data. Report files can be retained even after the log data has been deleted.

Working with Data Log Files

When log files grow large, reports are generated more slowly. If you review your logs frequently, setting limits will automatically break up logs to make them easier to view. The relog command can divide long log files into more manageable segments or you can use it to combine multiple log files.

The relog command has the following syntax. The parameters are detailed in the following sections.

```
relog [FileName [FileName ...]] [-a] [-c Path [Path ...]] [-cf FileName] [-f {bin
| csv | tsv | SQL}] [-t Value] [-o {OutputFile | DSN!CounterLog}] [-b M/D/YYYY
[[HH:]MM:]SS] [-e M/D/YYYY [[HH:]MM:]SS] [-config {FileName | i}] [-q]
```

`<FileName [FileName ...]>`

This parameter specifies the path name of an existing performance counter log. You can specify multiple input files.

`-a`

This parameter appends output file instead of overwriting. This option does not apply to SQL format where the default is always to append.

`-c <Path [Path ...]>`

This parameter specifies the performance counter path to log. To specify multiple counter paths, separate them with a space and enclose the counter paths in quotation marks (for example, "CounterPath1 CounterPath2").

`-cf <FileName>`

This parameter specifies the path name of the text file that lists the performance counters to be included in a relog file. Use this option to list counter paths in an input file, one per line. Default setting is all counters in the original log file are relogged.

`-f {bin| csv| tsv| SQL}`

This parameter specifies the path name of the output file format. The default format is bin. For a SQL database, the output file specifies the DSN!CounterLog. You can specify the database location by using the ODBC manager to configure the DSN (Database System Name).

`-t <value>`

This parameter specifies sample intervals in "N" records. Includes every nth data point in the relog file. Default is every data point.

`-o {OutputFile | DSN!CounterLog}`

This parameter specifies the path name of the output file or SQL database where the counters will be written.

`-b <M/D/YYYY HH:MM:SS[AM|PM]>`

This parameter specifies begin time for copying first record from the input file.

`-e <M/D/YYYY HH:MM:SS[AM|PM]>`

This parameter specifies end time for copying last record from the input file.

`-config {FileName | i}`

This parameter specifies the path name of the settings file that contains command-line parameters. Use *-i* in the configuration file as a placeholder for a list of input files that can be placed on the command line. On the command line, however, you do not need to use *i*. You can also use wildcards such as *.blg to specify many input file names.

`-q`

This parameter displays the performance counters and time ranges of log files specified in the input file.

`-y`

This parameter bypasses prompting by answering "yes" to all questions.

`/?`

This parameter displays help at the command prompt.

Viewing Reports

To help analyze collected data and identify trends, Reliability And Performance Monitor generates reports from Data Collector sets.

> **Note** To complete this procedure you must be a member of the Local Performance Log Users group or the Administrators group.

To view a Data Collector set report, follow these steps:

1. Open Windows Reliability And Performance Monitor/ Expand Reports and click User Defined Or System.
2. In the navigation pane, select the Data Collector set that you want to view as a report.
3. Click a report from the list of available reports. The report opens in the console pane, as shown in Figure 32-12.

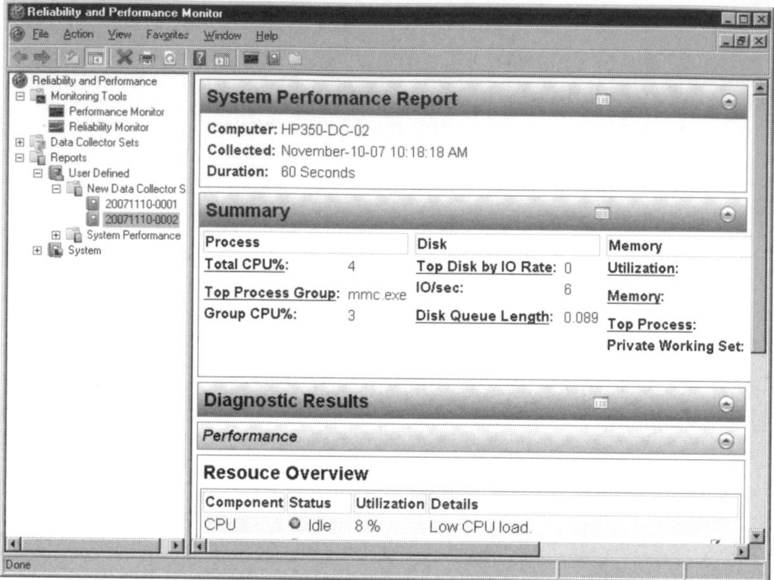

Figure 32-12 Viewing a Data Collector set report.

To create a new report for a Data Collector set, type **perfmon /report "Data_Collector_Set_name"** at a command prompt. Type **perfmon /report** without any other parameters to generate the System Diagnostics report.

Summary

In this chapter we covered the available tools for keeping track of your network's health and performance. The next chapter offers strategies for protecting your network from potential disasters.

Chapter 33

Disaster Planning

Smart drivers wear seat belts and shoulder harnesses; smart bicycle riders wear helmets. Racecar drivers do all of that and add special fire-resistant Nomex underwear and coveralls. All of them hope and expect not to ever be in an accident or need the protective gear they regularly use. Schools and businesses have fire drills even though the vast majority of buildings never burn down. Like all systems administrators, we sincerely hope we will never need our verified backups and detailed disaster recovery plans. Nevertheless, we keep them because there are only two types of networks: those that have experienced disaster and those that haven't. Yet.

Disaster can take many forms, from the self-inflicted pain of a user or administrator doing something really, really unwise to the uncontrollable, unpreventable results of a natural disaster such as a flood or earthquake. Whatever the source of the disaster, however, your competence as a system administrator will be judged by how well you were prepared and how well you and your team responded to–and recovered from–the consequences of that disaster.

This chapter covers emergency preparedness. It discusses creating a disaster recovery plan, with standardized procedures to follow in the event of a catastrophe. It also describes how to prepare for a disaster, including how to use the new, automated System Repair options in Windows Server 2008.

Planning for Disaster

Some people seem to operate on the assumption that if they don't think about disaster, it will never happen. This is similar to the idea that if you don't write a will, you'll never die–and just about as realistic. No system administrator should feel comfortable about a network's degree of preparedness without a clear disaster recovery plan that has been thoroughly tested. The plan is only the starting point, however. A good disaster recovery plan is one you are constantly examining, improving, updating, and testing. But understand your disaster plan's limitations: it isn't perfect, and even the best disaster recovery plan needs to be constantly examined and adjusted or it quickly gets out of date.

Planning for disaster or emergencies is not a single step, but an iterative, ongoing process. Systems are not mountains, they're rivers—constantly moving and changing. Your disaster recovery plan needs to change as your environment changes. To put together a good disaster recovery plan—one you can bet your business on—you need to follow these steps:

1. Identify the risks.
2. Identify the resources.
3. Develop the responses.
4. Test the responses.
5. Iterate.

Identifying the Risks

The first step in creating a disaster recovery plan is to identify the risks to your business and the costs associated with those risks. The risks vary from the simple deletion of a critical file to the total destruction of your place of business and its computers. To properly prepare for a disaster, you need to perform a realistic assessment of the risks, the potential costs and consequences of each disaster scenario, the likelihood of any given disaster scenario, and the resources available to address the risks. Risks that seemed vanishingly remote a few years ago are now part of our everyday life.

Identifying risks is not a job for a single person. As with all the tasks associated with a disaster recovery plan, all concerned parties must participate, for two important reasons: You want to make sure that you have commitment and buy-in from the parties involved, and you also want to make sure you don't miss anything important.

No matter how carefully and thoroughly you try to identify the risks, you'll miss *at least* one. You should always account for that missing risk by including an "unknown risk" item in your list. Treat it just like any other risk: Identify the resources available to address it, and develop countermeasures to take should it occur. The difference with this risk, of course, is that your resources and countermeasures are somewhat more generic, and you can't really test your response to the risk, because you don't yet know what it is.

Start by trying to list all the possible ways your system could fail. If you have a team of people responsible for supporting the network, solicit everyone's help in the process. The more people involved in the brainstorming, the more ideas you'll get and the more prevention and recovery procedures you can develop and practice.

Next, look at all the ways some external event could affect your system. The team of people responsible for identifying possible external problems is probably similar to a team looking at internal failures, but with some important differences. In a large industrial plant, for example, when you start to look at external failures and disasters, you'll want to involve the security and facilities groups, because they will need to understand your needs as well as provide input on how well the plant is protected from these disasters.

The risk identification phase is really made up of two parts: identification and assessment. *They are different tasks.* During the identification portion of the phase, you need to identify *every possible risk, no matter how remote or unlikely.* No risk suggested should be regarded as silly—don't limit the suggestions in any way. You want to identify every possible risk that anyone can think of. Then, when you have as complete a list as you can create, move on to the assessment task. In the risk-assessment task, you will try to understand and quantify just how likely a particular risk is. If you're located on a flood plain, for example, you're much more likely to think flood insurance is a good investment.

Identifying the Resources

Once you've identified the risks to your network, you need to identify what resources are available to address those risks. These resources can be internal or external, people or systems, hardware or software.

When you're identifying the resources available to deal with a specific risk, be as complete as you can, but also be specific. Identifying everyone in the IT group as a resource to solve a crashed server might look good, but realistically only one or two key people are likely to actually rebuild the server. Make sure you identify those key people for each risk, as well as the more general secondary resources they have to call on. So, for example, the primary resources available to recover a crashed Microsoft Exchange server might consist of one or two staff members who can recover the failed hardware and another one or two staff members who can restore the software and database. General secondary resources would include everyone in the IT group as well as the hardware vendor and Microsoft Premier Support.

An important step in identifying resources in your disaster recovery plan is to specify both the first-line responsibility *and* the back-end or supervisory responsibility. Make sure everyone knows who to go to when the problem is more than they can handle or when they need additional resources. Also, clearly define *when* they should do that. The best disaster recovery plans include clear, unambiguous escalation policies. This takes the burden off individuals to decide when and who to notify and makes it simply part of the procedure.

Developing the Responses

An old but relevant adage comes to mind when discussing disaster recovery scenarios: When you're up to your elbows in alligators, it's difficult to remember that your original objective was to drain the swamp. This is another way of saying that people lose track of what's important when they are overloaded by too many problems that require immediate attention. To ensure that your swamp is drained and your network gets back online, you need to take those carefully researched risks and resources and develop a disaster recovery plan. Any good disaster recovery plan has two important parts:

- Standard operating procedures (SOPs)
- Standard escalation procedures (SEPs)

Making sure that these procedures are in place and clearly understood by everyone before a disaster strikes puts you in a far better position to recover gracefully and with a minimum of lost productivity and data.

Standard Operating Procedures

Emergencies bring out both the best and worst in people. Unless you've been through an emergency, you can't really know how you will react. But if you're prepared for the emergency, trained for it, practiced it, and have a clear and unambiguous disaster recovery plan, your chances of being the hero instead of the goat are a whole lot better. If you're *not* prepared and let yourself get flustered or lose track of what you're trying to accomplish, however, you can make the whole situation worse than it needs to be.

Although no one is ever as prepared for a system emergency as they'd like to be, careful planning and preparation can give you an edge in recovering expeditiously and with a minimal loss of data. It is much easier to deal with the situation calmly when you know you've prepared for this problem, and you have a well-organized, *tested* standard operating procedure (SOP) to follow.

Because the very nature of emergencies is that you can't predict exactly which one is going to strike, you need to plan and prepare for as many possibilities as you can. The time to decide how to recover from a disaster is *before* the disaster happens, not in the middle of it, when users are screaming and bosses are standing around looking serious and concerned. Well, we hope the bosses are only standing around looking serious and concerned. When they start screaming too, it's a sure sign that all is not going well.

Your risk-assessment phase involved identifying as many possible disaster scenarios as you could, and in your resource-assessment phase you identified the resources that are available and responsible for each of those risks. Now you need to write up SOPs for recovering the system from each of the scenarios. Even the most level-headed system administrator can get flustered when the system has crashed, users are calling every 10 seconds to see what the problem is, the boss is asking every five minutes when you'll have it fixed, and your server won't boot. And that's the easy case compared to the mess that can be caused by an external disaster such as a flood or hurricane.

Reduce your stress and prevent mistakes by planning for disasters before they occur. Practice recovering from each of your disaster scenarios. Write down each of the steps, and work through questionable or unclear areas until you can identify exactly what it takes to recover from the problem. This is like a fire drill, and you should do it for the same reasons–not because a fire is inevitable, but because fires do happen, and the statistics demonstrate irrefutably that those who have prepared for a fire and practiced what to do in a fire are far more likely to survive a fire.

Your job as a system administrator is to prepare for disasters and practice what to do in those disasters–not because you expect the disaster, but because if you do have one, you want to be ready. After all, it isn't often that the system administrator gets to be a hero.

The first step in developing any SOP is to outline the overall steps you want to accomplish. Keep it general at this point–you're looking for the big picture here. Again, you want everyone to be involved in the process. What you're really trying to do is make sure you don't forget any critical steps, and that's much easier when you get the overall plan down first. You will have plenty of opportunities later to cover the specific details.

Once you have a broad, high-level outline for a given procedure, the people you identified as the actual resources during the resource-assessment phase should start to fill in the outline. You don't need every detail at this point, but you should get down to at least a level below the original outline. This will help you identify missing resources that are important to a timely resolution of the problem. Again, don't get too bogged down in the details at this point. You're not actually writing the SOP, just trying to make sure that you've identified all its pieces.

When you feel confident that the outline is ready, get the larger group back together again. Go over the procedure and smooth out the rough edges, refining the outline and *listening* to make sure you haven't missed anything critical. When everyone agrees that the outline is complete, you're ready to add the final details.

The people who are responsible for each procedure should now work through all the details of the disaster recovery plan and document the steps thoroughly. They should keep in mind that the people who actually perform the recovery might not be who they expect. It's great to have an SOP for recovering from a failed router, but if the only person who understands the procedure is the network engineer, and she's on vacation in Tahiti that week, your disaster recovery plan has a big hole in it.

When you create the documentation, write down *everything*. What seems obvious to you now, while you're devising the procedure, will not seem at all obvious in six months or a year when you suddenly have to use it under stress.

Real World Multiple Copies, Multiple Locations

It's tempting to centralize your SOPs into a single, easily accessible database. You should do that, making sure everyone understands how to use it. But you'll also want to have alternative locations and formats for your procedures. Not only do you not want to keep the only copy in a single database, you also don't want to have only an electronic version. Always maintain hard-copy versions as well. The one thing you don't want to do is create a single point of failure in your disaster recovery plan!

Every good server room should have a large binder, prominently visible and clearly identified, that contains all the SOPs. Each responsible person should also have one or more copies of at least the procedures he or she is either a resource for or likely to become a resource for. We like to keep copies of all our procedures in several places so that we can get at them no matter what the source of the emergency or where we happen to be when the call comes in.

Once you have created the SOPs, your job has only begun. You need to keep them up to date and make sure that they don't become stale. It's no good having an SOP to recover your ISDN connection to a branch office when you ripped the ISDN line out a year ago and put in a DSL line with three times the bandwidth at half the cost.

You also need to make sure that all your copies of an SOP are updated. Electronic ones should probably be stored in a replicated database. However, hard-copy documents are notoriously tricky to maintain. A good method is to make yet another SOP that details who updates which SOPs and who gets fresh copies whenever a change is made. Then put a version-control system into place and make sure that everyone understands his or her role in the process. Build rewards into the system for timely and consistent updating of SOPs—if 10 or 20 percent of your staff's bonus is dependent on keeping those SOPs up to date and distributed, you can be sure they'll be done at least as often as the review process.

Standard Escalation Procedures

No matter how carefully you've identified potential risks, and how detailed your procedures to recover from them, you're still likely to have situations you didn't anticipate. An important part of any disaster recovery plan is a standardized escalation procedure. Not only should each individual SOP have its own procedure-specific SEP, but you should also have an overall escalation procedure that covers everything you haven't thought of—because it's certain that you haven't thought of everything.

An escalation procedure has two functions–resource escalation and notification escalation. Both have the same purpose: to make sure that everyone who needs to know about the problem is up to date and involved as appropriate, and to keep the overall noise level down so that the work of resolving the problem can go forward as quickly as possible. The *resource escalation procedure* details the resources available to the people who are trying to recover from the current disaster so that they don't have to try to guess who (or what) the appropriate resource might be when they run into something they can't handle or something doesn't go as planned. This helps them stay calm and focused. They know that if they run into a problem, they aren't on their own, and they know exactly who to call when they do need help.

The *notification escalation procedure* details who is to be notified of serious problems. Even more important, it should provide specifics regarding *when* notification is to be made. If your print server crashes but comes right back up, you might want to send a general message only to the users of that particular server letting them know what happened. However, if your mail server has been down for more than half an hour, a lot of folks are going to be concerned. The SEP for that mail server should detail who needs to be notified if the server is unavailable for longer than some specified time, and it should probably detail what happens and who gets notified when it's still down some significant amount of time after that.

This notification has two purposes: to make sure that the necessary resources are made available as required, and to keep everyone informed and aware of the situation. If you let people know that you've had a server hardware failure and that the vendor has been called and will be on site within an hour, you'll reduce the number of phone calls exponentially, freeing you to do whatever you need to do to ensure that you're ready when the vendor arrives.

SEPs have one other important function–they set expectations to levels that everyone involved has agreed to and understands. This can significantly reduce the noise level when there are problems. And anything that reduces noise when you're in the middle of a major problem is a good thing.

Testing the Responses

A disaster recovery plan is nice to have, but it really isn't worth a whole lot until it has actually been tested. Needless to say, the time to test the plan is at your convenience and under controlled conditions, rather than in the midst of an actual disaster. It's a nuisance to discover that your detailed disaster recovery plan has a fatal flaw in it when you're testing it under controlled conditions. It's a bit more than a nuisance to discover it in a situation where every second counts.

You won't be able to test all aspects of all disaster recovery plans. Few organizations have the resources to create fully realistic simulated natural disasters and test their response to each of them under controlled conditions. Nevertheless, there are things you can do to test your response plans. The details of how you test them depend on your environment, but they should include as realistic a test as feasible and should, as much as possible, cover all aspects of the response plan. The other reason to test the disaster recovery plan is that it provides a valuable training ground. If you've identified primary and backup resources, as you should, chances are that the people you've identified as backup resources are not as skilled or knowledgeable in a particular area as the primary resource. Testing the procedures gives you a chance to train the backup resources at the same time.

You should also consider using the testing to cross-train people who are not necessarily in the primary response group. Not only will they get valuable training, but you'll also create a knowledgeable pool of people who might not be directly needed when the procedure has to be used for real, but who can act as key communicators with the rest of the community.

Iterating

When you finish a particular disaster recovery plan, you might think your job is done, but in fact your work is just beginning. Standardizing a process is actually just the first step. You also need to improve it.

You should make a regular, scheduled practice of pulling out your disaster recovery plan with your group and making sure it's up to date. Use the occasion to evaluate how you can improve on it. Take the opportunity to examine your environment. What's changed since you last looked at the plan? What servers have been retired, and what new ones have been added? What software is different? Are all the people on your notification and escalation lists still working at the company in the same roles? Are the phone numbers up to date?

Real World Understand and Practice Kaizen

Kaizen is a Japanese word and concept that means "small, continuous improvement." Its literal translation is, "Change (kai) to become good (zen)."

So, why bring a Japanese word and concept into a discussion about disaster recovery? Because a good disaster recovery plan is one that you are constantly Kaizening. When you really understand Kaizen, it becomes a way of life that you can use in many ways.

The first thing to understand about Kaizen is that you are *not* striving for major change or improvement. Small improvements are the goal. Don't try to fix or change everything all at once. Instead, focus on one area, and try to make it just a little bit better.

The second part of Kaizen is that it is continuous. You must constantly look for ways to improve and implement those improvements. Because each improvement is small and incremental, you can easily implement it and move on to the next one.

Kaizen is very much about teamwork. Good Kaizen balances the load on a team and finds ways to build the strengths of the team as a whole. If you practice Kaizen and continually look for small, incremental ways to improve your work, you will soon have a better and more enjoyable place to work. As a manager, if you find ways to encourage and reward those who practice Kaizen, your team and you will grow and prosper.

Another way to iterate your disaster recovery plan is to use every disaster as a learning experience. Once the disaster or emergency is over, get everyone together *as soon as possible* to talk about what happened. Find out what they think worked in the plan and what didn't. Actively solicit suggestions for how the process could be improved. Then make the changes and test them. You'll not only improve your responsiveness to this particular type of disaster, but you'll improve your overall responsiveness by getting people involved in the process and enabling them to be part of the solution.

Preparing for a Disaster

As Ben Franklin was known to say, "Failure to prepare is preparing to fail." This is truer than ever with modern operating systems, and although Windows Server 2008 includes a number of exceptionally useful recovery modes and tools, you still need to prepare for potential problems. Some of these techniques are covered in detail in other chapters and are discussed here only briefly, whereas others are covered here at length.

Setting Up a Fault-Tolerant System

A fault-tolerant system is one that is prepared to continue operating in the event of key component failures. This technique is very useful for servers running critical applications. Here are a few of the many ways to ensure fault tolerance in a system:

- Use one or more RAID arrays for system and data storage to protect you from hard disk failure. If a hard disk in the array fails, only that disk needs to be replaced–and no data is lost. See Chapter 19, "Implementing Disk Management," for information about using Windows Server 2008 to implement software RAID.
- Use multiple SAS adapters to provide redundancy if a SAS controller fails.

- Use an uninterruptible power supply (UPS) to allow the server to shut down gracefully in the event of a power failure.
- Use multiple network cards to provide redundancy in case a network card fails.
- Use multiples of everything that is likely to fail, including power supplies and so on.
- Use clusters to provide redundancy and failover in the event of a server failure. See Chapter 21, "Using Clusters" for information about implementing clusters in Windows Server 2008.

More Info For more on fault tolerance, see Chapter 35, "Planning Fault Tolerance and Avoidance."

Backing Up the System

Back up the system and system state regularly using a good Windows Server 2008 backup program. If a hard disk fails and must be replaced and you're not using some sort of RAID array, you can restore the data and system from backup. See Chapter 34, "Using Backup," for details on using the Windows Server 2008 backup program as well as suggestions on alternatives you might consider.

System Repair

A new feature in Windows Server 2008 is the Repair Your Computer option. This powerful new feature allows you to repair many problems automatically by booting from the original installation DVD. Once you've made your language selection, you'll see the Repair Your Computer option, as shown in Figure 33-1.

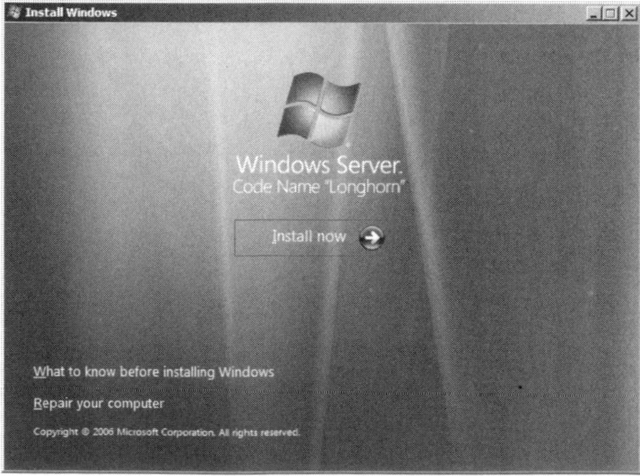

Figure 33-1 Use the Repair Your Computer option to begin automatic recovery.

If you select Repair Your Computer, Windows Server 2008 will try to identify an operating system it can repair, as shown in Figure 33-2. If you need to load drivers before you can see Windows Server 2008, you can click Load Drivers and provide the drivers.

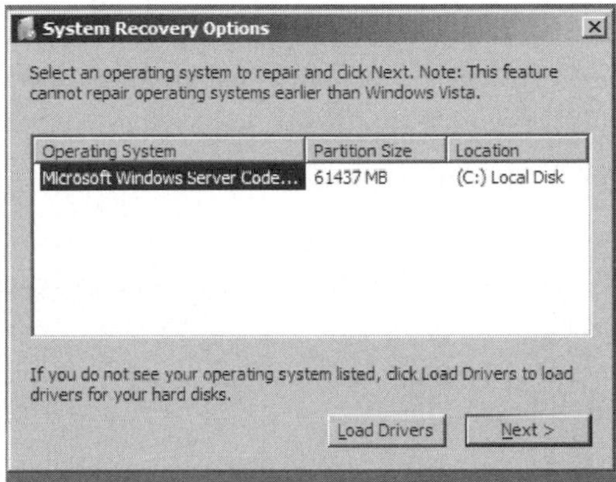

Figure 33-2 The System Recovery Options page of the Repair Your Computer Wizard

Once you click Next, System Recovery will try to identify problems with your system and repair them. The Startup Repair Wizard checks your system and attempts to correct errors it identifies. Once it has made its best attempt to repair, you can click Finish to end the repair and attempt to boot into the repaired server or click the Click Here For Diagnose And Repair Details link to see details on the tests performed and the repairs made.

If System Repair isn't able to completely repair the system automatically, it will offer the Choose A Recovery Tool page shown in Figure 33-3. On this page, you can select additional options, including a complete restore from backup, comprehensive memory testing, or a command prompt from which you can run manual repairs.

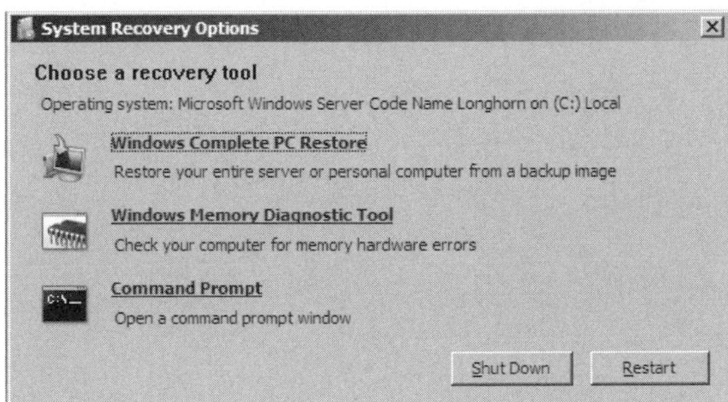

Figure 33-3 The Choose A Recovery Tool page of the Repair Your Computer Wizard

The Command Prompt option is essentially similar to the Windows Server 2003 Recovery Console–an enhanced, NTFS-enabled, secure command prompt that you can use to copy files, start and stop services, and perform other recovery actions.

Specifying Recovery Options

You can specify how you want Windows Server 2008 to deal with system crashes by changing a few options in the System tool in Control Panel. To do so, follow these steps:

1. Open the System tool from Control Panel and click Advanced System Settings in the Tasks pane.
2. Click Settings in the Startup And Recovery box to display the Startup And Recovery dialog box, shown in Figure 33-4.

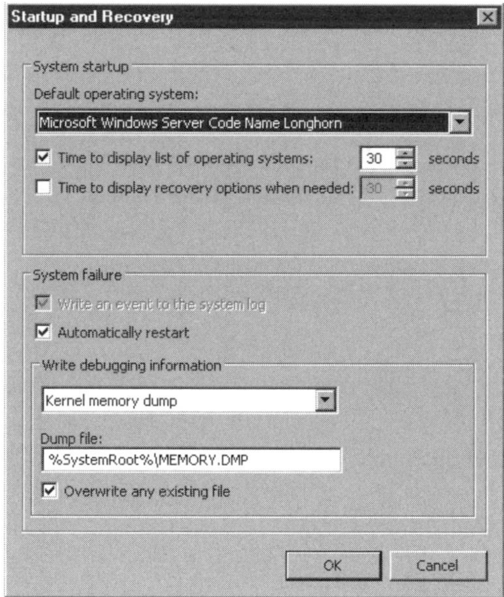

Figure 33-4 The Startup And Recovery dialog box

3. If you have multiple operating systems on the computer, select the operating system you want to have boot by default from the Default Operating System list box.
4. If you want to boot the default operating system automatically, without waiting, clear the Time To Display List Of Operating Systems check box. Otherwise, specify how long you want to display a list of options in the box provided.

5. If you want recovery options automatically displayed in the event of problems, select the Time To Display Recovery Options When Needed check box, and set the time for it.
6. Select the Write An Event To The System Log check box, if available, to record an entry in the event log when the system experiences a crash.
7. Select the Automatically Restart option to instruct Windows Server 2008 to reboot the system in the event of a crash. Otherwise, the system remains at a blue screen until an administrator manually reboots it.
8. Select how much debugging information you want to record in the Write Debugging Information list box. Note that if you have a large amount of RAM, you need the same amount of free disk space if you want to use the Complete Memory Dump option.
9. Enter the filename for the dump file in the Dump File text box, and select the Overwrite Any Existing File check box to maintain only a single dump file.

Real World Automatic Restart

Should you allow your servers to automatically restart in the event of a system crash? The obvious advantage is that in the vast majority of cases the system will recover and be back online in a matter of minutes without intervention. That's the good news. The bad news is that it becomes all too easy to ignore the problem unless it repeats often enough to be disruptive. And you really shouldn't be ignoring anything that causes Windows Server 2008 to crash. But having a server sitting at a "blue screen of death" (BSOD) isn't terribly helpful to production, either.

Our personal preference is to use the default of enabling automatic restart, but then change it for any situation where there has been more than a single unexplained crash.

Summary

Assume that a disaster will eventually occur, and plan accordingly. Create standardized recovery procedures, test them regularly, and keep them current. Emergencies create additional stress and lead to bad decisions. By having thoroughly tested standardized procedures and a staff that is trained in executing them, you provide a course of action without the need for on-the-spot decisions. The next chapter describes how to use the new Windows Server 2008 Backup utility.

Chapter 34

Using Backup

Windows Server Backup is an optional feature of the Windows Server 2008 operating system that provides a basic method for backing up and recovering the operating system and files and folders on the server. It consists of a Microsoft Management Console (MMC) snap-in and command-line tools.

> **Note** All backup processes require an account that is a member of the Administrators or the Backup Operators group.

Installing the Backup Service

Windows Server Backup isn't installed by default, so you need to add it using Server Manager. You must be a member of the Administrators group or the Backup Operators group to install and use Windows Server Backup.

To add Windows Server Backup, follow these steps:

1. Open Server Manager. In the left pane, click Features, and then in the right pane click Add Features to start the Add Features Wizard.
2. On the Select Features page, expand Windows Server Backup Features and select the box for Windows Server Backup (see Figure 34-1). (To schedule backups using Windows PowerShell scripts, select the box for command-line tools as well. PowerShell must be installed before you can add command-line tools.) Click Next.

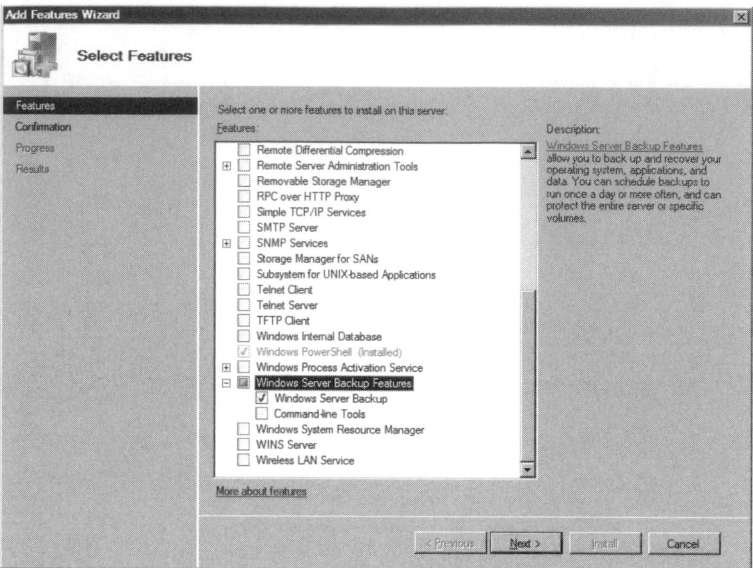

Figure 34-1 Selecting the Add Server Backup feature

3. On the Confirm Installation Selections page, review your choice, and then click Install. When the installation is complete, click Close. (If there is an error during the installation, it will be noted on the Installation Results page.)

Note The MMC snap-in isn't available on Windows Server 2008 Server Core. To manage backups for a computer with Windows Server 2008 Server Core installed, you must use the snap-in on another computer to manage the backups remotely or use command-line tools on the local computer.

Ntbackup Users

Current users of Ntbackup.exe who plan to switch to the new Windows Server Backup should consider the following:

- Settings for creating backups aren't upgraded when you upgrade to Windows Server 2008, so you'll need to reconfigure your settings.
- You need a separate, dedicated disk for running scheduled backups.
- Only NTFS-formatted volumes on a locally attached disk can be backed up.

- Windows Server Backup supports backing up to external and internal disks, DVDs, and shared folders. You can no longer back up to tape. (However, support of tape storage drivers is still included in Windows Server 2008.)

You can't recover backups created with Ntbackup.exe by using Windows Server Backup. However, a version of Ntbackup.exe is available as a download to Windows Server 2008 for users who want to recover data from backups created using Ntbackup.exe. The downloadable version of Ntbackup.exe is only for recovering backups for older versions of Windows and can't be used to create new backups in Windows Server 2008. To download Ntbackup.exe, see *http://go.microsoft.com/fwlink/?LinkId=82917*.

Scheduling a Backup

Before scheduling backups, you need to determine the following criteria:

- How many times a day and at what times you want to schedule backups
- Whether you want to back up the entire server or only selected volumes
- Whether the backup could potentially be used for system recovery
- Whether you will use one disk or multiple disks for storing backups

Choosing Volumes to Back Up

The volumes you choose to back up affect what can be recovered. Back up the entire server and you can recover the full server–all the files, data, applications, and the system state. Back up critical volumes (volumes containing operating system files) if you only want to be able to recover the operating system or system state. If you back up noncritical volumes you'll be able to recover files, applications, or data from that volume.

Designating a Storage Location

As detailed in Table 34-1, the location you choose for storing the backups will also have ramifications.

Table 34-1 Backup Locations

Storage location	What can be recovered	What cannot be recovered	Details
Local hard disk	Files, folders, applications, and volumes. System state and operating system if the backup contains all the critical volumes.	Operating system if the backup is on the same physical disk as one or more critical volumes.	The local disk you choose will be dedicated for storing your scheduled backups and will not be visible in Windows Explorer.
External hard disk	Files, folders, applications, and volumes. System state and operating system recoveries if the backup used contains all the critical volumes.		Backups can be easily moved offsite for disaster protection.
DVD, other optical media, removable media	Entire volumes.	Applications, individual files.	Media must have at least 1 gigabyte (GB) free space.

You can also back up to a remote shared folder, but your backup will be overwritten each time you create a new backup. To work around this, create subfolders in the shared folder to store your backups. Subfolders are advisable for another reason: If you back up to a folder that already contains a backup and the process fails, you will be left with no backup at all.

Creating the Backup Schedule

To create a backup schedule using the Windows Server Backup user interface, follow these steps:

1. Click Windows Server Backup on the Administrative Tools menu.
2. In the Actions pane, under Windows Server Backup, click Backup Schedule (see Figure 34-2). This opens the Backup Schedule Wizard.

Figure 34-2 Starting the Backup Schedule Wizard

3. On the Getting started page, click Next.
4. On the Select Backup Configuration page, select one of the following options, and then click Next:
   - Click Full Server to back up all volumes on the server.
   - Click Custom to back up just certain volumes, and then click Next. On the Select Backup Items page, select the check boxes for the volumes that you want to back up and clear the check boxes for the volumes that you want to exclude.

   Note Volumes that contain operating system components are included in the backup by default and cannot be excluded.

5. On the Specify Backup Time page, select and configure one of the time options (see Figure 34-3). Click Next.
   - Click Once A Day, and then enter the time to start running the daily backup.
   - Click More Than Once A Day. Under Available Time, click the time that you want the backup to start, and then click Add to move the time under Scheduled Time. Repeat for each start time that you want to add.

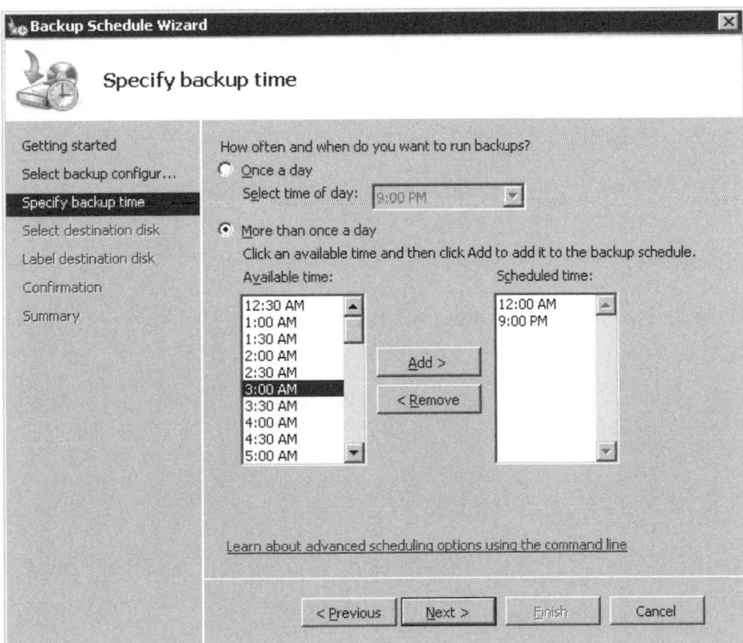

Figure 34-3 Selecting backup start times

6. On the Select Destination Disk page, select the check box for the disk that you attached for this purpose, and then click Next.

> **Note** By default, the likely disk or disks are shown in the list. These disks are external disks that can be used for moving backups offsite for disaster protection. If the disk that you want to use is not listed, click Show All Available Disks. Then select the check box next to the disk that you want to use to store the backups.

7. A message appears advising you that the selected disk will be formatted and any existing data will be deleted (Figure 34-4). Click Yes.

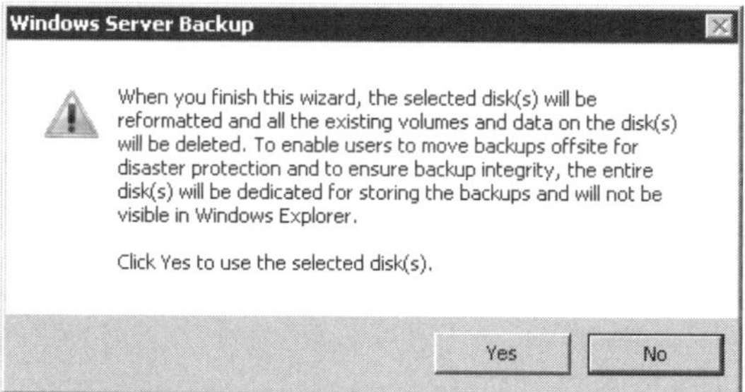

Figure 34-4 Destination disk warning

8. If there is any data that you need on the disk, do not proceed. Click No and select another disk. On the Label Destination Disk page, the disk that you selected is listed. A label that includes the computer name, the current date, the current time, and a disk name is assigned to the disk. Click Next.
9. On the Confirmation page, review the details, and then click Finish. The wizard formats the disk, which may take several minutes depending on the size of the disk.
10. On the Summary page, click Close.

The destination disk will no longer be visible in Windows Explorer—to prevent overwriting of stored data and the accidental loss of backups. It's a good idea to record and then physically attach the label information to the external disk. If you need to recover data from the backup, you will need this information to identify the disk.

Data Protection Manager 2007

If you depend on Microsoft Server–based platforms, including Microsoft SQL Server, Microsoft SharePoint Server, or Microsoft Exchange, to manage and deliver information within your organization, Microsoft Data Protection Manager 2007 is a better choice than Windows Server Backup. True, you'll have to purchase it, and it requires a dedicated stand-alone server. That's two licenses plus the cost of the hardware just to get started. So it's not as cheap as using the Windows Server Backup that comes as part of Windows Server 2008. However, Data Protection Manager (DPM) offers many benefits:

- Zero data loss recovery for Microsoft applications
- Shorter backup windows and smaller full backups thanks to patented Express Full technology. Scheduling a "backup window" is no longer necessary—a great advantage in environments where 24/7 uptime is required.
- Typical file recovery from tape can take hours; DPM performs the same function in minutes.
- DPM enables self-service user recovery, letting users access and retrieve files directly within Windows Vista. Windows XP, Microsoft Office 2007, and Microsoft Office XP applications without administrator intervention.
- Automates the scheduling of backups with Service Level Agreement–based policies.
- Advanced monitoring that alerts administrators only when an actionable error occurs.
- Efficiently uses standard hardware through innovative de-duplication technology, reducing the volume of disk needed, and providing disk-based backup at a fraction of the cost of proprietary hardware solutions.
- Customers can consolidate both disk- and tape-based backup infrastructure onto Data Protection Manager 2007, reducing the number of backup and recovery applications and managing both disk and tape from a single interface.

  DPM 2007 includes integrated support for both disk and tape media in a number of common configurations:

  - **Disk-to-Disk** Data can be moved from the source disk to the DPM-attached secondary disk using a very efficient block-level replication solution.
  - **Disk-to-Disk-to-Tape** After data is on a DPM-attached secondary disk, it can be moved to DPM-attached tape media, where it is written using the industry-standard MTF format. Data transfer rates capable of saturating an LTO3 drive are supported.
  - **Disk-to-Tape** In cases where the customer does not require secondary disk backup, data can be moved directly to DPM-attached tape drives.

Implementing a Rotating Backup Set

To increase the security of your backups, you can use multiple external disks to store backups, and rotate the disks between onsite and offsite storage locations. If your hardware is damaged, having an offsite backup allows for quick, more complete recovery.

For the best protection, visit the offsite location at regular intervals to drop off the most recent backup and retrieve the oldest backup. The disk with the oldest backup is then used for the next onsite backup.

To configure a backup schedule for multiple disks, follow these steps:

1. Click Windows Server Backup on the Administrative Tools menu.
2. In the Actions pane, under Windows Server Backup, click Backup Schedule to start the Backup Schedule Wizard.
3. On the Getting Started page, click Next.
4. On the Select Backup Configuration page, select one of the following, and then click Next:
   - Click Full Server to back up all volumes on the server.
   - Click Custom to back up particular volumes and then click Next. On the Select Backup Items page, select the check boxes for the volumes that you want to back up and clear the check boxes for the volumes that you want to exclude.

   Note Volumes that contain operating system components or applications are included in the backup by default and cannot be excluded.

5. On the Specify Backup Time page, select from the following options, and then click Next:
   - Click Once A Day and then enter the time to start running the daily backup.
   - Click More Than Once A Day. Under Available Time, click the time that you want the backup to start, and then click Add to move the time under Scheduled Time. Repeat for each additional start time.
6. On the Select Destination Disk page, select the disks to use to store backups, and then click Next.

   Note If the disks that you want to use are not listed on the Select Destination Disks page, click Show All Available Disks. Then select the check box next to each disk that you want to use.

7. A message appears, advising you that any one of the disks that you selected may be chosen to store the first backup. Click OK.
8. Another message advises you that the selected disks will be formatted and any existing data will be deleted. Click Yes.

> **Important** If there is any data that you need on the disk, do not proceed. Click No and select another disk.

9. On the Label Destination Disk page, each selected disk is listed. A label that includes your computer name, the current date, the current time, and a disk name is assigned to each disk. Click Next.
10. On the Confirmation page, review the details, and then click Finish. The wizard formats the disk, which may take several minutes depending on the size of the disk.
11. On the Summary page, click Close.

> **Note** Make a label recording the date, time, and contents and attach it to the external disk. If you need to recover data from the backup, you will need this information to identify the disk.

Modifying a Backup Schedule

The selections made when the backup schedule was created are reflected in the Backup Schedule Wizard when you run it again to make modifications.

To modify a backup schedule, follow these steps:

1. Click Start, click Administrative Tools, and then click Windows Server Backup. In the Actions pane, under Windows Server Backup, click Backup Schedule to start the Backup Schedule Wizard.
2. On the Scheduled Backup Settings page, click Modify Backup, and then click Next.
3. On the Select Backup Type page, select from the following types of backup and then click Next:
   - Click Full Server to back up all volumes on the server.
   - Click Custom to back up only certain volumes, and then click Next. On the Select Backup Items page, select the check boxes for the volumes that you want to back up and clear the check boxes for the volumes that you want to exclude from the scheduled backup.

Note Volumes that contain operating system components are included by default and cannot be excluded.

---

4. On the Specify Backup Time page, select and configure one of the following time options and then click Next:
   - Click Once A Day, and then enter the time to start running the daily backup.
   - Click More Than Once A Day. Under Available time, click the time that you want the backup to start, and then click Add to move the time under Scheduled Time. Repeat for each start time that you want to add.
5. On the Add Or Remove Backup Disks page, select one of the following options, and then click Next:
   - Do nothing
   - Add More Disks
   - Remove Current Disks
6. If you choose to add more disks to store backups, do the following:
   a. On the Select Destination Disk page, select the disk that you attached for this purpose, and then click Next.
   b. A message advises you that the selected disk will be formatted and any existing data will be deleted. Click Yes.

   Important If there is any data that you need on the disk, do not proceed. Click No and select another disk.

   c. On the Label Destination Disk page, each disk you selected is listed. A label that includes your user name, the current date, the current time, and a disk name is assigned to each disk. Click Next.
7. If you choose to remove disks, on the Remove Current Disks page, select the check box next to each disk that you want to remove from the disks used to store backups.
8. On the Confirmation page, review the details, and then click Finish. The wizard modifies the schedule and formats any added disks.
9. On the Summary page, click Close.

Stop Running Scheduled Backups

To stop running scheduled backups, follow these steps:

1. Open Administrative Tools and click Windows Server Backup.

2. In the Actions pane, under Windows Server Backup, click Backup Schedule to start the Backup Schedule Wizard.
3. On the Scheduled Backup Settings page, click Stop Backup to stop running scheduled backups and release the disk or disks where you were storing the backups. Click Next.
4. On the Confirmation page, review the details, and then click Finish. You will see a message asking you to confirm the change. Click Yes.
5. On the Summary page, click Close.

Using the Backup Once Wizard

The Backup Once Wizard is intended as a supplement to regularly scheduled backups, not as a substitution for them. For example, you can use the Backup Once Wizard for the following situations:

- Volumes that are not included in regular backups
- Volumes that contain important items before making changes, such as installing updates or new features
- Backups of regularly scheduled items to a location other than where scheduled backups are stored

Before starting the backup, review the information in "Choosing Volumes to Back Up" and "Designating a Storage Location" earlier in this chapter. If you are using a local disk, be sure the disk supports either USB 2.0 or IEEE 1394 and is internal or attached to the server. If using DVDs, make sure that a DVD writer is connected to the server and online, and that you have enough blank DVDs to store the contents of all the volumes that you want to back up. Backups to DVDs can span multiple DVDs if the backup is too large for a single DVD.

To create a manual backup on a local disk, DVD, or removable media, follow these steps:

1. Open Administrative Tools and click Windows Server Backup.
2. In the Actions pane, under Windows Server Backup, click Backup Once to start the Backup Once Wizard. On the Backup options page, click one of the following, and then click Next:
   - The Same Options That You Used In The Backup Schedule Wizard For Scheduled Backups
   - Different Options

3. On the Select Backup Configuration page, select one of the following, and then click Next:
   - Select Full Server to back up all volumes on the server.
   - Click Custom to back up only certain volumes, and then click Next. On the Select Backup Items page, select the check boxes for the volumes that you want to back up. Volumes that contain operating system components or applications are included in the backup by default to enable operating system recovery and system state recovery options. These recovery options can be excluded by clearing the Enable System Recovery check box (Figure 34-5).

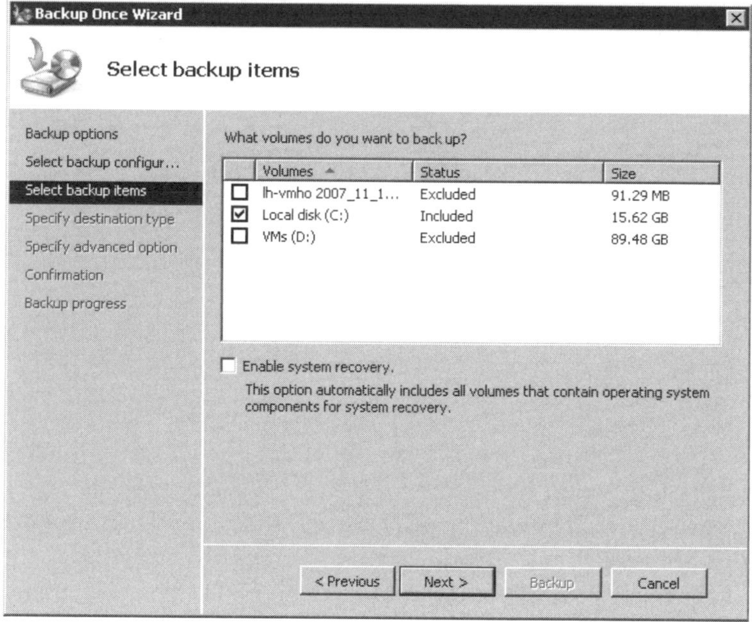

Figure 34-5 Selecting backup items

4. On the Specify Destination Type page, click Local Drives, and then click Next.
5. On the Select Backup Destination page, select the destination for the backup from the drop-down list. If you choose a hard disk, be sure that the disk has enough free space. If you choose a DVD drive or other optical media, indicate whether you want the contents to be verified after they are written to (Figure 34-6).

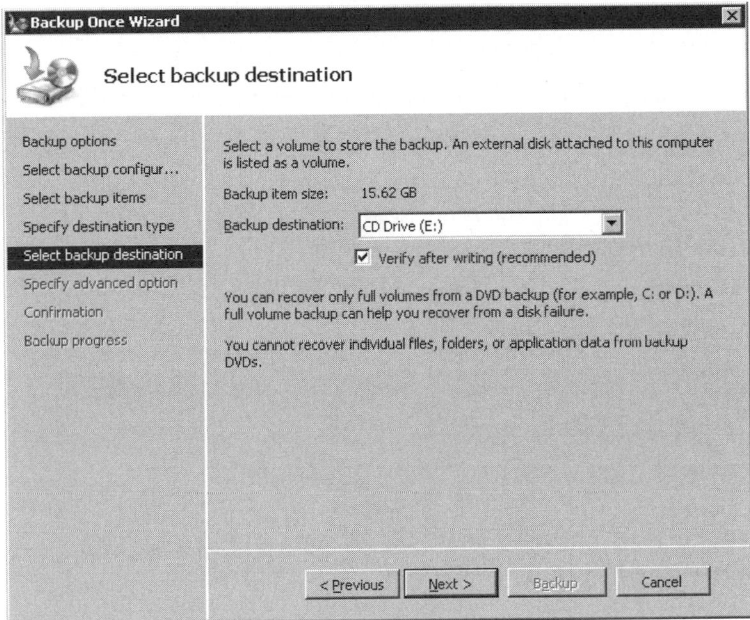

Figure 34-6 Selecting the backup destination

6. On the Specify Advanced Options page, choose whether you want to make a copy or full Volume Shadow Copy Service (VSS) backup. You should click VSS Full Backup if you are sure you are not using another product to create backups. Otherwise, click VSS Copy Backup. Click Next.
7. On the Confirmation page, review the details, then click Backup.
8. On the Backup Progress page, you can view the status of the backup. If you are backing up to a DVD, you are notified to insert the first DVD in the drive and then, if the backup is too large for a single DVD, you will be prompted for subsequent DVDs as the backup progresses.

Using the Wbadmin Command

The `Wbadmin` command allows you to back up and restore volumes and files from the command line. `Wbadmin` replaces the `Ntbackup` command released with previous versions of Windows. You can't use `Wbadmin` to recover backups created with `Ntbackup`. However, if you need to recover backups made with `Ntbackup`, you can download a version of `Ntbackup` usable with Windows Server 2008. This downloadable version of `Ntbackup` allows you to perform recoveries of legacy backups, but you cannot use it on

Windows Server 2008 to create new backups. To download this version of `Ntbackup`, see *http://go.microsoft.com/fwlink/?LinkId=82917*.

The next sections list `Wbadmin` commands and syntax. Table 34-2 lists and describes the parameters used with `Wbadmin`. For additional assistance, type **Wbadmin /?** at a command prompt.

Note Not all the `Wbadmin` commands are visible from the command line. Certain commands are available only from the Windows Recovery Environment, or are hidden but available for use. For the complete Command Reference see *http://go.microsoft.com/fwlink/?LinkId=93131*.

Wbadmin enable backup

The following enables or configures scheduled daily backup.

```
wbadmin enable backup
[-addtarget:{BackupTargetDisk | BackupTargetNetworkShare}]
[-removetarget:{BackupTargetDisk | BackupTargetNetworkShare}]
[-schedule:TimeToRunBackup]
[-include:VolumesToInclude]
[-allCritical]
[-user:UserName]
[-password:Password]
[-inheritAcl:InheritAcl]
[-quiet]
```

Wbadmin disable backup

The following disables running scheduled daily backups.

```
wbadmin disable backup
[-quiet]
```

Wbadmin start backup

The following runs a backup job.

```
wbadmin start backup
[-backupTarget:{TargetVolume | TargetNetworkShare}]
[-include:VolumesToInclude]
[-allCritical]
[-vssFull]
[-noVerify]
[-user:UserName]
[-password:Password]
[-inheritAcl:InheritAcl]
[-quiet]
```

Wbadmin stop job

The following stops a running backup or recovery job.

```
Wbadmin stop job
[-quiet]
```

Wbadmin start recovery

The following runs a recovery based on the specified parameters.

```
wbadmin start recovery
-version:VersionIdentifier
-items:VolumesToRecover | AppsToRecover | FilesOrFoldersToRecover
-itemtype:{Volume | App | File}
[-backupTarget:{VolumeHostingBackup | NetworkShareHostingBackup}]
[-machine:BackupMachineName]
[-recoveryTarget:TargetVolumeForRecovery | TargetPathForRecovery]
[-recursive]
[-overwrite:{Overwrite | CreateCopy | Skip}]
[-notrestoreacl]
[-skipBadClusterCheck]
[-quiet]
```

Wbadmin start systemstatebackup

The following creates a backup of the system state of a computer. A backup of the system state can be saved only to a locally attached disk (either internal or external). It cannot be saved to a DVD or to a remote shared folder. In addition, only the system state and system applications can be recovered from this backup–volumes and files cannot be recovered from this backup.

```
wbadmin start systemstatebackup
-backupTarget:<VolumeName>
[-quiet]
```

Wbadmin start sysstaterecovery

The following runs a system state recovery based on the supplied parameters.

```
wbadmin start sysstaterecovery
-version:VersionIdentifier
-showsummary
[-backupTarget:{VolumeName | NetworkSharePath}]
[-machine:BackupMachineName]
[-recoveryTarget:TargetPathForRecovery]
[-excludeSystemFiles]
[-quiet]
```

Wbadmin start sysrecovery

The following runs a system recovery based on specified parameters. This command can be run only from the Windows Recovery Environment, and it is not listed by default in the usage text of Wbadmin. (You can access the Windows Recovery Environment from a Windows Server 2008 installation DVD by inserting the DVD and following the steps in the wizard until you see the option Repair Your Computer. Click this link to open the System Recovery Options dialog box.)

```
wbadmin start sysrecovery
-version:VersionIdentifier
-backupTarget:{VolumeHostingBackup | NetworkShareHostingBackup}
[-machine:BackupMachineName]
[-restoreAllVolumes]
[-recreateDisks]
[-excludeDisks]
[-dfsAuth]
[-skipBadClusterCheck]
[-quiet]
```

Windows Recovery Environment

Windows Recovery Environment (Windows RE) is a recovery platform designed to automatically repair common causes of unbootable operating system installations. When the computer fails to start, Windows automatically fails over into this environment, and the Startup Repair tool in Windows RE automates diagnosis and repair. In addition, Windows RE is a starting point for various tools for manual system recovery.

Windows RE is a partial version of the operating system plus a set of tools you can use to carry out operating system or full server recoveries, using a backup that you created earlier using Windows Server Backup.

Wbadmin get versions

The following reports on the available backups.

```
wbadmin get versions
[-backupTarget:{VolumeName | NetworkSharePath}]
[-machine:BackupMachineName]
```

Wbadmin get status

The following reports the status of the current backup or recovery.

```
wbadmin get status
```

Table 34-2 Wbadmin Parameters

Parameter	Description
-addtarget	Storage location for backup. Disk is formatted before use and any existing data on it is permanently erased.
-allCritical	Automatically includes all critical volumes (volumes that contain system state data). Can be used along with the *-include* option.
-backupTarget	Storage location for this backup. Requires a hard disk drive letter (f:) or a Universal Naming Convention (UNC) path to a shared network folder (\\servername\sharename). If a shared network folder is specified, this backup will overwrite any existing backup in that location.
-dfsAuth	Marks the restore as authoritative. Can be used only when the server being recovered is hosting folders that are being replicated by Distributed File System Replication (DFSR). This parameter makes the recovered version of the replicated folders the authoritative copy, thereby overwriting the version stored on other members of the replication group. If this parameter is not used, the data is restored as a non-authoritative copy.
-excludeDisks	Can be used only with the *-recreateDisks* parameter. Must be input as a comma-delimited list of disk identifiers (as listed in the output of wbadmin get disks). Excluded disks are not partitioned or formatted. This parameter helps preserve data on disks that you do not want modified during the recovery.
-include	Comma-delimited list of volume drive letters, volume mount points, or GUID-based volume names to include in the backup.
-inheritAcl	If specified, the computer-name folder under the shared network folder inherits access control list (ACL) permissions from the shared network folder. Otherwise, the computer-name folder inherits ACLs for the user whose credentials were given when running the backup and access to the Administrators group and Backup Operators group on the computer with the shared network folder.
-items	Comma-delimited list of volumes, applications, and files to recover. If *-itemtype* is Volume, it can be only a single volume that is specified by providing the volume drive letter, volume mount point, or GUID-based volume name. If *-itemtype* is App, it can be only a single application. Applications that can be recovered include SQL Server and Windows SharePoint Services. You can also use the value *ADExtended* to recover an installation of Active Directory. If *-itemtype* is File, it can be files or directories, but it should be part of the same volume and it should be under the same parent.

Table 34-2 Wbadmin Parameters

Parameter	Description
-itemtype	Type of items to recover. Must be Volume, App, or File.
-machine	Specifies the name of the computer for which you want to recover the backup. Should be used when *-backupTarget* is specified.
-notrestoreacl	Can be used only when recovering files. Specifies to not restore the security access control lists (ACLs) of the files being recovered from backup. By default, the security ACLs are restored (the default value is true). If this parameter is used, the default ACLs for the location that the files are being restored to are applied.
-noVerify	If specified, backups written to removable media (such as a DVD) are not verified for errors. If not specified, backups written to such media are verified for errors.
-overwrite	Valid only when recovering files. Specifies the action to take when a file that is being recovered already exists in the same location. *Overwrite* causes the recovery to overwrite the existing file with the file from the backup. *CreateCopy* causes the recovery to create a copy of the existing file so that the existing file is not modified. *Skip* causes the recovery to skip the existing file and continue with recovery of the next file.
-password	Password for the user name that is specified by the parameter *-user*.
-recoveryTarget	Specifies the drive to restore to. Use if this drive is different than the one that was previously backed up. Can also be used for restorations of volumes, files, or applications. If you are restoring a volume, you can specify the volume drive letter of the alternate volume. If you are restoring a file or application, you can specify an alternate backup path.
-recreateDisks	Restores a disk configuration to the state that existed when the backup was created.
-recursive	Can be used only when recovering files. Recovers the files in the folders and all files subordinate to the specified folders. By default, only files that reside directly under the specified folders are recovered.
-removetarget	Storage location specified in the existing backup schedule.
-restoreAllVolumes	Restores all volumes from the selected backup. If this parameter is not specified, only critical volumes (volumes that contain system state data) are restored from the selected backup. Useful when you need to restore non-critical volumes during system recovery.
-schedule	Comma-delimited times of day specified as HH:MM.

Table 34-2 Wbadmin Parameters

Parameter	Description
-showsummary	Can be used only with Wbadmin start sysstaterecovery. Reports the summary of the last run of this command. This parameter cannot be accompanied by any other parameters.
-skipBadClusterCheck	Can be used only when recovering volumes. This skips checking your recovery destination disks for bad cluster information. If you are restoring to an alternate server or hardware, this switch should not be used. You can manually run the command chkdsk /b on your recovery disks at any time to check them for bad clusters, and then update the file system information accordingly.
-user	Specifies the user name with write access to the backup destination (if it is a shared network folder). The user needs to be a member of the Administrators or Backup Operators group on this computer.
-quiet	Runs the command with no prompts to the user.
-version	Specifies the version of the backup in MM/DD/YYYY-HH:MM format, as listed by wbadmin get versions.
-vssFull	If specified, performs a full backup using Volume Shadow Copy Service (VSS). Each file's history is updated to reflect that it was backed up. If this parameter is not specified, Start Backup makes a copy backup, but the history of files being backed up is not updated. Caution: Do not use this parameter when using a non-Microsoft program to back up applications.

Recovering Your Server

The backups you've created with Windows Server Backup can be used to recover your operating system, system state, volumes, application data, backup catalog, and local files and folders. Different tools are used to recover different objects. For example:

- The Recovery Wizard in Windows Server Backup can recover files, folders, applications, and volumes.
- Windows Setup disc or a separate installation of the Windows Recovery Environment can recover the operating system and the full server (all volumes).
- Wbadmin start systemstaterecovery can recover the system state.
- The Catalog Recovery Wizard can recover the backup catalog. This wizard is available only when the backup catalog is corrupted.

Note You can perform all of these recovery procedures using the *Wbadmin* command described earlier in the chapter.

Recovering Volumes

When you restore a full volume using the Recovery Wizard, all contents of the volume are restored—you can't select individual files or folders to recover. To recover just certain files or folders and not a full volume, see "Recovering Files and Folders from the Local Server" or "Recovering Files and Folders from Another Server" later in this chapter.

To recover selected volumes, follow these steps:

1. Open the Administrative Tools menu and click Windows Server Backup.
2. In the Actions pane, under Windows Server Backup, click Recover to start the Recovery Wizard.
3. On the Getting Started page, specify whether the volumes will be recovered from backups stored on this computer or another computer, and then click Next.
4. If you are recovering volumes from backups stored on another computer, do the following, and then click Next:
   a. On the Specify Location Type page, indicate whether the backup that you want to restore from is on a local drive or a remote shared folder.
   b. If you are recovering from a local drive, on the Select Backup Location page, select the location of the backup from the drop-down list. If recovering from a remote shared folder, type the path to the folder on the Specify Remote Folder page and then click Next. The path to the backup will be \\<RemoteSharedFolder>\WindowsImageBackup\<ComputerName>\<YourBackup>.
5. If you are recovering from this computer, on the Select Backup Location page, select the location of the backup from the drop-down list. If you are recovering from DVD or removable media, you are prompted to insert the device or first DVD in the series. Click Next.
6. For a recovery either from the local computer or another computer, on the Select Backup Date page, select the date from the calendar and the time from the drop-down list of backups you want to restore from.
7. On the Select Recovery Type page, click Volumes, and then click Next.
8. On the Select Volumes page, select the check boxes associated with the volumes in the Source Volume column that you want to recover. Then, from the associated drop-down list in the Destination Volume column, select the location that you want to recover the volume to. Click Next.

Important A message informs you that any data on the destination volume will be lost when you perform the recovery. Be sure the destination volume is either empty or doesn't contain information that could be needed later.

9. On the Confirmation page, review the details, and then click Recover to restore the specified volumes.
10. On the Recovery Progress page, you can view the status of the recovery operation and whether it was completed successfully.

Recovering Files and Folders from the Local Server

To recover files and folders, you must have at least one backup on an external disk or in a remote shared folder—you can't recover files and folders from backups saved to DVDs or removable media. The backup cannot be a system state backup—file and folder recovery isn't possible from a system state backup.

To recover files and folders from the current server, follow these steps:

1. Open the Administrative Tools menu and click Windows Server Backup.
2. In the Actions pane, under Windows Server Backup, click Recover to start the Recovery Wizard.
3. On the Getting Started page (Figure 34-7), select This Server and then click Next.

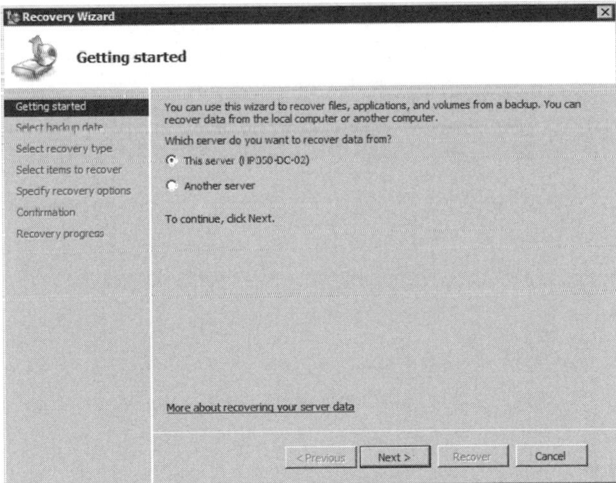

Figure 34-7 Getting started with the Recovery Wizard

4. On the Select Backup Location page, select the location of the backup from the drop-down list, and then click Next.
5. On the Select Items To Recover page, under Available Items, expand the list until the folder you want is visible. Click a folder to display the contents in the adjacent pane, click each item that you want to restore, and then click Next.
6. On the Specify Recovery Options page, under Recovery Destination, select one of the following, and then click Next:

- Original Location
- Another Location (Type the path to the location, or click Browse to select it.)

7. Under When Backup Finds Existing Files And Folders, choose one of the following options and then click Next:
   - Create Copies So I Have Both Versions Of The File Or Folder
   - Overwrite Existing Files With Recovered Files
   - Don't Recover Those Existing Files And Folders
8. On the Confirmation page, review the details, and then click Recover to restore the specified items.
9. On the Recovery Progress page, view the status of the recovery operation and whether it was completed successfully.

Recovering Files and Folders from Another Server

To recover files and folders from a backup on another computer, the backup must be on an external disk or in a remote shared folder–you can't recover individual files and folders from backups saved to DVDs or removable media. The backup cannot be a system state backup–file and folder recovery isn't possible from a system state backup.

To recover files and folders from the another server, follow these steps:

1. Open the Administrative Tools menu and click Windows Server Backup.
2. In the Actions pane, under Windows Server Backup, click Recover to start the Recovery Wizard.
3. On the Getting Started page, select Another Server and click Next.
4. On the Specify Location Type page, select one of the following and then click Next.
   - Local Drives
   - Remote Shared Folder
5. If you are recovering from a local drive, on the Select Backup Location page, select the location of the backup from the drop-down list.
6. If you are recovering from a remote shared folder, type the path to the folder on the Specify Remote Folder page and then click Next. The path to the backup will be \\<RemoteSharedFolder>\WindowsImageBackup\<ComputerName>\<YourBackup>.
7. On the Select Backup Date page, select the date from the calendar and the time from the drop-down list of backup you want to restore from. Click Next.

8. On the Select Recovery Type page, click Files And Folders, and then click Next.
9. On the Select Items To Recover page, expand the list under Available Items until the folder you want is visible. Click a folder to display the contents in the adjacent pane, click each item that you want to restore, and then click Next.
10. On the Specify Recovery Options page, under Recovery Destination, click one of the following, and then click Next:
    - Original location
    - Another location (Type the path to the location, or click Browse to select it.)
11. Under When Backup Finds Existing Files And Folders, click one of the following, and then click Next:
    - Create Copies So I Have Both Versions Of The File Or Folder
    - Overwrite Existing Files With Recovered Files
    - Don't Recover Those Existing Files And Folders
12. On the Confirmation page, review the details, and then click Recover to restore the files and folders.
13. On the Recovery Progress page, view the status of the recovery operation and whether it was completed successfully.

Recovering Applications and Data

The Recovery Wizard in Windows Server Backup can be used to recover applications and data from a backup provided that the application in question uses Volume Shadow Copy Service (VSS) technology so that it is compatible with Windows Server Backup. Also, the VSS writer for the application must have been enabled before you created the backup being used for recovery. Most applications do not enable the VSS writer by default. You will have to explicitly enable it. If the VSS writer was not enabled for the backup, you will not be able to recover applications from it.

To recover an application, follow these steps:

1. Open the Administrative Tools menu and click Windows Server Backup.
2. In the Actions pane, under Windows Server Backup, click Recover to start the Recovery Wizard.
3. On the Getting Started page, specify whether the application will be recovered from backups run on this computer or another computer, and then click Next.

4. If you are recovering applications from backups stored on another computer, do the following, and then click Next:

   a. On the Specify Location Type page, indicate whether the backup that you want to restore from is on a local drive or a remote shared folder.

   b. If you are recovering from a local drive, on the Select Backup Location page, select the location of the backup from the drop-down list. If recovering from a remote shared folder, type the path to the folder on the Specify Remote Folder page (Figure 34-8) and then click Next. The path to the backup will be \\<RemoteSharedFolder>\WindowsImageBackup\<ComputerName>\<YourBackup>.

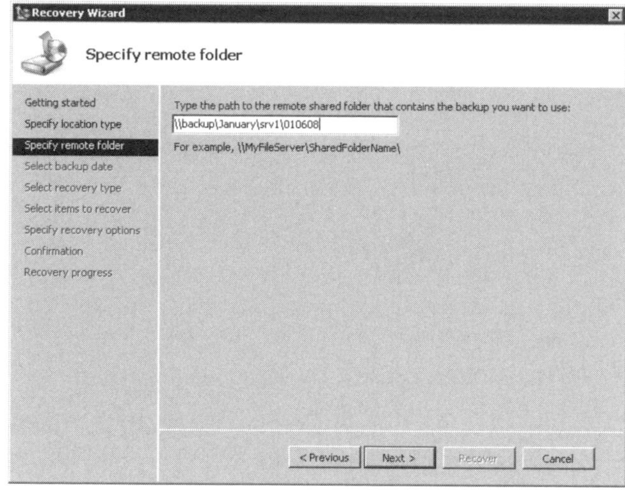

Figure 34-8 Specifying the remote shared folder

   c. If you are recovering from this computer, on the Select Backup Location page, select the location of the backup from the drop-down list, and then click Next.

5. On the Select Backup Date page, select the date from the calendar and the time from the drop-down list of the backup that you want to restore from, and then click Next.

6. On the Select Recovery Type page, click Applications, and then click Next.

7. On the Select Application page, under Applications, select the application to recover. If the backup that you are using is the most recent and the application you are recovering supports a "roll-forward" of the application database, you will see a check box labeled Do Not Perform A Roll-Forward Recovery Of The Application

Databases. Select this check box if you want to prevent Windows Server Backup from rolling forward the application database that is currently on your server. Click Next.

8. On the Specify Recovery Options page, under Recovery Destination, select one of the following options, and then click Next.
   - Recover To Original Location
   - Recover To Another Location (Type the path to the location or click Browse to select it.)
9. On the Confirmation page, review the details, and then click Recover to restore the listed items.
10. On the Recovery progress page, view the status of the recovery operation and whether it was completed successfully.

Note You can copy an application to a different location, but you cannot recover an application to a different location or computer of a different name.

Recovering the Operating System

You can recover your server operating system or full server by using a Windows Installation DVD and a backup created with Windows Server Backup. The Windows Installation disc allows access to the System Recovery Options page in the Windows Recovery Environment.

Before you start, you need to determine the following:

- Where you will recover to
- What backup you will use
- Whether you will perform an operating system–only or full server recovery
- Whether you will reformat and repartition your disks

Note When recovering to a new hard disk, the new disk must be least as large as the disk that contained the volumes that were backed up—no matter what size those volumes were. For example, if you backed up only one 50-GB volume on a 1-terabyte disk, you have to use a 1-terabyte or larger disk when restoring.

To recover the operating system or the full server using a Windows Setup disc, follow these steps:

1. Insert the Windows Setup disc into the DVD drive and turn on the computer. The Install Windows Wizard appears.
2. Specify language settings, and then click Next.
3. Click Repair Your Computer.
4. Setup searches the hard disk drives for an existing Windows installation and then displays the results in System Recovery Options. If you are recovering the operating system onto a separate computer, the list should be empty. (No operating system should be on the computer.) Click Next.
5. On the System Recovery Options page, click Windows Complete PC Restore to start the Windows Complete PC Restore Wizard.
6. Select Use The Latest Available Backup (Recommended) or Restore A Different Backup and then click Next.
7. If restoring a different backup, on the Select The Location Of The Backup page, select
   - The computer that contains the backup that you want to use, and then click Next.
   - On the Select The Backup To Restore page, click the backup you want to use. Click Next.
   - Click Advanced to browse for a backup on the network, and then click Next.

   Note If the storage location contains backups from multiple computers, be sure to click the correct row for the backups for the computer that you want to use.

8. On the Choose How To Restore The Backup page, do the following:
   a. Select Format And Repartition Disks to delete existing partitions and reformat the destination disks to be the same as the backup. This enables the Exclude Disks button. Click this button and then select the check boxes associated with any disks that you want to exclude from being formatted and partitioned. The disk that contains the backup that you are using is automatically excluded.
   b. Select the Only Restore System Disks check box to perform an operating system–only recovery.
   c. Click Install Drivers to install any needed device drivers for the hardware that you are recovering to.

   d. Click Advanced to stipulate whether the computer is restarted and the disks are checked for errors immediately after the recovery.

   e. Click Next.

9. Confirm the details for the restoration, and then click Finish.

Restoring a Backup Catalog

The details of your backups are stored in a file called a *backup catalog*. This file contains information about what volumes are backed up and where they're located. Windows Server Backup stores the catalog in the same place that you store your backups. If the catalog file is corrupted, Windows Server Backup sends you an alert and an event is added to the event log (Event 514). Before you can perform additional backups, the catalog must be restored or deleted.

If you have no backups that you can use to recover the catalog, the corrupted file must be deleted. This means information about previous backups is lost and the backups can't be accessed using Windows Server Backup. Therefore, it's important to create a new backup immediately after deleting the catalog file.

Note The Catalog Recovery Wizard is available only when Windows Backup Server detects that the catalog file is corrupted.

To recover a backup catalog, follow these steps:

1. Open the Administrative Tools menu and click Windows Server Backup.
2. In the Actions pane, under Windows Server Backup, click Recover to start the Catalog Recovery Wizard.
3. On the Specify Storage Type page, select one of the following:
   - If you don't have a backup to use to recover the catalog and you just want to delete the catalog, click I Don't Have Any Usable Backups, click Next, and then click Finish.
   - If you do have a backup that you can use, specify whether the backup is on a local drive or remote shared folder, and then click Next.
4. Do one of the following:
   - On the Select Backup Location page, if the backup is on a local drive (including DVDs), select the drive that contains the backup that you want to use from the drop-down list. If you are using DVDs, make sure the *last* DVD of the series is in the drive. Click Next.

- If the backup is on a remote shared folder, on the Specify Remote Folder page, type the path to the folder that contains the backup that you want to use, and then click Next.

5. A message informs you that backups taken after the backup that you are using for the recovery will not be accessible. Click Yes.
6. On the Confirmation page, review the details, and then click Finish to recover the catalog.
7. On the Summary page, click Close.

After the catalog recovery is completed or you have deleted the catalog, you must close and then reopen Windows Server Backup to refresh the view.

Summary

Windows Server Backup provides a basic but configurable backup and recovery tool for the server it's installed on. Scheduling backups and restoring backed-up information is easier and faster using the new Windows Server Backup.

In the next chapter, we cover the basics of fault tolerance and avoidance–important concepts in security.

Chapter 35

Planning Fault Tolerance and Avoidance

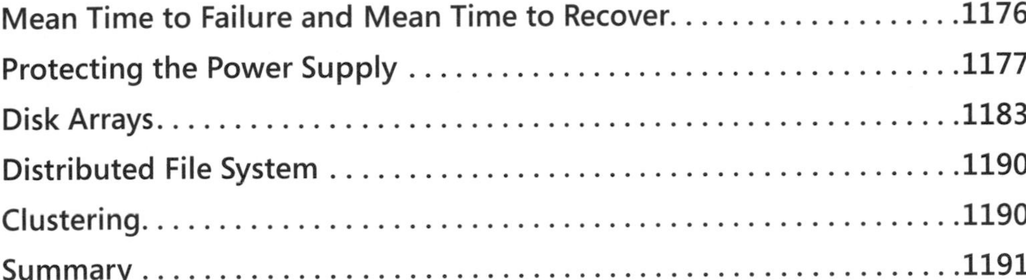

Every system administrator dreams of "five-nines" of availability (99.999 percent availability), but those who have actually committed to a five-nines Service Level Agreement (SLA) would probably describe those dreams as being closer to nightmares. Building highly available systems is hard work, and building a system that is unavailable for no more than about 5 minutes in a year is really hard work. And very, very expensive.

In this chapter, we won't cover everything you need to know to build a five-nines system—that is a very specialized task that could easily take up a whole book. We will, however, focus on some basic hardware and software tools that help you to build a more reasonable—but still highly available and fault-tolerant—Microsoft Windows Server 2008 environment. Remember, however, that even in our more reasonable three- or four-nines system, hardware and software are only a small part of the equation. Building and deploying for high availability and fault tolerance requires time, a clear understanding of the tradeoffs required, and—most important—discipline. We strongly recommend that if you're tasked with building or supporting a highly available system that you have a clear understanding of the Information Technology Infrastructure Library (ITIL) and the Microsoft Operations Framework (MOF).

More Info For more information on ITIL, see *http://en.wikipedia.org/wiki/ITIL* and *http://www.itil.co.uk*. For more information on MOF, see *http://www.microsoft.com/MOF*.

Building highly available and fault-tolerant systems involves discipline, commitment, and process. And money. The more highly available you want your systems to be, the more work is required–and the healthier your checkbook needs to be. You should have a clear understanding of the business needs you're trying to meet and a realistic assessment of the resources available to make informed decisions about what level of availability you're trying to achieve.

When planning for a highly available and fault-tolerant deployment, you should consider all points of failure and work to eliminate any single point of failure. Redundant power supplies, dual disk controllers, multiple network interface cards (multihoming), and fault-tolerant disk arrays (RAID) are all hardware strategies that you can and should employ. But whatever your hardware strategy, the single most important aspect of planning for fault tolerance is having clear, unambiguous policies and procedures that have been carefully thought out to ensure that you avoid failures–and the discipline to follow those policies and procedures.

Mean Time to Failure and Mean Time to Recover

The two most common metrics used to measure fault tolerance and avoidance are the following:

- **Mean time to failure (MTTF)** The mean time until the device will fail
- **Mean time to recover (MTTR)** The mean time it takes to recover once a failure has occurred

Although a great deal of time and energy is often spent trying to lower the MTTF, you should keep in mind that even if you have a finite failure rate, if your MTTR is zero or near zero, this may be indistinguishable from a system that hasn't failed. Downtime is generally measured as MTTR/MTTF, so increasing the MTTF will reduce the downtime. But increasing MTTF beyond a certain point can be prohibitively expensive, so you should spend both time and resources on managing and reducing the MTTR for your most likely and costly points of failure.

Most modern electronic components have a distinctive "bathtub" curve that represents their failure characteristics, as shown in Figure 35-1. During the early life of the component (referred to as the *burn-in* phase), it's more likely to fail; when this initial phase is over, a component's overall failure rate remains quite low until it reaches the end of its useful life, when the failure rate increases again.

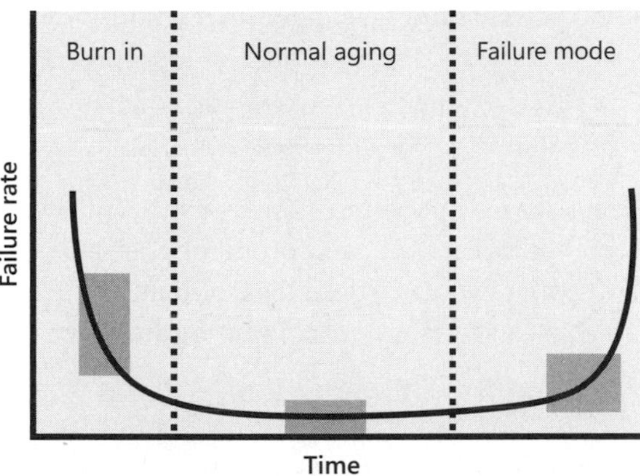

Figure 35-1 The normal statistical failure rates for mechanical and electronic components form a characteristic "bathtub" curve.

The typical commodity hard disk of 10 or 15 years ago had an MTTF on the order of three years. Today, a typical MTTF for a commodity hard disk is more likely to be 35 to 50 years, with MTTF ratings of server-oriented hard drives hitting 134 years! Do we actually believe those figures? No, we don't! A significant part of that difference is a direct result of counting only the portion of the curve in the normal aging section while taking externally caused failure out of the equation. Therefore, a hard disk that fails because of a power spike that wasn't adequately filtered doesn't count against the MTTF of the disk, nor does a disk that fails in its first week or two. This might be nice for the disk manufacturer's statistics, but it doesn't do much for the system administrator whose system has crashed because of a disk failure. As you can see, it's important to look at the total picture and carefully evaluate all the factors and failure points on your system. Only by looking at the whole system, including the recovery procedures and methodology, can you build a truly fault-tolerant system.

Protecting the Power Supply

The single biggest failure point for any network is its power supply. If you don't have power, you can't run your computers. This seems pretty obvious, and most of us slap an uninterruptible power supply (UPS) on the order when we're buying a new server, or we at least make sure that the current UPS can handle the extra load. However, this barely scratches the surface of what you can and should do to protect your network from power problems. You need to protect your network from four basic types of power problems:

- **Local power supply failure** Failure of the internal power supply on a server, router, or other network component
- **Voltage variations** Spikes, surges, sags, and longer-term brownouts

- **Short-term power outages** External power failures lasting from fractions of a second to several minutes
- **Long-term power outages** External power failures lasting from several minutes to several hours or even days

Each type of power problem poses different risks to your network and requires somewhat different protection mechanisms. The level of threat that each problem poses to your environment varies depending on the area where you are located, the quality of power available to you, and the potential loss to your business if your computers are down.

Local Power Supply Failure

Computer power supplies have made substantial gains in the last 10 years, but they are still one of the greatest risk points. All the power conditioning, uninterruptible power supplies, and external generators in the world won't help much if your server's only power supply fails. Most servers these days either come with a redundant power supply or have the option of including one. Take the option! The extra cost associated with adding a redundant power supply to a server or critical piece of network hardware is far less than the cost of downtime should the power supply fail.

If your server, router, or other piece of network hardware doesn't have the option of a redundant power supply, order a spare power supply for it when you order the original hardware. Don't count on the hardware manufacturer's "4-hour response" time, especially when you consider the cost to your business even if they actually repair the equipment in 4 hours. If you have a spare power supply in a well-marked cabinet where you can find it, you can quickly and with minimal disruption replace the failed power supply and return the equipment to full functionality. *Then* you can afford to wait patiently for the manufacturer's service response.

Real World **It's Only Useful if You Can Find It!**

Having a good supply of critical spares is a great idea, but sometimes reality intrudes. Storage can be the weak link here. Most server rooms are not nearly as spacious as administrators would like them to be, and all too often the spare parts end up jammed into a bin with inadequate identification. If your network is down and you need a power supply to get it back up, you don't want to be pawing through a jumble of spare parts looking for the right power supply.

Make every effort to develop a single, central, secure location for all spare parts. Then make sure the manufacturer's part number is visible, and clearly label the computer or computers each part is for. Finally, keep a master list of the spare parts you have and where they are located. It does you no good to have a spare power supply if you can't find it or don't know you have it.

Finally, *practice*! If you've never replaced a power supply before, and you don't have clear and detailed instructions, it will take you orders of magnitude longer to replace it when your mail server is down and everyone is yelling and the phone keeps ringing. By practicing the replacement of the power supplies in your critical hardware, you'll save time and reduce the stress involved. Document the steps you need to perform and include well-illustrated and detailed instructions on how to replace the power supplies of your critical hardware as part of your disaster recovery standard operating procedures. If you can change the power supply in a very short time, the cost of having it fail diminishes significantly. If you have to wait for your original equipment supplier to get a replacement to you, even if you're on a 4-hour response service contract, the cost can be much higher than the cost of keeping a spare around.

Voltage Variations

Even in areas with exceptionally clean power that is always available, the power that is supplied to your network inevitably fluctuates. Minor, short-term variations merely stress your electronic components, but major variations can literally fry them. You should never, ever simply plug a computer into an ordinary wall socket without providing some sort of protection against voltage variations. The following sections describe the types of variations and the best way to protect your equipment against them.

Spikes

Spikes are large but short-lived increases in voltage. They can occur because of external factors, such as lightning striking a power line, or because of internal factors, such as a large motor starting. The most common causes of severe voltage spikes, however, are external and beyond your control. The effects can be devastating. A nearby lightning strike can easily send a spike of 1000 volts or more into equipment designed to run on 110 to 120 volts. Few, if any, electronic components are designed to withstand large voltage spikes of several thousand volts, and almost all will suffer damage if they're not protected from them.

Protection from spikes comes in many forms, from the $19.95 power strip with built-in surge protection that you can buy at your local hardware store to complicated arrays of transformers and specialized sacrificial transistors that are designed to die so that others may live. Unfortunately, those $19.95 power strips just aren't good enough. They *are* better than nothing, but barely—they have a limited ability to withstand really large spikes.

More specialized (and more expensive, of course) surge protectors that are specifically designed to protect computer networks are available from various companies. They differ in cost and in their ability to protect against really large spikes. There's a fairly direct correlation between the cost of these products and their rated capacity and speed of action within any company's range of products, but the cost for a given level of protection can differ significantly from company to company. As always, if the price sounds too good to be true, it is.

In general, these surge protectors are designed to work by sensing a large increase in voltage and creating an alternate electrical path for that excessive voltage that doesn't allow it to get through to your server. In the most severe spikes, the surge protectors should destroy themselves before allowing the voltage to get through to your server. The effectiveness of these stand-alone surge protectors depends on the speed of their response to a large voltage increase and the mechanism of failure when their capacity is exceeded. If the surge protector doesn't respond quickly enough to a spike, bad things will happen.

Many UPSs also provide protection from spikes. They have built-in surge protectors, plus isolation circuitry that tends to buffer the effects of spikes. The effectiveness of the spike protection in a UPS is not directly related to its cost, however—the overall cost of the UPS is more a factor of its effectiveness as an alternative power source. Your responsibility is to read the fine print and understand the limitations of the surge protection a given UPS offers. Also remember that just as with simple surge protectors, large voltage spikes can cause the surge protection to self-destruct rather than allow the voltage through to your server. That's the good news; the bad news is that instead of having to replace just a surge protector, you're likely to have to repair or replace the UPS.

There are two basic kinds of UPS: the always-online kind that you should be buying for your server room, and the off-line kind priced for the consumer market. An online UPS has a battery that powers the circuit that your server is connected to, and a circuit that charges the battery. No direct power is ever applied to the server. An offline UPS has a battery, a circuit that senses when power is no longer available, and a circuit that supplies battery power when the power-sensing circuit decides it is necessary.

Finally, one other spike protection mechanism can be helpful—the constant voltage transformer. You're not likely to see one unless you're in a large industrial setting, but they are often considered to be a sufficient replacement for other forms of surge protection. Unfortunately, they're not really optimal for surge protection. They do filter some excess voltage, but a large spike is likely to find its way through. However, in combination with either a fully protected UPS or a good stand-alone surge protector, a constant voltage transformer can be quite effective. They also provide additional protection against other forms of voltage variation that surge protectors alone can't begin to manage.

Surges

Voltage surges and spikes are often discussed interchangeably, but we'd like to make a distinction here. For our purposes, a *surge* lasts longer than most spikes and isn't nearly as large. Most surges last a few hundred milliseconds and are rarely more than 1000 volts. They can be caused by many of the same factors that cause voltage spikes.

Providing protection against surges is somewhat easier than protecting against large spikes. Most of the protection mechanisms just discussed also adequately handle surges.

In addition, most constant voltage transformers are sufficient to handle surges and might even handle them better if the surge is so prolonged that it threatens to overheat and burn out a simple surge protector.

Sags

Voltage *sags* are short-term reductions in the voltage delivered. They aren't complete voltage failures or power outages and are shorter than full-scale brownouts. Voltage sags can drop the voltage well below 100 volts on a 110- to 120-volt normal line and cause most servers to reboot if protection isn't provided.

Stand-alone surge protectors provide no defense against sags. You need a UPS or a very good constant voltage transformer to prevent damage from a voltage sag. Severe sags can overcome the rating of all but the best constant voltage transformers, so you generally shouldn't use constant voltage transformers as the sole protection against sags. A UPS, with its battery power supply, is an essential part of your protection from problems caused by voltage sag.

Brownouts

A *brownout* is a planned, deliberate reduction in voltage from your electric utility company. Brownouts most often occur in the heat of the summer and are designed to protect the utility company from overloading. They are *not* designed to protect the consumer, however.

In general, a brownout reduces the available voltage by 5 to 20 percent from the normal value. A constant voltage transformer or a UPS provide excellent protection against brownouts, within limits. Prolonged brownouts might exceed your UPS's ability to maintain a charge at the same time that it is providing power at the correct voltage to your equipment. Monitor the health of your UPS carefully during a brownout, especially because the risk of a complete power outage increases if the power company's voltage reduction strategy proves insufficient.

The best protection against extended brownouts is a constant voltage transformer of sufficient rating to fully support your critical network devices and servers. This transformer takes the reduced voltage provided by your power company and increases it to the rated output voltage. A good constant voltage transformer can handle most brownouts for an extended time without problems, but you should still supplement the constant voltage transformer with a quality UPS and surge protection between the transformer and the server or network device. This extra protection is especially important while the power company is attempting to restore power to full voltage, because during this period you run a higher risk of experiencing power and voltage fluctuations.

Short-Term Power Outages

Short-term power outages last from a few milliseconds to a few minutes. They can be caused by either internal or external events, but you can rarely plan for them even if they are internal. A server that is unprotected from a short-term power outage will, at the minimum, reboot or, at the worst, fail catastrophically.

You can best protect against a short-term power outage by using a UPS in combination with high-quality spike protection. Be aware that many momentary interruptions of power are accompanied by large spikes when the power is restored. Further, a series of short-term power outages often occur consecutively, causing additional stress to electronic components

Long-Term Power Outages

Long-term power outages, lasting from an hour or so to several days, are usually accompanied by other, more serious problems. Long-term power outages can be caused by storms, earthquakes, fires, and the incompetence of electric power utilities, among other things. As such, plans for dealing with long-term power outages should be part of an overall disaster recovery plan. (See Chapter 33, "Disaster Planning," for more on disaster planning.)

Protection against long-term power outages really becomes a decision about how long you want or need to function if all power is out. If you need to function long enough to be able to gracefully shut down your network, a simple UPS or a collection of them will be sufficient, assuming that you've sized the UPS correctly. However, if you need to be sure that you can maintain the full functionality of your Windows Server 2008 network during an extended power outage, you're going to need a combination of one or more UPSs and an auxiliary generator.

If your situation requires an auxiliary generator to supplement your UPSs, you should carefully plan your power strategy to ensure that you provide power to all the equipment that the network will require in the event of a long-term power outage. Test your solution to make sure you didn't miss anything! Further, you should regularly test the effectiveness of your disaster recovery plans and make sure that all key personnel know how to start the auxiliary generator manually in the event it doesn't start automatically.

Finally, you should have a regular preventive maintenance (PM) program in place that services and tests the generator and ensures that it is ready and functioning when you need it. This PM program should include both static tests and full-load tests on a regular basis, and it should also call for periodically replacing the fuel to the generator. One of the best ways to do all this is to plan and execute a "disaster day," where your entire disaster recovery plan is tested in as close to real-world conditions as possible, including running your entire operation from the backup generator.

Disk Arrays

The most common hardware malfunction is probably a hard disk failure. Happily, it's one of the easiest to protect against. Even though hard disks have become more reliable over time, they are still subject to failure, especially during their first month or so of use. They are also vulnerable to both catastrophic and degenerative failures caused by power problems. Disk arrays are the norm for most servers, and Windows Server 2008 includes software redundant array of independent disks (RAID) as well supporting a wide range of RAID-specific hardware. The choice of software or hardware RAID, and the particulars of how you configure your RAID system, can significantly affect the cost of your servers. To make an informed choice for your environment and needs, you must understand the tradeoffs and the differences in fault tolerance, speed, configurability, and so on.

Hardware vs. Software

RAID can be implemented at the hardware level, using RAID controllers, or at the software level, either by the operating system or by a third-party add-on. Windows Server 2008 supports both hardware RAID and its own software RAID.

Hardware RAID implementations require specialized controllers and cost significantly more than an equal level of software RAID. However, for that extra price, you get a faster, more flexible, and more fault-tolerant RAID. When compared to the software RAID provided in Windows Server 2008, a good hardware RAID controller supports more levels of RAID, on-the-fly reconfiguration of the arrays, hot-swap and hot-spare drives (discussed later in this chapter), and dedicated, battery-backed caching of both reads and writes.

Implementing software RAID in Windows Server 2008 requires that you first convert your disks to dynamic disks. That means your disks will no longer be locally available to other operating systems, although this really shouldn't be a problem in a production environment because dual-boot is rarely used there. However, you should consider carefully whether you want to convert your boot disk to a dynamic disk. Dynamic disks can be more difficult to access if a problem occurs, and the Windows Server 2008 setup and installation program provides only limited support. For maximum fault tolerance, we recommend using hardware mirroring (RAID-1) on your boot drive; if you do use software mirroring, make sure that you create the required fault-tolerant boot floppy disk and test it thoroughly before you need it. (See Chapter 33.)

RAID Levels for Fault Tolerance

Except for level 0, RAID is a mechanism for storing sufficient information on a group of hard disks such that even if one hard disk in the group fails, no information is lost. Some RAID arrangements go even further, providing protection in the event of multiple hard disk failures. The more common levels of RAID and their appropriateness in a fault-tolerant environment are shown in Table 35-1.

Table 35-1 RAID Levels and Their Fault Tolerance

Level	Number of disks*	Speed	Fault tolerance	Description
0	*N*	Best	- - -	Striping alone. Not fault-tolerant—it actually increases your risk of failure—but does provide for the fastest read and write performance.
1	2*N*	Good	Better	Mirror or duplex. Slightly faster read than single disk, but no gain during write operations. Failure of any single disk causes no loss in data and minimal performance hit.
3	*N*+1	Better	Good	Byte-level parity. Data is striped across multiple drives at the byte level with the parity information written to a single dedicated drive. Reads are much faster than with a single disk, but writes operate slightly slower than a single disk because parity information must be generated and written to a single disk. Failure of any single disk causes no loss of data but can cause a significant loss of performance.
4	*N*+1	Better	Good	Block-level parity with a dedicated parity disk. Similar to RAID-3 except that data is striped at the block level.
5	*N*+1	Good	Better	Interleaved block-level parity. Parity information is distributed across all drives. Reads are much faster than a single disk but writes are significantly slower. Failure of any single disk provides no loss of data but results in a major reduction in performance.
0+1 and 10	2*N*	Best	Better	Striped mirrored disks or mirrored striped disks. Data is striped across multiple mirrored disks or multiple striped disks are mirrored. Failure of any one disk causes no data loss and no speed loss. Failure of a second disk could result in data loss. Faster than a single disk for both reads and writes.
Other	Varies	Best	Best	Array of RAID arrays. Different hardware vendors have different proprietary names for this RAID concept. Excellent read and write performance. Failure of any one disk results in no loss of performance and continued redundancy.

* In the Number of Disks column, *N* refers to the number of hard disks required to hold the original copy of the data. Good, Better, and Best show relative improvement or deterioration compared to a system using no version of RAID. The scale peaks at Best.

When choosing the RAID level to use for a given application or server, consider the following factors:

- **Intended use** Will this application be primarily read-intensive, such as file serving, or will it be predominantly write-intensive, such as a transactional database?
- **Fault tolerance** How critical is this data, and how much can you afford to lose?
- **Availability** Does this server or application need to be available at all times, or can you afford to be able to reboot it or otherwise take it offline for brief periods?
- **Performance** Is this application or server heavily used, with large amounts of data being transferred to and from it, or is this server or application less I/O-intensive?
- **Cost** Are you on a tight budget for this server or application, or is the cost of data loss or unavailability the primary driving factor?

You need to evaluate each of these factors when you decide which type of RAID to use for a server or portion of a server. No single answer fits all cases, but the final answer requires you to carefully weigh each of these factors and balance them against your situation and your needs. The following sections take a closer look at each factor and how it weighs in the overall decision-making process.

Intended Use

The intended use, and the kind of disk access associated with that use, plays an important role in determining the best RAID level for your application. Think about how write-intensive the application is and whether the manner in which the application uses the data is more sequential or random. Is your application a three-square meals a day kind of application, with relatively large chunks of data being read or written at the same time, or is it more of a grazer or nibbler, reading and writing little bits of data from all sorts of different places?

If your application is relatively write-intensive, you'll want to avoid software RAID if possible and avoid RAID-5 if other considerations don't force you to use it. With RAID-5, any application that requires more than 50 percent writes to reads is likely to be at least somewhat slower, if not much slower, than it would be on a single disk. You can mitigate this and even overcome it by using more but smaller drives in your array and by using an intelligent hardware controller with a large cache to offload the parity processing. RAID-1, in either a mirror or duplex configuration, provides a high degree of fault tolerance with no significant penalty during write operations–a good choice for the Windows Server 2008 system disk.

Important Mirroring won't protect you from data corruption caused by a catastrophic power interruption to a write-cached system disk. Disabling write caching on boot and system volumes is highly recommended if your system isn't protected by a UPS. And no UPS can protect you from tripping over the power cord. A good, battery-backed cache, however, will protect you even then.

If your application is primarily read-intensive, and the data is stored and referenced sequentially, RAID-3 or RAID-4 might be a good choice. Because the data is striped across many drives, you have parallel access to it, improving your throughput. And because the parity information is stored on a single drive rather than dispersed across the array, sequential read operations don't have to skip over the parity information and are therefore faster. However, write operations are substantially slower, and the single parity drive can become an I/O bottleneck during write operations.

If your application is primarily read-intensive and not necessarily sequential (a good description of most file servers), RAID-5 is an obvious choice. It provides a good balance of speed and fault tolerance, and the cost is substantially lower than the cost of RAID-1. Disk accesses are evenly distributed across multiple drives, and no one drive has the potential to be an I/O bottleneck. However, writes require calculation of the parity information and the extra write of that parity, slowing down write operations.

If your application provides other mechanisms for data recovery or uses large amounts of temporary storage (which doesn't require fault tolerance), a simple RAID-0 with no fault tolerance but fast reads and writes is a possibility.

Under the Hood Hot Spares

Most server class RAID controllers support one or more *hot spare* disks. A hot spare disk is one that is not used by the array, but is ready to go immediately in the event of a failure. Few hard disks fail instantly and catastrophically; they usually provide advance warning of impending failure. RAID controllers can monitor the health of the disks in the array, and if a failure is imminent, they will automatically remove a failing disk and replace it with the hot spare. This can save rebuild time and ensure that the maximum fault tolerance is maintained. If your array supports a hot spare, taking advantage of it is a good idea.

Fault Tolerance

Carefully examine the fault tolerance of each of the possible RAID choices for your intended use. All RAID levels except RAID-0 provide some degree of fault tolerance, but the effect of a failure and the ability to recover from subsequent failures can be different.

If a drive in a RAID-1 mirror or duplex array fails, you still have a full, complete, exact copy of the data. You have full-speed access to your data as well, because the remaining disk is treated just like a single, stand-alone disk. There is only a slight degradation caused by not being able to read from both disks simultaneously. So, everything is fine, right? Well, yes, except that until the failed disk is replaced, you have no fault tolerance.

None. Once you replace the failed disk, overall performance is *significantly* reduced while the new disk is initialized and the mirror is rebuilt.

Under the Hood Array Rebuilding

On most server-class hardware RAID controllers you can configure the speed at which an array is rebuilt. There is a direct tradeoff between the speed of rebuilding and the performance degradation of the array, and you can usually tune this to balance the need for fault tolerance with the need for disk speed.

If your RAID controller supports a command-line interface, you should be able to set the array rebuilding to favor data access performance during prime working hours, but then increase the speed of rebuilding during off-hours. For example, we have a pair of basic tasks in the Task Scheduler on our HP ML-350 G5 to change the rebuild priority of the P400 controller to high at 10:00 P.M. each night, and back to low at 6:00 A.M. By combining this with a built-in hot spare, the entire process is both automated and appropriately prioritized. The HP Array Configuration Utility Command Line Interface (HPACUCLI.EXE) command to set the rebuild priority to high is:

```
hpacucli.exe controller slot=5 modify rebuildpriority=high
```

If one of the data disks fails in a RAID-3 or RAID 4 array, performance degrades significantly and immediately if the failed disk is one of the data disks. Each read or write requires that the missing data be reconstructed from the parity information, and you'll have no fault tolerance until the failed disk is replaced. If the parity disk fails, you'll still have no fault tolerance until it is replaced, but performance will also be normal, with no degradation. Once you replace the failed disk, overall performance is significantly reduced while the new disk is initialized and the parity information or data is rebuilt.

In a RAID-5 array, the loss of any disk results in a significant performance degradation, and your fault tolerance will be gone until you replace the failed disk. Once you replace the disk, you won't return to fault tolerance until the entire array has a chance to rebuild itself, and performance is seriously degraded during the rebuild process.

RAID systems that are arrays of arrays can provide for multiple failure tolerance. These arrays provide for multiple levels of redundancy and are appropriate for mission-critical applications that must be able to withstand the failure of more than one drive in an array.

Under the Hood **Multiple Disk Controllers Provide Increased Fault Tolerance**

Spending the money for a hardware RAID system increases your overall fault tolerance, but it can still leave a single point of failure in your disk subsystem: the disk controller itself. Although failures of the disk controller are certainly less common, they do happen. Many hardware RAID systems are based on a single multiple-channel controller—certainly a better choice than those based on a single-channel controller—but an even better solution is a RAID system based on multiple identical controllers. In these systems, the failure of a single disk controller is not catastrophic but simply an annoyance. In RAID-1, this technique is known as *duplexing*, but it is also common with many of the proprietary arrays of arrays that are available from server vendors and in the third-party market.

Availability

All levels of RAID, except RAID-0, provide higher availability than a single drive. However, if availability is expanded to also include the overall performance level during failure mode, some RAID levels provide definite advantages over others. Specifically, RAID-1, mirroring/duplexing, provides enhanced availability when compared to RAID levels 3, 4, and 5 during failure mode. There is minimal performance degradation when compared to a single disk if one half of a mirror fails, whereas a RAID-5 array has substantially compromised performance until you replace the failed disk and rebuild the array.

In addition, RAID systems based on an array of arrays can provide higher availability than RAID levels 1 through 5. Running on multiple controllers, these arrays are able to tolerate the failure of more than one disk and the failure of one of the controllers, providing protection against the single point of failure inherent in any single-controller arrangement. RAID-1 that uses duplexed disks running on different controllers—as opposed to RAID-1 that uses mirroring on the same controller—also provides this additional protection and improved availability.

Hot-swap drives and hot-spare drives can further improve availability in critical environments; this is especially true for hot-spare drives. By providing for automatic failover and rebuilding, they can reduce your exposure to catastrophic failure and provide for maximum availability.

Performance

The relative performance of each RAID level depends on the intended use. The best compromise for many situations is arguably RAID-5, but you should be suspicious of that compromise if your application is fairly write-intensive. Especially for relational database data and index files where the database is moderately or highly write-intensive, the performance hit of using RAID-5 can be substantial. A better alternative is to use RAID0+1 or RAID10.

Whatever level of RAID you choose for your particular application, it will benefit from using more small disks rather than a few large disks. The more drives contributing to the stripe of the array, the greater the benefit of parallel reading and writing you'll be able to realize–and your array's overall speed will improve.

Cost

The delta in cost between RAID configurations is primarily the cost of drives, potentially including the cost of additional array enclosures because more drives are required for a particular level of RAID. RAID-1, either duplexing or mirroring, is the most expensive of the conventional RAID levels, because it requires at least 33 percent more raw disk space for a given amount of net storage space than other RAID levels.

Another consideration is that RAID levels that include mirroring or duplexing must use drives in pairs. Therefore, it's more difficult (and more expensive) to add on to an array if you need additional space on the array. A net 72-GB RAID10 array, composed of four 36-GB drives, requires four more 36-GB drives to double in size–a somewhat daunting prospect if your array cabinet has bays for only six drives, for example. A net 72-GB RAID5 array of three 36-GB drives, however, can be doubled in size simply by adding two more 36-GB drives, for a total of five drives.

Note The latest 2.5-inch SAS drive-array cabinets have substantially improved the overall space requirements for building large, wide, RAID arrays. In a space big enough for a pair of regular hard disks, you can fit an 8-drive, 2.5-inch, hot-swap SAS array.

Hot-Swap and Hot-Spare Disk Systems

Hardware RAID systems can provide for both hot-swap and hot-spare capabilities. A hot-swap disk system allows you to remove failed hard disks and insert a replacement disk into the array without powering down the system or rebooting the server. When the new disk is inserted, it is automatically recognized and either will be automatically configured into the array or can be manually configured into it. Additionally, many hot-swap RAID systems allow you to add hard disks into empty slots dynamically–automatically or manually increasing the size of the RAID volume on the fly without a reboot.

A *hot-spare* RAID configuration uses an additional, preconfigured disk or disks to automatically replace a failed disk. Older versions of these systems often don't support hot-swapped hard disks so that the failed disk can't be removed until the system can be powered down, but full fault tolerance is maintained by having the hot spare available.

Distributed File System

The Distributed File System (DFS) is primarily a method of simplifying the view that users have of the available storage on a network–but it is also, when configured appropriately, a highly fault-tolerant storage mechanism. By configuring your DFS root on a Windows Server 2008 domain controller, you can create a fault-tolerant, replicated, distributed file system that gives you great flexibility while presenting your user community with a cohesive and easy-to-navigate network file system.

When you create a fault-tolerant DFS root on a domain controller and replicate it and the links below it across multiple servers, you create a highly fault-tolerant file system that has the added benefit of distributing the load evenly across the replicated shares, giving you a substantial scalability improvement as well. See Chapter 12, "Managing File Resources," for more on setting up your DFS and ensuring that replication works correctly.

Clustering

Windows Server 2008 supports two different kinds of high-availability clustering, both of which can greatly improve your fault tolerance:

- For many TCP/IP-based applications, the Network Load Balancing service provides a simple, "shared nothing," fault-tolerant application server.
- Server clusters provide a highly available fault-tolerant environment that can run applications, provide network services, and distribute loads. Server clusters are available only with Windows Server 2008, Enterprise Edition and Windows Server 2008, Datacenter Edition.

Network Load Balancing

The Network Load Balancing service allows TCP/IP-based applications to be spread dynamically across up to 32 servers. If a particular server fails, the load and connections to that server are dynamically balanced to the remaining servers, providing a highly fault-tolerant environment without the need for specialized, shared hardware. Individual servers within the cluster can have different hardware and capabilities, and the overall job of load balancing and failover happens automatically, with each server in the cluster running its own copy of Wlbs.exe, the Network Load Balancing control program.

Failover Clustering

Failover clustering (generally called *server clusters* in earlier versions of Windows Server) uses a shared resource between nodes of the cluster. This resource can be a shared SAS or

Fibre Channel–attached disk array or iSCSI SAN. Each server in the cluster is connected to the shared resource, and the common database that manages the clustering is stored on this shared disk resource. Nodes in the cluster generally have identical hardware and identical capabilities. Although creating a failover cluster with dissimilar nodes is technically possible, this is not supported and not recommended.

Failover clusters provide a highly fault-tolerant and configurable environment for mission-critical services and applications. Applications don't need to be specially written to be able to take advantage of the fault tolerance of a failover cluster, although if the application is written to be clustering-aware, it can take advantage of additional controls and features in a failover and fallback scenario.

Summary

Building a highly available and fault-tolerant system requires you to carefully evaluate both your requirements and your resources to eliminate single points of failure within the system. You should evaluate each of the hardware subsystems within the overall system for fault tolerance, and ensure that recovery procedures are clearly understood and practiced to reduce recovery time in the event of a failure. Uninterruptible power supplies, RAID systems, distributed file systems, and clustering are all methods for improving fault tolerance. In the next chapter, we discuss the registry: what it is, how it's structured, and how to back it up and restore it.

Chapter 36

Managing the Registry

The registry is viewed with apprehension by many system administrators because it's the central repository of system configuration settings. Making mistakes while editing the registry can have undesirable consequences, but it's not so different from using power tools, which can cause powerful consequences if misused. If you know what you're doing and take a few simple safety precautions, you can take advantage of a powerful tool–like the registry–without accidentally cutting off something important.

Introducing the Registry

The registry is a binary database that organizes all of a system's configuration settings into a hierarchy. Applications, system components, device drivers, and the Windows kernel all use the registry to store their own preferences, read them back again, and obtain information about the system's hardware configuration, current user's preferences, and default settings that should be used when no predefined settings exist (such as when a new user logs on to the computer for the first time).

The Origins of the Registry

Back in the days of Windows 3.1, applications and Windows stored configuration information in .INI files. These files were simple to edit, which was both a blessing and a curse—users could easily make changes when needed, but they could also easily make changes when they *weren't* needed. The proliferation of Windows applications soon meant that computers were littered with dozens of .INI files, each with its own combination of settings—not all of which were documented or even understood by anyone other than the application programmers.

Windows NT 3.1 largely eliminated .INI files, replacing them with the registry. Indeed, the Windows NT 3.1 registry has some important features that have survived more or less intact to Windows Server 2008:

- Registry data is organized by category, so settings that pertain to a single user (such as a choice of default wallpaper) are kept separate from settings for other users or the system's own internal parameters. Each setting is stored as an independent piece of data.
- Registry data is stored in binary database files on disk; the only way to view or edit these files is to use special-purpose tools that call the registry access routines of the Win32 API.
- Each data item in the registry has a data type, such as REG_DWORD (a long integer) or REG_SZ (an ASCII string). The system's registry editors enforce these data types, so you can't put a string where a number belongs. This restriction helps weed out one class of mistakes—well-intentioned but misinformed attempts to put a round peg into a square hole.
- Like every other object in the system, each registry item has an owner, and it can have its own independent set of security access control lists (SACLs) and auditing controls.
- With appropriate permissions, administrators or programs on one computer can connect to, read, and modify the registries of remote computers.

A remarkable aspect of the Windows Server 2008 registry is how little it has changed from the Windows NT 4 version. The binary structures used to store the data remain the same, as do the structural underpinnings discussed later in this chapter.

Real World Being on Your Best Behavior

Microsoft continually warns us that editing the registry is dangerous. Is it really, or are they just covering themselves? The answer is somewhere between the two extremes. Because the registry is used by virtually every part of Windows, and because most programmers are lazy when it comes time to write code to check the validity of values that come from the registry, making an improper or ill-advised registry change can certainly harm your computer. Having said that, however, if you're careful and attentive, you don't need to be afraid of the registry. A few simple rules will keep you out of trouble:

- Don't edit a part of the registry for fun. If you don't know how a certain change will affect your system, don't make that change unless you can live with the consequences.
- Be careful about adding new values or keys. Software pays attention only to keys that have names it understands. Adding a new key or value in the hope that some component will recognize it and change its behavior is like adding a new switch labeled "Jet Boost" to your car's dashboard and expecting it to increase your car's speed. The exception to this rule is that Microsoft often uses code that can recognize a hidden (or at least under-documented) key and change its behavior accordingly.
- Maintain a current backup of your system state. Regedit.exe provides import and export functionality particularly suitable for maintaining backups and restoring them when needed. These two features are discussed in "Importing and Exporting Registry Data" later in the chapter.

How Registry Data Is Used

Now that you have a general understanding of what the registry's data is used for, it's time to get more specific. Registry data is used in five areas:

- Registry data is used during setup, installation, configuration, and removal of the operating system itself, of operating system components such as Internet Information Services (IIS) or Certificate Services, and of hardware devices. Any time you see an Add/Remove Something-Or-Other Wizard, you can bet that registry data is being used.

- The Windows Server 2008 kernel uses the information gathered at boot time to figure out which device drivers to load and in what order; it also stores information needed by those drivers in the registry.
- Device drivers use the data written by the recognizer and the kernel to configure themselves to work with the physical hardware in the computer.
- System tools and applications, such as control panels and some MMC snap-ins, read and write configuration data in the registry.
- Applications can store their own settings in the registry; in addition, they can read (and possibly write) the data gathered by other software that uses the registry.

Note that during the boot, kernel, and device-driver phases, the system can't use the disk. Until the device drivers are loaded, the system can't "talk" to the disk. We'll cover how the system works around this seemingly severe limitation in "Volatile Keys" later in the chapter.

Functional Changes in Windows Server 2008

While most of the registry is unchanged from Windows Server 2003, there are modifications that reflect new processes and structures in Windows Server 2008. Table 36-1 displays those registry changes

Table 36-1 Additions and Changes in Registry Functions in Server 2008

Category	Setting	Name	Default Value	Possible Values
Interface	Don't Open Server Manager At Logon	HKEY_LOCAL_MACHINE\SOFTWARE\Microsoft\Server Manager\DoNotOpenServerManagerAtLogon	0	0 causes the window to open normally, 1 prevents opening.
Interface	Don't Open Configuration Tasks At Logon	HKEY_LOCAL_MACHINE\SOFTWARE\Microsoft\Server Manager\oobe	0	0 causes the window to open normally, 1 prevents opening.
NDES (Network Device Enrollment Service)	Refresh	HKEY_LOCAL_ROOT\Software\Microsoft\Cryptography\MSCEP	7	Number of days that pending requests are kept in the NDES database.
NDES	Enforce Password	HKEY_LOCAL_ROOT\Software\Microsoft\Cryptography\MSCEP	1	1 means NDES requires a password for enrollment requests. 0 (zero) means passwords are not required.

Table 36-1 Additions and Changes in Registry Functions in Server 2008

Category	Setting	Name	Default Value	Possible Values
NDES	PasswordMax	HKEY_LOCAL_ROOT\Software\Microsoft\Cryptography\MSCEP	5	Maximum number of cached passwords.
NDES	PasswordValidity	HKEY_LOCAL_ROOT\Software\Microsoft\Cryptography\MSCEP	60	Number of minutes a password remain valid.
NDES	PasswordVDir	HKEY_LOCAL_ROOT\Software\Microsoft\Cryptography\MSCEP		If set, NDES accepts password requests only from the defined virtual directory. If the value is empty or not configured, NDES accepts password requests from any virtual directory.
NDES	CacheRequests	HKEY_LOCAL_ROOT\Software\Microsoft\Cryptography\MSCEP	20	Number of minutes certificates are kept in the database.
NDES	CAType	HKEY_LOCAL_ROOT\Software\Microsoft\Cryptography\MSCEP	Based on setup	Identifies the type of CA that NDES is linked to. The value 1 means it is an enterprise CA; the value 0 means it is a standalone CA.
NDES	SigningTemplate	HKEY_LOCAL_ROOT\Software\Microsoft\Cryptography\MSCEP		When set NDES uses this value as the certificate template name when clients enroll for a signing certificate.
NDES	Encryption Template	HKEY_LOCAL_ROOT\Software\Microsoft\Cryptography\MSCEP		When set, NDES uses this value as the certificate template name when clients enroll for an encryption certificate.

Table 36-1 Additions and Changes in Registry Functions in Server 2008

Category	Setting	Name	Default Value	Possible Values
NDES	SigningAnd Encryption Template	HKEY_LOCAL_ROOT\Software\ Microsoft\Cryptography\MSCEP		When set, NDES uses the value as the certificate template name when clients enroll for a signing and encryption certificate.
AD DS Auditing	MaximumString-BytesToAudit	HKEY_LOCAL_MACHINE\ System\ CurrentControlSet\Services\NTDS\ Parameters	1000	Minimum value: 0 Maximum value: 64,000

Understanding the Registry's Structure

In a file system, the root objects are disks, which contain folders and files. A single folder can contain an arbitrary number of other folders and files; each folder or file has a name. By combining the names of the folders that enclose a file, you can construct a path that unambiguously names only one file on the disk, so that C:\Windows\system32\Mapi32.dll and C:\Windows\SysWOW64\Mapi32.dll are completely separate files.

The registry is organized much like a file system, except that the vocabulary needed to describe it is somewhat different. At the root of the registry structure are the *root keys*, which can be likened to a disk in a file system. Each root key contains several *subkeys* (folders); in turn, these subkeys contain other subkeys and *values* (the registry equivalent of files). Like files, each value has a name that must be unique in the subkey or folder that encloses it; each value also has an associated data type that governs what kind of data it can hold.

Any registry value can be identified by specifying its full path, starting at the root. For example, the following path specifies a particular value in the Security subkey that belongs to Microsoft Exchange Server: HKEY_LOCAL_MACHINE\SOFTWARE\Microsoft\Exchange\Security\ObscureWireDataFormat. Figure 36-1 shows an annotated section of the Windows Server 2008 registry so that you can identify the root keys, subkeys, and values in it.

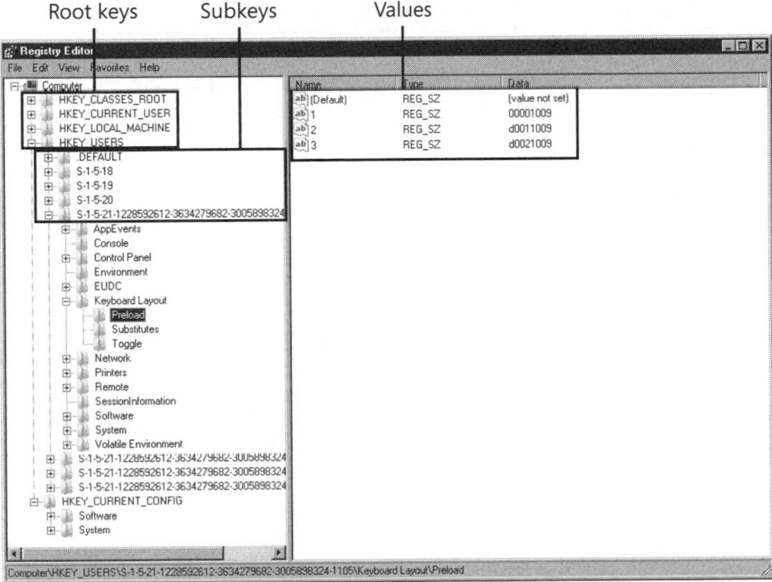

Figure 36-1 The three separate components of a registry value

Under the Hood 64-Bit and 32-Bit Side by Side

A 32-bit version of Windows Server 2008 has the five root keys described here. A 64-bit version of Windows Server 2008 has the same five root keys, but it has a special feature called Registry redirector. The Registry redirector presents 32-bit applications with a different view of the registry than a 64-bit application. This enables both 32-bit and 64-bit COM registration and application states to be supported side by side. The following keys are redirected for 32-bit applications:

- HKEY_LOCAL_MACHINE\SOFTWARE\MICROSOFT\SYSTEMCERTIFICATES
- HKEY_LOCAL_MACHINE\SOFTWARE\MICROSOFT\CRYPTOGRAPHY\SERVICES
- HKEY_LOCAL_MACHINE\SOFTWARE\CLASSES\HCP
- HKEY_LOCAL_MACHINE\SOFTWARE\MICROSOFT\ENTERPRISECERTIFICATES
- HKEY_LOCAL_MACHINE\SOFTWARE\MICROSOFT\MSMQ
- HKEY_LOCAL_MACHINE\SOFTWARE\MICROSOFT\WINDOWS NT\CURRENTVERSION\NETWORKCARDS

- HKEY_LOCAL_MACHINE\SOFTWARE\MICROSOFT\WINDOWS NT\CURRENTVERSION\PROFILELIST
- HKEY_LOCAL_MACHINE\SOFTWARE\MICROSOFT\WINDOWS NT\CURRENTVERSION\PERFLIB
- HKEY_LOCAL_MACHINE\SOFTWARE\MICROSOFT\WINDOWS NT\CURRENTVERSION\PRINT
- HKEY_LOCAL_MACHINE\SOFTWARE\MICROSOFT\WINDOWS NT\CURRENTVERSION\PORTS
- HKEY_LOCAL_MACHINE\SOFTWARE\MICROSOFT\WINDOWS\CURRENTVERSION\CONTROL PANEL\CURSORS\SCHEMES
- HKEY_LOCAL_MACHINE\SOFTWARE\MICROSOFT\WINDOWS\CURRENTVERSION\TELEPHONY\LOCATIONS
- HKEY_LOCAL_MACHINE\SOFTWARE\POLICIES
- HKEY_LOCAL_MACHINE\SOFTWARE\MICROSOFT\WINDOWS\CURRENTVERSION\GROUP POLICY
- HKEY_LOCAL_MACHINE\SOFTWARE\MICROSOFT\WINDOWS\CURRENTVERSION\POLICIES
- HKEY_LOCAL_MACHINE\SOFTWARE\MICROSOFT\WINDOWS\CURRENTVERSION\SETUP\OC MANAGER
- HKEY_LOCAL_MACHINE\SOFTWARE\MICROSOFT\SOFTWARE\MICROSOFT\SHARED TOOLS\MSINFO
- HKEY_LOCAL_MACHINE\SOFTWARE\MICROSOFT\WINDOWS\CURRENTVERSION\SETUP
- HKEY_LOCAL_MACHINE\SOFTWARE\MICROSOFT\CTF\TIP
- HKEY_LOCAL_MACHINE\SOFTWARE\MICROSOFT\CTF\SYSTEMSHARED
- HKEY_LOCAL_MACHINE\SOFTWARE\MICROSOFT\WINDOWS NT\CURRENTVERSION\FONTS
- HKEY_LOCAL_MACHINE\SOFTWARE\MICROSOFT\WINDOWS NT\CURRENTVERSION\FONTSUBSTITUTES
- HKEY_LOCAL_MACHINE\SOFTWARE\MICROSOFT\WINDOWS NT\CURRENTVERSION\FONTDPI

- HKEY_LOCAL_MACHINE\SOFTWARE\MICROSOFT\WINDOWS NT\CURRENTVERSION\FONTMAPPER
- HKEY_LOCAL_MACHINE\SOFTWARE\MICROSOFT\RAS
- HKEY_LOCAL_MACHINE\SOFTWARE\MICROSOFT\DRIVER SIGNING
- HKEY_LOCAL_MACHINE\SOFTWARE\MICROSOFT\NON-DRIVER SIGNING
- HKEY_LOCAL_MACHINE\SOFTWARE\MICROSOFT\CRYPTOGRAPHY\CALAIS\CURRENT
- HKEY_LOCAL_MACHINE\SOFTWARE\MICROSOFT\CRYPTOGRAPHY\CALAIS\READERS
- HKEY_LOCAL_MACHINE\SOFTWARE\MICROSOFT\WINDOWS NT\CURRENTVERSION\TIME ZONE
- HKEY_LOCAL_MACHINE\SOFTWARE\MICROSOFT\TRANSACTION SERVER
- HKEY_LOCAL_MACHINE\SOFTWARE\MICROSOFT\DFS
- HKEY_LOCAL_MACHINE\SOFTWARE\MICROSOFT\TERMSERVLICENSING

When a 32-bit application accesses one of these keys, it sees a special 32-bit version of it, allowing both 32-bit and 64-bit versions of an application to exist side by side.

Further, for those 32-bit applications that write REG_EXPAND_SZ keys containing %ProgramFiles% to the registry, WOW64 intercepts the write and substitutes "%ProgramFilesx86%". Thus, if the Program Files directory is on the C drive, "%ProgramFilesx86%" expands to "C:\Program Files (x86)".

For more information on how registry redirection behaves, see *http://msdn.microsoft.com/library/default.asp?url=/library/en-us/win64/win64/registry_redirector.asp.*

The Root Keys

When you click Computer on the Start menu, you always see certain items, such as icons that represent the logical disk volumes on your computer. The same is true of the registry. When you open it with the Registry Editor, you always see the same set of root keys. Each root key has a distinct purpose:

- HKEY_LOCAL_MACHINE (HKLM) stores all settings that pertain to hardware on the local computer. For example, the HARDWARE subkey of HKLM is where the system and its device drivers record and share information about the hardware devices that the system finds at boot time (as well as other Plug and Play devices you can add after the system is booted). Applications are supposed to store data here only if it pertains to everyone who uses a computer; for example, a printer driver might store a set of default print settings here and copy them to each new user's profile when he or she logs on.
- HKEY_USERS (HKU) contains one entry for each user who has previously logged on to your computer. Each user's entry is owned by that user's account, and it contains the profile settings that were in effect for that user. When you use Group Policy (discussed in Chapter 13, "Group Policy"), the policy settings you specify are applied to an individual user's profile here.
- HKEY_CURRENT_CONFIG (HKCC) stores information about the system's current boot configuration. In particular, it contains information about the current set of system services and which devices were present at boot time. This root key is actually a pointer to sections inside HKLM.
- HKEY_CURRENT_USER (HKCU) points to the currently logged-on user's profile inside HKU. Microsoft requires that Windows applications store any user-specific preferences in subkeys under HKCU; for example, HKCU\SOFTWARE\Binary Research\GhostSrv\Settings holds a user's personal preferences for Symantec's Ghost product. Another user's settings for the same product are available in the same key only when that user is logged on.
- HKEY_CLASSES_ROOT (HKCR) ties file extensions and OLE class identifiers together; it actually points to HKLM\SOFTWARE\Classes and HKEY_CURRENT_USER\SOFTWARE\Classes. System components such as Windows Explorer (and Microsoft Internet Explorer, for that matter) use these associations to determine which applications or components to use when opening or creating a particular type of file or data object. Because Windows Server 2008 relies heavily on the Component Object Model (COM), which in turn relies on the object identifiers stored in HKCR, this key and its subkeys are more important than you might think at first.

Note In the Windows documentation, Microsoft identifies only two registry root keys: HKLM and HKU. Because HKCU, HKCC, and HKCR are actually pointers to subkeys of HKLM and HKU, this is technically correct, but you might be confused if you're used to the idea of five separate root keys. To avoid that confusion, we use the old-style notation here.

Under the Hood HKCR in Windows Server 2008

If you've used Windows NT 4, you'll see a difference in the way Windows Server 2008 uses the HKCR tree. In Windows NT 4 and earlier, the data in HKCR is the same for all users. In some ways, this was a reasonable design decision for Microsoft to make—all users on the computer have access to the same set of installed OLE components and file mappings.

However, one common complaint from administrators whose users have to share computers is that two users' preferred associations might differ. If one user chooses Firefox as the preferred Web browser, that choice modifies HKCR; if another user later sets Internet Explorer as the preferred browser at the same computer, that choice undermines the original selection. More important, the ability for users to change these values reduces system security in two ways: It allows users to change associations for other users (increasing the risk of introducing malicious code), and it forces administrators to remove permissions from HKLM\SOFTWARE\Classes, because all users need access to it.

In subsequent server releases, Microsoft changed this. HKCR actually contains data from two sources: the user's profile (where user-specific customizations are stored) and HKLM\SOFTWARE\Classes, where system-wide settings live. Users can register and unregister COM components, change file associations, and so on without affecting other users. Administrators can adjust permissions on HKLM\SOFTWARE\Classes so that users can't tamper with the system-wide settings you want them to have. Each user's unique settings are stored in the Usrclass.dat file, which is treated like its own registry hive. (See "Where Data Goes on Disk" later in the chapter for more details about hive files.)

Major Subkeys

Within these root keys, several subkeys are noteworthy. Because each root key has so much information under it, you usually hear the following individual subkeys referred to—after all, HKLM\HARDWARE and HKLM\SOFTWARE don't have much in common except their root key.

HKLM\HARDWARE

The HKLM\HARDWARE subkey stores information about the hardware found in the system. All the values stored here are held only in RAM, not on disk, because of the device-driver ordering problem mentioned earlier. When the hardware recognizer starts, it enumerates every device it can find, both by walking the system buses and by searching for specific classes of devices such as parallel ports or keyboards. Three major subkeys live under HKLM\HARDWARE:

- The DESCRIPTION subkey contains descriptions of the CPUs, floating-point processors, and multifunction devices in the system. Users moving from Windows NT 4 to Windows Server 2008 will see big changes. For example, the CentralProcessor subkey now tracks a number of settings that aren't present in Windows NT 4. For computers that use multipurpose chipsets such as Intel's BX series, one of the multifunction devices listed in this key reflects the chipset's integrated controllers, with separate entries for disk, keyboard, and serial controllers.
- The DEVICEMAP subkey links a specific device to a specific driver. For example, DEVICEMAP\Video has a value named \Device\Video1 that contains a string, which is a pointer to the place where the driver for that video controller stores its parameters.
- The RESOURCEMAP subkey contains three primary subkeys: one for the hardware abstraction layer (HAL) to use when keeping track of the devices it finds, one for the Plug and Play Manager to record devices it knows how to handle, and one that reflects the amount of system resources (which is Microsoft-speak for memory and related resources) available on the computer.

Additional subkeys can exist, depending on the configuration of your computer. For example, systems that support the Advanced Configuration Power Interface (ACPI) have an ACPI subkey that contains information about the specific ACPI subfeatures that the computer supports.

HKLM\SAM

Even though Windows Server 2008 includes Active Directory Domain Services (AD DS), don't assume that no vestiges of the Security Accounts Manager (SAM) have survived. When you create local accounts or groups on a Windows Server 2008 computer, they are stored in HKLM\SAM, just as they were in Windows NT. However, you can't normally view or change data in this subkey, and it is mostly useful for compatibility with earlier Windows NT code that expects SAM to exist. The programming routines that access SAM data have all been revamped to use Active Directory data when it exists, or SAM when no Active Directory server is present.

HKLM\SECURITY

HKLM\SECURITY contains a lot of security information, as you might expect. Its format is hidden and undocumented, and you can't do anything in the subkey. However, the system caches logon credentials, policy settings, and shared server secrets in this subkey. The SECURITY\SAM subkey contains a copy of most of the data from HKLM\SAM.

HKLM\SOFTWARE

The HKLM\SOFTWARE subkey serves as the root location for applications and system components to store their computer-wide settings. For example, HKLM\SOFTWARE\Microsoft\ EnterpriseCertificates contains keys that hold the certificate trust lists (CTLs) and trusted CA certificates for this computer–individual users' CTLs and trusted CAs are stored elsewhere. Individual programs, control panels, and the like can create their own subkeys under HKLM\SOFTWARE; the de facto standard is for each vendor to create its own top-level key (for example, HKLM\SOFTWARE\Intel) and then create subentries beneath that key.

The most interesting parts of this subkey are HKLM\SOFTWARE\Microsoft \Windows\CurrentVersion (which stores much of the GUI preference data and is named the same as the corresponding key under Windows 95, Windows 98, and Windows Me) and HKLM\SOFTWARE\Microsoft\Windows NT\CurrentVersion. This latter subkey was significantly expanded in Windows 2000, adding new keys for automated system recovery handling, the Encrypting File System, the Security Configuration Editor, Terminal Services, and other goodies. Windows Server 2008, as you'd expect, maintains the Windows 2003 structure.

HKLM\Software\Wow6432Node

The HKLM\Software\Wow6432Node is present only on 64-bit versions of Windows. Its function is to provide a separate, 32-bit HKLM\Software subkey that is seen by 32-bit applications. When the registry is accessed by a 32-bit application, the application is redirected to this subkey when it looks for a key or value in HKLM\Software. This enables both 32-bit and 64-bit versions of the same application to coexist and have different settings and locations.

HKLM\SYSTEM\CurrentControlSet

When you boot your server, the last action in the boot phase is to update the registry to reflect which set of controls and services was last used for a successful boot. CurrentControlSet always points to the set of controls actually in use on the system. If you look under HKLM\SYSTEM, you usually see several ControlSetXXX keys. Each ControlSetXXX subkey represents a control set that existed at one time, whether or not it was successfully used to boot. CurrentControlSet is just a pointer to the most recent successful boot set, but because it isn't easy to determine *which* set that was, the operating system and applications use CurrentControlSet instead.

CurrentControlSet has four subkeys:

- **Control** Contains control information for services and system tools. For example, Control\BackupRestore\KeysNotToRestore contains a list of keys that the Backup

Utility shouldn't restore (including the contents of the Plug and Play subkey) when it restores the registry.

- **Enum** Contains one entry for every physical device or pseudo-device that the system can find. For example, Enum\IDE\DiskMaxtor_94098U8 contains information about the system's IDE disk drive. Because it was present at boot time, it is included in the enumeration list.
- **Hardware Profiles** Contains one entry for each hardware profile defined on a computer. Comparable with the numbering system seen in the HKLM\SYSTEM tree, each profile has a serial number, starting with 0001. HKLM\SYSTEM\Hardware Profiles\Current always points to the profile selected at boot time.
- **Services** Contains one subkey for each installed service. These subkeys, in turn, hold all the configuration information that the service needs. The exact set of subkeys on two computers is different if they have different services loaded on them.

HKLM\SYSTEM\MountedDevices

Windows Server 2008 dynamic disk volumes (discussed in Chapter 19, "Implementing Disk Management") are a neat technical achievement and a boon to administrators, but they depend on having information about the current configuration of the logical volumes on disk. Applications (and snap-ins such as the Disk Management snap-in) get this information from the Logical Volume Manager service; in turn, this service stores its list of mounted and available devices in the MountedDevices subkey.

How Data Is Stored

Although programs and services that use the registry don't have to understand how registry data is stored, administrators do—that way you know where data is stored, how the registry handles different types of data, and which files need to be safeguarded as part of your backups. You don't need to understand the internal format that the registry tools use, but you do need to understand the basic data types and storage locations.

Each value in the registry (Microsoft calls them *value entries*) has three parts: a name, a data type, and an actual value. For example, if you see a Microsoft Knowledge Base article that talks about some key—REG_DWORD: HKLM\SYSTEM \CurrentControlSet\Services\.NETFramework\Performance\FirstCounter, for example—you're seeing a complete definition of a value entry. (It's always nice to see a full path for values so that you know where to add or remove them.)

Useful Data Types

The following seven data types can be used to store data in the registry. (Actually, only two of these types are used for most registry data: REG_DWORD and REG_SZ.)

- REG_BINARY stores arbitrary binary data in raw form, without any reformatting or parsing. You can view binary data in binary or hex forms by using one of the Windows Server 2008 registry editors (described later in the chapter).
- REG_DWORD stores a 4-byte integer (or double word) value. This data type is usually used when a value indicates a count or interval, but it's also common to see REG_DWORD flags–0 means the flag is off, and 1 means it's on.
- REG_QWORD represents data by a number that is a 64-bit integer. This data is displayed in Registry Editor as a Binary Value and was introduced in Windows 2000.
- REG_SZ is an ordinary Unicode string. These strings can be of any length. This data type is usually used to store paths, human-readable messages or device names, and so on.
- REG_EXPAND_SZ is a REG_SZ with a twist–applications can embed a special token in the string and then expand the token when they read the value from the registry. The token is a variable name framed by the % character. For example, *Something* is a REG_EXPAND_SZ whose normal value is *%SystemRoot%*\System32\Something. When Windows Server 2008 reads the string, it expands *%SystemRoot%* to the full path where the operating system is installed.
- REG_MULTI_SZ is a collection of an arbitrary number of REG_SZ values. For example, the list of DNS servers you specify in the TCP/IP Properties dialog box is stored in a REG_MULTI_SZ value. Applications must know how to pick apart a single REG_MULTI_SZ into its component parts.
- REG_FULL_RESOURCE_DESCRIPTOR is a rare bird; it is used to encode information about the system resources required by a particular device. We've never seen it appear outside the subkeys of HKLM\HARDWARE.
- REG_NONE is just a placeholder. It is used to indicate that a registry value exists but doesn't contain any actual data. Some components look for the presence or absence of a specified key or value to control their behavior at run time; it's common for those components to look for an item of type REG_NONE–because this type doesn't hold any data, users can't mess these values up.

In day-to-day administration, what you need to know about these data types is mostly restricted to understanding the difference between REG_DWORD and REG_SZ values. A REG_DWORD value whose contents are 0 (the numeric value for zero) is different from a REG_SZ whose contents are "0" (the character "0"). If you need to add a new registry value (perhaps because a Microsoft Knowledge Base article recommends doing so), you have to ensure that you get the type right, or you might have problems with the components that use the value.

Volatile Keys

Some registry keys and values are *volatile*, in the original sense of the word—they aren't persistent and can evaporate at any moment. As an example, none of the data in HKLM\HARDWARE exists anywhere on disk; that entire subkey and all its contents reside entirely in memory. Every time you boot a Windows Server 2008 computer, that subkey is created anew, and when you shut it down its contents disappear.

Disk-Based Keys

Volatile keys are useful for data that doesn't need to stay around between reboots, but most of the data stored in the registry would be pretty useless if it weren't persistent. Imagine having to reconfigure all your preferences and settings after every reboot of your desktop computer—that would get old fast. The majority of registry keys are disk-based, meaning that their contents are held in structures on disk. When a key's contents are updated, the version on disk is updated too.

Even though disk-based keys are eventually stored on disk, Windows Server 2008 maps them into the paged memory pool (an area of memory whose contents can be written to the pagefile when not being used) to provide more efficient access. The registry size limit, discussed later in this chapter, regulates how much registry data can be stored in the paged pool.

Where Data Goes on Disk

Microsoft uses the term *hive* to refer to a group of keys and values that belong together. A hive can be a root key, or it can be a subkey. For example, HKCC is a hive (even though it's just a pointer to part of HKLM) and so is HKLM\SAM. The important concept to remember about hives is that a hive is a self-contained unit that can be loaded and unloaded independently of other hives.

Windows Server 2008 uses seven hives: DEFAULT (corresponding to HKU\.DEFAULT), SAM (HKLM\SAM), SECURITY (HKLM\SECURITY), SOFTWARE (HKLM\SOFTWARE), and SYSTEM (HKLM\SYSTEM). The sixth hive, which corresponds to the contents of HKCU, is better known as a user profile—a *user profile* is just a hive that is loaded into the registry when the user logs on and unloaded at logout. The final hive is HKEY_CURRENT_CONFIG, which was discussed previously.

Each hive exists in its own set of files on disk (with the files having the same names as the hives), along with a separate log file that acts as a journal of all changes made to that hive. (The only exception to this is HKEY_CURRENT_CONFIG, whose data is held with the HKLM\SYSTEM data in the files System and System.log.) Hive files don't have extensions, and the system keeps them open all the time—that's why you have to use a special-purpose backup tool such as the Backup Utility to back them up.

So, where do these hive files live? As with so many other Windows Server 2008–related questions, the answer is an emphatic "It depends." In this case, the answer depends on which hives you're talking about. The big five (DEFAULT, SAM, SECURITY, SOFTWARE, and SYSTEM), along with their .LOG files, are stored in the System32\Config subfolder of the %windir%.

Creating Registry Items with the Registry Wizard

Use the Registry Wizard to create multiple registry preference items. The Registry Wizard will organize the items you create in a folder that replicates the registry structure. Each item allows you to configure a value or key in the registry and deploy them as needed.

To create multiple registry items, follow these steps:

1. From the Administrative Tools menu, select Group Policy Management.
2. In the console tree, right-click the Group Policy object that will contain the new item and select Edit.
3. In the console tree, under Computer Configuration Or User Configuration, select Preferences and then select Windows Settings.
4. Right-click Registry, select New, and then select Registry Wizard (Figure 36-2).

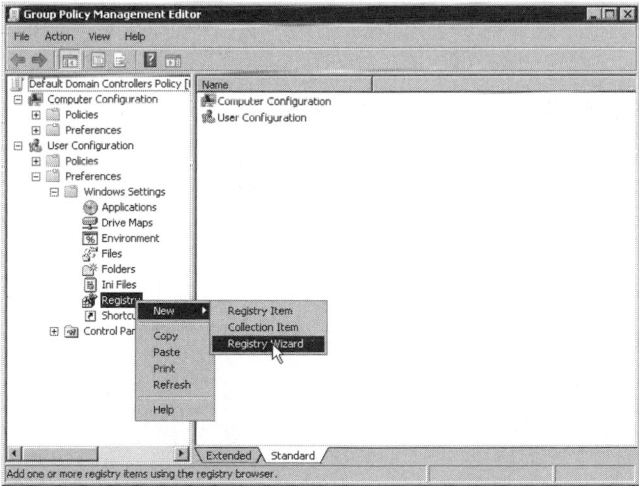

Figure 36-2 Starting the Registry Wizard

5. Select the computer with the registry settings you want to modify. Click Next.

6. In the Registry Browser, shown in Figure 36-3, use the check boxes to select the keys or values for which you want to create a preference item. Select a key only when you want to create a new registry item for the key as opposed to a value within a key.

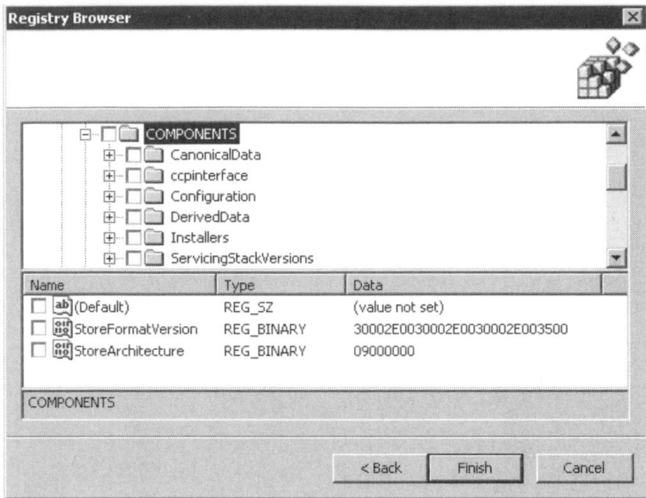

Figure 36-3 Browsing the registry

7. Click Finish.

8. The settings you chose appear in Registry Wizard Values. Right-click the collection, as shown in Figure 36-4. Select Rename and enter a descriptive title for the collection.

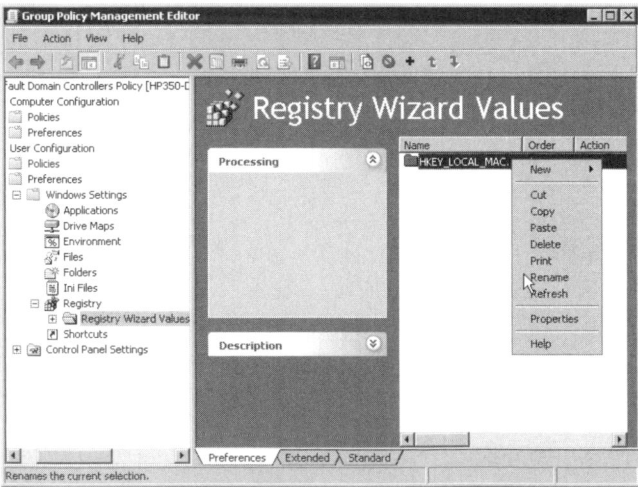

Figure 36-4 Renaming a collection of registry preference items

Using the Registry Editors

On occasions when you need to change values in the registry, you have to use some kind of registry editor. Many of the settings you can change with Control Panel items, Group Policy objects, or MMC snap-ins are actually stored in the registry, so you can think of these utilities as a kind of registry editor. Another kind is the custom-written script you use to make a specific change, perhaps as part of a logon script or a file you distribute to your users. However, most of the time when you need to make a change directly to the registry, you use one of the provided Windows registry editing utilities.

You can use two primary tools to edit your registry. You can always configure items in the MMC snap-ins, but for most of the changes you make, you'll probably choose the Registry Editor (Regedit.exe) or the command-line utility Reg.

What Happened to Regedt32?

If you are moving from a pre-Windows Server 2003 operating system, you probably noticed that when you run Regedt32.exe in Windows Server 2008, it starts Regedit.exe. Now, it's just a placeholder; the old Regedt32.exe has been removed.

Regedt32.exe was developed early in the life of Windows NT, and it reflected the Microsoft design standards of the day. Since Windows 95 was released, development of multiple document interface (MDI) applications has been frowned upon, and Microsoft has removed one of the last remaining applications–Regedt32.exe–of that type.

When Regedit32 was still a part of Windows, there were some things you couldn't do in Regedit.exe. Both tools were clearly needed. The missing functionality available in Regedt32 only (such as key security settings) has been rolled into Regedit. Now all your editing needs are satisfied in a single application.

A Whirlwind Tour of the Registry Editor

As a user of Windows Explorer (or any version of Windows), you already know about 85 percent of what you need to use the Registry Editor. This familiarity is entirely by design–Microsoft has tried to make it an easy-to-use tool by copying the user interface that you're already familiar with.

The Registry Editor's main window is shown in Figure 36-5. The important parts of the interface are fairly simple to understand. Notice the following features:

- The tree in the left pane of the Registry Editor window shows all the root keys and subkeys. What you see here depends on which keys and subkeys you expanded.
- The right pane shows the values associated with the selected key in the left pane. Each value is shown with three items: the value name (the name Default is used for the unnamed default value every key has), the value's type, and the value's contents or data.
- The status bar at the bottom of the window shows the full path to the currently selected key. (The Registry Editor can also copy this key's path to the clipboard for you, thanks to the Copy Key Name command on the Edit menu.)

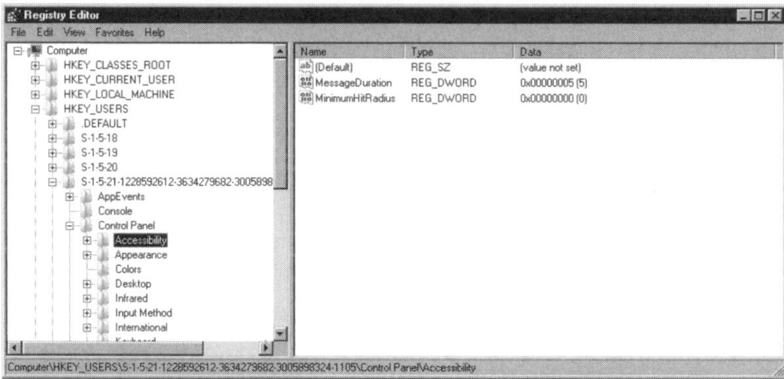

Figure 36-5 The Registry Editor user interface

Because these interface features are written with the standard Windows controls, all the keyboard navigation and control shortcuts you're accustomed to using with Windows Explorer work here. For example, you can jump to a particular key by clicking anywhere in the left pane and typing the first few letters of the key's name. And you can use the arrow keys to move around in either half of the Registry Editor window.

Searching for Keys and Values

The Find command on the Edit menu in the Registry Editor is worth its weight in gold when you need to find which key, or value, has a specific name or contents. The interface to this function is uncomplicated, as Figure 36-6 shows. Even with the simple interface, the tool is extremely valuable because it searches the entire registry for a specific value. Here's how to use the Find dialog box to get what you're looking for:

- Type the pattern you're looking for in the Find What box. You can search only for plain ASCII text—no wildcards are allowed. And no expansion of variables are allowed either—so if you search for %ProgramFiles(x86)%, it searches for that exact string, *not* what that variable would expand to. If you're searching for values, the

Registry Editor searches only string values (REG_SZ, REG_EXPAND_SZ, and REG_MULTI_SZ) for the pattern you give.

- Use the options in the Look At panel to control where the Registry Editor looks for the specified value. By default, it searches for key names (the Keys check box), value names (the Values check box), and value contents (the Data check box), but you can fine-tune it.
- The Match Whole String Only check box tells the Registry Editor to find the entire search string, not just a portion of it. For example, if you search for "Windows" with this check box selected, the search ignores HKLM\SOFTWARE\Microsoft\Windows NT.

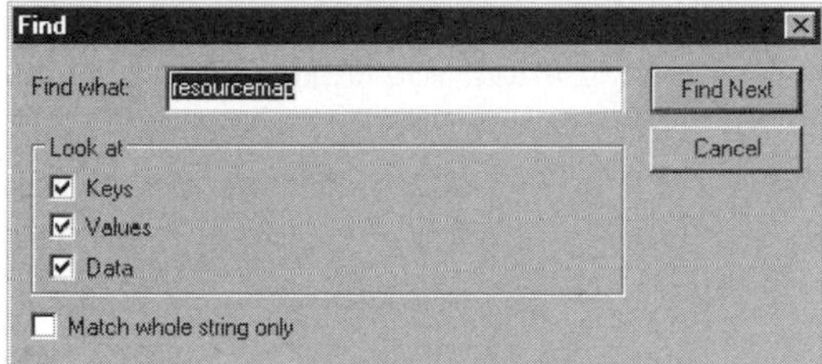

Figure 36-6 The Registry Editor's Find dialog box

When you make your selections in the Find dialog box, click Find Next and the Registry Editor begins searching. Eventually, one of two things happens: the Registry Editor either hits the end of the registry (in which case, it tells you it didn't find any matches), or it finds a match. In the latter case, the match is highlighted. If the match isn't what you were looking for, use the Find Next command on the Edit menu (or F3, its shortcut key) to continue the search.

Editing Value Contents

The Modify command on the Edit menu lets you change the contents of the selected value entry. (You can also edit a value by selecting it and pressing Enter.) What you see next depends on the type of value you're editing; separate editor dialog boxes exist for string values, DWORD values, and binary values. The Registry Editor lets you edit data types it doesn't support, such as REG_FULL_RESOURCE_DESCRIPTOR or REG_MULTI_SZ. For those types, it opens the binary editor dialog box. The editor dialog boxes themselves are straightforward—each presents the current value and lets you edit it. The keyboard shortcuts for the Cut, Copy, and Paste commands work in the editor dialog boxes, too.

Adding and Removing Keys and Values

The Registry Editor also allows you to add and remove keys, subkeys, and individual values. Now is a good time to reiterate the frequent warning from Microsoft: making unnecessary changes to the registry will likely damage your Windows installation. Be careful when you add data, and be doubly careful when you remove it. (See the sidebar "Being on Your Best Behavior" earlier in this chapter for more details.) To add a new key as a child of the selected key, open the Edit menu, point to New, and choose Key. The Registry Editor creates a new key and selects its name so that you can set it correctly. (It defaults to New Key #1.)

The new key automatically has an unnamed value attached to it. You can add more values using the six remaining commands on the New submenu: String Value, Binary Value, DWORD Value, QWORD Value, Multi-String Value, and Expandable String Value. Note that the Registry Editor can't create any other data types, and if you create a binary value, components interpret it as raw REG_BINARY data. Creating a new value adds it as a child of the selected key and gives it a default name (New Value #1, New Value #2, and so on), which you can immediately change. When you're done adding and naming the new values, you can use the standard editor dialog boxes to change their contents to the appropriate values.

Removing values and keys is simple. Select the item you want to zap, and choose Delete from the Edit menu or just press the Delete key. The Registry Editor asks you to confirm your command; after you confirm it, the value or key is immediately removed. (It's permanent, unlike most file commands–there's no Undo!)

Importing and Exporting Registry Data

You can import and export registry data from the Registry Editor into text files with the .reg extension that can be safely moved from computer to computer. In fact, the default association for .reg files automatically launches the Registry Editor and loads the contents of the file when you double-click it.

The Export Registry File command on the Registry menu lets you save the selected key to a file, and the Import Registry File command does the reverse. Note that importing a registry file from within the Registry Editor happens immediately–a confirmation dialog box appears that tells you whether the import succeeded or not, but you don't get a chance to stop it. If you launch a .reg file by clicking it, however, you *do* get a dialog box like the one in Figure 36-7 asking you to confirm that you want to continue.

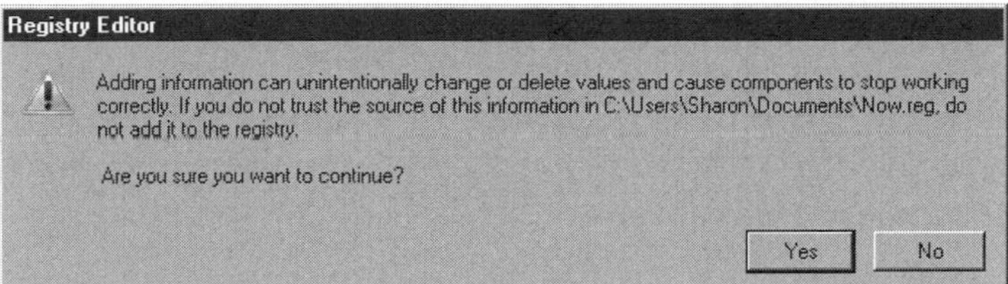

Figure 36-7 Confirming the import of a .reg file

Real World Creating Your Own .reg Files

If you need to distribute registry changes to your users, one way to do it is with the policy mechanisms discussed in Chapter 13. Another way is to use a .reg file. For example, sites that don't have direct access to Active Directory resources can't receive Group Policy updates. You can easily mail out .reg files and have your users double-click them. (Of course, that could create a potential security problem, so make sure all users are educated about proper and safe e-mail use.)

The easiest way to create .reg files for distribution is to use the Registry Editor to export the keys and values you want to pass around. Alternatively, create your own files using NotePad or any other text editor. Here's an example:

```
Windows Registry Editor Version 6.00

[HKEY_LOCAL_MACHINE\SOFTWARE\Microsoft\Windows NT\CurrentVersion
\AeDebug]
"Auto"="1"
"Debugger"="drwtsn32 -p %ld -e %ld -g"
"UserDebuggerHotKey"=dword:00000000
```

The first line tells the Registry Editor it's looking at a .reg file. (The blank line that follows is required, too.) After that, the format is easy to understand: define a key by putting its full path in square brackets, and then follow it with each value you want to import, one per line. Enclose value names and string value contents in straight double quotes. (Be sure to use straight double quotes instead of the "smart quotes" that are inserted by many word-processing systems, including Microsoft Office Word.) REG_DWORD values are specified using the DWORD: prefix; they don't have to be enclosed in quotes. You can bundle multiple keys into the same file, as long as you add a blank line before each key name. Each key can contain any number of values.

Until you become proficient with .reg files, practice using a harmless destination path. Create your own key (such as HKLM\SOFTWARE\Testing123), and import your .reg files under it until you're sure they make only the changes you want made.

Loading and Unloading Hives

You can load and unload hives for HKEY_USERS and HKEY_LOCAL_MACHINE. On the File menu, these options are enabled only when one of the two keys is selected. To either load or unload a hive, you must be a member of the Administrators group or you must have been given the authority to do so.

To load a hive, click Load Hive on the File menu and navigate to the folder that contains the hive you want to load. Select it and click Open. Provide a key name and click OK to save it. To unload a hive, select a hive in the Registry Editor and from the File menu, select Unload Hive.

> **Note** Loading and unloading hives is done while trying to recover from registry corruption. Do not do it on a production system that is running and not having problems.

Connecting to a Remote Computer's Registry

If you're logged on with sufficient permissions, you can use the Registry Editor to connect to another computer's registry and inspect or edit it. To accomplish this, your account must have administrative privileges on both the computer on which you're running the Registry Editor *and* the other computer whose registry you want to inspect or edit, and the remote registry service must be running on the target computer. You also have to be sure that Group Policy settings or Windows Firewall settings don't prevent you from gaining access.

Assuming your credentials are in order, you connect to the remote computer by choosing Connect Network Registry from the File menu. This command lets you browse your network to find the computer you want to connect to. After you successfully connect, the computer's name appears in the left pane on the same level as My Computer. You can expand its root keys, poke around in the subkeys, search, and modify data to your heart's content. When you're done, choose Disconnect Network Registry from the File menu and select the computer to disconnect.

Renaming Keys and Values

You can change the name of a key or a value by choosing Rename from the Edit menu. This command is not often needed because software looks for specific named values in the registry, and changing one of those names can produce unpredictable outcomes—none of them good. However, when you add keys or values based on advice from Microsoft Knowledge Base articles, you might misspell the name (or type it correctly and later discover that the name in the Knowledge Base article is wrong), and the Rename command is your only alternative to deleting and re-creating the key.

Managing Security on Registry Keys

Regedit allows you to adjust registry key security by selecting a key and choosing the Permissions command from the Edit menu. Everything you learned about setting permissions on files (discussed in Chapter 11, "Managing Users and Groups") is still true here, and the basic operations work exactly the same way: You select an object and then grant or deny specific privileges to specific users and groups. Figure 36-8 shows an example on a domain controller. The exact content you see on your computer varies according to the security template you applied; more restrictive templates might change these permissions significantly.

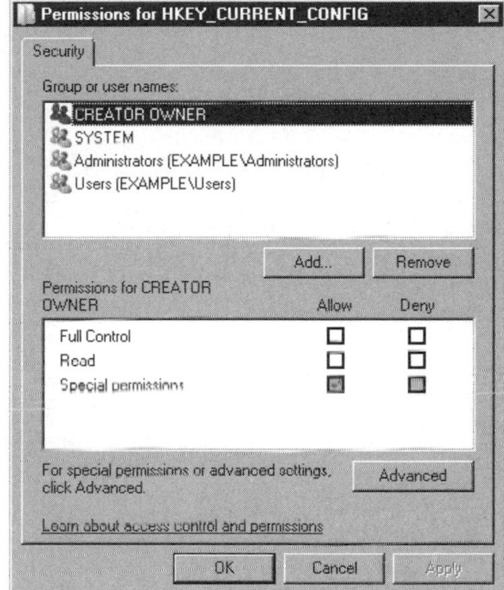

Figure 36-8 The standard Permissions dialog box for a registry key

On the Permissions dialog box, you can grant and deny the Full Control, Read, and Special Permissions options on keys. However, in general, don't do so on keys owned by the system–that's why Microsoft includes the security templates. It's easy to accidentally set permissions that are too restrictive (software that needs registry access can't get it) or too loose, raising security issues.

You can exercise advanced control by clicking Advanced, which brings up the Advanced Security Settings For... dialog box for the key you selected. The dialog box has four tabs: Permissions, Auditing, Owner, and Effective Permissions.

When you set permissions using the Permissions tab on the Advanced Security Settings For... dialog box, be sure to note whether you select the Replace All Existing Inheritable Permissions On All Descendants With Inheritable Permissions From This Object check box. If this check box is selected and you apply new permissions, permissions on this parent object will replace those on all subkeys of the selected key. Depending on the level at which you apply these permissions, inheritance might have unintended consequences–if you loosen permissions on a key, you might accidentally loosen permissions on a subkey that should remain secure. Before you change permissions on any keys, be sure to make a good backup of your registry *and* make a note of the changes you made so that you can reverse them later.

Settings that belong to applications, of course, are another matter altogether. The only way to determine appropriate permissions for most applications' keys is to tighten them as much as possible, and then gradually relax controls until the application starts working properly. It might not be easy, but it's effective. The control this method provides is absolute.

Here's a summary of what the various tab dialog box items allow you to do:

- The Permissions tab's Add/Edit button allows you to assign more granular permissions to individual users. For example, you can fine-tune who can create new values in a key by adjusting the setting for the Set Value permission. Table 36-2 shows the permissions you can grant or deny. Because most registry keys gain their permissions from inheritance, be aware that you might not be able to make changes here without turning inheritance off.
- The Auditing tab lets you set auditing permissions for the selected key. First, you specify the users or groups whose actions you want to audit; next, you specify which particular actions you want recorded. Note that the actions you can audit are the same as the permissions shown in Table 36-2. You can audit successful or failed attempts to exercise these permissions.
- The Owner tab lets you reassign ownership of the selected key, either with or without propagating that change to all subitems beneath it. Note that depending on your security settings, a change in ownership might result in an audit trail being generated.
- The Effective Permissions tab lets you see what permissions would be given to a particular user or group given the current settings.

Table 36-2 Registry Permissions

Permission	What happens when granted
Full Control	Allows user to open, edit, and take ownership for a specific key
Query Value	Allows user to query the registry for a specific value by providing the full path to that value
Set Value	Allows user to create new values beneath a key or to overwrite an existing value
Create Subkey	Allows user to create a new subkey beneath the specified key

Table 36-2 Registry Permissions

Permission	What happens when granted
Enumerate Subkeys	Allows user to get a list of all subkeys of a particular key; similar to directory traversal of an NTFS volume
Notify	Allows user to register a callback function that is triggered when the selected value changes
Create Link	Allows user to create a link to a specified key (just as HKCR links to HKLM\Classes)
Delete	Allows user to delete an individual value or key
Write DAC	Allows user to rewrite access controls on the specified key
Write Owner	Allows user to take ownership of the selected key
Read Control	Allows user to read the discretionary access control list (DACL) for the specified key

Real World Editing with PowerShell

You can use Windows PowerShell to view and edit the registry. Simply open an instance of Windows PowerShell and enter the root key followed by a colon. Figure 36-9 shows the steps.

- Change directory to HKLM.
- Open the subkey system\currentcontrolset.
- Display a directory.

```
Select Windows PowerShell
Windows PowerShell
Copyright (C) 2006 Microsoft Corporation. All rights reserved.

PS C:\Users\Sharon> cd HKLM:
PS HKLM:\> cd system\currentcontrolset
PS HKLM:\system\currentcontrolset> dir


   Hive: Microsoft.PowerShell.Core\Registry::HKEY_LOCAL_MACHINE\system\currentcontrolset

SKC  VC Name                           Property
---  -- ----                           --------
 67   6 Control                        {WaitToKillServiceTimeout, CurrentUser, PreshutdownOrder, System
 15  36 Enum                           {NextParentID.daba3ff.2, NextParentID.13c0b0c5.3, NextParentID.2
  3   0 Hardware Profiles              {}
365   0 Services                       {}
```

Figure 36-9 Using Windows PowerShell to explore the registry

Because PowerShell allows you to easily navigate through the Registry as if it were a file structure on a disk, you can use PowerShell to add, remove, or modify keys and values. This makes it possible to write PowerShell scripts to handle frequent tasks such as checking for the existence and set values in particular keys. For more on PowerShell, see Chapter 15, "Using Scripts for Consistent Administration."

A Whirlwind Tour of Reg

Reg (Reg.exe) is a utility that allows you to view, edit, or add registry entries from the command line. It's script-friendly and just as powerful as the Registry Editor, but it doesn't have the pretty interface. You can use it in batch files, for example, to repeatedly apply changes to your registry.

Using Reg takes a little getting used to if you're not familiar with the command line. A number of options are available, and you pass them as parameters to the executable. The format of Reg usage is

```
reg action [options]
```

where *reg* is the Reg executable, *action* is the Reg command you want to perform, and *options* is the list of command-specific parameters.

The primary commands of Reg are listed in Table 36-3. The return status of the commands is 0 if the command succeeded or 1 if a failure occurred, except where noted.

Table 36-3 Reg commands

Command	Purpose
Add	Adds a new subkey or entry to the registry.
Compare	Looks at the values for the two specified subkeys or entries, and returns the following: 0 if the comparison succeeds and there are no differences 1 if the comparison failed 2 if the comparison was successful and differences existed
Copy	Copies registry information to a new location in the local or network registry.
Delete	Removes registry information.
Export	Pulls information out of the registry, and writes it to a file. This file can be used to transfer the registry data to other computers using the Import command.
Import	Imports a registry file, and creates and modifies keys specified in the file into the local registry.
Load	Allows you to move registry data to a new position within the registry, enabling you to troubleshoot changes without the threat of doing permanent damage.
Query	Prints all the registry information beneath the specified key.
Restore	Restores registry information from a file created by the Save command.
Save	Saves specified registry information in a file. This is useful if you're planning to edit a key and want to make a backup of it first.
Unload	Removes the registry data that was added with the Load command.

Backing Up and Restoring the Registry

In Chapter 34, "Using Backup," you learned how to use Windows Server Backup and Wbadmin to back up and restore your system. To safeguard the registry, you can include it in scheduled backups or do manual backups from the command line.

Choosing a Backup Method

Because the registry is more than an ordinary file, it makes sense that you have to give your backup and restore procedures more than the ordinary amount of thought. You can back up and restore your registry in other ways besides making a complete backup of the entire system state. Of course, you should still perform regular backups of your data *and* the system state for each computer you administer. It is still useful to back up the registry by itself, because the registry is where most applications and system components store their preferences and settings.

Windows Server Backup

When you use Windows Server Backup to back up the server, a complete copy of the registry is included. The backup also includes copies of all volumes (or just the critical ones), certificate data, COM+ class registration information, and other information that is unrelated to what is in the registry. On the other hand, Windows Server Backup automates the process of backing up the registry, so it's easy to use and understand. In addition, keeping your registry data with the rest of your server data ensures that you're able to recover everything. Chapter 34 includes all the information necessary to do backups.

Wbadmin

You can create a backup of the system state from the command line using Wbadmin. System state backup isn't available in the Windows Server Backup snap-in. A backup of the system state can only be saved to a locally attached disk (either internal or external). It cannot be saved to a DVD or to a remote shared folder. In addition, only the system state and system applications can be recovered from this backup–volumes and files cannot be recovered from this backup. The command and syntax is as follows:

```
wbadmin start systemstatebackup
-backupTarget:<VolumeName>
[-quiet]
```

See "Using the Wbadmin Command" in Chapter 34 for more information.

Third-Party Products

Many Windows server sites use third-party backup tools. In general, these tools provide more sophisticated backup capabilities than the tools Microsoft ships. If you're using a third-party backup product, use it to back up your registry too. Be sure you have everything on hand that you need to restore data backed up with a third-party tool, and double-check to make sure your vendor's software is fully compatible with the version of Windows Server 2008 that you're running.

Do-It-Yourself Backups

Because Regedit allows you to export and import .reg files, you might think you can approximate what the backup utility does by manually saving to a hive file the keys you're most interested in, copying the resulting files someplace safe, and reloading them if you need them. This approach works fine and is most useful when you want to make changes to the registry while preserving a fall-back position, but it's labor-intensive because you have no way to automate the process of telling the Registry Editor which keys to save.

System Recovery

Using the command line, you can recover the system state as well as back it up. Chapter 34 describes Wbadmin start systemstate recovery and its parameters. A system recovery can be performed from the Windows Server Backup snap-in or from the command line. See Chapter 34 for details.

Summary

Windows Server 2008 depends on the registry for storing and retrieving vital configuration data. Knowing what's in it, how and when to edit the registry, and how to back it up and restore it is vital for system administrators. In particular, knowing how registry-editing utilities work and what they can do is a key skill you need to keep your Windows Server 2008 computers up and running. The next chapter is all about troubleshooting your server.

Chapter 37

Troubleshooting and Recovery

Many of the chapters in this book contain information and advice on keeping your network safe, organized, and available. Chapter 33, "Disaster Planning," Chapter 34, "Using Backup," and Chapter 35, "Planning Fault Tolerance and Avoidance," are all, in fact, dedicated to averting problems–and where problems can't be avoided, correcting them.

This chapter focuses on using available utilities to locate the causes of problems and fix them, but you'll also find details on recovering all aspects of a server.

Note Chapter 5, "Getting Started," Chapter 6, "Upgrading to Windows Server 2008," and Chapter 7, "Configuring a New Installation," are the places to look for tips on troubleshooting installations. Problems with printers? See Chapter 10, "Managing Printers." Additional help is available at the Microsoft Help and Support center (*http://support.microsoft.com*).

Determining Priorities

When a major problem is bearing down on you–or has already arrived–it's essential to get past the immediate response of

When in trouble or in doubt,
Run in circles, scream and shout.

Triaging the situation will calm the atmosphere and give everyone a focus.

- **Identify priorities** Single out the most important issues. If you are facing a natural disaster or other physical danger, human life and safety is the first priority. Protecting the organization's data is probably the second priority, followed by maintaining some level of service for the organization and customers.
- **Take steps to prevent further damage** Disable backup software to avoid overwriting good backups. If the problem involves an attacker or a virus, remove the server from the network immediately.
- **Set a timeline** Create deadlines for the goals you identify. In the event of physical danger, people can come to harm if you miss a deadline. Missing a deadline in more benign situations can result in lost data or revenue. Revise these deadlines as you gather additional information.
- **Identify available personnel** Ascertain who is available to perform troubleshooting or recovery. For important tasks, use two people when possible to reduce the potential for errors. This is particularly important during emergencies, when it is easier to make mistakes. If the available personnel don't have enough experience performing the task, get outside help.
- **Identify and secure available physical resources** Identify physical resources such as power for spare computers and lights, food, water, telephones, and toilet facilities. In a more dramatic emergency, you will also need to consider medical supplies, shelter, and security.
- **Review relevant procedures** Go over your disaster recovery or troubleshooting procedures. (See Chapter 33.) If you have no existing procedures, create simple procedures to guide troubleshooting.
- **Identify fallback plans** An important part of a disaster recovery procedure is a complete restore or replacement scenario, along with a time estimate for how long this should take and the possible effects it will have. Do not spend critical hours troubleshooting a crucial server that you can restore from backup quickly and with few negative consequences. Also, identify the fallback plan in case all recovery plans fail.
- **Take stock of available backups** Identify available backups, including disk images, full system backups, data backups, and online backups.
- **Identify available hardware and software** Identify what hardware and software resources are available. Use the following list as a guide:
  - Servers to take over roles from the affected systems

   - Spare servers and parts
   - External USB hard drives or spare internal drives
   - USB flash drives
   - Backup drives
   - Installation CDs, including old versions
   - Software licenses and keys
- **Expect the unexpected** With major disasters, priorities usually change before you are finished recovering. Organization priorities might change, and your own personal priorities might change.
- **Document *everything*** Document everything you do so that another administrator can take over if necessary. Taking notes also makes it easier to update procedures with anything you learn from the troubleshooting or recovery process.
- **Implement the plan** Decide on a reasonable amount of time for the triaging, and when it expires, implement the plan. Don't spend so much time triaging that the problems get worse.

Note When troubleshooting or recovering from a problem, try to increase the number of recovery options. If a server is failing, create a new backup before troubleshooting it. Do not overwrite an old backup—it might come in handy later, especially for computer forensics. If you have a single backup of important data, write-protect it and make a copy before restoring.

Recovering a System

This section discusses how to troubleshoot and recover a system that does not start. If you have a disaster recovery plan (as described in Chapter 33), follow those procedures. Use this section to supplement the plan as necessary, and make notes as you go on how you can update the plan.

The recovery steps outlined in this section proceed from modest measures to desperate ones. In any recovery procedure, adopt a minimalist approach. Start with the least invasive steps and move on to more drastic ones only if necessary.

Identifying Possible Causes

When a computer fails, there's always a reason. It may mot be immediately apparent, but contrary to popular belief, no magic is involved. The following list describes possible causes and the appropriate troubleshooting steps to take for each. Detailed procedures are located later in this chapter.

- **A device or driver** Start Microsoft Windows using the Last Known Good startup option, or start Windows in Safe Mode and use the Device Driver Rollback Wizard to revert to an older driver.
- **A program or software update** Start Windows using the Last Known Good startup option, or start Windows in Safe Mode and then uninstall the program.
- **Registry editing or changing system settings** Start Windows using Safe Mode, and edit the relevant system settings. If Windows does not start in Safe Mode, use wbadmin to perform a system state recovery. (See "Recovering the System State" later in this chapter.)
- **Failing hard drive** If a hard drive is making more or less noise than usual, it may be failing. A hardware RAID controller that beeps or clicks may have a failing drive. Open the RAID controller software and check the status of the drives. Check the Hardware Events log in Event Viewer for disk-related errors. Run chkdsk at the command line to scan the drive.

> **Note** Press F8 when the computer displays the Starting Windows text, and then choose the Enable VGA Mode option to resolve display malfunctions temporarily. After Windows starts, select a more conservative display setting (lower the resolution, refresh rate, or both) or choose a different display driver.

- **Failing hardware** A power outage or power surge may be the culprit. Also, be suspicious when a computer starts making noises that were hitherto unknown. Closely check the functioning of moving devices such as hard drives and power supplies. Verify that all fans are working. Check heat levels–processors running hotter than 50 degrees Celsius are on the verge of causing a failure.

Boot the system and verify that the power-on self test (POST) proceeds properly. If the POST fails or does not appear, the power supply, RAM, motherboard, display card, or CPU has failed. If the POST succeeds, use a hardware-monitoring tool in the BIOS, Extensible Firmware Interface (EFI), or third-party troubleshooting program to determine whether other devices are failing.

Rolling Back a Device Driver

Device drivers are one of the most common causes of system instabilities, so if the system becomes unstable after updating a device driver, revert to the previous driver. Windows

Server 2008 continues to make this easy by providing a simple rollback procedure. To use this feature, follow these steps:

1. Open Device Manager in Control Panel.
2. Right-click the device with a driver you want to roll back and select Properties from the shortcut menu.
3. Click the Drivers tab and then click Roll Back Driver.
4. In the Driver Package Rollback dialog box, click Yes.

Note The Roll Back Driver button is available only if a previous version of the driver was installed. If the current driver for the device is the only one that was ever installed on this computer, the Roll Back Driver button will not be enabled.

Recovering Your Server

You can use the backups you've created with Windows Server Backup to recover your operating system, system state, volumes, application data, backup catalog, and local files and folders.

Different tools are used to recover different objects. For example:

- The Recovery Wizard in Windows Server Backup can recover files, folders, applications, and volumes.
- Windows Setup disc or a separate installation of the Windows Recovery Environment can recover the operating system and the full server (all volumes).
- Wbadmin start systemstaterecovery can recover the system state.

Note You can perform all these recovery procedures using the Wbadmin command detailed in Chapter 35.

Recovering Volumes

When you restore a full volume using the Recovery Wizard, all contents of the volume are restored–you can't select individual files or folders to recover. To recover only certain files or folders and not a full volume, see "Recovering Files and Folders" later in this chapter.

To recover selected volumes, follow these steps:

1. Open the Administrative Tools menu and click Windows Server Backup.

2. In the Actions pane under Windows Server Backup, click Recover to start the Recovery Wizard.
3. On the Getting Started page, specify whether the volumes will be recovered from backups stored on this computer; skip to step 5 after clicking Next.
4. If you are recovering volumes from backups stored on another computer, do the following, and then click Next:
   a. On the Specify Location Type page, indicate whether the backup that you want to restore from is on a local drive or a remote shared folder.
   b. If you are recovering from a local drive, on the Select Backup Location page, select the location of the backup from the drop-down list. If you are recovering from a remote shared folder, type the path to the folder on the Specify Remote Folder page and then click Next. The path to the backup will be \\<*RemoteSharedFolder*>\WindowsImageBackup\<*ComputerName*>\<*YourBackup*>.
5. If you are recovering from this computer, on the Select Backup Location page, select the location of the backup from the drop-down list. If you are recovering from DVD or removable media, you are prompted to insert the device or first DVD in the series, and then click Next.
6. For a recovery either from the local computer or another computer, on the Select Backup Date page, select the date from the calendar and the time from the drop-down list of backups you want to restore from.
7. On the Select Recovery Type page, click Volumes, and then click Next.
8. On the Select Volumes page, select the check boxes associated with the volumes in the Source Volume column that you want to recover. Then, from the associated drop-down list in the Destination Volume column, select the location that you want to recover the volume to. Click Next.

   Important A message informs you that any data on the destination volume will be lost when you perform the recovery. Be sure the destination volume is empty or doesn't contain information that could be needed later.

9. On the Confirmation page, review the details, and then click Recover to restore the specified volumes.
10. On the Recovery progress page, you can view the status of the recovery operation and whether it completed successfully.

Recovering Files and Folders from the Local Server

To recover files and folders, you must have at least one backup on an external disk or in a remote shared folder—you can't recover files and folders from backups saved to DVDs or removable media. The backup cannot be a system state backup—file and folder recovery isn't possible from a system state backup.

To recover files and folders from the current server, follow these steps:

1. Open the Administrative Tools menu and click Windows Server Backup.
2. In the Actions pane under Windows Server Backup, click Recover to start the Recovery Wizard.
3. On the Getting Started page, select This Server and then click Next.
4. On the Select Backup Location page, select the location of the backup from the drop-down list, and then click Next.
5. On the Select Items To Recover page, under Available Items, expand the list until the folder you want is visible. Click a folder to display the contents in the adjacent pane, click each item that you want to restore, and then click Next.
6. On the Specify Recovery Options page, under Recovery Destination, select one of the following, and then click Next:
    - Original Location.
    - Another Location. Type the path to the location, or click Browse to select it.
7. Under When Backup Finds Existing Files And Folders, choose one of the following options and then click Next:
    - Create Copies So I Have Both Versions Of The File Or Folder
    - Overwrite Existing Files With Recovered Files
    - Don't Recover Those Existing Files And Folders
8. On the Confirmation page, review the details, and then click Recover to restore the specified items.
9. On the Recovery Progress page, view the status of the recovery operation and whether it completed successfully.

Recovering Files and Folders from Another Server

To recover files and folders from a backup on another computer, the backup must be on an external disk or in a remote shared folder—you can't recover individual files and folders from backups saved to DVDs or removable media. The backup cannot be a system state backup—file and folder recovery isn't possible from a system state backup.

To recover files and folders from another server, follow these steps:

1. Open the Administrative Tools menu and click Windows Server Backup.
2. In the Actions pane under Windows Server Backup, click Recover to start the Recovery Wizard.
3. On the Getting Started page, select Another Computer and click Next.
4. On the Specify Location Type page, select one of the following and then click Next.
    - Local Drives
    - Remote Shared Folder
5. If you are recovering from a local drive, on the Select Backup Location page, select the location of the backup from the drop-down list.
6. If recovering from a remote shared folder, type the path to the folder on the Specify Remote Folder page and then click Next. The path to the backup will be \\<*Remote-SharedFolder*>\WindowsImageBackup\<*ComputerName*>\<*YourBackup*>.
7. On the Select Backup Date page, select the date from the calendar and the time from the drop-down list of backups you want to restore from. Click Next.
8. On the Select Recovery Type page, click Files And Folders, and then click Next.
9. On the Select Items To Recover page, expand the list under Available Items until the folder you want is visible. Click a folder to display the contents in the adjacent pane, click each item that you want to restore, and then click Next.
10. On the Specify Recovery Options page, under Recovery Destination, click one of the following, and then click Next:
    - Original Location.
    - Another Location. Then, type the path to the location, or click Browse to select it.
11. Under When Backup Finds Existing Files And Folders, click one of the following, and then click Next.
    - Create Copies So I Have Both Versions of the File or Folder
    - Overwrite Existing Files With Recovered Files
    - Don't Recover Those Existing Files and Folders

12. On the Confirmation page, review the details, and then click Recover to restore the files and folders.
13. On the Recovery Progress page, view the status of the recovery operation and whether it completed successfully.

Recovering Applications and Data

You can use the Recovery Wizard in Windows Server Backup to recover applications and data from a backup, provided that the application in question uses Volume Shadow Copy Service (VSS) technology so that it is compatible with Windows Server Backup. Also, the VSS writer for the application must have been enabled before you created the backup being used for recovery. Most applications do not enable the VSS writer by default. You will have to explicitly enable it. If the VSS writer was not enabled for the backup, you will not be able to recover applications from it.

To recover an application, follow these steps:

1. Open the Administrative Tools menu and click Windows Server Backup.
2. In the Actions pane under Windows Server Backup, click Recover to start the Recovery Wizard.
3. On the Getting Started page, specify whether the application will be recovered from backups run on this computer or another computer, and then click Next.
4. If you are recovering applications from backups stored on another computer, do the following, and then click Next:
   a. On the Specify Location Type page, indicate whether the backup that you want to restore from is on a local drive or a remote shared folder.
   b. If you are recovering from a local drive, on the Select Backup Location page, select the location of the backup from the drop-down list. If recovering from a remote shared folder, type the path to the folder on the Specify Remote Folder page (see Figure 37-1) and then click Next. The path to the backup will be \\<*RemoteSharedFolder*>\WindowsImageBackup\<*ComputerName*>\<*YourBackup*>.

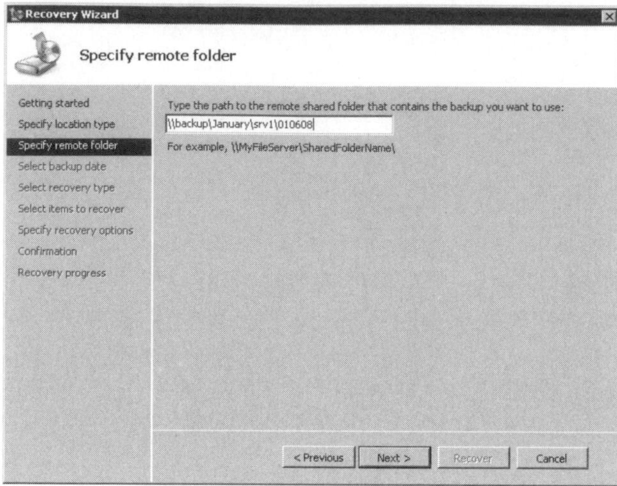

Figure 37-1 Specifying the remote shared folder

   c. If you are recovering from this computer, on the Select Backup Location page, select the location of the backup from the drop-down list, and then click Next.

5. On the Select Backup Date page, select the date from the calendar and the time from the drop-down list of the backup that you want to restore from, and then click Next.
6. On the Select Recovery Type page, click Applications, and then click Next.
7. On the Select Application page, under Applications, select the application to recover. If the backup that you are using is the most recent and the application you are recovering supports a roll-forward of the application database, you will see a check box labeled Do Not Perform A Roll-Forward Recovery Of The Application Databases. Select this check box if you want to prevent Windows Server Backup from rolling forward the application database that is currently on your server. Click Next.
8. On the Specify Recovery Options page, under Recovery Destination, select one of the following, and then click Next:
   - Recover to Original Location.
   - Recover to Another Location. Type the path to the location, or click Browse to select it.
9. On the Confirmation page, review the details, and then click Recover to restore the listed items.

10. On the Recovery Progress page, view the status of the recovery operation and whether it completed successfully.

Important You can copy an application to a different location, but you cannot recover an application to a different location or computer of a different name.

Recovering the Operating System

You can recover your server operating system or full server by using a Windows Setup disc and a backup created with Windows Server Backup. The Windows Setup disc allows access to the System Recovery Options page in the Windows Recovery Environment.

Before you start, you need to determine the following:

- Where you will recover to
- What backup you will use
- Whether you will perform an operating system–only or full server recovery
- Whether you will reformat and repartition your disks

Important When recovering to a new hard disk, the new disk must be least as large as the disk that contained the volumes that were backed up—no matter what size those volumes were. For example, if you backed up only one 50-GB volume on a 1-terabyte disk, you have to use a 1-terabyte or larger disk when restoring.

To recover the operating system or the full server using a Windows Setup disc, follow these steps:

1. Insert the Windows Setup disc into the DVD drive and turn on the computer. The Install Windows Wizard appears.
2. Specify language settings, and then click Next.
3. Click Repair Your Computer.
4. Setup searches the hard disk drives for an existing Windows installation and then displays the results in System Recovery Options. If you are recovering the operating system onto a separate computer, the list should be empty. (There should be no operating system on the computer.) Click Next.
5. On the System Recovery Options page, click Windows Complete PC Restore to start the Windows Complete PC Restore Wizard.

6. Select Use the Latest Available Backup (recommended) or Restore a Different Backup and then click Next.
7. If restoring a different backup, on the Select The Location Of The Backup page, select
   a. The computer that contains the backup that you want to use, and then click Next.
   b. On the Select The Backup To Restore page, click the backup you want to use. Click Next.
   c. Click Advanced to browse for a backup on the network, and then click Next.

   Important If the storage location contains backups from multiple computers, be sure to click the correct row for the backups for the computer that you want to use.

8. On the Choose How To Restore The Backup page:
   a. Select Format And Repartition Disks to delete existing partitions and reformat the destination disks to be the same as the backup. This enables the Exclude Disks button. Click this button and then select the check boxes associated with any disks that you want to exclude from being formatted and partitioned. The disk that contains the backup that you are using is automatically excluded.
   b. Select the Only Restore System Disks check box to perform an operating system-only recovery.
   c. Click Install Drivers to install any needed device drivers for the hardware that you are recovering to.
   d. Click Advanced to stipulate whether the computer is restarted and the disks are checked for errors immediate after the recovery.
   e. Click Next.
9. Confirm the details for the restoration, and then click Finish.

Recovering the System State

In Windows Server 2008, the System State consists of at least the following:

- Registry
- COM+ class registration database

- Certificate services database
- Active Directory Domain Services
- SYSVOL directory
- Cluster Service information
- Internet Information Services (IIS) meta-directory
- System files that are under Windows File Protection (WFS)

Depending on the computer configuration, additional data may be included.

Recovering the system state is performed by Wbadmin from the command line. The syntax for the command is:

```
wbadmin start sysstaterecovery
-version:VersionIdentifier
-showsummary
[-backupTarget:{VolumeName | NetworkSharePath}]
[-machine:BackupMachineName]
[-recoveryTarget:TargetPathForRecovery]
[-excludeSystemFiles]
[-quiet]
```

Table 37-1 describes the parameters of the Wbadmin command,

Table 37-1 Wbadmin Parameters

Parameter	Description
-version	Version identifier of the backup in MM/DD/YYYY-HH:MM format, as listed by WBADMIN GET VERSIONS.
-backupTarget	Specifies the storage location that contains the backups for which you want to do the recovery. Useful when the backups are stored in a different location than the normal location for backups of this computer.
-machine	Specifies the name of the computer for which you want to do the recovery. Useful when multiple computers have been backed up to the same location. Should be used when *-backupTarget* is specified.
-recoveryTarget	Existing directory path to restore to. Useful if you are restoring to an alternate location.
-authsysvol	Performs an authoritative restore of SYSVOL.
-quiet	Runs the command with no user prompts.
-showsummary	Reports the summary of the last run of reboot status of last successful online system state recovery. This option cannot be accompanied by any other options.

Note Use *wbadmin start systemstatebackup* as described in Chapter 35 to back up the system state.

Using System Information

The System Information utility (Msinfo32.exe) provides detailed information about the software and hardware environment of a system. To open the System Information utility, click Start, choose All Programs, choose Accessories, choose System Tools, and then choose System Information. As you navigate through the console pane, plenty of information about the system becomes available:

- Expand Hardware Resources to look for hardware conflicts.
- To look for device problems, expand Components and then expand Problem Devices. Make a note of any devices listed here, and then use Device Manager to disable or troubleshoot them.
- Expand Software Environment to view Startup programs. Disable any programs you suspect might be causing problems, and then reboot the computer.
- To view a list of Windows errors the system has reported to Microsoft, select Software Environment and then select Windows Error Reporting.
- To scan for unsigned system files, type **sigverif** in the Run dialog box and click OK. The File Signature Verification dialog box opens. Click Start and all system files will be scanned. Click Advanced and select options for logging the verification results to a file.

Verifying the Status of Services

Services that fail or don't start when they should can cause major problems on a server. To avoid this, set all important services to start automatically, disable any suspect services, and specify what actions to take if a service fails. To view the status of a service or change its options, launch Services (Services.msc) from the Administrative Tools menu.

The status of each service is shown in the Status column. To quickly change the status, right-click the service and make a selection from the shortcut menu, as shown in Figure 37-2.

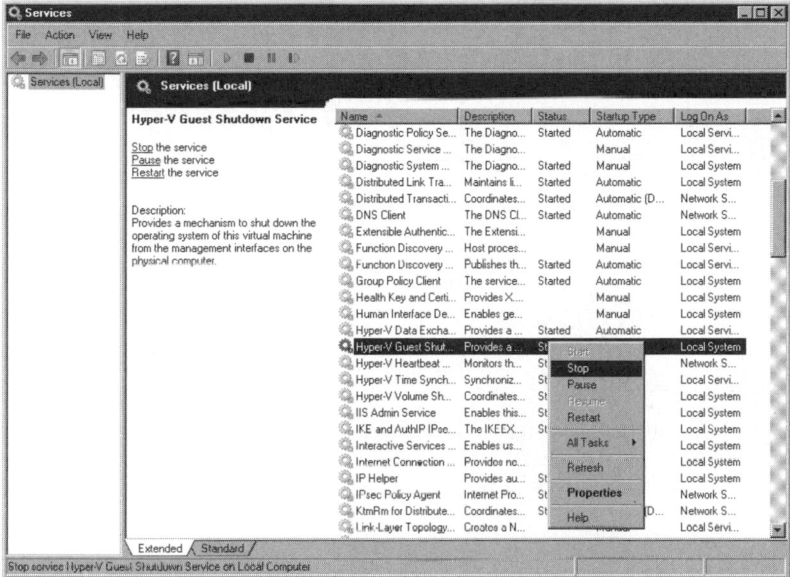

Figure 37-2 Changing a service status

To change advanced settings for a service, double-click the service or select Properties from the shortcut menu. In the Properties dialog box, shown in Figure 37-3, select the action you want to perform. To change when the service starts, select from the Startup Type list on the General tab.

- **Automatic** The service starts when the computer starts.
- **Manual** The service will start only when started manually.
- **Disable** The service is disabled.
- **Automatic (Delayed Start)** The service starts automatically but after other automatic services have started.

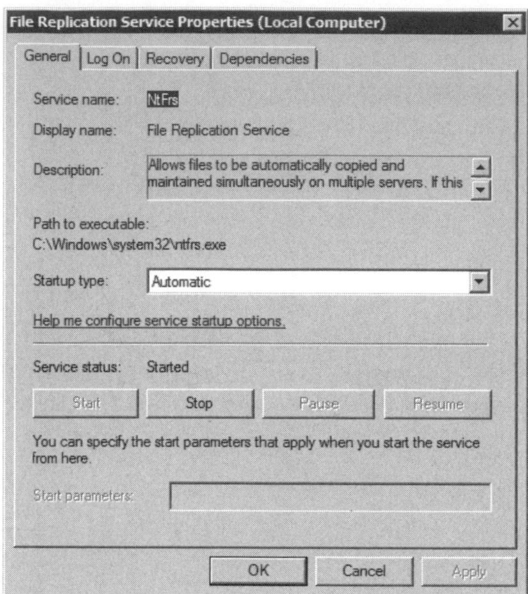

Figure 37-3 The General tab of the Service Properties

Real World **When to Use a Delayed Start**

Some services will benefit from being set for a delayed start. But how do you know which ones? Sometimes you'll get frequent messages that a service has failed to start, but when you start it in the Services MMC it starts without a problem. That's a clear indication that the service needs a delayed start.

Before changing the setting to Automatic (Delayed Start), click the Dependencies tab in the Properties dialog box. If items are listed in the lower box (The Following System Components Depend On This Service), scheduling a delayed start is not advisable. You will have to look elsewhere for the reason the service is failing. One place to look is at any services listed in the other dependencies box (This Service Depends On The Following System Components).

Note If you make changes to services and then have difficulty starting the computer, you can start the computer in Safe Mode. In Safe Mode, a basic set of services needed to start the operating system are started in a default scheme, regardless of any changes that are made to the service settings. After the computer is in Safe Mode, you can change the service configuration or restore the default configuration.

- To specify which account the service uses to log on, use the options on the Log On tab.
- To specify what actions to take when the service fails, use options on the the Recovery tab.
- To view the services on which the service is dependent and which services depend on it, click the Dependencies tab.

Using the System Configuration Utility

The System Configuration Utility provides access to virtually all startup parameters. To troubleshoot startup problems, start Windows in Safe Mode and then follow these steps:

1. Type **msconfig** in the Run dialog box and click OK to start System Configuration. The following list includes possible problem sources:
   - **Missing or damaged system files** Look for an error message during startup or in the boot log, or use the File Signature Verification Tool to determine whether all Windows files are intact and digitally signed. If a file is missing, damaged, or is the wrong version, boot from the Windows Server 2008 DVD and select Repair.
   - **Damaged registry** Restore the System State as described in "Recovering the System State" earlier in this chapter.
   - **Virus infection** Use a current virus scanner to find and remove viruses or other malware.
2. Select Diagnostic Startup on the General Tab. Click OK and then reboot the computer.
3. If the system starts properly using the Diagnostic Startup, start the System Configuration Utility, choose the Selective Startup option, and then select Load Startup Items.
4. Click OK and reboot the computer.
5. If the problem reappears, the Startup Items are the source. If it doesn't return, open the System Configuration Utility again, choose the Selective Startup option, check Load System Services, and clear Load Startup Items. Reboot.
6. When you identify generally where the problem lies, click the appropriate tab and troubleshoot the services, startup items, or lines in the file one by one until you locate the specific problem. Note the offending line or program.

7. Return the settings in the System Configuration Utility to normal startup, and then permanently disable the offending line or program. (Use the System Configuration Utility only to troubleshoot problems, not to fix them.) To disable the program or line, use the appropriate action based on the location of the problem:
   - For problems with services, use the Services MMC snap-in to change the service startup type to Disabled (as described earlier in the chapter in "Verifying the Status of Services").
   - For problems with startup items, make a note of the item's location, and then remove the program from the Startup Items folder on the Start menu (if the location of the item is Common Startup), or use Registry Editor to export the key and then delete it from the registry.
   - For problems in the System.ini or Win.ini files, type **Sysedit** in the Run dialog box or at a command prompt and then remove or comment out the offending line in the appropriate file. (Use a semicolon before the line to disable it.)

Using the System File Checker

The System File Checker is a command-line tool that verifies that the system has the correct versions of protected system files. If the System File Checker finds an incorrect version of a protected system file, it will retrieve the correct version from your Windows Server DVD or CD-ROM.

To use the System File Checker, log on locally as an administrator, open a Command Prompt window, and then type **Sfc** followed by the appropriate parameter. Table 37-2 describes the possible parameters.

Table 37-2 File System Checker Parameters

/Scannow	Scans all protected system files.
/Verifyonly	Scans integrity of all protected system files.
/Scanfile	Scans integrity of referenced file.
/Verifyfile	Verifies the integrity of the file with full path. For example, *sfc /verifyfile=c:\windows\system32\kernel32.dll* will check whether the kernel32.dll is valid and not corrupted.
/Offbootdir	For offline repair. Specify the location of the offline boot directory.
/Offwindir	For offline repair. Specify the location of the offline Windows directory.

Using the Shutdown Event Tracker

Server availability is of vital importance—a server that's off or restarting is not available to clients. Administrators can use the Shutdown Event Tracker tool to keep track of when and why a server restarts. Information about why a server shuts down is recorded in Event Viewer. If a user chooses the Start menu's Shut Down command, a dialog box prompts for an explanation for the shutdown. If the server shuts down unexpectedly (for example, because of a hardware failure), Windows prompts the next user with shutdown privileges who logs on to describe why the server shut down. Besides this user-provided information, any time a user shuts down the system and specifies in the Shutdown Event Tracker that the shutdown was unplanned, Windows records the system state data for later analysis. Administrators can then use this information to improve uptime. To view shutdown events, follow these steps:

1. Start Event Viewer from the Administrative Tools menu.
2. In the console tree, expand Windows Logs and select System.
3. In the Action pane, click Filter Current Log.
4. In the Filter Current Log dialog box, click the drop-down list for Event Sources and check the box next to USER32, as shown in Figure 37-4.

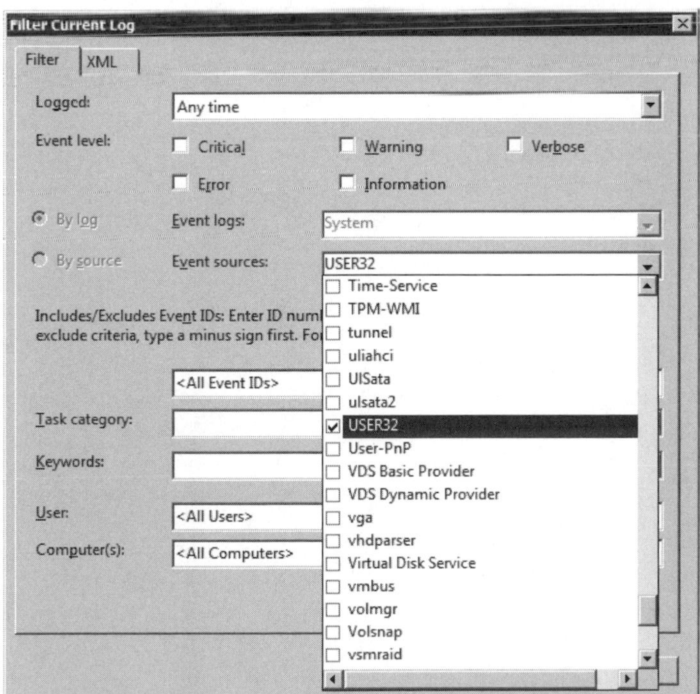

Figure 37-4 Filtering the system log for shutdown events

5. Click OK.
6. Double-click an event to view the details.

Summary

Using this chapter plus your own experience and judgment, you should now have the tools to troubleshoot whatever difficulties may come your way. There will probably be fewer than you imagine.

The next sections are appendices with helpful information about interface changes and additional tools.

Appendix A

Interface Changes from Windows Server 2003

At first glance, the interface of Windows Server 2008 appears to be completely different from the one in Windows Server 2003, and in some ways that's true. The new Server Manager console is a new and complete departure from earlier versions of Windows Server. For one thing, it's actually useful. But more important, it is *the* supported method for adding roles and features to Windows Server 2008. By integrating all the management and administration into a single interface, Server Manager changes the immediate look and feel of how Windows Server 2008 is managed. But underneath that major change, many of the underlying management consoles are essentially unchanged. As just one of a whole host of examples, DNS Management is the same. The executable, dnsmgmt.msc, is the same, and the look and feel are the same as they have been since Windows 2000 Server, at least. You can now get to that DNS Manager either as part of the Server Manager console or directly.

Other changes include:

- Event Viewer, covered in detail in Chapter 14, "Managing Daily Operations," which is vastly expanded and improved.
- Network And Sharing Center, the replacement for Network Connections, which is a major step backward. Fortunately, you can still get to the Network Connections dialog box–it just takes an extra click or two.
- Computer Management has been replaced by the Server Manager console. But you can still get to Computer Management using the command line: compmgmt.msc.

Table A-1 lists the changes since Windows Server 2003 R2, and, in some cases, the way to get to the old version. Table A-2 is a list of the administration consoles and their command lines.

Table A-1 Interface Changes Since Windows Server 2003 R2

Windows Server 2003 Name	Windows Server 2008 Name	Summary
Manage Your Server	Server Manager	Fully integrates all management into a single console, and includes adding roles and features.
Configure Your Server	Server Manager	Fully integrates all management into a single console, and includes adding roles and features.
Add/Remove Programs	Programs And Features	New interface, same basic functionality.
Add/Remove Windows Features	Server Manager	All Windows Components are added and removed through Server Manager.
Display Properties	Personalization	New Vista look. More clicks required to get the same functionality.
Accessibility Options	Ease Of Access Center	New interface.
Automatic Updates	Windows Update	New interface.
Stored User Names And Passwords	User Accounts	
Sounds And Audio Devices	Sound	The mechanics of the sound card and audio devices.
	Personalization	Windows system sounds.
Computer Management	Server Manager	Portions of this are also replicated in other places, but Server Manager is the place to go.
Terminal Services Manager Terminal Services Configuration Terminal Services Licensing	All Terminal Services Administration Tools have been moved one layer deeper. Open Adminstative Tools, then open Terminal Services.	Same tools are available, plus new ones for the many new features in Terminal Services.
Authorization Manager	Azman.msc	No link in Administrative Tools.
Cluster Administrator	Failover Cluster Management	
IP Address Management	Server Manager	
Remote Storage	Removable Storage Manager	

Table A-1 Interface Changes Since Windows Server 2003 R2

Windows Server 2003 Name	Windows Server 2008 Name	Summary
Routing And Remote Access	Network Policy Services	RRAS is a role service within NPS.
Telephony	Tapimgmt.msc	No icon in Administrative Tools.
Remote Installation Services (RIS)	WDS	Windows Deployment Services is now a server role.
Windows Services For NFS	Services For Network File System	
Performance	Reliability And Performance Monitor	Still uses Perfmon.msc, but major improvements and changes.
NT Backup	Windows Server Backup	All new.
Connection Manager Administration Kit	N/A	N/A

Table A-2 Command Lines for Administrative Consoles

Command Line	Console Name
AdRmsAdmin.msc	Active Directory Rights Management Services
Adsiedit.msc	ADSI Edit
Azman.msc	Authorization Manager
Certmgr.msc	Certmgr (Certificates)
Certtmpl.msc	Certificates Template Console
CluAdmin.msc	Failover Cluster Management
Comexp.msc	Component Services
Compmgmt.msc	Computer Management
Devmgmt.msc	Device Manager
Dfsmgmt.msc	DFS Management
Dhcpmgmt.msc	DHCP
Diskmgmt.msc	Disk Management
Dnsmgmt.msc	DNS Manager
Domain.msc	Active Directory Domains And Trusts
Dsa.msc	Active Directory Users And Computers
Dssite.msc	Active Directory Sites And Services
Eventvwr.msc	Event Viewer

Table A-2 Command Lines for Administrative Consoles

Command Line	Console Name
Fsmgmt.msc	Shared Folders
Fsrm.msc	File Server Resource Manager
Fxsadmin.msc	Microsoft Fax Service Manager
Gpedit.msc	Local Group Policy Editor
Lusrmgr.msc	Local Users And Groups
Napclcfg.msc	NAP Client Configuration
Nfsmgmt.msc	Services For Network File System
Nps.msc	Network Policy Server
Ocsp.msc	Online Responder
Perfmon.msc	Reliability And Performance Monitor
Pkiview.msc	Enterprise PKI
Printmanagement.msc	Print Management
Remoteprograms.msc	TS RemoteApp Management
Rsop.msc	Resultant Set of Policy
Secpol.msc	Local Security Policy
ServerManager.msc	Server Manager
StorageMgmt.msc	Share And Storage Management
Services.msc	Services
StorExpl.msc	Storage Explorer
Tapimgmt.msc	Telephony
Taskschd.msc	Task Scheduler
Tmp.msc	Trusted Platform Module (TPM) Management
Tsadmin.msc	Terminal Services Management
Tsconfig.msc	Terminal Services Configuration
Tsgateway.msc	TS Gateway Manager
Tsmmc.msc	Remote Desktops
Uddi.msc	UDDI Services Console
Wbadmin.msc	Windows Server Backup
Wdsmgmt.msc	Windows Deployment Services
Winsmgmt.msc	WINS
WmiMgmt.msc	WMI Control

Appendix B

Optional Components

Windows Server 2008 extends the Windows Server releases trend of including only the absolute essentials in the default release. Everything else is an optional component. In Windows Server 2008 that goes even further with the new Server Core versions, which don't include any of the GUI components that make up much of what we think of as "Windows." In both Server and Server Core, there are three types of optional components–Roles, Role Services, and Features. *Roles* are focused around the core functionality of a server, with Role Services being optional components of a Role. So, for example, the File Server Role is an optional component. But within that File Server Role, you have additional optional Role Services, including Distributed File System (DFS) and the DFS Role Services of DFS Namespaces and DFS Replication; File Server Resource Manager (FSRM); Services for Network File System; Windows Search Service; and the Windows Server 2003 File Services Role Services, including File Replication Service and Indexing Service.

Features are additional optional components that may be added to any server performing other roles, but doesn't define a role in and of itself. So Windows PowerShell is a Feature–one we install on every server we build except Server Core computers.

Table B-1 lists the Windows Server 2008 Roles and Role Services.

Table B-1 Windows Server 2008 Roles and Role Services

Role	Role Service	Install ID
Active Directory Certificate Services		AD-Certificate
	Certification Authority	ADCS-Cert-Authority
	Certification Authority Web Enrollment	ADCS-Web-Enrollment
	Online Responder	ADCS-Online-Cert
	Network Device Enrollment Service	ADCS-Device-Enrollment
Active Directory Domain Services		None (installed with dcpromo.exe)
	Active Directory Domain Controller	ADDS-Domain-Controller

Table B-1 **Windows Server 2008 Roles and Role Services**

Role	Role Service	Install ID
	Identity Management for UNIX	ADDS –Identity-Mgmt
	Server for Network Information Services	ADDS-NIS
	Password Synchronization	ADDS-Password-Sync
	Administration Tools	ADDS-IDMU-Tools
Active Directory Federation Services		
	Federation Service	ADFS -Federation
	Federation Service Proxy	ADFS-Proxy
	AD FS Web Agents	ADFS-Web-Agents
	Claims-aware Agent	ADFS-Claims
	Windows Token-based Agent	ADFS-Windows-Token
Active Directory Lightweight Directory Services		ADLDS
Active Directory Rights Management Services		
	Active Directory Rights Management Server	
	Identity Federation Support	
Application Server		Application-Server
	Application Server Foundation	AS-AppServer-Foundation
	Web Server (IIS) Support	AS-Web-Support
	COM+ Network Access	AS-Ent-Services
	TCP Port Sharing	AS-TCP-Port-Sharing
	Windows Process Activation Service Support	AS-WAS-Support
	HTTP Activation	AS-HTTP-Activation
	Message Queuing Activation	AS-MSMQ-Activation
	TCP Activation	AS-TCP-Activation
	Named Pipes Activation	AS-Named-Pipes

Table B-1 Windows Server 2008 Roles and Role Services

Role	Role Service	Install ID
	Distributed Transactions	AS-Dist-Transaction
	Incoming Remote Transactions	AS-Incoming-Trans
	Outgoing Remote Transactions	AS-Outgoing-Trans
	WS-Atomic Transactions	AS-WS-Atomic
DHCP Server		DHCP
DNS Server		DNS
Fax Server		Fax
File Services		
	File Server	FS-FileServer
	Distributed File System	FS-DFS
	DFS Namespaces	FS-DFS-Namespace
	DFS Replication	FS-DFS-Replication
	File Server Resource Manager	FS-Resource-Manager
	Services for Network File System	FS-NFS-Services
	Windows Search Service	FS-Search-Service
	Windows Server 2003 File Services	FS-Win2003-Services
	File Replication Service	FS-Replication
	Indexing Service	FS-Indexing-Service
Hyper-V		Hyper-V
Network Policy and Access Services		NPAS
	Network Policy Server	NPAS-Policy-Server
	Routing and Remote Access Services	NPAS-RRAS-Services
	Remote Access Service	NPAS-RRAS
	Routing	NPAS-Routing
	Health Registration Authority	NPAS-Health
	Host Credential Authorization Protocol	NPAS-Host-Cred

Table B-1 Windows Server 2008 Roles and Role Services

Role	Role Service	Install ID
Print Services		Print-Services
	Print Server	Print-Server
	LPD Service	Print-LPD-Service
	Internet Printing	Print-Internet
Terminal Services		Terminal-Services
	Terminal Server	TS-Terminal-Server
	TS Licensing	TS-Licensing
	TS Session Broker	TS-Session-Broker
	TS Gateway	TS-Gateway
	TS Web Access	TS-Web-Access
UDDI Services		
	UDDI Services Database	
	UDDI Services Web Application	
Web Server (IIS)		Web-Server
	Web Server	Web-WebServer
	Common HTTP Features	Web-Common-Http
	Static Content	Web-Static-Content
	Default Document	Web-Default-Doc
	Directory Browsing	Web-Dir-Browsing
	HTTP Errors	Web-Http-Errors
	HTTP Redirection	Web-Http-Redirect
	Application Development	Web-App-Dev
	ASP.NET	Web-Asp-Net
	.NET Extensibility	Web-Net-Ext
	ASP	Web-ASP
	CGI	Web-CGI
	ISAPI Extensions	Web-ISAPI-Ext
	ISAPI Filters	Web-ISAPI-Filter
	Server Side Includes	Web-Includes
	Health and Diagnostics	Web-Health
	HTTP Logging	Web-Http-Logging
	Logging Tools	Web-Log-Libraries

Table B-1 Windows Server 2008 Roles and Role Services

Role	Role Service	Install ID
	Request Monitor	Web Request Monitor
	Tracing	Web-Http-Tracing
	Custom Logging	Web-Custom-Logging
	ODBC Logging	Web-ODBC-Logging
	Security	Web-Security
	Basic Authentication	Web-Basic-Auth
	Windows Authentication	Web-Windows-Auth
	Digest Authentication	Web-Digest-Auth
	Client Certificate Mapping Authentication	Web-Client-Auth
	IIS Client Certificate Mapping Authentication	Web-Cert-Auth
	URL Authorization	Web-Url-Auth
	Request Filtering	Web-Filtering
	IP and Domain Restrictions	Web-IP-Security
	Performance	Web-Performance
	Static Content Compression	Web-Stat-Compression
	Dynamic Content Compression	Web-Dyn-Compression
	Custom Logging	Web-Custom-Logging
	Management Tools	Web-Mgmt-Tools
	IIS Management Console	Web-Mgmt-Console
	IIS Management Scripts and Tools	Web-Scripting-Tools
	Management Service	Web-Mgmt-Service
	IIS 6 Management Compatibility	Web-Mgmt-Compat
	IIS 6 MetabaseCompatibility	Web-Metabase
	IIS 6 WMI Compatibility	Web-WMI
	IIS 6 Scripting Tools	Web-Lgcy-Scripting
	IIS 6 Management Console	Web-Lgcy-Mgmt-Console

Table B-1 Windows Server 2008 Roles and Role Services

Role	Role Service	Install ID
	FTP Publishing Service	Web-Ftp-Publishing
	FTP Server	Web-Ftp-Server
	FTP Management Console	Web-Ftp-Mgmt-Console
Windows Deployment Services		WDS
	Deployment Server	WDS-Deployment
	Transport Server	WDS-Transport

Features are available across all Windows Server Roles, and provide functionality that can benefit a broad range of servers. One feature that stands out is Desktop Experience. This feature includes many of the optional programs and utilities that a normal Windows Vista workstation would use, but that aren't normally necessary on a server buried in a server room. These include Windows Media Player, Windows Mail, and the desktop themes that give Windows Vista its Aero look and feel. Table B-2 lists the features available in Windows Server 2008.

Table B-2 Windows Server 2008 Features

Feature	Install ID
NET Framework 3.0 Features	NET-Framework
.NET Framework 3.0	NET-Framework-Core
XPS Viewer	NET-XPS-Viewer
WCF Activation	NET-Win-CFAC
HTTP Activation	NET-HTTP-Activation
Non-HTTP Activation	NET-Non-HTTP-Activ
BitLocker Drive Encryption	BitLocker
BITS Server Extensions	BITS
Connection Manager Administration Kit	CMAK
Desktop Experience	Desktop-Experience
Failover Clustering	Failover-Clustering
Group Policy Management	GPMC
Internet Printing Client	Internet-Print-Client
Internet Storage Name Server	ISNS
LPR Port Monitor	LPR-Port-Monitor

Table B-2 **Windows Server 2008 Features**

Feature	Install ID
Message Queuing	MSMQ
Message Queuing Services	MSMQ-Services
Message Queuing Server	MSMQ-Server
Directory Service Integration	MSMQ-Directory
Message Queuing Triggers	MSMQ-Triggers
HTTP Support	MSMQ-HTTP-Support
Multicasting Support	MSMQ-Multicasting
Routing Service	MSMQ-Routing
Windows 2000 Client Support	MSMQ-Win2000
Message Queuing DCOM Proxy	MSMQ-DCOM
Multipath I/O	Multipath-IO
Network Load Balancing	NLB
Peer Name Resolution Protocol	PNRP
Quality Windows Audio VideoExperience	qWave
Remote Assistance	Remote-Assistance
Remote Differential Compression	RDC
Role Server Administration Tools	RSAT
Role Administration Tools	RSAT-Role-Tools
Active Directory Certificate Services Tools	RSAT-ADCS
Certification Authority Tools	RSAT-ADCS-Mgmt
Online Responder Tools	RSAT-Online-Responder
Active Directory Domain Services Tools	RSAT-ADDS
Active Directory Domain Controller Tools	RSAT-ADDC
Server for NIS Tools	RSAT-SNIS
Active Directory Lightweight Directory Services Tools	RSAT-ADLDS
Active Directory Rights Management Services Tools	RSAT-RMS
DHCP Server Tools	RSAT-DHCP
DNS Server Tools	RSAT-DNS-Server

Table B-2 Windows Server 2008 Features

Feature	Install ID
Fax Server Tools	RSAT-Fax
File Services Tools	RSAT-File-Services
Distributed File System Tools	RSAT-DFS-Mgmt-Con
File Server Resource Manager Tools	RSAT-FSRM-Mgmt
Hyper-V	Hyper-V
Services for Network File System Tools	RSAT-NFS-Admin
Network Policy and Access Services Tools	RSAT-NPAS
Print Services Tools	RSAT-Print-Services
Terminal Services Tools	RSAT-TS
Terminal Server Tools	RSAT-TS-RemoteApp
TS Gateway Tools	RSAT-TS-Gateway
TS Licensing Tools	RSAT-TS-Licensing
UDDI Services Tools	RSAT-UDDI
Web Server (IIS) Tools	RSAT-Web-Server
Windows Deployment Services Tools	RSAT-WDS
Feature Administration Tools	RSAT-Feature-Tools
BitLocker Drive Encryption Tools	RSAT-BitLocker
BITS Server Extensions Tools	RSAT-Bits-Server
Failover Clustering Tools	RSAT-Clustering
Network Load Balancing Tools	RSAT-NLB
SMTP Server Tools	RSAT-SMTP
WINS Server Tools	RSAT-WINS
Removable Storage Manager	Removable-Storage
RPC over HTTP Proxy	RPC-over-HTTP-Proxy
Simple TCP/IP Services	Simple-TCPIP
SMTP Server	SMTP-Server
SNMP Services	SNMP-Services
SNMP Service	SNMP-Service
SNMP WMI Provider	SNMP-WMI-Provider
Storage Manager for SANs	Storage-Mgr-SANS
Subsystem for UNIX-based Applications	Subsystem-UNIX-Apps

Table B-2 Windows Server 2008 Features

Feature	Install ID
Telnet Client	Telnet-Client
Telnet Server	Telnet-Server
TFTP Client	TFTP-Client
Windows Internal Database	Windows-Internal-DB
Windows PowerShell	PowerShell
Windows Process Activation Service	WAS
Process Model	WAS-Process-Model
.NET Environment	WAS-NET-Environment
Configuration APIs	WAS-Config-APIs
Windows Server Backup Features	Backup-Features
Windows Server Backup	Backup
Command-line Tools	Backup-Tools
Windows System Resource Manager	WSRM
WINS Server	WINS-Server
Wireless LAN Service	Wireless-Networking

Windows Server 2008 Core has a different subset of Roles, Role Services, and Features available, and they are all installed with the Ocsetup command-line tool. We list these in Table B-3 by their Install ID for Ocsetup.

Table B-3 Server Core Roles and Features

Install ID
BitLocker
BitLocker-RemoteAdminTool
ClientForNFS-Base
DFSN-Server
DFSR-Infrastructure-ServerEdition
DHCPServerCore
DirectoryServices-ADAM-ServerCore
DirectoryServices-DomainController-ServerFoundation
DNS-Server-Core-Role
FailoverCluster-Core
FRS-Infrastructure
IIS-WebServerRole

Table B-3 Server Core Roles and Features

Install ID
Microsoft-Windows-RemovableStorageManagementCore
MultipathIo
NetworkLoadBalancingHeadlessServer
Printing-ServerCore-Role
Printing-LPDPrintService
QWAVE
ServerForNFS-Base
SNMP-SC
SUACore
TelnetClient
WAS-WindowsActivationService
WindowsServerBackup
WINS-SC

Two Server Core Roles are not listed in detail—the IIS-WebServerRole and the WAS-WindowsActivationService role. Each of these has *many* Role Services that can be added as part of the role. Run Oclist at the command line on a Server Core computer to see a full listing.

Appendix C

Understanding TCP/IP v4

The protocol wars have ended, and TCP/IP is the winner. After years of proprietary protocols vying for popularity, TCP/IP has emerged as the only protocol needed by most networks. Every modern computer supports TCP/IP, as do a growing number of other devices such as printers, network appliances, personal digital assistants (PDAs), and cell phones. Additionally, Novell NetWare, Microsoft Windows, *and* Apple Mac OS have been using TCP/IP as their preferred network protocol for some time now. What is different is that version 6 of the TCP/IP protocols (IPv6) is beginning to enter our everyday world, and will eventually replace the ubiquitous version 4 of TCP/IP (IPv4).

Although the basics of setting up TCP/IP on a server are covered in Chapter 18, "Administering TCP/IP," we've included this appendix on the basics of IPv4 for those who wish to refresh their memories.

The TCP/IP Protocol Suite

Whole books have been written about TCP/IP, and justifiably so. Although most administrators don't need to know every detail of programming a TCP connection or what to expect as a return value from a *gethostbyname* call, they do need to understand enough to configure the protocol and make it work properly.

The key thing to remember about TCP/IP is that it *isn't a single entity*. TCP/IP is short for Transmission Control Protocol/Internet Protocol, but these are only two of the protocols included in the TCP/IP suite. A variety of other protocols exists, each with its own specialized area of importance and use.

TCP/IP isn't proprietary and isn't controlled by any one company or vendor, unlike other protocols such as Internetwork Packet Exchange/Sequenced Packet Exchange (IPX/SPX) and the now-obsolete NetBIOS Extended User Interface (NetBEUI) protocol. TCP/IP is an open standard controlled by the Internet Engineering Task Force (IETF) and by the users of the Internet itself in the form of RFCs (requests for comments). Anyone can submit an RFC for consideration and inclusion into the written definitions of the protocols and policies of the Internet and TCP/IP.

Internet Protocol

IP is the core protocol of the TCP/IP suite. To quote from RFC 791, "The Internet Protocol is designed for use in interconnected systems of packet-switched computer communication networks." IP performs only one basic function: It delivers a packet of bits (called a *datagram*) from point A to point B over any network "wire" it happens to encounter along the way.

> **Note** The term *wire* is used loosely here and elsewhere to indicate the actual—usually physical—network connection between two points. In fact, that wire can just as easily be a piece of optical fiber or even a radio or infrared signal. In all cases, it functions as the transmission medium through which the packets travel.

IP doesn't in and of itself know anything about the information in the datagram it carries, nor does it have any provision beyond a simple checksum to ensure that the data is intact or that it has reached its destination. That is left to the other protocols in the TCP/IP suite.

Transmission Control Protocol

According to RFC 793 (the defining RFC for the protocol), TCP is "a connection-oriented, end-to-end reliable protocol designed to fit into a layered hierarchy of protocols which support multinetwork applications." That's nice, but what does all that really mean? The following list should help you sort out these terms:

- **Connection-oriented** TCP provides for the communication of packets between two points, sending the datagram specifically from one computer or device to another, and sending an acknowledgment back to the sending computer on receipt of intact packets.
- **End-to-end** Each TCP packet designates a specific endpoint as its destination. Packets are passed along the wire and ignored except by the actual endpoint of the packet and any device that needs to direct it.
- **Reliable** This is the key point of TCP. When a program or application layer protocol such as File Transfer Protocol (FTP) uses TCP for its transport protocol, TCP

takes responsibility for the reliability of the communications. The protocol itself provides for interprocess communication to ensure not only that packets sent out get there, but also that they get there in the order in which they were sent. If a packet is missed, the protocol communicates with the sending device to ensure that the packet is resent.

Because TCP has to create a reliable connection between two devices or processes, each packet involves substantially more overhead than is needed with other, less reliable protocols within the suite. But by the same token, the programmer writing the application that uses TCP doesn't have to include a lot of error checking and handshaking in the application itself.

User Datagram Protocol

The User Datagram Protocol (UDP), another protocol in the TCP/IP suite, is a connectionless, transaction-oriented protocol designed to send packets with a minimum of protocol overhead. It provides no guarantee that its intended recipient received the packet, or that packets were received in the order in which they were sent. UDP is frequently used in broadcast messages that have no specific intended recipient, such as Boot Protocol (BOOTP) and Dynamic Host Configuration Protocol (DHCP) requests, but it can also be used by applications that prefer to ensure reliable delivery internally rather than in an underlying protocol. UDP is defined in RFC 768.

Many parts of the TCP/IP suite of protocols and programs can use either TCP or UDP as their transport protocol. The choice of which to use will depend on the reliability and security of the network you're on and whether it has routing issues. An example of a protocol that can use either TCP or UDP is the Network File System (NFS) Protocol.

Windows Sockets

Windows Sockets (commonly referred to as Winsock) is a Microsoft technology that provides a consistent way for application programs to communicate with a TCP/IP stack without having to consider any underlying variations in the TCP/IP stack implementation.

In the distant past, there were many vendors of TCP/IP protocol and applications suites for MS-DOS–based computers, each slightly different from the others. This situation made it extremely difficult to write an application that required TCP/IP and still worked with all the TCP/IP implementations that existed. Winsock was designed to get around this problem by providing a uniform set of application programming interface (API) calls that would be the same regardless of the underlying differences in the actual implementation of TCP/IP.

The original Winsock version 1 had a fair number of difficulties, and version 1.1 was released soon after its initial implementation. The current version of Winsock supported by Microsoft Windows Server 2008 and Windows Vista is version 2, which provides for full backward compatibility with earlier versions while offering improved functionality and support for additional features and expandability. Note that Winsock 2 has been around since Microsoft Windows NT 4, so applications are widely available that use this API.

NetBIOS

Network Basic Input/Output System (NetBIOS) is a networking API used by legacy applications and operating systems to communicate across a network using the NWLink (IPX/SPX compatible), NetBEUI, or TCP/IP protocols.

Until the advent of Microsoft Windows 2000, NetBIOS was the primary networking API used by all Microsoft operating systems. NetBIOS names were used for name resolution within Windows-based networks. Any time a computer wanted to communicate with another computer on the network, the computer had to resolve the NetBIOS name for the other computer either by querying a Windows Internet Naming Service (WINS) server, using a NetBIOS broadcast, or referring to the computer's local Lmhosts file.

With Windows 2000, Microsoft changed the Windows networking infrastructure to one based on TCP/IP, with no NetBIOS support required. Networks based on Windows Server 2003 or Windows 2000 can use DNS to resolve network names, and network applications can use the Winsock interface to communicate using a network.

Unfortunately, because earlier versions of Windows require NetBIOS support to function properly on a Windows-based network, most companies still need to support NetBIOS over TCP/IP and provide WINS services for earlier clients and servers. Even in a pure Windows Server 2008 and Windows Vista network, NetBIOS and WINS might be required, depending on other applications and servers on the network.

Requests for Comments

Requests for comments (RFCs) come in many guises, but they all have the same intent and a somewhat similar format. They are designed to provide a way for an extremely diverse group—the users of the Internet—to communicate and agree on the architecture and functionality of the Internet. Some RFCs are official documents of the IETF, defining the standards of TCP/IP and the Internet; some are simply proposals trying to become standards; and others fall somewhere in between. Some RFCs are tutorial in nature, others are quite technical, and some are even humorous (such as RFC 2324, "Hyper Text Coffee Pot Control Protocol"). But all are a way for the Internet—which is an essentially anarchic entity—to organize, communicate, and evolve.

We don't need to list all the RFCs here, and you certainly don't need to read them all, but you should know where to find them and be aware of the most important ones. You can find listings of RFCs in a number of places, including *http://www.ietf.org/rfc.html*. An excellent site that we find friendlier and more accessible for older RFCs is: *http://www.cse.ohio-state.edu/cs/Services/rfc/index.html*. The RFCs at this location are organized and linked logically to make the information you're looking for easy to find. Unfortunately, however, the site is no longer reliably updated, so you probably should just use the official RFC editor site, *http://www.rfc-editor.org*. Table C-1 lists some important RFCs and their subject matter.

Table C-1 Key RFCs and What They Cover

RFC Number	Subject
RFC 768	User Datagram Protocol (UDP)
RFC 791	Internet Protocol (IP)
RFC 792	Internet Control Message Protocol (ICMP)
RFC 793	Transmission Control Protocol (TCP)
RFC 821	Simple Mail Transfer Protocol (SMTP) (Made obsolete by RFC 2821)
RFC 822	Standard for the Format of Advanced Research Project Agency (ARPA) Internet Text Messages (Obsoleted by RFC2822)
RFC 854, 855	Telnet Protocol
RFC 959	File Transfer Protocol (FTP)
RFC 1001, 1002	Network Basic Input/Output System (NetBIOS) over TCP/IP
RFC 1011	Official Internet Protocols
RFC 1034	DNS Concepts and Facilities
RFC 1035	DNS Implementation and Specification
RFC 1166	Internet Numbers
RFC 1542	Clarifications and Extensions for the Bootstrap Protocol
RFC 1886	DNS Extensions to Support IP version 6 (Obsoleted by RFC 3596)
RFC 1918	Address Allocation for Private Internets
RFC 2131	Dynamic Host Configuration Protocol (DHCP)
RFC 2136	Dynamic Updates in the DNS System (Dynamic DNS)
RFC 2251	Lightweight Directory Access Protocol (LDAP)
RFC 2460 through 2463	Internet Protocol version 6 (IPv6) Specifications
RFC 2661	Layer Two Tunneling Protocol (L2TP)
RFC 2782	A DNS Resource Record (RR) for Specifying the Location of Services (DNS SRV)
RFC 3007	Secure DNS
RFC 3011	A DHCP server on one subnet can respond to an address from another subnet

Note Like any such list, some of these RFCs are currently standards, some are proposed, and some may never be fully adopted. An RFC is only a request for comment. The comments may lead to it becoming a standard, or may lead to it withering away.

IP Addresses and What They Mean

Your IP address is to the Internet (or to the other computers on your local network) what your street address is to your mail carrier. It uniquely identifies your computer by using a simple, 32-bit (or 128 bits with IPv6) addressing scheme. This scheme, which originated in the late 1960s and early 1970s, uses four octets (for IPv4) separated by dots, in the form *w.x.y.z*. Throughout this appendix, we'll use these letters to represent each octet–to describe both the network's address and the local computer's address on that network. Each octet is represented by a single decimal number but is called an octet because it requires eight bits to describe.

Note IPv6 addresses use hexadecimal notation, with blocks separated by colons. For IPv6 addresses, the first half (64 bits) of the address is a network and routing specific prefix, while the second 64 bits make up the actual address of the device. Each IPv6 device can have multiple, scope-specific addresses.

In terms of IPv4 addresses, all networks fall into one of three classes: A, B, or C. These different classes describe networks (sometimes referred to as *licenses*) of different sizes and complexities. The licenses to use a range of IP addresses are controlled by Internet Corporation for Assigned Names and Numbers (ICANN).

Note The use of the word *class* to describe the size of an IPv4 network is officially deprecated and we're not supposed to use it any more. But it's still commonly used and will undoubtedly continue to be used as long as IPv4 networks are in common use.

Class A Networks

A class A network has an address that begins with a number from 1 through 127 for the first octet–the *w* portion of the address. This octet describes the network itself, and the remainder of the address is the actual local device's address on that network. A class A network with the network address of 10 (the *w* portion) contains all IP addresses from 10.0.0.0 to 10.255.255.255.

The class A address 127 has a special meaning and isn't available for general use. This means that a total of 126 usable class A addresses in the world are possible (from 1 through 126), and that each class A network can contain more than 16 million unique network devices.

The class A addresses were spoken for long ago and are assigned to such entities as the United States Department of Defense, Stanford University, and Hewlett-Packard.

Real World 127: The Loopback Address

All IP addresses that begin with the network number 127 are special. Your network card interprets them as loopback addresses. Any packet sent to an address beginning with 127 is treated as though it got to its intended address, and that address is the local device. So packets addressed to 127.0.0.1 are treated the same as packets to 127.37.90.17. Both are actually addressed to your current computer, as are all the other 16 million addresses in the 127 class A network. (You, too, can have your very own class A network. Of course, you can talk only to yourself, but who cares?)

Class B Networks

A class B network uses the first two octets, *w* and *x*, to describe the network itself; the remainder of the address is the actual local device's address on that network. The first octet in a class B network must begin with a number from 128 through 191, resulting in 16,384 class B networks, each of which can have 65,534 unique addresses. This is still a pretty large network, and most of the class B networks were assigned long ago to large organizations or companies such as Rutgers University and Toyota Motor Corporation.

Many addresses in the class B address space have subsequently been divided into smaller groups of addresses and reassigned. Large Internet service providers (ISPs), for example, use this technique to more efficiently use the available address space.

Class C Networks

A class C network has an address that begins with a number from 192 through 223 for the *w* octet of the address and uses the first three octets (*w.x.y*) to describe the network itself. The last octet, *z*, describes the actual local device's address on that network. This arrangement makes for roughly 2 million class C networks, each of which can have a maximum of 254 devices on the network. That's enough for a small business or a department, but not for a major corporation.

Note Because Internet-accessible IPv4 addresses are in such short supply these days, a new method of dividing up Internet IP addresses was created—Classless Internet Domain Routing (CIDR). CIDR allows IP addresses to be leased out in smaller chunks than entire classes so that companies can lease a more suitable number of IP addresses than if they had to lease an entire class A, B, or C network. CIDR uses variable length subnet masks to accomplish these smaller address chunks.

Class D and Class E Addresses

An IP address with a number from 224 through 239 for the *w* octet of the address is known as a class D address, which is used for multicast addresses. With multicast addresses, a number of computers can share a single multicast address, in addition to their normal IP addresses. This makes it easy to send identical data to multiple hosts simultaneously–just send the data to the shared multicast address and every member of the multicast group receives it.

The IP address space that uses the numbers 240 through 247 for the *w* octet is referred to as a class E address. This space is reserved for future use.

Real World IP Addresses for Networks that Use Firewalls or Internet Gateways

Organizations and companies today use routers, proxy servers, and firewalls between the computers in their organization and the public Internet. The addresses of the computers within the organization are *translated* by that router or firewall, a process called Network Address Translation (NAT), and are never directly propagated onto the Internet. Addresses within the organization, therefore, need to be unique within the organization, but not necessarily globally unique, because no other organization will see them. Should you use just any old address then? No, you really shouldn't. A special set of network addresses is reserved for just such uses. These addresses are defined in RFC 1918, and by using these addresses you can comfortably employ a substantially larger address space than you are otherwise able to access.

Using these special network addresses also protects the integrity of the Internet. Because these special addresses are designated exclusively for private networks, they are automatically filtered at routers, protecting the Internet. The following is a list of these special addresses:

- 10.0.0.0 through 10.255.255.255 (a single 24-bit block of addresses or a class A network)
- 172.16.0.0 through 172.31.255.255 (16 contiguous 20-bit blocks of addresses or class B networks)
- 192.168.0.0 through 192.168.255.255 (256 contiguous 16-bit blocks of addresses or class C networks)

You should always use addresses from this group of addresses for your internal IPv4 network. Only computers directly connected to the public Internet should use globally unique IPv4 addresses. All other devices on your network should use these RFC 1918 addresses, which will be hidden by the router or firewall from public view using NAT. Microsoft Windows Server 2008 can provide NAT directly, or you can choose to use a full-featured firewall such as Microsoft Internet Security and Acceleration Server 2006 (ISA 2006). When you use a firewall or proxy server, you require "real" IP addresses only for computers that are outside your firewall and are visible to the Internet as a whole, which helps conserve the global IPv4 address space.

Routers and Subnets

If every computer on the Internet had to know the location of every other computer on the Internet and how to get from here to there, the entire Internet would have come to a grinding halt long ago. Early on, it became apparent that a method was needed to filter and route packets to allow users to not only print to their network printers easily, but also to reach any other computer on the Internet without having to know a whole lot about how to get there. Enter subnets, routers, and gateways.

What Is a Subnet?

A *subnet* is simply a portion of the network that operates as a separate network, without regard to what happens outside and without affecting the rest of the network. A subnet is usually a separate physical "wire" that has only a single point of contact with other areas of the network, through a router or bridge–although even when two subnets share the same physical wire, they still require a router to connect to each other.

Setting up a subnet involves using what is known as a *subnet mask* to allow computers in a subnet to see and directly communicate only with other computers in the same subnet. A subnet mask is a special number, again in *w.x.y.z* form, that masks or blocks areas outside the subnet from sight. The mask works by letting you see only those portions of the IP address space that aren't masked by a 1. (Remember that each octet is actually an 8-bit binary value. To *mask by 1* means to ensure that the appropriate bit has been set to a value of 1.) For example, if you have a class C address of 192.168.222.17, and your subnet mask is 255.255.255.0 (a typical class C subnet), as shown in Figure C-1, you can see only addresses in the last octet of the address (the *z* portion).

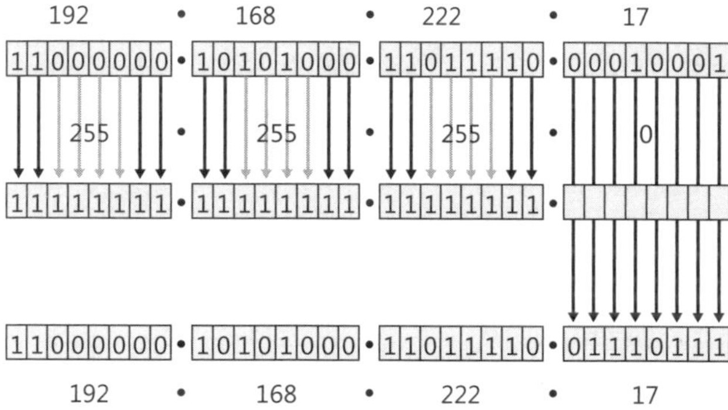

Figure C-1 Subnet masking

If your IP address is 192.168.222.17, the address at 192.168.223.25 is hidden from you by your subnet mask of 255.255.255.0. You can send a packet to that address only by first passing that packet to a gateway or router that knows both where you are and either where the other network is or how to find it. If, on the other hand, you send a packet to a printer with the IP address 192.168.222.129 or to a computer at 192.168.222.50, you have no problem. The system can see that address, and the packet goes directly to its destination.

If you can assign an entire class of addresses to a subnet, it's easy to figure out what your mask is; however, if you can assign only a portion of a class (as is the case when leasing Internet IP addresses using CIDR), you need to sit down with your binary-to-decimal conversion tables and determine exactly what the correct subnet mask should be. (Remember that this is all done in binary.) If you understand how it works, you can customize your subnet mask or figure out what the one you have is actually doing. Custom subnet masks are also called *variable length subnet masks*, and are often referred to in so-called slash notation, where the network number is specified, followed by the number of bits used in the subnet mask. For example, 192.168.1.0/26 has a subnet mask of 255.255.255.192, allowing a single class C network to be broken into 4 subnets, with a maximum of 62 hosts per subnet.

Note Use the default subnet mask for your network class unless you have a specific reason not to. For a class A network, this is 255.0.0.0; for a class B network, it's 255.255.0.0; and for a class C network, use 255.255.255.0.

All the subnet masks on a single portion of your network must be the same. If they aren't, this causes all sorts of problems. One computer might be able to send a packet to another, but the other might not be able to send the packet back.

Under the Hood Physical vs. Logical

Throughout this chapter, we talk about subnets as being separate physical segments on the network. And usually that is the case. But on certain occasions, different subnets need to share the same physical segment of "wire." Sometimes they're sharing an actual Ethernet cable, but it could also be a wireless network. You can have different physical networks even with wireless, by using different frequencies. For example, 802.11a and 802.11g are on different wireless frequencies and cannot see each other. Thus, an 802.11a and 802.11g network have some of the same characteristics as two separate Ethernet cables. Regardless of whether two subnets are on the same physical wire, however, they can't see each other without the intervention of a router because of the subnet masking. But in this case, the router would have two connections (virtual or physical) to the same physical network.

Often you'll have two different wireless networks sharing the same "wire"–that is, the same frequency and same general physical location. But even here, subnets and subnet masks help to hide one network from another. If you have a public, unsecured, 802.11g wireless network and a private, secured, 802.11g wireless network, you should assign a different subnet to each network. Traffic that must cross from one to the other will still need the services of a router.

Gateways and Routers

A gateway can have different functions on a network, but for the moment you're going to focus on the subnet and routing functions. As already mentioned, if you have a subnet mask of 255.255.255.0 and the *y* octet of your IP address is 222, you can't see an IP address on the network with a *y* octet of 223.

How, then, do you get to an IP address on another subnet? The answer is a *gateway*, or *router*. A router is a device (usually an external box, but sometimes a computer with more than one network adapter) that connects to more than one physical segment of the network and sends packets between those segments as required. It takes your packets from the 222 subnet and sends them over to the 223 subnet for delivery to the address on that subnet. Thus, it acts as a gatekeeper between the two separate portions of the network, keeping the traffic with 222 addresses in the 222 subnet and letting only traffic with 223 addresses cross over to the 223 segment.

If a router doesn't know where to direct a packet, the router knows which entity to ask for directions–another router. It constantly updates its routing tables with information from other routers about the best way to get to various parts of the network.

Note Although the terms *gateway* and *router* are often used interchangeably, strictly speaking a gateway is a device or computer that translates between networks of different architectures, such as IPX/SPX and TCP/IP. A router is a device or computer that sends packets between two or more network segments as necessary using logical network addresses (typically IP addresses).

In addition to gateways and routers, *bridges* are devices or computers that direct traffic between two network segments based on physical (media access control) addresses. They are generally used to isolate two sections of a network to improve performance. Bridges are cheaper and less capable than routers.

Address Resolution and Routing Protocols

Detailed information about how address resolution and routing protocols work and the algorithms involved in routing and address resolution are beyond the scope of this book, but it's useful to know what some of the protocols are, if only to recognize acronyms when they're thrown about. In that spirit, the following list consists of the most common TCP/IP address resolution and routing protocols:

- **Address Resolution Protocol (ARP)** ARP maps the IP address to the physical hardware address (the media access control, or MAC, address) corresponding to that IP address, permitting you to send something to an IP address without having to know what physical device it is.
- **Routing Information Protocol (RIP)** RIP is a distance vector-based routing protocol that is mostly provided for backward compatibility with existing RIP-based networks. As with most distance vector-based routing protocols (which make extensive use of broadcasts to discover which other devices and routers are nearby), RIP is being replaced by newer routing protocols that scale better and have lower network traffic overhead.
- **Open Shortest Path First (OSPF)** OSPF is a link-state routing protocol that is suitable for use in large and very large networks, such as those common in large enterprises. Link-state routing protocols maintain a map of the network topology that they share with other routers. As the topology changes, routers update their link-

state database and then inform neighboring routers of the topology change, reducing the amount of network bandwidth consumed when compared to vector-based routing protocols.

Real World Routing Flaps

The Internet has grown exponentially since the early 1990s and continues to grow, stretching the technology for resolving addresses to the limit, and sometimes past the limit. When a major router on the Internet goes down–even momentarily–all the other routers on the Internet have to tell one another about it and recalculate new routes that bypass that router. This adjustment results in large numbers of packets passing back and forth, causing traffic to become so heavy that the routing updates can't occur properly because the information doesn't make it through the traffic. Such a situation is called a *routing flap*, and it can cause a large portion of the Internet to come to a virtual halt.

Routing flaps don't happen very often, but they are becoming more and more of a problem. In addition, current router technology is reaching the limit of its ability to calculate the best route from all the possible routes when major changes are caused by the failure of a key router. The next generation of TCP/IP (IPv6, discussed later in this appendix) will help, as will new algorithms for performing the routing calculations.

Name Resolution

As useful as the 12-decimal–digit IP numbers (192.168.101.102) are when it comes to computers recognizing other computers, they're not the sort of information that human minds process very well. Not only is there a limit to how many 12-digit numbers one can memorize, but such numbers can also easily change.

Even worse, IP version 6 (IPv6) addresses are 128 bits expressed in strings that can have as many as 32 hexadecimal characters, although they're often shorter. (Actually, IPv6 addresses can even be written as 128 ones and zeroes, but that's not likely to catch on.)

Obviously, easy-to-remember names are preferable to strings of numbers or strings of characters and numbers. This section looks at how names are handled in the TCP/IP and Internet world.

The Domain Name System

The Domain Name System (DNS) was designed in the early 1980s, and in 1984 it became the official method for mapping IP addresses to names, replacing the use of hosts files. With Windows 2000, DNS became the method clients use to locate domain controllers using the Active Directory service. (Clients use LDAP to actually access the data stored in the Active Directory database.) Although the overall structure of DNS has been modified somewhat, the general result is still remarkably like the original design.

More Info See RFC 1591 for an overall description of DNS; see RFCs 1034 and 1035 for the actual specification. RFCs 3007, 4033, 4034, and 4035 provide the specification for dynamic updates (Dynamic DNS) with which Windows Server 2008 and Windows Vista comply.

The Domain Namespace

The domain namespace describes the tree-shaped structure of all the domains from the root ("." or "dot") domain down to the lowest-level leaf of the structure. It is a hierarchical structure in which each level is separated from those above and below with a dot, so you always know where you are in the tree.

Before the Internet moved to DNS, a single master file (Hosts.txt) had to be sent using FTP to everyone who needed to convert from numbers to names. Every addition or change required a revised copy to be propagated to every system. This obviously created enormous overhead even when the Internet was still quite small.

DNS overcomes the limitations of Hosts.txt files by maintaining a distributed database that is extensible to add information as needed. It permits local administration of local names while maintaining overall integrity and conformance to standards.

Top-Level Domains

The top-level domains are the first level of the tree below the root. They describe the kinds of networks that are within their domain in two, three, or now four letters, such as .com for commercial domains and .edu for educational domains. The original top-level domains were functionally based and had a decidedly American slant. That's not surprising, given that most of the namespace was originally set up and administered by the U.S. Department of Defense.

As the Internet grew, however, this approach made less and less sense, especially with a distributed database such as DNS that allowed for local administration and control. Geographical top-level domains were added to the functionally based ones, such as .ca for Canadian domains, .eu for European domains, and so on.

How Names Are Resolved into Addresses

When you click a link to *http://www.microsoft.com* and your browser attempts to connect to that site, what actually happens? How does it find *www.microsoft.com*? The short answer is that it asks the primary DNS server listed in the TCP/IP Properties dialog box on your workstation. But how does that DNS server know where the site is?

Real World Where Domain Names Come from and How You Get One

These days, virtually every business (and many individuals) wants its own domain. The keeper and distributor of domain names used to be Network Solutions, formerly called InterNIC. Recently this task was opened up to competition, and a myriad of companies will now register your domain name for you. The list is too big and volatile to include here—for a complete listing, visit the Internet Corporation for Assigned Names and Numbers (ICANN) Web site at *http://www.icann.org/registrars/accredited-list.html*. You can link to any of the accredited registrars from this site and perform a search to find out if your chosen name is taken.

Have alternative names in mind as well; you'll probably need them. After you research existing names and choose one that isn't taken, register the name with your chosen registrar. Pay between $15 and $35 (US) per year or you lose the name.

After you acquire a domain name from a registrar such as Network Solutions, you need to properly set up the DNS hosting for the domain name. If you acquire the domain name through your Web-hosting company, this is probably done automatically for you. Otherwise, follow the directions provided by your registrar to enter the addresses of two DNS servers that have DNS records for your domain name. If you're using a Web-hosting company, these are probably that company's DNS servers. If you're hosting your Web site on your own server or servers, you'll need to either host your own DNS records or contract with a company that specializes in DNS to host them for you. This could be your ISP, or a company such as ZoneEdit (*www.zoneedit.com*), which specializes in DNS.

Long ago, domain names were free and forever, but those days are gone. If you don't pay your bill from your chosen registrar, your domain name is put up for grabs, and chances are that someone else will claim it before you're able to reregister it. The available short names are disappearing at a rapid rate, and many people are finding that they need to think up longer versions to find something that isn't taken.

When a TCP/IP application wants to communicate with or connect to another location, it needs the address of that location. However, it usually knows only the name it's looking for, so the first step is to resolve that name into an IP address. The first place it looks for the name is in the locally cached set of names and their IP addresses that it has resolved recently. After all, if you asked about *http://www.microsoft.com* just a few minutes ago, why should it go through all the trouble of looking up that name again? It's not likely that the IP address will have changed in that time.

Suppose, however, that you haven't been on the Internet for a couple of days, and your computer doesn't have the address for *http://www.microsoft.com* cached. In this case, Windows queries your primary DNS server (specified in the connection properties for your Internet connection). If your DNS server doesn't have any recent information about *http://www.microsoft.com*, the DNS server asks around to see whether anyone else knows the IP address.

This can happen in a couple of ways. The default method is to use recursion, in which the DNS server queries the root server of the domain, which passes back the location of the DNS server that is authoritative regarding the next level down in the domain, which the original DNS server then queries. This process recurs until it reaches a DNS server that contains the IP address of the desired host in its zone data.

Note You might want to disable the use of recursion on your DNS server if it is in use on an internal network and you want your clients to fail over to a secondary DNS server that handles name resolution for hosts outside your local network.

If you disable recursion on the DNS server, or if the client doesn't request the use of recursion, the DNS entry for the desired host is found by iteration. When using iteration, the DNS server checks its zone and cache data, and when it finds that it cannot complete the request, it sends the client a list of DNS servers that are more likely to have the host name in their zones. The client then contacts those servers, which might in turn respond with their own list, possibly even to the point that the client might query the Internet root servers looking for the appropriate DNS server.

Reverse Lookups

In most cases, you have a host name for which you need to locate the IP address, but in some instances you might have only an IP address for which you need to look up the host name. Reverse lookup was added to the DNS specification for this reason. The only problem with creating reverse lookups is the difference between the way the DNS namespace is organized and the way in which IP addresses are assigned. DNS names go from specific to general, beginning with the host name and ending with the root of the domain (the period at the end of a fully qualified domain name, or FQDN). IP addresses work in reverse fashion, so to facilitate the lookup of a host name from an IP address, a special domain, the *in-addr.arpa* domain, was created.

In the in-addr.arpa domain, the octets of an IP address are reversed, with in-addr.arpa appended to the address. For example, the IP address 10.230.231.232 is queried as 232.231.230.10.in-addr.arpa.

The reverse lookup zone is maintained as a separate database within the DNS database. The resource records (RRs) in the reverse lookup zone are of the type PTR (pointer). Much like pointers in common programming languages, or shortcuts in Windows, these PTR RRs refer to a different record—the associated A (address) record in the forward lookup zone. For example, the following list describes two records that a host might have:

- **A record (forward lookup zone)** hp350-dc-02.example.local IN A 192.168.51.2
- **PTR record (reverse lookup zone)** 2.51.168.192.in-addr.arpa. IN PTR hp350-dc-02.example.local

You can perform a reverse lookup of an IP address by typing **nslookup** followed by the IP address you want to look up at a command prompt. For example, if you type **nslookup 192.168.51.2**, the DNS server responds with the name and address of the DNS server, followed by the name and address of the host.

Dynamic DNS and Active Directory Integration

Dynamic DNS, introduced in Windows 2000 Server, makes DNS more flexible by permitting clients to update their DNS records dynamically. This capability eliminates the need to update DNS entries manually when clients change IP addresses. Unfortunately, the standard dynamic DNS service described in RFC 2136 allows for only a single-master model, in which a single primary DNS server maintains the master database of zone data (the addresses and host names for a particular domain). This database can be replicated with secondary DNS servers, but only the primary server can manage dynamic updates to the zone. If the primary server goes down, client updates to the zone aren't processed.

The dynamic DNS server in a Windows Server can overcome the limitations of a single-master model and use Active Directory to store its zone data, permitting a multiple-master model. Because the Active Directory database is fully replicated to all Active Directory–enabled domain controllers, any domain controller in the domain can update DNS zone data. Using Active Directory to store the zone data also allows for added security features and simplified planning and management, as well as faster directory replication than is possible using a single-master model, because Active Directory replicates only relevant changes to the zone.

Zone Storage and Active Directory

A DNS server is required to support the use of Active Directory, so if a DNS server can't be found on the network when a server is being promoted to domain controller, the DNS service is installed by default on the domain controller. After Active Directory is installed, you can store and replicate your zones in one of two ways:

- **Standard zone storage using a text-based file** With this method, zones are stored in .DNS text files located in the *%SystemRoot%*\System32\DNS folder. The filename is the same as the zone name you chose when creating the zone. Figure C-2 shows part of a text DNS zone file.
- **Directory-integrated zone storage** Zones are stores in a *dnsZone* container object located in the Active Directory tree.

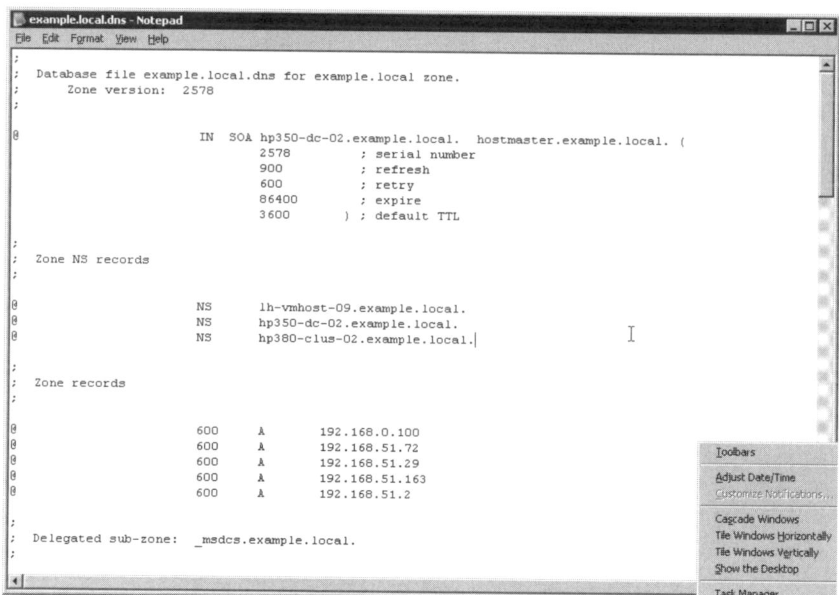

Figure C-2 Zone storage in a text file

The second method is preferred, not only because integrated zones are automatically replicated and synchronized whenever a new domain controller comes online, but also for reasons of administrative simplicity. Keeping a DNS namespace separate from the Active Directory namespace doubles your work (and your chances for error) when testing replication or modifying your domain, for example.

However, it is important to realize that using directory-integrated zone storage decreases the number of dynamic updates per second that the DNS server can process by a factor of two, and secure dynamic updates decrease this number by an additional 25 percent.

More Info DNS is one of the (many) subjects in this book that is a book-length topic in its own right. For more information on the configuration of DNS, consult the *Microsoft Windows Server 2008 Resource Kit* (Microsoft Press, 2008). For in-depth coverage of the subject, see *DNS and BIND, Fifth Edition*, by Paul Albitz and Cricket Liu (O'Reilly & Associates, 2006).

Lightweight Directory Access Protocol

LDAP is used to access data in the Active Directory database. Once again, DNS is used to locate domain controllers, and LDAP is used to access the Active Directory data. LDAP runs on top of TCP/IP, and Active Directory supports both versions 2 and 3 of LDAP. Any LDAP product complying with these specifications can be used to access data in Active Directory.

Dynamic Host Configuration Protocol

One of the problems traditionally faced by organizations using TCP/IP is deciding how to manage internal IP addresses. The chore of managing and maintaining all the IP addresses in an organization can quickly become an administrator's nightmare, especially with the number of intermittently connected computers such as laptops, PDAs, and remote computers. DHCP provides a simple way to manage addresses for computers, and it allows for greatly simplified administration and management of addresses and configuration. If you need to make a change to the TCP/IP settings for your entire organization, you need to make the change only to the DHCP server and it will be automatically propagated to all the DHCP clients. This is a *lot* simpler than having to change the settings of every computer in the organization.

DHCP allows the administrator to assign IP addresses only as required. A mobile user can connect a laptop to the network when necessary and be assigned an appropriate address automatically. Likewise, a dial-in user doesn't need a permanent IP address; one can be assigned when the connection is made to the network, and when the connection is broken the address is made available for someone else's use.

How DHCP Works

To receive an IP address, the client computer sends a DHCP discover broadcast, which a DHCP server picks up and responds to by offering the client an IP address for its use. The client responds to the first offer it receives and sends back to the DHCP server a request for the IP address offered. The DHCP server sends an acknowledgment telling the client that it succeeded in leasing the IP address for the amount of time specified by the DHCP server.

DHCP clients attempt to renew their leases at startup, as well as after 50 percent of the lease time has passed. In this renewal process, the discover stage is skipped and the client simply begins with a request. If the renewal of the lease fails at the 50 percent mark, the client waits until 87.5 percent of the lease has passed and then attempts to acquire a new IP address by sending out a DHCP discover broadcast and starting the IP lease process again.

Using Multiple DHCP Servers

Because DHCP uses UDP broadcasts, your DHCP servers don't see (and thus don't respond to) client requests on a different subnet unless the router between the two is configured to forward broadcasts. In most large establishments, this means separate DHCP servers for each subnet because broadcast traffic is an unnecessary burden on your routing capacity. If your DHCP server properly supports RFC 3011, it can handle requests from multiple subnets, assigning the correct address for each subnet. You can also configure a second DHCP server for each subnet to provide for redundancy and to give your network a way to issue addresses if the main DHCP server fails.

If you do opt to allow your routers to pass along broadcasts, they must support RFC 1542 and be configured to forward BOOTP broadcasts. Check the documentation for your router for configuration information; most new routers (and newer versions of router software) support this. If your router doesn't support RFC 1542 and you have clients that don't have access to a local DHCP server, you must configure a DHCP relay agent to forward client broadcasts to a DCHP server on another network segment.

Note Although you can use DHCP remotely with supported routers, it's best to situate your DHCP servers on-site. WAN failures do occur, and even a brief one can keep clients from being able to acquire or maintain an IP address. Letting a WAN be in a position to put your LAN out of business is a bad idea.

Windows Server 2008 supports integration of DHCP with dynamic DNS to facilitate the updating of a client's DNS record when the client receives a new IP address from a DHCP server.

DNS servers in a DHCP-managed network should support dynamic DNS. The Windows 2000 Server, Windows Server 2003, and Windows Server 2008 versions of DNS all properly support dynamic updates, as will BIND version 8 or later.

Note Zone transfers between Windows 2000 and BIND version 9.*x* DNS servers might not work unless the Windows 2000 server is running Service Pack 3 or later. Zone transfers between Windows Server 2003 or Windows Server 2008 and BIND version 9.*x* work fine.

Typically, you need one DHCP server for every 10,000 clients, though this number can be higher if you have large disk capacity and a fast CPU, or lower if your IP address class or network layout prevents this kind of server utilization. DHCP is very disk-intensive, so make sure that if your server will be handling a significant number of clients you have sufficient hardware, such as a large and fast redundant array of independent disks (RAID), adequate memory, and one or more fast CPUs.

More Info For more information about working with DHCP in Windows Server, see the Dynamic Host Configuration Protocol page on Microsoft TechNet at *http://technet.microsoft.com/en-us/network/bb643151.aspx*.

Real World **DHCP and Availability**

DHCP itself does not support synchronization with other DHCP servers. If your network demands increased reliability, have a backup DHCP server offline with the same scope as the primary server, so that if the primary server goes down you can bring the backup online immediately. (You can also use the Windows Server 2008 Failover Clustering to create a DHCP cluster.)

You might also want to split the address space between two DHCP servers, with the primary server handling 80 percent of the address space and the secondary server handling 20 percent. If the primary server fails, the secondary server handles all client leases from its 20 percent of the address space until the primary server is brought back online. If both servers are down, clients maintain their IP addresses until their leases run out.

If server reliability is a problem on your network, consider increasing the lease time to allow more time to bring servers back online before clients lose their addresses.

Windows Internet Name Service

NetBIOS is an interface originally developed to allow applications to access network resources in the Microsoft MS-DOS operating system. As such, it was the primary networking API and naming method for Microsoft networks until the release of Windows 2000.

NetBIOS host names are up to 15 characters long and part of a flat namespace, so all names on a given network must be unique. Normally, host names are resolved by broadcast—not the most efficient means in terms of either time or network bandwidth. Routers also usually do not forward NetBIOS broadcasts, eliminating the ability to resolve host names on a different subnet.

WINS was created to provide a solution to this problem by maintaining a dynamic database of IP addresses and their associated NetBIOS names. However, WINS is still limited in many ways by the underlying architecture of NetBIOS, and it is now an optional service in a Windows Server 2008 or Windows Server 2003 network.

Although many of us might be eager to do away with WINS, it is still used by many companies to provide NetBIOS name resolution services for pre-Windows 2000 Microsoft operating systems, and some current server applications still depend on it. However, if you have *any* computers running a version of Windows earlier than Windows 2000, it is more than time to get rid of them. They are no longer on support, no longer get security updates, and pose an active hazard to your network.

Note WINS is usually deployed in conjunction with DNS to provide optimal support for newer clients. Although BIND 8 and newer versions can be used adequately as a DNS server for Windows Server 2008 networks, BIND doesn't support WINS records, which can cause issues with DNS zone transfers. For this reason, stick with Windows 2000 or newer DNS servers if you need to use WINS servers on your network.

When deploying WINS servers on your network, deploy only the minimum number necessary to provide adequate service to your clients. WINS servers can be a pain to replicate, so keeping the number of servers down can be a big plus. (Microsoft itself, for example, used no more than about 12 WINS servers worldwide before moving to Windows 2000.)

Important Don't install WINS on a multihomed server. WINS has enough replication problems without complicating the situation by placing the server on two subnets.

To make WINS and Browsing (explained in the "Browsing vs. browsing" sidebar) work correctly when you are in an enterprise environment with subnets and multiple domains, keep a few tricks in mind. Three possible scenarios are listed here. Each is discussed in the sections that follow.

- Single domain across a subnet boundary
- Multiple domains within a subnet boundary
- Multiple domains across a subnet boundary

Single Domain Across a Subnet Boundary

To see the resources of a single domain across a subnet boundary, with only TCP/IP as your protocol, you need to set up WINS servers on both sides of the router or mess around with Lmhosts files. Avoid Lmhosts files like the plague: They're a pain to get right in the first place and have to be manually edited every time anything changes anywhere. They also don't deal well with DHCP, under which IP addresses are subject to change. However, if you're setting up a virtual private network with Internet-connected clients, you might not be able to avoid Lmhosts because these clients don't have an available WINS server.

In general, it's a good idea to have a domain on each side of your router. The alternative is much more traffic across the router than you want, because every authentication request has to cross over. The obvious choice is to put a WINS server in each domain. No special requirements need to be met for this to work because Browsing doesn't need to be told about another domain.

Real World Browsing vs. browsing

A source of possible confusion in any discussion about Microsoft networking is the subtle distinction between the common meaning of the word *browsing* and the very specific meaning that the word has in Microsoft networking. Many texts use *browsing* to mean looking for or at the resources available, which is a reasonable use of the word. However, *Browsing* in the Microsoft networking sense refers to the Computer Browser service used by Windows-based computers to maintain browse lists of all shared resources on the network. It's easy to get confused, so to avoid that here, *Browsing* is always capitalized when used in the Microsoft networking sense.

With the growth of networks and the introduction of directories such as Active Directory, Browsing has become much less important. Most networks are too large to browse for resources, and Active Directory helps alleviate this issue by permitting you to query Active Directory for the resources you want. This makes finding resources easier, and also reduces the network traffic caused by Browsing.

Multiple Domains Within a Subnet Boundary

If you're running a multi-domain forest within a single subnet, you might want a WINS server in each domain, but you don't need to do anything special with Browsing. You can set up and explicitly add the other domains to browse, but this step isn't required.

Multiple Domains Across a Subnet Boundary

Now you get to the tricky one. For everything to work in multiple domains across a subnet boundary, you need to set up everything very carefully. Because the Browsing packets don't cross the subnet boundary unless they know where they're going, you need to explicitly set the Computer Browsing service to browse the domain on the far side of the router. Each domain in the forest or tree needs to be configured to browse any domains on the far side of the router.

For the technical details of WINS and Browsing, see the *Microsoft Windows Server 2008 Resource Kit*. When you have a network free of Microsoft clients earlier than Windows 2000, you might be able to happily turn off WINS and make your life a lot easier. However, before disabling WINS on your network, you should carefully test your existing applications and servers to ensure that there isn't a dependency on NetBIOS names that you aren't aware of.

Summary

Although it's not necessary to become an expert on TCP/IP to run a network, some basic knowledge is required. TCP/IP and DNS in particular are worth studying in some depth because so many network difficulties can be traced to the misconfiguration of one or the other.

About the Authors

Charlie Russel and **Sharon Crawford** are co-authors of numerous books on operating systems. Their titles include *Microsoft Windows Small Business Server 2003 R2 Administrator's Companion, Microsoft Windows Server 2003 Administrator's Companion, 2nd Edition, Microsoft Windows XP Resource Kit, 3rd Edition*, and *Upgrading to Windows 98*.

Charlie Russel is a chemist by education; an electrician by trade; a UNIX sysadmin and Oracle DBA because he raised his hand when he should have known better; an IT director and consultant by default; and a writer by choice. Charlie is a Microsoft MVP for Windows Server and is the author of more than two dozen computer books on operating systems and enterprise environments, including *Microsoft Windows Small Business Server 2003 Administrator's Companion, Microsoft Windows XP Resource Kit, 3rd Edition*, and (with Robert Cordingley) the *Oracle DBA Quick Reference Series*. He has also written numerous white papers on microsoft.com.

Sharon Crawford began writing computer books in 1991 and prefers it to all her previous real jobs, which included driving a cab and repairing subway cars in New York. She has given up looking for legitimate employment.

Sharon and Charlie live in beautiful British Columbia with one dog, varying numbers of cats, and a delightful, if somewhat distracting, view of Pender Harbour.

Index

B

C

H

Q

R

U

V

W

X

Z

What do you think of this book?

We want to hear from you!

Do you have a few minutes to participate in a brief online survey?

Microsoft is interested in hearing your feedback so we can continually improve our books and learning resources for you.

To participate in our survey, please visit:

www.microsoft.com/learning/booksurvey/

...and enter this book's ISBN-10 or ISBN-13 number (located above barcode on back cover*). As a thank-you to survey participants in the United States and Canada, each month we'll randomly select five respondents to win one of five $100 gift certificates from a leading online merchant. At the conclusion of the survey, you can enter the drawing by providing your e-mail address, which will be used for prize notification only.

Thanks in advance for your input. Your opinion counts!

*Where to find the ISBN on back cover

Example only. Each book has unique ISBN.

Microsoft Press

No purchase necessary. Void where prohibited. Open only to residents of the 50 United States (includes District of Columbia) and Canada (void in Quebec). For official rules and entry dates see:

www.microsoft.com/learning/booksurvey/